The Good Hotel Guide 1988

The Good Hotel Guide 1988

Britain and Western Europe

Editor: Hilary Rubinstein

Continental Editor: John Ardagh

Contributing Editor for the British Isles: Wendy Arnold

Managing Editor: Caroline Raphael

Which? BOOKS

Published by Consumers' Association
and Hodder and Stoughton

Which? Books are commissioned by The Association for Consumer Research and published by Consumers' Association, 14 Buckingham Street, London WC2N 6DS and Hodder and Stoughton, 47 Bedford Square, London WC1B 3DP.

Editorial assistants: Sarah Thomas, Fay Amias, Philippa Carlile, Katinka Ardagh, Sue Carlile, Tiffany Arnold

British Library Cataloguing in Publication Data
The Good Hotel Guide: Britain and Western Europe.—1988
1. Hotels, taverns, etc.—Directories
I. Rubinstein, Hilary II. Consumers' Association
647'.94 TX907

ISBN 0 340 41359 X

Computer typeset by SB Datagraphics, Colchester, England

Printed and bound in Great Britain by
Hazell, Watson & Viney Ltd,
Member of the BPCC Group,
Aylesbury, Bucks

Acknowledgments: the extracts from John Fothergill's *An Innkeeper's Diary* in the Appendix are reproduced by permission of Faber & Faber.

Contents

A note for new readers 7
Introduction 9
The César awards 16
Special hotels 18
How to read the entries 21

PART ONE

Great Britain and Ireland

England 27
Wales 187
Scotland 203
Channel Islands 249
Republic of Ireland 255

PART TWO

The Continent

Austria 275
Belgium 297
Denmark 309
France 315
Germany 473
Greece 519

Hungary	531
Italy	535
Luxembourg	583
Malta (including Gozo)	587
The Netherlands	589
Norway	599
Portugal (including Madeira)	607
Spain (including Andorra, the Balearics and the Canaries)	625
Sweden	653
Switzerland	663
Turkey	687
Yugoslavia	705

Exchange rates	712
Good hotels — Czech and Bulgarian style	713
An Innkeeper's Diary, by John Fothergill	717
Alphabetical list of hotels	722
Maps	740
Hotel reports and champagne winners	767
Hotel report forms	769

A note for new readers

This is an annual guide to hotels and inns in Britain and the continent of Western Europe that are of unusual character and quality. The entries are based on reports from readers who write to us when they come across an establishment which has given them out-of-the-ordinary satisfaction, and who also send us their comments, critical or appreciative, when they visit places already included in the Guide. Our task is to collate these reports, check and verify them, making inspections where necessary, and select those which we consider make the grade. No cash changes hands at any point: contributors are not rewarded for writing to us; hotels do not pay for their entries; the editor and his staff accept no free hospitality.

The Guide operates on the same principle as *The Good Food Guide*, but is independently owned and edited. We have no say in the hotels and restaurants chosen by our sibling publication, nor are they involved in our choices. But we are keen to share our correspondence where appropriate: we pass on to *The Good Food Guide* reports on any British hotel where the restaurant is an important feature. Hotels listed in that Guide carry the notation [GFG] after their name.

The entries in the book cover a wide range. People want different things from a hotel according to whether they are making a single night stop or spending a whole holiday in one place, whether they have young children with them, whether they are visiting a city or staying in the remote countryside, and according to their age and means. We make no claims of universal compatibility or comprehensiveness, but we hope that our descriptions will help you to find good hotels that suit your tastes, needs and purse. If an entry has misled you, we beg you to use one of the report forms at the back of the book and tell us, in order that we can do better next time; and we hope that you will also write to us if you have found the Guide useful and a hotel has fulfilled your expectations: endorsement and criticism are both essential if the Guide is to achieve its purpose. A hotel is dropped unless we get a positive feedback.

INTRODUCTION

In 1986 a deep depression hung over the hotel industry. The previous year had seen European tourism, especially from the States, at an all-time high. Then came the Libyan bombing and Chernobyl and wholesale cancellation both of group and individual bookings. Hotels that relied heavily on their American trade – and that included many of the more expensive hotels in the Guide as well as all those urban monoliths, the multi-storey people parks catering for package tourism – faced onerous losses. The past 12 months have witnessed an unprecedented number of closures and changes of ownership. In Britain alone, this fall-out accounts for the following notable omissions among others: *Beechfield House*, Beanacre, *Riverside*, Helford, *Lodore Swiss*, Keswick, *Stone Green Hall*, Mersham, *The Priory*, Rushlake Green, *Shipdham Place*, Shipdham, *Thornbury Castle*, Thornbury, and *Balcraig House*, Perth. Partly for this reason, the 1988 edition of the Guide has a greater turnover of entries than ever before – no fewer than 236 hotels having been dropped from last year and their places taken by 184 newcomers.

At the time of writing, the 1987 season looks altogether brighter. But hotels at the upper end of the tariff scale are still worryingly dependent on a steady infusion of dollar income. A recession like that of 1986 could happen again for one of many unpredictable reasons. The only way a hotelier can insure against another bad year is to strive to give better value for money and by so doing seek to attract more visitors from the "home" counties.

Better value for money can be seen in hardware terms – better amenities outside, more appetising options in the restaurant, the upgrading of appointments in the public rooms and bedrooms, more freebies, more jacuzzis, more bidets. Some of the fashionable improvements are no better than frills, but others are real bonuses. Among the latter, I particularly welcome the installation of gas coal fires (much more convincing than the log variety) which can quickly turn the bleakest of bedrooms into a cosy den. Foolish virgins who fail to turn up their central heating early enough in an unexpected cold spell can get away with it now as they never could before.

Better value for money can also take less tangible forms. It can express itself through acts of kindness beyond the routine obligations of innkeeping hospitality. It often reveals itself instantly, the moment you cross the threshold. I had a good illustration of this in February when I stayed with a party of langlaufers at a small inn, the *Gasthof zur Rose*, in Oberammergau (see page 504). We had arrived cold and dispirited in heavy rain after a long coach ride from Munich Airport. We might have been treated as second-class citizens, being a group booking on modest half-board terms. But we were met at the door by the owner and his wife who insisted, even before we had been given our room keys, on serving us a complimentary glass of the local speciality, the Mozart chocolate liqueur. And that sort of spontaneous generosity and empathy showed itself often during our week's stay.

Hoteliers, however hard they work for most of the year, *do* take holidays themselves. They do stay in other people's hotels. They must notice the innumerable ways in which good hoteliers give satisfaction to their guests. And they also cannot fail to register the opposite: the meannesses and inefficiencies, the sloppiness, poor housekeeping and lack of imagination in many of the places they stay at when they travel abroad. Why are these lessons so hard to apply when they return home?

Why don't more hoteliers make a point of sleeping at least once a year in every one of their bedrooms? They would learn so much to their advantage. Poor lighting, missing bulbs, bare walls, noisy plumbing, uncomfortable beds, nowhere to put suitcases in the bedroom or toiletries in the bathroom, broken fittings, towels too thin or too small – all these errors of omission or commission recur constantly in our reports like some monotonous dirge.

The Crown on Trial

Three years ago we berated the Tourist Boards for their cumbersome system of classification and warned the innocent visitor that the notices displayed outside hotels and guest-houses and the entries in their *Where to Stay* handbooks gave the misleading impression that the establishments had been officially approved when it only meant that they had chosen to register themselves and pay the required dues. We urged long overdue reforms: a simpler, more readily intelligible system of grading hotels and regular statutory inspection.

Some of what we sought has come to pass: the three national Tourist Boards, English, Welsh and Scottish, after prolonged wrangling, have at last agreed on a common basis of classification. At the bottom of the pile are places which have details printed but remain unclassified; the next most basic kind of accommodation is described as listed; and above that category hotels are awarded between one and five crowns according to their range of facilities. The Welsh Tourist Board has had inspections for some years, and the English and Scottish Boards have now followed its good example. All establishments wishing to register with the Board send in details of their facilities, and in due course inspectors call and verify their accuracy.

Half a curate's egg is no doubt better than the dog's breakfast we had before, and I accept that these are early days. But a scrutiny of the three official *Where to Stay* guides in this, the first year of the crowns, reveals a stupefying variety of inadequacies.

For a start, there are the anomalies: crowns are awarded purely and inflexibly on a quantitative basis – things like the size of rooms, the ratio of guests to bathrooms, the presence or absence of bedside lights and luggage racks. No account whatever is taken of the quality of what is on offer. In consequence, hotels of wholly different character and tariff – sophisticated country house hotels and modest roadside lodgings – can find themselves put on an equal footing.

Only Scotland (and the Isle of Wight) make some attempt at qualitative grading. But there are many hotels in Scotland known to me personally as outstanding which aren't commended at all – and it can't be because they haven't yet been inspected because the book would say so. And – this is the final ignominy of the Scottish Guide – in these assessments no account whatever has been taken of the standard of food served. A hotel can be highly commended and serve only third-rate convenience food; another can have a distinguished chef whose cooking makes a huge contribution to guests' well-being, but whose virtues have been wholly overlooked. No wonder many hotels in Scotland are up in arms over this preposterous anomaly!

The crowning scheme suffers, too, because it is so far from being comprehensive. Some of the hotels not listed may be beneath contempt, but many of the omissions are of hotels which rate entries in this Guide but feel that registration with a Tourist Board is a waste of money or may bring them quite the wrong sort of customer. The biggest hotel group in Britain, Trusthouse Forte, along with the Crest and Rank chains, has boycotted the crowning scheme.

Finally, these *Where to Stay* guides are as user-unfriendly, as consumer-disoriented, as any guides that I have come across in a lifetime devoted to studying this sort of literature. The method of conveying information is largely through tiny hieroglyphics approximately one-tenth of an inch square. The Scottish Guide represents symbolism gone mad – there are no fewer than 50 of these exasperating little pictograms, informing you that a hotel has a residents' lounge or is heated throughout (gee, thanks) or that sea angling can be arranged. One symbol does tell you, however, that credit card(s) are accepted (which is more than Wales does) but not unfortunately which one or ones.

It may seem inappropriate for one Guide to knock another, but these works are a modest form of public disgrace. They bear the imprimatur of the National Tourist Boards, which are supported by public money, and their listings will inevitably be taken as an official seal of approval. Yet they have been prepared with so small a recognition of travellers' needs, and the contradictions in the method of awarding crowns are so abundantly absurd, that readers would be well advised to give them a miss. And of course the consumer would be better served if there was an acceptable form of grading and classification mandatory on all British hotels just as there is in almost every other country in Europe with a tourist industry.

A Depression of Deposits

We have had a spate of angry correspondence recently on the subject of deposits – not surprising after the torrent of cancellations the previous summer. Many visitors from abroad felt conned when they discovered that a substantial deposit was wholly forfeit even though they had cancelled some weeks before the date they were due to arrive. The subject is a lowering one from both the customer's and the owner's point of view. "When the hotel asked me for a deposit, I immediately felt distrusted and decided not to visit," wrote one correspondent, echoing a common discomfort at one's word not being one's bond. Individual hoteliers, too, frequently shrink from spelling out in detail their policy about forfeits and refunds because it introduces such a mercenary element into the relationship, often unnecessarily.

Practices vary enormously from hotel to hotel, and also depending on the length of stay and whether the booking is made from overseas. It is perfectly legal for a hotel to ask for full payment in advance, though in practice hotels are usually content to settle for something like 10% – enough to dissuade most customers from changing their minds or simply not showing up. Clearly, it is prudent for hotels to make quite clear how they play the deposit game when they confirm a reservation by post. But it is harder to do the right thing when someone books a room by telephone for the following night. An increasingly common custom is to ask the customer for his credit card number, without making clear how much, if anything, will be charged if the caller fails to show up.

We have much sympathy for hoteliers who lose thousands of pounds each year from no-shows. Some hotels which ask for deposits advise their customers to insure against cancellation – doubtless a good idea if you are booking well ahead for an extended stay. We don't altogether blame hotel-keepers for fudging the issue on some occasions, though their legal right to compensation may be damaged if they have failed to make clear the terms of their contract. We advise readers always to clarify this issue, along with any other topic that could give rise to disappointment later – early breakfasts, late dinners, pets, vegetarian diets or whatever – at the time of booking. Our complaints correspondence would then be a lot less voluminous.

Service Charges and Tipping

For several years past we have used these pages to campaign against hotels which impose a service charge automatically on their bills "without the option" and nudge their customers into giving something extra when nothing has occurred to make the visitor especially grateful. We believe that many owners and managers are at last beginning to question these dubious practices, and, as we said last year, we hope that readers who share our dislike of them will continue to let their views be known. Meanwhile, we have once again asked hotels to tell us their stand on these issues, and where they have divulged an answer we have printed it at the end of the entry in italics.

Stub It Out, Mr Ronay

Anti-smokers have been active for many years past, but the smoking lobby has been much less in evidence. Recently, however, Egon Ronay, doyen of British guidesmen, adopted a new persona – as the scourge of restaurants and hotels which have the nerve to curtail the freedom of smokers to light up as and when they please. If you read his article in the London *Sunday Times,* you might be forgiven for thinking that some important liberty of the subject was at stake as he extracted from his personal *Thesaurus* of abuse language normally reserved for really serious threats to the social fabric: "Intolerable imposition... Arrogance... Smacks of the mentality of obsessive do-gooders, spoilsports and guilt-ridden double-faced puritans who put on hair-shirts when eating lobster."

What has caused this normally urbane character to lose his cool? It isn't that he is addicted to cigarettes; on the contrary, he tells us that he is a non-smoker. Since I enjoy the occasional cigar myself, I should be the champion of the smoking classes, but in fact I applaud the growing number of hotels that have declared their dining rooms – and in many cases lounges and bedrooms as well – to be no-smoking areas, just as I am delighted that London Underground has banned smoking and that airlines allow you to choose whether to be polluted by your neighbours' smoke or to opt for relatively fresh air.

Although I am aware of recent evidence on the dangers of passive smoking, the nub of the matter for me is that smoke specifically affects those senses connected with eating – taste and smell. Even if you are not sensitive to its pollution, however, not smoking in restaurants should be a matter of simple consideration for fellow-eaters – on a par with not singing or playing a transistor radio in public places. It is of course entirely up to the proprietor whether to impose a ban on smoking – or, for that matter, on pets or children under 14 or men without jackets and ties at dinner – just as it is the customer's privilege to patronise an establishment or go elsewhere.

Egon Ronay would have us believe that the preference for restaurants without smoke is a fad, a *snobbisme*, a neurosis. The civilised French, he tells us, laugh at our attitude. But why should the French be the final arbiters on such matters? To defer to them on this issue is itself a *snobbisme* and a *conformisme*. And, for the record, the French *Michelin* guide itself has now declared itself a champion of non-smoking in restaurants, taking a lead from our sibling, *The Good Food Guide*, which has fought smoking since 1951.

Many years ago someone offered me a title for a book which he thought would be a surefire best-seller if only someone could be found to write it – *How to Avoid People Who Stop Smoking*. There is no copyright in titles, and maybe at long last it has found a fitting author in Egon Ronay. But I doubt it. His diatribe against smoking "nannies" reminds me of someone puffing too strenuously to keep alive the embers of a dying cigar. I am all in favour of ventilation – of spleen as well as of smoke – but hyper-ventilation can damage your health.

What's New This Year

We have new maps – a considerable improvement, we believe, on their predecessors.

Attentive readers of by-lines will have noticed a change on this year's title-page: John Ardagh, author of *France in the 1980s*, and, more recently, *Germany and the Germans*, having previously edited the French and German sections, now takes over responsibility for all the Continental entries. He is joined this year by Wendy Arnold, author of *The Historic Country Hotels of England* and *The Historic Hotels of London*, and a regular correspondent to the Guide for many years past, who has shared with the Editor a similar responsibility for the entries in Great Britain and Ireland. The policy of the Guide and its principles of selection remain unchanged – only the tone of voice may differ.

There has been a greater turnover of hotels in Part II this year, with more hotels disappearing for lack of feedback. For obvious reasons, inspections in remote areas are harder to achieve, and the less-travelled European countries suffer from reporting malnutrition. Two European sections, Finland and Cyprus, have had to be axed this year for these reasons, joining Northern Ireland which was sadly disenfranchised from these pages some years back. We should be delighted to hear from readers who have visited these areas recently and had rewarding hotel experiences. Meanwhile, by way of compensation, we offer at the end of the book some notes for visitors to Czechoslovakia and Bulgaria, and would be delighted to receive and publish similar bulletins from travellers to other countries in Eastern Europe. Whether the Eastern bloc will in due course enjoy full representation in these pages is impossible to say: we would like to think so, though a lot of privatising will have to take place first.

We have altered our policy about italicising entries this year. There are more such entries than previously, and they indicate hotels which we feel are worth considering, but which for various reasons – inadequate information, ambivalent reports, or lack of feedback – have not justified a full entry. Only brief details of tariff and facilities are given. We should be glad to hear from readers who already know and approve of these hotels or who try them out, and we hope that many will become fully-fledged entries next year, and that others will take their place.

In previous years, we have used the boxes which fill up empty spaces at the foot of pages with information or exhortation. This year, to vary the diet, we have added some stories of perfectly awful hotel experiences taken from recent correspondence. Further contributions to our little boxes of horror gratefully received.

Finally, a line about our concluding bonne-bouche, extracts from John Fothergill's *An Innkeeper's Diary*, which has just been brought back into print after many years. For the Editor, this is simply the most entertaining book about innkeeping ever written – a perfect bedside book for hotel nuts.

HILARY RUBINSTEIN

The César Awards 1988

Our annual awards of Césars – called after the celebrated hotelier, César Ritz – are given for different sorts of excellence among hotels in Britain and Ireland. The categories listed below show the wide range of hotels, inns and guest houses which appeal to us and afford some kind of definition of the scope of the Guide. As before, we have given a César for acceptable eccentricity, but otherwise categories change from year to year. Last year's Césars are indicated in the text by a small laurel wreath.

AWARD	WINNER
For country house hospitality at its luxurious best	Hintlesham Hall, Hintlesham, Suffolk Warmth of welcome is not always easy to maintain in a house of classical elegance. Ruth and David Watson, with no previous hotel experience but dedicated in their new profession, set the tone for relaxed but comprehensive cosseting.
For a notable contribution to architectural conservation and for first-rate hotel management	Bodysgallen Hall, Llandudno, Gwynedd Historic House Hotels deserve our gratitude for restoring the architectural and horticultural delights of a spectacularly beautiful building and for making it one of the best hotels in the Principality.
For enterprise and innovation in a city hotel	The White House, Glasgow The owners of *The White House* have rethought what visitors need in a city hotel. Their suites, simultaneously self-catering and offering full hotel services, set an example of a hybrid we hope others will copy.
For combining the best of two worlds – French flair with English dependability	The White House Hotel, Williton, Somerset Dick and Kay Smith have been welcoming guests to their Georgian country house for 20 years. Kay Smith's cooking owes much to French classical cuisine, but the house has quintessential English virtues.

For maintaining the highest standards of Irish hotelmanship

Cashel House Hotel,
Cashel Bay, Co Galway

Another vintage operation: Dermot and Kay McEvilly have been dependable hosts at their Irish manor house for 20 years – a civilised oasis in the rugged wilderness of Connemara.

For the family hotel of the year

Ard-na-Coille Hotel,
Newtonmore, Highland

The high-spirited hospitality of Alastair and Annie Murchie continues to delight their guests, young and old. Their hunting lodge, as Duncan said in other circumstances "has a pleasant seat; the air nimbly and sweetly recommends itself".

For outstanding farmhouse hospitality

Frog Street Farm,
Beercrocombe, Somerset

Peaceful surroundings, a lovely old house, delicious English home cooking, an unaffectedly welcoming atmosphere and exceedingly modest terms all combine to make Veronica Cole's 15th-century farmhouse/guest house deservedly popular.

For an island hotel in a class of its own

Isle of Colonsay Hotel,
Colonsay, Strathclyde

The most isolated registered hotel in Britain, two-and-a-half hours from the mainland on a ferry that runs only three times a week, is an unlikely place to find an exceptional hotel. But Kevin Byrne is a perfectionist and as caring a hotelier as any in the book.

For away-from-it-all delight in the doll's house class

The Woodmans Arms Auberge,
Hastingleigh, Kent

Only three quite small rooms, but Gerald Campion's tiny inn at the end of a cul-de-sac lane leading on to the North Downs is a haven of good cheer and Susan Campion's cooking is a superb bonus.

For utterly acceptable mild eccentricity

Huntsham Court,
Huntsham, Devon

Not so much a hotel, more an experience: the high Victorian Gothic architecture, the outsize eclectic furniture, the amazing bath tubs, the pre-war radios, the books, the records, provide a suitably outré backcloth for Mogens and Andrea Bolwig's convivial style of house-party entertaining.

Special hotels

City hotels with luxury and grandeur

England Priory, Bath; Connaught, London
Austria Schloss Mönchstein, Salzburg; Palais Schwarzenberg, Vienna
France L'Hôtel, Paris; Lancaster, Paris; Boyer "Les Crayères", Reims
Germany Vier Jahreszeiten, Hamburg
Italy Villa Cora, Florence; Residenza, Rome
Norway Continental, Oslo
Spain Landa Palace, Burgos; San Marcos, León; Reyes Católicos, Santiago de Compostela
Sweden Sara Hotell Reisen, Stockholm
Switzerland L'Arbalète, Geneva; Trois Couronnes, Vevey

Town hotels of character and/or value

England Bay Tree, Burford; Angel, Bury St Edmunds; L'Hôtel, London; Portobello, London; George, Stamford; Mount Royale, York
Scotland Mansion House, Elgin; Howard, Edinburgh; White House, Glasgow; Clifton, Nairn
Ireland Arbutus Lodge, Cork
Austria König von Ungarn, Vienna
France d'Arlatan, Arles; Diderot, Chinon; La Pérouse, Nice; L'Abbaye St-Germain, Paris; Scandinavia, Paris; Vieux Puits, Pont-Audemer; Colombe d'Or, St-Paul-de-Vence
Germany Mönchs Posthotel, Bad Herrenalb; Böttingerhaus, Bamberg; Sankt Nepomuk, Bamberg; Gehrhus, Berlin; Westend, Frankfurt-am-Main; Posthotel Partenkirchen, Garmisch-Partenkirchen; Hanseatic, Hamburg
Italy Umbra, Assisi; Villa Belvedere, Florence; Villa Mozart, Merano; Gregoriana, Rome; Casa Frollo, Venice
The Netherlands Ambassade, Amsterdam; Pulitzer, Amsterdam
Spain Parador, Carmona
Switzerland Rheinhotel Fischerzunft, Schaffhausen; Florhof, Zürich
Turkey Yeşil Ev, Istanbul

Rural charm in the luxury class

England Buckland Manor, Buckland; Gravetye Manor, East Grinstead; Hambleton Hall, Hambleton; Homewood Park, Hinton Charterhouse; Hunstrete House, Hunstrete; Chewton Glen, New Milton; Rookery Hall, Worleston; Sharrow Bay, Ullswater
Wales Bodysgallen, Llandudno
Scotland Inverlochy Castle, Fort William
Channel Islands Longueville Manor, St Saviour
Ireland Park Hotel Kenmare, Kenmare
Austria Schloss Dürnstein, Dürnstein
Belgium Scholteshof, Hasselt-Stevoort; Moulin Hideux, Noirefontaine
Denmark Falsled Kro, Falsled; Store Kro, Fredensborg

France Moulin du Roc, Champagnac-de-Belair; Château de Nieuil, Nieuil; Moulin de la Gorce, La Roche-l'Abeille; Mas de Chastelas, St-Tropez
Italy Villa Cipriani, Asolo; Villa Serbelloni, Bellagio; Certosa di Maggiano, Siena
The Netherlands Kasteel Wittem, Wittem
Portugal Palace, Buçaco
Sweden Halltorps Gästgiveri, Borgholm; Grythyttans, Grythyttan

Rural charm at medium price

England Farlam Hill, Brampton; Howfield Manor, Canterbury; Highbullen, Chittlehamholt; Summer Lodge, Evershot; Stock Hill House, Gillingham; Congham Hall, King's Lynn; Hope End, Ledbury; Plumber Manor, Sturminster Newton; Calcot Manor, Tetbury; Woodhayes, Whimple; White House, Williton; Old Vicarage, Witherslack
Wales Tyddyn Llan, Llandrillo
Scotland Polmaily House, Drumnadrochit; Ardsheal House, Kentallen; Achany House, Lairg
Ireland Cashel House, Cashel Bay; Drumlease Glebe House, Dromahair; Marlfield House, Gorey; Ballymaloe, Shanagarry
Austria Gams, Bezau
Belgium 't Convent, Renige
Denmark Steensgaard Herregårdspension, Millinge
France Pescalerie, Cabrerets, Lou Calen, Cotignac; Cro-Magnon, Les Eyzies-de-Tayac; Moulin, Flagy; Relais de la Magdeleine, Gémenos; Mas Candille, Mougins; Trois Roses, La Petite Pierre; La Source Bleue, Touzac
Germany Töpferhaus, Alt-Duvenstedt; Adler, Gutach im Breisgau; Erbguth's Landhaus, Hagnau; Zum Ochsen, Schönwald
Italy Castello, Gargonza; San Rocco, Orta San Giulio
Norway Utne, Utne
Portugal Quinta das Torres, Azeitão; Villa Hostilina, Lamego
Spain Es Molí, Deyá; Real Monasterio, Guadalupe
Sweden Åkerblads, Tällberg
Switzerland Ermitage, Kandersteg; Bella Tola et St-Luc, St-Luc; Stüa Granda, Soglio

Rural charm, simple style

England Glebe Farm, Diddlebury; Woodmans Arms Auberge, Hastingleigh; Hurstone, Wiveliscombe; Langley, Wiveliscombe
Scotland Riverside, Canonbie
Ireland Coopershill, Riverstown
France Auberge sans Frontière, Dégagnac; A Pastorella, Monticello; Rustica, Pons; Pélissaria, St-Cirq-Lapopie; Midi, St-Jean-du-Bruel

Seaside hotels, luxury style

England Marine, Salcombe
Denmark Sønderho Kro, Sønderho
France Métropole, Beaulieu-sur-Mer; Maquis, Porticcio; Caribou, Porticciolo; Plage, Ste-Anne-la-Palud
Greece Akti Myrina, Myrina
Italy Pellicano, Porto Ercole; Splendido, Portofino; Villa Politi, Syracuse
Malta Ta' Cenc, Sannat
Turkey Talya, Antalya; Kismet, Kuşadasi
Yugoslavia Sveti Stefan

Seaside hotels, medium priced or simple

England Island, Tresco
Wales Porth Tocyn, Abersoch; St Tudno, Llandudno
Scotland Isle of Colonsay, Colonsay; Airds, Port Appin

Channel Islands White House, Herm
France Menez-Frost, Bénodet; Chez Pierre, Raguenès-Plage; Ty-Pont, St-Jean-du-Doigt
Italy Casa Albertina, Positano; La Tonnarella, Sorrento
Spain Mar I Vent, Bañalbufar

Skiing or mountain hotels

England Seatoller, Borrowdale; High Greenrigg, Caldbeck
Wales Minffordd, Talyllyn
Austria Senger, Heiligenblut; Salome, Lech am Arlberg
France Albert Premier et de Milan, Chamonix; Bellier, Val d'Isère
Switzerland Flüela, Davos Dorf; Metropol, Zermatt

Small hotels with outstanding cuisine

England Bell, Aston Clinton; Mallory Court, Bishops Tachbrook; Uplands, Cartmel; Grafton Manor, Bromsgrove; Gidleigh Park, Chagford; Manoir aux Quat' Saisons, Great Milton; Hintlesham Hall, Hintlesham; Pool Court, Pool-in-Wharfedale; Miller Howe, Windermere; Rookery Hall, Worleston
Scotland Scarista House, Scarista
France Lameloise, Chagny; Prés d'Eugénie, Eugénie-les-Bains; Pyrénées, St-Jean-Pied-de-Port; Pic, Valence; Espérance, Vézelay; Georges Blanc, Vonnas
Netherlands De Swaen, Oisterwijk

Friendly informality/hotel run like a private house

England Little Hemingfold, Battle; Frog Street Farm, Beercrocombe; Little Hodgeham, Bethersden; Appletree Holme Farm, Blawith; Malt House, Broad Campden; Huntsham Court, Huntsham; Howe Villa, Richmond; Reeds, Poughill
Wales Rhyd-Garn-Wen, Cardigan; Penlan Oleu, Llanychaer
Scotland Ard-na-Coille, Newtonmore; Tiroran House, Tiroran
France Les Prouillacs, St-Amand-de-Vergt; Château de Roussan, St-Rémy-de-Provence
Italy Peralta, Camaiore; Rigatti, Florence; Cavarchione Toscanum, Gaiole in Chianti
Portugal Paço da Gloria, Arcos de Valdevez
Turkey Perili Köşk, Datça

Hotels with good amenities for children

England Crantock Bay, Crantock; Bedruthan Steps, Mawgan Porth; Penmere Manor, Falmouth; Dalmeny, St-Anne's-on-Sea; Tides Reach, Salcombe
Austria Madrisa, Gargellen
France Étrier Camarguais, Les Stes-Maries-de-la-Mer

How to read the entries

As in previous editions, entries are in two parts – a citation, usually endorsed by one or several names, followed by relevant information about accommodation, amenities, location and tariffs. We must emphasise once again that the length or brevity of an entry is not a reflection of the quality of a hotel. The size of an entry is determined in part by what we feel needs to be said to convey a hotel's special flavour and in part by the character and interest of the commendation. In general, country hotels get more space than city hotels because the atmosphere of the hotel matters more with the former and also because it is often helpful, when a hotel is in a relatively remote or little-known area, for the entry to say something about the location.

The names at the end of the citation are of those who have nominated that hotel or endorsed the entry that appeared in a previous edition. Some entries are entirely or largely quoted from one report; if several names follow such an entry, we have distinguished writers of quoted material by putting their names first. We do not give the names of those who have sent us adverse reports – though their contributions are every bit as important as the laudatory ones.

The factual material also varies in length. Some hotels provide a wide variety of facilities, others very little. But the paucity of information provided in some cases may derive from the fact that the hotel has failed to return our detailed questionnaire or send us a brochure. All hotels in the British Isles have completed our form, but the same is not true for continental hotels, even though we send out our questionnaire in five languages, and repeat the operation for any recalcitrants a month later. Around a quarter of the hotels in the second half of the book ignore our form or return it months later when the Guide has gone to press. In these instances, we have to rely on the information available from national tourist offices. The fact that no lounge or bar is mentioned in an entry does not mean that a hotel lacks public rooms – only that we can't be sure. The same applies to availability of parking, which we aim to mention in the case of town and city hotels. As to tariffs, in those cases where we have had no communication with a hotel, or where it was unable to give next year's rates, we print the 1987 tariffs, making it clear that these are last year's terms.

Our italicised entries are different this year. There are more of them, and they indicate hotels which we feel are worth considering, but which for various reasons – inadequate information, lack of feedback, ambivalent reports – do not at the moment justify a full entry. A hotel whose entry is in italics, with briefer information about its tariffs and facilities, need not be thought of as a half-good establishment, only as one about which we are eager to have more opinions. We hope that, with the help of such feedback, many will rate full entries next year.

There is a limit to the amount of "nuts and bolts" that can be given in any guide book, and we are against providing, as some other guide books do, a lot of potted information in complicated, hard-to-decipher hieroglyphic form. [GFG] after the hotel's name indicates that the hotel has an entry in the 1988 edition of our sibling publication, *The Good Food Guide*. Days and months are abbreviated, but virtually the only other shorthand we use is "B&B" for bed and breakfast and "alc" for à la carte; the "full alc" price is the hotel's estimate per person for a three-course meal and a half-bottle of modest wine, including service and taxes. Following a spate of complaints about hotels which refuse bookings of only one night we have asked hotels about their booking policy in our questionnaire and print their reply in the Terms section.

We try to give as much information as possible (ground-floor rooms, lifts, etc) to enable disabled people to judge whether or not a hotel will be suitable for them. If a hotel tells us it has special facilities for the disabled we give details; if we know it is not suitable we say so. But we do sometimes lack precise information; disabled people should *always* check with the hotel.

There is one crucial point that must be emphasised with regard to the tariffs: their relative unreliability. We ask hotels when they complete our questionnaire in the spring of one year to make an informed guess at their tariffs the following year. There are many reasons why this is a difficult exercise. Please don't rely on the figures printed. *You should always check at the time of booking and not blame the hotel or the Guide if the prices are wrong.*

Terms are difficult enough to cope with at the best of times. A few hotels have a standard rate for all rooms regardless of season and length of stay, but most operate a highly complicated system which varies from low season to high (and some have a medium-high season as well), according to length of stay, whether there is a bathroom *en suite* and, in the case of most British hotels, whether a room is in single or double occupancy. And, on top of all that, most British hotels offer breaks of one kind or another, but rarely of the same kind. When we can, we give a room rate rather than a rate per person and hope thereby to give a reliable idea of what people, especially those travelling on their own, can expect to pay. When figures are given without mention of single or double rooms they indicate the range of tariffs per person. Lowest rates are what you pay for the simplest room, or out of season, or both; highest rates are for the "best" rooms – and in high season if the hotel has one. Meal prices are per person. VAT and service are included unless we state otherwise.

If you are going for two days or more to a hotel in the British Isles, it will pay you to find out the exact terms of any special offers available. Sometimes these bargain terms are amazing value, and can apply throughout the year, not just in the winter, but they may call for some adjustment in your holiday plans in order to qualify. We also strongly advise you to check whether a hotel is open before making a long detour. We try in all cases to give accurate information, but hotels, particularly small ones, do sometimes close at times when they have told us they expect to be open. And hotels on the Continent often have a weekly closing date, but fail to make this clear when returning our questionnaire. Finally, they do not always give reliable information about whether or not they take credit cards. If it is vital to you, please check.

We end with our customary exhortation: we implore readers to tell us of any errors of omission or commission in both the descriptive and the informative parts of the entries. We make constant efforts to improve our information under "Location", especially with the more out-of-the-way places, but would be very grateful if readers would let us know of any cases where they have found our directions inadequate. We recognise what an imposition it is to be asking readers to write us letters or fill in report forms, but it is essential that people do let us know their views if the Guide is to meet consumer needs as well as it can.

Part one

England
Wales
Scotland
Channel Islands
Republic of Ireland

England

THE WOODMANS ARMS AUBERGE, HASTINGLEIGH

ABBERLEY Hereford and Worcester **Map 2**

The Elms Hotel
Abberley
Nr Worcester WR6 6AT

Tel Great Witley (029 921) 666
Telex 337105 ELMS

Our first entry in the Guide since its first edition – "a worthy opener" we used to say. Beautiful grand Queen Anne house, though with modern wings, in 13 acres of parkland with formal gardens, tennis, and exceptional herb garden. Hotel was privately owned till a few years back but was then bought by one company and in February 1987 sold to another. Rita Mooney, manager from way back, is still in charge, and all reports, without exception, speak warmly of staff. But many other details, heating of rooms, in particular, are criticised. There have been repeated changes of chef. No news as we go to press of the calibre of John Daniels, now wearing the toque. *We would welcome more reports – on the cooking and all else – and hope we can dub* The Elms *"worthy opener" once again next year. 27 rooms, 25 with bath. B&B £37–£52. Set lunch £11.95, dinner £18.*

Manor Arms at Abberley *Tel* Great Witley (029 921) 507
Abberley WR6 6BN

A traditional though superior village inn – offered as an alternative to the rich pastures of The Elms *above. All ten rooms have bathrooms* en suite *and* TV. *Trad English breakfast is said to carry most people until dinner. Closed at Christmas. B&B £18.25–£29.50. New nomination: reports please, including on the dinners.*

ALSTON Cumbria **Map 4**

Lovelady Shield Country House Hotel *Tel* Alston (0498) 81203
Alston CA9 3LF

A spate of enthusiastic letters endorses good reports of this late Regency house, set in a two-acre garden sheltered by a wooded hillside and bordered by the river Nent, high up in the lovely wild scenery of the Pennines. Picturesque Alston, England's highest market town, is nearby, and Hadrian's Wall, the Scottish Borders and the Lake District all within touring distance. Barry Rosier is an attentive host, and his French wife Annie's cooking, and use of fresh local produce in an interesting menu offering both English and French dishes, is much praised. "There is, clearly, an inspired cook in charge in the kitchen." The wine list is approved for balance and its good selection of half-bottles. "Service throughout was both friendly and efficient." There was one lone voice raised, liking the hotel, but objecting to too much pink in the decor, and lace cloths. (*Mr and Mrs Bailhache; also LT Silver, Ian and Anne Steel, WK Reid, RCJ Gordon, G and D Jones*)

Open Mid-Mar–mid-Dec.
Rooms 10 double, 2 single – 8 with bath, 4 with shower, all with TV and baby-listening.
Facilities Reception lounge/library, cocktail bar, drawing room, dining room. 2½-acre gardens on river bank with tennis and croquet. Golf, shooting, fishing and walking nearby.
Location From Alston take road for Stanhope; after 2½ m hotel signs appear on left; hotel is down long drive. Carpark for 20 cars.
Restrictions Not suitable for ♿. Very young children not allowed in dining room during dinner. Dogs by prior arrangement only; not in public rooms.
Credit cards Amex, Diners.
Terms (No service charge) B&B £25–£28; dinner, B&B £36–£40. Vegetarian diets catered for with prior notice. Reduced rates in early season (except Easter) for stays of 2 or more nights; weekly rates. Reduced rates for children sharing parents' room; special meals.
Service/tipping "No service charge is added to bills. All tips are pooled and divided among all staff at the end of the month in exact proportion to number of hours worked."

Hotels are dropped if we lack positive feedback. If you can endorse an entry, please do so.

Deadlines: nominations for the 1989 edition should reach us not later than 1 May 1988. Latest date for comments on existing entries: 1 June 1988.

AMBLESIDE Cumbria — Map 4

Kirkstone Foot Country House Hotel [GFG]
Kirkstone Pass Road
Ambleside LA22 9EH
Tel Ambleside (053 94) 32232

Reports this year have spoken well of this converted 17th-century manor house in two acres of pretty garden, sufficiently outside Ambleside to be peaceful and quiet. Readers have praised the comfortable and spotlessly clean accommodation, the service, the excellent five-course dinner (no choice until the dessert) using fresh local produce, and the welcome given them by Simon and Jane Bateman. (*Malcolm Cornford, and several others*) Only one indignant voice was raised, by a dog-owner banished to one of the Bateman's self-catering cottages, just vacated by a heavy smoker. *Note:* Half board terms only. More reports please.

Open 12 Feb–30 Nov.
Rooms 14 double, 1 single – all with bath and/or shower, telephone, radio, TV, tea-making facilities and baby-listening. Self-catering flats and cottages in the grounds.
Facilities Lounge, bar, restaurant. 2-acre garden with croquet. 1 m from Lake Windermere.
Location At Ambleside turn E off A591 Windermere–Keswick road towards Ullswater.
Restrictions Not suitable for ♿. No dogs.
Credit cards All major cards accepted.
Terms (No service charge) Dinner, B&B £24.50–£35. Set dinner £13.25. Spring and autumn breaks; "Wines of the World" weekends. Reduced rates for children; high tea for under 8s.
Service/tipping: "If we could wave a magic wand and eliminate all tipping that would be ideal! But as long as other hotels in our area solicit gratuities and distribute them to staff we are obliged to follow suit. Gratuities are invested and distributed (tax paid) to all staff at the end of the season."

Rothay Manor Hotel [GFG]
Rothay Bridge
Ambleside LA22 0EH
Tel Ambleside (053 94) 33605

Rothay Manor is a handsome Georgian house, once the home of a prosperous Liverpool merchant, and a scheduled building of historical importance for the grace of its design and detail. It is half a mile from Lake Windermere, in a valley surrounded by fine Lakeland mountain scenery, in one-and-a-half acres of garden. It has long been a favourite with readers, and this year is no exception. "The service was charming, the general atmosphere peaceful and relaxing, and excellent vegetarian food was provided for us on request each evening. Probably the highlight of our stay was the scrumptious tea provided each afternoon! Everything is home-made, from the quiche and savoury pastries, to the fruit bread, scones, strawberry jam and rich cakes. Make sure you walk at least ten miles a day." "I have never seen so many extras in a bathroom. The food was quite delicious, not ultra high cuisine, but extremely good and very plentiful." There were a few negative notes: over-heavy food, one bedroom overdue for redecoration, and disturbance from traffic on a busy one-way system close by. (Worth asking for quiet rooms when booking.) But most readers have continued to appreciate the atmosphere of a family-run, caring, comfortable hotel. (*B Watt and T Thorn, Julia Sharpe; also S Parsons, WF Johnson, and others*)

Open Mid-Feb–early Jan.
Rooms Honeymoon suite, 2 family suites (in annexe), 13 double, 2 single – all with bath, telephone, radio and TV; baby-listening in family suite, which is also suitable for ♿. 3 ground-floor rooms.
Facilities 3 lounges (1 with bar), 2 dining rooms. 1½-acre garden with croquet. Near river Rothay and Lake Windermere (¼ m). Steamer service, sailing and water-skiing nearby; also river and lake fishing, riding and golf.
Location On A593 SW of Ambleside towards Coniston. Garden-facing rooms quietest.
Restriction No dogs.
Credit cards All major cards accepted.
Terms (Service at guests' discretion) B&B: single £44–£50, double £62–£80, suite £84–£100; dinner, B&B: single £52–£68, double £82–£116, suite £102–£134. Buffet lunch Mon–Sat £6; set Sun lunch £10, dinner £18. Winter events such as wine-tastings; Victorian Christmas dinner and party; reduced rates Nov–Mar especially mid-week. Reduced rates for children sharing parents' room; special meals.

Wateredge Hotel *Tel* Ambleside (053 94) 32332
Borrans Road
Ambleside LA22 0EP

The eponymously-named *Wateredge* – originally a pair of 17th-century fisherman's cottages – has a choice position at the head of Windermere looking down the length of the lake as well as having views of Loughrigg Fells and other famous landmarks. It has been in the Guide for many years, and our reports seem to grow warmer each year. The good news for *Wateredge* regulars this year is that all rooms now have bathrooms *en suite* and five new luxury suites have been added to last year's complement. Small baskets of fruit are now being put in bedrooms. Bouquets from the 1986/87 postbag: "We have just returned from France where my wife repeatedly said: "Oh for the *Wateredge*, for its six-course dinners!" (*M Fagan*) "Our fourth visit – and we can't fault it. Everything home-made including breakfast croissants." (*Barbara Wooldridge*) "Its central location in the Lake District, its beautiful site and its reasonable rates especially in the spring – the best time in the Lakes – make us want to look no further for our regular place to stay. On our recent visit, we looked for any signs of slippage and all we found was that main-course plates were not hot enough on a couple of evenings. Otherwise it lived up to all our happy memories." (*JP Berryman; also JT Mills*) Lakeside traffic, heavy at weekends, passes close by; only two rooms, however, face the road.

Open Feb–Nov.
Rooms 5 suites, 16 double, 2 single – all with bath and/or shower, TV and tea-making facilities.
Facilities 3 lounges, TV room, bar, 2 dining rooms. 3-acre grounds with 200-ft lake frontage, private jetty, rowing boats and sailing boat available to guests free of charge; fishing and safe bathing. Good centre for walkers and climbers.
Location ½ m S of town; just off A591 at Waterhead on Kendal/Keswick road. (Front rooms can be noisy.)
Restrictions Not suitable for ♿. No children under 7. No dogs in public rooms.
Credit cards Access, Amex, Visa.
Terms (Service at guests' discretion) B&B £22.50–£39; dinner, B&B £29.50–£50. Reduced rates in low season. 1-night bookings sometimes refused. Half rates for children sharing parents' room.
Service/tipping: "No service charge. All tips are distributed equally to all staff."

ASTON CLINTON Buckinghamshire — Map 1

The Bell Inn [GFG]
Aston Clinton HP22 5HP

Tel Aylesbury (0296) 630252
Telex 83252 BELINN

The name suggests a rustic country pub. It was indeed an inn in 1650, on the estates of the Duke of Buckingham, a convenient point for a change of horses between his palaces at Stowe and on London's Mall. *The Bell* then became a coaching inn, on what is still a busy main road. All that remains of its humble beginnings are a small parlour with panelled walls, stone-flagged floors and an open fire. The rest has become a very grand restaurant, with a luxurious pavilion across the road for weddings and conferences, and 21 bedrooms, 15 of which are in the converted stables. There are tables to eat outside in the summer, a well-tended garden; in the stable courtyard hanging baskets of bright flowers, trees in tubs, and climbing plants give an almost Spanish air. The Harris family have been here since 1939, and run a smart wine business as well as the hotel and restaurant. The sophisticated dining room has painted murals of the four seasons, and other tables are in a long narrow room overlooking the garden. The original inn bedrooms – some with four-poster – have lovely antiques. "Most polite, efficient and quick service. Delightful bedroom charmingly decorated, plenty of space. Fresh fruit in the room, bed turned down at night, super clean bath towels at the same time." (*Mrs MD Prodgers*) But there have also been small irritations: ice cubes entombed in frozen fridge; twin beds pushed together purporting to be a double bed; a distracting tour of the murals while diners were eating; disappointing dishes for a vegetarian; and a vast breakfast tray arriving with the wrong items. As we go to press we learn of a new head chef.

Open All year. Limited menu on Sun evening and Mon.
Rooms 6 suites, 15 double (available as single) – all with bath, shower, telephone, radio and TV. 16 in annexe around courtyard. 7 ground-floor rooms.
Facilities Drawing room, bar, smoking room, restaurant; pavilion for conferences, banquets, etc. 3-acre grounds. Wine shop. Fishing nearby.
Location On A41, 4 m SE of Aylesbury (exit 8 off M1 for A41, or exit 11 for B489). Light sleepers should specifically request quiet rooms (some rooms double-glazed).
Restriction Dogs by arrangement, only in bedrooms with owners' blanket.
Credit cards Access, Visa.
Terms B&B (continental): single occupancy from £55, double from £77, suite from £97. English breakfast £5.20. Set lunch £12.50; special menu for residents' dinner Sun and Mon £15; alc lunch or dinner (excluding wine) £20–£34. Reduced rates for children sharing parents' room; special meals by arrangement.
Service/tipping: "A 12½% service charge is included, but guests sometimes give extra, which goes direct to staff, shared."

The Good Hotel Guide is published in the United States and Canada under the title *Europe's Wonderful Little Hotels and Inns.* Its success in North America has led to a sister publication on American and Canadian hotels based on the same principles. Readers with recent experience of good hotels in North America are urged to send their nominations to Sandra W Soule, *America's Wonderful Little Hotels and Inns,* PO Box 150, Riverside Avenue, Riverside Conn. 06878, USA.

BAGSHOT Surrey — Map 1

Pennyhill Park Hotel
College Ride
Bagshot GU19 5ET

Tel (0276) 71774
Telex 858841 PHPARK

A lavish country-club and hotel, well-equipped for conferences. Not perhaps our scene, but this large 1849 mansion does retain something of the atmosphere of the grand private house it was until only a few years ago. The bedrooms, recently refurbished, are large and comfortable, some with period bathrooms. The grounds are magnificent – 112 acres with a nine-hole golf course, tennis courts, stables, and fishing in an enormous private lake. Staff are friendly, and the hotel is well-placed for visits to Windsor or Epsom. Prices are high; there is very little competition in this area.

Open All year.
Rooms 10 suites, 38 double – all with bath, shower, telephone, radio, TV and baby-listening. 31 in 2 annexes. Some ground-floor rooms, some with wide doors.
Facilities Lounge, bar, restaurant; conference facilities. 112-acre grounds with country club: bar, lounge, restaurant; golf, swimming pool, tennis, fishing, clay pigeon shooting, riding.
Location ½ m SW of Bagshot village; take exit 3 off M3.
Restriction Dogs by arrangement only; not in hotel rooms.
Credit cards All major cards accepted.
Terms (No service charge) Rooms: single & double £68, suite £110–£150. Breakfast: continental £5.50–£6.50, English £4.50. Set lunch £18, dinner £25; full alc £40. Weekend breaks; Christmas programme. Children free if sharing parents' room; special meals on request.

"The breakfast room is a horror story unless you positively love making convivial conversation with complete strangers each morning. There is one large round table where all guests (about 12 when I was there) have to sit with elbows almost touching. Mrs . . . takes pleasure in ensuring that people who are staying together sit apart at breakfast. She enters regally at intervals to make tedious and repetitive comments about how absolutely wonderful her food is. She even had the impertinence to try to insist that I take sugar with my porridge."

"At the cocktail bar we were told that we would be invited to our table about 45 minutes after giving our order. My mother doesn't like to eat late, so she asked Mr . . . if there was anything on the menu which wouldn't take that long. Oh dear. Mr . . . drew himself up to his full considerable height and lectured us lengthily into submission on the virtues of freshly-prepared food and the sacrifices to be made thereto. We were hushed and shamed. 'But surely,' Mother bravely continued, 'the melon . . .' 'The melon, Madame,' intoned Mr . . .' is not simply a melon. It is in balls. It is cut up by a melon-balling machine. It is doused in blackcurrant liqueur and garnished with sprays of blackcurrant. Of course if you wish for another kind of meal altogether, you can always go into the bar and order a bar snack.'"

BARNSTAPLE Devon — Map 1

Downrew House
Bishops Tawton
Barnstaple EX32 0DY

Tel Barnstaple
(0271) 42497 and 46673

Downrew House was built around 1640, but enlarged during the reign of Queen Anne. It is a few miles from Barnstaple, facing south onto 15 acres of meadowland and gardens, with countryside views of up to 20 miles from all the windows. Desmond and Aleta Ainsworth, here since they opened *Downrew* in the mid-sixties, provide many facilities indoor and out, and the same standard of comfort in the main house, the West Wing annexe, and the Lodge. It has enjoyed flattering entries in the Guide for many years past, and has had its share of praise this year too. "Perfection is the word. I was the only guest on the first day of opening for the season but you wouldn't have known it – no corners cut in service, food etc, including having a huge log fire in the drawing room in spite of their being told I was going to bed early." "An outstandingly well-run hotel . . . deserves all your accolades." (*CT, and others*) But there has been criticism, too: hints of petty economies, pretentious decor, poor insulation between rooms and a lack of cordiality on the part of one of the owners. More reports please.

Open 26 Mar–27 Dec.
Rooms 2 suites, 14 double, – all with bath and shower, direct-dial telephone, radio and TV. 5 in West Wing, 2 in Lodge (with tea-making facilities). 2 ground floor rooms.
Facilities Drawing room, music room, bar, dining room; billiard room, card room, games room, solarium; laundry. 12-acre grounds with putting course, croquet, tennis and swimming pool (heated Easter–Sept). Free fishing 1¼ m; beaches 10-20 minutes' drive.
Location 4 m S of Barnstaple on A377, take unclassified turning signposted to Chittlehampton by BP filling station just S of Bishops Tawton. *Downrew* is 1¼ m further on.
Restrictions Not suitable for ♿. No children under 7. No dogs except in Lodge.
Credit cards None accepted.
Terms (No service charge) Dinner, B&B: single occupancy £44.90–£46.14, double £73.82–£77.50, suite £81.20–£89.12. Set dinner £16.60. Buffet lunch available. Reductions for long stays; 3-day Christmas package. Reduced rates for children sharing parents' room; special meals.
Service/tipping: "No service charge. If guests leave money for staff it is shared equally among all."

BARWICK Somerset — Map 2

Little Barwick House [GFG]
Barwick, Yeovil BA22 9TD

Tel Yeovil (0935) 23902

Further improvements to Christopher and Veronica Colley's Georgian dower-house restaurant-with-rooms, and further satisfied guests: "The Colleys gave us a friendly and warm welcome. Although the atmosphere is informal, their high professional standards are always evident. A tray of tea appeared each afternoon a few minutes after we arrived – most welcome. Dinners were eagerly awaited and fully up to expectations. Breakfasts first class." (*Mr and Mrs RJ Faircliff*) "The old village of Barwick is attractive, minuscule and tucked away down a lane carved through the rock. *Little Barwick House* looks out across the valley towards the village with its church and outlying obelisks on the skyline. A calm setting with a generous foreground of private garden. Our room on the top floor was very comfortable, pretty and well-equipped. The furniture was partly turn-of-the-century and partly modern. It included a sumptuous sofa." (*WH Bruton*) "This . . . is the sort of small hotel that a lot of people who read this Guide hope to find." (*A and J Lloyd; also D Neville-Jones, Dr and Mrs DS Wright*) Some bedrooms are small.

Open All year except Christmas.
Rooms 6 double – all with bath and shower, radio, TV and tea-making facilities.
Facilities Lounge, cellar bar, dining room. 3½-acre garden.
Location Follow signs from Yeovil to Dorchester (A37). Turn left off A37 at the Red House pub. Hotel is ¼ m on left.
Restrictions Not suitable for ♿. Dogs only with advance notice, not in public rooms.
Credit cards All major cards accepted.
Terms B&B: £27.50; dinner, B&B £42. Vegetarian and special diets catered for. Winter breaks; 1 night's accommodation free in any 2 days' stay if dinner taken both nights. 1-night bookings refused on Sun if hotel is empty. Reduced rates and special menus for children.
Service/tipping: "Service is included, but any money left is divided among the staff."

BASLOW Derbyshire — Map 4

Cavendish Hotel
Baslow, Bakewell DE4 1SP
Tel Baslow (024 688) 2311
Telex 547150 CAVTEL

Once a fishing inn, now an elegant hotel, on the edge of the beautiful parkland of the Chatsworth Estate, which all the rooms overlook. One of the few luxury hotels in the Peak District, the *Cavendish* is run with style by Eric Marsh. Rooms vary in size and style – worth discussing when booking – but all are warm and comfortable , and some have furniture made here by estate carpenters. Mrs Marsh is responsible for the beautiful flower arrangements in the public rooms. Improvements are reported in the food, with the bar snacks commended, especially the hotel's own venison sausage. No comments so far about the introduction last year of guests' ringside seats in the kitchen itself. Prices are high. More reports please. (*H Gholson, and others*)

Open All year.
Rooms 1 suite, 23 double – all with bath and shower, direct-dial telephone, radio, TV, tea-making facilities and mini-bar. 2 ground-floor rooms.
Facilities Lounge, bar, restaurant; private dining room for 10 people. Small grounds with golf practice (putting green and driving net); fishing in rivers Derwent and Wye.
Location On A619 in Chatsworth grounds (leave M1 at exit 29).
Restrictions Not suitable for ♿. No dogs.
Credit cards All major cards accepted.
Terms [1987 rates] (No service charge) Rooms: single occupancy £50-£57.50, double £60–£67.50. Breakfast from £3.50. Set lunch and dinner from £15; full alc £20. Cots/extra beds available for children; special meals by request. Winter bonus weekends.
Service/tipping: "No service charge. If a client wishes to leave a tip for staff it is gratefully accepted."

> Don't trust out-of-date Guides. Many hotels are dropped and new ones added every year.

BASSENTHWAITE LAKE Cumbria — Map 4

The Pheasant Inn
Bassenthwaite Lake
Cockermouth CA13 9YE

Tel Bassenthwaite Lake (059 681) 234

The Pheasant Inn, just out of sight of the lake, has kept something of the atmosphere of the 400-year old farm from which it grew. Using water from a pure spring on the hillside nearby, the farmers brewed beer which became so popular that the farm became an inn. Cumbrian owners Mr and Mrs Barrington Wilson still serve real ale, alas no longer brewed on the spot. One correspondent, himself a hotelier, arriving late, was impressed to find a substantial cold supper waiting for him in the dining room. He also appreciated his enormous breakfast, and *The Pheasant*'s good plain cooking. His report ended: "*The Pheasant*, to my mind, is the epitome of the traditional inn. It is surrounded by an old-fashioned country garden and some magnificent and peaceful scenery. The grounds and building are lovingly cared for, as are the customers. The beams in the ceilings, the sparkling copper and brass-ware, the crackling fires in the grates, the squeaking floorboards, compete with the ever-present buzz of conversation and local dialect, the hotel cat asleep on the best chair, the attentive staff always smiling and seemingly happy with their lot." (*Christopher Davy*) These impressions have been echoed by others though one reader was disappointed by a cramped and austere bedroom.

Open All year except Christmas Day.
Rooms 16 double, 4 single – 18 with bath, 2 with shower. 3 in bungalow annexe, all with tea-making facilities; ramps available.
Facilities 3 lounges (2 for residents), bar, dining room; facilities for private parties and small conferences. 1½-acre grounds. Sailing, fishing, pony-trekking and golf nearby.
Location 7 m NW of Keswick just off A66 (on W side of Bassenthwaite Lake).
Restrictions No dogs in bedrooms or dining room. No smoking in dining room.
Credit cards None accepted.
Terms Dinner, B&B: single £40, double £76. Set Sunday lunch £7.30; set dinner £12.80. Bar snacks available. Winter breaks. 1-night bookings for Sat sometimes refused.
Service/tipping: 10% service charge included in rates and distributed on a point system to all staff.

BATH Avon — Map 2

Holly Lodge
8 Upper Oldfield Park,
Bath BA2 3JZ

Tel Bath (0225) 24042

Unanimous approval from readers as far apart as Santa Barbara, California, and Truro, Cornwall, for Mrs Carolle Sellick's non-smoking, bed-and-breakfast hotel, with its fresh flowers and "immaculate taste . . . interiors match and surpass most top flight country house hotels". (*G Still*) Our inspector's impressions were just as favourable: "Another star in Bath's well-studded firmament. *Holly Lodge* is a large Victorian house, high up on the slopes opposite the city, with a wonderful night-time view across the valley. With luck and a little neck-craning you can see the floodlit Abbey from your bedroom window, and in the morning I realised I was looking straight across at the Royal Crescent . . . My bedroom was beautiful. Everything pale grey and blue, with biggish entrance lobby and bathroom taken off at the end, and archway leading into the bedroom, which was still really spacious . . . TV, trouser press, tea tray, wardrobe, dressing table, padded window seat for enjoying aforementioned view. Good towels, shampoos, shoe-cleaning sachets." She confirms the universally good impressions of a light, airy breakfast room, with its daffodil yellow and apple green decor, and of the excellent breakfast served there, with wholemeal toast, home-made jams, good coffee, fresh fruit and wide selection of cooked breakfasts. (*R Robins, RA Gale, JM Zimmer, CC Berlin*)

Open All year.
Rooms 5 double, 1 single – all with bath and/or shower, telephone, radio, TV and tea-making facilities.
Facilities Lounge, breakfast room. ½-acre garden.
Location ½ m W of town centre, 1st right off Wells Road (A367). Carpark.
Restrictions Not suitable for ♿. No dogs. No smoking.
Credit cards Access, Visa.
Terms B&B: single £25–£30, double £38–£48. Off-season reductions for 2 nights or more. Reductions for children sharing parents' room.

Number Nine Hotel *Tel* Bath (0225) 25462
Miles Buildings, Bath BA1 2QS *Telex* 449212 LANTEL ref 262

A distinguished early 18th-century house designed by John Wood the Elder, at the end of a quiet pedestrianised cul-de-sac off George Street, in the middle of Georgian Bath. Bedrooms are pretty and comfortable, even lavish – occasionally over the top, though we had one complaint of inadequate reading lights and the absence of a full-length mirror. There is a small garden, a nearby lock-up garage, opportunity for temporary membership of an upmarket health club for those working at being fit, and dinner provided by prior arrangement. More pricey than some of the other Bath B&Bs, but central and quiet. The owners, Sue and Paul Hayward, tell us that, in response to last year's criticism, they have upgraded their breakfasts: superior coffee and no more plastic containers for jams and butters. More reports please.

Open All year.
Rooms 1 suite, 8 double – 2 with bath and shower (1 has jacuzzi), 7 with shower only, all with telephone, TV and tea-making facilities. Suite and 2 rooms (1 on ground floor) in mews cottage close to main building.
Facilities Lounge, dining room. Small garden. Guests can use facilities of the Bath House, a nearby health club.
Location Central, near Assembly Rooms, but quietly situated on walkway on high pavement off George Street. Hotel will park guests' cars.
Restrictions No children under 16. No dogs.
Credit cards All major cards accepted.
Terms (No service charge) B&B: single occupancy £50–£55, double £60–£85, suite £80–£95. Dinner by arrangement, £25.
Service/tipping: "We do not agree with tipping; guests are paying for a service, they should not have to pay twice."

> We invited all British hotels to tell us of their policy on service charges and tipping. Many hotels ignored this question. Replies, when given, are printed at the end of an entry.

Paradise House Hotel *Tel* Bath (0225) 317723
86/88 Holloway, Bath BA2 4PX

A civilised bed-and-breakfast establishment, seven minutes by foot down to the Roman Baths, the Pump Room and the Abbey (rather longer and a steep uphill slog on the return journey), in a quiet cul-de-sac, formerly part of the old Roman Fosse Way. The house itself is c. 1720; it has fine views of the Georgian city, and a well-favoured three-quarter-acre garden. Recent visitors confirm an earlier report, and its writer has since returned on her honeymoon and found everything as much to her liking as before: "Lots of Laura Ashley and Designers Guild-type wallpaper and curtains. Rooms freshly decorated. Comfortable brass bed with duvet; good chairs for watching TV. Nice ornaments and mirrors. Residents' lounge with Habitat sofas and newspapers." (*Kathleen Kelly*)

Open Feb–Nov.
Rooms 2 suites, 6 double – 5 with bath, 1 with shower, all with TV, tea-making facilities and baby-listening. 1 ground floor room with good access for ♿.
Facilities Sitting room, breakfast room. ¾-acre garden with patios and croquet lawn.
Location 7 minutes' walk from centre. Entering city on A4 turn left at first main traffic lights onto A36, A367, Wells and Exeter ring road. At large roundabout (bisected by railway viaduct) take first left (A367 Exeter road). Continue up hill, the Wellsway, about ¾ m; turn left at small shopping area near Dewhurst butcher; continue left down hill into cul-de-sac. Hotel is 200 yds on left. Garages and parking.
Restriction No dogs.
Credit cards Access, Visa.
Terms B&B: single £28–£41, double £33–£48, suite £40–£48. Reduced rates for stays of 5 nights or more and for children sharing parents' room. (No restaurant; hotel can make dinner reservations in restaurants.) Advisable to book at least 2 months in advance Easter–end Oct. 1-night bookings may be refused for Saturdays.

The Priory Hotel [GFG] *Tel* Bath (0225) 331922
Weston Road, Bath BA1 2XT *Telex* 44612

The Priory is on the north-west side of Bath, a mile from the centre, high up on the hillside. It is close to the road in the front, but there are two acres of gardens at the back, with neat, green lawns, exuberant flower beds, huge old trees, and a heated swimming pool at the far end. The big grey neo-Gothic, 19th-century house is surprisingly light inside. There are beautifully carved decorative friezes round the high ceilings, and the decor is in pale pastels, peach, soft green and beige, with pretty floral curtains. Furnishings in the public rooms and the bedrooms are luxurious and comfortable. Service, if not always impeccable, is friendly and helpful. There are three different dining rooms, including a new Garden Room and adjoining Orangery. New head chef, Michael Collom, recently spent a sabbatical at Michel Lorain's renowned restaurant *À la Côte Saint-Jacques* at Joigny (q.v.) and this is reflected in many of the dishes he is now producing. Glasses have been raised to Collom's cooking; the menu prices have raised some eyebrows too.

Open All year.
Rooms 18 double, 3 single – 20 with bath and shower, 1 with shower only, all with telephone, radio and TV; some 4-poster.

Facilities Drawing room, morning room, restaurant in 3 rooms. 2-acre grounds with croquet and swimming pool (heated May–Oct).
Location ¾ m NW of centre of Bath, just beyond Royal Victoria Park. Detailed directions on brochure. Parking.
Restrictions Only public rooms suitable for ♿. No children under 10. No dogs.
Credit cards All major cards accepted.
Terms B&B (continental): single from £50, double from £92. English breakfast £7. Full alc £30. Weekend and mid-week breaks out of season; Christmas package.

Somerset House *Tel* Bath (0225) 66451 and 63471
35 Bathwick Hill
Bath BA2 6LD

Hotel or up-market guest house? Sometimes the distinction is hard to make, but we would put *Somerset House*, firmly in the latter category. That is in no sense to denigrate it, and in fact Jane and Malcolm Seymour's handsome Regency mansion a short drive or bus-ride or stiffish walk uphill from the city centre has much to recommend it, not least its reasonable tariff. Rooms are immaculately maintained, and nearly all have baths *en suite*. There are attractive public rooms and a particularly agreeable basement dining room. Moreover the Seymours take great pride in their traditional English cooking, grow much of their own produce and care about the quality of their suppliers. Dinners – breakfasts too – come in for many compliments. But it is an establishment very much with its own style – wholly congenial to many, irksome to some. It is a strict no-smoking house for a start; dinner is served between 7 and 7.30 pm; guests are expected to be punctual and may be invited to share tables. No TV or radio in the bedrooms. But *Somerset House* has never lacked enthusiastic endorsers, as many this year as before. (*ME Kirk, GM Morrison, John Hogg, Jane Butler*) The Seymours tell us they no longer accept B&B only bookings except for a minimum two-night stay when guests cannot arrive until late.

Open All year except Jan. Dining room open for lunch Sun only; closed Sun evening.
Rooms 8 double, 1 single – 8 with bath, 1 with shower, all with telephone and tea-making facilities. 1 ground-floor room.
Facilities 2 lounges (1 with TV), dining room. 1½-acre garden with trees, shrubs and 7¼-inch gauge model railway. 5 minutes from Kennet and Avon Canal – angling for temporary members at Bathampton Angling Club; canal boat trips. 15 minutes' walk from centre.
Location Junction of Bathwick Hill (which leads to Bath University) and Cleveland Walk. Carpark.
Restrictions Not suitable for ♿. No smoking. No children under 10. Small dogs allowed in bedrooms only.
Credit cards Access, Visa.
Terms (No service charge) Dinner, B&B £31. Set Sun lunch £7.65, dinner £11.50. Vegetarian and simple diets catered for. Mid-week breaks; special interest weekends: e.g. Georgian Bath, Roman Bath, Brunel, etc. Christmas and New Year packages. 1-night bookings sometimes refused. Reduced rates for children sharing parents' room; special meals.

> Always let a hotel know if you have to cancel a booking, whether you have paid a deposit or not. Hotels lose thousands of pounds and dollars from "no-shows".

Sydney Gardens Hotel *Tel* Bath (0225) 64818 and 445362
Sydney Road, Bath BA2 6NT

A handsome Italianate Victorian villa, ten minutes from the city centre; you can park your car in the grounds. B&B only, and a no-smoking hotel. We have had a shoal of letters praising, *The Sydney Gardens Hotel,* its location, and the kindness of the owners, Stanley and Diane Smithson. "A lovely, warm, welcoming, friendly, elegant house. The view from the enormous sash window was magical. We arrived at dusk and Bath looked like a gigantic pincushion starred with lights (I must add that the train rushes through a tunnel under here and gives you a bit of a fright, but you soon get used to it!) The owner is an artist of some repute, and his paintings and ceramic clocks adorn the walls. Everything is scrupulously clean and well-kept." (*Patricia Roberts; also many others*)

Open All year except 3–21 Jan.
Rooms 6 double, 1 single – 5 with bath and shower, all with TV and tea-making facilities.
Facilities Lounge, breakfast room. ¼-acre garden; private gateway to park and walk along adjacent Kennet and Avon canal.
Location From A4 turn left onto A36 ring road towards Exeter and Wells. Cross Avon; gateway to Sydney Gardens is directly ahead. Turn right, pass Holbourne Museum on left, turn left. Hotel is 200 yards up slope on left. From South the approach road (A36) takes you past the hotel.
Parking.
Restrictions Not suitable for ♿. No children under 4. Small dogs only. No smoking.
Credit cards Access, Visa.
Terms (No service charge) B&B: single £25–£28, double £35–£48. Extra bed £12. 1-night bookings sometimes refused. (No restaurant.)
Service/tipping: "As we run the business ourselves, we do not expect tips. However, anything left for the chambermaid is appreciated."

BATHFORD Avon — Map 2

Eagle House *Tel* Bath (0225) 859946
Church Street
Bathford BA1 7RS

This newcomer is an imposing listed Georgian building by John Wood the Elder, in a quiet conservation village three miles from Bath. All the rooms look out over either countryside or the one-and-a-half-acre garden. "Cool entrance hall leads towards the large and very handsome drawing room, with plenty of well-spaced chairs and sofas, tables with magazines, fine marble fireplace. Upstairs is a generous landing with sofas, chests of drawers etc, and bedrooms off. Mine was large (the largest in the house) with two lovely low windows over the garden; ample bathroom carved out with no real detriment to the room; nice cotton sheets on the bed, which had been turned down when I came back at night." No dinner is served, but there are plenty of small restaurants and pubs nearby, and in Bath. Both owners and decor were pleasant and unobtrusive, there were childrens' toys cheerfully about in the garden, and our inspector liked the lack of fuss and furbelows, finding this a refreshing alternative to staying in Bath itself, "provided you have a car".

Open 5 Jan–23 Dec.
Rooms 5 double, 1 single – all with bath and/or shower, direct-dial telephone, and TV, tea-making facilities; baby-listening on request.
Facilities Drawing room, sitting room, breakfast room. 1½- acre garden with croquet lawn, large sandpit for children.
Location 3 m E of Bath. 300 yards up Bathford Hill, turn first right into Church Street. Hotel is 200 yards on right behind high stone wall and wrought iron gates. Being in conservation area, hotel sign not permitted. Ample parking.
Restrictions Not suitable for ♿. No dogs in public rooms.
Credit cards None accepted.
Terms (No service charge) B&B: single £20–£26, double £30–£37.90. Children free in parents' room. (No restaurant.)
Service/tipping: "Service charge should be included in all tariffs in all hotels; if necessary legislation should be passed to enforce this – with the proviso that guests can leave a tip if they wish to ."

BATTLE East Sussex — Map 3

Little Hemingfold Farmhouse — *Tel* Battle (042 46) 4338
Telham, Battle TN33 0TT

"Farmhouse" may suggest a much more workaday sort of place than this part 17th-century, part early Victorian house filled with books, interesting pictures and fine furniture in an exceptionally tranquil and secluded setting. The buildings – there are rooms in an old coach-house and stables as well as in the farmhouse itself, all grouped round a flowery courtyard – are reached down a fairly steep half-mile track. There are large grounds with gardens, woods and pastures; ducks and moorhens breed on the two-acre lake which is used both for swimming and for fly fishing. The grounds have direct access to the thousand acres of Battle Great Wood, with footpaths to Battle. The Cinque Ports and Hastings are close by. Ann Benton, the resident owner, does the cooking, grows all her own soft fruit and vegetables and bakes her own bread. Evening meals are served communally round a large candle-lit Victorian table. Not a hotel and rather more than a guest-house, but certainly a highly sympathetic set-up." (*Marguerite Dickinson*)

That report was written in 1984, but 1987 guests continue to confirm its accuracy. Since last year, Ann Benton has acquired a further 13 acres to be used for conservation and woodland walks. The paths connect to public footpaths leading in all directions. Meanwhile: "The final bill was disconcertingly modest." (*Dennis Heyderman*) "First class value." (*Diana Rogers*) "An absolute pleasure." (*Christine Saunders*)

Open All year.
Rooms 10 double, 2 single – all with bath, hand shower, direct-dial telephone, radio, TV, tea-making facilities and electric blankets. 6 in converted coach-house and stables. 4 ground-floor rooms.
Facilities 2 lounges (1 for non-smokers), bar, dining room. 40-acre grounds with croquet and badminton; fields, woods, cows; 2-acre lake with trout fishing, swimming and dinghy.
Location 1½ m SE of Battle. From N, about 1½ m from Battle look for road sign indicating bend on left side of road. This sign is at the top of the farm lane. From S, about 1 m past Beauport Park, look for sign indicating bend. Proceed round corner and the farm lane is immediately on right.
Restrictions Not suitable for ♿. No children under 14. Dogs downstairs only.
Credit cards Access, Amex, Visa.
Terms (No service charge) B&B £24; dinner, B&B (including house wine) £30–£36. Set lunch £4; dinner £13. Spring, summer and winter rates for stays of 2, 5,

or 7 nights; Christmas and New Year packages. 1-night bookings sometimes refused at busy times.
Service/tipping: "No service charge. Any tips given are shared among all our staff."

Netherfield Place *Tel* Battle (042 46) 4455
Battle TN33 9PP

Country house hotel peacefully situated in 30 well-kept acres. Young, efficient staff, good food, many small extras. 12 rooms, all with bath and shower. Conference facilities. Double B&B £65–£70. Set dinner £16. New owners since previous entry. First reports favourable. More would be welcome.

BEAMINSTER Dorset Map 2

The Bridge House *Tel* Beaminster (0308) 862200
Beaminster DT8 3AY

Newly nominated as friendly, welcoming little hotel in a 16th-century house in small village. Good home cooking with fresh ingredients; period furniture; small walled garden. No children. 5 rooms with bath or shower. B&B £18. Set dinner £12. More reports welcome.

BEERCROCOMBE Somerset Map 1

Frog Street Farm *Tel* Hatch Beauchamp
Beercrocombe, Taunton (0823) 480430
TA3 6AF

César awarded for outstanding farmhouse hospitality

This "large, airy and beautifully kept" 15th-century farmhouse/guest house continues to bring in enthusiastic letters from readers, not least for its "incredibly modest terms". It stands in a 130-acre working farm, deep in rural Somerset, about 21 miles from the north and south coasts. It has fields and woods on one side, orchards on the other, a heated pool under the cherry trees, and a kind and generous hostess who is also an excellent cook. Two of the bedrooms have private facilities, and the house itself is welcoming. No licence, so you bring your own wine. "What a marvellous place! A pretty bedroom with very comfortable beds. Enormous breakfasts and later a delicious fresh salmon salad followed by rhubarb tart and clotted cream (described on our bill as a snack!)." "A most special and pleasurable experience . . . An unaffected atmosphere of traditional country charm." (*Mrs EF Roberts, Mr and Mrs EO Brown, Richard Porch; also Mrs PM Brooker, BW Ribbons, Mrs B Page, Mr and Mrs SGT England*) Mrs Cole who owns the farm has now decided, "after a lot of thought and consideration", no longer to accept children under 11, as she gets very few requests for family bookings.

Open All year, except Christmas and New Year.
Rooms 2 suites, 2 double, 1 single – 1 with bath, 1 with shower, all with tea-making facilities.
Facilities Lounge, dining room. Secluded garden with heated swimming pool. On 130-acre working farm with trout stream.

Location 7 m SE of Taunton. Leave M5 at exit 25; take A358 to Ilminster, then turning to Hatch Beauchamp. Turn at *Hatch Inn*, down Station Rd. Then left all way down no through road. Signposted.
Restrictions Not suitable for ♿. No children under 11. No dogs.
Credit cards None accepted.
Terms B&B £12–£16; dinner, B&B £22–£36. Set dinner £10. (Unlicensed – bring your own wine.)
Service/tipping: "I don't have any problems with tipping as this is a home rather than a hotel. My visitors love the fact that there are no extras: they come as friends as much as visitors."

BETHERSDEN Kent — Map 3

Little Hodgeham — *Tel* High Halden (023 385) 323
Bull Lane, Bethersden TN26 3HE

Erica Wallace, owner of this half-timbered Tudor cottage in Kent, was brought over from Australia by her mother to be presented at Court as a deb and stayed on to have a career in investigative journalism in London. She has English roots; a proud family heirloom is a receipt for £60 for the sale of New Place, Stratford-on-Avon, to Shakespeare, by an ancestor. When she bought Little Hodgeham in 1971, it was a tumbledown wreck in an overgrown weed patch. Largely with her own hands, she has transformed it into what one reader has called "a gem", removing tile-cladding to reveal ancient beams, laying new floors, hunting down and renovating antiques, creating a flower-filled garden, a pond stocked with carp and tench, and a swimming pool. Fine bone china, 1820s crystal, three double bedrooms with comfortable beds, one a fourposter, beamed ceilings, logfires, tasteful colour-schemes, with fresh flowers from the garden chosen to tone in, and many helpful extras have all been praised. Special diets are "effortlessly and deliciously managed". Erica Wallace, who makes a point of being present to keep dinner party conversation going, and welcomes visitors to the kitchen, says, "I have never had a cooking lesson, never measure anything, don't use recipes, but have a feel for food." This is a private house, with a house-party atmosphere appreciated by those who enjoy meeting their fellow guests. As when staying with friends, there is no choice of menu or wine list, though the menu changes every day. Those seeking full hotel amenities should look elsewhere; what *Little Hodgeham* aims to offer is a warmer welcome or better value for money. (*Mme Dibiffe, ME Burnheim, Lucy and Brian Clarke, Ralph Lambert, J Outram, B Solomon*)

Open Mid-Mar–Oct
Rooms 1 family, 2 double – 2 with bath, 1 with shower, all with radio, tea-making facilities and baby-listening; 1 4-poster.
Facilities Drawing room, TV room, small conservatory, dining room. ½-acre garden with unheated swimming pool. Fishing in pond stocked with carp and tench. Tennis and golf nearby.
Location 10 m W of Ashford. From Bethersden take Smarden road for 2 m.
Restrictions Not suitable for ♿. Small children not really welcome. Dogs by prior arrangement, not in public rooms.
Credit cards None accepted.
Terms (No service charge) Dinner, B&B £32. Reductions for stays of 4 nights or more. Reduced rates for children sharing parents' room, depending on age; special meals with advance warning.
Service/tipping: "The price is, and always has been, inclusive. Anyone who helps out during the season is told never to tout for tips."

BIBURY Gloucestershire — Map 2

Bibury Court — *Tel* Bibury (028 574) 337
Bibury
Nr Cirencester GL7 0NT

The Coln river – good fishing for trout – forms the boundary of the six-acre grounds of this splendid Tudor mansion, added to and improved in the 1660s, 1750s and 1920s. There are panelled rooms, four-posters and much fine antique furniture. Charles II and the Prince Regent are said to have visited *Bibury Court,* and celebrated litigation over it in the last century is thought to have inspired Charles Dickens' *Bleak House.* A gate leads through from the orchard to the churchyard of St Mary's Church, with fine Saxon carvings, and a footpath follows the river to Arlington Row, the 17th-century weavers' cottages now owned by the National Trust, and Bibury's Old Mill Museum. "A hotel of great individuality – the warmth and generosity of the Collier family were immediately evident, creating a wonderfully relaxed atmosphere. Our bedroom was enormous and well-furnished, the huge Victorian bath delighted my husband who is six foot three inches tall. Both food and wine interesting. Altogether a real gem!" (*Christine Gough; also Dr Janet Morgan, Sandy Berkley, Linda and Paul Duttenhaver*) Still no TV in bedrooms, though some signs of weakening resolve.

Open All year except 24–31 Dec.
Rooms 1 suite, 13 double, 2 single – 15 with bath, all with telephone and baby-listening; 8 with 4-poster.
Facilities TV lounge, residents' lounge, 2 bars, dining room. 6-acre grounds with croquet and dry-fly trout fishing. Golf courses nearby.
Location On edge of village.
Restrictions Not suitable for ♿. No dogs in dining room.
Credit cards All major cards accepted.
Terms (No service charge) B&B: single £27, double £45, suite £70. Full alc £18. 2-day breaks. Reduced rates and special meals for children.
Service/tipping : "We agree with your views on tipping and leave it to guests' discretion."

BIGGIN-BY-HARTINGTON Derbyshire — Map 4

Biggin Hall Farm Guest House — *Tel* Hartington (029 884) 451
Biggin-by-Hartington
Buxton SK17 0DH

New to the Guide last year, a former 17th-century manor house and still a working farm, offering hospitality superior to that which people tend to expect from a guest house in a particularly attractive location. Biggin-by-Hartington is a very quiet hamlet on the Derbyshire moors, with Dovedale, Chatsworth and Haddon Hall all within easy driving distance. Resident owners, Mr and Mrs Moffett, were away when our inspector paid a visit, but everything worked well under the locum. Nominators report that the Moffetts are "an exuberant youngish couple". There is one splendid large bedroom with a four-poster and great oak beams; other rooms are smaller, but all are pleasantly furnished. Dinner is at 7, a bit early for some tastes: the food, though not aiming too ambitiously, is imaginative and well-cooked and generous. Prices are reasonable. But could we have some feedback please?

Open All year.
Rooms 2 suites with 2 double bedrooms and bathroom, 1 suite with 2 singles and bathroom, 8 double – all with bath and/or shower; 7 with TV and tea-making facilities. 2 suites in building 30 yards from main building.
Facilities Lounge, TV lounge/library, dining room. 7-acre grounds.
Location ½m W of A515; turn off between Ashbourne and Buxton.
Restrictions Not suitable for ♿. No dogs in public rooms or any rooms in main building.
Credit cards None accepted.
Terms Dinner, B&B £18–£37.50. English breakfast £2 supplement per person. Set dinner £11.50. Bargain breaks; Christmas programme. 1-night bookings sometimes refused. Reduced rates for children sharing parents' room.
Service/tipping: "Service included, but guests sometimes tip individual members of staff for particularly good service. This is welcomed but not *expected."*

BISHOPS TACHBROOK Warwickshire — Map 2

Mallory Court Hotel [GFG]
Harbury Lane, Bishops Tachbrook
Leamington Spa CV33 9QB

Tel Leamington Spa (0926) 30214
Telex 317294 MALORY

"Beautiful setting. Our room was absolutely luxurious with everything at one's fingertips. Bathrobes, large bathroom with large selection of shampoos, bath gels etc, sewing kit, many books – including novels and a myriad of *useful* tourist books and maps. The hotel was attractively decorated. We had a wonderful dinner, the service was excellent." (*Isolde G O'Hanlon* and *P Jane Castle*) As usual, much unstinted praise for this luxurious country house in the Lutyens manner, in a large lovingly-maintained garden, with fine views. Owners Jeremy Mort and Allan Holland found it as a wreck, fell in love with it, and have gradually brought it to its present gleaming state. It is furnished with great taste, and is light, flower-filled and comfortable. Meals in the oak-panelled dining room are of the highest order earning Allan Holland a *Michelin* rosette. The setting is delightfully rural, only nine miles from Stratford-upon-Avon, and not much more from the National Exhibition Centre outside Birmingham. Not cheap – as you would expect.

Open All year.
Rooms 1 suite, 9 double – all with bath and shower, telephone, radio and TV; 1 4-poster.
Facilities Lounge, drawing room, garden room, dining room. 10-acre grounds with landscaped gardens, unheated swimming pool, hard tennis court, squash court and croquet. Golf 2 m.
Location 2 m S of Leamington Spa off A452. Take left turning signposted Harbury.
Restrictions Not suitable for ♿. No children under 12. No dogs.
Credit cards Access, Amex, Visa.
Terms B&B (continental): double £79–£121 in low season, £142–£182 in high season; suite £237 in low season, £300 in high season. Single occupancy rates on application. English breakfast £6.95. Set lunch £16.50, dinner £32.
Service/tipping: "We actively discourage all tipping. It is stated on all our literature that all prices include VAT *and service."*

> Set dinner refers to a fixed price meal (which may have ample, limited or no choice on the menu). Full alc is the hotel's own estimated price per person of a three-course meal taken à la carte, with a half-bottle of house wine.

BLANCHLAND Durham — Map 4

The Lord Crewe Arms Hotel *Tel* Blanchland (043 475) 251
Blanchland, Nr Consett
Durham DH8 9SP

Blanchland is on the river Derwent, about 30 miles south-west of Newcastle upon Tyne. It is surrounded by moors, fields, forests and a lake – some of the loneliest scenery in Britain. The name of the village comes from the white robes of the monks who inhabited Blanchland Abbey from its founding in the 12th century until its dissolution in the 16th. *The Lord Crewe Arms* was once the abbot's lodgings, guest-house and kitchen, before becoming a manor house and now, its latest transformation, a small country hotel. There is a Priest's Hole Lounge, a Crypt Bar and, reputedly, a ghost.

After changing hands in 1986, the hotel went through a bad patch, but recent reports have been more favourable. The dining room serves simple, well-cooked, traditional food. Bedrooms are comfortable and attractive, particularly perhaps those in a new wing (old cottages but newly converted) looking over a large, well-kept garden, once the Abbey cloisters, to the hills beyond. Breakfast is "hearty and excellent" apart from the coffee. We should welcome more reports on the new regime.

Open All year.
Rooms 15 double – all with bath and/or shower, telephone, TV and tea-making facilities; limited baby-listening. 7 in annexe across road.
Facilities 2 lounges, 2 bars, dining room; conference room. ½-acre garden; sailing and trout-fishing at nearby Derwent reservoir; golf and riding 10 m.
Location On B6306, 10 m S of Hexham. From E turn off A68; hotel signposted from main road.
Restrictions Not suitable for ♿. No dogs in public rooms.
Credit cards All major cards accepted.
Terms (Service at guests' discretion) B&B: single £34–£42.50, double £48–£64. Dinner £11.75. 2- and 4-day breaks; Christmas programme. Reduced rates and ½-portions for children.

BLANDFORD FORUM Dorset — Map 2

La Belle Alliance [GFG] *Tel* Blandford Forum (0258) 52842
Whitecliff Mill Street
Blandford Forum DT11 7BP

New to the Guide this year, *La Belle Alliance* (the name, given by the previous owners, is that of the inn where Napoleon stayed on the eve of Waterloo) is a Victorian house on the quiet outskirts of a pleasant market town in the heart of Hardy country. For the past three years, this restaurant-with-rooms has been run by Lauren and Philip Davison. Hearing it well spoken of, we sent an inspector who gave it an emphatic seal of approval: the rooms "pretty, feminine, restful, tending towards the pluche and ruche", with good lights and expensive thick towels; the food, cooked by Philip Davison, "very good indeed, with a short, modern interesting menu, using excellent local ingredients; rewarding wine list, concentrating on less expensive bottles and reasonably-priced halves; breakfasts as good as the dinners"; the tariff "excellent value for money, with everything included in the price, even a morning paper". Our inspector particularly appreciated the hospitable qualities of Lauren

Davison, endorsing a remark in last year's *Good Food Guide*, that she is one of life's hostesses: "That she most certainly is, but more than that – an incredibly sweet-natured charmer, who looked after with such kindness a decrepit old gentleman who sat hiccupping throughout his dinner." Her summing-up: "Thoroughly worth an entry, and because of the dedication and decent good nature of the Davisons, I'm sure the place will continue to be steadily worth an entry for years to come."

Open All year, except first 2 weeks of Jan.
Rooms 5 double (also available as single) – 4 with bath and shower, 1 with shower, all with telephone, radio, TV and tea-making facilities.
Facilities Lounge, restaurant. Small garden.
Location Go through town (1-way system); bear left onto Shaftesbury (Warminster) Road; restaurant is 300 yards on left.
Credit cards All major cards accepted.
Terms Single £22–£30, double £30–£40. Set lunch £8.50, dinner £15. Gourmet breaks.
Service/tipping: "We do not expect or encourage tips as we believe we pay our staff a fair wage for the good service they offer."

BLAWITH Cumbria — Map 4

Appletree Holme Farm — *Tel* Lowick Bridge (022 985) 618
Blawith, via Ulverston
LA12 8EL

Appletree Holme Farm is where owners Roy and Shirley Carlsen came in 1980, giving up the management of a large hotel in order to set, as their brochure puts it, "a fine example of living life the way it is meant to be lived". This secluded old stone farmhouse, with open fires and beamed ceilings, shines with loving care, and views from the window are of five acres of gardens and orchard with wooded slopes and fells beyond. There are many species of bird as well as foxes and deer to be seen. The four bedrooms are comfortable and well-equipped, though one room is reported to have had hot-water problems. Food is taken seriously: dinner orders are requested at tea-time, to allow for diets and personal preferences, and to prepare the wines. Local game, meats and trout and the Carlsens' own garden vegetables appear on the dinner menus, and Cumberland sausages, free-range eggs, oak-smoked kippers and goats-milk yoghurt are options for breakfast (orders taken after dinner, and this is no place for sluggards – 9 am being the latest, even on Sundays, that breakfast is served). The welcome is warm from the two border collies as well as the hosts, the food delicious, and the setting, in south Lakeland, magnificent.

Open All year except Christmas and New Year.
Rooms 1 suite, 3 double – all with bath, shower, telephone, radio, TV and tea-making facilities. Suite adjacent to main building with private entrance.
Facilities 2 sitting rooms, TV room, dining room. 5-acre grounds with gardens, woodlands and pasture; river with fishing 1¼ m; lake with fishing and bathing 2 m. Guests have access to pool and other facilities at Champneys Health Spa nearby.
Location 8 m N of Ulverston. Turn off A5084 up lane opposite church. ½ m turn right at farm sign.
Restrictions Not suitable for ♿. No babies or very young children. No dogs in bedrooms or public rooms.
Credit cards None accepted.

Terms Dinner, B&B £39–£44. Set dinner £12.50.
Service/tipping: "Tipping does not arise – one does not offer gratuities to one's hosts!"
Note: Mrs Carlsen adds this note to our questionnaire: "*Appletree* is a special place with an appeal limited to country lovers and those seeking peace and seclusion. In order to safeguard our guests' privacy, casual/chance callers are not encouraged and all reservations or requests to look around must be made in advance."

BLICKLING Norfolk — Map 3

The Buckinghamshire Arms — *Tel* Aylsham (0263) 732133
Blickling
Nr Aylsham NR11 6NF

A 17th-century inn a stone's throw from that jewel of the National Trust, Blickling Hall. Excellent bar snacks at lunchtime. Substantial home-made country food for full-scale meals. The hotel promises – and mostly delivers – "comfortable accommodation in a traditional pub ambience", but recent visitors, while confirming that the food was good and facilities adequate, complain of negligible, offhand service. 3 rooms, all with bath. B&B £23.25–£36.50. Set lunch £15, dinner £19. More feedback please.

BORROWDALE Cumbria — Map 4

Seatoller House — *Tel* Borrowdale (059 684) 218
Borrowdale, Keswick CA12 5XN

Seatoller House is at the head of the Borrowdale Valley, near the Honister Pass, close to the starting point of many spectacular fell walks. The house itself is over 300 years old, and it has been run continuously as a guest house for more than 100 years – almost certainly a record. Entries in the visitors' book start on 23 April 1886, when the house belonged to a Mrs Pepper, a great coincidence, since it has been run for several years now by David and Anne Pepper (no relation). Anne Pepper was not well last year, but reporters reassured us that "the high standards and special character of the place are being maintained". One frequent visitor protested that last year's grumble about small helpings at dinner were unfair, adding: "I have stayed in many hotels, most of them more expensive than *Seatoller House*, but in none of them have I experienced a homelier atmosphere, or met pleasanter guests, and a nicer couple managing the place." The willing and attentive service, excellent food, and the hotel's lovely setting won unanimous approval, as did the house-party atmosphere created by the communal tables where breakfast is served to everyone at 8.45 am and dinner at 7 pm. Private bathrooms for all the bedrooms have been promised for this year, though not all *en suite*. The hotel remains excellent value for money. (*MG Baron, W Ian Stewart, T Jeal, WJE Norton*)

Open Mar–Nov. Dining room closed Tue evening.
Rooms 9 double – all with bath or shower. 1 in converted bakehouse. 2 ground-floor rooms.
Facilities Lounge with open fire, library, dining room, tea-bar for guests to make hot drinks etc; small conference facilities; drying room, picnic shop. 2-acre grounds with fish pond. 6 m from Derwent Water and Buttermere.
Location 8m S of Keswick on B5289. Regular bus service from Keswick.

Restrictions Not suitable for severely ♿. No children under 5. No dogs in public rooms.
Credit cards None accepted.
Terms B&B: £14–£15.50; dinner, B&B: £20–£21.50. Set dinner £6 (at 7pm, not served Tue). Weekly rates; special rates for parties of 16 or more. 1-night bookings sometimes refused. Reduced rates for children under 12 sharing parents' room.

BOSHAM West Sussex — Map 1

The Millstream Hotel — *Tel* Bosham (0243) 573234
Bosham Lane, Old Bosham
Nr Chichester PO18 8HL

Conflicting reports for this hotel. It stands beside the millstream which runs parallel to the minor road into the tiny ancient village of Bosham, which is a favourite haunt of summer visitors and the sailing fraternity. Its church is pictured on the Bayeux Tapestry. Legend says this is where King Canute tried to turn back the tide, something visitors should remember before parking on the shore, as the sea rushes in swiftly to cover the road and lap the cottages. Some visitors, while expressing reservations about food and service, have found the bedrooms clean, bright and modern, the public rooms, with French windows opening on to the garden, very pleasant, the amazingly tame wild ducks which frequent the millstream enchanting, and staff very kind to elderly relatives. Others told us that their rooms were noisy, the decor poor, and the management unhelpful. More reports please.

Open All year.
Rooms 24 double (including 2 pairs inter-connecting), 5 single – all with bath and shower, telephone, radio, TV, tea-making facilities and baby-listening. 3 ground-floor rooms.
Facilities Residents' lounge, bar/lounge, cocktail bar, TV room, restaurant; conference facilities. Small garden with stream, pond and herb garden. Sailing, fishing, riding, golf nearby.
Location 4 m W of Chichester. Turn off A27 to Old Bosham, follow road to T-junction, turn right, hotel is 200 yds on right. Carpark.
Restriction No dogs in public rooms.
Credit cards All major cards accepted.
Terms (No service charge) B&B: single £35–£40, double £58–£75; dinner, B&B £25–£40 per person. Set lunch £4.50, dinner £11.50; full alc £15. Getaway breaks at most times of year. 1-night bookings sometimes refused. Reduced rates and special meals for children.
Tipping: "Completely at customers' discretion, although not encouraged. Any tips on accommodation are distributed evenly to all members of staff; in restaurant, shared among that department."

BOUGHTON MONCHELSEA Kent — Map 3

Tanyard Hotel — *Tel* Maidstone (0622) 44705
Wierton Hill
Boughton Monchelsea
Maidstone ME17 4JT

"I stayed at *Tanyard* after seeing it in the Guide. Superb setting, excellent food and friendly staff . . . By a long shot the best hotel in the area." (*SJ Rice*) This warm endorsement is for one of last year's newcomers, a lovingly restored medieval yeoman's house, later a tannery, which is enjoying a new lease of life as a very small personally-run country house hotel. It lies in a secluded position on the edge of the Weald of Kent, looking out over orchards and cottages. All the rooms are heavily beamed, and furnished with good antique pieces. Only five rooms, but one of them is a magnificent suite occupying the whole of the top floor with far-reaching views. The owner, Jan Davies, is an excellent cook and all our correspondents have praised the four-course dinners and their breakfasts the next morning. We are often asked to recommend small peaceful cosseting places within 50-mile radius of London, and *Tanyard*, four miles from Leeds Castle, and within easy driving distance of Sissinghurst, Knole, Bodiam and Canterbury, looks like an answer to many metropolitan weekenders' prayers.

Open Mar–Dec. Group bookings only Christmas and New Year, Jan–Feb. Restaurant closed for lunch.
Rooms 1 suite, 4 double (also let as singles) – all with bath and/or shower, telephone, radio, TV and tea-making facilities.
Facilities Hall/reception, lounge, restaurant. 1-acre garden with pond, stream and 4-acre orchard.
Location 5 m S of Maidstone. From B2163 at Boughton Monchelsea, turn down Park Lane opposite *Cock* pub. Take first right down Wierton Lane. Fork right; *Tanyard* is on left at bottom of hill.
Restrictions Not suitable for ♿. No children under 6. No dogs.
Credit cards All major cards accepted.
Terms (Excluding VAT. No service charge) B&B: single £37, double £45, suite £60–£80, depending on number of occupants. Set dinner £14.00.Surcharge for 1-night stay Sat or Sun.
Service/tipping: "Tips are not expected, but if given are distributed to all staff regardless of what job they do."

BRAITHWAITE Cumbria — Map 4

Ivy House Hotel — *Tel* Braithwaite (059 682) 338
Braithwaite
Nr Keswick CA12 5SY

A small hotel, 17th-century in origin but with a Georgian wing added in 1790, in the centre of the village, which lies between Derwent Water and Bassenthwaite Lake. *Ivy House* has suffered two changes of ownership in the past two years; the present owners, Mr and Mrs Peck, assisted by their sons, Robert and Nigel, only came into residence in February 1987. But one of our regular correspondents visited them shortly after and found the new set-up as good as the earlier one: beds comfortable, plenty of hot water, generous breakfasts (though the coffee might have been stronger and the packaged marmalade of better quality), excellent dinners (apart from tasteless frozen vegetables) decent inexpensive house wines, open fires and lots of books in the public rooms, first-rate drying facilities, and the Peck family and their staff all welcoming and friendly. (*SD*)

Open All year.
Rooms 10 double – 8 with bath, 1 with shower, all with TV and tea-making facilities; some with four-poster.
Facilities Entrance lounge, bar, lounge, restaurant. Small garden. Near lakes, fells.
Location Take A66 Keswick–Cockermouth road; after 2½ m turn left to Braithwaite. *Ivy House* is in middle of village at foot of Whinlatter Pass road.
Restrictions Not suitable for ♿. No children under 12. No dogs.
Credit cards Access, Visa.

Terms [1987 rates] (Service at guests' discretion) B&B £14.75–£25; dinner, B&B £24.25–£35.50. Set lunch £11.25. Off-season breaks.

BRAMPTON Cumbria — Map 4

Farlam Hall [GFG] — *Tel* Hallbankgate (069 76) 234
Brampton CA8 2NG

The comfort of *Farlam Hall* and the warmth of welcome of the Quinion family are again this year applauded by readers. Their part-17th-century Border manor house lies in unspoilt countryside close to Hadrian's Wall; it was visited by George "Rocket" Stevenson and preached in – so they say – by Wesley. The hotel has small, cosy front rooms, and vast, elegant high-ceilinged back ones. Its gardens are "especially lovely, with magnificent trees" and an ornamental lake. "We stopped here only to break a long journey, but it was a most relaxing episode. The Quinions' genuine hospitality has not flagged since our last visit four years ago," writes the owner of another fine hotel, *Scarista House* (q.v.), who goes on to describe the delicious meal, beautifully prepared and set out on a tray for their small daughter, and the Quinions' distress when not allowed to cook a special vegetarian meal for herself and her husband. "But the vegetables were so plentiful and well cooked and the cheeseboard so inviting we had no regrets. The decor is impeccable and extras many and well kept up: no nearly empty bottles of this or that by the bath". (*Alison Johnson, Geraldine Silver, Carole McQuarrie, and others*)

Open Mar–Jan. Closed Mon and Tue Nov–Jan.
Rooms 12 double, 1 single – all with bath and/or shower, telephone and TV. 2 ground-floor rooms.
Facilities 2 lounges, bar, dining room. 4½-acre grounds with croquet. 2 golf courses nearby.
Location On A689, 2½ m SE of Brampton (*not* in Farlam village).
Restrictions Not suitable for ♿. No children under 4. Dogs by arrangement only.
Credit cards Access, Amex, Visa.
Terms (Service at guests' discretion) Dinner, B&B £45–£60. Set dinner £16–£16.75. Winter and spring breaks late Oct–mid-Apr; New Year package. 1-night bookings refused over Easter and New Year.
Service/tipping: "Tipping is completely optional. We feel guests who wish to thank the staff should be allowed to do so. Tips are divided according to the amount of work done among all staff at the end of the season."

BRANSCOMBE Devon — Map 1

The Mason's Arms [GFG] — *Tel* Branscombe (029 780) 300
Branscombe, Nr Seaton EX12 3DJ

The village of Branscombe – a half-mile from the sea – is a picture-postcard sort of place, and lies at the end of a valley surrounded by National Trust land: good for coastal and inland walks, and riding too. And the *Mason's Arms* is your genuine Olde English inn, both outside, with bits of thatch and creeper, and garden benches in the flowery front garden, and inside, with polished wood and brass, and ingle-nook fireplaces. The inn dates from the 14th century and is a true local – warm and cosy, with a stone flag floor and huge open log fireplace in the bar – and a real ale pub at that. But it has moved with the times: most of the bedrooms (warning – some are tiny, and the ones in the main house are said to be preferred to the dozen in the cottages) have their own bathroom. The point is underlined by an American visitor who reported this year: "Our large room looked out over the hillside with sheep grazing there. It was the most scenic place we stayed at in England. Our companions had a very cramped room with no bath, though the price differential was substantial." There is also an attractive residents' lounge upstairs. Honest English fare. Most correspondents enjoyed their stay and endorsed the entry, but there have, as previously, been murmurs of discontent about slow service at meals, deterioration in the quality of the food, and some geriatric beds. (*Nancy and Walt Church; also April Young Glaze, A Laurence*)

Open All year.
Rooms 20 double, 2 single – 19 with bath, all with telephone, TV and baby-listening. 12 in cottages. 3 ground-floor rooms.
Facilities Residents' lounge, public bar, restaurant. Pebble beach with safe bathing and fishing ½ m.
Location 1½ m S of A3052, 5 m E of Sidmouth.
Restriction Dogs by prior arrangement (£2 per day); not in public rooms.
Credit cards Access, Visa.
Terms (No service charge) B&B: single £12.67–£19, double £25.33–£70; dinner, B&B: single £23.67–£30, double £47.33–£92. £23.17–£46.50. Set lunch £8, dinner £11; full alc £16. 1-night bookings refused at Christmas only. Special meals for children.
Service/tipping: "Entirely at customers' discretion. Split by staff among themselves."

BRATHAY Cumbria — Map 4

Grey Friar Lodge Country House Hotel
Tel Ambleside (053 94) 33158
Brathay, Ambleside LA22 9NE

A small hotel in the heart of the Lake District, fairly recently opened, gets an enthusiastic nomination from one of our regular correspondents. "*Grey Friar Lodge* is a typical Lakeland country house built in 1869 of green stone and slate. It is situated on the wooded flanks of Loughrigg Fell and has lovely far-reaching views. First a vicarage, then the rural retreat of the Bishop of Penrith, it now opens its doors to all comers, clerical or lay, and offers warmth of hospitality, comfort, and excellent cooking which uses fresh local produce with considerable flair. Our room was large, enjoyed spectacular views, and although it lacked a private bathroom, gave us virtually sole use of a commodious bathroom next door. There was ample provision for creature comforts, including well-sprung beds and a sofa . . . The style of furnishing throughout the house is eclectic and reassuring, and the proprietors, Tony and Sheila Sutton, spare no pains to cosset their guests. Besides sharing the kitchen duties, Tony is a mine of information on walking the fells and Sheila dispenses food and drink with unruffled good humour. Tom, their old English sheepdog, is usually on hand, and has a tireless capacity for retrieving rather soggy tennis balls." (*WH Bruton; endorsed in similar terms by WR Moss, A Gilbert*)

Open Mid-Apr–end Oct.
Rooms 8 double – 7 with bath and/or shower; all with TV and tea-making facilities.
Facilities 2 lounges, dining room; terrace. 1-acre garden with river valley and hill views. River and fishing ¼ m. Lake Windermere 1 m.
Location 1½ m W of Ambleside on A593.

Restrictions Not suitable for ♿. No children under 10. Dogs by arrangement only; not in public rooms.
Credit cards None accepted.
Terms (No service charge) Dinner, B&B: £23–£29. Set dinner £9.50. Packed lunch available on request. Special breaks. 1-night bookings sometimes refused if made far in advance. Reduced rates for children when sharing parents' room.
Service/tipping: "We believe that good service is an essential part of our establishment. It should be natural and automatic. Therefore we neither levy nor expect tips."

BRIGHTON East Sussex — Map 3

Topps Hotel
17 Regency Square,
Brighton BN1 2FG
Tel Brighton (0273) 729334

Most readers continue to appreciate this conversion of two terraced Regency houses in a sea-front square, and hosts Paul and Pauline Collins. "They are the most pleasant and accommodating people who seem always to be available when a guest needs them. The food was absolutely delicious both at dinner and at breakfast. We stayed there our first two nights in England and they spoiled us with their kindness." (*Nancy and Walt Church*) A vegetarian reader was delighted with the variety of dishes prepared – "the best balanced meals I have had when travelling". (*Mrs EH Prodgers*) *Elizabeth and Anthony Benger* felt that to describe the basement restaurant, *Bottoms*, as "offering unpretentious, home-cooked dishes" was "not doing justice to the admirable meals – the menu isn't changed very often but Mrs Collins will cook dishes to order, given reasonable notice." They also liked their "stately and comfortable bedroom with four-poster, settee, armchairs, fridge-bar etc and an equally sumptuous bathroom, including cupboards stocked with everything for the forgetful packer". An inspectorial party approved the thoughtful comforts provided, and enjoyed the vegetables and desserts, though not all the main dishes. The hotel has been well modernised – though not at all in Regency style.

Open 21 Jan–24 Dec. Restaurant closed Sun and Wed.
Rooms 7 double, 5 single – all with bath and/or shower, telephone, radio, TV and tea-making facilities.
Facilities Lift. Lounge, bar, basement restaurant. 100 yds from sea, safe bathing.
Location 200 yds from centre, opposite West Pier, but quietly situated. NCP carpark nearby.
Restrictions Restaurant not accessible for wheelchairs. No dogs.
Credit cards All major cards accepted.
Terms (No service charge) B&B: single £30–£50, double £60–£75. Set dinner £11; full alc £13.50. 10% reduction for any two nights Fri/Sat/Sun except public holidays. Reduced rates for children sharing parents' room; special meals.
Service/tipping: "Service is free."

The Twenty One [GFG]
21 Charlotte Street
Brighton BN2 1AG
Tel Brighton (0273) 686450 and 695560

Simon Ward and Stuart Farquharson's early Victorian town house in the fashionable Brighton suburb of Kemp Town (warning: no lifts and lots of stairs to the top floor), offers a sophisticated personally caring place to stay as an alternative to large impersonal hotels and mediocre look-alike guest-houses. A bonus for *21's* guests is that the owners serve ambitious gastronomic dinners in the French country cooking style. Indeed it is for many the occasion for the visit, since *21's* dinners are reserved for residents. These no-choice five-course *menus dégustation* are said to be on the generous side of *nouvelle cuisine*, so you should go easy on Sussex cream teas. Smaller appetites and special diets can be catered for with advance notice. In our entry last year we quoted from a report: "Not a hotel of great luxury," and the comment continued: "You get the door key and there are often times when the owners are out shopping or whatever. They operate with the minimum of outside staff, so you have the odd feeling at times that it is like home when all the family are out." The owners take polite exception to the no-great-luxury slur, mentioning their high standards of decoration, new orthopaedic beds, hairdriers, glossy magazines and many other features of luxury living. All true no doubt, but none of the rooms has a bath *en suite*, and some are quite small. We stand by our words.

Open All year except Christmas and New Year. Restaurant closed Wed and Sun.
Rooms 1 suite, 6 double – 5 with shower and WC, all with direct-dial telephone, radio and TV; 1 with 4-poster.
Facilities Lounge/bar, restaurant. Pebble beach with safe bathing 1 minute's walk.
Location Central. Off Marine Parade. Free street parking.
Restrictions Not suitable for ♿. No children under 12. No dogs in public rooms.
Credit cards All major cards accepted.
Terms (No service charge on rooms) B&B: single occupancy £25–£33, double £32–£44, suite £48. Set dinner £18 (plus 12½% service charge). Special 2-day breaks.
Service/tipping: "12½% added to restaurant bills and shared among kitchen staff, waiters and night porter."

BROAD CAMPDEN Gloucestershire — Map 2

The Malt House — *Tel* Evesham (0386) 840295
Broad Campden
Chipping Campden GL55 6UU

Some useful improvements are taking place in Mrs Pat Robinson's conversion of three mellow 17th-century Cotswold cottages in an unspoilt tucked-away Cotswold hamlet a mile from Chipping Campden. Bedrooms face a beautifully maintained, tranquil garden. A new wing is being added, which it is hoped will be ready for the 1988 season, to provide three more double rooms with baths *en suite*; there should be more space in the often over-crowded carpark; and a larger dining room can now take separate tables, though probably most guests will continue to sit communally for the four-course evening meal (no choice till the desserts) – always a lottery, more enjoyed by some than others. Meanwhile Mrs Robinson has won the Cotswold and Marches regional award for best bed-and-breakfast in a worldwide Bed and Breakfast Association competition. (How on earth do they judge such things?) Most visitors have appreciated their *Malt House* meals, which make use of fresh seasonal fruit and vegetables from its garden and orchards; there is an emphasis on game dishes in the season, though a vegetarian menu can be provided on request. "A lovely house and garden full of delightful things, and room, bed and linen all excellent," would sum up the consensus view

– though, as previously, there are occasional gripes about the communal eating. (*Dorothy Brining; also Susan Wolff, Dr W Davison, PH Freeman, Mrs G Heap*)

Open All year except Christmas week. Restaurant closed Sun evening.
Rooms 1 suite, 6 double, 1 single – 7 with bath and shower, all with TV and tea-making facilities.
Facilities Drawing room, bar, restaurant. 4½-acre grounds with large gazebo, small brook and pond, croquet lawn and orchard. Riding by arrangement.
Location Leave Chipping Campden by Sheep Street, turn first left after garage on left into Broad Campden; *Malt House* is second on left after Baker's Arms. Parking.
Restrictions Not suitable for ♿. Children over 12 preferred. No dogs (boarding at nearby kennels can be arranged).
Credit cards Access, Visa.
Terms (No service charge) B&B: single £25, double £58–£70, suite £90–£130. Set dinner £18. Reductions for children according to age; high teas.
Service/tipping: "Tipping is not expected; the staff are well paid. However if guests wish to show appreciation for a special service it is up to them."

BROADWAY Hereford and Worcester — Map 2

Collin House Hotel [GFG] *Tel* Broadway (0386) 858354
Collin Lane, Broadway WR12 7PB

A beautiful old Cotswold house in a lovely location, built of golden stone in the 16th century, roofed in the same stone, and with mullioned windows and leaded lights. There are small cosy public rooms, with carved stone fireplaces; some have flagstone floors. There is a huge inglenook in the bar, which has comfortable countrified furniture, wooden pews, tables and deep armchairs with floral upholstery. There are plans afoot to refurbish the dining room. The owners are warm and friendly, the service willing and pleasant. Not for the devotees of designer decor or *nouvelle cuisine*, it is comfortable, homely and occasionally shabby, with menus mixing the traditional and the creative, all home-cooked, with hearty portions and lavish puddings. There are plenty of books and magazines about. John and Judith Mills and their staff are unobtrusively attentive.

Open All year except 4 days over Christmas.
Rooms 6 double, l single – 5 with bath, 2 with shower; all with tea-making facilities; TV on request; 2 double with 4-poster.
Facilities Lounge bar, lounge with TV, restaurant. 8-acre grounds including ½-acre gardens and orchard and unheated swimming pool.
Location Off A44, 1 m NW of Broadway; turn right at Collin Lane.
Restrictions Only bar and dining room suitable for ♿. No children under 6 except by prior arrangement.
Credit cards Access, Visa.
Terms (No service charge) B&B: single £30–£36.50, double £63–£70. Set dinner £12–£14 depending on main course. Winter breaks Nov–Mar. 1-night bookings for Sat sometimes refused. Reduced rates for children sharing parents' room; special meals.
Service/tipping: "No service charge made. We do not forbid our staff to accept tips provided they are not solicited."

> "The TV was virtually useless since it was fixed to the wall *above* the bed. There was no convenient position from which to view it unless you fancied sitting on the wash-basin."

Lygon Arms
Broadway WR12 7DU

Tel Broadway (0386) 852255
Telex 338260 LYGON

*A show-place 16th-century hostelry in a show-place Cotswold village, offering luxurious accomodation to international travellers. Antique furniture in original part, good modern furniture in modern wing. Restaurant is in barrel-shaped Great Hall, with Minstrels' Gallery. Decor by Jean Munro. Hotel was taken over in 1986 by Savoy Group, more recently acquired as chef Michael Quinn, ex-*Gravetye, *ex-*Ritz, *ex-*Ettington Park. *Much refurbishment in train. 61 rooms, all with bath and shower. B&B double £105–£195. We lack feedback on new regime and kitchens.*

BROMSGROVE Hereford and Worcester — Map 2

Grafton Manor [GFG]
Grafton Lane
Bromsgrove B61 7HA

Tel Bromsgrove (0527) 31525

An architecturally splendid early 18th-century mansion which now dubs itself a country house hotel, albeit a small one, with just eight rooms, though one is an outsize suite occupying half of one wing on the first floor. All rooms are fitted with the mod cons appropriate to the grandeur of the house, including – a great bonus – gas-run coal fires. The linen, the beds, the bedside lighting, the towels, the soap – everything is of a standard which you would hope to find in any self-respecting country-house hotel. Only the decor may be though too sombre for some taste. Some turbulent episodes in English history have touched it since its pre-Norman beginnings: Jack Cade's rebellion, the Wars of the Roses, and the Gunpowder Plot, to name but three. Recently, it has enjoyed a halcyon phase in the hands of John and June Morris, assisted by all three of their children – an elder son and boy-and-girl twins – who have been busy with improvements since they became the lords of the manor. There is a large formal herb garden and a water garden bordering the lake in their eight acres of gardens. The kitchen garden provides as much as possible for the excellent restaurant in the *Manor*'s magnificent dining room. The Morris manor has a peaceful location down an isolated lane, but lies close beside the M5 motorway. Sadly, the section of the M5 nearest the hotel has recently been given a third lane, depriving the manor of an intervening bank and cover of trees. Rooms at the back facing the motorway have secondary glazing which keeps the traffic out of earshot if not out of sight. But if you like to open your window at night make sure you face the other way.

Open All year.
Rooms 1 suite, 6 double, 1 single – all with bath and shower, direct-dial telephone, radio, TV and teletext.
Facilities Lounge/bar, restaurant. 11-acre grounds with gardens, 2-acre coarse fishing lake, 2 golf courses nearby.
Location 1½ m from centre of Bromsgrove off B4090. From M5 (exit 4 or 5), take A38 towards Bromsgrove. Opposite Aston Fields Industrial Estate, take Charford Road, turn left into Worcester Road, right into Grafton Lane.
Restrictions Not suitable for ♿. No children under 7. Dogs in kennels only.
Credit cards All major cards accepted.

Terms (Service at guests' discretion) B&B (continental): single £52.50, double £71–£84, suite £111. English breakfast £5.75. Set lunch £13.75, dinner £23. Christmas package.

BROXTED Essex **Map 3**

Whitehall [GFG] *Tel* Bishops Stortford
Church End (0279) 850 603
Broxted CM6 2BZ

A beautiful old 12th-century timbered manor house, next to the village church in a pretty part of north Essex, and formerly the home of Lord Butler, *Whitehall* has been skilfully and tastefully converted by the Keane family into a luxurious hotel and restaurant. They have retained its original beams and character, adding modern furniture and bathrooms to the four luxurious bedrooms. Warm welcome, beautiful gardens, a peaceful location except for occasional flights overhead from Stansted, sophisticated decor, excellent breakfasts, and the *menu gourmand* at dinner have all delighted. The only small grumbles have been about limited space for hanging clothes – although there is ample drawer space – and not quite enough shelf space in the bathrooms, but these were only passing thoughts in otherwise enthusiastic comments. (*David Wooff, Pat and Jeremy Temple*)

Open All year except 1–23 Jan. Restaurant closed Mon.
Rooms 11 double, 1 single – all with bath, shower, telephone, radio and TV. 2 ground-floor rooms with easy access.
Facilities 2 lounge/bars, restaurant; conference facilities. 6-acre garden, tennis court, heated swimming pool. Ample parking.
Location On N edge of Broxted village.
Restrictions No children under 5. No dogs.
Credit cards Access, Amex, Visa.
Terms B&B: single £45, double £55. Set lunch £13, dinner £24. Special winter break: any 2 days – dinner, B&B from £110 per night; Christmas house party. *Service/tipping: "We believe very strongly that gratuities are entirely at our clients' discretion."*

BRYHER Isles of Scilly **Map 1**

Hell Bay Hotel *Tel* Scillonia (0720) 22947
Bryher, Isles of Scilly
Cornwall TR23 0PR

New owner since last year at this converted farmhouse on the tiny island (population 66) with its warm climate and rugged beauty. Hotel adjoins fine deserted beaches: many walks, much fishing, no traffic. Rooms surround grassed courtyard – fairly basic furnishings but new owner plans extensive refurbishment and redecoration. First report on new set-up strongly favourable: unpretentious but imaginative set menus; everything spotless; hotel responsive to special requests for children. 12 rooms, all with shower. Dinner, B&B £32–£35. We hope to hear more.

> Please write and confirm an entry when it is deserved. If you think that a hotel is not as good as we say, please write and tell us.

BUCKDEN North Yorkshire — Map 4

Low Greenfield [GFG] *Tel* Kettlewell (075 676) 858
Langstrothdale Chase
Nr Buckden, Skipton BD23 5JN

Built as a farmhouse in the 17th century, and extended in the late 1800s to accomodate shooting parties, this is now a modest-priced guest-house run by Austin and Lindsay Sedgley. High up – 1200 feet – in a secluded corner of the Dales National Park, it will appeal especially to walkers, naturalists and fishermen, and those in search of solitude. As the brochure says, it is for people who "enjoy life in the open, and a relaxing evening round an open fire". Our inspector last year reported: "I have never stayed in such a secluded hotel. You take a one-and-a-half-mile gated road into a remote valley. Four gates to open and shut . . . The Sedgleys' success is indubitable. On a cold April day we found a banked coal fire in the simply furnished but comfy sitting room. No TV. Bedrooms have bare spaces in them, but comfortable beds and a mug of tea at 7.45 am. Plenty of hot water. Splendid breakfast." Dinners also are warmly appreciated. There are plenty of books, novels, and information about the surroundings. "This remains the best place we have stayed in . . . for us a heaven on earth." (*Teresa Barker; also Drs H Roberts and R Barker*)

Open Easter–early Nov. Closed Aug. Dinner not cooked on Sun (snacks available 7.30–8.30 pm).
Rooms 1 triple, 1 double, 1 single – all with h&c. Also a self-catering wing.
Facilities Lounge, dining room; sauna. 1-acre garden and woodland; 27-acre nature reserve with fishing in beck. Fell walking, bird-watching.
Location 9 m SE of Hawes. From Buckden take left fork signposted Hawes. Approx. 5 m along road, cross river Wharfe over iron bridge on tight S bend. 1 m further take small left fork signposted Greenfield. Follow gated road to *Low Greenfield*.
Restrictions Not suitable for ♿. Dogs by special arrangement, not in public rooms.
Credit cards None accepted.
Terms (No service charge) B&B: £15; dinner, B&B £24.50. Set dinner £9.50 (residents only). Reductions for weekly bookings. 1-night bookings refused in peak periods. Reduced rates for children and tea in kitchen at 5.30 pm.
Service/tipping: "Tipping not encouraged or expected, but would not be refused."

BUCKLAND Hereford and Worcester — Map 2

Buckland Manor *Tel* Broadway (0386) 852626
Buckland, Nr Broadway
WR12 7LY

It is now five years since Barry and Adrienne Berman, newcomers to the hotel business, bought and renovated what has become for many a platonic idea of a luxury Cotswold Manor hotel. Buckland is one of those harmonious little Cotswold villages built of mellow honey-coloured stone, but, unlike nearby Broadway, it is an oasis of tranquillity. The ten acres of gardens and grounds are as beautiful as the house. The restaurant – like the cooking – is as elegant as the decor. "It is our aim," writes Barry Berman returning our questionnaire, "to provide an atmosphere of total well-being for our guests, to pamper them, and to provide a degree of service no longer encountered except on rare occasions." Editors of hotel guides are familiar with such claims, but in this case Berman's boast is supported by many warm tributes from his grateful guests. Only one complaint: inadequate (40 watt) bedroom lighting. (*The Marchioness of Tavistock, Jan Morris, Linda and Paul Duttenhaver, Theodore Wintner, Major JA Gardner*)

Open All year except 3½ weeks from mid-Jan.
Rooms 1 suite, 9 double – all with spring-fed bath (3 also with shower), direct dial telephone and TV; radio on request; 2 4-posters. Some ground-floor rooms.
Facilities 2 sitting rooms, dining room. 10-acre grounds with water and rose gardens, tennis court, croquet, putting green, heated pool; stables (riding available to guests). Walks and golf nearby.
Location E of A46, 1½ m SW of Broadway.
Credit cards Access, Visa.
Terms (Service at guests' discretion) B&B: double £105–£145, suite £182 for 4 people. Full alc £22.50. Winter breaks Nov–mid-Mar (min 2 days) except Christmas, New Year and Cheltenham Gold Cup week when there are special packages. 1-night bookings refused weekends and bank holidays.

BURFORD Oxfordshire — Map 2

The Bay Tree
Sheep Street
Burford OX8 4LW

Tel Burford (099 382) 3137 and 2188

The delectable – if over-touristy in the high season – town of Burford has been notable in the annals of inn-keeping for this splendid mansion in Sheep Street, built by Queen Elizabeth I's odious Lord Chief Baron of the Exchequer, which was an institution of a hotel for over 45 years in the hands of Sylvia Gray. When the present owners, the Kings, took it over a few years ago, it was palpably living on its reputation. But the Kings' reign has been enthusiastically acclaimed both by faithfuls of the *ancien régime* and by many new friends. Here is one report from this year's crop which speaks for all the others whose names appear below:

"The Kings keep *The Bay Tree* up to scratch. The full dining room reflects interest in the food – it is good, with some interesting puddings and starters. Service is very willing and the rooms, one feels, are improving each year. Somehow they have kept all the good things, and made the improvements slowly. There was so much to do; it still needs more really comfortable chairs in the lounges – the leather ones have character but not comfort. Despite the hordes that flock to Burford in the season, the garden of *The Bay Tree* remains as quiet as it was 30 years ago. The agelessness continues." (*Chris and Dorothy Brining; also RC Booth, Nancy and Walt Church, Dr J Morgan, and others*)

Open All year except Christmas.
Rooms 2 suites, 18 double, 2 single – all with bath, shower and TV. 2 ground-floor rooms. 12 in The Cottage (3 interconnecting buildings), 4 in garden annexe, all within 30 feet of hotel.
Facilities 2 lounges, library, bar lounge, bar, restaurant. Small grounds with terraced gardens, fishponds, summer house.
Location Central (but quiet). Go down hill from A40 roundabout and take first turn on left. Parking.
Restrictions Not suitable for ♿. No children under 7 in restaurant for dinner. Dogs in public rooms only, must be closely supervised.
Credit cards All major cards accepted.

Terms (No service charge) B&B £22–£30. Set lunch £7.50 (Sun £9.50); dinner £13.50 (Sat £15.50). Weekend breaks in off season, midweek breaks all year; special interest weekends. Reduced rates for children sharing parents' room; special meals by arrangement.
Service/tipping: "Our menus state that service is not included but our staff do not expect gratuities."

BURY ST EDMUNDS Suffolk **Map 3**

The Angel Hotel [GFG]
Angel Hill
Bury St Edmunds IP33 1LT

Tel Bury St Edmunds (0284) 3926
Telex 81630 ANGEL

The Angel Hotel has been an inn since at least 1452, and is still today very much part of the life of the town, so do not come here for a quiet rural excursion. Public rooms bustle with activity, as when Dickens, having given readings in the nearby Athenaeum, stayed overnight in "a fine room", said to be No 15, of the four-poster and gurgling bathtub. The Abbey Gardens, with trees, flowers and ruins beside the river Lark, the elegant shops of ancient Abbeygate Street, and Angel Hill itself, described as "the most perfect square in the land", are on the doorstep. The hotel received its classical facade in 1709, now softened by creepers. The rooms and bathrooms vary greatly in size and shape, as in all old buildings, and many have just been refurbished, together with the reception area. There have been a few mutters about lapses in housekeeping and minor repairs, all taken care of, we hope, during improvements. A couple returning from two years abroad, enjoyed their "pretty, chintzy, freshly-decorated room, with its comfortable sitting area, high old-fashioned bed, large modern bathroom, and windows surrounded by creepers overlooking the Abbey gatehouse". (The view at the front is more interesting, but cars pass: quieter at the back except during parties. One enraged letter from a reader whose back room overlooked a "function room", with revelry to 2 am.) One couple found the food "bland", another said the staff, "didn't seem interested", not the majority view. Breakfasts and delicious teas with a choice of tea were unanimously praised, and the single word most frequently used to describe the hotel, the service and the food, was "excellent." (*Bernice Spandorf, H Sharland, Stephan and Kate Murray-Sykes, HR, and others*)

Open All year.
Rooms 1 suite, 21 double, 14 single – all with bath and/or shower, telephone, radio and tv; 4-posters.
Facilities Lounge, bar, 2 restaurants (one conventional, one in arched basement); small conference facilities. Parking for 20 cars. Large Abbey gardens opposite.
Location Central (front rooms can be noisy). Parking.
Restrictions Not suitable for ♿, or young children. No dogs in restaurant; in rooms at management's discretion.
Credit cards All major cards accepted.
Terms Rooms: single £45, double £70, suite £95. Light breakfast £3, English breakfast £5. Full alc £13. Special weekend B&B rates. Special meals for children.
Service/tipping: "No stated policy – tipping is not actively encouraged."

> The length of an entry does not necessarily reflect the merit of a hotel. The more interesting the report or the more unusual or controversial the hotel, the longer the entry.

CALDBECK Cumbria — Map 4

High Greenrigg House *Tel* Caldbeck (069 98) 430
Caldbeck, Wigton CA7 8HD

This carefully restored 17th-century farmhouse is in the northern part of the Lake District, which is uncluttered even at the height of the season, and handy for visiting Hadrian's Wall and the Scottish Borders – that is, if you can tear yourself away from walking the northern fells. The hotel is three miles west of the nearest village, which boasts only one tiny shop – visitors don't come here for the bright lights. Walking is taken seriously: you are given weather information and asked to fill in details of your route plans before you set off. Robin and Fran Jacobs welcome guests warmly, exhort them to ask for anything (extra pillow, hot water bottle) they might need, and feed them plenty of decent home-cooking, sustaining packed lunches and well-cooked hearty breakfasts. The hotel interior with plain white walls, pine, and wood-burning stove, the informality (girls serve dinner wearing jeans), the shared interests and energetic days, the solitude, all create a special atmosphere of *camaraderie* as in ski-lodge or mountain cabin. Bedrooms are snug and comfortable, with warm duvets and firm beds. (*PD Austen*)

Open 1 Mar–31 Oct. Dining room closed for lunch.
Rooms 6 double, 2 single – 2 with bath and shower, 2 with shower only (2 more should have private facilities in 1988); some on ground floor with wide doors and *en suite* bathroom.
Facilities Residents' lounge with TV, games, tea-and coffee-making facilities, bar lounge, games room with darts, snooker and table-tennis, dining room with adjoining lounge with open fire. ¾-acre grounds. Birdwatching on the Solway coast.
Location From Caldbeck go W 3 m on B5299. Turn left at minor road signposted Greenhead, Branthwaite, Fellside. *High Greenrigg House* is ½ m along this road. Ordnance survey ref 288 376.
Restriction No dogs in bedrooms.
Credit cards None accepted.
Terms B&B £15–£18. Packed lunch £3, set dinner £10. Vegetarian meals available (£2 extra). Reduced rates for children sharing parents' room; special meals.
Service/tipping: "Tips are not expected or solicited, and guests obviously do not feel under any pressure as very few do tip. When tips are received they are distributed by staff to staff."

CALNE Wiltshire — Map 2

Chilvester Hill House *Tel* Calne (0249) 813981 and 815785
Calne SN11 0LP

"I cannot remember being more favourably impressed by any hotel of its size and type." (*DJ Williams*) "On our working trip round the south of England, we were lucky to save the best, *Chilvester House,* to the last. I would recommend the place to anybody (even my mother)." (*EA Rath*) Two all-out appreciations, among a raft of similar tributes for the welcome provided at this spacious Victorian mansion in seven acres, close to (but out of earshot of) the A4, run in a relaxed but thoroughly cosseting way by Dr and Mrs Dilley. When not entertaining their guests, Dr Dilley, recently retired from BP in Kuwait, does consultancies and Mrs Dilley breeds beef cattle. All reports confirm last year's commendation of the hospitality of the house – the spacious comfortable rooms, the silver, good glass, polished antiques and Mrs Dilley's excellent home cooking. "Breakfast what you like when you like", we had quoted the Dilleys as offering in last year's guide. Gill Dilley tells that this claim has proved somewhat burdensome; she has served breakfast at 5.30 am and 11.30 am and at every time in between, and some mischevious guests have enjoyed seeing how far she would go. We urge moderation on our readers or they may find strict breakfast times imposed when they return. Meanwhile, here is one reader's comment on that meal (her dinner had been pretty good too): "Breakfast was terrific – Mrs D's own damson and plum jam and marmalade, a huge pat of butter, excellent scrambled eggs, my own pot of coffee – all that and *The Times* and *The Independent* too." (*Caroline Currie*)

Open All year, except a week off-season (autumn or spring).
Rooms 3 double – all with bath, radio, TV, tea-making facilities and baby-listening.
Facilities Drawing room, sitting room with TV, dining room. 2½-acre grounds with swimming pool; also 5 acres used for cattle; golf and riding locally.
Location ½ m W of Calne; take A4 towards Chippenham, after ½ m take the right turn signposted Bremhill and immediately turn right into the drive marked by gateposts with stone lions.
Restrictions Not suitable for ♿. No children under 12. No dogs.
Credit cards Access, Amex, Visa.
Terms (No service charge) B&B: single occupancy £30, double £45. Set dinner £12.50–£18; full alc £17; packed lunches or pool snacks available. Reductions for stays of a week or more.
Service/tipping: "Tips not expected; but if anything is left it is put in a 'kitty' and shared out at Christmas."

CALSTOCK Cornwall — Map 1

Danescombe Valley Hotel [GFG] — *Tel* Tavistock (0822) 832414
Lower Kelly
Calstock PL18 9RY

The *Danescombe Valley Hotel*, new to the Guide this year, and a newish enterprise, has a glorious setting, on the steep wooded slopes of the river Tamar, facing south across a bend in the river where Saxons and Danes once fought a notable battle. Its four acres of woodland adjoin the grounds of Cotehele House, 15 minutes' walk away, now belonging to the National Trust, but owned once by Lord Mount Edgecombe, who built what is today the hotel at the beginning of the 19th century. Martin Smith and his half-Italian wife, Anna, bought the house in a run-down condition, and have worked hard to bring it to its current state. Our inspector was startled to be greeted by her first name by the owner, but loved the house, freshly redecorated throughout in Laura Ashley (country house fabrics, not small dotted ones) and furnished with a mixture of good antique, pleasant reproduction and comfortable modern furniture. Plenty of flowers, plants, magazines and books about, deep carpets, well-placed lighting, and generally a light, airy feeling about the place. Bedrooms are well-equipped with pretty duvets and huge pillows. Big fluffy towels and many extras in the bathrooms. Anna Smith cooks a four-course no-choice menu, which our inspector found excellent. The owners say the hotel is, "attractive to those who like tranquillity, scenery, river, birdlife, good food and wine; unattractive to those who require TV, as we don't have one".

Open Mar–Nov, also Christmas and New Year.
Rooms 6 double, 1 single – 2 with bath; tea-making facilities on request.
Facilities Lounge, bar, restaurant. 4 acres of steep woodland, with 2 limekilns, 3 wells and an incline railway. Hotel steps down to river Tamar. Fishing, walking, golf, riding and squash nearby.
Location ½ m W of Calstock village; under viaduct, past Methodist church; turn sharp right; follow road parallel to river Tamar for ½ m.
Restrictions Not suitable for ♿. No children under 12. No dogs in house.
Credit cards None accepted.
Terms B&B: single £27.50, double £40–£53. Set dinner £16.50.
Service/tipping: "Tips refused unless our refusal gives offence."

CAMBRIDGE Cambridgeshire — Map 3

May View Guest House — *Tel* Cambridge (0223) 66018
12 Park Parade
Cambridge CB5 8AL

A Victorian B&B – "a model of everything that this sort of place should be" – in a quiet position overlooking Jesus Green and the river Cam, and only a few minutes' walk from the town centre and the colleges. Bedrooms are attractively decorated, likewise the breakfast room, with antique furniture and paintings. The house has been in Roger Stock's family for more than half a century. It's only drawback: only two loos between the six bedrooms, and as one of these is in a bathroom "life can get a little hectic in the early mornings". But most guests are willing to put up with that minor inconvenience for the many pluses. "Sparkles with care and cleanliness . . . Breakfasts are superb." (*Patricia Roberts*) "Quiet, comfortable in a delightful position, with an excellent staff." (*Brian Williams; also MW Atkinson, Neil and Jacqueline Britton*) Since last year, Roger Stock tells us, he has added a four-poster in their largest room overlooking the Green.

Open All year except 18 Dec–2 Jan.
Rooms 6 double – radio and TV on request.
Facilities Breakfast room. River Cam 1 min; punting and fishing.
Location Overlooking Jesus Green and river. Multi-storey car park 1 min away.
Restrictions Not suitable for ♿. No children under 7. No dogs.
Credit cards None accepted.
Terms B&B: double room £28–£32. £7 added for child sharing parents' room. (No restaurant.)
Service/tipping: "I discourage tipping unless the housekeeper has done washing, ironing or shopping, and only then would I approve."

CANTERBURY Kent — Map 3

Howfield Manor — *Tel* Canterbury (0227) 738294
Chartham Hatch
Canterbury CT4 7HQ

The kitchen dates from 1181, when it was a chapel belonging to the Priory of St Gregory – the monks' well can still be seen by the dairy entrance. *Howfield Manor*, near the main road for Dover, and handy for the Channel ports, also has exposed beams, ingle-nooks, and a handsome red-brick gabled facade. Its owners, Clark and Janet Lawrence, (he American, she English) continue to feed their guests "exceptionally well", according to one of its original proposers for the Guide, who, returning two years later, enjoyed "baked fennel with garlic (delicious); salmon with vegetables (good); roquefort and salad (quite excellent); and a quite exquisite whisky soufflé". (*Charles Dewhurst*) The owners are welcoming, the five double bedrooms comfortable and well-equipped, and the hotel is well-placed for visiting Canterbury and exploring the many castles, villages, gardens and National Trust houses in the neighbourhood. (*DR Grossmark, E and B Guthrie*) *Note:* Meals, eaten family-style at one table, are no-choice, so discuss when booking.

Open Mid-Jan–mid-Dec. Dinner by prior arrangement only.
Rooms 5 double – all with bath and/or shower.
Facilities Sitting room, library with TV, dining room. 5-acre gardens. Golf, tennis, swimming nearby.
Restrictions Not suitable for ♿. No children under 14. No dogs.
Location 2 m SW of Canterbury on the A28 Ashford road. Directions given by telephone when bookings are made.
Credit cards Access, Amex, Visa.
Terms B&B: single occupancy £35–£45, double £45–£55. Winter breaks 1 Nov–31 Mar. Set dinner from £14.50.
Service/tipping: "We do not allow tipping, but since Howfield Manor *is run by us, it's an easily enforced rule."*

CARTMEL Cumbria — Map 4

Uplands Hotel [GFG] — *Tel* Cartmel (044 854) 248
Haggs Lane, Cartmel
Grange-over-Sands LA11 6HD

Tom and Diane Peters worked with John Tovey of *Miller Howe* (q.v.) fame, who helped them to set up their own hotel two years ago, unashamedly "in the *Miller Howe* manner", and maintaining the Tovey standards of cuisine, service and housekeeping. *Uplands* has won acclaim – *nem con* – both for its delicious food, impeccably served, and for the decor, which in the lounge and dining room is restful pastel greys and pinks, and upstairs in the four bedrooms bright and modern. The hotel is on a hillside, with views over the vast expanse of Morecambe Bay, in the uncrowded southern end of the Lake District. " Quite the best welcome we have ever had." "A gem." "A memorable weekend." "Outstanding decor" – and more in the same vein from *Michael and Thelma Goodger, Mrs JC Smye, William Rankin, Mrs LJ Hirst.*

Open End Feb–2 Jan. Restaurant closed Mon.
Rooms 4 double – 1 with bath, 3 with shower, all with telephone and TV.
Facilities Lounge, dining room. 2-acre garden. Golf nearby.
Location 2 m from Grange-over-Sands. From M6 exit 36 follow signs to Grange. Pass station on left, up hill bear right at Crown Hotel; go straight across cross-road into Grange Fell Road. Proceed up hill, past golf course on right. At T-junction take right for Cartmel. *Uplands* is on right.
Restrictions Not suitable for ♿. No children under 12. No dogs in public rooms.
Credit cards Access, Amex.
Terms (Excluding 10% service charge) Dinner, B&B: single £54, double £96. Set lunch £9, dinner £16. Mid-week breaks mid-Nov–mid-Mar. 1-night bookings refused for Sat. Reduced rates for children sharing parents' room.
Service/tipping: "As we charge 10% for service we refuse tips if offered."

CHADLINGTON Oxfordshire — Map 2

Chadlington House Hotel — *Tel* Chadlington (060 876) 437
Chadlington OX7 3LZ

A two-bedroomed cottage in 1650, *Chadlington House* has grown over the years into a modest-priced country house hotel in an Oxfordshire village, well away from Cotswold trippers. Owners Rita and Peter Oxford say, disarmingly, "We offer comfort, peace and welcome. We are not perfect, we just try very hard." Most readers appreciate the Oxfords' hospitality though one reported a slightly imperfect reception. More reports would be welcome.

Open End Feb–Nov. Closed Christmas.
Rooms 1 suite, 8 double, 2 single – 4 with bath, 7 with shower, all with radio, TV, and tea-making facilities; suite has 4-poster. Small cottage in grounds.
Facilities Lounge, coffee lounge, bar, dining room. 1-acre garden.
Location In village between Chipping Norton and Burford. From A34 take B4022. Parking.
Restrictions Only restaurant suitable for ♿. No children under 8. No dogs.
Credit cards Access, Visa.
Terms (Service at guests' discretion) B&B: single £25–£30, double £38–£50, suite £58–£65; dinner, B&B: single, £35.50–£45.50, double £50–£71, suite £79–£81. Set dinner £10.50; alc £15. Bar lunches. 2-day winter and 3-day summer breaks. Reduced rates and special meals for children.

CHAGFORD Devon — Map 1

Gidleigh Park Hotel [GFG] — *Tel* Chagford (064 73) 2367 and 2225
Chagford TQ13 8HH

Gidleigh Park, winner of numerous awards, member of the exclusive *Relais et Châteaux* organisation, continues to delight. It was built as a country retreat for an Australian shipping magnate, on the site of a 16th-century manor house at the edge of Dartmoor. If ever a house was well set back from the road, this is it, and you need the sign saying "take heart" to keep you going down the single-track lanes lined with huge granite boulders, moss and ferns, and overhung with trees. Once you arrive you will find yourself in an interior that combines tradition with unostentatious luxury and comfort: panelled walls, pretty elegant chintzes, deep armchairs, masses of fresh flowers, interesting maps and prints and roaring log fires. American owners Paul and Kay Henderson, having refurbished their main bedrooms (specially recommended are the large rooms on the first floor with a view), have created two new ones in a former chapel some 75 yards from the house. Other improvements include the installation of an all-weather surface to the tennis court, and the restoration of an elaborate water-garden in the already glorious 40-acre estate. Paul Henderson sets out to provide total comfort in a private house atmosphere for "affluent connoisseurs". For most he succeeds admirably; for others his perfectionist drive sometimes grates, though again some say the house loses warmth if he is away on his travels. Chef Shaun Hill, now settled in, has been acclaimed; *aficionados* of *Gidleigh Park* tell of joining him on a 15-mile hike over the moors before dinner. Perhaps this explains a sub-standard meal experienced by one connoisseur, though any fall from excellence is worrying at prices so geared to the affluent.

The majority echo *Andrena Woodhams'* "I wish we could have stayed longer," or *Bill Cutler's* "Can't wait to go back."

Open All year.
Rooms 14 double – all with bath and/or shower, telephone, radio and TV. 2 in converted chapel 75 yds from front door.
Facilities Front hall, large lounge, bar loggia, 2 dining rooms. 40-acre grounds and gardens with croquet lawn and hard tennis court. North Teign river 50 yds in front of house; 14 m of trout, sea trout and salmon fishing. Golf, riding and walking nearby.
Location Approach from Chagford, *not* Gidleigh. Take M4 or M5, then A30 to Whiddon Down. Then go to Chagford. From Chagford Square facing Webbers with Lloyds Bank on right, turn right into Mill Street. After 150 yds fork right and go downhill to Factory Crossroad. Go straight across into Holy Street and follow lane 1½ m to end.
Restrictions Not suitable for ♿. No dogs in public rooms.
Credit cards All major cards accepted.
Terms (Excluding VAT) Dinner, B&B: single occupancy £95–£175, double £126–£215. Set lunch £21.50, dinner £31.50 (including 25p cover charge per meal, donated to World Wildlife Fund). 5-day winter walking holidays. 1-night bookings sometimes refused. Special meals for children by arrangement.
Service/tipping: "We discourage tipping."

CHEDINGTON Dorset — Map 2

Chedington Court [GFG]
Chedington
Nr Beaminster DT8 3HY

Tel Corscombe (093 589) 265
Telex 417182 ENEL 103 CHE

A splendid fairly formal 1840 country house hotel in the Jacobean style – curved gables, mullioned windows – in a spectacular position high up in the Dorset hills, with panoramic views right across Dorset and Somerset. There are ten acres of parkland that match the grandeur of the building: balustraded and terrace gardens, lots of yews, a croquet lawn and a lake down below. The rooms are all fully equipped with the appropriate pamperings to be expected in this class of establishment.

Every prospect pleasing? Almost. The food in the restaurant is well cooked and presented, though not achieving – or perhaps aiming for – the higher reaches of *haute cuisine*. In the past, there have been complaints about the hotel's heating, but a new boiler has silenced these cool customers. UHT milk is still provided for tea in the bedrooms, but a jug of fresh milk can be had instantly on phoning reception. The ambivalence stems from the low-key character of Mr and Mrs Chapman's welcome – appreciated by some and continuing to disappoint others. Here is a report from a member of the pro-Chapman faction: "When we arrived, we were shown a more expensive room than we had booked and offered it for the price of the cheaper room. This gesture proved to be typical of the undemonstrative but extensive and thoughful hospitality at *Chedington Court*. The hotel may be quiet and formal, but it is not stuffy; ebullient dogs greet you in the hall, where walkers leave their muddy boots before padding upstairs. As for the atmosphere, there is certainly no hint of a holiday camp, but we found the owner the soul of courtesy and friendliness. I would recommend *Chedington* for the building and accommodation, gardens and surrounding countryside alone. It is ideal for anyone looking for peace and tranquillity with all the creature comforts." (*Giles O'Bryen; CH Eckert, Vera Alexander*)

Open All year, except Christmas, and 4 weeks Jan/Feb.
Rooms 10 double – all with bath and/or shower, telephone, radio, TV, tea-making facilities and baby-listening. 1 4-poster.
Facilities Drawing room, library, bar, billiard room, dining room; conservatory. 10-acre garden with croquet and putting. Golf, bird-watching, fishing nearby; coast 10 m.
Location ¼ m off A356 at Winyard's Gap, 4½ m SE of Crewkerne.
Restrictions Only restaurant suitable for ♿. No dogs.
Credit cards Amex, Visa.
Terms Dinner, B&B: £34–£68; B&B only, 20% less. Set dinner £18.50. Winter breaks 1 Nov–24 Mar excluding Christmas and New Year. 1-night bookings sometimes refused for Fri and Sat. Reduced rates for children sharing parents' room; special meals.
Service/tipping: "Prices include 10% service charge: any extras given are divided evenly among staff, but they are not sought or expected."

CHICHESTER West Sussex — Map 1

Suffolk House Hotel — *Tel* Chichester (0243) 778 899
3 East Row, Chichester PO19 1PD

Visitors to Chichester's Festival Theatre, unwilling to face a night drive home, will welcome the advent of the *Suffolk House Hotel.* The bedrooms in this 18th-century townhouse, which once belonged to the Dukes of Richmond, are comfortable, with bathrooms. Serge Paris, who owns the hotel, is welcoming and friendly, and the menu in the restaurant is sensibly priced, with a good choice of dishes: the cooking is apparently shared between several people, so may vary, but all reports so far have been favourable. There is a charming garden and a tiny bar, and arrangements of silk flowers throughout the hotel, even in the bathrooms.

Open All year.
Rooms 1 suite, 7 double (most with 4-poster), 3 single – all with bath and/or shower, telephone, radio, TV, tea-making facilities and baby-listening. Some ground-floor rooms.
Facilities Lounge, lounge/bar, restaurant. ¼-acre garden.
Location Central. Parking. Head for Quadrant; follow 1-way system into Little London for East Row
Restriction No dogs in public rooms.
Credit cards Access, Diners, Visa.
Terms B&B: single £42, double £58, suite £85. Set dinner £13; full alc £20. No charge for cot for child in parents' room.
Service/tipping: No service charge on hotel bills – left to guests' discretion; 10% added to restaurant bills and equally divided among staff.

CHIPPING CAMPDEN Gloucestershire — Map 2

The Cotswold House Hotel and Restaurant — *Tel* Evesham (0386) 840330, *Telex* 336810 CAMTEL
The Square
Chipping Campden GL55 6AN

Until this year, delectable Chipping Campden – 12 miles from Stratford-upon-Avon and an hour's drive from Oxford, in the heart of the Cotswolds – had but one entry in the Guide, the *Kings Arms* (see below). In Easter 1987, however, the latter's nextdoor neighbour, *Cotswold House,* a lack-lustre hotel under previous owners, reopened its imposing porticoed doors after a major refurbishment, and must now be regarded as the smartest place in town. The resident owners, Robert and Gill Greenstock, are no newcomers to the Guide: ten years ago they were running *Lower Brook House* at Blockley, three miles over the hill.

Cotswold House is a fine Regency building, centrally placed in the Market Square, with a particularly noble central staircase. The furnishings and decor throughout are a keen pleasure: the better-proportioned rooms face the street, and may be liable to some traffic disturbance at night; the ones at the back look over a beautifully manicured garden-cum-courtyard. The dining room faces the garden, too, and is a splendidly light, airy place to eat. Dinner, judging only from a single meal, was a mixed experience, with the à la carte seeming a better bet than the £13.25 [1987] set menu. Breakfast, with freshly-squeezed orange juice and an excellent home-made croissant, was an unalloyed pleasure. The rooms are nearly twice as expensive as their neighbour's, but all have bathrooms *en suite*, and are fitted out with more than adequate creature comforts. Duvets, but you can have sheets on request. Also recommended, the adjoining coffee house and snack bar – named, alas, *Greenstock's Eaterie*. Whatever next? God preserve us from a *Sleeperie*. (*HR*)

Open All year.
Rooms 12 double, 3 single – all with telephone, radio, TV and baby-listening.
Facilities Main hall lounge, sitting room, dining room, bar, coffee house.
Location Central (rear rooms quietest). Parking.
Restrictions Not suitable for ♿. No dogs.
Credit cards All major cards accepted.
Terms (Service at guests' discretion) B&B: single £35–£40, double £60.50–£80. Set Sun lunch £11.50, dinner £14.50; full alc £19–£21. 2-day breaks in low season. Reduced rates for children out of season; special meals on request.
Service/tipping: "We are against any form of tipping. But if we have done our job properly our guests will, if they are customary tippers, show appreciation. All tips are given to staff with instructions that everyone receives a share."

Kings Arms Hotel *Tel* Evesham (0386) 840256
Market Square
Chipping Campden GL55 6AW

The *Kings Arms*, like *Cotswold House* (see above), stands beside the old Market Square. Made up from two adjoining stone buildings, one 17th-century, the other Georgian, it has an exceptionally pleasant garden (excellent for bar lunches in the summer), open fireplaces and some good furniture. Unlike its neighbour, it has only two rooms with bath *en suite* and doesn't go in for "extras" like TV or radio in the bedrooms. Last year we asked for comments following a recent change of ownership. Most correspondents have appreciated its "laid-back, cheerful and kind welcome" and rooms that were "warm, clean and comfortable". Restaurant meals have had a mixed reception. One reader, who found her front room somewhat noisy and shabby, returned, and had an immaculate, quiet room overlooking the garden, which she loved – she plans to return again. Another summed up: "Loved the room, the view over the centre of the village, the bathroom, the hallways, the garden out back, the feel of the dining room. And simply to stay in Chipping Campden is an imponderable plus." (*Bill Cutler; also A Woodhams, T Bradbrook Smith*)

Open All year.
Rooms 2 suites, 9 double, 3 single – 2 with bath and shower.
Facilities Sitting room with TV, bar, dining room. ½-acre garden.
Location Central, in Market Square. Parking behind hotel.
Restrictions Not suitable for ♿. No dogs in public rooms.
Credit cards Access, Visa.
Terms (Excluding 10% service charge) B&B: £22. Bar lunches £1.25–£4.50, Sun lunch £10, dinner £14. Winter breaks Nov–Apr. Reduced rates for children sharing parents' room; special meals.
Service/tipping: "We find if we don't add 10% the staff get nothing – and we feel something is deserved."

CHITTLEHAMHOLT Devon — Map 1

Highbullen Hotel [GFG]
Chittlehamholt
Umberleigh EX37 9HD
Tel Chittlehamholt (076 94) 561

"Hugh and Pam Neil bought this large country house in Devon overlooking a valley with spectacular views, and steadily worked it up into a most comfortable and wholly individual country house hotel which is now much enjoyed by regulars, who appreciate its restfulness. Only 34 bedrooms, but two small, but delightful, heated indoor and outdoor swimming pools, jacuzzi, squash court, tennis court, nine-hole golf course (designed and built by Mr Neil with some fiendish holes, I am told by a golfer), herd of deer, and so on. We found a Norwegian diplomat and his wife wandering around the hall trying to find a reception desk. There is no reception desk. No waiters. No room service. Your room is cleaned by fairies while you are eating breakfast. It is like staying at rich friends' houses without any obligation at all to your host. There is only a snack lunch but a superb candle-lit dinner. This is an un-hotel-like hotel, run, very personally and efficiently, by its owners, and it might very well not be to your taste. In which case you will hate it. For those of us who like this sort of retreat it is quite superb." (*Frank Muir*)

Readers continue to testify to the accuracy of this earlier report, some lamenting the hiccups in the service, the tattiness of some of the rooms (if only, one reader said, Hugh Neil could have spent half of what it cost to drain the golf course on refurbishment) and inadequate heating; others cheerfully overlooking the weaknesses and being grateful for what *is* provided. *Gerald Campion*, of *Woodman's Arms*, Hastingleigh (q.v.) sends us this report: "As *Frank Muir* says, you either do or you don't. We do, but can see why people don't. We found the food excellent and the rooms nice *for the price*, which, I believe is rightly (in my opinion) going up a bit. I do not think customers should underestimate what it takes to run a very large hotel like this, especially in the way they do it, which reflects on the low prices they are able to charge. Believe me, you will miss them when they're gone." (*Endorsed by Jane Dorrell, PH Freeman, C Makoff, Ella and Tim May*)

Open All year.
Rooms 32 double, 3 single – all with bath, shower, telephone, TV and tea-making facilities. 23 in converted farmhouse and cottages. 7 ground-floor rooms.
Facilities Drawing room, library, bar with small dance floor, dining room, breakfast room, billiard room; hairdressing and massage facilities; indoor tennis court and swimming pool, sauna, spa bath, sunbed, exercise room. 50-acre grounds with 6-acre garden, 9-hole golf course, deer park, tennis and squash

courts, croquet lawn, putting green, 2 heated swimming pools. Fishing in river Mole ½ m.
Location Leave M5 at exit 27 – onto A373; at South Molton take B3225 for 5 m, turn right to Chittlehamholt; go through village for 500 yards to hotel.
Restrictions Not suitable for ♿. No children under 10. No dogs.
Credit cards None accepted.
Terms Dinner, B&B: single £37.50, double £70–£80. Sun lunch £8.50, set dinner £12.50. Midweek breaks Nov–Mar. 1-night bookings quite often refused for Fri and Sat. Reduced rates for children sharing parents' room; special meals by arrangement.
Service/tipping: "We make it quite clear that service is included and no tips are expected. Some people insist on leaving tips; they are distributed in proportion to individual staff earnings."

CIRENCESTER Gloucestershire — Map 2

The Fleece Hotel
Market Place
Cirencester GL7 4NZ

Tel Cirencester (0285) 68507
Telex 437287

In the absolute town centre, just up the road from the magnificent parish church, *The Fleece Hotel* has two different facades, one half-timbered Tudor, one Georgian coaching inn. Nowadays the great open passageway from the main road to the back leads to a patio with white tables and chairs for outside eating and drinking. The hotel has a wine bar with a bar counter section with Ronald Searle boozy prints and a middle section with railway-type compartments, curtains in case you wish for complete seclusion and wooden painted panels depicting persons of various ages and sexes desporting themselves with bunches of grapes. The bedrooms have been completely refurnished and redecorated this past year with a corresponding rise in prices which has raised some eyebrows. There has also been criticism of untrained, though cheerful, staff; and "fairly standard" food in the wine bar. In general, though, readers have appreciated the creature comforts of *The Fleece* and "its jolly, laid-back atmosphere". (*JT Sutton, RF Holmes*)

Open All year, except 24–26 Dec.
Rooms 5 suites, 18 double, 2 single – all with bath, shower, direct-dial telephone, radio, TV, tea-making facilities and baby-listening.
Facilities Lounge, bar, wine bar, dining room. Courtyard.
Location Central: follow signs to town centre. Parking.
Restrictions Not suitable for ♿. No dogs in public rooms.
Credit cards All major cards accepted.
Terms (Service at guests' discretion) B&B: single £50.95, double £61.90, suite £77. Set lunch £6.70–£8.25, dinner £13.45; full alc £17.45; snack meals also served. Weekend breaks; gastronomic festivals; honeymoon package; New Year's Eve package. Reduced rates for children sharing parents' room.
Service/tipping: "I do not encourage tipping, but many customers like to do it so we do not refuse."

> Don't keep your favourite hotel to yourself. The Guide supports: it doesn't spoil.

> We get less feedback from smaller and more remote hotels. But we need feedback on all hotels: big and small, far and near, famous and first-timers.

CLANFIELD Oxfordshire — Map 2

The Plough [GFG]
Clanfield OX8 2RB

Tel Clanfield (036 781) 222 and 494
Telex 449848 HT TRAN

This small Elizabethan manor house, *c.* 1560, in a rural setting opposite the village green, was in earlier editions of the Guide under previous owners. It now returns, refurbished, as an elegant if rather pricey restaurant-with-rooms. There are just seven smallish double rooms, five of which have a jacuzzi. Inspectors found their four-poster a little frilly, but no doubt frilliness is a matter of taste. In other respects their room was thoroughly comfortable and attractive, with adequate bedside lighting (just), trouser-press, bowl of fruit, pot-pourri and similar embellishments. Large carpeted bathroom, bath with gold taps. But £75 [1987], they felt, was on the steep side, especially when linen was not changed daily, there was neither radio nor clock, and soap had to be asked for on the second day. However, the restaurant is perhaps the important feature of *The Plough,* and was found wholly deserving its red "M" in *Michelin.* Their summing up: "Like a small bourgeois restaurant-with-rooms in France – comfortable, good food and enthusiastically run." Its proximity to London and Oxford, respectively 72 and 20 miles to the east, and also to the Cotswolds, is an added advantage.

Open All year.
Rooms 7 double – 5 with bath, shower and jacuzzi, 2 with shower, all with telephone and TV.
Facilities Lounge bar, 2 restaurants. Garden.
Location On A4095 between Witney and Faringdon.
Restrictions Not suitable for ♿. No children except infants in cot.
Credit cards All major cards accepted.
Terms B&B: single occupancy £49.50–£60, double £65–£75. Set lunch £10, dinner £17. Bargain breaks (min 2 nights) all year except Easter and Christmas when 3-day package is offered.

COATHAM MUNDEVILLE Durham — Map 4

Hall Garth Country House Hotel
Coatham Mundeville
Nr Darlington DL1 3LU

Tel Aycliffe (0325) 300400

A friendly, rambling sort of place, parts dating back to 1540, with Victorian and Georgian extensions, more of a small unpretentious family hotel writ large than the new super chic breed of country house hotel, and priced accordingly. There are large, spotlessly clean bedrooms, decorated with painted plates and embroidery, some "with an enchanting view of a sloping pasture picturesquely dotted with cattle". (*Bill Cutler*) It stands in ten acres, just off the A1(M), "ideally situated for seeing the maximum of Yorkshire and Northumberland in a short time, or for those travelling to Scotland". (*Pat Purvis*) Owners Ernest Williamson and Janice Crocker say they aim "to run a genuinely friendly establishment that welcomes all, children, babies, pets, etc (someone even brought the budgie!), and try to cater and care for all at an affordable price". One reader appreciated not being charged, as in other establishments, for "endless extras I don't need – I can have a refreshing bath without gold taps." (*Mrs MD Prodgers*)

There have been some criticisms of the standard of food and service in the restaurant, but readers found it a pleasant place to stay and enjoyed Ernest Williamson's bristling red beard and "lovable Dickensian eccentricity".

Open 2 Jan–22 Dec. Restaurant closed Sun evening (bar food available).
Rooms 1 suite, 15 double, 4 single – 16 with bath, 5 with shower, all with direct-dial telephone, radio, TV and tea-making facilities; 4 with 4-poster. 9 in annexe. 1 ground-floor suite.
Facilities 3 lounges, pub, dining room. 10-acre gardens with tennis court, putting, croquet, children's play area, heated swimming pool, sauna.
Location ½ m E of A1, 3½ m N of Darlington. Leave A1 at A167 junction, go towards Darlington, take first left at brow of hill signposted Brafferton; *Hall Garth* is 200 yds down the road.
Restriction No dogs in public rooms.
Credit cards All major cards accepted.
Terms (No service charge) B&B (continental): single £37–£41, double £51–£59, suite £65. English breakfast £3.75. Set 3-course lunch £9.50, 4 course dinner £12.95–£13.95. Bar lunches available. Weekend rates: 25% discount for 2 nights; honeymoon breaks. Reduced rates for children sharing parents' room; special meals on request.
Service/tipping: "No policy. Any tips are put into a pool that is divided fairly for the hours worked. Management leaves division to staff."

CONSTANTINE BAY Cornwall — Map 1

Treglos Hotel
Padstow PL28 8JH

Tel Padstow (0841) 520727
Telex 45795 WSTTLX TGS

This traditional seaside hotel, 400 yards from a sandy beach, with rock pools at low tide, has its own sheltered sunken gardens for sunbathing and an indoor heated pool. The National Trust coastal footpath is nearby, and maps are provided of walks from the hotel. Also close by are Trevose golf course, sea fishing and boat trips, tennis, surfing, and riding. Although the menu is in French, it is explained in English, and is as conventionally English as the brick fireplaces, patterned carpets and chintzy furniture, and as reassuringly homely for those disliking designer chic. One touch of formality: jackets and ties are expected at dinner, even if the weather is hot. Many of the guests return every year, and the welcome of owners Ted and Barbara Barlow, and the quality of the service, with shoes cleaned, baggage carried up, a smile with the morning tea, and any meal you like served upstairs, is gratefully praised. Nursery tea is provided for small children, and the Barlows point out that guests over 75 are included in their hotel insurance coverage. One reader found the food and service excellent, but would have liked to see the bedroom redecorated, and larger towels. Two guests from America felt the hotel was even better than they had expected: "The grounds kept up nicely, the food well prepared and presented . . . Our entire experience at this hotel was very positive and left us with nice memories." (*Nancy and Walt Church*)

Open 11 Mar–8 Nov.
Rooms 5 suites, 31 double, 8 single – all with bath and shower, direct-dial telephone, radio, TV and baby-listening. 1 suite on ground floor. 4 self-catering flats in grounds.
Facilities Lift. 4 lounges, cocktail bar, restaurant, bridge room, snooker room, children's den. 3-acre grounds with gardens, croquet, heated enclosed swimming

pool. Sandy beach (with lifeguard) 400 yds; golf, tennis, sailing, fishing, water-skiing, and riding nearby.
Location Avoid Bodmin and Wadebridge; hotel will send directions. From Padstow, follow signs to St Merryn, then Constantine Bay.
Restrictions No children under 3 in restaurant. Dogs at hotel's discretion, not in public rooms.
Credit card Access (for restaurant only).
Terms (No service charge) Dinner, B&B: single £37.50–£45.50, double £72–£88, suite £96–£115. Set lunch £6.95, dinner £11.95; full alc £16.75. Reduced rates for stays of 3 days or more in low season; special weekly rate Thur–Thur. 1-night bookings sometimes refused. Reductions for children sharing parents' room; special meals and games.
Service/tipping: "Tips left to guests' discretion."

CORSE LAWN Gloucestershire — Map 2

Corse Lawn House Hotel [GFG] — *Tel* Tirley (045 278) 479
Corse Lawn GL19 4LZ

A 1745 redbrick Queen Anne house, built as a coaching inn, and standing before a large pond into which the coaches were driven for washing. Enthusiastic reports this year from readers on the atmosphere, authentic-country-house rather than London-designer-concept, "grand without being pompous", and on the food, with meals highly praised, ditto the "tea-making facilities" – no teabags here, but ground coffee and leaf tea in closed jars, milk in a flask, home-made biscuits, and a bowl of fruit. There is a small dinner menu, "in the best traditions of modern British cooking with a few French accents", good bar snacks, and "splendid" breakfasts. The house is owned by Mr and Mrs Hine, and bedrooms are named after various of his family's brandies. Major refurbishments have taken place during 1987. Only complaints: a sagging mattress; noisy plumbing; audible staff discord on one occasion and rattle of cars crossing the cattle grid. Mention should also be made of a large house labrador, said by one reader to bark in the early morning and "wake people up like a cockerel", and by another to "snooze continuously on the landing or the doormat throughout one's stay". Verdict: "Good value for money" and "Wish I could take family or clients to such a hotel near London." (*Dr DL Cohen, IG Hall, Tessa Stuart, and others*)

Open All year.
Rooms 10 double – all with bath and shower, telephone, radio, TV and tea-making facilities. 2 ground-floor rooms suitable for ♿.
Facilities Large lounge bar, drawing room, restaurant, small dining room. 4-acre grounds, with croquet, ornamental pond and herb garden.
Location 5 m SW of Tewkesbury. Take A438 to Ledbury for 4 m. Turn left onto B4211 (signposted Corse Lawn) and continue for 1 m.
Restriction No dogs in public rooms.
Credit cards All major cards accepted.
Terms B&B: single £36, double £45. Set lunch £11.50, dinner £15.75; full alc £20–£30. Christmas breaks. Reduced rates for children in parents' room; special meals.
Service/tipping: "We make no charge for service, nor do we expect tips."

> "Whoever fitted the bidet has never used one. It was barely three inches from the lavatory basin. To sit astride it would be anatomically impossible, unless one sat with one foot in the lavatory bowl."

CRANBROOK Kent — Map 3

Kennel Holt Hotel — *Tel* Cranbrook (0580) 712032
Cranbrook TN17 2PT

In a beautiful part of Kent, a red-brick Elizabethan manor house, tile-hung and weather-boarded. It stands at the end of a long drive in immaculate grounds with well-tended lawns, clipped yew hedges with topiary birds, pond with irises and ducks, and pollarded walks. "Of the 61 hotels we have visited in the last 13 years, the *Kennel Holt* ranks among the top two or three in every classification . . . Our room was large, with comfortable beds, looking out over the beautiful gardens. The food is superior in every way, the service friendly and efficient, the library well-equipped with books current as well as books from the past, a good place to spend a rainy day." (*John R Sale*) Visitors from abroad appreciated introductions made all round by their host, and being treated as "an individual, not just another body to fill space". (*Pat Purvis*) Residents eat in one of two small beamed dining rooms; additional diners overflow into a less atmospheric but still pleasant room. Owners are Patrick and Ruth Cliff. Ruth taught for 16 years at a Cordon Bleu residential college, and has created the menu. Her use of fresh, seasonal ingredients, home-made bread and traditional puddings served with lashings of Jersey cream, has pleased readers, as has Patrick Cliff's "meticulous concern to see that all is in order" – though some felt it was a little too meticulous at times. (*M Berge, Dr J Morgan*)

Open 26 Mar–30 Oct.
Rooms 6 double, 2 single – all with bath and/or shower, radio and TV; 1 with 4-poster; telephone available. 3 more doubles planned for 1988.
Facilities 2 lounges with open fires, dining room. 5½-acre grounds with croquet lawn, duck pond. Golf nearby, at local club.
Location 1½ m NW of Cranbrook on A262 between Goudhurst and Cranbrook.
Restrictions Not suitable for ♿. Children under 6 at hotel's discretion. Dogs on lead, not in dining room.
Credit cards None accepted.
Terms (No service charge) B&B: single £26.50–£31.50, double £37–£77; dinner B&B: single £44–£49, double £72–£112. Sunday lunch £16, set dinner £18.50. Off-season weekend breaks; 4-day cooking courses. 1-night advance bookings sometimes refused.
Service/tipping: "Our service is free."

CRANTOCK Cornwall — Map 1

Crantock Bay Hotel — *Tel* Crantock (0637) 830229
Crantock, Newquay TR8 5SE

"We had a splendid bucket-and-spade hol there last year, and have booked up unreservedly for same room, same time this year. Perfect for children who can make their own entertainment and adults who prefer to put on a collar and tie in the evening. " (*I Morrison*) A very traditional seaside hotel, run for many years by David and Brenda Eyles, in a stunning and quiet setting facing the Atlantic on the Cornish coast, 200 yards from a sandy beach with rockpools round the edge. Six golf courses nearby, and Newquay the nearest big town. Decor is vaguely 1930s, food is conventionally English. It's the the sort of friendly place that welcomes your children and your dogs; easily addictive.

Open 1 Apr–mid-/end Oct.
Rooms 22 double, 9 single – 30 with bath, 1 with shower, all with radio, TV, tea-making facilities and baby-listening. 2 ground-floor rooms suitable for partially ♿.
Facilities 2 lounges, TV room, bar, games room, restaurant; dancing, table tennis, bar billiards, slide shows, children's parties 2-3 nights a week. 4½-acre grounds with putting green, croquet, children's play area. Sea with sandy beach and safe bathing (lifeguard service) 200 yards; tennis, riding, golf nearby.
Location On West Pentire headland, 1 m beyond Crantock; 5 m SW of Newquay. Guests met by arrangement at Newquay and Truro stations.
Restriction No dogs in public rooms.
Credit cards Access, Visa.
Terms (No service charge) Dinner, B&B £16–£27.50. Bar lunch from £1, set dinner from £7.75. 5-day packages; bargain breaks in spring and autumn. Reduced rates for children sharing parents' room; special meals.
Service/tipping: "We are against a service charge. However, as visitors do tend to show their 'appreciation', I hold a fund distributed to the staff at the end of the summer. An explanatory note appears in bedrooms."

DEDHAM Essex — Map 3

Dedham Hall — *Tel* Colchester (0206) 323027
Dedham
Nr Colchester CO7 6AD

Dedham Hall is in the heart of Constable country, with the river Stour a short stroll away, and Flatford Mill two miles further on. It stands in five acres with a carp pond, just outside the village of Dedham, and has changed little in outward appearance since it was built in 1400. Mr and Mrs Slingo run a mixture of farm, guest house and residential art school with dedication. We asked for feedback last year and received two striking testimonials from readers. "I stayed for a night as I liked the description of it in the Guide. I was so impressed by the friendly atmosphere, the fact that all the furniture is *real* and not hotel-ish, and – not least – the food, that I asked Mr Slingo whether I could go there to write a book. During the two-and-a-half months I was there I was never once disappointed. Perhaps there are some guests who don't like having to go through the kitchen in order to get to the dining room – I find it a remarkable bonus and doubt whether there are many hotels that could pass this very intimate inspection by the guests. I might say that while I lived in jeans for the entire time I was there, Mrs Slingo and the staff change into full gear to serve their guests dinner. There is absolutely nothing sloppy about their management. Bridge-playing, gardening and domestic farming are much in evidence. Not a place for *hippies* or the very young." (*Penelope Mortimer*) Another reader went there after emerging from hospital: " The Slingos could not have been nicer. They offered to cook me special meals, and of their own accord made special salt-free vegetables just for me. The food was almost like a museum-piece: everything was home-grown, home-reared and home-cooked, and the flavour, as a result, was like food half-remembered from childhood. The hotel itself was calm and beautiful, bathed in East Anglian gentle light, their garden brimming with flowers." (*Angela Lambert*)

Open 1 Mar–15 Dec. Closed Christmas and New Year. Restaurant closed for lunch and on Wed.
Rooms 10 double, 2 single – 3 with bath, 5 with shower (6 with WC), all with tea-making facilities. 3 ground-floor rooms in converted barn.

Facilities 2 lounges (both with TV), bar, 2 dining rooms. 6-acre grounds; river Stour within yards, coarse fishing, boating. Converted barn in grounds used as artists' studio; painting courses.
Location Just outside village, but 200 yds from road, so quiet.
Restrictions Not suitable for ♿. No children under 5. No dogs.
Credit cards None accepted.
Terms (No service charge) B&B: single £19–£30, double £28.50–£45; dinner, B&B single £30–£41, double £50–£67. Set dinner £11. Painting courses.
Service/tipping: "We make no compulsory charge, but if customers wish to show appreciation, the staff are pleased to receive it."

Maison Talbooth
Stratford Road, Dedham
Colchester CO7 6HN

Tel Colchester (0206) 322367
Telex 987083 LETALB
Reservations in USA:
(800) 323 3602 and (312) 954 2944

Dedham Vale Hotel [GFG]
Stratford Road, Dedham
Colchester CO7 6HW

Tel Colchester (0206) 322273

Two siblings of the entrepreneurial Gerald Milsom on or close to the banks of the Stour. You can stay in either *Maison Talbooth* or *Dedham Vale,* but the former only serves breakfast; for other meals, residents must take themselves to *Dedham Vale,* half a mile up the road, or to another Milsom offspring, *Le Talbooth,* a quarter of a mile further on, a *soigné* restaurant, though it lost its *Michelin* rosette last year, and some recent reports have been critical.

Maison Talbooth, a luxuriously equipped Victorian house, is a far cry from the modest connotation of a B&B: its ten outsize bedrooms are all kitted out with virtually every pampering extra your imagination can run to; the beds are king-size and the bathrooms are often as opulent as the bedrooms. *Dedham Vale* is also a fully modernised Victorian mansion set in three acres of landscaped garden, close by but out of earshot of the A12. The bedrooms are a bit smaller than at *Maison Talbooth* (the prices are substantially smaller, too) but are furnished with almost as many extras as those at the senior house. But the pride and joy of *Dedham Vale* is its conservatory-like rôtisserie Terrace Restaurant, "an amazingly exotic crystal palace". (*Susan Gillotti, and others*)

Maison Talbooth
Open All year.
Rooms 1 suite, 10 double – 9 with bath, 1 also with shower, all with telephone, TV and baby-listening; radio on request. 5 ground-floor rooms.
Facilities Large hall, drawing room. The hotel stands in 2 acres of grounds, the restaurant in 3 acres on the banks of the river Stour; fishing. 2 yachts for hire.
Location Off A12. 6 m NE of Colchester. Take Stratford St Mary–Dedham road.
Restrictions Not suitable for ♿. No dogs.
Credit cards Access, Amex, Visa.
Terms (Service included in room rates; 10% added to meals) B&B: single £60–£85, double £70–£110, suite £105–£110. Set lunch £12 (£12.95 on Sun), packed lunch available; full alc £31. Sailing holidays May-Sept (book a month in advance). 1-night bookings not accepted for Sat; min 3 nights at Christmas and Bank Holidays. Reduced rates for children sharing parents' room; special meals.

Dedham Vale Hotel
Open All year. Restaurant closed Sat lunchtime and Sun night.
Rooms 5 double, 1 single – all with bath, telephone and TV.

Facilities Drawing room, bar, restaurant; function facilities. 4-acre grounds; river 100 yards; fishing and sailing locally.
Location 5 m NE of Colchester on A12.
Restrictions Not suitable for ♿. No dogs.
Credit cards All major cards accepted.
Terms (Service included in room rates; 10% added to meals) B&B (continental): single £50–£55, double £65–£80, suite £80. English breakfast £4. Set lunch £8, Sun lunch £12; full alc £25. 1-night bookings refused for Sat. Special portions for children.

DIDDLEBURY Shropshire — Map 1

The Glebe Farm — *Tel* Munslow (058 476) 221
Diddlebury, Craven Arms
SY7 9DH

"It is always an intriguing problem, when touring with a play, to find congenial places to stay. The undersigned couple of vagabonds want to say what a splendid week they had at *Glebe Farm*. It is charming and comfortable, and surrounded by lovely countryside. Mr and Mrs Wilkes entertained us delightfully, and the food was excellent and plentiful – pheasant, Welsh lamb, fresh, lightly cooked vegetables and delicious puddings. We were made to feel like guests in their own home." (*Sir Anthony Quayle and Tony Britton*) Thus read last year's entry. *Tony Britton* has been back and sent us further praise – of the flasks of hot soup and sandwiches awaiting him before a carefully banked fire each night on his return from the theatre, and the "come down to breakfast whenever you're ready". *Glebe Farm* is still a working farm, its farmhouse Elizabethan, half-timbered, with oak beams and flagstones. It is near the Saxon village church with its fortified tower, which stands amid countryside made famous by AE Housman. Ludlow is nearby, and many other shamelessly picturesque towns along the Welsh border, as well as the Iron Age fort, Nordy Hill. Other readers enthusiastically endorse Mr and Mrs Wilkes' kindness and cooking, and the house's charm. (*Alan and Gillian Jacobs, Christine Elliott*) Only grouse: an elderly mattress.

Open 3 Mar–7 Nov. Closed first 10 days of June. Restaurant closed Mon nights.
Rooms 5 double, 1 single – 2 with shower and WC, all with tea-making facilities. 3 in cottage in garden.
Facilities Sitting room, bar with TV, dining room. 1-acre garden with stream, ducks and geese. Fishing on nearby river Corve; riding 5 m; walks on Wenlock Edge, Clee Hill etc (accompanied tours can be arranged).
Location E of B4368, 4 m NE of Craven Arms.
Restrictions Not suitable for ♿. No children under 10. No dogs.
Credit cards None accepted.
Terms (Service at guests' discretion) B&B £15–£19; dinner, B&B £25.50–£30.50. Set dinner £10.50. Mid-week breaks off-season. Reductions for children.
Service/tipping: "The matter of gratuities is left to guests' discretion."

> We asked hotels to estimate their 1988 tariffs some time before publication so the rates given are often arbitrary. Please always check terms with hotels when making bookings.

> If you have difficulty in finding hotels because the location details given in the Guide are inadequate, please help us to improve directions next year.

DORCHESTER Dorset — Map 2

Casterbridge Hotel — *Tel* Dorchester (0305) 64043
49 High East Street
Dorchester DT1 1HU

Dorchester is the city of Hardy's *Mayor of Casterbridge*, from which the *Casterbridge Hotel* (though perhaps guest house would suit it better) takes its name. There is plenty to see in and around the town: the best-preserved Roman amphitheatre in Britain is at Maumbury Rings, Maiden Castle is our finest earthworks and the mysteriously powerful priapic Giant at Cerne Abbas is also not to be missed. This Georgian has been in Stuart Turner's family for many years, and still has many of his grandfather's furniture and paintings. There is no restaurant, but two well-appointed public rooms, and a conservatory where tea is served in summer. Rooms vary in size: some are said to be too small for comfort, ditto the bathrooms. Breakfasts are generous and excellent. More reports needed. (*AMW; endorsed by KB Mowle*) More reports needed.

Open All year except 25/26 Dec.
Rooms 10 double, 5 single – all with bath and/or shower, telephone, TV and baby-listening; tea-making facilities on request. 6 in courtyard annexe (1 double and 1 single on ground floor).
Facilities Lounge, bar, dining room, conservatory. Small courtyard garden.
Location 100 yards from town centre. Parking.
Credit cards All major cards accepted.
Terms (No service charge) B&B: single £20–£28, double £34–£40. Buffet lunch and supper from £2.50. 10% reduction for 3-day stays in low season. Reduced rates for children sharing parents' room; special meals on request.
Service/Tipping: "Tips not expected."

DULVERTON Somerset — Map 1

Ashwick Country House Hotel and Restaurant [GFG] — *Tel* Dulverton (0398) 23868
Dulverton TA22 9QD

A small Edwardian country house, 900 feet up in the Exmoor National Park, in six acres of grounds with water-gardens and lily ponds, overlooking the valley of the river Barle. Flowers from the garden fill the house, there is the original "stunning" William Morris wallpaper still in the hall, the rooms are light, airy and comfortable, the food is delicious with a different menu every day, hand-written to take away, the walking is excellent, and the Sherwoods are welcoming hosts, declaring in their brochure that their aim is to make a stay at *Ashwick* a memorable one: our reports, this year at least, are evidence that they are succeeding. A returning guest, *Ann Webb*, writes: "We arrived in a blizzard and left in dense fog, but the comfort of the hotel and the warmth of the welcome almost compensated for the appalling spring weather. We had to spend more time than we wanted indoors, but this was no hardship. The log fire in the hall was burning from breakfast till bedtime, daffodils from the garden cheered the bedroom, the food was excellent, and as usual the Sherwoods were genuinely kind and concerned to make our visit a success – which it was!" Others agreed, with particular thanks for vegetarian meals well catered for, Easter eggs on the pillow on Easter

Saturday, the discreet, unobtrusive service. One reader pulled out all the stops: "Exceeded even the expectations raised by your entry. It was the most restful, relaxing two days we have ever spent anywhere." (*Isobel Kempton; and many others*) The Sherwoods now do dinner, B&B, and not B&B only.

Open All year. Dinner served only to residents on Sun and Mon.
Rooms 6 double (2 suites can be arranged) – all with bath, shower, radio and TV.
Facilities Hall, lounge, library, bar, dining room. 6-acre grounds with 2 ponds and croquet.
Location 2½ m NW of Dulverton. Take the B3223 Exford–Lynton road. Drive up to moor, over cattle grid; hotel signpost is ½ m further on, directing you left.
Restrictions Not suitable for ♿. No children under 8. No dogs.
Credit cards None accepted.
Terms (No service charge) Dinner, B&B £31–£40. Set Sun lunch £8, set dinner £12.50. Special rates for 2, 5 or 7 nights; Christmas and New Year packages. 1-night bookings refused over bank holidays.
Service/tipping: "No service charge added. We do not expect tips."

EAST BUCKLAND Devon — Map 1

Lower Pitt Restaurant and Guest House [GFG] — *Tel* Filleigh (059 86) 243
East Buckland
Barnstaple EX32 0TD

A delightful 16th-century whitewashed stone farmhouse, now a sophisticated restaurant-with-rooms, lying low in the fold of a hillside, surrounded by the walled fields of South Exmoor. *Lower Pitt*, run by Suzanne and Jerome Lyons, has a strong following among local gourmets. Its three bedrooms are thoroughly comfortable, with pine furniture, duvets and electric blankets. Breakfasts are as much appreciated as dinners: "Fresh orange juice (with bits in to prove it), super home-made muesli, non-stained smoked haddock, perfect scrambled eggs. Exquisite home-made marmalades, and decent coffee." (*Francine and Ian Walsh; also WH Bruton*)

Open All year except Christmas and New Year.
Rooms 3 double – 1 with bath and shower, 2 with shower, all with tea-making facilities.
Facilities Lounge/bar, 2 dining rooms. 2-acre grounds with gardens and terrace for drinks. Sandy beaches and North Devon coast within easy reach.
Location 3 m NW of South Molton. Turn off A361 at Stagg Head.
Restrictions Not suitable for ♿. No dogs.
Credit cards Access, Amex, Visa.
Terms (No service charge) B&B: single £35, double £60. Full alc £15. Mid-week reductions (3 nights min).
Service/tipping: "No service charge; tips are at customers' discretion and are divided equally among all staff. As owners, we do not expect a tip."

EAST GRINSTEAD West Sussex — Map 3

Gravetye Manor [GFG] — *Tel* Sharpthorne (0342) 810567
East Grinstead RH19 4LJ — *Telex* 957239 GRAVTY

Gravetye Manor was built in 1598 by Richard Infield for his wife Katherine, and their portraits are carved on the original overmantel of the master bedroom. Seemingly lost in the beautiful West Sussex countryside, it is in fact only 12 miles from Gatwick and 30 from London. William Robinson, pioneer of the English natural garden, lived here from 1884 for over 50 years, restoring the interior, panelling it in timber from the estate, and giving it a sedate, turn-of-the-century, club-like grandeur. He laid out the gardens, whose trees have reached magnificent maturity. "The driveway is every romantic's dream. In the house, crackling fires, peace and calm." (*Simon Offen*) There are also fresh flowers, patterned carpets, chintz and a feeling of continuity and tradition. As for the restaurant, fruit, vegetables, herbs, spring water, apple juice, watercress and free range eggs are from the estate; salmon, venison and duck breasts all smoked in the hotel's own smoke-house, while game is obtained locally. One visitor, who has known *Gravetye Manor* for over 25 years, regrets the opulence of the bathrooms: "We loved it better in its simpler phrase. There is now too much gilding of refined gold." Not the opinion of another reader, however. "Prices at Gravetye are high, but for treats like the apple juice pressed from fruit on the premises at breakfast, no price could be scandalous. The purest nectar, unlike anything I've ever tasted. Breakfast overall was on a level unmatched anywhere during our trip." (*Bill Cutler*) Dedicated long-time owner is Peter Herbert. His son Leigh Stone-Herbert, an apprentice of the Roux brothers who has also worked in France and Australia, is now taking over in the kitchens – let us hope he will restore *Gravetye*'s *Michelin* rosette, lost last year. (*J and M Bailey, Heather Sharland, H Gholson*)

Open All year. Restaurant closed to non-residents Christmas evening.
Rooms 12 double, 2 single – 12 with bath, 2 with shower, all with telephone, radio and TV.
Facilities 3 sitting rooms, club members' bar, restaurant; private dining room. 30-acre grounds with croquet, clock golf; private trout fishing in 3-acre lake.
Location 5 m SW of East Grinstead off B2110 at West Hoathly sign. Glyndebourne 40 minutes' drive; Gatwick Airport 9 m.
Restrictions Not suitable for ♿. No children under 7 except babies. No dogs. No smoking in restaurants.
Credit cards None accepted.
Terms (Excluding VAT) B&B: single £55–£75, double £98–£110; dinner, B&B: single £75–£95, double £138–£190. Set lunch £15, dinner £20; full alc £31. 1-night bookings refused Sat except mid-winter.

EAST STOKE Dorset — Map 2

Kemps Country House Hotel — *Tel* Bindon Abbey (0929) 462563
East Stoke, Wareham BH20 6AL

A Victorian rectory converted into a reasonably priced small hotel (bargain breaks especially good value), run by chef/proprietor Mike Kemp and his wife Valerie, *Kemps* retains a distinct Victorian atmosphere thanks to Sanderson's wallpapers, and bric-à-brac. The recently built dining room (which does a busy non-resident trade) is very pretty, with green and white colour scheme, a candle on each table and lighting muted. In the evening discreet taped classical music fills the dining room, bar and sitting room. The set dinner offers a good choice, as does the à la carte menu. Service is friendly and helpful but not fawning, housekeeping continues to be a bit wayward. There are five spacious bedrooms in the main building overlooking the Purbeck Hills, but also facing the

A352; light sleepers may prefer the four rooms in a converted coach house. The hotel is well situated for touring many of the Dorset sights. (*Mr and Mrs JW Taylor, AJ Golledge, Robert Sim, MJN Barnett*)

Open All year, except 15 Dec–10 Jan.
Rooms 1 family suite, 7 double, 1 single – 5 with bath, 3 with shower, all with telephone, TV, tea-making facilities and baby-listening. 4 in annexe. 2 ground-floor rooms.
Facilities 2 lounges, bar, restaurant. 1½-acre grounds with play area for children.
Location On A352 midway between Wool and Wareham.
Restrictions No children under 7 in dining room at dinner. No dogs.
Credit cards All major cards accepted.
Terms (No service charge) B&B £25–£35; dinner, B&B £35–£45. Set lunch £6.50, dinner £12.50; full alc £15–£20. Bargain breaks of 2-7 days; reduced rates in low season. Children under 7 sharing parents' room charged only for meals; 7-12 year-olds charged ½ adult rate if taking high tea, ⅔ if taking dinner; high teas provided.
Service/tipping: "Tipping optional; shared equally among all staff."

EASTON GREY Wiltshire — Map 2

Whatley Manor
Easton Grey
Malmesbury SN16 0RB

Tel Malmesbury (0666) 822888
Telex 449380 WHOTEL

A pleasing 17th-century manor house which was completely renovated by a wealthy sportsman in the 1920s. It stands on the banks of the fledgling Avon, between Tetbury and Bath, in ten acres of well-maintained grounds. Public rooms are spacious and flowery, and the bedrooms, some new, several upgraded this year, attractively and comfortably furnished. Prices, medium-to-high, are nevertheless still felt to be moderate considering the comfort and amenities. The restaurant, enlarged this year, has enterprising menus which include wild boar parfait, trout stuffed with pike and spinach, and sauces inspired by *nouvelle cuisine*, though you may have any dish served without the sauce if you prefer. One reader thought it should be pointed out that there is no room service in the attractive Court House, 70 yards from the main building, and that service of the excellent cooked breakfast stops at exactly 9.45 am, after which latecomers must settle for continental breakfast only. She felt the set meals and weekend breaks to be splendid value, and though she would have liked a few more extras perhaps (flowers, fruit?) in the bedroom, concluded: "We found everything well-run, and the staff very polite and helpful, the room spacious, clean and warm. I'm sure we will visit here again." (*Susan Cohen*)

Open All year.
Rooms 1 suite, 25 double – all with bath and/or shower, telephone, TV and baby-listening; radio on request. 11 in annexe also with tea-making facilities.
Facilities 2 lounges, library bar, dining room; sauna, solarium, jacuzzi, games room, snooker room. 10-acre grounds with croquet lawn, tennis court, putting green, golf practice net, heated swimming pool. Trout fishing in river Avon which forms part of boundary; riding nearby.
Location On B4040, 3 m W of Malmesbury.
Restrictions Not suitable for ♿. No dogs in public rooms.
Credit cards All major cards accepted.
Terms [1987 rates] (No service charge) B&B: single £49.50–£54.50, double £69–£79. Set lunch £9, dinner £17. Christmas and New Year packages. Reduced rates for children sharing parents' room; special meals.
Service/tipping : "Any tips left by guests are equally distributed to all staff."

EVERSHOT Dorset Map 2

Summer Lodge [GFG] *Tel* Evershot (093 583) 424
Evershot DT2 0JR

"Without doubt the friendliest place of our trip and the happiest atmosphere – we could not have enjoyed it more. Dinner and breakfast were delicious. I would love to spend a week there." (*The Marchioness of Tavistock*) "Just perfect. The Corbetts have the knack of making you feel perfectly at home as their guest while also preserving the sense that the staff are there to serve and help. Food delicious (with seconds!), flower arrangements a joy. Little things made such a difference – car windscreens cleaned in the morning, everyone calling you by name, a barrel of home-made biscuits in the room. *And* a goodbye wave which we felt was really sincere, though we had stayed only one night. At least, if it wasn't, why was Nigel still waving enthusiastically as we reached the end of the long, long gravel drive? Worth every penny." (*J and E Bailey*) "Attention to detail as good as ever. Last year we had told them how much we had enjoyed lamb en croûte on a previous visit: 'You shall have it next time.' And so we did, while everyone had a different dish that evening. No reminder needed either that we can't eat chocolate pudding – our special alternative came up unasked for." (*JP Berryman; also 24 others*)

Once again the peels of praise ring out in gratitude for the exceptional standards of hospitality maintained by Nigel and Margaret Corbett at their platonic idea of a country house hotel in the medium-price range incarnate in the Earl of Ilchester's former dower house in a pretty Dorset village. They won a César in 1985. Some readers would like them to have it in perpetuity.

Open 1 Feb–30 Nov.
Rooms 12 double (3 can be let as single) – all with bath, telephone and tea-making facilities. 1 ground-floor room suitable for ♿.
Facilities Large drawing room with log fire, TV room, bar, dining room. Garden with heated outdoor swimming pool, croquet lawn and stables. Golf, trout fishing nearby. 12 m from sea and pebble beach, good sea fishing; sandy beach at Weymouth and Lyme Regis, 20 m away.
Location 10 m S of Yeovil. (*Note:* the entrance on village street is for pedestrians only; cars must turn left on reaching village into Summer Lane and then right into drive to house.)
Restrictions No children under 8. No dogs in public rooms.
Credit cards Access, Visa.
Terms (Service at guests' discretion) Dinner, B&B £35–£60. Set Sunday lunch £8.50, dinner £16. 2- and 3-day bargain breaks. 1-night bookings sometimes refused for Sat night. 30% reduction for children sharing parents' room.
Service/tipping: "Tipping is left entirely *to our guests' discretion, and is* never *solicited by members of our staff who are fully and properly paid."*

EXETER Devon Map 1

White Hart Hotel *Tel* Exeter (0392) 79897
South Street, Exeter EX1 1EE

Characterful former coaching inn, parts dating from 14th and 15th centuries, centrally situated, close to Cathedral; many traditional features retained but bedrooms and public rooms comfortably modernised. Traditional English fare. Small garden. 61 rooms, most with bath or shower. B&B from £22.50. Set menus £8.75–£12 [1987]. *New nomination: more reports welcome.*

FALMOUTH Cornwall — Map 1

Penmere Manor Hotel
Mongleath Road
Falmouth TR11 4PN

Tel Falmouth (0326) 314545
Telex 45266 PMHTL

David and Rachel Pope, assisted by son Andrew and daughter Elizabeth, have been running this well-bred Georgian house as a family hotel for almost 20 years. It is the kind of unpretentious but dependable hotel that families often look for in vain, and its virtues bring it plenty of loyal regulars. It has five acres of sub-tropical gardens and woodland, and a large walled garden, supposedly built by French prisoners after the Napoleonic wars, which now frames the heated swimming pool. There is a snooker room, and a cellar games room with table tennis, bar billiards and the like; sandy beaches are a mile away. It is a thoroughly go-ahead place, organising special "House and Garden" breaks during the winter months, and golf holidays in the summer. The hotel was planning to introduce a new indoor leisure complex in the autumn of 1987, free to residents, including indoor swimming pool and jacuzzi ("both treated by ozone", whatever that may mean), mini-gym, sauna and solarium. Meanwhile, our first entry last year has swiftly been endorsed, with all correspondents singling out for special praise the quality of the Popes' service. "What makes the difference is not just the care to get everything right, but the cheerful amiable professionalism which goes with it. Hotel much used by superior reps who know a good place when they see it." (*JF Bowes; also Geoff Barratt, Mr and Mrs Blair Harrison*)

Open All year, except 21–27 Dec.
Rooms 28 double, 4 single – all with bath and/or shower, telephone, radio, TV, tea-making facilities and baby-listening. 5 in building in grounds.
Facilities 3 lounges, bar, dining room, games room, snooker room. Leisure complex with indoor swimming pool, jacuzzi, sauna, solarium. 5-acre sub-tropical gardens with golf net and heated swimming pool. Sandy beaches 1 m; safe bathing, reservoir fishing 3 m; golf 1 m.
Location 100 yards beyond traffic lights at Penryn Bridge turn right on B3291 to Constantine and Gweek. After ½ m bear left to Budock and Maenporth. Follow road for 1 m; look for hotel sign on left. Turn left into Mongleath Road.
Restriction Well-behaved dogs welcome, but not in public rooms (£1 per day).
Credit cards All major cards accepted.
Terms B&B: £26.50–£32; dinner, B&B £33.75–£37.50. Bar lunches. Set dinner £12. Reduced rates for children sharing parents' room; high tea.
Service/tipping: "Our staff are remunerated for the services they give willingly and there is no further obligation on guests."

FAUGH Cumbria — Map 4

The String of Horses
Faugh, Heads Nook
Carlisle CA4 9EG

Tel Hayton (022 870) 297 and 509

Exuberant kitschy olde worlde 17th-century pub ten minutes from the M6 (exit 43). Eclectic menu in restaurant: curry said to be best bet. 3 suites, 10 double rooms, with many fancy features including exotic Bonsack baths en suite. *Leisure centre and heated swimming pool. Not for all comers, but many appreciate its warm welcome and gimmicks. Double B&B £48–£58. Set dinner £11.25. Has it a place in the Guide? More views welcome.*

FELMINGHAM Norfolk **Map 3**

Felmingham Hall *Tel* Swanton Abbott (069 269) 228
Felmingham
North Walsham NR28 0LP

New to the Guide this year, Richard and Jennifer Joyce's comfortably modernised Elizabethan country house in unspoilt countryside is nominated by *Robert and Rosalind Plowright*: "There are many hotels in the UK that enable you to stay in the country, but few that make you feel part of it: *Felmingham Hall* does just that. As you head down the long drive you know that you are in the depths of rural Norfolk; and also that it is a substantial place, and has been since 1569. A bevy of outbuildings flank the main hall, beyond which lie a coach house and swimming pool. Beyond all this are several acres of mixed woodland containing a wide variety of birdlife and, in season, butterflies. Indoors are spacious rooms, log fires when necessary, loads of character (but not kitsch), and a varied and abundant menu complemented by a wine list reflecting the owners' joint careers in the wine trade. At the prices charged it is well worth exploring. A recent addition, part of a sensitive programme of restoration, is a cellar bar for serious boozing, while more discreet drinks are served upstairs in the main hall and drawing room. The bedrooms are in the main large and comfortable, with the extras one would expect – colour TV, tea-making apparatus and the like. On the first floor walls hang some perfectly awful watercolours by a local worthy which the owners have long since despaired of selling and now regard as something of a joke. An excellent base for exploring the unexpected delights of Norfolk; and also a most relaxing country hotel." A duet in 1987; can we expect a chorus of approval in 1988?

Open Mar–mid-Dec.
Rooms 10 double, 2 single – all with bath, TV and tea-making facilities. 2 more planned for 1988, accessible for ♿.
Facilities Reception hall, drawing room, cellar bar, dining room. 16-acre grounds with heated swimming pool, 8 acres woodlands; river.
Location 1 m S of Felmingham village, signposted from the church. Felmingham is off B145 W of North Walsham.
Restrictions No children under 12. No dogs (kennels nearby).
Credit cards Access, Amex.
Terms (No service charge) B&B £27.50–£33.80; dinner, B&B £32.50–£38.80. Full alc £12.50. Reductions for 3- and 7-day stays.
Service/tipping: "We accept tips if guests obviously feel that staff have gone out of their way to help. We accumulate them and distribute the total to all members of staff in relation to the number of hours worked. They can take money, or goods which we obtain for them through trade sources."

We need feedback on *all* entries. Often people fail to report on the best-known hotels, assuming that "someone else is sure to".

Our italicised entries are different this year. There are more of them and they indicate hotels which are worth considering, but which, for various reasons – inadequate information, lack of feedback, ambivalent reports – do not at the moment warrant a fully entry. We should particularly welcome comments on these hotels.

FLITWICK Bedfordshire — Map 3

Flitwick Manor [GFG] — *Tel* Flitwick (0525) 712242
Church Road, Flitwick MK45 1AE — *Telex* 825562 FM

A Grade II early 18th-century listed building, set in a 50-acre park (though only six-and-a-half acres of well-tended gardens belong to the hotel). Flitwick itself is "not a tremendously inspiring place" as one reader kindly put it, but the *Manor*, approached down an avenue of huge trees, has considerable pedigree and is well out of eyeshot of the village. And the resident owners, Somerset and Helene Moore, are clearly making a success of their new profession of country-house hoteliers as they previously did as restaurateurs. Service can sometimes be a little inexperienced in the restaurant, and the meals, too – with an emphasis on fish – can be erratic. But most correspondents would echo the couple who wrote after last year's nominating entry: "Enthusiastic endorsement! Extremely comfortable lavishly-furnished room and bathroom with every imaginable extra: flowers, fresh fruit, bath robe, slippers, shampoos, aftershave . . . everything except pyjamas. Also well-lit and quiet. The restaurant is generally very good. Wines are excellent and very fairly priced. Staff all very pleasant. Altogether very enjoyable!" (*Pat and Jeremy Temple; also WA, Hilary Leighter, Mrs EH Prodgers*) *Note*: prices of rooms and meals have shot up 20–40% since last year – perhaps to help pay for a new dining room and many new bedrooms. It is clear that the *Manor* is in something of a gastronomic and hotel desert, but can these price increases be justified?

Open All year.
Rooms 2 suites, 11 double, 2 single – all with bath and/or shower, direct-dial telephone, radio, TV and baby-listening. 3 on ground floor, 1 equipped for ♿.
Facilities 2 drawing rooms, bar, restaurant, private dining room. 6½-acre grounds with lake, tennis, 2 croquet lawns, 12th-century church and helipad. Set in a 50-acre park (not hotel's).
Location Take exit 12 from M1, then A5120 towards Bedford. Hotel is on outskirts of Flitwick.
Credit cards All major cards accepted.
Terms [1987 rates] B&B single £58, double £90–£105 (let as single £70–£120), suite £140–£150. Set lunch/dinner (excluding 10% service charge) £15.60–£19.50; full alc £26. Whitsun special break. Reduced rates for children sharing parents' room; special meals.
Service/tipping: "An optional 10% will be added to restaurant bills unless otherwise requested."

FRENCHBEER Devon — Map 1

Teignworthy [GFG] — *Tel* Chagford (06473) 3355
Frenchbeer, Nr Chagford
TQ13 8EX

A Lutyens-style 1920s house, built by the same expert craftsmen as Castle Drogo nearby, on a south-facing slope with glorious views, deep enough in Devon countryside for you to do your birdwatching from the window. "As comfortable and agreeable to stay in as ever, and the food is now of a very high standard: a new chef is doing splendid things. Breakfast excellent. The sitting room had a huge log fire burning as early as 9 am, so that on a wet morning we sat and read in real peace and comfort. Being there felt like staying with particularly thoughtful and attentive friends." (*Lady Marychurch*) Also praised were the fresh orange juice at breakfast, a vegetarian dish always on the menu, the good beds, and the generous selection of books and records. There was one complaint of a room being chilly in winter, though another letter applauded the refusal to super-heat. One guest found the decor dull, and the river fishing too informal (no paths cleared etc). Another complained of being chivvied. *Teignworthy* does not have the panache of nearby *Gidleigh Park*, nor the latter's outstanding restaurant. The rooms are smaller and less sophisticated in their decor. But the prices are a lot less steep, too. (*Richard and Betty Ireland, April Young, Richard Creed, Arleigh and Diane Kerr, and others*)

Open All year. House parties only Christmas and New Year.
Rooms 9 double – all with bath, direct-dial telephone, radio and TV. 3 in converted hayloft, 2 with shared sitting room.
Facilities Hall, drawing room with log fire, small bar, dining room; some conference facilities; sauna and sunbed. 14-acre grounds with woodland, heathland, lawned garden and croquet lawn; fishing in the river Teign at the bottom of the garden or in the Fernworthy Reservoir; golf at Moretonhampstead; riding available. Dartmoor on the doorstep.
Location 3 m SW of Chagford. Follow signs towards Fernworthy, then Thornworthy.
Restrictions Not suitable for ♿. No children under 12. No dogs.
Credit cards Access, Visa.
Terms (No service charge) B&B: single £48.50, double £85; dinner, B&B: single £56.50–£73, double £99–£133.50. Lunch from £15, dinner £25.75. Special winter rates (2 nights min); Christmas and New Year house parties.
Service/tipping: "We do not expect tipping. If anyone insists on tipping we distribute equally to all staff. But we feel that we are in a service industry to give service."

GILLINGHAM Dorset — Map 2

Stock Hill House Hotel [GFG] — *Tel* Gillingham (07476) 3626
Wyke, Gillingham SP8 5NR

An ovation for this 1987 newcomer, though its owners, Peter and Nina Hauser, became used to accolades from our readers in their previous incumbency at the *Aval du Creux* on Sark. They deserted Sark, which they felt had become too crowded and noisy, two years ago and installed themselves in this early Victorian manor house in ten acres of parkland – full, we are told, of old and rare trees and lots of wildlife. No shortage of showplace attractions in the area: Stourhead, Longleat, Shaftesbury, Wells, Bath *et al.*

Three features made *Aval du Creux* a favourite: the quality of Peter Hauser's cooking, the hospitality of both Hausers and Nina's sister Lorna, and a very reasonable tariff. The same features are displayed at *Stock Hill*. We offer one couple's appreciation, but all the names below would assent to their comments with similar enthusiasm. "One of the most pleasant weekends we have had for a long time. The house has been well renovated by the new owners, who are hard at work now successfully transforming the garden and grounds. What impressed us most was that they have done all the work themselves. Peter Hauser does all the cooking – he's just taken on some help for the washing up! Perhaps this is why prices are so reasonable. Our room charge of £80 [1987] included VAT, dinner (including half a lobster), full breakfast and morning paper. Our large bathroom had a raised section with a huge sunken oval bath –

great fun but it must be murder to clean, and a drain on the hot water supply. The food is superb. Everything fresh, with a small choice for each course. Many dishes are Austrian-based or influenced; the seafood ones are outstanding. The well-priced wine list is fairly short and mainly from Yapps, whose offices are only five miles away. All in all, an excellent addition to the country house scene." (*Pat and Jeremy Temple: also Sam and Sue Hall, HS, B Orman, Anthony and Elizabeth Tasker*)

Open All year except Feb. Restaurant closed Sun evening and Mon.
Rooms 6 double, 1 single – all with bath and/or shower, direct-dial telephone, radio and TV.
Facilities Large hall with drinks cupboard, lounge, breakfast room, restaurant; indoor heated swimming pool, sauna and solarium Apr–Oct. 10-acre grounds with stream, lake and croquet lawn.
Location On B3081 1½ m from Gillingham, just S of A303.
Restrictions Not suitable for ♿. No children under 7. No dogs.
Credit cards Access, Visa.
Terms (No service charge) Dinner, B&B: single £45, double £80–£90; full board: single £55, double £90–100. Set lunch £11, dinner £18. Reduced rates and special meals for children.
Service/tipping: "Tipping is between the guest and staff; we are much against service charges."

GITTISHAM Devon — Map 1

Combe House Hotel — *Tel* Honiton (0404) 2756
Gittisham, Nr Honiton EX14 0AD

Little feed-back this year on this very grand manor house, set in six acres of gardens in a 3,500 acre estate, owned by a descendant of James Boswell and filled with portraits, furniture and books from the ancestral home, Auchinleck House in Ayrshire. John Boswell, who worked for the P&O shipping organisation in the Far East, and his wife Thérèse took over the mainly Elizabethan house in a very run-down condition, but have restored its magnificence. It has a history going back to the Norman Conquest, and memorials to the family who owned it for 232 years are in the tiny towered church in the picturesque scheduled village of Gittisham. "The best smoked salmon since our own in the Outer Hebrides . . very reasonable and very good value." (*RA Dubery*) Another reader praised both the service and the food as excellent, but criticised the upkeep. More reports please.

Open End Feb to mid-Jan. Closed to non-residents for bar lunch and tea.
Rooms 1 suite, 11 double – all with bath and shower, telephone and TV.
Facilities Hall, sitting room, drawing room, cocktail bar, 2 dining rooms. 6-acre garden; croquet. Trout fishing on river Otter 1½ m. Sea 8 m; sandy beach at Exmouth 16 m; golf and riding nearby; shooting can be arranged.
Location Just off A30, 3½ m S of Honiton. Hotel is signposted in Gittisham.
Restrictions Only suitable for partially ♿. No young children in dining room at night. No dogs in dining room.
Credit cards All major cards accepted.
Terms B&B: single £45–£63, double £66–£85, suite £100. Set Sun lunch £13.50; full alc £21.50. Reductions out of season and for stays of over a week; winter breaks; Christmas package. Reduced rates for children sharing parents' room; special meals.

We depend on detailed fresh reports to keep our entries up-to-date.

GRASMERE Cumbria — Map 4

White Moss House [GFG] — *Tel* Grasmere (096 65) 295
Rydal Water, Grasmere LA22 9SE

Formerly three 18th-century cottages owned by Wordsworth's family, and lived in by his descendents until the 1930s, for many years past *White Moss* has been a small caring hotel, in the hands of the Butterworths. Now their daughter and son-in-law, Susan and Peter Dixon, have taken over. There are five rooms in the main house on the A591 (heavy lorries banned), and two rooms up a steep footpath in Brockstone cottage. Rooms are smallish and on the pricey side, but are extensively kitted out with cosseting extras - trouser press, sewing kit, hairdrier, bath essence, dried *White Moss* lavender, Crabtree and Evelyn soaps, and so forth. Correspondents all speak enthusiastically about the admirable – "very English and very good" – *White Moss* dinners: "7.30 for 8", five courses, with no choice until the dessert; the hotel boasts a particularly interesting selection of English cheeses and a wide-ranging reasonably-priced wine list with lots of halves. Breakfasts, too, get their share of praise. The Dixons' first year of full ownership seems a clear success, with readers appreciating Mrs Dixon's interest in plans and the sheets of advice for walks or drives. (*Dr John Lunn, RH Freeman, Christopher Carr, Dr JH Newton, DS*)

Open Mid-Mar–mid-Nov.
Rooms 7 double – 6 with bath, 1 with shower, all with radio and TV. 2 in cottage annexe.
Facilities Lounge, bar, dining room. 1-acre garden with terrace and hillside seats. Near Rydal Water and river Rothay; swimming and fishing.
Location On A591 between Ambleside and Grasmere.
Restrictions Not suitable for ♿. No children under 10. No dogs.
Credit cards None accepted.
Terms (Service at guests' discretion) Dinner, B&B £45–£49. Set dinner £17.95. Reduced rates for stays of 3 nights or more Mar, Apr and Nov. 1-night bookings sometimes refused, especially Sat and bank holidays.
Service/tipping: "Tipping is not expected. Sometimes guests insist on leaving something, which we put in a staff box."

GRASSINGTON North Yorkshire — Map 4

Ashfield House Hotel — *Tel* Grassington (0756) 752584
Grassington
Nr Skipton BD23 5AE

"Mrs Sugden's glowing personality represents an old-fashioned Yorkshire welcome." (*J Campbell*) "Mr Sugden is always cheerful and whistling." (*Margaret Ruth West*) Two tributes from this year's file on a dependably hospitable guest-house close by the village square in Upper Wharfedale. Correspondents continue to endorse this earlier report:

"A 17th-century tree-surrounded house, tucked away just off the main street. From it one can walk straight up through the village into the dales. The floors are uneven, the doorways low, the walls thick and the atmosphere delightful. A blazing fire is lit after dinner in the hall/sitting room where limitless fresh coffee is available for guests in the evenings. A 'mini-bar', run on a 'help-yourself' system, is in the other sitting room, along with TV but in our experience most people sit round the fire on the very uncomfortable settles and laundry baskets and high-backed old chairs and enjoy getting to know each other. Mrs Sugden is a real expert in the best of English fare. The only fixed point in the day is the high spot of 7 pm when dinner is served. We are by no means the only people who keep going back, because the home-like atmosphere, the sparkling cleanliness, make this an extremely pleasant place to stay." (*PS and HA; also Ian Barcroft*)

Open 1 Apr–31 Oct.
Rooms 7 double – 2 with shower, all with tea-making facilities.
Facilities 2 lounges (1 with open fire, 1 with bar and TV), dining room. ½-acre garden.
Location Central but secluded, off main square. Parking.
Restrictions Not suitable for ♿. No dogs.
Credit cards None accepted.
Terms (No service charge) B&B £13.70–£16.30; dinner, B&B £21.50–£25.80. 1-night bookings sometimes refused especially during bank holidays. Reduced rates and special meals for children.

GREAT AYTON North Yorkshire — Map 4

Ayton Hall — *Tel* Great Ayton (0642) 723595
Low Green
Great Ayton T39 6BW

North Yorkshire is not an area much blessed with good hotels. *Ayton Hall*, a pedigree Grade II listed country house, dating in part back to the 13th century, but mainly Elizabethan and Georgian, should perhaps be called a restaurant-with-rooms rather than an hotel. In the North Yorkshire Moors National Park, surrounded by its own park-like grounds, it was acquired six years ago by Melvin Rhodes and his wife, and thoroughly restored. The original nominator described the enormous bedroom in which he had stayed, with four-poster, easy chairs, a large bathroom, and "all the extras that one can expect to find in a luxury establishment". He commended the excellent breakfast, and enjoyed the dinner, which he however found slightly over-ambitious, the short set dinner menu to be preferred. He summed up: "Everything is in impeccable nick, the owners are friendly and concerned without obtruding, and the whole place exudes an atmosphere of modest success." (*DW; also FB Seward*) More reports please.

Open All year.
Rooms 2 suites, 5 double – all with bath and/or shower, telephone, radio, TV with video, and baby-listening.
Facilities Bar/reception, 2 lounges, restaurant; pianist in 1 lounge most nights. 6-acre parkland with landscaped garden and hard tennis court (advance booking necessary); trap shooting, archery and croquet available on request.
Location 9 m S of Middlesbrough.
Restrictions No children under 11. Dogs in kennels only (advance booking necessary).
Credit cards Access, Amex, Visa.
Terms B&B: single occupancy £50–£60, double £68–£79. Set lunch/dinner £9.95; full alc £30. Weekend breaks.

There are many expensive hotels in the Guide. We are keen to increase our coverage at the other end of the scale. If you know of a simple place giving simple satisfaction, please write and tell us.

GREAT MILTON Oxfordshire — Map 1

Le Manoir aux Quat' Saisons [GFG] — *Tel* Great Milton (084 46) 8881
Great Milton OX9 7PD — *Telex* 837552 BLANC

Le Manoir opened its doors in March 1984. With *Michelin* heralding the event with two rosettes, and with restaurant and hotel critics reaching for their *Thesaurus* to describe its qualities, it seemed destined to achieve instant immortality. Our entries for the past three years have indeed been adulatory: report after report paying tribute to Raymond and Jenny Blanc's triumphant realisation of the ideal country house hotel incarnate in a serene country mansion amid 27 acres of garden and parkland, just off the M40. Alas, as so often, instant fame carries its own penalty. Many reports *are* as unstinted as before. One reader, who recommends the mid-week winter breaks as particularly good value since rooms let in the ordinary way are often the cheaper ones and the winter breaker can often end up in the best room, wrote to tell us of his room – which was the best: it ran the full width of the building, with armchairs, sofas, a huge bed and an abundance of extras. "There is a feeling of generosity about the place, even for this price level. The bathroom is the answer to a *Dallas* fantasist's dreams, with its huge whirlpool bath on a carpeted plinth, a ledge to the left for the bottle of Bollinger and one to the right for the latest Jackie Collins. Breakfast is perfect. It goes without saying the dinners are memorable. Very expensive, but this place is a Centre of Excellence – we think it gives full value for money". (*David Wooff*)

If only all this year's reports could have smelled as sweet. Most indeed have spoken with awe of Raymond Blanc's brilliant innovative style of cooking, but there have been as many grouses about other matters as there have been compliments. Service in the restaurant has been erratic, rooms vary in size and agreeableness, and one visitor was outraged by a small double room over the kitchen for which the charge was £95. More than one reader complained about the way in which the hotel dealt with the tricky matter of deposits. People do expect something approaching perfection at the *Manoir*'s prices. We hope for better news in the coming year.

Open 21 Jan–23 Dec. Restaurant closed Sun evenings, all day Mon and Tue lunch; drinks, tea and pâtisserie available on these days.
Rooms 3 suites, 7 double – 2 with bath and shower, 8 with bath, all with direct-dial telephone, radio and TV; some with whirlpool bath; 2 with four-poster.
Facilities 2 sitting rooms, reception lounge, 2 restaurants; private restaurant, functions room. 27 acres of landscaped garden and parkland with tennis court, heated swimming pool, water garden and stables.
Location 1 m W of M40/A40, 8 m SE of Oxford. From London take M40: exit 7, 1 mile, 2nd right. From Oxford, take A40, then A329 at Milton Common towards Wallingford, 2nd right.
Restrictions No children under 5. No dogs in building – free kennel facilities in grounds.
Credit cards All major cards accepted.
Terms (No service charge) B&B: double £85–£185, suite £160–£235. Set lunch £19.50–£22.50 weekdays, £30–£40 Sun, dinner £36; full alc £40–£50. Special mid-week breaks Oct–Mar. 1-night bookings may be refused for summer weekends. Special meals for children.

> Please make a habit of sending in a report as soon as possible after a visit when details are still fresh in your mind.

GREAT SNORING Norfolk — Map 3

The Old Rectory
Barsham Road
Great Snoring
Fakenham NR21 0HP

Tel Walsingham
(032 872) 597 and 881

The Old Rectory at Great Snoring, once a manor house and probably built about 1500, is situated two miles from Walsingham, within easy reach of the North Norfolk coast. It started life hexagonal, but the Victorians squared it off, and it retains other curious architectural features: stone mullioned windows, for instance, bordered with frieze designs in terracotta tiles with heraldic devices of the Shelton family, and male and female Shelton heads. It offers "comfortable accommodation in this lovely old house to make your visit to this part of Norfolk pleasant and memorable during either the summer or the winter months", specialising in "traditional English food". Reactions: "A beautiful piece of architecture in a garden that is looked after but not manicured, very restful. A superb welcome, and a double-bedded room with a sizeable bathroom attached. Plenty of magazines and books. The food was good plain English – the spring cabbage done to a turn. The house was a joy to stay in. Lovely proportions, particularly the staircase. Most reasonably priced." (*Patricia Roberts; also WV and LE Shaw, R Thackrah, Antony Fletcher, Anne Oliphant*) One reader, however, found the rooms poorly furnished, and the traditional menu overly plain.

Open All year except 25/26 Dec. Dining room closed for lunch.
Rooms 6 double, 1 single – all with bath (5 *en suite*) direct-dial telephone and TV.
Facilities Sitting room, dining room. 1½-acre walled garden. 6 m from north Norfolk nature reserves. Bathing, fishing, sailing etc all within ½-hour drive.
Location Great Snoring is 3 m NE of Fakenham off A148 Cromer road. *Old Rectory* is behind church on Barsham road.
Restrictions Not suitable for ♿. Children not encouraged. No dogs.
Credit cards Amex, Diners.
Terms (No service charge) B&B: single £38–£42, double £55–£58. Set dinner £12–£15.
Service/tipping: "No service charge. If a guest wishes to tip this is given to the staff concerned."

GRIZEDALE Cumbria — Map 4

Grizedale Lodge Hotel
Grizedale, Hawkshead LA22 0QL

Tel Hawkshead (096 66) 532

Unpretentious, genuine small hotel run by Jack and Margaret Lamb in former shooting lodge in Grizedale forest, an untouristy area between Windermere and Coniston. Won the 1987 English Tourist Board award for Best Newcomer of 1987. Best rooms have valley views. Wholesome meals using local produce cooked by Mrs Lamb, an authority on Cumbrian food, who has presented her own cooking series on Border TV. *Reasonably priced. Closed Jan. Six double rooms, all with private facilities and* TV. *Dinner, B&B (double) £46–£58. New nomination: more reports please.*

> If you think we have over-praised a hotel or done it an injustice, please let us know.

GULWORTHY Devon — Map 1

The Horn of Plenty [GFG] *Tel* Tavistock (0822) 832528
Gulworthy, Tavistock PL19 8JD

The Horn of Plenty which has just celebrated its twentieth year as a distinguished restaurant, now becomes a restaurant-with-rooms. The six bedrooms in a nearby building are simple and modern in style and furnishing, with balconies and a lovely view over the Tamar valley. They have a fridge, telephone, lights in the right place, plenty of towels in the bathroom, and good beds. Breakfasts are ample and excellent, the main house has a vine-covered terrace, and a spectacular setting in a five-acre garden. The cooking of chef Sonia Stevenson is much acclaimed, as are her cookery courses, though sadly our inspectors found one of the two dinners they ate there somewhat disappointing. We should welcome more reports.

Open All year except Christmas. Restaurant closed Thur and Fri lunchtime.
Rooms 6 double – all with bath and/or shower, telephone, radio, TV, tea-making facilities and baby-listening. All in annexe adjacent to restaurant – 4 on ground floor, suitable for ♿.
Facilities Hall, restaurant; small conference room with TV; terrace. 5-acre garden. Fishing nearby.
Location 3 m W of Tavistock; follow roadsigns off A390.
Restrictions Children and dogs at management's discretion. No dogs in public rooms.
Credit cards Access, Amex, Visa.
Terms B&B: single £50, double £65. Set lunch £12.50, dinner £17.50–£28.50; full alc £25. Off-season rates for stay of 3 nights or more. Cookery courses Oct–Apr. Reduced rates for children sharing parents' room; special meals
Service/tipping; "We do not encourage tipping by bedroom guests. Tipping in the restaurant is optional."

HALIFAX West Yorkshire — Map 4

Holdsworth House Hotel [GFG] *Tel* Halifax (0422) 240024
and Restaurant *Telex* 51574 HOLHSE
Holmfield, Halifax HX2 9TG

Some differences of opinion on this 17th-century manor house extended to a 40-bedroom hotel, convenient for exploring West Yorkshire and the Brontë country. "Incredible value. A magnificent house, Grade I listed gazebo, Grade II listed barn – open fires, oak beams, oak panels. Pot-pourri-filled antique china. Incredibly friendly service, the head waiter insisted on *driving* my wheel chair down the two or three steps to the dining room. Complimentary sherry, gorgeous food, notably the tartare of marinaded salmon. Sumptuous rooms with antique furniture, fresh flowers, brass bed and well-stocked mini-bar; fabulous bathroom with all possible freebies." (*Sinclair Scobie; endorsed for the most part by AF Conradi, Rodney Cross, AJ Bruce*) But we have also had complaints of a meagre stock of warm drinks (where was the mini-bar?); a small room, poorly sound-proofed; over-efficient processing of the room during a 9 am breakfast (towels gone); food good but coolish; inefficient sending of a telex. The manager tells us of the arrival of a new French chef. More reports please.

Please make a habit of sending a report if you stay at a Guide hotel.

Open All year except Christmas and New Year. Restaurant closed Sat and Sun for lunch.
Rooms 4 split-level suites, 24 double, 12 single – 28 with bath and shower, 12 with shower only, all with direct-dial telephone, radio, TV, baby-listening and mini-bar. All in new building linked to the original house. 2 ground-floor rooms adapted for ♿.
Facilities Entrance lounge, reception lounge, reading lounge, bar, dining room, breakfast room, snooker room; 2 small functions facilities. 2½-acre grounds with grade 1 listed gazebo, grade 2 listed barn and ornamental gardens.
Location From Halifax go N on the A629 to Keighley, turn right at Ovenden where Holmfield Industrial Estate is indicated; continue 2 m. The hotel is set back from road on right opposite Holy Trinity school.
Restriction No dogs in public rooms.
Credit cards All major cards accepted.
Terms B&B: single £43–£53, double £55–£63, suite £65–£75; dinner, B&B: single £59–£69, double £87–£95, suite £81–£91; full alc £20. Half-board weekend rates. Reduced rates and special meals for children.

HAMBLETON Leicestershire — Map 4

Hambleton Hall [GFG]
Hambleton, Oakham
Rutland LE15 8TH

Tel Oakham (0572) 56991
Telex 342888 HAMBLE

"Superb. The warmth, comfort and wonderful food could not be bettered. And what a bargain, our mid-week winter break." (*Maggie Hunt*) *Hambleton Hall* is a model of the English country-house hotel in the luxury class, a stately Victorian mansion overlooking Rutland water, on what is almost an island. Its gardens are manicured, and have lovely mature trees, the interior has been beautifully decorated by Nina Campbell, and is always full of lovely arrangements of fresh flowers by Anne Taylor. The staff, the manager Jan Bos, who came from the *Connaught* in London (q.v.), and the owners, Tim and Stefa Hart, are all dependably welcoming. Since last year *Hambleton* has a new chef, Brian Baker, who was sous-chef for two years to Nicholas Gill. One recent visitor felt the new man was as good as, or even better than, his predecessor, another felt the meal had lacked something of Gill's flair but was still first-class. (*Sir Anthony Alment, P and J Temple, Hunter Gholson*)

Open All year.
Rooms 15 double – all with bath and shower, telephone, radio, TV and baby-listening.
Facilities Lift. Drawing room, bar, dining room; small conference facilities, private dining room. 17-acre grounds overlooking lake with walks, trout fishing and sailing; tennis court. Riding, shooting by arrangement.
Location Off A606 Stamford Road 1 m E of Oakham.
Restrictions No children under 9. Dogs only by arrangement, not in public rooms.
Credit cards All major cards accepted.
Terms B&B (continental): single £35.75–£77.50, double £41.25–£146.00. English breakfast from £3.50. Set lunch £15, dinner £25; full alc £28. Off-season discounts for stays of 3 nights or more. 1-night bookings refused for Sat.
Service/tipping: "Service is included in all prices, so very little tipping goes on."

> "The small chiming carriage clock in the bedroom was fine provided you remembered each night to put in the cupboard and cover it with a cushion."

HAROME North Yorkshire — Map 4

The Pheasant — *Tel* Helmsley (0439) 71241
Harome
Helmsley YO6 5JG

A new entry last year, *The Pheasant Hotel,* in a small village close to the North Yorkshire Moors, Castle Howard, etc, was originally created by converting the village smithy, two cottages and a shop. It has recently been renovated and extended. This year, Holly Cottage, a 16th-century beamed thatched cottage 350 yards away, with its own private garden, has been added. One reader, himself the owner of a Guide hotel, warmly commended it for a quiet break in a beautiful location. Another guest was put out to find a duvet on his bed instead of sheets and blankets. A third reader was totally delighted. " The hotel is a large house but has all the charm of a country cottage and has a good view of the surrounding countryside. The proprietors are a friendly couple who are always happy to give advice about local interests. The rooms are clean and simply furnished, the food is tasty and well presented, and there is a cosy bar where a log fire is very warming on cold winter evenings." (*Miss J Tucker; also RS Benson*)

Open All year except Jan and Feb.
Rooms 12 double (also let as singles), 1 single – all with bath, telephone, TV and tea-making facilities. 1 ground floor room equipped for ♿. Two cottages with self-catering facilities, one with private garden, let at rate per room, exclusive to party occupying them.
Facilities Bar, sitting room, dining room. ¾-acre garden with terrace overlooking village pond.
Location Leave Helmsley on A170 towards Scarborough. After ¼ m, turn right at Harome signpost. Village 2¼ m; hotel near church.
Restrictions No children under 12. No dogs in public rooms. No smoking in dining room.
Credit cards None accepted.
Terms (No service charge) Dinner B&B £37. Bar lunch up to £5; set dinner £12. Special 2-day minimum rates in low season (except bank holidays): dinner, B&B £28 per day; special Christmas and New Year rates. Children ⅔ adult rate if sharing parents' room.
Service/tipping: "Tipping is up to the guests if they feel they have received extra attention which deserves recognition."

HARROGATE North Yorkshire — Map 4

Russell Hotel [GFG] — *Tel* Harrogate (0423) 509866
Valley Drive
Harrogate HG2 0JN

Medium-sized well-run hotel within easy reach of the Conference Centre and overlooking the fine Valley Gardens. Run for past decade by the Hodgson brothers; the hotel's restaurant, Hodgson's, *is one of the city's best. 34 rooms, all with bath and/or shower. B&B (double) £47.50–52.75. Set dinner £11.50. Some ambivalent reports: more feedback please.*

> Don't let old favourites down. Entries are dropped when there is no endorsement.

HASSOP Derbyshire — Map 4

Hassop Hall Hotel
Hassop, Nr Bakewell DE4 1NS
Tel Great Longstone (062 987) 488
Telex 378485

Hassop Hall entered the Guide in 1985, with a notably mouth-watering account of its delights. Then it fell from favour with reports spelling out several serious fallings from grace: poor housekeeping, weaknesses in the cooking, amateur service. Now readers urge its reinstatement, endorsing the original nomination: "An imposing late Georgian stone building in spacious open grounds with splendid views, with a history that goes back centuries, though the present day hall was modernised in about 1820. Our room was very large with enormous windows, and a four-poster bed with a particularly beautiful canopy. Monogrammed linen sheets – with drawn-thread work! Both antique and really *good* reproduction furniture. Charming glazed chintz fabrics, sofa and easy chairs. A flower arrangement in a corner beside the vast Edwardian(?) bath, which, needless to say, was in immaculate condition. Loo, basin, bidet, WC all modern, very elegant. Bath *sheets* for once, *and* bath robes. A bottle of Buxton spring water on a shelf, nothing forgotten . . . Breakfast was wheeled in, and served on pale pink damask, with Doulton china. Hot croissants and some nice local baps. If one yearns for a spot of real luxury, these bedrooms were hard to beat. The only two main meals we had were excellent, and the service was pleasant and cheerful." (*Lady Elstub; also MRF Holmes*) More reports please.

Open All year except a few days at Christmas. Restaurant closed Christmas Eve; also Mon lunch and Sun dinner.
Rooms 12 double, also let as suite/single – 2 with bath and shower, 10 with bath, all with telephone and TV.
Facilities Lift. Bar, 2 sitting rooms (1 non-smoking), dining room. Chamber concerts in drawing room several times a year. 5½-acre garden, with all-weather tennis court, croquet and helipad. Access to 60-acre arboretum nearby (residents only).
Location 2½ m N of Bakewell. From M1, Chesterfield A619 to Baslow. A623 to Calver traffic lights. Left on B6001, Hassop 1 m.
Restriction Dogs at hotel's discretion, not in public rooms.
Credit cards All major cards accepted.
Terms Rooms: single £42.50–£52.50, double £54–£64, suite £145. Breakfast: continental £4.95, English £7.95. Set lunch £5.95–£8.95 (£9.50 weekends), dinner £14.50 (£16.50 on Sat). Reductions for 2-day stays Nov–Mar inclusive. Children sharing parents' room £10.

HASTINGLEIGH Kent — Map 3

The Woodmans Arms Auberge [GFG]
Hassell Street,
Hastingleigh, nr Ashford
TN25 5JE
Tel Elmsted (023 375) 250

César awarded for away-from-it-all delight in the doll's house class

"*The Woodmans Arms Auberge* is very small and not in the least hotel-like. It has only three double rooms and the restaurant can seat no more than ten. It has no staff, only the owner, Gerald Campion and his wife Susan.

By the end of our visit we found ourselves on first-name terms with the Campions and I imagine most visitors have the same experience. Those who like a decent formality to be observed between host and guest, give this place a miss! Other features which will repel some boarders: the *Woodmans Arms* does not accept children under 12 or dogs, and is a strict no-smoking house. An inn since the 17th century, it stands on a small lane leading to nowhere except the Downs, guaranteeing total peace and seclusion. For those with cars there is no shortage of showplaces in the neighbourhood: Leeds Castle, Chilham Castle, Dover Castle – and Canterbury itself is only ten miles away. It is conveniently situated for the Channel ports.

"The Campions are no amateurs of the arts of hospitality. Gerald is a part-time television actor, but he has always combined acting with restaurants or hotels. Recently he and Susan were the *patrons* at *Bassetts* in Frant, East Sussex. Since February 1986 they have nested in this delectable corner of the North Downs. Susan is the cook, and serves the sort of meal you may be lucky enough to get at a friend's house when that friend knows about food and is prepared to take enormous trouble to give you a treat. Caring is at the heart of their success. It shows in the furnishing and lighting of the bedrooms, the equipping of the bathrooms, and in particular in the way they make their guests feel at home. And the tariff is exceedingly reasonable." (*HR*)

Open All year except 1 week before Easter and 2½ weeks end Sept. Restaurant service may be restricted at weekends.
Rooms 3 double – all with bath (2 also have shower) and TV. 1 in adjacent cottage, with hall and patio.
Facilities Lounge, bar, dining room. Large grassed garden and paddock. Near sea at Sandgate and Hythe.
Location Off A28 Canterbury road. Hotel will send directions.
Restrictions Not suitable for ♿. No children under 12. No dogs. No smoking.
Credit cards None accepted.
Terms B&B £17.50–£35; dinner, B&B £30–42.50. 1-night bookings possibly refused Jul/Aug.
Service/tipping: "Tipping is unnecessary."

HAWKRIDGE Somerset — Map 1

Tarr Steps Hotel — *Tel* Winsford (064 385) 293
Hawkridge, Dulverton TA22 9PY

This former Georgian rectory, on Exmoor, 12 miles from the coast, is a sporting hotel *par excellence*, with four miles of salmon and trout fly-fishing, and 500 acres of rough shooting free to guests, who can stable their own horses here, and join local fox- or stag-hunts. It is also a pleasant place to stay, with eight acres of "slightly wild" garden and grounds, and the famous Tarr Steps (unhewn, probably Bronze Age) bridge only 200 yards away, over the river Barle. The hotel is 800 feet up, with lovely views down the river valley (wildlife and wildflowers); the river at night makes, "a soothing sound, like the sea". (*Colin Donald*) "Welcome by the proprietor was warm. Bedrooms small, but most comfortable. Superb views. Most attractive lounge, complete with fire (in August – it was cold!) A good relaxing atmosphere – here was a hotel owner who really cared for his guests." (*IC Dewey*) The only weakness –

remarked on by several correspondents – was with the cooking: generous portions but not up to the standard expected in a hotel of this class.

Open Mid-Mar–mid-Nov and Christmas.
Rooms 12 double, 3 single – 8 with bath. 3 in cottage annexe. 1 ground-floor room with bath and access for ♿.
Facilities Sitting room, bar, dining room. 8-acre grounds with garden; rough and clay pigeon shooting over 500 acres of privately owned land surrounding hotel. 4 m of fishing on river Barle (fly only – salmon and trout, licences from the hotel – free to guests); fox and stag hunting; stables and kennels for guests' horses and dogs. River bathing 100 yds, sea bathing 12 m.
Location Go towards Dulverton on B3222. Take left turn signposted Hawkridge. Follow signs to Hawkridge *not* Tarr Steps until the hamlet of Hawkridge. Then follow signs to Tarr Steps and hotel.
Restriction No dogs in public rooms: kennels available.
Credit cards Amex, Visa.
Terms (No service charge) B&B £21.50; dinner, B&B (3 nights min) £43. Set lunch £9.50, dinner £12.50. 4-day midweek breaks; 4-day Christmas package. 1-night bookings refused over bank holiday weekends. Children under 8 sharing parents' room, half price; high teas.
Service/tipping: "I do not add a service charge to my accounts. Anything left is shared between all the staff."

HAWKSHEAD Cumbria — Map 4

Field Head House — *Tel* Hawkshead (09666) 240
Outgate, Hawkshead LA22 0PY — *Telex* 64117 EKSPO

"A true gem" was the phrase of a Canadian journalist, *Ed Hailwood,* nominating this new Lakeland hotel, bought recently by a young Dutch couple. When Bob van Gulik was made redundant from Saudi Arabia, he and his wife Eeke decided that what they most wanted to do was to run a good hotel with high standards in a fine country house. In Lakeland, a mile outside the village of Hawkshead, where William Wordsworth attended grammar school, they found *Field Head House,* dating from the 17th century, and home from 1834 to 1843 to Wordsworth's friend, the artist John Harden. It stands in eight acres of woodland, old orchards, rhododendrons and azaleas, a few minutes' drive from Hill Top where Beatrix Potter wrote her tales. "We have a large vegetable garden," writes Bob van Gulik, "which makes us fully self-supporting in nearly all vegetables in summer, autumn and most of the winter (sometimes the deer or pigeons get in first). All food is freshly cooked by me with a strong emphasis on vegetables. My wife does the baking and jam-making, and we are blessed with excellent suppliers. We have a beautiful grand piano, much liked by professionals and amateurs alike." There are open log fires and wood-burning stoves, in addition to central heating. Our readers warmly approve: "Absolutely charming couple . . . huge garden . . . idyllic . . . total peace and quiet." (*EB*) "We arrived at 1 am. Not only were we greeted warmly but we were offered a drink by the two owners, which after a long drive from London made us feel extremely welcome. Breakfast was when we wanted it; the evening meals were beautifully cooked and presented. We could not have had a more pleasant and relaxing time." (*DEB Milner*)

Open All year.
Rooms 8 double – all with bath or shower and tea-making facilities; some with telephone; radio and TV on request.

Facilities 2 lounges (one with dispense bar), dining room. 6-acre grounds with flower and vegetable gardens, croquet lawn, stabling and orchard. Trout and coarse fishing, water sports, walking, golf nearby.
Location From Ambleside take B5286 to Hawkshead. ½ m past Outgate Inn take right turn signposted *Field Head*. From Hawkshead take B5286 to Ambleside. *Field Head* signposted 1 m N of Hawkshead.
Restrictions Not suitable for ♿. No smoking in bedrooms or dining room.
Credit cards Amex, Diners, Visa.
Terms B&B: £18–£22; dinner B&B : £25–£35. Set lunch £9, dinner £13. High-season surcharges made for single occupancy (£5) or 1-night stay (£2). 1-night bookings sometimes refused over bank holidays. Special breaks, gardening weekends, wildlife (birdwatching) safaris. Reduced rates. Children sharing parents' room £10; special meals.
Service/tipping: "Tips are not solicited, but if given are used for fund for outing by all staff."

HEADLAM Durham — Map 4

Headlam Hall — *Tel* Darlington (0325) 730238
Headlam, Nr Gainford
Darlington DL2 3HA

This Jacobean mansion, which stands in its own three acres at the centre of their large farm in a peaceful South Durham village, is run by John and Ann Robinson as a small hotel. In the formal gardens surrounding the house, which has Georgian additions, there are lawns, ancient yew and beech hedges, a brook and a hard tennis court. *Headlam Hall* is a relaxed sort of place, despite the imposing public rooms with their Doric columns and enormous fireplaces (and one has a grand piano) – you help yourself to a drink from the bar and write it down. In fact, although the staff are agreeably friendly and helpful, the atmosphere can be unstuffy to the point where it becomes a bit rough round the edges. The dining room is small and panelled, and the food acceptable. Reasonable cost, considering all that architectural splendour. More reports please.

Open All year except Christmas.
Rooms 4 suites, 12 double – 14 with bath and/or shower, all with telephone and TV; some with tea-making facilities.
Facilities Drawing room, bar, restaurant; private dining room; snooker room. 3-acre grounds with gardens, tennis court, small trout stream; surrounded by hotel's large farm.
Location 7 m W of Darlington off A67 Darlington to Barnard Castle.
Restrictions Not suitable for ♿. Dogs in suites only, not in restaurant.
Credit cards Access, Visa.
Terms B&B: single £30–£35, double £40–£45, suite £40–£65.Set lunch £7–£11, dinner £10–£15; full alc £15. Special weekend rates except Aug and Sept. Reduced rates and special meals for children.
Service/tipping: "We do not approve of tipping, but accept that it happens!"

HEDDON'S MOUTH Devon — Map 1

Heddon's Gate Hotel — *Tel* Parracombe (059 83) 313
Heddon's Mouth
Parracombe, Barnstaple EX31 4PZ

A turn-of-the-century Swiss-Victorian lodge with various eclectic extensions, looking over a luscious valley, with views over miles of moorland

and wooded hills. The 20 acres of grounds are surrounded by National Trust and Exmoor National Park land, and several private paths thread through the gardens – one directly on the South West Peninsular coastal path. The hotel has been owned by Robert and Anne De Ville for the past 20 years, and the steeply terraced gardens are clearly a source of pride. Coleridge wrote *Kubla Khan* a few miles up the road, and one reader thought he might have had *Heddon's Mouth* in mind when he wrote:

> "And there were gardens bright with sinuous rills,
> Where blossomed many an incense-bearing tree;
> And here were forests ancient as the hills,
> Enfolding sunny spots of greenery.
> But oh ! that deep romantic chasm which slanted
> Down the green hill athwart a cedarn cover !"

The emphasis in the cooking is on fresh food and some wholefoods, with everything home-made, including bread, jams and cakes. Breakfasts of the full English variety are strongly recommended. Help-yourself teas, included in residents' tariff, are also popular. The rooms are all named – Indian, Grandmamas, Nursemaids, Japanese, etc – and have a pronounced 1920s character. Poor insulation was mentioned in one report, with "urinary frequency problems next door keeping us up in the night". Decor, we wrote last year, is "catholic and a bit outré". One correspondent described it as "bizarre to put it kindly". Not to everyone's visual taste, but it's a stunning place if you like nature and walks and peace and quiet. And all correspondents continue to be impressed with the De Villes' care for their guests' comfort. (*PB Tadman, V Tan, JA Fisher, RH Freeman*)

Open Easter–1st week Nov.
Rooms 4 suites, 13 double, 1 single – all with bath and/or shower, telephone, radio, TV and tea-making facilities. 3 terraced cottage suites 70 yards from main building with wheelchair access.
Facilities Sitting room, library, bar, card room, dining room. 20-acre grounds with terraced gardens. Access to sea (¾ m) and river (¼ m) by private and National Trust footpaths. Riding, pony trekking, fishing nearby.
Location 4 m W of Lynton. From A39 2 m W of Lynton take Martinhoe/Woody Bay road; turn left towards Hunter's Inn; hotel sign is at next crossroads.
Restrictions No children under 10. Dogs by arrangement.
Credit cards None accepted.
Terms B&B £22–£33; dinner B&B £34.50–£45. Set dinner (at 8pm) £15. Reductions for stays of 3 or more days; weekly rates. 50% reduction for children sharing parents' room.
Service/tipping: "We never make any service charge and staff do not solicit tips; any that are given are collected, taxed and shared out among staff on basis of hours worked."

HENLEY-IN-ARDEN Warwickshire — Map 2

Ashleigh House — *Tel* Henley-in-Arden (05642) 2315
Whitley Hill
Henley-in-Arden B95 5DL

Ashleigh House, new to the Guide this year, is an elegant Edwardian house, in 1½ acres of grounds in quiet open country, with views over the Warwickshire countryside towards the Cotswolds. Only 15 minutes by car from Stratford-upon-Avon and its theatres, eight miles from Warwick and 14 from the National Exhibition Centre, it has spacious rooms furnished almost entirely with Victorian and Edwardian antiques. "Francisco Garcia is an enthusiastic and friendly host. Breakfast only: we all enjoyed it. A quiet place in open country with outstanding hospitality." (*JR Lloyd*) Light snacks can be provided, but co-owner Colin Eades points out that there are many good restaurants close by. More reports please.

Open All year.
Rooms 10 double – 1 with bath and shower, 9 with shower, all with TV and tea-making facilities. 4 in coach-house annexe.
Facilities Sitting room with TV, reading room, dining room. 1½-acre garden with flowers, fruit and vegetables.
Location On B4095 Warwick Road, 1 m from A34 traffic lights in Henley-in-Arden. Ample parking.
Restrictions Not suitable for severely ♿. Babies not encouraged. Dogs by arrangement only, not in public rooms.
Credit cards Access, Visa.
Terms B&B: single occupancy £20–£25, double £30–£35. No restaurant, but snacks available. Reduced rates for children sharing parents' room.
Service/tipping: "Tipping not encouraged."

HINTLESHAM Suffolk — Map 3

Hintlesham Hall [GFG]
Hintlesham, Ipswich
IP8 3NS

Tel Hintlesham (047 387) 268
Telex 98340

César awarded for country house hospitality at its luxurious best

This grandly beautiful mansion, dating from the 15th century but mainly Georgian, was bought by Ruth and David Watson three years ago from Robert Carrier, who had run it as a famous restaurant in the 1970s. Every year it gets better. "The renaissance has been effected in great style. It's a real pleasure to see the house looking its stunning best. Carrier's theatrical crimsons and veridians have been replaced with gentle pastels – mostly peach and white and grey, and the panelling and glorious plaster mouldings are doubly effective. Bedroom had ribbon-patterned chintz curtains and covers, and lots of ruching, the bathroom was splendid. Peaceful green views from the windows, space and taste, antiques. Mags and books to suit all moods." (*Patricia Fenn*) "Ultra-elegant but unstuffy, with a relaxed and friendly style of hospitality. Meals are in keeping. Good modern cooking using very fine and fresh ingredients." (*David Wooff*) "The nicest place to go, not only for the food which is excellent – inventive, attractive, mouth-wateringly delicious – but for the general ambience, the welcome, the attention to detail." (*Mary TA Woods*) This year the Tudor attics, with their oak beams, dormers and sloping eaves, have been transformed into bedrooms and spacious suites: bathrooms carpeted; thermostatic radiators installed; gas log-fires in bedroom fireplaces. Extra livestock will add interest in the grounds. The restaurant has been moved to the sunny side of the house. One or two grumbles: the hot water can run out; by a curious system one orders breakfast the night before, even when eating downstairs. Mere drops of dissent however in a sea of praise. (*HR, Heather Sharland, and others*)

Open All year. Restaurant closed Sat lunch.
Rooms 5 suites, 12 double – all with bath and shower, telephone, radio and TV.

Facilities Residents' drawing room, lounge bar, salon, reading room, 2 restaurants; private dining room, conference/function room; billiard room. 18-acre grounds with all-weather tennis court, small farm, orchard, lake with fountain, shooting. 20 minutes to sea; golf nearby.
Location 4 m W of Ipswich on the A1071 to Hadleigh. Parking.
Restrictions Only restaurant suitable for ♿. No children under 10 (except babies). No dogs in hotel, kennels provided.
Credit cards All major cards accepted.
Terms B&B: single £50–£75, double £70–£105, suite £120–£175. Set lunch £15, dinner £25; full alc £35. Weekend breaks Oct–end Mar; Christmas package. Any booking which includes a Sat must be for at least 2 nights.
Service/tipping: "We do not add a percentage to our prices, nor do we accept tips. Staff do not get or expect extra remuneration."

HINTON CHARTERHOUSE Avon — Map 2

Homewood Park Hotel [GFG]
Hinton Charterhouse
Nr Bath BA3 6BB

Tel Limpley Stoke (022 122) 3731
Telex 444937 HOMWOD

We gave *Homewood Park* a César in 1986 for "classic country house excellence" and Egon Ronay made it his Hotel of the Year in 1987. Stephen and Penny Ross have got it right with their blend of a warm welcome that makes you feel you have just dropped in on friends, meals of the highest quality and comfortable bedrooms, elegantly furnished and with good bathrooms, in which to relax at the end of the day. The house stands on what was probably the site of the Abbot's house for the now-ruined Hinton Priory. Mainly 18th century, *Homewood* was much added to in Victorian times, and again in the present century. The ten-acre garden is lovely, and getting better every year. "The hotel is perfect in every way – not overdone, just exactly right. Our room was delightful, the food worth a detour (and there were lots of guests who had come for exactly that) and the staff extraordinarily helpful . . . There are few hotels where one feels really comfortable doing needlepoint by the fire, in the late afternoon with tea, but at *Homewood Park* this is possible. A wonderful place to unwind in glorious countryside." (*Susan Gillotti; also KR Corcoran, PM Jackson, John Huntingford*).

Open All year 7 Jan–23 Dec.
Rooms 15 double – all with bath, shower, telephone, radio and TV. 2 ground-floor rooms.
Facilities Bar, drawing room, restaurant; private dining room, conference room. 10-acre grounds with tennis court, croquet and arboretum.
Location 5 m S of Bath opposite Hinton Priory. Turn left off A36 at village of Freshford.
Restriction No dogs.
Credit cards All major cards accepted.
Terms B&B (continental): single occupancy £45–£85, double £70–£95. Set lunch £15 weekdays, £16.50 Sun, dinner £22.50; full alc £30. 2-night winter breaks. Reduced rates for children sharing parents' room; special meals by arrangement.

"We were subjected to remarks that were out of place from a host to his guests, starting with 'Dinner is at 7.30. Don't be late'. 'You have dropped your napkin,' with no attempt to pick it up. And to the lady at the next table who inquired if there was any honey for breakfast: 'If you'd looked properly, you'd have seen it by the cereals.'"

HONITON Devon — Map 1

Colestocks House Hotel — *Tel* Honiton (0404) 850633
Colestocks
Nr Honiton EX14 0JR

Pink thatched 300-year-old house, nine miles from Devon coast and coastal footpath, five from M5. Traditional French and English recipes served by French proprietor Henri Yot and English wife Jacqueline. Wine personally chosen by M. Yot. 7 double rooms with bath or shower. Garden. B&B £15.25–16.75. Dinner £10.50. New nomination: more reports please.

HOVE East Sussex — Map 3

Courtlands Hotel — *Tel* Brighton (0273) 731055
19-27 The Drive, Hove BN3 3JE — *Telex* 87574 CHF

At first glance there is nothing much to distinguish this traditional, three-star hotel from many similar establishments. It stands on a broad avenue, 400 yards from the sea, and the front rooms may be noisy in summer, the back rooms to be preferred. It is in a series of period houses, and many of the rooms are large. Although conventional in many ways, it continues to give satisfaction to many regular guests, who endorse this earlier report: "The food is of good quality, with generous helpings, and reasonably priced. The hotel provides a good base for visiting the area and is a warm-hearted, unpretentious establishment that rises above its somewhat old-fashioned origins." (*Michael Appleby; and many others*)

Open All year.
Rooms 3 suites, 27 double, 25 single – all with bath and/or shower, direct-dial telephone, radio, TV and baby-listening. 5 in annexes with mini-bar and tea-making facilities. 8 ground-floor rooms.
Facilities Lift. 3 lounges, bar, games room, TV room, restaurant; conference facilities; spa and whirlpool bath. ½-acre garden with terrace, covered swimming pool and children's playground. Sea 400 yds, private bathing hut. Leisure complex nearby.
Location 400 yds from centre (back rooms quietest). Turn N on Grand Avenue at Queen Victoria statue. Parking.
Restrictions Not suitable for ♿. No dogs in public rooms, in bedrooms by arrangement.
Credit cards All major cards accepted.
Terms (Excluding 10% service charge) B&B: single £45–£47.50, double £57.50–£62.50: dinner, B&B (min 2 days) add £8.50 per person; full board add £10.50. Set lunch £8.50, dinner £11.50; full alc £16.50. Weekend, winter and summer breaks; 2-day Christmas programme. Reduced rates and special meals for children.
Service/tipping: "10% service charge added and distributed to all staff. We find it an added incentive to good service."

HUNSTRETE Avon — Map 2

Hunstrete House Hotel — *Tel* Compton Dando (076 18) 578
Chelwood — *Telex* 449540 HUNHSE
Nr Bristol BS18 4NS

It is now exactly ten years since Thea Dupays, who is responsible for the interior decor of *Hunstrete*, and her husband John, bought and converted this serenely beautiful Georgian mansion. The visual delight of the rooms, coupled with the sense the Dupays give of inviting you to be their country house guest, has rightly brought the house fame in the interim. The exterior scene is pretty stunning, too: the 90 acres of grounds contain not only the relatively standard provisions of expensive country house hotels – heated outdoor pool, tennis court and croquet lawn – as well as a lovingly-maintained flower and herb garden, but also, something of a rarity, a deer park. Readers enthuse about every aspect. "A standard of excellence which is hard to beat. After half-a-dozen visits, I have yet to find fault, which is quite an achievement on their part as things go wrong in the best of places. The furnishings never seem to be allowed to get tatty. The service gets better and better as one becomes a 'regular'. This must be one of the finest hotels in Britain." (*Lena Pycroft; also the Marchioness of Tavistock, Mrs JA Patterson, Mrs PC Bevan*)

Open All year.
Rooms 2 suites, 18 double, 1 single – all with bath and shower, telephone, radio and TV. 6 in Courtyard House, 1 suite in Swallow Cottage, adjoining main building. 4 ground-floor rooms (1 suitable for ♿).
Facilities Drawing room, library, bar, dining room. 90-acre grounds with walled garden, heated outdoor swimming pool, hard tennis court, croquet lawn, deer park; coarse fishing in grounds; trout fishing, riding and golf nearby. 4 racecourses within hour's drive.
Location On A368, 8 m SW of Bath.
Restrictions No children under 9. No dogs.
Credit cards All major cards accepted except for special breaks.
Terms (Excluding VAT) B&B: single £65–£80, double £85–£125, suite £110–£150. Set dinner £30. Special winter breaks Nov–Mar (min 3 days); Christmas programme. 1-night bookings sometimes refused for Sat.

HUNTINGDON Cambridgeshire — Map 3

Old Bridge Hotel
High Street
Huntingdon PE18 6TQ

Tel Huntingdon (0480) 52681
Telex 32706 OLBDG

"A rambling Georgian, ivy-clad building by the river. The bedroom was beautifully decorated with expensive fabrics and had a decent-sized bathroom and double-glazing. We only had breakfast, but it was really excellent. A large glass of fresh orange juice, good slices of succulent York ham with fresh scrambled egg (decorated with a spray of parsley) and little mushrooms freshly cooked in butter. Hot brown toast." (*JS and F Waters*) The restaurant has enjoyed an excellent reputation for many years past. In winter there are log fires to sit by, in summer there are tables out on the lawns sloping down to the river Ouse. The chief snag about the *Old Bridge*, hinted at in the reference to double-glazing above, is its location on Huntingdon's ring road; front rooms suffer from the traffic. *Note:* the hotel has recently opened a business centre. Will the conferees spoil the pleasure of the non-conferring traffic? More reports please.

Open All year. Restaurant closed Christmas and Boxing Day evenings.
Rooms 18 double, 9 single – all with bath and/or shower, telephone, radio and TV.
Facilities Lounge, bar, restaurant. ½-acre garden, on river Ouse with mooring and coarse fishing. Business centre with 4 boardrooms and conference room.
Location 300 yds from town centre.
Restrictions Not suitable for ♿. No dogs in public rooms.

Credit cards All major cards accepted.
Terms B&B: single £35–£47.50, double £58–£72.50. Full alc £25. Special meals for children by arrangement.
Service/tipping: "The service we offer is included in our prices. Tips are at the discretion of the guest."

HUNTSHAM Devon **Map 1**

Huntsham Court *Tel* Clayhanger (039 86) 210
Huntsham Valley
Nr Tiverton EX16 7NA

César awarded for utterly acceptable mild eccentricity

"*Huntsham* may look like just another country house hotel, but in fact it is providing an experience unique in the Guide. It is the creation of Mogens Bolwig, a Danish former travel agent, and his Greek wife Andrea, in a secluded setting in rural Devon, five slow meandering miles from the M5, roughly halfway between Taunton and Exeter. It is a choice example of High Victorian architecture, with awe-inspiring room dimensions. *Huntsham* is dedicated to making its guests forget that they are in a hotel at all. It eschews such mod cons as colour TV and direct-dial telephones or locks on bedroom doors. The furniture is eclectic: Victorian sideboards and outsize armchairs of the twenties and thirties which are out of favour these days. The bedrooms are all named after composers. Most have bathrooms *en suite* with free-standing old tubs with silver claws, which tend to be as big as other people's drawing rooms. Beethoven has two such baths side by side in the middle of the room, and a log fire. It recently acquired a seven-foot wide bed and a piano too! All the rooms have pre-war radio sets resurrected by some local enthusiast. Dinner is a five-course affair eaten communally, though you can opt to sit at a private table if you prefer. The hotel also has a huge musical repertoire, over 3,000 records and cassettes, mostly classical with a leaning towards the operatic, which are free for guests to play on a high hi-fi. There's also a sauna, a mini-gym and lots of bicycles. Tea and coffee are free for guests to help themselves to night and day in the butler's pantry. The bar can be help yourself, too, on the honour principle. Drink is really the only extra at *Huntsham*. A conventional hotel in this Gothic setting could only too easily be a morgue. But as soon as you enter the place, you feel its verve; it hums with life. The Bolwigs may appear laid-back; but they are also relaxedly attentive to their guests' needs and moods."

Huntsham is addictive: for those who enter into the spirit, it is an oasis among hotels, satisfying parts other hotels never reach. "A wonderful place . . . imposing, interesting, unusual, remote, relaxed and great fun, truly more like staying in a private if grand house than a hotel." (*Steve and Mary Watson*) Another reader described a typical *Huntsham* night: "As usual got acquainted with other guests at the self-service bar. Then we followed Mogens to the cellar and tried out three wines before dinner which was as superb as ever. Some dancing to Bill Haley, then the Last Night of the Proms, a game of snooker, a look at the thousands of books. Breakfast – fresh-squeezed orange juice, fresh rolls and croissants and everything else. Papers to read. The ladies had breakfast in bed served by some of the lovely Australian girls that always seem to be at *Huntsham*.

The experience has to be felt: it's a rest, it's a tonic: I just love it all." (*David Head*)

Open All year, except 1-14 Feb. Lunch by arrangement only.
Rooms 1 suite, 14 double – all with bath and shower, and pre-war wireless.
Facilities Hall, drawing room, library, music room, bar, dining room; sauna, mini-gym, table tennis room. 8-acre garden with croquet, bicycles, tennis courts, barbecue. Trout fishing in private lake, riding, golf nearby.
Location M5 to Taunton, then A361 towards Bampton; turn left to Huntsham when signposted. Or take exit 27 off M5, turn sharp right on bridge in Sampford Peverell and continue for 4 m.
Restrictions Not suitable for ♿. No dogs.
Credit card Visa.
Terms B&B: single £50, double £69, suite £79. Set dinner £17.50. House parties; mid-week and weekend breaks; occasional jazz, opera and special weekends; Christmas and New Year programmes. Reduced rates for children sharing parents' room.

HURSTBOURNE TARRANT Hampshire — Map 2

Esseborne Manor [GFG]
Hurstbourne Tarrant
Nr Andover SP11 0ER

Tel Hurstbourne Tarrant (026 476) 444

Esseborne Manor, new to the Guide this year, is mainly Victorian, though architects ponder earlier beginnings. Bits have obviously been added over the years to suit domestic demands, giving the house attractive bay windows with window seats, round windows, dormers, and a large room at the back, now the restaurant. Hurstbourne Tarrant (Hurstbourne from Hysseburn as in the Domesday Book, Tarrant after an order of Dorset nuns from Tarrant Crawford, given the lands by Henry III) is south of the M4, in pleasant countryside, a relaxing rural base for visiting Stonehenge, Bath and Oxford. The hotel is run by a group of friends who take it in turn to hold the fort, and our inspector was beguiled. "Met at the door by a smiling, bearded, stocky man in a cook's striped apron, who carried up our bags. The bedroom was fresh and attractive, white wicker furniture and blue curtains, snug and comfortable. Green plants, magazines, table and chairs, good bathroom with big white towels and efficient shower. Lovely view from window. Downstairs the sitting room proved small, pretty, heaped with fascinating books, comfortable. Bar ditto, plus fire, lit for us. Excellent wine list with interesting, good, less well-known vineyards explained, and at modest prices. Dinner superb, including wickedly rich puddings, cheese board in prime condition and good coffee. They have just finished a new building with six more rooms, all equally comfortable and bigger, and herb garden where you can sit. Altogether a charming small place, caring, attractive, and run with enthusiasm and pride." (*Endorsed by BEW Mace, and others*)

Open All year, except 2 weeks at Christmas.
Rooms 12 double – all with bath, shower, telephone, radio, and TV. 6 around courtyard, 30 yards from hotel.
Facilities Lounge, bar, restaurant; conference facilities. 2-acre grounds with all-weather tennis court, croquet, golf practice net, herb garden.
Location On A343 1½ m N of Hurstbourne Tarrant.
Restrictions Not suitable for ♿. No children under 10. No dogs.
Credit cards All major cards accepted.

Terms B&B: single occupancy £45, double £65–£75. Full alc £20. £5 discount for dinner for guests in double room staying 2 or more nights.

IPSWICH Suffolk — Map 3

The Marlborough
73 Henley Road
Ipswich IP1 3SP

Tel Ipswich (0473) 57677
Telex 81630 MARLBOROUGH

The Marlborough is a red brick hotel, a few minutes' walk away from the historic part of Ipswich, and all the quieter for it, with a garden and tranquil surburban setting. It is a reliable, professionally run hotel, with bedrooms verging on the luxurious and good bathrooms, and the one grouch about overcrowding in its public rooms has been dealt with this year by the addition of an extra study/library. Sadly, Dick Gough, owner both of this and of the *Angel* (q.v.) at Bury St Edmunds, died recently, but his wife has planned no changes in the *Marlborough*, which she hopes will continue its pursuit of excellence, and its active participation in the life of the town – organising competitions, making awards, and holding concerts, gastronomic events and special Explore Suffolk weekends, as well as fulfilling its municipal obligations for functions and banquets.

Open All year. Restaurant closed Christmas evening to non-residents.
Rooms 1 suite, 15 double, 6 single – 22 with bath, 8 also with shower, all with telephone, radio, TV and baby-listening; some with electric trouser press; 24-hour room service. Some ground-floor rooms.
Facilities Lounge, cocktail bar, library, restaurant; functions room. Small landscaped garden with patio for alfresco meals.
Location Henley Road is off the A12 to Felixstowe, Lowestoft, Great Yarmouth (Valley Road). Full details in brochure.
Restrictions No children under 5 in restaurant in the evening. No dogs in restaurant.
Credit cards All major cards accepted
Terms (No service charge) Rooms: single from £44, double from £60, suite £70. Breakfast: continental £3.50, English £5.75, champagne £11. Set lunch £8–£10.50; dinner £12.50–£15.50; full alc £22. Vegetarian menu. Reduced rates at weekend; special breaks of all kinds; Christmas and New Year packages; bargain holidays in Aug. Reductions for children sharing parents' room; special meals.
Service/tipping: "Actively discouraged."

JERVAULX North Yorkshire — Map 4

Jervaulx Hall
Jervaulx, Masham
Ripon HG4 4PH

Tel Bedale (0677) 60235

John and Shirley Sharp bought *Jervaulx Hall* in 1979; it appeared in the Guide for the first time two years later and has not been out of it since. It is an early Victorian mansion with much solid, reassuring Victorian furniture, on the site of one of the famous Cistercian abbeys. These ruins are less well known than Fountains and Rievaulx, but nonetheless impressive. The *Hall* adjoins the ruins, separated only by a ha-ha, and enjoys the run of the substantial Abbey Park. It makes an admirable base for a touring or walking holiday in the Yorkshire Dales.

Sadly, Shirley Sharp died after a long illness in October 1986, but her husband is carrying on. There were inevitably some adverse reports in the summer of 1986, but we are glad to say that an inspection in May 1987 makes it clear that the hotel is once again firing on all cylinders. Our inspector arrived with her husband and two babies in pouring rain. Mr Sharp provided a warm welcome and made at least three trips to the car helping with teddies and disposable nappies. *Jervaulx Hall* is not a family hotel, only a country house hotel willing to extend its hospitality to children as part of its overall service. And the services extended – except in one small respect – to all the things that matter most in a country house hotel: a large attractive room with many extras, an excellent meal of the honest English variety, and a convivial atmosphere that made guests comfortable in talking to each other. The only niggle: the room was cold in a chilly May because the hotel heating was turned off at night.

Open 1 Mar–end Nov.
Rooms 8 double – all with bath, 1 also with shower, all with tea-making facilities. 1 ground-floor room.
Facilities 2 lounges (1 with TV), dining room. 8-acre garden adjoining Abbey ruins; fishing by arrangement in nearby river Ure.
Location On A6108, 12 m N of Ripon, next to Jervaulx Abbey.
Restriction Dogs not to be left unattended in bedrooms.
Credit cards None accepted.
Terms (No service charge) Dinner, B&B £35–£40. Set dinner £12.50. 2-day winter breaks 1 Mar–Easter. 1-night bookings sometimes refused over bank holiday periods. Reduced rates and special meals for children by arrangement.
Service/tipping: "Tipping is purely optional, any money given is shared between all staff; full-time staff may get a larger share."

KILVE Somerset — Map 1

Meadow House — *Tel* Holford (027 874) 546
Sea Lane, Kilve TA5 1EG

Most readers again agree about the hospitality at this rectory, Georgian in style, in eight acres of gardens, with views of woodland, farmland, the Bristol Channel and the Welsh coast. This year's comments: "A particularly welcoming atmosphere." (*Mrs PC Bevan*) "Your existing entry has not done full justice to the management . . . the food is excellent and . . . of *Michelin* rosette standard; the wine mark-up is so very modest as to be both astounding and pleasurable." (*MJ Hedges*) "An enthusiastic and charming host . . . the peace and tranquillity we needed in idyllic conditions." (*Mr and Mrs P Ramage-Gibson*) "The bathroom – *en suite* – was enormous, and not only beautifully appointed but also had luxurious bathsheets as well." (*AJ Newall*) "Everything about the place, particularly the owners, David and Marion MacAuslan, was just right and made us feel very comfortable. We even enjoyed the rainy days . . . " (*Mr and Mrs G Churchard; also, in similar terms SW Cooper, Mr and Mrs DW Cox, Dr A Frank*)

Open All year except 24–26 Dec and New Year's Eve.
Rooms 1 suite, 5 double – all with bath and/or shower, radio, TV and tea-making facilities.
Facilities Drawing room, study, billiard room, dining room. 8-acre grounds with landscaped garden and stream. Rocky beach ½ m.
Location Off A39 Bridgwater–Minehead. In Kilve turn right down Sea Lane, just before pub. *Meadow House* ½ m on left.
Restrictions Not suitable for ♿. No children under 9. No dogs.
Credit cards Access, Visa.

Terms Double room: B&B £58–£76, dinner, B&B £92–£110. Set dinner £17. Special 2- and 3-day breaks except bank holidays.
Service/tipping: "Tips are not expected, and we do not levy a service charge. After all, service is part and parcel of what is offered in the accommodation and meal charges."

KINGHAM Oxfordshire **Map 2**

The Mill House Hotel and Restaurant [GFG] *Tel* Kingham (060 871) 8188
Telex 849041 SHARET
Kingham OX7 6UH

Last in the Guide in 1984, *The Mill Hotel* has been transformed in the past two years and is now a sophisticated country hotel, tucked away in a sleepy village five miles from Stow-on-the-Wold and Chipping Norton, and ten from Burford – well based for Cotswold touring. It is hard to discern its mill-house origins, though there's still an old baker's oven on display in the bar. All but one of the rooms have a bathroom *en suite* as well as the expected creature comforts like telephone and colour TV (those in the older part of the house can be smallish). The main change has been in the kitchens where 22-year-old Pascal Pommier from Lyon wears the *toque* and has brought an innovative modern style of cooking, much to the enjoyment of *DB Delaney, W Thomson, and others.*

Open All year.
Rooms 20 double – 19 with bath and shower, 1 with shower only, all with telephone, radio, TV and tea-making facilities.
Facilities Lounge, lounge bar, restaurant. 10 acre grounds with trout fishing in own stream. Walking, golf, swimming, squash and riding nearby.
Location Off B4450 on outskirts of Kingham village.
Restrictions Not suitable for ♿. No children under 5. No dogs.
Credit cards All major cards accepted.
Terms B&B: single £28–£40, double £46–£60; dinner, B&B: single £42.50–£54.50, double £60.50–£74.50; full board: single £51.50–£63.50, double £69.50–£83.50. Set lunch £8.95, dinner £14.50; full alc £22. Winter and summer breaks. Reduced rates and special meals for children.
Service/tipping: "All prices for the hotel include VAT *and service. Chance meal gratuities are optional."*

KING'S LYNN Norfolk **Map 3**

Congham Hall Country House Hotel [GFG] *Tel* Hillington (0485) 600250
Telex 81508 CHOTEL
Lynn Road, Grimston
King's Lynn PE32 1AH

"A really beautiful building set on a lawn that looked more like a Wilton carpet." Since *Congham Hall* is, as far as we know, the only hotel in England with its own cricket pitch, one can expect well-tended grass. *Congham* is an elegant Georgian manor house, with 40 acres of paddocks, orchards, country garden and parkland. Readers are enthusiastic. "A lovely house, well-furnished; particularly commendable are the sitting areas – a large beautiful drawing room, the hall and bar all pleasant places to be, with real fires." Bedrooms, including one with a four-poster, are well-appointed though they vary in size. Owners Christine and Trevor Forecast are "ever-attentive hosts as well as managers with a keen eye for detail", and their staff also come in for praise as "cheerful and courteous". There is a new chef this year, Robert Harrison, trained at *Le Gavroche* and, until recently, head chef at *The Priory*, Bath (q.v.). First verdict: "The new chef's food is exquisite." The eight-course "Hobson's Choice" menu remains, e.g. seasonal salad wih artichokes and bacon; chicken and rosemary consommé; quenelle of salmon with garden herbs and julienne of leeks; orange sorbet; roast pigeon breasts with red wine and wild mushrooms, stilton, exotic fruit salad, coffee and petits fours; but also now a shorter (cheaper) menu. The Forecasts tell us they have acquired the tenancy of the village pub, ¼ mile away, serving real ale and "good pub grub". Also, "we have now sorted out all our heating problems and are now nice and warm!" (*Patricia Roberts, Mary Lawrence, Bernadette Murray, Mr and Mrs AE Smith, Jack Watmough, RE Hands*)

Open All year.
Rooms 1 suite, 9 double, 1 single – all with bath and/or shower, telephone, radio and TV; some with 4-poster.
Facilities Hall, lounge, bar, restaurant; conference facilities. 40-acre grounds with heated swimming pool, jacuzzi, tennis court, cricket pitch, parklands and orchards; stabling for visiting horses. Coast with sandy beaches 10 m; nature and bird sanctuaries, fishing, golf, riding nearby.
Location 6 m NE of King's Lynn. Turn right off A148 to Grimston; *Congham* is 2½ m on left.
Restrictions Only restaurant suitable for ♿. No children under 12. Dogs in kennels only.
Credit cards All major cards accepted.
Terms (No service charge) B&B (light English): single £55, double £70, suite £105. Full English breakfast £2 added. Set lunch £10.50, dinner £21 (lighter dinner £15); full alc £15. Weekend breaks all year; 3-day Christmas break.
Service/tipping: "All our tariffs carry the statement 'No service charges are added to your account for any facilities offered in the hotel.' If guests do leave a tip it is all passed on to the staff who share it out."

KINGSTON BAGPUIZE Oxfordshire — Map 2

Fallowfields
Southmoor, Kingston Bagpuize
Nr Abingdon OX13 5BH

Tel Oxford (0865) 820416
Telex 83388 KINGS TG Attn FALLOWFIELDS

"A beautiful old house, with large, comfortable, spacious bedrooms, set in large grounds with a swimming pool and croquet lawn. Pictures, ornaments, floral displays, deep armchairs, no musak (thank heaven!) and a personal and kindly welcome by Mrs Crowther, the owner, makes the stay a happy one." (*Eric Adler*) Once the home of the Begum Aga Khan before her marriage, *Fallowfields* has for nearly ten years been run as a country guest-house by a sparky lady, Alison Crowther. "I've hunted with the old Berks, water ski'd in a ballet circus and exhibited paintings at the Royal Watercolour Society. I'm also deaf, so you've got to yell at me," she is quoted as saying in a *Guardian* article. The house is in 12 acres of well-kept grounds; as well as the swimming pool there is a hard tennis court, and much of the fresh fruit and vegetables for the "huge, delicious meals" grows here. Desserts are lavish, a jug of cream is left on the table; visitors leave feeling they have been thoroughly pampered.

Open 1 Apr–30 Sept. Winter weekend house parties for not fewer than 4 people – advance booking only. Dinner not served Wed.
Rooms 2 suites, 2 double – 2 with bath, 1 with shower, all with radio and tea-making facilities.

Facilities 2 lounges, TV room, dining room. 2-acre garden, 10-acre paddock; tennis, table tennis, croquet, heated swimming pool. Riding, golf, river and lake fishing, windsurfing, waterskiing at Stanton Harcourt Leisure Centre nearby.
Location On A420 8 m SW of Oxford, 6 m from Abingdon. Light sleepers may be disturbed by traffic on A420, in north rooms.
Restrictions Not suitable for ♿. No children under 10. Dogs at management's discretion, not in public rooms.
Credit card Access.
Terms (No service charge) B&B: single £19, double £31; dinner, B&B: single £31.50, double £56. Full alc £15.50.
Service/tipping: "We do not make a service charge. Any gratuities are divided by me amongst our part-time staff."

KIRKBY FLEETHAM North Yorkshire — Map 4

Kirkby Fleetham Hall [GFG] — *Tel* Northallerton (0609) 748226
Kirkby Fleetham
Northallerton DL7 0SU

Kirkby Fleetham Hall is a fine house, Elizabethan in parts, but substantially remodelled 200 years ago to give it its present Georgian appearance. A magnificently arrogant 18th-century squire of what was then a manor house demolished the village of Kirkby in order to enjoy greater privacy, so the house now sits in isolated splendour of 30 acres of grounds, with just a 12th-century Knights Templar church adjoining. The A1 is two miles to the west, with the dales beyond; the moors lie to the east; York and Castle Howard to the south. And the *Hall* is in a halcyon phase of its history as a country house hotel owned and run by David and Chris Grant.

Reports this year have been much the same as last. One dissenter who was disappointed with details of his dinner, and a rapturous chorus from all our other correspondents who single out for special praise the unobtrusive welcome of the host, David Grant; a "superb" wine list that "needs hours of reading" and has "many unusual though reasonably-priced half-bottles for the adventurous"; "the flowers, fruit, magazines and books and all the creature comforts" in the rooms; and "a whole library downstairs if that was not enough". (*Chris and Dorothy Brining, Denis Tate, Pat and Jeremy Temple, BH Jenkinson*)

Open All year.
Rooms 15 double – all with bath (2 also have shower), telephone, radio and TV.
Facilities 2 lounges, bar, dining room. 30-acre grounds; lake.
Location 1 m N of village of Kirkby Fleetham: follow sign to Kirkby Hall and Church.
Restrictions Not suitable for ♿. Dogs by arrangement; not in public rooms.
Credit cards Amex, Visa.
Terms B&B: single occupancy £55, double £69–£89. Set lunch £10.50; dinner £17.50. Reduced rates for children.
Service/tipping: "I do my costing without adding service, but say we include service because I do not expect people to tip. The whole concept of tipping is alien to me."

> Hotels often book you into their most expensive rooms or suites unless you specify otherwise. Even if all room prices are the same, hotels may give you a less good room in the hope of selling their better rooms to late customers. It always pays to discuss accommodation in detail when making a reservation.

KNOWSTONE Devon — Map 1

Masons Arms Inn *Tel* Anstey Mills (039 84) 231
Knowstone
South Molton EX36 4RY

This old-fashioned 13th-century thatched inn in the foothills of Exmoor, with just five smallish bedrooms furnished with antiques and books, was originally drawn to our attention by the editor of *The Good Pub Guide*. Readers have warmly endorsed the nomination. "The best inn within my experience – a real inn without pretentions or snobbery. The owner and staff provide plenty of good old-fashioned hospitality. The dining room is small but well furnished, and the bar has retained all of its original character – a *real* fire, wooden beams, stone floor and a quiet but friendly atmosphere. The food centres on 'farmhouse cooking' and is generally very good indeed. Huge English breakfasts are provided, and you can choose between bar snacks and a full meal in the evening. The immediate vicinity is typical Devon farmland with few diversions other than walking, but within five minutes' drive lies Exmoor with its many attractions. Overall, a hotel for people who enjoy peace, privacy and good food." (*DP Hearsum*) On the subject of the cooking, a Canadian visitor adds: "Excellently varied menu for such a small place: traditional English dishes and also some innovative ones. The traditional dishes are done fastidiously with none of the overpresentation that seems to be a common attempt to overcome the reputation of British food. Flavours are unmuddled. Vegetables are straightforward – fresh, colourful, crisp." (*Barbara Labranda; also Joyce and Geoff Tomlinson, William Grant*)

Open All year except Christmas. Restaurant closed to non-residents Sun (bar meals available).
Rooms 1 suite, 3 double, 1 single – 2 with shower, all with radio, TV and tea-making facilities. Suite on ground floor in cottage next door.
Facilities Small lounge with TV, public bar, restaurant. Occasional music in bar. ½-acre grounds.
Location 3 m NW of Rackenford; Knowstone signposted from B3221 ½ m W of Rackenford.
Restrictions Not suitable for ♿. Dogs at owners' discretion.
Credit cards None accepted.
Terms (No service charge) B&B £12.50–£19.50, dinner, B&B £20–£27.50. Set dinner £9.45; full alc £12.95. Special breaks all year. 1-night bookings sometimes refused over bank holiday weekends. Reduced rates for children sharing parents' room; special meals.
Service/tipping: "I am still theoretically opposed, but if service is friendlier or more willing than is normal, perhaps it is rational to reward it."

LACOCK Wiltshire — Map 2

At The Sign Of The Angel [GFG] *Tel* Lacock (024 973) 230
Church Street, Lacock
Chippenham SN15 2LA

A 14th-century half-timbered inn in the heart of the ancient wool village of Lacock now preserved by the National Trust, with lots of black oak panelling, log fires, polished brass and silverware. Honest English cooking with generous portions. Excellent breakfasts including home-made bread and thick-cut marmalade. This year's reports have all been enthusiastic, praising the food and the friendly service very highly.

Open All year except 22 Dec–1 Jan. Restaurant closed for lunch Sat and bank holidays, and for Sun dinner (cold meal available to residents).
Rooms 8 double – all with bath, telephone and tea-making facilities; 2 with TV. 2 in cottage across garden.
Facilities Lounge, 2 dining rooms. 1-acre garden with stream.
Location 7 m S of M4 (exit 17); E of A350 between Chippenham and Melksham.
Restrictions Not suitable for ♿. No children under 12. No dogs in public rooms.
Credit cards None accepted.
Terms (Service at guests' discretion) B&B (double room): £60–£65. Set lunch £14.50 (Sun £18), dinner £18. Winter breaks 1 Nov–1 Apr; mid-week breaks 1 Apr–31 Oct.

LAMORNA COVE Cornwall — Map 1

Lamorna Cove Hotel — *Tel* Penzance (0736) 731411
Lamorna Cove
Nr Penzance TR19 6XH

This cheerful family hotel lies at the foot of a long leafy valley on the sheltered southern coast of the Penwith peninsula – the rugged toe of Cornwall between Penzance and Land's End. It was created from a quarry-owner's house and an old chapel, with a modern extension. Some bedrooms and the dining room overlook the sea. There is a swimming pool, a rocky beach with some sand at low tide, access to the Cornish coastal path and surfing at Sennen Cove ten miles away. It was dropped from the Guide two years ago after a rash of ambivalent reports. Regulars have since been lobbying for its reinstatement, admitting weaknesses of decor and sound-proofing of rooms, but praising its cleanliness, the friendly and helpful owners, and the charming service. The chef went to a great deal of trouble to find imaginative dishes for some vegetarian readers, "consulting us as to personal preferences... as if we had presented him with an interesting diversion from his usual dishes". More reports please. (*T Thorn and B Watt; also David RW Jervois*)

Open All year.
Rooms 1 suite, 17 double – all with bath and shower, telephone, radio, TV and baby-listening.
Facilities Lift. 4 lounges, bar, dining room. 6-acre grounds, mainly woodland. Outdoor heated pool. Sandy beach at low tide – safe bathing, fishing. Golf nearby.
Location 5 m SW of Penzance. Take B3315 towards Land's End.
Restriction No dogs in public rooms.
Credit cards All major cards accepted.
Terms B&B: single £21.95–£37.50, double £39.90–£70, suite £65.90–£82; dinner B&B: single £29.95–£44, double £51.90–£85, suite £69.90–£97. Set lunch £7.50, dinner £11.25, full alc £13.50. Reduced rates and special meals for children.
Service/tipping: "If a guest wants to reward good food and service he or she should have that option. Any tips received are distributed to all members of staff."

> Wherever possible, we have quoted prices per room. Not all hotels are prepared to quote tariffs in this way. In these cases, we have given prices per person, indicating the range of prices – the lowest is likely to be for one person sharing a double room out of season, the highest for a single room in the high season.

LANGHO Lancashire — Map 4

Northcote Manor [GFG] *Tel* Blackburn (0254) 40555
Northcote Road, Langho *Telex* 635359 BASHEY
Nr Blackburn, BB6 8BE

A welcome newcomer, we hope, to a barren area for hotelophiles – 15 minutes from M6, junction 31. More a restaurant-with-rooms: excellent restaurant, rooms at present so-so and needing more investment. 6 rooms, all with bath. Double B&B £45. Full alc £20. Please send us more reports.

LASTINGHAM North Yorkshire — Map 4

Lastingham Grange *Tel* Lastingham (075 15) 345
Lastingham, York YO6 6TH

This modest country house hotel, built in the 17th century as a farmhouse in the heart of what is now the North Moors National Park, has appeared in the Guide since the first edition. It is an old stone, creeper-covered house, standing round a courtyard and surrounded by ten acres of garden and fields, with fine old trees and carefully tended flower-borders – the road stops here, becoming a bridle path to Rosedale and beyond. The village of Lastingham has an inscription in its main street telling of an abbey founded there in 654, and the whole area has a great atmosphere of peace and tranquillity.

Lastingham Grange is a thoroughly traditional hotel, in decor as well as in its style of cooking, maintaining the standards set in the fifties by the father of the present owner, Dennis Wood. Last year we quoted *John Timpson's* salute to Dennis Wood as Mr Faultless, the reverse of Basil Fawlty. And this year's guests also pay tribute to the enduring character of this hotel, with its 100-year-old editions of *Punch* rubbing shoulders with *Encounter*, Salman Rushdie, the *National Geographical Magazine* and books on squash. (*John Hopkins; David and Brenda Evans, CJK Fordham*)

Open Mar–Dec.
Rooms 10 double, 2 single – 1 with bath and shower, 11 with bath, all with telephone, radio, TV, tea-making facilities and baby-listening.
Facilities Entrance hall, lounge with log fire, dining room; sheltered terrace. 10-acre grounds with garden, croquet, swings, slides and adventure playground. In the heart of the National Park, near moors and dales; riding, golf and swimming nearby.
Location Off A170, 5 m N of Kirkbymoorside. Turn N towards Appleton-le-Moor 2 m E of Kirkbymoorside.
Restrictions Not suitable for ♿. Dogs by arrangement only, not in public rooms.
Credit cards Amex, Diners.
Terms (No service charge) B&B: single £35.25–£37, double £64–£67.25; dinner, B&B: single £42.25–£46.50, double £81.50–£85.50. Set lunch from £8.25, dinner from £12.75. Picnic lunches available. Reduced rates for long stays and winter breaks. Children under 2 sharing parents' room free; special meals.
Service/tipping: "Tipping is discouraged."

> Our italicised entries are different this year. There are more of them and they indicate hotels which are worth considering, but which, for various reasons – inadequate information, lack of feedback, ambivalent reports – do not at the moment warrant a fully entry. We should particularly welcome comments on these hotels.

LEAMINGTON SPA Warwickshire — Map 2

The Lansdowne Hotel
Clarendon Street
Leamington Spa CV32 4PF

Tel Leamington Spa (0926) 21313 and 450505
Telex 337556

"A long-time silent devotee of your guide, I simply had to write to you about this hotel. Infinite courtesy and patience during several phone calls about changing requirements (I had colleagues staying on various nights). It was everything I had expected from your entry and a good deal more besides. Food and wine such that none of us tired in a whole week and I regretted the one occasion I had to dine elsewhere. It was like being a guest in a well-ordered home. Quite an experience in really personal service." (*Frank Dennis*) "Each time we have been there we have been impressed with the excellence of the service and food – and the friendly welcome one receives is quite exceptional. The Allens are dedicated hoteliers – and the invaluable commodity of *time* is given freely and generously." (*Mrs GE Moore*) Two similar commendations to add to half-a-dozen others in this year's file on the special qualities of hospitality dispensed by David and Gillian Allen in their elegant town house in this once fashionable and still delightful watering place. It is convenient for Warwick Castle, but is also well placed for the National Exhibition Centre (25 minutes by car) and the National Agricultural Centre (10 minutes). Meanwhile, the enterprising Allens tell us that they have been awarded a red star by the AA – one of only six one-star hotels to receive this honour – and that they have come second in the Hotels Section of the local "Britain in Bloom" competition for their garden, and can now offer their guests discounts at various tourist attractions in the neighbourhood.

Open All year. Limited food service 24 Dec–12 Jan.
Rooms 6 double, 3 single – 6 with bath and shower, all with radio and double glazing; baby-listening by arrangement.
Facilities Residents' lounge with TV, bar, restaurant. Small garden. Personalised entry card for hotel guests offering discounts for local attractions such as Ragley Hall and Coventry Cathedral crypt; 10% discount on entry of Warwick Castle, 10 minutes' drive away.
Location Central, on A423. Parking.
Restrictions Only restaurant and bar suitable for ♿. No children under 5. No dogs.
Credit card Access.
Terms (No service charge) B&B £16.95–£22.85; dinner, B&B £26.60–£32.50. Set lunch £8.85, dinner £9.65. 2-night packages. Reduced rates for children sharing parents' room; special meals by arrangement.
Service/tipping: "We have always felt this to be an unnecessary impost. However if guests ask to recognise a particular service we try to get the member of staff together with the guest for a few personal words."

LEDBURY Hereford and Worcester — Map 2

Hope End Country House Hotel [GFG]
Hope End, Ledbury HR8 1JQ

Tel Ledbury (0531) 3613

"Can only use superlatives in describing Mrs Hegarty's food. Herbs, but not to excess, cream used, but not by the ladle, after-dinner truffles the best I've ever tasted. Her almond soup possibly the nicest but positively the most interesting I've ever had. Excellent wine list, including the lower end. Admirable locally bottled perry also available. And if you ask for a small helping, you are given one. Superb breakfast. Hotel's surrounding parkland contains a small lake, by which you can sit, and when we were there it was enlivened by huge clumps of semi-wild daffodils. Nearby countryside includes unspoilt stretches of the river Wye (whose salmon we ate) as well as the Malverns." (*Stephen Pyke.*) *Hope End* is all that remains of Elizabeth Barrett Browning's childhood home. Once a Moorish fantasy, like the Brighton Pavilion, most of the original was pulled down by later owners, leaving one lone minaret and huge stable gates. It is in a hidden valley, with big trees – a tranquil spot. The Hegartys tend a vast walled vegetable and fruit garden and keep chickens and goats. The bedrooms, mostly pine-clad, are pleasantly furnished, with woven covers on the beds, but make no attempt to be chic. *Hope End* doesn't conform to many people's notion of a hotel. As one reader put it this year: "Ideal for those who can't stand all the mod cons, drinks cabinet in the bedroom type of place. The Hegartys must be the most un-unctuous hoteliers in the country – one either likes it or one doesn't." (*Martyn Bainbridge*)

Open End Feb–end Nov. Closed Mon and Tue nights. Restaurant closed for lunch.
Rooms 1 cottage suite, 8 double – all with bath, telephone and tea-making facilities; TV in cottage. 1 ground-floor room.
Facilities 3 sitting rooms, dining room. Walled garden; 40 acres of wooded parkland and nature reserve.
Location 3 m from Malvern Hills N of Ledbury, ¼ m W of Wellington Heath.
Restrictions Not suitable for ♿. No children under 12. No smoking in dining room. No dogs.
Credit cards All major cards accepted.
Terms Dinner, B&B: single occupancy £78, double £110–£132, suite £132. Set dinner £20. Special breaks Mar–Nov (min 2 nights). 1-night bookings sometimes refused for weekends.
Service/tipping: "Our prices are fully inclusive. No tipping expected."

LEONARD STANLEY Gloucestershire — Map 2

The Grey Cottage — *Tel* Stonehouse (045 382) 2515
Leonard Stanley
Stonehouse GL10 3LU

Rosemary Reeves "likes to make things look nice". Helped by husband Andrew, she makes their cottage, built of grey Cotswold stone in 1807, look very nice indeed. It is spotlessly clean, with flowers everywhere: fresh flowers from the garden in vases, flowers on the china door knobs, on the Sanderson chintz sofa and chair covers, on the Portmeirion china, on the continental quilt covers, and in the very pretty framed botanical prints on the walls. There are comfortable beds, thick carpets throughout, and plenty of books everywhere. Guests are warmly welcomed, and pampered. "Being a husband and wife team," Rosie writes, "a 'them and us' situation does not exist. Our aim is to make guests comfortable and happy in our South Cotswolds home." You may well find a hot water bottle popped into your bed on a chilly night, tea, toast and freshly-baked flapjack waiting when you arrive back from a stroll, car windows magically cleaned: and all included in the modest charge. Breakfasts are delicious, freshly squeezed orange juice, warm brown bread, " the best damson jam I've ever tasted, scrambled eggs, bacon from real pigs –

lovely." Dinner can be provided at 24 hours' notice; simple generous good home cooking. The neat half-acre garden has yew hedges and a Wellingtonia planted in 1851. Points to note, plus or minus according to preferences: the Cotswold Way is only a mile away, Westonbirt Arboretum 13 miles, Slimbridge Wildfowl Trust eight miles; there is no drinks licence, but you may bring your own; a bathroom shower was not vastly powerful; there is excellent central heating; both owners smoke.

Open All year.
Rooms 2 double, 1 single – 1 with shower, all with telephone, radio, TV, tea-making facilities.
Facilities 2 lounges (1 with TV), dining room. ½-acre garden and patio.
Location 4 m SW of Stroud; 1 m off A419 between villages of Leonard Stanley and King Stanley.
Credit cards None accepted.
Restrictions No children under 10. No dogs.
Terms (Not VAT-rated) (No service charge) B&B: single £16, double £18; dinner, B&B: single £27, double £29. Dinners/suppers by prior arrangement only. Not licensed but guests may bring own drinks.
Service/tipping: "Tipping not expected."

LEW Oxfordshire — Map 2

The Farmhouse Hotel and Restaurant — *Tel* Bampton Castle (0993) 850297
University Farm
Lew, nr Bampton OX8 2AU

Pleasant, informal farmhouse hotel run by the family Rouse. The modernised 17th-century farmhouse is attached to a 216-acre working farm. Rooms, all with private facilities, are clean and have character. The barn restaurant is popular locally, but don't expect a gourmet experience. Possible snag is proximity to Brize Norton airfield, though disturbance limited. Prices are reasonable. 6 double rooms. B&B £15–£21. Dinner £9.95. More reports welcome.

LEWDOWN Devon — Map 1

Fox's Earth — *Tel* Lewdown (056683) 256/222
Lewtrenchard Manor
Lewdown, Nr Okehampton
EX20 4PN

A cautious welcome from our inspectors to a newcomer, *Fox's Earth*, the new name given to Lewtrenchard Manor by Americans Mary Ellen Keys and Greg Shriver. They have abandoned the world of computers to run this splendid Elizabethan manor house, with mullioned windows, grand staircase, long gallery and imposing fireplaces, a dovecote and impressive formal gardens. Restored in Victorian times by an avid collector of Tudor fine panelling and plasterwork, it has now been totally renovated, redecorated and refurnished with much panache. The blend is of antiques, good oil-paintings, Tudor four-posters, and comfortable modern furniture and lamps. "Our enormous bedroom included a recessed sitting area and had a superb gold leather frieze round the ceiling above the panelling; our bathroom was equipped with deep piled towels and de luxe his and hers bathrobes." Apart from a few small reservations, food lived up to the expectations raised by the menu, and service was "carried out efficiently and with great charm by a young local girl, extremely smart in her black and white uniform". The chief drawback was that the hotel was extremely cold during our inspector's visit in March. There were log fires, and fan heaters were provided for the bedroom, but the central heating was definitely not doing its stuff. Before booking, other than at midsummer, you should check the status quo. There were a few other niggles; containers not replenished in the rooms; a mattress which sagged; somewhat parsimonious portions of petits fours. All points which will no doubt be rectified when the hotel gets properly into its stride, and they do give you a complimentary quarter bottle of champagne.

Open All year except 4 Jan–13 Feb
Rooms 1 suite, 8 double – all with bath, shower, telephone, radio and TV.
Facilities 2 sitting rooms, bar, 2 dining rooms, gallery. 11-acre grounds with formal gardens, pond, 2-acre fishing lake with rowing boat, and 60-foot waterfall.
Location ¾ m S of A30. Turn left at Lewdown.
Restrictions No children under 12. Dogs by arrangement only, not in public rooms.
Credit cards Access, Amex, Visa.
Terms (Service at guests' discretion) B&B (continental): double £70–£80, suite £75–£85. Set Sun lunch £13.50, set dinner £18–£21.

LIFTON Devon — Map 1

The Arundell Arms [GFG] — *Tel* Lifton (0566) 84666
Lifton PL16 0AA

A much-creepered early 19th-century stone building, once a coaching inn, on the A30 (the five rooms in the front are sound-proofed and ventilated). It is very much a sportsperson's hotel: there are snipe- and pheasant-shooting weekends and hunting breaks in the winter, but Lifton is, above all, a popular resort for the fishing fraternity, and the *Arundell* has been a leading fishing hotel for the past half-century. It has 20 miles of its own water on the Tamar and four of its tributaries, and throughout the year it offers an extensive programme of fly-fishing courses for beginners and for the more advanced. The hotel has been run for a quarter of century with devotion and flair by Anne Voss-Bark who tells us that she has just completed a major refurbishment of the restaurant, sitting room and bedrooms, which should answer earlier reports of some rooms being "spartan" or "scruffy". And all readers attest to the excellence of Philip Burgess's cooking. "The hotel improves each time as Mrs Voss-Bark tries to iron out any complaints. Our bedroom had been recently redecorated, the lounge has new settees and the changes to the reception and bar area are an improvement. The food has always been copious and lovely, but now I would say it is *excellent*." "A delicious dinner; and the only hotel where we did not need our 100-watt bulb." (*Carol Jackson, the Marchioness of Tavistock, and others*)

Open All year except 4 days over Christmas.
Rooms 18 double, 11 single – all with bath and/or shower, TV and tea-making facilities; 24 with direct-dial telephone. 5 in annexe opposite. 1 self-catering flat.
Facilities Sitting room, 2 bars, 2 restaurants; conference suite, meeting rooms; games room, skittle alley. Small terraced garden. Exclusive fishing rights on 20 m of river Tamar and tributaries for salmon, sea trout and brown trout; also 3-acre lake. Cornish coasts within ½ hour's drive. Golf, riding, walks nearby.

Location 3 m E of Launceston on A30 (front rooms soundproofed). Parking.
Restrictions Not suitable for ♿. No dogs in restaurant.
Credit cards All major cards accepted.
Terms (No service charge) B&B £23.50–£37; dinner, B&B (2 nights min) £36–£51. Set lunch £9–£11, dinner £14–£16; full alc £24. Autumn, winter and spring breaks. Fishing, shooting, hunting, riding, golfing holidays. Children under 16 free in parents' room; special meals by arrangement.
Service/tipping: "No service charge made and no tipping expected. Any gratuities given are distributed monthly among all our staff."

LINCOLN Lincolnshire — Map 3

D'Isney Place Hotel — *Tel* Lincoln (0522) 38881
Eastgate, Lincoln LN2 4AA

Looks like the answer to many travellers' prayers: David and Judy Payne's elegant Georgian bed-and-breakfast, close to Cathedral, quiet and with many special touches: fresh fruit in rooms daily, two rooms with double *jacuzzi (a refinement new to us), one with four-poster, one with tester. Regrettably, reports have been mixed in recent years though better this past year. 18 rooms, all with private facilities. Double room with breakfast £48–£53. More reports would be welcome.*

LITTLE HORSTED East Sussex — Map 3

Horsted Place — *Tel* Uckfield (0825) 75581
Little Horsted — *Telex* 95548
Nr Uckfield TN22 5TS

An enthusiastic welcome from two hotelophiles for this recently opened lavish conversion of Lord Rupert Nevill's former home. In its previous incarnation members of the Royal Family stayed here, including the Queen – you can ask for the Windsor Suite which she apparently favoured. Its formal gardens were designed by Sir Geoffrey Jellicoe. "This would be my candidate for newcomer of the year in the luxury class; building, staff and service all a delight. An elegant mid-19th-century house set in well-tended grounds with pleasantly proportioned rooms and a striking long gallery. The public rooms are well lit and delightfully furnished. Most of the bedrooms have their own sitting room and lavish bathroom and all are, of course, equipped with all manner of extras. Breakfast consisted of excellent croissants, freshly-squeezed orange juice and a newspaper." (*WA*) "The dinner was generally very good, basically English with French overtones and smart presentation. We were told we could have anything else we wanted even it it was not on the menu. Breakfast was a weak point. No menu, brown toast was cold and of the Hovis variety, and butter rather 'portion controlled'. One niggle: a daily paper is included but when we ordered two on Sunday the extra one was charged! Staff were excellent, very friendly and welcoming with a high standard of service. We would return, but would try to go on a winter break as it is really very expensive." (*P and JT*)

Open All year except possibly first week of Jan.
Rooms 14 suites, 3 single – 16 with bath and shower, 1 with bath, all with direct-dial telephone, radio and TV. 4 suites in East Wing. Ground-floor rooms.

Facilities Lift. 2 drawing rooms, library, restaurant; indoor heated swimming pool. 23-acre grounds with tennis and croquet. Adjacent to small lake with fishing rights.
Location 3 m SW of Uckfield off A26.
Restrictions No children under 7. No dogs.
Credit cards All major cards accepted.
Terms B&B: single from £85, double £150–£250. Set lunch £15, dinner £27.50.
Service/tipping: "Tipping is not encouraged and staff are trained to refuse politely."

LITTLE SINGLETON Lancashire — Map 4

Mains Hall Hotel
Mains Lane, Little Singleton
Nr Poulton-le-Fylde FY6 7LE

Tel Poulton-le-Fylde
(0253) 885130

A small, friendly, distinctly unpricey kind of place, ten minutes inland from the gaudy life of Blackpool, but wholly pastoral, with rooms looking over meadows to the river Wyre and a pleasant garden in front. A house of character and history, too: the Hesketh lived here in Elizabethan times, and George IV, when Prince of Wales, courted Maria Fitzherbert in these rooms. And the owners, Bob and Beryl Owen, are as unpretentiously sympathetic as their hotel. Dinner is a home-cooked three-course no-choice event at 7 pm, mostly to guests' liking (mention your allergies, state your preferences when you book). Except by special arrangement, no evening meal is served on Sunday or during the Owens's own holidays. Here is one rapturous appreciation from this year's crop of compliments: "Without doubt the best hotel for value I have ever stayed in. It is quiet, the owners are delightful and accommodation and food left nothing to be desired. How they do it all for the price I just don't know. Love of the job I expect! They told me one man stayed for a year. I'm not surprised." (*JEH Wolff; also Heather Kirk, the Hon Mrs G Lascelles*)

Open All year except 31 Dec–2 Jan. Restaurant closed for lunch, on Sun and during owners' holiday (dates unspecified).
Rooms 7 double – 3 with bath, 4 with shower, all with radio and tea-making facilities; most with TV; telephone available; 1 4-poster, 1 half-tester.
Facilities Hall, lounge with TV, bar, dining room. 4-acre grounds with games room. Access to tidal river with fishing; birdwatching.
Location 5 m NE of Blackpool. Leave M55 at Exit 3; take A585 N following signs to Fleetwood. Hotel is ½ m past 2nd set of traffic lights.
Restrictions Not suitable for ♿. No dogs in public rooms.
Credit cards Access, Visa.
Terms (No service charge) B&B: single occupancy £18.50–£25, double £26–£45. Set dinner £9.75. 10% reduction for weekly bookings. Reduced rates for children sharing parents' room; special meals.
Service/tipping: "No service charge. We discourage tipping, but if tips are given they are shared equally among all employees."

LONDON — Map 3

Athenaeum Hotel
116 Piccadilly, W1V 0BJ

Tel (01) 499 3464
In USA (800) 223 5560
Telex 261589 ATHOME

The *Athenaeum* is the flagship hotel of the Rank chain. It has an enviable position overlooking Green Park (jogging maps and suits available for the energetic), and all the trimmings that one would expect from a de luxe West End hotel – 24-hour service, excellent restaurant, hyper-elegant decor and furnishings. All recent visitors confirm the impressions of a Rolls Royce of a hotel firing on all its well-lubricated cylinders.

Open: All year.
Rooms 22 suites, 80 double, 10 single – all with bath and shower, telephone, radio and TV; free in-house films; baby-listening; double-glazing. Also 33 1- and 2-bedroom apartments.
Facilities Lifts. Lounge, cocktail bar, restaurant; conference and functions facilities; resident pianist in restaurant and lounge Tue–Sat evenings.
Location Central (hotel is fully double-glazed); valet parking. (Underground Green Park.)
Restriction Guide dogs only.
Credit cards All major cards accepted.
Terms Rooms: single £115–£130, double £150–£170, suites £210–£250. Breakfast: continental £5.75, English £8. Set lunch £15.50–£17.50 (including wine), pre-theatre dinner £13.50–£15.50; full alc £35. Weekend packages. Reduced rates for children at weekends; special meals.
Service/tipping : "There is no service charge nor are tips expected. Clients who feel they have been well treated may wish to reward the staff."

Basil Street Hotel — *Tel* (01) 581 3311
8 Basil Street — *Telex* 28379
Knightsbridge SW3 1AH

Last year we were forced to italicise our entry for this traditional and traditionally well-regarded hotel in a quiet lane leading off Sloane Street (convenient for Hyde Park and Harrods). This year reports are altogether more favourable. Two typical 1987 comments: "The first impression one receives is one of the thirties. So much service with a genuine smile, and any orders from the bedroom executed promptly. It still retains its charm of 20 years ago – and seems to be the only bit of civilised life left in a rat-race city." (*Patricia Roberts*) "The Guide does not do justice to the unfailingly good *Basil Street*, a haven of peace in the busiest part of London. And I was the sort of customer so often overlooked – an elderly woman on her own." (*Mrs Anne S Wolff; Elizabeth Loder, Laura H Scott, Richard Creed, C and B Myles, and others*) Recurring niggles: one small lift, some rooms overlook an inner court (noisy with staff clattering in summer).

Open All year.
Rooms 1 suite, 44 double, 48 single – 69 with bath and/or shower, all with telephone, radio and TV.
Facilities 3 lounges, coffee shop, wine bar, dining room; ladies' club; facilities for conferences, functions and private meals.
Location Central; public carpark nearby. (Underground Knightsbridge.)
Restrictions Not suitable for ♿. No dogs in public rooms.
Credit cards All major cards accepted.
Terms [1987 rates] (Service at guests' discretion) Rooms: single £33–£72, double £60–£94, family £154. Breakfast: continental £3.50, English from £6.30. Full alc £15–£20. Weekend reductions Nov–Mar; 3-night Christmas stay. No charge for children under 16 sharing parents' room; special meals.

> We asked hotels to quote 1988 prices. Not all were able to predict them in the late spring of 1987. Some of our terms will be inaccurate. Do check latest tariffs at the time of booking.

The Beaufort Hotel *Tel* (01) 584 5252
33 Beaufort Gardens, SW3 1PW *Telex* 929200

A personally-run sophisticated bed-and-breakfast nestling in the shadow of Harrods. Most of the extras you would expect at a five-star hotel at half the price, even fax, telex, secretarial services and free membership of health club. Personal room keys approved by Control Risks Ltd. Breakfast served in bedrooms from 6.30 am. 29 rooms (including 3 suites). Double room with breakfast £90–£140. First reports sound highly promising. More would be welcome.

Blakes Hotel [GFG] *Tel* (01) 370 6701
33 Roland Gardens, SW7 3PF *Telex* 8813500

Don't let the prim Victorian exterior deceive you. *Blakes Hotel*, a few minutes' walk from South Kensington Underground, is a trendy, stylish hotel, somewhere to go if you want to be seen. Very laid-back staff, black-and-white decor in the downstairs dining room, cool ice-maidens at the reception desk, a parrot in a cage in the hall – that is unless owner/designer Anouska Hempel has decided to change everything as she often does. Some rooms have tremendous frills and flounces, others are severely plain, grey and white highlighted with a bright green plant. Best to discuss the style of room you prefer when booking. (*Paul Dwyer, and others*)

Open All year. Restaurant closed Christmas/Boxing Day.
Rooms 8 suites, 36 double, 10 single – all with bath and/or shower, telephone and TV; most with radio. 10 in annexe across road.
Facilities Lift. Lounge, bar, restaurant.
Location Central; no private parking. (Underground South Kensington or Gloucester Road.)
Restrictions Not suitable for ♿. No dogs.
Credit cards All major cards accepted.
Terms (Excluding 15% service charge on restaurant bills and for room service) B&B: single £96.90–£111.90, double £158.80–£173.80, suite from £198.90. Full alc £47. Special meals for children on request.
Service/tipping: "We do not levy a service charge on accommodation; tips are at guests' discretion. We add a 15% charge to restaurant and room-service bills which is included in the waiting staffs' wages."

Capital Hotel [GFG] *Tel* (01) 589 5171
22-24 Basil Street, SW3 1AT *Telex* 919042

A few doors away from the *Basil Street* (above) and under the same ownership as *L'Hôtel* (below), the smallish, thoroughly modern, privately-owned *Capital* is more sophisticated than either. Its rooms have been designed by Nina Campbell, and are double-glazed, air-conditioned and elegant in a country-house sort of way. What appear to be bookshelves turn out to be a deep, walk-in hanging cupboard, and bathrooms are lavishly marble and comprehensively equipped with bubble baths and the like as well as "wonderfully fluffy towels". The *Capital* is one of only four hotels in London to boast a *Michelin* rosette; the ladies' loo is said to be the most stylish in London. (*Stephan and Kate Murray-Sykes*)

Rooms 6 suites, 30 double, 20 single – all with bath, shower, telephone, radio, TV and baby-listening.

Facilities Lift. Lounge, cocktail bar, restaurant.
Location Central. Garage. (Underground Knightsbridge.)
Restriction Dogs at management's discretion, not in public rooms.
Credit cards All major cards accepted.
Terms (Service at guests' discretion) B&B: single £115.50, double £146, suite £166. Set lunch £17.50, dinner £25; full alc £35. Children if sharing parents' room free; special meals.

Claverly Hotel *Tel* (01) 589 8541
14 Beaufort Gardens, SW3 1PS

Yet another smart bed-and-breakfast newcomer in the streets behind Harrods. Our attention was drawn to it when we read that it had won a Certificate of Distinction awarded by the British Tourist Authority to the best B&B in Central London. Choosing a winner must be an arduous business for the SW3 assessor. Our inspectors, who don't pretend they have slept around comprehensively in the Knightsbridge area, were nevertheless approving of the *Claverly*, less expensive than some of its neighbours. The hotel had a good spick and span feel to it, their room was comfortable and warm and had all essential support systems without being over-luxurious. Everything was spotlessly clean. The staff were all as friendly as you could wish. Decent breakfasts with freshly-squeezed orange juice and Cona coffee. Only packaged jams and butter let the side down.

Open All year.
Rooms 23 double, 13 single - 2 with bath or shower, all with telephone, TV and baby-listening.
Facilities 2 lounges, breakfast room.
Location Central. Public carpark nearby. (Underground Knightsbridge.)
Restrictions Not suitable for ♿. No dogs.
Credit card Visa.
Terms B&B: single £45–£48, double £56–£61. (No restaurant.)

The Connaught [GFG] *Tel* (01) 499 7070
Carlos Place, W1Y 6AL

Still the *prima donna assoluta* of London hotels in the heart of Mayfair, a strolling distance from Piccadilly and Oxford Street, in a relatively unbusy street. "Preserved in amber, the last of the great hotels, running as smoothly as nostalgia would have us believe all such establishments did in the thirties. There seem to be more staff than guests. They appear as genii from bottles when one presses the relevant bell; they are totally obliging, endlessly helpful, extremely polite. The food is outstanding, a model for modern hotels to copy if they could, which I totally doubt. This plus a comfortable room, large bathroom, good shower, lots of big soft white towels, bed turned down at night, and linen mat, placed to step one's bare foot on to, beside the bed, a courtesy rarely still found in English hotels." (*AM, and others*)

Open All year.
Rooms 90, including suites – all with bath, direct-dial telephone and TV; 24-hour room service; air-conditioning. Some rooms suitable for ♿.
Facilities Lounge, cocktail bar, grill/restaurant (jacket and tie required; no jeans).
Location Central. No private parking. (Underground Bond Street.)
Restriction No dogs.

Credit card Access.
Terms [1987 rates] (Excluding 15% service charge) Rooms: single £110, double £132–£150, suite £300. Breakfast: continental £5.50, English alc. Full alc lunch/dinner £23–£45.

Cranley Place Hotel *Tel* (01) 589 7704
1 Cranley Place, SW7 3AB

Newly nominated reasonably priced B&B a few minutes' walk from South Kensington station. Rooms recently refurbished and pleasantly furnished. Small garden. Breakfast, with many options of menus, served in rooms or in dining room. 13 rooms, all with bath and/or shower. B&B £32.50–£55. More reports please.

Duke's Hotel [GFG] *Tel* (01) 491 4840
35 St James's Place, SW1A 1NY *Telex* 28283

Eighty years old this year, this sophisticated exclusive small hotel has the special attraction of being right in the centre, a stone's throw from St James's Palace and Fortnums, but also tucked unobtrusively away in a quiet cul-de-sac off a cul-de-sac, with an entrance still lit by gaslight as it presumably was when the hotel was built in 1908. For most readers – as previously – *Duke's* has been "an oasis of excellence", but two demurs reached us this year. One reader found the bar "smokey, stuffy and unpleasant" – perhaps a new extractor fan is needed? The other reported her profound disappointment, having reserved and paid for a room in advance and reconfirmed on arrival in England, in finding that the hotel had over-booked. To be "farmed out at a noisy business-man's hotel" at *Duke's'* expense, even accompanied by a bottle of champagne, was inadequate compensation . . .

Open All year.
Rooms 21 suites, 28 double, 8 single – all with bath and shower, telephone, radio and TV; 24-hour room service. Some suites on ground floor.
Facilities Lift. Lounge, bar, restaurant; banquet/conference facilities. Courtyard.
Location Central; off St James's Street, between Piccadilly and Pall Mall; 4 minutes' walk from Green Park Underground. NCP parking nearby.
Restriction No dogs.
Credit cards All major cards accepted.
Terms (Service at guests' discretion) Rooms: single £131, double £164 (4-poster £189), suite £241–£525. Breakfast: continental £6.75, English £8.75. Set lunch £19; full alc £40.

Ebury Court *Tel* (01) 730 8147
26 Ebury Street, SW1W 0LU

For almost half a century Diana and Romer Topham have been running this old-fashioned (in the most complimentary sense) and friendly hotel that rambles through five adjoining houses on the unseamy side of Victoria. The rooms are mostly small, the furniture the sort of mixture you find in a country house: a few antiques, including a Hepplewhite four-poster and a fine grandfather clock, comfortable chairs, inherited oddments, some modern pieces. Pretty ornamental china and chintzes, chosen with taste, and bathrooms fitted in where possible and functional.

Some rooms with no bathrooms (one down the corridor). Nothing brand-new or ultra-luxurious. The restaurant in the basement, all corners and crannies, cosy and low-ceilinged, serves decent traditional English fare. "Always quietly comfortable and reassuring, and friendly in a dignified way without being stuffy," was one tribute this year. Another reader wrote: "The art of making all comers feel at home is no mean one, and this is achieved with a remarkable sureness of touch." (*Eithne Scallan, Mrs Leslie Purdy, and others*) This year the Tophams contemplated retirement after Romer's 80th birthday and some ill-health, but now hope instead to work with daughter and friends on a programme of refurbishment.

Open All year.
Rooms 18 double, 21 single – 12 doubles with bath, 2 singles with shower, all with telephone and radio; TV for hire.
Facilities Lift. Sitting room, writing room with TV, Club Bar (visitors may become temporary members), restaurant; suppers served from 6.30pm for theatre-goers.
Location Central (front windows double-glazed) 3 minutes' walk from Victoria Station. Parking difficult. (Underground Victoria.)
Restrictions Not suitable for ♿. No children under 5 in restaurant. Small and well-behaved dogs only, not in public rooms.
Credit cards Access, Visa.
Terms (Service at guests' discretion) B&B: single £35.50–£37.50, double £55.50–£65.50. Full alc £20.

The Goring Hotel *Tel* (01) 834 8211
15 Beeston Place, SW1W 0JW *Tel* 919166

The Goring Hotel was built in 1910 by the present Mr Goring's grandfather, and was the first hotel in the world to have a private bathroom and central heating for each bedroom. The traditional standards of service and cleanliness are scrupulously maintained, and the present owner, Goring the Third, constantly sleeps his way round his bedrooms looking for weak spots. There's a high return ratio: guests appreciate the Englishness of the place as well as its useful location just round the corner from Buckingham Palace. Rooms are charmingly furnished, and there is a large comfortable bar which overlooks an inner courtyard garden and lawn (not, however, accessible to guests).

Open All year.
Rooms 5 suites, 48 double, 37 single – all with bath and shower, telephone, radio and TV; some with air-conditioning.
Facilities Lift. Lounge, bar, restaurant; 5 function rooms.
Location Central, near Buckingham Palace (front rooms are double-glazed). Garage and mews parking. (Underground Victoria).
Restriction No dogs.
Credit cards All major cards accepted.
Terms Rooms: single £87.50, double £125, suite £165. Breakfast: continental from £4.50, English from £7. Set lunch £15.50, dinner £18; full alc £28.
Service/tipping: "Guests are informed that no tipping is necessary."

Hazlitt's *Tel* (01) 434 1771
6 Frith Street W1V 5TZ

A new hotel, doors opened in October 1986, in the middle of Soho of all places. *Hazlitt's*, until recently a nurses' home, has been created from three terrace houses built in 1718. It takes its name from the famous essayist who died in one of the houses a century later. No restaurant, and the continental breakfast is served in the room: good coffee, but frozen-type croissants and rolls. Rooms have agreeable prints and plants as well as new firm beds and decent linen. Not luxurious, but the tariff is very reasonable for the area which otherwise offers little apart from mean, cramped, austere, shabby or sleazy accommodation. (*HR*)

Open All year except Christmas.
Rooms 2 suites, 20 double – 16 with bath, all with direct-dial telephone and TV. 3 ground-floor rooms.
Facility Lounge.
Location Central. NCP nearby. (Underground Tottenham Court Road.)
Restriction No dogs.
Credit cards All major cards accepted.
Terms Rooms: single £40–£50, double £55–£64, suite £95–£120. Breakfast £3.50. (No restaurant.)
Service/tipping : "Any tips are divided equally between staff."

The Knightsbridge Hotel *Tel* (01) 589 9271
10 Beaufort Gardens, SW3 1PT

A comfortable, cheery little hotel at the lower end of the price scale on this quiet tree-lined street a few minutes' walk past Harrods from Knightsbridge Underground. On checking in, you are given a room key and a front-door key, and from then on you come and go as though it were your own home. The atmosphere is bright, pleasant and casual. Readers continue to endorse an earlier report: "What was special about *The Knightsbridge* was the complete absence of the dreary run-down atmosphere so often encountered in lower-priced hotels. Obviously, at these prices this is not a place of great charm or style, but for those who would rather give their money to Harrods than to a hotel, it's a nice place to return to after an exhausting day running around the city." (*Donna Cuervo*) Sandwiches and light meals are served in the bar all day until 11 pm.

Open All year.
Rooms 11 double, 9 single – 9 with bath and shower, 4 with shower, all with telephone and radio; 4 with TV
Facilities TV lounge, bar/coffee room (open all day until 11 pm).
Location Central. Near Harrods. (Underground Knightsbridge.) Meter parking; public carpark 10 mins.
Restrictions Not suitable for ♿. No dogs.
Credit cards Amex, Visa.
Terms B&B (continental): single £26–£36, double £37–£59. Snacks from £1.50
Service/tipping: "Service charge is included in room rate."

Knightsbridge Green Hotel *Tel* (01) 584 6274 and 225 1635
159 Knightsbridge, SW1X 7PD

A £500,000 facelift is in train at this small family-run hotel close to Harrods and Hyde Park, unusual in having mostly suites. For many years it seemed to have been stuck in a timewarp of fifties furnishing: "Like entering the young Hubert Gregg's bachelor flat in a 1950s film; I was surprised not to have an immediate telephone call from Kay Kendall." Presumably that era will end as Dennis Marler and his sister Denise embark on their programme of renovation – installing double-glazing and new central heating and undertaking "full refurnishing". We hope the hotel won't entirely lose its unfashionable idiosyncratic charm, but the early reports from occupants of the improved eighties-style rooms are wholly complimentary. Prices have inevitably been raised, but we think the tariff is still remarkably good value for the neighbourhood, and all our correspondents speak well of the service and the breakfasts.

Open All year, except 4 days at Christmas.
Rooms 16 suites, 4 double, 2 single – all with bath, shower, telephone, TV and tea-making facilities.
Facilities Lift. Club Room on first floor for soft drinks, coffee and tea.
Location Central (front rooms double-glazed). NCP in Pavilion Road nearby. (Underground Knightsbridge.)
Restriction Not suitable for severely ♿. No dogs.
Credit cards Access, Amex, Visa.
Terms (Excluding VAT) Rooms: single £50, double £65, suite £80. Breakfast: continental £3.50, English £5. (No restaurant.)
Service/tipping: "Our rates include service charge; this is stated clearly in the bedrooms and guests are discouraged from further tipping."

L'Hôtel — *Tel* (01 589 6286
28 Basil Street, SW3 1AT — *Telex* 919042 HOTCAP attn L'HOTEL

A centrally located model city B&B in the upper-price bracket, owned by the Levins, who also own the neighbouring *Capital* (q.v.). Margaret Levin has been responsible for the decor, rustic in style, with French pine furniture and fabric wall coverings. Last year we cited one guest's appreciation: "The hotel is remarkable in that it provides a very personal big city experience. The young staff are relaxed, cheerful and chatty, but unfailingly professional under pressure. The *Métro* wine bar in the basement is a gem. The food is straightforward but interesting – not the usual wine bar clichés. There is a Cruover machine, which dispenses good wine by the glass, and an interesting reasonably-priced wine list. Breakfasts are served in the *Métro* – fresh orange juice, warm rolls and croissants and so-so coffee. All in all, a superb London base with a choice of unpretentiously excellent food or *haute cuisine* available at the *Capital* next door. Pleasant and efficient staff." The same correspondent has been back since, finding everything as good as before, but warning that you need to book well ahead to have a choice of rooms: some are smaller than others and lack the cosy benefit of a gas coal-fire. (*David Wooff; also Paul Dwyer, Pam Phillips*)

Open All year. Wine bar closed Sat evening, Sun and public holidays, except for residents' breakfasts.
Rooms 1 suite, 11 double – all with bath, shower, telephone, radio TV. 1 ground-floor room. (*Note:* no room service.)
Facilities Lift. Wine bar/brasserie.
Location Central. NCP opposite. (Underground Knightsbridge.)
Credit cards Amex, Visa.
Terms (Tipping at guests' discretion) B&B: double room £90, suite £120. Alc meal in wine bar (excluding wine) about £10; light meals also available.

> We invited all British hotels to tell us of their policy on service charges and tipping. Many hotels ignored this question. Replies, when given, are printed at the end of an entry.

Number Sixteen *Tel* (01) 589 5232
16 Sumner Place, SW7 3EG *Telex* 266638 WATSON

Discreetly elegant South Kensington B&B with pretty garden and new winter garden. Some top-floor rooms are on the small side. Taken over in 1987 by Granfel plc which owns Horsted Place *at Little Horsted, East Sussex (q.v.). We are assured its character will not change but there will be improvements to breakfasts, previously a source of complaint (fresh orange juice and croissants), and bedrooms (fancier soaps and the like). Prices also will rise. Former owner Michael Watson, though still associated, will no longer run the hotel. Hence the italics. 30 rooms, almost all with private facilities. B&B: single £40–£60, double £95–£110. Can we have reports on the new set-up please?*

The Portobello Hotel *Tel* (01) 727 2777
22 Stanley Gardens, W11 2NG *Telex* 268349 PORT

This six-floor Victorian terraced house, within strolling distance of the Portobello Road market and a little further to Kensington Gardens, is one of the few hotels in London with distinctive decor and life-style. Some of the rooms, called cabins, are pokey, even if they have essential elements of life-support like colour TV, tiny fridge and micro-bathroom. But there are also, as you work downwards, normal-sized rooms and ritzy suites. Some people can't take its easy-going approach to hospitality at all; others find its charms pall. But it has also had ardent champions. "Nothing changes here (fortunately). I now stay virtually every month – if my wife is with me in one of the Special Rooms (either the Round Room or the Bath Room), otherwise in one of the admittedly small singles. The prices are reasonable for central London. The place is relaxed, discreet and definitely to my taste. I wouldn't go near one of the bigger London hotels again." (*Iain Elliott*) Nothing essential has changed, we hope, but the owner, Tim Herring, tells us that a major room refurbishing programme is taking place in 1987, and that our reference last year to haphazard service was misleading: the *Portobello* doesn't claim to offer room service or a hall porter, but reception, bar and restaurant staff are on duty all day and all night and keen to help with theatre or restaurant advice or bookings.

Open All year.
Rooms 7 suites, 9 double, 9 single – 5 with bath and shower, 20 with shower only, all with telephone, radio, TV, tea-making facilities and fridge; baby-sitting can be arranged. 2 ground-floor rooms.
Facilities Lift. Lounge, bar/restaurant (open 24 hours a day to residents).
Location Central. Meter parking. (Underground Notting Hill Gate.)
Restriction Not suitable for ♿.
Credit cards All major cards accepted.
Terms (No service charge) B&B (continental): single £42–£55.50, double £66–£70, suite £12.75. Full alc £20. Special meals for children.
Service/tipping: "No service added to bill. Tipping not encouraged."

The Sandringham Hotel *Tel* (01) 435 1569
3 Holford Road, NW3 1AD

The Dreyer family have run this budget B&B for 33 years in their large Victorian house with a large leafy garden, near Hampstead Heath.

Readers continue to give it warm praise. "The next best place to stay if no friends with a house in London." (*JRM Crompton*) "Modest in scope, but so reasonable, and quiet. We've stayed at a number of hotels in London, always ruined by the fact that as soon as you open the window, all of London's traffic is at your feet. So the commute (20 minutes to somewhere more central) isn't too bad. The area round the hotel is quite *chic*, Chinese-y restaurants in high warehouse-y buildings with pink napkins – that kind of *chic*, but one doesn't have to commute to dinner. Everyone was friendly, breakfast was *comme toujours* eggsbaconsausage-mushroomtomatoestoast and tea. Good idea is downstairs fridge and hot beverage complex, serve yourself and pay on honour – fridge filled with cokes and juice and ribenas (heaven after a London trekking day and before a London town night)." (*A Gilbert*)

Open All year.
Rooms 10 double, 5 single – 4 with bath and shower.
Facilities Lounge with TV, breakfast room. Small walled garden.
Location 15 minutes by Underground from central London. (Underground Hampstead, close by.) Parking in forecourt of hotel or road.
Restrictions Not suitable for ♿. No dogs.
Credit cards None accepted.
Terms B&B: single £20–£22, double £39–£45. (No restaurant.)

Wilbraham Hotel *Tel* (01) 730 8296
1 Wilbraham Place, SW1X 9AE

No glossy, ultra-efficient hotel with marble bathrooms, but a sedate traditional establishment in three Victorian terrace houses, just off Sloane Street. Handsome staircases and archways and panelled walls remain from the original structure. Some rooms are small and the singles without bathrooms on the top floor are fairly basic. Plumbing can be tiresome. Despite some irritations, most readers want to give the *Wilbraham* the benefit of the doubt. One tells us how, coming back at 1.30 am, he was refused a cup of tea by the night porter: "I appealed to his decency, charity etc and he eventually relented." Last year a correspondent described kindness beyond the call of duty after she had been mugged. Prices are very reasonable for the area. *Note*: the hotel is embarking on a gradual refurbishment programme which we hope will deal with recurring complaints of poor insulation between bedrooms. (*Dr M Purshouse, Ian Morrison, Janette Bland*)

Open All year. Buttery closed Sun and bank holidays.
Rooms 40 double, 12 single – 40 with bath and shower, all with telephone and TV; baby-sitting available. 4 ground-floor rooms.
Facilities 2 lifts. Lounge, buttery/bar, TV room.
Location Near Sloane Square Underground. Public underground parking nearby.
Restriction No dogs.
Credit cards None accepted.
Terms (Excluding VAT; service at guests' discretion) Rooms: single £28–£39, double £48–£63. Breakfast: continental from £3, English from £5. Full alc £6–£10.

> "The welcoming fruit basket contained apples which were soft, bruised and full of worms. We asked for replacements which were brought to the room with the explanation that it was difficult to buy good apples at this time of year (September)."

LONG MELFORD Suffolk — Map 3

The Black Lion Hotel [GFG] *Tel* Sudbury (0787) 312356
Long Melford
Sudbury CO10 9DN

A well-modernised 17th-century coaching inn, recently taken over by Luke Brady, formerly in the wine trade, and wife Amelia. Overlooks the village green and is close by one of Suffolk's loveliest churches in a showplace village. Nominators gave general approval to the Brady enterprise – staff pleasant, food good, rooms excellent, everywhere bright and warm. 10 bedrooms, all with bath. B&B £20–£36. Full alc £18. More reports welcome.

LONGHORSLEY Northumberland — Map 4

Linden Hall Hotel *Tel* Morpeth (0670) 56611
Longhorsley *Telex* 538224
Morpeth NE65 8XF *Reservations* in US (800) 223 5581

Linden Hall is a mansion of considerable grandeur, built in 1812 in the classical style, and set in 300 acres. "Absolutely first-class" and "sheer unashamed luxury" were two of the compliments showered on *Linden Hall* last year, together with more specific appreciations of various cossetings and kindnesses: thoughtful facilities for small children, bath gel and shampoo replenished *twice* a day, fresh fruit in bedrooms every day, Bendick's mints left at night when beds turned down, etc, etc.

This year the hotel has had a mixed reception. There are still handsome compliments – "the place itself is gorgeous and beautifully appointed and there are plenty of smiling and helpful staff" and "accommodation and service excellent" – but also murmurs of discontent: "uncoordinated breakfasts – lack of senior staff seemed to be the problem" and substantial disappointment in the restaurant. Having scrutinised a number of sample menus we can only hope that the chef's cooking of French dishes is more literate than his spelling . . .

Open All year.
Rooms 44 double, 1 single – all with bath and shower, telephone, radio, TV, tea-making facilities and baby-listening. 10 ground floor-rooms. 2 equipped for ♿.
Facilities Lift. 3 lounges, 2 bars, conservatory, pub and snack bar, TV room, restaurant; functions/conference facilities; billiard room, table tennis room, sauna, solarium, hairdressing salon. 300-acre grounds with tennis, putting, croquet, clay pigeon shooting, children's playground and adventure woodland area.
Location 5 m N of Morpeth on A697; 30 m N of Newcastle.
Restriction No dogs in public rooms.
Credit cards All major cards accepted.
Terms [1987 rates] B&B: single £27.50, double £62.50–£73.50 Set dinner £14.50; full alc £24. 2- to 4- day While-a-Way breaks throughout year (Fri–Mon only Mar–Oct); special 7-day terms. Children under 12 if sharing parents' room free; special meals.
Service/tipping: "Service is included. Tipping is up to the customer (we are against it)."

Italicised entries are for hotels on which we need more feedback – either because we are short of reports or because we have had mixed or inadequate reports.

LOWER BRAILES Warwickshire — Map 2

Feldon House [GFG] — *Tel* Brailes (060 885) 580
Lower Brailes
Nr Banbury OX15 5HW

"This place is my find of the year," writes an enthusiastic nominator for this three-bedroom country guest house, with an excellent restaurant, whose owners enjoy entertaining a party which takes over the whole house, but are happy to have individual couples too. "Quieter, much more welcoming and vastly less expensive than the hotels in Stratford, it is a charming early 19th-century house set back from the Shipston-on-Stour to Banbury road. The house is furnished with taste and style – comfortable and relaxing. The Withericks know exactly how to make the visitor feel instantly at home. The bedrooms are well-appointed with electric blankets to make you feel snug on wintry nights. There are magazines and books that are worth reading. Perrier and sweets for the sleepless. No wash-basins, but two good bathrooms. Breakfasts are a joy, whether full or continental. And the tariff is a bargain – especially in the pricey Midlands!" (*A and B Freer; also Eleo and Peter Carson*)

Open All year.
Rooms 3 double.
Facilities Drawing room, study with TV, dining room. ⅔-acre garden with croquet.
Location In village on B4035 between Shipston and Banbury; near church. Parking.
Restrictions Not suitable for ♿. Dogs on leads only.
Credit cards None accepted.
Terms (Service at guests' discretion) B&B: £14.50. Set lunch £11, dinner £14.50 (both must be booked in advance). Reductions for 2-day stays.
Service/tipping : "We do not solicit or expect tips, but if people are kind enough to add something we are obviously appreciative."

LOWESWATER Cumbria — Map 4

Scale Hill Hotel — *Tel* Lorton (090 085) 232
Loweswater, Nr Cockermouth
CA13 9UX

Formerly a 17th-century coaching inn, and before that a farmhouse, this secluded hotel between Crummock and Loweswater is in one of the least trippery parts of the Lake District, and has spectacular views of lakes and fells. The National Trust land at Crummock Water is half a mile through the woods. The hotel has been in the Thompson family for several generations, and in its present incarnation is run by Michael Thompson, his wife Sheila and daughter Heather – the latter being responsible for "the simple food very well cooked". "No television – just peace, comfort and beautiful scenery" is what Michael Thompson promises and, judging from reports from long-time devotees, delivers. Rooms vary – best discuss options when booking. Only critical note – "can be chilly at times". (*Ellen Bentsen, Chris and Dorothy Brining*)

Open All year except Jan and Feb.
Rooms 12 double, 5 single – 14 with bath and/or shower; 1 with 4-poster. 2 double in annexe 10 yards from main door. 2 ground-floor rooms.

Facilities Entrance hall, 2 residents' lounges (1 non-smoking), 2 public lounges, bar, dining room. Small grounds. Walking and climbing, golf, pony-trekking nearby; 3 lakes with boating, fishing, swimming.
Location 12 m W of Keswick, just off B5289.
Restriction No dogs in public rooms.
Credit cards None accepted.
Terms Dinner, B&B £24–£40. Set dinner £11; bar lunches. Reduced rates for long stays; winter rates; Christmas and New Year packages. 1-night bookings sometimes refused. Reduced rates for children sharing parents' room; high tea provided.
Service/tipping : "Service is included in the rate; we do not expect any extra to be left."

LUNDY ISLAND Devon — Map 1

Millcombe House Hotel
Lundy, Via Bideford
EX39 2LY

Tel Woolacombe (0271) 870870
Reservations at Landmark Trust head office: Littlewick Green (062 882) 5925

For those who have never heard of Lundy Island, it rises 400 feet out of the sea in the Bristol Channel, and has wonderful views in all directions – England, Wales, the Atlantic. It is a birdwatcher's paradise – 425 different species have been recorded here – and there are also grey seals, Sika deer and Soay sheep. The island is only three miles long, and about half a mile wide, 24 miles and two hours by *MS Oldenburg*, which sails four times a week in summer, three times a week in winter, from Bideford or Ilfracombe in Devon.

To stay at *Millcombe House* – the only hotel on the island, though there are a dozen self-catering cottages owned, like the hotel, by the Landmark Trust – you must be fairly fit: it is set on a hill, and there are no roads. There is a tavern, a restaurant where you can eat with vouchers from the hotel, and a small shop for necessities. The house itself is snug and comfortable, and the views from the windows of the sitting room are amazing. The charge is all-inclusive at the hotel, only drinks are extra. Food is honest wholesome fare. Expect a few drawbacks like long-life milk and the electricity going off at midnight.

Our practice is to drop hotels from the Guide if we lack feedback. We have had no reports on *Millcombe House* for two years. We recognise that, with limited accommodation and restricted accessibility, few readers will have had the chance to visit Lundy. But could those who do please write to us? Otherwise this must be *Millcombe's* last appearance . . .

Open All year.
Rooms 4 double, 3 single.
Facilities Lounge, dining room. 1,000-acre grounds. Sea ¼ m with rock beach and safe bathing.
Location In the Bristol Channel. 24 m by boat from Bideford and Ilfracombe, whence the island's boat *MS Oldenburg* sails 4 times a week in summer, and 3 times a week in winter. Visitors making bookings to stay on Lundy automatically have places reserved.
Restrictions Not suitable for ♿. No dogs on Lundy.
Credit cards None accepted.
Terms (No service charge) Full board: single £22–£30, double £39–£53. Set lunch £4.50, dinner, £9.50. Vouchers for lunch/dinner available for use in island's Tavern or restaurant; packed lunches available. Reduced rates for children sharing parents' room; special meals.
Service/tipping: "Our staff do not expect or ask for tips."

MAIDEN NEWTON Dorset — Map 2

Maiden Newton House
Maiden Newton
Nr Dorchester DT2 0AA

Tel Maiden Newton (0300) 20336

"A place of patchwork fields, primroses and peace." (*Daphne Byrne*) So began one of several enthusiastic endorsements for last year's nomination of this honey-coloured Tudor-style mansion (17th-century rebuilt in the early 19th century) in 11 acres of parkland and gardens overlooking the river Frome. We are in Hardy country: Maiden Newton is Chalk Newton in *Tess of the d'Urbervilles*.

Maiden Newton House is one of the new hybrid breed – part hotel part private house taking guests. Bryan and Elizabeth Ferriss (he a migrant bird from Trusthouse Forte) sit down to dinner with their guests, an arrangement people find either fun or tiresome. It creates an instant house-party, so not for those wanting privacy. But our correspondents all kindled to the Ferriss style of hospitality. A regular reader writes: "The food is excellent – a four-course dinner with no choice but plenty of notice in case it is not to one's liking. All real food, fresh vegetables and much variety and ingenuity, though portions could be bigger (or, to continue the dinner party analogy, they could perhaps offer *seconds*). The Ferrisses do everything they can to make guests welcome. Our three children were treated with great kindness, an evening meal being served to them earlier in the library, and on very generous terms." Another has praised the attentiveness of the unobtrusive hosts, the log fires and warm bedrooms in winter, the tasteful colour schemes, the plethora of books and maps, and the very reasonable tariff, adding: "If you like dogs or cats, the house has an extremely friendly complement of them." One report ended: "Perhaps there should be a government health warning. When we were there, a young couple left the table after the main course to go for a walk and came back in time for the cheese to announce their engagement!" (*Stephen and Judy Parish, PH Freeman*)

Open All year except Jan.
Rooms 3 double, 2 single – all with bath, TV and tea-making facilities.
Facilities Drawing room, library with TV, dining room; functions facilities. 11-acre grounds with stabling for visiting horses, croquet, ¾ m fishing on river Frome. Golf, sailing, riding, hunting, walking nearby.
Location Maiden Newton is on A356 SE of Crewkerne. Hotel is on edge of village, next to church.
Restrictions Not suitable for ♿. No children under 12. No dogs in public rooms.
Credit cards Access, Visa.
Terms (No service charge) B&B £33–£65; dinner, B&B £43–£70. Set dinner £16.50. Lunches and packed lunches available by special request. 2- to 7-night special breaks; off-season breaks; Christmas package. Reduced rates for children; special meals by arrangement.
Service/tipping: "No service charge is added to bills and we discourage tipping."

> "Dominating the bedroom was a meaningless four-poster in white plastic with gold-coloured trim, of the self-assembly variety. And how do I know it was self-assembly? Well, when we entered the room and sat on the bed to take in the full horror of the surroundings the top corner of the bed collapsed and we spent the next 20 minutes reassembling it."

MALVERN WELLS Hereford and Worcester — Map 2

The Old Vicarage — *Tel* Malvern (068 45) 2585
Hanley Road
Malvern Wells WR14 4PH

New to the Guide, a rather splendid defrocked Victorian vicarage in the lovely countryside of the Malvern Hills. The rosetted *Croque en Bouche* restaurant is just up the road. Rooms are large, light, freshly redecorated and full of period character. Lots of stripped pine. The dining room has pale pink walls and traditional Victorian prints (*Gone But Not Forgotten* etc) The bedroom in which our inspector stayed had wallpaper on the ceiling with a flamboyant bird and flower print, which was also on the curtains. A good neat bathroom, an adequate breakfast, dinner not tried. The owner, Michael Gorvin, was friendly and helpful – there when you needed him, otherwise invisible. Heating goes off at night. Fatter bath towels and better linen would be appreciated, but are perhaps not possible at these extremely reasonable prices. More reports please.

Open All year.
Rooms 1 suite, 5 double, 1 single – 3 with bath, 3 with shower, all with tea-making facilities; TV by arrangement. Ground-floor room.
Facilities Lounge with TV, dining room. ¾-acre garden.
Location From Malvern take A449 Wells Road; turn left down B4209 Hanley Road – *Old Vicarage* on the right just before Green Lane turnoff.
Restriction No dogs in public rooms.
Credit cards None accepted.
Terms B&B: single £18, double £25–£28, suite £25–£30. Set lunch £6.50, dinner £8.50. Reduced rates and special meals for children.
Service/tipping: "Owners are rarely tipped, fortunately avoiding embarrassment on both sides."

MANCHESTER — Map 4

Etrop Grange — *Tel* Manchester (061) 437 3594
Bailey Lane, Etrop Green
Ringway, Manchester M22 5NR

12 minutes' drive from city centre and half a mile from the airport, a small Georgian country house down a leafy lane, with bedrooms "simple but tasteful in Laura Ashley fabrics". Meals said to be in Modern British style but on the bland side. In Manchester area. 3 rooms, all with private bath. B&B £22.50–£35. Set dinner £14.95 [1987]. We would welcome more reports.

MAWGAN PORTH Cornwall — Map 1

Bedruthan Steps Hotel — *Tel* St Mawgan (0637) 860555
Mawgan Porth
Newquay TR8 4BU

New last year to the Guide, a modern purpose-built hotel on a cliff with splendid sea views, specially geared to families with children, though one report this year from a retired hotelier noted that as there were separate areas for children, the standard of food and service made it perfectly acceptable for adults too. "We have visited *Bedruthan* since the children were really small. We go back each year because it is wonderful to find that holidays with children can at last be civilised . . . Their attitude seems to be, if the children are happy so are the parents. We've never had good weather at *Bedruthan* (we go before Easter) but we've always had a good time." (*Mrs P Finch; with similar endorsements from Mrs EM Strong, DB Abbott, and Mrs B Stratton*)

Open End Mar–early Nov.
Rooms 56 suites, 15 double, 4 single – all with bath and shower, tea-making facilities and baby-listening; 15 with TV. 10 de luxe suites in separate building with 4-poster, bathroom with jacuzzi, lounge with TV, kitchen.
Facilities 3 lounges, cocktail, bar, Grotto Pool bar, 2 restaurants; hydro spas, 2 indoor swimming pools, saunas, solariums, cinema, billiards; launderette and drying rooms; entertainments manager, discos, cabarets, jazz. 5-acre grounds with 3 swimming pools, tennis and squash courts, adventure playground and Cherokee Wigwam Club for children. 200 yards from sea with sand and rock beach and lifeguards May–Sept.
Location NE of Newquay. From A30 take road marked St Mawgan Airport and turn right past airport at T-junction.
Restrictions Not suitable for ♿. No dogs.
Credit cards None accepted.
Terms (Excluding VAT) Dinner, B&B (continental) £15–£28; full board £17–£30. Set lunch £5.50, dinner £7.50. 4-day breaks out of season. 1-night bookings may be refused in season. Reduced rates for children (1 child under 6 free in low season); special meals.
Service/tipping: "Guests are not expected to tip but if they do the staff keep their own tips."

MINCHINHAMPTON Gloucestershire — Map 2

Burleigh Court Hotel — *Tel* Brimscombe (0453) 883804
Minchinhampton
Nr Stroud GL5 2PF

A Pevsner-listed 18th-century Cotswold house with a five-acre garden designed by Clough Williams Ellis and a choice position looking over the Stroud valley. Hotel run by Hilary and Roger Benson assisted by two Benson daughters. Previously readers have specially appreciated elegant rooms and attentive service. 16 rooms, all with private facilities. Dinner, B&B £33–£39. In italics as no feedback in past year.

MUNGRISDALE Cumbria — Map 4

The Mill Hotel — *Tel* Threlkeld (059 683) 659
Mungrisdale, Penrith CA11 0XR

Dropped from the Guide last year after a change of ownership, this simple but civilised mill cottage dating from the 17th century is reinstated with many readers telling us of the "expert and caring" welcome provided by new owners Richard and Eleanor Quinlan. Mungrisdale is no more than a dozen miles from the Penrith exit of the M6, but well away from the tourist pack, and at the foot of the fells. *The Mill* stands in two acres of grounds with a mill-race, waterfall and trout stream. Readers single out for special mention: all-round warmth, large clean bath towels changed daily, generous home-made soups and bread, good use of fresh herbs in the "imaginative and well-presented" five-course dinners, attentive and friendly service – and, of course, "breathtaking scenery". (*Ben Whitaker, P and E Dunn, Audrey Eyton, and others*) Not to be confused with a nearby pub with rooms, *The Mill Inn* at Mungrisdale, though this might be a useful standby if *The Mill* is full.

Open Feb–Nov.
Rooms 9 double – 4 with bath and/or shower, all with tea-making facilities; 4 with TV; radio on request.
Facilities Lounge with log fire, TV lounge, sun lounge, dining room; games room; drying room. 2-acre grounds with mill-race, waterfall and trout stream. Ullswater 5 m with fishing and sailing; fell-walking, rock-climbing, pony-trekking, bird-watching, hang-gliding and golf nearby.
Location Leave M6 at Penrith (exit 40) and take A66 for Keswick. *The Mill* is 2 m N of A66; signpost for Mungrisdale is midway between Penrith and Keswick.
Restrictions Not suitable for ♿. Dogs at owners' discretion, not in public rooms.
Credit cards None accepted.
Terms (No service charge) B&B: single £19.50–£24.50, double £31–£41; dinner, B&B: single £51–£64, double £43–£56. Set dinner £10.50. Weekly rates. Reduced rates for children sharing parents' room; special meals.
Service/tipping: "Tipping not required or looked for."

NEWLANDS Cumbria — Map 4

Swinside Lodge — *Tel* Keswick (076 87) 72948
Newlands, Nr Keswick CA12 5UE

"A wonderful personal service. From the table to the door-mat all you see is spotless. And what a table! It's a shame to go home – but there's a waistline to consider." (*Mr and Mrs D Blackburn*) "I endorse all the comments in your 1987 entry. The food was imaginative and ample even for hungry fell walkers. The value for money is staggering. We don't know how they manage it." (*Michael Baron*) "Splendid accommodation, all supremely spic and span. Water really hot at all times. Everything is as fresh as the spring flowers in every room." (*Cyril Kitching*) Three typical thank-you reports from among many more for Lambert and Jeanne Dickinson's unassumingly friendly guest house, among the cheapest in the Guide. *Swinside Lodge* is a double-fronted Victorian lodge three miles from Keswick, the hub of northern Lakeland, in an idyllically beautiful location immediately at the foot of Cat Bells, one of the best easy fell walks. Everything is maintained immaculately: the bedrooms are well if simply decorated, and the food is straightforward cooking in the complimentary sense. No licence, but guests can bring their own bottles, with no charge for corkage.

Open Feb–Nov. Restaurant closed to non-residents.
Rooms 8 double – all with bath and/or shower.
Facilities Lounge with TV, dining room. ⅔-acre garden. 5 minutes' walk to Derwent Water.
Location 3 m SW of Keswick on A66. At Portinscale follow road to Grange.
Restrictions Not suitable for ♿. No dogs.
Credit cards None accepted.
Terms (No service charge) B&B £11.50–£14.90; dinner, B&B £17 – £20.50. Weekly rates. 1-night bookings for B&B refused in high season. Packed lunches on request. Reduced rates for children.

> Don't trust out-of-date Guides. Many hotels are dropped and new ones added every year.

NEWLYN Cornwall — Map 1

Higher Faugan Country House Hotel — *Tel* Penzance (0736) 62076
Newlyn, Penzance TR18 5NS

Higher Faugan was built at the turn of the century by the artist Stanhope Forbes to accommodate the first residential art school in Newlyn. It stands in ten acres of grounds, 300 feet up overlooking Penzance and Mount's Bay (sea views from the first floor) with its own heated outdoor swimming pool. The hotel is run by Michael and Jane Young. We had an entry for it in earlier editions, but left it out last year after criticisms of the food and upkeep. Two readers now urge its reinstatement, telling us of much refurbishment: all but one of the rooms now has a bathroom *en suite*, and the odd one out has a shower; towels, previously a cause of complaint, are now "large and fluffy", according to one, "not the plushest, but plentiful and adequate," according to the other; food is described as "honest and home-like, nothing too fancy or ambitious, but with plenty of choices and generous helpings". The owners offer "understated hospitality"; children are welcomed; and the attractive grounds have both a tennis court and a swimming pool. The verdict on *Higher Faugan*: it offers "unpretentious and comfortable value for money". (*V Tan, Bob and Abigail Kirby Harris*)

Open 1 Mar–end Oct.
Rooms 9 double, 2 single – all with bath and/or shower, direct-dial telephone, radio, TV, tea-making facilities and baby-listening.
Facilities 2 lounges, bar, restaurant. 10-acre grounds with heated swimming pool.
Location Take B3315 from Newlyn Bridge. Hotel signposted on right on hill.
Restrictions Not suitable for ♿. No dogs.
Credit cards All major cards accepted.
Terms (Excluding VAT) (No service charge) B&B £23–£30.80; dinner, B&B £30–£40.10. Set dinner £10.
Service/tipping: "All our staff are well paid and do not expect tips."

NEWMARKET Cambridgeshire — Map 3

Swynford Paddocks Hotel — *Tel* Six Mile Bottom (063 870) 234
Six Mile Bottom — *Telex* 817438 attn SWYNFORD
Newmarket CB8 0UE

Elegant country mansion, where Byron's half-sister Augusta Leigh carried on her famous incestuous affair with the poet, now a pricey country house hotel set in 60 acres of gardens and paddocks. In earlier editions under previous management, renominated by vegetarian who specially appreciated vegetarian menu as well as obliging service and beautiful room. Some conference business. Not many hotels in this area. 15 rooms, all with bath and shower. Double room with breakfast £70–£110. Full alc £25. More reports welcome.

> If you have had recent experience of a good hotel that ought to be in the Guide, please write to us at once. Report forms are to be found at the back (or use your own stationery if you prefer). Procrastination is the thief of the next edition.

NEW MILTON Hampshire — Map 2

Chewton Glen Hotel [GFG]
Christchurch Road
New Milton BH25 6QS

Tel Highcliffe (042 52) 5341
Telex 41456 CHGLEN
Reservations in US (800) 223 6800

"I was worried that *Chewton Glen* might be too hotelified and not countrified enough for us. But once we entered the door I felt as though I had entered my own private estate. The staff make *Chewton Glen*! Naturally they are accommodating, but in a very warm and personal way. Every whim or fantasy is catered for." (*Sukie Baxter*) A typical if slightly extravagant tribute (*every* whim? *every* fantasy?) to this *prima donna assoluta* of country house hotels at the southern fringe of the New Forest, run for the past 21 years by Martin Skan, assisted by a huge corps de ballet of staff, and with a splendid rosetted restaurant under Pierre Chevillard to add to its many other attributes. We read with awe an account by another leading hotelier, Kit Chapman of *The Castle*, Taunton (q.v.) of what he called "Martin Skan's uncompromising pursuit of perfection": "Housekeepers stalk the corridors dropping notes in bedrooms with extra tasks for the chambermaids during their morning routine. One such read: 'Be sure to scrub the edges of all window frames with a toothbrush.'" The only grouse – a perennial one in the case of this hotel – is the cost of so much perfection. It is among the half-dozen most expensive country house hotels in Britain. Some people don't turn a hair. Others look on it as the equivalent of a visit to Glyndebourne – and worth every penny if you want the full de luxe country hotel treatment with all the trimmings.

Open All year.
Rooms 11 suites, 33 double – all with bath and shower, direct-dial telephone, radio and TV. Some suites in coach house at side of hotel. Some ground-floor rooms.
Facilities Lounge, sun lounge, bar, private dining room, restaurant; snooker room, shop, terrace. 30-acre grounds with tennis court, croquet lawn, putting, jogging course and heated swimming pool; helipad. Sea 1 m walk through grounds with safe bathing from shingle beach; New Forest to the north. Fishing, riding, sailing nearby; 12 golf courses within radius of 20 m. Chauffeur service.
Location Do not follow New Milton signs. From A35, take turning to Walkford and Highcliffe; go through Walkford, then left down Chewton Farm road. Entrance is on right.
Restrictions No children under 7. No dogs; kennel facilities nearby.
Credit cards All major cards accepted.
Terms Rooms: single from £100, double from £125, suite from £225. Set lunch £16, dinner £30; full alc £38. Off-season rates; Christmas/New Year packages. 1-night bookings sometimes refused for Sat.
Service/tipping "Our prices are fully inclusive and all our guests are made aware of this."

NORTH HUISH Devon — Map 1

Brookdale House
North Huish
South Brent TQ10 9NR

Tel Gara Bridge (054 882) 402

Carol and Charles Trevor-Roper, well known among gourmets for their former restaurant Knights Farm, *Burghfield* (Michelin *Red "M". AA rosette, GFG rating of 13/20) recently opened this Tudor Gothic style Victorian rectory as an upmarket country house hotel and restaurant. Nominator applauds careful restoration and authentic country house feel to rooms, with outstanding food and wines. 8 rooms, all with bath. Double room with breakfast £60–£80. Set dinner £16; alc (without wine) from £20. More reports would be appreciated.*

NUNNINGTON North Yorkshire — Map 4

Ryedale Lodge — *Tel* Nunnington (043 95) 246
Nunnington
Nr Helmsley, York YO6 5XB

James Herriott country, and *Ryedale Lodge* is set in just the sort of quiet countryside he describes. Once Nunnington railway station, it has become privatised and civilised and is now a welcoming hotel in the hands of Jon and Janet Laird. "Very comfortable. As a single woman guest I was looked after very well by Mr Laird, though he had a full dining room. The hotel is peaceful – no other houses visible across the rolling farmland. My room had everything: fresh fruit, sweets, television, even a whirlpool bath, and I enjoyed my stay greatly. I suppose the lack of a residents' lounge might deter some, but there was a comfortable armchair in my room. The meals were good, served by very pleasant staff, who were delighted when one was complimentary. Forget about it being a railway station! It is a very delightful small hotel." (*Dorothy Brining; also Dr FM Halle, MD Hogg*)

Open All year except 3 weeks in Jan.
Rooms 7 double – all with bath, shower, telephone, radio, TV, tea-making facilities and baby-listening.
Facilities 2 lounges with bar service, restaurant. 4-acre grounds. River Rye 10 minutes' walk; trout fishing.
Location 1 m due W of Nunnington towards Oswaldkirk. Pass Nunnington Hall on left; after 400 yards turn right at crossroads. Pass church on right; hotel is 1 m further on right.
Restrictions Not suitable for ♿. No dogs.
Credit cards Access, Visa.
Terms (No service charge) B&B: single occupancy £35–£35.50, double £54–£58. Set dinner £17.50; full alc £20. Reduced rates for 2-night stays; Christmas package. Reduced rates and special meals for children.
Service/tipping: "Tipping at guests' discretion. Tips are shared weekly between all staff."

OAKHILL Somerset — Map 2

Oakhill House [GFG] — *Tel* Oakhill (0749) 840180
Bath Road, Oakhill
Bath BA3 5AQ

New to the Guide this year, though Cornish gourmets will be familiar with Ann Long's cooking from *The Count House*, Botallack. At present it is a restaurant with just three rooms, but the Longs hope to add another three or four in 1988. Here is part of a nominating report, strongly supported by our inspectors:

"A large Georgian house, run by the Long family, in lovely countryside 20 minutes south of Bath, and our stay there was a joy, just like visiting friends in the country, but paying the bill at the end. The Longs' home is delightful with beautiful antiques, paintings, squashy chairs, fresh flowers, pot pourri and a huge teddy in a straw hat keeping guard at the top of the stairs – nothing 'precious' about it at all. Rooms are very comfortable and bathrooms gorgeous. The main reason for going there is the delicious food. Freshly-squeezed orange juice for breakfast, followed by bacon and egg with *fried* potatoes (yum!), then wholewheat toast with home-made marmalade. Dinner, like breakfast, is a leisurely meal with sufficient choice. On our two nights at *Oakhill* we enjoyed such goodies as crab with mushrooms, smoked salmon mousse with strawberry sauce, crunchy asparagus, baked red mullet with leeks, slightly pink lamb in featherlight pastry. Mrs Long is an adventurous cook, careful of colour and presentation, and generous with portions. One lady dining there exclaimed it was the best meal she had ever eaten. Praise indeed, and we could be persuaded to agree with her about ours!.

"The Longs, Ian, Ann and daughter Suzanne, are delightfully informal but caring and courteous hosts, serving exquisite food and pleasant wine, though Mr Long's wine list isn't as adventurous as his wife's cooking. We were welcomed, cared for, well nourished, all at a reasonable price and as the Longs stood in the drive to wave goodbye, we didn't really want to leave. We shall return." (*Malcolm and Angela Reid*)

Open All year except 4 weeks Jan/Feb. Restaurant closed Sun evening and Mon.
Rooms 3 double – all with bath, TV and tea-making facilities.
Facilities Bar/lounge, restaurant. 4 acres of parkland.
Location On A367 2 m N of Shepton Mallet.
Restrictions Only restaurant suitable for ♿. No children under 12. No dogs.
Credit cards All major cards accepted.
Terms (No service charge) B&B: single £28, double £40. Set lunch £8; full alc dinner £17.75.
Service/tipping: "We do not encourage customers to tip."

OTLEY Suffolk — Map 3

Otley House — *Tel* Helmingham (047 339) 253
Otley, Ipswich IP6 9NR

Lise and Michael Hilton describe their home, *Otley House*, thus: "It sits in three acres of mature peaceful grounds with lake and really wild ducks. It is a listed Grade II house with Grade I staircase – Tudor period with Georgian aspect. Large light rooms furnished with antiques: Regency dining room with candle-lit chandelier. One very pretty four-poster bedroom." This is one of the Wolsey Lodge group of guest-taking private houses. The four-course dinners are taken communally. No choice but the owners are keen to be warned in advance of special diets or preferences. Prices are reasonable.

Open 1 Feb–1 Dec. Dining room closed for lunch.
Rooms 4 double – 3 with bath and shower, all with radio.
Facilities Hall, drawing room, TV and billiard room, dining room. 3-acre grounds, with tea terrace, small lake and croquet lawn. Golf, fishing and riding nearby.
Location In Otley village, 7 miles N of Ipswich, on B1079.
Restrictions Not suitable for ♿. No children under 12. No dogs.
Credit cards None accepted.
Terms B&B: double £28–£38. Set dinner £12; vegetarian meals by arrangement. 1-night bookings sometimes refused for Sat.

PAINSWICK Gloucestershire — Map 2

The Painswick Hotel — *Tel* Painswick (0452) 812160
Kemps Lane, Painswick GL6 6YB — *Telex* 43605

A noble old vicarage, converted to the country house hotel faith, in the back lanes of a picturesque Cotswold village. In earlier editions of the Guide under previous ownership, now run by Jacqueline Ash and daughter Kay Hardy. Early reports speak of excellent reasonably-priced meals, large comfortable rooms and friendly staff. 15 rooms, 14 with bath and shower, 1 with shower. B&B £28–£39. Set dinner £13.50. More reports please.

PENZANCE Cornwall — Map 1

The Abbey Hotel — *Tel* Penzance (0736) 66906
Abbey Street
Penzance TR18 4AR

The hotel won a César for utterly acceptable mild eccentricity in 1985; had to be dropped in 1986 as too many readers found the hotel's dependable unreliability had crossed the threshold and become intolerable; and appeared in italics in the 1987 edition. "Service is fitful," we wrote last year. Jean Cox writes to say that she has now installed tea and coffee machines in all the rooms "to help alleviate any problems", and that she no longer employs a manageress since, although "this kind of information takes quite a long time to filter through", she now realises that the lady was extremely reluctant to offer any reliable service to guests. (We fear she cannot have read the Guide these last four years!) Meanwhile, the latest report springs once more to the *Abbey*'s defence: "We had a wonderful bedroom, large enough and comfy enough to be a sitting room as well, full of faded splendour, with double wooden doors opening onto a marvellously old-fashioned bathroom. I can see that some people might not like the style, but it is a hotel with wkich we fell in love immediately. The food is first class and the atmosphere unique. It is one of the most romantic places we have ever stayed in." (*Richard and Ann Briers*)

Open All year.
Rooms 6 double – 3 with bath, 3 with shower, all with TV.
Facilities Drawing room, dining room. Small courtyard.
Location 100 yards from town centre. Courtyard parking.
Restrictions Not suitable for ♿. No children under 5. No dogs in public rooms.
Credit cards None accepted.
Terms (Service at guests' discretion) B&B: single £30–£40, double £40–£65. Set dinner £10.95. Reduced rates for stays of 2 nights or more Nov–Mar; 3-day Christmas package. Reduced rates for children sharing parents' room; special meals.

> "We went down to breakfast. The orange juice may have been freshly squeezed, but *when*? Not that morning, unless pre-dawn. I ordered croissants. I got *one*, so sour that it was inedible. I pointed this out. No apology, no substitute. The toast arrived cold. The porridge was nice. I asked for one fried egg, and was given two. The black pudding tasted off. Coffee was good. *Breakfast cost £10.* Nobody had pointed out it was not included."

PLUCKLEY Kent — Map 3

Elvey Farm Country Hotel
Elvey Farm, Pluckley
Nr Ashford TN27 0SU

Tel Pluckley (023 384) 442 and 726

In the triangle of Dover, Canterbury and Leeds Castle, restored and converted traditional oak-framed Kent farm buildings, including a yeoman barn and oast house in a family farm of 75 acres. At the end of a lane in complete seclusion, with views of the High Weald. Food mostly home-produced or naturally grown produce, including home-made bread. Nominator was awed by size of room with TV, *kitchenette, fridge, antiques, and modern bathroom* en suite *with thick fluffy towels. Substantial breakfasts taken communally. Tells us that Pluckley is reputed to be most haunted village in Britain and that* Elvey Farm *has a ghost in its oast house. 10 rooms, all with private facilities. Dinner, B&B £25.50–£27.75. We eagerly await further reports.*

POOL-IN-WHARFEDALE West Yorkshire — Map 4

Pool Court Restaurant with Rooms [GFG]
Otley LS21 1EH

Tel Arthington (0532) 842288 or 842414

"An absolute oasis of comfort and excellent food. Breakfast, too, up to gourmet standard. Staff could not do enough to please." (*Mary Woods*) Michael Gill's *Pool Court Restaurant* has been a gastronomic mecca for more than two decades and needs no embellishing. The four bedrooms were added five years ago. Since the restaurant seats 65, the rooms must necessarily take second place, and there is no residents' lounge. But the rooms themselves have been fitted out – each differently – with such consummate flair and style, and the breakfasts, too, are of such awesome generosity, that they almost overshadow the achievements of the restaurant. Here is another encomium: "There is such care, it's almost overdone; but since it is meant for guests' comfort and not a commercial stunt, it's accepted gratefully. A delicious basket of fruits (fresh and dried), lots of soaps, shampoos, bath gels, plus towelling robe – and slippers! At dinner there was the same friendly but professional care: lovely food most carefully presented. Only one sadness: no bedside lights despite a good selection of paperbacks in my room." (*Gillian Vincent; also Rosamund Hebdon*)

Open All year except 2 weeks from Christmas Eve and 2 weeks July/Aug. Rooms and restaurant closed Sun; restaurant generally closed Mon (limited room service or bookings made in alternative restaurants).
Rooms 4 double, 1 single – 3 doubles with bath and shower, single with shower, all with direct-dial telephone, radio/alarm, TV, bar, fridge, wall-safe and double-glazing.
Facilities Cocktail bar/lounge, restaurant; private dining room. ½-acre grounds.
Location 3 m N of Leeds airport on A658. Equidistant (9 m) from Leeds, Bradford and Harrogate.
Restrictions Not really suitable for ♿. No dogs.
Credit cards All major cards accepted.
Terms [1987 rates] (Service at guests' discretion) B&B (continental): single £55 (Mondays £40), double £65–£79 (Mondays £50–£59). Set dinner £10; full alc £28.

POOLE Dorset — Map 2

The Mansion House Hotel *Tel* Poole (0202) 685666
Thames Street, Poole BH15 1JN

"A really lovely building," writes a reader of this handsome Georgian town house in a quiet cul-de-sac close to the old parish church and to Poole's fashionable bustling Quay, with a grand sweeping staircase leading up from the hall. "A very good bedroom. No view of course, because it is on a street, but delightfully decorated wallpaper and curtains and unusually good furniture. Plenty of room in bedroom and bathroom; masses of 'goodies': books, magazines, sherry and so on. But my dinner was a bit of a shock. True I was told there was a dinner-dance that night and I must have my dinner in the bar. OK for a snack lunch, but dinner? With people milling in and out for a drink? The meal itself was patchy; a fair vegetarian dish and a superb sweet. Pleasant girls who did their best, but no sign of an owner or manager. Still I would come again, if only for the glories of the bedroom." Our correspondent was suffering from the fact that *The Mansion House*, is a fashionable Poole dining club (residents become temporary members). Another correspondent, luckier with the timing of his two-day stay, had no complaints.

Open All year except 25–31 Dec.
Rooms 10 double, 9 single – all with bath and shower, direct-dial telephone, radio and TV.
Facilities Lounge, 2 bars, breakfast room, dining club (residents are automatic members). Poole Quay 100 yds; fishing, boating, sailing.
Location Follow signs for town centre and Quay. Thames St is off Quay, between Fisheries Office and Maritime Museum – signposted to the parish church. 2 private car parks either side of hotel.
Restrictions Not suitable for ♿. No children under 11. No dogs.
Credit cards All major cards accepted.
Terms (Excluding 10% service charge) B&B: single £48, double £66–£95. Set lunch £9.50, dinner £13.50. Weekend rates throughout the year. Reduced rates for children sharing parents' room.
Service/tipping: "10% is added to bill and shared among all staff at end of month."

POUGHILL Cornwall — Map 1

Reeds [GFG] *Tel* Bude (0288) 2841
Poughill, Bude EX23 9EL

Margaret Jackson, a tiny, tremendously energetic lady, was already in her early sixties when she decided to make this turn-of-the-century house, close to the dramatic north Cornish coast, into a civilised sophisticated guest-house. She runs it with a perfectionist's attention to detail and warmth of welcome enormously appreciated by her guests. "Really felt as if we were going home on our second visit this autumn . . . the house has been repainted outside from top to bottom . . . the inside of the house is spic and span, warm and comfortable . . . two superb dinners." (*John and Padi Howard*) You can just see the sea over the moors from the top windows of the house, which was summed up last year as being "tastefully decorated and well kept". And the same writer added: "The gardens are lovely and lovingly cared for . . . So many places speak of being like a visit to a country house with friends. This is the genuine article." (*Donald Jurney; also Andrena Woodhams, Judith Edmondson*)

Open All year Fri pm–Tues am. Closed Christmas Day.
Rooms 3 double – all with bath, shower and tea-making facilities; radio on request.
Facilities Drawing room, hall with bar facilities, TV room. 4-acre grounds with landscaped garden and woodlands, sun terrace. Sea 1¼ m away with sandy beaches and coastal walks. Fishing and golf nearby.
Location Take Poughill Road from Bude. Turn left at Post Office towards Northcott Mount. *Reeds* is about 400 yards on left beyond garden centre.
Restrictions Not suitable for ♿. No children under 16. No pets.
Credit cards None accepted.
Terms (No VAT or service charge) B&B £27.50–£32.50; dinner, B&B £45–£50. Set dinner £17.50. Light lunch (cheese and fruit) on request £2.
Service/tipping: "I am totally opposed to the idea of tipping and actively (and I hope, politely) discourage it."

POWBURN Northumberland — Map 4

Breamish House Hotel [GFG] — *Tel* Powburn (066 578) 266
Powburn, Alnwick NE66 4LL

Something like a Hallelujah Chorus for this Georgian-style country house hotel at the foot of the Cheviot Hills and close to many tourist attractions – Floors Castle, Kelso, Holy Island, Farne Islands, etc. Report after report pulls out all the stops. "Just returned from three days in paradise. Never have we had such treatment in all our years of hotel visiting." (*J and SH Sprigg*) "We had driven 370 miles; my wife was seven months pregnant; supreme comfort and rest before continuing was the order of the day. These awaited us in superabundance. The style, the attention to detail, the informality combined with professionalism: all these, added to an unforgettable five-course meal, contributed to making this perhaps the most enjoyable night I have ever spent in a British hotel." (*Rev Michael Bourdeaux*) "The standard of housekeeping is exemplary. Bedroom appointments are perfection. Service is concerned but unobtrusive. The setting is delightful." (*PC Russell*) "The dinner has to be something of an economic miracle. And what sensibly-priced wine!" (*JC Cummins; and many others*)

Open All year except Jan.
Rooms 9 double, 1 single – 8 with bath and shower, 2 with shower, all with telephone, radio, TV and tea-making facilities.
Facilities Drawing room, sitting room (non-smoking), dining room. 5-acre garden.
Location On A697 about 23 m NW of Morpeth.
Restrictions Only restaurant suitable for ♿. No children under 12. Dogs only by special arrangement, not in public rooms.
Credit cards None accepted.
Terms (Service at guests' discretion) B&B £23–£32. Set lunch £8–£9, dinner £14–£15.50; vegetarian meals provided. Mini-breaks Oct–Apr inclusive, except Christmas and bank holidays. Reduced rates for children over 12 by arrangement.

RAVENSTONEDALE Cumbria — Map 4

The Black Swan [GFG] — *Tel* Newbiggin-on-Lune (058 73) 204
Ravenstonedale
Kirkby Stephen CA17 4NG

It is now four years since Christopher and Alison Davy bought this small country inn on the banks of Scandal Beck in a secluded and unspoilt village in the foothills of the Eden Valley. Junction 38 of the M6 is only seven minutes by car; ten minutes to the south lies the Yorkshire Dales National Park; half an hour to the west and you are in the heart of the Lakes. But this untouristy area of Cumbria has much to offer: superb walking and excellent fishing (the hotel has five miles of private brown trout fishing on the river Eden, lake trout fishing on Pinfold tarn, and tuition if required). And it is blessedly free from the crowds and traffic jams of the Lakes and Dales.

Major refurbishments have been taking place constantly during the Davy regime, and this year they have converted an old ballroom into three new bedrooms with *en suite* bathroom, created a new residents' lounge and transformed the lounge bar. Davy suggests that we should stop calling *The Black Swan* an inn and dub it henceforth a small country hotel. No doubt we should, but one reader told us how glad she was that all these improvements were in keeping with the Cumbrian inn that it still looks from the outside. In any event what has really endeared the hotel to many readers is not just the dependable comfort of the rooms, nor the remarkably high standards of the restaurant, but the particular qualities of welcome that the Davys offer. "The place is so friendly and professional. They remember your foibles with good humour. They enjoy life and make sure you enjoy your holiday." (*Dorothy Brining; endorsed with similar enthusiasm by P and J Temple, Janet Pell, KG Sayer, Gordon Provis*)

Open Mar–Dec inclusive. Restaurant closed Sun evenings (bar suppers served).
Rooms 9 double – 7 with bath (3 also have shower), all with tea-making facilities.
Facilities Residents' lounge with TV, lounge bar, dining room. Garden on banks of Scandal Beck. Trout and fly fishing; tennis and golf nearby.
Location About 10 minutes by car from exit 38 of M6. Take A685 from motorway towards Kirkby Stephen and Brough, then follow signs to Ravenstonedale.
Restrictions Not suitable for ♿. No dogs in public rooms (except lounge bar).
Credit cards None accepted.
Terms (No service charge) B&B: single £24, double £36; dinner, B&B: single £38, double £64. (£3 per person extra for *en suite* bath). Set lunch £8.50 (packed lunches available), dinner £14; full alc £16. Winter breaks; special 3-, 5- and 7-night rates throughout year. Walking holidays; fishing holidays with tuition; Christmas and New Year house parties. Reduced rates and special meals for children; early suppers if requested in advance.
Service/tipping: "We do not believe in or encourage tipping. Our staff are well paid for their duties. If, however, customers insist on an additional reward, their wishes will be complied with, to avoid offence being taken. Any gratuities are distributed to all staff."

RICHMOND North Yorkshire — Map 4

Howe Villa [GFG] — *Tel* Richmond (0748) 2559
Whitcliffe Mill
Richmond DL10 4TJ

"Our fifth visit. Surely a recommendation in itself. We know every inch of this beautiful area of Swaledale, but it is the thought of staying in such exquisitely-furnished surroundings, with every possible amenity and wonderful hospitality that compels our return. Where else could you enjoy a free drink whilst deciding among the infinite variety of starters. As to the meals, only a Cordon Bleu artiste could produce them. The candle-lit tables and the Wedgwood china complement the wonderful variety of the menus. The Greeks had their gods and goddesses – had

Anita Berry lived then, Zeus would have had no difficulty in choosing his spouse, for Hera, I'm sure, would have been unable to conjure up the infinite number of ambrosian delicacies which are second nature to the delightful hostess of *Howe Villa*." (*Olive H Charlton*) "Our bedroom, both in size and comfort, would put many larger hotels to shame. *Howe Villa* is all that can be asked of a small hotel. Anita Berry does everything possible to make you welcome and comfortable." (*NA Taplin*) And *Eileen Broadbent*, whose nomination brought this Georgian house, with its large elegantly-proportioned rooms and fine views over the river Swale, into the Guide two years ago, has been back and pronounces it "still perfection".

Open 1 Apr–1 Nov.
Rooms 4 double – 2 with bath, 2 with shower, all with radio and TV.
Facilities Large drawing room, dining room. ½-acre garden on river Swale.
Location ½ m from centre of Richmond – take A6108 signposted Leyburn and Reeth; at the ATS Tyre service station turn left, keep left following signs to Richmond Cleaners and Howe Villa.
Restrictions Not suitable for ♿. No children under 8. No dogs.
Credit cards None accepted.
Terms (No service charge) Dinner, B&B £25. Reduction for stays of 3 days or more. Reduced rates and special meals for children.
Service/tipping: "Guests do like to say thank you, perhaps with a small gift. I accept, enjoying the pleasure it gives them, but do not like service charges."

ROMALDKIRK Durham — Map 4

Rose and Crown Hotel — *Tel* Teesdale (0833) 50213
Romaldkirk
Nr Barnard Castle DL12 9EB

"Good old-fashioned English pub. Bedroom comfortable – a gabled room with heavy beams. Great fun if you remember to duck. Good dinner, a set four-course meal at £12.75, which we thought cheap for what we had. Very good breakfast." "Accommodation in the annexe was excellent, the food good and the service friendly and excellent. Wine list adequate but a little overpriced. Decent port to go with the local cheese. Overall verdict – as a two-day bargain break it would be hard to match." Continued enthusiasm in 1986/7 for this cheerful, well-modernised inn, much patronised by locals, on the village green of a picturesque Dales village, near High Force Waterfall and the rewarding Bowes Museum at Barnard Castle. (*Cynthia Archer, DA Lloyd, and others*)

Open All year.
Rooms 2 suites, 8 double, 1 single – all with bath and/or shower, telephone, radio, TV and baby-listening. 5 ground-floor rooms round courtyard, 1 specially designed for ♿.
Facilities 2 bars, 2 dining rooms. Fishing, golf, squash, sailing, pony-trekking, shooting, etc nearby. Barnard Castle 6 m; Raby Castle and Bowes Castle within easy reach.
Location 6 m NW of Barnard Castle on B6277.
Restriction No dogs in public rooms.
Credit cards All major cards accepted.
Terms [1987 rates] (No service charge) B&B: single £29, double £40–£45, suite £50–£60. Set lunch £3.50–£6.50, dinner £12.75. 2- and 4-day breaks; 3-day Christmas package; 2-day New Year package. Reduced rates for children; special meals.

ROWSLEY Derbyshire — Map 4

The Peacock Hotel — *Tel* Matlock (0629) 733518
Rowsley, Matlock DE4 2EB — *Telex* 8813387

The Peacock Hotel was originally built in 1652 as a manor house. After a short time as dower house to Haddon Hall a mile up the road, it became a farmhouse, and then in 1820 an hotel. Now owned by Embassy Hotels, a subsidiary of Allied Breweries, it is strong on creature comforts, and has some fine antique furniture in the public rooms. The lovely gardens go right down to the river Derwent, on which the hotel has rights for brown trout and grayling, as well as for rainbow trout on the adjacent river Wye. Rods are available from the hotel, for a small daily charge. "*The Peacock* has the feel of a family-run hotel, only some impersonality at the reception desk and the lack of the owner himself to greet you betrayed that it is not. The dining room is fairly formal, and correct dress is (perhaps too insistently) expected, but the atmosphere in the lounges and bar is very relaxed. Bedrooms are comfortable and well furnished . . . The hotel is ideally placed for the many attractions of the Peak District. Although it is on a main road, traffic did not trouble me." (*Jacqueline Matthew*) Food has steadily improved at the hotel, and vegetarian readers, having warned the hotel beforehand, "were delighted on arrival to be handed a letter from the chef with two proposed menus for our approval – the food was excellent, with a good balance of tastes and textures . . . attractively presented and imaginative". (*Jack Clarfelt*)

Open All year.
Rooms 17 double, 3 single – 11 with bath and shower, 4 with shower, all with telephone, radio, TV, tea-making facilities and baby-listening. 6 in annexe (2 on ground floor). Self-catering flat and cottage.
Facilities 2 lounges, bar, restaurant; private dining room. Large garden leading to river Derwent. Fishing rights on rivers Wye and Derwent.
Location On A6 between Bakewell and Matlock. Double-glazing; quietest rooms are at the back.
Restriction Dogs at management's discretion, not in public rooms.
Credit cards All major cards accepted.
Terms B&B: single £48.50–£54.50, double £68; dinner, B&B: single £31–£47, double £62–£70; full board: single £40.95–£56.95, double £81.90–£89.90. Set lunch £8.95, dinner £18.95. Hushaway breaks; gardeners' breaks; Christmas and New Year packages.
Service/tipping: "Service included; no additional gratuity expected."

RYE East Sussex — Map 3

The Old Vicarage Guest House — *Tel* Rye (0797) 222119
66 Church Square, Rye TN31 7HF

Ruth and Ernest Thompson won a César for "most civilised bed-and-breakfast" in 1986, but almost disappeared from last year's pages, having had a whim to sell up; they changed their minds just in time to achieve a three-line entry, and are now restored to the Guide with a full citation. Their pink, mostly Georgian guest house is in a secluded position in the old town, looking out across Church Square and the churchyard of ancient St Mary's. Mr Thompson is an enterprising fellow: he has incorporated an art gallery into his public rooms "to suit all pockets", and if you fancy the suite's four-poster he can arrange for a copy to be made for you. "This small establishment was the best value we encountered during our entire trip. Our room was in a garret with steeply sloping walls. The stairs up which we lugged our heavy suitcases might also have served as access to a crow's nest on board ship, and the loo and bathroom were down one flight of these treacherous steps. Notwithstanding our cramped quarters we found the place delightful and charming. Our view out over the churchyard was full of romance, and the location alone would justify including the guest house. Mr T came crashing in with wonderful strong wake-up tea early in the mornings, and the full English breakfasts we sat down to in his eccentrically cluttered parlour were exemplary, a standard against which we judged all subsequent breakfasts – and found the vast majority wanting. Mr T was a mine of useful information about places to visit and eat at – a most genial and helpful host." (*Bill Cutler; also Tracey Brett, RP Clarke, ES*) Not to be confused with *The Old Vicarage*, East Street, Rye.

Open All year except Christmas.
Rooms 1 suite, 4 double – 2 with shower, all with TV.
Facilities Lounge, dining room. Small walled garden. Safe bathing/sandy beach 2 m; golf nearby.
Location In town centre (but quietly situated) near St Mary's church. Parking nearby.
Restrictions Not suitable for ♿. No children under 12. No dogs.
Credit cards None accepted.
Terms B&B: single £20, double £30, suite £54. Only breakfast served but arrangements for meals made with local restaurants. Saturday-only bookings sometimes refused Apr–Sept. Off-season breaks.
Service/tipping: "We do not encourage tipping but if given it is given to staff."

SAFFRON WALDEN Essex — Map 3

The Saffron Hotel — *Tel* Saffron Walden (0799) 22676
10/18 High Street — *Telex* 81653
Saffron Walden CB10 1AY

The Craddock family acquired this 16th-century hotel – the only hotel in town, built round small patio garden – in 1980. Above-average food. Was in earlier editions, recommended by John Julius Norwich: "In my travels, I have seldom been so impressed with a small family-run hotel." Now recent visitors urge reinstatement. 22 rooms, 12 with private facilities. B&B £16–£35. Set lunch/dinner £11.95. More reports please.

ST ANNE'S-ON-SEA Lancashire — Map 4

Dalmeny Hotel [GFG] — *Tel* St Anne's (0253) 712236
19-33 South Promenade
St Anne's-on-Sea FY8 1LX

An energetic enterprising family hotel on the seafront of St Anne's, run by the Webb family since 1945. Richard Webb claims that the *Dalmeny* is unique in its flexible approach to the needs of families: their tariff is for rooms only so that families can choose their own "package" from any of the four restaurants within the hotel or use the small kitchens in the suites especially designed for families with babies or small children. One of their restaurants, *C'est la Vie*, which at midday serves reasonable budget lunches, offers a sophisticated à la carte menu in the evening. A veteran Guide hotel-watcher writes: "A real find! I have eaten here often and admired the thoughtfulness of the staff and skill of the chef. The mark-up on the best wines is exactly the same as on the house wines. It also works well as a hotel. There is an indoor swimming pool, sauna and squash court, a large lounge by the pool where children are not allowed in the evening, and a non-smoking sitting room." (*HBC*) More reports please.

Open All year except 24-26 Dec.
Rooms 51 suites, 32 double and family – all with bath, telephone, TV, tea-making facilities and baby-listening; many with radio; some with balcony; suites have kitchenette. Some ground-floor rooms.
Facilities Lifts. Foyer lounge, non-smoking lounge, lounge bar, TV room, 4 restaurants; indoor heated swimming pool, solariums, squash court, games room; organised crèche and family entertainments in holiday periods; children's outdoor play area. 4 championship golf courses nearby.
Location On seafront, 200 yards S of pier; 300 yards from town centre. Carparks and garages.
Restriction No dogs.
Credit cards Access, Visa.
Terms (Service at guests' discretion) Rooms: single from £20, double from £30, suite from £17 per person. Breakfast: continental £2, English £3.75, 3-course meal in Carvery £6.25, 5-course dinner £9.50; full alc £17. Reduced rates in low season. 1-night bookings refused in high season. Reduced rates and special menus/meals for children.
Service/tipping: "Any tips received are distributed among all staff."

ST AUSTELL Cornwall — Map 1

Boscundle Manor — *Tel* Par (072 681) 3557
Tregrehan
St Austell PL25 3RL

This is Andrew and Mary Flint's tenth year in their manor house hotel, medieval in part, 18th-century in the main, with a particularly attractive two-acre garden which has its own heated pool. The house lies in a bosky setting about a mile from the sea at Carlyon Bay. In their decade of tenure, the Flints have been continually active in improvements: this year, they tell us, they have carried out major renovations. All their rooms now have a bathroom, *en suite*, and when, in the winter of 87/88, they have made a new porch and recarpeted the ground floor their building programme will be complete.

Boscundle Manor has "mildly eccentric" characteristics, as we have said in the past. One visitor this year was surprised to be asked his profession when he registered. Some rooms are on the small side. But one guest summed it up: "A place of individuality and distinctive character." There are books everywhere, good pictures too. Andrew Flint is a welcoming host and is eager to share his extensive knowledge and love of the area. Readers mostly appreciate their meals – fish dishes in particular – though salads, according to one, are rather sparse and British. Breakfast is served in a sunny conservatory. (*JA Fisher; also Jane Castle and Isolde O'Hanlon, and Anthea Moore Ede*)

Open 1 Mar–end Oct. Restaurant closed for lunch, and Sun evening to non-residents.
Rooms 9 double, 2 single – all with bath and/or shower (2 with spa bath, 1 with jacuzzi), telephone, radio and TV. 2 in cottage in garden.

Facilities Sitting room, cocktail bar, lounge/breakfast room, dining room, conservatory; exercise room. 2-acre gardens and7 acres of woodland including an old tin mine; croquet lawn and heated swimming pool. Beaches 1 m and 6 m; golf, riding, fishing nearby; coastal walks.
Location 2 m E of St Austell, 100 yds off A390 on road signposted Tregrehan.
Restrictions Not suitable for ♿. No dogs in public rooms.
Credit cards Access, Amex, Visa.
Terms B&B: single £44–£55, double £66–£77, suite £120. Set dinner £16. Special meals for children by arrangement.
Service/tipping: "All rates include service. We actively discourage anyone leaving extra money."

ST IVES Cornwall — Map 1

Garrack Hotel *Tel* St Ives (0736) 796199
Burthallan Lane
St Ives TR26 3AA

We had our first entry last year for this family-owned and family managed three-star hotel (Mr and Mrs Kilby and sons – the elder, Michael, educated at *Claridge's*) in two acres of grounds overlooking St Ives' spectacular surfing Porthmeor Beach, well away from the hubbub of the town itself (the hotel is a *Relais du Silence*). Some of the rooms are in a characterful creepered older building, and others in a modern wing – the latter all enjoying a fine view over the bay. Its nominator had liked the friendliness of the place, decent food, fixed price mark-up on the wines making the expensive ones very good value, and the character of the rooms – "comfortable without being mod and trendy". (*DA Cash*) One couple reported this year that the *Garrack* had been less than welcoming to their three-year-old, but another gave it whole-hearted endorsement: "The spectacular view is matched only by the wonderful family that owns the hotel and their friendly staff who helped our party of six play fairly raucous *Trivial Pursuits* each evening." (*Deborah Kelly*)

Open All year.
Rooms 2 honeymoon suites, 13 double, 6 single – 13 with bath and/or shower, all with telephone, radio and baby-listening; TV on request (small charge). 2 with self-catering option in cottage in grounds.
Facilities Residents' lounge, bar lounge, restaurant. Small leisure centre with heated indoor swimming pool, whirl pool, sauna, solarium and bar (light meals are served all day). 2-acre grounds with heated swimming pool. Beach with safe bathing and surfing 7-8 minutes' walk.
Location ¾ m from centre of town. From Penzance on B3311 turn right on B3306 towards St Ives. Hotel is off this, to left (they will send a detailed map).
Restrictions Not easy for ♿. Dogs by arrangement in some bedrooms only, not in public rooms.
Credit cards All major cards accepted.
Terms (No service charge) B&B £18.50–£29; dinner, B&B £27.50–£38. Set Sun lunch £6.50, set dinner £16; full alc £16; light lunches available. Bargain breaks Apr–June and Sept–Oct; Christmas programme. Reduced rates and special meals for children.
Service/tipping: "The idea that 'service' should be an additional charge on the bill and the implications it carries are anathema to us but we do not feel we should actively discourage the guest from showing appreciation if he feels it is merited."

> Important reminder: terms printed must be regarded as a rough guide only to the size of the bill to be expected at the end of your stay. For latest tariffs, check when booking.

ST LAWRENCE Isle of Wight — Map 2

Woody Bank Hotel — *Tel* Ventnor (0983) 852610
St Lawrence, Ventnor PO38 1XF

St Lawrence is on the south coast of the island, in the fascinating area known as the Undercliff: a narrow coastal strip formed thousands of years ago by gigantic landslips. It has a particularly mild and equable climate where tender trees and shrubs flourish. It was much favoured by our Victorian forebears whose large houses with elaborate conservatories are all around. *Woody Bank* is just such a Victorian house in the pretty local grey stone, four square at the top of the Undercliff, looking southwards to France. It is run by Mr and Mrs Tindall, who write: "Although we are classified as a small hotel, we do in fact treat *Woody Bank* as an extension of our home. It is *very* informal, and full of our own personalia. We try to provide an atmosphere in which people feel they can relax, read, talk and walk. Guests often gravitate to the kitchen for a chat, and this we encourage. We doubt whether we could run the hotel any other way. Potential guests should not have formal four-star expectations!" Inspectors liked the feel of the place, found their rooms comfortable, enjoyed Mrs Tindall's home cooking, with plenty of imaginative touches "and a good nursery pud always on offer". They summed up: an excellent value unpretentious small hotel. More reports please.

Open Mar–Oct inclusive. Dining room open to residents only.
Rooms 7 double, 1 single – 4 with bath, 4 with shower.
Facilities 2 lounges (1 with TV), bar, dining room. ¾-acre terraced garden. Coastal path around the island ¼ m from hotel; coves and beaches within easy reach; golf and riding nearby.
Location 2 m W of Ventnor on coastal road A3055.
Restrictions Not suitable for ♿. No children under 5.
Credit cards None accepted.
Terms (No service charge) B&B: £16–£18; dinner, B&B £21.50–£23.50 per person. 1-night bookings refused Jul/Aug. Reduced rates for children sharing parents' room; special meals on request.
Service/tipping: "We have never believed in service charges. If a client expresses satisfaction financially, the money is pooled and our small staff shares equally in the proceeds. Naturally, we as proprietors take nothing."

ST MARY'S Isles of Scilly — Map 1

Star Castle Hotel — *Tel* Scillonia (0720) 22317
St Mary's, Isles of Scilly
Cornwall TR21 0JA

Readers continue to appreciate the hospitality of this modest but welcoming hotel, originally – 390 years ago – an Elizabethan fortress against a possible Spanish invasion after the defeat of the Armada. Built in the form of an eight-pointed star, with a dry moat and 18-foot wide ramparts, it enjoys a spectacular position overlooking the town and harbour and neighbouring islands; it has extensive grounds, with lawns enclosed by tall hedges forming welcoming suntraps. There is a covered heated swimming pool, and a tennis court. Some of the bedrooms are in the old building (one, popular with honeymooners, is in a guard-house on the ramparts); other, larger ones are in a modern annexe in the garden. There is an atmospheric dungeon bar where snack lunches are served, and the dining room is the former officers' mess, redolent of centuries of conviviality. Food is straightforward and good and there is an extensive wine list. The owners, Mr and Mrs Reynolds, are much in evidence, taking dinner orders, serving in the bar in the evening, and generally keeping a watchful eye on proceedings. St Mary's is easily reached by boat or helicopter from the mainland (the hotel will meet you) and is an excellent base for an island-hopping Scillonian holiday. "We had one of the garden rooms (for outcasts with dogs and kids), and it was very comfortable: lots of space and useful proximity to the pool and rambling gardens – still delightful even in October. Food well above hotel average, made more pleasant by friendly staff. Very modest bill – though it can't possibly be a cheap place to run." (*Alison Johnson; also PL Sugden*)

Open End Mar–mid-Oct.
Rooms 5 family, 17 double, 3 single – 22 with bath and/or shower, all with telephone, TV, tea-making facilities and baby-listening. 16 in annexe.
Facilities Reading lounge, garden lounge, games room, Dungeon Bar, restaurant. 4-acre grounds with grass tennis court and covered heated swimming pool. Sandy beaches, safe bathing and fishing nearby.
Location Central, overlooking town and harbour, but in large grounds so not noisy. Regular helicopter flights to Scilly Islands from Penzance.
Restrictions Not suitable for ♿. Dogs in garden rooms only (£1 per day).
Credit cards None accepted.
Terms (Service at guests' discretion) Dinner, B&B £28.50–£35.50. Set dinner £10. Packed and bar lunches available; vegetarian meals on request. Reduced rates for children sharing parents' room; high tea.
Service/tipping: "Tips are optional; they are given to staff who divide the money equally among themselves – including the gardener."

SALCOMBE Devon — Map 1

The Marine Hotel — *Tel* Salcombe (054 884) 2251
Cliff Road, Salcombe TQ8 8JH

A sophisticated modern hotel, superbly sited on the water's edge, offering a ringside seat on one of Devon's most colourful and busy sailing estuaries. It changed hands a few years back and recently underwent a major refurbishment; there is a new reception, cocktail bar, restaurant and library area; gone are the rather garish upholstery and curtains in public rooms and bedrooms, replaced by sophisticated pastel greens and pinks. The bedrooms have been given built-in wardrobes and dressing tables. It has also acquired a new manager. A visitor in April 1987 reports: "The redecoration is attractive and restful and we very much liked our bedroom with its balcony overlooking the lovely estuary. Reading lights good for the beds, but not the chairs, and no light above the dressing-table. Our son had a neighbouring single which was just as attractive and well-equipped at no extra charge. The restaurant has also gone upmarket and it was quite difficult to eat simply; we thought the fish dishes (excellent delicate sauces) better than the meat, and enjoyed a seafood terrine, good home-made tomato soup and a pretty salad of exotic fruits. There are two dinner menus at £15 and £18 (the former is included in the half-board rates). An enthusiastic pianist played throughout dinner and Sunday lunch, and was hard to escape as the sitting and dining rooms are open plan. Service depended on the luck of the draw; our first breakfast was impeccably served, the second was higgledy-piggledy. The hotel has put up a building with time-share apartments in its grounds and we wonder what its effect will be on the hotel as the occupants will have full use of the *Marine*'s smallish leisure complex as well as the swimming pool in the grounds, now covered to give it a longer season." Another Easter visitor praised the service and "the excellent pianist" but found the food "poor and very unattractively presented". More reports please.

Open All year.
Rooms 1 suite, 43 double, 7 single – all with bath and shower, telephone, radio, TV and baby-listening; most with balcony.
Facilities Lift. Lounge, bar, restaurant. Pianist in the evenings and Sunday midday. Relaxation and leisure centre with jacuzzi, sauna, massage, beauty parlour. ½-acre garden with covered heated sea water swimming pool. Safe sea bathing; fishing, sailing.
Location 400 yards from town centre. Parking.
Restrictions No children under 7 in dining room at night (children's supper at 7 pm or in room). No dogs.
Credit cards All major cards accepted.
Terms (No service charge) B&B £37–£60; dinner, B&B £37–£66. Bar lunches. Set dinner £15 and £18; full alc £22.50. Spring and autumn breaks; Christmas, New Year, Easter and Whitsun packages. Reduced rates and special meals for children.

Tides Reach Hotel *Tel* Salcombe (054 884) 3466
South Sands, Salcombe TQ8 8LJ

Tides Reach Hotel is a cheerful energetic modern family-run hotel, with a huge range of activities available for sporting folk, both outdoors and in the hotel's own leisure complex (see below). It has a choice location: South Sands is a mile to the south of Salcombe itself, well away from the crowded summer scene, facing across the estuary, and surrounded by spectacular National Trust land. In previous editions we have called *Tides Reach* a family hotel – something of a misnomer since the hotel only accepts children from eight upwards, and doesn't reckon to provide kiddy food. "Food OK, but nothing special," we wrote last year, and recent reports confirm – lots of fish and good cuts of meat, but poorly cooked vegetables and weak breakfast coffee. But everyone speaks well of the friendly attentive staff, the bright attractive bedrooms, lounges and restaurant – though, bad news for some, the public rooms have muzak. A shortish visitor found bathroom mirrors had been hung by someone tall; there was no shelf for toothcleaning etc, and nowhere to hang wet bathing suits.

Open Mar–Nov.
Rooms 3 suites, 36 double, 3 single – all with bath and/or shower, telephone, radio and TV; some with sea view and balcony.
Facilities Lift. Lounge, sun lounge, reading lounge, restaurant, cocktail bar with aquarium, pool bar; health and beauty salon, hairdressing salon, sauna, whirlpool bath, gym, games room, squash court with spectator lounge, snooker; heated swimming pool with sliding glass doors. Grounds with garden, pond, tea lawn. 10 yds from beach with safe bathing, windsurfing school, sea fishing, sailing and moorings for boats.
Location 1 mile S of Salcombe; follow signs to Bolt Head and South Sands.
Restrictions ♿ may find access to some facilities and movement outside hotel difficult. No children under 8. No dogs in public rooms.
Credit cards All major cards accepted.
Terms B&B (low season only) £34–£38, dinner, B&B £40–£58. Set dinner £14.50; full alc £18.25. Spring into summer bargain breaks; autumn breaks. 50% reduction for children sharing parents' room.

Service/tipping: "Service is included in our prices; it is part of the product we offer. However we do not discourage customers leaving tips when they feel the service they have received deserves the gesture."

SEAVIEW Isle of Wight — Map 1

Seaview Hotel [GFG] *Tel* Seaview (0983) 612711
High Street, Seaview PO34 5EX

One of the all-too-small class of reasonably priced seaside family hotels that offer good food and wine. *Seaview Hotel* is a three-storey bay-windowed Edwardian house at the foot of the High Street in this picturesque unspoilt sailing village. Front rooms have a fine view of the sea and coast. Nicholas and Nicola Hayward both come from a hotel background. "It is not a grand and impressive building," writes Mrs Hayward, "and will only ever have two stars. But we would like to think the rooms are exceptional for a hotel of this standard. We have a wonderful supply of delicious local fish, especially lobsters, crabs and prawns. The AA awarded us a rosette for the food . I do all the cooking myself and can only say that very few women win the AA rosette. Some comments: "Haywards make a superb team." "Delicious food – we particularly enjoyed real potted shrimps and excellent breakfast kippers." "Compared with our other 'away-breaks' over the past three years, *Seaview* came a comfortable first . . . The local draught beer from the wood was much appreciated!" (*DR Shorter, Lady Charles, Mrs John Hodges, Sarah Watkinson, and others*) Only cavil: small children not permitted to eat in dining room, but in "a rather dismal back room".

Open All year.
Rooms 2 suites, 13 double – all with bath, radio, TV and baby-listening.
Facilities Lounge, cocktail bar, public bar, restaurant; private dining/conference room. Sea and sandy beaches nearby with sailing, fishing and wind surfing.
Location In centre of village, near sea. Follow signs for sea front.
Restrictions Not suitable for ♿. No dogs in public rooms. No small children in dining room.
Credit cards Access, Amex, Visa.
Terms (No service charge) B&B: single occupancy £25–£27.50,double £42–£44, suite £48–£80; dinner, B&B (2 nights min) £30–£34. Set lunch £7.95, dinner £9.95; full alc £15.90. Breakaway, weekend and weekly tariffs all year. Reduced rates and special meals for children.
Service/tipping: "We do not levy a service charge, or expect our guests to leave tips."

SHEPTON MALLET Somerset — Map 2

Bowlish House Restaurant [GFG] *Tel* Shepton Mallet (0749) 2022
Wells Road
Shepton Mallet BA4 5JD

A spectacular Palladian Grade II* – the second highest category of preserved building – country house, built by rich wool merchants in the early 18th century and standing now in a National Conservancy Area. *Bowlish House* enjoys a considerable reputation as a restaurant and has a wine list remarkable for its length, its excellent coverage of lesser-known regions, its helpful comments and its very reasonable prices. The proprietors, the Jordans, make a point of stressing that they are no more than a restaurant with rooms (just four), though they add: "A visit to

Bowlish House is more like visiting acquaintances in the country than staying in a hotel in a conventional sense. We allow people to do whatever they want provided it is not destructive or disruptive to others." Readers continue to appreciate the Jordans' unsnobbish cordiality – as well as the considerable comforts of the rooms, the ambitious cooking (sometimes a bit over the top for some tastes) and the remarkable cellar.

Open All year except 4 days at Christmas. Closed for lunch.
Rooms 4 double – all with bath, radio and TV.
Facilities Sitting room, bar, restaurant, conservatory. Walled garden, croquet.
Location On main A371 Shepton Mallet to Wells road, ½ m from Shepton Mallet centre.
Restriction No dogs in public rooms.
Credit cards None accepted.
Terms (No service charge) B&B: single occupancy £29, double £32. Set dinner £14 and £17. Wine weekends.
Service/tipping: "Actively discouraged, but accepted if otherwise it would create embarrassment."

SHERBORNE Dorset — Map 2

The Eastbury Hotel — *Tel* Sherborne (0935) 813131
Long Street, Sherborne DT9 3BY

In earlier editions under previous management, a dignified Georgian town-house close to the Benedictine Abbey and castles, in attractive one-acre walled garden. David Lloyd-Jones has refurbished interior and given the en suite *bathroom and Laura Ashley treatment to bedrooms – trouser presses too. 12 rooms, all with bath and shower. B&B £33–£39.50. Set lunch £9.50, dinner £13.50 Reports please.*

SLAIDBURN Lancashire — Map 4

Parrock Head Farm Hotel [GFG] — *Tel* Slaidburn (02006) 614
Slaidburn, Clitheroe BB7 3AH

Winner of César last year for "best farmhouse hotel", but changed hands soon after. In remote and beautiful location at foot of Bowland Fells. New owner Richard Umbers, ex-Cambridge Rugby Blue, also ex-brewing; wife Vicky said to be "very positive and charming hostess". Dinners "English with French touches", breakfasts "kingsize". 9 rooms, all with bath. B&B £19.50. Set dinner £12.50. More reports needed.

****

" 'Drenched with' and 'smothered by' are two of Mr . . .'s favourite phrases, and they sum up his hotel. We were almost smothered by his effusive attentions and our appetites were drenched with the amount of cream in the cooking. This over-the-top, ponced-up, dollified and chi-chi flower-bedecked cuisine contrasts strangely with the under-the-top state of the bedrooms. My room (5′ by 10′) must have been converted from the end of a corridor. Every time I passed between the radiator and the bed to get to the bathroom I grazed my ankles. The windows were frosted over, and no wonder: they looked out on a dustbin and beer crate alley."

****

SOUTHWOLD Suffolk — Map 3

The Crown [GFG] — *Tel* Southwold (0502) 722275
The High Street — *Telex* 97223 ADNAMS
Southwold IP18 6DP

The *Crown* received special treatment in the 1987 edition with a long encomium which won its author a magnum of champagne for the best report of the year. The hotel is in the centre of this cheerful Suffolk resort, two minutes from the beach and within easy reach of Aldeburgh, the RSPB reserve at Minsmere, and other attractive venues. It is owned by Adnam's Wine Merchants, and is a showplace for their wine, as well as offering loss leader set meals. It is clearly a restaurant with rooms; the management tell us that the 12 bedrooms, "simple, decently old-fashioned, small but comfortable", have been refurbished this past year and now "complement the *Crown* rather than cause us to feel somewhat shamefaced". It is a go-ahead set-up, with lots of wine-tasting, musical and literary events in the off-season to enfranchise more than the local patrons. Much publicity attended the new Adnam's *Crown*, and the place has become fashionable with "shrieking Nigels and Amandas", to quote one jaundiced visitor. Clearly service has often been chaotic in the bar and restaurant, even though the cooking has been generally approved of. But the management seem to be working hard to order things better. Worth watching, but we would welcome more reports.

Open All year.
Rooms 1 family, 9 double, 2 single - 11 with bath, 1 with shower, all with telephone and TV.
Facilities Lounge, 2 bars, 2 restaurants. Patio. Classical music evenings, wine tastings. Sand and shingle beach 400 yards, bathing and fishing.
Location In town centre. Covered parking.
Restrictions Not suitable for ♿. No dogs in public rooms.
Credit cards Access, Amex, Visa.
Terms (No service charge) B&B (continental): single £22, double £35, family room £55. Set lunch £9–£11, dinner £11–£13. Bird-watching weekends. Christmas break. Children's meals half price.

> "As we passed the desk, the manager wished us a good night, 'If you can sleep . . .'. He assured us that the party starting in the courtyard would end at midnight. Warning bells began to ring in our heads. Soon they were accompanied by the whining and squealing of numerous untuned violins from a violinists' convention. For hours we listened to loud, atonal fiddle tunes, murdered over and over and over again. The racket did not end until 2.30 am, when, at the urging of several exhausted hotel guests standing at their courtyard windows, the last fiddlers left... But wait! The ringing in our heads began again at 6 am as the electric alarm clock, unbidden by us, came to life. Fumbling to find the 'off' switch, my exhausted, cursing husband finally unplugged it. Ten minutes later it rose from the dead and began clamouring again. This time we disembowelled it by yanking out the back-up batteries. By this time we felt like the dead, struggling to wake up from Hotel Hell."

SPARK BRIDGE Cumbria — Map 4

Bridgefield House [GFG] — *Tel* Lowick Bridge (022 985) 239
Spark Bridge
Nr Ulverston LA12 8DA

Spark Bridge is on the banks of the river Crake, a short drive to the fells and the Lakes themselves: the scenery is beautiful if less dramatic than further north, and has the advantage of being well away from the tourist hordes. *Bridgefield House* itself is on a quiet country lane – "one really does feel the peace of the countryside". The Glisters, David and Rosemary, bought this gentleman's residence of the late 19th century eight years ago, and all our recent reports have been warm in praise of their generous hospitality. There are only five rooms, all agreeably furnished, and there is no supplement for single people or one-night stays. Children are made particularly welcome: no charge is made for their high tea, and laundry service for children and babies is free. Most important, the standard of cooking is high and ambitious – and "astounding value". As last year, all our correspondents speak with enthusiasm about the Glisters' enterprise and commitment and the convivial atmosphere they engender. (*John and Lyn Spencely, Jane O'Leary, Gerald Campion, DS, Winifred Hurley, Peter McLeod, Brigadier and Mrs Peter Ferry*)

Open All year, but only for lunch on Christmas Day.
Rooms 1 suite, 4 double – 3 with bath and shower, all with radio.
Facilities Drawing room, bar, dining room (no smoking). 3-acre garden. Sea bathing 3 m; salmon and trout fishing and good fell walking nearby.
Location Off A5092. On back road (signposted) from Spark Bridge to Lowick Bridge.
Restrictions Not suitable for ♿. No dogs in public rooms.
Credit cards Access, Amex.
Terms [1987 rates] (No service charge) B&B £18.50–£25. Packed lunches available on request; set dinner £13. Spring and autumn breaks. Children aged 3 and under free, 50% reduction for under 12s; special meals; free laundry service for children and babies.
Service/tipping: "The inclusion of a service charge is iniquitous and should be banned by law. Let's face it, it is only an extra increase in the tariff."

SPREYTON Devon — Map 1

Downhayes — *Tel* Bow (036 33) 378
Spreyton, Crediton EX17 5AR

New to the Guide last year, a traditional Devon farmhouse dating from the 16th century, standing in its own 15 acres, high in the mid-Devon hills, 20 miles west of Exeter. It is in deep countryside – a car is essential. Readers unanimously commend "the imaginative, varied and plentiful diet [dinner £11 in 1987] with mouth-watering desserts and the entire bowl left on the table with masses of cream for seconds and thirds, the exceptional furnishings and comfort, and the extremely reasonable prices". (*Barbara Gill; also Mrs Richard Lethbridge*) More reports please.

Open All year except 20–29 Dec.
Rooms 3 double – 2 with bath. 1 ground-floor room.
Facilities Sitting room with TV, dining room. 15-acre grounds with flower garden and pasture.

Location 9 m SW of Crediton. Turn S off A3072 at Bow; drive entrance on right after 2¾ m. Or turn N off A30 at Whiddon Down, follow signs to Spreyton; *Downhayes* on left 1½ m N of Spreyton on Bow road.
Restrictions No children under 12. No dogs.
Credit cards None accepted.
Terms B&B: single £20–£24.50, double £32–£39. Set dinner £11.00. Weekly half board: £170–£192 per person.

STAMFORD Lincolnshire — Map 3

The George of Stamford [GFG] — *Tel* Stamford (0780) 55171
71 St Martins — *Telex* 32578
Stamford PE9 2LB

Stamford is a remarkably unspoilt medieval town, and *The George* is its historic coaching-inn, preserving plenty of innish features such as a flower-tubbed cobbled courtyard, but neither prettified nor self-conscious. A go-ahead management is always busy with improvements, and recently added a fully-equipped business centre. Compliments continue to be paid to the chef – good food and wine have always been a feature of the *George*. Most correspondents still appreciate the friendly staff, but hiccups in the service, mentioned last year, continue: one reader detailed several instances, including a disaster in the cocktail bar; another found staff at the reception too busy gossiping; a third, when checking out, asked whether the bill included a service charge, and was told: "There is a service charge added but the staff don't get any of it" . . .

Open All year.
Rooms 1 suite, 34 double, 12 single – 45 with bath and shower, 2 with shower only, all with direct-dial telephone, radio, TV (with teletext) and baby-listening; 24-hour room service; double-glazing.
Facilities Lounge, garden lounge, cocktail lounge, bar, restaurant; 4 private dining rooms, business centre. 1-acre grounds with patio and monastery garden with gravel walks and sunken lawn. Golf ½ m; fly fishing and sailing at Rutland Water 5 m.
Location In town centre (front rooms double glazed). Parking for 150 cars.
Restriction Only restaurant suitable for ♿. No dogs in public rooms.
Credit cards All major cards accepted.
Terms B&B: single £42.50–£45, double £68–£90, suite £80. Bar lunches; full alc £26. Antiques weekends; Christmas package; weekend breaks. Reduced rates for children sharing parents' room; special meals.
Service/tipping: "Staff are paid by the company for the service they provide, so guests are not expected to leave a tip."

STON EASTON Somerset — Map 2

Ston Easton Park [GFG] — *Tel* Chewton Mendip (076 121) 631
Ston Easton, Nr Bath BA3 4DF — *Telex* 444738

César awarded in 1987 for comprehensive excellence as a luxury country house hotel

The epitome of an English country house hotel, *Ston Easton* is a grand, immaculately-restored Palladian house, in 26 acres of parkland, designed by Humphrey Repton: the river Somer, which runs through the grounds, still flows over Repton's flight of shallow cascades, and other parts of the grounds are in the process of being restored according to Repton's original landscaping plans. The public rooms are high-ceilinged and imposing, with many distinctive architectural features, but are also welcoming with log fires and spectacular flower arrangements. Rooms individually designed by Jean Monro, are elegant in different ways. Those on the first floor have the huge windows and fine proportions of the original master bedrooms, but those on the floor above, though smaller, also pass the most exacting tests of civilised comfort. The kitchens are in the hands of a talented young chef, whose style of cooking suits the house – reasonably innovative and enterprising without excessive trendiness. *Ston Easton* is a decorous place: jacket and tie *de rigueur* at dinner, no children under 12. Given the grandeur of the house, some formality is unavoidable. But the open friendliness of the owners, Peter and Christine Smedley, and their staff help to dispel any tendency towards stuffiness so often found in the grander sort of hotel. The tariff is naturally high: the upkeep of such a seat must be enormous, and there is no stinting on service or appointments. But at *Ston Easton*, more than at other country house hotels, you feel you are being given the taste of an almost vanished style of living which most of us could not otherwise know. You may be only a paying guest, but you are also enjoying the benefit of the investment and dedication of the owners. (*HR; also the Hon Mrs G Holman, C Haward*)

Open All year.
Rooms 5 suites 14 double, 1 single – all with bath and/or shower, direct-dial telephone, radio and TV.
Facilities Drawing room with TV, library, salon, 2 restaurants; private dining room; billiards room, servants' room for chauffeurs etc. Recitals, entertainment groups occasionally. Terrace. 26-acre grounds with croquet, bowls, archery, riding, ballooning, helicopter pad, river with fishing.
Location On A37 from Bristol to Wells.
Restrictions No children under 12. No dogs in building (kennels on premises).
Credit cards All major cards accepted.
Terms (No service charge) B&B (continental): single £60, double £95–£135, suite £165–£190. Set lunch £15 (Sun lunch £16), set dinner £26. Vegetarian and low-fat meals on request. 4-day Christmas programme; winter breaks. 1-night bookings refused at Christmas and bank holidays.

STRATFORD-UPON-AVON Warwickshire — Map 2

Caterham House
58/59 Rother Street
Stratford-upon-Avon CV37 6LT

Tel Stratford-upon-Avon
(0789) 67309 and 297070

Stylish but very reasonably priced bed-and-breakfast guest house run by Dominique Maury, who is French, and his English wife, Olive, in two adjoining 1828 houses. Popular with Royal Shakespeare cast as well as visitors to Stratford. Despite French connection, full English breakfast served. 13 rooms, 2 with private bath. Double room with breakfast £21–£30. New recommendation: reports welcome.

If you feel we have done a hotel an injustice If we have failed to mention salient details If you consider we have got it about right	please let us know.

STRETTON Leicestershire — Map 4

Ram Jam Inn [GFG]
Great North Road
Stretton LE15 7QX

Tel Castle Bytham (078 081) 776
Telex 342888 HAMBLE ref RAM JAM

A maverick: an old coaching inn on the Great North Road converted into a motel by the owners of Hambleton Hall *(q.v.). All rooms face away from road. Perhaps a model for a new generation of discriminating motel-users. Nominator tells us of attractive decor, beautifully furnished rooms with best quality sheets and blankets and towels, and extra large bathrooms. Snack bar food original and interesting. Restaurant not tried. Service: un-servile, efficient, charming and English! 10 rooms, all with bath and shower. Rooms: single £35, double £45. Alc breakfast from £1.50; full alc lunch/dinner £11.30. A suitable establishment for the Guide? We await further reports.*

STURMINSTER NEWTON Dorset — Map 2

Plumber Manor [GFG]
Sturminster Newton DT10 2AF

Tel Sturminster Newton (0258) 72507

César awarded in 1987 for sustained excellence in a middle-price country house hotel

A handsome Jacobean house in the heart of Hardy countryside, which has been the family home of the Prideaux-Brunes since the early 17th century. It insists on calling itself a restaurant-with-rooms, but though the restaurant under Brian Prideaux-Brune's direction is admirable, the number and comfort of the rooms (six in a converted stable block) make it a far more attractive hotel than many others which boast that name. It contrives to be professional while maintaining a laid-back air. Also, perhaps because it has not had to pay back some huge mortgage, its prices are low for what is being offered.

Following our award last year, we have had an unusually large postbag. Many readers have supported the César with fresh superlatives. A vegetarian described her meal as "something to dream about: gourmet standard cooking for a vegetarian – unknown normally!" and appreciated the absence of "flunkies and flummeries". Others have been cooler in their response, missing flowers, and picking on small weaknesses in the housekeeping. One or two have mentioned shabby, faded furnishings – which other guests have felt gave the house a comfortable lived-in feel. Perhaps the Prideaux-Brunes are right to maintain the label of restaurant-with-rooms: the meals are dependably first-class, the service and decor incline to the "take-us-as-you-find-us" stance, which suits some but not all comers.

Open All year except 2 weeks in Feb. Restaurant closed for lunch and to non-residents on Sun Nov–Mar.
Rooms 10 double, 2 single – all with bath, shower, telephone, TV and tea-making facilities. 6 ground-floor rooms in adjacent coach-house annexe.
Facilities 2 lounge bars, portrait gallery, restaurant in main house; sitting/meeting room in converted barn. 4-acre gardens with tennis court, croquet lawn, trout stream; 600-acre farm. Golf, fishing, riding and clay pigeon shooting nearby.

Location 2 m SW of Sturminster Newton; turn S off A357 towards Hazelbury Bryan.
Restrictions No children under 12. No dogs.
Credit cards Access, Visa.
Terms [1987 rates) B&B: single £40–£50, double £50–£65. Set dinner £16–£19. Off-season discounts. 1-night bookings refused Christmas and bank holidays.

TALLAND-BY-LOOE Cornwall — Map 1

Talland Bay Hotel — *Tel* Polperro (0503) 72667
Talland-by-Looe PL13 2JB

This 16th-century Cornish country house enjoys a splendid position in two-and-a-half acres of sub-tropical gardens, 150 feet above sea-level, with unobstructed views of two headlands, the sea and, on clear days, the Eddystone Lighthouse on the horizon, 15 miles away. There is a wide variety of beaches from fine sand to rugged rocks nearby, or stay-at-homes can lounge by the hotel's own heated swimming pool. Out of season the management runs special-interest holidays for bird-watchers, painters and bridge-players.

Talland Bay had an entry in the early editions of the Guide but was dropped following critical reports. It is brought back by this commendation from *Susan Phillips* of the César-winning *Riverside Inn*, Canonbie (q.v.): "Situated in its own unspoilt bay with magnificent views, it's a place that 'puts its arms round you'. Staff are local, most friendly and chatty and nothing is too much trouble. Family treasures are in evidence in both lounges (one for non-smokers) and the garden is lovingly cared for. Breakfasts are very good. One night our dinner was excellent – not so good the second night, but we gathered it was the chef's night off." And a reader planning a fourth visit writes: "We have become devotees. Seeking a weekend sanctuary from business pressures we were welcomed with a natural charm which repeated visits prove not to have been affected. Rooms are very pleasantly furnished, if with a leaning towards four-posters and frilly trimmings. I am not qualified to comment learnedly about the cuisine, but we have been served a succession of very pleasant meals which were much as described in the menu and not pretentious or over-ambitious."

Open Mid-Feb–end Nov.
Rooms 1 suite, 18 double, 5 single – 8 with bath and shower, 13 with bath, all with telephone, radio, TV and baby-listening. 2 in hotel grounds, 2 across lane. 2 ground-floor rooms specially adapted for ♿.
Facilities Lounge, non-smoking lounge, bar, dining room. 2½-acre grounds with swimming pool, putting green and croquet. 5 min walk to beach with safe swimming.
Location 2½ m SW of Looe. Turn left at hotel sign on Looe-Polperro road.
Restrictions No children under 5 in dining room at night. Dogs in certain rooms only, not in public rooms.
Credit cards All major cards accepted.
Terms (No service charge) Dinner, B&B £31.50–£58. Full alc £19. 1-night bookings sometimes refused in high season. Reduced rates and high teas for children.
Service/tipping: "We do not encourage tipping. Anything given is distributed equally to all members of staff."

Report forms (Freepost in UK) will be found at the end of the Guide.

TAUNTON Somerset — Map 1

The Castle Hotel [GFG]
Castle Green
Taunton TA1 1NF

Tel Taunton (0823) 272671
Reservations in USA (800) 223 5581
Telex 46488

César awarded in 1987 for the best town hotel

Nothing seems to change – or if it does, only for the better – at the Chapman family's luxurious 300-year-old hostelry, which stands, creepered and castellated, in the centre of the town, though in a quiet oasis of higher ground on the site of the old castle, and with pleasant moated gardens at the back. For many years past, it has appeared in these pages as a model of the thriving, really well-run town hotel. The Chapmans are go-ahead in the best sense, constantly making improvements and also finding ways to fill their beds in the slack periods by devising special weekends – musical, ballooning, wine-tasting and the like. The major item of *Castle* news last year was that the head chef, Christopher Oakes, who won the hotel its *Michelin* rosette, was leaving and that his *toque* was being taken by Gary Rhodes, formerly at London's *Capital* (q.v.). Reports on the new kitchen regime have been enthusiastic, and we are delighted that Gary Rhodes has kept the *Castle*'s *Michelin* rosette – one of only six hotels in England outside London with that distinction.

Open All year.
Rooms 1 suite, 21 double, 13 single – all with bath and shower, telephone, radio, TV and baby-listening.
Facilities Lift. Lounge, bar/lounge, restaurant; private dining/meeting rooms. ½-acre grounds with Norman moat, keep and well. Musical weekends, hot-air balloon trips, Exmoor safaris etc.
Location Central (follow signs for castle), but quietly situated. Garages and parking.
Restriction Dogs by arrangement, not in dining room.
Credit cards All major cards accepted.
Terms (Service at guests' discretion) B&B: single from £49, double from £85, suite from £155. Set lunch £9.50–£10.90, dinner £19.90; full alc £33. Weekend and mid-week breaks; 4-day Christmas package. Special meals for children.

TAYNTON Oxfordshire — Map 2

Manor Farm Barn
Taynton, Burford OX8 4UH

Tel Burford (099 382) 2069

César awarded in 1987 for best rural B&B

"The Good Hotel Guide, bought for the first time this year, provided us immediately with the best bed-and-breakfast we have ever enjoyed – at the *Manor Farm Barn*. The accommodation is absolutely charming, and Mrs Florey anticipated our every need from hairdrier to vacuum flask. Though within easy reach of the busy A40, it affords that absolute peace and tranquillity that is so elusive nowadays. We are already planning our next visit." A warm endorsement for this truly rural, though comfortably modernised bed-and-breakfast in a typical unspoilt Cotswold hamlet near Burford – a lovely old church, but no shop, pub or post office. It is run by the hospitable Floreys, whose guests have also praised the warmth of their welcome, the grateful comforts of the furnishings, the dishes of fresh fruit and serried toiletries in the bedrooms and the large and varied breakfast served at the long table in the sunlit dining room. (*Isobel W McNeillie*)

Open All year, except Christmas and New Year.
Rooms 3 double – all with bath and shower, radio, TV and tea-making facilities. 1 self-catering cottage.
Facilities 2 lounges with TV, dining room. 8-acre garden and paddocks.
Location 1½ m NW of Burford; from Burford, take A361 towards Stow-on-the-Wold; turn left towards Taynton at roundabout, then left by church (car or personal transport essential).
Restrictions Not suitable for ♿. No children under 8. No dogs.
Credit cards None accepted.
Terms [1987 rates] B&B: single occupancy £25, double £35. 1-night bookings refused Sat. (No restaurant.)
Service/tipping: "Tipping not required or looked for."

TETBURY Gloucestershire — Map 2

Calcot Manor [GFG] — *Tel* Leighterton (066 689) 227
Beverston — *Telex* 437105
Nr Tetbury GL8 8YJ

Brian and Barbara Ball, with son Richard and a pair of decorous labradors, bought an old Cotswold farmhouse four years ago and turned it into *Calcot Manor*, now one of the most dependable of Cotswold country house hotels. It opened its doors in August, 1984, won a *Michelin* red "M" for above-average cooking just over a year later, and is now one of only eight hotels in the British Isles outside London to boast a *Michelin* rosette. Such awards are not won lightly: to have achieved one so rapidly is a rare tribute to the chef's gifts and dedication.

Calcot Manor is a timeless, mellow Cotswold house with a range of venerable outbuildings, including a fine 14th-century tithe barn. There is also a heated outdoor pool. Accommodating the 13 bedrooms, each with its own large and luxurious bathroom, has been accomplished with little punishment to the proportions and a lot of thought and money. The rooms are all admirably comfortable. No errors of taste, though the choice of furnishings could have been more adventurous. A major pleasure is the quality of the young chef Ray Farthing's cooking. He took over the *toque* in 1986, having been sous-chef at the rosetted *Castle Hotel*, Taunton (q.v.). The set dinner is £22 and no *minceur* feast; for the more robust gourmet there is also a six-course gastronomic surprise menu at £28. Farthing is a naturally innovative cook; everything we ate had been prepared in the Manor's kitchens – from the rolls and walnut bread to the home-made biscuits with the cheese and the chocolate-covered Montélimar served with the coffee. The wine list was catholic, well-described and with an unusually modest mark-up. Everything about *Calcot Manor* displays professionalism at its best. (*HR; also many others*)

Open All year. Restaurant closed to non-residents Sun night.
Rooms 1 suite, 12 double – all with bath and shower (3 have whirlpool bath), telephone, radio and TV; 1 4-poster. 5 ground-floor annexe rooms, 1 equipped for ♿.
Facilities Lounge, drawing room, dining room; private dining room, conference facilities. 4-acre grounds with croquet lawn, heated outdoor swimming pool. Fishing, golf and riding nearby.

Location 3 m W of Tetbury on A4135. Parking.
Restrictions No children under 12. No dogs.
Credit cards All major cards accepted.
Terms B&B: single occupancy from £50, double £70–£110. Set lunch £10.50 and £18.50 (£12.50 on Sun), dinner £22 and £28. Reduced rates for longer stays. Weekend or mid-week breaks; Christmas package; gourmet and wine weekends in Autumn. 1-night bookings refused during Badminton, Gold Cup week, Gatcombe horse trials and some bank holidays.

TREBARWITH STRAND Cornwall — Map 1

The Old Millfloor — *Tel* Camelford (0840) 770234
Trebarwith Strand
Tintagel PL34 0HA

No hotel, but a small secluded guest house – three rooms in the house and a couple of self-catering chalet/bungalows in a picturesque location by a mill-stream. Not for the disabled or infirm, since there is a steep path down from the road, but perfect for families: lots of pets, ten acres of grounds and the beach ten minutes' walk away; and the prices are ridiculously modest. "A wonderfully relaxing place, set in a fern-filled glen by an old mill-stream. Very romantic atmosphere: old beams, gleaming wood and fresh flowers everywhere. Janice Waddon-Martin is a delightful and enthusiastic hostess. She creates a welcoming feeling with clever use of fabric, light and colour. Dinner by candlelight with different crystal each night! Lovely food: home-made soups, ice-creams and lots of home baking (e.g. breakfast croissants), fresh vegetables, boozy sauces and lashings of clotted cream; excellent tea and coffee. No TV, radio or papers (except Sunday) – a real treat! Cats and books available by the fire for wetter days. Rooms very comfy with friendly touches like supplies of tissues, cotton wool, bath 'smellies' etc. We loved everything about it (except the plumbing which was unpredictable) and thought it excellent value." (*Allison Bretherton; also CT, M Nicholson, and others*)

Open Easter–30 Nov.
Rooms 3 doubles with h&c and tea-making facilities. 2 self-catering bungalows.
Facilities Restaurant with lounge. 10 acre grounds with garden, orchard, paddocks and stream. Beach 10 mins walk. Riding centre 2½ m.
Location 2 m S of Tintagel.
Restriction Not suitable for ♿.
Credit cards None accepted.
Terms (No VAT or service charge) B&B £12; dinner, B&B £22. Dinner £10. (Unlicenced – bring your own wine). No charge for 1 child sharing parents' room; special meals.
Service/tipping: "Tipping is not my policy."

TREGONY Cornwall — Map 1

Tregony House — *Tel* Tregony (087 253) 671
Tregony, Truro TR2 5RN

A typical hybrid Cornish village house, part 17th-century and part Victorian, in "that rare thing – an inland Cornish village of charm and distinction". Tregony lies at the entrance to the Roseland Peninsula, about five miles from the sea. In 1986, under the ownership of Mr and Mrs Lock, it won a César for "best value" and we were sorry to learn in

October 1986 that the Locks were leaving. But a flurry of reports in the spring of 1987 have reassured us about the qualities of the new incumbents, Mario and Verna Marin. Welcome was "warm and genuine"; "fresh snowdrops in our delightful room"; "much enjoyed a slightly tart apple and parsnip soup and delicious stuffed chicken"; "nice touches like daily change of towels". And the best news: prices are still extremely reasonable. (*John and Sheila Heather, N Sugarman, Paul Hoddinott, U Needland*)

Open Mar–Oct inclusive.
Rooms 5 doubles (2 can form a family suite), 1 single – 1 with bath, 1 with shower.
Facilities Lounge with TV, bar area with seating, dining room. Cottage garden with seats on terrace. Beaches and Cornish coastal path 6 m.
Location In centre of village main street. Private carpark. Front rooms double-glazed.
Restrictions Not suitable for ♿. No children under 7.
Credit cards None accepted.
Terms (No VAT or service charge) Dinner, B&B £20. Reduced rates for stays of 7 days or more. 1-night bookings sometimes refused in high season if made very far in advance. Half price for children 7-12; special meals on request.

TRESCO Isles of Scilly — Map 1

The Island Hotel — *Tel* Scillonia (0720) 22883
Tresco, Isles of Scilly
Cornwall TR24 0PU

Continued applause for the only hotel on Tresco, a private island, two miles by one, renowned for the Abbey Gardens, and filled with exotic plants from all over the world. No cars are allowed – there are bicycles for hire, and guests of *The Island Hotel* are met on arrival (by boat or helicopter) by a tractor and trailer – so Tresco (day trippers apart) is exceptionally peaceful. *The Island Hotel* is a modern building with five acres of grounds beside the sea, and a private beach. It enjoys dramatic views of the rocky coast and other islands and a peaceful and beautiful setting. "Absolute tranquillity. Very pleasant dining room. This was our fifth visit and the food has improved each time. The cooking is inventive and unusual, especially for a hotel with a more or less captive clientele. Mr and Mrs Pyatt offer a warm welcome and the service is unobtrusive but faultless." "We met people who had been returning for more than a decade, and many of the staff had been there for years, which speaks for a happy hotel." (*Mrs CJ Stephens, James Pell; also A and H Hosford*)

Open Mid-Mar–mid-Oct.
Rooms 1 suite, 25 double, 5 single – 28 with bath and shower, all with telephone, radio, TV and baby-listening; 6 with tea-making facilities. Some groups of 1 double and 1 single, with shared bathroom. 3 ground-floor rooms.
Facilities Lounge, bar, bar lounge, TV room, dining room, games room for adults with table tennis and bar billiards, children's playroom; laundry facilities. 5-acre grounds with heated swimming pool, bowls, croquet and outdoor badminton; private beach with safe bathing. Hire of rowing boats, sailing dinghies and small motor boats can be arranged.
Location Tresco is reached by scheduled helicopter flight (British International Helicopters Ltd – approx. 20 minutes) or by boat (approx. $2\frac{1}{2}$ hours) from Penzance; not Sun. It is essential to book in good time. Hotel meets guests on arrival.
Restrictions Island not suitable for ♿. No dogs allowed on Tresco.

Credit cards None accepted.
Terms (No service charge). (Prices vary according to season and to type of room, view, etc) Dinner, B&B: single £40–£57; double £44–£71, suite £72–£82. Set lunch £10, dinner £17. Bar lunches available. Discounts for pre-booked stays of over 5 nights. Tresco gardeners' 7-day holiday in spring and autumn. Reduced rates for children in bunk beds or cots; special meals.
Service/tipping: "No service charge made or tips expected. If guests wish to reward courtesy and good service or a particular person for some extra service it is entirely up to them."

TWO BRIDGES Devon — Map 1

Cherrybrook Hotel — *Tel* Tavistock (0822) 88260
Two Bridges
Yelverton PL20 6SP

"Our haven in a storm. Dartmoor was impossible during the year's worst weather. Our two-month-old son, our dog and our sodden clothes were all accepted with equal graciousness by John Reynolds. The breakfast set us up to face our stormy days and were the best we have had anywhere. The atmosphere of a true house-party is quickly engendered by the delightful informality of the public rooms." One of several reports this year in praise of this family-run, modest-priced hotel, formerly a farmhouse, centrally placed for a Dartmoor holiday, with splendid views of the moor. *Cherrybrook* was built in the last century by a friend of the Prince Regent, which doubtless accounts for its rural elegance. Today it is pleasantly and comfortably furnished. The four-course dinner menu (with some choice) is straightforward and wholesome, and "much too generous" according to one report. Another commented that his room was "a bit pokey", with no table and little space for a suitcase, "but the excellent value compensated for the strictures above; we shall return". (*Rev Michael Bourdeaux; R Lee, Mr and Mrs Jenks, and others*)

Open All year except Christmas and New Year and proprietor's holiday in winter.
Rooms 6 double, 1 single – all with shower, 6 with WC, all with tea-making facilities; TV available.
Facilities Lounge, bar, dining room (no smoking). 4-acre grounds with access to open moorland. Golf, trout fishing, riding and pony-trekking nearby.
Location On B3212, ½ m NE of Two Bridges crossroads.
Restrictions Not suitable for ♿. No dogs in public rooms.
Credit cards None accepted.
Terms (No service charge) B&B £17.50–£18; dinner, B&B £25.50–£26. Set dinner £8. Off-season breaks and activity breaks; weekly rates. Reductions for children sharing parents' room; special meals.
Service/tipping: "Tips are not accepted."

ULLINGSWICK Hereford and Worcester — Map 2

The Steppes Country House Hotel — *Tel* Hereford (0432) 820424
Ullingswick
Nr Hereford HR1 3JG

Ullingswick is a tiny Domesday-old hamlet in the Wye valley, and the *Steppes* is a Grade II listed 17th-century country house, rich in exposed beams, ingle-nook fireplaces and other period features. It is a highly personal guest house, owned and run by Tricia Howland. Most readers have responded gratefully to Mrs Howland's style of hospitality, and to her excellent individualistic and eclectic four-course dinners, which tend to the high cholesterol end of the scale unless otherwise requested. One reader, whose parents' 60th wedding anniversary celebrations were held at the *Steppes*, was full of praise for the helpful friendly service and excellent buffet dinner, which had made the occasion a resounding success. Dinner is normally at 7 pm by candlelight and with taped classical music. "Ties for gentlemen please." As a reader wrote last year, "Not for everyone, but a pleasure if you are on the right wavelength." More reports please.

Open All year except 2 weeks from 4 Jan.
Rooms 3 double – all with shower and wc, telephone, radio, TV and tea-making facilities. 1 ground-floor room.
Facilities Lounge with open fire and TV, dining room/bar with open fire. 1½-acre garden with sheep, rabbits and chickens; riding and fishing nearby. Tours round Royal Worcester porcelain works arranged.
Location 7 m NE of Hereford off A417 Gloucester to Leominster road.
Restrictions No children under 10. No dogs in public rooms.
Credit cards None accepted.
Terms (No service charge) B&B: double £35–£44; dinner B&B single £30–£35, double £52–£70. Set dinner £15. Bargain breaks available throughout the year; Christmas and New Year 3-day house parties.
Service/tipping; "We do not make a service charge of any description, but many guests automatically leave tips for the chambermaid in the bedroom."

ULLSWATER Cumbria — Map 4

Howtown Hotel — *Tel* Pooley Bridge (085 36) 514
Ullswater, Penrith CA10 2ND

Sharrow Bay (below) and *Howtown* share the same place name on the map – *Howtown* is two miles further along the lakeside road – but they could not be more different. They represent almost polar extremes of the Guide's parameters: *Sharrow Bay* provides a kind of ultimate in pampering, with prices to match; *Howtown* eschews excessive indulgences and its tariff is astoundingly low. We were worried last year at the absence of feedback – had all their guests got lost, we asked. The owner Michael Baldry tells us that his guests have indeed not gone missing – his hotel enjoys 99% bed occupancy without advertising, but many of his guests tend to keep it a closely guarded secret for fear of not being able to get in next time. And that view is confirmed by the reports we now have received after last year's appeal: "The best hotel in Lakeland – if you can get in!" (*W Ian Stewart*) Another view: "Beautiful home-cooked food by Mrs Baldry, great comfort and ridiculously low prices . . . You won't get reports – the sort of people who stay here prefer to keep it to themselves." (*Stephanie Sowerby*) Be warned though: this comfortable old farmhouse is not a high gloss establishment. The furnishings are homely rather than elegant, the food too. But it probably has as high a return rate as any hotel in the Guide.

Open End Mar–1 Nov.
Rooms 13 double, 3 single – 2 with bath. 4 in 2 annexes in grounds.
Facilities 4 lounges, 2 bars, TV room, dining room. 1-acre garden. 300 yds from lake with private foreshore; yachting, boating, fishing, wind-surfing, walking and climbing. Riding and golf nearby.

Location *Howtown* is on E shore of lake 4 m S of Pooley Bridge.
Restrictions Not suitable for ♿. No children under 7. Dogs at management's discretion, not in public rooms.
Credit cards None accepted.
Terms (No service charge) Dinner, B&B £22 (£18.30 for 4 nights or more). Self-catering cottages £45–£140 per week. Set lunch: cold table on weekdays £4.50, on Sun £5.50, dinner £7.50. 1-night bookings sometimes refused. Reduced rates for children sharing parents' room.
Service/tipping: "Any gratuities offered are distributed equally amongst the staff."

Sharrow Bay Country House Hotel [GFG]
Ullswater, Penrith CA10 2LZ

Tel Pooley Bridge (085 36) 301 and 483

This is Brian Sack's and Francis Coulson's fortieth anniversary at their rightly celebrated country house hotel on the eastern shore of Ullswater – the longest-running show in the Guide – and the reviews this year are as usual of the rave variety. "Our annual treat, and as superb as ever; if anything the meals are even better." (*P and J Temple*) "The ultimate in genuine hospitality." (*Eric Marsh*) "Sumptuous . . . an institution to which others should aspire . . . An experience to remember." (*Ken and Mildred Edwards*) "We thought we could do without lunch and get through till dinner, but the lure of afternoon tea was irresistible! Never in my life have I found tea to come up to my wildest dreamy expectations, but I did at *Sharrow Bay*. Everything about every detail is attended to, every whim anticipated. The staff were all so friendly – an attitude they must pick up from Brian and Francis; they are such extremely nice people – there is no malice in them, just a real desire to make their guests feel wanted and welcome. They apologised for the place being so cluttered with bits and pieces, which it undoubtedly is, but the 'clutter' consists of beautiful pieces of china, clocks and mirrors they have collected over the years, and lots and lots of flowers and plants, and why not fill their home/hotel with what they want? But I'm glad I don't have to do the dusting! The food we found to be consistently of the highest standard. The coffee the best I have drunk in a hotel." (*Lady Macdonald*) Long may these great old troupers continue to draw such notices!

Open Early Mar (or possibly mid-Feb)–early Dec.
Rooms 6 suites, 23 double, 7 single – 24 with bath and shower, 2 with shower, all with telephone, radio and TV; some with tea-making facilities. 18 rooms in cottages, Lodge annexe and Bank House. 2 ground-floor rooms.
Facilities 4 lounges, breakfast room, 2 restaurants. 12-acre grounds at Sharrow, 5 at Bank House; garden and woodlands; ½ m of lake shore with private jetty and boathouse; lake bathing (cold!) and fishing from shore; boats for hire nearby; steamer service in season across lake; magnificent walking/climbing country.
Location On E shore of Ullswater, 2 m S of Pooley Bridge. Turn by small church in Pooley Bridge and take Howtown Lane. (M6 exit 40.)
Restrictions Not suitable for ♿. No children under 13. No dogs.
Credit cards None accepted.
Terms (No service charge) Dinner, B&B £54–£95. Set lunch £15–£21 (light lunches also available weekdays), dinner £28.50–£30. 10% mid-week reductions in Mar and Nov. 1-night bookings sometimes refused, especially at weekends.
Service/tipping: "No tipping!"

> Before making a long detour to a small hotel, do check that it is open. Some are known to close on impulse.

UNDERBARROW Cumbria **Map 4**

Greenriggs Country House Hotel *Tel* Crosthwaite (044 88) 387
Underbarrow, Nr Kendal LA8 8HF

Converted mainly 18th-century farmhouse in the secluded Lyth Valley, three miles west of Kendal – a specially peaceful location. In earlier editions of the Guide, but omitted after a change of ownership. Readers report well of new owners, the Smithsons: improved comforts, superior cooking, unobtrusive friendliness. 14 rooms, 10 with bath and shower. Open Mar–Dec inclusive. Dinner, B&B £29.50–£39.50. More reports would still be welcome.

VERYAN Cornwall **Map 1**

The Nare Hotel *Tel* Truro (0872) 501279
Carne Beach, Veryan TR2 5PF

New to the Guide, a traditional, professionally-run seaside hotel, with a particularly agreeable location on the Roseland Peninsula entirely surrounded by National Trust land and 50 yards from a safe, sandy NT beach; there is also an outdoor pool. Built in the mid-fifties the hotel is furnished with bright, modern furniture, and its bedrooms (ask if you want a sea view) have modern bathrooms and plenty of storage space. The dining room has big Moorish-arched windows, with fine views over the sea and coastline. Our nominator speaks warmly of the unobtrusive, friendly service and well-prepared meals, making good use of local produce. There is a games room with snooker and table-tennis, a hard tennis court, and many delightful villages and National Trust gardens and houses nearby to explore. Not a specially sophisticated hotel (though jackets and ties for dinner and whites for tennis preferred), but a dependable base for a seaside holiday. (*Dr K Robinson; also Deborah Murdoch*)

Open All year.
Rooms 32 double, 5 single – 32 with bath and/or shower, all with radio, tea-making facilities and baby-listening; TV on request. 3 in annexe. Some ground-floor rooms.
Facilities Bar, 2 lounges (1 with TV), games room, restaurant; sauna, gym and solarium. 5-acre grounds with childrens' play area, tennis court and swimming pool (heated May–Sept). National Trust beach 50 yards with swimming, fishing and wind-surfing. Riding, golf, sailing and bowling nearby.
Location 1 m W of Veryan, signposted Carne Beach.
Restriction No dogs.
Credit cards All major cards accepted.
Terms (Service at guests' discretion) B&B £22–£30; dinner B&B £32.50–£41.50. Set dinner £13.50; full alc £16. New Year and Christmas tariffs. Reduced rates and special meals for children.

WAREHAM Dorset **Map 2**

The Old Granary *Tel* Wareham (092 95) 2010
The Quay, Wareham BH20 4LP

"The best feature of the hotel besides its pretty location on the river Frome was the helpful and friendly service of the owner and his staff. They made every effort to ensure that we were well looked after. The full

English breakfast deserves a mention – the best I have had in years. The current report is too harsh on the food – there was no evidence of the tin-opener. Excellent value." A recent comment on the rather qualified first entry in last year's Guide for this 200-year-old grain store in an idyllic situation on the banks of the river Frome overlooking the Purbeck Hills which, however, praised "the rooms, two looking over the water, pretty, beamy, well-equipped, two with good modern bathrooms", and the owners as "helpful kindness personified – chatty, smiling, incredibly hard-working". The proprietor, Mr Sturton, also feels that our reference to the tin-opener is unfair: "The only item we may use from a tin is tomatoes; 90% of our vegetables are fresh and our meat and fish are all bought fresh locally. As you can appreciate from our vast menu, some items may be frozen and we use the microwave to defrost." Another reader found the cooking over-ambitious, with "glutinous sauces", and also mentioned thin walls. (*Mr ST Pearson, Patricia Fenn*) More reports welcome.

Open All year. Restaurant closed Christmas Day.
Rooms 4 double – 2 with bath and shower, all with TV and tea-making facilities.
Facilities Lounge, bar area, 2 restaurants, riverside terrace. On river Frome; private moorings, fishing (permits from local council).
Location 2 mins' walk from centre. Take A351 Wareham to Swanage road.
Restrictions Not suitable for ♿. Dogs at managements' discretion, not in public rooms.
Credit cards All major cards accepted.
Terms [1987 rates] B&B £16–£25. Set lunch £4.95, dinner £9.75; full alc £12. Reductions for children in cots.
Service/tipping: "A 10% service charge is added to business accounts and parties of 6 or more unless otherwise requested. This is distributed between all staff pro rata to hours worked."

WARMINSTER Wiltshire — Map 2

Bishopstrow House [GFG] — *Tel* Warminster (0985) 212312
Warminster BA12 9HH — *Telex* 444829

Expensive sophisticated late Georgian country house hotel in 25 acres bordering river Wylye. Luxurious furnishings. Indoor swimming pool with pillars and palms. Should be idyllic but readers disagree about warmth – both literally and metaphorically. Some appreciate comprehensively; others express disappointments about heating, restaurant and service. 26 rooms, all with bath. B&B double from £70. Set dinner £25. More reports please.

WATERMILLOCK Cumbria — Map 4

The Old Church Hotel — *Tel* Pooley Bridge (085 36) 204
Watermillock
Penrith CA11 0JN

"An attractive, comfortable and well-situated hotel with friendly and helpful owners who continue to improve the decoration, service and food which are now of high standard. We suggest next improvements should be: a course on vegetables for the chef; a different phone system; different dining room chairs. There would then be no fault." "Full of warmth both from the staff and from the open fires and efficient central heating. We had a room overlooking the lake and the hills beyond. The bathroom was small but perfectly adequate. One drawback: the beds had very firm mattresses and my wife was unable to have hers changed for a softer one. Dinner was imaginative and varied and the wine list extensive for a small hotel. The public rooms were cosily furnished and impeccably maintained. The Whitemores have clearly found the secret of providing a hotel with character and warmth. Long may they flourish." Just two of many endorsements of last year's entry for this quietly-situated hotel in a spectacular position on the edge of Ullswater, an 18th-century house on the site of a 12th-century church, reached by a long private drive off the A592. Its gardens go right down to the water and there are fine views. Only a few light brickbats: correspondents who appreciated comfortable rooms and excellent food, but felt the hotel at times was run more for the convenience of its owners than its guests. (*David M Laing, RA Devin, and others*)

Open Mid-Mar–mid-Nov.
Rooms 9 double, 2 single – 7 with bath, all with baby-listening.
Facilities 2 lounges, TV lounge, bar, dining room (no smoking). 4-acre grounds with extensive lake frontage with mooring and fishing; sail boards and rowing boat available for guests' use.
Location 3 m S of Pooley Bridge; 5 m from junction 40 on the M6.
Restrictions Not suitable for ♿. No dogs.
Credit cards None accepted.
Terms Dinner, B&B £45–£53. Set dinner £17.50. 1-night bookings refused during bank holiday weekends. Reduced rates and special dining room for children.
Service/tipping: "We hope service charge and tipping will disappear. We normally suggest that money offered should be spent on the guests' next visit."

WEOBLEY Hereford and Worcester — Map 2

Red Lion Hotel — *Tel* Weobley (0544) 318220
Weobley HR4 8SE

"We highly recommend the *Red Lion* for a quiet, restful stay in the heart of Herefordshire, its central location permitting fascinating trips to Ludlow, Hay on Wye and other places of historical interest and picturesque setting. Our hosts, Edward Townley-Berry and Judith Weedon, struck just the right note of easy-going friendliness without being intrusive. The food was good, well presented and ample, without the exaggerated attempt at *haute cuisine* that one sometimes runs across, to one's discomfiture, at such establishments. The house wines were most satisfactory. Exactly the kind of place we had hoped to find from the Guide and we were not disappointed." (*T Bradbrooke Smith*) This 14th-century inn, at the centre of a medieval village famous for its many half-timbered black-and-white houses was first brought to our attention by *Robert Robinson*: "Part of the delightful black-and-white architecture of Weobley, backing rather agreeably on to the bowling green, and with (if our accommodation was typical) small unfussy bedrooms, the pleasantest of dining rooms and the most conventional of menus." Only criticism: the bedrooms "could benefit from a little more refinement in the decor".

Open All year.
Rooms 7 double – 2 with bath, 5 with shower, all with telephone, TV, tea-making facilities and baby-listening.

Facilities 2 lounges/bars, wine bar, carvery, restaurant; terrace. 2-acre grounds, bowling green. Golfing at Wormsley Golf Course nearby.
Location In centre of village, but quiet; next to church. 10 miles NW of Hereford. Parking.
Restrictions Not suitable for ♿. Dogs in one lounge only.
Credit cards Access, Visa.
Terms (No service charge) B&B double £39.50. Full alc £16.50. 3-day Christmas package. Reduced rates for children sharing parents' room; special meals.
Service/tipping: "We feel it quite unnecessary to tip for good service. However, most people do."

WEST BAGBOROUGH Somerset — Map 1

Higher House
West Bagborough
Taunton TA4 3EF

Tel Bishops Lydeard
(0823) 432996

Newly-nominated unpretentious country guest house – part 17th-century farmhouse, part 19th-century, built round two courtyards, in six acres of gardens with heated swimming pool. Spectacular views towards Brendon Hills and Exmoor. Owners, William and Jo Beaumont, have run it for five years and renovations are still in progress. Set time for dinners eaten communally, breakfast times staggered. Home-cooked plentiful meals. 7 rooms (no private facilities). B&B £14–£15, dinner, B&B £22–£25. More reports please.

WEST BEXINGTON Dorset — Map 2

The Manor Hotel [GFG]
West Bexington
Dorchester DT2 9DF

Tel Burton Bradstock
(0308) 897616 and 897785

"A 16th-century stone manor house, with reassuringly massive walls which wears the Jacobean oak panelling in its hallway with accustomed ease. Our room was on the whole comfortable and well equipped but the decorative scheme did not inspire praise. The bathroom had a sharply sloping ceiling and a window which was stuck ajar." "Our room, probably the best one, was very simple, but pretty, large with all manner of extras. Everywhere was spotless. The food was all excellent quality and I do not think I have been anywhere quite so generous except *Sharrow Bay*. Breakfast, too was a feast. It has faults: we gather some of the rooms are very small indeed and 'on the tilt', but the staff were charming, the proprietors very helpful and pleasant, the garden pretty and the other guests very nice indeed. I imagine it would be cold in winter as none of the windows fitted properly and the central heating is only partial." Other readers are more critical of the food, and consider fish dishes better than meat ones. One was disturbed by "clearly heard family discord" in the kitchen during breakfast; another described his breakfast as "hearty but rich with a hit and miss directness, a hit with the scrambled eggs, a miss with the poached." But the consensus seems to be that despite faults it offers good food, comfortable beds and good value for money. West Bexington itself is unprepossessing; but it is within easy reach of Dorset beauty spots. (*WH Bruton, Heather Sharland; also N Spencer, and others*)

Open All year except Christmas and New Year.
Rooms 10 double – all with bath and shower, radio, TV, tea-making facilities and baby-listening.
Facilities Lounge, cellar bar, dining room, grill room. 3-acre grounds with childrens' play area. 500 yds from sea; Chesil beach, unsafe for swimming, is famous for fishing. Sandy beaches within easy reach.
Location 5 m SE of Bridport on B3167.
Restrictions Not suitable for ♿. No dogs in bedrooms or public rooms except bar.
Credit cards Access, Amex, Visa.
Terms (No service charge) B&B £20–£22.95; dinner, B&B £30.95–£33.35. Set lunch £9.95, dinner £12.95; bar meals. 2- to 7-day breaks. 50% reduction for under 10s; special meals.
Service/tipping: "Left to guests discretion; distributed on a points system according to number of shifts worked."

WEST CLIFFE Kent — Map 3

Wallett's Court Country Guest House [GFG] — *Tel* Dover (0304) 852424
West Cliffe, Dover CT15 6EW

A hybrid establishment – bed-and-breakfast from Monday to Friday (though with simple farmhouse-style evening meals available at about £9.50) but transformed on Saturday night into a serious restaurant. The building itself would merit the journey: a 17th-century listed manor house, the home of Prime Minister William Pitt in 1804, set in rural surroundings on the white cliffs of Dover, a mile from St Margaret's Bay; inside, there are intricately carved honey-coloured beams, huge open fireplaces, plenty of good antiques, flowers everywhere. Major restoration has taken place under the supervision of Lea Oakley, wife of the chef/*patron*, Chris Oakley, who trained with the Roux brothers at *Le Gavroche* and was then chef at *Le Poulbot* in London. Four of the bedrooms are in a converted barn at the back of the house and are pine-furnished, adequate but rather basic: "Slightly cool," writes a reader, in October, "and wardrobe space very limited." "An ideal place to stay if you are going through Dover." "Refreshingly simple and unpretentious, offering excellent value for money." "Our evening meal was very good and the breakfast was excellent." Even a vegetarian who was served "the type of main course I dread" enjoyed her soup and dessert and vowed to return. (*Richard Whiting, Stephan and Kate Murray-Sykes; also Kay and Neville Varley, and others*)

Open All year except Christmas. Restaurant closed Sun.
Rooms 2 family suites, 5 double – 3 with bath and shower, 4 with shower, all with tea-making facilities; radio and TV in suites. 4 rooms in converted barn 10 yards from main building.
Facilities Lounge, TV lounge, dining room. 4-acre grounds with orchard, badminton, and children's play area. 1 m from St Margaret's Bay with bathing, windsurfing, tennis club; golf 2 m.
Location 3 m N of Dover, 1 m down B2058 off A258 Dover–Deal road. Hotel is on right.
Restrictions Not suitable for ♿. No dogs.
Credit cards None accepted.
Terms (No service charge) B&B: single £22, double £30–£40. Gourmet dinner on Sat £17; set dinner on weekdays £9.50; private functions (lunch or dinner) by arrangement every day. Children £8 when sharing family suite; special meals.

WEST STOUR Dorset — Map 2

The Ship Inn — *Tel* East Stour (074 758) 640
West Stour
Nr Gillingham SP8 5RP

Modest and reasonably priced country pub – a traditional 18th-century coaching inn with listed exterior. One-acre grounds. In beautiful unspoilt part of Dorset. Recently modernised and refurbished. Friendly welcome from proprietors Mr and Mrs Cumming; simple but interesting dinners and substantial breakfasts. 6 double rooms, 4 with private facilities. B&B £14.50–£19. Set dinner £6.50; full alc £14. New nomination: more reports please.

WHIMPLE Devon — Map 1

Woodhayes Hotel — *Tel* Whimple (0404) 822237
Whimple, Nr Exeter EX5 2TD

Our last half-dozen entries for John and Alison Allan's demure Georgian country house hotel in a peaceful apple orchard village handy for the A30 have been full of effusive compliments. Last year's was no exception, and doubtless a little over the top ("if you're looking for perfection and divine decadence . . .") but this year's file has been distinctly cooler. The compliments still roll in, but they are sometimes muted and express a number of reservations. Last year we mentioned complaints that service was slow at dinner, and John Allan tells us that he has shortened the meal from five to three courses, and reduced the choices (also the price), and has speeded up the serving process. In other respects, we don't believe anything much has changed, only that perhaps Guide entries have aroused too great expectations. The Allans are welcoming and attentive to guests' needs, but they are not hearty extrovert hosts and more than one guest has commented on a quiet or over-quiet dining room. The bedrooms are endowed with a cornucopia of extras, but some readers have commented adversely on old-fashioned beds and bathroom equipment – which we imagine have been appreciated by others. But we also heard about a cold room when the weather was inclement, an uncomfortable mattress, some decoration in need of attention, inadequate bedside lighting. We hope that *Woodhayes* may return to a *nem con* entry next year.

Open All year except Jan.
Rooms 7 double – all with bath, telephone, radio and TV.
Facilities 2 lounges, dining room. 3-acre grounds with paddock, lawns, arboretum, gazebo, croquet, bowls and kitchen garden. 11 m from sea; trout fishing nearby.
Location On the edge of Whimple village, which is just N of A30, 9 m E of Exeter.
Restrictions No children under 12. No dogs.
Credit cards All major cards accepted.
Terms B&B: single occupancy £45–£55, double £65–£75. Set lunch/dinner £18.50. Reduced rates for winter breaks and longer stays in summer; 3-day Christmas programme.
Service/tipping: "Service included; no tipping expected."

WICKHAM Hampshire — Map 2

The Old House Hotel [GFG] *Tel* Wickham (0329) 833049
The Square, Wickham PO17 5JG

A creepered early Georgian house in a picturesque, part-medieval, part-Georgian village square, converted by Richard and Annie Skipwith 16 years ago, and now a flourishing highly prized French restaurant (Annie Skipwith has spent some time with Vergé and Guérard) as well as "a splendid small hotel". All recent correspondents endorse last year's praise of the food, but one is extremely critical of a bedroom: "It had cheaply-constructed cupboards and a diminutive bathroom with inadequate handbasin. There was a damaged ceiling light and exposed electric cables. Not up to the standard one would expect for these prices. Our second room was considerably better; the size of bedrooms varies enormously. The owners' greatest kindness was to provide a very late supper long after the restaurant had closed, to round off our weekend in France." Other readers have found the bedrooms comfortable, with an excellent selection of reading matter and describe the food as "memorable" and "superb". (*Susanna Backhurst, Blair and Dinah Harrison, and others*)

Open All year, except 10 days Christmas, 2 weeks Easter, 2 weeks July/Aug. Bedrooms closed Sat and Sun; restaurant closed Mon and Sat lunch and all Sun.
Rooms 7 double, 3 single – all with bath, shower, telephone, radio, TV and baby-listening.
Facilities 2 lounges, bar, restaurant. Small garden. River Meon nearby.
Location In village centre (front rooms double glazed). Parking. Wickham is at junction of B2177 and A32, 3 m N of Fareham.
Restrictions Not suitable for ♿. No dogs.
Credit cards All major cards accepted.
Terms B&B: single from £50, double from £70. Full alc £23. Reductions for children according to age; special meals.
Service/tipping: "We feel that in a service industry it is not right to ask for extra payment for service. The tariff should cover the amount we need to run our organisation satisfactorily. However, we print on the menus 'service included' even though no extra amount is added."

WIDEGATES Cornwall — Map 1

Coombe Farm *Tel* Widegates (05034) 223
Widegates, Nr Looe PL13 1QN

Alexander and Sally Low's small, welcoming country house (not a working farm) in large grounds with lawns, meadows and ponds and magnificent views over unspoiled valley to the sea. Outdoor swimming pool. Attractively and comfortably furnished; spotlessly clean and polished. Substantial traditional English food on no-choice dinner menu. Generous cooked breakfasts. Open Mar–Oct inclusive. 8 rooms, none with private facilities. Dinner, B&B £17.50–£29. New nomination: more reports please.

> Our italicised entries are different this year. There are more of them and they indicate hotels which are worth considering, but which, for various reasons – inadequate information, lack of feedback, ambivalent reports – do not at the moment warrant a fully entry. We should particularly welcome comments on these hotels.

WILLERSEY Gloucestershire — Map 2

The Old Rectory — *Tel* Broadway (0386) 853729
Church Street, Willersey
Nr Broadway WR12 7PM

John and Helen Jones' homely, friendly B&B in pretty, lovingly restored 17th-century country house with walled garden, built in mellow Cotswold stone and retaining original beams and fireplaces. Quietly situated in uncommercialised village a mile from Broadway. 6 individually styled rooms, all with private facilities, direct-dial telephone and TV. *B&B double: £39–£65. New nomination: more reports please.*

WILLITON Somerset — Map 1

Curdon Mill [GFG] — *Tel* Stogumber (0984) 56522
Lower Vellow
Williton TA4 4LS

Small country hotel – previously just a catering business – at foot of Quantocks in 200 acres of Richard and Daphne Criddle's own farmland. Water wheel still works; mill shaft hangs across restaurant's ceiling. Lots of flowers around, books too. Nominator speaks well of whole set-up. 6 rooms, all with private facilities. B&B £11.50–£17.50, dinner, B&B £19.50–25.50. Could we hear from other Mill *visitors?*

The White House Hotel and Restaurant — *Tel* Williton (0984) 32306
Williton TA4 4QW

César awarded for combining the best of two worlds – French flair with English dependability

1987 was an anniversary year for Dick and Kay Smith – 20 years since they became proprietors of *The White House Hotel* (on 22 May 1967). Just cause for congratulation and celebration both for them and for the Guide, as they had an entry in our first edition in 1978 and *The White House* is precisely the kind of hotel the Guide hopes to foster and propagate. High standards of accommodation, decor, service and food are perhaps not very difficult to achieve if one charges extortionate prices, but the Smiths achieve them for most reasonable sums. Their enthusiasm has not waned over the years. They still close for the winter months to replenish their gastronomic ideas, and to think up new decors for the bedrooms. Strong emphasis on style throughout. A reporter this year offers the following encomium: "There's the feel of a Mediterranean artist's retreat about the place, from the palm and fig trees in the forecourt and garden, to the brown cork walls and old wine auction prints in the bar. The style has been achieved through dedication rather than cash. Almost all the lovely old paintings, prints and furniture have been bought at auctions. Each bedroom has been individually thought out. "It is not a place for sybaritic luxury – of the 13 bedrooms four do not have their own bathroom – nor is it a house-party hotel. But the owners are friendly and the atmosphere very relaxed; if you do want to get on an intimate footing with your host, talk to Dick Smith about the wine list, which is extensive and very strong on the lesser-known regions that purvey the more reasonably-priced wines. Clearly he is dedicated to increasing the number of wine enthusiasts in the world. "The food is so good that it might be more accurate to describe *The White House* as a restaurant-with-rooms. The cooking is basically French provincial, with excursions into traditional British *and* into *nouvelle cuisine*. The short menu might include charter pie (chicken and parsley), cheese soufflé suissesse, quails with grapes, filet de boeuf sauce anchois, pineapple vacherin, or rich chocolate praline loaf. Whatever the style of the dish, the cooking always presents good, strong, clear tastes based on excellent raw materials. The fourth course is always the cheeseboard, with home-made oatcakes and local English cheeses as well as French ones. "Let's hope the Smiths will continue along the same lines for at least another 20 years." (*Catherine Steele-Kroon*)

Open Mid-May–early Nov; weekends only in Nov. Restaurant closed for lunch.
Rooms 1 family suite, 11 double, 1 single – 9 with bath (3 also have shower), all with TV. 5 in courtyard annexe, some on ground floor, suitable for ♿.
Facilities Lounge, bar, dining room. 2 m from coast; shingle beach 3 m, sandy beach 4 m.
Location On A39 in centre of village. Parking in courtyard.
Restriction Dogs by arrangement, not in public rooms.
Credit cards None accepted.
Terms (No service charge) B&B £20–£26; dinner, B&B £33.50. Set dinner £17.50. Bargain breaks for 3 or 4 days. Reduced rates for children.
Service/tipping: "We do not make a service charge. Some guests do leave money for staff which is distributed proportionately to all the staff that were involved."

WILMSLOW Cheshire — Map 4

The Stanneylands Hotel
Wilmslow SK9 4EY

Tel Wilmslow (0625) 525225
Telex 8950511 ONEONE attn 16616001

A substantial 1920s red-brick hotel owned and run by the Beech family, with Anton Mosimann-trained chef, Iain Donald, in charge of the kitchens. It is just down the road from Manchester Airport, but far enough away not to be troubled by low-flying aircraft; it is also handy for the M6, M52, M62 and Manchester itself. This years postbag contains warm endorsements of last year's recommendation which ran: "Delightful to stay in, not only because of the impressive surrounding Cheshire countryside, but also for the gardens. The Beech family take great pains to compete with Kew, particularly with their choice of trees – they say there are 36 different kinds of tree and shrub from all around the world in the grounds, but I haven't counted. All I know is that the grounds are idyllic, when it isn't raining. But it *is* local to Manchester . . . The restaurant is extremely good, if expensive, but the prices are in accordance with others of a similar quality. The menu is mainly contemporary English, but they'll serve steak-and-chips without complaint if asked. The main dining room is quiet and peaceful, even when full (and it is always full, for the *Stanneylands* enjoys a high reputation among the better-off Mancunian gastronomes). Just the place for a romantic, confidential evening, because the service is absolutely impeccable. You can witter on as long as you like without being disturbed. There is a modern wing with the usual accoutrements." (*Sean O'Connell*)

Open All year except Boxing Day, New Years' Day and Good Friday.
Rooms 27 double, 6 single – all with bath, shower, direct-dial telephone, radio and TV. 1 ground-floor room suitable for ♿.
Facilities Lounge, cocktail bar, restaurant; 2 private dining rooms, conference facilities. 3-acre grounds.
Location Go N of Wilmslow on A34. Turn left at first traffic lights into Stanneylands Road. Manchester International Airport 3 m.
Restriction No dogs.
Credit cards All major cards accepted.
Terms (No service charge) Rooms: single £35–£50, double £45–£60. Breakfast: continental £4, English £6. Set lunch £7; gourmet dinner £17; full alc £22. Gastronomic festivals. Off-season and weekend rates.
Service/tipping: "No service charges of any kind. If customers leave a gratuity it is accepted as an appreciation of services received above expectation and is therefore the incentive to personnel that was originally intended."

WINDERMERE Cumbria — Map 4

Miller Howe [GFG] — *Tel* Windermere (096 62) 2536
Rayrigg Road
Windermere LA23 1EY

Once more a bulging file of appreciation, with no more than a single dissenting note, for John Tovey's celebrated hotel perched above Lake Windermere with an awesome view to the great peaks across the water. In place of a string of pearls culled from a dozen oysters, we offer the experiences of a single woman who had booked at the last moment, had been offered and accepted the last room, which faced the back, but had confessed to the man on the telephone, who turned out to be Tovey himself, her dream of waking in a room with *the* view. She arrived to find a letter from the *patron*, who had had to go into hospital suffering from a painful neck condition, to say that he had succeeded in upgrading her room, at no extra cost, to make the dream come true. She continues: "His thoughtfulness at such a time, and the friendly but impeccable attention from all the staff were typical of everything at *Miller Howe*. My rooms contained all one could possibly want, including two gents' umbrellas, hairdrier, shampoo, Dabitoff, soapflakes and small clothes drying rack, cassette player with cassettes to suit all musical tastes, books, magazines, Scrabble, fresh flowers – even an electric trouser press! No TV – who needs it, with the sunset over the Langdales and a chance to watch it while eating the wonderful food for which *Miller Howe* is so justly famous? More delightful surprises the next morning: an outline drawing of the mountains opposite, with their names and heights, accompanied early morning tea and lemon biscuits. And Buck's Fizz, poured for each guest upon arrival downstairs, preceded breakfast. After the 'Platter of Hearty Lakeland Fare' (a mixed grill plus!) there was no need for more than a cup of coffee during the day, or afternoon tea with special scones while sitting on the terrace, with that incredible view again. Altogether, you might gather that I'm enthusiastic about *Miller Howe*. The 'Tovey Touch' is sheer magic." (*Miss Gillian S Berry; also countless others*)

Open End Feb–early Dec.
Rooms 13 double – all with bath and/or shower and radio; telephone and TV on request.
Facilities 4 lounges, 2 dining rooms; terrace. 4-acre grounds with landscaped garden. Walking, climbing, tennis, sailing, fishing and water sports nearby.

Location On A592 N of Bowness. Lake-facing rooms quietest.
Restrictions Not suitable for ♿. No children under 12. No dogs in public rooms.
Credit cards Access, Amex, Diners.
Terms (Excluding 12½% service charge) Dinner, B&B £52–£95 per person. Set dinner £22. Packed lunches £5.50. Spring and autumn breaks; residential cookery courses in Mar and Nov. 1-night bookings sometimes refused for Sat.
Service/tipping: "A surcharge of 12½% is added to all final accounts in lieu of gratuities."

Quarry Garth Hotel *Tel* Windermere (096 62) 3761
Windermere LA23 1LF

In eight acres of attractive grounds set back from Windermere–Ambleside road. Owner-chef is Rudolf Schaefer, originally from Germany, and menus have Austro-Germanic overtones. Comfortable rooms and prices very reasonable for the Lake, but recent reports highlight some weaknesses in housekeeping and service. 11 rooms with bath or shower. Dinner, B&B £22.50–£45. More reports please.

WINSFORD Somerset — Map 1

Royal Oak Inn *Tel* Winsford (064 385) 455
Winsford, Nr Minehead TA24 7JE *Telex* 46529 ROAK

"This is a charming old thatched pub with hanging baskets of flowers, set in a picture village in beautiful Lorna Doone country. The comfort, food, friendliness and quietness are perfect. Special pluses for me: log fires; no DIY tea/coffee gear in bedrooms (early tea is brought to you); no net curtains; no duvets. Superb chintz soft furnishing; colour TV in bedrooms. Food imaginative and excellent. Home-made granary rolls and good roast for dinner; no frozen vegetables. I look forward to my next visit." A new nomination for this handsome 14th-century thatched inn, oak-beamed and with an ingle-nook fireplace, and opposite a cobblestoned packhorse bridge over the river Winn. There are seven more bridges and a ford in this village whose other claim to fame is that it is the birthplace of Ernest Bevin. It is in on the edge of the Exmoor National Park; the hotel provides a guide to walks and proprietor Charles Steven can arrange riding, hunting, shooting and fishing for guests. The menu offers *inter alia* Exmoor Pie, poached local salmon, haunch of venison and roast goose. (*Mrs MJ Currie*) More reports please.

Open All year.
Rooms 1 suite, 11 double, all with bath, shower, telephone, radio and TV. 5 ground-floor rooms in courtyard annexe.
Facilities 3 lounges, bar, restaurant. Small garden. Hotel owns 1 m of fishing on river Winn.
Location SW of Minehead off A395
Restrictions Not suitable for ♿. No dogs in dining room.
Credit cards All major cards accepted.
Terms (Service at guests' discretion) B&B: single £40–£50, double £50–£60; dinner, B&B: single £50–£60, double £70–£80. Set lunch £8.50, dinner £12; full alc £22. Off-season rates.

****
"The 'lounge' is a horrid drab room with faded fabrics – even the cat has dandruff."
****

WITHERSLACK Cumbria — Map 4

The Old Vicarage [GFG] — *Tel* Witherslack (044 852) 381
Witherslack
Grange-over-Sands LA11 6RS

"We visited *The Old Vicarage* in 1982 and thought it was good, but it's even better now. Imaginative but comfortable decor, and plenty of thoughtful extras. Very friendly welcome and patience shown with our child and dog to a saintly degree. Dinner and breakfast both excellent. I was most disinclined to leave. A very revivifying place." Thus *Alison Johnson* of *Scarista House* (q.v.). And there is much more in the same vein in praise of this little Georgian hotel situated in beautiful walking country south of Lake Windermere, and, though only 15 minutes from the M6, quiet and secluded, away from the heart of the village. Roger and Jill Burrington-Brown and Stanley and Irene Reeve run the hotel informally as a joint enterprise. The rooms are delightfully furnished – William Morris curtains, Heal's lampshades, lots of pine and cane in the bedrooms, ample reading light. The emphasis is on quality – a few rooms beautifully equipped and furnished; nothing flash, but first-rate and imaginative. The hotel's cooking is warmly commended. "Very fine English food, imaginative, high quality." Home-made rolls are a speciality. There is a five-course set menu dinner – no choice except at the dessert stage where both a hot and cold sweets are offered, and you are warmly encouraged to have both.

This year a reader says "I don't think the breakfasts have been mentioned: excellent, everything freshly cooked and the home-made brioche delicious. The dinners were superb but I enjoyed the breakfasts more." (*Alexandra Webb*) A few criticisms also this year: public rooms and dining room cold during a February visit; one correspondent disliked "the discreet music during dinner – Chopin all three nights". Another commented: "Slightly pretentious clientele, slightly prissy food, and no other outdoors people there." (*Mrs C Foy, M and T Goodger, DS, and others*)

Open All year except Christmas week. Restaurant closed for lunch.
Rooms 7 double – all with bath or shower, telephone, radio, TV and tea-making facilities.
Facilities Lounge, bar lounge, restaurant, breakfast room; private dining room. 5 acres of gardens and woodlands. Sea 5 m, Lake Windermere 6 m, river fishing 6 m. Fell-walking.
Location From M6 take exit 36; follow route to Barrow-in-Furness. Turn off A590 signposted Witherslack and take first turn left past phone-box. Hotel is ½ m along this lane on left.
Restrictions Not suitable for ♿. Children under 10 by arrangement only. Dogs by arrangement only, not in public rooms.
Credit cards All major cards accepted.
Terms (Service at guests' discretion) Dinner, B&B £41.50–£46. Set dinner £16.50. Special 2-day breaks 1 Nov–31 Mar; 3-day breaks 1 Apr–15 Nov. Reduced rates for children; special meals.
Service/tipping: "We do not encourage or expect tips. However, it would be dishonest to say that we do not appreciate the extras we occasionally receive."

> Most hotels have reduced rates out of season and for children, and some British hotels offer "mini-break" rates throughout the year. If you are staying more than one night, it is always worth asking about special terms.

WIVELISCOMBE Somerset — Map 1

Hurstone Farmhouse Hotel — *Tel* Wiveliscombe (0984) 23441
Waterrow, Wiveliscombe TA4 2AT

This far-off-the-beaten-track Georgian farmhouse hotel has fine views down the combe and up the far hillside from its windows. It is a great place for walkers, both within the farm's 65 acres and beyond. From its first entry, the "tremendously courteous" John Bone has come in for special mention, and among this year's crop of reports, one mentions a special meal cooked for a three-year old followed by an entirely different menu for the parents, another speaks of the imaginative vegetarian meals and of an extra room provided for a restless child without charge. John Bone's cider is still being appreciated, and he is now making his own cheese, "Hurstone", Dunlop-style from a Scottish recipe of his father's. "Perfect unpretentious quiet hotel – not tarted up. Service very good and informal. Food delicious and original," read one report this year, endorsing this earlier one: "The highlight of our six-week honeymoon in Europe. Such warm, intelligent, kind-hearted people, and so beautiful their Georgian farmhouse atop lush rolling Somerset hills. We cried when we had to leave. We once tried leaving, drove to Wales for a day and drove back because we missed our 'adopted family'. Were welcomed back with open arms. Lovely place. Very homey!" (*Tom and Jodi Homann; also AS and DI, DL Cohen, SGT England*)

Open All year.
Rooms 1 suite (1 double, 1 single), 4 double – 4 with bath, 1 with shower, all with telephone, TV, tea-making facilities and baby-listening. Self-catering flat.
Facilities Sitting room with TV and log fire, dining room with sitting area and bar. Terrace and gardens; 65-acre farmland bordered by small trout river. Wimbleball Lake (10 m) provides sailing and fishing. Riding, tennis, golf nearby.
Location ¼ m off A361 at Waterrow.
Restrictions Not suitable for ♿. Dogs by arrangement only.
Credit cards None accepted.
Terms (No service charge) B&B: £15.50–£27.50, dinner, B&B: £25–£37. Set lunch £5–£7.50, dinner £8.50–£11.50. Weekend breaks Oct–April except public holidays; generous discounts for stays of 5 nights or more; Christmas programme. Reduced rates for children; special meals by arrangement.

Langley House Hotel and Restaurant [GFG] — *Tel* Wiveliscombe (0984) 23318, *Telex* 46648 WILSCO
Langley Marsh
Wiveliscombe TA4 2UF

The young owners of Langley House, Peter and Anne Wilson, he formerly of the *Lygon Arms* and *Ston Easton* (both q.v.) she of the BTA, have been highly praised by readers, who have greatly enjoyed their visits to this quiet rural corner of Somerset. The house was built in the 16th century, altered and enlarged in the 18th, and stands in three acres of landscaped gardens. The food is reported as imaginative and delicious, five courses served at a sensible pace, not rushing people along; a "lovely" room with a four-poster and view, ample wardrobe and drawer space. Service is described as friendly and efficient, the welcome as warm, the decor as attractive, the restaurant as elegant and with good quality silverware. There are fresh flowers in all the rooms, and Anne Wilson provides guests with maps and advice on touring. Somebody requiring a special diet commented on the obliging willingness to adapt the set menu to her needs. Peter Wilson's cooking, *nouvelle cuisine* at its best, beautifully presented, provoked two mumbles about a slightly heavy hand with the pepper, and two contradictory comments of, "puds out of this world", and a cross, "mine are much better" from a culinary professional, but most people liked everything, the Wilsons, the house and the food. (*C Makoff, F Cummins, E Chatten, B Horrocks, JN Bowen, H Cox, T Withers, EL Harte*)

Open All year.
Rooms 1 family suite, 7 double, 1 single – 8 with bath and shower, all with telephone, radio, TV and baby-listening.
Facilities 2 lounges, bar, restaurant. 4-acre grounds. Croquet lawn.
Location ½ m N of Wiveliscombe. Turn right at town centre, signposted Langley Marsh.
Restrictions Not suitable for ♿. No children under 7. No dogs in public rooms.
Credit cards Access, Amex.
Terms (No service charge) B&B £25.20–£34; dinner, B&B £40.70–£52.25. Set lunch £15.50, dinner £18.75. 2-day breaks in off-season; Christmas programme. 1-night bookings sometimes refused. Reduced rates for children sharing parents' room; special meals.
Service/tipping: "Service is an essential part of a stay in any hotel. We do not levy a service charge or expect gratuities."

WOODSTOCK Oxfordshire — Map 2

The Feathers Hotel [GFG]
Market Street
Woodstock OX7 1SX

Tel Woodstock (0993) 812291
Telex 83138 TELKAY

We had an entry in earlier editions of the Guide for this 17th-century building in the centre of the show-place village, and within a few minutes' stroll of the breath-taking vista of Blenheim. But things didn't go smoothly in the early days of its new incarnation (it changed ownership – and name – in 1982). This year *Mr JH Bell* persuades us to reconsider: "Having noticed that your entry for *The Feathers* had disappeared from the latest issue of the Guide we booked in with some trepidation. We need not have worried. Friendly receptionists greeted us and we had a most comfortable and quiet room reached by two back flights of stairs. There were no frills but the bed was comfortable and the hotel warm, which was much appreciated on an unseasonably cold night. The water was really hot – something not found in all hotels. Dinner, and breakfast next morning were both enjoyable, and we liked the dining room and the various small but comfortable lounges. Altogether a most pleasant small hotel with a friendly atmosphere and efficient young staff. We intend to return." Other views: "Very professional and English; lovely old house, lots of concussion-low beams." "Superb food with excellent selection and good presentation." "The restaurant was full of affluent foreigners and expense account businessmen. Good food in comfortable surroundings, but clearly not aimed at the natives. We were the only two women in the dining room, neither young, beautiful nor obviously rich, but we received excellent service." Two complaints: the chlorinated taste of the water; the at times haphazard waiting. And we wonder whether anyone can explain to us a dish on the Sunday lunch menu: "Fillets of Witch served with strips of Leek and a Herb Butter Sauce"? (*Abigail Kirby Harris, and others*)

Open All year.
Rooms 14 double, 2 single – all with bath and/or shower, telephone, radio and TV.
Facilities 2 lounges, bar, restaurant. Gravelled courtyard. Fishing in Blenheim Park Lake ¼ m.
Location In town centre, but quiet at night.
Restrictions Not suitable for ♿. Dogs by prior arrangement only.
Credit cards All major cards accepted.
Terms (No service charge) B&B: single £45, double £68–£88. Set lunch £10.50, dinner £16.50; full alc £20–£25. Winter breaks; Christmas package.

WOOLER Northumberland — Map 4

Ryecroft Hotel [GFG] — *Tel* Wooler (0668) 81459
Ryecroft Way, Wooler NE71 6AB

Small welcoming, enterprising hotel run by Patricia and David McKechnie in quiet Northumbrian market town. In area rich in historical sites and good for birdwatching, cycling, angling, gliding. Open fires in public rooms; bedrooms clean, warm and well-equipped. Food fresh and well presented with change of menu every day. Reasonably-priced wine; real ale. Closed 2 weeks in Nov, and Christmas. 11 rooms, none with private facilities. Double room with breakfast £36 (£28 for 3-day stay). Dinner £12. Newly nominated: feedback please.

WOOLHOPE Hereford and Worcester — Map 2

The Butchers Arms [GFG] — *Tel* Fownhope (043 277) 281
Woolhope HR1 4RF

A spate of reports this year, following last year's appeal, on this "example of that disappearing species, an honest old-fashioned country inn". Woolhope is a small village, equidistant from Hereford, Ross and Ledbury, and three miles from the river Wye. *The Butchers Arms*, a black-and-white half-timbered building, dating from the 14th century, is a popular village pub, with low beams and log fires in the bars (good bar snacks), but it also has three small but comfortable rooms, and an enterprising à la carte menu in its restaurant. "I was astonished that you are considering omitting this hotel from future editions of the Guide. We visited it first in 1983; on our second visit we found the standard of interior decoration and bedroom comfort vastly improved. One of the joys of the hotel is the complete silence; apart from bird-song and country noises, which induce perfect relaxation and sound sleep." (*JS MacLachlan*) "Accommodation and service are all you would expect in a country inn. Pity there are not more of them." (*Mr G Benjamin*) But one correspondent was disappointed with the quality of the accommodation and warned of very steep steps which would be awkward for the elderly or disabled. "A good pub, but that's it."

Open All year. Restaurant closed Christmas Day lunch (guests go to another hotel), also Sun–Tue though open for residents during winter months. Bar lunches and dinners served every day.
Rooms 3 double – all with mono TV and tea-making facilities.

Facilities Lounge bar, public bar, restaurant. Patio garden leading to small stream.
Location 8 m SE of Hereford, take B4224; at Mordiford turn left to Woolhope; at T-junction take left turn; *Butchers Arms* is $\frac{1}{4}$ m outside village.
Restrictions Not suitable for ♿. No children under 14 in bar in evenings. No dogs.
Credit cards None accepted.
Terms (No service charge) B&B £14.50–£18.50. Full alc £12.25 (in bar £7.75). Bargain breaks Oct–Mar (except Easter), any 2 days; reductions for stays of 7 nights or more. Reduced rates for children sharing parents' room; special meals on request.
Service/tipping: "We do not add a service charge to bills. Some residents do leave a tip for the restaurant staff in the same way as non-resident diners do."

WORFIELD Shropshire — Map 1

The Old Vicarage Hotel
Worfield
Nr Bridgnorth WV15 5JZ

Tel Worfield (074 64) 497
Telex 35438

New to the Guide – and the more welcome for being in an area sparsely represented on our map, close to the M54 and the confluence of the M5 and M6, and also handy for the Coalport Museum complex: a redbrick Edwardian country rectory converted about five years ago into a small country hotel by Peter and Christine Iles. It is a *Relais du Silence* and is situated on a hill just outside the pretty village of Worfield with extensive views over the Worfe Valley. Our nominator appreciated comprehensively: "Delightful and peaceful location. Rooms beautifully furnished. Great care in blending of furnishings, even down to matching soaps, towels and bathrobes. TV in a discreet cabinet, electric overblankets, a bowl of fruit . . . Plenty of choices on menu, and instead of the usual rolls we were offered delicious home-made mint and poppyseed bread. No pretentions to *nouvelle cuisine*, but an imaginative menu well-executed. Reasonable wine list with many half-bottles . . . Not a hotel for those seeking a bright lively atmosphere, but difficult to fault for a peaceful stay in comfortable surroundings." (*Victor Coles*) More reports please.

Open All year.
Rooms 8 double, 2 single – all with bath and/or shower, telephone, radio, TV and tea-making facilities. 6 more rooms to be built in 1987/8.
Facilities Lounge bar, conservatory, dining room; private dining room. 2-acre grounds. Near river; fishing can be arranged.
Location 1 m N of A454 from Bridgnorth to Wolverhampton.
Restriction Not suitable for ♿. No dogs in public rooms. Smoking in bar only.
Credit cards All major cards accepted.
Terms (Service at guests' discretion) B&B: single £36, double £52.50. Set lunch £9.95, dinner £10.95 and £15; full alc £21. Leisure breaks.
Service/tipping: "We leave it entirely to guests. A surprisingly large number do leave a tip."

> "The place was very cold when we arrived (in October). When I complained they just said that the heating switches on at 4 pm . . . During the night, the water tank started to make noises and at 4 am my husband was up trying to fix it. I spent the night falling out of bed. In the morning, I pulled back the covers and found one of the bed legs was broken and propped up with a milk crate."

WORLESTON Cheshire — Map 4

Rookery Hall [GFG]
Worleston, Nr Nantwich
CW5 6DQ

Tel Nantwich (0270) 626866
Telex 367169 ROOKHALL

Much praise in 1987 for this Victorian Gothic château, with parts dating back to Georgian times, set in 28 acres of garden and parkland, with fountains, statuary and a small lake thick with water lilies. "Serene country house of the non-designer breed of English hotel. Quietly posh, with food to match. The public rooms have aquamarine or yellow painted walls; furniture is of varying interest and there is a mixture of good and mediocre pictures. Service is formal but pleasant. Expensive, but worth it." (*David Wooff*) "One of the most agreeable places to stay in the United Kingdom. Welcome and service outstanding, food as good as any in the land, a great wine list, though expensive. Excellent rooms with many extras – fruit, biscuits, champagne, towelling robes and so on. Most welcome of all a *proper* breakfast in the bedroom – not the trouble-free sort called continental – all beautifully cooked and piping hot." (*MA Pelham*) Audrey and Peter Marks, now joined by their son David, were new to the hotel business when they bought *Rookery Hall* three years ago; since then they have been continually upgrading the bedrooms and have spent much time and effort restoring the gardens. The original vegetable garden now supplies much of what is served in the beautiful panelled dining room where the food is "English, cooked in the modern manner".

Open 27 Jan 1988–4 Jan 1989.
Rooms 2 suites, 7 double, 2 single – all with bath, shower, telephone, radio and TV. 2 de luxe Coach House rooms 60 yards from front entrance.
Facilities Hall, 2 sitting rooms, 2 dining rooms. 28-acre garden and parkland with brook, croquet, putting, hard tennis court, coarse fishing, clay pigeon shooting, riverside and woodland walks. Riding and golf nearby.
Location From the north, take junction 18 from M6; from the south, junction 16. Hotel is on B5074, 2 m N of Nantwich (avoid town centre if possible).
Restrictions Not suitable for ♿. No children under 10. No dogs.
Credit cards All major cards accepted.
Terms (Service at guests' discretion) Dinner, B&B £70–£100 per person. Set lunch £12.95, dinner £25. £7.50 reduction per person per day for stay of 2 nights or more Oct–Mar. 1-night bookings sometimes refused during public holiday periods.
Service/tipping: "No service charge. All tips divided amongst all members of staff."

WYKE see GILLINGHAM — Map 2

YATTENDON Berkshire — Map 2

The Royal Oak Hotel [GFG]
The Square
Yattendon, Nr Newbury
RG16 0UF

Tel Hermitage (0635) 201325

A new entry this year, warmly recommended by our Continental editor who chose this redbrick, part 17th-century pub in a pretty village for his honeymoon night. "Cosy and informal, but also sophisticated and relatively expensive. Its young owners, Kate and Richard Smith, belong to the new breed of English hoteliers, mixing enthusiasm with a continental-style professionalism (they worked in Lausanne), and they have given their five-bedroom hotel the feeling of a private house. You enter straight from the street into a lavishly-furnished sitting-room where a log fire blazes (no reception desk anywhere.) To one side is the old pub part where locals drink and good bar snacks are served – all very spruce and inviting with red-tiled floors, open brickwork and newspapers hanging on sticks as in the cafés of old Vienna. Our pleasant bedroom looked onto the walled rose-garden at the back where you can drink in summer. Nice old 19th-century furniture, quilt bedspread, brass bath-fittings and other such touches, but the water could have been hotter. Discreetly elegant restaurant – just eight tables gleamingly appointed – where Mr Smith's Anglo-French cooking is ambitious and interesting but not too fussy: he worked with Richard Shepherd at *Langan's Brasserie*, and the influence shows . . . copious crab salad, the vegetables *al dente*, and marvellous beignets soufflés with hot lemon sauce. Lavish breakfast, and friendly service from a young local team in white blouses." (*Warning*. Bedrooms directly above the pub can be noisy.) (*John and Katinka Ardagh*)

Open All year except 2–3 weeks in Jan/Feb.
Rooms 5 double – all with bath and shower, telephone, radio, TV and baby-listening.
Facilities Restaurant, lounge, bar. ½-acre garden.
Location Just N of M4 between exits 12 and 13.
Restrictions Only restaurant suitable for ♿. Dogs by arrangement only.
Credit cards Access, Amex, Visa.
Terms (No service charge) B&B: single £45–£55, double £55–£65. Full alc £14.50 in bar, £21 in restaurant. Reduced rates for children sharing parents' room; special meals on request.
Service/tipping: "All gratuities are pooled among all staff. Guests are under no obligation to tip, but if they feel they have had special attention they may like to express thanks."

YORK North Yorkshire — Map 4

Mount Royale Hotel — *Tel* York (0904) 28856
The Mount, York YO2 2DA — *Telex* 57414

"Another enjoyable stay. Comfortable, friendly and well-kept." "Food well-prepared and served. The portions are enormous; clearly the Oxtobys cater for Yorkshire appetites; breakfasts equally gargantuan and set one up for the day." "Lovely room overlooking the gardens; we were delighted with the view. I commented on the flowers and a lovely arrangement soon appeared in the room. The Sunday evening buffet was impressive, with a dessert cart to send one to heaven." "My room was equipped with everything including a very glamorous bed. I was very satisfied with all, especially the welcome – they were actually pleased to see a single lady!" Comments this year on Richard and Christine Oxtoby's characterful hotel, Gothic in appearance, William IV in the main though with a modern extension, near the racecourse, a few minutes' walk from Micklegate Bar and three-quarters of a mile from the Minster. One of its great attractions is its garden with heated swimming pool. And readers appreciate the solid comforts of the bedrooms, with their trouser-presses, hairdriers and so forth. Only quibbles: the lack of an alternative, for those of less robust appetite, to the generous table d'hôte; the bedroom and dining-room cold on a winter's night; and the traffic noise in the front rooms, though this is mitigated by double glazing. (*Pat and Jeremy Temple, Jean and Eric Lace, Mr and Mrs Victor Isenberg, Dorothy Brining, and others*)

Open All year except 23 Dec–4 Jan.
Rooms 2 suites, 15 double, 2 single – all with bath, shower, telephone, radio, TV, baby-listening and tea-making facilities. 2 ground-floor rooms.
Facilities 2 lounges, TV room, bar, dining room with conservatory. 1½-acre grounds with heated swimming pool.
Location On A1036 from Tadcaster (front rooms have double-glazing). Hotel is on right just before traffic lights at junction with Albemarle Road opposite sign to Harrogate (A59). Parking for 24 cars.
Restrictions Not suitable for ♿. Dogs by arrangement only.
Credit cards All major cards accepted.
Terms (Service at guests' discretion) B&B: single £49.50–£55, double £60–£65, suite £85–£95. Set dinner £17.95; light lunch by arrangement. 2-day breaks (excluding bank holidays). 1-night bookings refused over some bank holiday periods. Reduced rates for children sharing parents' room; special meals by arrangement.
Service/tipping: "People tip if they wish; we don't think it degrading for staff to accept. Tips are added to wages each week."

Wales

FAIRYHILL COUNTRY HOUSE HOTEL, REYNOLDSTON

ABERSOCH Gwynedd **Map 4**

Porth Tocyn Hotel [GFG] *Tel* Abersoch (075 881) 2966
Abersoch LL53 7BU

This consistently popular family hotel (run by the family Fletcher-Brewer and for families as well as other nuclear units) has a particularly choice position on a headland overlooking Cardigan Bay and Snowdonia. It is surrounded by its own 250-acre farm sloping down to the sea a few minutes' stroll away. Comments this year have been much as before: mostly pro, with a few cavils. "The food is now better than ever – in our view one of the best restaurants in Wales. Value for money also very good, and the wines reasonably priced." "The food, especially the fish, quite superb, and the atmosphere, carefully stage-managed by Mr F-B, perfectly relaxing and laid-back." And similar tributes in the same vein, with more than one mentioning "the sheer value for money". A minority, even while praising the cooking and the ambience, have queried the prices with respect to the accommodation. Nicholas Fletcher-Brewer tells us that he has carried out major refurbishment of his middle-wing bedrooms this past winter, so we hope that if they were responsible for moans about "a well-worn room and a simply shabby bathroom" and "a bed that had seen much better days" we'll get a unanimous vote of approval next year. (*R Inns-Wyatt, Deborah Kelly, and others*)

Open Week before Easter–early Nov.
Rooms 14 double, 4 single – all with bath, telephone and TV; radio and tea-making facilities (no extra charge) on request; baby-listening. 3 ground-floor rooms with easy access for ♿.
Facilities 6 lounges, bar, TV room. Garden with hard tennis court and heated (mid-May to end Sept) swimming pool; rock garden, lawns set within the hotel's 25-acre farm; 3 minutes' walk from sea, Heritage coastal walk; sailing, bathing, water-skiing, windsurfing, sea fishing, walks, golf and riding nearby.
Location 2½ m S of Abersoch, through the hamlets of Sarn Bach and Bwlchtocyn. From Abersoch take Sarn Bach road; follow three signs marked "Gwesty/hotel".
Restrictions No children under 7 in dining room at night. Dogs in bedrooms only – bring dog basket.
Credit card Access.
Terms (No service charge) B&B: single £27–£33, double £41–£62; dinner, B&B: single £38–£48.50, double £63–£93. Buffet Sun lunch £8.25, dinner £11.75 (2 courses) or £15.50 (4 courses). Bargain breaks out of season. 1-night bookings sometimes refused. Reduced rates and special meals for children.
Service/tipping: "Tips are not expected at any time but, if given, are shared amongst staff."

CARDIGAN Dyfed — Map 1

Rhyd-Garn-Wen [GFG] — *Tel* Cardigan (0239) 612742
Cardigan SA43 3NW

A secluded Victorian house, one-and-a-half miles from the sea in a remote and historic area of north Pembrokeshire, is the setting for this highly personal establishment run with flair and dedication by Huw and Susan Jones. Their aim, they say, is to help people to discover, as they have done, "the utter tranquillity of Pembrokeshire, the fantastic scope of its sporting facilities and its wonderful, interesting scenery". Readers continue to testify as warmly as ever to the special pleasures of a visit. In returning our questionnaire, Susan Jones writes: "I try to respond in minute detail to the aspirations of guests, to entertain in any other style is alien and useless. I find out, through letters sent in advance of a visit, what people like and because the numbers are small and the diners (usually!) an eager band of hungry devotees, I am able to prepare food to an even more exacting standard than ever – which is honestly sheer bliss. We no longer serve meals to non-residents, and our guests respond avidly to the extra attention. A really happy relaxed guest who is enjoying his holiday is the goal of our house." And the names that follow would all say "amen" to that – *Lady Briggs, William Grant, EA Rath, Bernadette Murray, A and B Freer*

Open Easter to Sept. Restaurant closed to non-residents.
Rooms 3 double – 2 with shower, 1 with private bathroom opposite. Suite for 2 in stable block: bedroom, bathroom, sitting room with mono TV, cooking facilities.
Facilities Drawing room, bar, dining room. 18-acre grounds with rookery. Hunting, shooting, fishing by arrangement; stabling for visiting horses; excellent walking country; 2 m from coast; safe swimming, boating, golf; historical sites, lectures and music festivals in vicinity.
Location On A487 Cardigan–Fishguard road on Gilgerran; turn 2¾ m from Cardigan at Croft crossroad.

Restrictions Not suitable for ♿ or children under 12. No dogs.
Credit cards None accepted.
Terms (Not VAT-rated) (No service charge) Dinner, B&B £38 per person in a double room; single rates by arrangement.
Service/tipping: "If people are kind enough to offer, we first say no, but if they insist we accept gracefully. They usually buy plants for me and perfume for our helper Amelia."

CONWY Gwynedd — Map 4

Sychnant Pass Hotel — *Tel* Conwy (0492) 596868
Sychnant Pass Road — *Telex* 61155 Ref SI
Conwy LL32 8BJ

An unpretentious, well-run hotel in a beautiful part of the county, very near Conwy's marvellous castle, and close to the north coast resorts. "It doesn't have the extensive grounds and elegant decor (nor the high prices) of *Bodysgallen* nearby (q.v.), but the atmosphere is relaxed and the service caring under the vigilant eye of proprietor Brian Jones. Don't be put off by the coy names of the courses in the *Four Seasons Restaurant* – Spring, Summer, Autumn and Winter – (with a sorbet 'to clear the palate' between the first two, if you like that sort of thing). The food is decently prepared and well presented. There's a modest wine list (no half-bottles). At breakfast everything was brought in the right order - no tea and toast cooling on the table while you wait for your eggs and bacon." The Joneses particularly recommend spring and autumn visits, when the countryside and the weather are often at their best. (*CR; endorsed by L Gaffield*)

Open Feb–Dec. Restaurant closed for lunch.
Rooms 1 suite, 11 double, 1 single – all with bath and shower, telephone, radio, TV, tea-making facilities and baby-listening. 1 room specially designed for ♿.
Facilities 2 lounges, bar, restaurant. 3-acre grounds with woods, pond and stream. 3 coastal resorts, golf, riding, fishing, walking etc nearby.
Location Proceed through Conwy until you see Bangor Arch ahead; turn sharp left into Upper Gate Street, through arch at the top and turn right into Sychnant Pass Road. Hotel is 1½ m on right.
Restriction No dogs in public rooms.
Credit cards All major cards accepted.
Terms (Service at guests' discretion) B&B £19.50–£29.50; dinner, B&B £29.50–£37.50. Set dinner £12.50. 2-night winter breaks; Christmas house party. Reduced rates for children.

CRICKHOWELL Powys — Map 1

Gliffaes Country House Hotel — *Tel* Bwlch (0874) 730371
Crickhowell NP8 1PH

This is the Brabner family's fortieth year running a hotel that regularly enchants most of our correspondents and invariably succeeds in infuriating a minority. Utterly acceptable mild eccentricity? That would certainly be a fair description of the building, an imposing Italianate mansion, built just over a century ago, with a striking campanile at either end, plonked down in the valley of the Usk midway between the Brecon Beacons and the Black Mountains and surrounded by 29 acres of magnificent garden and parkland – "a miniature Kew". There are glorious views from the dining room and terrace, and many of the rooms, too.

There is a real country-house feel to the place, with fishing tackle everywhere; the hotel has two stretches on the Usk and there are eight fishable reservoirs in the vicinity. As usual our postbag is full of appreciative comments: on the service, the standards of cleanliness, individual acts of kindness, the abundant flower arrangements, the magnificent spread of tea. Many reports come from regulars who find the hotel addictive. One wrote to express her surprise that a guest, quoted in a previous edition, had found rudeness and a semi-clean room – "this must be an aberration." Unfortunately, these complaints recur; one correspondent told us this year of finding a pair of panties under his bed. Service can certainly be amateurish at times. A standard complaint for many years was about the food. It has clearly improved recently – "not quite *haute cuisine*, but would please most British people", was one slightly back-handed compliment this year. Our inspector, who much appreciated the atmosphere of the house, called the cooking well-intentioned but amateurish and the ingredients not consistently good. She summed up – and so probably would most of the Brabners' guests: "It's a place where you enjoy yourself very much and the food is not too bad."

Open Mid-Mar–end Dec.
Rooms 19 double (5 also let as singles) – 16 with bath, 3 with shower, all with radio and tea-making facilities; baby-listening by arrangement.
Facilities 2 sitting rooms, bar, TV room, billiard room, sun room, dining room. 29-acre grounds with gardens, croquet lawn, putting green, golf practice net, hard tennis court (£2 per hour). Brown trout and salmon fishing in river Usk; bird-watching, riding, boating, squash and golf nearby.
Location 3½ m W of Crickhowell, 1 m S of A40. Turn left at "Gliffaes" sign.
Restrictions Not suitable for ♿. No dogs in hotel (kennels available).
Credit cards All major cards accepted.
Terms B&B £20.50–£28; dinner, B&B £30.50–£38; full board £33.50–£42. Set lunch £6.80, dinner £10. Weekly rates.
Service/tipping: "Service is an integral part of the bill. It is 10%. Total hours worked are calculated and then a rate per hour calculated and that amount shared every month. If a tip is offered it is gracefully refused; if pressed it is accepted and handed in to be shared."

EGLWYSFACH Dyfed — Map 1

Ynyshir Hall Country House Hotel
Eglwysfach
Machynlleth SY20 8TA

Tel Glandyfi (065 474) 209

Lovely 16th-century manor house in specially choice 11-acre garden on southern shore of Dovey estuary and backed by the famous Ynyshir Bird Reserve. Was in earlier editions and came out after ownership changed. New owners, Jane and Richard Allison, have done extensive refurbishing. Recent reports speak warmly of the hotel's comforts and cooking. Open Mar–mid-Nov. 9 rooms, 8 with private facilities. B&B £17–£26. Set lunch £9.50, dinner £11.50. More reports would be welcome.

> Wherever possible, we have quoted prices per room. Not all hotels, especially in Britain, are prepared to quote tariffs in this way. In these cases, we have given prices per person, indicating the range of prices – the lowest is likely to be for one person sharing a double room out of season, the highest for a single room in high season.

GLAN CONWY Gwynedd — Map 4

The Old Rectory — *Tel* Glan Conwy (049 268) 611
Llanrwst Road
Glan Conwy LL28 5LF

In secluded grounds, with views over the river Conwy estuary to Conwy Castle to Snowdonia, *The Old Rectory* is a family house – a member of the Wolsey Lodge consortium – with only three guest bedrooms. The house is Georgian in origin, furnished with antiques, and Wendy and Michael Vaughan have worked hard on restoring and extending it. Welsh lamb and salmon from the Conwy figure on the three-course dinners eaten communally. A convenient stop on the way to the Holyhead or Liverpool crossing to Ireland. In our nominating report last year, we quoted a Californian visitor's commendation of "this near perfect small inn". He was of course using "inn" in the American sense. A visitor this year calls it "a small gracious house with a beautiful well-equipped bedroom . . . superb dinner . . . excellent breakfast". (*Barbara M Wooldridge*)

Open 1 Feb–18 Dec.
Rooms 3 double – all with bath and/or shower, and TV; telephone on request.
Facilities Lounge, dining room. 2-acre grounds. Sea with safe bathing 2 m; fishing in trout lakes 6 m; golf, riding, sailing nearby.
Restrictions Not suitable for ♿. No children under 10 except at hotel's discretion. No dogs. No smoking in bedrooms or dining room.
Credit cards None accepted.
Terms (Not VAT-registered. No service charge) B&B £19.50–£29.50, Set dinner £13.90. 50% reduction for children sharing parents' room.

HARLECH Gwynedd — Map 4

Castle Cottage Hotel [GFG] — *Tel* Harlech (0766) 780479
Pen Llech, Harlech LL46 2YL

*A family-run hotel in one of Harlech's oldest houses, 300 yards from the castle, run by Jim and Betty Yuill. Jim Yuill is chef/*patron *and his eclectic cooking and discerning wine list have been recognised elsewhere. A nominator speaks warmly of the accommodation too, and the friendly welcome. 6 rooms, 4 with bath and shower. B&B £14–£15. Set lunch £10, dinner £14. More reports please.*

LLANARTHNEY Dyfed — Map 1

Golden Grove Arms Hotel [GFG] — *Tel* Dryslwyn (055 84) 551
Llanarthney
Nr Carmarthen SA32 8JU

An old coaching inn on the back road between Llandeilo and Carmarthen in the Tywi valley. Stunning views. Has feel of inexpensive family-run hotel in rural France – accommodation clean and comfortable but fairly functional and can be pokey and tatty. Bar popular as local pub, but dining room something else: outstandingly good for area – fish specially recommended. Owner admits "nothing much to do except fishing, shooting, riding, sailing, walking, eating and drinking". Open 30 Jan–10 Jan. 8 rooms, 2 with bath, 4 with shower. B&B £15–£25. Full alc £16. In italics as new enterprise, needing more feedback.

LLANBERIS Gwynedd — Map 4

Pen-y-Gwryd Hotel — *Tel* Llanberis (0286) 870211
Nantgwynant LL55 4NT

A newcomer to the Guide, but famous in the annals of mountaineering. It has been an inn since the early 1800s, and stands in the middle of the Snowdonia National Park, ideally situated for climbers, walkers and fishermen. It was used as a training base for the successful 1953 Everest team. Many momentos of this and other expeditions can be seen in the smoke room (residents' oak-panelled bar) and in the Everest room (the public bar), where many famous people have signed the ceiling. Bedrooms are small and old-fashioned and one has a special Victorian bathroom with a canopied bath containing sprays and a shower. In the evening, the owner tells us, coffee is served in the smoke room or residents' lounge where "the atmosphere generates good conversation, and lasting friendships are formed". Our nominator, *Simon Winchester*, writes: "It is, I realise, a rather basic place. The charms of John Hunt's string vest and Sherpa Tensing's oxygen tank may not outweigh the frayed carpets and noisy plumbing. But I love the place, regard it as a second home, and look upon all who stay there as friends, even before I meet them. The Briggs family have been running it for years, and it is without a doubt, a truly *good* hotel." What else? Wonderful views; if you want to swim you can – in a natural mountain pool; the food is good, of the steak-and-kidney pie, jam roly-poly variety; and the hotel bakes its own bread.

Open All year except 1 Nov–29 Dec; weekends only Jan and Feb.
Rooms 17 double (1 on ground floor across courtyard, with bath) , 3 single.
Facilities 3 public rooms for non-residents, residents-only bar, lounge, games room, dining room. 1 acre grounds with natural swimming pool; lake and river fishing.
Location From Nantgwynant signposted to Pen-y-Gwryd.
Restriction No dogs in restaurant.
Credit cards None accepted.
Terms (No service charge) B&B £13 (£1 extra with bath), double £14–£26. Bar lunches from £1.60; set dinner £9.50. Reduced rates and special meals for children.
Service/tipping: "There is a staff gratuity box available only if guests wish to contribute to the staff. They usually like to!"

LLANDDERFEL Gwynedd — Map 4

Palé Hall Hotel [GFG] — *Tel* Llandderfel (067 83) 285
Llandderfel, Bala LL23 7PS

A grand Victorian edifice, built with no expense spared by a Scottish building engineer in 1870. Queen Victoria stayed here, and it certainly looks regal: her bathroom is at your disposal, and the lavish bedroom adjoining with an antique half-tester bed. The daunting exterior belies the warmth of the panelled hall, and the elegance of painted ceilings, tall windows, marble fireplaces, and lavishly furnished bedrooms, one with a round bed and jacuzzi behind a gauzy curtain. The original kitchen range is still there in the breakfast and coffee kitchen, if without dawn-rising scullery maids to tend it. The menu is of a piece with the sophistication of the setting. But, oddly, no recent reports.

Open All year.
Rooms 2 suites, 14 double, 1 single – all with bath, shower, telephone, radio, TV; 2 with private jacuzzi.
Facilities Lift. Hall/lounge, boudoir (non-smoking lounge), bar, 2 restaurants; ballroom/conference room; gymnasium, sauna, solarium. 16-acre grounds, heated plunge pool-jacuzzi, near river Dee with salmon and coarse fishing; sailing, canoeing, rowing and windsurfing on Lake Bala.
Location 4 m from Bala village.
Restriction No dogs in bedrooms or public rooms.
Credit cards All major cards accepted.
Terms (Service at guests' discretion) B&B: single £35–£45, double & suite £55–£75; dinner, B&B single £50–£65, double & suite £85–£95. Set lunch £8.50, dinner £15; full alc £12.50. Vegetarian meals available. Winter breaks; special musical weekends, gourmet weekends in winter; 4-day Christmas package. Reduced rates for children; special meals.

LLANDRILLO Clwyd — Map 4

Tyddyn Llan Country House Hotel and Restaurant [GFG] — *Tel* Llandrillo (049 084) 264
Llandrillo
Nr Corwen LL21 0ST

Peter and Bridget Kindred, both ex-television, continue to improve on their lovingly restored 18th-century grey stone country house. All bedrooms now have their own bath or shower though they are still refreshingly free of those cluttering extras which bump up the prices in so many establishments. And, despairing of finding furniture that went with the period of the house, Peter Kindred has been creating new designs in mahogany and oak which are being made by local craftsmen. The Kindreds have made an Elizabethan-style kitchen garden where vegetables and herbs are grown for the restaurant, an agreeable room with well-spaced tables, French windows onto the garden and log fires in cold weather. Mrs Kindred believes in keeping her food simple, using fresh ingredients and finding the right herbs and spices to bring out flavours. "Old-fashioned hospitality in well-designed surroundings, imaginative food . . . Exactly the kind of hotel that deserves all the encouragement it can get." (*Miss VA Creed; also Heather Sharland, and others*)

Open All year except Feb. Restaurant closed to non-residents Mon and Tue 1 Nov–1 Mar.
Rooms 9 double – all with bath and/or shower, radio and tea-making facilities.
Facilities Lounge with TV, bar, dining room; drying room. 3-acre grounds. River fishing nearby; windsurfing and sailing on Bala Lake 8 miles.
Location Through Corwen on A5 take B4401 to Llandrillo.
Restrictions Not suitable for ♿. Small dogs by arrangement, not in public rooms.
Credit cards Access, Visa.
Terms (No service charge) B&B single £25, double £43; dinner, B&B single £32–£35, double £57–£64. Set lunch £3–£7.50, dinner £10.50–£12. Mini-breaks (2 or more nights) all year except July–Sept and bank holidays; painting courses; wine-tasting weekends; Christmas and New Year house parties. Reduced rates and special meals for children.
Service/tipping: "Guests are not expected to tip the staff, but if they wish to do so it will be equally divided amongst them."

> Hotels are dropped if we lack positive feedback. If you can endorse an entry, please do so.

LLANDUDNO Gwynedd Map 4

Bodysgallen Hall [GFG] *Tel* Deganwy (0492) 84466
Llandudno LL30 1RS *Telex* 617163 HHH

César awarded for a notable contribution to architectural conservation and for first-rate hotel management

"The most spectacular hotel any of us (we were a party of four) had ever stayed in. Our room was very large, complete with king-size bed, ginger cookies, Malvern water, welcoming champagne, views over the rose garden nearby Conwy Castle and Snowdonia. The food was excellent. We felt we had left the hustle of life and retired to a glorious relaxed country manor. A perfect visit, worth the five-and-a-half-hour drive from London." (*Deborah Kelly*)

For those who collect country house hotels, *Bodysgallen* is a must. It is a building rich in architectural and horticultural delights: a 13th-century tower, splendid Elizabethan and Jacobean rooms with oak panelling, great fireplaces, mullioned windows, a 17th-century knot garden, an 18th-century walled rose garden – and many other atmospheric features too numerous to mention here. Snowdonia is a handsome backdrop. Fine castles and gardens abound in the neighbourhood. Since it opened its doors to paying guests six years ago, it has been attracting a plethora of compliments similar to the above – alike for the palpable creature comforts of the house and for the attentive service. This year has been no exception. The success of *Bodysgallen* is the more remarkable in that it isn't an owner-occupied establishment, but is run by a private company, Historic House Hotels, dedicated to restoring and giving the kiss of life to buildings of architectural merit. Renovating decayed houses is one kind of operation, running a country house hotel is quite another: to be succeeding on both counts is a considerable achievement.

Open All year.
Rooms 9 cottage suites, 18 double, 1 single – all with bath and/or shower, radio, telephone and TV; tea-making facilities in cottages. 2 cottages with ramps for ♿.
Facilities Hall, drawing room, dining room, library, cocktail bar; conference centre. 47-acre gardens and parkland with tennis and croquet. Sandy beaches 2 m. River and sea fishing nearby.
Location Off A470 1½ m S of town centre; parking. (Guests coming by train can be met at Llandudno Junction.)
Restrictions No children under 8. No dogs except in cottages and parkland.
Credit cards All major cards accepted.
Terms B&B: single £55–£75, double £65–£110, suite £95–£120, dinner, B&B: single £77.50–£92.50, double £105–£145, suite £135–£155. Set lunch £9.30, dinner £18.50 (excluding 10% service charge); full alc £30. Out of season champagne breaks; special interest weekends; Christmas packages. 10% discount for stays of 7 nights or more.

The St Tudno Hotel [GFG] *Tel* Llandudno (0492) 74411
North Parade
Llandudno LL30 2LP

César awarded in 1987 for best seaside resort hotel

"I was pleased to see the César award to this hotel and decided to spend a few days at the *St Tudno* to enjoy all that it offers. We were not disappointed in any way. Mr and Mrs Bland are not the sort of proprietors to rest on their laurels, the food and service were excellent and there were many little touches that mean so much for a good stay, for example a different shape of toast for me as I was having a boiled egg for breakfast. I can entirely confirm the 1987 entry." (*Richard Whiting*) We were glad to get this endorsement for the *St Tudno* as every other fulsome letter we received in 1987 was written on a photostatted copy of our report form on page 799 or else on page 82 of the *Good Food Guide*; clearly the hotel had been handing them out to consenting departing guests. We should be glad, in 1988, to receive genuine unsolicited reports on this smart modern seafront hotel (though much of the interior decor is Victorian in character) opposite Llandudno's pier and ornamental gardens, which boasts of its connection with Alice Liddell, the original "Alice in Wonderland"; she stayed here in what was then a private house in 1861, at the age of eight. Meanwhile we see no reason to retract on the compliments we paid it last year based on genuine commendations.

Open Mid-Jan–end Dec.
Rooms 1 suite, 19 double, 1 single – all with bath and/or shower, direct-dial telephone, radio, TV, tea-making facilities and fridge; baby-listening by telephone. 1 ground-floor double room with shower.
Facilities Lift. Non-smoking residents' sitting room, coffee lounge, bar lounge, restaurant; indoor heated swimming pool; small front patio. Hotel is on promenade; safe sandy beaches, pier, boat rides, fishing, sailing, wind-surfing; 3 golf courses close by.
Location Central, opposite pier. Free promenade parking and small carpark at rear of hotel.
Restrictions Not suitable for ♿. No dogs.
Credit cards Access, Visa.
Terms (No service charge) B&B: single £28–£45, double £40–£75. Set Sun lunch £8.50, dinner £15.50. Long and short breaks all year; winter weekend breaks. Reductions according to age for children sharing parents' room; high tea.
Service/tipping: "We do feel that if customers enjoy kind, considerate and personalised service and feel inclined to tip, that they should be allowed to do so. As hoteliers, we would never dream of adding a service charge automatically."

LLANRWST Gwynedd — Map 4

Meadowsweet Hotel [GFG] — *Tel* Llanrwst (0492) 640732
Station Road, Llanrwst LL26 0DS

It is now seven years since John and Joy Evans turned their Victorian home on the outskirts of this tiny market town from a first-class restaurant into a small hotel. With the river Conwy 200 yards away, and Snowdonia a few miles up the road, *Meadowsweet* would make a good base for a fishing or walking holiday or as a centre for exploring "the ravishing landscape and history-rich towns of northwest Wales"; it is also a handy stopover for the Anglesey–Ireland ferries. Don't be put off by the immediate environs of the house or the fact that it is right on the road; the distant prospects – of meadows and mountains – greatly please, and traffic dies away during the night.

Michelin still dubbs *Meadowsweet* a restaurant-with-rooms, and we think this is probably correct. The restaurant scores high with nearly all our correspondents, and readers approve of the new set menu options – a regular three-courser, included in the dinner, B&B rates, at £14.50 and a five-course gastronomic treat at £22 [1987 prices]. The wine list, too, comes in for much awed appreciation ("it takes ten minutes just to read"). The accommodation side gets some applause too: "The most beautifully decorated and furnished hotel I have ever stayed in" was one unrestrained report. But others have been less impressed, mentioning a guest-housey feel to stairs and entrance, occasional sloppy service and a cramped room. Rooms at the front, we gather, are to be preferred. (*G Fownes Norman; also Professor and Mrs Frank Harrison, Dudley Wilson, Timothy Burrill, and others*)

Open All year.
Rooms 10 double – all with shower, direct-dial telephone, TV and baby-listening.
Facilities Bar lounge, residents' lounge, both with log fire, dining room. Salmon/trout fishing, horse-riding, golf within easy reach; sea 10 m.
Location ¼ m N of town centre on A470. Car park. (Rooms at back are quietest.)
Restrictions Not suitable for ♿. No dogs in dining room. No smoking in dining room.
Credit cards Access, Amex, Visa.
Terms (No service charge) B&B £17–£28; dinner, B&B £32–£37. Set dinner £15.50 and £24; full alc £20. Special rates for stays of 2 days or more; Christmas and New Year house parties; gourmet weekends for parties of 10 couples. Children sharing parents' room charged for meals only.
Service/tipping: "Tipping optional. Anything left is shared amongst all staff."

LLANYCHAER Dyfed — Map 1

Penlan Oleu — *Tel* Puncheston (034 882) 314
Llanychaer, Fishguard SA65 9TL

Penlan Oleu (the name means "Light above the Church") is a converted Welsh farmhouse. It is five miles above and behind Fishguard, 800 feet up in the Preseli Hills; be warned: winds can howl in these hills. On a clear day, you can look across Fishguard Bay to the mountains of Wicklow. No telephones, no TV, no radio. It may be used as a staging post for the Fishguard ferry, but also makes a fine centre for a walking holiday; the Pembrokeshire coastal path is four miles away. "Don't expect anything very sophisticated in the decor," we wrote last year. Andrew Stuart-Lyon tells us that, while all rooms have been redecorated and all beds re-mattressed, the plain decor is a deliberate wish to keep the house simple and uncluttered. Ruth Stuart-Lyon is the cook: all herbs and many of the vegetables are home-grown, ditto the eggs and goat-milk products; fish is bought locally direct from the boats. "Mrs Stuart-Lyon is a professional cook of high and original standard. In 14 days she never had an 'off' day or let her perfection slip. Every meal was freshly cooked and beautifully presented. Husband and wife are an excellent team. Absolute cleanliness, organisation and friendliness; and wonderful value for money." (*Mona Bourn*)

Open All year except Christmas and Boxing Day.
Rooms 4 double, 1 single – 3 with bath, 2 with shower, all with tea-making facilities. 1 in annexe. 3 ground-floor rooms.
Facilities Lounge, bar, garden room in summer, dining room. Several acres of garden. 4 m from sea and Pembrokeshire coastal path. Safe bathing and sandy beaches 4½ and 6 m.
Location Leave Fishguard by B4313 (signposted Maenclochog). Through Llanychaer beyond Bridge End Inn for 2 m. At top take road to Puncheston. Hotel drive well signposted off this road.

Restrictions No children under 11. Dogs in cars only, and must be kept on a lead.
Credit cards Access, Visa.
Terms (No service charge) B&B £16; dinner, B&B £28. Full alc £10–£12.

MAENAN Gwynedd — Map 4

Maenan Abbey Hotel — *Tel* Dolgarrog (049 269) 247
Maenan, Llanrwst LL26 0UL

Tipped off by a much-travelled industrial relations adviser, we asked an inspector to try out this early Victorian country house hotel in the Conwy Valley and on the edge of Snowdonia, run by Michael Kerridge (ex-British Airways chief steward) and wife Cheryl. The brochure speaks about "olde worlde charm", but don't be put off: our inspector found plenty of contemporary appeal. "The grounds are imposing with huge topiary yews clipped in the shape of chess pawns, tall cedars, a huge copper beach, a safe garden for children with swings and a super log play house with chute. Well-spaced picnic tables on the terraces. Most bedrooms are set round a gallery looking down into the hall, cosy with log fires (which are reset and glowing in time for breakfast). The back lounge is pretty with a red Turkish carpet and much greenery from healthy potted plants no doubt from Bodnant Gardens just down the road. The management is young, unstuffy but very much on the ball. No stinting anywhere. Our room had fresh Laura Ashley-type bedspreads, lamps, and draped cradle-style swags over the bed. Lots of big fluffy towels. Quality soap and Twining's tea and coffee; thermos jug, hairdrier etc. Pink and maroon dining room. Imaginative very reasonable dinner menu with huge servings – a challenge suitable for heavy walkers. A sweet trolley groaning with lemon cheese cakes, fresh fruit salad, raspberry charlotte and *loads* of cream. Very good coffee. Comprehensive wine list. House wine fades a bit. First class beer. The breakfast was one of the best we've had in years. Excellent service. You get the feeling that if you ask for something it will be attended to gladly. The atmosphere in the hotel is relaxed; the Kerridge family very friendly. The young master of the house, just four weeks old, was proudly displayed to all. A very nice place to stay indeed. Good for children because of the tolerant management. Welsh singing in the bar Saturday nights. Only complaint: a very thin partition meant much disturbance from neighbours' snores."

Open All year.
Rooms 1 suite, 10 double, 1 single – all with bath and/or shower, telephone, radio, TV, tea-making facilities and baby-listening.
Facilities Lounge, coffee lounge, 2 bars, restaurant; Welsh singing in public bar on Sat; occasional dinner-dances. 7½-acre grounds with childrens' play area. Fishing rights on river Conwy nearby.
Location On A470 2½ m N of Llanrwst.
Restrictions Not suitable for ♿. No dogs in areas where food is served.
Credit cards All major cards accepted.
Terms B&B: single £22–£34, double £34–£44; dinner, B&B: single £31–£36, double £54–£64. Set lunch £6.95, dinner £9.95; full alc £18. Bar lunches and suppers. Bargain breaks off season;Christmas breaks.
Service/tipping: "Tipping not encouraged. Anything given is divided every couple of months between all staff."

> We don't lack *Michelin*-rosetted hotels in France but would be glad of more nominations at the more modest end of the price scale.

NEWPORT Dyfed — Map 1

Cnapan Country House for Guests [GFG] — *Tel* Newport (0239) 820575
East Street, Newport SA42 0WF

A friendly place, more than a guest house, and less than an hotel, *Cnapan Country House for Guests* is a pink-washed corner house owned and run by John and Eluned Lloyd, and their daughter and son-in-law, Judith and Michael Cooper. "One of the finest listed houses in Newport," is their brochure's proud claim. A Welsh dresser crowded with family treasures stands in the hall, and the five bedrooms are comfortably cluttered with whatever a guest might want, bunk-beds in one for children. There is a woodburning stove to sit beside if the weather does not tempt you out, with plenty of books to read, though you can be exploring the rock pools on Parrog beach after a ten-minute walk, or building castles on Newport Sands in 15. Inland there is the Nevern Estuary with wooded walks, a Celtic Cross, the blue-stone ridge of the Preseli Hills, source of some of the stones of Stonehenge. Mother and daughter cook the meals: plenty of choice for the main course, including vegetarian dishes. Bread is home-made, portions are generous, breakfasts serve-yourself-as-much-as-you-like. Everywhere spotlessly clean, plenty of hot water, and first names all round. More reports please.

Open All year except Christmas and Feb. Restaurant closed Tue.
Rooms 5 double – all with shower, mono TV, tea-making facilities and baby-listening.
Facilities Residents' sitting room with TV, bar, dining room. Small garden. 10 minutes' walk to estuary and sea; small yachting rock beach and large sandy beach.
Location Central (traffic light at night). Parking.
Restrictions Not suitable for ♿. No dogs.
Credit cards Access, Visa.
Terms (No service charge) B&B £15; dinner, B&B £23; £5 surcharge for single occupancy. Set dinner £14.50 to non-residents. Reduced rates and high teas for children.
Service/tipping: "Gratuities at customers' discretion; divided amongst staff."

REYNOLDSTON West Glamorgan — Map 1

Fairyhill Country House Hotel and Restaurant [GFG] — *Tel* Gower (0792) 390139
Reynoldston, Gower
Swansea SA3 1BS

Five minutes inland from the Gower peninsula's lovely beaches, where the cockle pickers still go out with cart and pony, *Fairyhill*, a new entry this year, stands in 24 acres of park and woodland, with half a mile of trout stream meandering through its grounds. John and Midge Frayne had retired from a shoe business when they saw a derelict mansion in their village, and decided to buy it and turn it into a hotel. The work is still not over, and the wild ponies get into the gardens, defying efforts at order. But the main part of the house is in use, simply furnished, with good paintings. "The owners bought the house to restore it and live in it, so the atmosphere is that of a house and home first, and of a hotel second. It is not often that a guest is welcome to walk into the kitchens and talk to the cook. The public rooms are gracious, and like the bedrooms furnished to match the style of the house. The beds were very comfortable, and of the best quality. Our bathroom's fittings would have been a Victorian's pride – and they worked . . . The young cook, Kate Spring, is a 'natural'." (*JEJ Hayward; also Heather Sharland, DS, and others.*) Some criticisms among the commendations: bedroom furnishings a bit sparse, poor bathroom fittings, and intrusive muzak in restaurant.

Open All year except Boxing Day–New Year's Eve and possibly first week of Jan. Meals only Christmas and New Year.
Rooms 11 double, 1 single – 2 with bath and shower, 10 with shower, all with telephone, TV and tea-making facilities. 3 in coach house.
Facilities Drawing room, bar, 2 dining rooms, conservatory; conference facilities. 24 acres park and woodland, stream and lake. 2 m from sea; golf, sailing, windsurfing, riding, hang-gliding and nature walks nearby.
Location At traffic lights in Gowerton take B4295 North Gower coastal road through Penclawdd, Crofty and Oldwalls. Pass *Greyhound Inn* on left; 1 m to Fairyhill.
Restrictions Not suitable for ♿. No children under 12 in restaurant at night. No dogs in public rooms.
Credit cards All major cards accepted.
Terms B&B : single £45, double £55. Sunday lunch £9.95; full alc £20. Reduced rates for child sharing parents' room; special meals on request.
Service/tipping: "Our prices do not include service. I feel it's a cheek to include it. Some people get pleasure from leaving tips for good service. If anyone feels strongly against it they do not have to leave anything. I object strongly to restaurants that add service."

ST-BRIDE'S-SUPER-ELY South Glamorgan — Map 1

Guest House St-y-Nyll — *Tel* Cowbridge (0446) 760209
St-Bride's-super-Ely CF5 6EZ

Neo-Georgian country guest house overlooking Vale of Glamorgan with magnificent trees in 14-acre wild garden. Nominators who only took B&B found it "delightful" and "a most useful find" in a part of Wales lacking in such havens. 6 rooms (no private facilities). B&B £15-£20. Set dinner £10-£12.50. More reports welcome, including on St-y-Nyll's *meals.*

TALSARNAU Gwynedd — Map 4

Hotel Maes-y-Neuadd [GFG] — *Tel* Harlech (0766) 780200
Talsarnau LL47 6YA

This beautiful old house, *Maes-y-Neuadd* (pronounced Mice-er-Nayeth), is tucked into a wooded hillside smothered in rhododendrons, looking out across Snowdonia National Park. It dates originally from the 14th century, though it was enlarged in the 16th and 17th centuries, and the beamed bar has links with Cromwell and the Civil War. Seven-and-a-half acres of lawns, orchards and paddocks surround it, the renowned Royal St David's golf course is only three miles away, and Portmeirion village and magnificent Harlech castle nearby. The owners, the Horsfall and Slatter families, respectively a nurse, an engineer, an accountant and an architect, have spent several years refurbishing and restoring this attractive grey granite and slate mansion. They have furnished it with good antique and modern furniture, the plain clear colour-washed walls show the pretty patterned chintzes to advantage: there is a log fire in the dining room. When we dropped their entry for a year after ambivalent reports on rooms and cooking, indignant former guests leapt to their defence, leading us to reinstate them last year. This year's crop of reports supports that decision. "The food is superb and the treatment of guests outstandingly good. The owners have done everything possible to make a visit delightful and memorable." (*JG Dumoulin*) "An extremely comfortable well-fed and well-looked-after stay: our second visit this year. A lovely house, delightful owners, excellent food – what more could one want?" (*Major WF Garnett; also Alan Johnston, Ruth Warner*)

Open All year except 3 Jan–4 Feb. Lunch by reservation only Mon–Sat.
Rooms 1 suite, 12 double, 3 single – 14 with bath and/or shower, all with direct-dial telephone and TV. 1 ground-floor double room suitable for ♿. 1 suite in Coach House and 1 detached cottage.
Facilities Lounge, bar, restaurant; small conference/private dining room. 8-acre grounds with sun terraces, landscaped lawns, orchard and paddock. Sea 3 m with safe bathing from sandy beaches; Royal St David's golf course 3 m; riding, sailing, climbing nearby; fishing in rivers and lakes.
Location Off B4573, 3 m NE of Harlech. Hotel sign at junction.
Restrictions No children under 7. Dogs at management's discretion, not in public rooms.
Credit cards Access, Visa.
Terms (No service charge) B&B: single £26–£28, double £56–£66, suite £70–£75; dinner, B&B: (2 nights min) single £31–£38, double £76–£88, suite £90–£96. Set lunch £9.50, dinner £15. 2-day breaks Nov–Mar; 3-day Christmas house party. Children under 12 sharing parents' room half price.
Service/tipping: "No service charge. Tips not solicited in any way. If a guest does add a gratuity it is divided among restaurant and kitchen staff."

TALYLLYN Gwynedd — Map 4

Minffordd Hotel [GFG] — *Tel* Corris (065 473) 665
Talyllyn, Tywyn LL36 9AJ

The footpath to the top of Cader Idris starts by the front gate, Talyllyn lake is half a mile away, and some of Wales' most beautiful scenery lies all round the *Minffordd Hotel*, a former coaching inn. Mr and Mrs Bernard Pickles have owned the hotel for ten years now, and their son Jonathan is the chef. Here is a characteristic letter from a grateful regular: "My husband and I have recently spent a very happy week at this hotel, our eighth visit since 1981. So lovely to return to such a genuinely warm welcome from everyone. The Pickles are a delightful family, and the friendly atmosphere is radiated to all their guests. A great deal of time and thought is given to preparing and attractively serving food, which continues to be of a very high standard and delicious. There are several additional improvements for the convenience and comfort of guests, which are much appreciated by us both, especially my husband who is disabled." (*K Webster*) "We had a marvellous time. A place that does all the things the mega-stars of your Guide do, and more." (*David Taylor*)

Open Mar–Nov inclusive and Christmas; restaurant closed lunchtime, also Sun and Mon.
Rooms 6 double, 1 single – all with bath and/or shower, telephone, radio and tea-making facilities. 2 ground-floor rooms.
Facilities Sun lounge, lounge bar, dining room; laundry facilities. 3 acres of paddock and garden; the peak of Cader Idris rises from here, path to summit 100 yards away; river at the bottom of paddock; Talyllyn lake ½ m; sea 12 m; lake fishing by arrangement.

Location 12 m SW of Dolgellau. At junction of A487 with B4405.
Restrictions Not suitable for severely ♿. No children under 3. No dogs. No smoking in dining room.
Credit cards Access, Diners, Visa.
Terms (No service charge) B&B £21–£31; dinner, B&B £33–£43. Set dinner £11.95; packed lunches on request. Off-season breaks; reductions for stays over 2 nights June–Sept; Christmas package. 1-night bookings sometimes refused in high season. Children under 12 sharing parents' room free, otherwise 25% reduction; special meals on request.
Service/tipping: "Service is free and part of the caring family-run atmosphere, which tries to make guests feel wanted. Tips are not part of our arrangements."

Scotland

THE ROMAN CAMP HOTEL, CALLANDER

ACHARACLE see GLENCRIPESDALE **Map 5**

ACHILTIBUIE Highland **Map 5**

Summer Isles Hotel [GFG] *Tel* Achiltibuie (085 482) 282
Achiltibuie by Ullapool
Ross and Cromarty IV26 2YG

The road to the *Summer Isles* is in itself quite an experience, single track and following the outline of the rugged countryside, here climbing up high, there down low beside a dark brown peaty loch. All well worth the effort for the marvellous views you will have over the sea, and a great scattering of little islands, once you arrive at what is one of Britain's most remote hotels. A splendid base for bird-watchers, walkers and fishermen (the hotel holds fishing rights in the area), its comforts previously were modest, except in the dining room. But this year there have been changes. Mark Irvine and Geraldine Deller, who have been running the hotel for the past two years, have married, and bought it from Mark's father Robert, who now concentrates on growing produce in his hydroponicum. A programme of refurbishment has begun. The public bar has been separated from the resident's bar, bathrooms have been added to bedrooms in the main hotel, new chairs bought for a totally redecorated dining room, and furniture generally revamped. Two bedrooms have been furnished in antique pine, more will follow as business permits. First reports on the new Irvine régime are wholly favourable: less idiosyncratic maybe, but the spirit of the place for *Summer Isles* addicts is still intact and the cooking better than ever – specially commended the nursery puds among the desserts, which "evoke sheer greed in almost all guests". (*Margaret Box*)

Open Easter–Oct.
Rooms Loghouse suite (available for self-catering Oct–May – sleeps 2-5), 12 double, 1 single – 12 with bath and/or shower. Suite and 7 rooms in annexe. Ground-floor rooms.
Facilities 2 lounges (1 with TV), 2 bars, dining room, restaurant; hydroponicum – daily lecture tours. Sea 50 yards, sandy beach 4 m; loch fishing, walking nearby.
Location 10 m N of Ullapool; take twisting single-track road that skirts lochs Lurgain, Badagyle and Oscaig. After 15 m you reach Achiltibuie. Hotel is a few hundred yards past the post office.
Restrictions Not suitable for ♿. No children under 8, except in Loghouse. No dogs in public rooms.
Credit cards None accepted.
Terms B&B: single £17, double £40–£56, suite £30–£60. Set dinner £19. 10% reduction for stays of 6 nights or more.
Service/tipping: "We make it very clear that service is included in all prices and do not expect our customers to tip. However, if guests insist on showing their special appreciation, the money is divided evenly between all members of staff."

AMULREE Tayside — Map 5

Amulree Hotel — *Tel* Amulree (03505) 218
Sma' Glen, By Dunkeld
Perthshire PH8 0EF

Martin and Cecily Hill abandoned merchant banking to move family and two horses 500 miles to this 18th century droving inn at a river crossing. Having been first a "King's House" on a Wade Military Road, then a coaching inn, it now gives a friendly welcome to passing travellers and resident walkers, fishermen, and tourists wishing to take advantage of the lovely unspoilt countryside. A newcomer last year, it has received strong endorsement since from a correspondent who particularly appreciated the courtesy with which the demands of an eight-month-old daughter were met. "An unpretentious but very comfortable and warm family hotel. Splendid food, especially dishes made from local fish. Will return for more walking!" (*JN Clogstoun-Willmott*)

Open 1–15 Jan, 1 Mar–31 Dec. Closed Christmas Day.
Rooms 12 double, 1 single – 4 with bath and/or shower, all with tea-making facilities.
Facilities Residents' lounge, lounge bar, public bar with games room, 2 dining rooms; occasional ceilidhs. 4-acre grounds along river Braan with fishing for trout and pike (free to residents). Golf, riding, walking nearby.
Location On A822 10 m SW of Dunkeld. (Road is quiet at night.) Parking.
Restrictions Not suitable for ♿. No dogs in bars or dining rooms.
Credit cards All major cards accepted.

Terms (No service charge) B&B £15 (with continental breakfast £2 less). Set dinner £9.50–£10. Teas, high teas and bar meals available. Reductions for stays of more than 1 night; weekly rates. Reduced rates and special meals for children; no charge for under-2s.
Service/tipping: "A service charge is not included. Tips go into a pool which is shared among the staff."

ARDVASAR Skye, Highland — Map 5

Ardvasar Hotel — *Tel* Ardvasar (047 14) 223
Ardvasar, Sleat, Isle of Skye
Inverness-shire IV45 8RS

An unassuming early 18th-century coaching inn, a mile from the Armadale Ferry on the Isle of Skye. Some bedrooms have views over the Sound of Sleat to the mainland. Owners Bill and Gretta Fowler describe the *Ardvasar* as, "a small cosy country inn, with truly personal caring service, in warm unpretentious surroundings". More than one reader felt "unpretentious" was a euphemism – that both the accommodation and the cooking lacked character. There may be nothing special about the decor, but most visitors have appreciated the hotel's hospitality: "Welcoming hosts, lovely staff, comfortable accommodation, and some catalyst that allows the disparate guests to enjoy each others' company. All this and Skye's superb scenery too!" (*AJ Phillipson; also Jack Waddell, Mary Lawrence*)

Open All year except Christmas and New Year.
Rooms 1 suite, 8 double, 2 single – 8 with bath and/or shower, all with tea-making facilities; 2 with TV; radio and baby-listening on request.
Facilities Lounge, TV lounge, 2 bars, dining room. Small garden. Safe but rocky bathing ½ m.
Location In tiny village. 2 ferries to island, Kyle of Lochalsh–Kyleakin and Mallaig–Armadale, operate all year round but latter will not take vehicles in winter. Also car ferry Glenelg–Kylerhea in summer.
Restrictions Not suitable for ♿. Dogs at discretion of the management.
Credit card Visa.
Terms (No service charge) B&B: single, £15–£19, double £28–£38, suite £45; dinner, B&B: single £28–£31, double £54–£63, suite £69. Set lunch £7, dinner £13.15; full alc £20; picnic lunches and bar meals available. 3-day breaks Feb to Apr. Reduced rates for children sharing parents' room; special meals.
Service/tipping: "We are pleased when anyone wishes to give, as we have very good staff and it is nice to see that guests also think so!"

ARISAIG Highland — Map 5

Arisaig Hotel [GFG] — *Tel* Arisaig (068 75) 210
Arisaig, Inverness-shire
PH39 4NH

A Jacobite coaching inn on the seashore in Arisaig village, on the Road to the Isles. It is a small family enterprise, with George and Janice Stewart assisted by their son sharing nearly all the work between them, and the tariff is accordingly modest. "Warm friendly hosts and all the staff delightful. We had an excellent week's family holiday." "Public rooms extremely comfortable and bedrooms and general facilities excellent. Food was excellent – beautiful quality fish and meat and everything

cooked to perfection. Delicious sauces and home-made soups." "Huge breakfast, I felt I was eating the profits. Food in the bar excellent: fish and chips like Granny used to make." "Good selection of medium-priced wines, all at the right temperature." The only criticism came from a reader who felt the setting was not what he had been led to expect by the brochure and our description. Last year we commented that some of the rooms could do with renovation; the Stewarts tell us that extensive redecoration has been done during the winter and more improvements are planned. (*CJH Kelnar, Ann Meek, C Robertson, JE Goodford, and others*)
Note: Do not confuse with *Arisaig House*, the sophisticated country house hotel three miles from village.

Open Apr–end Oct.
Rooms 4 family suites, 9 double – 3 with bath, all with telephone, radio, tea-making facilities and baby-listening.
Facilities Residents' lounge with open fire, TV lounge, public bar, lounge/bar, dining room; ceilidhs and music some weekends in public bar. ½-acre garden. Rocky beach by hotel but sandy beaches 5 minutes' drive away, with safe bathing, yachting. Fishing permits arranged. Cruises to Hebrides from the village.
Location Take A830 for Mallaig, which is off A82 just N of Fort William. Hotel is on outskirts of village.
Restrictions Not suitable for ♿. No dogs in public rooms.
Credit cards None accepted.
Terms (No service charge) B&B £22, dinner, B&B £44. (£3.50 added for private bathroom and for single occupancy). Bar lunch £3–£7; set dinner £15; full alc £18. 5% reduction for stays of a week or more. Reduced rates for children under 14; special meals.
Service/tipping: "If guests wish to tip, we distribute the money equally to staff."

AUCHTERHOUSE Tayside — Map 5

The Old Mansion House Hotel — *Tel* Auchterhouse (082 626) 366
Auchterhouse
By Dundee DD3 0QN

The Old Mansion House, new to the Guide this year, is a far more exciting building than its name leads you to suggest, a tall whitewashed 15th-century stronghold on a knoll, surrounded by enormous trees. Ten carefully-tended acres, with a small stream, enormous ancient clipped yew hedge and bright herbaceous borders, lawns, orchards and vegetable gardens, slope down in terraces to a watergarden and woodland walks. Inside there are a lot of steps to climb, from the stone undercroft by the front door up to the hall, then up again to the residents' fine library bar. The bedrooms are up still higher, some enormous attics under the eaves. Back rooms are smaller, the furniture plain with some antiques, bathrooms are modern. Nigel and Eva Bell are welcoming and attentive hosts. The dining room is magnificent, with one of the several ornate plasterwork ceilings and huge fireplaces acquired during 17th-century improvements. A ruined tower in the grounds is named for William Wallace, said to have stayed here. In spite of its great age, the house is warm and comfortable, clean and has friendly staff. There is a cheerful courtyard bar, with bar snacks and tables outside in good weather. It is mainly a restaurant-with-rooms (the restaurant seats 50) but the quality of the house and the quiet leafy surroundings often tempt people to stay. (*WA; also BH Jenkinson*)

Open 4 Jan–24 Dec.
Rooms 2 suites, 4 double – 5 with bath, 1 with shower, all with telephone, radio, TV, tea-making facilities and baby-listening.
Facilities Library bar, courtyard bar. 10 acre grounds with squash court, tennis court, croquet lawn and heated swimming pool. Golf, shooting, fishing and skiing nearby.
Location 7 m NW of Dundee. Take A923; fork right at Muirhead. Hotel is on left after 3 m.
Restrictions Not suitable for ♿. No children in dining room in evening. No dogs in bedrooms.
Credit cards All major cards accepted.
Terms (No service charge) B&B : single £46–£50, double £55–£70, suite £65–£75. Set lunch £10; full alc dinner £20. Weekend rates. Reduced rates and special meals for children.
Service/tipping: "Tipping is left to the guests' discretion."

BALLATER Grampian — Map 5

Craigendarroch Hotel and Country Club [GFG] — *Tel* Ballater (0338) 55858, *Telex* 739952
Braemar Road, Ballater
Aberdeenshire AB3 5XA

A sophisticated hotel in the Scottish baronial style and an elaborate sports complex are part of this ambitious time-sharing enterprise in Royal Deeside, which opened in June 1985. In due course there will be more than 80 luxury lodges surrounding *Craigendarroch Hotel*, and both sorts of lodgers will have the run of the extensive facilities of the Country Club (see below). The chef at the hotel's restaurant, *The Oaks*, Bill Gibb, aged 27, has two years running been named "Scottish Chef of the Year". *The Oaks* is for *soigné* meals: crystal glasses, bone china and silverwear. There is also the *Café Jardin*, which shares the chef and kitchens and provides simpler meals and snacks at much lower prices.

Our sort of place? we asked last year when *Craigendarroch* had its opening entry. Very much so, according to reports. No tipping allowed, notes one visitor, "but service excellent; not cheap, but prices, if you use the facilities, understandable". Another, commenting on Bill Gibb's *cuisine moderne* meals writes: "We have never eaten superbly presented wonderful food at such *inexpensive* prices anywhere." And the standard of accommodation, everyone agrees, is exceptional. (*Captain N Clogstoun-Willmott, DS and LM Maclean*)

Open All year.
Rooms 29 double – all with bath and shower, direct-dial telephone, radio, TV, tea-making facilities and baby-listening.
Facilities Lift. Lounge with bar, café, restaurant. Guests have use of Club facilities including swimming pool, spa pool, squash, snooker, children's room with games and pool table, health and beauty salon, sauna and solarium. 29-acre grounds with tennis courts, putting green and dry ski slope; bowls and golf at Ballater Golf Club; fishing, climbing and winter sports nearby.
Location On A93 ½ m W of Ballater.
Restriction No dogs.
Credit cards All major cards accepted.
Terms (No service charge) B&B: single £49, double £105. Set dinner £22; full alc £30. Reduced rates for children sharing parents' room; special meals.
Service/tipping: "Staff encouraged to hand back/refuse tips. We pay our staff and don't expect the guests to do so too."

BEATTOCK Dumfries and Galloway — Map 5

Auchen Castle Hotel
Beattock, Moffat
Dumfriesshire DG10 9SH

Tel Beattock (068 33) 407
Telex 777205 AUCHEN

As you drive north from Beattock on the A74, you can see the *Auchen Castle* on the left. Built in sandstone in 1849, it has an impressive appearance with its tower and porticoed entrance; there is a fine terraced garden, and beautiful views over the upper Annandale. But don't expect another *Inverlochy Castle*! The *Auchen* has not the trappings nor anywhere near the prices of that august establishment. This is a hotel in the traditional style. "A very warm welcome from the owner, a good mix of friendliness and efficiency from the staff, excellent dinners and breakfasts and a comfortable room in the annexe. Exceedingly good value. The slight noise from the A74 is not their fault." (*Erasmus Barlow; also General Sir Timothy Creasey, RS White, DA Turner*) Since last year Robert Beckh has added five new luxury rooms in the annexe and carried out extensive redecorations.

Open All year except 3 weeks over Christmas and New Year.
Rooms 23 double, 2 single – all with bath and/or shower, telephone, radio, TV, baby-listening and tea-making facilities. 15 in Cedar Lodge annexe.
Facilities Lounge, TV lounge, bar, dining room; conference unit. Sat dinner-dance Oct–Mar. 50-acre grounds with trout-stocked loch; boat. Permits for fishing on river Annan can be obtained. Golf, riding, tennis, sailing nearby.
Location 1 m N of Beattock village with signed access from A74 (east-facing rooms could get traffic noise from A74).
Restrictions Not suitable for ♿. No dogs in restaurant.
Credit cards All major cards accepted.
Terms B&B £18–£30. Set dinner £9–£12.50; bar lunches. Discounts for stays of more than 1 night. "Border Breaks"; "Dine, Dance and Stay-the-Night" breaks; family holidays; golf holidays. Reduced rates and special meals for children.
Service/tipping : "We do not expect but cannot prevent tips. All tips are distributed in full to all staff on an hours worked basis."

BELLOCHANTUY Strathclyde — Map 5

Putechan Lodge Hotel
Bellochantuy by Campbeltown
Kintyre, Argyllshire PA28 6QE

Tel Glenbarr (058 32) 323

Views from this former hunting lodge of the Dukes of Argyll, 50 yards from the shore of the Atlantic, are over the Inner Hebrides and, on a clear day, to the mountains of Donegal. The area all round it is protected by the Nature Conservancy Council, because of shore nesting birds and rare wildflowers, and the Mull of Kintyre is off the usual tourist route. Ferries nearby go to Gigha, Jura, Islay and Arran. A reader criticised our last year's remarks about the food, which he found excellent, but regretfully endorsed the mention of weaknesses in the housekeeping. However, owner Peter Moll has now remarried, and his wife Irene is helping to run the *Lodge*. There is also a new chef. More reports, please, on what one reader has called "an oasis in a place of some wilderness". (*Dr James Mair*)

Open 1 Mar–6 Jan.
Rooms 12 double – 10 with bath and shower, all with radio, TV, tea-making facilities and baby-listening. 6 on ground floor. 6 self-catering cottages in grounds.

Facilities 2 lounges, lounge bar, 2 games rooms, 2 dining areas. 7½-acre garden. Rocky pebbled beach in front of hotel with safe bathing and swimming; fishing, golf and pony-trekking nearby. Sea and loch fishing by arrangement. Occasional dances and ceilidhs.
Location 9 m NW of Campbeltown, off A83.
Restriction No dogs in dining rooms.
Credit cards Access, Diners, Visa.
Terms (Service at guests' discretion) B&B: single £20–£22, double £38–£40. Full alc £14–£16. Dinner, B&B mini-breaks (2-day minimum) £60 per person. Cookery weekends; theme weekends (e.g. medieval Scots banquets). Reduced rates for children; special meals.

BLAIRGOWRIE Tayside — Map 5

Kinloch House Hotel [GFG] — *Tel* Essendy (025 084) 237
By Blairgowrie
Perthshire PH10 6SG

An ivy-covered country house hotel in a 25-acre estate, complete with Highland cattle. It is popular with shooting parties, having a game larder, drying facilities and kennels for the gun-dogs, and with fishermen and golfers also (there are 40 golf courses within about an hour's drive). David and Sarah Shentall bought *Kinloch Lodge* in a very run-down condition, and have been busy with restoration ever since. This year they added telephones in the bedrooms. The bedrooms are comfortable, the house has charm, the food is highly praised, and the only grumble was from an American visitor who found his bed sub-standard. But we should welcome more reports.

Open All year except 7-28 Dec.
Rooms 12 double, 1 single – 8 with bath, 5 with shower, all with telephone, radio and tea-making facilities.
Facilities Large hall, lounge, residents' lounge, TV room, cocktail bar, breakfast room, dining room. 25-acre grounds with highland castle and croquet lawn. ½ m to loch with coarse fishing. Shooting and stalking; golf nearby.
Location 3 m W of Blairgowrie on A923 Dunkeld road.
Restrictions Not suitable for ♿. No dogs in public rooms.
Credit cards Access, Amex, Diners.
Terms B&B single £32.50, double £42–£54. Set dinner £14.50; bar lunches available. Reductions for stays of 3-6 nights. 1-night bookings occasionally refused in peak season. Reduced rates and special meals for children by arrangement.
Service/tipping: "Not encouraged; all prices inclusive. If people insist on tipping, the money is distributed among staff."

BUNESSAN Mull, Strathclyde — Map 5

Ardfenaig House — *Tel* Fionnphort (068 17) 210
Bunessan, Isle of Mull
Argyllshire PA67 6DX

A haven of quietly polished civilisation, *Ardfenaig House* stands at the head of a small loch where you may often see seals, in a garden as flowery as the deer will permit. Pink clematis smothers the porch, and there is a neatly mown lawn. Mull is an enchanting island, full of wildflowers and birds, and the island roads (you must adjust to single-track driving and blind corners) lead through beautiful scenery, especially round the coastline. You come to Bunessan to take the ferry to Iona, or to stay with Robin Drummond-Hay and Ian Bowles. They were both librarians at Oxford, so their house, built in the 1700s and formerly belonging to the Duke of Argyll, is full of books, as well as antiques inherited from their families. It is a real country house, with wellington boots by the door, portraits on the stairs, decent but not lavish bathrooms and no fewer than three grand pianos; also a friendly King Charles spaniel. The owners take it in turns to cook excellent four-course, no-choice dinners, and bake bread daily. "There are only five rooms for guests who share three bathrooms, and it all felt more like a house-party than a hotel. We were reminded of childhood visits to grandparents before inflation had made such luxurious living impossible." This earlier commendation by *Lt-Cdr and Mrs R Kirby Harris* continues to be endorsed by recent visitors. (*WF Johnson, and others*)

Open May–Sept inclusive. Maximum 6 guests at a time. Restaurant closed for lunch, and to non-residents on Sun.
Rooms 4 double, 1 single – all with tea-making facilities.
Facilities Lounge, bar, music room, sun room, dining room. 18-acre grounds sloping down to loch with shingle beach (plenty of sandy beaches nearby). Fishing, safe bathing.
Location 3½ m W of Bunessan on Iona ferry road. The hotel's long drive is on the right.
Restrictions Not suitable for ♿. No children under 12. No dogs in public rooms.
Credit cards None accepted.
Terms Dinner, B&B £55. Set dinner £18. Discount for 3 or more nights' stay. *Service/tipping: "Our prices are structured to include a service charge which is distributed each week to the staff. Even so guests sometimes leave extra, but we try to discourage this."*

BUSTA Shetland — Map 5

Busta House — *Tel* Brae (080 622) 506
Busta, Brae, Shetland ZE2 9QN

Claims to be the oldest continuously inhabited building in Shetland, parts dating back to 16th century, 27 miles north of Lerwick. Omitted from last year's Guide, after receiver called in, but now in hands of partners Robin Black and Gordon Stark, formerly catering manager and chef at Sullom Voe Oil Terminal. First report on new set-up wholly favourable: first-rate cooking, with mostly fresh vegetables (not easy on Shetland), decent wine list (inevitably pricey), plus 115 malt whiskies, warm comfortable accommodation, pleasant service. 21 rooms, all with private facilities. B&B £24–£33. Set dinner £16. More reports welcome.

CALLANDER Central — Map 5

The Roman Camp Hotel [GFG] — *Tel* Callander (0877) 30003
Callander, Perthshire FK17 8BG

A pink-painted hunting lodge in a bend of the river Teith, looking like a miniature château, built for the Dukes of Perth in 1625. There are 20 acres of lovely formal gardens, especially glorious in the spring, and walks along the river where you may well spot a kingfisher. The entrance hall has ancient panelling and an open log fire. There is a pair of elegant high-ceilinged rooms, one a library hung with a collection of modern Scottish artists, the other with an oval ceiling with fine plasterwork. The restaurant has modern décor, with plain European maple tables with mats, lamps hanging low over them, and painted beams which look Swiss, like owner Sämi Denzler, but are in an old Scottish tradition. The *Roman Camp Hotel* has had a good postbag this year: "Returned for our second holiday." "A most excellent and comfortable hotel." "The staff enormously friendly and helpful and the setting idyllic." There was praise for the comfortable bedrooms, with easy chairs, well-placed reading lamps and gas-log fires. Most readers appreciated the food, though one expressed disappointment with desserts and cheeses. (*Miss EJ Robinson, Mrs C Smith, Mr and Mrs RB Gardner*)

Open Early Mar–mid-Nov. Restaurant sometimes closed for lunch on low season weekdays.
Rooms 3 suites, 11 double – all with bath and/or shower, radio, TV, tea-making facilities and baby-listening. 7 ground-floor rooms, 1 adapted for ♿.
Facilities 2 lounges, cocktail bar, library, sun lounge, dining room (non-smoking). 20-acre grounds with walled and formal gardens. Trout and salmon fishing free to residents in river Teith (bring your own rod). Callander golf course ½ m; tennis, squash, pony-trekking and water sports nearby.
Location ½ m from centre of Callander; take driveway between two pink cottages on Main Street (east end).
Restrictions Not suitable for severely ♿. Dogs at management's discretion, not in public rooms.
Credit cards None accepted.
Terms B&B: single £38–£50, double £53–£80, suite £70–£86. Set lunch £10.50–£12, dinner £18–£20. 2-day breaks Oct–Nov and Mar–May, 3-day breaks in summer. 1-night bookings refused to large groups. Reduced rates for children sharing parents' room; special meals on request.
Service/tipping: "All prices are inclusive of VAT and service. No further tipping is expected unless you wish to reward outstanding service."

CANONBIE Dumfries and Galloway — Map 5

Riverside Inn [GFG] *Tel* Canonbie (054 15) 295 and 512
Canonbie
Dumfriesshire DG14 0UX

Robert and Susan Phillips' 17th-century fisherman's retreat on the banks of the Esk is well placed for touring Hadrian's Wall and the Solway coast, or as a staging post on long-haul journeys. Meals in the restaurant continue to be, by inn standards, uncommonly enterprising, as do the bar snacks. Breakfasts, too, are specially recommended. All the rooms are full of generous extras. The Phillips are houseproud innkeepers, and take us to task for not mentioning in last year's entry their new residents' lounge, "especially as we sent extra photographs of it". They go on to report on their latest renovations: "The two rooms that were criticised as being pokey have been refurnished to give more space, one room has acquired a four-poster, double beds have matching bed-spreads, canopies and curtains; even shower curtains and spare loo-roll covers now match up!" We are happy to report these *Riverside* events, though it would still be sensible to discuss rooms when booking: they vary considerably in size. But in any event the restaurant is the more important concern for many visitors. One reports: "A comfortable simple room, but an exceptional restaurant! Perhaps the best breakfast selection in all of Scotland: fresh trout, lambs kidneys and two kinds of kipper – even haggis for the patriot." (*William Grant; also Gillian Seel*)

Open All year, except Christmas and Boxing Day, New Year's Day, and two weeks in Feb.
Rooms 6 double – 4 with bath, 2 with shower, all with radio, TV and tea-making facilities; 1 with 4-poster. 2 ground-floor rooms in cottage annexe.
Facilities Lounge bar, residents' lounge, TV/coffee lounge, sitting room, dining room. Small garden with children's play area. River Esk 100 yds; salmon and sea trout fishing (permits available from hotel). Good centre for visiting Hadrian's Wall.
Location M6 exit 44. 12 m N on A7; well signposted.
Restriction No dogs.
Credit cards Access, Visa.
Terms (No service charge) B&B: single occupancy £34, double £44. Set dinner £14.50. Bar lunches from £3. 2-day winter breaks Nov–Apr. Weekly rates.
Service/tipping: "We don't charge for service. Tipping is discouraged."

COLONSAY Strathclyde — Map 5

Isle of Colonsay Hotel [GFG] — *Tel* Colonsay (095 12) 316
Argyllshire PA61 7YP

César awarded for an island hotel in a class of its own

Just going to Colonsay is in itself an adventure. The ferry threads slowly between the islands, on a 2½ hour journey, only three times a week (Monday, Wednesday, Friday) so that you are automatically marooned on Colonsay for at least two days. Everyone on the island seems to come down to the pier to meet the ferry, a scene of enormous excitement, repeated when it departs again. Kevin Byrne is always there. Owner of the 250-year-old *Isle of Colonsay Hotel*, the most isolated registered hotel in Britain, he has a bristling red beard, and endless perfectionist energy. Many of his guests are keen naturalists or walkers, and he can tell you where to go to see seals or wildflowers, and when to wade safely over to the Isle of Oronsay without getting caught by the incoming tide.

The hotel is the social centre of the island, and its bar stays open twice a week until 1 am for ferry arrivals. At other times people gather there to chat, drink, and eat the excellent bar lunches. Dinners in the restaurant are also good, with generous portions, home-made bread, local seafood and vegetables from the hotel garden. Bedrooms vary in size, are conventionally furnished, and some have views. There is an occasional grumble about a sagging mattress or seized-up shower, though niggles seem churlish given the logistics of running such a place. Service is friendly and caring. After working hard on refurbishments for nearly ten years, Kevin Byrne and his wife Christa view with apprehension the "improved" ferry service due to begin in 1989, and its even more difficult timetable. But as one reader put it: "I shall be returning, I know. This place (hotel and island) will draw me back again." (*AJ Bowen; also Andrew and Ros MacDowall, Janet Weir, Peter Macklin*)

Open All year, except New Year.
Rooms 1 garden bungalow for family accommodation, 7 double with bath, 3 single – all with radio and tea-making facilities; TV available, but poor reception; telephone and baby-listening on request.
Facilities Residents' lounge, cocktail bar (for lunches, bar meals etc), public bar, sun room, restaurant. 1-acre grounds including vegetable gardens; lawns, pleasure

garden with burn. ½ m to sandy beach and lochs. Fishing and bicycles, free to all adult guests.
Location 400 yards west of harbour. Access by car/passenger ferry from Oban Mon, Wed, Fri – 37 m crossing (2½ hours) – hotel courtesy car to/from all sailings.
Restrictions "Handicapped guests welcome but facilities not perfect." No dogs in public rooms.
Credit cards All major cards accepted.
Terms (No service charge) B&B £26; dinner, B&B £27.50. Set lunch £3, dinner £12.25. Vegan, vegetarian meals if requested. Reductions for long stays. Special rates Sept–Apr and Apr–mid-May. Children normally charged only for meals when sharing parents' room, except in high season.
Service/tipping: "Any gratuities go into a tronc *– actually a teapot – and are distributed equally by our domestic staff amongst themselves."*

CRAIL Fife — Map 5

The Golf Hotel — *Tel* Crail (0333) 50206
4 High Street, Crail
Fifeshire KY10 3TD

"I wish I could pick up this little hotel, lock stock and barrel, complete with Mr and Mrs Rennie and their staff, and bring them nearer home so that I could stay there more often." Thus our inspector in decidedly uninspectorial language, recommending this spruce black and white-washed inn in an unspoilt fishing village which has just won an award for the best kept village in Fife. Despite its name, it is in fact a mile from the local golf course; it is also within easy reach of St Andrews, Carnoustie and Gleneagles. Mr Rennie supplies some background details: "Historic 18th-century inn on site of older 14th-century one. Inaugural meeting of Crail golfing society held here Feb 1787 and was club-house for many years – all recorded in minutes. Regarded by architects as one of finest examples of Fife domestic architecture – very little altered since built (all mod cons naturally!). Often used on calendars by BBC Scotland." Be prepared for chips with everything and a walk down the corridor for your bath. But for our inspector, virtually every prospect pleased: window boxes with tulips, hyacinths and daffodils, pots of steaming Scotch broth served in the public bar, lots of locally caught fish, plenty of piping hot water, crisp white cotton sheets and embroidered pillow cases, wonderfully generous breakfasts. Her report ends: "The *Golf* is simple but very competent. Sticking to high quality, radiating friendliness, with traditional cooking for local people. It is very busy and nearly always full. You need to reserve well ahead. Just look at the rates! And what a breakfast!"

Open Apr–Oct inclusive.
Rooms 5 double – all with H&C, and tea-making facilities.
Facilities Lounge bar with TV, public bar, dining area. Many golf courses nearby; also bowling, putting, beaches, swimming and tennis.
Location In centre of Crail. Parking.
Restrictions Not suitable for ♿. No children under 5. No dogs in public rooms.
Credit cards None accepted.
Terms (No service charge) B&B: £12–£13; dinner, B&B: £17–£18. Full alc £12. Reduced rates and special meals for children. *Service/tipping: "Very much up to the customer. No set policy."*

> Don't keep your favourite hotel to yourself. The Guide supports: it doesn't spoil.

CRINAN Strathclyde — Map 5

Crinan Hotel [GFG] *Tel* Crinan (054 683) 261
Crinan, by Lochgilphead
Argyllshire PA31 8SR

The *Crinan* has an incomparable location: it lies at the seaward end of the eight-mile Crinan Canal looking across to the mountains of Mull and the Isle of Jura. At closer quarters, it has a ringside seat over a yacht basin and the constant movement of craft, big and small, bound for the Inner and Outer Hebrides. A major fire gutted much of the original Victorian building, so the present hotel offers all the 1980s mod cons, including a lift; and there was a further refurbishment recently after a fire sprinkler erupted by mistake. All is fresh and floral in the decor, every room different. The hotel also prides itself on its restaurants: a relatively conventional main dining room, and a more expensive seafood restaurant called *Lock 16* on the top floor. "My favourite hotel. The Ryans were, as ever, present and keeping an eye on everything, and this very personal attention must be one of the main reasons for the consistent high standards. This time I was in a blue-striped room, with a pink-striped bathroom. The place is full of yachtsmen getting ready for the Tobermory race. I also hear Irish, Swiss and American voices ('I'll have kippers and an egg once over lightly, wholewheat toast and do the cornflakes come out of a packet?') Seafood, wine and sea views are as good as ever, but prices have risen steeply. Dinner is now £20 (£25 in *Lock 16*) and B&B for one is now £35. *Crinan* is still Paradise, but will it soon be Paradise Lost?" (*CC; also WA, Barbara Wooldridge, Robert Gould*)

Open End Mar–mid-Oct.
Rooms Family room, 19 double, 2 single – all with bath, and/or shower, telephone and radio.
Facilities Lift. Lounges, TV lounge, 3 bars, ground-floor restaurant (*Telford Room*), roof-top bar (with pianist 3 nights a week), roof-top restaurant (*Lock 16*). 1-acre grounds; on sea loch: fishing, boat trips, sailing, windsurfing.
Location On B841, 8 m NW of Lochgilphead.
Restriction No dogs in restaurant.
Credit cards Access, Visa.
Terms (Service at guests' discretion) B&B £30–£37.50. Set dinner £20 in *Telford Room*, £25 in *Lock 16*; bar lunches available. Reduced rates and special supper at 6.15 pm for children.

DERVAIG Mull, Strathclyde — Map 5

Bellachroy Hotel *Tel* Dervaig (068 84) 225 and 314
Dervaig, Isle of Mull
Argyllshire PA75 6QW

Stone-built white-washed drover's inn, with plain but clean rooms. No bathrooms en suite, *but plenty to go round. Local produce used for simple meals, with home-made jams, freshly baked bread and much crayfish, salmon, venison etc. Comfortable sitting room for bad weather. Bars popular with island characters. Nominator appreciated wholesome decor, brisk friendly service and "amazing value". 8 rooms. Dinner, B&B £18.50–£19.50. More reports please.*

Please make a habit of sending a report if you stay at a Guide hotel.

Druimnacroish Hotel *Tel* Dervaig (068 84) 274 and 212
Dervaig, Isle of Mull
Argyllshire PA75 6QW

Instead of putting his feet up when he retired from the Ministry of Defence in 1975, physicist Donald McLean and his wife Wendy bought a ruined farmhouse, and have turned it, largely with their own hands, into an impeccably neat small hotel. Camellias bloom in their large conservatory, peace in this isolated spot is complete. Rooms are comfortable, with duvets and modern bathrooms, food is traditionally British, using local produce and vegetables from the garden. No smoking in the dining room – a lounge is set aside for smokers. Donald McLean has a passion for detail which some have found irksome – but "My admiration goes out to a couple who can serve a well-cooked breakfast, offer a weather forecast, advise on midge-bites, book one party on a pony-trekking trip and another on a boat trip to Fingal's Cave, and more – all at the same time!" (*Rosemary Dunn*)

Open 1 May–30 Oct.
Rooms 6 double – all with bath, radio, TV and tea-making facilities. 2 double rooms on ground floor.
Facilities 2 lounges (1 smoking, 1 non-smoking), garden room, dining room. 5-acre grounds with natural rock gardens. Swimming pool planned for 1988. Boating, fishing, deer-stalking, golf, pony-trekking, bird-watching nearby.
Location On A849 between Dervaig and Salen, 1½ m S of Dervaig. Car ferry from Oban.
Restrictions No children under 12. Dogs by arrangement, not in public rooms. No smoking in dining room.
Credit cards All major cards accepted.
Terms (No service charge) Dinner, B&B £49. Set dinner £17.50. Long weekend and 5- and 7-day package including golf and fishing holidays.
Service/tipping: Any gift from a guest is equally divided among the staff. We do not encourage the idea.

DRUMNADROCHIT Highland — Map 5

Polmaily House [GFG] *Tel* Drumnadrochit (045 62) 343
Drumnadrochit
Inverness-shire IV3 6XT

Widely differing reports this year on *Polmaily House,* a rambling Edwardian mansion set in 18 acres, a few miles to the west of Loch Ness – a tranquil rural setting, though the dramatic landscape of Glen Affric is only a short drive away. It is run by Nicholas and Alison Parsons; she is an excellent innovative cook, he a friendly thoughtful host. The rooms, both the public ones and the bedrooms upstairs, have a comfortable lived-in feeling. There is very little about the house that suggests it is a hotel – and that, for many visitors, is the key to its success. "Impossible to be too enthusiastic. Rooms comfortable without being luxurious – there was a slight noise insulation problem in the bathroom but the water was always hot and the heating efficient." "The essence of what a Scottish country hotel should be." "We were cordially welcomed and treated throughout like pampered cousins. Delightful setting, interior decoration full of charm. One of our rooms was on the second floor and had lovely wall-paper and a cosy feel; the other, on the third resembled a maids' dormitory with something of an unfinished look, a slight mustiness in the air – even that mitigated by a delightful view and commodious, well-equipped bathroom. Dinner was splendid and breakfast divine." (*Caroline Campbell, Elizabeth Loder, Bill Cutler*) But on the reverse side two reports written in 1986 describe the hotel as "seedy and in need of refurbishment", the bedrooms as "cramped and furnished with depressing junkshop pieces" and the service as "lacking in finesse". Returning our questionnaire, the Parsons tell us that they have replaced the bed "past its prime" mentioned in last year's entry. Perhaps the time has come for further changes?

Open April–mid-Oct.
Rooms 7 double, 2 single – doubles with bath, all with radio; 1 with 4-poster; baby-listening on request.
Facilities Drawing room, bar, reading room, restaurant. 18-acre grounds with hard tennis court, unheated swimming pool, croquet lawn, boating pond and trout stream; fishing, shooting, stalking and pony-trekking can be arranged.
Location 2 m W of Drumnadrochit on A831 Cannich road.
Restrictions Not suitable for ♿. No smoking in main part of dining room. No dogs.
Credit cards Access, Visa.
Terms (No service charge) B&B: single £28, double £62. Full alc £17.50. Reduced rates for children sharing parents' room; high teas on request.
Service/tipping: "No service charge. Tips are not solicited."

DUNBLANE Central — Map 5

Cromlix House — *Tel* Dunblane (0786) 822125
Dunblane, Perthshire FK15 9JT

Cromlix House is a very grand, very comfortable house, built in 1880, altered and extended in 1903 giving its Victorian solidity an added spaciousness. The large entrance hall is panelled, the drawing room has comfortable chintz chairs and a giant log basket beside the elegant fireplace, the dining room is candle-lit at night and has stiffly starched white tablecloths, flowers, and formally served fish and game, much of it from the 5,000 acre estate. There is a well-filled conservatory, a well-stocked library, a chapel, one fishing loch within strolling distance, others nearby, a grouse moor, complete peace and quiet and lovely views over wooded grounds where deer, pheasants, wild duck and rabbits abound. There are large bedrooms with even bigger bathrooms, and spacious suites with pretty and elegant decor. The house is perfectly suited to the sort of formal shooting party that Edward VII attended here, and which still takes place today; in between times it provides a comfortable home-from-home for pampered travellers. The family of the Hon Ronald Eden has owned the estates for 450 years, and *Cromlix House* has only been an hotel for the last five, so that it still has the feeling of being somebody's home. Grant Howlett, a most professional manager, keeps everything running smoothly for the owner, who now lives elsewhere on the estate. The staff are charming and invisible unless required. Formal grandeur is the keynote.

Open All year.
Rooms 8 suites, 6 double – all with bath and shower, telephone, radio and TV.
Facilities Morning room, library, dining room, breakfast hall; functions facilities; conservatory. 5,000-acre grounds with fishing, tennis, riding and shooting (advance booking advisable). Wine tutorials, master chef's dinners, musical evenings.

Location ½ m N of Kinbuck, 4 m S of Braco. Take A9 out of Dunblane; turn left on to B8033; go through Kinbuck village, and take second left after a small bridge.
Restrictions Not suitable for ♿. No dogs in public rooms.
Credit cards All major cards accepted.
Terms (No service charge) B&B: single £60–£85, double £100, suite £130–£145. Set lunch £15, dinner £27.
Service/tipping: "Our staff do not expect to be tipped."

DUNOON Strathclyde — Map 5

Enmore Hotel — *Tel* Dunoon (0369) 2230
Marine Parade, Kirn
Dunoon, Argyllshire PA23 8HH

Dunoon is no longer the popular seaside resort it was in Victorian times, but it makes a useful base for exploring the Isles of Arran and Bute, and the Mull of Kintyre. It can also lie on the route to the Highlands – up the Ayr coast and across the ferry, thus avoiding Glasgow. The *Enmore*, a whitewashed turn-of-the-century house, overlooks the Clyde Estuary a mile out of Dunoon, and has its own gravel beach just across the road. David and Angela Wilson are an enterprising couple. They are keen on beds and have four four-posters and a water-bed, the latter with a whirlpool bathroom *en suite*. They organise Normal and Luxury Breaks, the latter with "complimentary fruit, flowers, 'bubbly', and even a heart-shaped box of chocolates . . . breakfast in bed with heart-shaped eggs". There are two squash courts on the premises and the Cowal golf course is a mile away. Here is one all-out appreciation: "Extraordinary transformation of a rather ordinary Victorian villa into a tiny luxury hotel. The ultimate in spacious comfort is achieved with imagination and taste. Apart from creature comforts like the bowl of perfect fruit, the his and hers shampoos, and hairdrier in the bathroom and electric blanket in the four-poster, three well-chosen books lie temptingly to hand by the armchairs and plenty more abound throughout the house. Food is to match: a savoury peach (with blue cheese, hot, on toast) and a wonderful mint and pea soup, with new young pear added at the last minute, were particularly memorable. All this, with the glory of the Highlands only minutes away." (*Dr F Peter Woodford, and many others*)

Open All year except early Jan.
Rooms 1 suite, 8 double, 2 single – all with bath, shower and TV; radio, tea-making facilities and baby-listening on request; 1 with waterbed and whirlpool bath. 3 in annexe. 2 ground-floor rooms.
Facilities 2 lounges, games room, cocktail bar, dining room; 2 squash courts, 1 with video playback facilities. 1-acre grounds with private shingle beach across road; safe bathing and boating. Golf, swimming pool, tennis and pony-trekking nearby.
Location On Marine Parade between 2 ferries, 1 m N of Dunoon.
Restriction Not suitable for ♿. No dogs in public rooms.
Credit card Visa.
Terms B&B: single £18–£31, double £38–£46, suite £70. Set dinner £13; bar meals £2–£6. Luxury Breaks and Normal Breaks (min 3 nights). Reduced rates and special meals for children.
Service/tipping: "If tips are are offered they are distributed fairly amongst staff at end of season."

Report forms (Freepost in UK) will be found at the end of the Guide.

EASDALE Seil, Strathclyde — Map 5

Easdale Inn — *Tel* Balvicar (085 23) 256
Easdale, by Oban
Argyllshire PA34 4RF

16 miles south of Oban on the island of Seil (joined to mainland by Telford's Clachan bridge), small Victorian inn 25 yards from rocky sea shore. New nomination: report speaks well of whole set-up – fresh fruit and flowers in room, good firm beds, towels oversize, hospitable owners, the Atkinsons, flexible about children and mealtimes, and admirable home cooking. Open Easter–Oct. 7 rooms, 4 with bath. Dinner, B&B £22–£28. More reports please.

EDINBURGH Lothian — Map 5

The Howard Hotel — *Tel* (031) 557 3500
32–36 Great King Street — *Telex* 727887
EH3 6QH

In the handsome Georgian area of Edinburgh that lies to the north of Princes Street, the *Howard Hotel* was built in 1820 as part of the New Town. Those who dislike staying in large establishments may prefer this smaller 25-room option. "The *Howard Hotel* is small, quiet, clean and centrally located. I would plan to stay there whenever I visited Edinburgh. It is a five- to ten-minute walk from the city centre. The meals are delicious and the staff courteous and helpful. The hotel is far enough away that you don't have the noise of the city, but close enough to walk in." (*Laura H Scott*) Bedrooms are comfortable, with modern bathrooms, but get smaller the higher up you go in the hotel. There is a pleasant modern lounge, and the hotel has its own parking area.

Open All year except Christmas and New Year. Restaurant closed for lunch Sat and Sun (bar food available).
Rooms 17 double, 8 single – all with bath and/or shower, direct-dial telephone, radio, TV and tea-making facilities.
Facilities Lounge, cocktail bar, pub, restaurant; conference/functions facilities.
Location Central, near Royal Circus (some front rooms could be noisy). Carpark at rear.
Restrictions Not suitable for ♿. No dogs in public rooms.
Credit card All major cards accepted.
Terms (Excluding 10% service charge) B&B: single £35–£50, double £50–£80. Set lunch £8, dinner £12.50. Winter rates. Reduced rates for children sharing parents' room; special meals by arrangement.
Service/tipping: "We add a 10% service charge to discourage tipping."

Prestonfield House — *Tel* (031) 668 3346
Priestfield Road, EH16 5UT — *Telex* 72396

"Driving through the semi-detached suburbs of Edinburgh, look out for a sudden pair of grand iron gates. They're a bit of a surprise in themselves, but they lead to an even bigger surprise. At the end of a long drive there is a tiny fairytale castle. You'll still wonder if it really is a hotel as you mount the Cinderella staircase to the (hidden) reception. The frequent 'just like staying in a country house' is just as frequently not quite true; but at *Prestonfield* it's partially true. Not many hotels would supply you with a few yards of bare scrubbed stone to tiptoe across to the nearest bathroom but *Prestonfield* dares to because it has only five eccentric rooms and doesn't want to spoil any of them by installing bathrooms – quite rightly [actually two have showers - Ed]. My room was old-fashioned and very comfortable. There was a polished brass fender and hefty mantelpiece with illuminated oil painting, and a green washbasin, also illuminated, in a panelled cupboard. Armchair, desk and huge mahogany wardrobe completed the warm, nursery-like appearance. Windows on two sides looked out over the mountains and parklands and I was further privileged with a bagpipe practice and peacocks on the lawn. But enter the dining room and you join the grown-ups. Chandeliers, swagged curtains, polished tables, silver and flowers are all very formal and the diners and service match. Formal, too, is the management – polite, efficient and professional. I understand that *Prestonfield* is booked from one Festival to the next and I'm not surprised; it really is a hotel for living in." (*Gillian Vincent*)

This report brings back to the Guide a hotel that was omitted a few years ago following some poor reports. An inspector was rather more critical: she noticed some worn carpets and paintwork in need of renewal, felt that you had to tread carefully through the menu, and pointed out that it is primarily a restaurant-with-rooms, and often busy with conferences and receptions. But she was beguiled by the *Cupid* bedroom, smallish but with a splendid plasterwork ceiling, reported that her breakfast (served only in the bedroom) was on the whole good, apart from packets of jam and sliced white bread, and pronounced *Prestonfield* "an architectural treasure not to be missed".

Open All year.
Rooms 5, 2 with shower, all with TV and tea-making facilities; baby-listening can be arranged.
Facilities 2 lounges, 2 public bars, 2 restaurants; 2 private dining rooms. Round stables for conferences, weddings, exhibitions etc. 16-acre grounds with heated swimming pool and helipad; loch and bird sanctuary nearby.
Location 10 minutes' drive from city centre. Signposted off A68 going S out of Edinburgh. Parking.
Restriction Only restaurant suitable for ♿.
Credit cards Some accepted.
Terms (Service at guests' discretion) B&B: single £42.50–£58.50, double £52.50–£72.50. Set lunch £9–£10.50. Full alc dinner £20.

Teviotdale House *Tel* (031) 667 4376
53 Grange Loan, EH9 2ER

Victorian B&B in quiet residential area (free street parking) one-and-a-half miles south of the city, just off A7, two minutes from bus stop, 10 minutes bus ride to city centre. Elaborate extensive breakfast menu. As last year, many appreciative reports – some clearly inspired by Mrs Riley's nudging – but also complaints of defective lighting, inadequate heating and hot water, and small meannesses. 6 rooms, 5 with shower. B&B £19.50–£37.50. More dispassionate witnesses please.

Deadlines: nominations for the 1989 edition should reach us not later than 1 May 1988. Latest date for comments on existing entries: 1 June 1988.

ELGIN Grampian — Map 5

The Mansion House Hotel — *Tel* Elgin (0343) 48811
The Haugh, Elgin
Moray IV30 1AW

An imposing Scots baronial mansion, complete with castellated tower and stair turret, in five acres of rather splendid grounds overlooking the river Lossie. It was rescued from demolition a few years back by the exuberant Fernando Oliveira, who comes from Portugal, and his Scottish wife. One returning visitor this year, while still appreciating many of the comforts of the hotel, felt the menu was somewhat over the top and in danger of providing a contribution to Pseuds' Corner. Another, however, had virtually no reservations and provided a prize-winning entry for the Rave of the Year award: "It would be difficult to find any fault with this hotel – it was the closest I've ever come to perfection. It is beautifully furnished and spotlessly clean and sparkling. We were given the room with the four-poster bed which is truly spectacular and, even better, charged for an 'ordinary' room. The writing pad and pencil by the phone, the fruit, the glasses of sherry, and all the sachets in the bathroom were very impressive. The food was equally good: wild mushroom soup, a sea-food starter, game perfectly presented and meringues cooked in the shape of mushrooms with fresh fruits. A 1979 bottle of St-Émilion at £15 made it all a delightful experience. The service provided by Mr Oliveira was very good – he is charming, as are the staff. Trying *very* hard to be critical: (1) I would have liked a glass of Sauternes/muscat wine with dessert and there was none. (2) Glasses in the dining room could be improved." (*Prudence Perry; also NM Laing*)

Open All year.
Rooms 1 suite, 11 double – all with bath, shower, telephone, radio, TV, tea-making facilities and baby-listening; 2 4-posters.
Facilities Residents' lounge, lounge-bar, bar, dining room; conference/function room. 5-acre grounds with children's playground. Close to river, low-cost fishing permits available; hotel is member of local squash club.
Location Coming E from Inverness or W from Aberdeen on A96 turn off Elgin High St into Alexandra Rd; take turning into Haugh Rd, then first turn on left. Parking.
Restrictions Not suitable for ♿. No dogs.
Credit cards All major cards accepted.
Terms (No service charge) B&B: single £30–£45, double £45–£65, suite £65–£70. Set lunch £6.90, dinner £12.50; full alc £20. Weekend and weekly breaks. Reduced rates for children under 12; special meals.
Service/tipping: "Payment for service is not expected. When tips are received they are shared out equally between all staff except management."

ERISKA Strathclyde — Map 5

Isle of Eriska Hotel [GFG] — *Tel* Ledaig (063 172) 371
Eriska, Ledaig, Connel — *Telex* 777040 ERISKA
Argyllshire PA37 1SD

Imposing Victorian mansion on islet rich in natural history, linked by bridge to mainland. Owned and run by Robin Buchanan-Smith, a minister of the Church of Scotland, and his wife Sheena, on private house lines. Sophisticated in style and has never lacked support, but continuing mumbles of discontent necessitate these italics. 16 double rooms, with bath, shower and other mod cons. Advance bookings min 2 nights. Dinner, B&B from £65. More reports please.

FORT WILLIAM Highland — Map 5

The Factor's House [GFG]
Torlundy, Fort William
Inverness-shire PH33 6SN
Tel Fort William (0397) 5767
Telex 776229 attn FH

Off to a good start is the verdict on *The Factor's House*, built in the early part of the century for the factor or estate manager of what is now *Inverlochy Castle*. It is owned and run by Peter Hobbs, son of *Inverlochy*'s owner, Grete Hobbs, and, though an entirely independent enterprise, will not be found unworthy by frustrated would-be *Castle* guests, who will be further mollified by its prices, half those of the *Castle*. Opened in Spring 1986, the house has a fresh, light, airy feeling to it. Bedrooms are modern, with duvets and colour TV, and bathrooms "generously tiled". "The restaurant, looking out at Ben Nevis, has an effective extractor fan, so there was no smell of cigarette smoke. A daily blackboard menu has four or more choices at each course. Imaginative and interesting menu. Excellent gravlax, good soups, main courses which always include a form of steak or fish. Excellent desserts as well." Guests from the USA said that a be-kilted Peter Hobbs had "made them feel like members of the family". Friendly black labrador, Pancho, meets and greets guests, accompanied by hotel manager Ranald Duff. (*WA Low, Hamish Osborne*)

Open Mar–20 Dec. Restaurant closed Mon.
Rooms 8 double – all with bath and/or shower, telephone and TV. Some ground-floor rooms.
Facilities 2 lounges, dining room. 50-acre grounds with tennis and clay-pigeon shooting. Sailing 3 m; fishing in nearby lochs and rivers.
Location 3 m NE of Fort William on A82 Inverness road, just after turnoff to *Inverlochy Castle*.
Restrictions No children under 6 in restaurant. No dogs.
Credit cards All major cards accepted.
Terms (No service charge) B&B single £40.25, double £69. Lunch £5 (residents only), dinner £12.75. Special meals for children on request.
Service/tipping: "We do not have a service charge and no tips are expected. However, we do not decline if offered. Tips distributed to all members of staff."

Inverlochy Castle [GFG]
Fort William
Inverness-shire PH33 6SN
Tel Fort William (0397) 2177
Telex 776229

This spectacular example of Scottish baronial architecture was built by the first Lord Abinger 125 years ago this year. Ten years later, Queen Victoria came to stay and wrote in her Diary: "I never saw a lovelier or more romantic spot" – a plug that the hotel naturally appreciates. It stands in 50 acres of grounds, rich in rhododendrons, on the lower slopes of Ben Nevis in the heart of the West Highlands. *Inverlochy Castle* is not, in its present incarnation, under royal appointment, but for many years it has been in a class of its own as a country house hotel under its warmly welcoming *châtelaine* Grete Hobbs and her manager Michael Leonard. It won a César, in our first year of those awards, for "incomparable grandeur", and one reader told us this year: "*Inverlochy* should have your highest award every year." Another wrote: "I wouldn't trade our stay here for anything." No wonder the hotel gets booked up months, even a year or two, in advance. The only change of consequence this year was the departure of chef François Huguet, whose fine cooking had brought the hotel a *Michelin* rosette. His *toque* was taken in February 1987 by Graham Newbould, formerly chef to the Prince of Wales, who reports that his ambition is to win a second star for *Inverlochy*. First reports of Newbould's performance: "Stunning." We await more detailed appreciations. (*Michael O'Donnell, Elizabeth Loder, Donald Hackler*)

Open 1 Mar to 1 Nov.
Rooms 2 suites, 14 double – all with bath, shower, telephone, radio, TV, baby-listening; 24-hour room service.
Facilities Great hall, drawing room, 2 dining rooms, billiard room; facilities for small (25) conferences out of season. 500 acres of farmland and 50-acre grounds with rhododendron gardens; all-weather tennis court; trout fishing on nearby private loch. Several golf courses within easy driving distance; pony-trekking. Chauffeur-driven limousines can be hired.
Location Take turning to NW off A82, 3 m N of Fort William just past golf club. Guests met by arrangement at railway station or airports.
Restrictions Not suitable for ♿. No dogs.
Credit cards Access, Visa.
Terms [1987 rates] (No service charge) B&B: double from £125, suites from £145. Set dinner £29.33. Light lunch available on request. Reduced rates for children sharing parents' room; special meals.
Service/tipping: "Our guests are advised that there is no charge and tipping is not expected."

GLASGOW Strathclyde — Map 5

One Devonshire Gardens [GFG] — *Tel* Glasgow (041) 339 2001 and 339 9494
1 Devonshire Gardens G12 0UX

"An oasis among the bedroom factories," writes a nominator for this new trendy opulent hotel one mile from city centre in the fashionable West End suburb. Its restaurant is claimed to have the same chic as the decor. 8 suites, all with bath and/or shower. Suites £75–£95. Set lunch £13.50, dinner £19.50. May give The White House (*below*) *a run for its money, but we should welcome more reports.*

The White House — *Tel* Glasgow (041) 339 9375
11-13 Cleveden Crescent — *Telex* 777582 attn The White House
G12 0PA

César awarded for enterprise and innovation in a city hotel

Elsewhere there are hotels and self-catering apartments. *The White House* has thought carefully about varied visitors' needs in a city hotel and come up with a flourishing hybrid. The hotel is in the centre of a classical Georgian crescent about a mile from the city centre: in its setting it reminds one of the *Royal Crescent*, Bath; though not of the same scale of grandeur, it is still a pedigree building, designed by John Burnet Senior, who designed Glasgow's imposing Stock Exchange. It is a set of three adjoining terrace houses, comprising 32 handsome suites and rooms at prices which compare favourably with the tariff at the city's conventional five-star establishments. All the rooms have fully-fitted kitchenettes, but the hotel also offers full room service for all meals not just breakfast, and has a tie-in with three down-town restaurants, *Rogano's*, the *Buttery* and the *Colonial*; a courtesy Mercedes is provided and guests can charge their restaurant bill to their hotel account. The rooms themselves are for the most part immodestly large by the standard of other hotels and have dining table and chairs as well as easy chairs and sofas. There are all the usual conveniences, such as remote-control TV with teletext, and trouser press. Bathrooms, though lacking some luxury frills available elsewhere, have all the essentials to comfort. The hotel is not without faults: accommodation varies in quality and poor standards of housekeeping have been reported by more than one visitor. More effective extractor fans are needed to dispel pervasive smells of cooking. But *The White House* still sets several examples which other city hotels could copy to advantage. (*HR; also Ellen Bentsen, Andrew and Ros Macdowall, WA*)

Open All year.
Rooms 11 suites, 9 double, 12 single – all with bath and shower, direct-dial telephone, radio, remote-control TV with in-house video, kitchenette; baby-sitting arranged. 4 ground-floor rooms.
Facilities Room service for meals; conference suite. Small garden.
Location ½ m W of Glasgow town centre; 10 minutes' drive from airport. From centre take Great Western Road (A82). From 2nd set of traffic lights past Botanic Gardens turn right, then first left into Cleveden Crescent. From airport take A739 Clyde tunnel turn-off to Anniesland Cross. Courtesy car to town centre between 8.15 and 8.30 am Mon–Fri.
Restrictions Not suitable for ♿. Dogs by arrangement only.
Credit cards All major cards accepted.
Terms [1987 rates] (No service charge) Single £48.50–£56, double £59.50–£70, suite £89. Room service meals: breakfast £4.25–£5.75; set lunch/dinner £11.50–£13.50. Champagne weekends; reductions for weekend stays of 2 or 3 nights; reduced Christmas rates 14 Dec–12 Jan. No charge for children sharing parents' room; cots (£5) and special meals on request.
Service/tipping: "We prefer guests not to tip. If they should then it is always pooled amongst all members of staff both full time and casual."

GLEN CANNICH Highland — Map 5

Cozac Lodge — *Tel* Cannich (04565) 263
Glen Cannich by Beauly
Inverness-shire IV4 7LX

If somewhere remote is what you are after, *Cozac Lodge*, built by the Chisholm of Chisholm as a hunting lodge in 1912, may answer your need. New to the Guide this year, it is about an hour from Inverness, lost in the Highlands, down a single track road which winds and twists through woodland and over moors, surprising the sheep, and brings you, after some eight miles or so, to a dam ahead, a loch, and a large white-painted Edwardian house. Inside there is a mahogany panelled hall, with shallow stairs leading up to agreeable bedrooms with modern bathrooms, a large dining room and smaller breakfast room, and a sitting room with comfortable chairs, a bay window over the loch view, and masses of books to read. It is the sort of place where, if you arrive tentatively and famished at 2.30 pm, not to stay but to look round, they ask if you would like a hot lunch! A happy surprise. Food, in generous portions, proves tasty. Ideal for walkers; trout fishing a few steps away in the loch; for more professional fishermen, trout and salmon rivers nearby. If you get soaked, there is a large drying room. A most delightful place, run by Pam Hall, ex-racehorse trainer, and John Wood, ex-producer of golden discs, now both busy in the kitchens. (*Dr and Mrs DAJ Neden, Mr and Mrs RJ Clough, Mr and Mrs B Spratt*)

Open 26 Mar–31 Oct, Christmas and New Year.
Rooms 1 suite, 6 double – 3 with bath, 4 with shower, all with TV and tea-making facilities. 1 ground-floor room suitable for ♿.
Facilities Sitting room, dining room, breakfast room. 3-acre grounds on loch; boat available for fishing – serious salmon/trout fly fishing can be arranged locally. Golf, walking, stalking and riding nearby.
Location From Cannich village follow signs for Mullardoch and Glen Cannich. *Cozac Lodge* is first and only house on left after 8 m.
Restrictions Dogs by arrangement only. No smoking in dining room.
Credit cards Access, Amex, Visa.
Terms B&B £21–£25; dinner, B&B (3 nights or more) £30.50–£34.50. Set lunch £5.50, dinner £14. Reduced rates Mar, Apr and Oct for parties of 4 staying 2 or more nights. Reduced rates for children sharing parents' room or in family suite.
Service/tipping : "We do not expect any extra reward for service and hospitality."

GLENBORRODALE Highland — Map 5

Glenborrodale Castle Hotel — *Tel* (097 24) 266
Glenborrodale, Acharacle
Argyllshire PH36 4JP

This fairy-tale late-Victorian castle, embellished with turrets, battlements and balconies, and set in grounds of 113 acres on the shores of Lake Sunart, lies 40 winding miles south-west of Fort William. It has had a chequered history in the Guide. Until 1986 it was owned by Trusthouse Forte; some years we had an entry as this most distant outpost of the THF empire seemed to escape the worst effects of chain management, and other years the long arm of head office caused it to be omitted. Now it is in the hands of Mr Brown: reports speak of clean decent rooms, sometimes shabby, short on bathrooms, "the worst wine list we've ever seen", but also of loyal and enthusiastic staff, often interesting food, lovely formal gardens and "quite simply one of the two most outstanding situations in Britain". More reports please. (*Richard Gollin; also WA*)

Open Easter–Oct.
Rooms 3 suites, 14 double – 10 with bath (4 also have shower), all with telephone, radio, TV, tea-making facilities and baby-listening. 3 ground-floor rooms.
Facilities 2 lounges (1 with TV), cocktail bar, dining room. 113-acre grounds with croquet and putting. 150 yds to sea loch with safe bathing, and fishing.
Location 40 m W of Fort William. On B8007 7 m W of Salen.
Restriction No dogs.
Credit cards All major cards accepted.
Terms Dinner, B&B: single £38.50, double £44–£48.50. Bar lunches £2–£5. Set dinner £14.50. Reductions for stays of 3 nights or more. Reduced rates for children; special meals.
Service/tipping: "In its original meaning of an advance payment – To Insure Proper Service – we do not agree with it. We try to ensure that everyone is served as well as possible with no extra reward. However we cannot prevent or object to gratuities being given by customers who feel they have had very special help." [Can any reader authenticate this surprising etymology of "tips"? – Ed.]

GLENCRIPESDALE Highland **Map 5**

Glencripesdale House *Tel* Salen (096 785) 263
Glencripesdale, Loch Sunart
Acharacle, Argyllshire
PH36 4JH

Glencripesdale entered our Guide last year, and the nominating report could hardly have been more extravagantly enthusiastic: "It is no cliché when I say that this is a hotel in a million – but perhaps more like a second home for anyone lucky enough to stay there. For Bill and Susan Hemmings, their home is also the hotel; it is one of the most remote in Britain, standing, as it does, by Loch Sunart and at the end of an eight-mile rough track through forest and wildlife sanctuary that takes an hour to drive. (For those not having a car Bill will collect from Fort William, the railhead.) Here, with deer grazing on the front lawn, is tranquillity for the jaded that has to be experienced. The bedrooms are spacious and comfortable (one had a Victorian bath; another a sky-light allowing one to lie abed and watch the stars) and the meals, personally cooked by Susan and served by Bill, are out of this world. I had nettle soup, lamb cooked with garlic leaves and home-produced vegetables with sage jelly and mint jelly and blackberry and hazelnut crumble with cream. The Hemmings' book-lined lounge is available to all who require rest and quiet; there is abundant walking, fishing, boating, and bird/animal observation for the more active visitor. The terms are ridiculously low for a sojourn that is an unbelievable experience in an environment beautiful beyond compare, remote but not desolate, wild without savagery." (*Christopher Portway*)

Could any hotel live up to that sort of introduction? To our awed surprise, *Glencripesdale* can. All the signatories below, one himself an owner of a Guide hotel in the Outer Hebrides, have endorsed Portway's paean in terms no less eloquent. (*Richard Gollin, EJ Woodward, Bunty Smith*)
Important note: Acharacle is only a postal address; it is a two-hour drive from the house.

Open All year.
Rooms 4 double – 2 with bath, 2 with shower.
Facilities Library/lounge, dining room, children's playroom. ½-acre grounds and access to hundreds of acres; nature reserve ¼ m; sea trout and occasional salmon nearby; rock and shingle beaches; windsurfing board and boat with outboard motor for hire.
Location Do *not* go to Acharacle. Hotel is on S side of Loch Sunart. Take A861 towards Strontian; fork left on A884. Hotel is through Laudale estate. (They will send detailed directions.)
Restrictions Not suitable for ♿. Dogs by arrangement, usually not.
Credit cards None accepted.
Terms B&B £18; dinner, B&B (including packed lunch) £33. Bar lunch £4. Set lunch/dinner £12.50.
Service/tipping: "Tips not sought; any money given goes to Cancer Research."

> "We arrived in an October gale after a 3-hour drive and rushed to the lounge to take tea by the fire. We were coolly welcomed both by staff and silk flowers in the grate. When I commented on the lack of fire, they said: 'Oh, it's not cold enough yet.'"

INVERNESS Highland — Map 5

Dunain Park Hotel [GFG]
Inverness
Inverness-shire IV4 6JN

Tel Inverness (0463) 230512
Telex 75446

An enthusiastic renomination for this Italianate early 19th-century country house in its six acres of gardens and woodlands overlooking the Caledonian canal. It was in earlier editions under previous management: now three reporters urge its reinstatement. "Inverness is food- and hotel-wise a desert, but this is a lovely little hotel with superb food and accommodation. The owners, Mr and Mrs Nicoll, have been there only a year, and it was a lucky break for us that we found it. We had intended only staying one night but stayed two, we were so comfortable. There are only eight bedrooms (six in the main house and two in a garden cottage), all decorated in the most delightful fashion and all different. It is the warmest hotel I have ever visited: excellent central heating, and in the bedrooms a fan-heater and electric blankets. There are books everywhere. The lounges have log fires and fantastic views from all the windows. The food lives up to the ambience. Perhaps the only minor complaint I have is that the breakfasts, which I would have expected to be very lavish, are not, but as Mrs Nicoll has a five-course dinner to prepare every night it is perhaps understandable. The hotel is not keen on children (understandable as there are antiques everywhere) but they welcome dogs with open arms." (*Susan Chait; also John Fryman, Alistair Sunderland*)

Open All year.
Rooms 2 suites, 6 double – all with bath, telephone, radio and TV. Suites (1 with kitchenette) in garden cottage, 100 yards from hotel.
Facilities 2 lounges, dining room. 6-acre grounds with garden, badminton and croquet.
Location 1 m S of Inverness off A82 to Fort William. Turn left shortly after Craig Dunain hospital which is on right.
Restrictions Not suitable for ♿. Not ideal for children. No dogs in public rooms.
Credit cards All major cards accepted.
Terms (Service at guests' discretion) B&B £22–£40. Set lunch £12.75, dinner £17.50. Low season breaks.
Service/tipping: "Any tips received are shared equally among all staff."

IONA Strathclyde — Map 5

Argyll Hotel
Isle of Iona
Argyllshire PA76 6SJ

Tel Iona (068 17) 334

Our first entry for the tiny pilgrim island of Iona (three-and a half-miles long and one-and-a-half wide) and reached by a five-minute ferry from the Isle of Mull.

"Islands off islands are special. And Iona is special not only because of this but by reason of its light, often contrasting with the mountains of Mull glowering darkly under rain, and its numinous quality, apparent not in the later red granite abbey but rather in the small, starkly simple St Oran's chapel, said to have been built by one of Columba's monks. I went for one night and stayed four, seduced by the island itself, the drawbridge-up pleasure of seeing the last ferry leave in the evening bearing the day's visitors away, and not least by the particular attraction of the *Argyll Hotel*. This consists of three converted cottages (one of which was an inn in the 19th century, visited by RL Stevenson) and an annexe, right by the sea, whose sound lulls one to sleep at night. The bedrooms are smallish, cottagey, each with an original water colour or etching of real merit (and, despite the Gulf Stream, an electric blanket). There are two sitting rooms with open fires and no TV, full of local history and bird books, and a built-on sun lounge with creaking wicker chairs. The dining room has a piano round which the girls who serve at table sometimes gather after dinner to try out a little Mozart or Bach. There are two menus, one vegetarian and one not, and you can dodge, as I did, between the two. Both were delicious, accompanied by home-made bread and making full use of the vegetables organically grown in the hotel plot and salmon from mainland Mull. The atmosphere is extraordinarily peaceful. There is a wholly attractive air of wholesome good living and high thinking; the table next to yours may have a visiting man of God bound for the abbey, a birdwatcher, a walker or a poet – I met all four." (*Rosemary Davidson*)

Open 1 May–1 Oct.
Rooms 10 double, 9 single – 8 with bath, shower and tea-making facilities. Some in annexe.
Facilities 2 lounges, sun lounge, dining room. ½-acre grounds on seashore with rocks, sand, safe bathing; sea and loch fishing.
Location In the village, near jetty. Iona is reached by direct steamer from Oban in summer or by car or bus across Mull to Fionnphort and then passenger ferry. No cars on Iona. Carparks at Oban and Fionnphort.
Restrictions Not suitable for ♿. No dogs in dining room.
Credit cards Access, Visa.
Terms (No service charge) B&B £15–£21; dinner, B&B £20.50–£30. Set lunch (including wine) £6.80, dinner (not including wine) £9.
Service/tipping: "We agree with your policy, but any tips given are distributed equally among all staff."

JEDBURGH Borders — Map 5

Ferniehurst Mill Lodge — *Tel* Jedburgh (0835) 63279
Jedburgh, Roxburghshire
TD8 6PQ

John and Beryl Tough (pronounced Tew) specialise in trail-riding, but their purpose-built Cheviot lodge, with well-equipped if smallish rooms, also cheerfully caters for non-horsey folk. 25 acres grounds beside river Jed, unpolluted, fishable. Standard hotel food. 11 rooms, all with bath or shower. B&B £18.50. Set dinner £11.50. In earlier editions, now freshly nominated. More reports please.

KENTALLEN Highland — Map 5

Ardsheal House [GFG] — *Tel* Duror (063 174) 227
Kentallen of Appin
Argyllshire PA38 4BX

Ardsheal House, historic home of the Stewarts of Appin, was built in the 1500s, sacked in 1745, and rebuilt in 1760. It featured in Robert Louis Stevenson's *Kidnapped*, and stands in a garden full of superb mature trees, in a commanding position overlooking Loch Linnhe and the Morvern hills. The interior has charm, with aged pine and antiques. It is owned and run by two Americans, ex-banker Bob Taylor, and his ex-advertising wife Jane, with polish and professionalism. They divide their lives between wintering in the USA and running the house in the summer. It is clearly on a circuit for visiting Americans, who have remarked on their enjoyment of the twice-baked goat cheese soufflé, and the Cheddar cheese soup, and called *Ardsheal* "our favourite spot". British guests, too, have appreciated the conviviality of the house, but there have been strong criticisms this year of poor upkeep, lack of space for clothes, shabby bathrooms and suchlike. More reports please.

Open Apr–Nov.
Rooms 12 double, 1 single – all with bath and/or shower.
Facilities Reception lounge, TV/snooker room, library with view of loch, dining room. 900-acre grounds with tennis court; rocky beach behind hotel, trout stream nearby, coarse fishing from dinghies on loch; riding, hill-walking.
Location 17 m S of Fort William. From Ballachulish roundabout take A828 towards Oban; hotel is 4 m further on, on right. Parking for 18 cars.
Restriction Only dining room suitable for ♿
Credit cards Access, Amex, Visa.
Terms (No service charge) Dinner, B&B: single occupancy £65, double £92–£117. Set lunch £7–£8, dinner £20. 15% discount in Apr. 1-night bookings sometimes refused if requested far in advance. Reduced rates for children sharing parents' room; high teas at 6 pm.
Service/tipping: "We do not ask for gratuities. If guests want to contribute something to the staff, money goes into a 'kitty' and is distributed to everyone on a work-done basis twice during the season."

KILCHRENAN Strathclyde — Map 5

Cuil-na-Sithe Guest House — *Tel* Kilchrenan (086 63) 234
Kilchrenan, by Taynuilt
Argyllshire PA35 1HF

Unpretentious modest-priced late-Victorian guest house on the banks of lovely Loch Awe, run by a welcoming young couple, Margaret and Dave Mutter. They have 300 feet of loch frontage and fishing rights, and the name of their house means "corner of tranquillity". Robust meals and 3½ acres of garden to stroll in, complete with peacocks, guinea fowl and the occasional deer. 6 rooms, 3 with private facilities. Dinner, B&B £21–£27. More reports please.

Taychreggan Hotel [GFG] — *Tel* Kilchrenan (086 63) 211
Kilchrenan, by Taynuilt
Argyllshire PA35 1HQ

Many readers again pass a vote of thanks to John and Tove Taylor (now joined by son Nicholas) at their admirably-converted old coaching inn peacefully located at what was once the main ferry point across Loch Awe from Inverary to Oban. "The Taylors are model hosts. They are always about, and their staff is charming and efficient. The food is almost all locally produced, and is simple and delicious. At lunch they provide a wide choice of bar snacks, very useful for families, as well as the delicious *koldt bord* (Tove Taylor is Danish) – an amazing and most generous spread of meats and salads, fresh prawns and Scandinavian delicacies. The bedrooms are Laura Ashley in the main, with impeccable bathrooms, and there are lovely family antiques, prints, maps, stuffed fishes, porcelain and Scandinavian rugs everywhere. If the day gets the least chilly they light the fire in the hall, and there are big log-burning stoves in the public rooms. The views over gardens and loch are superb." (*WA; also David Laing, R Redock, W Kelly*)

Open 25 Mar–mid-Oct.
Rooms 1 suite, 14 double, 1 single – 15 with bath, 6 also with shower, all with radio and baby-listening.
Facilities Lounge/hall, 2 lounges, TV lounge, all with log fires, bar, dining room. 25-acre grounds on the loch, with fishing, bathing, boating. Riding, shooting, walking; fine scenery.
Location On N shore of Loch Awe, 7 m S of Taynuilt, off B845.
Restriction Not suitable for ♿.
Credit cards All major cards accepted.
Terms (No service charge) Dinner, B&B: £40–£62. Lunch (Danish cold table) £10, dinner £15. 1-night bookings occasionally refused. Reduced rates and special meals for children.
Service/tipping: "It is up to hoteliers to charge their guests a realistic amount; they should have nothing to do with private appreciation shown by guests to staff."

KILFINAN Strathclyde — Map 5

Kilfinan Hotel [GFG] — *Tel* Kilfinan (070 082) 201
Kilfinan, Nr Tighnabruaich
Argyllshire PA21 2AP

We heard good things about this century-old black-and-white coaching inn in the remote and tiny clachan of Kilfinan and sent along an inspector who reports:
Welcome A most hearty one from the 20-stone kilted Tony Wignell who runs the hotel with his wife Gina. An amiable host and a superb story-teller.
Lounge/bar Rather tiny, but with a log fire and lots of magazines. Not a place to relax in for long, but ideal for a pre-dinner drink.
Dining room Two rooms with rich burgundy wall coverings. Immaculate napery. Fresh flowers. Exceptionally good four-course dinners, with three choices at each course except for soup. First-rate mousseline of salmon; breast of duck (cooked pink) served with a sauce of fresh oranges and Grand Marnier; and crème brûlée. The stilton was in excellent condition. Plentiful breakfast with top-class kippers. Wine list fairly short – about 30 bottles – but reasonably priced. In quality of food, value and presentation the dining room scores highly.
Bedroom We had the honeymoon suite which overlooks the graveyard . . . Large bright room, with the largest bed I have ever slept in – easy to lose your partner in it! Housekeeping of high standard and adequate lighting. Bathroom well-stocked with extras, even indigestion pills and Andrew's Liver Salts, but bath was short and narrow and wouldn't suit the tall or over-weight.
Recommendation Definitely worth an entry. It is popular as a base for the hunting, fishing and shooting brigade but would also be a most restful place to spend a few days, and ideal for birdwatchers, painters, photographers and walkers.

Please make a habit of sending a report if you stay at a Guide hotel.

Open All year.
Rooms 11 double – all with bath, 2 also have shower, all with telephone, TV and baby-listening.
Facilities Public bar, bar lounge, dining room; function room. Private sandy beach on Loch Fyne 1 m. Fishing on Kilfinan Burn; sea angling, golf, deerstalking, clay pigeon shooting nearby.
Location In tiny village, next to church. On B8000 9 m NW of Tighnabruaich road.
Restrictions Not suitable for ♿. No dogs in dining room.
Credit cards All major cards accepted.
Terms (No service charge) B&B £22–£28; dinner, B&B £36–£42. Set dinner £15; full alc £20. Reduced rates for children sharing parents' room; special meals.

KILLIECRANKIE Tayside — Map 5

Killiecrankie Hotel and Restaurant [GFG] — *Tel* Pitlochry (0796) 3220
Killiecrankie by Pitlochry
Perthshire PH16 5LG

Once more, many contented guests at this unpretentiously welcoming small hotel, originally a dower house, in an area of great natural beauty – autumn tints specially recommended – close to the Pass of Killiecrankie, and a short distance from Pitlochry with its Festival Theatre. "The best food, value and bedroom (in spite of lack of bath) of the whole trip." "Our room was very pretty and practical, with everything you might require – even to 14 colours of thread in the mending basket. The personal attention of the owners was outstanding and reflected in the qualities of the staff who always referred to you by name and gave service with a smile." "The food as always was delicious and imaginative and a very generous choice." (*WF Johnson, Mr and Mrs RB Gardner, Joan Williamson; also CT and Rosamund Hebdon*)

Last year we had one aggrieved report from an American who felt that his host had gone out of his way to be disobliging. No such complaint this year, we are glad to say, but another visitor, having booked a room with a bathroom was dismayed to find that the "bathroom" only contained a shower, especially since the shower didn't work and she was forced to trek upstairs through the main hall. And, though she accepts no-smoking rules in restaurants, she objected to being told officiously "to put it out", when she lit up unaware of the house ruling. We are sure these are not everyday happenings in *Killicrankie*, but record another report that "the two men in our party enjoyed Mr Hattersley Smith's sense of humour, but my friend and I found him rude".

Open Easter–mid-Oct.
Rooms 11 double, 1 single – 5 with bath, 5 with shower. 4 ground-floor rooms, 1 with bathroom suitable for partially ♿.
Facilities Lounge with TV, bar-lounge, cocktail bar, dining room. 6-acre gardens and woodlands; putting, croquet. Golf, fishing, stalking, shooting, skiing, walking, mountaineering nearby.
Location Just off A9 3½ m N of Pitlochry. Follow Killiecrankie signs.
Restrictions No small children in dining room at dinner-time. No dogs in dining room. No smoking in dining room.
Credit cards Access, Visa.
Terms (No service charge) B&B £18.20–£22.80; dinner, B&B £29.60–£37. Set dinner £13–£13.50; bar lunches. Mid-week breaks; weekly rates. Reduced rates for children sharing parents' room; high teas.

KINCLAVEN Tayside — Map 5

Ballathie House Hotel — *Tel* Meikleour (025 083) 268
Kinclaven, by Stanley
Perthshire PH1 4QN

Turreted Victorian residence in French baronial style in 15 acres on west bank of the Tay. Popular for its fishing and shooting. Some rooms in annexe 100 yards from house. Rooms light and attractive, but entry in italics after criticisms of the cooking. Open Mar–Nov. 34 rooms, all with private facilities. Dinner, B&B £32.75–£38.50 in annexe, £41.25–£55.50 in main building. More reports welcome.

KINGUSSIE Highland — Map 5

The Osprey Hotel — *Tel* Kingussie (054 02) 510
Kingussie
Inverness-shire PH21 1EN

"More a very comfortable guest house than a hotel maybe, but the better for it. Food is generous, imaginative without being at all fussy – more like the kind of food you get at a friend's dinner party than a hotel kitchen doing fancy tricks for the sake of being different. Breakfast was a treat. Although the place is obviously in the business to make a profit, there were no corners being cut for the sake of higher percentages." (*Isobel MacKenzie; also Robert Young, Owen Sims, and others*) *The Osprey* has long been popular with Guide readers as a small welcoming hotel on a moderately quiet village street, very reasonable in its price, and offering remarkably good cooking (it won the 1985 Scottish Taste of Britain Award), an excellent wine list (more half-bottles than ever this year) and the agreeable company of Duncan and Pauline Reeves as hosts. It is also well placed in the heart of the Spey Valley for all the leisure activities of the region – walking, fishing, golf, riding, skiing. Aviemore is 12 miles off, the Cairngorms 30 minutes by car. The public rooms, like the bedrooms, are small and it is not much of a place to hang around in during the day if the weather is poor. But correspondents continue to express their appreciation of the care taken by the hosts to create a convivial house-party atmosphere both at dinner (couples may be asked to share tables) and then post-prandially, and of the very reasonable prices. Only complaint: a gregarious hotel cat may upset those allergic to the species.

Open 27 Dec–31 Oct.
Rooms 7 double, 1 single – 1 with bath, 3 with shower.
Facilities Lounge, TV room, dining room. Small garden. Most sports within easy reach: golf; salmon and trout fishing in river Spey ¼ m, trout fishing in loch 1 m; gliding at Glen Feshie; sailing, canoeing, windsurfing 6 m; sports facilities at the Aviemore Centre 12 m; bird-watching, walking, hill-climbing; skiing in Cairngorms (usually Dec–May), 30 minutes by car.
Location Near A9, about 12 m SW of Aviemore and 200 yds from village centre; parking for 10 cars. Rail: on main London/Inverness line with good services.
Restrictions Not suitable for ♿. No dogs in public rooms.
Credit cards All major cards accepted.
Terms (No service charge) B&B £13–£27; dinner, B&B £26–£40. Set dinner £14. Reduced rates for children.

Service/tipping: "If people wish to tip – and some definitely do – the gratuity is accepted with thanks and given to staff as bonus at Christmas."

KINLOCHBERVIE Highland — Map 5

The Kinlochbervie Hotel *Tel* Kinlochbervie (097 182) 275
Kinlochbervie, by Lairg
Sutherland IV27 4RP

Modern hotel in far northwestern corner of Scotland, only 27 miles from Cape Wrath. The most northerly mainland entry in the Guide, with beautiful views over the fishing ports of Lochs Clash and Bervie. No frills, but dependable comforts in rooms. David and Geraldine Gregory are hospitable owners. Local single-track roads along the coast and beside lochs are a notable scenic experience. New nomination, so more reports welcome. 14 double rooms, all with bath. Dinner, B&B £56.90–£110.90.

KNIPOCH Strathclyde — Map 5

Knipoch Hotel *Tel* Kilninver (085 26) 251
Knipoch, by Oban
Argyllshire PA34 4QT

A smart, well-furnished, fairly pricey country house hotel, run by the Craig family. *Knipoch* is a long low building, modernised or neo-Georgian, in a particularly beautiful and tranquil setting beside Loch Feachan, an arm of the sea stretching four miles inland just south of Oban. A nominator last year described it as one of the best hotels he had stayed at during a ten-day Scottish tour. A reporter this year confirmed that impression, had especially appreciated the night life ("listening to the water on the loch lapping on the shore") and the cooking ("presentation, quality and quantities all 'just right'") Value for money? "I think so. Even at £62 per person for dinner, B&B, we will return." (*Wilson Phillips*)

Open 15 Feb–2 Jan.
Rooms 21 double – all with bath and shower, telephone, radio and TV; tea-making facilities and baby-listening on request.
Facilities Lounge, bar, restaurant. 3-acre grounds. On sea loch; trout and salmon fishing, sea fishing, sailing, yachting, golf, tennis, squash, bowls, hill walking, pony-trekking, winter sports.
Location 6 m S of Oban on A816.
Restrictions Not suitable for ♿. No dogs.
Credit cards All major cards accepted.
Terms (No service charge) B&B £22.50–£41.50. Alc lunch about £7. Set dinner £23.50. Children under 5 half price.
Service/tipping: "No service charge. Any tips given are divided equally among staff unless it was for something 'beyond the call of duty'. We too would like to see tips fade, but to refuse them can offend."

> Our italicised entries are different this year. There are more of them and they indicate hotels which are worth considering, but which, for various reasons – inadequate information, lack of feedback, ambivalent reports – do not at the moment warrant a fully entry. We should particularly welcome comments on these hotels.

LANGBANK Strathclyde — Map 5

Gleddoch House Hotel
Langbank, Renfrewshire
PA14 6YE

Tel Langbank (047 554) 711
Telex 779801

If you are visiting Glasgow, and are not inconvenienced by staying outside the city centre, this would be a natural choice. *Gleddoch House* is five miles from Glasgow airport and 20 minutes by the M8 from the city centre, but it stands in a 250-acre estate, its outlook wholly rural with lovely views across the Clyde to the hills of Loch Lomond. The house was built in the twenties by the late shipping magnate, Sir James Lithgow, but its conversion to a relatively small country hotel took place only in the seventies. A plus for golfers is that the Gleddoch Golf and Country Club is within the grounds and available to hotel residents at no extra charge – also a squash court, a snooker table, riding stables and trout fishing. Prices, as one reader points out, are comparable to those in central Glasgow, while the standard of accommodation is much higher. The restaurant, too, has much to recommend it. "We vote for this place – and we do not even play golf. We thought it a fine urban hotel in a park-like setting: not as intimate as some country house hotels, but the staff were extremely helpful, and we liked our lovely spacious room overlooking the Clyde, and the fine dinner." (*H Richard Lamb; also Derek Cooper, WA, and others*)

Open All year except 26 Dec and 1/2 Jan.
Rooms 12 double, 8 single – 18 with bath, 2 with shower, all with direct-dial telephone, radio, TV, tea-making facilities and baby-listening.
Facilities Lounge, cocktail bar, restaurant; conference facilities. 250-acre grounds with Golf and Country Club, riding school.
Location Leave M8 at Langbank. Follow signs on B789.
Restrictions Not suitable for ♿. No dogs in public rooms.
Credit cards All major cards accepted.
Terms (No service charge) B&B: single £63–£70; dinner, B&B £85–£120. Set lunch £9.50, dinner £21; full alc £28. Weekend Golf and Leisure break. Reduced rates for children; special meals.

NAIRN Highland — Map 5

Clifton Hotel [GFG]
Viewfield Street, Nairn
Nairnshire IV12 4HW

Tel Nairn (0667) 53119

César awarded in 1987 for utterly acceptable mild eccentricity

"A hotel hand-crafted for lovers of theatre and the theatrical. With the Moray Firth as a backdrop, impresario Gordon Macintyre has filled his old family hotel with paintings, sculptures, bas reliefs, *objets trouvés*, long-gones, bygones, far-gones, the indifferent nestling happily against the tasteful, the tasteless complementing the outrageous. Centrepiece of the whole establishment is the large sea-facing dining room with tables placed upon podiums of varying heights. You feel as you climb the steps to your particular table that on some other night Macbeth may well have climbed up here or Hamlet's pa's ghost may have stalked these lime-lit battlements. Nor is this fancy. Mr Macintyre's principal preoccupation, apart from haunting salesrooms and country-house auctions whence the whole house has been assembled, is the production of plays. The amateur cast is assembled from a 40-mile catchment area, the grand piano is rolled aside and drama happens. The food is elaborate and as ambitious as the theatrical productions . . . "(*Derek Cooper*)

That description of *Clifton*, a collector's piece for connoisseurs of the eccentric, was written in 1980, but everything happily remains the same from year to year. Some recent comments: "As eccentric as you say and as delightful. Definitely not to be missed." (*Carole McQuarrie*) "The best singles I have ever seen – mine looked over the water and was in such a shade of pink as only *Clifton* would dare use." (*Andrena Woodhams*) "A great treat. Breakfasts truly perfect and Gordon Macintyre is an accomplished mind-reader: no sooner did a thought for more coffee, jam etc spring to mind than he was at my side with the required item. His clothes are *wonderful* if a little shabby at times." (*GM Leach*)

Open Mar–end Oct.
Rooms 9 double, 7 single – 15 with bath, 1 with shower; beds have continental quilts, but conventional bedding available on request.
Facilities Drawing room, lounge bar, writing room with TV, 2 restaurants. Hotel licensed as theatre: concerts, plays, recitals in winter. 1-acre grounds. Fishing, shooting, riding, beach, tennis courts, swimming pool, golf nearby.
Location 500 yds from town centre; coming from Inverness turn left at roundabout on A96. Parking for 20 cars.
Restrictions Not suitable for ♿. No dogs in dining room.
Credit cards All major cards accepted.
Terms (No service charge) B&B: single £43, double £68–£76. Full alc £18–£22. 10% discount for stays of 5 days and over. Children's special meals by arrangement.
Service/tipping: "Service charge not imposed; tipping not expected. It is very difficult to convince the public that this is the case."

NEWTONMORE Highland — Map 5

Ard-Na-Coille Hotel [GFG] — *Tel* Newtonmore (054 03) 214
Kingussie Road, Newtonmore
Inverness-shire PH20 1AY

César awarded for the family hotel of the year

Ard-na-Coille means "High in the Woods", an apt description for this unstuffy and welcoming Edwardian shooting lodge, in two acres surrounded by pine trees, with magnificent views over Strathspey towards the Cairngorms. Left in peace by the A9 bypass, it is nevertheless only 15 miles from all the sporting facilities of Aviemore. Unanimous approval from readers for the way in which Annie and Alastair Murchie have created a relaxing and caring small hotel. "Bedrooms are individual with the important extras like a selection of books. The bathrooms are interesting, and they have real baths, that I can lie in stretched-out. Very comfortable sitting room. The wine list is a work of art, makes interesting reading and offers some good wines. The Murchies as always charming, and certainly individual. Where else would the 'breakfast cook' (Mrs Murchie) dress in size ten green wellies and a bowler hat to cook breakfast? Along with the excellent hosts, the other amazing thing is the incredible value for money." (*W Andrew Low; also Frank Kerr, Hon Mrs G Lascelles, Leon T Silver, W Ian Stewart, JS d'Angibau*)

Open Easter–31 Oct and New Year.
Rooms 8 double, 2 single – 1 with bath and WC, 4 with shower (3 also have WC), all with radio and baby-listening.
Facilities 2 lounges, dining room; table-tennis room; drying room; terrace. 2-acre grounds. Salmon/trout fishing on river Spey (licence obtainable from local angling club), golf, pony-trekking, sailing, gliding, shooting, walking, bird-watching; skiing at Aviemore (15 m).
Location Leave A9 at Newtonmore/Kingussie signs. Hotel is at northernmost edge of Newtonmore, just outside speed restriction signs (London–Inverness trains stop at Newtonmore main line station).
Restrictions Not suitable for ♿. No dogs in public rooms.
Credit cards None accepted.
Terms (No service charge) B&B £15.50–£23.50; dinner, B&B £25.50–£33.50. Set dinner £12. Ski packages and golf breaks. 50% reduction for children sharing parents' room; special meals.
Service/tipping: "We make clear that nothing is expected, but quite a number of people like to leave a token of appreciation."

PEEBLES Borders — Map 5

Cringletie House Hotel [GFG] — *Tel* Eddleston (072 13) 233
Peebles, Peeblesshire EH45 8PL

Pedigree pink stone mansion in the Scottish baronial manner with turrets and dormers, two miles north of Peebles, surrounded by garden, woodland, and a 28 acre estate, offering tennis and croquet. Owners, the Maguires, have run the hotel for 17 years, providing traditional comforts and superior cooking, but this year, among compliments from grateful regulars, some criticisms of meals and service. 16 rooms, 10 with bath. B&B £24. Dinner £16.50. More reports please.

PITCAPLE Grampian — Map 5

Pittodrie House Hotel — *Tel* Pitcaple (046 76) 444
Pitcaple, Aberdeenshire AB5 9HS — *Telex* 739935

A promising newcomer to the Guide in the fertile Aberdeenshire plains, with Bennachie as a dramatic backdrop – a country house dating back to the 17th century, but mostly Victorian, acquired by the present owner's grandfather in 1900. It has been a hotel for just over a decade, but the family portraits and the library are part of Theo Smith's inheritance: our inspector told us that he felt as though he was staying with "real" people instead of hoteliers who have bought an old house to run as a hotel. He liked everything about the place. The location: totally secluded and peaceful in a setting prettier than much of this eastern part of Scotland. Grounds: three and a half acres, with a magnificent walled garden. The house: an agreeable twisty-and-turny interior with fine rooms, including a large billiard room, good antique furniture, decent old pictures, much-read old books on the shelves. Comfort: duvets a bit too thick, but beds comfortable and room had armchairs and ample wardrobe space; bathrooms of pre-1920 vintage, with original fittings – plenty of hot water. Food: excellent fresh ingredients, perhaps a bit heavy on the cream. Chef has special gourmet evenings once a month – not tried. Service: consistently efficient and welcoming, without being intrusive. We look forward to more reports.

Open All year.
Rooms 6 double, 6 single – all with bath and/or shower.
Facilities Bar, lounge, restaurant, snooker room, library/private dining room. 3½-acre walled gardens with tennis, squash, croquet and clay pigeon shooting.
Location On A96 Aberdeen–Inverness road. Turn left 2 m N of Inverurie to Chapel of Garloch.
Restrictions Not suitable for ♿. No dogs in public rooms.
Credit cards All major cards accepted.
Terms B&B: single £35–£50, double £70; dinner, B&B: single £53.50–£68.50, double £107. Set lunch £10 (bar lunches also available), dinner £20. 2-day winter breaks. Reduced rates for children sharing parents' room; special meals.

PORT APPIN Strathclyde — Map 5

The Airds Hotel [GFG] — *Tel* Appin (063 173) 236
Port Appin, Appin
Argyllshire PA38 4DF

As usual a bumper crop of appreciation for the hospitality offered by Eric and Betty Allen who this year celebrate their tenth year at this early 18th-century ferry inn overlooking Loch Linnhe, the islands of Lismore and the mountains of Morvern – an enchanting prospect. What readers appreciate is the welcome of the Allens and their staff, the care in the presentation of meals, the skill and assurance of Betty Allen's cooking, Eric Allen's commendable wine list, and the generally high standards that are maintained dependably from year to year, bringing back many regulars. There were, however, among the cries of "faultless" and "perfection", some niggles: only one telephone for the use of residents, in a public place under the stairs; a paucity of extras in rooms: "not even a hook on the bathroom door; no heating in a bathroom, and towels not changed in a five-day visit"; and "it is a pity that Mr Allen can't get just a little more drawer space and depth to drawers in Room 10". We hope that Eric Allen, dedicated hotelier, will be able to deal with these mini-complaints by the time the next Guide comes out.

Open Mid-Mar–mid-Nov.
Rooms 15 double, 2 single – all with bath and/or shower and radio. 2 in annexe.
Facilities 2 lounges, small residents' bar, dining room. Small garden; near loch with shingle beach, bathing, fishing, boating; pony-trekking, forest walks.
Location 2 m off A828, 25 m from Fort William and Oban. Parking for 30 cars.
Restrictions Not suitable for ♿. No children under 5. No dogs.
Credit cards None accepted.
Terms (No service charge) Dinner, B&B £62. Set dinner £22. Reductions for children sharing parents' room; special meals.
Service/tipping: "We do not expect tips. When guests insist the money is distributed to all members of staff."

PORTPATRICK Dumfries and Galloway — Map 5

Knockinaam Lodge Hotel — *Tel* Portpatrick (077 681) 471
Portpatrick
Wigtownshire DG9 9AD

Knockinaam Lodge was built as a holiday house for Lady Hunter Blair in 1869, and enlarged in 1901. It is hidden away in a wooded glen with steep cliffs, which shelters it on three sides, while on the fourth it faces the sea, looking towards the coast of Ireland. It is so secluded that you can sometimes see deer grazing among the trees on the slopes beside the hotel. In spring there are carpets of bluebells and primroses in the woods.

The hotel changed hands last year, so was left out of the Guide, but has come back on a strong tide of approval: "Excellent food, delightful decor, pleasant, fairly formal French service. Well-furnished elegant bedrooms with good bathrooms. Lovely flowers. Enthusiastic and welcoming hosts. Countryside charming." Marcel Frichot, the young Frenchman who with his English wife, Corinna, owns the hotel, was raised in the Seychelles. Both have worked in large continental hotels, but wanted a place of their own, and have already made many improvements. Despite the beach, sandy at low tide, this is no bucket-and-spade place, but an exclusive small hotel with imaginative, sophisticated cooking by a French chef. (*RCJ Gordon, Elizabeth Bushill, Dr Stewart Rae*)

Open Easter–Jan.
Rooms 10 double, 1 single – all with bath and shower, direct-dial telephone and TV; radio on request.
Facilities Small cocktail bar, morning room, drawing room. Downstairs WC equipped for ♿. 30-acre grounds, croquet and sea-fishing. Private beach 100 metres, swimming "for the brave". Wildlife, walks, golf nearby.
Location 8 m SW of Stranraer. Turn left off A77 after Lochans, before Portpatrick.
Restrictions No dogs in public rooms, and only in 2 of the bedrooms.
Credit cards All major cards accepted.
Terms Dinner B&B £40–£80. Set dinner £18–£19; bar lunches available. Off-peak breaks. High tea and reduced rates for children.
Service/tipping: "Tipping not encouraged; any money left is distributed among all staff."

PORTSONACHAN Strathclyde — Map 5

Portsonachan Hotel [GFG] — *Tel* Kilchrenan (086 63) 224
Portsonachan, by Dalmally
Argyllshire PA33 1BL

The setting is superb, on the banks of Loch Awe, in lovely wooded Argyll scenery, with deer browsing the hillsides, and wonderful views. Savoy-trained Christopher Trotter and his wife Caroline have now been six years in this small inn, and bedrooms and public rooms have been gradually upgraded. Most reports endorse the warmth of welcome that gained them a 1985 award of "Most welcoming hotel in the Highlands and Islands", praising the excellent and original food, and use of local ingredients. Few of the bedrooms have bathrooms *en suite*, and complaints persist about poor insulation, lumpy mattresses and inadequate heating. However, most guests feel the setting and welcome far outweigh any niggles. (*RD Burnell, Gillian Seel, Jane Sinclair, Mr and Mrs DS Rampton, PJ Forrest*)

Open Mar–mid-Nov, Christmas and New Year.
Rooms 18 double, 1 single – 6 with bath and shower, all with radio, tea-making facilities and baby-listening.
Facilities 2 lounges, TV room, public bar, residents' bar, dining room. Large garden. Hotel has own jetty on Loch Awe and 10 rowing boats (engines available). Safe bathing and fishing in Loch Awe. River and sea loch fishing.
Location 10 m S of Dalmally. On B840 off A819 Dalmally–Inverary road. (Portsonachan often shown on maps as Southport.)
Restrictions Not suitable for ♿. No dogs in public rooms.
Credit cards Access, Visa.

Terms [1987 rates] Dinner, B&B £29.50–£37.50. Buffet lunch £1–£5.50. Set dinner £13 (£14 to non-residents). Reductions for stays of 3 nights or more; off season tariffs. Reduced rates and high teas for children.
Service/tipping: "No charge made – left to guests' discretion. Tronc *system."*

RAASAY Skye, Highland — Map 5

Isle of Raasay Hotel — *Tel* Raasay (047 862) 222 and 226
Isle of Raasay
by Kyle of Lochalsh, Skye
Inverness-shire IV40 8PB

Raasay is a tiny (4 miles by 15 miles) island reached by a 15 minute ferry from Sconser on Skye, and described by our inspector as "one of the Inner Hebrides' most enchanting islands – a world set apart from the increasingly crowded roads of Skye, with breathtaking views of the Cuillin Hills on Skye and the Torridon Hills on the Scottish mainland. Walkers and birdwatchers should not miss beautiful, wild Raasay and an opportunity to see its golden eagles. The useful *Isle of Raasay* sits 300 yards from the Sound of Raasay looking towards Skye. It is run by Mrs Nicholson and her charming daughter Sheena, an excellent cook whose substantial breakfasts could carry you through a day in the hills with ease. Bedrooms in the new wing are well fitted and comfortable. The decor of the hotel can only be described as latter-day Edwardian Scottish, which gives an impression of formality, even coldness, leavened by the friendliness of the Nicholsons." A report this year fully confirms our inspector's impressions: "Very good value. Highly recommended, especially to those who like an open-air life with walking and peace and quiet." (*Harold Purser*)

Open Apr–Sept inclusive.
Rooms 11 double, 1 single – all with bath, radio, TV and tea-making facilities. 6 ground-floor rooms, 1 specifically designed for ♿.
Facilities 2 residents' lounges (1 with TV), lounge bar, dining room. Small garden in front of hotel. Good walking country; trout fishing in lochs; 5 minutes' from sea.
Location Travel to Kyle from Inverness or to Mallaig from Glasgow; take the ferry to Kyleakin or Armadale respectively. Proceed to Sconser village on Loch Sligachan; there are three ferries daily (except Sun) to Raasay, taking about 15 minutes. Hotel is signposted from ferry terminal.
Restriction No dogs in public rooms.
Credit cards None accepted.
Terms (No service charge) B&B £20; dinner, B&B £32. Bar and packed lunches available. Set dinner from £12. 3-day Holiday Special in conjunction with Skye Hotel Association; 6-day Two Island package May–Sept. Weekly rates. Reduced rates for children under 10.

ST OLA Orkney — Map 5

Foveran Hotel — *Tel* Kirkwall (0856) 2389
St Ola, Nr Kirkwall
Orkney KW15 1SF

Dropped after a change of ownership last year, the *Foveran* is back after favourable reader comments. A modern hotel, designed by its previous owner, an architect, it is half a mile inland from the sea, overlooking

Scapa Flow and has a pleasant Scandinavian interior. The new owners, David and Norma Gerrard, he a former British Airways executive and she an adopted Orcadian, tell us that there are short-eared owls and hares to be seen on their 18 acres, a tempting thought for naturalists. Recent visitors have appreciated the dependable comforts of the house, and, in particular, the gregarious welcome of the hosts – "such warmth, humour and genuine kindness are not easily forgotten". (*Suki Skidmore; also Donald Hackler, Mary Lawrence.*) A car is advisable: the sandy beach at Scapa, five minutes' drive away, is usually cleaner than the local pebble beach.

Open All year except Feb and Oct. Restaurant closed Sun.
Rooms 5 double, 3 single – all with bath and/or shower, radio and tea-making facilities; all on ground floor, suitable for ♿.
Facilities Lounge with open fire, TV room, dining room. 18-acre grounds with beach. Loch and sea fishing, archaeological sites, bird reserve, swimming, golf and squash nearby.
Location SW of Kirkwall on A964 Orphir Road, 2½ m from where it leaves the A963. Hotel is signposted.
Restriction No dogs in public rooms.
Credit cards Access, Visa.
Terms (No service charge) B&B: single £21, double £31. Set dinner £12.50; full alc £15. Special meals for children.

SCARISTA Western Isles — Map 5

Scarista House Hotel — *Tel* Scarista (085 985) 238
Scarista, Isle of Harris PA85 3HX

"Outstanding in every way – the best hotel I've ever visited." (*John Hamp*) "We liked everything about the house: we still feel the glow of the place." (*R Lamb*) "Run by charming perfectionists in a spectacular setting. Food quite exceptional." (*Virginia Godfrey*)

Three fulsome expressions of appreciation to add to the scores we have published in the past, about Andrew and Alison Johnson's "House by the Shore" (the title of Alison Johnson's recent book) – a Georgian manse overlooking a magnificent stretch of Atlantic beach on the western, gentler part of Harris. *Scarista* won a César in 1984 for "civilised living in the wilds": no TV, no radio, but an individual and highly innovative standard of cooking, a first-rate library, specially strong in the wildlife and nature-studies section, and a passion for excellence in every aspect of hotelmanship.

For some time past, it has become clear that the Johnsons weren't going to be at *Scarista* for ever. At one time it seemed likely that they would pack it in, but they are now to run the hotel more as a cooperative venture with two long-time members of their staff, Lena Maclennan and Morag Macleod: the Johnsons won't be around all the time, but Alison Johnson assures us that guests won't much notice the difference – the food will be simpler but the two new co-venturers will keep to the same general style. Naturally, in such a very personal establishment, any change of this kind is likely to alter guests' experience. We should be glad to get reports on the new set-up.

Open Easter–early Oct. May be closed occasional weekends.
Rooms 7 double – all with bath (5 also have shower), all with tea-making facilities. 4 in annexe.

Facilities Drawing room with peat fires (and central heating), library, 2 dining rooms. 2-acre grounds. Access to miles of sandy beach; sea-fishing.
Location 15 m SW of Tarbert on A859, 50 m SW of Stornoway. Regular ferries from Ullapool to Stornoway and from Uig to Tarbert; daily flights to Stornoway from Glasgow and Inverness. Hotel will arrange car hire.
Restrictions No children under 5. Dogs by special arrangement, not in public rooms.
Credit cards None accepted.
Terms (No service charge) B&B £28. Set dinner £16.
Service/tipping: We don't have a policy. We try not to press either way. If people leave something, we share it out according to the proportionate amount of work done in a particular week by each employee. I can't see why you make such a fuss about it: if people are weak-witted enough to tip against their better judgment, more fool them. If they're too mean to want to show appreciation in any *circumstances by giving a present, stuff them!"*

SLEAT Skye, Highland — Map 5

Kinloch Lodge — *Tel* Isle Ornsay
Sleat, Isle of Skye IV43 8QY — (047 13) 214 and 333

Lord and Lady Macdonald are the owners of *Kinloch Lodge*, built on the Macdonald estates as a farmhouse in 1680, but later used as a shooting lodge. It stands at the head of Loch Na Dal, looking across to the mainland mountains and Skye's famous Cuillin Ridge. The gardens go down to the sea, which is on two sides of the hotel. The land behind it rises steeply to 1200 feet. *Kinloch Lodge* is very much a family house, with two drawing rooms with log fires, furnished in pleasant autumnal browns and golds, a formal dining room, painted dark green, with family silver and portraits, modest-sized bedrooms with their own bathrooms, plain but decent, and lovely views over the loch or out towards the wooded hillside. The setting is isolated and peaceful: the rough track leading to the hotel is happily being repaired this year.

The Macdonalds have run the hotel for 14 years, but only moved in as a family four years ago, since when they have extensively redecorated and made it a home. Our description of them in previous years as a "genial couple" led readers to expect elderly hosts. In fact they are spry 39-year-olds who carry suitcases, serve wine, and cook, helped by their children when present. Lady Macdonald also writes successful cookbooks. Reports: an elderly guest appreciated ground floor bedroom, "friendly, delightfully kind atmosphere, food imaginative and delicious"; disappointment from some who had come expecting food to be more *nouvelle*, and higher standards in bedrooms and bathrooms; pleas for direct-dial not coin-box phones; praise for beds turned down, electric blankets turned on; "superb" breakfasts. As usual, there has been a variety of opposition views, but the "ayes" have it by a comfortable margin. (*Caroline Robertson, Susan Coombs, John Hamp, and others*)

Open 28 Dec–5 Jan, 1 Mar–12 Dec.
Rooms 9 double – all with bath, shower and tea-making facilities. 1 ground-floor room.
Facilities 2 drawing rooms, TV room, dining room; games room. 60-acre grounds, superb hill-walking and climbing; sea at bottom of garden; swimming; bird, seal and otter watching, stalking and rough shooting. Fishing (trout, salmon and sea trout) available. Boats for hire. Pony-trekking, golf, sailing all within 20 m.
Location 1 m off A851, 6 m of S of Broadford, 10 m N of Armadale ferry. 4 flights weekly from Glasgow. Through-train London to Mallaig, then Armadale Ferry.
Restrictions Children under 8 not encouraged. No dogs in public rooms.

Credit cards Access, Visa.
Terms B&B £30–£45. Set dinner £20. High tea for children.
Service/tipping: "We actively discourage the leaving of tips; the staff do not expect it."

STRATHTUMMEL Tayside **Map 5**

Port-An-Eilean Hotel *Tel* Tummelbridge (088 24) 233
Strathtummel, by Pitlochry
Perthshire PH16 5RU

The *Port-an-Eilean Hotel,* a newcomer this year, was built as a sporting lodge in 1865 for the sixth Duke of Atholl. It stands beside Loch Tummel in the geographic centre of Scotland, with glorious Highland scenery all round it. You must have good brakes to get down the drive, which plunges steeply through 21 acres of rhododendrons and silver birches to the shores of the loch, and to the hotel. If you arrive in August there will be house-martins nesting under the eaves. Mr and Mrs Gordon Hallewell who own the hotel are very welcoming, and totally unobtrusive. Having made sure you have settled in, they vanish. There is a bell in the hall, to which they respond promptly with tea and fresh scones if required. All the main public rooms have lofty ceilings, though there is also a modern pine sun-lounge. There are bedrooms of various sizes, some overlooking the loch, all with their own *en suite* bathrooms, easy chairs, good reading lights and wardrobe space. There is a fine collection of modern Scottish artists on the walls: prints, oils, tapestries, collages. Mrs Hallewell is an artist, and her daughter designs knitwear, available here. Everywhere is spotlessly clean and warm. The bar is fairly plain. Meals are simple, unpretentious, good home cooking, cooked by the owner, with fresh ingredients. A relaxing and tranquil place: we look forward to more reports.

Open Late Apr–mid-Oct.
Rooms 2 suites, 7 double – all with bath and tea-making facilities.
Facilities Lounge, sun lounge, lounge bar, dining room. 21 acres natural woodland and formal gardens. On loch shore; bathing, fishing, and sailing; walking, shooting, golf nearby. Pitlochry Festival Theatre 10 m.
Location On B8019 9 m W of Pitlochry.
Restrictions Not suitable for ♿. No dogs in public rooms.
Credit cards None accepted.
Terms B&B: single £22.50, double £40; dinner, B&B : single £32.50, double £60. Set dinner £10, bar and packed lunches available. Reduced rates and special meals for children.
Service/tipping: "At guests' discretion: tips go into a tronc.*"*

TIMSGARRY Lewis, Outer Hebrides **Map 5**

Baile-na-Cille *Tel* Timsgarry (085 175) 242
Timsgarry, Uig
Isle of Lewis PA86 9JD

A converted 18th-century manse, run with flair by Richard and Joanna Gollin on the wild west coast of Lewis – "the most remote hotel in Britain," they say, though some other Guide entrants would make the same claim. The village is 34 miles from Stornoway, the last 15 on a single track road. Most rooms face a spectacular seascape; there are three sitting rooms (for TV, music – the Gollins have first-rate stereo – or peace and quiet); and guests regularly praise Joanna Gollin's "bountiful" cooking. Since last year, the hotel has at last acquired a licence – not easy if you are an ex-Church of Scotland manse. Richard Gollin offers this sales pitch: "Right out of the door into 240 square miles of hills, lochs, white sand beaches, birds, wild flowers, clean and total peace and quiet. If this is all too hectic, we also do boat trips to uninhabited islands off the shore!"

Holiday Which? recently voted *Baile-na-Cille* the best hotel on Lewis: it doesn't mean much, Gollin tells us, since most of the others are bars for local drinkers. More important, our readers continue to write enthusiastically: "A superb guest house magnificently situated on the edge of a sandy bay looking across to mountains and islands, run by a very friendly young couple. Joanna Gollin is a super cook – I remember particularly lamb baked in cranberry and rosemary sauce, poached salmon, profiteroles, home-baked scones and bread – all in generous quantities. (I am now on a diet.)" (*Erica Kendall; also JV Salinsky, B Raven*)

Open Mar–mid-Oct.
Rooms 2 family suites, 5 double, 2 single – suites and 3 doubles with bath, all with tea-making facilities. 6 in 2 converted stable blocks by main entrance. Some ground-floor rooms.
Facilities 3 lounges (1 with TV), dining room. 3-acre grounds with walled garden and direct access to beach. Near 7 sandy beaches with safe bathing; trout and sea fishing; sailing, trips in hotel's boat to see seals and birds.
Location 34 m W of Stornoway. Take A858 from Stornoway or Tarbert to Garynahine, B8011 towards Uig; at Miavaig follow signs to *Baile-na-Cille*.
Restriction Not suitable for ♿.
Credit cards None accepted.
Terms B&B £13–£19; dinner, B&B £24–£30. Set dinner £11–£12 (packed lunches about £3.50). Special weekly packages for walkers, bird-watchers, trout fishermen and sea anglers. Reduced rates and special meals for children.
Service/tipping: "Service included. We are 100% against tipping, but if people insist, the money goes straight to the girls."

TIRORAN Mull, Strathclyde — Map 5

Tiroran House — *Tel* Tiroran (068 15) 232
Tiroran, Isle of Mull
Argyllshire PA69 6ES

This is Wing-Commander and Mrs Blockey's tenth year at their well-bred modernised shooting lodge above Loch Scridain, with 13 acres of gardens and woodlands sweeping down to the loch on which the hotel has its own dinghies and a boat for day trips. It is very much the Blockeys' own elegant private home which they open as a hotel in the summer. No TV, room phones, muzak, or even newspapers. One reader this year commented on "a slight inflexibility in administration", but most appreciate the very personal style of the Blockeys' hospitality as well as Mrs Blockey's cooking ("her puddings are a dream"). Here are the views of one comprehensive appreciator: "An immaculate and delightful house with marvellous views, set in a trim and well manicured garden, through which a small river flows down in a series of waterfalls. The Blockeys work very hard indeed, and the results are spectacular. The house is filled with lovely furniture, the dining room is partly an inner room, partly a conservatory in which, when I was there, great bunches of purple grapes were hanging above our heads. Bedrooms are elegant, with matching glazed chintz interlined curtains and bedcovers, comfortable armchairs, and many thoughful extras. Food is delicious and imaginative, mainly locally produced, and the house is run efficiently and thoughtfully, guests being introduced to one another, gathering for drinks before a 7.45 pm dinner to exchange the day's news as in a house party. Most people spend the day exploring Mull, which is a fascinating and beautiful island. They should however be warned that the roads leading to the hotel are single track, and mainly follow the coast, so while providing breath-taking veiws, cannot be taken fast, and guests should allow plenty of time from leaving the ferry to arriving at the hotel. As well as rugged mountains, Mull has leafy glades, many waterfalls, charming small ports, seals, and a ferry to historic Iona." (*WA; also BD Kingston, Allen and Beryl Freer*)

Open Early May–early Oct.
Rooms 8 double, 1 single – 8 with bath (1 also with shower), all with radio and tea-making facilities. 2 in cottage 30 yards from hotel. 1 ground-floor room.
Facilities 2 drawing rooms, dining room, games room. 13-acre gardens and woodland; croquet lawn; immediate access to sea loch safe for bathing, sailing, canoeing.
Location Oban–Craignure car ferry (45 minutes) bookable with Caledonian McBrayne, The Pier, Gourock PA19 1QP. (Lochaline–Fishnish car ferry is not bookable – but much cheaper, and necessitates a longish but superb drive through Morvern.) From Craignure ferry terminal take A849 to Fionnphort. At head of Loch Scridain turn right on to B8035; after 5 m turn left to Tiroran (1 m).
Restrictions Not suitable for severely ♿. No children under 10. Dogs at manager's discretion, not in public rooms.
Credit cards None accepted.
Terms B&B £32–£47, dinner, B&B (min 3 nights) £50–£60. Set (light) lunch £7.50 (packed lunch also available), dinner £18.50. 5- and 7-day all-inclusive holidays including reimbursement of car ferry ticket. Reductions for stays of 3 nights or more.
Service/tipping: "People staying for some time often wish to leave 'a little something'. I make it clear it's entirely up to them. I refuse tips otherwise."

TOBERMORY Mull, Strathclyde — Map 5

The Tobermory Hotel — *Tel* Tobermory (0688) 2091
53 Main Street
Tobermory, Isle of Mull
Argyllshire PA75 6NT

Michael and Christine Ratcliffe are an enterprising couple. They bought their colour-washed fisherman's cottages overlooking the harbour of this unspoilt village in 1984, and have been busy refurbishing and improving. They organise a special motorists' holiday package with reduced rate car ferry to and from Oban and tickets to visit various sites on or near Mull, and this year they are introducing trips on their specially built yacht, *Sea Topaz*, to include dinner, bed and breakfast on an overnight cruise in the waters of Mull. The same boat will take guests on day cruises of the Sound and Loch Sunart. Meanwhile, many readers have written appreciatively of the pleasures of a stay at the hotel, the excellence of the cooking, the high standard of accommodation, the profusion of flowers everywhere, even in the bathrooms, and the "extremely professional and pleasant hosts". Only one or two caveats: room 5 is said to be extremely cramped and "it's not easy for a man to use the loo in room 16". (*IB and CE Pearson, M and N Adler, Isobel Whyte, and others*)

Open 1 Apr–31 Oct.
Rooms 12 double, 3 single – 3 with bath, 2 with shower, all with tea-making facilities.
Facilities 2 lounges (1 with TV), dining room. Small beach nearby; sea and loch fishing; bathing 12 m. 43-foot yacht; cruises.
Location Near centre of Tobermory, on waterfront.
Restrictions Not suitable for ♿. No dogs in dining room.
Terms (No service charge) B&B £15.50–£17; dinner, B&B £23.50–£25. Full alc lunch £6.50; set dinner £8. Motorists' holiday package; overnight sailing trips. Reduced rates for children (under 2 free).
Service/tipping: "We have a 'pot' at reception marked 'staff gratuities' – no coercion on guests to contribute. Money shared among all staff at end of season according to time worked."

ULLAPOOL Highland — Map 5

Altnaharrie Inn [GFG] — *Tel* Dundonnell (085 483) 230
Ullapool, Wester Ross IV26 2SS

César awarded in 1987 for away-from-it-all delight in the featherweight class

"One of the most magic places I have ever stayed in. The food was delicious, certainly the best in Scotland, the simplicity and quiet utterly beguiling. I dream of returning." (*WA*) And so, once again, say many other of our correspondents about this very special uncategorisable establishment, an old drover's inn, with just five bedrooms, that lies across the waters of Loch Broom, virtually inaccessible by land, but reached most romantically, and in bad weather dramatically, in Fred Brown's ferry from Ullapool harbour. As usual our files are full not just of appreciation of the comforts of the room or the wonderful, endlessly inventive cooking of Fred Brown's Norwegian wife, Gunn Eriksen, but of the many different ways in which the couple practise, almost Zen-like, the art of hospitality. One writer this year tells of missing his plane connection, arriving at 11.30 pm and finding to his astonishment a table set with candles and a three-course "snack" waiting for him – watercress soup, a generous portion of local salmon and a rhubarb tart with a delicious sauce. Another contributor mentioned Fred's sympathetic seating arrangements in the dining room: "a master of tact and intuition". The same writer had written in advance that she didn't like shellfish – "I was amazed at Fred's instant ability to realise that I wasn't allergic to shellfish, I just didn't care for the idea of it. So he tempted me with a miniature portion of everyone else's dish. To my surprise I discovered that scallops can be wonderful – at least the very fresh ones that Gunn so expertly presented." And much more in the same vein from *R Lamb, Jan Edwards; also Verena Keable, D Quirk, Mr and Mrs RB Gardner*

Open Easter–mid-Oct.
Rooms 5 double – all with bath and/or shower. 2 in small annexe 30 yards from main building.
Facilities Residents' lounge, dining room. 15-acre grounds with gardens, hills and mountains; on sea loch shore; pebbled beach, safe (but cold) bathing; deep sea fishing free; trout and salmon fishing by arrangement.

Location On western shore of Loch Broom. Access by private launch from Ullapool harbour. Private parking in Ullapool. Guests requested to telephone for launch on arrival in Ullapool.
Restrictions Not suitable for ♿. Children under 8 by arrangement only. Dogs by arrangement, not in public rooms.
Credit cards None accepted.
Terms (No service charge) Dinner, B&B £60. Set dinner £27.50. Reduced rates for children sharing parents' room; special meals.
Service/tipping: "We do not accept tips. Guests should receive good service in return for the fee they have agreed for staying here."

The Ceilidh Place *Tel* Ullapool (0854) 2103
14 West Argyle Street
Ullapool
Wester Ross IV26 2TY

Jean and Robert Urquhart (he, a TV actor when not running the *Place*) continue to do their own thing with splendid verve in their hotel/club-house/restaurant/coffee shop/bookshop complex near the centre of Ullapool. The *Ceilidh Place* won a César for acceptable mild eccentricity in 1986 and, as often happens with this particular award, there is a backlash from the anti-eccentric brigade the following year. The hotel has not lacked supporters, but, not for the first time, some visitors have felt the *Place* too laid-back for comfort, and others have resented its radical propaganda. Here is a characteristic report from this faction:

"Well, unfortunately I am well to the right of Genghis Khan so all the left-wind literature and the unilateral disarmament stuff gets right up my nose. The ageing hippy atmosphere of peace, love and lots of brotherhood in a place very successful at separating tourist from money also grates. They are very busy and this shows as the general rush reduces the service to a farce at times. Hectic music doesn't help at all. However without grudge one has to support their entry in the book. There is plenty of enthusiasm, charming staff and hostess, very interesting if somewhat trendy food and a good atmosphere among guests (I lost 40 pence at Cribbage to an American – most of the anti-American literature was, somewhat pragmatically, quite well hidden!) The place is well designed and a pleasant environment, even if the annexe bedrooms are a mixed lot. All in all, very enjoyable, even for Genghis Khan."

Open All year (limited restaurant service Nov–Feb).
Rooms 12 double, 3 single – 8 with bath. 11 extra rooms (simpler, with bunk beds etc) in Clubhouse in annexe.
Facilities Lounge, Clubhouse bar with live music, coffee shop, games room, dining room; ceilidhs, jazz, classical and folk music evenings at least once a week in summer. Small garden. Rocky beach, boat trips, sea angling, waterskiing, diving; pony-trekking, climbing.
Location First right after pier at W end of Main Street. Large car park.
Restrictions Not suitable for ♿. No dogs in public rooms.
Credit cards All major cards accepted.
Terms (No service charge) B&B £14.50–£26. In Clubhouse £9.50 for bed; continental breakfast £3.75, English breakfast £4.95. Packed lunches available. Coffee shop buffet service from £3.50. Set dinner £12. Special rates for 6 days or more. Occasional courses; activity holidays. Reduced rates and special meals for children.
Service/tipping: "We discourage/disapprove of tipping. In our opinion 'service' is what you pay for on the bill – included in the price of the meal: wages are paid for 'service'.

Tips are of course left however and they are shared equally among everybody. (NB. We encourage staff to support the caterers' union whose policy is against tips.)"

WALLS Shetland Map 5

Burrastow House *Tel* Walls (059 571) 307
Walls, Shetland ZE2 9PD

Built in 1759 and bought early this century by owners of the Black Dyke mill, who then used wool from the Shetland sheep which grazed the land, *Burrastow House*, along with seven acres of land, was acquired in 1981 by Mr and Mrs Harry Tuckey. It entered the Guide in 1984 and has never lacked readers' support. Here is the latest report: *"Burrastow House* is in one of the more remote parts of the Shetland mainland. The views from the house are very fine: looking in one direction across the sound to the island of Vaila, and in another across Lera Voe towards the small community of Walls. Despite its remoteness, there is nothing primitive about the food, service or accommodation. The rooms are spacious, airy and well-appointed. Mr and Mrs Tuckey have furnished the house so that its 18th-century character is enhanced. The food, which is such an important part of each holiday, is superb at *Burrastow House*. Home-made soups and pâtés feature regularly as starters. Fresh home-grown vegetables in season and local fish are used in imaginative dishes, and all the baking, including granary bread, is done daily by Mrs Tuckey. Classical music, peat fires, garden room, the unspoilt character of the building and the warm hospitality all contribute to the very special atmosphere of *Burrastow*." (*Nigel Morries*)

Open 1 Mar–30 Sept.
Rooms 3 double (2 forming a connecting family unit) – all with bath, TV, tea-making facilities and baby-listening.
Facilities Residents' sitting room (TV available on request), diners' sitting room, dining room. 7-acre grounds laid out for golf practice and croquet; private beach with safe (but cold) swimming and pier; sea trout fishing, free dinghy available.
Location 3 m W of Walls.
Restrictions Not suitable for ♿. No dogs in public rooms.
Credit cards None accepted.
Terms B&B £24.75; dinner, B&B £34. Set dinner £13.50–£20; full alc £18. Weekend breaks and reductions for long stays. 1-night bookings occasionally refused. Reduced rates and special meals for children.
Service/tipping: "Most of our guests know that they have been served by the proprietor and therefore the problem of tipping seldom arises."

WHITEBRIDGE Highland Map 5

Knockie Lodge [GFG] *Tel* Gorthleck (045 63) 276
Whitebridge
Inverness-shire IV1 2UP

Knockie Lodge was built in the 18th century as a hunting lodge for the Chief of Clan Fraser. It has a beautiful wild position, in unspoilt countryside, in the high, lightly wooded area of hidden valleys and small lochs, to the eastern side of Loch Ness. Ian and Brenda Milward had never been hoteliers, but had done a great deal of entertaining. They searched for a long time before finding *Knockie Lodge*, and immediately knew this was where they wanted to live. They have treated it as though it were their own home, making the sitting room comfortable, with books and magazines, building on a sun-trap porch, making the dining room elegant with silver and candlelight, and keeping the bedrooms unfussy and snug, with fitted carpets and good hanging space, and immaculate modern bathrooms. "One of the pleasures that one hopes, often in vain, to find in a country house hotel is to be treated as a guest and not a customer. At *Knockie Lodge* one is a guest indeed. Mr and Mrs Milward take an immense amount of trouble to be with their guests and talk to them. A really restful place . . . Fixed-menu dinners were excellent and so well balanced that one never felt bloated." (*JV Armstrong; also Jim Hough, Patricia Featherby*)

Open End Apr–end Oct.
Rooms 9 double, 1 single – all with bath (4 also have shower); tea-making facilities if required.
Facilities Drawing room, dining room; patio. 10-acre grounds. Walking; 2 lochs with free trout fishing for guests; deer-stalking and golf nearby.
Location 2 m down single-track private road W off B862, 8 m N of Fort Augustus.
Restrictions Not suitable for ♿. No children under 10. No dogs in public rooms.
Credit cards Access, Amex, Visa.
Terms (No service charge) B&B: single £30, double £50–£75. Set dinner £15. Bar lunches. Reduced rates out of season.
Service/tipping : "We do not charge for service but if guests particularly want to leave something for the staff it is put in a kitty and divided up amongst staff equally at the end of the month."

Channel Islands

LA SABLONNERIE, SARK

HERM **Map 1**

White House Hotel *Tel* Guernsey (0481) 22159
Herm, via Guernsey

César awarded in 1987 for best family hotel away from it all

"Although it was the worst Easter weather possible, we were warm and snug around the open fires and enthralled by the raging seas only yards from the hotel windows. After the storm, three days of blissful sunshine enabled us to enjoy the beauty of this enchanted island. All the cares of the world are forgotten. Decent food and wine, and all at a reasonable price." "Like a good welcoming country house. We were looked after like old friends, though we had never been before." "Comfort, cleanliness, friendly staff were as good as before, and the food (though one would not make a pilgrimage to Herm for the cuisine) had gone up a notch or two." (*Brian and Di Jobson, Rev and Mrs D Chaning-Pearce, KB Mowle, and others*) Thus the latest report on the only hotel on this tiny island, one-and-a-half miles long and one mile wide, with a native population of 36 including children, though it has to meet an invasion of 1,000 or more day-trippers from Guernsey in August. Herm is a unique family-run fief, with one hotel, one pub, one church. There are no cars, no TV, no clocks on any of the buildings. An earlier visitor called it the most perfect island he had ever clapped eyes on, a paradise. The official brochure dubs it "heaven on earth".

One reader this year, however, offered a contrary view: the decor had "faded chintzy fifties charm", the food was standard boarding-house fare, the pool was unheated and, perhaps worst of all, though the day trippers leave at 5.30, there is an evening boat from Guernsey in the season and aliens carouse in the bars and restaurant till 10.45 pm. More reports please!

Open 31 Mar–7 Oct.
Rooms 7 family suites (each with 2 bedrooms), 23 double, 2 single – all with bath, radio, tea-making facilities and baby-listening. 22 in 3 cottages in grounds. 7 ground-floor rooms.
Facilities 2 lounges, 2 bars, 2 restaurants. 3-acre garden with unheated swimming pool and tennis court. Sandy beaches with safe bathing; private harbour and mooring facilities; fishing.
Location Travel via Guernsey (hourly ferry service from St Peter Port taking 20 minutes). Hotel meets guests at airport or ferry. (No cars on Herm.)
Restriction Herm not really suitable for ♿. No dogs.
Credit cards Access, Visa.
Terms (No service charge) Dinner, B&B £28.50–£38; full board £31–£40. Set lunch £7, dinner £9.25; full alc £14. Christmas and New year programmes. Children under 6 free in family suites, other children 25%–75% discount except July and Aug; special meals.
Service/tipping: "Guests tip only if they wish. These monies are shared equally among all *staff monthly."*

ST PETER PORT Guernsey — Map 1

La Frégate Hotel — *Tel* Guernsey (0481) 24624
Les Cotils

Once an 18th-century manor house, though you would hardly guess that from its present appearance, *La Frégate* has a fine location in its own terraced garden high on a hill above St Peter Port harbour, about five minutes' walk from the town. Some rooms have double-glazed patio windows leading onto a private balcony. A bonus is *La Frégate*'s esteemed French restaurant. "This thoroughly modernised hotel, in which 11 of the 13 rooms enjoy splendid views over St Peter Port and its harbour, is a haven of luxurious tranquillity. Everything one could possible anticipate is provided, down to shower caps and an elegant sewing bag. The rooms are spacious and well furnished. Above all, no one bothers you, though the continuously-manned reception desk courteously and promptly fulfils any request. The French restaurant is still of a very high standard, even though we were disappointed with the main courses and especially their sauces." (*CJ McFeeters*) The restaurant is fairly formal – ties and jackets *de rigueur* – and the table d'hôte for residents must be ordered and begun between 7 and 7.30 pm. Also the hotel is not fully licensed – there is no bar for non-residents.

Open All year.
Rooms 9 double, 4 single – all with bath and shower, telephone and tea-making facilities; 6 with private balcony; TV on request.

Facilities Residents' lounge, lounge bar, air-conditioned restaurant. 2-acre grounds with terraced gardens. 5 minutes' walk to harbour with fishing, 10 minutes to indoor leisure centre; easy access to all island beaches.
Location Near Candie Gardens. 5 minutes' walk from town centre. Difficult to find: the hotel suggests you telephone for directions on arrival on the island. Private carpark.
Restrictions Not suitable for ♿. No children under 14 in hotel, under 9 in restaurant. No dogs.
Credit cards All major cards accepted.
Terms (Service at guests' discretion) B&B: single £27.50–£37.50, double £50–£75; dinner, B&B: single £39–£49, double £73–£98; full board: single £46.50–£56.50, double £88–£113. Set lunch £7.50, dinner £11.50; full alc £20.

Midhurst House *Tel* Guernsey (0481) 24391
Candie Road

We continue to reeive warm comments on this small personal establishment, in an elegant Regency town house quietly located ten minutes' walk up from the harbour. Prices are very reasonable. Two characteristic comments: "A modest but immaculate hotel with truly caring owners. Only drawback is the early dinner in the evening, but the food is very good, fresh, original, with delicious vegetables (not overcooked!) and puddings. The friendly atmosphere leads to easy chatting among the other guests who on both occasions were unanimous in their warm approval of the establishment."(*C Haward*) "Brian and Jan Goodenough gave our young children and us a wonderful holiday, and even had enough patience to show our youngsters how to make home-made ice-cream and sorbets. This hotel deserves to thrive. When the Guernsey April winds blew hard, we were snug, warm and well fed at *Midhurst*." (*Neil Riley; also M Crick, AE Stockvis*)

Open 26 Mar–29 Oct.
Rooms 8 double – 2 with bath, 6 with shower, all with TV and tea-making facilities. 3 in cottage-style annexe. 4 ground-floor rooms.
Facilities Lounge, dining room. Small garden. 5 minutes' walk from bathing pools and fishing.
Location 5 minutes' walk from town centre, near Candie Museum and Cambridge Park. Public free parking nearby.
Restrictions Not suitable for ♿. No children under 8. No dogs.
Credit cards None accepted.
Terms (No service charge) B&B: single occupancy £17–£20, double £30–£36; dinner, B&B (high season only): single £22–£25, double £40–£46. Set lunch/dinner £5; special meals (lobster etc) on request £8 extra. Special packages including transport. 50% reductions for children 8-10 yrs if sharing with 2 adults. *Service/tipping: "Tipping is not expected. Some guests insist and these tips are distributed between all employees in proportion to hours worked."*

ST SAVIOUR Jersey — Map 1

Longueville Manor Hotel [GFG] *Tel* Jersey (0534) 25501
Telex 4192306 LMH

Longueville Manor has long been the most recommendable place to stay in Jersey for those who like a sophisticated country house style for their vacations. It stands in 15 acres of grounds at the foot of a wooded valley, one-and-a-half miles inland from Jersey's capital, St Helier, well away from the tourist hubbub, and, a plus for golfers, only two-and-a-half miles from the Royal Jersey Golf Club. There is a large heated swimming pool (which one reader this year found somewhat murky), where lunch may be taken in fine weather. It has been a family-run enterprise for more than a quarter of a century, and the only complaint of any substance over the years has been that the cuisine did not match the luxury of the setting. In the past two years, however, the restaurant has dramatically improved under the *toque* of John Dicken. Now there is a new *chef de cuisine,* Barry Foster, who has been working with Michael Quinn at the *Ritz* and then at *Ettington Park.* There has also been a major refurbishment – at a cost of £500,000 we are told – of half the bedrooms. We should welcome reports on the new kitchen regime and the bedroom facelifts.

Open All year.
Rooms 2 suites, 23 bed-sitters, 8 double, 2 single – all with bath, shower, direct-dial telephone, radio and TV.
Facilities Lift. Bar/lounge, 2 sitting rooms, dining room; conference facilities. 15-acre grounds with swimming pool (heated in season) and putting green. Golf, bowls, squash, tennis within easy reach. 1½ m from sea, sandy beaches, surfing, sailing and water-skiing. Coaches call by arrangement for excursions.
Location 1½ m E of St Helier; bus stops near main hotel gates. From airport, take main roads to St Helier; near harbour follow sign A17 to Georgetown. Then take A3 for 1½ m; hotel is on left.
Restrictions Only restaurant suitable for ♿. No children under 7. No dogs in public rooms.
Credit cards All major cards accepted.
Terms (10% service charge added to meals) B&B: single £48–£53.50, double £80–£123.50, suite £155–£175; dinner, B&B: single £63.50–£69, double £111–£154, suite £186–£206. Set lunch £13.50, dinner £16.50; full alc £25. Winter weekend breaks; Christmas–New Year package. Reductions for children sharing parents' room; special meals.
Service/tipping: "No service charge on room rates. 10% mandatory on restaurant bills; shared between all restaurant and kitchen staff.

SARK — Map 1

Hotel Petit Champ

Sark, via Guernsey — *Tel* Sark (048 183) 2046

The *Petit Champ* has the admirable virtue of maintaining its character and quality from year to year. Two typical comments from this year's mailbag: "Up to its excellent standard in every way." And: "Have stayed here for 12 years running and will probably continue to do so." It is a pleasant late 19th-century granite building, in a secluded part of the island, well away from the day-trippers' tracks, but within half-an-hour's walk of any part of Sark. Most of its rooms have superb views of the sea and the neighbouring islands of Guernsey, Herm and Jethou; there's a well-tended sheltered garden and, about 50 yards from the hotel, a solar-heated swimming pool built into a disused quarry – a fine sun-trap out of the wind. It will take you ten minutes to walk down to a secluded bay with sand at low tide – but allow half an hour for the climb back. There is also, *mirabile dictu,* a first-rate restaurant. It seemed to have gone through a bad patch a couple of years ago, but recent reports have been unreservedly favourable. Only gripes this year: the swimming pool not as immaculately clean as hitherto and – a generalised complaint: "Does no hotel expect its guests ever to write a letter? Even in this quite excellent hotel, the only writing table is occupied by a huge and beautiful bowl of flowers which I have had to move in order to write to you." (*Tim Brierly, RA Nisbet, SC Gibson; also Margaret Crick, J Douglas Noble*)

Open Mid-Apr–early Oct.
Rooms 2 family suites (doubles with adjoining singles), 11 double, 3 single – 13 with bath and/or shower. Some ground-floor rooms.
Facilities 3 sun-lounges, lounge (no smoking), TV lounge, bar, restaurant. 1-acre grounds. 5 minutes' walk down to sea with sandy beach and safe bathing; fishing.
Location 10 minutes' walk from centre. Head for Beau Regard and turn right just before duck pond.
Restrictions Sark not suitable for seriously ♿. Children must be old enough to sit with parents at dinner. No dogs.
Credit cards All major cards accepted.
Terms Dinner, B&B £26–£30. Set lunch from £7.50, dinner £10.50. One-third reduction for children sharing parents' room.
Service/tipping: "Our tariff clearly states that service is included. Many guests still leave something. We explain that it is unnecessary, but if they insist we accept graciously rather than cause offence."

La Sablonnerie *Tel* Sark (048 183) 2061
Sark, via Guernsey

This more-off-the-beaten-track hotel in the quieter, less commercialised southern peninsula of the island is owned by the Sark-born Perrée family. It came into the Guide for the first time last year with the following inspectorial report: "Set in a picturesque rural part of Little Sark and reached by the dramatic isthmus of La Coupée, the hotel is surrounded by interesting walks and striking scenery. Consisting of a farmhouse and a handful of cottages, the hotel has converted the old buildings to provide the 22 rooms, each individual in size and decor, sprinkled about the tiny hamlet. Simple in style and facilities, they all have a charm that makes the hotel very appealing. That charm is carried through to the public rooms – small but very cosy, and pretty in their style. The main building has attractive flowerbeds and a croquet lawn. Opposite is the tea garden with well-kept lawns and gardens and suntraps with tables and chairs. Service was as friendly as I can recall anywhere. The food was interesting and competently prepared. Overall a quite enchanting hotel." More reports please.

Open Easter–Oct.
Rooms 1 suite, 14 double, 6 single – 12 with bath and/or shower. All in cottages in courtyard and garden 50 yards from main building.
Facilities Lounge, cocktail bar, dining room, public bar in tea garden, sun lounge and 2 smaller lounges in annexe. 5-acre grounds with gardens and croquet lawn; surrounded by hotel's 100-acre farmland. Small coves and pebble beaches suitable for bathing nearby; sandy bay 15 minutes' walk. Hotel boat for trips round island; fishing.
Location At southern tip of island. Guests are met by tractor or horse and carriage if they arrive by afternoon boats.
Restrictions Sark not suitable for severely ♿. Dogs at hotel's discretion only.
Credit cards Access, Amex, Visa.
Terms (Excluding 10% service charge) B&B £16–£25; dinner, B&B £25.50–£37.50; full board £27.50–£39.50 Set lunch £9, dinner £12.
Service/tipping: "10% added; distributed between all the staff."

There is no VAT in the Channel Islands.

Stocks Hotel *Tel* (048 183) 2001
Sark, via Guernsey

The family Armorgie are the hosts at this old-established characteristically granite Sark hotel in the Dixcart Valley, which made its first appearance in the Guide last year, the nominator singling out for special mention: "A big sunny room overlooking the garden. Special soap, talc in bath and lots of nice extras. Divine food – good sauces, decent wine and a table full of desserts to make a strong man weep: the best food I had on a three-week trip." (*Joan Marble Cook*) A recent visitor warmly supports the entry – "marvellous value for money . . . The family Armorgie and all their staff are a happy lot and this is infectious" – though she would have liked some heating in the bedroom (in early May) and mentioned some shabby furniture and furnishings. More reports please.

Open Apr–Oct.
Rooms 2 family, 18 double, 4 single – 14 with bath and/or shower. 8 in Dower House annexe.
Facilities Lounge, TV lounge, library/games room with TV, residents' bar, restaurant, buffet/bar; terrace. 1½-acre grounds with unheated swimming pool. Beach 10 minutes' walk; fishing, cycling.
Location 5 minutes' walk from centre.
Restrictions Sark not suitable for seriously ♿. No dogs.
Credit cards None accepted.
Terms (No service charge) Dinner, B&B £22.50–£28. Set lunch £11.50, dinner £12.50; lunch and evening buffet from £7.50. Reduced rates according to age for children sharing parents' room; special meals.
Service/tipping: "Service is optional. Tronc *split equally regardless of position – Armorgie family excluded!"*

Republic of Ireland

CASHEL HOUSE, CASHEL BAY

BALLINDERRY Co Tipperary **Map 6**

Gurthalougha House *Tel* Borrisokane (067) 22080
Ballinderry, Nenagh

"Yes, this is a lovely old house, and beautifully furnished. Pigeons coo in the courtyard. The setting is perfect, and evening views across Lough Derg are utterly peaceful and calm. Michael Wilkinson's cooking is delicious. I just hope the Wilkinsons will continue to do their own thing in their own way . . . Their house has a unique quality." (*Ruth West*) The place with these halcyon qualities is an early 19th-century country house in 150 acres of forest, on the shores of Lough Derg, the largest lake on the Shannon. Ruth West endorses the nomination from *Myrtle Allen* (of *Ballymaloe House*): "Very quiet and peaceful – much more attractive than the write-up in the brochure. Michael Wilkinson loves cooking and this shows through with everything that comes out of the kitchen. His wife, Bessie, is perfect in the front of house. The place is very professionally run, with an authentic country house style and atmosphere. I arrived on a chilly May evening and was delighted with the warm log fires and large but cosy bedroom. Don't expect a posh decor. The house is decorated with a lot of taste and a little money (*much* better than the other way round). A lovely area for a holiday and of course excellent for fishermen." (*Also Sheila Young*)

Open All year except Christmas.
Rooms 8 double – 4 with bath, 1 with shower; baby-sitting can be arranged.
Facilities Sitting room, library, dining room. 150-acre grounds with forest walks, ornamental gardens and ½-m lake shore with private quay, safe bathing, boats for guests' use, ghillie available; windsurfing, pony-trekking.
Location On shores of Lough Derg, W of Ballinderry village, which is 16 m N of Nenagh. (Signposted from Ballinderry.)
Restriction Not suitable for ♿. No small children in dining room.
Credit cards None accepted.
Terms (No service charge) B&B: IR£25; dinner, B&B IR£41. Set dinner IR£16. Weekend breaks. 33% reduction for children under 10.

BALLYLICKEY Co Cork — Map 6

Sea View House Hotel — *Tel* Bantry (027) 50073 and 50462
Ballylickey, Bantry

A former Guide hotelier, *John Naismith* (ex-*Bear* of Nayland), gives his own professional appreciation of Kathleen O'Sullivan's comfortable, friendly establishment three miles north of Bantry, with good views over Bantry Bay and distant mountains: "*Sea View* is really in between a guest house and a hotel as the bedrooms are quite small, mostly *en suite*, and individually decorated. They are also very comfortable and very clean, in fact spotless, and while you are having dinner your room is tidied and the beds folded down. Dinner embarrasses me as I thought I was good changing my six main course menu every couple of weeks; Kathleen, as she is known, changes the menu every night and there are normally six to eight starters and eight main courses with a middle course of soup normally from a choice of two or three. The wine list is only average but I think that is an Irish seasonal problem with not enough customers, too short a season and lousy distribution. Kathleen and her staff are very friendly and a packed lunch or tea and cakes in the afternoon is never a problem." (*Endorsed by Amanda Garrett, and Professor DA Webb*)

Open Mid-Mar–31 Oct.
Rooms 12 double, 1 single – all with bath or shower, telephone, tea-making facilities and baby-listening. Family accommodation in cottage in garden.
Facilities Lounge, reading room, TV room, cocktail bar, dining room. 5-acre grounds. Game fishing, sea fishing, pony-trekking, boating, beaches and golf nearby.
Location 3 m N of Bantry towards Glengarriff, 70 yds off main road.
Restriction Not suitable for ♿.
Credit cards Access, Amex, Visa.
Terms B&B IR£25–IR£30. Set lunch IR£8.50–IR£9, dinner IR£17.50. Mid-week and weekend breaks.
Service/tipping: "Service charge included; any extra is shared equally among all staff."

> "The very large dressing table had a large marble top and was situated in the recess, thus making it quite impossible to see to make up. A colour TV stood on this but it would be difficult to watch it, unless you perched beside it."

BALLYVAUGHAN Co Clare — Map 6

Gregans Castle Hotel

Tel Ennis (065) 77005
Telex 70130

Stony seabord, far and foreign,
Stony hills poured over space,
Stony outcrop of the Burren,
Stones in every fertile place,
Little fields with boulders dotted.
Grey-stone shoulders saffron-spotted,
Stone-walled cabins thatched with reeds.
Where a Stone Age people breeds
The last of Europe's stone age race.

The poet, paying his tribute to the Burren, is the late and lamented John Betjeman, but *Gregans Castle*, the only hotel in the heart of the 100 square miles of this botanists' and ornithologists' paradise, is no stone-walled cabin. It is a welcoming country house hotel hosted by Peter and Moira Haden, who have done much to add to the comforts of their guests in their tenure of more than a decade. The setting, with views over the Burren and Galway Bay is "beyond price" on a fine day, and the area around is touristically very rich, especially for Yeats enthusiasts, with his house, Thoor Ballylee, and Lady Gregory's home, Coole Park, within easy driving distance. But one visitor this year, while appreciating the comforts of the house and liking the family feel of the place, found the cooking, both at dinner and breakfast, decidedly disappointing. More reports welcome.

Open 31 Mar–end Oct.
Rooms 4 mini-suites, 12 double, 1 single – 14 with bath and/or shower. Some ground-floor suites.
Facilities Hall with fireplace, 2 lounges (1 with TV), bar, dining room. 12-acre grounds with parkland and gardens. Safe, sandy beach with excellent shore fishing 4½ m; harbour with swimming and boating 3½ m.
Location On road N67 between Ballyvaughan and Lisdoonvarna, 3½ m SW of village, at foot of "Corkscrew Hill".
Restriction No dogs.
Credit card Visa.
Terms (No service charge) Dinner, B&B: single IR£60–IR£70, double IR£100–IR£110. Set dinner IR£19.50. Reduced 3-day rates. Reduced rates for children; special meals.
Service/tipping: "We find most guests want to tip. That is their prerogative."

CASHEL Co Tipperary — Map 6

Cashel Palace Hotel

Tel Tipperary (062) 61411
Telex 26938

Cashel itself is no great scenic attraction with its 21 bars and its dreary high street. But the *Palace* is something else – a magnificent Palladian episcopal residence built in 1730 for Archbishop Bolton by Sir Edward Lovett Pearce (the architect of the old Parliament House in Dublin, now the Bank of Ireland), with a noble red-brick Queen Anne facade and a garden bordering on the Rock of Cashel, also a fine picture collection. Under its present owner, Ray Carroll, it has become a sophisticated 20th-century country house hotel, albeit at the upper end of the price spectrum. Readers continue to appreciate the handsome dining room overlooking a well-tended garden and the friendly service. (*Mary Purdy, Edward Harvey*)

Open All year except Christmas and Boxing Days. Restaurant closed Fri in winter.
Rooms 3 suites, 15 double, 2 single – all with bath, shower, telephone, radio, TV and baby-listening.
Facilities Drawing room, cellar bar, 2 restaurants. 20-acre grounds with landscaped gardens. Golf, shooting and fishing nearby.
Location 2 minutes' walk from centre of Cashel which is on main Dublin–Cork road. Ample parking.
Restrictions Not suitable for ♿. No dogs.
Credit cards All major cards accepted.
Terms (Excluding 10% service charge) Room: single IR£59–IR£65, double IR£90–IR£95, suite IR£120. Breakfast: continental IR£5.50, English IR£8. Set dinner IR£25; full alc IR£30. Special meals for children on request.
Service/tipping: "10% is added to room and restaurant bills if customer is satisfied. It is distributed to all staff via their wages. Other tipping discouraged."

CASHEL BAY Co Galway — Map 6

Cashel House Hotel

Tel Clifden (095) 31001
Telex 50812

César awarded for maintaining the highest standards of Irish hotelmanship

"One of the most pleasant hotels I have ever visited. It was like being at home with turf fires, exquisitely comfortable rooms and furniture, refreshingly personal and friendly service and delicious food. The restaurant is a treasure. I love fresh, well-cooked food and this is exactly what you get at *Cashel House*. The portions are enormous and without fail we were asked if we would like more." (*Mike Dormer*) "We adored *Cashel House* – the warmth and hospitality to my wife and four children. Can there be a better-run restaurant in the world? The memory of the smoked salmon!" (*Harrison Gardner; with similar tributes from Margaret M DeVine, Ruth West*)

Judging by our reports *Cashel House*, like a vintage wine, gets better each year. It is a civilised former manor house, with a 50-acre prize-winning garden run by two veteran hoteliers, Dermot and Kay McEvilly – an oasis in the rugged wilderness of Connemara. In filling up our questionnaire, Dermot McEvilly adds a few further bonuses: "Antiques, fluffy towels, orthopaedic beds, freshly-squeezed orange juice, hot water bottles on cool nights. No music, no noise, no functions."

Open Mid-Mar–end Oct.
Rooms 13 suites, 17 double, 3 single – all with bath (whirlpool baths in 4 garden suites); TV in suites on request. 6 ground-floor rooms.
Facilities Bar/lounge with conservatory, 2 lounges, TV room, library, dining room. 50-acre gardens with woodland walks; hard tennis court; small private sandy beach for residents; grounds lead to Cashel Hill. Many other beaches within easy reach; golf, lake and river fishing, bird-watching, riding, deep-sea fishing.
Location Take N59 from Galway. Turn left to village 1 m after Recess.
Restrictions No children under 5. No dogs in public rooms.
Credit cards All major cards accepted.

Terms (Excluding 12½% service) B&B: IR£33–IR£36; dinner, B&B (3 days min) IR£51–IR£55. Set dinner IR£17–IR£18; full alc IR£12–IR£15. Reduced rates for children by arrangement.
Service/tipping: "Service charge made to counteract 'Good tippers got good table or service' syndrome instead of good service being rewarded by tip. No need for further tips, though graciously accepted by staff."

CORK Co Cork — Map 6

Arbutus Lodge Hotel [GFG] — *Tel* Cork (021) 501237
Montenotte — *Telex* 75079 ARBU

Two items of good news for *Arbutus* fans: first, the hotel has recovered the *Michelin* rosette which it lost several years back. Several readers have sent us glowing accounts of their recent meals: "A memorable experience", "food – and service, too – better than ever", etc. Secondly, major renovations – not before time – have been put in hand in the bedrooms. *Arbutus Lodge* stands in the posh suburbs of Montenotte, 15 minutes' walk or five minutes' drive from the centre. The *Lodge* was built *c*.1802, a master cooper's house, and some rooms still reflect the solid virtues of its origins. Others, in the modern extension grafted on either side of the main building have been no more than functional. Many, however, have a spectacular view over the river Lee to the city beyond; it's well worth asking for a room with a view when booking. Downstairs there is a large comfortable bar, a residents' lounge and the restaurant with large bay window, starched white table cloths, good china and glass, flowers, candles and so on. There is a splendid wine list, reflecting Declan Ryan's zeal in tracing uncommonly good wine at uncommonly low prices. The same personal flair is shown in the public rooms, filled with the work of contemporary Irish artists. (*Janess McLaren Irving, Patrick Skene Catling, Sydney Carpenter*)

Open All year, except Christmas. Restaurant closed Sun (bar meals available).
Rooms 11 double, 9 single – all with bath and/or shower, telephone, radio, TV.
Facilities Lounge, bar, 2 dining rooms. 1-acre garden with patio.
Location 1½ m up hill from town centre. Parking.
Restrictions Not suitable for ♿. No dogs.
Credit cards Amex, Diners, Visa.
Terms (No service charge) B&B: single IR£30-IR£55, double IR£60-IR£96. Set lunch IR£16.75, dinner IR£19.95; full alc IR£28.50. Weekend rates; gourmet weekends.
Service/tipping: "Guests should tip only if they receive exceptional service."

Lotamore House — *Tel* (021) 822344
Tivoli

We had our first entry last year for this Grade A guest house B&B in a splendid Georgian manor. It lies just east of the city on the N25 dual carriageway towards Dublin and Waterford. Not an ideal location perhaps, though there are fine views across the main road to the river Lee. Its nominator was welcomed with much kindness, had a spacious room away from any traffic noise, with good fluffy towels and orthopaedic beds, enjoyed an excellent breakfast with freshly-squeezed orange juice – "in front of our eyes!" – and delighted in "a lovely quiet atmosphere and very kind, smiley staff". (*Wendy Hillary*) A report just received describes the nomination as "correct in every detail". (*Janess McLaren Irving*)

Open All year.
Rooms 20 double, 2 single – all with bath and shower, telephone and TV. Some ground-floor rooms.
Facilities Lounge with TV, breakfast room. 4-acre grounds.
Location 3 m E of city centre; on N25 towards Dublin and Waterford.
Credit cards Access, Amex, Visa
Terms (No service charge) B&B IR£16.50–IR£20. Children under 12 IR£7.50. (No restaurant but light snacks available.)
Service/tipping: "We leave it to customers. Anything given is distributed amongst the staff monthly."

CULLEENAMORE Co Sligo — Map 6

Knockmuldowney Country House and Restaurant — *Tel* Sligo (071) 68122
Culleenamore, Nr Strandhill

Georgian country house in the heart of Yeats country, at the foot of Knocknarea Mountain and with views over Ballisodare Bay. Good sandy beach two miles. Sligo five miles. New this year, and recommended for its caring cooking, the quiet, friendly welcome of Mr and Mrs Cooper and their staff. Open Mid-Mar–early Nov. 6 double rooms with bath and shower. B&B: IR£25–IR£30. Set dinner IR£12.50. New this year: more reports please.

DROMAHAIR Co Leitrim — Map 6

Drumlease Glebe House — *Tel* Sligo (071) 64141
Telex 40301 DLSTEI

This Georgian country house stands in ten acres of grounds bordering on the River Bonet, in the heart of Yeats country, close to Sligo. It's a great place for fishing, and the hotel owns salmon and trout fishing rights on Lough Melvin and can provide boats, ghillies, tackle etc. The hotel recently changed hands but kept its place in the Guide since it was clear that standards had only improved under the new American owners, Andrew and Barbara Greenstein – he a lawyer for 27 years, and she a former singer and actress. Good reports continue to reach us: "The owners could not have been more accommodating. The hostess even played the harp for us. We borrowed their dogs to hike with round the beautiful countryside. The food was outstanding and we were served like royalty. We felt that we had taken a step back in time in this manicured fairy-tale setting." (*Beverly and Michael Henning*) The friendliness of the Greensteins' dogs and their chaperoning qualities also feature in another report which concludes: "A lovely home, outstanding food and service, wonderful ambience . . . The best of Irish country house living." (*Elaine Doolittle*). An inspector gives it a seal of approval too. Of her dinner she writes: "It would be possible to criticise aspects of the meal, but it was prepared and served with such elaborate care and attention to detail that it really shouldn't be faulted in any circumstances. To produce it for three guests at the back end of a dismal summer season in the depths of Leitrim deserves an Order of Merit."

Open 1 Apr–2 Oct.
Rooms 8 double, – 3 with bath, 5 with shower.
Facilities Drawing room, library/TV room, dining room; antique shop. 10 acres of wooded parkland, unheated swimming pool, private salmon and trout fishing in river Bonet and Lough Melvin. Deep-sea fishing nearby; ghillie, boats, engines, tackle etc available. Championship golf course 12 m.
Location 2 m E of Dromahair; take the school road out of Dromahair village.
Restrictions Not suitable for ♿. No children under 15. No dogs.
Credit cards Access, Amex, Visa.
Terms (No service charge) B&B IR£33–IR£36. Set dinner IR£18; picnic lunch IR£6.50.
Service/tipping: "We do not have a service charge; any tips are distributed equally among all staff."

DUBLIN — Map 6

Buswells Hotel
Molesworth Street, Dublin 2

Tel Dublin (01) 764013 and 613888
Telex 90622

Reinstated after several years in the Guide wilderness, this "creaky but comfortable" amalgamation of two Georgian red-brick terrace houses overlooks Leinster House, where Dail Eireann, Ireland's Parliament, convenes. An inspector reports: "Noel Duff, the amiable and discreetly attentive proprietor, says his establishment is the oldest family-owned and -managed hotel in Dublin. Eamon de Valera was among its early distinguished patrons. Members of the Dail and journalists often congregate in the Georgian Bar, especially before, or instead of, lunch. Eavesdropping in the comfort of the bar is a popular sport, enjoyed even by Dubliners. For those who prefer to take their refreshment more tranquilly, there are many secluded corners for intimate tête-à-têtes. Visitors say they appreciate the hotel's central location, an architectural oasis, only a few minutes walk from St Stephen's Green, Trinity College, the National Gallery and the better shopping streets. The hotel was entirely refurbished in 1987 in harmony with its past, with the friendly staff blessedly unaltered and modern innovations mainly restricted to the bathrooms and a welcome new lift. The bedrooms are small, immaculate and comfortable. The restaurant, with a lot of red plush and two handsome glass-dome skylights, provides a comprehensive, conventional à la carte menu, most notable for seafood, steaks and chops. The chef is cautious and sound. There is an adequately representative list of decent wines at reasonable prices. Overall, the hotel gives an impression of soft carpets, warmth and sympathy."

Open All year. Restaurant closed Sat, and Sun lunchtime.
Rooms 3 triple, 51 double, 21 single – all with direct-dial telephone, radio, TV and tea-making facilities; baby-listening by arrangement.
Facilities Lift. 2 bars, restaurant; 4 conference rooms.
Location Opposite Dail; between Trinity College and St Stephen's Green.
Restrictions Not suitable for ♿. Small dogs only, not in public rooms.
Credit cards All major cards accepted.
Terms (Excluding 12½% service charge) Rooms: single IR£43, double IR£66. Breakfast IR£6. Full alc IR£17.
Service/tipping: "Tips left to customers' discretion."

We are particularly keen to have reports on italicised entries.

Kilronan House *Tel* Dublin (01) 755266,751562
70 Adelaide Road, Dublin 2 and 782841

New this year, an upmarket guest house in the heart of Georgian Dublin, ten minutes' stroll to Grafton Street and St Stephen's Green. Recommended for the fairly small but well-maintained rooms, the charm of the staff and the excellent home-made bread and preserves for breakfast. Open l Jan–23 Dec. 11 rooms, 10 with shower. B&B IR£21–IR£28. More reports please.

Mount Herbert *Tel* Dublin (01) 684321
Herbert Road, Ballsbridge *Telex* 92173 GLMH
Dublin 4

A large guest house – once the home of Lord Robinson – in the select suburb of Ballsbridge, within walking distance of the Royal Dublin Society's show-grounds. Recommended for its convenient location, very reasonable tariff and friendly service. Rooms are fairly simple but dependably well maintained. Restaurant for residents, but no bar. 107 rooms, all with bath and shower, 6 specially adapted for ♿. B&B IR£16.50–IR£20. Set dinner IR£10. More reports please.

GOREY Co Wexford — Map 6

Marlfield House [GFG] *Tel* Gorey (055) 21124
Telex 80757

"This was probably the best of all the hotels we stayed at on this visit," writes *Kathleen Edwards* of Mary Bowe's noble three-storey Regency house, formerly the dower-house of the Courtown estate, now a sophisticated admirably-run country house hotel, with a particularly attractive conservatory dining room, with white trellis, a profusion of plants, subtly placed mirrors and subdued lighting – "a fairyland appearance". Mary Bowe tells us proudly of the host of awards her hotel has won this past year: two national awards for her breakfasts and her garden, a regional award for cheese, and, for the eighth time, an Irish Tourist Board award for the excellence of her restaurant. *Marlfield* was also chosen by Andrew Harper's Hideaway Report as the most enchanting Irish small hotel. Apart from the comforts of the hotel and its acclaimed restaurant, it is in a choice position for touring – a mile from the sea with sandy beaches, close to a golf course, and with plenty of the beauty spots of Co Wicklow at hand. Only grumble: no credit cards accepted.

Open All year, except 3 days at Christmas.
Rooms 1 suite, 11 double – all with bath, shower, telephone, and TV. 1 ground-floor room.
Facilities Drawing room, library, lounge bar, restaurant; conservatory, veranda. 36-acre grounds with tennis court. Sea with sandy beaches and safe bathing 2 m.
Location 1 m from Gorey on the Courtown road.
Restrictions No children under 5. No dogs.
Credit cards None accepted.
Terms (Excluding 10% service charge) B&B: single IR£55–IR£70, double IR£70–IR£100, suite IR£80–IR£100. Set lunch IR£16, dinner IR£23; full alc lunch IR£20. Weekend rates in off season. 1-night bookings sometimes refused for off-season weekends. High teas for children on request.

Service/tipping: "10% added; included with wages. I am considering doing away with service charge and leaving tips optional."

KANTURK Co Cork — Map 6

Assolas Country House — *Tel* Kanturk (029) 50015

An elegant and serene 17th-century manor house, set in beautiful grounds beside a river, the home of the Bourke family for the past 70 years. It made its first appearance in the Guide last year. No feedback at the time of going to press – not surprising since the hotel is closed through the winter. We repeat part of our inspector's report: "Even before we arrived, everything denoted care and good housekeeping – the gravel *outside* the gate is raked, and the grass verges and hedges are neat and trimmed along the driveway. The house, with white paint and green creeper, is very beautifully proportioned and excellently maintained and decorated throughout. There is a meticulously well-kept stable-yard with quaint stone figures on the gate pillars. Lawns and tennis court and gravel slope away down to the river which comes complete with wooden bridge, weir, small boat and swans. It is utterly quiet and peaceful, there is only bird-song. Our bedroom was in soft gold colours with white; spotless, bright and comfortable - and big enough to hold a dance in. The public rooms are equally attractive: wonderfully polished furniture, lovely ornaments, lots of books and candles, flowers, sparkling glass and damask napkins in the dining room. Service was quiet, efficient and friendly. Restricted menu might not suit everyone, but most dishes were well-cooked. Obviously both the family and the guests are happy here – it is probably the most attractive of the Irish country house hotels we have visited."

Open Easter–end October.
Rooms 2 suites, 8 double, 1 single – 9 with bath (7 also have shower). 3 de luxe rooms in Garden Court.
Facilities 2 lounges, TV room, restaurant. 7-acre grounds with gardens, tennis, croquet; river with boating and fishing. Salmon fishing and golf nearby.
Location NE of Kanturk; turn off road towards Buttevant.
Restrictions Not suitable for ♿. No dogs.
Terms B&B: single occupancy: IR£40–IR£45, double IR£70–IR£80; dinner, B&B: single IR£59.50–IR£64.50, double IR£109–IR£119. Set dinner IR£19.50. 1-night bookings refused for more than 2 months ahead.
Service/tipping: "Service is included. If guests ask we tell them it is not necessary to tip. Any tips given are pooled and shared by staff."

KENMARE Co Kerry — Map 6

Park Hotel Kenmare — *Tel* Killarney (064) 41200
Telex 73905

The *Park Hotel* goes from strength to strength. It is a substantial mansion, built at the turn of the century and furnished in period style, set in a large, splendidly maintained park. It is one of only two establishments in the Republic to earn a *Michelin* rosette – *Arbutus Lodge*, Cork (q.v.) is the other. "A formidable contender for the best country house in Ireland," we wrote last year. Our readers agree. "The friendliest luxury hotel of its size I've ever stayed in." (*Sheila Young*) "Absolutely perfect. Everyone so friendly and anxious to please. The meals were superb and well worth the journey. We spent the day wondering what to have for dinner – scallops, salmon, mussels, the best you could have; and the chocolate mousse was an absolute dream." (*Mary Purdy*)

Open Apr–Jan.
Rooms 6 suites, 32 double, 12 single – 42 with bath and shower, 8 with shower, all with telephone, radio and baby-listening; TV in suites. 1 suite adapted for ♿. Some ground-floor rooms.
Facilities Lift. 3 lounges, drawing room, TV/games room, cocktail bar, restaurant. 11-acre grounds, with all-weather tennis court, 9-hole golf course and croquet. Sea and river fishing available locally.
Location 60 m west of Cork, adjacent to village. Parking.
Restriction No dogs.
Credit cards Access, Visa.
Terms [1987 rates] (Service at guests' discretion) B&B: single IR£57–IR£66, double IR£110–IR£136, suite IR£155–IR£186; dinner, B&B: single IR£84.50–IR£92.95, double IR£163–IR£189.90, suite IR£220–IR£250. Set lunch IR£13.50, dinner IR£26.95; full alc IR£32. Christmas programme. Reduced rates for children; special meals on request.
Service/tipping: "All gratuities are held in bank account belonging to staff, used towards a vacation for all."

KILLARNEY Co Kerry — Map 6

Cahernane Hotel — *Tel* Killarney (064) 31895
Muckross Road — *Telex* 73823

Built a century ago, *Cahernane*, new to the Guide this year, is an imposing mansion on the outskirts of Killarney, with 13 acres of attractive grounds against a backdrop of lakes and mountains. With 52 rooms, it is no bijou establishment, and group bookings are probably the basis of its trade. But here is the nominating report: "We found this a charming place to stay with very good food and a large menu. Bedrooms had views of mountains or park, and ours, in the original part of the 19th-century mansion, was spacious, well-furnished and comfortable. The bathroom was modern and well-equipped. The modern extension, built to blend, has smaller but equally comfortable rooms. There is a modern sun lounge and old-fashioned reception rooms. Our only complaint was dim lights in the bedroom so that one had to remove the lampshade between the beds in order to read. This does seem to be a problem in Ireland – cost of electricity perhaps? We were the only English people there and the visitors' book showed only one other, some way back. A German party came, later a French one (and were fed in a separate dining room). Otherwise guests were American, German, Belgian and, unusually, a Canadian couple. We felt the British were missing a good thing." (*Lady Maddocks*)

Open Easter–Oct inclusive; also 20 Dec–4 Jan.
Rooms 8 master, 47 double, 5 single – all with bath and/or shower, direct-dial telephone and baby-listening. 36 in annexe.
Facilities Foyer, 2 lounges, conservatory, cellar bar, TV/video room, dining room. 13-acre grounds with tennis, croquet and mini-golf. Lakes with private fishing for brown trout and salmon 5 minutes' walk.
Location ½ mile from town centre; turn right off Kenmare road.
Restrictions Not suitable for ♿. Dogs in grounds only.
Credit cards All major cards accepted.

Terms (Service at guests' discretion) B&B IR£30–IR£47.50; dinner, B&B IR£50–IR£67.50. Set dinner IR£20; full alc IR£30.

MOUNTRATH Co Laois — Map 6

Roundwood House — *Tel* Portlaoise (0502) 32120

An intriguing newcomer near the centre of the Republic, *Roundwood House* lies in the shadow of the unspoilt and beautiful Slieve Bloom Mountains. On our questionnaire, the owner, Frank Kennan, writes: "This is a truly purist Palladian house, built in 1742. Everything here dates from then or earlier. We have an extensive library and the house is furnished in keeping with the period." Our inspector's report explains the purism of this "architectural gem" of a house. Her room had authentic 18th-century furniture and Georgian colours. No curtains on the window, only shutters. The carpet was quite threadbare, but accurately chosen, she felt, for the old-world look. However, her bed was extremely comfortable, and there was central heating and plenty of piping hot water. The sitting room was beautifully furnished, with many books on Irish architecture, and had a fine crackling fire. Dinner was a no-choice affair: a good starter of avocados and kiwi fruit dressed in oil, a perfectly cooked steak followed by a decent ice-cream – "a careful amateur meal". There was freshly-baked soda bread for breakfast. The service was faultless, prices very reasonable. Her only reservation: might it be possible to maintain the look of the 18th century rooms while making them – perhaps with curtains and wall-to-wall carpeting – look a little more comfortable to live in?

Open 1 Feb–31 Dec.
Rooms 6 double – all with bath.
Facilities Drawing room, library, dining room. 17½-acre grounds with croquet and swings.
Location 3 m from main Dublin/Limerick road. Follow signs for Slieve Bloom.
Restrictions Not suitable for ♿. No dogs.
Credit cards Access, Amex, Visa.
Terms B&B: single occupancy IR£19, double IR£32. Set Sun lunch IR£9, dinner IR£14. Reduced rates and special meals for children.
Service/tipping: "We and our staff sometimes get tips. We notice that we are pleased when we do so. However the bulk of our customers never tip us (because they feel it might offend us) and we would like to keep it this way."

NEWPORT Co Mayo — Map 6

Newport House Hotel — *Tel* Newport (098) 41222
Telex 53740

We welcome this fine Georgian country house back to the Guide after an interval of several years following the death of the previous owner. It stands in 20 acres of grounds along the Derrydeevagh river where it flows into Clew Bay, and its extensive private salmon and sea trout fishing brings many visitors; sea angling can also be arranged nearby. The hotel has attractive architectural features, and plenty of good antiques. Our original nomination, which dates back to 1981, had commented: "Ramshackle in best Irish style . . . Authentic (unselfconscious) Irish (shabby) atmosphere," a description which found favour with the then proprietor ("I wouldn't alter a single word of it"). The present owners, Kieran and Thelma Thompson, have changed the old image: the house is thoroughly well furnished and freshly decorated. There's a brightly-lit dining room (too well lit for our inspector's liking), and decent cooking. A sophisticated fishing hotel with country house attributes.

Open 20 Mar–30 Sept.
Rooms 2 suites, 15 double, 2 single – 17 with bath, 2 with shower. 2 ground-floor rooms in courtyard and Gate Lodge.
Facilities Bar, lounge, sitting room, dining room. 20-acres grounds. River, lough and sea fishing; sandy beach 5 km.
Location Just outside the town of Newport; clearly visible from Westport–Achill road. Parking.
Restriction Dogs in annexe only.
Credit cards Amex, Diners, Visa.
Terms (No service charge) B&B IR£26–IR£41; dinner, B&B IR£45–IR£61. Set dinner IR£21.
Service/tipping: "Tipping not encouraged. Guests are advised it is not expected or necessary. If they insist, it is held by staff in a fund and divided among themselves."

OUGHTERARD Co Galway — Map 6

Currarevagh House — *Tel* Galway (091) 82313

Faithful returners continue to extol the "relaxed and gracious living" to be had at the Hodgson family's mid-Victorian house on the banks of Lough Corrib. *Currarevagh* has been in the same family for five generations and is particularly popular with fishermen, though the beautiful wild country around is also excellent for walking and riding. One correspondent this year singled out the "old-fashioned and rare comforts of finding, when you go to bed, the bedside lights on, curtains drawn, bed turned down and hot-water bottle installed on a chilly autumn evening". She also appreciated the large help-yourself sideboard at breakfast, offering porridge, ham, kedgeree as well as eggs, bacon and sausages. The food is as traditional as the decor and the service: Corrib trout, roast pork, beef or mutton with the usual trimmings, followed by golden syrup pudding or lemon sponge – old favourites all. Another veteran comments: "You will over-eat, as second helpings are available for almost everything and a trolley laden with wickedly tempting calories is pushed into the drawing room at tea-time. Fortunately, the hotel is in good walking country." (*Val Watson, Professor DA Webb*)

Open Easter to early Oct.
Rooms 14 double, 1 single – 13 with bath, 2 with shower. 4 ground-floor rooms in mews.
Facilities Drawing room, sitting room, TV room, dining room. 150-acre grounds with lakeshore fishing, boating, swimming, tennis, croquet.
Location 4 m NW of Oughterard on lakeshore road.
Restrictions Not ideal for ♿. Children tolerated but not encouraged. Dogs by arrangement, only on lead in public rooms.
Credit cards None accepted.
Terms (Excluding 10% service charge) B&B: single IR£29–IR£39, double IR£58; dinner, B&B (min 3 days): single IR£42–IR£52, double IR£84; full board (min 3 days): single IR£50–IR£60, double IR100. Set lunch IR£7, dinner IR£14.25. Weekly rates. 1-night bookings occasionally refused in high season. Reduced rates for children sharing parents' room.

Service/tipping: "10% is added for service; it is divided among all staff. Guests are asked not to tip individual members of staff."

RATHNEW Co Wicklow — Map 6

Hunter's Hotel

Tel Wicklow (0404) 40106

One of Ireland's oldest coaching inns, which has been in the Gelletlie family for five generations. "*Hunter's* has cleverly managed to combine the homeliness of staying at one's grandmother's country house with the attributes of a clean, comfortable, well-run hotel and a good table, all within less than an hour's drive from central Dublin, even on a busy evening. There is a welcome timelessness about the yard and its archway, still with the feel of a coaching inn (which it was 200 years ago), the tiled hallway with its ticking clock and shining brass, the engagingly crooked floors and walls, and the tranquil garden. There is nothing timeless, though, about the cheery, helpful, efficient local staff, or the tight control of owner, Mrs Gelletlie. The house is clean and freshly decorated, the bar well stocked. There is quite a good menu, and a fresh pot of tea at the log fire for the traveller arriving on a cold wet winter evening." (*ES*) More reports please.

Open All year.
Rooms 18 – 10 with bath. 2 ground-floor rooms accessible for ♿.
Facilities Residents' lounge, lounge bar, TV lounge, dining room. 2-acre gardens by river; fishing for brown and sea trout. Golf, tennis, riding, sea fishing, sandy beaches nearby.
Location 28 m S of Dublin. Turn off the main Dublin-Wexford road at Ashford.
Credit cards Access, Amex, Diners.
Terms (Excluding 10% service charge) B&B: single IR£24, double IR£46. Set lunch IR£10, dinner IR£15.50. 10% reduction for children sharing parents' room; special meals.

Tinakilly House Hotel

Tel Wicklow (0404) 69274 and 67227
Telex 80412

Hearing good things about this fairly grand Victorian house 30 miles south of Dublin, we sent along an inspector who reports: "When Captain Robert Halpin retired from laying transoceanic cables in the 1860s, a grateful British Government rewarded him with enough money to build *Tinakilly House*. Having once commanded Brunel's *Great Eastern*, which in her day was the biggest ship in the world, the great navigator had a highly developed sense of stylish grandiosity. His retirement home, in seven acres of bosky pleasure gardens, overlooking the Irish Sea (you can just see it) near Wicklow town, is a grey-stone mansion of Victorian monumental splendour. William and Bee Power, a friendly, efficient couple, introduced modern comforts when they converted the place into a hotel five years ago, yet successfully retained its period atmosphere. The rooms, including the 14 bedrooms, which are outnumbered by the staff, are large and high-ceilinged with tall windows. There is a 'Superior Room' (IR£15 extra) with a four-poster bed of imperial dimensions. The general impression is of old-fashioned opulence – golden chandeliers and sconces, polished dark wood, rococo fireplaces, softly upholstered, formal sofas and chairs, red carpets, potted plants, and a magpie miscellany of glittering bric-à-brac. There is a quiet, comfortable bar. Meals are served in three dining rooms, each with only a few discreetly separated tables. The ambitious and imaginative cuisine could be called *Nouvelle Hibernian*: the excellent Irish ingredients, notably sea-food, are presented picturesquely in sauces that seem French. The chef is careful not to over-cook the vegetables. The wine list is unusually comprehensive, and particularly strong in clarets. Mrs Power herself bakes brown bread for the full Irish breakfast."

Open 10 Feb–23 Dec
Rooms 1 suite, 13 double – 13 with bath and shower, 1 with bath only, all with direct-dial telephone, TV and tea-making facilities.
Facilities Large reception hall, bar, residents' lounge, dining room. 7-acre grounds.
Location Coming from Dublin on N11, go through Rathnew village on R750. House is signposted on left after about ¼m.
Restrictions Not suitable for ♿. No children under 8. No dogs.
Credit cards Access, Visa.
Terms [1987 rates](Excluding 10% service charge) B&B IR£30–IR£60. Set lunch IR£11, dinner IR£21. Discounts for stays of 3 nights or more.

RIVERSTOWN Co Sligo — Map 6

Coopershill

Tel Sligo (071) 65108
Telex 40301 attn Coopershill

César awarded in 1987 for outstanding Irish country hospitality

Coopershill has a spectacular position, with the Bricklieve mountains and vast peat bogs to the south, and the town of Sligo and the sea to the north. This is Yeats country, and the poet himself is buried at Drumcliff not far from Riverstown. It is a place of enchantment whose special qualities were evoked in this report last year: "One of the grand houses built by the landed Anglo-Irish families in the 18th century. It is situated in a huge estate and in complete silence. The atmosphere is that of a country house of 50 years ago; the main door stands open, the Irish Chippendale chairs in the hallway are strewn with the riding regalia of the O'Hara family (whose daughter trains showjumpers). The rooms are tall and gracious, the furniture old-fashioned and well used. Mrs O'Hara, whose family has always lived in the house, is the most charming old lady and greets her guests with obvious pleasure and welcome attention. Do not expect a smart hotel – this is the home of an old Irish family in which you are a welcome guest." (*Robert McNicol*)

One major change has taken place since last year: *châtelaine* Joan O'Hara has retired to the Coach House, though she is still very much part of the scene, and her son Brian and his wife Lindy have taken over the day-to-day running of the house. Meanwhile eulogies of an unrestrained variety continue to reach us: "We just arrived at *Coopershill*, Mrs O'Hara could take us and we never budged. The only word to describe this hotel is HEAVEN. We could have stayed for ever. The food is beautiful and *so fresh*, and so elegantly served. The size of the house and the rooms are an experience in themselves. The drawing room with its huge chairs covered in pink damask and the peat fire makes you want to stay in it and enjoy it just for its own sake! I could go on for ever about this beautiful house, and it beats me to hear that people complain about the lack of central heating.

Where on earth are their priorities? It is a privilege to stay in *Coopershill* just as it is, and long may it remain so." (*Ruth West*)

Open Mid-Mar–end Sept.
Rooms 6 double – all with bath and/or shower and tea-making facilities; most with 4-poster.
Facilities Hall, drawing room with TV, dining room; playroom for children with mono TV, piano, record-player, table tennis, etc. Large garden within 500 acres of farmland. A river runs through grounds, with coarse fishing; trout fishing nearby; sandy beach at Sligo, also golf – both 17 m.
Location 2 m from Riverstown; on Dublin/Sligo road (N4), take 2nd right turn towards Riverstown. After about 1 m, by black post and rail fence, turn left; turn right by ruined lodge, cross stone bridge and 2 cattle grids.
Restrictions Not suitable for ♿. No dogs in public rooms.
Credit cards Access, Amex, Visa.
Terms IR£25–IR£28. Light lunch IR£6, set dinner IR£15. Reduction for children under 12 sharing parents' room; special meals on request.
Service/tipping: "We do not expect guests to leave a tip. However, if they should wish to do so, such money will be distributed entirely among the staff."

ROSSNOWLAGH Co Donegal — Map 6

The Sand House Hotel

Tel Bundoran (072) 51777
Telex 40460

A modern hotel four-square on a two-mile stretch of sandy beach on the edge of the Atlantic Ocean – "the clearest waters in Europe" – overlooking Donegal Bay, run for many years past by Mary and Vin Britton and their son Conor. Major refurbishments have been taking place in the past two years, and Mary Britton tells us that the new facade has transformed the "airport terminal" appearance of the building. *Sand House* specialises in golf and fishing holidays (there are two 18-hole championship courses within five miles) but water sports and riding are also available and the hotel has its own hard tennis court. Readers continue to appreciate the Brittons' hospitality: "Their attention to detail is evident everywhere: ratio of one staff to two guests even in the height of the season: bedrooms need no pictures when the wide windows are moving panoramas on the ever-changing seashore vista. Highly recommended for lovers of the sea or for those who want to recharge their batteries in great comfort." (*John O'Neill*)

Open 1 May–5 Oct.
Rooms 2 suites, 32 double, 6 single – all with bath and/or shower, telephone and baby-listening.
Facilities 3 residents' lounges, TV lounge, lounge bar, residents' cocktail bars, restaurant. Folk music Fri and Sat in high season. 2-acre grounds with hard tennis court, miniature golf, croquet and paddock; on 2-mile safe sandy beach with swimming, canoeing, windsurfing (boards and canoes available at hotel). Salmon and trout fishing, golf, riding, water sports nearby.
Location On Donegal Bay; N of Ballyshannon on coast road.
Restrictions Not suitable for ♿. No dogs in public rooms.
Credit cards Access, Amex, Diners.
Terms B&B IR£25–IR£35; dinner, B&B (3 days min) IR£35–IR45. Set lunch IR£8.50, dinner IR£1.50; full alc IR£15. Golf and fishing holidays.
Service/tipping: "10% added to room rates which is distributed to all staff on a 3-monthly basis on a point system."

SCOTSHOUSE Co Monaghan — Map 6

Hilton Park — *Tel* Emyvale (047) 56007
Scotshouse, Clones

John and Lucy Madden's family mansion for eight generations of the Madden family, in the heart of 600 acres of parkland including golf course, and trout and pike fishing. Wonderful vistas of lakes and hills. Owners cultivate house-party hospitality. Traditional Irish cooking with bread, biscuits, cheeses and ice-cream all made in-house. Nominator warns that, as with other old Irish country house hotels, standards of upkeep not always maintained to highest standard. Open Easter–end Oct. 6 rooms, 3 with bath. B&B IR£27–IR£33. Set dinner IR£16. A new nomination, so we should welcome more reports.

SHANAGARRY Co Cork — Map 6

Ballymaloe House [GFG] — *Tel* Cork (021) 652531
Shanagarry, Nr Midleton — *Telex* 75208 BHI

"I first went to this hotel years ago, when we dropped in for lunch and found ourselves staying several days. I went there for my honeymoon, and whenever we feel we deserve a treat, we go there again. It's a beguiling place. The Allen family who run it are in evidence everywhere – Mrs Allen is in the kitchen, various children driving tractors on the Home Farm, helping in the office, etc, and grandchildren eating in the dining room. The service is efficient and relaxed. On our way here for our honeymoon, we were delayed by a meandering Irish cow on the road, and rang the hotel who sympathised and promised that they would have a cold meal waiting for us when we arrived very late at night. There was a beautifully arranged cold supper with a half-bottle of Pommard waiting for us in our room." (*Mirabel Cecil*)

That encomium was written more than a decade ago and appeared in the first edition of the Guide. Many similar tributes have been paid to it since – and this year again: "Thoroughly delightful in every way." (*Eithne Scallan*) "The food was everything we had heard it could be." (*Kathleen Edwards*) *Ballymaloe*, for the uninitiated, lies 20 miles east of Cork. It is a gracious rambling house, more Georgian than anything else though somehow ageless, with a Norman keep built into the fabric on one side, and relatively modern pink-washed cottages on the other, overlooking the courtyard. Close to the house are a swimming pool and tennis court; beyond lies a 400-acre farm; and beyond that, at two or three miles distance, is the sea with good sandy beaches, and the charming little fishing port of Ballycotton. Virtually everything you eat, apart from the wonderful fish, is home-grown or raised on the Allen's farm. It is an exceptionally convivial house, reflecting the Allens' confidence, pride and pleasure in what they are doing.

Open All year except 24-26 Dec inclusive.
Rooms 5 suites, 26 double, 3 single – all with bath and/or shower, telephone and baby-listening. 11 in converted stable, 4 on ground-floor suitable for ♿. Gate

> When telephoning Ireland from abroad, omit the 0 at the beginning of the dialling code.

Lodge has double-bedded room and kitchen/living room.
Facilities 2 sitting rooms, TV room, playroom, 5 inter-connecting dining rooms; conference facilities. 400-acre farm and grounds with tennis court, heated swimming pool, 9-hole golf course, trout pond, children's play area; craft shop; riding by arrangement. Sea 3 m, with safe sandy beaches; sea and river fishing by arrangement.
Location 20 m E of Cork; 2 m E of Cloyne on Ballycotton road, L35.
Restriction No dogs in bedrooms or public rooms.
Credit cards All major cards accepted.
Terms (Excluding 10% service charge) B&B (continental): single IR£41.40–IR£46, double IR£60.80–IR£70.60. Set lunch IR£10.50, dinner IR£20. Special weekend rates; winter and spring breaks. Reduced rates and high teas for children.
Service/tipping: "10% mandatory charge used for annual bonuses and weekly extras in pay packets. Customers and staff seem to like this arrangement as it is quite clear."

Part two

Austria
Belgium
Denmark
France
Germany
Greece
Hungary
Italy
Luxembourg
Malta
including Gozo
The Netherlands
Norway
Portugal
including Madeira
Spain
including Andorra, the Balearics and the Canaries
Sweden
Switzerland
Turkey
Yugoslavia

Austria

HOTEL MADRISA, GARGELLEN

ALPBACH 6236 Tyrol **Map 15**

Hotel Alpbacherhof *Tel* (05336) 5227
Telex 051160

Alpbach, scene of the European forum since the end of World War II, ranks "amongst the prettiest villages in the country". Skiing is good and the air is remarkably clear. All the rooms at this hotel have a balcony with fine views. "Indoor pool, garden, wonderful terrace where they serve any meals you want from breakfast on (which you can also have in your room). Dinner is by candlelight and owner Andreas Bischofer is willing to replace items on the half-pension menu you don't like. Service is superbly friendly and helpful - they will even look after an aged parent for you." (*Gitta Sereny*)

Open Dec–Mar, mid-May–Sept.
Rooms 12 suites, 30 double, 5 single – all with bath or shower, telephone, radio and balcony; TV on request. 1 suite in annexe.

Facilities Lift. Bar, 2 lounges, TV room, 2 restaurants; conference facilities; indoor heated swimming pool; terrace (where meals are served in fine weather). Garden. Winter sports; climbing, swimming and tennis in summer. English spoken.
Location Alpbach is in a valley S of Innsbruck–Kufstein main road. Hotel is central. Parking.
Credit card Diners.
Terms B&B 600-1,100 Sch; dinner, B&B 700-1,200 Sch; full board 130 Sch added. Set lunch 190 Sch, dinner 200 Sch; full alc 280 Sch. Reduced rates for children sharing parents' room; supper at 6 pm.

Romantikhotel Böglerhof — *Tel* (05336) 5227
Telex 051160

An attractive old inn, built in 1470 to house workers at the nearby silver and copper mines. Large lounge, 3 dining-rooms, excellent food served by dignified waitresses. Nice bedrooms; splendid views from their balconies. Open Dec–Mar, mid-May–Sept. 47 rooms, all with bath. B&B 600-1,000 Sch. Set meals 190-200 Sch. New nomination: more reports please.

ANIF 5081 Salzburg — Map 15

Hotel Friesacher — *Tel* (06246) 2075
Telex 632943

Surrounded by mountains and woods, the attractive village of Anif is an all-season resort just outside Salzburg. Here the *Friesacher* is a sizeable modern chalet-style hotel with large neo-rustic bedrooms and scenic-view balconies, and readers again speak well of it this year: "Good value and very peaceful. A lovely room with balcony looking over meadows to the mountains. Waitresses in pretty national costume serve good basic food either in the rather airless restaurant or in the garden." "Friendly service, warm and cosy room with large bathroom." The set breakfast is considered dull. Besides the hotel's own more formal restaurant, the Friesacher family own two other cheaper ones next door with buffet-style meals that one reader found "a major bargain". (*Pamela Pierce, RJ Stubberfield, and others*)

Open All year except 23 Dec–15 Jan. Closed Wed mid-Sept–mid-July.
Rooms 2 suites, 36 double, 7 single – 38 with bath, 7 with shower, all with telephone, radio and TV; many with balcony. 18 in annexe. Ground-floor rooms.
Facilities Lift. Lounge, bar, dining room; conference facilities. Garden with children's play area and café. Disco, swimming, tennis, skiing, skating etc nearby. English spoken.
Location 4 km S of Salzburg. Leave *Autobahn* at Salzburg, go to the right at Anif (1km) and turn ½km on road to Hellbrunn. Parking.
Restriction Not suitable for ♿.
Credit card Diners.
Terms B&B: single 510-540 Sch, double 730-810 Sch, suite 990 Sch. Set lunch 120 Sch, dinner 180 Sch. Reduced rates for children; small portions.

> Our italicised entries are different this year. There are more of them and they indicate hotels which are worth considering, but which, for various reasons – inadequate information, lack of feedback, ambivalent reports – do not at the moment warrant a fully entry. We should particularly welcome comments on these hotels.

BERGHEIM 5101 Salzburg — Map 15

Hotel-Gasthof Gmachl

Tel (0662) 52124
Telex 632771

Converted from an old *Gasthof*, this breezy and rather stylish modern holiday hotel stands in a village on the northern fringe of Salzburg. Renewed praise this year ("delightful, with courteous staff, comfortable beds and excellent food") backs up this earlier account: "There are several chalets interconnected by a long and airy corridor – the smaller ones containing a ground-floor apartment, and two rooms upstairs with balconies. There are 60 modern and luxurious bedrooms, double-glazed to cut out the noise of the nearby road and railway line. All rooms have timber-panelled ceilings and wooden panelling all round the room to waist height; even a frieze of Austrian dancers running around the top. Bathrooms are superb. We enjoyed staying here. Our only reservation is the cuisine, which in our opinion is not quite up to the general high standards – even though the hotel owns the butcher's shop next door." Lovely swimming pool opening onto the garden. (*J Van Brimer, Francine and Ian Walsh; also HC Robbins Landon*)

Open All year.
Rooms 3 suites, 29 double, 8 single – 17 with bath and shower, 23 with shower, all with telephone and TV; some with tea-making facilities; many with balcony. Some ground-floor rooms.
Facilities Lounge, salons, bar, restaurant; conference facilities. Indoor heated swimming-pool; sauna. Garden with tennis court and children's play area; fishing, riding and golf nearby. English spoken.
Location 2 km N of Salzburg on road 156 towards Oberndorf. Take Salzburg Nord exit from motorway E14.
Credit cards All major cards accepted.
Terms [1987 rates] B&B: single 665-930 Sch, double 1,105-1,555 Sch; half board: 205 Sch per person added to B&B rates. Set lunch/dinner 290 Sch. Special meals for children.

BERWANG 6622 Tyrol — Map 15

Singer Sporthotel

Tel (05674) 8181

Just off the main Innsbruck–Stuttgart road, a few miles west of the towering Zugspitze, the Singer family's chalet-style hotel is set on a pine-studded hillside in the "enlarged but not much spoiled" summer and ski resort of Berwang. "One of our favourite holiday locations – Gunter and Gerti Singer are welcoming hosts who speak good English and always welcome us like old friends." So runs a report this year from satisfied regulars, who go on to praise the "efficient staff, first-rate cuisine, spacious apartment bedrooms, reasonable prices and delightful village." An earlier account: "The food was excellent, and we revelled in a large room with balcony. The facilities of bathing, sauna, massage, jacuzzi etc did not impinge on those looking merely to enjoy strolling in the countryside. The serious walkers have a wonderful time. And for those who prefer lazing by the pool, life is good too. " (*John Bell, Jenny Garrett*)

Open 18 Dec–10 Apr, 12 May–9 Oct.
Rooms 25 suites, 35 double, 10 single – all with bath and/or shower and telephone; many with balcony; radio and TV in suites.

Facilities Lift. Lounge, *Stübe*, TV room, 2 bars, 2 restaurants; fitness/sports centre with whirl pool, sauna and massage. Small garden with 2 big terraces. Heated open-air swimming pool, mini-golf, tennis; winter sports nearby. Bathing and fishing in Lake Heiterwanger 8km. Dancing in the bar each night in winter. Tyrolean evenings in summer. English spoken.
Location 80 km NW of Innsbruck. Parking.
Credit card Diners.
Terms B&B 360–910 Sch; half board 430–980 Sch; full board 480–1,030 Sch. Set lunch 80–150 Sch, dinner 130–250 Sch; full alc 170–300 Sch. Weekend packages; ski packages. Reduced rates and special meals for children.

BEZAU 6870 Vorarlberg — Map 15

Gasthof Gams

Tel (05514) 2220
Telex 59144 VVWALD-GAMS

Bezau is a sleepy little town on the edge of the Bregenz forest. The road on one side winds down to the busy resorts of Lake Constance; on the other, it loops over the mountains to the big sophisticated ski-stations of Lech and St Anton. *Gasthof Gams* is a sizeable 17th-century coaching inn, with modern additions such as jacuzzi (in the basement) and heated outdoor swimming pool. "Excellent in every way, especially the food (large helpings) and the remarkable service." That is one report this year. Despite its size, this is a genuinely personal family hotel, with one of the *Familie* Nenning usually around (when they are not, service may suffer). "Unsophisticated family ambience." "Rooms vary considerably in size; the under-floor heating is rather nice. The public rooms are quite *gemütlich*, furnished in traditional Austrian style." The hotel bus takes guests to and from the ski-slopes in season. (*Ian and Anne Steel, Frank Mattinson, and others*)

Open All year except 1–18 Dec.
Rooms 6 suites, 24 double, 10 single – 15 with bath, 25 with shower, all with telephone; TV on request; some with balcony. Some ground-floor rooms.
Facilities Lift. Lounge, dining rooms; conference/functions rooms; games room, sauna, solarium, hot whirl pool; terraces. Large garden with swimming pool (heated May–Oct) and 3 tennis courts. Skiing, climbing, walking. English spoken.
Location 35 km SE of Bregenz, 37 km NW of Lech. Central. Parking.
Credit cards None accepted.
Terms B&B 320–500 Sch; dinner, B&B 480–660 Sch; full board 560–740 Sch. Set lunch/dinner 160–320 Sch; full alc 300 Sch. Reduced rates and special meals for children.

DÜRNSTEIN 3601 Lower Austria — Map 15

Richard Löwenherz

Tel (02711) 222
Telex 071199 LÖWE

The romantic old village of Dürnstein is on the northern bank of a particularly luscious stretch of the Danube, about 50 miles west of Vienna. Richard the Lionheart was imprisoned here in 1192 – hence the name of this hotel, which stands at the end of a narrow street and continues to be much admired: "An excellent dinner, elegantly served by courteous staff." "Quite splendid – our room overlooked the Danube and dinner was taken on the terrace with gorgeous river views." "The large swimming pool is attractive; local wines excellent." The helpfulness with luggage, laundry and securing tickets for the Opera are this year much commended, and so is the quiet lounge "where you can sit in a relaxed atmosphere and listen to taped classical music". The hotel is built on the site of an old abbey and incorporates some of its buildings; there are flowery gardens and a bar-terrace on a cliff with a view of the Danube. (*J van Brimer, George D MacDonald, A Wilcock, and others*)

Open Mar–Oct.
Rooms 2 suites, 44 double, 4 single – 36 with bath, 10 with shower, all with telephone.
Facilities Hall, TV room, bar/terrace, dining room. Large garden with heated swimming pool. On river with bathing and fishing. English spoken.
Location 50 m W of Vienna.
Restriction Not suitable for ♿.
Credit cards Amex, Diners.
Terms [1987 rates] B&B 495-950 Sch; dinner, B&B 745-1,200 Sch.

Hotel Schloss Dürnstein *Tel* (02711) 212
Telex 71147

The much-admired *Schloss Dürnstein* stands inside the village, perched above the Danube, with spectacular views of this lovely winding river from its dining-terrace and from most bedrooms. Built in 1630, it was for centuries owned by the Princes Starhemberg, and was used as a refuge by the Emperor Leopold I when fleeing from the Turks. Some 50 years ago, it was reincarnated by the Thiery family, who still own and run it. Rather a formal place, it has beautiful antique furniture in both the public rooms and the bedrooms. One eulogy this year: "Captivating views, and the best head waiter I have ever met in Europe. The Fürstenzimmer is well worth paying extra for - like staying in Emperor Franz Joseph's bedroom in the Hofburg in Vienna, only twice the size. Breakfast arrived on two huge trays and was placed on a genuine 16th-century table in our room. Go there just for the history and romance." Fine cooking and some of the wine comes from the castle's own vineyards. (*P Sennett, and others*)

Open 25 Mar–6 Nov.
Rooms 2 suites, 32 double, 4 single – 34 with bath and shower, 3 with shower, all with telephone and radio; TV and baby-listening on request. Some ground-floor rooms.
Facilities Lift. Lounge, TV room, bar, restaurant and private dining room, grill room with dance floor. Courtyard with heated swimming pool. Barbecue evenings, candle-lit dinners once a week. Terrace overlooking Danube; fishing and boating. English spoken.
Location At end of main street in village. Parking.
Credit cards All major cards accepted.
Terms B&B: single 820-860 Sch, double 1,000-1,640 Sch, suite 2,300 Sch; dinner, B&B: single 1,140-1,180 Sch, double 1,740-2,280 Sch, suite 2,940 Sch. Set lunch 280 Sch, dinner 350 Sch; full alc 450 Sch. 10% reduction in low season. Reduced rates for children.

FIEBERBRUNN 6391 Tyrol — Map 15

Schlosshotel Rosenegg *Tel* (05354) 6201 and 6211
Telex 51332 HOROS

Recently renovated, with a modern annexe, this castle in the Kitzbüheler Alps was built in 1555. It is recommended as "ideal for family skiing" because of the special attention given to children: but it is over a mile from the hamlet of Rosenegg to the ski-slopes and the après-ski entertainment of the lively resort of Fieberbrunn itself, so it might be best for those with a car. "Ossie Eberhardt and his charming English wife, Jane, offer a unique service for families at this delightful hunting lodge. Their attention to detail is excellent. Heated tiled floors in the sparkling *en suite* bathrooms. Beautiful wooden beds, antique furniture and modern comfort. The Eberhardts personally sort out their guests' problems. The hotel also has an enchanting wine bar. Service in the large restaurant is slow." (*Nicola Hayward, AR*)

Open All year.
Rooms 69 double (48 can be triple), 10 single – all with bath, telephone and radio; many with balcony. 48 in annexe connected by a covered bridge to main building.
Facilities 2 lifts. Hall, lounge/hall, TV room, cocktail bar, wine bar, restaurant; children's playroom; disco. Garden with sun terrace. Evening entertainments. Winter sports (free hotel bus to main skiing areas); indoor swimming pool nearby. English spoken.
Location 9 km E of St Johann, on route 164 to Saalfelden.
Restriction Not suitable for ♿.
Credit cards None accepted.
Terms Dinner, B&B 465–615 Sch; full board 80 Sch per person added. Set lunch/dinner 100–150 Sch; full alc 130 Sch. Reduced rates and special menus for children.

FREISTADT 4240 Upper Austria — Map 15

Gasthof Deim zum Goldenen Hirschen — *Tel* (07942) 2258 and 2111
Böhmergasse 8

This old town with its traces of ramparts, towers and gateways stands on a wild granite plateau between Linz and the Czech frontier. The *Deim* is a genuine old inn within the ramparts and has a pretty garden. It was left out of last year's Guide through lack of feedback, but this year a regular visitor tells us: "It is still very good - from the individual character of the bedrooms to the excellence of the food (dining rooms get crowded at weekends). All the modern conveniences and luxuries combined with old-world charm." An earlier account was more exuberant: "A glimpse of the flower-bedecked facade compels the weary traveller through the medieval gateway and into the gay warmth and welcome of the life within. Everything afterwards is a dream – a dream of (princesses in) canopied (but firm and comfortable) beds, of ancient walls and arched roofs (ceilings is too dull a word), of foaming (locally brewed) beer pots, of superb Upper Austrian (lighter than Viennese) cuisine and wine, of happy laughing waitresses in simple local costume. Antique furniture and etchings, and discreet hyper-efficient modern plumbing. They speak enough English to entrance but not enough to encourage linguistic sloth. Best of all, I shall remember the strains of the local chamber orchestra drifting across the castle into my bedroom."(*RM Sparkes; TJW*) This Meaulnian vision in Julie Andrews territory requires yet more endorsement, please.

Give the Guide positive support. Don't just leave feedback to others.

Open All year.
Rooms 1 suite, 17 double, 6 single – 9 with bath, 8 with shower (2 without WC), all with telephone and radio; 3 with TV.
Facilities Lounge, TV room, restaurant. Garden (meals can be taken outside).
Location Central. Parking. Town is 40 km NE of Linz.
Credit card Diners.
Terms B&B: single 290 Sch, double 510-520 Sch; dinner, B&B: single 360 Sch, double 650-660 Sch. Set lunch 120 Sch; full alc 260 Sch. Reduced rates and small food portions for children.

FUSCHL-AM-SEE 5330 Salzburg — Map 15

Pension Rupertihof — *Tel* (06226) 447

The Fuschlsee is the nearest of the Salzburg lakes to Salzburg, though not the loveliest of them. Here by the lakeside is a clean modern *pension*, in chalet style with flower-decked balconies. It is just outside the village, an easy walk to several hotels for dinner. "Excellent in every way," is one recent verdict; another: "Still as good as ever! Comfortable beds, many rooms with a balcony; excellent varied breakfasts (muesli, eggs, cheese etc). Hans Stöllinger speaks good English." (*AGW Holloway, David Regan*)

Open All year.
Rooms 12 double – all with bath or shower; some with balcony.
Facilities Breakfast room, lounge with TV. Small garden. Lake Fuschl 50 metres (beach and safe bathing, sailing etc). Walks arranged. English spoken.
Location 25 km E of Salzburg on road to Bad Ischl. Hotel is central. Parking.
Restriction Not suitable for ♿.
Credit card Amex, Diners, Visa.
Terms Double room: B&B 180–220 Sch. Reduced rates for children. (No restaurant.)

GARGELLEN 6787 Vorarlberg — Map 15

Hotel Madrisa — *Tel* (05557) 6331
Montafon — *Telex* 52269 MADRIS

Again in 1986-7 readers have written glowingly about this traditional family ski hotel, enlarged and modernised, in the beautiful Montafon valley. "Excellent value, well run." "The breakfasts were a wonderful array, and the evening meals were imaginative." Others have spoken of "a chef well above average for a small hotel in the mountains". The enthusiastic reports continue: "We spent five marvellous days here, it's a great place for children." "As well as for winter holidays, it's splendidly situated for spring and summer in a beautiful valley." "At Christmas, we arrived late at the hotel but the Rhomberg family welcomed us, carried our bags and gave us extra bedding. The staff had finished for the night but a cold buffet was waiting. The hotel exuded warmth – at the end of a hard day on the slopes it was bliss to return to. Days slip away in this cosy retreat and mountains of food appear regularly. We had rooms in the old part, ample, warm, rustic. Those in the new extension have balconies. The value for money makes me blink when I think of other ski resorts." (*Rosemarie Powell, Ian and Anne Steel, John H Bell, and others*)

Open 18 Dec–16 Apr, mid-Jun–end Sept.
Rooms 5 suites, 48 double, 12 single – 50 with bath and/or shower, all with telephone; 38 with radio and TV.

Facilities Lift. Hall, lounge, reading room, games room, *Stüberl*, dining room; children's playroom (with children's films); disco; indoor swimming pool, sauna. Large grounds with terrace, lawn, ski lift. English spoken.
Location 28 km S of Bludenz. In centre of Gargellen. Parking.
Credit cards Access, Amex.
Terms Dinner, B&B 640–1,180 Sch. Full alc 300–350 Sch. In skiing season bookings are normally for 1 week (Sat–Sat). Weekly and Christmas packages. Reductions for children sharing parents' rooms; special meals.

GRAZ 8010 Styria — Map 15

Schlossberg Hotel — *Tel* (0316) 702557
Kaiser-Franz-Joseph-Kai 30

"A recently renovated 400-year-old inn which provides country house atmosphere in a quiet side street near the centre of this historic city, Austria's second largest. Rambling corridors and a modern lift lead to large rooms (and even larger bathrooms) all individually furnished with antiques – not to mention colour television and direct-dial telephone. The staff speak excellent English, the receptionist doubles as barmaid and breakfast is served from 7 am onwards. Unfortunately, there is no restaurant but most of the better eating houses in the city are within five minutes' walk." (*David Phipps*) More reports please.

Open All year.
Rooms 3 suites, 30 double, 10 single – all with bath or shower, direct-dial telephone, TV and radio.
Facilities Lift. Bar, salon, TV room; conference room; rooftop terrace with swimming pool. English spoken.
Location Central (most rooms are quiet). Parking.
Credit cards Access, Amex, Diners, Visa.
Terms B&B: single 850–1,100 Sch, double 1,350–1,600 Sch. Weekend reductions. No charge for children under 12 in parents' room. (No restaurant.)

HEILIGENBLUT 9844 Carinthia — Map 15

Hotel Haus Senger — *Tel* (04824) 2215
Grossglockner

"Heiligenblut is a beautiful place, and this is a very *gemütlich* hotel, friendly and helpful, where we had an excellent apartment." One of two accolades this year for the family-run *Senger*, just above the village in high, wild mountainous countryside, excellent for walking or skiing. Comfort, excellent food and the kind of personal attention that makes everyone feel relaxed and good-humoured; it's a typical old mountain chalet with a new house skilfully added. Most of the rooms have balconies. "The food is so copious," ran an earlier report, "that almost everyone opts for breakfast and dinner and skips lunch, though the cook bakes cheesecakes, Sachertorte and apfelstrudel almost every day and there is always the temptation to try them warm from the oven after a day out on the mountains." One reader this year was less enthusiastic about the food. (*Ian and Anne Steel, JD Macdonald, Hella Pick, and others*)

Open Christmas–Easter, Jun–early Oct.
Rooms 6 suites, 6 double, 3 single – all with bath and/or shower, telephone and radio; TV on request.

Facilities 3 salons, bar, TV room, restaurant; games room, fitness room, sauna. Garden and terraces. Winter sports. English spoken.
Location On the edge of Heiligenblut, which is on 107, 40 km N of Lienz. Parking.
Credit card Amex.
Terms Dinner, B&B 450-570 Sch; full board 90 Sch added. 10% added for bookings of 1 night only. Set lunch 150 Sch, dinner 170 Sch; full alc 150-250 Sch. 30% reduction for children sharing parents' room; special meals.

HOF BEI SALZBURG 5322 Salzburg — Map 15

Hotel Schloss Fuschl

Tel (06229) 22530
Telex 633454

"Probably the most elegant hotel in Austria," one visitor calls this former hunting lodge of the prince-archbishops of Salzburg. Still distinctly regal, but now a wholly lay establishment, it overlooks Lake Fuschl with the mountains as backdrop; Salzburg is 20 kilometres away. "Romantic, luxurious and superb," was an earlier verdict, echoed more recently: "Beautifully situated, with an elegant and interesting interior. The set meals were extremely good and the staff outstandingly welcoming and helpful." Some rooms are in the main building facing the lake, but even better are the chalets in the garden. One lunches or dines overlooking the lake, and at dinner in summer there are spectacular sunsets. The food is Austrian international at its best. Clientele international too. Swimming both in an indoor pool and in the lake. (*AGW Holloway, also Ian and Anne Steel*)

Open All year.
Rooms 23 suites, 54 double, 5 single – all with bath and/or shower, telephone and radio; most with TV. 60 in buildings in the garden. Some ground-floor rooms.
Facilities 3 salons, bar, dining room, conservatory; conference facilities; beauty farm; indoor heated swimming pool. Large park with terrace for outdoor meals; private beach and swimming area on lake, fishing, boating, refreshments, tennis, 9-hole golf course. English spoken.
Location 20 km E of Salzburg; take 158 road to St Gilden; turn left 1 m after village of Hof.
Restriction Not suitable for ♿.
Credit cards All major cards accepted.
Terms B&B: single 1,000–1,400 Sch, double 1,400–2,800 Sch, suite 2,600–4,500 Sch. Set lunch 380 Sch, dinner 460 Sch. Full alc 550 Sch. Children under 12 sharing parents' room free; special meals on request.

INNSBRUCK 6020 Tyrol — Map 15

Weinhaus Happ

Herzog-Friedrich Strasse 14
Tel (05222) 22980
Telex 533511

Innsbruck's Herzog-Friedrich Strasse is flanked with arcades (*Lauben*) leading directly to the Goldene Dächl or Golden Roof. For 200 years it has been possible to glimpse the reflection of this roof in the restaurant window of the *Happ*, a very old *Weinhaus* indeed. "This small hotel offers comfortable accommodation, a good welcome and excellent food at a reasonable price. Our room was well equipped with a bathroom *en suite* and big feather bolsters on the beds. The hosts speak English – with great pleasure it seems – as do the staff." (*Bonnie Wilson*) The restaurant is well known for its wild game specialities in the autumn. More reports would be welcome on the accommodation.

Open All year. Restaurant closed Sun.
Rooms 10 double, 5 single – all with bath and/or shower, telephone and radio.
Facilities Lift. 3 restaurants; conference facilities. Garden. English spoken.
Location Central, in pedestrian zone. Hotel garage 3 minutes' walk.
Credit cards Amex, Diners, Visa.
Terms B&B 320–500 Sch. Set lunch/dinner from 75 Sch; full alc 160 Sch. Reduced rates for children under 12; special meals on request.

KITZBÜHEL 6370 Tyrol — Map 15

Hotel Montana — *Tel* (05356) 2526
Hahnankammstrasse 5 — *Telex* 51551

A family-owned hotel, well equipped with saunas, solarium and indoor pool, close to the main cable car and a few minutes' walk from the town centre. Dropped from the 1987 Guide for lack of feedback, now reprieved by a reader who thought it "ideal for families, groups or couples, a wonderful place with a friendly informal atmosphere, attentive service, plenty of space; food good but not spectacular." An earlier visitor had a comfortable room: "The bathroom was a masterpiece of ceramic and chromium plate. Doors opened onto a wide terrace." (*Sophie Horniman; also WHB*)

Open Dec–Mar, May–Sept.
Rooms 45 double – all with bath and/or shower and telephone; most with balcony; TV and baby-listening on request.
Facilities Lift. TV room, salon, bar; children's playroom; terrace, sauna, solarium, heated indoor swimming-pool. English spoken.
Location 3 minutes' walk from town centre, close to cable car. Parking.
Restriction Not suitable for ♿.
Credit cards Amex, Diners.
Terms B&B: 400-630 Sch; half board 470-700 Sch. Reduced rates for children; special meals.

KRIMML 5743 Salzburg — Map 15

Gasthof Krimmlerfälle — *Tel* (06564) 203

A sizeable holiday hotel much frequented by coach parties, about 50 kilometres east of Innsbruck. It is near the spectacular Krimml waterfalls, but far enough distant for their mighty roar to be muffled. "A typical Austrian building with timber-clad upper floors and carved wooden flower-filled balconies – a simple, unpretentious place but spacious and full of character. Our bedroom was palatial, with solid pine furniture, folk-weave rugs and goat skins. It was comfortable, had a balcony with table and chairs and faced the famous falls. Summer coach-tour guests are kept firmly separate from individual guests, who are fed in a characterful dining room with a striking three-foot high frieze of Tyrolean dancers. The food was simple but good and the prices very reasonable." A couple this year also found it "enjoyable and good value", but were surprised to see no sign of the Schöppl family owners – "We think it was the cook who signed us in and the waiter who made out our bill when we left." (*F and IW, Ian and Anne Steel*)

Open All year.
Rooms 6 suites, 50 double, 10 single – 16 with bath, 11 with shower. 12 in annexe. Some ground-floor rooms.
Facilities Lounge, TV room, 2 bars, restaurant; musical evenings. Large garden. Swimming pool, tennis courts and winter sports nearby. English spoken.
Location Central. Krimml is on A5743 between Gerlos and Mittersil. Parking.
Credit cards None accepted.
Terms [1987 rates] B&B 180-260 Sch; full board 310-395 Sch. 10% reduction for children under 12; special meals.

LANS 6072 Tyrol — Map 15

Gasthof Zur Traube — *Tel* (05222) 77261

Lans, Nr Innsbruck

This pretty village amid farmland overlooks Innsbruck, with a fine view of the mountains. The *Zur Traube*, recorded as an inn since 1313, is as Tyrolean as they come, with flowered balconies, traditional furnishings and cooking provided by the Raitmayr family, who have owned and cared for it for 15 generations. This hospitality continues: "We were given a warm welcome, a comfortable bedroom and a delicious dinner," say visitors this year. (*Ian and Anne Steel*)

Open All year except 15 Oct–5 Nov.
Rooms 21 double, 4 single – 3 with bath, 22 with shower, all with telephone; some with TV; many with balcony.
Facilities Lift. Salon, TV room, 3 dining rooms. Garden with terrace and lawns. Winter sports; golf, tennis and swimming in summer. English spoken.
Location In village centre. Parking. Lans is 6 km S of Innsbruck.
Credit cards None accepted.
Terms B&B: single 390-420 Sch, double 680-740 Sch; dinner, B&B single 490-520 Sch, double 880-940 Sch; full board: single 590-620 Sch, double 1,080-1,160 Sch. Set lunch/dinner 150 Sch; full alc 220-250 Sch. Reduced rates for children.

LECH AM ARLBERG 6764 Vorarlberg — Map 15

Hotel Post — *Tel* (05583) 22060

Telex 5239118 PHOT

Once a small village in the Arlberg mountains, Lech is now one of Europe's finest ski resorts. This sophisticated resort hotel for all seasons, run by three generations of the Moosbrugger family, receives an unreserved accolade from a loyal veteran: "We have been coming here for 25 years. Nowhere else in the world have I met this mixture of perfection and casual charm of a *pension de famille*. It would be worth staying here for the hotel itself, but it is also in the middle of the most charming village and the centre of wonderful mountain walking. When we lightly remarked to the chef that we thought the food less perfect this year, we were immediately asked what we would like to eat and were given it impeccably cooked and served for the next few days (including fresh girolles!)" (*Stefan and Yvette Wiener*) Warmly endorsed this year: "Combines efficiency with the personal charm of a family operation. First-class food." (*Tim Hart*) Only complaint: double beds replaced by twins. All those for doubles please protest.

Please make a habit of sending a report if you stay at a Guide hotel.

Open 28 Nov–22 Apr, June–Oct.
Rooms 10 suites, 25 double, 6 single – 35 with bath, 6 with shower, all with telephone, radio and TV. 2 suites in separate building across the road.
Facilities Lift. Hall, bar, TV room with video facilities, dining room, restaurant; conference facilities; children's playroom; indoor heated swimming pool, sauna, massage. Large grounds with landscaped gardens, meadows, café. English spoken.
Location Central. Garage and parking.
Credit cards None accepted.
Terms B&B: single 1,220-2,100 Sch, double 950-1,650 Sch, suite 1,460-2,500 Sch; dinner, B&B: single 1,590-2,300 Sch, double 1,320-2,020 Sch, suite 1,830-2,870 Sch. Set lunch 100 Sch; full alc 400-600 Sch. In winter only reservations for 1 week or more accepted. Christmas and touring packages. Reduced rates for children; special meals on request.

Hotel-Gasthof Salome — *Tel* (05583) 23060
Oberlech — *Telex* 52588 SALHO

The *Salome* is a comfortable, fairly pricey ski hotel perched on the mountainside at Oberlech with mountain views all around and a nursery slope at its front door (in winter the hotel is probably best approached during daytime as you have to drive up a narrow winding snow-covered road). It is a 600-year-old farmhouse, renovated in Alpine style with wooden ceilings and carved beams. This year a family with three children had "a happy and comfortable week, with delicious food and a welcoming atmosphere". Earlier visitors have felt likewise: "The pine cupboards, coloured rugs, ornaments and books made the hotel feel lived in. We were taken to the nicest room we have ever had in a ski hotel." "The food was very pleasant without being gastronomically outstanding." Guests have a large and comfortable sitting room, a sun terrace, sauna, solarium and whirlpool. Some of the larger bedrooms are divided into sleeping and sitting areas and have a balcony. (*Mrs JG Nutting, Barbara von Klipstein, and others*)

Open 5 Dec–12 Apr, 25 June–5 Sept. Closed to non-residents for dinner.
Rooms 11 suites, 4 double, 1 single – all with bath and/or shower, telephone, radio and TV.
Facilities Lift. Lounge, bar, restaurant, residents' dining room, sun terrace; sauna, solarium, whirl pool, massage. Fishing 3 km. English spoken.
Location On the mountain above Lech; take road to Oberlech. Parking.
Credit cards None accepted.
Terms Half board winter rates: 905-1,480 Sch; summer rates: half board 450-550 Sch, full board 550-650 Sch. Set lunch/dinner: winter rates: 250-450 Sch; summer rates 150-250 Sch. 1-week ski packages in winter low season. 50% reduction for children sharing parents' room; special meals.

Hotel Tannbergerhof — *Tel* (05583) 2202 and 2239
Telex 5239117

A visitor this year who was "warmly welcomed", and had "an extremely elegant room decorated à la Eaton Square", endorses this earlier account of the *Tannbergerhof*: "It is right in the thick of things on the main street of Lech, looking over the little river with its bridges, and only a few minutes' walk from the ski school and many of the lifts. At five o'clock every day there is *thé dansant* in the downstairs bar, and skiers gather to drink glühwein in front of the hotel in the sun or snow. At night there is a disco in the bar. But the bedrooms are peaceful and comfortable. We had a good bed – though the lighting was so poor it was almost impossible to read in bed. Service excellent: Frau Hilde Jochum keeps a close eye on things, as does the young *maître d'hôtel.* The food was delicious, beautifully presented, and not too heavy. Meal-times were flexible. Breakfast was a generous self-service spread – quite enough to keep us going all day without much lunch." (*Jane Nissen, A and CR; also Adam Ruck*) Frau Jochum tells us that she has now made a lounge for residents only.

Open 25 June–25 Sept, 28 Nov–16 Apr.
Rooms 4 suites, 17 double, 9 single – 27 with bath and shower, 3 with shower only, all with telephone, radio and TV. Annexe (*Chalet Hilde*) with self-catering apartments 8 minutes' walk.
Facilities Lift. Reception, hall, 3 lounges, bar 2 restaurants, downstairs bar where disco is held daily in winter; terrace. River nearby with trout fishing. Swimming pool, whirlpool in annexe. Winter sports. English spoken.
Location Central. Parking.
Credit cards None accepted.
Terms (Minimum prices in summer, maximum in winter) B&B 460-1,600 Sch; half board 590-1,700 Sch. Set lunch 230-290 Sch, dinner 280-520 Sch; full alc 590 Sch. Only half and full board available in winter. Reduced rates for children in parents' room; special meals.

MAYRHOFEN 6290 Zillertal — Map 15

Hotel Elisabeth — *Tel* (05285) 2929
Einfahrt Mitte 432 — *Telex* 534145

Mayrhofen is a skiing and mountaineering resort in an out-of-the way Tyrolean valley, the Zillertal: international holiday courses of Innsbruck University are held here in summer, engendering much liveliness and folklore activity. "A wonderful hotel, quite pricey but worth every penny," says a nominator of the *Elisabeth* this year. "Good for skiers and English spoken. There's a nightclub and ski store in the basement, and a fitness centre and indoor pool all beautifully maintained. The 'standard' bedrooms are as luxurious as the suite. The open-plan public rooms have a lovely spacious feel and the food is delightful. It's a family-run hotel and the staff are tremendously kind and helpful – I had a skiing accident and there was the hotel taxi at my disposal to take me to and from the doctor."(*Alison Patey*)

Open All year
Rooms 2 suites, 24 double, 10 single – all with bath and shower, telephone, radio, TV and baby-listening.
Facilities Lift. Bar, hall with open fire place, 4 restaurants; conference room; indoor swimming pool, sauna, hot whirl pool, beauty farm. Dancing. Garden, children's playground with games, barbecues. English spoken.
Location In centre of village, 68 km E of Innsbruck.
Credit cards Probably most major cards accepted.
Terms B&B 750–945 Sch; dinner, B&B 850–1,045 Sch. Set meals120–500 Sch; full alc 300 Sch. 50% reduction for children in parents' room; special meals.

> Do you know of a good hotel or country inn in the United States or Canada? Nominations please to our sibling publication, *America's Wonderful Little Hotels and Inns,* PO Box 150, Riverside Avenue, Riverside, Conn. 06878, USA.

MUTTERS 6162 Tyrol — Map 15

Hotel Restaurant Muttererhof — *Tel* (05222) 27491
Nattererstrasse 20
Mutters, bei Innsbruck

A picturesque village on a ledge just south of Innsbruck. "Every chalet turns into a *Gasthof* during the skiing season, but in the summer it is redolent of cow byres. The hotel is the last building on the road to Natters and faces the most breathtaking landscape. The *pièce de résistance* is the good-sized, well-heated swimming pool, solarium and sauna. Decor and furniture of bedrooms uninspiring, though our room had a balcony (many of them do not, and they face north, getting no sun). Beds were comfortable. The dining room was absolutely beautiful, panelled in dark wood with ecclesiastical-style carvings. Our appetite was well satisfied by the meal, and the *carte* contained Austrian specialities. Service was really friendly and efficient all round. A good, reasonably priced base to explore the area." (*Francine and Ian Walsh*) Confirmed by *Rosemarie Powell* this year, though another reader found the service lacking warmth and the lighting dim. He was made to pay extra for use of the pool, though others were not – can any other visitor shed light on this?

Open 20 Dec–10 Apr, 1 May–25 Oct.
Rooms 1 suite, 18 double, 1 single – all with bath or shower; many with balcony.
Facilities Bar, *Stübe*, restaurant; indoor swimming pool, sauna and solarium. Garden. Tennis and winter sports nearby. English spoken.
Location 6 km SSW of Innsbruck, S of Natters, E of Gotzens.
Restriction Not suitable for ♿.
Credit cards Amex, Visa.
Terms B&B 320–370 Sch; full board 460–540 Sch. Set lunch/dinner 100–140 Sch; full alc 160-200 Sch. Reduced rates and special meals for children.

SALZBURG — Map 15

Hotel Elefant — *Tel* (0662) 843397
Sigmund-Haffnergasse 4, — *Telex* 632725 ELHOT
Salzburg 5020

In a quiet pedestrian street in the historic heart of Salzburg, a typical town house, tall and medieval. Public rooms are splendid, even grandiose, with old paintings, fine antiques, chequered marble floors. Upper floor bedrooms have in the past been found cramped and ordinary: but this year the hotel says it has extensively renovated them, likewise the cellar restaurant on which our reports had been variable. 36 rooms, all with bath and/or shower. B&B double 880-1,100 Sch. Set dinner from 180 Sch. No reports this year: more badly needed on whether this has now ceased to be a white Elefant.

Hotel Kasererbräu — *Tel* (0622) 842445
Kaigasse 33, Salzburg 5010 — *Telex* 633492

In the heart of old Salzburg, a very elegant hotel in a 14th-century building near the cathedral, some rooms furnished in baroque or Biedermeier styles, others more up-to-date. Friendly service and good, fairly priced food at the hotel restaurant, Mozart Inn. *Closed Feb. 37 rooms, all with bath or shower. B&B double, 940-1,500 Sch. No recent reports: more welcome.*

Pension Nonntal *Tel* (0662) 841427 and 846700
Pfadfinderweg 6-8
Salzburg 5020

Recommended again this year as a "small homely *pension* set in a pretty garden" in residential south-east Salzburg, with a spectacular view of the Hohensalzburg fortress and only ten minutes' walk from the centre. "Herr Otto and his wife were most helpful. Good Austrian cooking." Earlier reports: "Most gracious and warm." "An old converted house in a quiet area. Rooms overlook greenery; comfortable twin beds; bath is generous in size and modern." Some readers have praised the evening meals, served out on the terrace when fine, but one visitor disliked the lack of choice and commented on instant coffee and a cramped room. (*Joan Stanton, Laura Wiese, Janet Merutka, Thomas J Loran*)

Open All year except Nov. Restaurant closed to non-residents.
Rooms 2 suites, 10 double, 6 single – all with bath and/or shower, telephone. 6 rooms and 2 flats in annexe. 2 ground-floor rooms.
Facilities Breakfast room, restaurant; functions room. Garden with terrace and lawns. Bicycles available. English spoken.
Location In SE suburbs. Leave *Autobahn at Salzburg-Süd*, take Friedensstrasse, Hellbrunnerstrasse, Hofhaymer-Allee, Nonntaler Hauptstrasse. Frequent buses to city centre.
Credit cards Access, Amex, Visa.
Terms B&B: single 580-650 Sch, double 800-850 Sch, suite 950-1,400 Sch. Set lunch 135-170 Sch, dinner 180-200 Sch; full alc 250-300 Sch.

Hotel Schloss Mönchstein *Tel* (0662) 848555
Am Mönchsberg 26 *Telex* 632080 MOEHO
Salzburg 5020

This dun-coloured *Schloss* with its creepers and red gabled roofs, now a rather smart hotel, stands high on the Mönchsberg just above central Salzburg. Once the guest-house of an archbishop, it is today admired by many modern lay tourists (including our own readers) for its fine location and other qualities. "It is a haven, tucked away from the central city, yet easily accessible. Our room had a lot of space, but was cosy; antiques in the halls and dining room. Linen changed daily. The food was delicious and the service excellent." "Not more than 15 minutes by foot from the *Festspielhaus* and yet remote from the tourist hurly-burly. Thanks to an efficient lift service which runs until two in the morning, you can be whisked to the top of the mountain in a mere 30 seconds. It is beautifully quiet and the air is fresher than down in town." "Breakfast ranged from brioches to fruit salad to cheese and cold cuts, and was served on our flower-filled terrace." Others have commented on the big tidy garden, the lawns, flowerbeds and dense trees. (*Kathie Walker, G Sharp, Vicki Turner, and others*)

Open All year.
Rooms 9 suites, 7 double, 1 single – 15 with bath, 2 with shower, all with direct-dial telephone, radio, TV and mini-bar; 24-hour room service. Some ground-floor rooms.
Facilities Lift. Hall, salon, bar, restaurant; chapel for weddings; terrace with café; monthly concerts. Large garden with tennis court. English spoken.
Location Above Salzburg on Mönchsberg – hotel is signposted. 3 minutes by car from city centre, 7 minutes by the Mönchsberg lift. Parking and garages.
Credit cards All major cards accepted.

Terms [1987 rates] B&B: single 1,200-1,400 Sch, double 1,800-3,000 Sch, suite 3,000-16,200 Sch. Set lunch/dinner 450 Sch; full alc 510 Sch. Reduced rates and special meals for children on request.

Hotel Schöne Aussicht *Tel* (0662) 78226 and 78449
Heuberg 3, Salzburg 5023 *Telex* 631153

A big white modern chalet, set on a green hillside just outside the city - and the view of Salzburg from its terrace is *schön* indeed. The pool, tennis courts, red parasols on the panoramic terrace, and cosy beamed bar, all add to the holiday ambience. "Excellent food with delicious Austrian wines, served on the wide terrace. Waitress service remains bucolic, though willing. We soaked up the heavenly scent of the first haymaking, just below our windows." That report this year endorsed earlier accounts of this popular place: "Visiting Salzburg with the car is difficult as most of the old town is pedestrianised: a better idea is to stay out of town and then drive in to one of the large car parks. This we did. We had a lovely room with balcony, service was courteous and friendly, and the food was delicious. Glorious walks in the countryside." Two small caveats. One, front bedrooms may suffer from late evening noise from the bar. Two, although the brochure mentions public transport, the walk from the bus stop is up three steep hills, so a car is advisable. (*F Peter Woodford, Bettina and Sacha Dudkin, and others*)

Open 1 Mar–end October.
Rooms 3 suites, 24 double, 1 single – all with bath or shower, telephone and radio; TV on request.
Facilities Lounge, bar, TV room, restaurant; conference/function facilities; sauna; terrace. Garden with swimming pool. English spoken.
Location 3 km NE of city centre, off N158 to Bad Ischl.
Restriction Not suitable for ♿.
Credit cards Amex, Diners.
Terms B&B: single 500–700 Sch, double 800–1,200 Sch, suite 1,200–1,700 Sch. Full alc 245 Sch. Reduced rates and special meals for children.

SCHLOSS ROSENAU 3924 Lower Austria Map 15

Museumsverein Schloss Rosenau *Tel* (02822) 8221

Less than two hours' drive west from Vienna, and not far from the Czech border, the village of Schloss Rosenau lies quietly amid rolling country-side, good for walking and cross-country skiing. The *Schloss* is a baroque palace, most of it now housing a spectacular 18th-century Masonic museum. The rest is a hotel, outwardly very grand but offering quite simple accomodation at a reasonable price: bedrooms are plain, with simple pine furniture. The extensive dinner menu offers food that is tasty, plentiful, fairly imaginative and good value. *Note*: the *Schloss* has close links with the *Pension Weissenhofer* next door, and guests who book may find themselves sleeping at the *Pension*, unless they specify. (*K and SM-S; also Professor HC Robbins Landon*) More reports welcome.

Open All year except 25 Jan–28 Feb.
Rooms 1 suite, 17 double – all with shower and WC. Guests also accommodated in *Pension Weissenhofer* nearby.

Facilities Lift. TV room, dining room, 2 *Stüberl;* conference and banqueting rooms; sun terrace. Masonic museum and baroque church. Park with covered heated swimming pool, sauna, hard tennis court and miniature golf. Riding and fishing available. English spoken.
Location 6 km SW of Zwettl.
Credit cards All major cards accepted.
Terms B&B: 330-380 Sch; half board 415-465 Sch; full board 480-540 Sch. Set lunch/dinner 100-150 Sch; full alc 100-250 Sch. Reduced rates and special meals for children.

SCHRUNS 6780 Vorarlberg — Map 15

Hotel Krone — *Tel* (05556) 2255
Schruns, Montafon

A delightful cattle-market and *Loden*-manufacturing town in the Montafon valley. Five minutes' walk from its centre is the *Krone*, a *gemütlich* little hotel run by the Mayer family for four generations. This year, as in the past, readers have responded to their hospitality. "Excellent room, food and service, nice furniture," is one new report. "The Mayers maintain a keen interest in the running of their hotel and the behaviour of the staff reflected their simple kindness. Our meals were beautifully planned, delightfully cooked and served with great charm." (*Frank Mattinson, A Wilcock; also Ian and Anne Steel*)

Open Mid-Dec–Apr, end May–mid-Oct. Restaurant closed Thur.
Rooms 8 double, 1 single – all with bath, shower, telephone and radio; TV for hire.
Facilities Lounge, bar, TV room, wine cellar, dining room. Garden terrace; river frontage with trout fishing. English spoken.
Location Central, near the Kronen bridge. Parking. 12 km SE of Bludenz.
Restriction Not suitable for ♿.
Credit cards None accepted.
Terms B&B 290-380 Sch; dinner, B&B 420-510 Sch; full board 500-620 Sch. Set lunch 140 Sch, dinner 160 Sch; full alc 180 Sch. Ski packages with reduced rates in Jan. Reduced rates for children; special meals.

STEYR 4400 Upper Austria — Map 15

Hotel Minichmayr — *Tel* (07252) 23410
Haratzmüllerstrasse 1-3 — *Telex* 28134

In an industrial town with a picturesque old quarter, this attractive hotel stands opposite the confluence of two rivers, and some rooms have fine views of them. Comfortable rather than elegant, the hotel has modern bathrooms, a wood-panelled breakfast room, and a good restaurant with original nouvelle-*ish dishes, copiously served. Service friendly. 50 rooms, almost all with bath or shower. B&B 365–535 Sch. Full alc 250 Sch. No recent reports: more needed.*

VIENNA — Map 15

Hotel Amadeus — *Tel* (0222) 638738
Wildpretmarkt 5, Vienna 1010 — *Telex* 111102

"Comfortable and charming, flowers everywhere, fine prints on the walls, staff all helpful and pleasant." That new report reprieves the

Amadeus, dropped from last year's Guide because of noisy building work in progress in its small street near St Stephan's in old Vienna. "The bedrooms and public rooms are decorated in red and white like the Austrian flag, the hotel is fully carpeted with rich red rugs; crystal chandeliers are scattered throughout." An earlier visitor found the atmosphere "pure Maria Theresa and delightful". Another reader voiced delight about breakfast – "ambrosial coffee and a basket of newly baked rolls". One reader even had "a delicious chocolate cake" for breakfast one day. (*Donna Cuervo; also Ruth Luborsky, F and IW*)

Open All year except 23–27 Dec.
Rooms 18 double, 12 single – all with bath and/or shower, telephone and radio; 22 with TV.
Facilities Breakfast room. English spoken.
Location Central, down a small turning off Tuchlauben.
Restriction Not suitable for ♿.
Credit cards Amex, Diners, Visa.
Terms B&B: single 935-1,260 Sch, double 1,620 Sch. Reduced rates for children. (No restaurant.)

Hotel Kaiserin Elisabeth *Tel* (0222) 515260
Weihburggasse 3 *Telex* 112422 ELIHO
Vienna 1010

Traditional demure B&B in historic building near St Stephan's cathedral. Well-equipped bedrooms, which vary in size and price. Some a bit claustrophobic. Public rooms all face away from the street. No restaurant, but snack meals served. 71 rooms, all with private facilities. B&B double 1,050–1,500 Sch. More reports please.

König von Ungarn *Tel* (0222) 5265200
1 Schulerstrasse 10, Vienna 1010 *Telex* 116240

A beautifully restored 18th-century building, only a stone's throw from St Stephan's cathedral. Its inner courtyard has been converted into an attractive Art Nouveau-style lounge "where an inspired variety of cocktails are served". Warm praise again this year for the help-yourself breakfasts, the spacious and attractively furnished rooms, the central but quiet location, and the friendly staff. "The reception area is off to one side so that when you go through the fine bevelled glass doors you have the feeling of entering an exclusive club." "Our quite sizeable attic room had a large walk-in cupboard. I felt I could have lived there with all my wardrobe. The restaurant is under separate ownership. It is very elegant and a well-known place to go among the Viennese society. The service is all one could wish for and the food excellent." "The nicest hotel we've been in in a long while." One typically pleasant touch is that the hotel provides its guests with daily reports in three languages, on places to visit and other suggestions for the day. (*H Langenberg, Bill Appelman, Jim Rose, C and W Bagshawe, and others*)

Open All year.
Rooms 70 beds – 28 rooms with bath, 4 with shower, all with telephone.
Facilities Lift. Lounge, bar, restaurant, TV room, children's room.
Location Central, near St Stephan's Cathedral. Parking.
Terms [1987 rates] B&B: single 1,000-1,300 Sch, double 1,400-1,600 Sch.

Pension Nossek *Tel* (0222) 5337041
Graben 17, Vienna 1010

Dr Renato Cremona's old-world *pension*, established by his grandmother before World War I, has recently been renovated and upgraded. It is very centrally situated in one of Vienna's most fashionable streets, now a pedestrian precinct – five minutes from the Opera, the Hofburg and the Riding School – and occupies the top floors of a stately office building. "I returned with pleasure to its immaculate, high-ceilinged and well-lit accommodation," is one report this year. Another visitor adds: "Comfortable, quiet, service friendly and efficient." But an anonymous reader, while agreeing that it offers very good value, with "outstanding" beds and cleanliness, thought the lighting poor and the service unreliable and casual, "sometimes garnished with that dreadful Viennese 'charm' which cuts no ice with me". (*F Peter Woodford, Peter Cook, Lesley Heal*)

Open All year.
Rooms 3 suites, 22 double, 3 single – 21 with bath and/or shower, all with telephone, baby-listening and tea-making facilities.
Facilities Lift. Reading room, breakfast room. English spoken.
Location Central, but quiet. Underground car park 1 minute's walk.
Credit cards None accepted.
Terms B&B: single 300 Sch, double 580 Sch, suite 740 Sch. Reduced rates for children. (No restaurant.)

Hotel im Palais Schwarzenberg *Tel* (0222) 784515
Schwarzenbergplatz 9 *Telex* 136124 HPS
Vienna 1030

Prince Karl Johannes von Schwarzenberg is the owner of this stately pile, which has been his family's home since the early 18th century. It was bombed during the war, but has been faithfully reconstructed. Although only 15 minutes' walk from the Opera, it has its own 19-acre park and is a discreet, quiet and impressively elegant place – a visitor this year found the food excellent and the service very smooth, without a hint of the condescending arrogance sometimes found in a princely hotel of this kind. Guests do not stay at the Palace itself, but are accommodated in what was formerly the stables and servants' quarters. Of course, prices are high, but most readers think them reasonable for what is offered. "Our room was comfortably large, with fabric-covered walls, antique furniture, crystal chandelier and plush carpeting. Forgetting the price, this was definitely one of the nicest rooms we have stayed in. Surprisingly, there was no buffet at breakfast and all except the basic rolls, jam and coffee were charged as extras – rather mean, we felt. All the staff were helpful and polite." There have been occasional complaints about muddles over bookings or demands for large deposits, but we still hear comments like: "This hotel alone is worth a visit to Vienna – on our final night there was a garden ball in the palace with dancing and fireworks in the garden. I felt as if I had visited 19th-century Vienna." (*Uli Lloyd Pack, JA Thomas, and others*)

Open All year.
Rooms 4 suites, 34 double – all with bath, telephone and radio; TV on request; 1 suite with kitchenette. Some ground-floor rooms.

Facilities 3 lifts. Hall, salons, bar, restaurant with summer and winter terraces; large conference halls, function facilities. 19-acre private park. Tennis, swimming and sauna nearby. English spoken.
Location Entrance at bottom of Prinz-Eugen-Strasse. Unlimited parking.
Credit cards All major cards accepted.
Terms B&B double 3,000-4,500 Sch, suite 6,000 Sch. Full alc 800 Sch. Christmas and New Year packages. Children under 12 free in parents' room; special meals for children on request.

Pension Suzanne *Tel* (0222) 5132507
Walfischgasse 4, Vienna 1010

The Walfischgasse is 100 yards from the Opera House and the start of the pedestrianised Kärntnerstrasse. As in other Viennese *pensions*, the entrance of the *Suzanne* is unimpressive; the bedrooms are on the upper floors, some facing the street (double-glazed) and some a parking lot in the rear, while there is even a sex-shop next door. A breakfast-room/salon has just been built, which adds to the rather sparse amenities. But what distinguishes the *Suzanne* is its agreeable Viennese furnishings – handsome beds, chairs and tables, fine mirrors, decent pictures – that, and friendly efficiency on the part of the English-speaking staff. "We had a pleasant room on the eighth floor, with a small kitchen and our own balcony overlooking the Opera House." (*Uli Lloyd Pack, Mr and Mrs DPG Weizmann; also Hugh Verity*)

Open All year.
Rooms 36 beds – 16 rooms with bath, 3 with shower, all with telephone; some with kitchenette; some with balcony.
Facilities Lift. Breakfast room. English spoken.
Location Central, near Opera House.
Restriction Not suitable for ♿.
Credit cards None accepted.
Terms [1987 rates] B&B 355-550 Sch; suite with kitchenette 810-860 Sch. (No restaurant.)

WAGRAIN-MOADÖRFL 5602 Salzburg — Map 15

Hotel-Gasthof Moawirt *Tel* (06413) 8818
Schwaighof 123

Backed by forested hills, this spruce modern flower-bedecked chalet stands just outside Wagrain, an all-year resort 25 miles south of Salzburg, just off the *Autobahn* to Villach. "Large excellent rooms, good bathroom and balcony, good local food and friendly service," is a typical comment this year. The hotel is owned and run by the delightful *Familie* Maurer. The surrounding countryside is lovely, perfect for summer walking and for winter skiing (a chair lift is opposite the hotel). (*Harry Robinson, FC Parker*) One visitor has warned of traffic noise from front rooms.

Open All year.
Rooms 23 double, 4 single – all with bath and/or shower, telephone, radio, TV and balcony.
Facilities Lift. Lounge/bar, TV room, breakfast room, dining room; folk music once a week. Sun terrace and garden. Winter sports. English spoken.
Location About 25 m S of Salzburg, just off Salzburg/Villach *Autobahn*.
Credit cards Access, Amex, Diners.
Terms [1987 rates] B&B 280-300 Sch; full board 395-460 Sch.

WEIZ 8160 Styria — Map 15

Modersnhof *Tel* (03172) 3747
Büchl 32

Weiz is a pleasant little town in lovely wooded hill country north-east of Graz – a bit out of the way, but it could make a useful stop on the route from Vienna to northern Italy. Here the *Modersnhof* is a most elegant Romantikhotel, a low white building with balconies beside a swimming-pool. "Expensive but worth it," is a comment this year. "Food and service were exceptional." Earlier visitors have also spoken warmly of the Maier family's personalised service and good continental cooking. (*Rosemarie Powell; also John G Peetz*)

Open 15 Mar–15 Jan.
Rooms 7 double – all with bath and shower, direct-dial telephone, radio and TV; many with balcony.
Facilities Lobby, salon, bar, reading room, 2 restaurants. Large grounds with terrace restaurant, tennis, swimming pool with bar. English spoken.
Location 3 km SE of Weiz which is 25km NE of Graz.
Restriction Not suitable for ♿.
Credit cards All major cards accepted.
Terms B&B: single 850 Sch, double 1,250 Sch; dinner, B&B: single 1,130 Sch, double 1,810 Sch. Set lunch 290 Sch, dinner 390 Sch; full alc 420 Sch. Reduced rates for children sharing parents' room; special meals.

WINDISCHGARSTEN 4580 Upper Austria — Map 15

Hotel-Pension Schwarzes-Rössl *Tel* (07562) 311 and 8282

This popular 15th-century family inn stands in the middle of a pleasant town in the Garstner valley north of Liezen, and again this year it has been commended for the friendliness and courtesy of the owners, the Baumschlagers, and their staff. All around are woodlands, pastures, rocky hills. Most summer visitors come for walking, climbing, riding or fishing, though the hotel has the use of a heated swimming pool and a tennis court, five minutes' walk away. In winter it's a centre for skiing, both cross-country and downhill. Thick walls and double-glazing keep out local traffic noise. The hotel has all the virtues of its age: its rooms are larger and more characterful than in many modern hotels, the beds more spacious, the bed linen better quality, lighting adequate (just). There are plenty of local dishes and the helpings cater for large appetites. "The mushroom season was in full swing (October) and fresh mushrooms including chanterelles were served daily. We found the cooking light and imaginative." Other visitors also much appreciated the Baumschlagers' other Windischgarsten hotel, the *Sport Hotel* (four stars to this one's three). (*J ter Haar*)

Open All year except Nov. Closed Wed out of season.
Rooms 2 suites, 16 double, 5 single – 18 with bath and shower.
Facilities Lounge, reading room, TV/playroom for children, restaurants. Entertainment (zither and concertina playing, folklore evenings and dancing) can be arranged. Indoor and outdoor games for children. All facilities of the nearby *Sport Hotel* are available to guests at the *Schwarzes-Rössl* – large grounds, tennis courts, heated outdoor swimming pool, riding hall, ski school, tobogganing, squash courts, and terrace where coffee, cakes and pastries are served. Gleinkersee lake 5 km. English spoken.

Location Central (double-glazing). Parking.
Restriction Not suitable for ♿.
Credit cards None accepted.
Terms B&B: 242-270 Sch; dinner B&B: 290-320 Sch; full board: 310-340 Sch. Set lunch 100-120 Sch, supper 120 Sch; full alc 160-210 Sch. 25% reduction for children under 12, 50% reduction for children under 6 sharing parents' room; special meals.

HOTEL DE ORANGERIE, BRUGES

AS 3668 Limburg **Map 9**

Hotel Mardaga *Tel* (011) 65.70.34 and 65.72.34
Stationstraat 89

Situated in north-east Belgium, not far from Maastricht and close to the Brussels–Cologne motorway, this solid hostelry lies amid forests and has its own five-acre wooded garden. Its facade is 1900-ish and it has been run by the Mardaga family since about then. Our inspectors give high marks to the restaurant, and average marks to the bedrooms which come in two styles: white 1960s vinyl or 1920s veneer. Some are immense, with sitting areas and comfortable armchairs. Linen is white and crisp and central heating admirable. Spacious lounge downstairs overlooking lawn and forest, filled with good pictures and Delft porcelain. The dining room is lovely and light with spotless napery, elegant pleated cream curtains, engraved glassware and monogrammed house china. Fresh tulips grace each table. M. Mardaga is the chef and the food is excellent, as is the service. Breakfast includes freshly-squeezed orange juice, eggs, cheese, and home-made rhubarb jam with lots of strong fresh coffee. The hotel has the air of having known better days, but everything is gleaming. (*Ron and Jan Davidson, and others*)

Open All year except 1–15 Jan, 15–30 Jun. Restaurant closed Wed.
Rooms 20 double – 15 with bath, 5 with shower, all with telephone and TV.
Facilities Lift. Salon, bar, 2 restaurants; banqueting room. Large garden. English spoken.
Location 2 km N of As which is 22 km NE of Hasselt, 29 km NW of Maastricht.
Restriction Not suitable for ♿.
Credit cards Amex, Diners, Visa.
Terms B&B: single 950-1,700 Bfrs, double 1,200-2,100 Bfrs; half board 1,800-2,500 Bfrs per person; full board 2,000-2,700 Bfrs per person. Set lunch 950 Bfrs; dinner 1,450-2,300 Bfrs; full alc 1,500 Bfrs.

BRUGES 8000 Flanders — Map 9

Hotel Adornes — *Tel* (050) 34.13.36
St Annarei 26

This small reasonably-priced B&B hotel is a 17th-century house close to the *Markt*. It is quite peaceful and was recently renovated. "My room overlooking a canal was well appointed, with bathroom *en suite* and nice touches such as fresh flowers and fruit. The owners could not have been more helpful." (*Norman W Turner*)

Open 11 Feb–3 Jan.
Rooms 20 double (also let as single) - 18 with bath, 2 with shower, all with telephone and radio; 15 with TV. 2 ground-floor rooms.
Facilities Lift. 2 lounges. English spoken.
Location Central. Go from *Markt* to theatre; hotel is signposted. Parking.
Credit cards Access, Amex, Visa.
Terms B&B: single 1,700-2,700 Bfrs, double 1,900-2,900 Bfrs. Special winter packages, including tickets for museums. Reduced rates for children.

Hotel Anselmus — *Tel* (050) 34.13.74
Riddersstraat 15

A small B&B, run by Lode and Yvette Dutoit-Schoore: "An attractive old Flemish-style gabled house, entered through a massive wooden door of vast proportions. It takes its name from an eminent humanist of Bruges who lived here and was possibly a contemporary of Erasmus. The interior has been skilfully and beautifully converted into a comfortable little hotel. The owner was most attentive and helpful. Our spacious and spotless room had a well-equipped bathroom. The breakfast room is attractive. The hotel is in a quiet street, close to the central market." (*Michael Appleby; also Barbara Wolfe, NM Williamson, and others*)

Open All year.
Rooms 1 suite, 8 double, 1 single – all with bath and/or shower, telephone, radio and TV. 2 ground-floor rooms.
Facilities Hall, lounges, breakfast room. English spoken.
Location 5 minutes' walk from the market square. Parking in street.
Credit cards Access, Amex, Visa.
Terms B&B: single 1,500 Bfrs, double 1,900-2,100 Bfrs; suite 2,500 Bfrs, for 3 people 2,800 Bfrs, for 4 3,200 Bfrs. 1-night bookings sometimes refused. Reduced rates for children.

Hotel de Orangerie *Tel* (050) 34.16.49
Kartuizerinnenstraat 10 *Telex* 82443 ORANGE

"Set in the heart of Bruges, overlooking the Dijver, this creeper-covered 16th-century house has recently been immaculately converted into an elegant small hotel (three red gables in *Michelin*). No restaurant, but there is a charming bar with an open fireplace and period furniture giving the impression of a private drawing room. In the summer breakfast and drinks are served on a terrace overlooking the canal. The hotel is managed by two charming and attractive sisters, Beatrice and Christine Strubbe, who looked after us with care and attention far beyond the call of duty." (*Jacintha Alexander*)

Open All year.
Rooms 5 suites, 14 double – all with bath and shower, direct-dial telephone, radio, TV and mini-bar; baby-sitting on request. Some ground-floor rooms.
Facilities Lift. Lounge/bar, TV room, breakfast room. 2 terraces, garden. English spoken.
Location Central, on canal near Belfry. Valet parking.
Credit cards All major cards accepted.
Terms B&B: single 3,500 Bfrs, double 3,950-4,950 Bfrs, suite 5,500-6,800 Bfrs. (No restaurant.)

Die Swaene *Tel* (050) 34.27.98
Steenhouwersdijk 1 *Telex* 82446 SWAENE

Warm words again this year for this very central B&B hotel in a 15th-century house on a canal, almost opposite the Belfry. "A quietly elegant hotel with a comfortable family atmosphere and a pleasant outlook over a quiet canal," says a reader who enjoyed her lavish breakfast and the cream-and-pink colour scheme of her comfortable bedroom. A visitor from Dallas was thrilled with the warmth of his late-evening welcome from the owners "who make you feel like a part of the family". Others have lauded the "big, airy modern rooms" and "helpful service, wonderful breakfast". The owners, the Hessel family, tell us that their lounge, with open fire and a fine painted ceiling, is the restored meeting room of the Guild of Tailors, dating from 1779, and free coffee and tea are still served in this guildhall every afternoon from two till four. (*K and S Murray-Sykes, Prof RS Harmon, and others*)

Open All year.
Rooms 2 suites, 24 double – all with bath and shower, telephone, radio, TV and mini-bar; 4 with open fire. 6 ground-floor rooms.
Facilities 2 Lifts. Lobby, lounge, bar, breakfast room. Terrace and garden. English spoken.
Location Central (but quiet): signposts from the market square. Garage.
Credit cards All major cards accepted.
Terms B&B: single 2,600 Bfrs, double 4,000 Bfrs, suite 6,800 Bfrs. Reduced rates for children. (No restaurant.)

Hotel Ter Duinen *Tel* (050) 33.04.37
Langerei 52

A small, unassuming and inexpensive hotel on a canal, about 800 metres from the centre, run by a dedicated and very friendly young couple, and now a firm favourite with readers. Reports this year: "More caring owners would be hard to find. Lovely breakfasts, fresh orange juice; rooms old-fashioned but very clean. A little gem." "I took a party of seven very fussy German ladies, all pleasantly surprised, it really was spotless. Drinks in the lounge till 11 pm, nicely served with nuts, bits of salami etc." Last year another visitor enthused: "It's a beautiful walk along canals from the centre of town, and if you forget the exact address, just look for the masses of flowers on each of its three tiers. The young owners would bend over backwards to help you choose a restaurant, to serve you a whole second pot of coffee at breakfast, load you with keys to get in the door after 10. The rooms are spacious and uncluttered, but tastefully furnished with subtle printed fabrics and period furniture. We enjoyed moonlight over the canals at night from our two big windows. I would recommend this place to everyone, from students to countesses. It's simply beautiful, just like the city it lives in." But front rooms are said to be a little noisy. (*S Phillips, Mrs BI Coppack, J and AW, Mr and Mrs Earl McCleave*) Ten new bedrooms were being added in 1987.

Open All year.
Rooms 20 – 18 with bath and/or shower, all with telephone.
Facilities Lift. Lounge/bar with TV. English spoken.
Location On canal 10-15 minutes' walk from centre. Street parking in front of hotel; private garage available (100 Bfrs 1st night, 50 Bfrs thereafter). Windows are double-glazed.
Restriction Not suitable for ♿.
Credit cards All major cards accepted.
Terms B&B: double 2,000 Bfrs. Reduced rates for children. (No restaurant.)

BRUSSELS — Map 9

Hôtel Agenda
6 rue de Florence
1050 Brussels

Tel (02) 539.00.31
Telex 63947 AGENDA

Our request last year for news of budget hotels in Brussels has now been answered – well, almost answered – by a reader's nomination of this small modern medium-priced hotel just off the Avenue Louise: "It looks very conventional from the outside, but its charm lies in its comfort and tranquillity and the genuinely warm greeting. Our spacious room had big windows, lots of cupboards, soft chairs, and a kitchenette. Breakfast was delicious, served in a pretty room. No restaurant, but we ate well at reasonable cost at *Les Cadets de Gascogne* down the block." (*Kathleen Ashley*) More reports please on what seems like remarkable value in this pricey Euro-capital.

Open All year.
Rooms 2 suites, 23 double, 13 single – all with bath and shower, telephone, TV and kitchenette. 2 ground-floor rooms.
Facilities Lounge, breakfast room. Small garden. English spoken.
Location Fairly central: in side street, off Avenue Louise, 700 metres S of Place Louise. Garage.
Restriction Not suitable for ♿.
Credit cards All major cards accepted.
Terms B&B: single 2,750 Bfrs, double 3,300 Bfrs, suite 3,800 Bfrs. Week-end, Christmas and Easter packages.

Hôtel Amigo *Tel* (02) 511.59.10
Rue de l'Amigo 1–3 *Telex* 21618
1000 Brussels

The preferred choice of many visiting diplomats, marketeers and tourists, the modern and spacious *Amigo* occupies a prime site close to the Grand' Place, and again this year has been described as "delightful", "charming and quiet, especially rooms at the back". The airy lobby has a fine flagstone floor. The restaurant is wholesome rather than enterprising, but there are many exciting eating-spots in the Grand' Place area, and the hotel's ambience is unrushed, personal and agreeably old-world. (*AL, DS McGuire, and others*)

Open All year.
Rooms 11 suites, 157 double, 26 single – all with bath and/or shower, telephone, radio and TV. Some ground-floor rooms.
Facilities Lift. Salons, TV room, bar, restaurant; conference rooms and banqueting facilities. English spoken.
Location Central, behind the Grand' Place. Garage.
Credit cards All major cards accepted.
Terms B&B: single 3,950-5,100 Bfrs, double 4,550-5,550 Bfrs, suite 8,900-18,500 Bfrs. Set meals 1,090 Bfrs; full alc 1,600 Bfrs. No charge for children under 12 sharing parents' room; special meals on request.

Residence Rembrandt *Tel* (02) 512.71.39
57 rue de la Concorde
1050 Brussels

Quite a discovery, this small and inexpensive family-run pension *in a stylish 19th-century house, in a quiet central street just off the Avenue Louise. Warmly solicitous owners, rooms simple but clean (two are virtual suites). No restaurant, but some room service. 10 rooms, some with bath or shower. B&B double 1,145-1,655 Bfrs. New nomination: more reports please.*

DURBUY 5480 Luxembourg Belge — Map 9

Hostellerie le Sanglier des Ardennes *Tel* (086) 21.10.88 and 21.32.62
Telex 42240 SANDUR
Rue Comte Théodule d'Ursel

Set amid lovely forests in the valley of the river Ourthe, Durbuy is a pretty little village, overcrowded in summer. Here three small hotels, the *Sanglier, Cardinal* and *Vieux Durbuy,* are under the same ownership (Maurice Caerdinael) and are run jointly, with the *Sanglier* serving as the restaurant for all three. Its cooking is highly reputed (two *Gault Millau toques*) and this year one of our readers too thought it excellent (good grilled frogs' legs and sole poached in vermouth, though poor Belgian cheese). He also stayed at the *Sanglier,* and found it quiet and reasonably furnished, with some antiques. Another new report: "Nicely welcomed, we enjoyed our room with its pleasant fabrics; breakfast was a dream except for tea." Others in the past have praised the bedrooms in all three hotels and the views of the river and medieval castle. There were some complaints last year about poor room standards and lack of private toilets, but we understand that some rooms are now being refurbished. (*E Allfrey-Pizer, Gabriele Berneck and Dr Christine Herxheimer, and others*)

Open All year except Jan. Restaurant closed Thur.
Rooms 7 suites in the *Cardinal;* 30 double – most with bath (but not all bathrooms have WC); some with telephone, radio, TV and mini-bar; baby-sitting on request. Some ground-floor rooms.
Facilities Lounge, TV room, bar, restaurant; banquet room; conference facilities; terrace. The *Cardinal* has a large garden. Fishing, park, children's play area nearby. Swimming 3 km. English spoken.
Location 45 km S of Liège. Hotels are central; the *Cardinal* has private parking.
Restriction Not suitable for ♿.
Credit cards Amex, Diners, Visa.
Terms Rooms: single 895–2,200 Bfrs, double 1,195–2,200 Bfrs, suite 3,200–4,200 Bfrs. Breakfast 275 Bfrs. Reduced rates for children under 10.

ESSENE 1705 Brabant — Map 9

Hostellerie Bellemolen — *Tel* (053) 66.62.38
Stationstraat 11

Converted with flair from an old Flemish watermill, this very smart restaurant-with-rooms lies not far from Brussels in the lush Brabant countryside. Its restaurant serves some of the best dishes (*Michelin* rosette) in the area. "The wrought iron gates give the impression of entering a château, but the mill is a low timber structure. The main door is on a balcony straight above the mill stream which runs right under the cocktail lounge to operate the wheels, visible through a glazed hole in the floor. The lounge and restaurant are tucked away at various levels beneath the timbers. The bedrooms are at all kinds of levels and feature the timber structure clearly exposed. Some are very spacious. The furniture is dark oak rustic at its best. Bathrooms are smartly decorated. The restaurant has an elegant and sophisticated city ambience. A wood fire burned, the service was skilful and the food was served with panache. We woke next morning to the sound of clucking and crowing. The breakfast table was nicely set and we had fresh eggs from our feathered friends outside." There are a few jarring notes: some bedrooms are small with no central heating, dark rooms (but compensated for by extra lighting), but the hotel has "bags of character and atmosphere". (*I and F Walsh; also Pat and Jeremy Temple*)

Open All year except 6–31 July and Christmas/New Year period. Closed Sun evening and Mon.
Rooms 6 – all with bath, shower and frigobar. Some ground-floor rooms.
Facilities Lounge, bar, restaurant; conference room. Garden and courtyard.
Location 18 km NW of Brussels, just N of motorway to Ostend, and 10 km SE of Aalst. Leave motorway at Aalst turning, or take old N10 from Brussels to Aalst and turn off S. Hotel is on river at edge of village. Parking.
Credit cards Access, Amex, Diners.
Terms [1987 rates] B&B: single: 1,850 Bfrs, double 2,500 Bfrs. Alc (excluding wine) 1,450-2,130 Bfrs.

GENT 9000 East Flanders — Map 9

Hôtel St Jorishof — *Tel* (091) 24.24.24
Botermarkt 2 — *Telex* 12738

Belgium's fourth largest town is quite an industrial place, but it also possesses a famous medieval quarter, with many historical buildings and museums and the splendid cathedral of Saint Bavon, with Van Eyck's masterpiece *The adoration of the Mystic Lamb.* The *Hôtel St Jorishof* (also known as *Hôtel Cour St George*) is in the centre of the old town, and dates from the 13th century. It claims – we can't remember how many other claimants there are – to be the oldest hotel in Europe. But is is certain that many famous people such as Charles V and Napoleon stayed here; and the hotel, while adding modern accommodation in an annexe, has maintained in fine order many of the original rooms, including a spacious Gothic hall. Readers this year have found the service and ambience "delightful"; it is said to be spacious and clean, with excellent food. Some bedrooms are on the simple side. (*R Butterworth, Ann Price, and others*)

Open All year except 12 July–3 Aug. Restaurant closed Sun and public holidays.
Rooms 5 suites, 26 double, 5 single – some with bath or shower. 26 in annexe across road.
Facilities Lift. Bar, Gothic hall, restaurant; conference facilities. English spoken.
Location Central, opposite Town Hall. Garage and car park.
Credit cards All major cards accepted.
Terms [1987 rates] B&B: single 1,735-2,470 Bfrs, double 2,260-3,570 Bfrs. Set lunch/dinner 960 and 1,375 Bfrs.

HASSELT-STEVOORT 3512 Limburg — Map 9

Scholteshof — *Tel* (011) 25.02.02
Kermtstraat 118 — *Telex* 39684 TESHOF

"By Hasselt, Dirk groaned," recalls Browning – but joyfully do two of our own veteran travellers continue each year to bring the Guide more good news of what they call "one of the nicest hotels in Europe". This year they had an "excellent" breakfast and dinner and found that changes in the restaurant decor made it more attractive than ever. Roger Souvereyns, one of the leading Belgian chefs (two *Michelin* rosettes), has created this luxurious venture from an 18th-century manor house built round a small inner courtyard. It is set in green countryside just outside the pleasant town of Hasselt; the grounds have been landscaped, and there is a large herb and vegetable garden.

"Guests are shown into the flag-stoned entrance hall with its old beams, lit by modern spotlights. 'Would you like a glass of champagne while you fill in this form . . . ?' Each room is named after a plant or flower in Latin; all are stylish. Mr Souvereyns practises 'open cooking', and he and his staff work in full view of everyone. His food is fantastic. His restaurant, beautifully decorated with plants and flowers and old kitchen implements, has a country atmosphere. Staff are friendly. Considering the quality, the hotel is not too expensive." (*P and J Temple*) Another visitor this year, however, while enjoying the food and setting, found the service imperfect.

Open All year except 2–31 Jan. Restaurant closed Wed.
Rooms 5 suites, 13 double – all with bath and/or shower, telephone, radio, TV, frigobar and air-conditioning.
Facilities Lounge, bar, dining room, restaurant; conference facilities. Garden and courtyard.
Location On edge of Stevoort village, 7 km W of Hasselt; turn left at church. Parking.
Restriction Not suitable for ♿.
Credit cards All major cards accepted.

Terms [1987 rates] Rooms: single 1,900 Bfrs, double 4,300 Bfrs. Breakfast 300 Bfrs. Set lunch/dinner 1,250–2,300 Bfrs. Special meals for children.

HERBEUMONT 6803 Luxembourg Belge — Map 9

Hostellerie du Prieuré de Conques — *Tel* (061) 41.14.17
Route de Florenville 176

Mixed reports have reached us this year on the *Prieuré*, which stands on the banks of the river Semois in the heart of the vast forest of the Ardennes. It is a stylishly converted 18th-century priory, long, low and white, surrounded by coiffeured gardens. "The park-like scene is helped by open fields which stop the dark forest pressing too close. There are long lawns set with apple trees running down to the curving river. Inside are two connected vaulted lounges. The deep comfortable armchairs surround large tables and the lighting is kind. Beyond the hall with its curving staircase are two dining rooms, elegant and comfortable. The bedrooms on the first floor are large, those higher up are a little smaller but more romantic with an attic ambience and exposed beams. Everything has the stamp of cleanliness and order." One recent visitor writes: "Dinner is worth a special mention . . . Splendid food, beautifully served and all quite modestly priced." Another thought the owner/manager, Florimond de Naeyer, most helpful and added: "He is straight out of a film Jacques Tati should have made." But this year one reader found the management much less concerned and the food below par, so we'd be glad of more reports. (*Dr R L Holmes, A Wilcox; also Lucille de Marinis, and others*)

Open 1 Mar–27 Dec. Restaurant closed Tue in low season.
Rooms 11 double – all with bath, telephone and radio.
Facilities 2 salons, bar, 2 restaurants. Garden. English spoken.
Location 3 km from Herbeumont, between Florenville and Bouillon.
Restriction Not suitable for ♿.
Credit cards All major cards accepted.
Terms B&B: single occupancy 2,500 Bfrs, double 3,000 Bfrs; half board: single 3,400 Bfrs, double 3,800 Bfrs. Set lunch/dinner 990-1,900 Bfrs; full alc 2,250 Bfrs. 1-night bookings for Sat sometimes refused. Reduced rates for children under 10; special meals.

LISOGNE 5501 Namur — Map 9

Moulin de Lisogne — *Tel* (082) 22.63.80
Rue des Fonds de Leffes

This Relais du Silence *is a tastefully converted water-mill in an idyllic setting, four miles north-east of Dinant above the Meuse valley. Run by a young couple. Food very good but not cheap. Open mid-Feb to mid-Dec. 8 rooms, all with bath. Dinner, B&B double 2,500 Bfrs. New nomination: more reports welcome.*

"Dogs (3) and cats (2) run loose through the hotel. At breakfast one 'did what it should' on the carpet one yard from the table."

LO 8180 West Flanders — Map 9

Oude Abdij — *Tel* (058) 28.82.65
Noordstraat 3

Not far inland from Dunkerque and Ostend, this Augustinian monastery dating from the 11th century is now an elegant little restaurant-with rooms, owned and run by Jan and Nelly Clement (he is a graduate of the *Ritz* in Paris). A reader this year extols the "fine food, attractive rooms, friendly atmosphere", thus endorsing earlier praise: "We enjoyed Flemish hospitality at its best, all details presented with a touch of the *Ritz*." "Bedrooms delightful, with furniture made from local cherry wood and little extra touches like fresh fruit, free mineral water, chocolates." And of the restaurant: "We had an excellent meal. During our dinner we observed the kitchen boy rush seven times out to gather fresh herbs, which Jan says must never be more than minutes old before use!" "Although we arrived later than expected, Monsieur took the trouble to go into his garden to pick in the dark all the necessary ingredients for a big salad." The Clements have written to tell us about the Lo cheese festival beginning the last week of July. (*Mr and Mrs Robert E Koretz, Norma Wagner, JL Andrews, and others*) This year one visitor detected some un-*Ritz*-like signs of dirt and dust.

Open All year except annual holiday (dates unspecified). Closed Sun evening and Mon except public holidays.
Rooms 1 suite, 5 double – all with bath and shower, telephone, TV and baby-listening.
Facilities Salon, bar, 2 restaurants; solarium, terrace. Small grounds with herb garden and orchard. Small lake (with eel-fishing); beach 15 km. English spoken.
Location 15 km S of Veurne, just off the Veurne–Ieper motorway. Behind the church, down a lane of linden trees.
Restriction Not suitable for ♿.
Credit cards All major cards accepted.
Terms [1987 rates] B&B: single occupancy 1,250 Bfrs, double 1,800 Bfrs, suite 2,500 Bfrs. Set lunch/dinner (including wine) 1,250-1,750 Bfrs; full alc 1,500 – 2,000 Bfrs. Christmas, New Year and Easter parties; cheese festival end July/early Aug. Babies free, 50% reduction for under-7s; special children's meals.

MALMÉDY 4891 Liège — Map 9

Hostellerie Trôs Marets — *Tel* (080) 33.79.17
1 Mont

Not far from the German frontier, in lovely hilly country north-east of the pleasant little town of Malmédy, this Guide newcomer is a sleek modern hostelry with a neat garden set amid trees: "Off the winding road amid Ardennes pine-forests, the *Trôs Marets* nestles on a steep slope - immaculate, elegant and comfortably welcoming. Very well-furnished bedrooms with 16 TV channels – imagine watching *Popeye* in Italian on a Sunday morning, after a swim and walk in the forest and *before* a delicious breakfast with Ardennes ham, fresh croissants, home-made jam. The beautiful dining-room has food to match: on the gastronomic menu we had very imaginative, light little courses – cubes of warm goose-liver, turbot lasagne, quail with wild mushrooms, etc. The wine is decanted into enormous glasses with a lip to let it breathe before being poured out." (*Minda and Stanley Alexander*)

Open All year except 15 Nov–24 Dec.
Rooms 4 suites, 7 double – all with bath and shower, telephone and TV. Suites in garden annexe.
Facilities Lounge/bar, restaurant; conference room; indoor swimming-pool and solarium. Garden, terrace. English spoken.
Location At Mont, 5km NE of Malmédy on N28 to Eupen. Parking.
Credit cards All major cards accepted.
Restriction Not suitable for ♿.
Terms Rooms: single occupancy 2,250-3,750 Bfrs, double 3,750-5,500 Bfrs, suite 6,500-12,000 Bfrs. Breakfast 300 Bfrs. Set lunch/dinner 1,875 Bfrs.

NOIREFONTAINE 6831 Luxembourg Belge — Map 9

Auberge du Moulin Hideux — *Tel* (061) 46.70.15
Route de Dohan 1 — *Telex* 41989 HIDEUX

"Everything this year was wonderful, as usual" at this exceptional country hotel in the Ardennes, near the French border – exquisitely furnished, internationally renowned, gastronomically memorable (two *Michelin* rosettes, two *Gault Millau toques* for inventive specialities), owned and run by a young couple who are steeped in the traditions of good hotel-keeping. There are 13 luxurious bedrooms, and a spacious garden complete with floodlit waterfall. Our readers remain in love with the place. "It really is a trip to Utopia. The moment you enter the gates and see the beautifully-manicured lawns and flower beds and M. Lahire and his charming wife greet you, you experience a great sense of well-being. Even the ducks in the ornamental lake are thoroughly hedonistic, spurning French bread left over from lunch in preference to the sponge cake served with tea. The house looks delightful with its Virginia creeper. The bedrooms have every possible essential to comfortable living." The restaurant serves dinner to residents only: "The leisurely gathering of guests in the lounge or conservatory, for pre-dinner drinks and an invariably delicious appetizer, is a time to savour for its own sake. Autumn is one of our favourite times to visit, partly for the game on the menu, partly for the warm and cossetted feeling inside the hotel." (*Stephan and Kate Murray Sykes, John and Padi Howard, and others*)

Open Mid-Mar–mid-Nov. Restaurant closed Wed Mar–Jun.
Rooms 3 suites, 10 double – all with bath (2 also with shower), telephone, radio and TV.
Facilities Sitting room, loggia, restaurant. Garden with tennis court. Golf 40 km, riding 10 km. Trout fishing nearby. Fine walking country. English spoken.
Location 22 km N of Sedan, 8 km N of Bouillon.
Restriction Not suitable for ♿.
Credit cards All major cards accepted.
Terms [1987 rates] B&B: single occupancy 4,200 Bfrs, double 5,000 Bfrs. Set meals 1,750-2,100 Bfrs. Special meals for children on request.

DE PANNE 8470 West Flanders — Map 9

Hostellerie Le Fox — *Tel* (058) 41.28.55
Walckierstraat 2

In a popular coastal resort near Ostend, a family-run restaurant-with-rooms, reputed for its fish and good regional dishes (Michelin *rosette*). *Good but simple bedrooms, at modest cost. Closed October, 15-31 Jan, and Thurs. 7 rooms (6 more from spring 1988), some with bath or shower. B&B double 1,500-1,1950 Bfrs. Set meals 1,295-1,800 Bfrs. Some noise from main road and adjacent nightclub: more reports please.*

RENINGE 8981 West Flanders — Map 9

't Convent — *Tel* (057) 40.07.71
Halve Reningestraat 1

This "bucolic" hotel, 40 minutes' drive inland from either Dunkerque or Ostend, "is really a medieval barn right in the middle of a field. Some rooms are fairly small, but others are the reverse and retain a convent flavour: canopied painted bed, stone floor, icons and other such medieval trinkets surround the fireplace and a bathroom like a private chapel with the basin in an arched alcove. Our room was wood-panelled with French *petit-point* chairs. The bubble bath supplied by the hotel threatened to take over the bathroom. The service was cool, but efficient. The evening meal was elegant and elongated. Lots of food, but you didn't notice because it was so luxuriously long in coming. Monkfish in hollandaise sauce was perfect. Charming loft bar for drinks or after-dinner coffee. Fresh red roses at every opportunity. The rooms are a bargain, but then dinner costs twice as much. Both well worth it." Other recent visitors agree, though one found the rooms "rather cramped, if quaint". One visitor was impressed by the care taken by the hotel when she became ill, rushing her family back and forth to the hospital. (*J and AW, Madeleine Westlake*)

Open All year except Feb and 1 week in Sept.
Rooms 7 double – all with bath and shower, telephone and radio. Some ground-floor rooms.
Facilities Bar, restaurant in separate building; conference facilities. English spoken.
Location On edge of village, 15 km NW of Ieper (turn off N65 at Oostvleteren).
Credit cards All major cards accepted.
Terms B&B: single 1,250 Bfrs, double 2,000-3,000 Bfrs. Set lunch/dinner 1,400-1,880 Bfrs; full alc 2,200 Bfrs. Reduced rates and special meals for children.

RONSE 9681 East Flanders — Map 9

Hostellerie Shamrock — *Tel* (055) 21.55.29
Ommegangstraat 148 — *Telex* 86165 SHAMRO
Nukerke, Maarkedal

Wagner is said to have been inspired by the wooded hilly area around Ronse, a textile town between Brussels and Lille. The *Shamrock* itself seems to be of mixed British and French inspiration (not to mention its Irish name). Up a long drive in a well-tended garden, it has the air of a sizeable private house in 1910 mock-Tudor style, whereas the large and airy bedrooms are furnished à la Louis XV. This is really a restaurant with rooms, boasting a *Michelin* rosette and two red *Gault Millau toques* for its modern French-style cooking served in moderate quantities. An inspector found this excellent, though the wines were "fiendishly priced" and the waits between courses rather long. "The main dining room is quietly elegant, in shades of turquoise with impeccable white napery. The main staircase with carved wooden banister descends directly into this room, giving residents the opportunity for a spectacular entry. Service is pleasant and courteous and everyone speaks good English. The rooms are good value for money, with large carpeted bathrooms." (*F and IW*) According to the management, changes were taking place in the hotel and garden during 1987, so we should welcome up-to-date reports.

Open All year except 25 Dec–8 Jan and 15–31 July. Closed Sun evening to Tue midday except public holidays.
Rooms 1 suite, 5 double – all with bath and shower, telephone and TV.
Facilities Salon, bar, restaurant; small conference room. 5-acre shady garden. Swimming pool and tennis 4 km; golf 15 km; fine walking country. English spoken.
Location 5 km NE of Ronse, to E of Ronse-Oudenarde road in Schorisse direction, near hamlets of Louise-Marie and Muziekbos.
Restriction Not suitable for ♿.
Credit cards All major cards accepted.
Terms B&B: double 5,200 Bfrs, suite 6,000 Bfrs. Set lunch/dinner 1,500-2,100 Bfrs; full alc 2,500 Bfrs.

STAVELOT 4970 Liège — Map 9

Hostellerie Le Val d'Amblève
7 route de Malmédy — *Tel* (080) 86.23.53

The surrounding Ardennes countryside is attractive, and though the immediate setting is suburban, on the edge of a small town, this little hotel is discreetly screened by venerable trees. In the past the bedrooms have been found somewhat shabby, but recent extensive renovations will, we hope, silence these complaints. In any event, it is the cuisine provided by the excellent Focquet family that really matters here (*Michelin* rosette, *Gault Millau* red *toque* for e.g. raviolis de langoustines au fruits de la passion). The large modern restaurant has views of the distant pine-clad mountains from its huge picture-windows, and here the food ranges from an ample menu for those on *pension* terms through five different fixed-price menus, to an interesting *carte*. "We enjoyed a most relaxed and civilised dinner. Apart from the normal wine list, they have a smaller list of 'bin-ends' which represents particularly good value." Service is said to be very good, though there tend to be long waits between courses, and the dining-room sit-up chairs are less comfortable than the deep armchairs in the lounge. Excellent breakfasts with plentiful butter, cheese and ham, "and a proper pot of jam". (*P Grimsdale, JM Beaton, Dr P Marsh, and BW Ribbons*) More reports please.

Open Easter–15 Nov. Restaurant closed to non-residents on Mon.
Rooms 18 double – 11 with bath and shower, 5 with shower, all with telephone and TV; baby-listening on request. 6 in garden building. 4 ground-floor rooms.
Facilities 2 lounges, breakfast room, restaurant. Garden with tennis court (no charge). Golf, fishing and swimming pool nearby. English spoken.
Location On outskirts of Stavelot, SW of Malmédy. Parking.
Credit cards All major cards accepted.
Terms Rooms: single occupancy 890-1,640 Bfrs, double 1,185-2,185 Bfrs. Breakfast 210 Bfrs. Dinner, B&B: single 2,340-2,850 Bfrs, double 3,525–4,350 Bfrs; full board: single 3,240-3,750 Bfrs, double 5,175-6,000 Bfrs. Set lunch/dinner 1,080, 1,490 and 1,875 Bfrs. Reduction for stays of 4 or more days. Special meals for children on request.

Denmark

STORE KRO, FREDENSBORG

COPENHAGEN **Map 7**

Hotel Ascot *Tel* (01) 12.60.00
Studiestræde 57 *Telex* 15730
Copenhagen 1554

A converted 18th-century house, very central, close to Tivoli, in a fairly quiet street. Staff very friendly, breakfast good, many rooms attractively modernised, impressive central stairway. 70 rooms, all with bath and/or shower, some with kitchenette. B&B double 690-870 Dkr. Upkeep and fittings of some rooms criticised this year: more reports needed.

---

71 Nyhavn Hotel *Tel* (01) 11.85.85
Nyhavn 71, Copenhagen 1051 *Telex* 27558 NYHHOT

Hans Christian Andersen lived next door to this converted early 19th-century warehouse on the *Nyhavn* (New Harbour) in the heart of the old city. Readers have enjoyed especially the "lively bustle" (though no traffic noise) and the adjacent canal with its mixture of restaurants and bars. The building was restored about 15 years ago as a smart hotel, with the sea motif much in evidence. Its *Pakhuskælderen* restaurant has an excellent reputation, with its smorgasbord specially recommended ("but it is worth trying some of the new ones which have sprung up along the north side of the Nyhavn"). The cheapest bedrooms are very small; the dearer ones have a view over the canal. But the staff are helpful and welcoming and the hotel is not so big as to be impersonal. A couple this year had a small room "fabulously decorated" and enjoyed the "generous and delicious" breakfast (it includes hot table of bacon, eggs, etc). (*Isabel Meyer, J and L Spencely, and others*)

Open All year.
Rooms 6 suites, 39 double, 37 single – 19 with bath, all with shower, telephone, radio and TV; baby-listening on request.
Facilities Lift. Lounge, bar, 2 restaurants; 2 conference/function rooms. English spoken.
Location In town centre, facing Nyhavn Canal and harbour. Parking.
Restriction Not suitable for ♿.
Credit cards All major cards accepted.
Terms B&B: single 828-1,198 Dkr, double 1,078-1,498 Dkr; half board 265 Dkr per person added; full board 410 Dkr added. Set lunch 160 Dkr, dinner 280 Dkr; full alc 325 Dkr. Christmas package. Children under 12 sharing parents' room free; special meals on request.

Hotel Vestersøhus — *Tel* (01) 11.38.70
Vestersøgade 58 — *Telex* 15708
Copenhagen 1601

A modest and friendly bed-and-breakfast hotel, ten minutes' walk from the old town. Spacious rooms: some are flatlets with kitchens, and most have views over the Skt Jørgens lake. Double-glazing; rooms at back quietest. 44 rooms, most with bath and/or shower. B&B double 800-850 Dkr. Few recent reports: more needed.

FALSLED 5642 Funen — Map 7

Falsled Kro — *Tel* (09) 68.11.11
Telex 50404

"Wonderful, wonderful *Falsled Kro* . . ." On the south-west coast of the central island of Funen, in the 15th century a smugglers' inn and now an outstandingly sympathetic little luxury hotel. This year and last, two of our most experienced husband-and-wife teams have awarded it the highest marks. "The old thatched buildings are grouped round a small cobbled courtyard with a fountain. The outbuildings are converted to rooms with some in cottages across the road, each differently decorated. The hotel garden runs down to the sea and the local yacht harbour. The welcome was warm and friendly. The whole hotel has been tastefully and originally decorated, and our room was excellent and spacious. Floors were covered with lovely Spanish tiles. The restaurant is the main attraction and we were not disappointed. It must be the best, or one of the best, in Denmark. Cooking is modern and French-inspired, and there are open kitchens on one side of the restaurant where you can see your meal being prepared. Breakfast was superb – crème fraîche with honey, freshly-squeezed orange juice, quails' eggs served on bacon and endless excellent coffee! If *Michelin* discovered Denmark, *Falsled* would be awarded one if not two rosettes." "The most delicious meal I have tasted outside Eugénie-les-Bains – delicious langoustines in a cream sauce, monkfish au beurre blanc, moist breast of guinea-fowl (but wine mark-ups fearfully high). Our room in the converted stables was a warm and comfortable haven . . . candles for the truly romantic . . . the place oozes care and attention to detail . . . marvellous!" "Rooms enchanting, dinner superb, but *very* expensive." (*P and JT, Ian and Francine Walsh, D Steven McGuire*)

Open 1 Mar–10 Dec. Restaurant closed Mon.
Rooms 3 suites, 9 double, 2 single – 12 with bath, 2 with shower, all with telephone; 5 with TV; some 4-posters. 3 suites in *Ryttergåarden* farmhouse opposite the hotel (all with bathroom, sitting room, mini-bar and TV). Some ground-floor rooms.
Facilities Lounge, salon with TV, bar, café, restaurant. Garden. Sea 100 metres. English spoken.
Location 10 km NW of Millinge; S of Odense on Fåborg/Assens road.
Restriction Not suitable for ♿.
Credit cards Access, Diners, Visa.
Terms [1987 rates] B&B: single 548 Dkr, double 1,086-1,146 Dkr, suite 1,646 Dkr. Set lunch 300 Dkr, dinner 600 Dkr; full alc 500 Dkr.

FREDENSBORG 3480 Seeland — Map 7

Store Kro — *Tel* (02) 28.00.47
Slotsgade 1 and 6 — *Telex* 40971 STORKRO

Under its new owners Margit and Erik Brandt, well-known Danish fashion and fabric designers, the *Store Kro* has re-established itself as one of the most attractive country house hotels in the kingdom. And indeed it has royal connections. Close to Fredensborg Castle (the Danish Queen's spring and autumn residence), it was built by Frederik IV in 1723 at the same time as he was putting up his royal palace next door; he was, we are told, the first innkeeper here. There are other castles worth visiting in the vicinity, also the marvellous Louisiana Museum of Modern Art.

Inspectors recently visiting the newly-renovated hotel were impressed with every aspect: they had a large comfortable room with a huge bed and big armchairs. All the public rooms were equally spruce and cosseting; dinner in the attractive restaurant was well-presented; the fish was excellent, served from a great silver salver, with second helpings; there was a good wine list, and a home-made fresh fruit tart for dessert. Breakfasts were of the same standard, with four types of Danish pastry.

Open 14 Jan–18 Dec.
Rooms 6 suites, 17 double, 26 single – all with bath and/or shower, telephone and radio. 16 in annexe. Some ground-floor rooms. Double-glazing.
Facilities Lift. Lounges, bar, coffee room, restaurant, games room; banqueting rooms, conference facilities. Large garden. Riding and tennis nearby; near Esrum lake with fishing, water sports and bathing; sea at Hornbaek 16 km away. English spoken.
Location 9 km NE of Hillerød. Hotel central, next to Castle. Parking.
Credit cards All major cards accepted.
Terms B&B: single 725 Dkr, double 970 Dkr, suite 1,450-1,650 Dkr. Full alc from 300 Dkr. Reduced rates and special meals for children.

LØNSTRUP 9800 Hjørring — Map 7

Pension Kirkedal — *Tel* (08) 96.02.97 and 08.96.00.45
Mårup Kirkevej 30

Facing the Skagerrak near Hjørring in northern Denmark, an attractively converted farmhouse with comfortably furnished rooms, pleasant lounge, small bar, and good Danish food. Warmly hospitable. Games facilities for children; monthly folk music concerts in the former cowshed. 14 rooms, most with bath and shower. B&B double 240-395 Dkr. Alc meals about 200 Dkr (excluding wine). New nomination: more reports please.

MILLINGE 5642 Funen — Map 7

Steensgaard Herregårdspension — *Tel* (09) 61.94.90
Steensgågard 4

A half-timbered manor house dating back to 1310 and furnished with Italian rococo, Louis XIV and English antiques. It is set in a 27-acre park on the middle island of Funen (Fyn), amid countryside that is possibly the prettiest in Denmark – an area of small hills and fields dotted with long low farmhouses. *Steensgaard*, run by two talented young people, is very much a part of this countryside. It's built on three sides of a cobbled courtyard. On one side lies a working farm; on the other a garden, a tennis court and an enclosure full of deer and boar.

"Inside, *Steensgaard* has a delightful country house atmosphere. The grand entrance hall is decorated with hunting trophies, the library is lined with leather-bound volumes, all three lounges are spacious. And the number of guest rooms is so few that it's quite possible to have one of these grand reception rooms to yourself, even when the hotel is full. The double rooms are handsomely furnished, most with modern bathroom." Dinner is served in the candle-lit dining room promptly at 7 o'clock. Reports vary on the food. "Not outstanding but adequate . . . a superb ice-cream cake." And: "Breakfast a splendid buffet, food excellent." Some bedrooms can be noisy, especially when a late party is in progress. (*J Goeller, Alexander Dow, NB, CRA Jackson*)

Open 14 Feb–31 Dec.
Rooms 13 double, 2 single – 8 with bath, 2 with shower, all with telephone.
Facilities Hall, 5 salons, library, dining room; billiards, piano, chess. Large park with deer and wild boar; lake (fishing), tennis and riding. Rocky beach 2 km. English spoken.
Location NW of Millinge, between Assens and Fåborg on the Middlefart road.
Restriction Not suitable for ♿.
Credit cards Access, Amex.
Terms [1987 rates] Rooms: single 260-470 Dkr, double 415-840 Dkr. Breakfast 50 Dkr. Set lunch 115 Dkr, dinner 180 Dkr. Reduced rates for 3 or more nights; 12% reduction during low season. Reduced rates for children.

> Wherever possible, we have quoted prices per room. Not all hotels are prepared to quote tariffs in this way. In these cases, we have given prices per person, indicating the range of prices – the lowest is likely to be for one person sharing a double room out of season, the highest for a single room in the high season.

RIBE 6760 Jutland — Map 7

Hotel Dagmar — *Tel* (05) 42.00.33
Torvet 1

Ribe lies on the windy west coast of Jutland, in typically flat Danish countryside, and with its 800-year-old cathedral and narrow cobbled streets it is an old town of great charm. It has now being preserved as a national heritage "and has a unique atmosphere". In spring you can see the celebrated storks' nests on the rooftops. The *Dagmar* too has much character. Standing opposite the cathedral, it was built in 1581 and is in keeping with the rest of the town. Very different from the usual modern functional Danish hotel, it gives a good idea of what a traditional Danish posting-inn was like before the 20th century. The picturesque building consists on the ground floor of a series of inter-connecting rooms, hung with splendid paintings, and filled with antique and repro furniture. Front bedrooms have tiny windows overlooking the church. "Ours," says one reader, "was without a view, but it had lovely paintings and was quiet. The *Dagmar* is a nice friendly family-run place." One visitor this year enjoyed the "superb and varied" help-yourself breakfast and the "beautiful" candle-lit restaurant (food is of good quality, with copious helpings) but found the bedroom not totally quiet at night. " (*I and FW, M Brummel, B and R Kenyon Glover, Angela Pearse*)

Open All year.
Rooms 50 double – all with bath and/or shower, telephone, radio, TV, video and mini-bar.
Facilities 2 bars, 2 restaurants; conference facilities; 2 night clubs (dances on Fri and Sat). Fishing 3 km. English spoken.
Location Central; Ribe is 34 km SE of Esbjerg.
Restriction Not suitable for ♿.
Credit cards All major cards accepted.
Terms B&B: single 420 Dkr, double 620 Dkr; dinner, B&B: single 560 Dkr, double 900 Dkr. Children under 12 sharing parents' room half-price.

SØNDERHO 6720 Fanø — Map 7

Sønderho Kro — *Tel* (05) 16.40.09

"An extremely charming small hotel" at the southern tip of the island of Fanø, off the west coast of Denmark near Esjberg: "In a picturesque old fishing village of low thatched cottages, the *Sønderho Kro* is one of the oldest inns in Denmark, dating from 1772. It has been owned by the same family for three generations, and Olga and Erik Jensen are very proud of their traditions and the atmosphere of the past. But modern comforts have not been overlooked - they have a new extension where the bedrooms are large and very comfortable. The entrance hall has a large open fireplace with a roaring fire in cold weather; antiques, modern paintings and flowers abound. The comfortable sitting room looks out over the beach. Cooking is excellent, in traditional style but with French influence: fresh local produce and large helpings. Breakfast was also excellent. Altogether a pleasant, friendly unassuming place." (*Pat and Jeremy Temple*)

Open All year except 1–26 Dec and 1 Jan. Closed Mon and Tue 1 Nov–31 Mar.
Rooms 7 double – all with bath. 5 ground-floor rooms.

Facilities Hall, salons, restaurant. Garden. By the sea with sandy beach and safe bathing; golf course and tennis nearby.
Location 20 minutes by ferry from Ejsberg.
Credit card Diners.
Terms [1987 rates] Rooms: single 350-500 Dkr, double 460-650 Dkr. Breakfast 50 Dkr. Set lunch/dinner 150-320 Dkr.

VEJLE 7100 Jutland — Map 7

Munkebjerg Hotel — *Tel* (05) 71.35.00
Munkebjergvej 125 — *Telex* 61103 MUNKEN

Larger than most establishments in the Guide, *Munkebjerg* is a resort hotel in a lovely setting of beechwoods, a few kilometres outside Vejle (free hotel bus) and 90 metres above the Vejle fjord. It is a good area for walking or cycling (free hotel bikes), and would make a useful base for touring Jutland. Not our sort of place perhaps, but correspondents have repeatedly enthused about the excellent food and exceptional service. Inspectors initially felt the place was too large and impersonal for the Guide, but after an extremely pleasant meal in the hotel's small restaurant, "Tree Tops", with a French-influenced menu, accompanied by delicious home-made bread and a long if expensive wine list, and a comfortable night in a well-equipped modern room with large picture windows and a small balcony overlooking woods, they changed their minds. Their conclusion: the hotel has lots of facilities and is extremely well run, and the management are clearly trying to please individuals as well as groups. In fact, a visitor this year found no coach parties, but adds: "Breakfasts are glorious, but rather a free-for-all as you battle with Teutonic matrons for delicious sliced meats etc." (*P and JT, Mrs GM Leach*)

Open 3 Jan–21 Dec.
Rooms 3 suites, 128 double, 16 single – 87 with bath, 62 with shower, all with telephone, radio and TV.
Facilities Lift. Lounge, TV room, bar with live music, wine cellar, restaurant; banqueting rooms, conference facilities; nightclub open nightly except Sun; billiard room; heated indoor swimming pool, sauna, solarium. Large grounds with tennis court and children's playground; bicycles; hotel is adjacent to golf course; beaches and fishing nearby. English spoken.
Location 6 km from town centre. Drive along S side of Vejle fjord from Vejle, follow serpentine road up the hill.
Restriction Not suitable for ♿.
Credit cards All major cards accepted.
Terms [1987 rates] B&B: single 495 Dkr, double 760 Dkr, suite 1,230-1,990 Dkr. Set meals from 88 Dkr. Reduced rates and special menu for children.

France

MOULIN DE VILLERAY

AGDE 34300 Hérault — Map 10

La Tamarissière *Tel* 67.94.20.87
21 quai Théophile-Cornu

The old fishing-port of Agde, with its fortified ex-cathedral made from the tufa-ash of a nearby extinct volcano, lies just inland from the new resort of Cap d'Agde, built in the style of a Provençal fishing-village, as pretty and contrived as an operetta stage-set; close by is Europe's largest nudist holiday-town. *La Tamarissière* competes with these exotica by being a fishermen's *buvette* stylishly transformed into a chic waterside inn, at the mouth of the river Hérault, south-west of Agde. "A pleasant surprise," says a recent visitor. "It combines the charms of a quiet river with those of a little seaside town. We had an excellent large room overlooking the river. Bouillabaisse, beautifully presented, was served in an elegant dining-room." On the flower-filled terrace facing the river and fishing-boats, you can also enjoy inventive variations on classic Languedoc dishes (two red *Gault Millau toques*). (*Mr and Mrs RB Tait*)

Open 15 Mar–30 Nov. Restaurant closed Sun evening and Mon 15 Mar–15 June and 15 Sept–30 Nov.
Rooms 35 – 28 with bath, 7 with shower, all with direct-dial telephone, radio, TV and mini-bar; most with balcony or terrace.
Facilities 2 lounges, restaurant. Garden. Sandy beach and river with fishing rights in front of hotel. English spoken.
Location 4 km SW of Agde by D32.
Restriction Not suitable for ♿.
Credit cards All major cards accepted.
Terms Dinner, B&B 250–490 frs; full board 330–560 frs. Set lunch 99–210 frs; full alc 300–350 frs. Reduced rates and special meals for children.

AIGUES-MORTES 30220 Gard — Map 10

Hostellerie des Remparts — *Tel* 66.53.82.77
Place Anatole-France

A famous medieval walled town on the marshes, built by St Louis when he set sail from here for the Crusades. "It is now something of a delectable tourist trap and best visited out of season. The hotel is within the walls, in a stone 17th-century building, beautifully adapted and furnished. Our room was a huge stone-walled chamber with compatible furniture, comfortable, and quiet after the trippers had departed (this was Easter). We did not eat in the hotel (the *carte* looks adequate) but in the nearby *Camargue* restaurant which can be thoroughly recommended for local specialities (portions of unsuccessful bulls) and gipsy guitar music." "A marvellous six-course set-meal blow out, and euphoric ambience, at *La Camargue.*" Hotel endorsed this year: "Staff very helpful and friendly." (*HE Emson, JA, AD*)

Open 15 Mar–31 Oct. Restaurant closed Mon 15 July–15 Sept and public holidays.
Rooms 19 – most with bath or shower, telephone and TV.
Facilities Salon, restaurant. Garden where meals are served.
Location Central, in the old walls. Parking.
Credit cards All major cards accepted.
Terms [1987 rates] B&B: single 240 frs, double 420 frs.
Set lunch/dinner 105-195 frs.

AIRE-SUR-LA-LYS 62120 Pas-de-Calais — Map 9

Hostellerie des Trois Mousquetaires — *Tel* 21.39.01.11
Château de la Redoute

Forty miles from Calais and with easy access to the motorway, a small late-19th-century château in a garden beside a pond. Booking is essential, for the place is very popular - too much so maybe, for standards seem to be erratic and our numerous reports reflect this. "What a lovely hotel!" says a returning visitor this year. "It was like coming home to see the family, and refreshing glasses of cold cider were waiting for us in our comfortable rooms, overlooking the gardens and stream. In the spotless restaurant we had a very good meal – filet de sole au champagne, etc." Another reader had one of the new rooms in the lodge, "furnished in the Japanese style with maize-coloured grass wallpaper and antiques", while others have spoken of "delectable food" and "Madame charming". But the much-loved Madame Venet *mère* is not always present, and when she is absent the ambience suffers and the service is slow. Some visitors this year have had poor meals and have found the up-market excursions into *nouvelle cuisine* not so successful. (*HR Michaels, Susan and Russell Flint, CJ Frost, Frank Mattinson, and others*)

Open 20 Jan–20 Dec. Closed Sun evening, and Mon.
Rooms 1 suite, 11 double – all with bath, shower, telephone and TV. 3 in pavilion in park. 15 more planned for 1988.
Facilities 2 salons, TV room, garden room in summer, 2 restaurants. 7-acre garden. English spoken.
Location On N43 between St-Omer and Lillers, 2km from centre of Aire on Arras side. Private parking.
Restriction Not suitable for ♿.
Credit cards Access, Amex, Visa.
Terms Rooms: 170-315 frs, suite 370 frs. Breakfast 29 frs. Set lunch/dinner 68, 104 and 155 frs. Special meals for children.

AIX-EN-OTHE 10160 Aube — Map 9

Auberge de la Scierie — *Tel* 25.46.71.26
La Vove

An unusual *auberge* just outside the little town of Aix, in the rolling Othe country between Troyes and Auxerre. It has recently been extended (it is very popular) but keeps its warm rural quality: it consists of four farmhouse-type buildings, two modern and two conversions, 18th- and 19th-century (one a former sawmill as the name implies). The buildings are scattered around a big pleasant garden beside a trout-stream; there are ducks, geese, peacocks, a donkey, and horses for hire. The rooms are in chalets in the garden, round a small swimming pool.

Though the fairly sophisticated cooking seems to be of variable quality, most reports continue to be appreciative. "A delightfully quiet spot, with friendly and efficient service and comfortable rooms; food very good, save that portions were too large." "A wonderful place, dinner was excellent." "The children enjoyed the horses." Others have praised the rustic bar with its wooden beams, horse-brasses etc. "On a summer evening we dined in the garden: local cured ham, rabbit pâté, marinated salmon." (*Mr and Mrs BN Wilson, Carole McQuarrie, T Keniston, and others*)

Open All year. Closed Mon evening and Tue 15 Oct–1 Apr.
Rooms 15 double – 10 with bath, 5 with shower, all with telephone, radio, TV and baby-listening. All in chalets in garden. Some ground-floor rooms.
Facilities Lounge with TV, bar, 2 dining rooms; functions room. Large park with terrace/alfresco dining area; swimming pool. English spoken.
Location 1 km S of Aix-en-Othe on N374 after the camp site. Parking.
Credit cards All major cards accepted.
Terms Rooms 280-300 frs. Breakfast 38 frs. Half board 320 frs per person. Set lunch/dinner 108 and 195 frs; full alc 200-280 frs. Reduced rates for children under 6; special menu.

Hotels often book you into their most expensive rooms or suites unless you specify otherwise. Even if all room prices are the same, hotels may give you a less good room in the hope of selling their better rooms to late customers. It always pays to discuss accommodation in detail when making a reservation.

AIX-EN-PROVENCE 13100 Bouches-du-Rhône — Map 11

Hôtel Le Manoir — *Tel* 42.26.27.20
8 rue d'Entrecasteaux — *Telex* 441489

In the heart of old Aix, down a narrow street, a 14th-century cloister beautifully restored: large, fairly simple rooms with period furniture, pretty wallpaper. Very quiet. Parking. Open 15 Feb–15 Jan. 43 rooms, all with bath or shower; B&B double 289-448 frs. New nomination: more reports welcome.

Hôtel Pullman le Pigonnet — *Tel* 42.50.02.90
5 avenue du Pigonnet

Readers this year have again enjoyed the spacious gardens, the elegance and the "delicious" food at what is probably Aix's most attractive hotel (previously just *Le Pigonnet*) – a handsome creeper-covered mansion, set in its own large garden full of chestnut trees, in a quiet residential district south of the city's historic centre. Bedrooms have antique furniture and cheerful wallpaper, and some have a balcony with views of Cézanne's Mont Ste-Victoire. The garden, which has a swimming pool set amid flowers, is unusual, with rose-bowers, fountains and ornamental pools. There is a formal dining room, but you can lunch under the chestnut trees. The cooking, with variations on local dishes, is mostly praised. Some readers have found the ambience a little impersonal. (*K Carlson, Robert Stevens and Alexa Grace, and others*)

Open All year. Restaurant closed Sun dinner Nov–Mar inclusive.
Rooms 1 suite, 44 double, 6 single – 38 with bath, 12 with shower, all with telephone, radio, TV, baby-listening and room service. 14 in annexe.
Facilities Lifts. Lounges, bar, TV room, 2 restaurants; conference facilities; terrace. Small garden with swimming pool. Rocky and sandy beach 25 km. English spoken.
Location Coming from Nice or Toulon, leave *autoroute* at Aix-Ouest exit; coming from Lyons or Paris, leave it at Aix-Sud exit. Hotel is 800 metres from city centre, in a quiet side street. Parking.
Credit cards All major cards accepted.
Terms B&B: single 570-600 frs, double 750-785 frs; dinner, B&B: single 730-765 frs, double 1,070-1,105 frs. Set lunch/dinner 160 frs; full alc 250 frs. Children free when sharing parents' room.

AJACCIO 20000 Corsica — Map 11

Dolce Vita — *Tel* 95.52.00.93
Route des Sanguinaires — *Telex* 460854

The Route des Sanguinaires stretches west along the coast from Ajaccio, Corsica's lively capital and the birthplace of Napoleon. Five miles out is the modern *Dolce Vita*, where the sweet life centres round a beautiful swimming pool and dining terrace right by the sea and is only somewhat soured, indoors, by some loud-coloured decor. "A slightly pretentious place, but we ate well," says a visitor this year. Earlier praise: "A low two-storey building between the road and the rocky shore, where the coastline is lovely. The better rooms on the first floor are very large and beautifully furnished. A large balcony overlooks the lawns and the sea sparkles through the oleander blossoms. Breakfast is perfect, eaten to the soft sound of the sea. The large terrace built over the rocks is shaded with palm-trees, and here lunch was a pleasant surprise. The hotel is popular with French families." The small sandy beach is covered at high tide, but there is an iron ladder from the rocks into the sea which is superb to swim in. (*DIK Evans, Angela and David Stewart*)

Open 15 Mar–end Oct.
Rooms 32 – all with bath and/or shower, telephone, TV, refrigerator, air-conditioning and terrace.
Facilities Lounge, bar, restaurant; private night-club. Garden with terraces and swimming pool; bathing from rocks; slipway for boats.
Location 8 km W of Ajaccio, on the coast.
Restriction Not suitable for ♿.
Credit cards All major cards accepted.
Terms [1987 rates] Rooms: single 360 frs, double 600 frs. Breakfast 36 frs. Set meals 185 frs.

Eden Roc *Tel* 95.52.01.47
Route des Sanguinaires *Telex* 460486

A fairly smart and very pleasant family-run hotel overlooking the sea, next to the Dolce Vita *and preferred by* Michelin (*red print*). *Large bedrooms all with canopied balconies facing the sea. Outdoor terrace, open dining room with good* en pension *food. Garden and swimming pool. Open May–Sept. 30 rooms, all with bath. Full board 600-660 francs* [1987]. *New nomination: more reports please.*

ALBERTVILLE 73200 Savoie — Map 10

Hôtel Philippe Million *Tel* 79.32.25.15
8 place de la Liberté

The 1992 Winter Olympics are to be centred on this dullish town in a sub-alpine valley, no doubt bringing millions (of people and francs) to Philippe Million's graceful and sophisticated hostelry, just off the main street. Between now and then, we have four years to savour in relative peace his "original cooking in the modern style" (e.g. lake fish with snails) which is rated among the finest in Savoy (two *Michelin* rosettes, two red *Gault Millau toques*). One reader this year found the food and rooms "pleasant, but not exciting", but earlier praise was less equivocal: "Traditional atmosphere with modern comforts. Rooms not very large but pleasantly decorated: most are in a modern extension behind the building. There is a comfortable lounge and bar in traditional style. Plentiful breakfasts, and a good wine list with delicious local Savoie wines at low prices. The superb cooking is reasonably priced for the quality." The savoury pastries and sweets and home-made chocolates are especially praised. In summer you can dine in elegance on a flowery terrace facing the small and pretty garden. One reader adds: "Sadly the hotel is now surrounded by apartment blocks, so there are only fleeting views of the mountains. But 20 minutes' walk up the hill is the medieval walled hill-village of Conflans, where the views are superb." (*Pat and Brian Lloyd, Pat and Jeremy Temple, Bernadette Murray*)

Open All year except 24 Apr–12 May, 25 Sept–11 Oct. Restaurant closed Sun evening and Mon.

Rooms 24 double, 4 single – all with bath and/or shower, direct-dial telephone and TV.
Facilities Lift. Salon/bar, TV salon, dining room. Small garden terrace for dining. English spoken.
Location Central. Parking. Albertville is 45 km SE of Annecy.
Credit cards Amex, Diners, Visa.
Terms Rooms: single 220-300 frs, double 250-300 frs. Breakfast 40 frs. Set lunch/dinner 150-400 frs; full alc 340 frs.

ALBI 81000 Tarn — Map 10

La Réserve — *Tel* 63.60.79.79
Route de Cordes — *Telex* 520850 LA RESERVE

A smart modern hotel, three kilometres out of town, owned by the Rieux family. "We had a lovely room with balcony, overlooking pool and river, a perfect setting. Superb bathrooms, splendid food, and Mme Rieux was charming." Other recent visitors concur ("perfect lunch", "friendly staff"), though some found the food uninteresting. "The extensive grounds slope down to the Tarn on which you may venture in a pedalo; the swimming pool is large." (*Judith Kendrick, Mr and Mrs RB Tait, and others*)

Open Apr–Oct.
Rooms 2 suites, 16 double, 2 single – 20 with bath and shower, all with telephone, TV and mini-bar.
Facilities 2 salons, TV room, restaurant. Large garden with heated outdoor swimming pool and tennis court; near river with pedalo and boat-fishing rights. English spoken.
Location 3 km N of Albi on the Cordes road.
Restriction Not suitable for ♿.
Credit cards All major cards accepted.
Terms [1987 rates] Rooms: single 390 frs, double 630 frs. Breakfast 45 frs. Dinner, B&B: 450-600 frs per person. Set lunch/dinner 130-240 frs. Reduced rates and special meals for children.

AMBOISE 37400 Indre-et-Loire — Map 10

Hostellerie du Château de Pray — *Tel* 47.57.23.67

If you'd like to stay in a real château when visiting the Loire château country, then try this small 13th-century one just outside Amboise (fine château there too). Turreted, part creeper-covered, and set in its own 25-acre park beside the Loire, it has belonged to major families of the area since 1244. That ambience remains, according to readers. "Everything one would expect from a French château. Faintly intimidating Madame, efficient black-jacketed waiters with a quiet sense of humour, lovely five-course meals, suits of armour – and a concierge with a dog, both of whom seemed to be over 80. Friendly and totally relaxing." "A commanding view across terraces and the river, and a small farm that appears to have changed little since the Middle Ages. Comfortable bedrooms. Not the place for a long stay, as there was no lounge." "In fine weather meals were taken on the outside terrace facing the river; aperitifs were served in the formal garden. Excellent food, especially local fish." (*FM and GE Hunter, Mark Dumont, and others*) An American visitor this year however, himself an hotelier, thought the food poor and the service inadequate. More reports please.

Open 8 Feb–31 Dec.
Rooms 16 double – all with bath and/or shower and telephone.
Facilities Salon, bar, restaurant. Garden with terrace on the Loire.
Location 2.5 km NE of Amboise, on S bank of Loire; take D751 in direction of Chaumont-sur-Loire.
Credit cards All major cards accepted
Terms Dinner, B&B: single occupancy 465 frs, double 700-816 frs. Set meals 180-190 frs. Reduced rates for children.

AMIENS 80000 Somme — Map 9

Le Grand Hôtel de l'Univers — *Tel* 22.91.52.51
2 rue de Noyon — *Telex* 145070

"Helpful staff, breakfast good", "comfortable, excellent bedrooms", are the latest comments, backing up earlier praise:"Amiens' best hotel. It is pleasantly quiet, despite a central situation, on a main street between the station and the vast and splendid Gothic cathedral that is the jewel of this otherwise rather sombre northern city. The hotel's interior has a high central foyer with galleries running round on three floors – rather Spanish, though I doubt it's the result of the former Spanish occupation of this part of France! I had a snug room at a reasonable price. No restaurant, but you can eat well in town at *Joséphine.*" (*JA, Richard Whiting, BJ Barry*) Some top-floor rooms are rather small.

Open All year.
Rooms 34 double, 7 single – all with bath and/or shower, direct-dial telephone, TV and mini-bar; double-glazing.
Facilities Lift. Lounge with TV, cellar bar; conference/function facilities. English spoken.
Location Central. Quietest rooms at rear. Parking opposite.
Credit cards All major cards accepted.
Terms [1987 rates] Rooms 265-320 frs. Breakfast (with newspaper) 27 frs. 10% off stays of 3 nights or more 15 July–end Aug; group rates. Children under 15 sharing parent's room free. (No restaurant.)

ANDUZE 30140 Gard — Map 10

Les Trois Barbus — *Tel* 66.61.72.12
Générargues

Remote in the wooded southern foothills of the Cévennes, this is an attractive modern hotel built in the local style. It is in a splendid situation, on a steep slope overlooking a gorge and a branch of the river Gardon, with lovely views in all directions. Terraced gardens slope down to a magnificent swimming pool. One visitor this year found it "a friendly family-run place that would suit children, nice unpretentious atmosphere and delicious half-board meals", but another thought the meals lacking in choice and the ambience not so welcoming. An earlier report ran: "When I asked the presiding matriarch who the 'three bearded men' were, she said, *'Ce sont mes fils.'* Our room was comfortable, if not spacious. Very quiet, the only sound at night being a waterfall down in the gorge.

Charming Limoges china. Good food: marvellous sauces, light and original." (*J and A McGlashan, and others*)

Open 20 Mar–3 Nov. Closed Mon except 15 Jun–15 Sep.
Rooms 34 double – all with bath or shower, most with WC; 10 with TV; many with balcony. 20 in separate building in garden. 5 ground-floor rooms.
Facilities 2 salons, bar, restaurant; conference facilities; disco dancing Fri in July and Aug; covered terraces. Small garden with unheated swimming pool with bar and grill. On river with fishing rights. English spoken.
Location 4.5 km N of Anduze towards Mialet on D50.
Credit cards All major cards accepted.
Terms Rooms: single 170 frs, double 350 frs. Breakfast 30 frs. Full board 420-460 frs per person. Set lunch/dinner 130-220 frs. 1-night bookings without dinner refused in July and Aug. 50% reduction for children under 12 sharing parents' room; special meals.

ANTIBES 06600 Alpes-Maritimes — Map 11

Mas Djoliba — *Tel* 93.34.02.48
29 avenue de Provence — *Telex* 461686

In a quiet street in the southern suburbs, near the beach, a villa-hotel in a lovely garden, with a little of the air of a private house. Friendly staff, pretty bedrooms. Meals served in a vine-arbour when fine. Swimming pool. 14 rooms, some with bath and shower, 260-450 frs [1987]. New nomination: more reports welcome.

ARDRES 62610 Pas-de-Calais — Map 9

Grand Hôtel Clément — *Tel* 21.82.25.25
91 esplanade du Maréchal Leclerc — *Telex* 130886 RES CLEMENT

On the edge of a small town near Calais, a small family-run hotel much frequented by the British. Garden with swings, log fire in bar in winter. Excellent well-known restaurant (Michelin *rosette,* Gault Millau *red* toque), *with* nouvelle-*ish cooking done by the son of the house, François Coolen. But many bedrooms tend to be sub-standard: small, dingy, fusty, unkempt. Closed 15 Jan–15 Feb and Mon. 17 rooms, 16 with bath or shower. B&B double 235-335 frs. Set meals 100–300 frs. If you do test those bedrooms again please let us know.*

Hôtel-Restaurant Le Relais — *Tel* 21.35.42.00

A useful and inexpensive halt outside Calais: a modernised auberge *with sizeable rooms (front ones can be noisy). Friendly, considerate service; fairly good food in a beamed dining-room. Garden. 11 rooms, 10 with bath or shower. B&B double 170-255 frs. Set meals 59–165 frs. Reinstated in Guide: more reports welcome.*

If you feel we have done a hotel an injustice
If we have failed to mention salient details } please let us know.
If you consider we have got it about right

We asked hotels to estimate their 1988 tariffs. About a quarter of the hotels in Part Two failed to reply, so prices in that section are often more approximate than those in Part One.

ARGELÈS-SUR-MER 66700 Pyrénées-Orientales Map 10

Hôtel Le Cottage *Tel* 68.81.07.33
21 rue Arthur-Rimbaud

Not far from Perpignan, and close to the pretty fishing-port of Collioure, Argelès is a busy popular resort whose long sandy beach is backed by huge forests of pine and cork-oak. In high summer the scores of camping-sites are full to bursting; but this unpretentious *Logis de France* stands apart in a quiet road 1,500 metres from the beach. It is a new nomination this year: "One of those friendly small places where you instantly feel at home. Madame does the cooking (it was superb), while her attractive daughter is receptionist, waitress etc (she speaks good English, having done hotel training in Devon). Bedrooms are clean and adequate. The place is an oasis of quiet, with its own garden (fairly basic, but with barbecue and outdoor eating facilities)." (*Patricia Mitchell*) More reports welcome.

Open Apr-Oct.
Rooms 22 double – all with bath and shower, telephone, TV and baby-listening. 1 ground-floor room.
Facilities Lounge, bar, restaurant, TV room; terrace. Garden, swimming pool. English spoken.
Location Between village and *Le Centre Plage.* Argelès is 21 km SE of Perpignan.
Credit cards Access, Diners, Visa.
Terms Rooms: single occupancy 180-230 frs, double 250-280 frs. Breakfast 25 frs. Dinner, B&B: single 285-335 frs, double 460-490 frs. Set lunch 55 frs, dinner 85 frs; full alc 150 frs. Reduced rates and special meals for children.

ARLES 13200 Bouches-du-Rhône Map 11

Hôtel d'Arlatan *Tel* 90.93.56.66
26 rue du Sauvage *Telex* 441203 ARLATAN

A hotel of unusual character and beauty, run by the cultivated Desjardin family. The building, dating from the 15th century, was the ancestral home of the Counts of Arlatan; it fronts a quiet street in the heart of old Arles, and has a special secretive quality. Its idyllic little garden is enclosed on one side by the high wall of the palace of Constantine. "Lovely and picturesque," runs one recent account. "You enter through a fine courtyard with palm trees and an interesting stone fountain. The public areas and bedrooms carry out the theme of old Provence, with antiques, colourful print fabrics and art objects." Most others are also appreciative ("a gem", "pretty bedroom", "delicious breakfast"), though one reader found the garden unkempt and another suffered at night from creaking floorboards. "M. Desjardin takes a great deal of interest in every guest," says one visitor, though another found him and his staff rude and unhelpful. (*David and Patricia Hawkins, Dr John Morgan, Donna Cuervo, and others*) No restaurant, but try the *Jules César* (see below) or the cheaper *Lou Gardian* or *La Paillotte.*

Open All year.
Rooms 1 suite, 40 double, 6 single – all with bath and/or shower and telephone. 5 in annexe.
Facilities Reading room, Louis XIII salon, salon with TV; conference room. Garden with courtyard patio for outdoor refreshments. English spoken.

Location Central, near place du Forum, but quiet (rooms overlook garden and patio). Garage parking.
Restriction Not suitable for ♿.
Credit cards Amex, Diners, Visa.
Terms Rooms: single 270-350 frs, double 350-465 frs, suite 680 frs. Breakfast 38 frs. (No restaurant.)

Hotel Jules César *Tel* 90.93.43.20
Boulevard des Lices *Telex* 400239 JLCESAR

The phoney "imperial Roman" porticoed facade gives a misleading impression of the very real quality of Arles' leading hotel, brought back to the Guide by a reader's report this year after some years' absence: "A converted 17th-century convent built of soft gold stone. It is right in town, but the terrace-garden with cypress hedge shuts out the bustle and is most pleasant for a drink. Pretty Provençal printed cloth covered the walls of our room, whose thick outer walls kept it cool on a blazing hot day. There is a grand lobby, and a wide terrace for lunch or dinner as well as a handsome dining-room. Owner Michel Albagnac and his wife give guests a warm greeting and he speaks perfect English. Their chef is impressive for meals." (*Elisabeth Lambert Ortiz; also JA*) *Michelin* rosette and *Gault Millau toque* for subtle variations on classic Provençal dishes, such as raie en raito and baudroie en aïgo sau.

Open 22 Dec–early Nov.
Rooms 3 suites, 42 double, 10 single – all with bath and/or shower and telephone; 35 with TV; 20 with air-conditioning. 15 ground-floor rooms.
Facilities Salon, TV room, bar, restaurant; terrace. Garden with swimming-pool. English spoken.
Location Central, near main post office. Parking.
Credit cards All major cards accepted.
Terms Rooms: single 400-600 frs, double 500-800 frs, suite 900-1,400 frs. Set lunch/dinner 150, 200 and 250 frs; full alc 300 frs. Reduced rates for children; special meals

---

ARPAILLARGUES 30700 Gard **Map 11**

Hôtel d'Agoult, Château d'Arpaillargues *Tel* 66.22.14.48
Telex 490415
Arpaillargues, Uzès

Uzès (q.v.) is one of the most lovely and fascinating old towns in Provence. Five kilometres to the west, on the edge of the village of Arpaillargues, stands this 18th-century château, formerly the home of the d'Agoult family (Marie d'Agoult was a mistress of Lizst). "It is lovely, and beautifully maintained and modernised," runs a recent report. "Our large room was good value, and so was dinner, which we took once in the courtyard and once in the atmospheric dining-room – outstanding escargots and roast lamb." Others have added: "Luxurious and a bit grand, with the best swimming-pool facilities I've ever come across"; "a finely furnished room more like a suite, and a perfect dinner that included terrine de rascasse and magret de canard." There is a library, a park, and views over the rolling hills. (*J McGlashan, Robin and Dietmar Schiel, Mr and Mrs RB Tait*)

We are particularly keen to have reports on italicised entries.

Open 15 Mar–1 Nov. Restaurant closed Wed in low season.
Rooms 25 – all with bath or shower and telephone.
Facilities Salon, library, restaurant; conference facilities; courtyard. Large grounds with tennis courts and swimming pool.
Location 4.5 km W of Uzès.
Credit cards All major cards accepted.
Terms [1987 rates] Rooms: single 390 frs, double 520 frs. Breakfast 38 frs. Full board 540-730 frs per person. Set lunch/dinner 170 frs.

AUXERRE 89000 Yonne — Map 10

Le Parc des Maréchaux — *Tel* 86.51.43.77
6 avenue Foch

"Just the kind of place that Guide readers would relish," writes an inspector this year after visiting "this idiosyncratic little bed-and-breakfast hotel" in a quiet street of this dignified cathedral city. "It is run in an appealing and very personal way by its lovely bubbly patronne, Espérance Hervé, a doctor's wife. Where there's Hope there's life - and certainly she has given a new lease of life to this genteel 1856 mansion, set in its own big garden amid lovely and unusual trees. This was formerly known as the Parc des Maréchaux, so the comfortable bedrooms are now all named after French marshals such as Lyautey (but not Pétain). The American bar, all plush red velvet, is called L'Araucaria, after the 100-year-old African monkey-puzzle tree in the garden. These may be gimmicks: but there is nothing forced about the private-house atmosphere, especially in the comfortable sitting room where under chandeliers I took a pleasant breakfast to the strains of Chopin. Even the large party of cyclists from Lucerne, jabbering away in *Schwyzer-Dütsch*, did not unduly break the spell. Breakfasts and drinks are served on the lawn in summer."

Open All year except Sun 1 Nov–1 Apr.
Rooms 23 – all with bath or shower, telephone and TV.
Facilities Lift. Lounge, bar; conference room. Garden.
Location 500 metres W of town centre. Parking.
Credit card Visa.
Terms Rooms: single 175 frs, double 259 frs. Breakfast 22 frs. (No restaurant.)

AVALLON 89200 Yonne — Map 10

Hostellerie de la Poste — *Tel* 86.34.06.12
13 place Vauban — *Telex* 351806

In the centre of Avallon, a famous and dignified old hostelry dating from 1707. Napoleon spent a night here on his way back from Elba. Well-appointed rooms, stylish service, beautiful restaurant, flowery cobblestoned courtyard for summer dining (good traditional cooking). Open mid-Mar–end Nov. 23 rooms, almost all with bath or shower. B&B double 750 frs. Set meals 150–350 frs. Change of owners, no reports since then: more needed.

Le Relais Fleuri — *Tel* 86.34.02.85
In this much-visited and heavily-hotelled area, the *Relais Fleuri* could make a useful modern alternative to our more "picturesque" Avallon

entries. Outside the town on the Saulieu road, it is a new Guide nomination: "A cut above other main-road-stopover hotels and good value. Originally an old *auberge*, it has recently been extended; behind it, well away from the road, are ranges of single-storey motel rooms separated by lawns. Our large well-equipped room faced fields and was very quiet. The hotel has comfortable seating areas, a bar and a smoke-soaked card room. The large and attractive new restaurant is nicely lit and had a welcoming feel: friendly multilingual waiter, an open fire in October, and a good meal for 84 francs [1986]. Open-air solar-heated swimming pool with pleasant poolside bar." (*Don and Maureen Montague*)

Open All year except 24 and 31 Dec.
Rooms 48 double – 45 with bath and shower, 3 with shower, all with telephone, radio and TV. All on ground-floor, 2 specially equipped for ♿.
Facilities 2 lounges, bar, restaurant; 3 conference rooms. Garden with heated swimming pool. English spoken.
Location 4 km E of Avallon on N6 to Saulieu.
Credit cards All major cards accepted.
Terms Rooms: single 245-260 frs, double 265-290 frs. Breakfast 30 frs. Set lunch/dinner 90-140 frs; full alc 200 frs.

Le Moulin des Templiers *Tel* 86.34.10.80
Vallée du Cousin

An idyllically-situated old watermill, attractively converted into a small bed-and-breakfast hotel beside the quiet-flowing Cousin, in a pastoral valley outside Avallon. Breakfast served on a terrace by the water's edge or in a tiny but pretty salon. Bedrooms though charming are very small and washing facilities cramped: best for a night stop, not a long stay. Open 15 Mar–31 Oct. 14 rooms, all with bath and/or shower, 170-250 frs [1987]. More reports please.

AVIGNON 84000 Vaucluse — Map 11

Hôtel d'Angleterre *Tel* 90.86.34.31
29 boulevard Raspail

On a fairly quiet street within the ramparts. A cut above the average utility town-centre hotel, and much cheaper than the Europe (*below*). *Pleasant, clean, sprucely modernised. Connection with Angleterre unknown. Closed 12 Dec–18 Jan. 40 rooms, almost all with bath or shower. B&B double 154-329 frs. No restaurant, but try* Patio *or* Fourchette. *New nomination: more reports please.*

Hôtel d'Europe *Tel* 90.82.66.92
12 place Crillon *Telex* 431965

Most Avignon hotels are modern and functional; this one has classic character: a former 16th-century aristocrat's house, it was already an inn when Napoleon stayed here in 1799. It is in a small square just inside the old city walls, a mere 300 metres from the Papal Palace, and has won praise again this year: "Ambience delightful, dinners excellent." An earlier report: "The courtyard and public rooms are a feast to the eye and spirit, cool, peaceful, filled with flowers and antiques. My comfortable room was decorated with simplicity and good taste. When there was a muddle over a booking (not the hotel's fault), the staff went out of their way to accommodate me." However, readers do warn that a few of the bedrooms are "pokey" and badly lit. The Provençal cuisine in the hotel's *Vieille Fontaine* restaurant is admired. You can eat in a rather formal dining room or, preferably, under the plane trees beside a fountain in the graceful courtyard ("a magical experience"). (*T and J Campbell, Constance Ellison; also Kate Currie*)

Open All year.
Rooms 6 suites, 37 double, 10 single – all with bath and/or shower, telephone and TV.
Facilities Lift. 2 salons, bar, TV room, restaurant; conference facilities. Courtyard. 5 minutes' walk from Papal Palace. English spoken.
Location Enter inner city by Porte de l'Oulle on W side; place Crillon is just inside. Private garage (40 frs).
Restriction Not suitable for ♿.
Credit cards Amex, Diners, Visa.
Terms [1987 rates] Rooms: single 250 frs, double 390-790 frs. Breakfast 45 frs. Set lunch 200 frs; full alc from 170 frs.

BANNEGON 18210 Cher — Map 10

Auberge du Moulin de Chaméron — *Tel* 48.61.83.80

A converted 18th-century watermill, very romantic, prettily lit at night – in the geographical and spiritual heart of *la douce France*, south-east of Bourges in the rolling Berry country. American readers have spent very rich hours here, adding their voice to the flurry of red-print praise in the French guides: "Yes, yes! Worth the detour for the food alone. Our room modest but bathroom large. Pool was great. Walks on country lanes. Museum of former mill implements. Dining room charming and romantic – *nouvelle cuisine*." Endorsed this year: "We enormously enjoyed dining outside by the stream." "Very peaceful, comfortable, dinners good." *Relais du Silence.* (*Marie Earle, Geoffrey Sharp, Dr RL Holmes and Dr MW Atkinson*)

Open 4 Mar–15 Nov, 15 Dec–4 Jan. Closed Tue off-season.
Rooms 3 suites, 10 double – all with bath and/or shower, and telephone; 4 with TV. All in separate building. 4 ground-floor rooms.
Facilities Lounge, bar, 2 dining rooms; facilities for small conferences. Garden with river, swimming pool and old watermill converted into museum. English spoken.
Location Between Thaumiers and Sancoins off D41; hotel is signposted.
Credit card Visa.
Terms Double room: 180-350 frs, suite 420 frs. Set lunch/dinner 170 frs; full alc from 150 frs. Children's menu.

BASTELICA 20119 Corsica — Map 11

U Castagnetu — *Tel* 95.28.70.71

A simple but modernised little hotel, in a village high up in the wooded and mountainous interior of the island, to the east of Ajaccio. "Very much a mountain place. Bedrooms simple but comfortable. Our welcome was a bit surly, but later the staff were friendly and the food delicious – wild boar, home-made soups, mountain cheese, with the emphasis on honest home cooking and fresh local produce. A good base for people with a car who like peace and quiet." (*Joan Williamson*) Good skiing nearby.

Open All year except Nov. Closed Tue Oct–May.
Rooms 15 double – all with bath and/or shower, 8 with wc, all with telephone.
Facilities Salon/bar, dining room; terrace.
Location 41 km NE of Ajaccio; on D27.
Credit cards Amex, Diners, Visa.
Terms Rooms: single occupancy 130-160 frs, double 150-180 frs; dinner, B&B: single 200-250 frs, double 290-320 frs; full board: single 250-280 frs, double 390-420 frs. Set lunch/dinner 60-120 frs. No 1-night bookings in high season.

BASTIA 20200 Corsica — Map 11

Hotel Pietracap — *Tel* 95.31.64.63
Pietranera

A modern bed-and-breakfast hotel, well located up a quiet road two miles north of Bastia, near the very scenic Cap Corse peninsular. Decor ugly but rooms comfortable, many with sea-facing balcony; clean swimming pool amid trees. Open 1 Apr–12 Dec. 22 rooms, all with bath or shower. Double 350-450 frs. Reinstated in Guide: more reports welcome.

LES BAUX-DE-PROVENCE 13520 Bouches-du-Rhône — Map 11

Oustaù de Baumanière — *Tel* 90.54.33.07
Telex 420203

The ruined hill village-cum-castle of Les Baux, on a spur of the Alpilles, is one of the show-places of Provence. In the Middle Ages this was the seat of a great feudal family and a leading "court of love" where troubadours played. Then it came under the rule of a sadistic viscount who would kidnap his neighbours and laugh as he forced them to jump to their deaths from the clifftop. In 1632 Richelieu had the castle demolished. Today it is a ghost realm, where coachloads daily pick their way across the jagged rocks of bauxite (hence its name) and through the spooky remains of medieval grandeur. It is best visited by moonlight.

The *Baumanière,* in the valley below the village, is still owned by 90-year-old Raymond Thuilier, the doyen of great French restaurateurs, and is run by his son-in-law; their chef Alain Burnel still wins *Michelin*'s top rating of three stars and five red knives and forks, and he sticks to the classic style, eschewing *nouvelle cuisine*. Prices are in the top bracket, but this may not always ensure perfection: one visitor this year thought the food indifferent and the atmosphere less than indigenous ("It used to be said that when Americans die they go to Paris. Well, those committed to Purgatory presumably go to the *Baumanière*; the place is full of the poor things. Not a Frenchman in sight . . ."). But others have at least been impressed by the setting and the very real beauty of the place. One "poor thing", from Nashville, found that her Purgatory consisted of "a large garden with peach, fig and olive trees, roses and a plethora of flowers. Dinner was memorable and breakfast was served in our own garden." "At night, the crescent moon, starlight and floodlit château, the eerie white rocks, the discreetly lit pool . . ." (*Vicki Turner, Wendy Arnold, Adrian Turner, and others*) But we would welcome more reports.

Open All year except 20 Jan–6 Mar. Closed Wed, and Thur afternoon from 1 Nov–15 Mar.
Rooms 11 suites, 14 double – all with bath, telephone, and air-conditioning; 16 with TV. 16 in 3 annexes. 8 ground-floor rooms.
Facilities Salon, arcaded restaurant. Garden, swimming pool, tennis courts, riding stables. English spoken.
Location 19 km SW of Arles; 60 km NW of Marseilles.
Credit cards Access, Amex, Visa.
Terms Rooms: single 725 frs, double 770 frs, suite 1,050 frs. Breakfast 70 frs. Alc lunch/dinner (excluding wine) 280-405 frs.

La Benvengudo *Tel* 90.54.32.54

In the valley south-west of the village, a creeper-covered farmhouse considerably cheaper than the Baumanière. *Lovely swimming-pool in a charming orchard-garden, all quite glamorous. Dinners in a cosy room with antiques or on a floodlit patio (no lunches). Open 15 Feb–31 Oct. 20 rooms, all with bath or shower. B&B double from 350 frs. Set meals 170–220 frs. Much admired in past, but recent criticism of food, rooms and welcome: more reports please.*

BAYEUX 14400 Calvados — Map 8

Hôtel d'Argouges *Tel* 31.92.88.86
21 rue St-Patrice *Telex* 170234 ARGOUGES

Quite close to the cathedral and famous tapestry, an 18th-century private town house now converted into a charming and elegant little family-run hotel, warm and welcoming, with beamed bedrooms and small garden. 25 rooms all with bath or shower. B&B double 200-305 frs. No restaurant. More reports welcome.

Hôtel Restaurant du Lion d'Or *Tel* 31.92.06.90
71 rue St-Jean *Telex* 171143

The *Lion d'Or* is an old coaching-inn right in the town centre but very quiet (a *Relais du Silence*) because its rooms are set back from the street around a long paved courtyard set with trees, flowers and lawns. It has been much admired by 1986/7 visitors: "Unchangingly excellent, we shall always return. We had a small room on the top floor, OK for one night, and the best meal of our holiday (notably the cheeseboard, left on the table)." Another reader had "a bedroom as large as a sitting room, well decorated in French taste, and with a huge bed. The food was delicious and memorable, with perfect service – our waiter was an enthusiast, who gave us a running commentary on the merits of Norman cheeses. Of 17 cars in the courtyard, 12 bore GB plates." Others too have praised the food and service – "Don't be put off by *Michelin*'s rosette." In fact we are not, nor by the *Gault Millau toque* awarded for andouille chaude à la Bovary and other local dishes that Emma might have enjoyed. (*BW Forster, Colin Pilkington, CS Granger, and others*)

Open All year.
Rooms 28 double, 2 single – 16 with bath and shower, 10 with shower, all with telephone and TV.
Facilities Salon, bar, restaurant, TV room. Courtyard. English spoken.
Location Central, near Halle aux Grains but quietly situated. Courtyard parking.
Restriction Not suitable for ♿.

Credit cards All major cards accepted.
Terms Rooms: single 200 frs, double 220 frs. Breakfast 25 frs. Dinner, B&B 250-420 frs. Set lunch/dinner 80-220 frs; full alc 220 frs. Reduced rates and special meals for children.

BAZINCOURT-SUR-EPTE 27140 Eure — Map 8

Château de la Râpée — *Tel* 32.55.11.61

Usefully located between Paris and the Channel ports, just inside Normandy, this *Relais du Silence* makes its Guide debut this year. Set beside woods in its own ten-acre park, it is an Anglo-Norman manor. "It looks a bit like a Hammer House of Horror from outside, but is a very Edwardian country house inside, with fires etc, and very comfortable. Best croissants for years at breakfast, and very careful individual cooking" (local dishes such as douillon normand and caneton rouennais, betoqued by *Gault Millau*). Elegant upholstery and wallpaper patterns; beamed ceilings; chandeliers. (*ECM Begg*)

Open 1 Mar-16 Aug. 1 Sep-12 Jan. Closed Wed.
Rooms 1 suite, 7 double, 2 single – all with bath and/or shower, telephone and TV.
Facilities Salon, bar, TV lounge, restaurant; conference room. Garden. English spoken.
Location 5 km NW of Gisors, which is 32km SW of Beauvais, 58km E of Rouen.
Restriction Not suitable for ♿.
Credit cards Amex, Diners, Visa.
Terms B&B: single 250 frs, double 410 frs; dinner, B&B: single 380 frs, double 470 frs. Set lunch 120 frs, dinner 155 frs; full alc 250 frs. Special meals for children.

BEAULIEU-SUR-MER 06310 Alpes-Maritimes — Map 11

Hôtel Métropole — *Tel* 93.01.00.08
15 boulevard Maréchal Leclerc — *Telex* 470304

Beaulieu with its casino and floodlit palms is still sedately elegant, though no longer as fashionable as in pre-war days. *Le Métropole*, a well-known hotel of the old style, is set back from the road, surrounded by a pretty garden and terrace; it overlooks the glorious coast and is right by the sea. Bedrooms are furnished in cool blue/white, pink/white, green/white schemes, rather Scandinavian, with bathroom tiles to match. Smart David Hicks-style carpets. Several readers this year have appreciated the impeccable old-style service and the notable cuisine (*Michelin* rosette, two *Gault Millau toques*), though one found it lacking in innovation "maybe because of the slightly elderly clientèle". One presumably not-so-elderly couple found the staff "nice about our baby" (true, babies seldom expect innovative cuisine) and thought the heated salt-water pool "a dream". "In May, the gardens were immaculately ablaze, stretching down to the sea. One snag is that you have to accept *demi-pension*, and extras are outrageous. The cheapest rooms are small and face on to the town; medium-priced ones are at the side, facing over the pool; those facing the sea are de luxe price." (Rooms facing the main road may be a little noisy). During winter, the normally outrageous prices are halved, making it not unreasonable.(*Mrs H Langenberg, Nathan Waks, EF Snelgar, PF*)

> We depend on detailed fresh reports to keep our entries up-to-date.

Open 20 Dec–31 Oct.
Rooms 3 suites, 36 double, 10 single – 41 with bath, 9 with shower, all with telephone and TV; some with balcony.
Facilities Lift. Bar, lounges, terrace restaurant, dining room, air-conditioning. Garden with terrace, swimming pool heated throughout winter, private beach. English spoken.
Location 10 km E of Nice on N559. Parking.
Credit cards None accepted.
Terms Dinner, B&B: single 1,585 frs, double 2,900 frs; full board: single 1,720 frs, double 3,170 frs. Large reductions out of season. Set lunch/dinner 390 frs.

BEAUNE 21200 Côte-d'Or — Map 10

Hôtel le Cep — *Tel* 80.22.35.48
27 rue Maufoux — *Telex* 351256 CEPHOTL

A charming 17th-century house in the centre of Burgundy's wine capital. Now under new ownership and reported to be as good as ever – antique furnishings, lounge, lovely bathrooms; back rooms face quiet courtyard, front ones could be noisy. Restaurant due to open by 1988. Open 14 Mar–30 Nov. 46 rooms, all with bath and/or shower. B&B double 510-880 frs. Set meals 150 frs. More reports please.

LE BEC-HELLOUIN 27800 Eure — Map 8

Auberge de l'Abbaye — *Tel* 32.44.86.02

"A splendid place, with very good rooms"; "outstanding in the area"; "a perfect French inn, dinner very good" - so runs the enthusiasm this year and last for this *auberge*, which has simple but clean rooms, modest prices, and no lounge but a dining room offering excellent meals at a cost considerably lower than the English equivalent. Le Bec-Hellouin was the home of one of Europe's great Benedictine monasteries, and no fewer than three archbishops of Canterbury came from here in medieval times. The monastery, formerly a ruin, has now been substantially restored and once again houses a religious community; it is only a stroll from the *auberge* across the tranquil village green. The Gregorian chant in the abbey is worth hearing: but its resonant bells do tend to start ringing early. (*P Coleman, William A Howard, Laura Berish and others*)

Open 27 Feb–10 Jan. Closed Mon evening and Tue out of season.
Rooms 1 suite, 7 double – all with bath, shower and telephone.
Facilities Restaurant, breakfast room; courtyard. English spoken.
Location 5 km from Brionne; SW of Rouen, W of N138. Parking.
Restriction Not suitable for ♿.
Credit cards Diners, Visa.
Terms Rooms 240 frs, suite 400 frs. Breakfast 30 frs. Set lunch/dinner 120-220 frs; full alc 150 frs.

BELLEGARDE-SUR-VALSÉRINE 01200 Ain — Map 10

Hôtel Le Fartoret — *Tel* 50.48.07.18
Éloise

This unusual family-run hotel, in a hamlet near the Swiss frontier, continues to find fluctuating favour with readers. Last year no fewer than five letters of praise reached us: but this year a visitor felt that *pension* guests were less well treated than the local business trade, and like others he found that the set menus were dull and repetitive. With some hesitation we reprint a glowing earlier account:

"*Fartoret* is the Savoyard word for a shelter for workers in the vineyards and this shelter in Éloise is one of the most welcoming we have found in many years of touring France. High up on the south side of the Rhône, amid magnificent scenery, Éloise is a dead-end hamlet where *la famille* Gassilloud have run an inn since the 1890s. *Le Fartoret* has since been modernised and extended, and its steeply-sloping site tactfully exploited so that most rooms have splendid views. Pale pink linen, some big locally-made wooden dressers and cupboards displaying old pottery are some of the many homely touches. The excellent *carte* has many Savoyard specialities – e.g. a type of feral trout caught only in Savoy lakes." (*Eileen A Michie; endorsed by Thomas J Loran, Mrs A Sennett, SD Carpenter, Professor JM Mitchison*) More reports please.

Open All year.
Rooms 35 double, 7 single - all with bath and/or shower and telephone. 20 in new building in garden. 6 ground-floor rooms.
Facilities 2 lifts. 3 lounges (1 with TV), bar, restaurant; conference facilities. Large grounds with garden, tennis court and heated swimming pool. English spoken.
Location Éloise is 5 km SE of Bellegarde, off N508 to Annecy (36 km to SE).
Credit cards All major cards accepted.
Terms B&B: single 193 frs, double 241–351 frs; dinner, B&B: 205–265 frs per person; full board 250–314 frs. Set lunch/dinner 89–208 frs; full alc 200 frs. Reduced rates for children.

BÉNODET 29118 Finistère — Map 8

Hôtel Menez-Frost — *Tel* 98.57.03.09
4 rue Charcot

Close to Quimper and Concarneau, at the mouth of the quiet river Odet studded with pleasure-boats, Bénodet is an attractive and bustling resort in South Brittany. Its season ends early, so that a September visitor found it "sleepy and rather genteel". The *Menez-Frost* has again been warmly recommended this year: "A well-run hotel, lovely for a family holiday as it has so many facilities – heated swimming pool, tennis, ping pong – and is near very good beaches. And – a plus point for us – it is only B&B, so you can eat around (though there is an elegant restaurant in the grounds, with outstanding food). Our bedroom had dull decor but a balcony overlooking the pool; in our building the rooms were grouped in pairs, useful for a family. Breakfast was very good, though marred by packaged butter and jams. The manager was wonderful, keeping an eye on everything in a charming fashion." Last year's praise: "Exceedingly comfortable. My only gripes concern the incessant piped music (but we did have one breakfast to a Brandenburg). The garden restaurant, *Le Parc*, was excellent value, especially the fish." (*Adam and Caroline Raphael, Mrs RB Richards*)

Open 1 Apr–15 Oct.
Rooms 7 suites, 46 double, 8 single – all with bath and shower, and telephone; some with balcony. 15 ground-floor rooms.

Facilities Salon, bar, restaurant; conference facilities; billiards and table tennis. Garden with heated swimming pool (lessons available), solarium and sauna; tennis. English spoken.
Location Central, near post office, port and ferry. Parking.
Credit cards Access, Visa.
Terms Rooms: single 230–280 frs, double 240–325 frs, suites 440–613 frs. Breakfast 25 frs. Set meals from 75 frs. Reduced rates for children.

BEUZEVILLE 27210 Eure — Map 8

Auberge du Cochon d'Or and Le Petit Castel

Tel 32.57.76.08 and 32.57.70.46

Place du Général-de-Gaulle

An old Norman *auberge* and adjacent small modern hotel, both owned and run by the Folleau family, in a little town near Honfleur, only 48 km from Le Havre. Most guests sleep at the *Castel*, a *Logis de France*, recently renovated, and everyone seems to like it a lot – comfortable, pretty rooms, a nice walled garden, and a good breakfast at very modest cost. As for the *Cochon d'Or*, where you eat, one returning visitor this year felt that it had deteriorated badly and found the service again painfully slow. But others consider that it still deserves its *Michelin* red "R" for good value - "Normandy cooking at its best"; "a dozen oysters as a starter on the 120-franc [1987] set menu"; "an enjoyable meal in a relaxing atmosphere - trout stuffed with smoked salmon, guinea-fowl in a grapefruit and orange sauce." Madame is said to be "most welcoming". (*Kay and Neville Varley, Richard O Whiting, Denis and Kathleen Perry, and others*)

Open 15 Jan–15 Dec. Restaurant closed Mon.
Rooms 24 double - 17 with bath, 7 with shower; 16 with telephone; 5 with TV. 16 in *Petit Castel*.
Facilities Lounge, TV room, restaurant; conference room. Garden. English spoken.
Location In centre. Quietest rooms in *Petit Castel*. Beuzeville is 15 km SE of Honfleur, just N of Paris/Caen motorway.
Credit cards Access, Visa.
Terms Rooms: single occupancy 150 frs, double 270 frs. Breakfast 21 frs. Set meals 80, 130 and 180 frs; full alc 200 frs.

BEYNAC 24220 Dordogne — Map 10

Hôtel Bonnet

Tel 53.29.50.01

Beynac dominates a curve in the Dordogne river, with four medieval castles in full view. The Bonnet, *an old favourite with British visitors, has comfortable rooms, spacious bathrooms and a flowery creeper-covered terrace. One snag: the hotel is on a busy main road – rooms at the back are quieter. Open Easter to Oct. 22 rooms with bath or shower. Single 90–130 frs, double 155–210 frs. Breakfast 22 frs; lunch/dinner 90–175 frs. No recent reports, hence these italics.*

> Set dinner refers to a fixed price meal (which may have ample, limited or no choice on the menu). Full alc is the hotel's own estimated price per person of a three-course meal taken à la carte, with a half-bottle of house wine.

LES BÉZARDS 45290 Loiret — Map 9

Auberge des Templiers — *Tel* 38.31.80.01
Boismorand — *Telex* 780998 TEMPLIE

An old posting house, gastronomically distinguished, very expensive and luxuriously renovated, on the busy N7 about 90 minutes' drive south from Paris. Some 20 bedrooms are in new buildings scattered in the grounds, where there are pretty gardens and tennis courts. "A truly wonderful place," runs a report this year. "We had a lovely room and found the food excellent as ever. We took breakfast under leafy trees." Others have praised the "lovely welcoming interior, with an open fire and lots of big wooden beams", and the prettily decorated bedrooms "with bowls of fresh flowers and live plants". Everyone agrees that the food is remarkable (two *Michelin* rosettes, three red *Gault Millau toques,* for inventive dishes such as fricassée of sole and frogs). But there have been some reports of offhand service, incorrect room bookings, a heated swimming pool "heated with ice cubes" and prices a little *too* extravagant. (*Stephan and Kate Murray-Sykes, Mrs Henry, Dr RL Holmes*)

Open Mid-Feb–mid-Jan.
Rooms 8 suites, 22 double – all with bath and/or shower, telephone and TV; baby-sitters available. About 20 rooms and suites in buildings in grounds. Some ground-floor rooms.
Facilities Salons, bars, smoking room, 2 restaurants; conference facilities. Garden with heated swimming pool and 2 tennis courts. English spoken.
Location 138 km S of Paris – take N7 towards Nevers (69 km E of Orléans).
Credit cards Access, Amex, Visa.
Terms Rooms: single 550 frs, double 900frs, suite 950-1,950 frs. Breakfast 55 frs. Set lunch/dinner 270–400 frs.

BIOT 06410 Alpes-Maritimes — Map 11

Hôtel-Restaurant Galerie des Arcades — *Tel* 93.65.01.04
16 place des Arcades

An idiosyncratic 15th-century inn/café/bistro/art gallery in a picturesque hill village. Engagingly Bohemian patron, *ex-coiffeur André Brothier, has lined the dining room with Braques and Mirós. Bedrooms are olde worlde, but the plumbing, happily, is not. The inn's hyper-relaxed ambience may not suit all tastes: loud pop music may resound from the café while you eat your aïlloli or tripes niçoise. 12 double rooms, all with bath or shower. Rooms 150–280 frs. Breakfast 25 frs. Set meals 120 frs. In italics as no recent feedback.*

BOUILLAND 21420 Côte d'Or — Map 10

Hostellerie du Vieux Moulin — *Tel* 80.21.51.16

This "small village in the middle of nowhere, not easy to find "lies amid the little hills and valleys of the so-called "Swiss Burgundy", just west of the famous golden slope of the great vineyards and due north of Beaune. Here, in a big garden beside a mill-stream, the *Vieux Moulin* is a small, very elegant restaurant-with-rooms where you can dine out under the trees in the summer. A new bedroom annexe has just been added, and readers this year have found its rooms "perfect" and "very comfortable" and the breakfasts "unusually good", though the limited lounge space might make the place unsuitable for a long stay.

Cuisine here is a very serious matter: owner Jean-Pierre Silva cooks interesting dishes in a modern way but based on traditional Burgundian recipes (e.g. meurette of frogs' legs with leeks), and innovation-loving *Gault Millau* is so enthusiastic that since 1984 it has put up the rating from one red *toque* to three (*Michelin* more prudently stays at one rosette). Our readers likewise continue to find the food "excellent", though servings can be wee and twee in the *nouvelle* manner (a "second helping" consisted of one slice of carrot, one button mushroom, one thumb-length bone of quail leg, largely bare). And the setting and ambience? "A little too exquisite for our taste, though others might find its charms irresistible," says one visitor this year. "The restaurant's big picture-windows look directly onto evergreen trees which are floodlit at night with dramatic effect, and maybe it was this, the large number of staff and the contrived elegance of the decor that served to intimidate the diners and hush their chatter." Or, as another reader puts it: "Food delicious, but the atmosphere was too 'holy' and unrelaxed for our taste. Food is served with a recital of the components of each dish delivered in an unenthusiastic monotone." (*Don and Maureen Montague, Mr and Mrs GA Jones, Bernadette Murray, and others*) More reports please.

Open 26 Jan–19 Dec. Closed Wed, and Thurs midday except holidays.
Rooms 2 suites, 9 double – all with bath or shower, direct-dial telephone, radio and TV. All in 2 annexes 5 and 20 metres from restaurant. 1 ground-floor room suitable for ♿.
Facilities Salon/bar, breakfast room, restaurant. English spoken.
Location On edge of village, 15 km N of Beaune.
Credit card Visa.
Terms Rooms: double 350-500 frs, suite 700 frs. Breakfast 40 frs. Set lunch/dinner 140, 200 and 300 frs; full alc 300 frs. Special meals for children.

LA BOUILLE 76530 Seine-Maritime — Map 8

Hôtel-Restaurant le Saint-Pierre — *Tel* 35.23.80.10

"The setting is dramatic, the rooms were large and the food quite exceptional," runs a report this year on this restaurant-with-rooms in a picturesque Norman hamlet by the banks of the Seine near Rouen; it has a terrace for outdoor meals and drinks in summer. Earlier praise: "The owners, the Huets, are charming and have spent a lot of time in England. You enter the hotel through the bar which is very colourful, open to the public and very French in atmosphere. Our bedroom, overlooking the river, had oriental touches in the decor. It was quiet, but some rooms on the road side might be less so. The dining room, light and airy, had a great ambience of pure enjoyment of food and wine. The cooking, a mix of traditional and *nouvelle*, was excellent (rosette in *Michelin*), though not cheap. On the 190-franc menu [1987] we especially enjoyed the salade d'huîtres et St-Jacques, and panaché de ris de veau et rognons de veau. The place was a real breath of France." One caveat this year about a pre-paid booking not properly honoured. (*Robert CC Sandys, PH; also Else Robbins Landon*)

Report forms (Freepost in UK) will be found at the end of the Guide.

Open All year, except Tue evening and Wed 1 Nov–31 Mar.
Rooms 7 double – all with bath, shower and telephone; 1 with TV.
Facilities Bar, restaurant. Garden terrace. English spoken.
Location 20 km SW of Rouen; take Maison Brûlée turning off Paris/Le Havre *autoroute.*
Restriction Not suitable for ♿.
Credit card Visa.
Terms Rooms: single occupancy 220-300 frs, double 250-300 frs. Breakfast 35 frs. Set lunch/dinner 120-190 frs; full alc 250-300 frs. Reduced rates for children sharing parents' room; special meals.

BOULOGNE-SUR-MER 62200 Pas-de-Calais — Map 9

Hôtel de la Plage — *Tel* 21.31.45.35
124 boulevard Sainte-Beuve

A clean, cheerful family-run little place, very cheap, opposite casino and near beach. Stairs steep, but rooms large and warm. Quiet, save for noisy British tourists. Good breakfast. Closed 20 Dec–27 Jan. 10 rooms, some with shower. B&B double 160 frs. Restored to Guide this year: more reports please, especially on restaurant.

BOURBON-L'ARCHAMBAULT 03160 Allier — Map 10

Hôtel des Thermes — *Tel* 70.67.00.15
Avenue Charles Louis Philippe

Talleyrand used to take the cure for rheumatism at this small spa town on the northern edge of the Auvergne. Here the *Thermes* is suitably sedate and very spruce, and its *patron*-chef, M. Barichard, tells us that his Guide entry has brought him many British visitors. He has won the First Prize for Welcome and Friendliness for the Allier *département,* and again this year our readers have had no cause to query that verdict: "M. Barichard was most charming," says one, "and he gave us a memorable dinner of omelette, sole meunière and steak in a special sauce." M. Barichard wins a *Michelin* rosette for the kind of orthodox dishes that *curistes* probably prefer. His hotel has a garden-terrace facing the cure centre and a private lake for fishing. One visitor had a spotless room overlooking a flowery patio, with a large tiled bathroom. (*PW Barratt, Mr and Mrs JMA Lang, and others*)

Open 25 Mar–31 Oct.
Rooms 1 suite, 17 double, 4 single – 9 with bath, 6 with shower, all with direct-dial telephone. 4 in annexe.
Facilities Salon with TV, dining room. Large grounds, with terrace, garden and private lake; fishing.
Location 100 metres from town centre. Town is 23 km W of Moulins. Garage.
Restriction Not suitable for ♿.
Credit cards Amex, Visa.
Terms B&B: single 129 frs, double 264 frs, suite 283 frs. Set lunch/dinner 73-270 frs; full alc 170 frs.

> Important reminder: terms printed must be regarded as a rough guide only to the size of the bill to be expected at the end of your stay. For latest tariffs, check when booking.

BOURDEILLES 24310 Dordogne Map 10

Hostellerie Les Griffons *Tel* 53.05.75.61

In the heart of the Périgord Noir, one of the most historic and seductive regions of south-west France, Bourdeilles is a medieval village on the river Dronne, crowned by a feudal castle on a rocky hill; the townlet of Brantôme, even lovelier but touristy, is only ten kilometres away. The *Griffons*, a 16th-century building recently converted, is in the village by the river and continues to win praise, alike for its good local cuisine (Madame is chef), comfort, and rural character: "Most comfortable and welcoming, excellent food"; "a beautifully furnished bedroom with timbered ceiling"; "a lovely room with view across river"; "a pleasant terrace where drinks are served, a comfortable rustic dining-room with beamed ceiling and good food" – confit of duck, pink trout with cèpes, etc. One reader this year found Madame a little domineering, and disliked having to pay 20 francs extra for orange juice at breakfast. (*CE Warner and JEA Garnett, DAC Cartwright, Consuelo Phelan, and others*)

Open 10 April–10 Oct. Closed Tue 10 Apr–1 Jul.
Rooms 10 double – all with bath, shower and telephone.
Facilities Salon, TV room, bar, 2 dining rooms; 2 terraces. River fishing, swimming pool and riding nearby. English spoken.
Location Bourdeilles is 10 km SW of Brantôme and 25 km NW of Périgueux.
Restriction Not suitable for ♿.
Credit cards All major cards accepted.
Terms Rooms: single 250 frs, double 290 frs. Breakfast 30 frs. Set lunch/dinner 90-200 frs.

LE BOURGET-DU-LAC 73370 Savoie Map 10

Hôtel Ombremont *Tel* 79.25.00.23
Telex 980832 CHAMBERY

A handsome gabled hotel in country-house style, secluded in its big garden by the lovely Lac du Bourget, just outside this smart resort. Elegant furnishing, fine views, lovely dining room with open terrace for summer eating. Excellent inventive cooking (Michelin *rosette, two red* Gault Millau toques). *Sympathetic young owners. Swimming pool. Open 7 Feb–19 Dec. 18 rooms, all with bath. B&B double 500-950 frs. Set meals 160–400 frs [1987]. No recent reports: more urgently solicited.*

BRANTÔME 24310 Dordogne Map 10

Le Châtenet *Tel* 53.05.81.08

Brantôme is a beautiful, but consequently very trippery, little town on the river Dronne, north of Périgueux. Just outside it, away from the crowds and by the river, stands this small 17th-century manor house, recently converted by its English-speaking owners, the Laxtons – "We seek to share a calm family life with our guests," they have told us, and this year one guest at least has written warmly of the results: "Mrs Laxton is a darling and her staff are wonderful. A gem of a place." Others have spoken of "a lovely old house with luxurious and comfortable bedrooms in a delightful setting". Bed-and-breakfast only: but there are no fewer than three *Michelin*-rosetted restaurants nearby (see Champagnac-de-Belair). (*N French, Osmond Edwards*)

Open All year, except possibly a short while in low season.
Rooms 2 suites, 5 double – all with bath, shower, telephone, TV and baby-listening. 2 rooms in annexe. Suites on ground floor, suitable for ♿.
Facilities Lounge with bar, TV room, summer lounge; terrace. 10-acre grounds with heated swimming pool. Tennis court planned for 1988. Fishing nearby. English spoken.
Location 1/2 m W of Brantôme, off D78.
Credit cards Access, Visa.
Terms B&B: double 420 frs, suite 600 frs. (No restaurant.)

BRINON-SUR-SAULDRE 18410 Cher — Map 10

Auberge de la Solognote — *Tel* 48.58.50.29
Grande Rue

This unremarkable village by a river, south-east of Orléans, stands on the edge of the strange haunting forests and marshlands of the Sologne. It is close to Alain-Fournier country – to his birthplace at La Chapelle-d'Angillon and the nearby château of Loroy that helped to inspire his novel *Le Grand Meaulnes. La Solognote*, outwardly unprepossessing, is in the village but quiet (a *Relais du Silence*), and all bedrooms face the little patio-garden at the back where drinks and breakfasts are served when it's fine. It is a typical down-to-earth country *auberge*, a bit cramped, with not much of a lounge, but it remains popular with readers, especially for the *nouvelle*-ish cuisine of owner/chef Dominique Girard, which wins a *Michelin* rosette and *Gault Millau toque* for such dishes as paupiette of quail with wild mushrooms. "There is a magical quality about this charming *auberge*, where the Girards are friendly and hospitable. Exquisite cooking, and a very comfortable dining room with rustic touches. The young waitresses were proper but sweet." "Our rooms were attractively furnished including on our bed the largest pillow (or was it the smallest duvet?) we have ever seen." (*H Michaels, Peter McLeod; endorsed this year by Carol E Lindenmeyr*)

Open All year, except Feb, 10 days in May, 10 days in Sept. Closed Wed, also Tue evening except July/Aug.
Rooms 13 rooms – all with bath or shower and telephone. 2 ground-floor rooms.
Facilities Salon, bar, dining room. Garden and terrace. Tennis 200 metres, bathing and sailing at nearby lake. English spoken.
Location 57 km SE of Orléans, on D923. Hotel is central.
Credit card Visa.
Terms Rooms 180-270 frs. Breakfast 30 frs. Set meals 140-200 frs; full alc 250 frs.

BRIOUDE 43100 Haute Loire — Map 10

Hôtel de la Poste et Champanne — *Tel* 71.50.14.62
1 Boulevard Docteur Devins

Midway between Le Puy and Clermont-Ferrand, Brioude is a good centre for touring the Massif Central. It is a market town with narrow medieval streets and a splendid 12th-century romanesque basilica. Here on a broader main street is this down-to-earth little hotel, run by the septuagenarian Albertine Barge. It was dropped from the Guide after what may have been a bad patch, and still today its "rough-and-ready atmosphere" may not appeal to those who expect fine frills. But recent visitors have urged re-instatement: "Inexpensive, comfortable and clean rooms with balconies in a modern annexe, dinner in the old building – excellent menus, tremendous verve and atmosphere." "Good plain meals with generous portions, but beware of the higher-priced menus." Both *Michelin* and *Gault Millau* award their "good value" red print for the cheaper menus (good local dishes such as potée de lentilles and tripoux d'Auvergne). (*G Heap, Peter Stattersfield*) The hotel has just been enlarged and modernised, and now has better lounge facilities.

Open All year. Restaurant closed Sun evening Nov–Apr.
Rooms 20 double – 14 with bath and shower; 2 with TV. 14 in annexe.
Facilities 2 lounges (1 with TV), bar with terrace, 4 dining rooms. Small garden. English spoken.
Location Central. Brioude is 69 km S of Clermont-Ferrand, on N102.
Credit cards None accepted.
Terms Rooms: 90-170 frs. Breakfast 18 frs. Half board 160 frs per person; full board 200 frs. Set lunch/dinner 60, 80 and 120 frs. Reduced rates for children.

CABRERETS 46330 Lot — Map 10

La Pescalerie — *Tel* 65.31.22.55

"Luxe, calme et volupté!" The delightful and ever-admired *Pescalerie* stands alone at the foot of a rocky hill, just outside the village. It is an 18th-century Quercy country house, restored and decorated in exquisite taste. A large semi-formal garden stretches away to the wooded banks of the Célé where you can swim if you wish and where jays call and kingfishers arrow through the shadows. "The atmosphere," says one reader this year, "is rather like that of an English country house hotel with splendid French overtones. We were all made so welcome by Hélène Combette and her surgeon husband. Our room was small but the cream marble bathroom was palatial. Food very good and different, and the ambience in the dining-room one of total enjoyment." "Our room prettily furnished with antiques." "Breakfast on the terrace, attended by a friendly cat, was a joy – fresh orange juice, honey in the comb." "The luxury of the bedrooms was almost sinful, the elegance of breakfast on the terrace under a huge magnolia tree, with oleanders in bloom, was unforgettable." One blot on this idyllic landscape: again this year we have received news of silly muddles over bookings. (*Angela and David Stewart, Mrs RB Richards, Mrs R Goeller, and others*)

Open 1 Apr–1 Nov.
Rooms 10 double – all with bath, telephone and TV.
Facilities Lounge with TV, bar, dining room; breakfast terrace. Garden leading to river with swimming, fishing, boating. English spoken.
Location 35 km from Cahors, 2.5 km after Cabrerets on D19 to Figeac.
Credit cards Amex, Diners, Visa.
Terms B&B: single 445 frs, double 570-640 frs; dinner, B&B: single 630 frs, double 940-1,010 frs. Set lunch/dinner 195 frs; full alc 290 frs. Special meals for children on request.

We don't lack *Michelin*-rosetted hotels in France but would be glad of more nominations at the more modest end of the price scale.

CABRIS 06530 Alpes-Maritimes — Map 11

Hôtel Horizon — *Tel* 93.60.51.69

Camus, Sartre, Leonard Bernstein and other luminaries have stayed at this modest creeper-covered auberge *on the edge of a famous and fashionable hill-village near Grasse. Fabulous views of hills and valley; lovely patio-garden; friendly and cultivated proprietor. But lounge and bedrooms are small and set meals unexciting. Open Apr–mid-Oct. 18 double rooms, 17 with bath and shower. B&B double 260-290 frs. Set meals 80 frs. Some recent criticisms: more reports needed.*

CAGNES-SUR-MER see HAUT-DE-CAGNES — Map 11

CAHORS 46000 Lot — Map 10

Hôtel Terminus — *Tel* 65.35.24.50

5 avenue Ch-de-Freycinet

The traveller from the north will feel that he has truly arrived in the Midi by the time he gets to Cahors, a pleasant and dignified old town of narrow streets and shady squares, built above a great loop of the river Lot. The *Terminus*, just across from the station, has been recommended this year and last as a pleasant and unpretentious hotel in the old French style, but well modernised, with an excellent restaurant. (*G Morrison, Lady Engle, John Cliffe, Anne Stott*)

Open All year.
Rooms 31 double – all with bath and/or shower and telephone.
Facilities Lift. Bar, TV room, restaurant; terrace. English spoken.
Location Central; near station. Parking.
Credit card Visa.
Terms Rooms 165-255 frs. Breakfast 23 frs. Set lunch/dinner 80, 160 and 220 frs; alc (excluding wine) 200-250 frs.

CALVI 20260 Corsica — Map 11

Hôtel Résidence "Les Aloës" — *Tel* 95.65.01.46

Quartier Donatéo

On a hill 1 kilometre outside this popular summer resort, an unpretentious modern hotel with erratic plumbing, small but attractive and comfortable rooms, and friendly staff. Some rooms have fine views of the bay; quieter rear ones face the maquis. *Terraces and garden; no restaurant, but there are plenty down town. Open end Apr–1 Oct. 26 rooms, all with bath and/or shower. B&B double 270-310 frs. No recent reports: more welcome.*

> If you have had recent experience of a good hotel that ought to be in the Guide, please write to us at once. Report forms are to be found at the back (or use your own stationery if you prefer). Procrastination is the thief of the next edition.

CAMBRAI 59400 Nord — Map 9

Hôtel Beatus — *Tel* 27.81.45.70
718 avenue de Paris — *Telex* 820211

A low white building set back from the road, a mile out of town on the N44 to Paris and St-Quentin. Quiet, comfortable and welcoming, with good service; rooms furnished in Louis XV/XVI styles; elegant little bar; good breakfast; parking easy. No restaurant, but there are several in town. 26 rooms, all with bath or shower. B&B double 245-320 frs. New nomination: more reports please.

CANDÉ-SUR-BEUVRON 41120 Loir-et-Cher — Map 10

Hostellerie de la Caillère — *Tel* 54.44.03.08
36 route des Montils

A restaurant-with-rooms in a Loire valley village near Blois, new to the Guide this year: "A wholly charming small country house, set in its own lovely garden. It is supervised carefully by a lady of taste; our room was beautifully furnished, and breakfast included brioches, yoghurt and fresh fruit."(*LW St John-Jones*) The renowned restaurant (where you can dine outdoors in summer) sounds controversial: *Michelin* this year has withdrawn its rosette, but *Gault Millau* has increased its rating from one red *toque* to two (for brochet aux morilles, pigeon rôti à l'ail doux, etc), so we should welcome *your* verdicts.

Open All year, except 15 Jan–1 March. Restaurant closed Wed.
Rooms 6 double – 2 with bath, 4 with shower.
Facilities Salon, 2 restaurants. Large garden and terrace. English spoken.
Location Candé is 14 km SW of Blois, S of Loire on road to Amboise; La Caillère is just E of village, on road to Les Montils.
Restriction Not suitable for ♿.
Credit cards All major cards accepted.
Terms B&B: 232 frs; dinner, B&B: 280 frs. Set lunch/dinner 120 frs; full alc 150 frs.

CAP D'ANTIBES 06600 Alpes-Maritimes — Map 11

Hôtel du Cap d'Antibes and Restaurant Eden Roc — *Tel* 93.61.39.01 — *Telex* 470763
Boulevard Kennedy

Not just a very famous hotel but a monument to Riviera social history. Ever since its opening in 1870 it has been the grandest and most stylish of all the Côte d'Azur's luxury palaces, and was the original for the Hôtel des Étrangers in Fitzgerald's *Tender is the Night*. Regular visitors ranged from Haile Selassie to Betty Grable, from JF Kennedy to GB Shaw, while Scott himself, champagne glass in hand, would watch his mad wife Zelda diving from the rocks beside the fabulous pool of the *Eden Roc*.

Not quite Guide material, you might think – and indeed we have only one recent report on this stately palace in its great park, secluded at the southern tip of the Côte's loveliest peninsula: "Impeccable. A grand high-ceilinged reception room with marble floors, tapestries and great bowls of roses. We weren't staying in one of the best rooms, our medium-sized one cost 1,400 francs a night but the staff showed no trace of condescension.

The room was charming and dignified, the bathroom was marble. The *Eden Roc*, the hotel's main restaurant, has a lounge decorated with *trompe l'oeil* paintings. Here the view of the coast, sea and islands is such a knockout that it hardly matters if the food fails to match its culinary pretentions (four red *couverts* in *Michelin*, but no rosette). And in any case, unlike other luxury hotels, you are not required to take a meal here. My only caveat is that the hotel does attract some doozies [*sic*] both British and American who talk in strident voices in the lounge. French and German guests may be as boring but at least they talk quietly." (*Carolyn Mathiasen*)

Open Apr–end Oct.
Rooms 10 suites, 100 double – all with bath and/or shower and telephone.
Facilities Lift. Reception, bar, restaurant with terrace; conference facilities. Large park with beach, swimming pool and tennis.
Location Near Pointe de l'Ilette. Parking.
Terms [1987 rates] Rooms: single occupancy 1,950 frs, double 2,400 frs. Breakfast 90 frs. Alc meals in *Eden Roc* (excluding wine) 350-450 frs.

CARCASSONNE 11000 Aude — Map 10

Domaine d'Auriac — *Tel* 68.25.72.22
Route St-Hilaire — *Telex* 500385

Set peacefully amid its own woods and vineyards, this imposing old creeper-covered mansion lies three kilometres out of hectic, dusty modern Carcassonne; only a motorway (out of earshot) separates it from the vast medieval hilltop fortress, magically floodlit at night. Approached down an impressive driveway, it is a beautiful house, well furnished, and has been praised again this year as "very enjoyable". An earlier view: "Our bedrooms were smallish but attractive, with balcony and view. Swimming pool and tennis court approached down lengthy flight of steps. Good restaurant: à la carte best. Superb local wines. All staff made us feel welcome." (*G Godfrey-Isaacs, Richard and Susan Faulkner*) Innovative cuisine (e.g. monkfish in vermouth) wins *Gault Millau* red *toque*. A blazing fire in winter in the dining room's huge chimney-piece.

Open All year except 10-31 Jan. Closed Sun evening and Mon midday 1 Oct–Easter.
Rooms 23 double – all with bath, telephone, radio, TV, tea-making facilities and baby-listening.
Facilities Lift. Salons, restaurant; conference facilities. Garden with unheated swimming pool and tennis court.
Location Leave *autoroute* (A61) by Carcassonne Ouest exit. 2.5 km SE of town by D118 and D104. Parking.
Credit cards All major cards accepted.
Terms [1987 rates] Rooms: single 480 frs, double 850 frs. Breakfast 40 frs. Set meals 160-210 frs. Special meals for children.

CARTERET 50270 Manche — Map 8

Hôtel de la Marine — *Tel* 33.53.83.31
11 Rue de Paris

Really good stopover places south of Cherbourg have tended to prove fickle in their standards, so readers have dealt with them fickly in turn, and the various entries have been ebbing and flowing in and out of the Guide like the spring-tides on this attractive west Normandy coast. But here at last, nominated this year, is a possible answer to our hopes – a sturdy family-run hotel by the sea, in a small resort and fishing-port with a direct ferry to Jersey and 37 kilometres south of Cherbourg. *Michelin* rosette and *Gault Millau toque*: excellent local fish dishes on the 85 franc and 135 franc menus. "Dinner was superb, rooms small but adequate; the well-furnished lounge overlooks the water, and there's a patio/balcony for drinks. Sand dunes within easy walk. We shall return – I can still smell that fish soup." (*IC Dewey*)

Open All year except 15 Nov–25 Dec.
Rooms 27 double, 1 single – all with bath and/or shower, direct-dial telephone and TV (with English programmes).
Facilities Salon, lounge, bar, dining room; terrace. English spoken.
Location In village of Carteret, which is part of Barneville-Carteret; 37 km S of Cherbourg.
Credit cards Access, Diners, Visa.
Terms Rooms: single occupancy 200 frs, double 250-350 frs. Breakfast 28 frs. Set lunch/dinner 85-260 frs.

CASTELPERS 12170 Aveyron — Map 10

Château de Castelpers — *Tel* 65.69.22.61

In deep countryside far from anywhere, ten kilometres off the main N88 from Rodez to Albi, an old stone mansion set in its own wooded park, turned into a small unpretentious hotel/restaurant by the family who have owned it for generations. Comfortable smallish bedrooms, total quiet, friendly welcome, good food. Open 1 Apr–1 Oct. 9 rooms all with bath or shower. B&B double 265 frs. Set meals 95–160 frs. New nomination: more reports welcome.

CAUDEBEC-EN-CAUX 76490 Seine-Maritime — Map 8

Le Normandie — *Tel* 35.96.25.11
19 quai Guilbaud

Caudebec, with its big 15th-century Gothic church, stands beside a great loop of the Seine between Le Havre and Rouen. Here this *Logis de France* stands on the banks of the river, with fine views: "It is more satisfactory in our experience than either of the other two *Michelin*-listed hotels in Caudebec" (both formerly listed here, but now dropped). "Excellent *prix fixe* dinner, with oysters as one of the starters. The kind of simple, modern, comfortable, unpretentious and wholly professional hotel/restaurant which Britain so singularly lacks but is still common enough in France. I have seen no explanation convincing to me as an economist why the French can make what appears to be a good living at these prices, whereas I scan every page of your UK section and find nothing that can begin to compare." (*Professor Alan Day*) And so say all of us.

Open All year except Feb. Restaurant closed Sun evening except holidays.
Rooms 15 double, 1 single – 3 with bath, 13 with shower, all with telephone and TV.
Facilities Salon, restaurant. English spoken.
Location Central. Parking.
Credit cards Access, Visa.

Terms Rooms: single 125 frs, double 170 frs. Breakfast 18.50 frs. Set lunch/dinner 50.20, 79 and 132 frs. Special meals for children.

CENTURI PORT 20238 Corsica — Map 11

Le Vieux Moulin — *Tel* 95.35.60.15

Cap Corse is one of the most scenic parts of the island, and near its northern tip is this attractive fishing-village where the characterful *Vieux Moulin* has a pleasant terrace with views. "A lovely, quiet, friendly hotel. The main house is decorated with guns, antiques etc. Bedrooms vary in size and type: those in bungalows by the terrace are fairly plain but very comfortable. The Corsican/French food is good value, and the local wines are cheap and very drinkable, especially the red. The stylish and somewhat Gauguinesque paintings on the walls are by the *patron*." A more recent visitor found those paintings "gloomy" but the food excellent. (*Joan Williamson, RG*)

Open 15 Apr–30 Oct.
Rooms 14 – all with shower.
Facilities Restaurant. Garden with tennis court.
Location Centuri Port is 59 km NW of Bastia.
Credit cards Amex, Diners, Visa.
Terms [1987 rates] Rooms: single 145 frs, double 160 frs; full board 255-265 frs per person. Breakfast 17 frs. Set lunch/dinner 95-180 frs.

CÉRET 66400 Pyrénées-Orientales — Map 10

La Terrasse au Soleil — *Tel* 68.87.01.94
Route de Fontfrède

In a splendid position in the Pyrenean foothills, south of Perpignan, a small modern hotel built in Catalan style; fine views of the mountains and distant sea from its terrace and pool. Friendly owners, relaxed atmosphere; attractive bedrooms, especially those in new annexe. Food variable. Open 20 Mar–3 Nov. 18 rooms, all with bath and/or shower. Half board: double 700 frs. Set meals 160 frs; they have been criticised: more reports please.

CHABLIS 89800 Yonne — Map 9

Hostellerie des Clos — *Tel* 86.42.10.63
Rue Jules Rathier

The former almshouse of this famous little north Burgundy wine town has just been converted by *patron*/chef Michel Vignaud into an elegant and select little restaurant-with-rooms, with the aim of its becoming a showcase and focal point for Chablis and its products. Within the space of two years he has won a *Michelin* rosette and *Gault Millau* red *toque* for his regional cooking (crayfish cooked in Chablis, kidneys and grapes cooked in chablis, etc) and now gets an entry into our Guide too: "Our best new find in France for some years," writes a connoisseur. "It's a restaurant that is totally professional, serving light creative cookery that perfectly complements the great wines of Chablis. The rooms are carefully decorated and furnished in the modern style. Lack of bidets and mirrors, and failure to replace blown light bulbs, indicates that the place was designed and is run by a restaurateur rather than a hotelier. But it is in a quiet position with a small neat garden and some swings." (*T Keniston*)

Open All year, except Jan. Closed Wed and Thur midday except 1 May–30 Sep.
Rooms 26 double – all with bath, telephone, radio, TV and baby-listening. Some specially adapted for ♿.
Facilities Lift. Hall, salons, bar, restaurant; garden restaurant. English spoken.
Location Central, parking. Chablis is 19 km E of Auxerre.
Credit cards All major cards accepted.
Terms Rooms: 178-305 frs. Breakfast 38 frs. Set lunch/dinner 130, 210 and 320 frs; full alc 300 frs. Extra bed for child 40 frs; special meals.

CHAGNY 71150 Saône-et-Loire — Map 10

Hôtel Lameloise — *Tel* 85.87.08.85
36 place d'Armes — *Telex* 801086

An elegantly converted 15th-century mansion, renowned for its cuisine which is arguably the best in Burgundy (three *Michelin* rosettes and three *Gault Millau* red *toques*). It stands in the main street of a dullish little town amid woods and vineyards. Returning visitors this year found a smart new modern lift to all floors and renovations in the bedrooms which are now very comfortable, with superb bathrooms. But they felt that the cuisine, though still good, was "not as brilliant as we have come to expect", nor the service so efficient, though still friendly. But this is to judge the place by the very high standards it has set itself. Others have spoken recently of "the best cuisine we've had in France", "elegant rooms, with antiques, beamed ceilings and fireplaces", "a quietly luxurious atmosphere, attentive and courteous service", and "the top *sommelier* of France, Georges Pertuiset, is a charming and modest man". (*Pat and Jeremy Temple; also Rosamund V Hebdon, and others*)

Open All year, except 21 Dec–21 Jan. Closed Wed and Thur midday.
Rooms 20 double – all with bath or shower, telephone and TV.
Facilities Lift. Salon, restaurant.
Location Central. Parking.
Credit cards Access, Visa.
Terms [1987 rates] Rooms: single 280 frs, double 750 frs. Breakfast 45 frs. Alc (excluding wine) 250-390 frs.

CHALLES-LES-EAUX 73190 Savoie — Map 10

Hôtel du Château — *Tel* 79.85.21.45

A restored 13th-century fortress, outside a small spa town south-east of Chambéry. Impressive entrance, large terrace with views, dull salon but cosy English-style bar. Rooms very modestly priced for a château hotel: those in annexe simplest, but comfortable. Attractive candle-lit restaurant with beamed ceiling and open fire: good, simple food, pleasantly served; nice atmosphere. Open 3 Feb–31 Oct. 63 rooms, most with bath or shower. B&B double 215-315 frs. Set meals 85-250 frs [1987]. New nomination: more reports welcome.

> If you have kept brochures and tariffs for foreign hotels, *please* enclose them with your reports.

CHÂLONS-SUR-MARNE 51000 Marne — Map 9

Hotel d'Angleterre and Restaurant Jacky Michel — *Tel* 26.68.21.51
19 place Monseigneur Tissier

Traditional hotel in the town centre, small but soignée, *praised for owner Jacky Michel's innovative cooking* (Gault Millau *red* toque). *Friendly staff, comfortable rooms, beautiful dining room, shady terrace with trees, where meals are also served. Closed 2–26 Jan, 20 Dec–3 Jan. 18 rooms, all with private facilities. Dinner, B&B 298–423 frs.*

CHALON-SUR-SAÔNE 71100 Saône-et-Loire — Map 10

Hôtel St-Georges — *Tel* 85.48.27.05
32 avenue Jean-Jaurès — *Telex* 800330

"A superb hotel. Rooms comfortable, spacious and air conditioned; excellent evening meal, one of the finest we've ever had in France." "A marvellous recommendation – a civilised hotel with tremendously friendly welcome, *un*patronising waiters, best dinner of our whole holiday." So run two reports this year on a place that is now an old favourite with readers – in the best French tradition, a commercial hotel next to the railway station in a biggish town, splendidly refreshing the parts (i.e. palates) of tired travellers that similar hotels in Britain so signally fail to reach. *Michelin* rosette, and *Gault Millau toque* for young Yves Choux's cooking, described as "non-eccentric *nouvelle*" (vinaigrette de rouget, poêlée d'escargots en meurette). (*RT Johnson, Mrs HR Jones; also DC Eastwood, and others*)

Open All year.
Rooms 48 – most with bath or shower, all with direct-dial telephone, TV, mini-bar and air-conditioning.
Facilities Lift. Bar with TV, restaurant; conference facilities.
Location Central, near railway station; parking.
Credit cards All major cards accepted.
Terms Rooms: single 195-270 frs, double 195-290 frs. Breakfast 30 frs. Set lunch 75 frs, dinner 250 frs (both plus 15% service charge); full alc 295 frs.

CHAMONIX 74400 Haute Savoie — Map 10

Aiguille du Midi — *Tel* 50.53.00.65
Les Bossons

Two miles outside Chamonix on the St-Gervais road, an attractive family-run holiday hotel with a flowery orchard/garden and splendid views of Mont Blanc. Affable service, good food, large rustic-style rooms, some with balcony. Large swimming pool, tennis court. Open 20 May–20 Sept, Easter and Christmas holidays. 50 rooms, most with bath or shower. B&B double 292 frs. Set meals 80-150 frs [1987]. *New nomination: more reports welcome.*

"It was the first time that I had had boiled potatoes in a restaurant that I was unable to cut with a knife."

Hôtel Albert Premier et de Milan *Tel* 50.53.05.09
Telex 380779
119 impasse du Montenvers

Apart from one sharp criticism of the food from veteran travellers, there has again this year been plenty of praise for this sizeable chalet-type ski-hotel, set in its own big garden near the middle of the resort: "Very professionally run, good atmosphere, good value." "A marvellous place with excellent food; our nice room had a view of Mont Blanc and we used the pool, jacuzzi, sauna." An earlier visitor found it "roomy and comfortable, full of well-heeled skiers enjoying their *après-ski*. Log fire and piano in the salon; huge bedrooms, with views from their windows of the white peaks all round. A large sophisticated dining room, and ambitious, interesting cooking by the son of the *patron*, Pierre Carrier" (*Michelin* rosette, two red *Gault Millau toques*). Several others have praised the food both for quality and quantity: but this year a reader found the 125 franc set *pension* menu very poor and lacking in choice. (*Tom and Linda Baldwin, John George, DE Jennings, Anthony Steen MP, and others*). When fine, it's well worth taking the téléphérique (the world's highest, they claim) to a point just below the summit of Mont Blanc.

Open All year, except 4–26 May, 12 Oct–4 Dec. Restaurant closed Mon out of season.
Rooms 2 suites, 31 double, 2 single – all with bath and shower, telephone, TV and mini-bar.
Facilities Lift. Bar, lounge, 3 dining rooms, table tennis room; sauna, whirl pool, solarium. Large garden with tennis court, swimming pool (heated in summer), children's play area. Winter sports, walking. English spoken.
Location In side road, 150 metres from station; 500 metres from town centre. Parking and garages.
Credit cards Amex, Diners, Visa.
Terms B&B: single 301-391 frs, double 361-542 frs, suite 652-722 frs; dinner, B&B 300-450 frs per person; full board 350-500 frs. Set meals 125 frs; full alc 300 frs. Reduced rates and special meals for children.

CHAMPAGNAC-DE-BELAIR 24530 Dordogne — Map 10

Moulin du Roc *Tel* 53.54.80.36
Telex 571555

Still one of the Guide's favourite places in rural France – a gracefully converted 17th-century walnut mill, with a quiet pastoral setting beside a stream, in a Périgord village north-east of the pretty little town of Brantôme. *Michelin* (two rosettes) and *Gault Millau* (three *toques*) have long considered that the cuisine of the owner's wife, Solange Gardillou, is as brilliant as any in this region: her forte is variations on local dishes, e.g. foie gras poêlé à la ciboulette. This, and the idyllic setting, have led the *Moulin* to be much publicised in the glossy press and the rich international tourists have arrived *en masse*, but our readers this year do not feel that ambience has suffered unduly: "Fabulous food, attentive service. Agreed, it's getting a bit conscious of its cult-status, but while standards don't drop, why shouldn't it?" And: "Despite extensions to the hotel and restaurant, there was no sign of an 'up-market tripper' atmosphere. M. Gardillou was still there in person, meeting and talking to guests, not off somewhere writing a book! His wife's cooking is as inventive as ever and the service was attentive, the waiters with eyes downcast like novices in a culinary convent." An earlier report: "Tiny hotel, small rooms, everywhere cluttered with flowers, *objets*, old walnut-mill equipment. Small sitting areas amid the museum pieces. Our room with four-poster bed, dim lights. Lots of small courses, even an extra pudding. Silver-tray breakfast: strawberries, home-made jams. View from our window of maids and waiters crossing the yard with plates and trays and chairs; rinsing a bin in the mill stream . . ." Bucolic this may seem, but ties must be worn at dinner. (*N French, DAC Cartwright; also Linda and Paul Duttenhaver, and others*)

Open All year except 15 Nov–15 Dec, 15 Jan–15 Feb. Restaurant closed all Tue and Wed midday.
Rooms 12 double – all with bath, telephone, radio and TV.
Facilities Salons, restaurant. Small garden. English spoken.
Location 6 km NE of Brantôme by D78 and D83. Parking.
Credit cards All major cards accepted.
Terms [1987 rates] Rooms: single 400 frs, double 600 frs. Breakfast 50 frs. Set lunch/dinner 190-250 frs.

CHAMPILLON 51160 Marne — Map 9

Hôtel Royal Champagne — *Tel* 26.51.11.51
Champillon, Épernay — *Telex* 830111

An 18th-century coaching-inn, smartly modernised, set on a hillside with sweeping views over the champagne vineyards and the Marne valley. It consists of a grand restaurant (*Michelin* rosette), and superior chalet accommodation in the grounds; most rooms, but not all, have their own veranda and view. But the views of our own readers are not unanimous. Some have written in warm praise of the food, the staff, the bedroom decor, the huge bathroom, the excellent breakfast. But others have criticised the mock-baronial decor and felt that the quality did not quite match the very high prices. More reports please. *Note:* Some front rooms may be a little noisy until traffic subsides.

Open All year except 3 weeks in Jan.
Rooms 23 suites – all with bath and/or shower, telephone, radio and private veranda; 3 with TV. All in bungalows.
Facilities Salon, TV room, bar, restaurant; conference/functions facilities. Park and garden. Tennis, riding, swimming pool and golf nearby. English spoken.
Location On N51, 7 km N of Épernay on road to Reims.
Credit cards Amex, Diners, Visa.
Terms [1987 rates] Rooms: single occupancy 370 frs, double 700 frs, suite 1,100-1,200 frs. Breakfast 35 frs. Set lunch/dinner 210-340 frs; full alc 350-450 frs. Reduced rates for children in parents' room; special meals.

CHÂTEAU-ARNOUX 04160 Alpes-de-Haute-Provence — Map 11

La Bonne Étape — *Tel* 92.64.00.09
Chemin du Lac — *Telex* 430605 BONETAP

Michelin has this year restored a second rosette, and *Gault Millau* continues to award three red *toques*, to this sympathetic family-run *auberge* that provides some of the best cooking in Provence, a mixture of the traditional and the inventive – gâteau de mostèle, pigeon aux gousses d'ail, and the local speciality, Sisteron lamb, whose subtle aromatic flavour comes from its being reared on the herbs of Provençal upland pastures. The little town is in a dull part of the Durance valley, and the inn stands on the main road from Grenoble into Provence – a rather cramped and unpromising setting (front rooms can be noisy). But it looks onto open hills and fields at the back, and this 17th-century coaching-inn has been converted into a stylish and very comfortable little hotel, owned and run by the delightful Gleize family who are strongly anglophile – father created the restaurant at the *Capital* in London, while son Jany worked at the *Connaught*. One couple "had an attractive bedroom in Louis XV style, with a balcony facing the hills, and enjoyed lazing on the pretty patio beside the swimming-pool". (*Hadley and Heather Buck; also Kitty and Art Chester, Jean Bates*)

Open All year except 3 Jan–15 Feb, and last week Nov. Closed Sun evening and Mon out of season.
Rooms 7 suites, 11 double – all with bath and shower, direct-dial telephone and radio; 12 with TV; some with balcony.
Facilities Salon, bar, 2 dining rooms; small conference room. Air-conditioning. Garden with heated swimming pool and patio. Lake 200 metres. English spoken.
Location Near centre of town, which is 14 km S of Sisteron; front rooms can be noisy. Garage and parking.
Credit cards All major cards accepted.
Terms [1987 rates] Room 360 frs, suite 650 frs. Breakfast 60 frs. Set lunch/dinner 190-400 frs.

CHÂTEAUNEUF-DU-PAPE 84230 Vaucluse — Map 11

Hostellerie Château des Fines Roches — *Tel* 90.83.70.23

A betowered and creeper-covered Gothic mansion, set on a hill above its own vineyards. Excellent food (Michelin *rosette*). *Comfortable bedrooms, lovely lounge, antique furniture – but the piped jazz and rock jars. Good breakfasts served on a terrace with splendid views. Closed Christmas–end Feb, and Sun and Mon out of season; restaurant closed Mon. 7 rooms, all with bath. B&B double 490-690 frs. Set meals 190 frs [1987]. No recent reports: more needed.*

CHÂTEAUNEUF-EN-AUXOIS 21320 Côte d'Or — Map 10

Hostellerie du Château — *Tel* 80.33.00.23

A friendly and charming little rural hotel, well modernised, in a picturesque medieval fortified hill-village west of Dijon. Very quiet (Relais du Silence). *Bedrooms small. Good Burgundian food served in beamed restaurant or in courtyard. Open 15 Mar–15 Nov. 19 rooms, all with bath and/or shower. B&B double 230-470 frs. Set meals 110-250 frs. No recent reports: more requested.*

CHÂTEAUNEUF-SUR-SARTHE 49330 Maine-et-Loire — Map 8

Hôtel de la Sarthe — *Tel* 41.69.85.29

1 rue du Port

This modest but pleasant little restaurant-with-rooms has long been popular with readers for its good food and the charm of its setting – when fine, grills are served on a terrace by the river. "A lovely little place built at the turn of the century, furnished in 17th-century style"; "my pretty room overlooked the river with its slow boats and relentless fishermen"; "the charming Houdebines and their staff gave us two excellent dinners." Rooms vary in quality (some are a little basic) and this year one visitor was put into more expensive rooms than those he had pre-booked. (*JF Holman, RD Gooder, endorsed this year by Brian Beves, Linda and Paul Duttenhaver*)

Open All year, except 15-31 Oct and 11-29 Feb. Restaurant closed Sun evening and Mon except July and Aug.
Rooms 7 double – 4 with bath, 2 with shower; 2 with TV.
Facilities Salon, bar, rustic dining room overlooking river; riverside terrace. Public swimming pool 1 km; tennis and fishing nearby. Some English spoken.
Location 31 km N of Angers. Hotel is near bridge. Parking.
Credit card Visa.
Terms Rooms 90-180 frs. Breakfast 18 frs. Set lunch/dinner 55, 80, 130 and 175 frs; full alc 180 frs.

CHAVOIRE 74290 Haute-Savoie — Map 10

Pavillon de l'Ermitage — *Tel* 50.60.11.09

Maurice Tuccinardi's distinguished and formally elegant restaurant-with-rooms occupies a white villa beside the lovely lake of Annecy, looking across to the town of that name three kilometres to the west. In summer you can dine by the water's edge on a smart terrace under the trees. The Bressane cooking is regarded as deserving its *Michelin* rosette and *Gault Millau toque*: "Excellent fish soufflé, guinea-fowl, etc. But little choice on the set menus. Most rooms face the lake and are quiet, with splendid views. Small garden by the lake." (*J and O Lloyd*)

Open 1 Mar–1 Nov.
Rooms 2 suites, 11 double – 10 with bath and shower, 9 with WC, all with telephone.
Facilities Lounge, bar, restaurant. Terrace and lakeside garden. English spoken.
Location 3 km E of Annecy on Lake Annecy, near *téléphérique*.
Restriction Not suitable for ♿.
Credit cards Amex, Diners, Visa.
Terms Double room with breakfast 330-370 frs; dinner, B&B 260-300 frs per person; full board 330-350 frs. Set lunch/dinner 150, 200 and 280 frs; full alc 250 frs.

CHEFFES 49125 Maine-et-Loire — Map 10

Château de Teildras — *Tel* 41.42.61.08, *Telex* 722268 TEILDRA

Cheffes is a peaceful and untrippery village on a pretty stretch of the river Sarthe, 19 kilometres north of Angers. *Teildras*, a graceful little 16th-century château, white-walled, grey-roofed, is the family home of the Comte de Bernard du Breuil, who some years ago decided that the best way to preserve his estate was to turn it into a hotel. This he has done, meticulously. You can ride, fish or go for walks in the large park. "A lovely place, excellent food, friendly service" and "magnificent atmosphere, delicious food", are recent verdicts, echoing earlier praise: "The public rooms are beautifully decorated with tapestries, paintings and plants, and the lighting is subdued. Our bedrooms had antiques and a beamed ceiling, the beds were comfortable, and our windows looked on to the park with its lovely trees and three cows munching in the sunlight." One recent visitor however thought the ambience pretentious and mercenary, and there has been some dissent about the cooking of the new young chef, François Pascal. (*Sandy Berkley, Arleigh and Diane Kerr, Gordon Bond, and others*)

Open 1 Apr–4 Nov. Restaurant closed Tue midday.
Rooms 11 double – all with bath, shower, telephone and TV.
Facilities 2 salons, 2 dining rooms; conference/functions facilities. Wooded park, river nearby: fishing, riding, boat hire. English spoken.
Location 19 km N of Angers; château is well signposted; turn out of Cheffes towards Juvardeil. Parking.
Credit cards All major cards accepted.
Terms [1987 rates] Rooms: single 390-710 frs, double 540-895 frs. Breakfast 50 frs. Set lunch/dinner 200-260 frs.

CHÊNEHUTTE-LES-TUFFEAUX 49350 Maine-et-Loire — Map 10

Hostellerie du Prieuré *Tel* 41.67.90.14
Telex 720379 PRIEURE

This smart and famous hostelry, once a priory dating from the 12th century, stands in a splendid position on a bluff above the Loire, amid 60 acres of private wooded park. Several recent visitors have praised it profusely. "The location is beautiful, the multiple terraces and flower-gardens are wonderful, and the staff are friendly and helpful. Not all bedrooms overlook the Loire, but ours did and the view was superb. The room itself was delightfully furnished with matching material, and well equipped: there was even a fly-spray, not in fact needed. The dining room and lounge also look over the river. Here the food (*Michelin* rosette, two red *Gault Millau toques*) was just a little 'over the top' and *too* highly priced: delicious, but fussily garnished, and helpings minute. This was the hotel's only major fault." Others however have found this *nouvelle*-ish *cuisine* "excellent". But on one occasion service slowed down when two busloads of tourists arrived for dinner. (*Dr TJ David; also Brian and Ruth Kenyon Glover, Kate and Steve Murray-Sykes, Group-Capt E Shipley*) It is well worth visiting the nearby caves in the tufa rocks. Some are used for growing mushrooms (300 tons per day!), some have ancient sculptures recently discovered, and some are still occupied as troglodyte dwellings (open to tourists).

Open 1 Mar–5 Jan.
Rooms 3 suites, 34 double, 2 single – all with bath, shower and telephone; 10 with TV. 15 in pavilion in park.
Facilities Lounge, bar with TV, restaurant. Large grounds with mini-golf, tennis court, heated swimming pool; fishing in the Loire. English spoken.
Location 7 km NW of Saumur off D751.
Restriction Not suitable for ♿.
Credit cards Access, Visa.
Terms B&B: single 502-602 frs, double 654-1,404 frs; dinner, B&B 540-590 frs per person. Set lunch/dinner 250-370 frs; full alc 400-600 frs. Reduced rates and special meals for children.

CHINON 37500 Indre-et-Loire — Map 10

Hôtel Diderot
4 rue Buffon — *Tel* 47.93.18.87

A lovely old town near the Loire, with a half-ruined fortified hilltop castle, where Joan of Arc first met the Dauphin. The *Diderot* is an unassuming bed-and-breakfast hotel of unusual charm, run by a friendly and helpful Cypriot, M. Kazamias, and his French wife, and this year it has continued its long run of popularity with readers. "Good value, and quiet. Excellent beds, newly-done tiled bathroom, quite luxurious; nice breakfast, especially the home-made jams." Earlier praise: "We were entranced by the the beauty and atmosphere. The staff were pleasant and helpful, and our bedroom windows opened onto the quiet courtyard." "A beautiful old pale stone building, much of it covered by a vine, with an enchanting wrought-iron balcony on the second floor, reached by a spiral staircase. Inside are exposed beams, and a pretty salon where we were offered Madame's 13 different home-made jams" (including green tomato with ginger, greengage with mint, apricot and myrtle). "We think courtyard-facing rooms are quieter, as the other side overlooks a road. Be warned, too, that rooms vary greatly in size." (*Betty Silander, Carol E Lindenmayr, D Dutton, and many others*)

Open All year.
Rooms 20 double, 2 single – 10 with bath, 12 with shower, all with telephone. 4 ground-floor rooms with bath suitable for ♿.
Facilities Lounge, salon with TV, breakfast room; limited conference facilities. Courtyard. English spoken.
Location Near place Jeanne d'Arc; hotel is well signposted. Parking in courtyard.
Credit cards Access, Visa.
Terms Rooms: single 110–210 frs, double 180–250 frs. Breakfast 20 frs. (No restaurant.)

Château de Marçay
Tel 47.93.03.47
Telex 751475 MARCAY

Quite a familiar species of hotel in this Loire Valley area – a 15th-century stone château with neat pepper-pot towers and formal garden, converted into a smart and stylish hotel, consecrated by *Michelin* with its full panoply of rosette, red gables and red rocking-chair. One reader has had reservations about the service and decor, but other recent visitors have been full of admiration."Set in open country four miles south of Chinon, and offering peace and comfort. We were captivated. Our room was large, with balcony, sitting-room recess with elegant chairs, magazines on the coffee table. The public rooms are gracefully furnished. An evening swim in the sheltered outside pool was followed by dinner by candlelight on the terrace: very good service, and food a mixture of *nouvelle* and traditional (e.g. foie gras de canard aux abricots secs)" (*DJS*) "Excellent food in charming restaurant." (*David Blum, Carol Lindenmeyr, and others*)

Open 10 March–31 December.
Rooms 4 suites, 32 double, 2 single – all with bath and/or shower and telephone; 12 with radio and TV. 11 in pavilion annexe.
Facilities 2 salons, TV room, bar, restaurant; 2 terraces; conference facilities. Night club at weekend. Gardens with tennis court and heated swimming pool. English spoken.

Location 7 km S of Chinon by D116.
Credit cards Amex, Visa.
Terms B&B: single 470-520 frs, double 615-1,150 frs, suite 1,045-1,280 frs. Set lunch/dinner 120-285 frs; full alc 300 frs.

CHONAS L'AMBALLAN 38121 Isère — Map 10

Domaine de Clairefontaine — *Tel* 74.58.81.52

This fine old stone house in splendid grounds makes a cheaper alternative to the *Marais St-Jean* (see below). It has an outdoor terrace, pretty dining room, good food, and has been recommended by a discerning francophile: "An ideal spot to break your journey, or for a longer stay to sample the many delights of the region. It has large and airy rooms, somewhat temperamental plumbing and lighting, and is reasonably priced. Interesting and well-presented food served in a *salle à manger* (rather than a restaurant), with somewhat stodgy atmosphere. Tennis court, but no pool. Expansive views across open fields." (*GS*) Another admirer of this family-run venture adds: "Sleep at the *Domaine* for peace, friendly service, solid comfort and excellent value; eat at the *Marais St-Jean* if you can afford it." (*Eileen Broadbent*) More reports would be welcome.

Open 1 Feb–15 Dec. Closed Sun evening and Mon midday out of season.
Rooms 18 double – 12 with bath, all with telephone; some with TV. 6 ground-floor rooms in annexe next to main building.
Facilities Salon, 2 dining rooms; terrace. Garden, tennis court. English spoken.
Location Off N7, 9 km S of Vienne; turn off A7 motorway at Vienne Sud. Parking.
Restriction Not suitable for ♿.
Credit card Visa.
Terms [1987 rates] Rooms: single 90 frs, double 250 frs. Breakfast 15 frs. Set lunch/dinner 80-200 frs.

Hostellerie Le Marais St-Jean — *Tel* 74.58.83.28

In pretty countryside above the Rhône valley south of Vienne, this is a big pink farmhouse, rather Provençal in style, converted into a stylish modern hotel by two enthusiasts, Christian and Suzette Heugas. Recently it has won fulsome praise from several readers. "Every course on the 165 franc [1987] menu was quite exquisite both in taste and presentation, including duck in a sharp fruit sauce and the prettiest and most interesting petits fours I've ever seen. The bedrooms are luxurious, the owners charming, and it was pleasant to sit in the hillside garden." "Outstanding. We had two beautiful rooms and the finest meal we had in France. Our teenage children had great fun with the owners' dogs." In their cool and sober dining room, with beamed ceilings and tiled floor, the Heugas provide enterprising dishes such as fresh frogs with chives and raspberry soufflés. (*RNH Robertson, Mrs D Curtis, and others*) One correspondent reported a disastrous dinner – the worst meal of their holiday. The chef's night off? More reports welcome.

Open All year except 2–10 Nov, Feb, Tue evening and Wed.
Rooms 10 double – all with bath, shower and direct-dial telephone. 1 ground-floor room with easy access.

Facilities 2 salons, bar, restaurant; conference room. Garden with terrace for alfresco meals. English spoken.
Location Off N7, 9 km S of Vienne; turn off A7 motorway at Vienne Sud.
Credit cards All major cards accepted.
Terms B&B: single 455 frs, double 490 frs. Set lunch/dinner 120-270 frs; full alc 230 frs. Reduced rates and special meals for children.

CLUNY 71250 Saône-et-Loire — Map 10

Hôtel de Bourgogne — *Tel* 85.59.00.58
Place de l'Abbaye

The old town of Cluny contains the remains of the mighty Romanesque abbey that in the Middle Ages was one of Europe's leading religious, artistic and intellectual centres. Today little of it remains; but the medieval town of narrow streets is still well worth a visit. The *Bourgogne* stands in the main square facing the abbey – a dignified old mansion that has been an inn since the 18th century (Lamartine often stayed here and guests can still sleep in his bed). Most of the bedrooms look out onto green hills or to the towers of the abbey.

One reader this year was sharply critical of food, service and management, but most others remain enthusiastic about the Gosse family owners, the food (*Michelin* rosette) and the decor: "A rambling old hotel, well run with a courteous staff; our top-floor room was the size of a small flat." "About the best meal we had in two weeks in France, notably the foie de veau au vinaigre de framboise." (*Brian Beves, Mrs EH Prodgers, and others*)

Open 10 Mar–15 Nov. Closed Tue except holidays.
Rooms 2 suites, 13 double, 1 single – 11 with bath, 4 with shower, all with telephone.
Facilities Salon with TV, bar, restaurant. Small courtyard where drinks and breakfasts are served in fine weather. English spoken.
Location On N79, 27 km from Mâcon. Hotel is opposite the abbey (back rooms quietest). Garage parking
Restriction Not suitable for ♿.
Credit cards Amex, Diners, Visa.
Terms Rooms: single 170 frs, double 330 frs, suite 980 frs. Breakfast 32 frs. Set lunch 140, 180 and 280 frs, dinner 180, 280 and 320 frs. Reduced rates for children; special meals.

LA COLLE-SUR-LOUP 06480 Alpes-Maritimes — Map 11

Hostellerie de l'Abbaye — *Tel* 93.32.66.77
Route de Grasse — *Telex* 462304

This hulking 12th-century monastic abbey, with vaulted 10th-century chapel attached, has been carefully converted into yet another of those sophisticated little luxury hotels that crowd the lyrically lovely but sadly over-built hinterland of Nice and Cannes. It is only a few minutes' drive (traffic jams permitting) from the Galérie Maeght at St-Paul-de-Vence and the Renoir museum below Haut-de-Cagnes, and it comes new to the Guide this year: "Tremendous atmosphere, romantic and very Provençal, magical central courtyard. All rooms different with interesting views and good modern bathrooms. Food can be excellent and imaginative, but drinks not cheap and service can be erratic. Many of the staff are women with strikingly good looks." Beamed ceilings, and a large shady patio for summer dining. (*Paul Dwyer*) More reports welcome.

Open 1 Mar–1 Jan.
Rooms 13 double, 1 single – all with bath and/or shower, telephone, radio and TV. All in 3 separate buildings.
Facilities 2 salons, 2 dining rooms, chapel. Courtyard. Garden with swimming pool. English spoken.
Location On Grasse road outside village of La Colle, which is 3 km SW of St-Paul-de-Vence, 10 km W of Nice airport.
Restriction Not suitable for ♿.
Credit cards Amex, Diners, Visa.
Terms Rooms: single 300-520 frs, double 460-720 frs. Breakfast 40 frs. Set lunch 120-180 frs, dinner 180-250 frs; full alc 300 frs. Reduced rates for children.

COLLIOURE 66190 Pyrénées-Orientales — Map 10

Hôtel Madeloc — *Tel* 68.82.07.56
Rue Romain-Rolland

The famous and picturesque fishing-port-cum-trendy-resort of Collioure, south-east of Perpignan, is mainly for those who really enjoy noise and bustle – at least in high season. But ten minutes' walk up a steepish hill, away from the hurly-burly, is this Guide newcomer, a cool white-walled hotel in local Catalan style with a spacious foyer: "We had a delightfully warm welcome, and our third-floor room had a balcony with table, chairs, umbrella and a view over the hills, so that we could enjoy the sunset and watch the various floodlit towers light up. A rosebud in a vase was a nice touch. Bathroom efficient; breakfast run-of-the-mill; no lift, so the ascent to the scenic top-floor rooms could be taxing. Quiet apart from distant traffic hum." (*Mrs RB Richards*) No restaurant, but there are lots down town.

Open 1 Apr–15 Oct.
Rooms 4 trible, 17 double – 10 with bath, 11 with shower, all with telephone, baby-listening and balcony or terrace.
Facilities Salons, TV room. Garden, terrace. Beach 600 metres. English spoken.
Location 10 mins walk from centre; turn right off avenue Maillol; parking.
Restriction Not suitable for ♿.
Credit cards Diners, Visa.
Terms Rooms 175-280 frs. Breakfast 28 frs. Reduced rates for children. (No restaurant.)

COLLONGES-LA-ROUGE 19500 Corrèze — Map 10

Relais de St-Jacques de Compostelle — *Tel* 55.25.41.02

A very beautiful 16th-century village, built of local purple-red stone, carefully restored, set in lush green valleys a few miles north of the Dordogne. It was used as a weekend retreat by the courtiers of the Vicomte de Turenne, former lord of the region, whose ruined château stands just to the west. Many fine buildings, including a 12th-century church. The *Relais*, modest and simple but "delightful and friendly", is again praised this year, especially for the warm welcome by M. Castèra and his wife and for the qualities of his cuisine (*Michelin* red "R") – "Generous helpings, incredible value – trout, duck with peaches, good cheeses and profiteroles on the 74-franc menu." "Bedroom small, but very clean and bright, with charming view over orchards." "M. Castèra loves to chat with his guests after dinner, even if their French is poor." One reader comments on "a shortage of lavatories". (*Mr and Mrs Bernard Dunstan, A Morris, K and N Varley, and others*)

Open 1 Feb-1 Dec, Wed Oct–Mar.
Rooms 11 double, 1 single – 7 with bath and/or shower, all with telephone. 5 in annexe.
Facilities Salon, bar, 2 dining rooms, dining terrace. English spoken.
Location 21 km SE of Brive; follow signs to Meyssac. Hotel is central. Parking.
Restriction Not suitable for ♿.
Credit cards Amex, Visa.
Terms Rooms: single 80 frs, double 90 frs; dinner, B&B: single 150 frs, double 140-190 frs. Set lunch/dinner 70-190 frs; full alc 230 frs. Reduced rates for children.

COLROY-LA-ROCHE 67420 Bas-Rhin — Map 9

Hostellerie La Cheneaudière — *Tel* 88.97.61.64
Telex 870438 CHENEAU

"A delightful experience" is a verdict this year on this imposing and luxurious modern hostelry, built in local chalet style and set amid wooded hills on the edge of a flowery Alsatian village. A winding hill-road takes you in a few minutes to such places as Riquewihr and Colmar. "Magnificent bathroom (circular bath), service friendly, food splendid and plentiful" (two *Michelin* rosettes, two *Gault Millau toques*). An earlier account: "Very superior and most enjoyable, this 'Oak Grove'. The decor verges on kitsch-de-luxe, but the rooms are comfortable, and the hotel is run with superb professional self-confidence by a stylish and friendly Lorrain family, the François. Their young son-in-law, Jean-Paul Bossée, provides cooking that we found delicious and inventive without being chi-chi: from the à la carte menu we especially enjoyed the ris de veau and the unusual tartare of diced raw salmon. Very sophisticated restaurant; service assured but slowish. A notable feature is the copious help-yourself breakfast, including smoked ham, cheese, eggs, cereals, fruit salad – most un-French. Nice sunny terrace for drinks, but garden minimal for so posh a place." (*DW Tate, Pat and Jeremy Temple, JA*)

Open 1 Mar–31 Dec.
Rooms 4 suites, 23 double – all with bath and shower, telephone, radio, TV and terrace (suites have mini-bar and video). Some ground-floor rooms.
Facilities Salon, bar, 2 restaurants. Garden with children's play area; outdoor meals in fine weather. English spoken.
Location 62 km SW of Strasbourg on N420. Parking.
Credit cards All major cards accepted.
Terms B&B: double 609-871 frs, suite 976-1,386 frs; dinner, B&B 525-662 frs per person; full board 735-872 frs. Full alc 350-400 frs.

> Don't let old favourites down. Entries are dropped when there is no endorsement.

> Deadlines: nominations for the 1989 edition should reach us not later than 1 May 1988. Latest date for comments on existing entries: 1 June 1988.

COMPIÈGNE 60200 Oise — Map 9

Hostellerie du Royal-Lieu *Tel* 44.20.10.24
9 rue de Senlis

Joan the Maid was captured and sold to the English in this historic town with its huge royal palace; then first the Germans in 1918 and later the French in 1940 signed ignominious armistices in a clearing in the nearby forest. In today's age of EEC amity British, French and German tourists rub shoulders in this very pleasant hostelry just outside the town. "That rare thing, a good first-night stop in France that seems not to have been discovered by motorists coming from the Channel ports. The road is unattractive and full of traffic, but at the back all is different: the bedroom wing has a flowery lawn on one side and a vegetable garden on the other. The rooms are cool, comfortable and simply furnished – they bear names like 'Madam Butterfly' instead of numbers, but nothing else is gimmicky. The staff are friendly and the food is outstandingly good." "Nice rooms, a lovely dinner, and superb raspberry juice and coffee at breakfast," runs a 1987 endorsement. Spacious outdoor terrace for dining in fine weather. (*Jean Rowntree, Mrs EH Prodgers*)

Open All year.
Rooms 3 suites, 15 double – all with bath, direct-dial telephone and TV. 1 ground-floor room suitable for ♿.
Facilities Salon, bar, restaurant; terrace for meals in fine weather. Garden. English spoken.
Location 3 km SW of town, on Senlis road (D932A).
Credit cards All major cards accepted.
Terms Rooms: double 275 frs, suite 385 frs. Breakfast 25 frs. Set lunch/dinner 180 and 230 frs; full alc 350 frs.

CONDRIEU 69420 Rhône — Map 10

Hôtellerie Beau Rivage *Tel* 74.59.52.24
Telex 308946 BORIVAG

An old family hotel beside the *beau rivage* of the Rhône, in Côte du Rhône vineyard country. In summer you can take drinks under white parasols on the "wonderful" terrace right by the river, or dine out on the stone-flagged patio. "The most considerate luxury – everything is done with good humour," runs a report this year. "It's a real bargain, and the demi-pension allows you to eat anything on the *carte* at the price of the cheapest menu." But this is no cut-price place: it wins two *Michelin* rosettes and two *Gault Millau toques* for the "excellent" cooking of *patronne*/chef Paulette Castaing (e.g. fish with ginger, onions with chanterelles). One English food writer was much disappointed, but others are still full of praise. "A nice bedroom with interesting antique furniture." "Our spacious and comfortable room had its own terrace with view of the river (petro-chemical works half a mile away)." (*Paul Cheshire, Mrs EH Prodgers, and others*)

Open All year except 5 Jan–15 Feb.
Rooms 4 suites, 22 double – all with bath and/or shower, direct-dial telephone, radio and TV. Some in separate building opposite. 1 ground-floor room.
Facilities Salon, bar, dining room; conference/banqueting facilities; terrace restaurant overlooking the Rhône. Garden by river, fishing. Swimming 2 km.

Location 40 km S of Lyon. Leave A7 at Condrieu exit (coming from N), or Chanas exit (coming from S). Condrieu is on N86.
Restriction Not suitable for ♿.
Credit cards All major cards accepted.
Terms [1987 rates] (Excluding 15% service charge) B&B: single 245–295 frs, double 500–570 frs, suite 740 frs; dinner, B&B: single 640 frs, double 1,190–1,260 frs, suite 1,430 frs. Set lunch/dinner 180–265 frs.

CONQUES 12320 Aveyron — Map 10

Hôtel Sainte-Foy — *Tel* 65.69.84.03

The famous old village of Conques lies between Figeac and Rodez and was a leading staging-post on the pilgrimage to Santiago. It straggles along a steep wooded hillside above a gorge, and its slate-roofed houses and cobbled streets surround a massive and awesome abbey church, famous for the masterly Romanesque stone carving on the west doorway and for its rich gold and silver treasure. The *Sainte-Foy* is called after the martyred girl whose weird gold relic is still to be seen in the abbey museum. It's a fine medieval house, facing the abbey, with a shaded courtyard in the rear and handsome old furniture in the public rooms. Again in 1986/7 it has remained popular with readers – "restful atmosphere, good food and service"; "a delightful place to stay"; "very comfortable". The food has long enjoyed a well-merited *Michelin* red "R" for good value: try the local Rouergue dishes such as crêpes aux herbes. Not a place for an extended stay, but Conques itself is so remarkable, especially in the evening when the abbey is floodlit and the sightseers have gone. Readers warn that some rooms are small (but well fitted, apart from one account of a sagging bed) and that church clocks can be irritating at night. (*Jane and William Dorrell, JM Chandler, FR Hilborne, and many others*)

Open 1 Apr–1 Nov.
Rooms 18 double, 2 single – all with bath and/or shower, and telephone.
Facilities Reading room, TV room, bar, dining room; interior patio. English spoken.
Location Off D601 and not far from N662 between Figeac (54 km) and Rodez (37 km). Hotel is central, opposite cathedral. Garage and car park.
Restriction Not suitable for ♿.
Credit card Visa.
Terms [1987 rates] B&B: 162–212 frs. Set lunch 98 frs, dinner 160 frs; full alc 180 frs.

CORDES 81170 Tarn — Map 10

Hôtel Le Grand Écuyer — *Tel* 63.56.01.03

Rue Voltaire

The old fortified village of Cordes was built by the Counts of Toulouse in the 13th century as a defence against Simon de Montfort and his anti-Albigensian crusade. With its ramparts, ancient houses and museums, it sits on a high spur above a valley north-west of Albi (Cordes-in-the-sky, it is called). The *Grand Écuyer*, a former hunting-lodge of Raymond, Count of Toulouse, is now a very select little hotel in the village, with distinguished antique furniture and spacious bedrooms, many with four-poster beds. It is known above all for its cuisine which tends towards the *nouvelle* (oeufs de caille au foie gras, salade de rougets) and wins a rosette from *Michelin* and two red *toques* from *Gault Millau*. "The staff are courteous and well trained, each meal was a delight, and our bedroom with its high beamed ceiling looked over the red roofs of Cordes and the green rolling country beyond." So runs a recent report, backing up an earlier one: "An outstanding hotel. The chef is one of France's first 50. The sweets are inspired." (*Rosamund V Hebdon, CN Janson*)

Open 1 Apr–end Oct. Restaurant closed Mon Apr–Jun, Sept–Oct.
Rooms 15 double – all with bath and telephone; some with 4-poster.
Facilities 2 lounges, bar, 3 dining rooms. English spoken.
Location In centre of village which is 25 km NW of Albi. Parking nearby.
Restriction Not suitable for ♿.
Credit cards Access, Amex, Visa.
Terms [1987 rates] Rooms: 300–550 frs. Breakfast 40 frs. Set lunch/dinner 160–310 frs; full alc 250–300 frs.

CORDON 74700 Haute-Savoie — Map 10

Hôtel des Roches Fleuries — *Tel* 50.58.06.71

A pleasant, spacious and informal chalet-style hotel, in a small ski-resort west of Chamonix. All rooms have a balcony, many with splendid grandstand view of Mont Blanc. Fondue party and dancing once a week; garden with chalet-bar; swimming pool. New owners: first reports on their food and service are positive. Open 19 Dec–30 Sept. 29 rooms, all with bath or shower. B&B: double 336 frs. Set meals 120–220 frs. More reports welcome.

CORPS-LA-SALETTE 38970 Isère — Map 10

Hôtel de la Poste — *Tel* 76.30.00.03
Place de la Mairie

A village near the summit of a zig-zag section of the N85 Grenoble to Gap highway in the Dauphiné Alps. This is the Route Napoléon, and here Bonaparte rested on his triumphant journey from Elba to Paris and then on to Waterloo. Today many tourists trek this way too, on their way to or from Provence, and might well be glad to rest at the *Poste*, recommended again this year, above all for its "richly deserved" *Michelin* red "R" for good value. "On the 100 franc menu [1987] we enjoyed a large tray of hors d'oeuvre, cold salmon, very good wild duck with delicious gratin dauphinoise, expertly cooked raspberry tart and delicious mini-profiteroles. Our room was fair sized, with unremarkable furniture, but its walls were covered in gold silk damask and the shower room was all new in lilac pink with gold taps." (*Kay and Neville Varley*) Nearby, the famous Pont du Sautet spans the deep Drac gorge.

Open 15 Jan–15 Nov.
Rooms 24 double or triple – 20 with bath, shower and telephone; 4 with radio and TV. 4 in annexe opposite.
Facilities Salon with TV, bar, restaurant. Lake 1 km, with sailing and fishing. English spoken.
Location In centre of village. Garage parking.
Credit cards Access, Visa.
Terms B&B: single 185 frs, double 230-250 frs; dinner, B&B 240-250 frs per person; full board 280-350 frs. Set meals 75-100 frs; full alc 150 frs.

COTIGNAC 83850 Var — Map 11

Hostellerie Lou Calen

1 cours Gambetta — *Tel* 94.04.60.40 — *Telex* 400287

Cotignac, in the hills of the Var hinterland, is oddly situated at the foot of a brown cliff holed with caves, some of them once lived in. Potters and other craftsmen abound in the village, and their wares are on sale. The *Lou Calen* (Provençal for "the place of the oil-lamp") remains popular – an admirable little family-run hotel, very friendly, with rooms furnished in local country style and modern plumbing. You eat on a beautiful terrace with a wide view, and here the Provençal cooking is always reliable and sometimes excellent: one reader enthuses over the "fantastic array of help-yourself hors d'oeuvre with delicious dressings", another over the "pieds et paquets and sinful great hunks of tarte aux fraises on the 80-franc menu [1986]". Large swimming pool (sometimes out of action) reached through an exquisite garden filled with exotic plants. Only drawback: some traffic noise at night, heard in front rooms. Much of interest to visit in the area: the majestic Gorges du Verdon, the lovely Cistercian abbey of Thoronet and, less well known, the château at Entrecasteaux, housing a most original museum created by the Scottish surrealist artist/diplomat, the late Ian McGarvie-Munn. (*Kay and Neville Varley, Eileen Broadbent, NH Robertson, and others*)

Open 26 Mar–2 Nov. Restaurant closed Wed in low season.
Rooms 7 suites, 8 double – 15 with bath, 1 with shower, all with telephone; 8 with TV. 2 suites in garden annexe.
Facilities Salon with TV, bar, 2 restaurants; conference facilities. Garden with terrace and swimming pool. English spoken.
Location On Route des Gorges du Verdon. For Cotignac take exit Brignoles or Le Luc-Toulon off N7. Central (3 rooms might have traffic noise). Parking.
Credit cards All major cards accepted.
Terms Rooms 184-398 frs. Breakfast 29 frs. Set lunch/dinner 90-200 frs; full alc 250 frs. Reduced rates for children sharing parents' room; special meals.

COULANDON 03000 Allier — Map 10

Le Chalet

Tel 70.44.50.08

More tributes have arrived this year for this former hunting lodge set peacefully (it is a *Relais du Silence*) in its own spacious park with a pond full of fish. Offering rural tranquillity at modest prices, it stands half-way between the market town of Moulins and the village of Souvigny with its fine priory church. "Good value in the old style; a lush pastoral setting with nightingales." "Excellent value, lovely grounds with a lake; some rooms have exposed beams." "A very restful and pretty hotel. The staff very pleasant and the food good, and there is a comfortable library" (what a rarity in a modest French hotel). Breakfasts however have been criticised and one reader found the food dull. The wall fabrics of some rooms are said to be amazing. (*JP Berryman, David Wurzel and others*)

Open 1 Feb–31 Oct. Restaurant closed midday.
Rooms 21 double – all with bath and/or shower, telephone and mono TV.
Facilities Lounge, dining room with terrace; functions room. Large park with pond. English spoken.
Location 6 km W of Moulins, down side-road just off D945 towards Savigny.
Credit cards All major cards accepted.

Terms Rooms: single occupancy 145 frs, double 185 frs. Breakfast 20 frs. Set lunch/dinner 70 and 110 frs; full alc 150 frs.

COULON 79510 Deux-Sèvres — Map 10

Au Marais *Tel* 49.35.90.43
46-48 quai Louis-Tardy

"The Poitevin is a low marshy region inland from La Rochelle, bisected by numerous canals. Here the 'Venise Verte' has become sadly decadent and depopulated, with the smaller waterways falling into disrepair through neglect; the local punts, once the sole means of transport, are now used to carry tourists. But *Le Marais* is delightful – a simple two-storey whitewashed building in local style, run by a young couple, the Mathés (he cooks, she serves). All rooms are furnished in rustic wooden style with folkweave curtains, but with modern bathrooms. Ours was cosy and quiet, attractive in its simplicity and clean and sparkling. Breakfast came with good strong coffee. The restaurant, on two floors in the house opposite, is spacious, with exposed beams, a wrought-iron staircase and tiled floors. The food, leaning towards *minceur*, was very good and not pricey: on the most expensive menu [110 francs in 1987], we enjoyed moules florentine, an exquisite feuilleté de boudin noir, very fresh goat's cheeses and a superb hot apricot tart. The place was amazing value." (*Francine and Ian Walsh*)

Open All year. Restaurant closed 21 Dec–31 Jan and Sun evening, also Mon except July and Aug.
Rooms 11 double – all with bath, shower, telephone and TV.
Facilities Salon with TV, restaurant. English spoken.
Location From Niort follow signs for Marais Poitevin; hotel is on the river.
Restriction Not suitable for ♿.
Credit card Visa.
Terms Rooms: single occupancy 175–225 frs, double 199–249 frs. Breakfast 20 frs. Dinner, B&B: single 298–343 frs, double 438–488 frs. Set lunch/dinner 70 and 130 frs; full alc 220 frs.

CRÈCHES-SUR-SAÔNE 71680 Saône-et-Loire — Map 10

Hostellerie du Château de la Barge *Tel* 85.37.12.04

Just off the N6 south of Mâcon, a handsome creeper-covered 18th-century mansion, now a traditional family-run hotel, slightly old-fashioned but comfortable; quietly set in its own large well-kept garden, away from the road. Friendly service, prettily decorated bedrooms, set menus with a good choice. Closed 20 Dec–5 Jan, 23 Oct–6 Nov. 23 rooms, most with bath or shower, 150-220 francs. Set meals 70–155 frs. New nomination: more reports please.

DÉGAGNAC 46340 Lot — Map 10

L'Auberge sans Frontière *Tel* 65.41.52.88

Unspoilt rural simplicity in the heart of the Dordogne/Lot area. South-west of Gourdon, Dégagnac is "a quiet sleepy village surrounded by woods, hoopoes and flowers – lovely walking country". And the *auberge*:

"A village *logis* with simple but comfortable rooms furnished most charmingly. Excellent *pension* rates and so cheap that everyone comes again. Madame Hauchecorne speaks good English and is delightful, helpful, and an exciting chef, with husband and friends helping out. The bar-cum-dining room welcomes locals, kittens and bar footballers – *sans frontière*!" (*Heather Dauncey, endorsed this year by A Frank*) Madame writes to us: "Our hotel is the family type, and we need people trying to mix with the life of the village." This is not just sales talk, for one couple report: "As we were the only guests, we were asked by our hosts to join them for an afternoon's grape-picking in a nearby farm. After a few hours' easy and sociable work, all 15 of us adjourned to the farmhouse for dinner, where we were treated as honoured guests by people we had never met before. That's *entente cordiale*! The hotel's only snag: our bed was the squeakiest we have ever slept in . . . and we were on our honeymoon." (*Mike and Sally Hardy*)

Open All year except 19-29 Oct, end Nov–end Dec. Closed Mon in winter.
Rooms 1 4-bedded, 6 double, 2 single – 1 with bath, 5 with shower (no private WC).
Facilities Bar, 3 dining rooms; patio for drinks. Fishing nearby. English spoken.
Location Dégagnac is on main Cahors/Sarlat road, 10 km SW of Gourdon (*Michelin* map 79). Hotel is central. Parking in village square.
Credit card Diners.
Terms B&B 85-75 frs. Set lunch/dinner 42-105 frs; full alc 110 frs. Half and full board rates (3 nights min). 1-night bookings sometimes refused in high season. Cookery lessons. Children under 6 half price; special meals.

DIEPPE 76200 Seine-Maritime — Map 9

Hôtel de l'Univers — *Tel* 35.84.12.55
10 boulevard de Verdun — *Telex* 770741

Facing Dieppe's elegant esplanade, this solid hotel with old-fashioned virtues remains popular with readers on their way to or from Newhaven. Rooms at the back are quieter (as well as cheaper) than front ones with balcony and sea views. The restaurant is quite good, not more, but possibly the best buy in a town short of good eating-places. Several reports comment on the courtesy and helpfulness, but some rooms are said to be shabby: "To prevent rattling, our window shutter had been wedged by a page of the *Guardian* from 1952." The *Manchester Guardian*, surely? (*Colin Pilkington, Shirley and Alan Day, and others*)

Open All year except 10 Dec–5 Feb.
Rooms 28 – all with bath or shower, telephone and TV; some with balcony.
Facilities Lift. Restaurant; conference facilities.
Location Central, near casino. Parking.
Credit cards All major cards accepted.
Terms [1987 rates] Rooms: single 215 frs, double 375 frs. Breakfast 30 frs. Full board 325-490 frs per person. Set lunch/dinner 90-185 frs.

> When hotels have failed to return their questionnaire, we have quoted 1987 prices, with a note to that effect.

> If you have difficulty in finding hotels because the location details given in the Guide are inadequate, please help us to improve directions next year.

DIGOIN 71160 Saône-et-Loire — Map 10

Hôtel Commerce et Diligences — *Tel* 85.53.06.31
14 rue Nationale

"Exceptional value: the food was wonderful, everything was spotlessly clean, bedrooms were small but adequate." So runs a report this year on this classic hostelry, which keeps up the old solid traditions even though Peugeots and Audis have now replaced the eponymous stagecoaches in its courtyard. "Things so often lacking today in French hotels here stand out in contrast – thick, plentiful towels, the delightful breakfast tray, the help with luggage. Some older bedrooms need modernising – but they are inexpensive. In the charming beamed dining room Felix Beck's food is beautifully prepared and served and well deserves its *Michelin* rosette." (*RCJ Gordon, Norman Brangham*) The hotel prefers its guests to dine there. Digoin, on the upper Loire, is only nine kilometres from the majestic 12th-century basilica at Paray-le-Monial.

Open All year except 2-11 May, 3 Nov–4 Dec; closed Mon evening and Tue.
Rooms 10 double – 3 with bath, 5 with shower, all with telephone.
Facilities Salon with TV, dining room. Courtyard.
Location Central, between the church and the Loire (quietest rooms overlook courtyard). Digoin is on N79 between Moulins (60 km) and Mâcon (80 km). Parking.
Credit cards All major cards accepted.
Terms Rooms: single occupancy 100 frs, double 120 frs. Breakfast 25 frs. Set lunch/dinner 80, 110, 180, and 270 frs; full alc 300-350 frs. Reduced rates and special meals for children.

DINAN 22100 Côte-du-Nord — Map 8

Hôtel d'Avaugour — *Tel* 96.39.07.49
1 place du Champs-Clos

A spacious Breton mansion, comfortable and characterful, on the summit of the ramparts in this handsome medieval hilltop town. Front rooms can be noisy: rear ones are quieter and look over the hotel's lovely flower garden. Dining room with outdoor terrace. But the cooking does not always live up to its reputation (two red Gault Millau toques), *and despite the beauty of the hotel and its setting, the bedroom upkeep and service continue to provoke controversy. 27 rooms, all with bath and shower. B&B double 350-410 frs. Set meals 90–140 frs. More reports badly needed.*

DOMME 24250 Dordogne — Map 10

Hôtel l'Esplanade — *Tel* 53.28.31.41

"Domme, overlooking the Dordogne valley, is tastefully restored, in the tradition of Viollet-le-Duc, and is full of expensive antique shops and foie gras. M. and Mme Gillard (he the chef, she the front-of-house manager) have refurbished this hotel which has always enjoyed a superb view. The rooms are individually decorated in a variety of floral wallpapers in the best tradition of the French country hotel. Gillard's table can be recommended not only for the skill he brings to it, but also for the size of the dishes in which that skill is revealed. The dining room is large and airy." (*Frederic and Sylvia Raphael*)

The Raphaels, who sent this description a few years ago, still frequent this *Logis de France* and say it is as good as ever. Recent reports have all been enthusiastic. "Our room had an enchanting small balcony overlooking the wonderful valley. Superb food (try the salmon stuffed with mousseline of trout) and the best café au lait of our holiday." "Splendid meal and dining room, stunning view, *patronne* rather bossy." "When you arrive in Domme at midday, it is awful – a tourist trap. But in the late afternoon it quietens. On a midsummer evening, when it is still and you stroll along the cliff-top path after dinner, magic is in the air." (*Marilyn and Conrad Dehn, Mr and Mrs Bernard Dunstan; endorsed this year by P Talbot-Smith*)

Open All year except Feb and Nov. Restaurant closed Mon out of season.
Rooms 20 double – all with bath and/or shower, and telephone; some with balcony. Some in 2 annexes in the village. Some ground-floor rooms.
Facilities Salon with TV, bar, restaurant; terraces. River 2 km, swimming pool 10 km. English spoken.
Location 13 km S of Sarlat.
Restriction Not ideal for ♿.
Credit card Amex.
Terms B&B double 228-438 frs. Set lunch/dinner 100 frs. Special meals for children.

DUCEY 50220 Manche — Map 8

Auberge de la Sélune — *Tel* 33.48.53.62
2 rue St-Germain

More praise this year for the hearty Norman good cheer at this spruce little hotel, with its garden and terrace above the river, in a dullish village not far from Mont-St-Michel. "A little jewel. Try the truite duceyne – pink, tender, stuffed with a light calvados mousse." "Bedrooms very clean and pretty: ours was Rechitto blue, with white furnishings. Best rooms are those at the back, facing garden and river. Josette Girres looks after front of house with quiet charm; her husband is chef, and his freshly made pâtisserie is perfect. Crab pie is a speciality. Lots of fresh fish; good breakfast with Normandy butter." (*Eileen Broadbent; also Bernadette Murray, Jan Morris, Carol E Lindenmeyr, and others*)

Open All year except Feb, Mon Oct–Mar.
Rooms 19 double, 1 single – 19 with bath and shower, all with telephone. 3 in garden pavilion.
Facilities TV lounge, bar, restaurant; seminar room. Garden with terrace. Salmon fishing in river Sélune; tennis nearby. English spoken.
Location On N176, 11 km SE of Avranches (garden rooms quietest). Private car park.
Credit cards Access, Diners, Visa.
Terms Rooms: single 120 frs, double 180 frs. Breakfast 15 frs. Set lunch/dinner 50-95 frs. Reduced rates and special meals for children.

"We decided to pass on the hotel restaurant for dinner when a fish floated dead in the trout aquarium and the rest were evidently sick."

ÉPERNAY 51200 Marne **Map 9**

Hôtel des Berceaux *Tel* 26.55.28.84
13 rue des Berceaux

The *Berceaux*, cradled into a side-street of this champagne capital, yet very central, is run by *patron*-chef Luc Maillard and his English wife Jill, who will organise visits to the local champagne firms and their *caves*. Readers continue to endorse accounts of Jill Maillard's charming welcome and of pleasant simple rooms with well-equipped bathrooms at fair prices. M. Maillard's dishes are expensive, of the turbot au champagne type: but you can eat lighter and cheaper dishes in the new wine bar (this bar has a pianist three nights a week and is described intriguingly by readers as "a hoot" and "attempts charm, hits bordello"). The "lavish" help-yourself buffet breakfast is praised. One visitor adds: "Mattress on double bed left a lot to be desired – probably because desire had asked a lot of the mattress." Some rooms can be noisy. (*TJ Kenny, Ayse Gilbert, Arthur Hopcroft*)

Open All year. Restaurant closed Sun evening.
Rooms 29 double – 19 with bath, 10 with shower, all with telephone and baby-listening; 5 with TV.
Facilities Lift. Lounge, TV room, bar, restaurant, wine bar (pianist 3 times a week). English spoken.
Location Central, near place de la République. No special parking facilities.
Credit cards All major cards accepted.
Terms Rooms: 220-300 frs. Breakfast 30 and 45 frs. Set lunch/dinner 130-300 frs; light meals in wine bar 90 frs.

L'ÉPINE 51460 Marne **Map 9**

Aux Armes de Champagne *Tel* 26.68.10.43
Telex 830998

This old coaching-inn, restored and modernised, stands in the village square of L'Épine (east of Châlons-sur-Marne), opposite the huge basilica of Notre-Dame, a pilgrimage centre in the Middle Ages and now floodlit at night. Most bedrooms, all prettily furnished, overlook it. Recent comments: "Extremely good value for money." "The picturesque garden at the back, with a small stream, is an ideal spot for an aperitif. Meals are excellent (*Michelin* rosette, *Gault Millau toque*) and good value. The floodlighting of the basilica makes a fine backdrop for diners at the window tables." (*KW George*) "Clean and comfortable, without the firework-night-in-Hawaii wallpaper that usually tells you that you are in a French hotel. Staff friendly and obliging, cooking a dream. The hotel is in the champagne district and three-quarters of the long wine list is devoted to the stuff (much of the menu too – you can have either snails or pigeon cooked in it)." (*A and SL; also Pat and Jeremy Temple*) One visitor this year found the food disappointing.

Open All year except 4 Jan–8 Feb, evening 24 and 31 Dec.
Rooms 38 double, 2 single – all with bath and/or shower, and telephone; 8 with TV. 16 in 2 annexes 150 metres from main building. Ground-floor rooms.
Facilities Bar, TV room, 2 restaurants; functions facilities. Concerts in summer. Small garden with mini-golf. English spoken.
Location Central; village is 8.5 km E of Châlons, on N3. Parking.
Credit cards Access, Amex, Visa.

Terms Rooms 435 frs. Breakfast 36 frs. Dinner, B&B 380 frs per person. Set lunch/dinner 90, 170, 250 frs. Full alc 400 frs.

ERDEVEN 56410 Morbihan — Map 8

Hostellerie Château de Keravéon — *Tel* 97.55.68.55

On the south Brittany coast, near Carnac, an exquisitely restored creeper-covered 18th-century château complete with dovecote and moat, set in its own park. Stylish period furniture in public rooms and bedrooms. Food plentiful (demi-pension *obligatory in season*). *Sandy beach two miles away. Open 15 May–15 Sept. 20 rooms, all with bath or shower. Half board 488-548 frs per person. No recent reports: more, please.*

EUGÉNIE-LES-BAINS 40320 Landes — Map 10

Les Prés d'Eugénie — *Tel* 58.51.19.01
Telex 540470

Michel Guérard's very superior establishment, in a Second Empire mansion north of Pau, is world-famous as the home of *cuisine minceur*: dishes low on calories but gastronomically refined. But not everyone makes the pilgrimage to Eugénie's meadows to be fed on sprigs of cress and creamless *sauces déglacés*: robust appetites are catered for too. In the main restaurant, the cuisine may be what is loosely known as *nouvelle*, but it is *gourmande* rather than *minceur*. And next door is the thermal centre and health farm where guests pay huge sums to reduce on diets devised by this three-star chef: for this, you must have a doctor's certificate and you eat at different times from the gourmand guests.

A connoisseur who visited the hotel/restaurant this year had mixed feelings: "The food prepared for the wealthy gourmets is totally exquisite, and its accent is on subtlety of taste, not calorie control. Presentation is impeccable, and service is on oiled castors by waiters clearly proud of the masterpieces coming from the kitchen. The Great Man himself was there, he and his wife deeply in conversation with VIP guests. This said, the place seems to have serious flaws as a hotel. The bedrooms are comfortable and spacious, but they are not serviced properly and have lacunae that seem odd amid so much expensive luxury – no writing paper, an elderly and tatty TV set, very few bathroom goodies and nowhere to hang one's rinsed undies. Breakfast is idiosyncratic and expensive. Staff are cheerful and relaxed, but reception was somewhat casual." Others have been less critical: "We lapped up the comfort. Elegant buildings in very pretty grounds where fountains play, lions lie and a semi-nude lady stands in the courtyard. Our bedroom was a gentle and luxurious dream in pale dusky pink and white, looking on to a sun-bathed terrace, blue pool and green fields. The decor in the public rooms was a pale champagne; fires burned brightly on a chilly day, and at the edge of each table in the elegant dining room was a most unusual candelabra. The menus to our minds were better than the à la carte. Each course arrived looking like a painting. Soft background music." Top ratings in the French guides, needless to say. (*Francine and Ian Walsh; JL, and others*)

Open 2 Mar–30 Nov.
Rooms 7 suites, 28 double – all with bath, telephone, radio and TV.
Facilities Salon, smoking and billiard room, TV room, gallery, bar, dining rooms, restaurant. Beauty salon, thermal baths, sauna. 2 tennis courts, *boules*, unheated swimming pool. Garden and river. Golf 25 km. English spoken.
Location Off D944 St-Sever–Aubagnan, 53 km N of Pau.
Credit cards Amex, Diners.
Terms [1987 rates] (Excluding 15% service) Rooms 880 frs, suites 1,155 frs. Breakfast 70 frs. *Menu minceur* (residents only) 160-280 frs; alc meals in *Restaurant Michel Guérard* 380-400 frs (excluding wine).

LES EYZIES-DE-TAYAC 24620 Dordogne — Map 10

Hôtel Cro-Magnon

Tel 53.06.97.06
Telex 570637

Les Eyzies, France's leading "centre of prehistory", is dominated by steep cliffs riddled with paleolithic caves. In its outskirts is this handsome creeper-covered old hotel, still in the main very popular with readers (part of its special atmosphere comes from the fact that its founder was a 19th-century prehistorian who first identified the skeleton of Cro-Magnon Man and discovered the cave drawings). One recent report: "Just like Grasmere, overflowing with tourists and knick-knackery, Les Eyzies is bedlam at the height of the tourist season, but it all quietens down dramatically of an evening, and once the mists settle the town acquires an eerie magical feeling. The hotel's main building stands against the stone face of the cliff; down the road and across a railway line is the annexe, in a large garden with a swimming pool and children's paddling pool. The entrance hall has an English coaching-inn feel, with wood-panelled walls, pretty flowers, brasses polished daily; there is a delightful and quiet residents' lounge upstairs. Our room was a fair size, spotless, furnished and wallpapered in rustic style; plumbing noises were the only snag. The hotel's family owners, Jacques and Christiane Leyssalles, chat warmly with their guests while at the same time keeping a close eye on their bright and efficient staff. The whole ambience is friendly and personal. And the food deserves its *Michelin* rosette for quality and presentation, especially the hot salmon, terrine de foie d'oie and the desserts." (*Ian and Francine Walsh*)

Others write in similar vein. The annexe rooms are probably the most pleasant, but both here and in the front rooms of the main building there can be some early morning noise from traffic and trains. As for food, "the gastronomic *demi-pension* dinner was magnificent", according to one visitor, but some others have found the *en pension* meals dull and one reader this year thought the cuisine pretentious and the service unhelpful. (*Mrs RB Richards, Conrad Dehn, Harry Singer, KC Turpin, and many others*)

Open Apr–mid Oct.
Rooms 3 suites, 24 double – 25 with bath, 2 with shower, all with telephone. 12 in annexe. 1 ground-floor room.
Facilities 2 lounges, 2 dining rooms. Garden restaurant. 5 acres of parkland with heated swimming pool and river. English spoken.
Location 600 metres W of town centre. Parking.
Restriction Not suitable for ♿.
Credit cards All major cards accepted.
Terms B&B: single 298 frs, double 388-418 frs. Set lunch/dinner 110-300 frs; full alc 200-300 frs.

Les Glycines *Tel* 53.06.97.07

"I rate *Les Glycines* a better buy than the *Cro Magnon* (q.v.). It is similarly creeper-covered, and beautiful in autumn, and it is further from the railway, with that dreaded level-crossing out of earshot. There is a vine-shaded terrace for drinks or lunch, and a huge, quiet though untidy garden at the back; by the river lies the kitchen garden, leaving one in no doubt as to the freshness of the vegetables. Our room in the new annexe was quiet but small, with doors opening onto our own table and chairs in the sunny courtyard; rooms in the main building may be a little dark and cramped. The menus had the usual regional dishes (cèpes with everything) and the *carte* had interesting variations: pea soup with sorrel was delicious. Service attentive and informal." (*SM Whitehead*) More reports welcome.

Open End Mar–early Nov
Rooms 25, of which 6 are single – all with bath, shower and telephone. Some rooms accomodating 4 in separate building in garden. 5 ground-floor rooms.
Facilities Reading room, bar, restaurant; terrace for alfresco meals. Large garden with swimming pool. English spoken
Location On road to Périgueux, by the river. Parking.
Credit cards Amex, Visa.
Terms Rooms 270-290 frs; dinner, B&B 295 frs per person; full board 350 frs. Breakfast 35 frs. Set lunch/dinner 100, 130, 160 and 270 frs; full alc 220 frs. Reduced rates for children under 5; special meals on request.

Le Moulin de la Beune *Tel* 53.06.94.33

This big converted mill stands next to the National Museum of Prehistory and beside the river Beune which flows through its garden. "Owners friendly, breakfast good, bedrooms attractive with good modern plumbing." That is this year's view, endorsing previous ones: "Tastefully restored. There is a large old fireplace in the lounge/reception which is attractively furnished as are the bedrooms. Inviting breakfast room, with glass doors leading out to tables by the river. Breakfast exceptional, with home-made jams, hot croissants, coffee ad lib. Smart chairs in the garden. Warm welcome from the owners, the Dudicourts." No restaurant, though the millwheel building may become one soon and there are superb ones nearby. (*Noel and Sheila Marriott, Kay and Neville Varley*)

Open End Mar–3 Nov.
Rooms 20 (6 for 3 people, 1 for 4) – 14 with bath, 6 with shower, all with direct-dial telephone. 4 ground-floor rooms with separate entrance.
Facilities Salon, bar, TV room, breakfast room. Garden. River (fishing), swimming pool and tennis nearby. English spoken.
Location Central, near the National Museum of Prehistory. Parking.
Credit cards Access, Visa.
Terms Rooms 180-240 frs. Breakfast 28 frs. (No restaurant.)

ÈZE-BORD-DE-MER 06360 Alpes-Maritimes Map 11

Le Cap Estel *Tel* 93.01.50.44
Telex 470305

Once the home of a prince, this stately white Italianate villa is now an elegant luxury hotel, family-run, and it stands on a promontory between

Beaulieu and Monaco, just below the eyrie-village of Èze. Two of our readers like it so much that they have taken their holidays here every year since the mid-60s, and this year they again endorse their earlier view: "It's rather like a club with the same people returning. We have a room with sitting room leading onto a patio – you can lie in your bath and watch boats go by. There is a comfortable public lounge and poolside bar. A magnificent hors d'oeuvre table is served at lunch outdoors under the trees, and dinner is often served there too. Food and comfort excellent." (*Tom and Rosemary Rose*)

Open 1 Mar–end Oct.
Rooms 43 – all with bath and shower, telephone, terrace or loggia, and air-conditioning. 7 in annexe.
Facilities Lift. 2 salons, cocktail bar, TV room, restaurant; sauna, solarium, indoor and outdoor swimming pools. Garden with restaurant, private beach with water sports. Tennis and sailing nearby. English spoken.
Location Just off Lower Corniche (N98), 3 km NE of Beaulieu; 4 km from Monaco.
Restriction Not suitable for ♿.
Credit cards All major cards accepted.
Terms Dinner, B&B: double 1,400–2,250 frs, suite 2,750 frs; full alc 285–400 frs. 1-night bookings might be refused in high season.

ÈZE-VILLAGE 06360 Alpes-Maritimes — Map 11

Château de la Chèvre d'Or — *Tel* 93.41.12.12
Rue du Barri — *Telex* 970839 CHEVDOR

The best-known and most densely tourist-infested of all the Côte d'Azur's hill-villages stands in a spectacular site beside the Middle Corniche, on a rocky outcrop almost sheer above the sea (Èze-Bord-de-Mer, see above, is just below). It has been scrupulously restored, and its many souvenir shops are not too vulgar; when the tourists have departed, it can be hauntingly quiet at night. There is no motor-traffic, but a short walk along its main alley leads to the celebrated *Chèvre d'Or*, a medieval château artistically converted into a small luxury hotel, run with suave efficiency by its Swiss owner, Bruno Ingold. Soft music plays as you sip your champagne cocktails by the pool, gazing at Cap Ferrat far below; even the telephones in the lavishly furnished bedrooms are Edwardian museum-pieces. If some bedrooms are cramped, blame the 11th-century architect, though the 20th-century redesigners have done their ingenious best. Rooms near the kitchens may be noisy. The panoramic restaurant, frequented by famous and beautiful people, wins a well deserved *Michelin* rosette and two red *Gault Millau toques* for such *nouvelle*-ish cuisine as hot oysters in champagne.

Several readers this year have enjoyed the service and the cooking – "delicious, light and elegant". An American reader comments: "Each room is unique. All have sea views, some have terraces too. Breakfast in bed comes with fresh roses and Limoges china. The fire in the bar is welcome, and the new grill room offers excellent food in a less formal setting than the main restaurant. A lovely romantic hotel." (*Douglas S Coleman; also Wendy Arnold, David Wooff*)

Open 1 Mar–30 Nov. Restaurant closed Wed Mar–Easter.
Rooms 2 suites, 6 double – all with bath, shower, telephone, and TV.
Facilities Bar/salon, restaurant, grill room. Garden with terrace and small swimming pool; alfresco meals in summer. English spoken.

Location 10 km E of Nice on "Moyen Corniche" road.
Restriction Not suitable for ♿.
Credit cards All major cards accepted.
Terms (Excluding 15% service) Rooms: single occupancy 900-1,100 frs, double 1,300-1,600 frs, suites 1,600-2,000 frs. Breakfast 55 frs. Set lunch 280 frs; full alc 400-500 frs. Reduced rates and special meals for children.

LA FAVÈDE 30110 Gard — Map 10

Auberge Cévenole — *Tel* 66.34.12.13

La Favède is a hamlet in the lovely wooded southern foothills of the Cévennes, just off the Alès–Florac road. Here the *Auberge Cévenole* wins *Michelin*'s red rocking chair and two red gables for secluded tranquillity and pleasant charm, and from our reporter the comment: "Very relaxing, in a beautiful setting with a well-kept garden and swimming pool. Rooms well furnished, tasty food, service of a high standard." It is a neat, white-walled, red-roofed building in local style, very sprucely and prettily decorated. The dining room, with its big picture windows facing the garden, offers Cévenol specialities – on its 135 franc menu [1987], starters such as soupe de moules, main dishes such as stuffed quail with grapes. (*Mr and Mrs GH Russell*) More reports please.

Open 15 Mar–15 Nov.
Rooms 2 suites, 16 double – all with bath, shower and direct-dial telephone; suites have mini-bar and TV. 6 bungalow rooms, suitable for disabled. 12 ground-floor rooms.
Facilities Salon, TV room, dining room. Terrace where meals are served in summer. Garden with unheated swimming pool. English spoken.
Location 3 km W of La Grand-Combe, on D283.
Credit card Access.
Terms B&B: single 230 frs, double 280 frs, suite 560 frs; dinner, B&B: single 370 frs, double 550 frs. Set lunch/dinner 140-220 frs.

FAVERGES-DE-LA-TOUR 38110 Isère — Map 10

Le Château de Faverges — *Tel* 74.97.42.52
La Tour-du-Pin — *Telex* 300372 FAVTOUR

In winter, hoteliers Jo and Catherine Tournier run ski-hotels in Courchevel; in summer, they turn their attention to this imposing château topped by a circular turreted tower. It stands high in large grounds, just off the A43 *autoroute* between Lyon and Chambéry, with fine views towards the Alps. The cooking, new style with regional overtones (e.g. roast pigeon with cabbage and foie gras), wins a *Michelin* rosette and *Gault Millau* red *toque*, while the hotel has other merits, too, so our readers say: "Public rooms are beautifully restored, with a superb marble staircase. The lower floors, almost cellar-like, provide the restaurant, attractive, though some decor is a bit kitsch. There is an outdoor terrace for summer eating, a swimming pool, sauna and tennis. Our bedroom was large, comfortable, with a mix of antiques and good French rural repro. The food was very good, and the staff friendly and efficient." (*Pat and Jeremy Temple*). More reports please.

We are particularly keen to have reports on italicised entries.

Open 14 May–23 Oct. Restaurant closed Mon.
Rooms 3 suites, 37 double, 3 single – all with bath and shower, direct-dial telephone, TV and baby-listening; 20 with radio. 23 rooms in less luxurious but pretty annexes.
Facilities 2 salons, bar, dining rooms; conference/function room. Grounds with terrace, swimming pool, sauna, fitness room, 2 tennis courts, jogging track, golf. English spoken.
Location Leave Lyon/Chambéry *autoroute* (A43) at La Tour-du-Pin or Abrets exits and follow signs for Faverges-de-la-Tour on N75. Parking.
Restriction Not suitable for ♿.
Credit cards Amex, Diners, Visa.
Terms Double rooms 550-1,200 frs, suite 1,700 frs. Breakfast 65 frs. Set lunch 280-420 frs; full alc 350 frs. Reduced rates for children sharing parents' room.

FÈRE-EN-TARDENOIS 02130 Aisne — Map 9

Hostellerie du Château — *Tel* 23.82.21.13
Telex 145526 OTELFER

A luxurious manor house, part-Renaissance, part 19th-century, that stands in its own sizeable park within a forest, 45 kilometres west of Reims, owned, run and cooked for by the Blot family. Rooms vary greatly; older ones in the main house have more personality, newer ones are larger and plainer but with superior bathrooms. Serious nouvelle cuisine *raved about in* Gault Millau; Michelin *rosette. But continuing disappointments in the cooking and hotel upkeep have necessitated these italics. Open Mar–Jan inclusive. 23 rooms, with bath/shower, 550–660 frs. Set meals 275 and 420 frs.*

FLAGY 77130 Seine-et-Marne — Map 9

Hôtel-Restaurant au Moulin — *Tel* (1) 60.96.67.89
6 rue du Moulin
Flagy, Montereau-Faut-Yonne

Readers remain as delighted as ever with this 13th-century mill, beautifully converted into a restaurant-with-rooms, in a village south-east of Fontainebleau. "We loved it and would gladly have stayed for weeks: grounds well cared for, food simple and delicious," runs one report this year. Others have mentioned the "delightful" staff and the setting – the meals in summer under weeping willows beside a stream, the sight and sound of rushing water, the charming lounge with some of the old mill-wheels and pulleys. "This charming hotel retains the feel of an old mill but with all modern comforts. A warm and friendly greeting and an excellent dinner in the attractive dining room with a blazing log fire (in February). Our room was delightful, with a beamed ceiling." (*GG Klima, P Tyler, Peter Earl, Dr and Mrs S Lovejoy, and others*)

Open All year, except 15–25 Sept, 18 Dec–22 Jan, Sun evening and Mon.
Rooms 10 double – all with bath and telephone.
Facilities Lounge, bar, beamed restaurant. Large garden beside river, fishing (permit issued in the village). English spoken.
Location 23 km S of Fontainebleau by N6 (18 km), then turn right by D403, and immediately left by D120.
Restriction Not suitable for ♿.
Credit cards All major cards accepted.

Terms [1987 rates] Rooms: single 130 frs, double 200 frs. Breakfast 25 frs. Full board 293-310 frs person. Set lunch/dinner 110-170 frs. Reduced rates for children.

FLORIMONT-GAUMIERS 24250 Dordogne — Map 10

La Daille — *Tel* 55.28.40.71
Florimont-Gaumiers, Domme

The British love-affair with the Dordogne finds a very personal fulfilment here in this secluded farmhouse about nine miles south of Domme, which Derek and Barbara Brown have been running for the past ten years as a tiny four-bedroom hotel-restaurant. Set in the hills above the Céou valley, the house is built in local stone with an external stone staircase and pigeon tower, but internally it has been sensitively modernised. The distinguished British restaurateur *Kenneth Bell*, now retired, who has a country home nearby, has sent this nominating report: "Very small and individual, in an attractive unspoilt rural setting. The bedrooms have modern baths. Excellent food served by Derek and cooked by Barbara – in my opinion the best cooking for 30 miles around. No lunches served, but you can buy your own delicatessen and wines and enjoy them under the walnut trees in the pretty garden." We look forward to more reports.

Open Easter–2 Nov. Restaurant closed for lunch.
Rooms 3 double, 1 single – 3 bath, 1 with shower. Single room in annexe.
Facilities Restaurant. Garden, terrace. Swimming-pool, tennis and Dordogne river with canoeing and swimming nearby. English spoken.
Location La Daille is signposted SE of Gaumiers village, which is just W of the D46, 13 km S of Domme and 5 km NW of Salviac.
Restrictions Not suitable for ♿. No children under 7.
Credit cards None accepted.
Terms Dinner, B&B: 270-300 frs. Set dinner (by reservation only) 100–110 frs (excluding wine).

LA FLOTTE 17630 Charente-Maritime — Map 10

Le Richelieu — *Tel* 46.09.60.70
44 avenue de la Plage — *Telex* 791492
La Flotte, Ile de Ré

Ré, a long flat island near La Rochelle, is noted for its clear sparkling light, its sandy beaches (crowded in summer) and its asparagus; some women still wear the local white headdresses known as *quichenotte*, originally used as a defence against amorous English soldiers ("kiss not"). This year an English group-captain came peacefully to the smartest hotel (three red gables and a rosette in *Michelin*, two red *Gault Millau toques*) and found the food expensive but excellent, the heated pool good and his room in the main building small but comfortable. (*Group-Capt Edwin Shipley*) An earlier invader reported: "Beautiful and comfortable; de luxe. We had the best room, huge balcony, good breakfast. Lovely heated swimming pool. Dinner was marvellous – langoustine tails on red peppers, a large fish from the bay, a divine pudding of solid cream – that sort of thing, coupled with *no vegetables or salad at all*, just about finished us every night. A delightful island, quite impossible in season we'd imagine. Best to avoid hurricanes." (*Gerald Campion*) The bungalows in the garden are thought to be larger than the rooms in the hotel.

Open 15 Mar–15 Nov, 15 Dec–5 Jan.
Rooms 30 – all with bath, shower, telephone and TV; some with balcony. 16 in bungalows in garden, suitable for families.
Facilities Bar, 2 lounges (1 with TV), restaurant; conference facilities; billiard room; terrace. Garden with heated swimming pool, tennis. English spoken.
Location On N coast of island, at harbour entrance facing bay; frequent ferry service to La Pallice/La Rochelle.
Credit card Possibly Visa.
Terms Rooms: single 300-550 frs, double 400-800 frs. Breakfast 50 frs. Dinner, B&B: 450-800 frs per person; full board 500-900 frs. Set lunch/dinner 190-350 frs; full alc 350 frs. Children half price; special meals.

FOIX 09000 Ariège — Map 10

Hôtel Lons — *Tel* 61.65.52.44
6 place Georges-Duthil

A high triple-towered medieval château rises romantically above this charming and historic little town of narrow winding streets, near the foothills of the Pyrenees and on the main Toulouse/Barcelona road. The *Lons* (formerly *Audoye*) is worthy of this setting: "Delightful hotel facing a small square, with fountain and half-timbered buildings. Our room was large, overlooking the river Ariège and also (alas) the road: it might be wiser to forego this view for the peace of a room facing the square. Restaurant was very good, built out over the river with huge sliding windows, so that you feel suspended. The fixed-price menus include magnificent help-yourself hors d'oeuvre." Endorsed this year: "Old fashioned, but good value, with excellent food." (*Elizabeth Hill, GM Morrison*)

Open 15 Jan–15 Dec.
Rooms 19 double, 16 single – most with bath or shower, 25 with WC, all with telephone. 9 in annexe in front of hotel.
Facilities Lift. Salon, TV room, bar, snack bar, restaurant and terrace; functions facilities. Swimming, tennis, fishing, riding nearby. English spoken.
Location Central (back rooms quietest). Parking.
Credit cards All major cards accepted.
Terms Rooms: single 135 frs, double 160 frs. Breakfast 18 frs. Set lunch/dinner 55-100 frs; full alc 83 frs.

FONTAINEBLEAU 77300 Seine-et-Marne — Map 9

Hôtel Aigle Noir — *Tel* (1) 64.22.32.65
27 place Napoléon — *Telex* 600080

Fontainebleau's grandest hotel, in the centre, facing the gardens of Napoleon's favourite palace. Recent accounts of it vary somewhat. One visitor had a good meal with excellent service, and found the bedrooms large but plain; another was shown to a "wonderfully Victorian room" with the TV set hidden in the wall, and had a dinner that was "not good" (*Michelin* however awards a rosette, and *Gault Millau* a *toque*, for such dishes as terrine de caille et pigeonneau aux morilles). Previous visitors have admired the efficient service and a certain "*ambiance napoléonique*". The hotel combines classic Louis XVI and Empire decor with all the latest mod cons – glass-fibre sound-proofing, etc. (*Wendy Arnold, Roger Bennett, Mrs MD Prodgers*)

Open All year.
Rooms 4 suites, 26 double (all available as singles) – 28 with bath, 2 with shower, all with telephone, radio, TV, mini-bar and sound-proofing.
Facilities Lift. Salon, bar, 2 restaurants; conference and function facilities. 2 small gardens (meals served there weather permitting). Near château park; swimming pool nearby, river 7 km, riding 10 km. English spoken.
Location Central, opposite the château gardens. Parking.
Restriction Not suitable for ♿.
Credit cards All major cards accepted.
Terms [1987 rates] Rooms 695-845 frs, suite 1,015 frs. Breakfast 65 frs. Set lunch/dinner 190-260 frs. Children under 12 years sharing parents' room free; special meals.

FONTVIEILLE 13990 Bouches-du-Rhône — Map 11

Auberge La Régalido — *Tel* 90.97.60.22
Rue Frédéric Mistral — *Telex* 441150

Fontvieille, a small town in the foothills of the Alpilles, makes a good excursion centre for the Arles and Les Baux areas; Daudet's famous windmill is on a hill close by. Again highly admired this year, *La Régalido* is a former oil-mill in a side street, now converted into a most welcoming little *auberge*, luxurious yet unpretentious. It is run by the Michel family: Madame's hand is evident in the flowers which grace all the rooms, and Monsieur's in the cooking (*Michelin* rosette), which our readers continue to find excellent (try the feuilleté de morilles et ris d'agneau). A report this year: "A wonderful place with *really* charming staff, not just put on. Mme Michel a powerhouse of efficiency and strikingly beautiful; Monsieur a delight, aimiable, slightly potty, the perfect host. Not cheap, neither *should* it be." A visitor in October found "a fire blazing in the sitting-room". Bedrooms have individual charm, and there is a flowery garden with neatly-cut lawn. (*N French, Robin Schiel, and others*)

Open 1 Feb–end Nov.
Rooms 14 double – all with bath and/or shower, telephone; some with TV. 1 ground-floor room.
Facilities 3 small salons (1 with TV), restaurant; salon for functions. Garden. English spoken,
Location 5 km NE of Arles. Leave *autoroute* A7 at Cavaillon, direction St-Rémy-de-Provence, or at Nîmes, direction Arles. Parking.
Credit cards All major cards accepted.
Terms B&B: single 400-550 frs, double 550-1,100 frs. Breakfast 60 frs. Set lunch/dinner 200-290 frs. Special meals for children on request.

GÉMENOS 13420 Bouches-du-Rhône — Map 11

Relais de la Magdeleine — *Tel* 42.82.20.05

Again very warmly praised this year as a family-run hotel that welcomes children, the *Magdeleine* is described as "a charming 17th-century *bastide*, set in a large walled garden with lovely bathing pool – a peaceful and luxurious oasis on the outskirts of the small town of Gémenos" (which is within easy reach of the coast at Cassis or Marseilles, and the wild and strange *massif* of La Sainte-Baume). "The owners, the Marignanes, made us feel like welcome guests in their own home. The service was faultless by charming young girls, and the food was delicious, with good breakfasts too." This backs up an earlier encomium: "The public rooms and large bedrooms were attractively furnished with antiques; the beds were high quality. The dining rooms were cool and spacious, with some walls covered with silk or damask. But in spite of this luxury there was nothing pretentious or formal about the atmosphere, which was friendly and happy. There was an aura of peace, especially on the terrace in the early evening when drinks were served under floodlit plane trees. Provençal cooking par excellence, plus a large selection of pâtisseries and wonderful cheese. At breakfast, freshly-made hot brioches." (*Mr and Mrs Michael Mackie, Drs D and T Wardle; also Dennis and Peggy Coombs, J and A McGlashan*)

Open 15 Mar–1 Nov.
Rooms 4 suites, 16 double – all with bath and/or shower, telephone and TV.
Facilities 3 salons, 2 restaurants. Garden, swimming pool. English spoken.
Location On outskirts of Gémenos, which is 23 km E of Marseilles. Exit Pont de l'Étoile from Aix–Toulon motorway.
Restriction Not suitable for ♿.
Credit card Visa.
Terms B&B 360-380 frs; half board 385-410 frs. Set lunch/dinner 160 frs; full alc 280-300 frs. Reduced rates and special meals for children.

GENNES 49350 Maine-et-Loire — Map 8

Aux Naulets d'Anjou — *Tel* 41.51.81.88
18 rue Croix-de-Mission

A modern white-fronted country hotel in a village on the Loire between Angers and Saumur. The rooms are in white with large windows, pine furniture and fresh flowers; a large airy dining room and terrace overlook the distant Loire. Colette Maudonnet, the *patronne*/chef, offers classic regional dishes as well as her own lighter low-calorie variations, and our readers this year have been contented: "A pleasant welcome and an excellent dinner." "I was put off at first by the inn's modern look, but we thoroughly loved it. The meals were delicious and the rooms spacious, airy and beautifully decorated. The owner's artistic eye was evident." Perhaps this will pacify the Maudonnets, who had been incensed by a reader's comment in our 1987 Guide that the decor was "dull". Paul Maudonnet, himself an artist, wrote to point out that the ceramics in the bedrooms were his own work and the tapestries that of his wife, and that he was the author of 14 illustrated art books and had won a prize from the Académie Française. He also gives annual painting courses at the hotel. (*GG Klima, Mrs JC Smye, MA, Gordon Bond*)

Open Easter–1 Nov. Closed Mon out of season.
Rooms 20 double – all with bath, shower and direct-dial telephone. 5 ground-floor rooms.
Facilities Salon, dining room, picture gallery; functions facilities; exhibitions and concerts. Garden with terrace for alfresco meals. Tennis, riding, sailing and bathing nearby.
Location Coming from Saumur (15 km) turn left just before Mairie, then right into rue Croix-de-Mission; hotel is on right.
Credit card Visa.
Terms B&B: single occupancy 230 frs, double 280 frs. Dinner, B&B 280 frs per person; full board 320 frs. Set lunch 85 frs, dinner 125–170 frs; full alc 150 frs.

GÉRARDMER 88400 Vosges — Map 9

Chalet du Lac *Tel* 29.63.38.76
Route Épinal

On the edge of this serene lakeside resort in the Vosges foothills, an old chalet by the lake, quiet and picturesque. Charming and helpful owners; rooms simple but adequate; excellent food, admired locally, served in a restaurant facing the lake. Closed Oct. 11 rooms. B&B double 215 frs. Set meals 55–200 frs. New nomination: more reports please.

GIEN 45500 Loiret — Map 10

Hôtel du Rivage *Tel* 38.67.20.53
1 quai de Nice

"The cheap menu provided one of our best meals ever in ten years of touring France." "Excellent food and a charming bedroom overlooking the Loire." "Superb house wine – a very soigné little hotel." So run three reports this year on the *Rivage*, a very spruce little hotel that carries a *Michelin* rosette for such dishes as fricassée of sweetbreads with cider vinegar and honey. It has modernised rooms and tiled bathrooms, and it stands off the main road in this pleasant Loireside town on one of the main routes south from Paris. Gien's 15th-century castle contains an impressive museum of hunting. (*Peter Stattersfield, Sheila Shaw, PH Freeman and others*)

Open All year except 9 Feb–2 Mar.
Rooms 15 double – all with bath and shower, telephone, TV. 3 suites and 4 more doubles planned for 1988.
Facilities Salon, TV room, dining room; functions room. River with fishing, bathing; riding, tennis nearby. English spoken.
Location On road to Nevers, on banks of the Loire. Parking.
Restriction Not suitable for ♿.
Credit cards Amex, Diners, Visa.
Terms [1987 rates] Rooms 220-250 frs. Breakfast 23 frs. Set lunch/dinner 135-245 frs. Special meals for children on request.

GIGONDAS 84190 Vaucluse — Map 11

Les Florets *Tel* 90.65.85.01
Route des Dentelles

This small country hotel, near to some of the best Côtes du Rhône vineyards, is an enticing new nomination this year: "It is immediately below the spectacular Dentelles de Montmirail, a mile east of Gigondas in an otherwise empty valley. It consists of a smallish main house and an annexe on the hill behind, all gravel yard, blossom and sunshine. The service is pleasant, the food a bit boring, but the glory of the place is the deliciously tree-dappled, fountain-rilled, Pernod-supplied, chaise-longued terrace, which looks over vineyards and mountains, is absolutely silent except for the clinking of ice in glasses, and seems to me about as happy a place as anywhere in Europe for the writing of books." (*Jan Morris*) The owners write to say that they also possess a Gigondas vineyard.

Open 1 March–31 Dec. Closed Wed.
Rooms 13 double, 2 single – 13 with bath and/or shower, all with telephone. 4 bungalows 50 m from hotel.
Facilities Salon/bar, restaurant, TV room, terrace.
Location 1.5 km E of Gigondas, which is 18 km E of Orange.
Restriction Not suitable for ♿.
Credit cards Amex, Diners, Visa.
Terms Dinner, B&B: single 200 frs, double 500 frs; full board: single 300 frs, double 600 frs. Set lunch/dinner 100–160 frs. 1-night bookings may be refused in high season.

GIVRY 71640 Saône-et-Loire — Map 10

Hôtel de la Halle — *Tel* 85.44.32.45
Place de la Halle

A modest but very friendly little hotel in a pleasant Burgundy village west of Chalon; it is a venerable building with a fine spiral staircase, facing the former market hall. Accommodation is somewhat basic, but reports this year and last are full of praise for the charming owners, the Renards, and the "excellent old-fashioned Burgundian food, unbelievable value". "Bedrooms may be simple, but they are spotlessly clean, and have an interesting conflict of different textile patterns. We had a warm reception from M. Renard in his snowy apron and from his wife. It was a pleasure to sit in his very good restaurant watching the locals come and go, most of them close friends of M. Renard, judging by all the kissing going on. He introduced us to a wine-growing friend of his, and we piled up our car with bottles." Some front rooms may be noisy. (*BW Ribbons, Ian and Agathe Lewin, Peter McLeod, JSL, and others*)

Open All year. Closed Sun evening and Mon.
Rooms 10 double – 2 with bath, 3 with shower, all with telephone.
Facilities 2 salons, restaurant. Garden. Swimming pools 5 and 8 km, also swimming in nearby river; walks in woods and vineyards. English spoken.
Location Givry is 9 km W of Chalon-sur-Saône on D69. Hotel is central (front rooms may be noisy). Parking.
Restriction Not suitable for ♿.
Credit cards All major cards accepted.
Terms B&B 168-196 frs; dinner, B&B: 290-390 frs; full board 320-490 frs. Full alc 230 frs.

GORDES 84220 Vaucluse — Map 11

La Mayanelle — *Tel* 90.72.00.28

The large and very well-known hill-village of Gordes, much used as a summer resort by the Parisian intelligentsia, stands on a steep rocky outcrop above the Coulon valley. Victor Vasarély's extraordinary "*musée didactique*", which he has installed in the local château as a shop-window for his own ego, is well worth a visit; so is the nearby Cistercian abbey of Sénanque, and the unusual *Village des Bories*, a group of primitive beehive-shaped huts converted into a museum. All this and much more can be explored by using as a base *La Mayanelle*, a small and elegant hotel perched on the cliff edge, and admired again this year: "Very French and exquisitely decorated with antiques. Our room was in subtle shades of red and gold. Every window opened onto a breathtaking view of the countryside, the staff were most welcoming and the restaurant was a gourmet's delight." It is worth asking for rooms overlooking the Lubéron valley. (*Lee Bennett, SD Carpenter*)

Open 3 Mar–3 Jan. Restaurant closed Tue.
Rooms 10 double – all with bath and/or shower.
Facilities 2 salons (1 with TV), 2 restaurants (1 with terrace). Garden and terrace. English spoken.
Location 38 km E of Avignon; hotel is central.
Credit cards All major cards accepted.
Terms Rooms 250-275 frs. Breakfast 30 frs. Alc (excluding wine) 150-190 frs. Reduced rates for children; special meals.

GOUMOIS 25470 Doubs — Map 10

Hôtel Taillard — *Tel* 81.44.20.75

Right by the Swiss border between Belfort and Neuchâtel, and secluded on the slope of a wooded valley, the Taillard family's spacious and gracious chalet is much reputed for its cooking (*Michelin* rosette). Experienced travellers enjoyed it this year: "A typical French country hotel, looking a little seedy from outside but with a large terrace which must be lovely in mid-summer. We can understand the obvious affection that regulars have for it. The food is French country cooking at its best with very ample portions – we remember especially the poached salmon." (*Angela and David Stewart*) As careful students of this annual Guide will know, the *Taillard* has one especially affectionate regular among its readers, and she too has been back this year and found it as good as ever: "We had a large bedroom and tiny sitting room with French windows overlooking the Alps and a balcony where we could have had breakfast had it not been lashing with rain. All was comfortable and cosy. The food is always the high spot, and this year we specially enjoyed the escalope de foie gras poché, the truite au bleu au vinaigre de champagne (I always have trout here and it never fails to delight), the delicious sorbets and excellent wines. The setting is beautiful, with lovely country walks." Earlier she had written: "Not a sound all night save the gurgling of the little stream in the gardens. The service is always cheerful. I cannot explain the magic generated by the Taillard family." (*Padi Howard*)

Open 1 Mar–early Nov. Closed Wed Oct and Mar.
Rooms 3 suites, 14 double – 14 with bath or shower, all with telephone.
Facilities Salon, TV room, bar, 2 dining rooms; terrace. River with trout fishing and canoeing; riding and winter sports nearby. English spoken.
Location 50 km SE of Montbéliard, 18 km E of Maiche on D437A and D437B. Leave *autoroute* A36 at Montbéliard Sud exit. The hotel is near the church. Parking.
Restriction Not suitable for ♿.
Credit cards All major cards accepted.
Terms [1987 rates] Rooms: single 110 frs, double 250 frs; full board 250-300 frs per person. Breakfast 24 frs. Set lunch/dinner 90-250 frs.

> We don't lack *Michelin*-rosetted hotels in France but would be glad of more nominations at the more modest end of the price scale.

> We need feedback on *all* entries. Often people fail to report on the best-known hotels, assuming that "someone else is sure to".

LA GRAVE 05320 Hautes-Alpes — Map 10

Hôtel La Meijette — *Tel* 76.79.90.34

This skiing and mountaineering resort stands 5,500 feet up near the Col du Lauteret, on the N91 Grenoble–Briançon road. It is somewhat drab in aspect, but the scenery and the skiing are great. *La Meijette* is on the main road, on a ledge above the Romanche torrent: its modern restaurant, finely built in wood, has been cantilevered out over the river and has spectacular views, shared by the bedrooms, over the valley and the snow-capped mountains.

Several recent visitors have written eagerly about the "spectacular" view from the restaurant and sun terrace, the "almost unbelievably beautiful" mountain flowers in June and early July, and the "charmingly helpful" Juge family owners. A few of the older rooms are small and dull, and those by the road can suffer from lorry noises in the early morning. One devotee has confirmed his earlier praise: "This is as near a perfect hotel for us as any we know – for its combination of setting, unostentatious comfort, very good, homely food, friendly family and possibly the best area for wild flowers known to us. Most of the bedrooms are chalet-type and very comfortable. There is a five-course meal each evening and a different menu on a two-week cycle." (*AS; also Peter McLeod, Pat and Brian Lloyd, BW Ribbons*)

Open Mar–mid-Apr, Jun–Sept. Closed Tue out of season.
Rooms 22 – all with bath and/or shower and telephone.
Facilities Lounge with bar and TV, restaurant; sun terrace. Winter sports. English spoken.
Location On N91, 77 km from Grenoble, 39 km from Briançon. Hotel is in centre of village. Parking.
Restriction Not suitable for ♿. Children over 10 preferred.
Credit cards None accepted.
Terms B&B: single 170 frs, double 230 frs. Set lunch 80-110 frs, dinner 110 frs; full alc 130 frs. Reduced rates for children under 7.

GRIMAUD 83360 Var — Map 11

Hostellerie du Coteau Fleuri — *Tel* 94.43.20.17

Place des Pénitents

Like some other hill-villages in the St-Tropez area, Grimaud is now fashionable with Parisians and others who have smartly converted its old stone houses into summer homes. This trend has at least given it a new lease of life. The *Coteau Fleuri*, on the edge of the village, is a 12th-century chapel converted into a neo-provençal *auberge* in local style, with tiled floors and plenty of flowers. There is a piano for guests to use, and a log fire for chilly days. Bedrooms are rather small – some are cell-like – but modern, with pretty furnishings and Provençal prints. A terrace leads to a delightful rambling garden slope, with olive trees. Bedrooms and dining room alike have fine view over the Maures mountains, but the sea is not visible. Hot water can be haphazard. The cooking is fairly sophisticated (e.g. veal cooked with langoustines) and has been admired. Previous reports have spoken of the friendly atmosphere, but this year a reader found the service slow and unhelpful, so we should welcome more reports. (*Mr and Mrs RB Tait, LH, and others*)

Open 1 Apr–31 Oct. Restaurant open mid-May–mid-Oct. Closed Wed except July and Aug.
Rooms 14 double – 9 with bath, 5 with shower, all with telephone. Ground-floor room.
Facilities Lounge/bar, 3 dining rooms; terrace. Small garden. Sandy beach nearby. English spoken.
Location 3 km from Port Grimaud; 10 km from St-Tropez. On edge of village. Parking.
Credit cards All major cards accepted.
Terms Double room with breakfast 318-408 frs. Set lunch 120 frs, dinner 170 frs; full alc 150-230 frs. Special meals for children on request.

GUÉTHARY 64210 Pyrénées-Atlantiques — Map 10

Hôtel Brikétenia — *Tel* 59.26.51.34
Rue de l'Empereur

On a hillside above this old fishing-port near Biarritz, a 17th-century Basque coaching-inn, run by the charming and talented Ibarboure family. Their Basque cuisine is very highly praised by our readers and the French guides (Michelin *rosette, two red* Gault Millau toques). *But bedrooms rank a poor second and have been found uncomfortable and fusty. Closed Nov and early Dec. 21 rooms, almost all with bath and shower. B&B double 300-330 frs. Set meals 38–140 frs. More reports needed.*

Hotel Pereria — *Tel* 59.26.51.68
Rue de l'Église

This old Basque house in a big, slightly unkempt garden is much admired as "a seaside hotel where families resort in an old-fashioned way, run by youngish, good-looking and friendly owners, with an attractive and demure staff". The annexe, across a busy road, is possibly more comfortable than the hotel itself, and bedrooms in both are large. Several readers this year have enjoyed the friendly efficiency and the good meals (e.g. ttoro, a Basque fish soup) served out on the terrace."Dishes of plum jam and warm croissants at breakfast, well-cooked and varied dinner menu. The ambience in fine weather is beautiful – there are hills and the distant sea, and you can watch the sunset from the outdoor dining terrace." (*Eileen and Ernest Greenwood, Dr IA Campbell, EB*)

Open 1 Mar–1 Nov.
Rooms 28 double, 2 single – all with bath, shower and telephone. 11 in annexe across the road.
Facilities Salon, 2 restaurants; terrace where meals are served. TV room. Garden with tables, *boules* and swings. Beach nearby with swimming, wind-surfing, sailing and fishing. English spoken.
Location On the coast between Biarritz and St-Jean-de-Luz.
Restriction Not suitable for ♿.
Credit card Visa.
Terms single 56-80 frs, double 183-190 frs. Breakfast 13.50 frs. Dinner, B&B (off-season only) 140 frs. Set lunch/dinner, 65, 100 and 140 frs; full alc 100 frs. Reduced rates for children.

> Many hotels put up their prices in the spring. Tariffs quoted in the text may be more accurate before April/May 1988 than after.

HAUT-DE-CAGNES 06800 Alpes-Maritimes — Map 11

Le Cagnard — *Tel* 93.20.73.21
Rue du Pontis-Long — *Telex* 462223

The sizeable town of Cagnes-sur-Mer is divided, like Caesar's Gaul, into three parts: the ugly sprawling resort of Cros-de-Cagnes; just inland, Cagnes-Ville, unremarkable save for the inspiring Renoir museum on its outskirts; and, higher up, Haut-de-Cagnes, one of the region's most sophisticated hill villages (fascinating museum in the château). Here *Le Cagnard*, a well-known and very *soigné* little hotel, has been artfully converted out of some 13th-century houses by the ramparts and virtually clings to the side of a cliff. Most readers continue to be enthusiastic: "As comfortable and enjoyable as ever." "Our room was the whole floor of a medieval house, with superb antique furniture and picture window." "Highly romantic." Rooms, however, vary considerably in size and comfort: one visitor this year felt that his had been insensitively modernised and was poorly maintained. It is worth asking for a room with a view of the coast (but these may be the costlier ones).

The cuisine, sometimes criticised in the past, is now "outstandingly good" according to a visitor this year, and has won back its *Michelin* rosette and gained a second *Gault Millau toque* for inventive adaptation of local dishes (despite these *nouvelle* influences, portions are large). The set menu is very expensive, but they do not mind if you take a light snack from the *carte*. You eat either on the beautiful terrace, with fine views, or in a graceful candle-lit room, former guardroom of the château. Breakfast is "outstanding". (*John Cliffe, David Wooff, Pat Clinch, HR, P and JT, and others*) Parking has always been a nightmare in the village, but planning permission has now been obtained for a public car park for 500 cars, to be located below *Le Cagnard* with a lift available for *Cagnard* residents, to be completed maybe by 1988.

Open All year except 20 Nov–15 Dec. Restaurant closed 20 Nov–18 Dec, 5–20 Jan and Thur midday.
Rooms 9 suites, 10 double – 18 with bath, 1 with shower, all with telephone and baby-listening; 12 with TV. 8 in annexe.
Facilities Lift. Bar, restaurant, crêperie; terrace; night club, disco. Small garden. Sea and rocky beach 3 km, sandy beach 10 km. English spoken.
Location On the ramparts, 2 minutes from château. Parking.
Restriction Not suitable for ♿.
Terms [1987 rates] Rooms: single occupancy 310 frs, double 600 frs, suites 660-1,000 frs. Breakfast 45 frs. Set lunch/dinner 300-380 frs.

LE HAVRE 76600 Seine-Maritime — Map 8

Hôtel de Bordeaux — *Tel* 35.22.69.44
147 rue Louis-Brindeau — *Telex* 190428 BOROTEL

A modern utility bed-and-breakfast hotel only five minutes' drive from the car ferry (ferry-catchers can get early breakfast). Friendly service, reasonable prices; bedrooms variable. 31 rooms, all with bath and/or shower. B&B double 380-485 frs. Some criticisms: more reports please.

> Don't keep your favourite hotel to yourself. The Guide supports: it doesn't spoil.

HENNEBONT 56700 Morbihan — Map 8

Château de Locguénolé et Résidence de Kernavien — *Tel* 97.76.29.04
Route de Port-Louis — *Telex* 950636 CHATEL

Stately home in south Brittany, family seat of the de la Sablières since 1200, in 250 acres of wooded parkland, with meadows stretching to the banks of a quiet river estuary. Cuisine is highly-priced and highly-rated (two Michelin *rosettes, three* Gault Millau *red* toques). *Some visitors have found the ambience cool and formal, the food not so special and the high prices* too *high but for others it was "a dream" with "truly magnificent cooking". 36 rooms, all with bath, 530–980 frs. Set meals 185–430 frs. No recent feedback, hence these italics.*

HONFLEUR 14600 Calvados — Map 8

La Ferme St-Siméon — *Tel* 31.89.23.61
Rue du Marais — *Telex* 171031

On the outskirts of the most picturesque and hence touristy of Norman fishing-ports, this is not the simple farmhouse that its name might imply but a very luxurious little hotel of considerable charm, fame and character. It is a much-gabled half-timbered 17th-century Norman house, which used to be a meeting-place of Impressionist and other painters (Monet, Corot and Boudin all worked at Honfleur). The *Ferme St-Siméon* was dropped from the Guide in 1984, as some readers felt it was over-priced and pretentious, but an expert hotel-watcher this year has no such qualms, so back it comes:

"The Boelen family owners have found ancient huge timbers for their new rooms downstairs, so they blend perfectly with the rest of the house. In the old timbered style they have converted a *pressoir* with large very elegant bedrooms, lavishly decorated, and superb modern marble bathrooms. A third building, an ancient manor house, also has bedrooms. We were warmly welcomed and had a delicious dinner, pleasantly served. One of the Boelen sons has a charming English wife, so no language problems for those with no French. Flowery gardens, and a lovely setting overlooking the sea." (*Wendy Arnold*)

Open All year.
Rooms 5 suites, 31 double, 2 single – all with bath and/or shower, telephone and TV. Rooms in three different buildings.
Facilities Lift. Lounge, restaurant. Garden with tennis court. English spoken.
Location 1 km NW of centre of Honfleur; near St Catherine's church.
Credit cards Access, Visa.
Terms Rooms: single 590 frs, double 1,000-1,400 frs, suite 2,400-3,000 frs. Breakfast 65 frs. Dinner, B&B 1,030-2,050 frs per person. Set lunch 200 frs; full alc 450 frs. Special meals for children.

HOSSEGOR 40150 Landes — Map 10

Les Huîtrière du Lac — *Tel* 58.43.51.48 and 58.43.51.26
1187 Avenue du Touring-Club

Many of Wellington's soldiers settled in this part of south-west France on their return from the Spanish campaign and they have left many souvenirs – among them, the name Hossegor which is said to be a local corruption of "horseguards". Today it is one of the larger family resorts on the Landes coast north of Biarritz: lovely long beaches, backed by pine forests and lakes. On one of these lakes is the *Huîtrière*, a restaurant-with-rooms new to the Guide this year and much reputed locally for its excellent fish (*Gault Millau toque*). "The spacious and airy restaurant was packed with French people, and our *demi-pension* terms included half a lobster as a starter at one meal. We had a simply furnished but large room with a balcony facing the lake. The staff were more than helpful and Madame Cotis speaks good English. We shall go back." (*S and T Philips*)

Open 1 Mar–1 Dec. Closed Wed in Mar, Sept and Oct.
Rooms 3 triple, 6 double – 3 with bath and shower, 6 with shower, all with telephone.
Facilities 2 lounges, bar, 2 restaurants; terrace. Beach 1 km with safe bathing, surfing and waterskiing. Tennis, riding and golf nearby.
Location In resort, 1 km from sea. Parking. Hossegor is 20 km N of Bayonne.
Restriction Not suitable for ♿.
Credit cards None accepted
Terms Rooms: single occupancy 160 frs, double 180-220 frs. Breakfast 20 frs. Dinner, B&B 200-220 frs per person; full board 290-310 frs. Set lunch/dinner 120, 160 and 240 frs; full alc 180 frs. Reduced rates for children sharing parents' room.

IGÉ 71960 Saône-et-Loire — Map 10

Château d'Igé — *Tel* 85.33.33.99
Telex 351915

A "beautiful little medieval castle", former hunting lodge of the Dukes of Mâcon, now a luxurious hotel set beside a stream on the edge of the Mâcon hills in Burgundy. Igé itself is a small village away from the main roads, with pleasant country lanes for walking or cycling. As for the hotel: "A proper castle with rounded turrets, grey ivy-covered walls and stone-flagged floors and staircases. It is full of character. We had a sizeable room in one of the turrets – the bedroom was circular, which felt slightly odd at first – with a large *en suite* bathroom. Food was good and the service friendly." A visitor this year enjoyed breakfast on the terrace and a suite of rooms full of antiques. Another has praised the home farm's goat's cheese and liked being able to select his own trout from a holding pond. Food is not cheap, but straightforward rather than fancy modern. (*GG Klima, K and SM-S, Clay Leitch, Mrs MD Prodgers*)

Open 5 Feb–5 Nov. Restaurant closed Thur midday.
Rooms 6 suites, 6 double – all with bath and/or shower and telephone; some with balcony. 1 in annexe.
Facilities Salon, 2 dining rooms. Garden, terrace. English spoken.
Location 6.5 km N of N79; 14 km NW of Mâcon, 11 km SE of Cluny.
Restriction Not suitable for ♿.
Credit cards Access, Visa.
Terms [1987 rates] Rooms: double 360-500 frs, suite 600-750 frs. Breakfast 45 frs. Full alc 250 frs. Set lunch/dinner 180 frs.

> Do you know of a good hotel or country inn in the United States or Canada? Nominations please to our sibling publication, *America's Wonderful Little Hotels and Inns*, PO Box 150, Riverside Avenue, Riverside, Conn. 06878, USA.

JARNAC 16200 Charente — Map 10

Domaine de Fleurac — *Tel* 45.81.78.22

An attractive 16th-century château, rebuilt in the 19th century, set in its own pleasant grounds amid the rolling Cognac vineyards. "We thoroughly enjoyed our stay," says a visitor this year. "The food was delicious, though expensive and slowly served. Michel Guichemerre, the English-speaking owner, gives a friendly welcome." Another reader found the place "very pretty inside, with a marvellous *trompe l'oeil* floor in the lounge (and there *is* a lounge, a leg-up on most French hotels). Altogether very civilised, almost luxurious. Rooms very pleasant, all different – ours, with a marvellous bed, was newly decorated all in jet black, which sounds awful but wasn't." (*Diana Holmes, Gerald Campion*) M. Guichemerre prides himself on his collection of Cognacs.

Open All year except Nov. Closed Mon 15 Sept–15 May.
Rooms 1 suite, 9 double, 6 single – 10 with bath, 6 with shower, all with telephone. Singles in annexe.
Facilities Bar, Cognac lounge, TV room, 3 dining rooms. Garden. English spoken.
Location At Fleurac, 9 km NE of Jarnac: take N141 towards Angoulême, then D 384.
Credit cards Access, Visa.
Terms [1987 rates] Rooms: single 180 frs, double 430 frs. Breakfast 29 frs. Alc (excluding wine) 170-240 frs.

JOIGNY 89300 Yonne — Map 9

À la Côte Saint-Jacques — *Tel* 86.62.09.70
14 faubourg de Paris — *Telex* 801458 SAINJAC

Patron/chef Michel Lorain has long been reputed for his fine cooking at this old coaching inn beside the river Yonne, on the edge of a little town north of Auxerre. Now, by dint of various improvements, he has succeeded in making his way into the topmost bracket of small hotels serving exquisite cuisine in luxury surroundings with bedrooms and prices to match – to be mentioned in the same reverential breath as Boyer at Reims, Blanc at Vonnas, Guérard at Eugénie-les-Bains (qq.v.). He now belongs to *Michelin*'s select band of 19 three-rosette places, while *Gault Millau* too has upgraded him from three *toques* to four (red ones, of course, for "inventive cuisine").

Two of our most fastidious experts have stayed there twice in the past two years: "Excellent food, needless to say, with many unusual combinations and flavours. The newly renovated restaurant is attractive, and Jacqueline Lorain points out unusual bottles from her large wine list, including many outstanding burgundies. As for the bedrooms, the family have made a huge investment in modernising and have created some magnificent rooms from old houses across the noisy N6, overlooking the river. To provide access to them, they have tunnelled under this road, with a lift each end and a paved tunnel decorated with Roman remains from the excavation, plus antique urns and heads. The rooms and apartments are probably among the finest in France: all have huge window walls over the river and many have a small terrace. The bathroom, marble from floor to ceiling, was as large as many hotel bedrooms." (*Pat and Jeremy Temple, endorsed by RS Ryder*)

Open All year except Jan.
Rooms 8 suites, 7 double – all with bath and shower, telephone, radio, TV and baby-listening. All in annexe linked to main building by underground passage.
Facilities Salon/bar, bar, breakfast room, 3 restaurants; conference room; indoor heated swimming pool. Garden. English spoken.
Location 27 km NW of Auxerre on N6; leave at Sens exit.
Restriction Not suitable for ♿.
Credit cards Amex, Diners, Visa.
Terms (Excluding 12% service charge) Rooms 980-1,250 frs. Breakfast 60 frs. Set lunch/dinner 400 frs. Full alc 450 frs.

KAYSERSBERG 68240 Haut-Rhin — Map 9

Hôtel Résidence Chambard — *Tel* 89.47.10.17
13 rue du Général de Gaulle — *Telex* 880272

Albert Schweitzer was born in this picturesque Alsatian wine-village, and in its main street is a small museum devoted to him. Down the road is the *Chambard*, whose *patron/chef* Pierre Irrmann has taken two buildings and renovated them radically, preserving the pretty facades. His smartish restaurant-with-rooms puts its accent on serious eating: "It's *nouvelle* but not too much so," says an inspector, "and I think it merits its *Michelin* rosette and two red *Gault Millau toques*, though it's of course expensive. The marinated raw salmon and garlicky ragout of lamb were delicious; puddings were lavish and the Alsatian wines reasonably priced for once. But the bedroom annexe lacks the personality of a hotel, though the modernised rooms are comfortable. Breakfast, served in a foyer with dubious repro decor, included freshly-squeezed orange juice. It might be worth paying the 100 francs extra to secure the one special room, which has a big canopied bed and a quaint round salon in a 15th-century tower. Rooms at the back have small balconies overlooking the vineyards." (*Jonathan Williams, and others*)

Open All year except 1–20 Mar and 1–15 Dec. Restaurant closed Sun evening and all day Mon.
Rooms 2 suites, 16 double, 2 single – all with bath and shower, direct-dial telephone, radio and TV; some with balcony.
Facilities Lounge, TV room, bar, breakfast room, restaurant; cellar for conferences/functions. 3-acre grounds. English spoken.
Location 10 minutes NW of Colmar on D4. Hotel is central, but quiet. Parking.
Restriction Not suitable for ♿.
Credit cards All major cards accepted.
Terms (Excluding 3% tax per person) Rooms: single 330 frs, double 350-400 frs, suite 450-470 frs. Breakfast 35-40 frs. Set lunch/dinner 160-280 frs.

LACAVE 46200 Dordogne — Map 10

Le Pont de l'Ouysse — *Tel* 65.37.87.04

Not far from Rocamadour, a restaurant-with-rooms in a charming situation by a river, with a château looming above and a dining terrace for fine weather. Reputed regional cooking (Gault Millau toque), *fairly expensive. Open 1 Mar–11 Nov. 12 rooms, recently renovated, all with bath and shower. B&B double 360-380 frs. Set meals 120–160 frs. No recent reports: more welcome.*

LAMASTRE 07270 Ardèche — Map 10

Hôtel du Midi/Restaurant Barattero — *Tel* 75.06.41.50
Place Seignobos

A hotel in the market square of a pleasant little town in ravishing country on the edge of the Rhône valley, 40 kilometres west of Valence on the road to Le Puy. One faithful fan returning this year finds it close to his ideal of what a small French provincial hotel should be. "Very pleasant room with tremendous bathroom," runs another report. "Excellent service, food possibly a little expensive, although some dishes were superb, notably the raie with special sauce and the pigeon de Bresse served with honey and two cabbages." Clearly the *Midi*'s star asset is the cooking of owner/chef Bernard Perrier (*Michelin* rosette, red *Gault Millau toque*), though one visitor found it too *nouvelle cuisine* for his taste, with small portions. Bedrooms are spacious and clean, but "the fittings may have dated from the 1930s and reminded me of the Queen Mary". Another reader had a room at the front, dully furnished and noisy with traffic, but he thought the restaurant most attractive – "each dish was introduced and described in great detail by our waiter as he served it". Back rooms, or those in the annexe, are the quietest. (*John Cliffe, M Berge, and others*)

Open 1 Mar–15 Dec. Closed Sun evening and Mon except July, Aug, and public holidays.
Rooms 18 – 13 with bath, 2 with shower, all with telephone.
Facilities 2 salons, 3 restaurants. Garden. Fishing nearby.
Location Central. Parking.
Credit cards Access, Visa, Diners
Terms [1987 rates] Rooms: single 150-200 frs, double 200-250 frs; full board 280-330 frs. Breakfast 30 frs. Set lunch/dinner 135-300 frs; full alc 250-300 frs. Reduced rates and special meals for children.

Château d'Urbilhac — *Tel* 75.06.42.11
Route de Vernoux

Very different from our other Lamastre entry, this Guide newcomer is a beautifully converted 19th-century château in Renaissance style, complete with pepperpot tower, and it stands high on a hillside in its own 150-acre wooded park just outside the town. "A small gem of a château with a most charming *châtelaine*, "write experienced travellers. "It has a fine swimming pool and a glass conservatory dining-room where food was excellent and service quietly efficient. Public rooms are furnished in heavy French provincial style, but our bedroom was prettily decorated and well fitted." (*Angela and David Stewart*)

Open 1 May–10 Oct.
Rooms 2 suites, 10 double, 2 single – all with bath or shower and telephone. 2 apartments in annexe.
Facilities Bar, salon, 2 dining rooms; terrace. Garden, heated swimming pool. English spoken.
Location 2 km S of Lamastre on D2 to Vernoux.
Credit cards All major cards accepted.
Terms Rooms: single 250 frs, double 400-450 frs, suite 650 frs. Breakfast 40 frs. Dinner, B&B: single 400 frs, double 380-400 frs per person. Set lunch 150 frs; full alc 200 frs. Reduced rates and special meals for children on request.

LANGRES 52200 Haute-Marne — Map 9

Grand Hôtel de l'Europe — *Tel* 25.87.10.88
23-25 rue Diderot

Langres is an interesting town set high on a ridge, with fine ancient ramparts, an old cathedral, and many 17th-and 18th-century buildings. Near its centre is this traditional stone-fronted hostelry, a useful *étape* on the way to Switzerland and this year more popular with readers than ever: "Exceptional value for money. We had a large room, comfortable and quiet, and after dinner spent a pleasant time in the bar talking to the charming manager." "A wonderful four-course meal for 85 francs [1987]" (red *Michelin* "R" for good value). Rooms vary in size and facilities: those at the front are the best, and all are quiet. (*Sally and Curtis Wilmot-Allistone, RCJ Gordon, MS Thornton, and others*)

Open All year except 1–15 May, 1–24 Oct and Sun evening. Restaurant closed midday on Mon.
Rooms 2 suites, 25 double, 1 single – all with bath and/or shower, and telephone; 9 with TV. 8 (with shower) in annexe.
Facilities Salon, bar, TV room, 2 restaurants. English spoken.
Location Between Chaumont (35 km) and Dijon (66 km). Hotel is central (rooms overlooking garden are quietest). Garage facilities for 20 cars.
Restriction Not suitable for ♿.
Credit cards All major cards accepted.
Terms Rooms: single 70 frs, double 140 frs, suite 180 frs. Breakfast 20 frs. Set lunch/dinner 50, 85 and 130 frs; full alc 160 frs.

LAPOUTROIE 68650 Haut-Rhin — Map 9

Hôtel-Restaurant Les Alisiers — *Tel* 89.47.52.82
5 Faudé

Unlike our other Alsatian entries, mostly smart, this Logis de France *is cheap and rustic: an old farmhouse with beamed ceilings, secluded up in the Vosges but only 19 km from Colmar. Good food, friendly* patron, *wonderful value. Some rooms small, others bigger with glorious mountain views. Open 1 Jan–8 Mar, 15 Mar–15 Nov, 25–31 Dec. 15 rooms, a few with bath or shower. B&B double 248 frs. Set meals 80–164 frs. Few recent reports: new ones, please.*

LESTELLE-BÉTHARRAM 64800 Pyrénées-Atlantiques — Map 10

Le Vieux Logis — *Tel* 59.71.94.87
Route des Grottes

New to the Guide this year, this simple flower-girt country *auberge* could make an excellent excursion centre, for it is near to Lourdes and within easy reach of the high Pyrenees and the delightful city of Pau, while the interesting Bétharram caves are right next door. "It is peacefully situated, with extensive grounds, peacocks in the courtyard, and pleasant views of the Pyrenean foothills. Two large friendly Pyrenean dogs bounded up to greet us. The staff were pleasant, too. For a ridiculously low price [120 francs, 1986], we had a comfortable room in a wooden chalet in the grounds. The restaurant was spacious and attractive, with good food (*Michelin* red 'R'), and breakfast (very good coffee) was served in a cosy room with an open fireplace." (*Kay and Neville Varley*) More reports welcome.

Open 1 Mar–1 Nov. Restaurant 1 Mar–15 Jan.
Rooms 15 double – all with bath, shower and telephone. 5 chalets in the park.
Facilities Lounge, restaurant. Garden.
Location 12 km W of Lourdes and 3 km E of Lestelle-Bétharram, on N637.
Restriction Not suitable for ♿.
Credit cards Access, Visa.
Terms B&B: single 150–180 frs, double 170–200 frs; dinner, B&B: single 200–210 frs, double 300–320 frs; full board: single 260–280 frs, double 410–440 frs. Set lunch/dinner 70–140 frs; full alc 250 frs.

LIVERDUN 54460 Meurthe-et-Moselle — Map 9

Hostellerie des Vannes et sa Résidence — *Tel* 83.24.46.01
6 rue Porte-Haute

The Moselle curves majestically just below the panoramic windows of the dining-room, and only 16 kilometres away is the city of Nancy (where the 18th-century Place Stanislas is also majestic, and very lovely). New to the Guide this year, this *hostellerie* is a rather elegant restaurant-with-rooms, where Jean-Loup Martin's ambitious cooking (especially the fish dishes such as duo de rouget et de rascasse) is very well thought of (*Michelin* rosette, two red *Gault Millau toques*). "Up a rather dingy staircase, we were shown into a remarkably pretty and well-equipped bedroom, with antique chairs, a very comfortable bed, and large windows overlooking the river which changed its colour between sunset and sunrise. It was all very peaceful and we enjoyed our meal served in the glassed-in veranda, though it was possibly not as good as the *Michelin* rosette would indicate." (*Angela and David Stewart*)

Open All year except Feb. Closed Mon except bank holidays.
Rooms 2 suites, 6 double, 3 single – all with bath, shower and telephone. 6 in annexe. 2 ground-floor rooms.
Facilities Lounge, 3 dining rooms. Garden. English spoken.
Location On river bank on edge of town which is 16 km NW of Nancy.
Credit cards All major cards accepted.
Terms Rooms: single 210 frs, double 350 frs, suite 420-450 frs. Breakfast 35 frs. Set lunch/dinner 135-275 frs; full alc 350-400 frs. Special meals for children on request.

LOUVIE-JUZON 64260 Pyrénées-Orientales — Map 10

La Forestière — *Tel* 59.05.62.28
Route de Pau

Towards the Pyrenean foothills south of Pau, a small, trim and attractive little hotel in shady gardens, backed by wooded hills (good walking country). Charmingly furnished bedrooms, some with mountain views. Elderly owners assisted by young staff, somewhat sedate ambience; good traditional local cooking. 13 rooms, all with bath. B&B double 250-310 frs. New nomination: more reports please.

LUYNES 37230 Indre-et-Loire — Map 10

Domaine de Beauvois — *Tel* 47.55.50.11
Telex 750204

In a stretch of the Loire valley where the grander hotels look indistinguishable from the châteaux visited by tourists, here is a typical grace-and-favour establishment set in a 450-acre park: "A well-kept manor with genuine 15th-century tower. It is in a nice rural setting up a hill beyond the village of Luynes, 13 kilometres from Tours. Our sizeable bedroom, with its matching fabrics, had a lovely light and warm feel, with a view from its windows down over a lake to wooded hills beyond. The restaurant was a little large and impersonal, but the food was excellent and plentiful (not always the case in a place of this kind, that carries a *Michelin* rosette and two red *Gault Millau toques*) and the service good: on the 230 franc menu [1986] we especially enjoyed the sole in a peppery sauce and veal in a ginger sauce." (*Kate and Steve Murray-Sykes; also Tony Woollard*)

Open Mid-March–Mid-Jan.
Rooms 9 suites, 28 double – all with bath and shower and telephone; some with TV. 1 suite in villa on estate. 4 ground-floor rooms.
Facilities Lounge, bar, TV room, restaurant; conference rooms. 350-acre grounds with heated swimming pool, hard tennis court and wooded park. English spoken.
Location NW of Luynes off D49; watch for "Beauvois" signs.
Credit cards Access, Visa.
Terms [1987 rates] Rooms: single 740 frs, double 1,175 frs, suite 1,290–1,735 frs. Set lunch/dinner 220-310 frs.

LYON — Map 10

Hotel Bayard — *Tel* 78.37.39.64
23 place Bellecour
Lyon 69002

Very central, in big main square, a tiny unassuming hotel recommended for budget travellers. Humdrum entrance but comfortable and cheerfully decorated rooms; breakfast in a kind of outdoor patio. No restaurant, but try the little bouchons *(bistros) in the St-Paul and Vieux Lyon areas. 15 rooms, most with bath and/or shower. B&B double 175-220 frs. New nomination: more reports please.*

La Cour des Loges — *Tel* 78.42.75.75
2468 rue du Boeuf — *Telex* 330831
Lyon 69005

France's second city is as short on really attractive hotels as it is rich in excellent restaurants. But at last a high-class hostelry of individual character has opened in 1987, in the St-Jean quarter of Vieux-Lyon, just across the Saône from the centre. It has been formed by restoring four adjacent Renaissance buildings, all with Florentine galleries, giving onto a central courtyard. Lavish decor including marble corridors; superior bedrooms; swimming pool. No restaurant, but the Michelin-*rosetted* Tour Rose *is almost next door. 63 rooms, all with bath, 850-1,250 francs. New nomination: more reports please.*

LYS-CHANTILLY 60260 Oise — Map 9

Hostellerie du Lys — *Tel* 44.21.26.19
Rond-point de la Reine — *Telex* 150298 HOTELYS

Attractive discovery this year, just 45 kilometres north of Paris off the road to Chantilly: "Lys-Chantilly is a stockbroker-belt estate of prosperous villas spaced out neatly amid woodlands. Here we rather liked this low-gabled hostelry, serenely fronted by a big lawn and tall trees; it is very quiet and has a pleasant outdoor terrace where you can drink or take a meal. Popular with Parisian weekenders, the hotel has an intimate, civilised ambience; reception and dining-room staff were smiling and efficient. Good classic dishes on the 130-franc set menu. Bedrooms perfectly adequate for a night or two's halt, though the upkeep was not perfect and the wallpaper usual French garish. Breakfast so-so." (*J&KA*)

Open All year except 21 Dec–5 Jan.
Rooms 35 double – all with bath and/or shower, telephone and TV. Ground-floor rooms.
Facilities Lounge, restaurant, salon with TV; 3 functions rooms. Garden and terrace for outdoor meals and drinks. English spoken.
Location Turn W off N16 at Lamorlaye (signposted).
Credit cards All major cards accepted.
Terms [1987 rates] Rooms: single 230-340 frs, double 285-360 frs. Breakfast 29 frs. Set lunch 130 frs, dinner 145 frs; full alc 150-200 frs. Reduced rates for children; special meals.

MAILLY-LE-CHÂTEAU 89660 Yonne — Map 10

Le Castel — *Tel* 86.40.43.06

A *Relais du Silence* in a village between Auxerre and Avallon: "We found the setting, the village and the hotel itself with its attractive decor all quite charming. Madame is attentive and the food is good, with many imaginative dishes – e.g. snails in garlic butter with an addition of chopped hazelnuts, and calves' liver in a cream sauce, all delicious." This year one visitor was disappointed by the food, but another thought it "excellent"; several have praised the peace and quiet, and the large comfortable bedrooms, though some are said to be pokey. Pleasant views to the river Yonne and pretty country beyond. (*Susi Pennycard, Alison Symonds, and others*)

Open 15 Mar–15 Nov.
Rooms 2 suites, 10 double – all with bath and/or shower, and telephone. 2 ground-floor rooms.
Facilities Lounge, restaurant; functions facilities. Garden with terrace. English spoken.
Location 30 km S of Auxerre, 30 km NW of Avallon. Turn off N6 at either of these towns or at Nitry. Hotel is in centre of quiet village. Parking.
Credit cards Access, Visa.
Terms Rooms: single 130-200 frs, double 210-280 frs, suite 300 frs. Breakfast 20 frs. Set lunch 72 frs, dinner 135 frs.

> The length of an entry does not necessarily reflect the merit of a hotel. The more interesting the report or the more unusual or controversial the hotel, the longer the entry.

LA MALÈNE 48210 Lozère — Map 10

Château de la Caze — *Tel* 66.48.51.01

Visitors this year to the "fantastic landscape" of the Tarn gorges have warmly endorsed these two earlier reports: "In this wild and unique natural setting one comes upon a 15th-century château rising out of spacious grounds with the hills of the gorges surrounding it and the river rushing past its side. All the rooms are furnished in 15th-century style, with tapestries and painted ceilings. There is an annexe with a terrace where one can enjoy the view and where the bathrooms have huge sunken Roman baths. The food is extremely good and the dining room (the château's former chapel) is comfortable, with fine service." "A sympathetic conversion, so the castle still looks as it must have done hundreds of years ago. Our bedroom was vast, with genuine antiques, polished wood floor, modern bathroom. The sheltered terrace overlooks a moat, now a trout stream, providing one of the hotel's specialities. Light, beautifully-prepared food, fully deserving its *Michelin* rosette and pleasantly served by young girls." (*M and GS, A and DS; also J and A McGlashan*)

Open 2 May–15 Oct. Restaurant closed Tue.
Rooms 6 suites, 8 double – all with bath, telephone and TV. Suites in annexe.
Facilities Salons, dining room; terrace. Large grounds with garden and stream.
Location 5.5 km NE of La Malène which is equidistant from Mende and Millau.
Restriction Not suitable for ♿.
Credit cards Access, Diners, Visa.
Terms [1987 rates] Rooms 420-620 frs. Breakfast 45 frs. Alc meals (excluding wine) 230-350 frs.

MARSEILLES — Map 11

Résidences Le Petit Nice et Marina Maldormé — *Tel* 91.52.14.39, *Telex* 401565 PASSEDA
Corniche JF Kennedy
Marseilles 13007

Small, stylish, and superior, *Le Petit Nice* is the last place you might expect to find in noisy, dusty proletarian Marseilles. It stands aloof. Though well inside the conurbation, it is secluded on an isolated strip of rocky coast (access down a narrow alley is not easy if your car is large) and has fine views across the bay. The house was built in the last century by the Passédat family who turned it into a hotel in 1917 and still own and run it today. The restaurant is a richly-decorated Hellenic-style villa with a pretty garden: a curving picture-window overlooks the sea. The *Marina Maldormé* is a curiously named bedroom annexe with elegant classical-style rooms. A recently returning visitor enjoyed "modern Provençal cuisine of a very high standard" (two *Michelin* rosettes, two red *Gault Millau toques*) on the terrace by the pool - "juicy pink fillets of lamb with whole cloves of garlic, superb pastry work and an aïoli which cried out to be photographed. The cooking is shared by father and son Passédat." (*David Wooff*)

Open 8 Feb–31 Dec. Restaurant closed Mon, and 1 May.
Rooms 2 suites, 15 double – all with bath and shower, telephone and TV. 8 in annexe.

Facilities Lift in annexe. 2 lounges, bar, restaurant. Garden with sea-water swimming pool, solarium and terrace; rocky beach. English spoken.
Location 4 km SW of city centre, off Corniche Kennedy. Take small street called Traverse de la Cascade by No 160 on the Corniche. Parking.
Credit cards Amex, Visa.
Terms [1987 rates] Rooms 500-1,000 frs, suite 1,100-1,600 frs. Breakfast 63 frs. Set lunch/dinner 428-489 frs; full alc 550-600 frs.

MARTIN-ÉGLISE 76370 Seine-Maritime — Map 9

Auberge du Clos Normand — *Tel* 35.82.71.01
22 rue Henri IV

Just inland from Dieppe, on the edge of a forest, this former 16th-century *relais de poste*, now a restaurant-with-rooms, is as redolent of Normandy as its name implies. The bedrooms are in a separate vine-covered building, once stables or a hayloft, with a romantic garden which has a pavilion for eating out in summer and a stream; it's very quiet except for farmyard noises. The accommodation until recently was defiantly unmodernised, and we used to receive reports of sagging beds, gouty chairs, sinister *armoires*, and even flooding toilets and rotten balconies. But all that seems to have changed, for the bedrooms (say the management) have just been renovated, and our own 1987 postbag bears this out: "I was expecting something much more ramshackle, but our room was lovely, with pink bedspreads, clean and well appointed." "We had a good room with a newly-installed bathroom." But what has been the effect of the transformation on the "Chekhovian atmosphere" and the "wayward and personal charm" that used to appeal to so many readers? Has the baby gone out with all this newly-installed bathwater?

Dinner has long been admired – generous helpings of Norman cooking with lashings of cream, butter and calvados. Several readers this year were again pleased, especially with the duck terrine and sole meunière, though one was disappointed. "Service was conducted with charm and aplomb by Madame," says one reader, though some have found her "chilly". Above all, the setting delights – "farmhouse sounds and smells" and "a selection of cats, a stick-retrieving dog and the river abounding in young frogs". (*Deborah Newman, Mrs Allfrey-Pizer, Robert CC Sandys, and others*)

Open 1 Mar–15 Nov. Restaurant open 1 Feb–15 Dec. Both closed Mon evening and Tue.
Rooms 1 family, 8 double – all with bath and/or shower and telephone. All in separate building in garden.
Facilities Lounge with TV, restaurant; functions room/ballroom. Garden with large lawn and stream; pavilion for outdoor summer meals. Some English spoken.
Location 5 km from Dieppe; off D1 to Neufchatel.
Restriction Not suitable for ♿.
Credit cards Access, Amex, Visa.
Terms Double room 214-278 frs, family room 278 frs. Full alc 147.50 frs. Guests are expected to dine in the restaurant.

> We asked hotels to estimate their 1988 tariffs some time before publication so the rates given are often arbitrary. Please always check terms with hotels when making bookings.

MENDE 48000 Lozère — Map 10

Hôtel de France — *Tel* 66.65.00.04
9 boulevard Arnault

"The Lozère, France's least populated department, has far more sheep than human inhabitants. But tourists come crowding in summer to its beautiful forests and valleys. The river Lot winds along one of these, past the tiny capital city of Mende, and here in the town centre this *Logis de France*" (new to the Guide) "would make a good one-night stop or excursion centre (the Gorges du Tarn are nearby). It is run with friendly professionalism by the Brager family and has been thoroughly modernised – almost too much so, for a near-Germanic degree of neatness is more in evidence than wayward rural charm. My efficient modern bedroom was remarkable value for 123 francs [1987]. But the cuisine in the tidy beamed dining-room remains happily traditional, and the 60-franc menu left me feeling that *Michelin*'s red 'R' is deserved. Breakfast so-so." (*JA, endorsed by Yves and Ghislaine Gonssard*)

Open 1 Feb–15 Dec. Restaurant closed Sun evening and Mon.
Rooms 28 double – 22 with bath and shower, 2 with shower only, all with telephone. 5 ground-floor rooms.
Facilities Bar, salon, restaurant, TV lounge. English spoken.
Location Central.
Credit card Visa
Terms B&B: single 140-200 frs, double 240-260 frs. Dinner, B&B: single 210-270 frs, double 380-400 frs. Set lunch/dinner 70-150 frs; full alc 170 frs.

MERCUREY 71640 Saône-et-Loire — Map 10

Hôtellerie du Val d'Or — *Tel* 85.45.13.70
Grande Rue

Visitors continue to speak well of this hostelry in the main street of a village producing one of Burgundy's great wines (there are several *caveaux de dégustation* close by). Here the "courteous and efficient" Cogny family provide jovial cohorts of Burgundians with generous helpings of *nouvelle*-ish *cuisine* (*Michelin* rosette, two *Gault Millau toques*). Bedrooms are comfortable and charmingly decorated, if a little cramped. Light and colour in the garden, armchairs in the salon, and sociable chatter in the attractive restaurant with its stone-tiled floor, flowers and lamps. The middle-priced set menu is said to be good value and there is a decent range of Mercurey wines.

Open 8 Jan–25 Aug, 7 Sept–8 Dec. Closed Mon, also Tue midday 16 Mar–15 Nov, and Sun evening 15 Nov–15 Mar.
Rooms 1 suite, 10 double – all with bath, 8 with WC, all with telephone and TV.
Facilities Reception, salon, bar, 2 restaurants. Garden, swings. English spoken.
Location 13 km from Chalon-sur-Saône. Leave *autoroute* at Chalon Nord and take D978 Autun/Nevers road, then turn right to Mercurey. Parking.
Credit card Visa.
Terms Rooms: single occupancy 100 frs, double 280 frs, suite 365 frs. Breakfast 27 frs. Set lunch/dinner 130-280 frs; full alc 250-300 frs. Reduced rates and special meals for children.

MIMIZAN 40200 Landes — Map 10

Au Bon Coin du Lac — *Tel* 58.09.01.55
34 avenue du Lac

The long flat Atlantic coast south-west of Bordeaux has splendid sandy beaches, lined by a number of dullish resorts. Just inland are freshwater lakes amid the Landes forest, also with resort facilities, and here is *Au Bon Coin du Lac*. Its emphasis is on cuisine (*Michelin* rosette, two red *Gault Millau toques*), though its recently modernised bedrooms are of good quality too, according to this year's visitors. An earlier account: "At first sight the hotel resembles a seaside café, rather off-putting: but the setting is idyllic, and *patron-chef* Jean-Pierre Caule's cuisine fully merits its awards, especially the fish. Best stick to the set menus. The atmosphere is excellent, with a smiling Madame Caule leading a friendly team. The hotel lies by the lake shore, six kilometres inland, surrounded by pine trees and with Monet-style bridges leading off into forest walks – an oasis of tranquillity. The only sound to disturb us at night was a cat fight." Rooms alike in the annexe and the main building are now fairly luxurious. (*EH, AJ Flaherty, I and FW*)

Open All year.
Rooms 4 suites, 5 double – all with bath and shower, telephone, radio, TV and baby-listening. Suites in annexe, with kitchenette. Ground-floor rooms.
Facilities Lounges, bar, dining room; functions rooms; terrace. Garden with children's games. English spoken.
Location 2 km N of Mimizan, which is 111 km SW of Bordeaux. Parking.
Credit cards Amex, Visa.
Terms Rooms: single occupancy 250-350 frs, double 350-550 frs. Breakfast 45 frs. Set lunch/dinner 120-260 frs; full alc 260 frs. Reduced rates and special meals for children.

MIRAMAR 06590 Alpes-Maritimes — Map 11

Le Tour de l'Esquillon — *Tel 93.75.41.21*

Back in the Guide this year, after an inspector's report: "A fine purpose-built holiday hotel, dating back to 1926, on the red-rocked Esterel corniche west of Cannes, with a spectacular location high up facing the bay of Cannes like a set for Coward's *Private Lives*. All rooms are decently furnished and face the sea, and most have a balcony: but oddly these adjoin the bathrooms, so you get a breathtaking view if you take a shower but not from your bed. The pleasant restaurant faces the view, but our dinner lacked distinction and was poor value for money. A *cabine-téléférique* swoops you down over beautiful gardens to a small private rock lido (bar and snacks available): a lovely place to swim and sunbathe, but you have to pay 80 francs for it even as a resident. In sum, a good hotel with a friendly air, spoilt only by the dullish food. The genial owner, M. Derobert, says his is the last privately owned hotel in the area."

Open 1 Feb–18 Oct.
Rooms 25 – all with bath and shower.
Facilities Lounge, bar, restaurant. Garden. Private beach. English spoken.
Location 15 km NE of Cannes, on N98. Garage parking.
Restriction Not suitable for ♿.
Credit cards All major cards accepted.

Terms [1987 rates] Single 500 frs, double 650 frs. Breakfast 50 frs. Set lunch/dinner 150 frs. Reduced rates for children.

MOLINES-EN-QUEYRAS 05390 Hautes-Alpes — Map 10

Hôtel l'Équipe — *Tel* 92.45.83.20
Route de St-Véran

A small chalet-hotel in a broad high valley south-east of Briançon, with ski-slopes and wooded hills all round. Nearby is the 13th-century fortress of Château-Queyras, and the isolated village of St-Véran, which at 2,040 metres claims to be the highest in Europe. Here a rough narrow road runs into Italy via the Col Agnel. Two recent commendations of *l'Equipe*: "Fantastic value for money. We had a comfortable bedroom with a balcony giving magnificent views. The set meals show an imaginative streak – as well as cheese fondue and raclette, there is sometimes even couscous and (for a supplement) quail with grapes." And: "There's no night life around here, but interesting 'happenings' in season, such as folk-singing, and fireworks displays on the hills. The *Équipe,* no architectural gem, is an unpretentious, comfortable and relaxed place, run with quiet and kindly efficiency by the Catalins. Monsieur leads excursions into the mountains. Our *en pension* meals were copiously served, and breakfast came with very light fluffy croissants." Sometimes the Catalins throw all the guests together for a fondue party. (*Ursula Price, Pat and Brian Lloyd*)

Open 19 Dec–17 Apr, 11 June–18 Sept.
Rooms 22 – all with bath and telephone. 11 with 2-4 beds in annexe. Some ground-floor rooms.
Facilities Salon, TV room, bar, restaurant; dancing once a week in winter. Terrace. Winter sports (ski lifts 50 metres).
Location 1 km from village of Molines on road to St-Véran.
Restriction Not suitable for ♿.
Credit cards All major cards accepted.
Terms B&B: double room 267 frs; dinner, B&B 196 frs per person; full board 252 frs. Set lunch/dinner 52, 81, 108 frs; full alc 120 frs.

MONTBAZON 37250 Indre-et-Loire — Map 10

Château d'Artigny — *Tel* 47.26.24.24
Route d'Azay-le-Rideau — *Telex* 750900

This most seigneurial hotel stands in its own 60-acre park above the valley of the Indre, south of Tours. It looks like a peerless 18th-century château, but in fact is a pastiche: it was built in the 18th-century style in 1919 by the famous *parfumier* François Coty. He spared little expense: there is a huge staircase in polished limestone, an imposing gallery, a brass-inlaid marble floor in the dining room, delicate wood-carving in the library and so on. Heated swimming pool, tennis, wooded walks; sophisticated Parisian clientele. Chamber music concerts of some quality are held from October to March. The restaurant wins a *Michelin* rosette and two *Gault Millau* red *toques* for such innovative dishes as poached eggs with ragoût of coxcombs and cocks' kidneys (!).

One reporter this year had her mind boggled: "It made me feel splendidly decadent – and splendid was indeed the word for the huge hall: its Versailles-ish feeling made the reception hall look like the postcard stall at a stately home. Vitrines display the latest Baccarat etc. Our room, furnished with lovely antiques, was in the annexe – no ordinary annexe but the chapel converted, and it gave me a slightly sacrilegious feeling to bath and besport myself scantily dressed amongst clearly religious pillars. In the very, very smart restaurant, dinner was most enjoyable as the sunset through the huge windows gave way to scores of real candles in the candelabra. The food, exceptionally served, was all one would have wished in such surroundings. An idyllic walk in the grounds to the Belvédère (concert hall) where a vernissage was in progress – we were offered champagne and ladies with miniature poodles shook our hands." Two other recent visitors were slightly less impressed: one had a poor mattress on her four-poster bed and the other found the service "not very friendly". (*Francine Walsh; and others*)

Open 10 Jan–28 Nov.
Rooms 7 suites, 46 double – all with bath and/or shower and telephone. 23 in converted chapel and pavilions near main building. 6 ground-floor rooms.
Facilities Lift. 2 salons, TV room, bar, 2 dining rooms; conference and functions facilities. Large garden with 2 tennis courts, heated swimming pool with grill in summer, ping-pong, putting; fishing, riding, rowing, private flying courses nearby; golf 12 km. English spoken.
Location 13 km S of Tours. Leave N10 at Montbazon; turn right on D17 towards Azay-le-Rideau. 2 km on left is private road leading to the Château.
Credit card Visa.
Terms [1987 rates] Room: 520-1,020 frs, suite 695-1,160 frs. Breakfast 55 frs. Set lunch/dinner 210-350 frs. Children under 6 half price, under 12 30% reduction; special meals on request.

MONTICELLO 20220 Corsica — Map 11

Hôtel A Pasturella — *Tel* 95.60.05.65
Monticello, L'Ile Rousse

Monticello is a medieval hamlet high on a hill above the smart resort of L'Ile Rousse. For some years now, visitors have been succumbing to the charm of the modest *A Pasturella* ("lively atmosphere, good country cooking, friendly family owner"), to which *Frank Muir* first introduced us: "It can be a bit noisy, but it is clean, bright and happy, and the food is plentiful and cheap." Other praise has since flowed in: "Food enjoyable, with a wide choice of cheeses, some fiercely Corsican." "A cool white dining room with polished dark furniture, bright daisies on the tables and glorious views. M. Martini is a cheerful and gentle host who murmurs the menu of the day confidentially to the diners, no menu appearing on paper. The children work efficiently in the dining room and Grandfather Martini grows the vegetables, besides minding his sheep. The silence at night was lovely – no luxury here, but a perfect base for the hill-walker." Red "R" in *Michelin* for good value. *Warning:* some rooms are very small, and those in the converted cellar annexe can be stuffy: it is best to book early and get a room which "opens on a stupendous view". (*D Hammond, LH, WH Bruton*) We have had no reports this year, and would much like new ones.

Open Open all year except Nov.
Rooms 15 double – all with bath and shower. 5 in annexe 20 metres from main building.

Facilities Salon with TV, bar, restaurant. Beach 4 km.
Location 3 km SE of L'Ile Rousse.
Restriction Not suitable for ♿.
Credit cards None accepted.
Terms Rooms: single occupancy 150 frs, double 180 frs. Breakfast 25 frs. Set lunch/dinner 75 frs. Reduced rates and special meals for children.

MONTMORILLON 86500 Vienne — Map 10

Hôtel de France — *Tel* 49.91.00.51
Restaurant Mercier
2 boulevard de Strasbourg

A comfortable family-run hostelry in a pleasant little town between Limoges and Poitiers. Spacious rooms, courteous staff, attractive dining room and good cooking (popular with locals) all praised by readers, though one report this year was critical of plumbing, service and food. Open 2 Feb–31 Dec. 25 rooms, 10 with bath or shower. B&B double 220-250 frs. Set meals 95–225 frs. More reports welcome.

MONTPELLIER 34000 Hérault — Map 10

Hôtel de Noailles — *Tel* 67.60.49.80
2 rue des Écoles-Centrales

This 17th-century mansion is not easy of access by car (without a good street map, at least), for it lies in the heart of the *vieille ville*, a network of quiet alleys, some closed to traffic, that forms the kernel of this graceful southern city. The hotel too is graceful, in a cool classical style, and again in 1987 has been strongly commended: "Charming and comfortable, with good breakfasts." Another reader found the staff caring and the contrast with modernism quite blissful. But there are warnings that front rooms can be noisy, especially from the bell tower next door. No restaurant, but you can eat well at the *Chandelier* (medium/upper price) or *La Gabelle* (cheap). (*Maureen Montague, Mary Yeigh, RG and E Tennant*)

Open Mid-Jan–mid-Dec.
Rooms 27 double, 3 single – 20 with bath and shower, 10 with shower only, all with telephone and TV. 1 ground-floor room.
Facilities Reception, salon/TV room. English spoken.
Location Central, near church of Notre Dame de Tables. Nearby parking not easy; the hotel advises guests to use the underground car park in place de la Comédie, entrance opposite Monoprix (300 metres S).
Restriction Not suitable for ♿.
Credit cards All major cards accepted.
Terms Rooms: single 250 frs, double 300–360 frs. Breakfast 30 frs. (No restaurant.)

MONTREUIL 62170 Pas-de-Calais — Map 9

Château de Montreuil — *Tel* 21.81.53.04
4 chaussée des Capucins — *Telex* 135205 HOTEUIL

A large old house set in a lovely walled garden, close to the ruined citadel in a quiet part of the medieval hilltop town of Montreuil. It is the first really stylish and ambitious hotel along the main road going south from

Calais and Boulogne; nearly all the guests are British, as is *la patronne*, which of course influences the atmosphere, even though the cooking, the decor and the building itself are essentially French. So tourists arriving in search of their first true taste of *la douce France* may be disappointed – "more London Home Counties than French", as one put it.

The rooms are furnished in a variety of styles: all have polished tiled floors with rugs, some have panelled walls and fireplaces, and some are adorned with plaster casts of parrots and monkeys. The resident owners, Christian Germain, former *chef de cuisine* at Bray, and his English wife Lindsay, are *protégés* of the famous Roux brothers of the *Gavroche* in London and the *Waterside Inn* at Bray. *Michelin* has awarded them a rosette, and *Gault Millau* again bestows two red *toques* (wild duck with ginger and paupiette de sole à l'indienne are specialities). Again in 1986/7 most readers have been delighted, alike with the food and the hotel itself; just one or two, however, have found their meals disappointing, the ambience pretentious, and weaknesses in the housekeeping. (*PW Barratt, Rosamund V Hebdon, Mrs J Cookson, Dr RL Holmes and Dr MW Atkinson, and many others*)

Open All year except mid-Dec–1 Feb. Restaurant closed Thur lunchtime in low season.
Rooms 11 double, 3 single – 12 with bath, 2 with shower, all with telephone and baby-listening; 24-hour room service. 3 ground-floor rooms in garden annexe, 1 suitable for ♿.
Facilities Sitting room, bar, breakfast room, restaurant; conference facilities. 1-acre garden. 18 km from sandy beach at Le Touquet. English spoken.
Location 38 km S of Boulogne, just off N1. Hotel is 450 metres from centre of Montreuil, opposite the citadel. Parking.
Credit cards All major cards accepted.
Terms Rooms: single 350 frs, double 480-550 frs. Breakfast 43 frs. Set lunch 240 frs; full alc 300 frs. Cookery courses. Mid-week off-season breaks. Reduced rates and special meals for children.

MONTRICHARD 41400 Loir-et-Cher — Map 10

Hôtel Bellevue — *Tel* 54.36.06.17
Quai du Cher

In an attractive old town on the Cher near Chenonceaux, a modern hotel with fine views of the river. Large, well-furnished rooms (front ones can be noisy), welcoming Madame, good simple country cooking. Closed 15–21 Dec, Mon evening and Tue in winter. 29 rooms, most with bath or shower, 125–245 frs. Set meals 78–200 frs [1987]. *Few recent reports: more needed.*

Hotel de la Tête Noire — *Tel* 54.32.05.55
24 rue de Tours

Nominated this year by a regular visitor to France as a useful alternative to the *Bellevue*: "We could not fault this splendid place, solid and old-fashioned, and quite cheap. Our room and bathroom were spacious, with the decor one might expect in this setting. The dining room was lively and full of locals, with food average to good. The eye of La Direction was everywhere, keeping the large and youthful staff on its toes. Long corridors beside the windows are used as a kind of sun-parlour, with comfortable armchairs." (*Mrs RB Richards*)

Open 7 Feb–3 Jan. Closed Fri 15 Oct–18 Mar.
Rooms 38 – 20 with bath, 11 with shower. 9 in 2 annexes (1 by river).
Facilities Salon, TV room, residents' bar, 3 dining rooms; conference facilities. Terrace, garden. Fishing in river Cher 100 metres. English spoken.
Location Central. Parking.
Restriction Not suitable for ♿.
Credit cards Access, Visa.
Terms Rooms: single 138-192 frs, double 138-220 frs, suite 145-260 frs. Breakfast 23 frs. Set lunch/dinner 70-200 frs.

MONT-ST-MICHEL 50116 Manche — Map 8

Hôtel La Mère Poulard — *Tel* 33.60.14.01
Telex 170197

No other site in France outside Paris attracts more tourists than Mont-St-Michel, that offshore granite pyramid linked to the coast by a causeway at low tide and capped by a towering ramparted Benedictine monastery. An overnight stay is well worth it, for then you can appreciate the aura of the place when the milling crowds have left in the evening, and visit the abbey early the next morning before they arrive, "an unforgettable experience". *La Mère Poulard,* facing you as you pass the rampart gates, is not the only hotel, but it has the most character and tradition, also a restaurant long famous for its omelettes and praised too for its classic Norman and Breton cooking (*Michelin* rosette, one *Gault Millau toque*). "The food was some of the best we had in France and the omelette-making ritual is clearly more than a gimmick," runs one report this year. Another: "An unforgettable stay. The experience of staying Easter Saturday and visiting the Abbey at midnight for the service was perfectly complemented by the hotel. Service was excellent. The food even better." Not a hotel for the elderly as the stairways to the rooms are steep and narrow. (*Gordon Bond, Geraldine Cox, GG Klima, John Ring*)

Open All year.
Rooms 3 suites, 15 double, 4 single – 17 with bath and/or shower, all with telephone.
Facilities Lounge, bar with TV, games room, restaurant, omelette room. Fishing and bathing nearby. English spoken.
Location Just inside walls of Mont St-Michel. Large car park across causeway.
Restrictions Not suitable for ♿. No babies in restaurant.
Credit cards All major cards accepted.
Terms Half board (obligatory): single 590-690 frs, double 830-1,030 frs. Set lunch 150 frs, dinner 300 frs; full alc 350 frs. Special meals for children.

MONTSALVY 15120 Cantal — Map 10

Auberge Fleurie — *Tel* 71.49.20.02
Place du Barry

The lovely upper Lot valley, the Truyère gorges and amazing Conques (q.v.) are all within easy reach of this typical Massif Central village where the *Fleurie* has been commended: "Delightful, also cheap – a creeper-covered building in a village amid marvellous wooded country. Comfortable rooms; no private bathrooms, but we had our own shower and bidet. Charming owners and dining room with red check tablecloths and good bourgeois food. Breakfast in the bar where the postman drops in for a chat. For those who want not luxury but a typical French atmosphere." (*June Bullough*) In Montsalvy, Mrs Bullough recommends also the *Hotel du Nord*, slightly larger and smarter, also with a red *Michelin* "R" for its value-for-money regional cuisine (e.g. tripoux d'Auvergne). More reports needed.

Open All year. Restaurant closed 15 Nov–15 Feb (only breakfast served).
Rooms 17 double, 1 single – 6 with shower, 1 with WC. 5 in old house 1 km away.
Facilities Salon with TV, bar, 2 dining rooms; banqueting facilities. Small grounds; annexe has 5-acre grounds. Lake 1 km for fishing and wind-surfing. English spoken.
Location 35 km of S of Aurillac by D920 towards Rodez.
Restriction Not suitable for ♿.
Credit cards All major cards accepted.
Terms [1987 rates] Rooms 93-113 frs. Breakfast 17 frs. Dinner, B&B 160-173 frs per person. Set lunch/dinner 42, 64 and 95 frs; full alc 130 frs. Reduced rates and special meals for children.

MOUGINS 06250 Alpes-Maritimes — Map 11

Le Mas Candille — *Tel* 93.90.00.85
Boulevard Rebuffel — *Telex* 462131 MASCAND

An Englishman, Alan Kimber, former manager of the *Carlton* in Cannes, now runs this graceful and very attractive *auberge* in the fashionable hill-village of Mougins, just behind Cannes (it has more good restaurants per square metre, including Vergé's mighty *Moulin*, than any other place in France, but few good hotels). Converted from a 17th-century farmhouse, the white-walled *Mas Candille* stands peacefully in its own flowery park, on a wooded hillside, looking out across the valley – a blessed retreat from the tumult of the Côte. "A lovely old hotel, the cooking was perfection and all services impeccable," runs a comment this year, echoing earlier ones: "Wonderful hospitality", "food and comfort excellent, we had a splendid time", "comfortable though not de luxe, cuisine of a high standard", are among recent reports. Most rooms are "rural" in style, a bit cramped, but well appointed, with old beams and fireplaces: front ones have balconies with good views. You can eat either in the cool dining room or out in the flower garden above the valley where at night the mood is wistfully poetic. The cuisine has *nouvelle* touches (red *Gault Millau toque*) but most dishes are classical (e.g. ris de veau aux morilles), and cheaper light meals are served in the bar or bar terrace. The swimming pool is small but in a lovely setting, amid firs and olive trees. Recent modernisation of the hotel has brought in some air-conditioning and other benefits. (*JA and KA, P Roberts, Donna Chiaro, Robin Schiel, and others*)

Open All year, except 2 weeks in Jan and mid-Nov–mid-Dec. Restaurant closed Tue midday; also Tue night in low season (light meals always available).
Rooms 1 suite, 22 double – all with bath, shower and telephone; some with balcony or terrace; some with air-conditioning. 1 in small house, *La Fermette*.
Facilities Bar, salon with TV, 2 restaurants; terrace with bar. Large garden with swimming pool. Golf, tennis, riding and beaches nearby. English spoken.
Location 800 m W of the village, which is 6 km N of Cannes. Parking.
Restriction Not suitable for ♿.
Credit cards All major cards accepted.

Terms Rooms: 550-720 frs, suites 850-1,100 frs. Breakfast 50 frs. Set lunch/dinner 220, 270 and 310 frs; full alc 375 frs; light meals served in bar. 1-night bookings sometimes refused in high season.

MOULINS 03000 Allier — Map 10

Hôtel de Paris — *Tel* 70.44.00.58
21 rue de Paris — *Telex* 394853

Near the centre of this attractive old market town, a small and select hotel, fairly smart and expensive. Comfortable rooms, personal service, "period" decor in variable taste. In the panelled restaurant, excellent and imaginative cooking (Michelin *rosette, two red* Gault Millau toques)*: some cheaper menus, good value. Closed Sun and Mon out of season. 28 rooms, all with bath or shower, 228-420 frs* [1987]. *Set meals 80–310 frs. No recent reports: more welcome.*

NAJAC 12270 Aveyron — Map 10

Hôtel Belle-Rive — *Tel* 65.29.73.90
Au Roc du Pont, Route 039

In this remote but scenic part of the Massif Central, Najac is a beautiful medieval village above the gorges of the Aveyron, with a fairy-tale castle high on a hill above the river. The *Belle-Rive* has a choice traffic-free position by a bridge a short distance from Najac; it is run by the Mazières family and again in 1987 has won praise for its fair prices and good food: "Service was cheerful in the large, busy dining-room where generous helpings of plain, nourishing fare made our 55 franc [1987] set meal a bargain." Others have enjoyed dining on the terrace, listening to the river and gazing across at the floodlit castle. If you ask, you can choose between a small older-style bedroom with a view of the castle and a larger modern one. This year a regular on his *ninth* visit writes: "The new feature, brought about no doubt by a surge of Eperon-inspired clients, is a mid-Atlantic speaking lady who takes away some of the fun of trying one's French on the Mazières." Another recent report warns that if you are on full *pension*, you will be allocated a table in the dining room and miss the pleasures of a table with a view on the terrace. (*P Stattersfield, Dr A Frank, H Morris, and others*)

Open 26 Mar–15 Oct.
Rooms 42 double – 9 with bath, 31 with shower, all with telephone. 8 in annexe, 4 ground-floor rooms.
Facilities Lift. Salon with TV, bar, 4 dining rooms; terrace. Large garden with children's play area and heated swimming pool. Fishing. English spoken.
Location 2 km N of Najac on D39, on edge of village. Parking.
Credit card Visa.
Terms [1987 rates] Rooms 135-180 frs. Half-board. (3 days min) 170-180 frs per person; full board 210-220 frs. Breakfast 17 frs. Set meals 55, 90, 140 frs; full alc 130 frs. 1-night bookings may be refused in high season. Reduced rates and special meals for children.

> We get less feedback from smaller and more remote hotels. But we need feedback on all hotels: big and small, far and near, famous and first-timers.

Hôtel Miquel: l'Oustal del Barry *Tel* 65.29.74.32
Place du Bourg

A welcoming little hotel on the village square, with white chairs and tables outside. Readers this year agree that this central position makes it possibly a better option than the *Belle-Rive* for a short stay. "Our room was large and clean if rather bare, with a tiny balcony and wonderful view. Hot croissants and delicious home-made jam atoned for the awful coffee. Cheerful service except for Madame la Réceptioniste who never once smiled." "Comfortable, and a good main restaurant, even if the *pension* menus are boring and served in a separate room." An earlier report: "There is a private well-tended garden nearby for sunbathing and for children to let off steam, complete with climbing frame, roundabouts. At dinner, generous helpings of well-cooked regional food." (*RA Mayon, PS, JH; also P Talbot-Smith*)

Open Early Apr–end Oct. Closed Mon Apr and Oct except holidays.
Rooms 18 double, 3 single – all with bath and/or shower and telephone. 7 in annexe.
Facilities Lift. Salon with TV, reading room, bar, 2 restaurants; 2 terraces. Large garden with play area and small swimming pool for children, *boules*. Tennis courts nearby; river Aveyron 2 km with fishing and canoeing. English spoken.
Location Coming from Villefranche de Rouergue or Cordes on D122 hotel is on right at entrance of village. Parking.
Credit card Visa.
Terms [1987 rates] Rooms: single 129-157 frs, double 157-180 frs; dinner, B&B: 173-203 frs per person; full board 203-233 frs. Breakfast 20 frs. Set lunch/dinner 90, 150 and 220 frs; full alc 200 frs. Reduced rates for children; special menu.

NANTILLY 70100 Haute-Saône Map 10

Le Relais de Nantilly *Tel* 84.65.20.12
Telex 362888

An elegant 1830s château standing in its own wooded park to the west of Gray, which is midway between Dijon and Besançon on a useful cross-country route from the coast to Switzerland. It has a tranquil rural setting, the trees of its gardens busy with birds and a slow stream running along its boundary. "The flowers and decor were fresh and beautiful," runs a report this year, "the courtesy of the staff was outstanding; food very much *nouvelle cuisine* but of high quality." Others have liked the "pretty dining room" and "relaxed atmosphere". The food is traditional and copious but not cheap, and one or two visitors have been disappointed by the lowest-priced set menu – worth paying extra for one of the others. All rooms have just been renovated. (*PH Freeman, BH Jenkinson, Dr Bill and Lisa Fuerst, and others*)

Open 1 Apr–20 Oct.
Rooms 3 suites, 11 double – all with bath, telephone and TV. 5 simpler but well-equipped rooms in annexe 50 metres from château.
Facilities Bar, salons, breakfast rooms, restaurant; conference facilities; terrace. Grounds with outdoor swimming pool, tennis court and heliport. 4 km from river Saône with beach, boating, waterskiing and fishing. English spoken.
Location 4 km W of Gray by D2. Parking.
Credit cards All major cards accepted.
Terms [1987 rates] Rooms: 450-560 frs, suite 1000 frs. Breakfast 45 frs. Set lunch/dinner 175 and 230 frs.

NARBONNE 11100 Aude **Map 10**

Hôtel la Résidence *Tel* 68.32.19.41
6 rue du Premier Mai *Telex* 500441 SOMARES

In a quiet street in the shadow of Narbonne's great fortified cathedral, an unusual little hotel in Victorian boudoir style, very feminine: Louis XV furniture, gilt mirrors, gold draperies, silk flowers in vases. Rooms very comfortable, breakfast excellent. No restaurant, but several good ones close by. Closed 3 Jan–1 Feb. 26 rooms, all with bath or shower. B&B double 360 frs. No recent reports: more welcome.

NICE 06300 Alpes-Maritimes **Map 11**

Hotel La Pérouse *Tel* 93.62.34.63
11 Quai Rauba, Capeu *Telex* 461411

Ejected from the 1986 Guide because of a change of ownership, the splendid *Pérouse*, upper-medium-priced, now regains its rightful place: "In a resort with 350 hotels, nearly all dull,this is much the best, apart of course from the super-luxury *Negresco*." Its setting is its strongest feature, for it is perched half-way up the castle rock at the east end of the promenade, with "breathtaking" views of the bay. "The jewel in the crown of Nice, and entirely charming," write experienced travellers this year. "Our room was spacious, equipped to the last detail. On our balcony facing that view, we shared our breakfast with half the pigeons of Nice – too late we saw the sign telling us not to feed them." "The pool area is attractive, at the side of the mountain amid a garden with lemon trees. Breakfast, drinks and snacks are served in the comfortable bar." Rooms vary greatly in price, but even the cheaper ones without sea views are said to be well furnished and comfortable. The hotel is quiet, because of its high position. No restaurant, but grills and snacks are served by the outdoor swimming-pool in summer; and there are scores of candle-lit bistros close by in the Vieille Ville. (*Jean and Eric Lace, Donna Cuervo, GB Morrison*)

Open All year.
Rooms 2 suites, 59 double, 3 single – all with bath and shower, telephone and TV; 14 with radio.
Facilities Lift. Bar/lounge, terrace. Garden with patio; 2 swimming pools with grill. English spoken.
Location At E end of Promenade des Anglais, by château. Parking 20 metres.
Credit cards All major cards accepted.
Terms Rooms: single 260-630 frs, double 340-860 frs, suite 945-1,300 frs. Breakfast 30 frs. Reduced rates for children. (No restaurant but light snacks and room service.)

NIEUIL 16270 Charente **Map 10**

Le Château de Nieuil *Tel* 45.71.36.38
Telex 791230

Between Angoulême and Limoges, this grand old Renaissance château complete with moat and 350-acre wooded park is a former hunting-lodge of François I, full of antiques and Aubusson tapestries and with an imposing marble staircase – and of course it is not cheap. Readers continue to praise its beauty and comfort, the kindliness of M. Bodinaud, the owner, and the qualities of the cuisine (*Michelin* rosette). Here is one recent report by a true connoisseur of this kind of place: "The gardens are lovely, and the château bears the stamp of several generations of French nobility. Yet the atmosphere is not pretentious. It is both friendly and sophisticated, and M. Bodinaud is truly affable with his guests. Dinner, a mixture of trad and modern, was good but not outstanding, with generous helpings, imaginative salads, and a choice of 46 different fruit tarts. Each course was decorated with fresh flowers. The dining-room, panelled, had napery so well starched that it could stand up unaided. We were somewhat embarrassed, however, by M. Bodinaud's gimmick of putting a flag of the appropriate nation on each guest's table. There was an amazing cold buffet lunch alfresco by the pool, served with stately deference to bikini-clad beauties, some of them topless. M. Bodinaud is also an art buff, and in the former stables he exhibits and sells expensive prints, modern paintings and sculptures. Lastly, eight of the young female staff are British, sent to M. Bodinaud by the cream of British domestic science colleges – 'Everything here,' said one, 'has to be ten times better than what would be considered normal in an English hotel.'" (*Francine and Ian Walsh; also Dr TJ David, Susan Welch, and others*)

Open 29 Apr–12 Nov.
Rooms 3 suites, 12 double – all with bath and/or shower, and telephone; some with mini-bar; TV and baby-listening on request. 1 in converted chapel 40 metres from main building. 2 ground-floor rooms.
Facilities Salon/bar with TV, restaurant; conference facilities. 350-acre wooded park with swimming pool, tennis court, fishing in pond, archery and art gallery. English spoken.
Location Off D739, between Nieuil and Fontagie; 42 km NE of Angoulême.
Credit cards Access, Amex, Visa.
Terms Rooms: single occupancy 400 frs, double 700 frs, suite 1,300 frs. Breakfast 45 frs. Set meals 175 and 220 frs.

NONTRON 24300 Dordogne — Map 10

Grand Hôtel Pélisson — *Tel* 53.56.11.22
3 place Alfred Agard

An old walled town on a hill, roughly midway between Angoulême and Périgueux, in the so-called "Périgord Vert". The *Pélisson*, a *Logis de France*, is a former coaching-inn on the main square, with a spacious rear courtyard, good for parking, and again this year it has won warm praise: "Food of high quality beautifully cooked with complete simplicity – the best of French country cooking" and "Wonderful peaceful countryside, friendly, helpful people, and our double room for 150 francs was an incredible buy. Attentive cuisine, big portions, e.g. ris de veau, magret de canard" (red "R" in *Michelin* for good value). Earlier reports: "Not a luxury place, but all you expect a French hotel to be: bright, welcoming and '*correct*'. The rooms are large and sparkling, the service attentive but unfussy, the menu and wine list outstanding value." (*Peter Norton, Mark Ottaway, Pamela Pierce, and others*)

Open All year.
Rooms 22 double, 4 single – 16 with bath, 2 with shower, all with telephone.

Facilities Lift. Salon with TV, bar, dining room; functions facilities; terrace. Garden. Swimming pool, tennis courts and doll museum nearby.
Location 45 km SE of Angoulême. Centre of town. Garage.
Credit card Visa.
Terms [1987 rates] Rooms 85-210 frs. Breakfast 18 frs. Dinner, B&B 160-180 frs per person; full board 200-220 frs. Set lunch/dinner 50-180 frs; full alc 130 frs. Special meals for children.

NOUAN-LE-FUZELIER 41600 Loir-et-Cher — Map 10

Le Moulin de Villiers — *Tel* 54.88.72.27
Route de Chaon

Between Orléans and Bourges, this long low building is an old millhouse lost in the silent Sologne forests beside its own lake full of ducks. An unassuming, informal hotel with large adequate bedrooms; in the beamed dining room, good food at modest price but with little choice. Open 20 Mar–30 Aug, 14 Sept–3 Jan. 20 rooms, some with bath or shower. B&B double 140-240 frs. Set meals 75 frs. Few recent reports: more welcome.

NOVES 13550 Bouches-du-Rhône — Map 11

Auberge de Noves — *Tel* 90.94.19.21
Telex 431312

A 19th-century manor amid pleasant open country south-east of Avignon, now owned and run by André Lalleman as a stylish and luxurious hotel, well-known for its cuisine (*Michelin* rosette, two red *Gault Millau toques*). Dropped from the 1987 Guide for lack of news, it is now freshly recommended by three correspondents. All praise the rooms, the food, and M. Lalleman's charming attentive presence: but like others in the past they have found the gardens ill cared-for. "A friendly and helpful atmosphere. M. Lalleman presided over the tree-covered *terrasse* where dinner is served, and proved an amusing, intelligent and multi-lingual host. The cuisine is quite *nouvelle*: our noisettes d'agneau were unbelievably rare even by French standards. Excellent antiques in the bedroom, elegant pink marble bathroom – but we could have done with a mini-bar in the heat! An expensive place, marginal value for money." "We can recommend the duck en papillote. M. Lalleman, who talks perfect English with a cultured accent, personally advised us on our choice of dishes. A magnificent breakfast on our balcony, served to us with a rose. The waitresses treat you like honoured guests. The hotel even has its own well, with refreshing spring water: but the pool and gardens were untidy and the public rooms have too much flowery wallpaper." Many rooms have a balcony with pastoral views. (*Pat and Jeremy Temple, J and A McGlashan; also G Godfrey-Isaacs*)

Open All year except early Jan–early Mar. Restaurant closed Wed midday.
Rooms 20 – all with bath and/or shower, and telephone; some with TV; some with balcony.
Facilities Lift. Salon, dining room; conference facilities. Garden with swimming pool and tennis court. English spoken.
Location Off D 28, 2km NW of Noves, which is 13km SE of Avignon.
Credit cards Access, Amex, Visa.
Terms [1987 rates] Rooms: 550-920 frs. Breakfast 50 frs. Set meals 300-330 frs.

NUITS-ST-GEORGES 21700 Côte d'Or — Map 10

Hôtel La Côte d'Or — *Tel* 80.61.06.10
37 Rue Thurot

A classic hostelry in a famous little wine town, now a sophisticated restaurant with beamed ceiling and red walls, where owner-chef Jean Crotet provides some of the best traditional cooking in Burgundy (two rosettes in *Michelin*, two *toques* in *Gault Millau*). As so often at this kind of place in France, the handful of bedrooms are entirely secondary to the main gastronomic purpose: but they too are very stylish. Nominated for the Guide this year by a party of exuberant eaters: "What a revelation – this is *haut* French food, served *haut*, but *not* stuffy. The hotel is small and on a busy *rue* – but large rooms, high ceilings, charming decor and *real* flowers – tiled baths, tons of hot water. A comfortable and livable room. We go down to dinner. A bottle of good, steely Chablis. Lamb, beef, fish – all so beautiful, so classic that the first forkful is heresy, the next heaven. Exquisite. One member opts for the chocolate puff pastry stuffed with banana sorbet, another for the hot lime soufflé. Madame serves with ultimate skill. Breakfast is simple, French and hot, includes an odd butter-based fruit cake. M. Crotet is always immaculate and slightly worried looking." (*A Gilbert*)

Open All year except 5–20 Jul, 10 Feb–5 Mar. Closed Sun evening and all Wed.
Rooms 1 suite, 6 double – all with bath, telephone and TV.
Facilities Salon, 2 restaurants. English spoken.
Restriction Not suitable for ♿.
Location Central; public parking. Nuits-St-Georges is 22 km S of Dijon, on N74.
Credit cards Access, Visa.
Terms Rooms: single occupancy 350 frs, double 480 frs, suite 600 frs. Breakfast 40 frs. Set lunch/dinner 250-450 frs; full alc 450 frs.

ORVAULT 44700 Loire-Atlantique — Map 8

Le Domaine d'Orvault — *Tel 40.76.84.02*
Chemin des Marais du Cens — *Telex* 700454 DOMDO

The growth of Nantes, north-west France's biggest city, has turned Orvault village, to the north-west, into a residential suburb. Here the *Domaine* is "surrounded by a tangle of dual carriageways", which hardly sounds promising. But in fact this smart modern hostelry stands quietly in a big wooded garden. "An oasis of tranquil greenery," says one visitor. "The public rooms are pleasingly plush, bedrooms are small but comfortable, looking over a garden. The hotel's supreme virtues are the charm of its *patron-chef* Jean-Yves Bernard and the excellence of his cooking" (*Michelin* rosette and two red *Gault Millau toques* again this year, for such inventions as salad of duck's liver and crayfish). Puddings and cakes are "served with enthusiasm". (*Gordon Bond, Mrs Howard L Miller, Martin Gilbert*)

Open All year. Restaurant closed 3 weeks in Feb, and Mon midday.
Rooms 1 suite, 30 double – all with bath and shower, direct-dial telephone, radio, TV and mini-bar. Some ground-floor rooms.
Facilities Lift. Bar, salon, TV room, restaurant; conference facilities. Garden with children's play area and tennis court. English spoken.
Location 7 km NW of centre of Nantes off N137 to Rennes. Parking.

Credit cards Amex, Diners, Visa.
Terms [1987 rates] Rooms: single 345–380 frs, double 420–500 frs. Breakfast 40 frs. Set lunch/dinner 160–380 frs; full alc from 300 frs. Special menu for children.

PARIS **Map 9**

Hôtel de l'Abbaye St-Germain *Tel* (1) 45.44.38.11
10 rue Cassette, 75006

"Excellent – very clean and comfortable, beautiful decor, friendly staff." So runs an endorsement of last year's entry for the ever-popular *Abbaye*, a former monastery delightfully restored and decorated with simple elegance. Wide windows open on to a lovely little flagged courtyard with palms, pot-plants and flowers, where breakfast or refreshments can be taken (no other meals served). The hotel is in a busy street near St-Sulpice, and though it is a *Relais du Silence*, front rooms are not entirely noise-free: best ask for one at the back. "An oasis of calm and peace," says a visitor this year. "Bedrooms are not large but exquisitely furnished. Our bathroom was tiled with genuine marble. We slept well and woke to the sound of church bells and birdsong." (*Ian and Francine Walsh, and others*) One critic this year found his top-floor room and its bathroom far too small.

Open All year.
Rooms 45 double – all with bath and shower, telephone and radio. Baby-sitting.
Facilities Lift. 2 salons (1 with TV), bar, breakfast room. Interior courtyard/garden. English spoken.
Location Central, near St-Sulpice church. (Métro St-Sulpice.)
Restriction Not suitable for ♿.
Credit cards None accepted.
Terms B&B: double room 500-630 frs. (No restaurant.)

Hôtel Châtillon *Tel* (1) 45.42.31.17
11 square de Châtillon, 75014

This very cheap and intriguing little hotel is in the Alésia district, about four kilometres south of the centre of Paris, and good for access to the Boulevard Périphérique and the Autoroute du Sud. "A charming and quiet place where we awoke to birdsong in the trees. The floorboards creak, the toilets flush like Niagara, the furniture was bought at a fire sale in 1941 . . . *but* the staff are delightful, the beds comfy, the rooms cosy, and breakfast is deliciously fresh, with *hot* coffee. Run by real easy-come-easy-go Parisians." (*Paul N Palmer*) Returning this year, Mr Palmer enjoyed it all just as much, and adds that there is now an underground car park near by.

Open All year except Aug.
Rooms 31 double – 24 with bath, 7 with shower, all with direct-dial telephone. 1 ground-floor room.
Facilities Salon with TV, bar, breakfast room.
Location Near Porte de Châtillon and Porte d'Orléans. Underground parking nearby. (Métro Alésia.)
Credit card Visa.
Terms Rooms: single occupancy 200 frs, double 230 frs. Breakfast 20 frs. (No restaurant.)

Hôtel des Deux-Iles *Tel* (1) 43.26.13.35
59 rue St-Louis-en-l'Ile, 75004 *Telex* 375974

An elegant 17th-century house has been prettily converted into a small hotel. Being in the middle of the Ile-St-Louis it has no views of the Seine, but there is a small flowery courtyard. Readers continue to be enthusiastic. "Charming atmosphere and decor", runs one report this year; "the staff were helpful and polite, the blue-and-white-tiled bathroom and the Provençal fabrics in the bedroom were attractive. We enjoyed our stay." Others have referred to the "cosiness and good taste" and "breakfast delicious and prettily served in blue and white china". There is also an attractive cellar-bar. Some readers have found the front rooms noisy in the early morning and the bedrooms a little airless in hot weather. And an American visitor told us of a booking that the hotel had failed to honour. (*Jean and John Ervasti, Jacques Visick, and others*)

Open All year.
Rooms 13 double, 4 single – all with bath and/or shower, telephone, TV and baby-listening.
Facilities Lift. Salons, bar. Garden. English spoken.
Restriction Not suitable for ♿.
Location Central. Parking nearby. (Métro Pont Marie.)
Credit cards None accepted.
Terms Rooms: single 425 frs, double 535 frs. Breakfast 30 frs. (No restaurant.)

Hôtel des Grands Hommes *Tel* (1) 46.34.19.60
17 place du Panthéon, 75005 *Telex* 200185 PANTEON

The "great men" are André Breton and other surrealist painters and writers who used to stay at this little hotel in the heart of the Latin Quarter. It has been praised again this year as a very clean and characterful place with helpful and friendly staff: "Our room had a stylish canopy bed, and its view of the lighted dome of the Panthéon was the most beautiful nightlight we've ever had." Each room is separately furnished in period style; breakfast is served in a stone-vaulted 18th-century cellar. But an oddly jarring note is struck by the radio playing loudly in the lobby and the recorded rock music at breakfast - would Breton have approved? (*JT and JH Ervasti; also Mary and Mike Dettrich*)

Open All year.
Rooms 32 double (also let as singles) – all with bath, direct-dial telephone, radio, TV, mini-bar.
Facilities Lounge with bar, breakfast room. Small garden. English spoken.
Location Opposite Panthéon. Underground paying car park 100 metres. (Métro Luxembourg.)
Restriction Not suitable for ♿.
Credit cards Amex, Diners, Visa.
Terms Rooms: single 320-520 frs, double 480-600 frs. Breakfast 26 frs. (No restaurant.)

L'Hôtel *Tel* (1) 43.25.27.22
13 rue des Beaux-Arts, 75006 *Telex* 270870

Discreet in its name but in nothing else, this famous little place was a sleazy joint when Oscar Wilde died here, broke. In 1967 it was smartened up by its owner, Guy Louis Duboucheron, to become the highest-priced small hotel on the Left Bank, much patronised by the likes of Mick Jagger and Julie Christie. "Elegant, expensive but worth it," writes our own nominator this year. "Very small rooms except for the penthouse suite which was superb." You can ask for the room (and bed!) that Wilde died in, or the one containing Mistinguett's Art Déco furniture. Velvet and antiques everywhere, pink Venetian marble in the bathrooms; winter garden converted into a chic and cosy little restaurant with resident pianist and illuminated fountain full of goldfish. (*Tony Woollard*) M. Duboucheron would agree that there is only one thing in the world worse than being talked about, and that is not being talked about – so do send us some reports.

Open All year. Restaurant closed in Aug.
Rooms 2 suites, 24 double, 1 single – all with bath and/or shower, telephone, radio, TV and tea-making facilities.
Facilities 3 salons, bar, restaurant. English spoken.
Location Central. (Métro St-Germain-des-Prés.)
Credit cards Access, Diners, Visa.
Terms Rooms: single 1,300 frs, double 850-1,700 frs, suite 2,300-2,700 frs. Breakfast 70 frs. Set lunch 150 frs. Full alc 250 frs.

Hôtel Lancaster *Tel* (1) 43.59.90.43
7 rue de Berri, 75008 *Telex* 640991 LOYNE
Reservations in UK (01) 439 2365

This exclusive and luxurious hotel just off the Champs-Élysées is owned by the Savoy group which also owns London's *Connaught* (q.v.), and it might be called its Paris equivalent. It maintains old-style traditions of service and has been praised again for this in 1987: "Room service was alarmingly swift." "The friendly staff take an obvious pride in their work." Another Lancastrian writes: "Of all the hotels I've ever stayed in, this is the one I'd most like to *live* in. Anything you might need to feel at home is there – towelling robes, plenty of writing paper, lots of table lamps to vary the lighting. Breakfast included superb pain au chocolat, fruit and fragrant coffee. The service is remarkable almost by its invisibility, and when it *is* visible it is accompanied by real smiles and courtesy. There are paintings and flowers, and the furnishings are quietly beautiful, from the soft lounges downstairs to Louis XIV beds with linen sheets, and inlaid desks and huge mirrors in the bedrooms." (*GV*) "Like putting the clock back to what I used to envisage a grand hotel to be." The restaurant has also been praised. One reader adds a sting this year: "The hotel's only drawback was the other guests, many of them loud-mouthed show-offs." (*Esme Walker, John Tovey, and others*)

Open All year.
Rooms 10 suites, 42 double, 14 single – all with bath and shower, telephone, radio and TV; baby-sitting by arrangement; some air-conditioning.
Facilities Lift. Hall, large salon, small salon, bar, restaurant; private dinner party/functions rooms; conference facilities. Garden patio which many rooms overlook, used for meals in fine weather. English spoken.
Location Central (garden rooms quietest), off Champs-Élysées and near Arc de Triomphe. Parking. (Métro Georges V.)
Restriction Not suitable for ♿.
Credit cards All major cards accepted.
Terms (Excluding 15% service charge) Rooms: single 1,200-1,400 frs, double 1,600-1,800 frs, suite 2,600-6,000 frs. Breakfast 85 frs. Set lunch/dinner 185 frs;

full alc 380 frs. Special weekend rates Jul–Aug, Nov–Mar. Reduced rates for children sharing parents' room; special meals on request.

Hôtel La Louisiane *Tel* (1) 43.29.59.30
60 rue de Seine, 75006

Those who saw Tavernier's wonderful recent movie *Round Midnight* may have noticed that this was the simple little Left Bank hotel where his Negro jazz musician hero lived in the 1950s. That is historically accurate. This is probably the most distinguished cheap hotel in Europe, for it is hallowed in literary and artistic history: Sartre, Hemingway, Connolly and others used to stay here (it's mentioned in *The Unquiet Grave*). Today the plumbing may be better and the geniuses, alas, far fewer: but basically it's unchanged, and this year again it has appealed to readers in search of blissful Rive Gaucherie at very low cost. "This is not a place for those seeking chic, and you may be put off by the cramped foyer and tiny lift: but the young staff are affable and the bedrooms, though very plain, are well modernised and amazing value at 230 francs with bath (1987). Front rooms look straight onto the colourful Buci street market; but there's double glazing, and upper or back rooms are very quiet." One reader this year suffered a muddle over a booking, but otherwise enjoyed the place – alike for the panoramic view of the Buci market from his window and, at breakfast, for that of the cosmopolitan clientèle – "a group of precocious child fashion-models were demanding croissants". This demand was because the help-yourself breakfast (in a very drab room) features not croissants but a kind of brown soda-bread (as well as good coffee ad lib). (*JA, Francis Durham, Sally and Christopher Davis, and many others*)

Open All year.
Rooms 79 – all with bath and/or shower, and telephone.
Facilities Lift. Breakfast room. English spoken.
Location Near St-Germain-des-Prés. (Métro St-Germain-des-Prés, Odéon.)
Credit cards Access, Diners, Visa.
Terms B&B: single 230 frs, double 300-350 frs. (No restaurant.)

Hôtel de Lutèce *Tel* (1) 43.26.23.52
65 rue Saint-Louis-en-l'Ile, 75004

"Small, charming and reasonably priced, in a great location." So runs a report this year on the sister hotel to the *Deux-Iles* (q.v.), in the long road that runs down the middle of the Ile. Rooms are minuscule, but comfortable and very clean and warm. A comfortable sitting area with a log fire. No food, but an excellent restaurant (*Les Chimères*) next door. "The staff are friendly, helpful people for whom speaking English is not a disgrace; breakfast wonderful." (*L and P Duttenhaver, David Mathiasen, and others*)

Open All year.
Rooms 23 double – all with bath and/or shower, direct-dial telephone, radio and TV.
Facilities Lift. Sitting room.
Location In centre of Ile-St-Louis. (Métro Pont-Marie.)
Restriction Not suitable for ♿.
Credit cards None accepted.
Terms [1987 rates] Rooms 550 frs. Breakfast 30 frs. (No restaurant.)

Hôtel le Pavillon *Tel* (1) 45.51.42.87
54 rue St-Dominique, 75007

Formerly a nunnery, now a simple but attractive little hotel just west of the Invalides, set back from the street with a small courtyard. Rooms small but clean and cheerful, recently renovated; friendly staff; no lounge; breakfasts good. 19 rooms, all with bath or shower, 190-390 frs. No recent reports: more welcome.

La Résidence du Bois *Tel* (1) 45.00.50.59
16 rue Chalgrin, 75116

Elegant Paris B&B – a Third Empire mansion in quiet position near the Étoile with charming garden. Small, de luxe, exclusive, furnished with period pieces. No restaurant, but light meals and breakfast provided on request. It has had many commendations in the past but lacks recent feedback. 19 bedrooms with bath and/or shower. Rooms: single 910 frs, double 1,320 frs.

Hôtel Scandinavia *Tel* (1) 43.29.67.20
27 rue de Tournon, 75006

A characterful hotel in a converted 17th-century building near the Luxembourg Gardens. Some bedrooms have Louis XIII antiques, red plush and velvet; a few have a balcony. Upper rooms reached by steep narrow staircase and can be very small. Service good and friendly. Closed Aug. 22 double rooms, all with bath and shower, 350 frs. Some criticism, few recent reports: more welcome.

Hôtel St-Merry *Tel* (1) 42.78.14.15
78 rue de la Verrerie, 75004

In the Marais, near the Pompidou Centre, a tiny medium-priced hotel whose mild eccentricity has delighted some, dismayed others. Housed in the former presbytery of the next-door church (one bedroom contains a flying buttress), it has antique furniture and fine matching fabrics. No lounge, no lift; charming patron *with German shepherd dog. Good breakfasts; some street noises. 13 rooms, all with bath or shower. B&B double 510-610 frs. No restaurant. More reports welcome.*

Hôtel de Suède *Tel* (1) 47.05.00.08
31 rue Vaneau, 75007 *Telex* 200596

In the heart of the old Faubourg St-Germain, aristocratic in Proust's day, governmental in ours. A smallish medium-priced hotel, approved again this year as being quiet, comfortable and good value for Paris. Rooms at the back overlook the gardens of the Hôtel Matignon, the prime Minister's residence and office. "Stylish in a somewhat formal way, and with a discreet, private feel to it. An adequate breakfast is served in the big salon, furnished in Directoire style with yellow-green upholstery. Here you can also get 'mini-snacks' such as omelettes. Service efficient, though night porter a bit bossy. Clientèle of young men in modish dress – is the hotel named after their footwear rather than any Nordic connection?" (*JA*) "An interior courtyard where they serve breakfast and drinks in summer. The police with machine-guns in the street, protecting Chirac etc, may not exactly create a holiday atmosphere, but they do make this a very safe part of Paris at night." (*Jane Dorrell*)

Open All year.
Rooms 1 suite, 33 double, 7 single – 37 with bath and/or shower, all with direct-dial telephone; baby-listening on request. 7 in pavilion in courtyard.
Facilities Lift. Lounge where drinks and snacks are served 6.30 am–10 pm. Small garden. English spoken.
Location 10 minutes' walk from Seine and St-Germain-des-Prés. (Métro Varenne.)
Credit cards Access, Amex, Visa.
Terms B&B: single 393 frs, double 431 frs, suite 723 frs. (No restaurant.)

Hôtel de l'Université — *Tel* (1) 42.61.09.39
22 rue Université, 75007 — *Telex* 260717 OREM 310

A 17th-century town house converted into an intimate small hotel, near the Seine and St-Germain-des-Prés: "We were delighted," runs a report this year. "It is very peaceful, our bedroom was furnished with antiques, and the staff welcomed our two-year-old son." This backs up earlier praise: "Classy, tasteful and stylish – it's what I come to Paris for. Brass street lamps light up the entrance. Inside, the public areas are beautifully decorated with antiques and tapestries. Beautiful touches were everywhere, from the scented soaps in my shower each day to the Limoges china with breakfast. This meal is taken at small marble tables looking out onto a charming tiny courtyard." (*Alison Symonds, Donna Cuervo*)
Back rooms are quieter.

Open All year.
Rooms 1 suite, 17 double, 10 single – 20 with bath, 8 with shower, all with telephone; baby-sitters available.
Facilities Lounge, bar. English spoken.
Location 5 minutes from St-Germain-des-Prés. Underground parking nearby. (Métro Rue du Bac.)
Restriction Not suitable for ♿.
Credit cards None accepted.
Terms Rooms: single 370-400 frs, double 450-750 frs, suite 950 frs. Breakfast 38 frs. 1-night bookings refused in high season. Reduced rates for children sharing parents' room. (No restaurant, but snacks served in bar.)

Hôtel de Varenne — *Tel* 45.51.45.55
44 rue de Bourgogne, 75007 — *Telex* 260717 abon 439

"One of my favourite little Left Bank hotels in this price range, is a regular visitor's comment this year on this converted mansion with a pretty courtyard, very near the Invalides. Others have written: "Very clean, but new bedspreads would brighten the rooms." "Peaceful, with a friendly and efficient staff. Nice comfortable rooms. Breakfast on patio or in lounge area." (*Vivienne Menkes-Ivry, Deborah Kelly, Dr Bill and Lisa Fuerst, and others*) *Warning:* occasional late night disco parties nearby.

Open All year.
Rooms 17 double, 7 single – all with bath and/or shower, direct-dial telephone and TV.
Facilities Lift. Lounge, patio. English spoken.

Location Within walking distance of the Champs-Élysées and St-Germain-des-Prés. Parking in quiet street, 5 minutes' walk away. (Métro Varenne.)
Credit card Amex, Visa.
Terms Rooms: single 350 frs, double 400-450 frs. Breakfast 30 frs. (No restaurant.)

PASSENANS 39230 Jura — Map 10

Auberge du Rostaing — *Tel* 84.85.23.70

This modest but enticing little *auberge* lies tucked away in unspoilt countryside, yet is easy to get at, for major tourist routes are close by. "A charming place, family-run by a Franco-Swiss couple, the Eckerts (she cooks, he is a most courteous and helpful host). It is on the outskirts of Passenans, an attractive sleepy village of beige-ochre stone houses and beautifully-tended vegetable gardens, in a remarkably untouristy area between, as the blurb says, 'the rich market gardens of the Bresse to the west, and the Jura hills to the east with their forests, waterfalls and picturesque castle'. Good walking country – and walking is what many of the guests do. Then they come drifting in to sit in the courtyard under a tree or parasol, sipping a drink – all very relaxed. The white 18th-century main building contains a spacious dining room with open fireplace, large peasant cupboards and modern art, and a 'parlour' upstairs with a piano, records, books and games. Some of the rooms are in an attractive vine-balustraded building with an outside staircase and open walkway balcony. Rooms are simple but pleasant; excellent showers and even an electric hair drier. The food is good and varied, with local specialities and once a week Swiss dishes such as fondue and raclette. The 47-franc menu [1987] is good value, as is the whole place; breakfast included the best marmalade we've ever had." (*Ian and Agathe Lewin, endorsed by James Kempson*)

Open 1 Feb–30 Nov. Closed Tue except school holidays.
Rooms 10 double – 6 with bath and/or shower, 3 with WC.
Facilities Salon with library, 2 dining rooms. Courtyard and garden. Bicycles for hire. English spoken.
Location Off N83, 11 km S of Poligny, which is where the Dijon–Geneva road crosses the Lyon–Besançon road.
Restriction Not suitable for ♿.
Credit cards Diners, Visa.
Terms Rooms: single 59-109 frs, double 65-122 frs. Breakfast 25 frs. Full board (min 3 days): single 138-195 frs, double 226-294 frs. Set lunch/dinner 47-87 frs. 1-night bookings sometimes refused during peak holiday periods. Reductions for stays of over 7 days. Reduced rates and special meals for children.

PÉGOMAS 06580 Alpes-Maritimes — Map 11

Hôtel le Bosquet — *Tel* 93.42.22.87
Quartier du Château

Britons especially, also Germans, Dutch and others continue to love this idiosyncratic little hotel in the scruffy outskirts of a village in the mimosa country between Cannes and Grasse. "Calm and comfort, courtesy and character." "Very friendly, charming and good value - but don't expect smartness." "The ebullient *patronne*, Simone Bernardi, *vaut le détour*. We were beguiled by the convivial spirit, the happy communal breakfasts in the courtyard, the home-made jams. We enjoyed the *piscine*, even though you pay extra for it. The garden is unkempt but spacious and there are nice views of the hills." No restaurant, the best places to eat nearby are the *Nossi-Bé* at Auribeau and the *Lou sans l'Ail*. (*JA, Gerald Campion, Richard Binns*)

Open All year, except Nov.
Rooms 17 double, 7 studios – 2 with bath and shower, 22 with shower, all with telephone. All in 2 annexes. Studios have kitchenette.
Facilities Salon, breakfast room with TV; courtyard. Garden with *boules* and unheated swimming pool. English spoken.
Location On road to Mouans-Sartoux, in northern outskirts of Pégomas, which is 11 km NW of Cannes.
Restriction Not suitable for ♿.
Credit cards None accepted.
Terms Rooms: double 165-210 frs, suite 240-285 frs. Breakfast 18 frs. (No restaurant.)

PEILLON 06440 Alpes-Maritimes — Map 11

Auberge de la Madone — *Tel* 93.79.91.17

Only ten kilometres from Nice, yet remote in the silent hills, this very civilised *auberge* stands on the edge of one of the most striking *villages perchés* of the area. It is run by the sympathetic Millot family who create a warm atmosphere and have many regulars, mainly "the nicer kind of Parisian". With much use of Provençal herbs, Christian Millot prepares interesting local dishes such as daube de boeuf à l'orange et aux cêpes (*Gault Millau toque*). His *Madone* was venerated by readers for some years, then came silence so it left the Guide, but this year two visitors have written warmly ("a memorable stay", "good comfortable rooms, very clean, the food was delicate and very good"). A third however, during what we can only hope was a bad patch, found the food poor and the service slow and inept "by a sort of Jacques Tati waiter". Some bedrooms have a large balcony. One reader regretted the absence of a swimming pool, but a terrace has just been added. (*Rosemary Gilbey, P Roberts, JA*) More reports please.

Open 15 Dec–15 Oct. Restaurant closed Wed.
Rooms 3 suites, 15 double – 15 with bath, 3 with shower, all with telephone; 3 with TV.
Facilities Salon, bar, TV room, dining room; conference facilities. Large garden; sea (at Nice) 15 km. English spoken.
Location 18 km NE of Nice on D21.
Restriction Not suitable for ♿.
Credit cards None accepted.
Terms Rooms: 246-350 frs. Breakfast 35 frs. Dinner, B&B: 250-380 frs per person. Set lunch/dinner 85-150 frs; full alc 200-240 frs. Reduced rates for children.

LA PEINIÈRE-ST-DIDIER 35220 Ille-et-Vilaine — Map 8

Hotel Pen'Roc — *Tel* 99.00.33.02

In eastern Brittany, off the main road from Rennes to Vitré (lovely feudal castle), this attractive modern hotel has been built in local style, with grey slate roof, and lies in a quiet rural setting. "Not easy to find, but worth the effort. It's used during the day for business gatherings, but in the evening we found it delightful and peaceful: there's even a perfect little Romanesque church alongside. Family-run by the Frocs. Madame is immensely tall and (even at 8 am) as elegant as the dishes her husband produces – *cuisine naturelle,* with the fish especially delicious. The restaurant space is graceful, and the huge kitchen garden at the back lived up to its promise. Large, comfortable bedrooms, and a staff who were not only helpful but much impressed by our having bicycled 100 kilometres that day to reach them." The odd-sounding specialities include fisherman's choucroute and méli-mélo de la mer à la badiane. (*Diana Holmes*)

Open All year except 2 weeks Feb, 2 weeks Nov. Restaurant closed Sun evening.
Rooms 15 double – 8 with bath or shower, 7 with WC, all with telephone, radio-alarm and TV.
Facilities Bar, restaurant; conference facilities. Garden with children's play area. Service lift can be used by ♿. English spoken.
Location 6 km E of Châteaubourg. Turn off D857 at St-Jean-sur-Vilaine, towards St-Didier, then L to La Peinière.
Credit cards All major cards accepted.
Terms B&B: single 173-218 frs, double 214-261 frs. Half and full board rates on request. Set lunch/dinner 65, 99.50 and 180 frs (children's menu 47.50 frs); full alc 210 frs.

LA PETITE PIERRE 67290 Bas-Rhin — Map 9

Hôtel aux Trois Roses — *Tel* 88.70.45.02
Telex 890308

Renewed praise in 1987 for this fine 18th-century *auberge,* white-walled, flower-bedecked, all cosy inside. It is in the main street of an ancient hill-top village (front rooms can be noisy), with remains of ramparts, and hilly forests all around; the dining room has a fine view of the castle, romantic on summer evenings when it is floodlit. "A very typical Alsatian *auberge,* sympathetic, informal and lively, run hectically by a whole bevy of Alsatians, chattering away in their dialect. It's very much a local social centre, less in the French than the Central European tradition – several comfy salons, and a big *Stübe* where snacks are served all day, as well as a lavish array of cakes and tartlets. The food is pleasant if unexciting – good soups and fresh trout, run-of-the-mill civet de sanglier. Our bedroom, the last, was cramped but with comfy bed and a valley view. The heated indoor pool, reserved for residents, was super in chill November." "A splendid warm welcome." "Charming, excellent value, and in a marvellous walking area." One dissenter this year found the dinner excellent but his bedroom somewhat unkempt. (*JA, KA, Patrica Hawkins, Pat and Richard Neumann, and others*)

Open All year except Jan. Restaurant closed to non-residents Sun evening and Mon.
Rooms 16 suites, 21 double, 11 single – 45 with bath and shower, all with telephone; 16 with radio and TV.
Facilities Lift. 3 lounges (2 with TV), bar, 5 dining rooms; indoor swimming pool. Garden with terrace, children's play area, tennis courts. Small lake 3 km with fishing. English spoken.
Location 60 km NW of Strasbourg; hotel is central. Parking.
Credit cards Access, Visa.
Terms Rooms: single 60-185 frs, double 130-280 frs, suite 380 frs. Breakfast 25 frs. Set lunch/dinner 75-175 frs; full alc 180 frs. Reductions for children under 8; special meals on request.

PEYRAT-LE-CHÂTEAU 87470 Vienne — Map 10

La Caravelle — *Tel* 55.69.40.97
Lac de Vassivière

In the forested and gently hilly Limousin country east of Limoges, a modern and friendly holiday hotel beside the big artificial Vassivière lake (good for boating, bathing). No beauty outside, but nicely furnished inside; excellent food, served on outdoor terrace by lake when fine. Closed 1 Jan–12 Mar. 21 rooms all with bath, many with balconies facing lake. B&B double 300 frs [1987]. Set meals 120–200 frs. New nomination: more reports please.

PIANA 20115 Corsica — Map 11

Capo Rosso — *Tel* 95.26.82.40

A charming hotel high up above the bay of Porto on the west coast, with spectacular views over the sea and the Calanches (dramatic red rocks). Rooms are neither large nor luxurious, but all have balcony with views. Nice garden, pleasant atmosphere, imaginative cooking. Open 1 Apr--15 Oct. 6 rooms, most with bath or shower. B&B double 350-400 frs. Set meals 85-185 frs. New nomination: more reports please.

PLÉHÉDEL 22290 Côtes-du-Nord — Map 8

Château Hôtel de Coatguelen — *Tel* 96.22.31.24
Telex 741300

This elegant little 19th-century château stands serenely in its own 170-acre park of woodlands, meadows and lakes – not to mention a nine-hole golf-course. It is on the main Lanvollon–Paimpol road, just south-west of Pléhédel, seven kilometres from the sea and near to good north Brittany beaches and interesting old towns such as Tréguier. A recent report: "Such a peaceful and lovely place. Do not miss the *menu dégustation* – especially the dessert." Earlier visitors have spoken of "delightful large rooms with pleasant furnishings." And: "The hotel is all repro – beautifully done. It must have cost a fortune to restore. We had the Bridal Suite in the tower and it was most attractive. The welcome could not be better." A red *toque* in *Gault Millau* for "modern Breton cooking", e.g. hot fried oysters. (*J Ring, and others*)

Open 1 Apr–5 Jan. Restaurant closed Tue, and Wed lunchtime.
Rooms 3 suites, 11 double, 2 single – all with bath (3 also have shower), telephone and baby-listening.
Facilities Salon with TV, salon/bar, restaurant; conference rooms; children's playroom; ping-pong, bridge tables. Large park with unheated swimming pool, tennis, children's play area, horses and ponies, trout fishing, 9-hole golf course. Beach 7 km; sailing, windsurfing and sea fishing 10 km. English spoken.
Location On D7 between Lanvollon and Paimpol (no need to go to Pléhédel). Parking.
Credit cards All major cards accepted.
Terms Rooms: single 460-590 frs, double 620-970 frs, suite 720-1,240 frs Breakfast 45 frs. Dinner, B&B: 540-870 frs per person. Set lunch/dinner 130, 185, 230 and 300 frs; full alc 350 frs. Special meals for children.

LE POËT-LAVAL 26160 Drôme — Map 10

Les Hospitaliers — *Tel* 75.46.22.32

A medieval village in fine wooded countryside where the foothills of the Alps descend to the Rhône valley, on the borders of Dauphiné and Provence. Again admired this year, *Les Hospitaliers* is a very *soigné* country hotel in the village, with a swimming pool and flowery terrace. "One of my secret paradises, and truly quiet," ran an earlier report. "There are no passing cars: the streets of this former Protestant stronghold are too narrow or bumpy to accept them, though the hotel can be reached by road and has ample parking space. Cumbrian-like hills are in view from its windows. Its creator, M. Morin, has achieved great feats of building and engineering. A few years ago there was no water, electricity or telephone system in the village. He bought old stones to restore and blend his reconstruction with the 12th-century deserted chapel towering above." Others this year and last have enjoyed the friendly service, the views of the valley, and the antique furniture in the larger rooms. One reader complained that the pool was still unheated in a late May heatwave. Another felt that the *nouvelle*-style cooking had deteriorated, but there was no lack of praise for, e.g., the carré d'agneau and potage of wild mushrooms (*Michelin* rosette and *Gault Millau* red *toque*). (*John Cliffe, Anne Stott, Kenneth E Smith, and others*)

Open 1 Mar–15 Nov.
Rooms 19 double, 1 single – 19 with bath and shower, 1 with shower only, all with telephone. 9 in annexe adjacent to main building.
Facilities Salon, TV room, bar, 2 restaurants; conference facilities. Garden with terrace and heated swimming pool. Tennis, riding, fishing nearby. English spoken.
Location On D540, E of La Bégude-de-Mazenc; Montélimar 25 km.
Restriction Not suitable for ♿.
Credit cards All major cards accepted.
Terms Rooms: single 250 frs, double 360-600 frs. Breakfast 55 frs. Set lunch/dinner 160-360 frs; full alc 350 frs. Reduced rates for children; special meals.

PONS 17800 Charente-Maritime — Map 10

Auberge Pontoise — *Tel* 46.94.00.99
23 avenue Gambetta

Just outside this medieval town above the river Seugne, dominated by a castle with a vast rectangular keep, the old hospice used by pilgrims on their way to Compostela is still extant, and open to sightseers. Modern gastronomic pilgrims have found somewhere better than the hospice: the *Pontoise*, in the town centre, has this year won a rosette from *Michelin* for such dishes as brochette of langoustines with pasta. "A truly excellent little hotel, unpretentious, clean, comfortable and quiet, with attentive staff. The plain dining room had magnificent fresh flowers and the cuisine was first class . . . pleurotte mushrooms in a delicious cream sauce, fresh hake in a champagne sauce." (*Jean Hayward*) Front rooms may be noisy. More reports, please.

Open 27 Jan–22 Dec. Closed Mon.
Rooms 1 suite, 21 double – 16 with bath, 6 with shower, all with direct-dial telephone and TV. Some ground-floor rooms.

Facilities Lounge, bar, 2 dining rooms; conference facilities. Swimming pool and tennis courts nearby. English spoken.
Location Central (front rooms could be noisy). Parking. Pons is 96 km N of Bordeaux.
Credit cards Access, Visa.
Terms B&B: single 200 frs, double 280 frs; suite 500 frs. Set lunch/dinner 90-230 frs; full alc 260-300 frs.

Le Rustica *Tel* 46.96.91.75
St-Léger

Much liked again this year for its homely simplicity and value-for-money, this small restaurant-with-rooms lies off the beaten track in a vineyard-girt hamlet north-west of Pons. "Superb food." "The staff were charming." "Our room was creaky, sloping and quaint but very comfortable. Excellent French provincial cuisine." "The bar was very simple, but the dining room was most attractive with large open fireplace, wooden beams, tables with flowers. The dinner was one of the best we have had in that price range [56 frs, 1987]: first mouclade (mussels in cream sauce, delicious) then steak au poivre, then home-made plum tart. We had an enormous, very comfortable bed: the loo and shower were both new." Many visitors have found the place quiet, but there was a report this year of noise on a Saturday night. " (*Keith Perry, ECM Begg, Bill and Kathy Reece, and others*)

Open All year except 7–29 Oct, 5–16 Feb. Closed Tue evening and Wed out of season.
Rooms 7 double.
Facilities TV room, public bar, 2 dining rooms. Garden.
Location In St-Léger, just W of N137, 5 km NW of Pons. Parking.
Credit card Visa.
Terms Rooms 76 frs. Breakfast 17 frs. Dinner, B&B 56 frs per person added to B&B rate. Set lunch/dinner 56-210 frs; full alc 170 frs.

PONT-AUDEMER 27500 Eure — Map 8

Auberge du Vieux Puits *Tel* 32.41.01.48
6 rue Notre-Dame du Pré

Few other hotels in France arouse such sustained enthusiasm among readers as the *Vieux Puits*, which is a collection of three 17th-century buildings around a courtyard. Originally a tannery, it is mentioned by Flaubert in *Madame Bovary*. A digest from this year's crop of reports: "A thoroughly delightful inn, with welcoming hosts, ancient timbered charm, and memorably delicious food by a vast fire (try their aged calvados). The owners speak excellent English and all the nice ladies who help were utterly polite." "A delightful place full of character, and run so professionally by Jacques and Hélène Holtz. The two dining rooms are small and crowded, but this adds to the cosiness of the wonderfully enjoyable atmosphere: dinner was delicious, breakfast above average, and service excellent." "Nice grounds, very good dinner, excellent breakfast (best hot chocolate ever)." Others have commented that "the owners take evident pleasure in serving Norman dishes the proper way" and "the cooking, especially the truite Bovary, well deserves its *Michelin* rosette". Six new bedrooms, all with bath, have just been added, and the eight original ones by the courtyard – prettily decorated but small and without baths – are now used only in high season. Some readers prefer the comfort of the new rooms, others the charm (and lower prices) of the old ones. The Holtzes expect their room guests to take at least one meal, though under French law they cannot insist on this. (*Wendy Arnold, Maurice E Southon, Bernadette Murray, and many others*)

Open 15 Jan–29 Jun, 9 Jul–15 Dec. Closed Mon evening and Tue.
Rooms 11 double, 3 single – 6 with bath, 5 with shower; 12 with telephone; 6 with TV. 2 ground-floor rooms, specially equipped for ♿.
Facilities 2 small salons, 2 restaurants. Small garden. English spoken.
Location 300 metres from town centre (hotel is signposted), but quiet. Parking.
Credit cards Access, Visa.
Terms Rooms: single 90 frs, double 120-310 frs. Breakfast 25 frs. Set lunch/dinner 210 frs; full alc 210-250 frs. Guests expected to dine at the hotel.

PONT-DE-LARN 81660 Tarn — Map 10

La Métairie Neuve — *Tel* 63.61.23.31

"Comfortable bedrooms, good food and wine, and Madame most helpful," runs a report this year on this converted 18th-century farmhouse just north of Mazamet (the leading sheep-shearing and leather-dressing town in France, between Albi and Carcassonne). Now a rural restaurant-with-rooms, it has an air of spacious comfort and elegance. "The exterior is a bit tatty," ran an earlier account, "but once you step inside the picture is very different – cool rough-cast walls, gleaming tiles, old exposed beams, the 'antique rustic' style at which the French are unbeatable. Bedrooms are simple and plainly decorated, but some are very large. Our table at dinner overlooked the inner courtyard, yet felt very cosy with its lamp, pretty Limoges china and fresh flowers. Our meal, the *menu touristique*, was good, especially the confit de foie de canard which melted in the mouth. Service is efficient and the owners charming." (*I and FW*)

Open All year, except 20 Dec–20 Jan, 1–15 Aug. Restaurant closed Sat and for lunch on weekdays.
Rooms 7 double – all with bath, shower and telephone; 3 with TV.
Facilities Salon, dining room; terrace. Garden. Golf 2 km, tennis and swimming pool 1 km; lakes with beaches and sailing 25 km. English spoken.
Location 2 km N of Mazamet on N112 Béziers–Castres road. Parking.
Credit cards Diners, Visa.
Terms Rooms: single occupancy 200 frs, double 300 frs. Breakfast 30 frs. Dinner, B&B: single 380 frs, double 560 frs. Set meals 75-240 frs; full alc 180 frs. Special meals for children.

PORTICCIO 20166 Corsica — Map 11

Le Maquis — *Tel* 95.25.05.55
Telex 460597

Various eulogies recently for this sophisticated hotel right on the water, across the bay from Ajaccio. "A beautiful hotel in a lovely place, small, very French and absolutely marvellous. It's run by a family – Madame Salini is always dressed in leather. It has a very pretty swimming pool and its own private beach: our lovely room overlooked it. The decor, really delightful, is white and black beams and red-tiled floors. Cheeses and seafood are super." (*Claire Rayner*) "If you have a ground-floor room, your balcony literally meets the sand. The food is good, especially the huge help-yourself hors d'oeuvre table. One of our happiest memories will be eating lunch on the terrace – pink tablecloths, umbrellas, silver, fine china and glass and the bright blue sky and sea below, wonderful fresh seafood and delicious Corsican wines. Not cheap, but one has to pay for such perfection."(*J and NH; endorsed this year by Colonel RC Sidwell*)

Open All year. Restaurant closed 4 Jan–4 Feb.
Rooms 3 suites, 14 double, 2 single – all with bath and/or shower, telephone, TV and video.
Facilities Lounge, bar, dining room; terrace for alfresco meals. Garden with tennis court, heated swimming pool, and children's play area. On private beach with safe bathing.
Location On the coast 15 km SE of Ajaccio, on the D55. 12 km from airport.
Credit cards All major cards accepted.
Terms [1987 rates] Dinner, B&B 790-1,150 frs. Full alc 215-365 frs.

PORTICCIOLO 20228 Corsica — Map 11

Hôtel Le Caribou — *Tel* 95.35.02.33 and 95.35.00.33

(*Correspondence between Oct 1987 and May 1988 should be addressed to the sister hotel, Le Caribou, 38 place Thiars, 13001 Marseilles*)

A warm endorsement for this "find" by two veteran correspondents whose report we reprint: "The most delightful atmospheric hotel we have found in two Corsican holidays. It lies on the road north from Bastia to Cap Corse, in a colourful garden of flowers and trees. As you go up the steep drive, you find a swimming pool set into the garden and an extensive restaurant overlooking both and out to sea. Splendid old trees have been interlaced with vines to make a cool shady place for aperitifs or coffee. Our suite across the road, overlooking the sea, was one of several *pavillons* built in to the rocks just above the water's edge, each with a small sun-terrace.

"The restaurant looked so inviting we decided to have one simple course – hors d'oeuvre for one of us, a lobster for the other. The request for hors d'oeuvre triggered off the most amazing response: a series of generous platefuls of luscious melon, ham, platters of hors d'oeuvre, a sunburst of moules, generously and most deliciously sauced, pâtés and sausages, hot, fresh-from-the-oven feather-light feuilletés. And my lobster, when it came, was superb. Fresh flowers had been put in our room when we retired for a siesta. Later we swam from the breakwater: there are facilities for boating, fishing, windsurfing. There is a wonderful atmosphere in the restaurant, full of noise and animated French. The chefs were outstanding." (*Angela and David Stewart*) Confirmed this year by visitors who also enjoyed the "informal house-party atmosphere", the "cornucopia of food in a constant stream", and the "evening animation in the courtyard, with melodic mandolin music", but found the local wines overpriced and bedrooms a little small. (*Eric and Jean Lace*)

Open 18 June–22 Sept.
Rooms 10 *pavillons* (bungalows with bath and kitchen) for 3-8 people, 20 double – all with bath or shower, telephone; some with balcony.

Facilities Lounge, bar, restaurant; terraces. Swimming pool, tennis courts, private harbour, fine sandy beach with bathing, waterskiing, windsurfing, sailing, fishing, skin-diving and volley-ball. English spoken.
Location On east coast, off N198.
Credit cards All major cards accepted.
Terms Dinner, B&B 450 frs; full board 500 frs. Set lunch/dinner 220 frs. Reduced rates and special meals for children.

PORT-MANECH 29139 Finistère — Map 8

Hôtel Restaurant du Port — *Tel* 98.06.82.17
30 rue de l'Aven

An unpretentious and inexpensive modern inn by the harbour, in a charming south Brittany fishing-village. Simple rooms, some with fine coastal views (avoid those in the ugly annexe). Kindly owners, good breakfasts. Excellent seafood. Open Easter–end Sept. 36 rooms, a few with bath or shower. B&B double 178-273 frs. Some criticisms: more reports welcome.

PORTO-VECCHIO 20137 Corsica — Map 11

Grand Hôtel de Cala Rossa — *Tel* 95.71.61.51
Cala Rossa — *Telex* 460394

This old harbour town, now quite a smart summer resort, lies amid cork forests at the head of a deep gulf. Ten kilometres to the north-east (you would need a car), the modern *Cala Rossa* stands in a beautiful and tranquil position by the sea, in its own 100-acre park. "Good value," says a reader this year. "A superb beach, friendly service, excellent *demi-pension* dinner (*Gault Millau toque*). Seaward-facing rooms see only greenery, the back ones are smaller and face the none-too-quiet road." An earlier visitor liked the lush garden and had a spacious room with excellent bathroom. Lunch, served by the sandy beach under the pines, is a big buffet of salads and grills. (*PJ Forrest, LH*)

Open May–Oct.
Rooms 58 double – all with bath and direct-dial telephone.
Facilities Salon, TV room, bar, dining room; conference facilities. Large park with garden; direct access to sandy beach, where lunch is served; ping-pong; bathing, windsurfing and waterskiing. Nightclub nearby. English spoken.
Location On peninsula 10 km NE of Porto-Vecchio by N198, D568, D468.
Restriction Not suitable for ♿.
Credit cards Amex, Diners, Visa.
Terms [1987 rates] B&B: 150–720 frs. Set meals 200–280 frs. Reduced rates and special meals for children.

Hôtel San Giovanni — *Tel* 95.70.22.25
Route d'Arca

A recent visitor spent "five nights very happily" at the *San Giovanni*, a "small and delightful family-run hotel in rural surroundings", three kilometres south-west of the town, just inland. An earlier report: "You need a car here, but some beautiful beaches are within ten minutes' drive. We had a pleasant bungalow room in a newly-built outside block. The only noise in the daytime was the sound of the cuckoo and at night we could hear a nightjar singing. Open-air swimming pool. The lowest-priced menu seemed rather limited and we think we ate better in town." (*Joan Williamson, LH, David G Sefton*)

Open 1 Apr–15 Oct.
Rooms 26 double – all with bath and telephone; TV on request. Some in bungalows. Some ground-floor rooms.
Facilities Bar, restaurant (entertainment twice a week). Garden with tennis court, sauna and swimming pool.
Location 3 km SW of Porto-Vecchio on D659.
Credit cards Amex, Diners, Visa.
Terms B&B: single 237 frs, double 287 frs; half board: double 507-573 frs. Set dinner 84 frs. Children under 2 free.

PULIGNY-MONTRACHET 21190 Côte d'Or — Map 10

Le Montrachet — *Tel* 80.21.30.06

A big traditional stone building in the pretty main square of one of the classic Burgundy wine-villages. Delightful local atmosphere, tasteful decor, pleasant bedrooms. Excellent regional cooking, lauded in the French guides: cheaper menus are good value, but wines are dear. Closed 2 Dec–8 Jan. 22 rooms, all with bath and shower. B&B double 364-444 frs. Set meals 120-300 frs. Warmly nominated this year: more reports please.

QUINÉVILLE 50310 Manche — Map 8

Château de Quinéville — *Tel* 33.21.42.67

Whereas most French converted-château hotels are so expensive, this one is very modestly priced; it also has the merit of being only 35 kilometres south-east of Cherbourg, useful as a stopover. A solid grey building in its own park, it looks a little austere from outside but is very pretty within. "We have known it for some years, as we have a house nearby," write nominators this year, "and friends often stay there at our suggestion. We have stayed there, too. It is classic 18th-century and very beautiful, with the ruins of an earlier château in the grounds. Despite its elegance it is not manicured: you will find Muscovy ducks on the lawns, and dandelions. The staff and the owner seem just one big family. Room 14 remains our favourite, and as it lacks a bathroom it is still the cheapest. It has a Louis XV settee and a magnificent bureau bookcase at which I worked for four blissfully happy days. Two huge windows look onto the park with a distant view of the sea; a third overlooks a moat with ducks in it. The public rooms are rather lovely. The dining room looks onto the attractive courtyard and the park behind, with steps going down to the drinks terrace and lawns. After several years of sampling their various menus, we think their best dishes are the mussels à la crème, the duck (they must be the muscovies from the moat, they are so huge and tasty), and the local oysters done hot in champagne. We don't really want the English to know about it, but it's really unfair to the hotel not to tell them!" (*G Still*)

Open 1 Apr–31 Dec.
Rooms 12 double or triple – 6 with bath, 6 with shower.
Facilities Restaurant, bar, TV room. Park with pond (fishing). Sea 600 metres.
Location 35 km SE of Cherbourg, 7 km E of Montebourg by D42.
Restriction Not suitable for ♿.

Credit cards Access, Visa.
Terms Rooms 220-250 frs. Set lunch/dinner 65, 15 and 140 frs.

RAGUENÈS-PLAGE 29139 Finistère **Map 8**

Hotel Chez Pierre *Tel* 98.06.81.06

The superb sandy beaches, excellent for bathing and rarely too crowded, are one of the main attractions of this very sympathetic seaside hotel, within easy reach of Concarneau and Pont-Aven (where Gauguin painted). It has been owned and run for many years by the Guillou family. They tend to get overstretched in August when standards may drop a little, and the ensuing criticisms led to *Chez Pierre* losing its place in the Guide after 1985. It is now restored enthusiastically by several new reports, with the caveat that rooms in the modern annexe are better than the older ones. Xavier Guillou's cooking (*Michelin* red "R" for good value) is strongly admired by readers, especially the fish and shellfish: the set lunches are better than the dinners. This year's mailbag: "A spacious room in the annexe and a cordial reception. Madame Guillou Jr was charm itself, making sure our needs were met. Food was excellent, with memorable fruits de mer. Drinking chilled Muscadet in the garden was a daily must." "Reasonably priced, comfortable, near a safe beach. Garden a bit run-down, in a pleasant informal way." Attractive courtyard, bar and lounge. Not a place for those who want to avoid their fellow-Britons on holiday. (*BW Forster, Dr IA Campbell, and others*)

Open 10 Apr–28 Sept. Restaurant closed Wed 17 Jun–9 Sept.
Rooms 31 – all with bath and/or shower and telephone; some in annexe. 1 ground-floor room.
Facilities Salon, bar, 2 dining rooms. Garden. English spoken.
Location 12 km SW of Pont-Aven. Parking.
Credit card Access.
Terms [1987 rates] Rooms: single 140 frs, double 290 frs. Breakfast 19 frs. Set lunch/dinner 90-180 frs.

RAMATUELLE 83350 Var **Map 11**

Hostellerie Le Baou *Tel* 94.79.20.48
Avenue Georges Clémenceau *Telex* 462152

The charming hill-village of Ramatuelle is within easy reach of the best St-Tropez beaches; Gérard Philippe lies buried in its cemetery, and the noble elm in its main square was planted in 1598. Plenty of rich, sophisticated people visit this fabulous peninsula, and quite a few of them nowadays make for *Le Baou*, a very swish hotel on a hillside, with fine views over woods and vineyards to the sea. After a recent bad patch it has been taken over by the Sarraquigne family and is much improved: "The new owners have tastefully revived the place and they treat their guests with care. Most rooms have a balcony, and from these and the dining terrace there are lovely views. Grills are served during the day by the pleasant swimming pool. Good house wine, and excellent cuisine." "Food superb, ambience magical," adds a visitor this year. Pretentious-looking menu, 60x40 centimetres, features bouillabaisse with langouste for 280 frs. (*David Swift, Mary Woods*)

Open Early Apr–end Oct.
Rooms 12 suites, 24 double – all with bath and shower, telephone, TV and balcony; some with private garden.
Facilities Lift. 2 lounges, 2 bars, 2 restaurants; indoor garden. Garden with terrace, grill, swimming pool, jacuzzi, solarium. Sea 3 km. English spoken.
Location At entrance of village. Garage and parking.
Restriction Not suitable for ♿.
Credit cards All major cards accepted.
Terms B&B: single 595-725 frs, double 640-740 frs, suite 930-980 frs; dinner, B&B: single 850-960 frs, double 1,100-1,250 frs, suite 1,400-1,550 frs. Set lunch 235 frs, dinner 320 frs; full alc 350 frs. Reductions for long stays. l-night bookings sometimes refused in high season.

REIMS 51100 Marne — Map 9

Boyer "Les Crayères" — *Tel* 26.82.80.80
64 boulevard Henry-Vasnier — *Telex* 830959

"Awe-inspiring" remains the word for this very stylish and civilised little hotel in the city's south-east outskirts, converted from a graceful 18th-century-style château by Gérard and Elyane Boyer (he is one of France's most renowned chefs). The French guides continue to give their top accolades (*Michelin*'s three rosettes and four red gables, *Gault Millau*'s three red *toques*), while our own readers remain equally impressed. "It reminded me of the *Connaught*," says a report this year. "No more expensive than other luxury establishments, and to my mind far better value and enjoyment. The building may be grand, but all the staff are smiling and wholesome-looking. Excellent food, cooked with a marvellously light touch, beautifully presented. The rooms large, comfortable and elegant, but with more the feeling of cherished house than a soulless hotel." (*WA*) "A mansion of pale creamy stone, its perfect proportions set against the mature trees and sweeping lawns of its park. The use of subtle muted colours, blending harmoniously, gives the impression of a whole scheme designed together. Our spacious and elegant bedroom overlooked the park; off it was the best-designed dressing room we've ever met. Dinner was superb: the cuisine was *nouvelle* but unfussy, with light sauces and delicate portions." (*Angela and David Stewart*)

"Truly deserves its *Michelin* rating. The Boyers, friendly and efficient, seem to be in all places at all times. The beautiful building is approached through massive wrought-iron gates; entrance hall and staircase are imposing, made of pale beige marble, with huge tapestries. Our large bedroom had enormous windows giving a feeling of light and space." (*Padi and John Howard; Pat and Jeremy Temple, RA Malt*) Best to book way ahead.

Open All year except 21 Dec–11 Jan. Restaurant closed for lunch Mon and Tue.
Rooms 1 suite, 15 double – all with bath and/or shower, direct-dial telephone, radio, TV and baby-listening.
Facilities Lift. Hall, bar, restaurant; private dining-room. Park and gardens with tennis and helipad. English spoken.
Location Leave motorway at St-Rémy exit. Travel towards Luxembourg for ½ km, then towards Châlons-sur-Marne on N44. Hotel is 3 km from town centre. Parking.
Credit cards All major cards accepted.
Terms (Excluding 15% service charge) Rooms: single 783–1,243 frs, double 826–1,287 frs; suite 1,113 frs. Breakfast 60 frs. Full alc 530–560 frs.

REPLONGES 01750 Ain — Map 10

La Huchette — *Tel* 85.31.03.55

A red-roofed *auberge* on the edge of a village east of Mâcon, ornately decorated in warm colours and long admired for its friendly welcome, good service and pretty dining-room. "Not just a hotel *en route* to the South, but a delightful green oasis full of civility and charm. It has lovely spacious lawns with tall trees and a large swimming pool, equipped with luxurious mattress loungers. The owner, Yolande Gualdieri, soft-spoken and efficient, makes you feel welcome. Our rooms were large and attractive, in pink and dark green, with lovely airy bathrooms. Cooking was careful: *carte* somewhat limited, but included delicious local Bresse chicken and tempting sweet trolley. In the big lounge were magazines and books in various languages." One visitor complained of traffic noises and a not very clean swimming pool. (*C and DB, and others*) More reports please.

Open All year.
Rooms 1 suite, 12 double – all with bath and shower, telephone and TV. 4 ground-floor rooms with wide doors.
Facilities 2 lounges, dining room. Garden with swimming pool. Fishing and golf nearby. English spoken.
Location 4 km E of Mâcon off N79. On edge of village. Parking.
Credit cards All major cards accepted.
Terms B&B: single occupancy 342 frs, double 534 frs, suite 600 frs. Set lunch/dinner 140 frs; full alc 180 frs.

RIBEAUVILLÉ 68150 Haut-Rhin — Map 9

Le Clos Saint-Vincent — *Tel* 89.73.67.65
Route de Bergheim

Energetic walkers can climb up to the three ruined castles that stand above this picturesque little Alsatian wine town. On its outskirts is the *Clos Saint-Vincent*, anything but ruined – a sophisticated chalet-style restaurant-with-rooms, superbly set among Riesling vineyards and garlanded with a *Michelin* rosette and more Guide praise this year: "Expensive, but an idyllic place to stay, with management and staff constantly attentive." "Wonderful rooms, superb meals, though the wines are very dear and the menus stay unchanged too long." The hotel's interior is spacious and elegant, with decor in soft muted golds and browns. "Our room was large and airy, with French windows opening onto a small terrace and attractive gardens, with views of the gently rolling countryside and the lights of Colmar in the distance. The dining room was again very elegant, with tables well spaced, and that same stupendous view. The food was mostly superb (foie gras de canard, ris et rognons de veau). Fine Alsatian wines, and good breakfast on our terrace." (*RA Devin, Dr TC and Mrs IE Barker*)

Open 15 Mar–15 Nov. Restaurant closed Tue/Wed.
Rooms 3 suites, 8 double – all with bath and shower; TV on request.
Facilities Lift. Salon, bar, restaurant. Garden. English spoken.
Location In NE outskirts of town, which is 15 km N of Colmar. Parking.
Credit card Access, Visa.
Terms [1987 rates] B&B: single 455 frs, double 777 frs, suite 900 frs. Alc meals (excluding wine) 150-300 frs.

RIGNY 70100 Haute Saône — Map 10

Château de Rigny — *Tel* 84.65.25.01 *Telex* 362926

Like the nearby *Relais* at Nantilly (q.v.), this is a small and select country house hotel, with three red gables in *Michelin* for attractive charm: but whereas the *Relais* is a 19th-century house, this one dates from 1286, rebuilt in its present form under Louis XIII. It is set quietly in its own grounds bordering the Saône and has a 12-acre *jardin anglais* and a large baronial salon. Dropped from the 1987 Guide as some readers felt it was becoming run-down, it has now been refurbished and is back in favour with three reporters this year. "Totally rehabilitated, lovely terrace, rooms vary in size but all well furnished (ground floor ones in the annexe look the best). Jacques and Brigitte Maupin are excellent hosts; a delightful dining-room serves above-average food." "Food very good, chairs reupholstered." "The hotel is still a bit spartan, but the tennis court and swimming pool are now in order." (*Richard H Proctor, Denis Tate, PH Freeman*)

Open All year except Christmas.
Rooms 24 double – all with bath, shower, telephone and TV. 11 in annexe. 4 ground-floor rooms.
Facilities Salon, bar, dining room; conference/function facilities. 12-acre park with tennis court and swimming pool, pond for fishing, access to Saône river. English spoken.
Location 5 km NE of Gray on Rigny road; Gray is 49 km NE of Dijon. Parking.
Credit cards All major cards accepted.
Terms [1987 rates] Rooms: single occupancy 250 frs, double 320 frs. Breakfast 35 frs. Full board 450-500 frs per person. Set meals 160-230 frs.

ROCHEGUDE 26790 Drôme — Map 11

Château de Rochegude — *Tel* 75.04.81.88 *Telex* 345661

This gracefully-restored stone château, dating in part from the 12th century, is set on a rocky bluff above the vineyards of the Rhône plain north of Orange. It is now a very swish hotel, which this year has gained a rosette from *Michelin* for its cooking. Our own recent reports are just as enthusiastic: "In a private park with the largest private swimming pool I've ever seen. Most of the rooms are quite grand, but we opted for a lower-priced courtyard one. Antiques everywhere, and all is elegant, from breakfast on the terrace (with home-grown plums) to the lovely dining room with its first-rate chef." "Service impeccable, like being in a private house. Food was the best I've had in France. They make their own wine and olive oil." (*Susan Welch, Joannie Kennedy*)

Open Mar–Jan. Restaurant closed to non-residents for lunch on Mon.
Rooms 4 suites, 23 double, 2 single – all with bath and shower, telephone and TV. Some ground-floor rooms.
Facilities Lift. 3 salons, TV lounge, bar restaurant. Large grounds with heated swimming pool and tennis court. English spoken.
Location 14 km N of Orange. From N leave A7 motorway at Bollène and go towards Carpentras. From S leave at Orange and go towards Gap on N7.
Credit cards All major cards accepted.

Terms B&B: single 330-1,050 frs, double 370-1,050 frs, suite 1,350 frs; dinner, B&B: single 550-1,270 frs, double 590-1,270 frs, suite 1,570 frs. Set lunch 120 frs, dinner 240 frs.

LA ROCHE-L'ABEILLE 87800 Haute-Vienne — Map 10

Moulin de la Gorce — *Tel* 55.00.70.66
La Roche-l'Abeille
St-Yrieix-la-Perche

The cascades of 1986/7 enthusiasm for Jean Bertranet's enchanting *Moulin* bring it firmly into the top bracket of our most-loved French rural hotels. It is in a hamlet in pleasant hilly Limousin country between the two porcelain centres of Limoges (large and ugly) and St-Yrieix-la-Perche (small and lovely). The *Moulin*, also small and lovely, is the kind of place that warmly appeals to lovers of French rural simplicity plus high gastronomic complexity (two *Michelin* rosettes and two red *Gault Millau toques*, but don't let that put you off). Very quiet and off the beaten track, it consists of two very old buildings, one with the restaurant, one with nine bedrooms, beside a small lake with waterfall. The bedrooms have antiques; in one is a fine four-poster bed.

"An enchanting setting, especially if you can watch the sun rise over the lake. Our small room was comfortable and the bathroom luxurious. Breakfast was expensive but wonderful – home-made jam, croissants and rolls straight from the kitchen. Food magnificent." "The best hotel we have been to for a long time." "A gem of a place." "Dinner was delicious, service impressive. Expensive, but value for money." Just one dissenter found his dinner disappointing. And everyone agrees that you would need an MIT degree in engineering to master the modern high-tech system of mixer taps in the bathrooms. (*Diana Holmes, CJ Rae, PL Sugden, BH Jenkinson, CE Warner and JEA Garnett, and others*)

Open All year, except 16 Nov–2 Dec, 25 Jan–20 Feb, Sun night and Mon 30 Sept–31 Mar.
Rooms 9 double – all with bath, direct-dial telephone and TV. 6 in annexe.
Facilities Salon, dining room. Garden. Near river and lake, fishing available; tennis, swimming and riding nearby. English spoken.
Location 2 km S of St-Yrieix, on the D17. Parking.
Restriction Not suitable for ♿.
Credit cards Amex, Diners, Visa.
Terms [1987 rates] Rooms: single occupancy 250 frs, double 450 frs. Breakfast 45 frs. Full board 550-700 frs per person. Set lunch/dinner 200-400 frs. Reduced rates and special meals for children.

LA ROCHELLE 17000 Charente-Maritime — Map 10

Hôtel les Brises — *Tel* 46.43.89.37
Chemin de la Digue de Richelieu — *Telex* 790754 LES BRISES

"Stunning views over the bay, friendly people, firm bed, huge breakfast" – so runs one of this year's many positive reports on this efficient and stylish modern hotel in a prime position overlooking the islands, the estuary, and the outer harbour of enchanting La Rochelle (see below). Others speak of "breakfast a delight", "a pretty room overlooking the sea"; and of car windows being "cleaned religiously every night of our stay". "The hotel is right on the sea front, with a vast terrace on which one can sun oneself over a drink, and two luxurious lounges. A very warm welcome. Utterly quiet." (*Veronica Chamberlain, S Rogers, Jan Morris, William S Rogers, and many others*) No restaurant. La Rochelle has a number of clip-joints, but you do eat well at *Richard Coutanceau* (expensive) and at *Serge* (upper-medium).

Open All year.
Rooms 41 double, 5 single – all with bath and/or shower and telephone.
Facilities Lift. Salon, TV room/library, breakfast room, bar; terrace with direct access to sea. Park and Casino nearby. English spoken.
Location On sea front 1½ km from town centre. Underground garage and carpark.
Restriction Not suitable for ♿.
Credit cards Access, Visa.
Terms [1987 rates] B&B: single 325 frs, double 480 frs. Reductions for children. (No restaurant.)

Hôtel de France et d'Angleterre *Tel* 46.41.34.66
22 rue Gargoulleau *Telex* 790717 FRATEL ROCHL

Virginia Woolf stayed here in 1931 and found it "exactly right". Though it has been much modernised since her day, our readers mostly feel as she did about this clean and spruce hotel in a quiet street: "Modern but not too modern, highly comfortable, efficient and friendly service, very good value." One reader this year had "a lovely meal" (*Gault Millau* awards a *toque* for interesting regional dishes). The ancient fishing port of La Rochelle is described as "outstandingly attractive – a kind of maritime Bruges. Its narrow streets have been beautifully paved and closed to traffic, and all summer this area is splendidly animated." (*S Rogers, and others*)

Open All year. Restaurant closed 15 Dec–15 Jan, Sun, and Mon midday.
Rooms 76 double – 32 with bath, 35 with shower, all with telephone and radio; 36 with TV. Some in 2 annexes. 6 suitable for ♿.
Facilities Lift. Salon, TV room, breakfast room, restaurant; conference facilities. Interior garden for meals or drinks. English spoken.
Location Central, near place de Verdun. Parking (at a price) in nearby street.
Credit cards All major cards accepted.
Terms [1987 rates] Rooms: single 136 frs, double 310 frs. Breakfast 33 frs. Full board 409-583 frs per person. Set lunch/dinner 120-160 frs; full alc 250 frs. 30% reduction for children sharing parents' room; special meals on request.

LES ROCHES-DE-CONDRIEU 38370 Isère — Map 10

Hôtel Bellevue *Tel* 74.56.41.42

In a riverside village south of Lyon where the Rhône makes a splendid curve, backed by vine-clad hills, here is a typical French provincial hotel with pleasant bathrooms and bedrooms (apart from inadequate lighting). With picture windows facing the river, the restaurant is very popular with the French: fairly good food, excellent wines. Closed 3-14 Oct, 15 Feb–11 Mar, Sun evening in winter, Tue lunch in summer, and Mon. 18 rooms, most with bath or shower, 145-235 frs. Set meals 95-235 frs [1987]. New nomination: more reports please.

Hotels are dropped if we lack positive feedback. If you can endorse an entry, please do so.

ROLLEBOISE 78270 Yvelines — Map 9

Château de la Corniche — *Tel* (1)30.93.21.24
5 route de la Corniche — *Telex* 695544 CHAROL

Rolleboise is a village on the Seine between Paris and Rouen, some 12 kilometres from the splendid Monet museum and garden at Giverny. The *Château de la Corniche*, built by Leopold II of Belgium, is perched splendidly above a bend in the Seine (front bedrooms have fine views of countryside and river) and has been admired recently by a Californian travel expert: "An idyllic location, set amid five acres of gardens. The restaurant is done in pretty pink napery with bouquets of flowers on each table and the view is dreamy. The food includes artfully arranged salads and superlative desserts. Each bedroom is different and the management are very thoughtful." (*Pamela Lechtman*)

Open 23–30 Dec. Closed Sun evening and Mon 1 Oct–30 Apr.
Rooms 28 – 21 with bath, 7 with shower, all with telephone, radio and TV. 8 in 2 separate buildings in grounds.
Facilities Lift. Salons, bar, TV room, 2 restaurants; conference facilities; terrace. 5-acre grounds with swimming pool, tennis court and walks. English spoken.
Location Just W of Rolleboise, overlooking the Seine. Leave A13 to Rouen at Bonnières exit.
Restriction Not suitable for ♿.
Credit cards All major cards accepted.
Terms Rooms: single 220-260 frs, double 300-450 frs. Breakfast 40 frs. Set lunch 190 frs, dinner 300 frs. 1-night bookings sometimes refused.

ROMANÈCHE-THORINS 71570 Saône-et Loire — Map 10

Les Maritonnes — *Tel* 85.35.51.70
Telex 351060

At the foot of the vine-clad slopes of the Beaujolais, between Fleurie and the N6 highway, here is a rather formal and sophisticated little hotel, with plenty of parasols and lilos around the swimming pool in its garden and a *Michelin* rosette for its ambitious Burgundian cuisine (a huge *carte* featuring, e.g., escalope de saumon au Fleurie). "Absolutely superb. Beautifully furnished rooms and a warm welcome from Madame Fauvin. Her husband's cooking deserves the awards it has won. The gardens are a delight." (*David Lodge*)

Open All year, except 15–25 Dec, 9–16 June. Closed Sun evenings Oct–June. Restaurant closed Mon, and Tues midday 1 Jul–30 Sept.
Rooms 20 double – 18 with bath, 2 with shower, all with telephone and TV.
Facilities Lounge, bar, restaurant. Garden with heated swimming pool. English spoken.
Location Near station. Parking.
Restriction Not suitable for ♿.
Credit cards All major cards accepted.
Terms B&B: single 340 frs, double 460 frs. Set lunch/dinner 160, 210 and 290 frs; full alc 280-300 frs.

> We asked hotels to estimate their 1988 tariffs. About a quarter of the hotels in Part Two failed to reply, so prices in that section are often more approximate than those in Part One.

ROQUEFORT-SUR-SOULZON 12250 Aveyron — Map 10

Grand Hôtel — *Tel* 65.59.90.20
Rue de Lauras

The village straggles along the side of a limestone cliff, where the noblest of French cheeses are matured in their deep cool caves (well worth a visit). The *Grand,* a classic hostelry in the main street, is noted for its cooking (*Michelin* rosette and *Gault Millau toque* for such dishes as scrambled eggs with crayfish). "We were given a friendly welcome and a good-sized traditionally furnished and comfortable room. Our dinner was delicious, especially the truite à l'estragon and tourte au Roquefort." In summer you eat in the cool vaulted depths of a former cheese-cellar. (*DJ Cheeseman*)

Open 1 Apr–30 Sept. Closed Sun evening, and Mon, except July and Aug.
Rooms 14 double, 2 single – 11 with bath and/or shower, all with direct-dial telephone.
Facilities Bar, TV room, dining room; 2 function rooms. English spoken.
Location In village, parking. Roquefort is 24 km SW of Millau.
Restriction Not suitable for ♿.
Credit cards Amex, Diners, Visa.
Terms [1987 rates] Rooms: 190-325 frs. Breakfast 27 frs. Full board 190-300 frs per person. Set lunch/dinner 90-180 frs; full alc 250 frs.

LES ROSIERS-SUR-LOIRE 49350 Maine-et-Loire — Map 10

Auberge Jeanne de Laval — *Tel* 41.51.80.17
Route Nationale

A recent visitor had "an excellent dinner" at this much reputed restaurant-with-rooms where *patron*/chef Michel Augereau specialises in local beurre blanc fish dishes and wins a *Michelin* rosette and two *Gault Millau toques.* It is a handsome creeper-covered house, all very *soigné* inside, both the public rooms and bedrooms; simpler, more rustic bedrooms (and at least one uncomfortable bed) are in a nearby annexe, the *Ducs d'Anjou,* a converted manor. "When we had persuaded the rather scatty Madame that we actually *had* booked, we enjoyed a very pleasant overnight stay. We stayed in the annexe, a short car ride from the hotel: it is a very pretty house in a big walled garden, and the rooms were prettily decorated and adequate. Breakfast, with good home-made jam, was taken by an open window facing the garden. At dinner, the chicken in a gentle sauce was delicious." (*Gillian Vincent; endorsed this year by PHM Vischer*)

Open All year except 12 Nov–27 Dec, and Mon except public holidays.
Rooms 7 double – some with bath or shower, all with telephone. 8 double in annexe, *Ducs d'Anjou,* nearby – some with bath or shower .
Facilities Restaurant; functions facilities. Garden. Tennis, swimming, riding and golf nearby.
Location 15 km NW of Saumur, on banks of the Loire.
Credit cards All major cards accepted.
Terms [1987 rates] Rooms: single 220 frs, double 420 frs. Breakfast 36 frs. Alc (excluding wine) 280-300 frs.

> Please make a habit of sending in a report as soon as possible after a visit when details are still fresh in your mind.

ROUEN 76000 Seine-et-Marne — Map 9

Hôtel de la Cathédrale — *Tel* 35.71.57.95
12 rue St-Romain

Very centrally situated on a pedestrian walkway near the cathedral, this efficient and modest-priced hotel dropped out of last year's Guide for lack of new reports but is now borne back by a returning visitor: "From the moment you go through the heavy wooden doorway and into the courtyard with its geranium pots, busy lizzies and bits of statuary, you feel the delicious Frenchness of it all. Our room with flowered wallpaper overlooked the courtyard with a view of the cathedral spire; comfortable beds and very quiet at night. Good coffee for breakfast but no croissants. No restaurant, but we had a good fairly-priced meal at the popular *Petite Auberge* nearby." (*Caroline Raphael*) To another reader, however, the hotel was "a bit too old and shabby" and the beds "saggy". But he too appreciated the staff, the courtyard and the location.

Open All year.
Rooms 24 double – 8 with bath, 16 with shower, all with telephone.
Facilities Entrance hall, salon. Courtyard. English spoken.
Location Central. Public carpark nearby.
Credit cards Access, Visa.
Terms Rooms: single 115-195 frs, double 155-235 frs. Breakfast 18 frs. (No restaurant.)

SABRES 40630 Landes — Map 10

Auberge des Pins — *Tel* 58.07.50.47
Route de la Piscine

In the heart of the Landes pine-forests, an attractive chalet-like building in local style, half-timbered, with a huge gently-sloping roof. In the hands of the Lesclauze family, it has won first prize for the best flower-decked hotel in Aquitaine. "This friendly *Logis de France* in an unspoilt village has a super local flavour and is also very suitable for young families – *piscine*, sand-pit, swings, table-tennis, while a miniature railway takes you to the Marquèze Eco-Museum. Our room in the attractive annexe was nice and warm, and the cuisine was good and regional" (cassoulet, salmis de palombes etc). (*JC Gillett*)

Open All year.
Rooms 14 double – 4 with bath, 8 with shower, all with direct-dial telephone. 4 in annexe 50 metres away, with balcony overlooking the park.
Facilities Salon, bar, restaurant; conference facilities. Garden with children's play area. English spoken.
Location 30 km NW of Mont de Marsan.
Restriction Not suitable for ♿.
Credit card Visa.
Terms Rooms: single 90 frs, double 200 frs; half board 220 frs per person. Set lunch/dinner 60-180 frs; full alc 180 frs. Children's menu.

> "'Gorgeous home-made sweets' promised on the brochure included tinned melon, which was accompanied – and this was in Devon – by artificial cream."

SAILLAGOUSE 66800 Pyrénées-Orientales **Map 10**

Auberge Atalaya *Tel* 68.04.70.04
Llo

The Cerdagne, an hour's drive from Andorra and two from Perpignan, is one of the most appealing corners of France – an upland plain of meadows and pine forests, backed by the snowy Pyrenees. It is surprisingly lush and pastoral for such an altitude (1,066 metres) and has France's highest sunshine level. There's much of interest – the fortress of Mont-Louis, the big ski-resort of Font-Romeu, and the strange black Romanesque Madonna at l'Hermitage.

The *Atalaya,* a converted farmhouse in the hamlet of Llo, two kilometres from the resort of Saillagouse, is run by Hubert Toussaint, London born and bred. "Interesting auberge and attractive village, comfortable room and excellent dinner, though the menus tend to get repeated." So runs a report this year, following up earlier approval: "Very attractive – a stone building with dark wood but light and spacious bedrooms. Ours had a balcony. The Toussaints have a civilised attitude to their guests. A quiet and relaxing place to stay – out of season at least." (*PL Sugden, RJG*)

Open 20 Dec–5 Nov. Restaurant closed Mon in low season.
Rooms 1 suites, 9 double – all with bath, shower and telephone; TV on request.
Facilities Lounge, bar, restaurant. Garden. English spoken.
Location In Llo, on D33 2 km E of Saillagouse, which is 91 km W of Perpignan.
Restriction Not suitable for ♿.
Credit cards Diners, Visa.
Terms B&B: double 424–484 frs; dinner, B&B 640–700 frs; full board 860–920 frs. Set lunch/dinner 120 frs; full alc 220 frs.

ST-AMAND-DE-VERGT 24380 Dordogne **Map 10**

Manoir Les Prouillacs *Tel* 53.54.96.61

South of Périgueux, a stone-built 18th-century manor now run by an Englishwoman, Mrs Audrey Summerskill-Brontë, as a small private hotel in house-party style. "I arrived very tired to find peace and beauty," runs a report this year, "with a lovely swimming pool and a piano on which I could play. Our charming hostess gave us excellent value with five-course dinners and wine ad lib – superb cooking. I fell in love with my comfortable, pretty bedroom and its view across the fields." Others have extolled "this lovely crumbly old manor", "the dinners taken by candle-light in the stone-floored dining-room" and "the sitting-room with shelves full of books in English". (*Mrs Hilary Kunzru, IG Griffiths, and others*) However, with only five bedrooms, the success of the house-party style depends largely on who the guests are: last year, readers were pleased with the results, but this year one visitor found the international mix much less congenial – please send more reports.

Open End May–Nov. Other times by arrangement.
Rooms 1 suite, 4 double – 1 with bath, 4 with shower. Suite and 1 double on ground floor suitable for slightly ♿. 1 self-catering cottage.
Facilities Lounge, dining room; courtyard, terrace. Garden, swimming pool (unheated). Tennis, riding and lake with beach, boats, sand, fishing nearby. English spoken.

Location Just outside hamlet of St-Amand-de-Vergt, 7 km S of Vergt and 24 km from both Bergerac and Périgueux.
Restriction Children discouraged.
Credit cards None accepted.
Terms (Service at guests' discretion) Dinner, B&B (including wine) double £60 per night, £360–£400 per week.

ST-CIRQ-LAPOPIE 46330 Lot — Map 10

Hôtel de la Pélissaria — *Tel* 65.31.25.14

More and more readers each year are now being drawn to this paradise in one of the loveliest corners of rural France. St-Cirq is a famous *village perché*, set spectacularly on a cliff high above the river Lot. One of its old houses is now a tiny hotel, lovingly restored by its owner, François-Charles Matuchet, and on such a steep slope that you enter at the top with bedrooms on the floor below. "We adored the place", "delightful", "it even surpassed your description", are some of this year's comments. So we repeat that description: "M. Matuchet, a man of infinite charm who speaks excellent English, is a musician and singer and during the evening will usually play the tape he has made of his own settings of the poems of Ronsard. The music is not obtrusive but has the same elegance that characterises the hotel and his conduct of it. The beautiful dining room with its beamed ceiling is furnished with simplicity and grace. Highlights of Madame Matuchet's cooking were the trout soufflé, crêpe aux cèpes, gratin of pike, brochette of beef with superb sauce au poivre, and the gâteau au chocolat et aux noix which combines lightness with incredible richness." "There's an open fireplace and immense views. Bedrooms, cool and spacious, have tiled floors, white walls, pine doors, rough-woven white curtains and bedspreads, flower-beds outside and the most wonderful peace." "The dining room with its rustic furniture is reached by passing through a warm country kitchen redolent of robust soups and stews. The beamed bedrooms overlook the ancient church, and way below beyond the apple trees is the Lot river." (*CP, B and JS, M and GS; also N French, FR Hilborne, and others*) Madame Matuchet is now serving two set menus (120 and 200 frs) which need to be ordered in advance, and no lunches.

Open 1 Apr–3 Nov. Restaurant closed midday.
Rooms 6 – 3 with bath, 3 with shower, all with telephone.
Facilities Salon, dining room. Poetry recitals on Sat. Garden. English spoken.
Location Central. Parking at some distance from hotel. Village 30 km E of Cahors.
Restriction Not suitable for ♿.
Credit cards None accepted.
Terms Rooms 200–300 frs. Breakfast 30 frs. Set dinner (by arrangement) 120–200 frs.

Auberge du Sombral — *Tel* 65.31.26.08

Already praised in the French guides for its rural charm and good regional cooking, the *Auberge du Sombral* is for us a recent discovery by an American reader: "At this beguiling ten-bedroomed inn, our carpeted room was cosily charming in soothing blue, beige and cream, with floral wallpaper, view of rustic cottages and modern bathroom. The softly-lit rose-fragrant dining room was pleasant. Our 70-franc [1987] set menu offered little choice, but the gigot d'agneau was excellent." (*H Morris*) More reports welcome.

Open 15 Mar–15 Nov.
Rooms 10 double – all with bath or shower, and telephone.
Facilities Restaurant.
Location In village. St Cirq is 33 km E of Cahors.
Restriction Not suitable for ♿.
Credit cards None accepted.
Terms Rooms 200 frs. Breakfast 30 frs. Set lunch/dinner 70-220 frs; full alc 300 frs.

ST-CYPRIEN 24220 Dordogne — Map 10

Hôtel l'Abbaye — *Tel* 53.29.20.48

Sarlat and Les Eyzies-de-Tayac are both quite close to this pleasant village in the Dordogne valley, where the comfortable *Abbaye* remains a favourite with most readers. "The owners, the Schallers, are charming and prepared to help in any way," runs a report this year, "and their staff reflect their friendliness and professionalism. Our comfortable bedroom had fine views of the valley, but we were a little disturbed by village noises and the clock marking every half-hour. One can sit on the terrace or by the lovely pool all day. The salon is rustic, the dining room large and airy – *en pension* four-course meals included delicious lemon chicken, braised ham and duck." Other readers agree, but felt the menus did not change often enough, and that cooking was patchy. Poor insulation in some bedrooms. (*Chris and Dorothy Brining, T Keniston, and others*) The Schallers are said to have bought an 18th-century house nearby, to convert into a luxurious annexe - does anyone have news of this?

Open 15 Mar–15 Oct.
Rooms 1 suite, 23 double – 14 with bath, 10 with shower, all with direct-dial telephone and baby-listening. Some in 2 annexes. 2 ground-floor rooms.
Facilities Hall, 2 salons (1 with TV), restaurant. Garden, terrace, heated swimming pool; tennis 500 metres. English spoken.
Location Near town centre. Parking.
Credit cards All major cards accepted.
Terms [1987 rates] Rooms: 228-500 frs. Breakfast 26 frs. Set lunch/dinner 110-275 frs. Reduced rates and special meals for children.

ST-DYÉ-SUR-LOIRE 41500 Loir-et-Cher — Map 10

Manoir Bel Air — *Tel* 54.81.60.10

Right by the banks of the broad Loire between Blois and Orléans, and not far from Chambord, this is a low, creeper-covered manor house converted into an unpretentious, inexpensive hotel. "A casual but friendly reception, and a modern, very comfortable bedroom with spacious bathroom and lovely view of the river. It was very peaceful. House martins were flying around. Charming exterior stone staircase. An enjoyable dinner – rillettes de saumon, coq au vin, etc." Endorsed this year: "Spacious, nicely-decorated dining room with views of the Loire. Walks beside the river. Good value: we will go again." (*DJ Cheeseman, JN Jolly*)

Open All year, except 10 Jan–20 Feb.
Rooms 38 – most with bath and/or shower and telephone.

Facilities Salon, TV room, restaurant; conference facilities. Garden. English spoken.
Location 200 metres from village which is 4 km W of Chambord.
Credit card Visa.
Terms [1987 rates] Rooms 180-280 frs. Breakfast 22 frs. Full board 240-260 frs. Set lunch/dinner 65-170 frs. 50% reduction for children under 10.

ST-FÉLIX-LAURAGAIS 31540 Haute-Garonne — Map 10

Auberge du Poids Public — *Tel* 61.83.00.20
Telex 532477

An attractive village of timbered houses, perched on a hill in the rolling countryside east of Toulouse. The view from it is magnificent, taking in the snowy Pyrenees to the south and the darker Dordogne hills to the north. The *Poids Public* is a low building much extended from the original village inn where produce was weighed (hence its name) before the proceeds were split between landlord and tenant. Our reporter: "*Michelin* accurately describes the interior as *bel aménagement* – interesting pictures everywhere, and bedrooms furnished with great taste and comfort. Most have that splendid view. *Patron*/chef Bernard Augé is a bit of a showman, but produces wonderful food based on local produce (red *Michelin* 'R'and *Gault Millau* laurels for regional cuisine) – our five-course 85-franc [1987] menu included brochet mousseline with walnut sauce and his grand-mère's way of dealing with pig's trotters (interesting!). We sat at our window table watching the setting sun light up houses in Puy Laurens 20 kilometres away. The fresh flowers on the table were all wild. Thoroughly recommended." (*Diana Holmes*) A returning visitor this year was mildly disappointed: "Our room was charming but ultra-twee, with one big bed and one wooden 'Goldilocks' truckle bed. Dinner was good value but nothing remarkable and breakfast a cheek. M. Augé is fun in a larger-than-life way and his wife is a poppet. But for a few details, that place would be a dream." (*PP; also Bernard Dunstan*)

Open All year except 6 Jan–10 Feb. Closed Sun evening 15 Oct–15 Mar.
Rooms 13 double – all with bath and/or shower and telephone.
Facilities Salon/bar, TV lounge, restaurant; terrace. Garden. English spoken.
Location On N622 43 km E of Toulouse. Back rooms quietest.
Restriction Not suitable for ♿.
Credit cards Amex, Visa.
Terms Rooms 188-205 frs. Breakfast 22 frs. Dinner, B&B 190-220 frs. Set lunch/dinner 47-157 frs; full alc 200 frs. Reduced rates for children sharing parents' room; special meals.

ST-FLORENT 20217 Corsica — Map 11

Hôtel Dolce Notte — *Tel* 95.37.06.65
Route de Bastia

St-Florent is a busy little bathing resort on a lovely stretch of coast west of Bastia, at the base of the gorgeous Cap Corse peninsula. Above it stands an old citadel, reminder of its past as a Genoese strongpoint. The modern *Dolce Notte*, just outside the town, is a recent nomination: "It is set in prettily landscaped grounds and the rooms are immaculate in wood and white plaster. Ours overlooked the sea, whose ebb and flow on the pebbles filled the air with gentle noise. The management were helpful; and, unusual for hotels in Corsica, here everything *worked*, including the plumbing in the large tiled bathroom. We took breakfast on our small balcony." (*WH Bruton*)

Open Mar–Nov.
Rooms 1 suite, 24 double – all with bath or shower, direct-dial telephone and TV; some with balcony. 5 ground-floor rooms (with shower) in annexe 5 metres away.
Facilities Terrace where breakfasts are served. Garden.
Location 23 km W of Bastia; near village centre. Private parking.
Credit cards None accepted.
Terms Rooms 320–340 frs (180 frs in annexe). Breakfast 25 frs. (No restaurant.)

ST-FLORENTIN 89600 Yonne — Map 9

Hôtel La Grande Chaumière — *Tel* 86.35.15.12
3 rue des Capucins

New to the Guide this year, and newly modernised, this long pink building, really a restaurant-with-rooms, could be useful for anyone touring northern Burgundy: "It is just off the main square of a pleasant small town near Auxerre. The church has fine 16th-century glass and carvings. Our large and well-furnished room was at the back and very quiet: it needed redecorating, but the renovated rooms we saw were quite chic. Madame was charming and welcoming and the hotel seemed efficiently run. The restaurant was very attractive and the food well presented and served by Madame's 'corps de ballet' of four smart young ladies. The quality of the food was superb."(*BN Wilson*) Interesting Burgundian dishes on a 43 cm-high menu, pretentiously printed.

Open 16 Jan–20 Dec. Closed first week in Sept.
Rooms 1 suite, 10 double – all with bath and shower, telephone and TV.
Facilities Reception, salon, restaurant; terrace. Garden. Fishing nearby.
Location Central, parking. Town is 31 km N of Auxerre, on N77 to Troyes.
Restriction Not suitable for ♿.
Credit cards Amex, Diners, Visa.
Terms B&B: single 310 frs, double 340 frs, suite 390–410 frs. Set lunch/dinner 90, 170 and 260 frs; full alc 280 frs.

ST-GERMAIN-EN-LAYE 78100 Yvelines — Map 9

Cazaudehore and La Forestière — *Tel* 34.51.93.80 and 39.73.36.60
1 avenue du Président Kennedy — *Telex* 696055

In the depths of the forest of St-Germain, a bare 19 kilometres from Paris, the Cazaudehore family run a famous and distinguished restaurant that bears their name, and next to it a stylish little hotel, *La Forestière*. Both for some years have caused the French guides to wax lyrical (rosettes, *toques*, red print), but oddly they come new to ours in 1988: "Tasteful modern rooms and suites, elegantly decorated with interesting antiques and prints. Tiled bathrooms, friendly service, and a pleasing outlook onto the oak and beech forest. The restaurant has fresh flowers, gleaming silverware, an excellent menu, and on our visit its clientèle was sophisticated and international." (*WA; also Richard H Proctor*) The Cazaudehore family are Basque, and their cuisine is inspired by the south-west: tripes à la paloise, terrine de canard aux pistaches, etc.

Open All year. Restaurant closed Mon (light meals available for hotel guests).
Rooms 6 suites, 24 double – all with bath and shower, telephone, radio, TV and mini-bar.
Facilities 2 salons, restaurant; conference facilities. Garden. Swimming pool, tennis courts and golf course nearby.
Location 2.5 km NW of St-Germain, by N 284 and route des Mares.
Restriction Not suitable for ♿.
Credit card Visa.
Terms Rooms: single 540 frs, double 620 frs, suite 720 frs. Breakfast 40 frs. Full alc 280–330 frs. Reduced rates for children sharing parents' room; special menu.

ST-HIPPOLYTE 68590 Haut-Rhin — Map 9

Hôtel Munsch: Aux Ducs de Lorraine — *Tel* 89.73.00.09
16 route du Vin

St-Hippolyte is a village on the much-visited *route du vin* north of Colmar. The *Munsch*, a gabled and half-timbered mansion on the outskirts, adjoins the owner's own vineyards and typifies the high standards of hostelry in this serene sector of Alsace. Several visitors have admired it this year: "The food is good and plentiful; our warm and comfortable room had a balcony overlooking the vineyards." "We were courteously received; agreeable, well-served dinner." Popular with locals, the dining-room serves Alsatian food, with the owner's own wine. (*Brian Beves, Eric Dodson, and others*)

Open 1 Mar–1 Dec, 20 Dec–10 Jan. Restaurant closed Mon.
Rooms 2 suites, 39 double – all with bath and/or shower, telephone, radio and tv; many with balcony. Some ground floor rooms.
Facilities Lift. 3 reception rooms, breakfast room with TV, dining room; small conference room. Garden and terrace with children's play area. English spoken.
Location At entrance to village, but quietly situated. Ample parking.
Credit card Amex, Diners, Visa.
Terms Rooms: single 280-380 frs, double 340-440 frs, suite 750-900 frs; Breakfast 35 frs. Dinner, B&B 340-540 frs per person. Set lunch/dinner 100, 170 and 290 frs. Reduced rates for children under 11; special meals on request.

ST-JEAN-DU-BRUEL 12230 Aveyron — Map 10

Hôtel du Midi — *Tel* 65.62.26.04

The Papillon family's unpretentious *Logis de France* in the western Cévennes remains one of the most warmly-praised of all our French rural entries. It is in an old village on the river Dourbie between Millau and Le Vigan, a good centre for walking holidays or for visiting the Gorges du Tarn. "Many regulars find this hotel irresistible and spend weeks here every year. Monsieur cooks and Madame looks after everything with friendly and charming efficiency. Rooms are freshly decorated and spotless." Another report this year: "This is for the country-lover – dead quiet after 9.30 pm except for the chorus of nightingales in the fruit trees." Others enjoy the "informal atmosphere" and Madame's "buoyant and elegant personality". Bedrooms vary in quality, some well modernised, some a bit cramped, but all adequate. The food (red "R" in *Michelin*) is a star attraction, as so often in this kind of French hotel – "a five-course dinner beautifully cooked and prepared", "little boudins of sea fish, glazed roast rabbit (or hare?)", "the fresh vegetables, crudités and salads are a delight". *Pension* meals vary daily. "Incredibly good value" is the overall verdict. The clientele is largely French, though the British have now arrived too (average of four GB cars at a time). (*Prof Charles Thomas, JP Berryman, Noel and Sheila Marriott, and others*)

Open 26 Mar–11 Nov.
Rooms 17 double, 2 single – 11 with bath, 2 with shower, all with telephone. 2 pairs of communicating rooms in nearby annexe.
Facilities Salon, TV room, bar, 3 restaurants; terrace. On banks of river Dourbie, with small beaches; bathing, fishing. English spoken.
Location 40 km SE of Millau on D991; 20 km E of N9. Garage and open parking.
Restriction Only restaurant suitable for ♿.
Credit cards None accepted.
Terms B&B: single 80 frs, double 112-185 frs; half board: single 154-164 frs, double 260-352 frs; full board: single 179-189 frs, double 310-404 frs. Set lunch/dinner 61-160 frs; full alc 100 frs. Reduced rates for children under 6.

ST-JEAN-DU-DOIGT 29228 Finistère — Map 8

Le Ty-Pont — *Tel* 98.67.34.06
Plougasnou

A down-to-earth seaside hotel in northern Brittany, removed from last year's Guide for lack of reports, but now brought back by a family who enjoyed "a memorable holiday" here, thus endorsing this earlier portrait: "Incredible value. For about £16 each [1987 rates] we had full board in high season, and the food was staggering: honest cooking and the freshest possible ingredients, with excellent seafood. Lunch might start with crab-claws and slices of melon, then a fish in a delicate sauce, then a meat course (perhaps guinea-fowl), then cheese, fromage blanc or yoghurt, then ice-cream (home-made) or a good selection of fresh fruit or crème caramel. The scene in the dining-room was astonishing – working-class French families, a baby drinking potage out of its bottle, a two-year-old having fromage blanc spooned into it. It was very noisy, but the young waitresses were never flustered. Breakfast was a rushed affair that could involve long waits.

"Bedrooms were adequate. There is a garden by a stream, where you can sit in the sun and recover from *la bouffe*. St-Jean is a pretty village amid farmlands, with good views: the church is lovely, but its bell strikes every 30 minutes, so we had less sleep than we'd have liked. Lovely beach at Primel-Tregastel nearby." (*CAR*) One reader this year dared to find *Le Ty-Pont* "nothing special and a bit basic", but another agreed with *CAR* about the food, and admired the "impeccably clean rooms" and the amenities for children. (*Alan K Fowler*)

Open Apr–mid-Oct. Closed Sun and Mon.
Rooms 29 double – 2 with bath, 12 with shower; 17 with telephone.
Facilities Bar, TV room, 2 restaurants. Garden. English spoken.
Restriction Not suitable for ♿.
Location 17 km NE of Morlaix, 1.5 km E of Plougasnou village.
Credit cards None accepted.
Terms Rooms 104-153 frs; dinner, B&B 132-152 frs per person. Set lunch/dinner 47-170 frs.

We are particularly keen to have reports on italicised entries.

ST-JEAN-PIED-DE-PORT 64220 Pyrénées-Atlantiques Map 10

Hôtel des Pyrénées *Tel* 59.37.01.01
Place du Général de Gaulle

St-Jean, at the foot of the Roncesvalles pass into Spain, used to be a major resting-place for pilgrims about to cross the Pyrenees on their way to Santiago. Today it is one of the most picturesque of Basque towns (15th-century ramparts, hilltop citadel) and a capital of Basque folklore (summer festival and *pelota* championships). Its other distinction is the *Pyrénées*, its main *auberge*, which has been owned and run by the Arrambide family for four generations and today has one of the most highly-rated kitchens in the south-west (two *Michelin* rosettes, three red *Gault Millau toques*). A reader this year has confirmed, with minor reservations, an earlier visitor's enthusiasm: "Exceptionally good food, with interesting set menus and seasonal specialities. In October, we had: a warm first course of assorted wild mushrooms (including delicious black 'trumpets of death'), beautifully arranged; a whole hare, boned and stuffed with foie gras; noisette of roe deer; excellent local wine. There was a sense of occasion about the entire restaurant, packed with interesting and lively well-heeled locals." Another visitor has lyricised over "the joy of eating on the terrace on a fine day". (*Noel and Barbara Buxton, WB, and others*) Many bedrooms are still no more than "adequate", but there are now luxury suites on the first floor.

Open All year. Closed Mon evening Nov–Mar and Tue except July–Sept and public holidays.
Rooms 2 suites, 25 double – all with bath, shower and telephone; 7 with TV.
Facilities Lift. 2 salons, TV room, 2 dining rooms; conference rooms; terrace. Tennis, swimming, fishing, pigeon-shooting. English spoken.
Location 54 km SE of Bayonne on D933. Parking.
Credit cards Amex, Visa.
Terms Rooms: double 260-290 frs. Breakfast 30 frs. Set lunch/dinner 140-130 frs.

ST-JUNIEN 87200 Haute-Vienne Map 10

Relais de Comodoliac *Tel* 55.02.27.26
22 avenue Sadi-Carnot *Telex* 590336

West of Limoges, in a small glove-making town with a fine old Romanesque church, a comfortable and welcoming hotel, family-run, efficient patronne. *Good food, well served; covered terrace for drinks. Front rooms could be noisy. 28 rooms, with bath and shower, 190-250 frs [1987]. New nomination: more reports please.*

ST-LATTIER 38160 Isère Map 10

Le Lièvre Amoureux *Tel* 76.36.50.67
Telex 308534 LIEVRE

In the Isère valley between Valence and Grenoble, this "amorous hare" is a very pleasant old creeper-covered *auberge*, really a restaurant with rooms, given three knives-and-forks in *Michelin* for comfort-plus-attractiveness. The cooking is regional, served outside in summer on a terrace under lime-trees, or indoors in a panelled room where a fire blazes in winter. The hare was chased out of the Guide in 1986 as it had not been fed with feedback, but now it returns well nourished by this report: "We stayed in the new annexe by the new open-air heated swimming-pool: these rooms are quiet and well-appointed with sliding 'patio' windows. We were staying *en pension*, but Madame Breda, the *patronne*, allowed us the run of all the menus including the *carte* at no extra cost. The food was excellent, especially the local trout, and the local wines were good too. Breakfasts included optional orange juice, yoghurt and eggs at no extra charge. The staff were competent and friendly, and on our last evening we received a free bottle of champagne over dinner." Rooms in the old building are smaller and simpler but have pretty views through the trees to the Vercors mountains. (*GE Samson*)

Open Feb–Dec. Closed 24 Dec.
Rooms 6 suites, 6 double, 2 single – 12 with bath and shower, all with telephone; 5 with radio; 6 with TV. 5 in annexe. 2 ground-floor rooms.
Facilities 2 small salons, 2 restaurants. Garden with terrace for meals in summer, swimming pool and bar. River with fishing nearby. English spoken.
Location Halfway between St-Marcellin and Romans on N 92.
Credit cards Amex, Diners, Visa.
Terms Room: 120-380 frs. Breakfast 35 frs. Set lunch/dinner 150-220 frs; full alc 160-170 frs. Reduced rates for children; special meals.

ST-LÉONARD-DES-BOIS 72590 Sarthe — Map 8

Touring Hôtel — *Tel* 43.97.28.03
Telex 722006

In southern Normandy, south-west of Alençon, a modern chalet-style tourist hotel with a pleasant garden and sun-terrace beside the river Sarthe, and rolling wooded country all round. Very helpful staff, attractive rooms, good country cooking. Mini-golf, children's games, seminar facilities. Open 15 Feb–15 Nov. 33 rooms, all with bath. B&B double 220-360 frs. Set meals 80–180 frs. New nomination: more reports please.

ST-MALO 35400 Ille-et-Vilaine — Map 8

Hôtel Le Valmarin — *Tel* 99.81.94.76
7 rue Jean XXIII

"Very good, though a bit too formal for my taste," is this year's verdict on this modern hotel, converted from an 18th-century house in the suburb of St-Servan, just south of St-Malo harbour and about two kilometres from the old walled city. Another recent view: "Fabulously comfortable and civilised, with a discreet atmosphere. The proprietor brings you a glass of chilled Muscadet on a silver tray, covered with lace, while you sit in the impressive gardens." An earlier visitor had a room beautifully decorated in white, green and gold. No restaurant, but there are several good cheap fish places in the harbour area. (*Carol E Lindenmeyer, Stephen and Flo Bayley*)

Open 1 Mar–31 Dec. Restaurant closed New Year.
Rooms 10 double – all with bath, telephone, radio and TV.
Facilities Salon, bar. Garden. 100 metres from safe sandy beach; swimming, sailing, tennis nearby. English spoken.

Location Centre of St-Servan near Port Solidor; 2 km from old St-Malo. Parking.
Restriction Not suitable for ♿.
Credit cards Amex, Visa.
Terms B&B: single 318-428 frs, double 346-496 frs. (No restaurant.)

ST-MARTIN-DU-FAULT 87510 Haute-Vienne — Map 10

La Chapelle-St-Martin — *Tel* 55.75.80.17

In the countryside north-west of Limoges, the chief tourist sight is a tragic one – Oradour-sur-Glane, where on 10 June 1944 the SS massacred the entire village population of some 650 men, women and children. A new village has been built: the ruins of the old one are kept as a memorial, with a sign in German, "Do not forget." Today German tourists and others stay at the smart country hotels of the area: *La Chapelle* has much the same qualities and high prices as its neighbour at Nieuil (q.v.) and is new to the Guide this year: "A very pretty *gentilhommière* set in a park; elegantly and newly refurbished in a very French style with bright royal-blue carpets. Comfortable bedrooms and bathrooms. The dining-room is more like a series of drawing-rooms with the occasional table in the corner – all very elegant. The food is served with panache but we did not think it very good and the wines are expensive." The French guides beg to differ, bestowing rosette and *toque*. (*Jane and William Dorrell*) More reports please.

Open All year, except Jan, Feb and 1–8 Aug. Restaurant closed Mon.
Rooms 10 – all with bath and/or shower and telephone.
Facilities Lounge, restaurant. Park with lake and tennis-court.
Location 12 km NE of Limoges, by N147 and D35; near Nieuil.
Credit card Visa.
Terms [1987 rates] Rooms: single: 370 frs, double 690 frs. Breakfast 43 frs. Alc (excluding wine) 205-310 frs.

ST-MOREIL 23400 Creuse — Map 10

Moulin de Montalétang — *Tel* 55.54.92.72

St-Moreil, Bourganeuf

Remote in the wooded undulating Limousin countryside between Aubusson (tapestries) and Limoges (porcelain), this converted millhouse (a *Relais du Silence*) has a somewhat severe exterior but is full of rewards for those who appreciate simple French rural hospitality – as a nominator reports this year: "In an area that is a blank space in your Guide, the hotel is several miles from any main road, down narrow tortuous lanes, in a soft and friendly countryside of conifer woods, lakes and farmland. Christian Lagrue and his wife took the place over in 1985: he is the front man, a cheerful extrovert who works hard to make his guests welcome. About half the guests were British (thanks to R. Binns). We found the *demi-pension* meals interesting and the à la carte dishes delicious. One day we hired excellent bikes from the hotel, which provided us with a big picnic." So who needs a limousine in Limousin? (*Peter Hancock*) Fanciful decor; some four-poster beds.

Open All year, except Christmas; New Year by prior reservation only.
Rooms 14 double – all with bath and/or shower, and telephone.
Some ground floor rooms.

Facilities Salon, bar, TV room, restaurant; terrace. Garden. Fishing, riding, tennis, golf nearby.
Location 13 km SW of Bourganeuf, towards Limoges.
Credit card Visa.
Terms B&B (double room): 230–280 frs; dinner, B&B 358–398 frs; full board 508–548 frs. Full alc 120 frs.

ST-MARTIN-VALMEROUX 15140 Cantal — Map 10

Hostellerie de la Maronne — *Tel* 71.69.20.33
Le Theil

A dawn symphony of bells ringing on local cows, complained of by one reader, seems to be the only drawback to the Auvergnat rural bliss to be found in plenty at this simple little hotel outside the hamlet of Le Theil, midway between St-Martin-Valmeroux (on the Mauriac–Aurillac road) and the lovely Renaissance hill-village of Salers. "A *Relais du Silence* with real distinction, in the lush upper valley of the Maronne, where rocky outcrops give promise of the volcanic mountains to come. The hotel stands in its own informal garden and grounds. Alain de Cock, his Malagasy wife and a small, well-trained staff provide comfort and a choiceless but excellent evening meal (e.g. rève d'escargots and tripoux flambés au cognac). Good stock of wines. Walkers may dislike the unavailability of breakfast before 8.30 am." Recent visitors enjoyed swimming in the new pool and had "excellent" food, but were not so keen on being obliged to sit down to dine before 8 pm. "Not more than half the guests are British", is semi-reassuring news this year. (*Jack and Helen Thornton; also Peter Hancock, JF Holman*)

Open 1 Apr–4 Nov.
Rooms 2 suites, 22 double – all with bath, shower, telephone and mini-bar. 8 rooms in annexe. Some ground-floor rooms.
Facilities Salon, games room, dining room. Garden with heated swimming pool, tennis and archery. English spoken.
Location 3 km E of St-Martin-Valmeroux on D37 to Fontanges.
Credit cards Access, Visa.
Terms [1987 rates] Dinner, B&B: 200-290 frs. Reduced rates for children sharing parents' room.

ST-PAUL-DE-VENCE 06570 Alpes-Maritimes — Map 11

La Colombe d'Or — *Tel* 93.32.80.02
Telex 970607

Our readers have mixed feelings about this famous little luxury hotel in a show-village behind Nice. Undoubtedly it suffers from its popularity as a tourist attraction in its own right, for it houses a private collection of modern art that would be the envy of any museum – Braque and Calder by the swimming pool, César and Miró in the lounge, Matisse, Picasso and Utrillo in the dining room, and much else. Many of these works were given to the former owner, the late Paul Roux, in payment by artists who stayed or ate there. It's a beautiful old house, with many fine pieces of furniture, and is still owned and run by the Roux family. Each room has a distinctive character – some with original beams, others all in white stucco with window-seats overlooking gardens. Many have a lovely terrace and outside bathroom. There is a splendid veranda, decorated with a fine Léger mural, where lunch is served; dinner is taken indoors in a large sophisticated rustic dining room. The swimming pool is surrounded by cypress trees. But it is not a place that is going to suit everyone. An inspector this year found the service slapdash (so it usually is) but the food itself he judged better than its low reputation. Another recent visitor was enchanted with "this idyllic hotel". (*Mrs JN Hicks*)

Open All year, except 5 Nov–20 Dec.
Rooms 8 suites, 16 double – all with bath, direct-dial telephone, radio and TV; many with terrace. 1 ground-floor room.
Facilities Salon, restaurant; terrace for lunch or refreshments; sauna. Garden with swimming pool. 10 km from sea. English spoken.
Location 10 km from Nice; take road to La Colle and Hauts de St-Paul. Parking.
Credit cards All major cards accepted.
Terms [1987 rates] Rooms: 650 frs, suite 750 frs. Breakfast 30 frs. Full alc 190-320 frs.

ST-PIERRE-DU-VAUVRAY 27430 Eure — Map 8

Hostellerie Saint-Pierre — *Tel* 32.59.93.29

2 chemin des Amoureux

"This excellent establishment lies pleasantly on the banks of the Seine where one can enjoy the leisurely plying of the barges. It is an undistinguished 1912 Le Touquet version of an old half-timbered Norman farmhouse; but this does not matter in the least as old Norman houses are draughty, creaky and cold, whereas this hotel was nicely warm, with excellent beds, and very quiet. We were delighted by the delicious pâté, and the turbot served on a bed of noodles - sounds extraordinary, but they know what they are doing. Service a bit slow." The restaurant's wide windows give views of the river. Bedrooms in various styles, some "empire" with river views, some heavily beamed with four-poster bed. In England, in plushy hostelries of this mock-Tudor kind, the food is usually mock-French: here it is real French. (*CFC*) More reports please.

Open 1 Mar–31 Dec. Restaurant closed Tue.
Rooms 3 suites, 11 double – all with bath, shower, telephone, TV and mini-bar.
Facilities Lift. Salon, restaurant; conference facilities. Garden by river; fishing. Riding, sailing, water-skiing, golf nearby.
Location Leave A13 motorway at Louviers if coming from Rouen, and Louviers Sud if coming from Paris; follow signs to St-Pierre-du-Vauvray.
Credit card Visa.
Term B&B: single 292 frs, double 327-442 frs, suite 382-572 frs. Set lunch/dinner 145-225 frs; full alc 250 frs.

ST-PONS-DE-THOMIÈRES 34220 Hérault — Map 10

Château de Ponderach — *Tel* 67.97.02.57

Route de Narbonne

Deep in the Haut Languedoc Nature Reserve, this splendid 17th-century manor-house lies in its own 400-acre wooded park and has been the owner's family home for some 300 years. It is at the edge of wild heavily-forested country, above a river, in the rocky foothills of the Montagne

Noire, just outside the pleasant old town of St-Pons (fine 12th-century cathedral). "Warm reception, excellent food and service, flowers everywhere," is one recent comment. Another: "Superlative. Complete peace and quiet. Charming reception by the aristocratic lady owner, Madame Counotte. Particularly elegant dining room. Our bedroom, up an old stone staircase, was spacious and lovely. Superb breakfast." (*John Hills, SS-B*) More reports please.

Open 1 Apr–mid-Oct.
Rooms 9 double – all with bath, shower and telephone.
Facilities Salon with TV, bar, restaurant; conference facilities. Large garden where meals are served in good weather. Small lake nearby. English spoken.
Location 1 km S of town on Narbonne road.
Credit cards Access, Diners, Visa.
Terms Rooms 330 frs. Breakfast 50 frs. Dinner, B&B 600 frs; full board 780 frs. Full alc 300 frs.

ST-RÉMY-DE-PROVENCE 13210 Bouches-du-Rhône — Map 11

Hôtel Les Antiques — *Tel* 90.92.03.02
15 avenue Pasteur

St-Rémy is the quintessential small Provençal town, with the bonus of possessing some of the most curious Roman remains in France (at Glanum, just to the south); nearby is the mental home of St-Paul-de-Mausole where Van Gogh spent a year as a patient after cutting off his ear in Arles. "Our fourth visit to *Les Antiques*, and we found it as delightful as ever," runs this year's report from two veteran francophile travellers. "A most restful hotel, with amazingly well-tended grounds and good breakfast including fruit and brioches." The hotel is a 19th-century mansion, gracefully converted, and it stands by a main road near the town centre, with its own big garden at the back. You can stay in the main building, or in a *pavillon* with its own terrace." Another report: "Lovely people, charming atmosphere: it was like being guests in a private home. On my husband's birthday they gave him a cake. Beautiful gardens, and a grand entrance with marble floors, tapestries, Italian painted ceiling." (*Kay and Neville Varley, H Emson*) No restaurant, but the *France* and the *Arts* in town are both good value.

Open 26 March–15 Oct.
Rooms 26 double, 1 single – all with bath, shower and telephone. 10 in bungalow in park. 2 ground-floor rooms with ramps.
Facilities Large salon, TV room, bridge room; functions room; Large grounds with unheated swimming pool; riding centre. English spoken.
Location In town centre.
Credit cards Amex, Diners, Visa.
Terms (Excluding tax) B&B: single 344 frs, double 440 frs. (No restaurant.)

Hôtel-Château de Roussan — *Tel* 90.92.11.63
Route de Tarascon

This stately pink 18th-century château, secluded outside St-Rémy in its own big park, has been the country home of the Roussel family for over a century; today they accept bed-and-breakfast clients to keep it going. This year it has been more popular than ever: many readers find it an unusual and civilised experience, more like being the house-guests of cultured friends than staying in a hotel. "Totally charming and our room was fabulous." "Our enormous room was full of antiques; good breakfast under the chestnut trees." "An ideal place for writing. You can set your table and chair in a far corner of the park and be disturbed only by the house dogs who take a well-behaved interest when picnic lunchtime has arrived." Bathrooms are modern, but the rooms are in careful period style, with Louis XV furniture. "Louis Roussel was a courteous host, showing us the 16th-century farmhouse in the grounds where Nostradamus once lived and inviting us to browse in his library. We enjoyed the sprawling garden, full of pools and fountains." No restaurant, but try the *Café des Arts* or the *France* in town, both quite cheap. (*Jane and William Dorrell, Robert Stevens and Alexa Grace, Nina Bawden and Austen Kark, and others*)

Open 20 Mar–20 Oct.
Rooms 12 double – 10 with bath and shower, 2 with bath only, all with direct-dial telephone. 1 ground-floor room.
Facilities 2 salons. Large park. English spoken.
Location 3 km W of centre of St-Rémy, off Tarascon road. Parking.
Credit card Visa.
Terms Rooms: single occupancy 330 frs, double 380-540 frs. Breakfast 42 frs. (No restaurant.)

ST-SYMPHORIEN-LE-CHÂTEAU 28700 Eure-et-Loir — Map 8

Château d'Esclimont — *Tel* 37.31.15.15
St-Symphorien-le-Château — *Telex* 780560 ECLIMON

This stately moated Renaissance château, typically Ile-de-France, stands in a 150-acre wooded park, between Chartres and Rambouillet. On its facade is a motto of la Rochefoucauld: "C'est mon plaisir." Ours? "Truly glorious, and luxuriously appointed," writes a visitor this year, "and rescued by the notable Frenchman, René Traversac, who has created lovely hotels from French châteaux in various stages of decrepitude. Even on a bitter winter's day, everywhere was deliciously warm. The views are amazing, over park, river and woods; the food is delicious and served in generous portions from an inspired menu (two *Gault Millau toques*). One group arrived by helicopter, landing on the snow." Our own more terrestrial readers have enjoyed the beamed high-ceilinged dining room, the spacious bedrooms, the swimming pool, and the wide terrace where aperitifs can be taken under the sun umbrellas. (*WA; also Mrs Robert A Goeller Jr, and others*)

Open All year.
Rooms 6 suites, 48 double – all with bath, shower, telephone and TV. 24 in 3 separate annexes.
Facilities Salon, bar, 4 restaurants; conference facilities. Wooded park with small lake, river, tennis court, heated swimming pool and helipad. English spoken.
Location 6 km NW of Ablis. Leave A11 or N10 at Ablis; go towards Prunay; turn left on D101.
Restriction Not suitable for ♿.
Credit card Visa.
Terms Rooms: single occupancy 495 frs, double 780-1,145 frs, suite 1,350-1,975 frs. Breakfast 60 frs. Set lunch/dinner 235-430 frs; full alc 420 frs.

ST-TROPEZ 83990 Var — Map 11

Le Mas de Chastelas — *Tel* 94.56.09.11
Route de Gassin — *Telex* 462393

For some years now this old *mas* has been described as *the* most sympathetic and tasteful hotel in the St-Tropez area (where tranquil charm and good taste are not always in evidence). It's a converted 17th-century farmhouse, once used for silkworm breeding, and it stands secluded in vineyards a little west of St-Tropez and 500 metres from the sea. Guests tend to include French stars of stage, screen and fashion, fleeing the *paparazzi* of the frenzied port area. "One of the most delightful places we know in France," write discerning travellers. "It is beautifully run in a very personal way, with superb service. Our suite in an annexe in the woods was luxurious; flowers were changed daily. Fine breakfast, with cherries and brioches; good food pleasantly served by the pool, but the menus don't change often enough." A visitor this year found the dinners very good, while others have admired the buffet lunches by the heated pool, the dinners served on a candle-lit terrace, and the pine furnishings. "Outstanding comfort and food, friendly staff and atmosphere." Two *Gault Millau toques* for Jean-Louis Vosgien's cooking.(*Stefan and Yvette Wiener, Nicola Hayward, Vicki Turner*)

Open End Apr–early Oct. Restaurant closed to non-residents for lunch.
Rooms 10 suites, 21 double – 27 with bath and shower, 4 with shower, all with telephone and TV. Suites are in annexe.
Facilities Lounge, bar, TV room, indoor and outdoor restaurant; terrace. Garden with heated swimming-pool and 4 tennis-courts. English spoken.
Location 3 km SW of St-Tropez, just off Gassin road.
Restriction Not suitable for ♿.
Credit cards All major cards accepted.
Terms Rooms: double 480-1,050 frs, suite 1,500-1,800 frs. Breakfast 60 frs. Set lunch 120-150 frs, dinner 260-350 frs; full alc 320 frs. Special meals for children.

Hôtel du Treizain — *Tel* 94.97.70.08
Domaine du Treizain, RN 98

It is never easy to choose between the scores of rustic-style hotels that circle St-Tropez, so we were delighted this year to receive a New Yorker's nomination of the *Treizain*. Like the *Mas de Chastelas* (above), it is outside the town, aloof from the garish hurly-burly; it is cheaper, however, and could make a useful alternative. "Lovely stucco and tile *mas*, built recently in charming traditional style. Sprawling structure set around a beautiful swimming pool, astride a hill with breathtaking views of the gulf. Both our rooms were wonderful – tile floors, spacious modern bath, patio and balcony, flowering trees framing every window view. Breakfast by the pool was a delight; the large sitting room had comfortable couches. A friendly Dutch family run this casual but sophisticated hotel. St-Tropez is about ten minutes by car, and fabulous beaches are closer." (*MA Mikulich*) Though the *Treizain* has no restaurant it does provide lunch, and dinner is served three times a week by the pool in summer. Alternative eating places are *Le Cabichou*, the smart place to eat in town, and there are middle-price outdoor restaurants in the little *port de pêche* by the Place Révelin, east of the main port.

Open End Mar–31 Oct.
Rooms 17 double – all with bath and/or shower, telephone. Some on ground floor.
Facilities Lounge with TV; sauna. Garden with swimming pool and bar.
Location 2 km SW of town, off D98A coast road to Cogolin.
Credit cards All major cards accepted.
Terms B&B: single 340–370 frs, double 485–525 frs. Set lunch 60 frs, dinner (3 times a week, summer only) 140 frs. 1-night bookings sometimes refused in high season. Reduced rates and special meals for children.

ST-VAAST-LA-HOUGUE 50550 Manche — Map 8

Hôtel de France et des Fuchsias — *Tel* 33.54.42.26
18 rue Maréchal Foch

Before the battle of Crécy, Edward III landed his troops at St-Vaast, an attractive old oyster-breeding fishing port 27 kilometres east of Cherbourg. And other Britons, on "winter mini-breaks" and the like, are today landing regularly at the *Fuchsias*, a small, family-run holiday hotel, exuberant, down-to-earth and very pretty, much festooned with eponymous red blossoms. One recent winter-breaker reports: "Yes, very pleasant and pretty, with public rooms furnished handsomely and comfortably. The service by beautiful young girls was discreet and friendly; tea and drinks were brought to our room when we asked. Rooms all pretty colours and bathrooms well equipped, but walls thin – the flushing of neighbours' loos and all those five o'clock morning starts were a bit of a bore. Our package put us on the 80-franc menus: fish soup, local oysters, guinea-fowl with grapes, excellent cheeses – all generous, worthy and good value. I thought I was going to be awash with Normandy cream sauces, but for that we would have needed the tantalising à la carte. The hotel *is* run to a formula – it's become a kind of club for the English middle classes." (*Mary Clark*) Others this year and last have admired the garden, cobbled courtyard, thatched canopy and "superb" meals including breakfast. No lounge, but plenty of sitting space. There is now a new annexe. (*John and Earl McCleave, CS Grainger, Jane Temperley, and others*)

Open 15 Feb–3 Jan. Closed Mon Oct–May. Restaurant also closed Tue midday Oct–May.
Rooms 30 double, 2 single – 29 with bath and/or shower, and telephone. 3 suites, 9 double in new annexe near port.
Facilities Bar, reading room, 2 dining rooms; conference facilities. 2 salons in annexe. Garden. Sandy beach 2 km.
Location Central.
Restriction Not suitable for ♿.
Credit cards Access, Diners, Visa.
Terms B&B: single 215 frs, double 240 frs, suite 350 frs; full board 245-375 frs per person. Full alc 165 frs. Guests expected to dine in the hotel in summer. Children under 8 half-price in parents' room; special menu.

ST-VALLIER-DE-THIEY 06460 Alpes-Maritimes — Map 11

Hostellerie Le Préjoly — *Tel* 93.42.60.86
Place Rougière

In a bracing summer resort on a fine open plateau behind Grasse, an unpretentious family-run hotel/restaurant with its accent firmly on the food, which is very good value (Gault Millau toque), *lavishly and exuberantly served, very popular with locals who convivially crowd the big rustic* salle. *The bedrooms are second best, some with balcony and pleasant rural views but some poorly insulated and graceless. OK for a night stop. Closed 25 Oct–6 Nov, 20 Dec–6 Jan and Tue in winter. 20 rooms, most with bath, 200-350 frs. Set meals 80-170 frs [1987]. Criticised but reinstated: more reports please.*

STE-ANNE-LA-PALUD 29127 Finistère — Map 8

Hôtel de la Plage — *Tel* 98.92.50.12
Plomodiern — *Telex* 941377

St Anne's chapel by the beach is the venue of one of the largest and most colourful of Breton *pardons*, held on the last Sunday of August. The busy fishing port of Douarnenez and the pretty village of Locronan are both within 20 kilometres. Near the chapel is the *Plage*, not an ordinary seaside hotel as its Hulot-ish name might imply, but stylish and expensive – and warmly approved again this year: "Superb – the Le Coz family owners and their staff were charming, helpful and welcoming, our room was delightful if a little small, and the food outstanding." "A good meal, a good tennis court, and a stunning situation, above all with the light of the setting sun reflected on the wet low-tide sands." Others have enjoyed the heated swimming pool and lovely gardens. Not least, the cooking is highly rated, especially the fish (*Michelin* rosette, two red *Gault Millau toques*). (*Brian Beves, A and CR; also Tom and Rosemary Rose, and others*)

Open 1 Apr–15 Oct.
Rooms 3 suites, 27 double, 2 single – nearly all with bath and shower, all with telephone; 16 with TV. 2 ground-floor rooms.
Facilities 2 lifts. Salons, bar, TV room, restaurant; conference facilities. Tennis, sauna. Safe, sandy beach.
Location On coast, 16 km NE of Douarnenez.
Terms Rooms: single occupancy 520-600 frs, double 620-800 frs, suites 950-1,100 frs. Breakfast 48 frs. Full board 550-680 frs per person. Set lunch/dinner 150-300 frs.

STE-FOY-LA-GRANDE 33220 Gironde — Map 10

Domaine de Loselly — *Tel* 57.46.10.59
38 avenue Georges Clémenceau
Pineuilh

On the edge of a small town on the Dordogne west of Bergerac, a handsome family house in shady park on the banks of the river. Stylishly renovated, it is now a comfortable small hotel with large rooms, run in a personal style by manager Michel Macq. Regional cooking, very reasonably priced; good local wines. Closed 20 Dec–3 Jan. 9 rooms, all with shower. B&B double 200-270 frs. Set dinner 80 frs. New nomination: more reports please.

> Set dinner refers to a fixed price meal (which may have ample, limited or no choice on the menu). Full alc is the hotel's own estimated price per person of a three-course meal taken à la carte, with a half-bottle of house wine.

SAINTES 17100 Charente-Maritime — Map 10

Relais du Bois St-Georges — *Tel* 46.93.50.99
Rue de Royan — *Telex* 790488 STGEOR

Saintes with its ruined Roman amphitheatre and fine Romanesque churches is one of the most attractive and historic towns of south-west France. The *Bois St-Georges*, by contrast, is decidedly modern, but elegantly so. It is in the western outskirts, not far from the *autoroute*, and has a garden with wide lawns and views of the quiet countryside. "Delightful, in a rural setting, with flowers everywhere," runs a recent report on this *Relais du Silence*, while others have admired the simple but tastefully decorated bedrooms with their impeccable modern bathrooms. The open-plan dining room, lounge, bar and reception are carefully divided up; several open fires add to the ambience. The food is said to be excellent, though not cheap, and the owner to be "very anglophile". He is enterprising, too, for he has recently added nine large rooms with sun-terraces, built a lake and an indoor heated swimming pool, and extended the grounds to 14 acres. More reports please.

Open All year.
Rooms 3 suites, 27 double – all with bath, shower, telephone, radio, TV and baby-listening. Some with balcony. 3 ground-floor rooms specially adapted for ♿.
Facilities Lounge, 2 bars, TV room, restaurant; indoor swimming pool; terrace where meals are served in season. 14-acre grounds with lake. English spoken.
Location On W outskirts – 1.5 km from exit 25 of *autoroute* A10. Garage parking.
Terms Rooms: single occupancy 290-380 frs, double 360-500 frs, suite 700-850 frs. Breakfast 45 frs. Dinner, B&B 385-550 frs per person. Set lunch/dinner 115 frs; full alc 160-260 frs. Special meals for children.

LES STES-MARIES-DE-LA-MER 13460 Bouches-du-Rhône — Map 10

L'Étrier Camarguais — *Tel* 90.47.81.14
Chemin bas des Launes — *Telex* 403144

The *Étrier* stands in its own big garden on the edge of the Camargue, that strange flat land of lagoons and wild white horses, bulls and flamingoes. Three kilometres north of the unusual seaside town of Les Saintes-Maries where the gipsies hold a festival every 23-27 May, it is one of several modern ranch-like hotels in the area that cater for riding enthusiasts: it has its own herd of local white horses, which it hires to guests by the hour (at a price!). "Very pleasant, with good straightforward cooking. The horses were good too: stables owned by the hotelier's daughter." So runs a recent report, endorsing this previous one: "An excellent holiday hotel, spacious and informal, with log-cabin style decor, a breezy youthful ambience, lots of children, incessant music, and jokey staff – sub-Club Méditerranée, you could say. Our bedroom, simple but serviceable, was in a chalet in the garden. Especially we enjoyed the big swimming pool and sun-terrace, prettily lit at night. The hotel runs a lively disco just far enough away to avoid keeping us awake." (*Vicki Turner, LK Carlson, JACA*)

Open 1 Apr–15 Jan. Restaurant closed Mon in low season.
Rooms 31 double – all with bath, telephone and TV. 6 ground-floor rooms with private bath/WC and wide entrances.

Facilities Bar, dining room, breakfast room, terrace; conference room; night club/disco. Garden with swimming pool, tennis court and *boules*; horses for hire. Beach 3 km. English spoken.
Location 3 km N of the town, just off N570 to Arles.
Credit cards All major cards accepted.
Terms Half board: single 529–569 frs, double 710–750 frs; full board: single 675–715 frs, double 1,000–1,040 frs. Set lunch/dinner 145 frs; full alc 170 frs.

Hôtel Le Mas de la Fouque *Tel* 90.47.81.02
Telex 403155

This Guide newcomer is similar in style to the *Étrier* (see above), but smaller and much more up-market: "Quite delightful – a modern whitewashed ranch, very comfortable, set in the Camargue with wildlife all around and a stable full of white horses. Fishing and duck-shooting can be arranged. Each room has a small private balcony, like a sort of private deck built over the lagoon. The pool is lovely, heated but not over-heated, with good beach chairs. The hotel is in superb good taste, and the welcome from owner Jean-Paul Cochat is warm. His wife runs the kitchen, his daughter the bar and dining-room (food satisfactory). It is all very informal and relaxed. If one is lucky, one sees flights of white flamingoes around sunset taking off from the marsh, and in the morning the white horses will come thundering down the narrow path outside one's bedroom – a wonderful sight." (*Elisabeth Lambert Ortiz; also JA*)

Open 25 Mar–2 Nov. Restaurant closed Tue.
Rooms 2 suites, 12 double – all with bath and/or shower, direct-dial telephone and tea-making facilities; some with TV. Ground-floor rooms.
Facilities Salon, bar, 2 restaurants; terrace. Garden with heated swimming pool, tennis, putting. Beach 4 km. English spoken.
Location 4 km NW of Les Saintes-Maries by D38.
Credit cards All major cards accepted.
Terms Dinner, B&B: single 950 frs, double 1,200 frs, suite 1,200-2,000 frs. Set lunch 160-180 frs, dinner 200-260 frs; full alc 310-330 frs. Reduced rates and special meals for children.

SALON-DE-PROVENCE 13300 Bouches-du-Rhône Map 11

Abbaye de Sainte-Croix *Tel* 90.56.24.55
Route du Val de Cuech *Telex* 401247 STECROI

Again warmly commended in 1987, this venerable 12th-century abbey stands on a hillside north-east of Salon, approached down a private road. It has been sumptuously and carefully restored after long neglect and appeals to lovers of luxury-cum-tradition. A letter this year ("dinner of a high standard, tea wonderful with large cakes, a small pool with a wall of vivid flowers as a backdrop") endorses an earlier description: "The Cistercian monks slept in small cells and enjoyed the space of their gardens, ambulatories and refectories. And this is rather what the hotel offers: mostly small rooms (but a few with terraces), a large wooded park, and a dining room giving onto a terrace with a stunning view south across the plain towards Arles. The monastic bedrooms can be claustrophobic, but one can't have it all ways. Dinner by candlelight under the mulberry trees is an unforgettable experience, especially as the service is *soigné* yet relaxed and the food of a standard worthy of the setting." A *Gault Millau toque*, in fact, for cooking that is both inventive and classically Provençal, on which another visitor comments: "Splendid – home-smoked fish of many kinds, steak in blueberry sauce, pork in a wild mushroom sauce, a battery of cheeses, as well as that chariot of puddings." (*J and A McGlashan, GS, JJ Wüthrich, and others*)

Open 1 Mar–31 Oct. Restaurant closed Mon midday.
Rooms 5 suites, 19 double – all with bath and/or shower and telephone; some with terrace; TV in suites. Some ground-floor rooms.
Facilities Reception, salon, bar, restaurant; functions facilities; covered terrace. Wooded grounds and garden with unheated swimming pool and summer restaurant. Tennis and riding nearby. Sea 40 km. English spoken.
Location 3 km NE of Salon, off D16; sign in Salon after exit from *autoroute*.
Credit cards All major cards accepted.
Terms [1987 rates] Rooms: single 520 frs, double 760 frs, suite 1,360 frs. Breakfast 52 frs. Full board 960-1,800 frs per person. Set lunch/dinner 200-305 frs.

SARLAT 24200 Dordogne — Map 10

La Couleuvrine — *Tel* 53.59.27.80
1 place de la Bouquerie

In one of the loveliest old towns in the Dordogne area, a small modern hotel, inexpensive, in a beautiful ancient building forming part of the ramparts. Rooms furnished in antique style with great taste. Attentive patronne. *Meals served in traditional dining room or courtyard: service a little slow, but good regional specialities offered on 70-franc [1987] menu. No salon. Closed Jan. 18 rooms, some with shower, 135-210 frs. Set meals 70-140 frs [1987]. New nomination: more reports requested.*

SAULIEU 21210 Côte d'Or — Map 10

Hôtel de La Côte d'Or — *Tel* 80.64.07.66
2 rue d'Argentine — *Telex* 350778

This venerable old coaching-inn stands in the main street of a dullish little Burgundy town on the old winding Paris–Lyon highway. It was for long famous, for its former owner Alexandre Dumaine was one of the greatest French chefs of his day (****Michelin*). Then it fell into eclipse, with Dumaine's death and the coming of the *autoroute* which stole most of the through traffic. Today, despite its unpromising location, it is again in form under a new *patron*/chef, Bernard Loiseau, who has brought it up to the standard where it wins two *Michelin* rosettes and no fewer than four red *Gault Millau toques* – recently endorsed by two of our experts: "Both dining rooms are attractively decorated and well spaced. Cooking is modern and light, but soundly based on traditional Burgundy dishes. The wine list, long and mostly expensive, contains some house wines at reasonable prices. Breakfast included excellent bread and home-made jams. Our room was comfortable, furnished in rather heavy traditional style, with a large modern bathroom." (*Pat and Jeremy Temple*) Some of the older rooms are rather small, but an annexe of lavish suites has just been added.

Open All year.
Rooms 9 suites, 15 double – 15 with bath, 6 with shower, all with telephone;

some with radio and TV; baby-listening on request. Suites in annexe.
Facilities Salon, bar, restaurant. Garden. Near Morvan National Park with tennis, riding, lakes, fishing and watersports. English spoken.
Location Central. Garage parking.
Credit cards All major cards accepted.
Terms Rooms: single occupancy 150-253 frs, double 391-529 frs, suites 863-1,495 frs. Breakfast 60 frs. Set lunch 235, 295 and 448 frs, dinner 295, 305 and 448 frs; full alc 400-450 frs.

SÉGURET 84110 Vaucluse — Map 11

La Table du Comtat — *Tel* 90.46.91.49

Terraced on a hillside above the Rhône vineyards, the picturesque old village of Séguret is within easy reach of Orange and Vaison-la-Romaine and has fine views of the startling jagged peaks of the Dentelles de Montmirail. Here this fine old 15th-century house, now a sophisticated restaurant-with-rooms (*Michelin* rosette), is magnificently situated just above the village and again this year has been much admired: "The setting is superb, and the restaurant feeds the eye with its view, as well as the body. A warm welcome, a pleasant room, and food and wines of high quality." "Lovely hotel, breakfast divine." A regular correspondent adds: "A memorable meal, especially the sole with lobster mousseline, the goats' cheeses and the sweets. The dining room furniture, Provençal rustic, is very striking; reception rooms are light and airy; and from our bedroom we could gaze at the famous rock outcrops of the Dentelles. Madame, harrassed at first, was charming by the time we left." The small curving *piscine* beneath its high rock is a delight. (*AD, Claire Enders, I and FW, and others*)

Open All year except end Nov–beginning Dec and Feb. Closed Tue evening and Wed except July, Aug, Easter and Christmas holidays.
Rooms 1 suite, 7 double – 4 with bath, 4 with shower, all with direct-dial telephone.
Facilities Salon, dining room; terrace. Small garden with unheated swimming pool. English spoken.
Location 8 km S of Vaison-la-Romaine off the D23; at entrance to Séguret; hotel is signposted. Parking.
Restriction Not suitable for ♿.
Credit cards All major cards accepted.
Terms Rooms 290-500 frs. Breakfast 45 frs. Set lunch/dinner 180-320 frs. Special children's menu.

SEILLANS 83440 Var — Map 11

Hôtel des Deux Rocs — *Tel* 94.76.87.32
Place Font d'Amont

An 18th-century mansion converted into a very personal little hotel, in an enchanting old hill-village west of Grasse, much frequented by artists and writers. Prettily decorated rooms, some spacious. Summer dining by the fountain under the plane trees in a tiny cobbled square: food fairly good on the à la carte (*avoid* pension *menu*). *Service slow. Open 20 Mar–13 Oct. 15 rooms, all with bath or shower, 160-330 frs. Set meals 120-180 frs [1987]. No recent reports: more welcome.*

SEPT-SAULX 51400 Marne — Map 9

Hôtel du Cheval Blanc — *Tel* 26.03.90.27
2 rue du Moulin — *Telex* 830885 CHEBLAN

On the eastern fringe of the champagne country, this old coaching inn has been run by the Robert family for five generations. The hotel straddles the main road of the village – on one side a modern block of bedrooms, on the other the charming creeper-covered old inn beside a big garden. It has long been praised both for its pastoral setting and for its food (*Michelin* rosette, *Gault Millau toque*) and this year it has been more popular than ever – with the caveat that rooms on the road side, noisy from lorries, hardly justify the hotel's rating as a *Relais du Silence* (rooms facing the garden are quieter and more attractive). "A warm atmosphere, Madame Robert very charming, dinner excellent especially poulet de Bresse in a tarragon sauce." "We were delighted with the food and excellent breakfast. Service competent if not swift – but who wants to rush a good French meal?" "A peaceful hotel, beautifully warm, with cordial reception. Good meal, presided over by efficient Madame Robert, who is rather like Sybil in *Fawlty Towers*". We hope this is the only resemblance to Fawltyland – save that one dissenter this year found his annexe room shabby and cold and his lamb tough. (*Mrs J Cookson, Eric Clyne, Mrs Allfrey-Pizer, Mr and Mrs BN Wilson, and others*)

Open All year except 15 Jan–15 Feb. Closed Christmas Eve.
Rooms 2 suites, 19 double – 9 with bath, 12 with shower, all with direct-dial telephone, TV and mini-bar; baby-sitter on request. All on ground floor in building opposite restaurant.
Facilities 2 salons, TV room, restaurant; functions room; billiard room. Large park bordered by river Vesle; tennis, mini-golf, table tennis, volleyball, fishing. Heated swimming pool 12 km. English spoken.
Location 25 km E of Reims, on D37 off N44 in direction of Châlons.
Credit cards Amex, Diners, Visa.
Terms [1987 rates] B&B: single 235 frs, double 365 frs; dinner, B&B (min 4 days) 430-490 frs per person; full board 550-600 frs. Set lunch/dinner 160 and 250 frs.

SERRES 05700 Hautes-Alpes — Map 10

Hôtel Fifi Moulin — *Tel* 92.67.00.01
Route de Nyons

Recently redecorated, this useful halt on the main Grenoble to Provence road (the Route Napoléon) remains very popular, especially for its restaurant (*Michelin* red "R") which is strongly patronised by locals. "Tremendous value, excellent set menus, breakfast with good home-made jams"; "hot soup served at 2.30 pm (and not charged for) when we arrived wet and bedraggled." An inspector adds: "Totally unpretentious, not everyone's cup of tea, but good value, with pleasant, efficient staff; the owner is a cheerful and dynamic man who speaks good English. The hotel is on several levels, rather like a beehive, with kitchens next to guest bedrooms: for this reason, some rooms may be a little noisy in late evening. Terrace and back bedrooms on upper levels have excellent views over the mountains in the background and blocks of council flats in the foreground. Our room was very clean and the bathroom modern and spacious." Upper rooms at the back are best. (*HC Clifford, JJ Wüthrich, I and FW, and others*)

Open Beginning of Feb holidays–end Nov. Closed Wed except in season.
Rooms 25 double – all with bath and shower, telephone and baby-listening. 12 in garden annexe.
Facilities Bar, restaurant; terrace. Large garden with swimming pool. Near river with bathing and fishing. English spoken.
Location 107 km S of Grenoble, 64 km from Nyons on N75.
Credit cards All major cards accepted.
Terms Rooms: single 175 frs, double 185 frs. Breakfast 22 frs. Dinner, B&B: single 270 frs, double 375 frs. Set lunch/dinner 80 and 130 frs; full alc 150 frs. Special meals for children.

SEURRE 21250 Côte d'Or — Map 10

Le Castel — *Tel* 80.21.15.07 and 80.20.45.07
Avenue de la Gare

A pleasant Logis de France *in a small town in eastern Burgundy, on the Beaune–Dole road. Comfortable rooms with modern bathrooms. No lounge but a bar and flowery terrace. Big, bright dining room: excellent local cooking at reasonable prices by the* patron/chef *who worked for 13 years in England. Closed Feb and Mar. 20 rooms, most with bath and/or shower. B&B double 190-240 frs. Set meals 68-160 frs. New nomination: more reports welcome.*

SEYSSEL 01420 Ain — Map 10

Hôtel du Rhône — *Tel* 50.59.20.30
Quai de Gaulle

Geneva, Annecy and Aix-les-Bains are all within a 50 kilometre radius of this "characterful little town" on the upper Rhône, where the eponymous hotel faces the river, with a broad and pretty terrace for summer meals and drinks. Long popular with readers, it is described this year as "a modest, comfortable and faintly eccentric country hotel, fine for a night or two's stay. It has a handsome view over the great river to hills sunlit in the evening. Dinner was quite good but not exciting; breakfast was delicious with lovely bread and home-made jams." Previous reports have mentioned the "delightful owners" and excellent service and food – patron-chef Robert Herbelot wins a *Michelin* rosette for such dishes as poularde de Bresse aux morilles and his way with a local salmon-like fish called lavaret; try, too, the local Seyssel wines. The hotel has its own landing-stage, for boating and wind-surfing. There have been complaints of noise from traffic crossing a temporary Bailey-type bridge, but this will stop when the new bridge is finished. (*Ann Lawson Lucas; also HC Clifford, and others*)

Open 1 Feb–15 Nov. Closed Sun evening and Mon lunch. Restaurant open 2 May–15 Nov (except Sun evening and Mon).
Rooms 15 – 5 with bath, 4 with shower, all with telephone. 5 in annexe.
Facilities Salon with TV, bar, restaurant; terrace on the Rhône. Tennis, fishing, windsurfing, bathing, canoeing nearby. English spoken.
Location Outside Seyssel on left bank of Rhône between the 2 bridges. Garage.
Restriction Not suitable for ♿.
Credit cards Amex, Diners, Visa.

Terms Rooms: 100-250 frs; dinner, B&B 190-240 frs per person. Breakfast 24 frs. Set lunch/dinner 90-260 frs.

SOMMIÈRES 30250 Gard — Map 10

Auberge du Pont Romain — *Tel* 66.80.00.58
2 rue Emile-Jamais

Sommières is a big, fairly typical old Languedoc village on the edge of the hilly *garrigue* country, just off the Nîmes-Montpellier road. Here a regular visitor has made "a find", to which she returned twice in 1986/7: "Great fun. It's a 17th-century carpet factory turned into the most unusual hotel. Lovely large bedrooms with huge windows and prettily tiled floors. Delightful staff. A vegetarian dinner out of this world." The more carnivorous may enjoy *patron*/chef Bernard Michel's enterprising specialities such as foie gras of duck served half-cooked and – most notably – saumon Lawrence Durrell, named after Sommières' most famous inhabitant who is a regular customer. Large, attractive garden. (*Mrs MD Prodgers*)

Open 16 Mar–14 Jan. Restaurant closed Wed.
Rooms 14 double – all with bath and/or shower and telephone.
Facilities 2 salons, bar, 3 restaurants; conference facilities. Garden with children's play area. River with fishing nearby. English spoken.
Location 300 metres from town centre. Private parking.
Credit cards Amex, Diners, Visa.
Terms B&B: single 180 frs, double 270–325 frs; dinner, B&B 305 frs per person. Set lunch/dinner 135–185 frs; full alc 180 frs. 1-night B&B only bookings may be refused in high season. Reduced rates for children.

STRASBOURG 67000 Bas-Rhin — Map 9

Nouvel Hôtel Maison Rouge — *Tel* 88.32.08.60
4 rue des Francs-Bourgeois — *Telex* 880130

In this Euro-capital where most hotels are expensive, here is a medium-priced one that is both quiet and very central, 30 metres from the main square, the place Kléber. The staff are multi-lingual, efficient. "Very pleasant and good value," says a visitor this year. "Delicious croissants on the breakfast tray of charming modern porcelain. Our high room at the back was quiet and overlooked the rooftops of old Strasbourg." Others have written in similar vein, praising the friendly staff and copious buffet breakfasts. "Magnificent furniture"; "a place of Victorian comfort" – but redecoration is taking place. No restaurant, but you can eat very well all over Strasbourg – for example, expensively at the *Crocodile*, medium-pricewise at *l'Ancien Horloge* and cheaply at *l'Ancienne Douane*. (*Dr F Peter Woodford, GB Brook, Mr and Mrs J Sennett, and others*)

Open All year.
Rooms 6 suites, 70 double, 60 single – all with bath and/or shower, direct-dial telephone and sound-proofing; some with radio; some with TV.
Facilities Lift. TV room, bar, breakfast room. English spoken.
Location In town centre. Underground parking in place Kléber nearby.
Credit cards All major cards accepted.
Terms Rooms: single 270 frs, double 380 frs, suite 460-650 frs. Breakfast 35 frs. (No restaurant.)

Hôtel des Rohan *Tel* 88.32.85.11
17 rue Maroquin *Telex* 870047

The *Rohan* is small and upper-medium priced – that is, rather cheaper than the nearby Hiltons and Sofitels. It is newly modernised, but lies in the heart of the old quarter, in a cobbled pedestrian area only 50 metres from the cathedral. All recent visitors have found it quiet, friendly and efficient. It is a family hotel, traditional, discreet and "a joy to stay in". Though modern, it has "repro" furniture in the current French taste and is warm and comfortable; direct-dial telephone even in the bathroom. (*JA, JT, Aileen Hall*)

Open All year.
Rooms 36 – 24 with bath, 12 with shower, all with direct-dial telephone, radio, TV and mini-bar.
Facilities Lift. Salon, breakfast room.
Location Central, near cathedral. Parking nearby.
Credit card Visa.
Terms [1987 rates] Rooms: single 235 frs, double 420 frs. Breakfast 30 frs. (No restaurant.)

TALLOIRES 74290 Haute-Savoie Map 10

Hôtel de l'Abbaye *Tel* 50.60.77.33
Telex 385307

"Baby Doc" Duvalier and his entourage stayed here for some weeks in 1986 in the lap of luxury, after fleeing from Haiti. If this does not turn you off, you might well enjoy this gracefully converted old abbey with its lovely setting beside the Lake of Annecy; it has a fine cloister, vast oak-panelled rooms, and a charming garden and shady dining terrace by the water. "Ultimate luxury, and a superb setting, peaceful and relaxing. We were delighted by the quality of the food and service, down to the beachboy who looks after the hotel's private jetty. Most water sports are available next to the hotel." Modernised regional cooking: e.g. trout with cabbage, duck with raspberries – and even scrambled eggs with frogs. (*Iain Elliott*)

Open 16 Jan–15 Dec. Restaurant closed Sun evening and Mon in low season.
Rooms 31 double – all with bath, shower and telephone. 1 ground-floor room.
Facilities Salon, cloisters salon, bar, restaurant; conference facilities; concerts and exhibitions in cloisters; medical centre with hydrotherapy, whirl pool, massage etc. Garden and terrace; private lakeside beach. English spoken.
Location On E shore of Lake Annecy, 12 km SE Annecy.
Credit cards All major cards accepted.
Terms [1987 rates] Rooms 1,025 frs. Breakfast 45 frs. Set lunch/dinner 250-300 frs. Reduced rates for children.

Hôtel Beau-Site *Tel* 50.60.71.04
Much commended again this year, this unpretentious family-run hotel offers an alternative to the high prices of the famous *Père Bise* (no longer in the Guide) and the *Abbaye*, and is also set serenely by the shores of the glorious lake of Annecy. Everyone finds the owners, the Conans, a delightful, cultured and very professional family; everyone enjoys the location and the food; everyone likes the rooms, with the caveat that

those in the venerable old annexe are somewhat austere. "A place of quiet charm, with lovely views from the terrace across the brilliantly clear lake. The light dining-room, also with lake views, serves *en pension* meals that are carefully prepared but not as robust as the à la carte dishes." "Delightful hotel, superb garden, good cooking." (*Harriet and Lucy Clark, Elizabeth Robey, JD McDonald, Brian Beves, and others*)

Open 20 May–1 Oct.
Rooms 34 double, 4 single – 26 with bath and shower, 2 with shower, all with telephone. 28 in 3 garden annexes. 4 ground-floor rooms.
Facilities 3 salons, TV room, dining room; terrace. Garden with private beach on lake, tennis court. English spoken.
Location Central, on Lake Annecy. Parking.
Credit cards All major cards accepted.
Terms B&B: single 165-215 frs, double 250-325 frs; dinner, B&B 248-319 frs per person; full board 275-341 frs. Set lunch/dinner 120 frs; full alc 200-250 frs. Reduced rates for children sharing parents' room; special meals on request.

Hôtel Les Prés du Lac *Tel* 50.60.76.11
Telex 309288 PRESLAC

According to *Michelin*'s red-print classification, tiny Talloires (pop. 931) has more hotels of special charm and character (five) than *any* other resort in France, and as many as Paris itself. So it is not surprising that our Guide, too, now allots this lakeside village several entries. The newest comer is *Les Prés du Lac*, a very select ultra-modern little villa, highly-priced, but a nominator thought it worth it: "We were warmly welcomed by the daughter of the house, and were given a lovely room with patio, terrace, parasol and sun loungers. The views were superb, and we could walk across the hotel lawns to bathe in the lake at the hotel's private beach. The very good breakfast came on trays decorated with posies of flowers." (*Mrs J Cookson*) Another praised the outstanding design of the hotel and his "extremely comfortable high tech room". (*J McGlashan*) No restaurant, but you can eat at the nearby *Beau Site* (see above) which is owned by the same family.

Open All year except 11 Nov–20 Dec and 1 Jan–5 Feb
Rooms 1 suite, 9 double – all with bath, shower, direct-dial telephone, mini-bar, balcony or terrace; 9 with radio and TV; 2 with jacuzzi.
Facilities Lounge. Garden, private beach; tennis. English spoken.
Location On lake, near Sailing Club. 12 km S of Annecy. Parking.
Credit cards Amex, Diners, Visa.
Terms B&B: double 700-950 frs, suite 1,400-1,520 frs. Off-season rates.

TAMNIÈS 24620 Dordogne Map 10

Hôtel-Restaurant Laborderie *Tel* 53.29.68.59

A "delightful" and truly rural hotel on the edge of a tiny hilltop village between Les Eyzies and Sarlat, facing out over rolling wooded country. With its facade of rough yellowish stone, it could be in the Cotswolds (like so many buildings in this area); inside are beamed ceilings and a log fire in winter. Visitors this year and last have continued to find the staff friendly, the restaurant attractive and the food good and generously served: "It is a popular eating-place for locals, many of whom were being greeted as old friends." "Absolute tranquillity for a song. A warm welcome from the Laborderie family, who are good with children. Bar and lovely terrace. In the large dining room, fine rustic Périgourdin food with delicious hors d'oeuvre. Boating lake a kilometre away." The best rooms are in the annexe, with good views. A swimming pool has just been completed - "perhaps with the aim of increasing the appeal of the hotel to a younger clientèle: on recent visits we had found it patronised mainly by the over-sixties." (*PM Bower, TK, Kay and Neville Varley, and others*)

Open 26 Mar–14 Nov.
Rooms 32 double – all with bath, shower and telephone. 16 in garden annexe. Some ground-floor rooms.
Facilities Bar, 2 salons, TV room, 2 dining rooms; functions rooms; terrace. Garden with swimming pool. Lake nearby with swimming, fishing, windsurfing, sandy beach. English spoken.
Location In centre of Tamniès which is 14 km NE of Les Eyzies. Parking.
Restriction Not suitable for ♿.
Credit cards Access, Visa.
Terms Double room 90-280 frs. Breakfast 23 frs. Half board 140-250 frs per person; full board 190-300 frs. Set lunch/dinner 65, 85, 120 and 210 frs; full alc 100 frs. Reduced rates for children.

THIZY 69240 Rhône — Map 10

Hôtel La Musardière — *Tel* 74.64.03.15
12 rue du Bois-Semé

"Thizy, on the western side of the Beaujolais hills, towards Roanne, is a tight-cornered little town with an eccentric way of dealing with its steep contours. Nothing in it is more eccentric than the very amiable *Musardière*, which is a peach of a folly in the mini-château style. Two alarming Alsatians are housed in an ornate aviary. Hotel customers are no less oddly accommodated, but in a most agreeable way. A four-sided gallery high above a rather drab lounge gives grand access to bedrooms whose big, blocked-in marble fireplaces extend the feeling of faded airs and graces. The food is seriously Lyonnais, served in two very different dining-rooms, one light and bright, one sombrely dignified. An entirely individual little hotel, very quiet, with a charm that stays in the memory." (*Arthur Hopcraft*) A Guide newcomer: please tell us more.

Open All year. Closed Sun evening.
Rooms 11 double – 6 with bath, 5-with shower, all with telephone.
Facilities Lounge, 2 restaurants. Garden.
Location Thizy is 21 km E of Roanne.
Credit card Visa.
Terms B&B: double 200 frs; half board (min 3 days) 350 frs. Set lunch/dinner 70, 120 and 150 frs; full alc 130-180 frs. Guests are expected to dine at the hotel. Extra bed 50 frs.

TOULOUSE 31000 Haute-Garonne — Map 10

Grand Hôtel de l'Opéra — *Tel* 61.21.82.66
1 place du Capitole — *Telex* 521998 ESPI

Surprisingly, this is our first-ever downtown entry for France's fourth largest city and the capital of the European aviation and aerospace industries. The heart of the old rose-pink town is the 18th-century place du Capitole, and here stands Toulouse's most attractive hotel, stylishly modernised and new to the Guide this year: "The salons are very comfortable, and the bedrooms are furnished prettily in patterned curtains and covers. Air-conditioning very quiet and efficient." The beautiful new garden-restaurant, with terrace and ornamental pool, is *the* smart place to eat in town: chef Dominique Toulousy (local boy made good) has won a *Michelin* rosette and two red *Gault Millau toques* for inventive dishes such as grouper fish with oysters and kidneys with madeira and ginger (the fixed price menus are not cheap, but fair value). (*Eileen Spencer; JA*)

Open All year. Restaurant closed 14–23 Aug.
Rooms 7 suites, 34 double, 9 single – 48 with bath and shower, 2 with shower, all with telephone, radio, TV, and air-conditioning; baby-sitting on request. 4 in separate building.
Facilities Lobby, salon, bar, restaurant; conference facilities; terrace. Garden, swimming-pool. English spoken.
Location Central (double-glazed windows). Public garage nearby.
Credit cards All major cards accepted.
Terms Rooms: single 330-360 frs, double 480-680 frs, suite 880-1,050 frs. Breakfast 48 frs. Set lunch/dinner 160-220 frs; full alc 370 frs. Reduced rates for children sharing parents' room; special meals.

TOURTOUR 83690 Var — Map 11

Auberge St-Pierre — *Tel* 94.70.57.17

The medieval hill-village of Tourtour ("village in the sky" it cutely calls itself) is today a fashionable residential centre and quite a showpiece: its lovely facades of golden-brown stone have been scoured clean. There are wide vistas on all sides, and the Gorges du Verdon are within easy reach. The *St-Pierre*, a fine 18th-century manor converted into an unusual country hotel, stands alone in rolling country just east of the village and has nearly 200 acres of farmland. "It is pleasant to sit on the terrace and watch horses, cows, goats and gazelles graze in the meadow," runs a recent report. The hotel is owned and run by a dedicated Provençal couple, the Marcellins, who believe in keeping up local traditions and furthering ecology. "The stone floors and low ceilings we found a little austere, but we were intrigued by such oddities as the chapel turned into a TV salon, the mossy fountain in the dining-room, and the *tableaux vivants* of Provençal clay dolls (*santons*) representing agricultural tradition. To prove his point, M. Marcellin gets his meat, poultry and cheese fresh from his home farm. Pleasant bedrooms." (*Mrs JA Patterson, JA*)

Open 1 Apr–15 Oct. Restaurant closed Thurs, and to non-residents for dinner.
Rooms 15 double – 5 with bath, 10 with shower, all with telephone.
Facilities Salon, bar, TV room, games room, 2 restaurants. Garden with children's play area, solar-heated swimming pool and sauna. Riding and fishing nearby.
Location At St-Pierre-de-Tourtour, 3 km E of Tourtour, which is 20 km NW of Draguinon.
Restriction Not suitable for ♿.. No children under 6.
Credit cards None accepted.
Terms Double room: B&B 350 frs; dinner, B&B 570 frs; full board 650 frs. Set lunch/dinner 170 and 200 frs.

TOUZAC 46700 Lot — Map 10

Moulin de la Source Bleue — *Tel* 65.36.52.01

"I could complain about being kept awake by the nightingales – but I won't! This is a really lovely place run by a charming young couple. Perfect for honeymoons?" The couple are Jean-Pierre and Siàn Bouyou, he local, she from Cardiff – and they run a most romantic little stone-walled, creeper-covered hotel, converted from a 14th-century paper-mill in the lovely Lot valley. It is next to a large garden, a bamboo forest, and the eponymous bright-blue spring, and *Michelin* garlands it with red-print praise for its peaceful charm. "Guests can wander round the gardens which are right by a beautiful stretch of the Lot," our report goes on. "At the side of other old buildings is the blue source, bubbling up and flowing into the river with great vigour. The 90-franc [1986] dinner menu provided little choice, but was memorable, especially the avocado and salmon mousse, and a light-as-a-feather gâteau filled with apricots. Madame Bouyou was most kind." Candle-lit dinners by an open fire; swimming in the river in summer. (*Diana Holmes*)

Open 1 Apr–15 Oct.
Rooms 2 suites, 9 double – all with bath, shower and telephone.
Facilities Lounge with TV, restaurant. Large garden with children's play area. River Lot with small beach – bathing in summer. English spoken.
Location By D911, 8 km E of Fumel towards Cahors, on the left bank of the river.
Credit card Visa.
Terms Double room: B&B 250 frs, dinner B&B 490 frs; full board 730 frs. Set lunch/dinner 100–190 frs; full alc 150 frs. Reduced rates for children.

TREBEURDEN 22560 Côtes-du-Nord — Map 8

Hôtel Ti al-Lannec — *Tel* 96.23.57.26

Allée de Mezo Guen — *Telex* 740656

Rocks in strange shapes alternate with sandy coves along this delightful stretch of the North Brittany coast, where Trebeurden is an appealing family bathing resort. Here the *Ti al-Lannec*, a handsome grey-and-white mansion, stands high above the sea in its quiet garden. It is becoming a Guide favourite. "Hosts charming *and* efficient – a truly professional hotel with a human face," is one of several favourable reports this year. "Food exceptional (red *Gault Millau toque*) and a double bed of generous proportions." "Our room was beautiful, with a small sitting room between the bedroom and sliding French windows on to a balcony. The hotel faces south and our view on to the bay with its boating activities was just perfect. Trebeurden is ideal for a spring holiday but probably crowded in summer." Big light dining room with sea views; snug, elegant lounge with period decor; white tables and chairs under parasols and trees on the lawn. (*James Kempston, Gordon Bond, BH Jenkinson, and others*)

Open Mid-Mar–mid-Nov. Restaurant closed Mon lunchtime.
Rooms 21 double, 2 single – all with bath, shower and direct-dial telephone; TV on request.
Facilities Salon, TV/games room, bar, restaurant; conference facilities. Garden with outdoor chess, table tennis and *boules*; path leading down to sandy beach, safe bathing and fishing. Tennis, sailing and windsurfing nearby. English spoken.
Location In centre of village. Signposted from Lannion.
Restriction Not suitable for ♿.

Credit cards Access, Amex, Visa.
Terms B&B: single 275-310 frs, double 440-550 frs; dinner, B&B 345-430 frs per person; full board 460-545. Set lunch/dinner 145, 198 and 250 frs; full alc 270 frs. Reduced rates for children under 8; special menus.

TRIGANCE 83840 Var — Map 11

Château de Trigance — *Tel* 94.76.91.18

More praise this year for this boldly battlemented medieval pile on a hilltop, only about ten kilometres from the dramatic Gorges du Verdon in Upper Provence: "Trigance is a hamlet with a church (handsome polychromatic roof to its tower) perched on a rocky hill above a river. In the Middle Ages the local baron built a small castle on the crag above, then around 1965 a Paris ex-businessman, Jean-Claude Thomas, bought the site and restored the castle, making it into a small hotel. It is a brave sight in the middle distance (access is by a steep rocky path and stone stair). From the terrace roof there are wide views over the encircling rocky hills: one evening I watched a flock of sheep being herded over the slopes and felt a great sense of pastoral peace. Rooms comfortable though not *grand luxe;* food good; proprietor very agreeable." Confirmed this year and last by visitors who warmed to M. Thomas' bonhomie and enjoyed the "lovely canopied bed" as well as the "excellent food and service" in the "romantic vaulted restaurant". (*April and Michael Corner, M and DR Blakemore*)

Open 21 Mar–1 Nov.
Rooms 1 suite, 8 double – all with bath, shower and telephone; some with TV.
Facilities Salon, dining room, large terrace. English spoken.
Location 20 km SW of Castellane, 12 km NW of Comps-sur-Artuby.
Restriction Not suitable for ♿.
Credit cards All major cards accepted.
Terms Rooms: double 400 frs, suite 500 frs. Breakfast 40 frs. Set lunch/dinner 135–200 frs; full alc 250 frs. Reduced rates and special meals for children.

UZÈS 30700 Gard — Map 10

Hôtel d'Entraigues — *Tel* 66.22.32.68

8 rue de la Calade
Place de l'Évêché

In the rolling *garrigue* country of western Provence, an enchanting little old town of narrow streets and lofty towers: the tallest belongs to the massive turreted ducal castle. Secluded in one of the alleys just below it is the *Entraigues,* a 16th-century mansion once the home of a general. Its recent conversion into a select little hotel is supremely aesthetic but not cosy – soft-hued stone and dim-lit low-vaulted ceilings. It is under the same ownership as the *Château* at Arpaillargues (q.v.) and makes its Guide debut as a useful and cheaper alternative: "We were warmly welcomed. Room was comfortable. Restaurant quite good for lunch (simple dishes), but for dinner try the excellent *Alexandry* nearby." (*AD, JA*) Uzès has a classical music festival in July, and quaint country fairs in the main square all the year - e.g. pig fair in February, garlic fair in June.

Open All year. Restaurant closed Jan, all day Tue, and Wed midday.
Rooms 18 double – all with bath, shower and direct-dial telephone.

Facilities Salon with TV, tea room, restaurant. Courtyard. English spoken.
Location Central, opposite cathedral, but quietly situated. Uzès is 25 km N of Nimes. Parking.
Restriction Not suitable for ♿.
Credit cards Diners, Visa.
Terms B&B: single 248-275 frs, double 271-402 frs; dinner, B&B: single 342-368 frs, double 457-578 frs. Set lunch/dinner 70 and 102 frs; full alc 170 frs. Special meals for children.

VAL D'ISÈRE 73150 Savoie — Map 10

Hôtel Bellier — *Tel* 79.06.03.77

"Val d'Isère, the most dedicatedly *sportif* and international of French ski stations, fills up with more and more British skiers every winter." So writes an inspector, himself very *sportif*: "The *Bellier* stands tall and square, its concrete facade little softened by martial-looking shields bearing coats of arms. It's a friendly place, traditional in atmosphere and distinctly retro in decor and style of cooking. The bar is cheerful, decorated with antique snowshoes. Bedrooms are simple, but large and bright enough; most have a small balcony with views of the ski-slopes. Many British families return year after year, and they are well pleased with the *pension* menus, geared to the needs of energetic skiers who want solid, wholesome refuelling." (*AR*) "We ski twice a year, and it's one of the very few skiing hotels where we have felt really comfortable in a caring atmosphere. Breakfast always good – fruit, cereals, ham, etc. Food best at the price in Val d'Isère." (*Miranda Macintosh*)

Open 1 Dec–5 Apr.
Rooms 1 suite, 21 double, 1 single – 17 with bath and shower, 4 with shower, all with telephone.
Facilities Salon, TV/video room, bar, restaurant; sauna.
Location Central. Parking.
Credit cards Amex, Diners, Visa.
Terms [1987 rates] B&B: single 130–140 frs, double 210–240 frs, suite 510 frs; dinner, B&B 220–420 frs per person. Full alc 180 frs. Reduced rates in some cases for children; special meals.

VALENCE 26000 Drôme — Map 10

Restaurant Pic — *Tel* 75.44.15.32

285 avenue Victor-Hugo

In the southern outskirts of dusty Valence, in the Rhône valley, Jacques Pic and his charming wife run one of France's most illustrious restaurants, triple-rosetted, four-red-knife-and-forked. They offer a shady garden, just four pretty bedrooms, and *nouvelle cuisine* at its least affected, fully worth the high prices. "Splendid food, perfect and charming service. We were invited to the kitchen after dinner," writes an American visitor. "Everything marvellous – helpful staff, incredible (but simple) comfort in the bedrooms and total luxury in the dining room. The whole place is so undaunting, the atmosphere is charming and there's no snootiness by anyone, unlike at many other prestigious places. Breakfast a dream of warm fresh lemon brioche etc." (*Carolyn Mathiasen*) We should welcome more reports.

Open All year. Closed Wed and Sun evening.
Rooms 2 suites, 2 double – all with bath and shower, telephone and TV.
Facilities Sitting room, dining room. Courtyard and garden. English spoken.
Location 1 km from town centre. Take *autoroute* exit for Valence Sud, then go towards centre. Parking.
Restriction Not suitable for ♿.
Credit cards Amex, Diners, Visa.
Terms Rooms 350-600 frs, suites 750 frs. Breakfast 50 frs. Set lunch 220 frs (Mon, Tue, Thur and Fri except holidays), 350 and 450 frs; dinner 350-450 frs; full alc 450-500 frs. Special meals for children.

VAL SUZON 21121 Côte d'Or — Map 10

Hostellerie du Val Suzon — *Tel* 80.35.60.15
Val Suzon Fontaine-lès-Dijon

Chalet de la Fontaine aux Geais — *Tel* 80.35.61.19

Nearly all our other entries for the much-visited Dijon/Beaune area are rather grand and expensive: here, by contrast is simple Burgundian rusticity at a more moderate price. It is a double entry – a restaurant-with-rooms and a small chalet-hotel close by, both new to the Guide, both owned by the same family. A correspondent explains: "The hamlet of Val Suzon, north-west of Dijon, is a good base for visiting the city and places nearby such as Fontenay and Vézelay. The best bet is to book a room at the *Chalet*, a two-minute walk up the hill above the *Hostellerie*: its rooms are quieter and more spacious, and have a nice outlook across the gardens to the hills beyond. The grounds are well manicured and contain two aviaries (geai=jay). The *Hostellerie* is the restaurant for both buildings; the food is almost one-rosette standard, far better than at many similar country places around, and you can eat outside on fine days or by the fire in winter. The whole place has an air of unpretentious efficiency and relaxed charm." (*Geoffrey Sharp*) Another reader this year, who stayed at the *Hostellerie* itself, had a nicely decorated room with a small hip-bath and also liked the food (*Gault Millau* gives it a *toque* for such dishes as oysters with asparagus in hollandaise sauce). (*Harry Robinson*)

Open All year except Jan. Closed Wed and Thur lunchtime.
Rooms 16 double, 1 single – 9 with bath and shower, 8 with shower, all with telephone. 10 in the *Chalet*.
Facilities Lounge, bar, restaurant, TV room. Garden. English spoken.
Location 16 km NW of Dijon, just off N71 to Châtillon.
Restriction Not suitable for ♿.
Credit cards All major cards accepted.
Terms Rooms: single 150 frs, double 200-250 frs. Breakfast 30 frs. Set lunch/dinner 100, 170 and 260 frs.

VARETZ-EN-LIMOUSIN 19240 Corrèze — Map 10

Château de Castel-Novel — *Tel* 55.85.00.01
Telex 590065 CANOVEL

A handsome old grey-turreted, ivy-covered, stone-walled feudal castle, set on a hill above the valley of the Vézère gorges and the château of Pompadour. Distinguished restaurant: Michelin *rosette,* Gault Millau toque. *Lavishly refurbished in traditional style – grander bedrooms have canopied four-poster.*

Big swimming pool, tennis courts. Open May–Oct inclusive. 38 rooms, all with bath and shower. Dinner, B&B 555-1,050 frs. No recent reports.

VENCE 06140 Alpes-Maritimes — Map 11

Hôtel Diana — *Tel* 93.58.28.56
Avenue des Poilus

"Excellent", "clean and comfy", "very well run", are among this year's reports on this efficient modern hotel near the centre of a lively little Provençal town. The rooms, although small, are beautifully designed and furnished, with well-equipped *cuisinettes* (washing up is part of the hotel's service). The underground garage is not easy to operate: take advice. Breakfasts are variously described as "generous" or "adequate". The hotel has no restaurant, but it will prepare snacks such as omelettes, or downtown you could try the romantic *Les Portiques* (expensive) or the more down-to-earth *Farigoule*. Do not miss Matisse's lovely Chapel of the Rosary in Vence itself (open Tuesdays and Thursdays only), nor the mountain drive to the north, the *circuit des clues*. (*Kay and Neville Varley, Ann Carpenter, GM Morrison, and others*)

Open All year.
Rooms 25 double – all with bath and telephone; most with kitchenette.
Facilities Lift. 2 salons with TV, bar, library, 2 breakfast rooms; terrace. Garden. English spoken.
Location 200 metres from town centre. Garage.
Restriction Not suitable for ♿.
Credit cards Amex, Diners, Visa.
Terms Rooms 265–290 frs. Breakfast 30 frs. (No restaurant.)

VENDEUIL 02800 Aisne — Map 9

L'Auberge de Vendeuil — *Tel* 23.66.85.22

A trim white-walled modern auberge, *beside a wood just off N44 Laon-St-Quentin road. Rooms small but comfortable and very attractive. Staff friendly, but service a bit slow. Very pleasant beamed restaurant, popular with locals: à la carte (regional dishes, praised by* Gault Millau) *probably better than set menus. Very good breakfasts. 22 rooms, all with bath and shower. B&B double 300-330 frs. Set meals 76.80–200 frs. Some criticisms this year, so more reports welcome.*

VERDUN 55100 Meuse — Map 9

Hostellerie du Coq Hardi — *Tel* 29.86.36.36
8 avenue de la Victoire — *Telex* 860464

As strategically situated for the tourist today as it was for the generals of 1914-18, Verdun lies just off the *autoroute* from Paris to Strasbourg and Frankfurt. The main battlefields, well worth a visit, are in the hills some five kilometres to the north-east; others are to the north-west, and there is the big American cemetery of Romagne-sous-Montfaucon with its 14,000 white marble tombstones. The *Coq Hardi*, very central, close to the Meuse, was approved again in 1987 as a solid hostelry with notable food (*Michelin* rosette, *Gault Millau* red *toque*): "Our meal was superb –

amazing what the French can do with kidneys and rabbit," says one reader, though another thought his expensive meal was poor value. "Seen from outside, usual French scruffy. But the picturesque quality of the public rooms is achieved by the lavish use of what a priestly friend calls 'ecclesiastical tat', including three misericord seats just outside the ground-floor loos. Our front room was comfortable, spacious, and quiet." One visitor this year found the hotel a little impersonal, another wished the breakfast room could have been less gloomy. (*MS Thornton, Angela Pearse, Dr F Peter Woodford, Ian and Anne Steel*)

Open 1 Feb–21 Dec. Restaurant closed Wed except public holidays.
Rooms 3 suites, 40 double – 20 with bath, telephone and TV.
Facilities Lift. Hall, restaurant; conference facilities.
Location Central, near river; front rooms may be noisy. Parking.
Credit cards Amex, Diners, Visa.
Terms [1987 rates] Rooms: single 120 frs, double 270 frs, suite 500 frs. Breakfast 28 frs. Set lunch/dinner 140-275 frs.

VERVINS 02140 Aisne — Map 9

La Tour du Roy — *Tel* 23.98.00.11
45 rue du Général Leclerc

This ever-popular hotel, redecorated throughout this past year, is a converted manor house built on the ramparts of a small town near the Belgian border, and readers this year have some invigorating experiences to report. "The owner and his staff were kindness itself to our three children, aged 11, eight and six, who were given a special early meal, and the food converted my previously vegetarian daughter into a committed carnivore. Our own meal was excellent, but breakfast surpassed all as the motherly waitress kept asking us if we wanted anything more. The night cost us slightly less than a terrible one at a Holiday Inn in England where we were crammed into one room and the food was truly awful." Another account: "When we asked for a 'nice' room, Madame said, 'We will put you in the Tower', and opening its front door we found ourselves in an enormous circular bathroom with a large near-circular bath, and a toilet which was literally a throne, made of decorative porcelain, with chair back and arm rests. We then climbed the spiral staircase to another circular room with a very high domed ceiling, a small decorative sink, and our bed. It was kitschy but comfortable – and dinner was good quality traditional French."

It should be added that the other bedrooms are more "normal", and several adult carnivorous readers have waxed lyrical about the quail, rabbit, river fish and other dishes (*Michelin* rosette). The hotel is run with warmth and skill by Claude and Annie Desvignes (she cooks, using local produce, he is a helpful front-of-house) and service is "quietly professional". The only gripe is over some noise from the main road (but there is double glazing). Vervins is the capital of the Thiérarche, a pastoral stretch of apple orchards, streams and little green hills. (*JA Smithson, Kate and Steve Murray-Sykes, BW Ribbons, and others*)

Open All year except 15 Jan–15 Feb.
Rooms 14 double, 1 single – 11 with bath, 4 with shower, all with direct-dial telephone, radio, TV and baby-listening. 2 ground-floor rooms in annexe.
Facilities Salon bar, TV room, restaurant; functions rooms. Lake and river fishing and bathing nearby. English spoken.

Location Vervins is off N2, 71 km N of Reims. Hotel is central. Parking.
Credit cards All major cards accepted.
Terms B&B: single 210 frs, double 360 frs; half board: single 350 frs, double 600 frs; full board: single 490 frs, double 800 frs. Set lunch/dinner 140 frs; full alc 300 frs. Reduced rates and special meals for children.

VÉZAC 24220 Dordogne — Map 10

Manoir-Hôtel Rochecourbe — *Tel* 53.29.50.79

Set amid lush meadows and backed by gentle wooded hills, this small manor house lies in one of the loveliest parts of the Dordogne valley, between Beynac and Domme, and again this year it has been much admired: "The old house has been restored with great care. Our spacious room looked out on three castles. Breakfasts are excellent with delicious home-made jam, and for dinner there is a *carte* which expands as Madame Roger gets to know you" (there is no restaurant, but Madame serves light evening meals to residents, à la carte). Others have remarked on the peace and tranquillity – "Our room looked across the valley to Beynac château, and the loudest noise was the bleating of sheep and the singing of birds." A spiral staircase in the tower leads from the garden (reclining chairs for drinks) to the large dining room and then up again to the seven bedrooms (60 steps in all – not for the infirm). (*Chris and Dorothy Brining, William Howard, Clare Harvey, and others*)

Open 8 May–1 Nov.
Rooms 1 suite, 5 double, 1 single – 6 with bath and shower, 1 with shower, all with telephone. 2 in annexe.
Facilities Salon, TV room, dining room. Garden. English spoken.
Location 8 km from Sarlat on D57 between Sarlat and Beynac.
Restriction Not suitable for ♿.
Credit card Visa.
Terms Rooms: single occupancy 130 frs, double 260-340 frs, suite 360 frs. Breakfast 27 frs. (No restaurant, but light meals available in evenings.)

VÉZELAY 89450 Yonne — Map 10

L'Espérance — *Tel* 86.33.20.45
St-Père — *Telex* 800005

Just as the hilltop Romanesque basilica of Vézelay, in northern Burgundy, is one of the 20 finest buildings in France, so today the *Espérance* is one of the 20 finest restaurants (three *Michelin* rosettes, four red *Gault Millau toques* for inventive new-style cuisine). It is down in a dip just east of the little town, on the Avallon road - small, chic and expensive, gracious yet unpretentious. Antique furniture, strikingly pretty bedrooms; a garden with a rose arbour, and a stream with ducks lit up at night.

Again this year the approval is intense. "Sipping pre-dinner drinks on the terrace by the garden or in the glass-domed cocktail bar to the music of a grand piano is a delight. The gleaming cutlery, sparkling glasses and impeccable damask of the dining-room are visible beyond. *Patron*-chef Marc Meneau greets diners with a modest charm; service is polished yet friendly and the food the best I have ever tasted – wonderful saumon sauvage sauce champagne and feuilleté de roquefort chaud. Our room was in a converted mill nearby, peaceful, cool and spacious, with dark beams and antiques and a large modern bathroom *en suite*. The room was efficiently serviced by seemingly invisible maids – a fused light-bulb replaced without our having to mention it. Breakfast, a laden tray with cheeses, brioches, three types of jam, etc, is ferried out from the hotel by Renault 4." "The restaurant is housed in three big greenhouse-like structures, full of house plants, behind the manor house/hotel. Our meal fully confirmed M. Meneau's reputation as one of the most exciting of the younger French chefs and his wife Françoise supervises with dignity and charm. Our bedroom in the manor house was impeccable but small and hot (we know that those in the mill-annexe are larger and better)". (*Rosamund V Hebdon, Eric and Jean Lace; also Tom and Linda Baldwin, Wendy Arnold*)

Open All year except early Jan–early Feb. Restaurant closed Tue, and Wed midday.
Rooms 4 suites, 17 double – 16 with bath, 4 with shower, all with telephone; 10 with TV. 5 in annexe. 3 ground-floor rooms.
Facilities Salon, restaurant. Garden with river. English spoken.
Location 3 km E of Vézelay on D957.
Credit cards Amex, Diners, Visa.
Terms [1987 rates] Rooms: single occupancy 480 frs, double 900 frs, suite 1,800 frs. Breakfast 65 frs. Set lunch/dinner 400 frs.

Résidence Hôtel Le Pontot *Tel* 86.33.24.40
Place de la Mairie

A handsome old stone house near the town centre, with a fine Louis XVI salon. It has long been the home of an American architect, Charles Thum, who with the help of his manager, Christian Abadie, has now turned it into a very select bed-and-breakfast hotel: "Expensive, but worth it. I cannot praise these two charming gentlemen highly enough. They were friendly and courteous, and are running a hotel that is more like a private home. You enter through an arched doorway into a lovely walled garden, immaculately manicured. A stone-flagged spiral stairway leads up to the bedrooms which are furnished in exquisite taste and very spacious: opposite ours was a delightful lounge with views across Vézelay and the country below. We took breakfast in the salon before a log fire – the most beautifully prepared breakfast I have ever seen, with deep blue and gold Limoges china and excellent jams resting on dainty dishes with doilies. M. Abadie was fired with enthusiasm to help us create a really artistic photograph of it. Plenty of good restaurants in the area." (*PH*) More reports please.

Open 25 Mar–15 Nov.
Rooms 3 suites, 7 double – 9 with bath, 1 with shower, all with telephone, radio and coffee-making facilities. 1 suite in separate wing.
Facilities Entrance hall with boutique, lounge, bar, breakfast room. Walled garden with breakfast and bar service in fine weather. English spoken.
Location Centre of town, but quietly situated. Parking.
Restriction Not suitable for ♿.
Credit card Visa.
Terms Rooms: double 500-650 frs, suite 650-850 frs. Breakfast 55 frs. Reduced rates for children sharing parents' room. (No restaurant.)

Sterling and dollar equivalents of foreign currencies at the date of going to press will be found on page 712.

Hôtel de la Poste et du Lion d'Or *Tel* 86.33.21.23
Place du Champ-de-Foire *Telex* 800949

A former 18th-century coaching inn, with the characterful ambience of a handsome country house, at the foot of the hill below the cathedral. Bedrooms look onto the countryside. Friendly service; good but expensive food. Open 13 Apr–15 Nov. 46 rooms, most with bath, 220-500 frs. Set meals 180-230 frs [1987]. *Few recent reports: more welcome.*

VILLARD-DE-LANS 38250 Isère Map 10

Hôtel Le Christiania and Restaurant Le Tétras *Tel* 76.95.12.51
Telex 320125 OTVILAR
Avenue Nobécourt 3

The beautiful and rugged Vercors massif, west of Grenoble, was a major stronghold of the French Resistance and the scene of fierce fighting in 1943/44. Today it peacefully welcomes Germans, British and others to its high slopes, excellent for cross-country skiing and other sports. Villard-de-Lans is its main resort, alike in summer and winter, and here the *Christiania* is a very *soigné* hotel in chalet style, with a big outdoor swimming pool and mountain views from its terrace. "We enjoyed its cosiness and comfort, the warmth and hospitality of the owners, the Buissons, and the high quality of the meals, even on *demi-pension* terms – warm oysters with ginger, ray with asparagus and excellent home-made desserts." (*Richard A de Bono*)

Open 12 Dec–20 Apr, 1 June–30 Sept.
Rooms 24 double, 2 single – all with bath and/or shower, telephone and TV.
Facilities Lift. Salon, bar, 2 restaurants; conference facilities; terraces. Garden with heated swimming pool. Winter sports. English spoken.
Location Central, near municipal tennis courts. Parking.
Restriction Not suitable for ♿.
Credit cards All major cards accepted.
Terms B&B: single 285 frs, double 370-460 frs; dinner, B&B (min 3 days): single 320-420 frs, double 600-710 frs; full board: single 370-470 frs, double 700-810 frs. Set lunch/dinner 120, 175 and 280 frs; full alc 300 frs. Skiing packages. 1-night bookings refused in high season. Reduced rates for children.

VILLEFRANCHE-DU-PÉRIGORD 24550 Dordogne Map 10

Hôtel du Commerce *Tel* 53.29.90.11

This attractive village lies in wooded country between the Dordogne and Lot rivers, and would make a good base for exploring either of these glorious valleys. "Excellent value – a local meeting place with atmospheric bar and terrace," runs a recent comment on this unassuming family-run hotel whose cooking wins a *Michelin* red "R" for good value ("helpings over-generous at times," says a visitor this year). "An old building fronted by a deep arcade as so often in this area, it has been modernised and has a new top storey of rooms surrounding a small sun room. We had one of these which was spacious, with a good-sized bathroom. M. and Mme Fays and their family are welcoming. The food is good, the size of the helpings prodigious. The house wine too is excellent." (*Sir Douglas Franks, David J Alston, FR Hilborne*)

Open 1 Mar–15 Nov.
Rooms 28 double – 22 with bath and shower, all with telephone.
Facilities Salon, TV room, bar, 2 restaurants; terrace. Small lake nearby with fishing rights and swimming; tennis, riding, walking. English spoken.
Location In village on D60 between Fumel and Sarlat. 40 km NW of Cahors. Parking.
Restriction Not suitable for ♿.
Credit cards None accepted.
Terms Rooms: single 150 frs, double 200 frs. Breakfast 20 frs. Dinner, B&B 170-200 frs per person; full board 200-230 frs per person. Set lunch/dinner 55-200 frs. Reduced rates and special meals for children.

VILLENEUVE-LÈS-AVIGNON 30400 Gard — Map 11

Hôtel Résidence les Cèdres — *Tel* 90.25.43.92
39 boulevard Pasteur

A small and friendly family hotel in a flowery cedar-shaded garden in the western outskirts. Some bedrooms are in attractive well-equipped bungalows; others, bright and airy, are in the handsome main building, furnished partly in Louis XV style. Amusing cigar-smoking patronne; *good food, served outdoors by swimming pool when fine. Some criticisms of service and upkeep. Open 15 Mar–15 Nov. 25 rooms, all with bath or shower. B&B double 250-280 frs. Set dinner 92 frs. Few recent favourable reports: more welcome.*

Hostellerie le Prieuré — *Tel* 90.25.18.20
7 place du Chapitre — *Telex* 431042

The town of Villeneuve contains almost as much of interest as Avignon itself, directly across the Rhône. Relics of the great age when the popes held sway in their palace include the gigantic Chartreuse, the Fort St-André, the municipal museum (superb painting by Charenton) and the church of Notre-Dame with its remarkable carved ivory statuette of the Virgin. Next to this church is the *Prieuré*, a 14th-century priory, well converted and run with panache by the Mille family as an elegant and luxurious little hotel. It is quiet and looks out over fields and an ugly school building. You can choose between a "characterful" bedroom in the old building (antique furniture, tiled floors, but very modern bathrooms) or a larger, more expensive one in the new annexe (wide balconies, big sofas). Amenities include a lovely garden with rose arbours, a tennis court, and a swimming pool and lido amid trees. Food is served either on the lawn or in the lovely beamed dining room. Our readers are mostly satisfied: "Elegant and sophisticated but intimate, and very professionally run." "Food superb, attentive help, altogether charming." But one visitor thought the place "pretentious and over-priced" and found fault with the service and general upkeep. What is more, the food is poorly rated in the French guides (*Michelin* has this year withdrawn its rosette), so we would welcome more reports. (*Sarah Curtis, HC Robbins Landon, Jane and Bob Goeller*)

Open 10 Mar–10 Nov. Restaurant closed 1 May.
Rooms 10 suites, 20 double, 6 single – all with bath, shower, telephone, radio and TV. 24 in 2 annexes. 1 ground-floor room and 15 with access for ♿.Double glazing and air-conditioning.

Facilities Lift. 2 salons, bar, breakfast room, bridge room, dining room and dining patio. Garden with 2 tennis courts and swimming pool. English spoken.
Location 3 km N of Avignon. In village centre, behind the church. Car park.
Credit cards All major cards accepted.
Terms B&B: single 460-760 frs, double 510-1,120 frs, suite 1,220-1,720 frs. Set lunch/dinner 200 and 250 frs; full alc 300-400 frs. Special meals for children.

VILLERAY 61110 Orne — Map 8

Moulin de Villeray — *Tel* 33.73.30.22

Villeray is a hamlet well off the beaten track, north of Nogent-le-Rotrou in the Perche district of southern Normandy, a pleasant region of wooded hills and wide green valleys, studded with fine old manor houses. Here is the *Moulin*, a stylish and expensive restaurant-with-rooms: "A beautifully converted old mill, in attractive grounds. Its ten bedrooms are havens of peace, save for the one directly above the rushing waterfall beside the mill-wheel. Our room was tastefully furnished, with a balcony overlooking the garden. The dining room is outstandingly beautiful, with the old wooden mill-wheel visible through a large window and illuminated at night. Food was memorable, service very friendly, and for after dinner there is a large and comfortable lounge with an open log fire. A nice place for a quiet romantic evening with someone special, but not quite the place for small children, for there are plenty of spots where they could fall into the water and quietly disappear." (*Dr TJ David*) In summer you can dine out on the terrace above the river, on such dishes as lobster cooked in champagne.

Open All year except 1 Dec–1 Feb, and Tue; restaurant also closed Wed midday.
Rooms 10 – all with bath, shower and telephone; some with balcony.
Facilities Lounge, dining room. Garden. Fishing. English spoken.
Location 11 km N of Nogent, off road from Condé to Rémalard.
Restriction Not suitable for ♿.
Credit cards All major cards accepted.
Terms Rooms: double 640-740 frs; half-board 1,250-1,450 frs for two. Breakfast 35 frs. Set lunch/dinner 200-300 frs; full alc 280 frs.

VINAY 51200 Marne — Map 9

Hostellerie La Briqueterie — *Tel* 26.54.11.22

Route de Sézanne — *Telex* 842007 BRICTRI

Recommended for its comfort, excellent food and lovely rural setting, this is a big modern *auberge*, stylish and sophisticated, lying amid the rolling vineyards of the champagne district, just south of Épernay. Red-jacketed waiters, breakfast in a lofty patio, pleasant swimming pool and well-kept gardens. The food, *Michelin*-rosetted, not at all cheap, comes arranged on the plate with artistic symmetry: "My turbot steak lay across one semi-circle of white champagne sauce and another of rich red champagne sauce. Splayed out north, south, east and west were small pieces of beautifully shaped potatoes, carrots, mange-tout and courgettes. It seemed a pity to touch it!" (*WC Meigh*) More reports please.

Open All year except Christmas.
Rooms 4 suites, 38 double – 32 with bath, 10 with shower, all with telephone and TV; baby-sitting by arrangement. Some ground-floor rooms.

Facilities Salon, bar, restaurant; 2 private dining rooms; terrace. Garden, children's play area and *boules*. English spoken.
Location 6 km S of Épernay towards Sézanne.
Credit cards All major cards accepted.
Terms [1987 rates] Rooms: single occupancy 310-350 frs, double 370-450 frs, suite 500-600 frs. Breakfast 40 frs. Set meals 220-290 frs; full alc 300 frs. Special meals for children.

VONNAS 01540 Ain — Map 10

Hôtel-Restaurant Georges Blanc

Tel 74.50.00.10
Telex 380776 GEBLANC

M. Blanc's famous and sophisticated little hotel/restaurant, half-timbered and pink-bricked, stands in pretty countryside beside the river Veyle on the edge of a quiet *village fleuri* between Mâcon and Bourg-en-Bresse. He remains pre-eminent among the great *patron*-chefs of France (three rosettes and four red gables in *Michelin*, four red *toques* in *Gault Millau*), and readers this year have seen little reason to quibble, save that the service is always slow – but who wants to be hurried through such a meal? "Georges Blanc *is* Vonnas, with two shops in the village selling his provisions and souvenirs. But there's a refreshing candour about his enterprise. His chefs can be seen at work as you walk through the kitchen to the large elegant dining room with its beamed ceiling, antiques and tapestries. The food lived up to its reputation – delicious roulade of sea bass and potato crêpes stuffed with salmon and caviar, and an extensive choice of Beaujolais." "Rooms vary in grandeur, some are small and plain, some huge with marble bathrooms." "The menus were superb and the sommelier was British – but why does a hotel spend all this money on glamour and then not provide a proper shower or shower curtain?" (*Rosamund V Hebdon, Wendy Arnold, Tom and Linda Baldwin; also Pat and Jeremy Temple, and others*)

Open All year except 2 Jan–10 Feb. Restaurant closed Wed and Thur (except 15 June–15 Sept when open Thur evening).
Rooms 4 suites, 26 double – all with bath and/or shower, telephone and TV.
Facilities Lift. 2 lounges, breakfast room, dining room; terrace on river Veyle. 2½-acre grounds with tennis court, putting green, swimming pool and helipad. English spoken.
Location 20 km E of Mâcon. From N leave *autoroute* at Mâcon Nord; from S leave *autoroute* at Villefranche, then direction Châtillon-sur-Chalaronne, Neuville-les-Dames and Vonnas.
Credit cards Amex, Diners, Visa.
Terms (Excluding 12% service charge) Rooms: double 450-1,000 frs, suite 1,100-1,850 frs. Breakfast 58 frs. Set meals 280-420 frs; full alc 450 frs.

WIERRE-EFFROY 62720 Pas-de-Calais — Map 9

Ferme-Auberge du Vert

Tel 21.92.82.10

Quite a number of French farms nowadays have turned themselves into small *auberges* while retaining their farming activities. This one, just off the Boulogne to Calais road, provides British visitors with a marvellous opportunity to move straight from the hassle of ferries and hovercraft into the bosom of French peasant life. "Tucked away in the lanes near Marquise, this is not exactly a hotel, but the standards of the rooms fashioned from converted barns is high and excellent value. We made our way across the farmyard with its scores of ducks and geese into a simple restaurant-cum-bar where plain food was served at a fair price. Our small daughter, too tired to stay up for dinner, was given eggs, ham, chocolate gâteau and cool glasses of milk; breakfast was as substantial as required, with coffee drunk in traditional bowls. A really warm welcome with lots of handshaking." (*TK*) The farmers, the Bernards, write: "We have kept our 70 goats, and our son makes cheeses here. Our English guests like to visit the goat-folds and buy cheese to take back home. The pork, kid and poultry we serve is from the farm." A salutary antidote, some might feel, to the onrush of Eurotunnel technology just down the road.

Open All year except Jan. Restaurant closed Mon.
Rooms 1 suite, 13 double, 1 single – 2 with bath and shower, 13 with shower, all with direct-dial telephone; suite with TV. 12 in 2 farm buildings. 4 ground-floor rooms.
Facilities Salon with TV, bar/restaurant, breakfast room.
Location Off N1 between Calais (N) and Boulogne (S); SE of Marquise. Follow signs "Ferme H** Auberge" from Marquise and from Hypermarket Auchan.
Credit card Visa.
Terms B&B: single 195 frs, double 260 frs, suite 470 frs; dinner, B&B: single 250 frs, double 480 frs, suite 750 frs. Set lunch 140 frs, dinner 165 frs. Reduced rates and special meals for children.

Germany

HOTEL BADISCHER HOF, AMORBACH

ALT-DUVENSTEDT 2371 Schleswig-Holstein **Map 13**

Hotel Töpferhaus *Tel* (04338) 3 33
Am Bistensee Restaurant (04338) 2 22

"What a find!" wrote an inspector after visiting this stylish rural hotel in the flattish Schleswig countryside just east of the Hamburg/Flensburg *Autobahn*; "It's a lovely white-painted building with thatched roof, on a bluff above a lake and reached down a drive through woods. Everything inside superbly chosen and arranged – Persian rugs on the floor etc. Biggish bedroom, a real charmer. A faultless meal in the restaurant, including Labskaus, the traditional sailors' dish of North Germany – a hash of pickled meat, herring and potato with fried eggs, tasting a bit like a pickled shepherd's pie. Supremely comfortable lounge with a sort of boudoir feel." "Excellent game dishes in season," comments a visitor this year. "A memorably pleasant place, despite a certain lack of professionalism in the detail, i.e. poor ventilation in the bathroom." Another reader felt the place was a little run-down. (*SAL; Guy and Phoebe Atkins*)

Open All year. Restaurant closed Mon.
Rooms 8 double, 4 single – 10 with bath, 2 with shower, all with telephone.
Facilities Hall, lounge, breakfast room, restaurant in annexe. Garden with terrace and lawns. On lake; swimming and sailing; riding and golf nearby.
Location 12 km N of Rendsburg; leave *Autobahn* at Rendsburg-Nord if coming from S, at Owschlag if coming from N. Hotel is at S end of Bistensee. *Note*: do not go towards town of Bistensee on N side of lake.
Credit cards None accepted.
Terms B&B: single 75-85 DM, double 130-155 DM. Set lunch from 27.50 DM; full alc 28-53 DM. Reduced rates for children under 15; special meals.

AMORBACH 8762 Bayern — Map 13

Hotel Badischer Hof — *Tel* (09373) 12 08 or 39 62
Am Stadttor 4

Lying in a lush wooded valley of north-western Bavaria, between Würzburg and Heidelberg, Amorbach is a pleasant little summer resort with a fine 18th-century baroque church. The *Badischer Hof*, where the physician Max Planck often used to stay, is praised as a typically neat and cosy German hostelry in the heart of town: "Has been run by the same family for nearly 200 years. Pleasant welcome. Dinner and breakfast good. Our bedroom and bathroom looked freshly decorated, and though not large had every convenience. Large balcony where one could breakfast in good weather and a lovely courtyard full of flowers. Quiet soothing atmosphere." (*D R and A Besson*)

Open 25 Jan–15 Nov.
Rooms 18 double, 14 single – 3 with bath, 20 with shower and WC, all with telephone; some with radio; some with balcony. 7 in annexe 50 metres from main building.
Facilities Drawing room, TV room, café, restaurant. Garden. English spoken.
Location In town centre. Carpark and garage.
Restriction Not suitable for ♿.
Credit card Amex.
Terms B&B: single 32-49 DM, double 64-100 DM. Full alc 50 DM.

ASPERG 7144 Baden-Württemberg — Map 13

Hotel Adler — *Tel* (07141) 6 30 01
Stuttgarter Strasse 2 — *Telex* 7264603

Situated in a small town near Ludwigsburg, this heavily half-timbered old hostelry with modern extensions has been in the same family hands since its foundation in the 1850s. Today Richard Ottenbacher serves some of the best food in the Stuttgart region (*Michelin* rosette) in his *gemütlich* dining-rooms – lobster terrine, snail soup and various Swabian specialities. One visitor enjoyed his ragout of venison and found the place comfortable and friendly. Rooms vary in style but all are nicely furnished. (*HL Fenn*)

Open All year. Restaurant closed Mon and 3 weeks in summer.
Rooms 3 suites, 24 double, 38 single – all with bath and/or shower, direct-dial telephone, radio and mini-bar; most with TV. Some on ground floor.
Facilities Lift. Bars (with wine tastings), 2 restaurants; conference facilities; indoor heated swimming pool, sauna and solarium. Tennis and golf nearby. English spoken.

Location Asperg is 5 km NW of Ludwigsburg – turn off Autobahn at Ludwigsburg-Nord. Hotel is central. Garage and parking place.
Credit cards All major cards accepted.
Terms B&B: single 95-145 DM, double 148-208 DM. Full alc 45-55 DM. Reduced rates for children sharing parents' room.

BAD BERGZABERN 6748 Rheinland-Pfalz — Map 13

Hotel-Pension Pfälzer Wald — *Tel* (06343) 10 56
Kurtalstrasse 77

This neat little spa town lies in a lush valley amid the rolling wooded hills of the Palatinate (Pfalz). It is at the southern end of the Pfalz "wine road" and only ten kilometres from Wissembourg across the border in Alsace; there are some fine old castles nearby. The *Pfälzer Wald,* a small traditional family hotel, stands serenely alone beside a lake, with green hills behind, and in 1987 was again much admired: "The building is old-fashioned and rather plain, but our rooms were spacious and clean, the welcome was warm and the staff helpful, and we enjoyed the plain home cooking. The copious buffet breakfast was marvellous." Other readers have concurred, though one found the plumbing noisy and suggests that rooms at the back would be quietest. Another found the place a bit *too* quiet and sleepy – as at many spa towns, the hotel's clients are often elderly. (*JS; also Sandra Martin, AR Waller*)

Open All year.
Rooms 15 double, 12 single – all with bath or shower and telephone.
Facilities Lounge/TV room, wine bar, dining room, restaurant; functions room; terrace. Large garden on lake. English spoken.
Location About 1 km S of town centre; 38 km NW of Karlsruhe. Parking.
Restriction Not suitable for ♿.
Credit card Access.
Terms B&B: 35-50 DM; half board 52-67 DM; full board 59-74 DM. Set lunch/dinner 9-25 DM; full alc 25-30 DM. Reduced rates and special meals for children.

BAD HERRENALB 7506 Baden-Württemberg — Map 13

Mönchs Posthotel — *Tel* (07083) 74 40
Doblerstrasse 2 — *Telex* 7245123

"Just as you say – expensive and elegant, yet intimate and cosy. And today better than ever." So writes a regular visitor returning this year to this smart and stylish old half-timbered flower-decked post-hotel, at a crossroads in the centre of a Black Forest spa town. The setting is less urban than this may suggest, for the hotel also has an outdoor swimming pool and large and graceful gardens leading to a river. A previous account: "Our large bedroom was superbly equipped. The lovely dining room has beamed ceilings, wood panelling and several discreet alcoves. The food, beautifully prepared and presented, tended towards *nouvelle cuisine* and was worthy of its *Michelin* rosette. Service was smooth and affable. The breakfast buffet was the most lavish we have found in Germany – and that's saying something. All in all, a romantic place – despite the prevalence of rich businessmen." Other readers concur, but point out that front rooms facing the noisy road should be avoided, and that service can be slow. (*RS McNeill, Daphne Borton, JA and KA*)

Open All year.
Rooms 10 suites, 25 double, 15 single – 40 with bath, 10 with shower, all with telephone and TV. 9 in adjoining annexe.
Facilities Hall, salon, TV room, bar, restaurant, dining room, breakfast terrace; conference facilities; beauty parlour. Garden with heated swimming pool; tennis and 9-hole golf course close by. English spoken.
Location Central. (*Warning:* rooms on the road can be noisy.) Parking.
Restriction Not suitable for ♿.
Credit cards Amex, Diners.
Terms B&B: single 125–145 DM, double 180–195 DM, suite 230–270 DM; half board 35 DM added to room rate; full board 45 DM added. Set lunch from 35 DM, dinner from 45 DM; full alc 60–90 DM.

BAD HERSFELD 6430 Hessen — Map 13

Hotel Zum Stern — *Tel* (06621) 7 20 07
Am Markt

A Romantik Hotel, formerly part of Benedictine monastery, in the pedestrian zone of picturesque spa town near GDR border. Courteous owners, comfortable rooms, good food, swimming pool. 49 rooms, all with bath and shower. B&B 72.50-110 DM. More reports please.

BAD RAPPENAU 6927 Baden-Württemberg — Map 13

Schloss Heinsheim — *Tel* (07264) 10 45
Gundelsheimer Strasse 36 — *Telex* 782 376
Heinsheim

Heinsheim is a village in the lovely Neckar valley, near the small spa resort of Bad Rappenau and the city of Heilbronn. Here the *Schloss*, a serene red-roofed mansion, has been the home of the aristocratic von Racknitz family since 1730. In 1956 they converted it into a smart little hotel, today managed by Monica von Racknitz. Two recommendations bring it new to the Guide this year. "A taste of gracious living! Hotel set in its own beautiful grounds; bedrooms in the old house, public rooms in a newer building. Our room was light and furnished with genuine antiques; it overlooked an apple orchard, as do most rooms, with a hill rising behind. Bathrooms were large. The restaurant, managed by a Scot, was exceptionally good and the service perfect. The Neckar valley is a beautiful hilly wine-growing area." (*EB Schaffer*) "One of my very favourite places in Baden-Württemberg. Freifrau von Racknitz genuinely gives you the feeling that you are guests in her own home; her touch is truly personal yet effortlessly patrician. Often I have enjoyed lolling under the pink parasols in the idyllic garden. The hotel is popular with weddings, as the family has its own chapel." (*Katinka Ardagh*)

Open All year except 23 Dec–31 Jan.
Rooms 1 suite, 26 double, 13 single – all with bath or shower, and telephone; some with TV.
Facilities Lounge, salon with open fire place, restaurant; conference facilities. Garden, unheated swimming pool.
Location 6 km NE of Bad Rappenau, 25 km NW of Heilbronn.

Credit card Visa.
Terms B&B: single 95-125 DM, double 135-155 DM, suite 280-300 DM; dinner, B&B: single 135-155 DM, double 215-235 DM; full board single 160-180 DM, double 265-285 DM. Set lunch/dinner 30 DM; full alc 35-65 DM.

BADEN-BADEN 7570 Baden-Württemberg **Map 13**

Hotel "Der Kleine Prinz"
Lichtentaler Strasse 36
(entrance Du-Russel Strasse)

Tel (07221) 34 64
Telex 722123 PRINZ

Possibly the most beautiful of Baden-Baden's many small hotels, this Romantik hotel is a converted Victorian building in the town centre, nicely balancing old and new in its furnishings. Its owners, Norbert and Edeltraud Rademacher, spent 22 years in America (he was food director of the *New York Hilton* and the *Waldorf Astoria*). "A real charmer, with excellent food," says our inspector, while an American visitor has written: "All the rooms we saw were lovely. Ours, overlooking the town and ruined *Schloss*, was large, with pine furnishings and a fireplace; prints from *The Little Prince* hung on the walls. The bed was the most comfortable I slept on in Europe, and the bath the largest I have seen outside those marvellous tubs in England. The buffet breakfast was copious and the service excellent." (*SL, SB*)

Open All year.
Rooms 11 suites, 11 double, 7 single – 20 with bath, 9 with shower, all with telephone, radio, TV and mini-bar; some with whirl pool. Each room has a "special feature" e.g. open fire or balcony. Some ground floor rooms.
Facilities Lift. Lobby, bar, restaurant. Golf, tennis, swimming and riding nearby. English spoken.
Location Central, near Kurpark and convention hall. On corner of Lichtentaler Strasse and Du-Russel Strasse; hotel is signposted. Parking.
Credit cards All major cards accepted.
Terms B&B: single 125-175 DM, double 175-275 DM, suite 275-450 DM; half board 35 DM added per person, full board 70 DM added. Set lunch/dinner 49-59 DM; full alc 55 DM. Reduced rates and special meals for children.

BAMBERG 8600 Bayern **Map 13**

Böttingerhaus and Gästehaus Steinmühle
Judenstrasse 14

Tel (0951) 5 40 74
Telex 662946 BOETT

Another jewel in the fairytale heart of old Bamberg has been unearthed this year, to cap the splendours of the *Sankt Nepomuk* (see below). The *Böttingerhaus* is a Baroque mansion of great beauty, built in 1713 as the home of a rich merchant and diplomat, recently acquired and renovated by a Hamburg architect and now run by his daughter, Maria, and her Parisian husband, Victor Orsenne, as a distinguished restaurant and cultural centre. In 1983/4 they renovated a lovely old millhouse on the river beside the *Sankt Nepomuk* and opened it as a guesthouse annexe, the *Steinmühle*. Our field despatch:

"A dream hotel in a dreamy maze of cobbled streets, wonderful churches, enchanting old houses, delicious *Konditorei* and plenty of antique shops. When you stay at the *Steinmühle*, you have superb views of the 15th-century Rathaus set on its tiny island; light sleepers who might be disturbed by the roar of the millstream can take rooms facing the street. Our room though smallish was charming and furnished elegantly with an *en suite* bathroom. All meals – including the generous buffet breakfast – are taken amid the splendours of the *Böttingerhaus*. Dinner was very good and beautifully served. There is a grand *dégustation* menu which looked as if it might take hours to get through, but dishes on the normal menu were delicious, and not at all heavy and over-copious as is often the case in Bavaria. Windows look out onto ancient roofs, or onto the delightful terrace garden where you can take aperitifs; the sound of Mozart drifts gently in the distance." The cuisine includes local Franconian specialities with French influences coming from M. Orsenne; there is also an informal bistro for lighter meals. Live piano music at weekends and classical concerts fill out the scenario, as do official banquets of all kinds. Henry Kissinger has been a guest. A second bedroom annexe, next to the *Steinmühle*, is due to open in 1988. (*Eileen Spencer; also Franz Münsterer*)

Open All year.
Rooms 2 suites, 18 double, 3 single – all with bath, shower, telephone, radio and TV; kitchenette in suite. All in 2 houses about 80 yards from main building. 2 ground-floor rooms suitable for ♿.
Facilities Lift. Lounge, restaurant, bar, tea-room, wine cellar; (piano player nightly); conference facilities. Garden terrace. English spoken.
Location Central. Garages.
Credit cards All major cards accepted.
Terms B&B: single 95 DM, double 150 DM, suite 260-330 DM. Set lunch 30 DM, dinner 65 DM; full alc 90 DM. Reduced rates for children; special meals.

Hotel Sankt Nepomuk *Tel* (0951) 2 51 83
Obere Mühlbrücke 9

An enchanting and unusual hotel, newly converted from a half-timbered 17th-century millhouse, standing on stilts on the river Regnitz between two rushing millraces. It is next to the old quarter of Bamberg, one of the loveliest of Bavarian towns, its narrow streets and Baroque palaces marvellously unscathed by wartime bombing. Visitors this year endorse this earlier account of the *Sankt Nepomuk*: "It belongs, surprisingly, to an affluent Catholic foundation which has managed the conversion with fastidious taste. Everything is open-plan, stylish and spacious, notably the big restaurant on two floors, with handsome fireplace, curving stone stairway, and picture-windows where we gazed at the river as the light faded. Here the cooking is ambitious and varied but not pretentious, and very good, with the accent on local Frankish specialities. We enjoyed Bamberg's curious 'smoky beer' made from smoked malt. The bedrooms are stylish. The special glass of our bathroom window gave out a dazzling prismatic light effect; glow-worms darted and shone above the river; and we were lulled to sleep by the therapeutic roar of the millrace – to awaken next day to a sumptuous buffet breakfast that included cherries, strawberries, smoked ham and Camembert, served in a lovely room with cheerful modern murals of local scenes. The young couple who own and run the place, the Grüners (he chef, she manageress), were most welcoming, as were all their young staff. An original, magical hotel, like a lovely dream – and with very reasonable prices." (*JACA, KS*) "Superb cooking and excellent service." (*D Quirk; also Mr and Mrs Neil Biggs*)

Open All year.
Rooms 10 double, 2 single – 6 with bath, 6 with shower, all with telephone, radio, TV and mini-bar.
Facilities Lift. Bar, café, 2 restaurants; conference facilities. Some English spoken.
Location Central. Do *not* try to drive car up to hotel (narrow streets); leave it in public car park in Geyerswörthstrasse just across river.
Credit card Diners.
Terms B&B: single occupancy 72-95 DM, double 122-145 DM. Full alc 40-50 DM. Children under 6 free; special meals on request.

BAYREUTH 8580 Bayern — Map 13

Bayerischer Hof — *Tel* (0921) 2 20 81
Bahnhofstrasse 14 — *Telex* 642737

A visitor this year confirms earlier views that this is probably the best of Bayreuth's hotels: "This post-war building opposite the station is unprepossessing from outside, but the hotel has many qualities: large, well-furnished and well-insulated rooms (we never heard a train at night); a fine large heated indoor swimming-pool, and attractive rooftop restaurant and bar with outdoor terrace for summer; pleasant staff and good help-yourself breakfast. The hotel has been in the Seuss family since 1918." "The luncheon and dinner menus include plenty of local dishes and go well with the Franconian wines. During the *Wagnerfest* the hotel is likely to be full of visiting notables, but at other times the town resumes its normal quiet rhythm, with music in the old churches and the baroque opera house." (*HR, John and Eileen Spencer, endorsed by Alan Blyth*)

Open All year. Restaurant closed Sun Sept–June.
Rooms 36 double, 26 single – all with bath, shower, telephone and TV.
Facilities Lift. Hans Sachs Room, TV room, Spanish-style cellar restaurant, roof-garden terrace and restaurant; conference room; indoor swimming pool, sauna. Tiny garden. English spoken.
Location Central, 50 metres from station. Garage.
Restriction Not suitable for ♿.
Credit cards All major cards accepted.
Terms B&B: single 65-110 DM, double 110-180 DM. Alc dinner (excluding wine) 21-50 DM.

BAYREUTH-SEULBITZ 8580 Bayern — Map 13

Waldhotel Stein — *Tel* (0921) 90 01

Seulbitz (follow the signs to Eremitage) is a pretty farming village six kilometres east of Bayreuth and on higher ground, so you see the floodlit *Festspielhaus* from your window. "As good as ever and the food even better," writes one devotee this year who confirms his earlier nomination of Frau Stein's peaceful modern hotel: "It is like a well-run private house. One chambermaid was in the *Meistersinger* chorus, and this shows the standard of all the staff. Two swimming pools and acres of grass and trees to laze in. Many rooms are bedsitters with balcony; bathrooms luxurious." Some rooms are bungalows in the big garden. (*D Quirk*) More reports please.

Please make a habit of sending a report if you stay at a Guide hotel.

Open 1 Feb–30 Nov.
Rooms 8 suites, 35 double, 5 single – all with bath or shower, telephone, TV and mini-bar; many with balcony; suites have kitchenette. Many in bungalows in grounds. Some ground-floor rooms with large bathrooms.
Facilities Lounge, breakfast room, restaurant; conference facilities; indoor heated swimming pool, sauna, solarium and massage. Large grounds with unheated swimming pool, adjoining extensive forest. English spoken.
Location 6 km E of Bayreuth, near Seulbitz village; follow signs for Eremitage and *Waldhotel.*
Credit cards All major cards accepted.
Terms B&B: single 58-78.50 DM, double 68-98 DM, suite 120-140 DM. Set lunch/dinner 25 DM; full alc 45 DM. Reduced rates for children.

BEILSTEIN 5591 Rheinland-Pfalz — Map 13

Hotel Haus Lipmann — *Tel* (02673) 15 73

Beilstein is an attractive fortified village in the Mosel valley, famous for its last overlord, Metternich, whose castle stands on the hill above. To the south is the wooded plateau of the Hunsrück where Edgar Reitz set and filmed his 16-hour masterpiece *Heimat.* For this 1988 Guide there has been nothing but praise for the *Lipmann*, a cheap and unpretentious little family-run village inn, half-timbered and full of old-world atmosphere. The "superb" wines and the "excellent" food with its generous portions, served in a baronial hall, are all again praised. But the bedrooms are of uneven quality. Those in a modern annexe set amid trees are the most comfortable; rooms in the older "Alte Zollhaus" annexe are quaint but small. (*RT Johnson, J and B Flowers, R Barratt, and others*)

Open 15 Mar–15 Nov.
Rooms 20 double, 4 single – 1 with bath, 20 with shower. 18 in annexe.
Facilities Restaurant; conference/functions facilities; wine cellar (wine tastings held); terrace on Mosel. English spoken.
Location Central, near market place. Parking.
Credit cards None accepted.
Terms B&B: single 35-45 DM, double 62-85 DM. Alc meals (excluding wine) 20-45 DM.

BERLIN 1000 — Map 13

Hotel Belvedere — *Tel* (030) 826 10 77

Seebergsteig 4, Grunewald
Berlin 33

The smart residential suburb of Grunewald, aptly named, is some four kilometres from the city centre and next to a forest that leads to the Havel lake. It's a setting that puts paid to the false image of West Berlin as a claustrophobic city without space or greenery (in fact, it has 80 farms). Here, in a quiet and leafy side-street, this turn-of-the-century villa in its own garden has proved more popular than ever with visitors, in Berlin's 750th anniversary year. One new report praises the buffet breakfasts, another the thickness of the feather duvets, a third their welcome to small children; one reader had a room that was "adorable but tiny". "Stylish bedrooms with antique cane and wood furniture. Public rooms have the air of a bourgeois private house. Peaceful, relaxed, unpretentious. Breakfast in a funny conservatory-like annexe." (*Gerhard Cohn, JT Ervasti,*

Linda Rose) Evening meals may be had on request, but you would do better to eat out. Bus 19, five minutes' walk, will take you to the city centre. Visit the fabulous Dahlem museums, quite close by.

Open All year. Restaurant open to residents only.
Rooms 11 double, 6 single – 10 with bath and shower, 2 with shower only, all with direct-dial telephone, radio and TV. Some ground-floor rooms.
Facilities Salon, breakfast room, small restaurant. Sauna, solarium.
Location In Grunewald, 4 km SW of city centre.
Credit cards Access, Diners.
Terms Rooms: single 55-100 DM, double 85-140 DM. Breakfast 8 DM. Light cold meals 8-18 DM. Reduced rates for children.

Hotel-Pension Dittberner *Tel* (030) 881 64 85 and 881 39 63
Wielandstrasse 26, Berlin 15

In a quiet street just off the hectic and glittering Ku'damm, here's the kind of quaint and very Berlinesque little *pension* that the late Herr Issyvoo might have enjoyed, and it's new to the Guide this year: "On the fourth floor of an amusingly old-fashioned building with a creaky old elevator. The delightful Frau Lange greeted me warmly and gave me a simply furnished but very comfortable room. The window looked onto a yard with lots of trees and birds singing – a touch of nature in the *Grossstadt* just off the Ku'damm. Breakfast was good, served in a homey room full of plants and curios from many countries." (*Donna Cuervo*) Nearby are the delightful bohemian *Kneipe* (pubs) of the Savignyplatz area: try especially the quirky *Zillemarkt* and the cosy *Dicke Wirtin*, both of them lively centres of the social scene where you can enjoy a cheap snack and just be a camera.

Open All year.
Rooms 12 double, 9 single – 18 with bath and/or shower, all with telephone.
Facilities Lift. Breakfast-room, lounge, TV room. English spoken.
Location Central: between Kurfürstendamm and Olivaer Platz, 800 metres from Memorial Church. Parking.
Credit cards None accepted.
Terms B&B: single 54-62 DM, double 80-110 DM. Extra bed for child 25 DM. (No restaurant.)

Schlosshotel Gehrhus *Tel* (030) 826 20 81
Brahmsstrasse 4-10, Berlin 33

Also set in quiet park-like Grunewald (see above), this most unusual hotel evokes the splendours of a Berlin long vanished. It was built as a private palace in 1910 by the rich society lawyer W. von Pannwitz to house his distinguished collection of art and china. He was personal attorney to the Kaiser, and the house was a rendezvous of high society. Today the sumptuous public rooms are largely unchanged – the great hall in Italian renaissance style, the picture gallery and the beautiful library with its hand-painted ceiling. "An atmospheric hotel of charm and style. It has its own sizeable garden, so it is quiet, with lots of birds. Dinner was quite good and breakfast first-rate. Locals use the elegant function rooms for parties and weddings." (*R Duncan Luce, endorsed this year by Gabriele Berneck*)

Report forms (Freepost in UK) will be found at the end of the Guide.

Open All year.
Rooms 5 suites, 14 double, 16 single – 27 with bath and shower, all with telephone; some with radio and TV.
Facilities Lift. Salons, bar, restaurant; conference facilities. Garden. English spoken.
Credit cards Amex, Diners, Visa.
Location 4 km SW of city centre. Garage and parking place.
Terms B&B: single from 65 DM, double from 110 DM, suite from 220 DM. Set lunch/dinner 35 DM; full alc 45 DM.

BONN 5300 Nordrhein-Westfalen — Map 13

Schlosshotel Kommende Ramersdorf

Tel (0228) 44 07 34

Oberkasselerstrasse 10
Bonn 3–Beuel

This converted *Schloss* lies across the Rhine from Bonn, about three kilometres from the city centre and government area: "An alternative to the soulless and expensive down-town hotels. The original *Schloss* was built in 1220 and it is slightly incongruous to see this huge ancient building surrounded by a motorway network. This does, however, make it a convenient base for business or official visitors, and it is quiet. Our room was sizeable, warm and comfortable, with antique furniture and a modern bathroom. Corridors were a little cool and impersonal, but service was helpful. Part of the *Schloss* is a museum of furniture, carpets and paintings, some items being for sale. The restaurant serves good Italian food and seems to be very popular locally." (*K and S M-S*)

Open All year. Restaurant closed Tue and 3 weeks in July.
Rooms 10 double, 8 single – all with bath and shower, direct-dial telephone and radio; some with TV.
Facilities Bar, TV room, breakfast room, restaurant; terrace-café; 2 functions/conference rooms. Courtyard and garden. English spoken.
Location Take A59 motorway in direction of Königswinter, leave it at Niederholtorf exit; turn left, and after 300 metres left again. Bedrooms have double-glazed windows to cut out motorway noise.
Restriction Not suitable for ♿.
Credit cards All major cards accepted.
Terms B&B: single 85–100 DM, double 150–170 DM. Set lunch 20 DM, dinner 30 DM; full alc 65 DM.

Hotel und Restaurant Mertens

Tel (0228) 47 44 51

Rheindorferstrasse 134
Bonn 3–Beuel

"If you want to escape the diplomatic cocktail-party chatter of Bad Godesberg, and the high prices of central Bonn where government is a mono-industry, then just cross the river to the tidy suburb of Beuel and you could be in any little convivial Rhineland town," writes an inspector, who was quite content with this unassuming and friendly little modern family-run hotel. Although front rooms can be noisy, it is quiet at the back, except when local singing-clubs use the hotel's back restaurant. You may feel that this adds to local colour or – as another visitor did this year – that it's a bit tiresome. The place is very clean, tidy and practical in the best German manner: honest German home cooking and good Kölsch beer, the kind they drink in millions of gallons at the Cologne carnival. *(JA and KA; endorsed, except for the club life, by GM Morrison)*

Open All year. Restaurant closed for lunch and on Tue.
Rooms 10 double, 4 single – 5 with bath, 8 with shower, all with direct-dial telephone.
Facilities Salon/bar, TV room, dining room; conference room. Rhine 500 metres. English spoken.
Location In Beuel, E of Rhine; 2 km from centre of Bonn. Parking.
Restriction Not suitable for ♿.
Credit card Diners.
Terms [1987 rates] B&B: single 48 DM, double 85 DM. Alc 20-32 DM (excluding wine).

Hotel Schaumberger Hof *Tel* (0228) 36 40 95
Am Schaumberger Hof 10
Bonn 2–Bad Godesberg

A solid, spacious, pleasantly old-fashioned hotel, formerly a wine tavern, in a splendid position right on the Rhine at Bad Godesberg – a paved promenade along this famous stretch of river goes right past the hotel, with views of the Siebengebirge and the Drachenfels. "A pity that my bed was so hard and the pillow so small; breakfast too was uninteresting, by German standards. Otherwise, the place makes a good choice for anyone seeking to avoid the soulless modernism and high prices of down-town Bonn." That view is backed up this year by a family who enjoyed the food and service in the attractive panelled dining room overlooking the river. *(JA, also Linda Kay Rose)*

Open 15 Jan–19 Dec.
Rooms 2 suites, 18 double, 14 single – 10 with bath and shower, all with telephone.
Facilities Hall, lounge, TV room, restaurant; conference facilities; terrace. English spoken.
Location On river, 1 km NE of central Bad Godesberg, 2 km SE of central Bonn. Private parking.
Restriction Not suitable for ♿.
Credit cards Amex, Diners.
Terms [1987 rates] B&B: single 57-80 DM, double 99-140 DM. Alc meals 25-52 DM (excluding wine); children's menu.

BREITNAU 7821 Baden-Württemberg — Map 13

Hotel Kaiser's Tanne-Wirtshus *Tel* (07652) 15 51
Am Wirbstein 27

Pleasantly secluded, here is yet another radiant chalet-like Black Forest hotel, all gables and flowery balconies outside, all folksy *Gemütlichkeit* within. It is newly nominated this year: "Set in pleasant rolling country a few miles outside the big resort of Hinterzarten and thus away from the tourist crowds. Not cheap, but rooms are well appointed: ours had a balcony with rural views. Indoor swimming pool and attractive garden. The restaurant was excellent, the staff friendly." *(RM Sparkes)* More reports welcome.

Open All year except 15 Nov–20 Dec. Restaurant closed Mon.
Rooms 24 double, 6 single – all with bath or shower, telephone, radio and TV.

Facilities Lift. Lounge, bar, 2 restaurants, indoor heated swimming pool; terrace. Garden, playground for children. English spoken.
Location Just SW of Breitnau, which is 30 km E of Freiburg, off route 500.
Credit card Diners.
Terms B&B: single 65-70 DM, double 110-160 DM; dinner, B&B: single 95-105 DM; double 190-240 DM. Set lunch 24-35 DM, dinner 30-65 DM; full alc 45 DM.

BREMEN 2800 — Map 13

Landhaus Louisenthal — *Tel* (0421) 23 20 76
Leher Heerstrasse 105, Bremen 33 — *Telex* 246925 HOTEL

Hanseatic Bremen has a splendid breezy, quirky atmosphere: do not miss the beautiful Renaissance *Rathaus*, better than Bruges', or the stylish boutiques of the Böttcherstrasse, a highly original traffic-free alley. The *Louisenthal* is an 18th-century mansion in a garden, converted into a stylish little family-run hotel with a cream-coloured Italianate facade. It is in Horn, a north-east suburb of Bremen, near the *Autobahn* and with bus and tram services passing the door, but quiet. "Excellent value and comfort and attractive grounds." "We ate a delicious light supper on a terrace overlooking the garden." One note of caution: "Menu fairly basic (vegetables tinned) but adequate." (*Betty Hooper, Paul Harris, Iain Elliot, Angela Pearse*)

Open All year.
Rooms 2 suites, 31 double, 31 single – 5 with bath, 59 with shower, all with telephone and baby-listening; some with radio and TV. Some suitable for ♿. 20 in annexe.
Facilities Salon, TV room, dining room; conference facilities. Garden with terrace. English spoken.
Location In the suburb of Horn-Lehe 6 km NE of centre of Bremen, just off E71/A27 *Autobahn*.
Credit cards All major cards accepted.
Terms [1987 rates] B&B: single 50 DM, double 86 DM, suite 175 DM; dinner, B&B: single 65 DM, double 116 DM, suite 205 DM; full board: single 75 DM, double 126 DM, suite 225 DM. Set lunch 18 DM, supper 16 DM; full alc 30 DM. Reduced rates for children.

BÜSINGEN 7701 Baden-Württemberg — Map 13

Alte Rheinmühle — *Tel* (07734) 60 76
Junkerstrasse 93 — *Telex* 793788 HOTEL

Only four kilometres from the handsome old Swiss town of Schaffhausen, the village of Büsingen is a German enclave inside Switzerland (either Swiss or German currency can be used). Here the *Alte Rheinmühle*, a converted 17th-century mill on the Rhine, is reputed to serve some of the best food in Baden-Württemberg (*Michelin* rosette):"The dining hall, with its big wooden beams and lots of windows overlooking the river, is large but has a cosy atmosphere, enhanced on our visit by a roaring log fire. Delicious food: in the game season we had pheasant terrine and ragout of venison with spätzle. The Schaffhausen red wine was light but pleasant. It was lovely to have breakfast (including air-dried meat) in this same room facing the river and the bird sanctuary opposite. The bedrooms and sitting areas are dotted around on various levels in a higgledy-piggledy but homely fashion: our room was slightly ramshackle but comfortable, with a four-poster bed and traditional painted wooden wardrobe. Lighting was a bit limited." (*Stephan and Kate Murray-Sykes*)

Open All year, except 20 Dec–10 Jan.
Rooms 16 double – all with bath or shower and telephone.
Facilities Hall and sitting areas, restaurant; conference facilities. Garden.
Location 4 km E of Schaffhausen.
Restriction Not suitable for ♿.
Terms [1987 rates] B&B: single 80-90 DM, double 150-170 DM. Alc meals (excluding wine) 52-85 DM.

CELLE 3100 Niedersachsen — Map 13

Fürstenhof – Restaurant Endtenfang — *Tel* (05141) 20 10, *Telex* 925293 CEHOG
Hannoversche Strasse 55

The stylish and rather formal *Fürstenhof*, a pink-fronted mansion, stands on a main road near the centre of the historic old city of Celle where the Guelph princes ruled (imposing *Schloss*, lovely *Altstadt* of timbered houses undamaged in the war). "The hotel successfully combines traditional character and modern amenities. One part is a 17th-century palace, housing the public rooms; bedrooms are in a new glass-fronted building, and between the two is a little garden where drinks are served. Our room was pleasant, with floral wallpaper and a big balcony. The lounge, very comfortable, is in 'baroque' style. There are two restaurants – a cheaper *Kutscherstube* and the more formal *Endtenfang* where we found excellent service and food, especially the duck dishes." (*K and S M-S*) More reports welcome.

Open All year. *Kutscherstube* closed midday and Sun.
Rooms 75 – all with bath and shower, telephone, radio, TV and baby listening.
Facilities Lift. Lounge, bar, beer-cellar, 2 restaurants; conference and functions facilities; indoor swimming pool, solarium, sauna. Garden and terrace; bowling.
Location Central, near *Schloss*. Parking.
Credit cards Access, Amex, Diners.
Terms [1987 rates] B&B: single 95-190 DM, double 170-330 DM. Alc meals (excluding wine): *Kutscherstube* 35-52 DM, *Endtenfang* 47-80 DM.

COLOGNE 5000 Nordrhein-Westfalen — Map 13

Hotel Bristol — *Tel* (0221) 12 01 95
Kaiser Wilhelm Ring 48, Köln 1 — *Telex* 8881146 HOBR

Family-run bed-and-breakfast hotel (but snacks also available), quite central (700 metres west of cathedral). Some rooms with carved wooden furniture and four-poster. Upper rooms quiet, lower front ones may be noisy. 43 rooms, all with bath or shower. B&B single 78-150 DM. More reports welcome.

Haus Lyskirchen — *Tel* (0221) 23 48 91
Filzengraben 26-32, Cologne 1 — *Telex* 08885449

In a quiet street just off the Rhine bank, 700 metres from the cathedral and its magnificent adjacent museums, here is a six-storey modern hotel, functional but quiet: excellent swimming pool, also garage, bowling-alley and conference facilities. Restaurant with limited menu (lots of better ones nearby). Service rather erratic. Closed 23 Dec–2 Jan. 95 rooms. B&B double 176-210 DM. Set meals 26-39 DM. Reinstated after previous criticisms of staff: more reports please.

DEIDESHEIM 6705 Rheinland-Pfalz — Map 13

Deidesheimer Hof — *Tel* (06326) 18 11
Am Marktplatz

In a wine village in the Pfalz vineyards, a Romantik Hotel full of Germanic warmth, prettiness and good cheer, with red Michelin *symbol for good food at fair prices (Pfalz dishes). Rooms at back are best. 26 rooms, some with bath or shower. B&B [1987 rates] 42-115 DM. No recent reports: please send some.*

DORTMUND 4600 Nordrhein-Westfalen — Map 13

Romberg-Park Hotel — *Tel* (0231) 71 40 73
Am Rombergpark 67
Dortmund 50–Brünninghausen

Idyllically sited in a park by a lake in the south Dortmund suburbs (decaying steel-mills just out of sight), a pleasant modern hotel (part of a hotel school): bedrooms spacious, with balconies facing lake. Outdoor dining-terrace; excellent cooking by the students. 32 rooms, all with bath or shower. B&B 72.50-92.50 DM. Set meals from 17 DM. No recent reports: please send some.

DÜSSELDORF 4000 — Map 13

Hotel Schnellenburg — *Tel* (0211) 43 41 33
Rotterdamerstrasse 120 — *Telex* 8581828 BURG
Düsseldorf 30

A visitor this year, who had a spacious room and good breakfast, confirms this earlier account: "In a commercial city with few hotels of character, this one at least is a bit unusual. It's not central but it's in a fine position on the Rhine, almost next door to the Trade Fair centre and ten minutes' drive from the airport. It's a low white building by the main road, with iron grilles on the windows, and looks more Spanish than German; a sort of superior motel. Cheerful service and a good buffet breakfast." (*Andrew Palmer, and others*) A new restaurant has just been built and opened, under separate management.

Open All year except Christmas and New Year period.
Rooms 3 suites, 38 double, 11 single – all with bath and shower, telephone, radio and TV.
Facilities Lounge, residents' bar, restaurant (under separate management). Small garden. English spoken.
Restriction Not suitable for ♿.
Location 4 km N of city centre, opposite Nord Park, on the Rhine. Parking.
Credit cards All major cards accepted.
Terms B&B: single 120-160 DM, double 160-220 DM, suite 250-280 DM. Full alc 25 DM. Reduced rates and special menu for children.

EISENSCHMITT-EICHELHÜTTE 5561 Rheinland-Pfalz Map 13

Hotel Molitors Mühle *Tel* (06567) 5 81

A village in wooded hilly country between the Eifel massif and the Mosel valley. Here the *Mühle*, a converted white-walled millhouse, has been owned and run for over 100 years by the Molitor family. "Not at all smart, but delightful and relaxed; excellent food," is a recent report. Another: "The setting is idyllic, by a small lake, with marvellous forest walks (signposted) winding their way along a stream near the garden. The ultimate delight is to sit on the terrace by the lake and watch the sun set and the trout rise while enjoying a bottle of local Mosel. The food is imaginatively cooked, not expensive, and is eaten in the former iron foundry. The owner and his son speak English and will lend you rods for fishing." One reader was irritated by the overhead flights from the USAF base at nearby Bitburg. (*Duncan Graham, SAL*)

Open 1 Feb – 10 Jan.
Rooms 3 suites, 22 double, 10 single – 5 with bath and shower, 30 with shower only, all with telephone and TV; some with balcony. 2 suites and 3 double in separate building in grounds.
Facilities 3 lounges, TV room, bar, dining rooms; indoor swimming pool; sauna, solarium, massage. Garden by lake; boating, fishing, tennis, mini-golf, barbecues in summer. English spoken.
Location In the hamlet of Eisenschmitt-Eichelhütte, between Wittlich (17 km) and Bitburg; 1 km W of Himmerod.
Restriction Only restaurant suitable for ♿.
Credit cards Access, Amex, Visa.
Terms B&B: single 50–55 DM, double 80–108 DM, suite 130 DM; dinner, B&B: 15 DM per person added; full board: 25 DM per person added. Set lunch/dinner 20–25 DM; full alc 30–40 DM.

ETTLINGEN 7505 Baden-Württemberg Map 13

Hotel Erbprinz *Tel* (07243) 1 20 71
Rheinstrasse 1 *Telex* 782848

Ettlingen is a pleasant little town between Karlsruhe and the edge of the Black Forest, where the *Autobahnen* from Frankfurt and Stuttgart converge on their way to Basle. In this workaday setting, in fact in the town centre, is the anything but workaday *Erbprinz*, worthy indeed of a Crown Prince and one of south Germany's most luxurious smaller hotels. "Old fashioned in the grand style, with comfortable bedrooms, friendly staff, and excellent food in the *Michelin*-rosetted restaurant," runs our latest report. Another visitor had a room with a balcony and a large marble bathroom, and enjoyed the "excellent, beautifully-presented food in the large, well-known restaurant, wood-panelled, decorated with fine paintings." "Just before Christmas, the management apologised for the absence of snow." (*Pat and Jeremy Temple, Christine Herxheimer, Gabriele Berneck, and others*)

Open All year except 24 and 31 Dec.
Rooms 6 suites, 19 double, 25 single – all with bath, shower, telephone, radio and TV.
Facilities Lift. Lounge, bar, 4 restaurants; conference and function facilities. Garden with terrace restaurant. English spoken.
Restriction Not suitable for ♿.

Location Central. Ettlingen is 8 km S of Karlsruhe. From *Autobahn* A5 take Karlsruhe-Rüppurr or Karlsruhe-Rheinhafen exit. Parking.
Credit cards Access, Amex, Diners.
Terms B&B: single 120-180 DM, double 180-250 DM, suite 300-340 DM.

EUTIN-FISSAU 2420 Schleswig-Holstein — Map 13

Hotel Wiesenhof — *Tel* (04521) 27 26
Leonhardt-Boldtstrasse 25

Eutin, with its moated castle, is a characterful old 18th-century town of brick buildings, and it lies close to the Baltic, in an area known as the Holsteinische Schweiz. It has a number of lovely lakes – and close to one of these, surrounded also by woods and meadows, lies the most attractive *Wiesenhof*, a scattering of modern white-walled buildings in local style. All very spruce and airy, with plenty of amenities such as sauna and ping-pong, and something of a Scandinavian feel. "This part of Germany is neglected by British tourists, but it's attractive and quite close to Lübeck and Hamburg. The hotel is pleasantly furnished, our bedroom was delightful and the breakfast excellent. Drinks are served on a trust-the-guest basis." (*Richard O Whiting*) More reports please.

Open 5 Apr–3 Nov.
Rooms 9 suites, 17 double, 9 single – 30 with bath, 5 with shower, all with telephone and tea-making facilities. Suites in building 10 metres from main house. Ground-floor rooms.
Facilities 2 TV rooms, library, wine bar, 2 dining rooms. Indoor swimming pool with jetstream; sauna, solarium, fitness room; table tennis. Garden. Sea and fishing 20 min by car. Some English spoken.
Location 2 km N of the centre of Eutin, towards Malente.
Credit cards None accepted.
Terms B&B: single 49-64 DM, double 86-118 DM, suite 94-128 DM. 1-night bookings sometimes refused. Reductions for children sharing parents' room. (No restaurant.)

FEUCHTWANGEN 8805 Bayern — Map 13

Greifen-Post — *Tel* (09852) 20 02
Marktplatz 8 — *Telex* 61137

American readers this year add their words of praise ("The dining room was superb, and our bedroom very pretty") to this earlier account: "Feuchtwangen is a pleasant little north Bavarian town with some picturesque houses and an interesting Frankish folk museum. It is close to medieval Rothenburg, that tourist show-piece, and lies on the so-called Romantikstrasse that runs across Bavaria, while the *Greifen-Post*, in its attractive main square, belongs to the Romantik association of old hotels of character. But there's no need to fear a surfeit of romanticism, even though Lola Montez and Catherine the Great were among past guests: today it is a solidly down-to-earth coaching inn, spacious and rambling, with parts dating back to 1450 or earlier. Wide corridors full of antiques are part of the charm, but the bedrooms are comfortably modernised." Those in the front may be noisy, those in the newer extension are quieter but have less charm.

"The Lorentz family have owned the *Greifen* for three generations, and they provide a personal touch. Their cooking is especially good –

interesting specialities, Frankish and other, served in old beamed dining rooms. Dandelion and mushroom salad, trout fillet in a wine sauce, and spicy Nuremberg sausage." (*Barbara and Jim Flowers, JACA*)

Open All year. Restaurant closed 2 Jan–15 Feb.
Rooms 2 suites, 35 double, 6 single – 40 with bath and shower, all with telephone, radio and TV. 1 specially adapted for ♿.
Facilities Lift. Bar with open fire place, 3 restaurants; conference facilities; indoor heated swimming pool, sauna, solarium; garden terrace for summer use. English spoken.
Location Central. Garage parking.
Credit cards All major cards accepted.
Terms B&B: single 65-100 DM, double 90-250 DM, suite 230-250 DM. Set lunch 35 DM, dinner 90 DM; full alc 40 DM. Reduced rates for children.

FRANKFURT-AM-MAIN 6000 Hessen — Map 13

Westend — *Tel* (069) 74 67 02 and 74 50 02
Westendstrasse 15, Frankfurt 1

This "small hotel of charm and character" lies in a quiet residential district that has somehow survived the metallic frenzy of post-war rebuilding: yet it is very central, only five minutes' walk from the Fair centre, the *Hauptbahnhof* and the banking district. "Quite a discovery – select, serene, rather old-fashioned, such a contrast to the skyscraper banks that tower above it. The late 20th century has been carefully excluded from the *Westend*, which is tastefully furnished throughout with antiques and old pictures; gracious old-world service by discreet middle-aged men in black suits who address lady guests as 'Gnädige Frau' ('Esteemed Madame'). Very comfortable rooms; lavish German breakfasts; light evening meals on request; a leafy garden for summer; prices very reasonable for central Frankfurt." (*JA and KA*)

Open All year.
Rooms 9 double, 11 single – 5 with bath, 2 with shower, all with telephone.
Facilities Lift. 3 lounges (1 with TV). Garden and terrace where light meals and drinks are served. English spoken.
Location Central; 5 minutes' walk from station. By car approach from Westkreuz. Private parking.
Credit card Amex.
Terms [1987 rates] Rooms: single 90-140 DM, double 130-180 DM. Breakfast 14 DM. (No restaurant but light evening meals served on request.)

FREIBURG IM BREISGAU 7800 Baden-Württemberg — Map 13

Zum Roten Bären — *Tel* (0761) 3 69 13
Oberlinden 12 — *Telex* 7721574 BAER

In the quiet medieval heart of this lovely old university city, the *Roten Bären*, according to its owners, is "authentically proved to be" the oldest inn in Germany, dating from 1120. Blue-and-pink diamond-shaped fresco designs adorn the facade; inside, all is spruce *Gemütlichkeit* in the best Baden tradition. Two recent reports: "Perfectly charming, with a good restaurant and comfortable rooms." "We spent eight nights here, using it as a base for Black Forest walking. The hotel has 'new' sections which have been skilfully integrated into the old parts. Our room was in the new part, very comfortable and furnished to a high standard, as were all the public rooms. All the right touches – old prints on the walls, plants and flowers, and so on. The daily menu in the restaurant was excellent (e.g. smoked salmon, smoked trout, braised venison), breakfast was a feast and the service was friendly."*(Pat and Richard Neumann, Colin and Sally Spensley; also William Goodhart)*

Open All year. Restaurant closed 24 Dec.
Rooms 2 suites, 23 double, 5 single – 30 with bath and/or shower, all with telephone and radio; some with TV.
Facilities Lift. Reception, lounge, TV room, restaurant; conference room. Courtyard and boulevard café. English spoken.
Location Central; in old part of city. Underground carparks. From Basle highway take exit Freiburg Mitte; follow signs for Stadtmitte, Schwabentor, *Hotel Bären*.
Credit cards All major cards accepted.
Terms B&B: single 75–135 DM, double 120–180 DM, suite 200–250 DM; dinner, B&B 30 DM per person added; full board 50 DM added. Set lunch 25 DM, dinner 39–60 DM; full alc 55 DM. Reduced rates and special meals for children.

FREUDENSTADT 7290 Baden-Württemberg — Map 13

Hotel-Restaurant Gut Lauterbad

Tel (07441) 74 96

Dietrichstrasse 5, Lauterbad

Freudenstadt, one of the larger Black Forest resorts and spa towns, lies on a pine-clad plateau, astride the old hill-road from Stuttgart to Strasbourg. The *Gut Lauterbad*, a modern building in traditional style, lies just outside the town, amid meadows, woods and streams. "A charming setting, a warm welcome and excellent food," is one recent verdict. Another: "Lovely hotel. Large, modern, very comfortable rooms, all tastefully furnished. A garden terrace overlooks a trout pond and stream. Good restaurant, friendly staff and owners. Plenty of good paths for walking close by." (*Dr Bill and Lisa Fuerst, Ted and Vera Baker*)

Open 1 Feb–13 Nov, 12 Dec–9 Jan. Restaurant closed Wed.
Rooms 16 double, 4 single – all with shower, telephone, radio and TV. 4 double, 1 apartment in annexe.
Facilities Lounge, bar, TV room, restaurant; conference room; indoor heated swimming pool. Park with children's playground, small lake and stream; trout fishing. English spoken.
Location 3 km SE (B294) of Freudenstadt. From town centre, follow directions to Freiburg then to Dietersweiler/Lauterbad. Hotel is at end of road on left. Garage and parking.
Restriction Not suitable for ♿.
Credit cards All major cards accepted.
Terms B&B: single 48-52 DM, double 76-98 DM; dinner, B&B: 17.50 per person added; full board 27 DM added. Set lunch 12.50 DM, dinner 18.50 DM; full alc 25 DM. Children under 2 free; under 12, 50% reduction; special meals.

FRIEDRICHSRUHE 7111 Baden-Württemberg — Map 13

Wald-und Schlosshotel Friedrichsruhe

Tel (07941) 70 78
Telex 74498 WAFRI

Öhringerstrasse 11

The 1987 *Varta* guide, a German equivalent of *Michelin*, awards its highest ratings to this imposing castle in the hilly, wooded Hohenlohe country, and our own recent reports tend to agree ("the best hotel we have stayed at in Germany"). It was built in 1712 by the Fürsten of that ilk and is still owned today (after conversion into a very grand hotel in 1953) by the Prinz Kraft zu Hohenlohe-Öhringen. His chef/manager, Lothar Eiermann, runs it in lordly style and has also built a reputation for serving some of the best food in south Germany (*Michelin* rosette). Rooms are in the old castle or, along with the restaurant, in an extension built in 1969. "All rooms we saw were nicely decorated, some in traditional chintzy style or with country pine. Ours had a good view. On our return from dinner, everything had been tidied up, including putting the newspaper back together in the right order. Everything we ate was excellent, especially the saddle of venison. Good breakfast too. Service, food and accommodation all faultless." "Very luxurious, beautiful gardens and rural setting, two lovely swimming pools." (*Kate and Steve Murray-Sykes, Katinka Ardagh*)

Open All year.
Rooms 7 suites, 31 double, 10 single – 45 with bath, 3 with shower; most with telephone; radio and TV on request. 22 rooms in hunting lodge.
Facilities Lifts. Lounge/bar, 2 restaurants; functions room. Large grounds with outdoor and covered swimming pools, tennis court, 9-hole golf course, playground for children. English spoken.
Location 30 km E of Heilbronn; leave the Nürnberg motorway at Öhringen exit, drive through Öhringen till Friedrichsruhe is signposted.
Credit cards All major cards accepted.
Terms B&B: single 160-175 DM, double 258-278 DM, suite 298- 508 DM. Set lunch 105 DM, dinner 160 DM; full alc 108 DM. 1- night booking might be refused over bank-holiday weekends.

FÜSSEN-WEISSENSEE 8958 Bayern — Map 13

Seegasthof Weissensee — *Tel* (08362) 70 95

Nominated this year as a pleasant little gasthof *by a lake, with lovely mountain views, in a village just west of the big resort of Füssen. Two modern buildings in traditional modern style (lots of stripped pine); lavish breakfasts, average main meals. Closed 10 Nov to 20 Dec. 22 rooms, all with shower and* WC. *B&B double 41-56 DM. Set meals 15-20 DM. More reports please.*

GARMISCH-PARTENKIRCHEN 8100 Bayern — Map 13

Posthotel Partenkirchen — *Tel* (08821) 5 10 67
Ludwigstrasse 49 — *Telex* 59611

The *Posthotel*, sizeable and very stylish, has been in the hands of the Stahl family for four generations and a hotel has stood on this site since the 15th century. It is in the unsmart eastern part (Partenkirchen) of Bavaria's largest and smartest resort (Garmisch), but an inspector found that to be no drawback: "A smashing place – a three-storey building with paintings on the walls outside, Bavarian-style. A feeling of antiquity pervades the place – oil portraits, and dark wood furniture set on Persian carpets or stone flags. Ceilings are beamed, with stucco motifs, and bedrooms have wood panelling. Our spacious room had a balcony too. There's a roof garden, and you can see Germany's highest mountain, the Zugspitze, on a clear day. The panelled restaurant was popular, especially with

Americans (there's a big US base nearby), and food and service was excellent." (*JS*) More reports, please.

Open All year.
Rooms 1 suite, 38 double, 21 single – all with bath and shower, telephone and radio; some with balcony; TV on request.
Facilities Lift. Lounge, TV room, bar, wine bar (piano daily), coffee shop, restaurants; conference and function facilities. Roof garden. English spoken.
Location In Partenkirchen, near *Kurhaus*, opposite the main church. Parking.
Restriction Not suitable for ♿.
Credit cards All major cards accepted.
Terms B&B: single 110 DM, double 145-195 DM. Set lunch from 20 DM, dinner from 65 DM; full alc 50 DM. Discounts for long stays. Reduced rates for children; special meals.

GEISLINGEN AN DER STEIGE 7340 Baden-Württemberg — Map 13

Burghotel — *Tel* (07331) 4 10 51
Burggasse 41
Weiler ob Helfenstein

This attractive modern two-storey building, in superior motel style, lies in the rolling hills of Schwäbische Alb, between Ulm and Stuttgart, and is reached from Geislingen via two miles of hairpin bends. It has an indoor swimming pool, jacuzzis and a large garden. "Very friendly welcome," say regular visitors. "A pleasant modern room with balcony, and a varied breakfast. On each of our pillows was a little sack with fruit, nuts and a chocolate Father Christmas" (this is south Germany and it was St Nicholas night). "No restaurant, but the hotel has an arrangement with the *Burgstüble*, 300 metres away: very warm and welcoming in a Germanic way, and delicious home cooking, for example breast of pheasant in passion-fruit sauce, and Swabian dishes such as Spätzle baked with cheese." (*K and S M-Š*) Opposite the hotel are the castle ruins.

Open All year except 3 weeks in summer (check with hotel). Closed Christmas–3 Jan.
Rooms 11 double, 12 single – 4 with bath and shower, 19 with shower, all with telephone, radio, TV and baby-listening.
Facilities Lounge, bar, reading room/TV lounge, breakfast room; indoor swimming pool, sauna. Large garden with terrace. English spoken.
Location 3 km E of Geislingen; turn by station towards Helfenstein castle ruins. Garage (6 DM).
Restriction Not suitable for ♿.
Credit cards None accepted.
Terms Rooms: single 48–91 DM, double 82–135 DM. Breakfast 6–18 DM. Half board arrangement (3 days min) with meals at *Burgstüble*).

GÖTTINGEN 3400 Niedersachsen — Map 13

Hotel zur Sonne — *Tel* (0551) 5 67 38
Paulinerstrasse 10 — *Telex* 96787 SONNE

In a famous university city, a useful budget halt on the edge of the downtown pedestrian zone. Spacious rooms with twin and (rare in Germany) double beds. Yugoslav restaurant next door. Closed Christmas/New Year. 41 rooms, most with bath and/or shower. B&B 49-85 DM. No recent reports: please send some.

GRAINAU 8104 Bayern — Map 13

Hotel Alpenhof *Tel* (08821) 80 71
Alpspitzstrasse 22

Just west of Garmisch, the village of Grainau is a popular little resort on the way to the Eibsee and the Austrian frontier, at the foot of the high Alps. Here the *Alpenhof* is "recommended without hesitation", says a recent visitor. "It is in a quiet side street, and half the rooms have a balcony looking on to the Zugspitze massif, a breathtaking view. The rooms are clean and well equipped and the food is excellent, particularly the buffet breakfasts that include a heated covered dish of bacon, scrambled eggs and sauté potatoes." (*PE Roland*)

Open All year except 9 Nov–15 Dec, 27 Apr–9 May.
Rooms 38 – most with bath and/or shower, telephone and TV; some with balcony.
Facilities Lift. Salons, restaurant; conference facilities; indoor heated swimming pool, sauna and indoor tennis court; terrace.
Location 6 km SW of Garmisch-Partenkirchen. Hotel is central, but quietly situated. Parking.
Credit cards Access, Amex, Diners.
Terms [1987 rates] B&B: single 68-115 DM, double 140-195 DM. Alc (excluding wine) 26-53 DM.

GUTACH IM BREISGAU 7809 Baden-Württemberg — Map 13

Hotel-Restaurant Adler *Tel* (07681) 70 22
Landstrasse 6

Gutach, a village north-east of Freiburg, is a key centre of Black Forest folk tradition, with an attractive folk museum. Here the splendid *Adler* typifies the high average quality of hotels in the area and has been much admired recently: "A new building in traditional rustic style, with oak-beamed ceilings, tiled floors. Our bedroom was airy and attractive, furnished in repro rococo style with pretty pictures and central chandelier. It was at the back, quiet, looking on to a steep pine-clad hillside with huge rocks. The gardens are well tended: you can eat outside on warm days. One dining room has an open log fire and beautiful Victorian oil-lamps. The other has an original 19th-century mechanical organ with moving military statuettes, playing hum-pah-pah music. We enjoyed the frogs' legs, wild duck, venison with spätzle. Good Bodensee wine. Dogs permitted in restaurant: we were treated to a howling concerto for poodle, dachshund and mongrel. Breakfast buffet included two sorts of muesli. We'd go back with pleasure." (*Ian and Francine Walsh; also KA*)

Open All year except 2 weeks in Jan. Closed Sun, and Mon until 5pm.
Rooms 1 suite, 10 double, 3 single – 13 with bath, 2 with shower, all with telephone; some with radio and TV.
Facilities Lounge/bar, TV room, 2 restaurants. Garden terrace with outdoor meals and barbecues in summer. English spoken.
Location In village, 21 km NE of Freiburg. Ample parking.
Restriction Not suitable for ♿.
Credit cards None accepted.
Terms B&B: single 50-60 DM, double 78-100 DM. Set lunch from 25 DM, dinner from 45 DM.

HAGNAU 7758 Baden-Württemberg — Map 13

Erbguth's Landhaus — *Tel* (07532) 62 02
Neugartenstrasse 39 — *Telex* 733811

"A hotel of considerable personality, run by a young couple, the Erbguths, with a great deal of flair. He cooks, she hostesses." It is a converted private house on the edge of a pretty village by the Bodensee and is typical of the small hotels of character along this holiday lakeside. "The entrance hall with its white marble floor has an aura of cool elegance, in contrast to the warm traditional interiors of the dining areas, where you dine in the glow of candlelight, amid masses of flowers and modern 'antiques'. The only flaw is the loud piped music. Food was pleasant and original, much of it smoked and preserved in the hotel's own kitchens – we had sensational home-smoked caviar from local fish, fantastic tender rinderfilet, good local wine. Excellent buffet breakfast. Bedrooms and bathrooms could not be faulted, either, in taste or comfort, save that lighting was dimmish. Our room had original pictures and prints. Frau Erbguth has panache and artistry: she dresses smartly, is charming, modern and slick, and the same could be said of her clientele. Not a cheap place, but the quality is superb." "A lovely place, very smart, but with a real local atmosphere and tradition" (*Francine and Ian Walsh; warmly endorsed this year by Katinka Ardagh*) In 1988 there will be four new rooms in an annexe on the edge of the lake.

Open All year except Jan and Feb. Restaurant closed Tue.
Rooms 14 double – 2 with bath and shower, 12 with shower, all with telephone, radio and TV. 4 in lake-side annexe. Ground-floor rooms.
Facilities Bar, restaurant, lounge, TV room; fitness room with sauna and solarium. Garden and terrace. Private beach on lake. English spoken.
Location On Lake Constance (Bodensee), just E of Meersburg. Parking.
Credit cards All major cards accepted.
Terms B&B: single 70-110 DM, double 120-300 DM; half board 35 DM per person added to B&B rates. Alc dinner (excluding wine) 35-45 DM. Reduced rates for children.

HAMBURG 2000 — Map 13

Hotel Abtei — *Tel* (040) 44 29 05 and 45 75 65
Abteistrasse 14, Hamburg 13 — *Telex* 2165645 ABHA

A small elegant bed-and-breakfast hotel with big, well-lit attractive rooms in a quiet residential district two miles north of the centre, near Alster. "The service from the Lay family is splendid. The rooms are elegant, clean and airy. Lovely bathroom – the best we experienced in three weeks. And after many self-service breakfasts, what a pleasure to be served with tasty and novel combinations of breakfast food. The hotel has an ingenious device which provides a fresh toilet seat for each customer: more economical than it sounds, but hard to explain without recourse to a working model." (*Keith and Mary Weller*)

Open All year except Christmas and New Year.
Rooms 4 suites, 8 double, 6 single – 12 with bath and/or shower, all with telephone, radio and TV.
Facilities Lounge, TV room, breakfast room. Small garden. Near Alster lake, boating. English spoken.
Location Just W of Alster lake. Parking. Easy access to centre by underground.

Restriction Not suitable for ♿.
Terms B&B: single 150–167 DM, double 180–280 DM. (No restaurant.)

Hotel Bellevue — *Tel* (040) 24 80 11
An der Alster 14, Hamburg 1 — *Telex* 2162929 bell

Almost next door to the Prem *(q.v.), with the same lake view but rather cheaper, the* Bellevue *is a stylish and efficient hotel with big comfortable rooms and friendly staff; double-glazing keeps noise down. Basement restaurant offers large interesting meals; large buffet breakfasts, too. Conference facilities. 80 rooms, most with bath or shower. B&B double 165-200 DM. Set dinner 25 DM. New nomination: more reports please.*

Hotel Hanseatic — *Tel* (040) 48 57 72
Sierichstrasse 150 — *Telex* 213165 HANSE
Hamburg 60

A select little 12-bedroom hotel, said to be Hamburg's smallest, in a residential area just north of the big Alster lake, between the city centre and the airport. The personal atmosphere created by owner/manager Wolfgang Schüler is "like that of a private house", and it is not surprising that some film, theatre and opera people visiting Hamburg prefer to stay here rather than at the larger and more expensive *Vier Jahreszeiten* (q.v.). Herr Schüler spends much of his time cosseting his guests and keeping all spick and span, in this pink-fronted patrician villa that he has converted with great taste: well-chosen paintings and furniture in the very comfortable bedrooms. His breakfasts, including the breads and marmalades that he makes himself, are wonderful and he serves them personally in a high style verging on the camp. "We now have a fitness room and sauna - my dreams become reality," he writes this year. Small garden, too. (*J and KA*)

Open All year.
Rooms 2 suites, 10 double – all with bath and shower, telephone, radio and TV; babysitting on request.
Facilities Lounge/bar, breakfast room; fitness room and sauna. Small garden. Alster lake and city park both 2 blocks away. English spoken.
Location In Winterhude, 4 km N of city centre. Parking in street, but difficult.
Restriction Not suitable for ♿.
Credit cards Access, Amex, Diners.
Terms Rooms: single 140 DM, double 160 DM, suite 220 DM. Breakfast 18 DM. Children under 12 sharing parents' room free. (No restaurant.)

Hotel Prem — *Tel* (040) 24 54 54
An der Alster 9, Hamburg 1 — *Telex* 2163115

A smallish and elegant hotel, fairly expensive and recently renovated, facing the Alster on its eastern shore, a mile from the city centre. Rooms vary in size: some look over the lake, some over gardens and those facing the street can be noisy. Courteous and efficient staff, good breakfasts; the hotel's French restaurant, La Mer, *is reputed. 48 rooms, all with bath and shower. B&B double 220-290 DM* [1987]. *No recent reports: more welcome.*

Hotel Vier Jahreszeiten *Tel* (040) 3 49 41
Neuer Jungfernstieg 9-14 *Telex* 211629
Hamburg 36 *Reservations* in UK: (01) 583 3050
in USA (800) 341 8585

This superlatively gracious hotel for all seasons stands on a quay of Hamburg's gracious inner lake, the Alster. Founded in 1897, it has no connection with the other Vier Jahreszeiten hotels (e.g. in Munich), being privately owned and still run by the Haerlin family who have carefully amassed its antique furnishings over the years. "Despite its splendour, it is somehow totally unpretentious." "Although fairly large, with conference facilities, it is neither bustling nor impersonal and has something of the calm atmosphere of a private club. The elegant rooms have antiques and splendid tapestries. Some, with balcony, look over the lake. Nice extras included a shoe-horn, and a thermometer for checking the bathwater – but you might well expect this at £90 a night." "Super-efficient German service dished up with a smile. Huge classy rooms with glittering chandeliers and gilt carved mirrors – all thoroughly plush and decadent. Best venison I've ever eaten – the restaurant (*Michelin* rosette) is one of Hamburg's best." The restaurant is beautiful, in a modern style; so is the *Konditorei Condi* that serves light lunches. (*Gitta Sereny, K and S M-S, Harold Philpot*)

Open All year.
Rooms 11 suites, 69 double, 95 single – all with bath and shower, direct-dial telephone, radio and TV.
Facilities Lounge, 2 bars, tea-room, restaurant and grill; conference facilities; night club, barber's shop, wine shop. English spoken.
Location Central, on W side of Alster lake. Parking.
Restriction Not suitable for ♿.
Credit cards All major cards accepted.
Terms Rooms: single 230-295 DM, double 335-425 DM, suite 545-930 DM. Set lunch/dinner 60-80 DM; full alc 60 DM.

HEIDELBERG 6900 Baden-Württemberg — Map 13

Hotel zum Ritter St Georg *Tel* (06221) 2 02 03 and 2 42 72
Hauptstrasse 178 *Telex* 461506 RITHD

In the main street of the old town (pedestrian zone: car access difficult), this 1592 building has an ornate five-storey Renaissance facade, much-photographed, and it delights lovers of the olde-worlde picturesque. International tour groups frequent it heavily. Some rooms are splendid (e.g. vaulted ceilings), others less so. Good restaurant. 36 rooms, most with bath or shower. B&B double 145-250 DM.

HINTERZARTEN 7824 Baden-Württemberg — Map 13

Pension Hotel Sassenhof *Tel* (07652) 15 15
Adlerweg 17

A very attractive and friendly hôtel garni, *in a stylish resort high in the Black Forest, popular alike with skiers and walkers. Comfortable, flower-filled, well furnished; swimming pool, sauna, garden; lavish breakfasts. Several good restaurants nearby. 22 rooms, all with bath or shower. Double room 116-156 DM. New nomination: more reports welcome.*

HOHENAU 8351 Bayern — Map 13

Romantik-Hotel Bierhütte — *Tel* (08558) 3 15
Bierhütte 10 — *Telex* 57446 BIERH

In the hilly Bavarian Forest, north of Passau near Czech border, this former glassworks and brewery is now a very attractive inn, modern but folksy. Extrovert owner, pretty waitresses, good local dishes. Rooms in annexe have balcony; 29 rooms, all with bath or shower. B&B 45-90 DM; full alc 40-50 DM.

HORBEN-LANGACKERN 7801 Baden-Württemberg — Map 13

Hotel zum Engel — *Tel* (0761) 2 91 11

High up in a Black Forest village ten kilometres south of Freiburg, this traditional inn lies close to the valley station of the cable car up to the Schauinsland heights. "Food excellent, staff friendly and efficient," runs a recent report. Earlier ones: "Everything very clean and well kept. Salmon trout brought to table by Herr Hagenmeier before being cooked; superb béarnaise sauce. A good centre for walking or trout fishing." A visitor arriving late on a Friday was given a warm welcome and a "sumptuous" dinner at 10 pm, but the next night found the place crowded out with local private parties, so recommends avoiding weekends. More reports please.

Open All year except 12 Jan–12 Feb. Restaurant closed Mon.
Rooms 27 – some with shower; some with telephone; some with balcony.
Facilities Bar, restaurant. Garden and terrace. Winter sports, walking.
Location 10 km S of Freiburg. Garage.
Credit cards All major cards accepted.
Terms [1987 rates] B&B: single 40-70 DM, double 76-140 DM; full board 80-110 DM per person. Alc meals (excluding wine) 26-53 DM.

IMMENSTAAD AM BODENSEE 7997 Baden-Württemberg — Map 13

Strandcafé Heinzler — *Tel* (07545) 62 88
Strandbadstrasse 10

"Not a café, but a charming little lakeside hotel/restaurant, lively and unpretentious – a modern chalet built in traditional style, with long wooden balconies, in one of the most attractive smaller resorts on Lake Constance. It is run with aplomb by a large family of large Swabians, the Heinzlers, and in late July it was packed with holiday-makers come for the excellent local cooking, modestly priced. We sat under chestnut-trees on the wide terrace by the lake, watching the pleasure-boats, the multi-coloured windsurf-sails and the sunset glowing on the Swiss pre-Alps, as we enjoyed fresh fish from the lake (*Felchen* – dace) in a subtle mustard sauce, and a full-bodied tawny-gold Hagnau Spätburgunder from nearby vineyards. In the bedroom areas, the decor is 'superior rustic kitsch' – painted cupboards, folksy giant candles, old farm implements, etc. Our room was quite comfortable, though slightly ramshackle. The Heinzlers seem to put the accent on the food, rather than on household neatness – unusual for Swabia. But the buffet breakfast was good, and we'd gladly return." (*JA and KA*)

Open All year.
Rooms 3 suites, 16 double – all with shower and telephone; suites have cooking facilities.
Facilities Salons, restaurants; sauna. Garden terrace with café.
Location On lake, 1 km W of centre of Immenstaad which is 10 km W of Friedrichshafen. Parking.
Terms [1987 rates] B&B: double 60-95 DM, suite 120 DM. Alc lunch/dinner (excluding wine) 17.50-48 DM.

ISMANING 8045 Bayern — Map 13

Hotel Fischerwirt — *Tel* (089) 9 61 53
Schlossstrasse 17

In an attractive commuter town on the northern edge of Munich. A typical modern German inn, clean friendly and efficient, set back in a quiet courtyard. Nice lounge, small garden; lavish breakfasts; useful restaurant. Closed 2 weeks Christmas/New Year. 44 rooms, most with bath or shower. B&B 35-74 DM [1987]. No recent reports: send us some, please.

KETTWIG 4300 Nordrhein-Westfalen — Map 13

Hotel Schloss Hugenpoet — *Tel* (02054) 60 54
August-Thyssen-Strasse 51

"It continues to be one of our favourite stopping-off points in Germany," runs a recent report from regular visitors to this stately, moated 16th-century castle. It stands on the banks of the river Ruhr in a wooded valley, yet is close to the Ruhr industrial conurbation. It is within the borders of Essen (Germany's fifth largest city) but 11 kilometres from its centre and just outside the residential suburb of Kettwig (where you should visit the Krupp family mansion, now a museum; also, in downtown Essen, the Folkwang Museum of local history – both provide poignant reminders of the splendours and horrors of the Ruhr's mighty past). "Fresh flowers in our room, and fresh fruit including a fresh strawberry in January. The hotel and restaurant cater for meetings and functions but this did not intrude during our stay. Our room was large, well furnished with antique pieces. There is a very grand entrance hall/lounge area with a magnificent black marble staircase. The main attraction is the restaurant – a rosette in *Michelin*. The food is French, superbly cooked and presented." (*Kate and Steve Murray-Sykes, and others*)

Open All year. Restaurant closed 24 Dec.
Rooms 1 suite, 13 double, 5 single – 18 with bath and shower, 1 with shower – all with telephone, radio and mini-bar; doubles have TV.
Facilities Lift. Large hall, salon, wine cellar, restaurant; conference facilities; chapel for weddings and christenings; terrace. Large grounds with tennis court.
Location 11 km SW of Essen off A52, near A2 and A3 motorways. Parking.
Restriction Not suitable for ♿.
Credit cards All major cards accepted.

Terms B&B: single 150-225 DM, double 210-330 DM, suite 360 DM. Set lunch/dinner 50-80 DM; full alc 100 DM. Reduced rates for children sharing parents' room.

KÖNIGSTEIN IM TAUNUS 6240 Hessen — Map 13

Hotel Sonnenhof — *Tel* (06174) 29 08
Falkensteinerstrasse 7-9 — *Telex* 410636

Visitors on business to little-loved Frankfurt might well prefer, if they have a car, to stay in one of the pleasant resorts in the Taunus mountains, rather than at one of the city hotels, mostly over-priced. Königstein is a mere 20 minutes' drive, though more at rush hour. It is a small town in the foothills, just below a ruined feudal fortress, and here the *Sonnenhof* stands attractively on a hill in its own 20-acre park, with giant trees – a big Victorian hunting-lodge, spacious and gracious, well converted, rather grand in an old-fashioned way. It used to belong to Baron Rothschild. "We were affably received and served a nice breakfast amid the German upper crust," runs a report this year. Earlier ones: "Smart, with good but not outstanding food; notable desserts." "My small bedroom was in a modern annexe with pleasant view of the park from the balcony." (*James Shorrocks, Jenny Towndrow, Kate and Steve Murray-Sykes*)

Open All year.
Rooms 24 double, 21 single – 40 with bath and shower, all with telephone, radio, and TV. 20 in annexe. 9 ground-floor rooms.
Facilities Hall, salon, bar, restaurant; function rooms; heated indoor swimming pool, sauna, solarium; sun terrace. Large park with gardens and tennis. Königstein spa and therapy centre nearby. English spoken.
Location On edge of town which is 23 km NW of Frankfurt.
Credit cards Amex, Diners.
Terms B&B: single 100-129 DM, double 136-212 DM; dinner, B&B: single 133-162 DM, double 202-278 DM; full board: single 155-184 DM, double 246-322 DM. Set lunch 35 DM, dinner 60-80 DM; full alc 80 DM. Reduced rates and special meals for children.

KRONBERG IM TAUNUS 6242 Hessen — Map 13

Schlosshotel Kronberg — *Tel* (06173) 70 11
Hainstrasse 25 — *Telex* 415424 SHLO

This vast grey towered and gabled *Schloss*, eminently Victorian, was built for Queen Victoria's eldest daughter after the death of her husband, Kaiser Friedrich III. It is now a classy hotel (though still sometimes also used privately by visiting royalty) and in its grounds is an 18-hole golf course. It is no more expensive than the leading hotels in down-town Frankfurt, 17 kilometres away. "Our bedroom overlooking the beautiful grounds was lovely, with a less impersonal feel than in many grand hotels," is this year's comment by returning regulars. "The main rooms are imposing, with wood panelling and huge tapestries. Bedrooms on the lower floors tend to be larger and grander, but upper ones could be quieter. Staff are polite and efficient; the dining rooms are attractive and the food good but nothing special." (*S and K M-S*)

Give the Guide positive support. Don't just leave feedback to others.

Open All year.
Rooms 5 suites, 20 double, 29 single – most with bath and/or shower, all with telephone and TV; some with radio.
Facilities Lounge, lounge/bar, 2 restaurants; functions facilities; casino. "English" park with 18-hole golf course. English spoken.
Location 15 minutes' walk from the centre of Kronberg. Parking.
Restriction Not suitable for ♿.
Credit cards All major cards accepted.
Terms B&B: single 210-235 DM, double 320-365 DM, suite from 485 DM. Set lunch/dinner 50-125 DM; full alc 100 DM. Special meals for children on request.

LIESER-AN-DER-MOSEL 5550 Rheinland-Pfalz — Map 13

Hotel Mehn "Zum Niederberg" — *Tel* (06531) 60 19
Moselstrasse 1-2

A sturdily-gabled little roadside hotel in the Mosel valley, new to the Guide this year: "A charming, neat little village buried in vineyards, just three miles from picturesque but busy Bernkastel. The *Mehn* is unpretentious, comfortable and inexpensive: we liked its quiet simplicity and its lovely setting on one of the more peaceful stretches of the Mosel. Dinner, taken outdoors, was ambitious rather than a triumph, but breakfast was one of those sumptuous buffets that goes on and on. Most other guests were clearly walkers who have been coming for years." (*Dr F Peter Woodford*)

Open All year except 17 Dec-31 Jan.
Rooms 9 suites, 18 double, 6 single – most with shower, WC and telephone. Suites in annexe 20 metres from main building with TV and tea-making facilities.
Facilities 2 restaurants, TV room; terrace; sauna. Wine tasting. Fishing in the Mosel. English spoken.
Location Central; village is 4 km W of Bernkastel, upstream.
Restriction Not suitable for ♿.
Credit cards None accepted.
Terms B&B: single 33-50 DM; dinner, B&B 10 DM per person added to B&B rate; full board 20 DM added. Set lunch 12-25 DM; full alc 25 DM. Reduced rates and special meals for children.

LIMBURG AN DER LAHN 6250 Hessen — Map 13

Hotel Zimmermann — *Tel* (06431) 46 11
Blumenröderstrasse 1 — *Telex* 0484782

Dull looking from outside, but inside richly furnished with antiques, this modern hotel behind the station is only a short walk from Limburg's picturesque old quarter and hilltop Gothic cathedral. Prices moderate, service very thoughtful; dinner for residents only. 30 rooms, all with bath and/or shower, 90-168 double [1987]. *No recent reports: more welcome.*

LINDAU IM BODENSEE 8990 Bayern — Map 13

Bayerischer Hof — *Tel* (08382) 50 55
Seepromenade — *Telex* 54340

A large, smart hotel on the front, facing the harbour, in this picturesque old island-town that was for five centuries a Free Imperial City and is now Lake

Constance's sleekest resort. Rooms are quiet, and even small ones may have lake views. Lovely flower-girt swimming pool. Good fish dishes at the restaurant with its terrace open to the lake. Open Easter–Oct. 95 rooms, all with bath or shower. B&B double 168-296 DM. Set meals 35-70 DM. Few recent reports: more welcome.

MANDERSCHEID 5562 Rheinland-Pfalz **Map 13**

Hotel Zens *Tel* (06572) 7 69
Kurfürstenstrasse 35

A pleasant hotel on the main road of an old village in the southern part of the wooded Eifel massif, close to some ruined castles. A 19th-century coaching-inn, still run by the same family, it has several lounges, a big garden, lovely courtyard and indoor heated swimming pool. Comfortable rooms, good food. Closed 5 Jan–25 Feb, 9 Nov–19 Dec. 46 rooms, 26 with bath or shower. B&B double 70–160 DM. No recent reports: more welcome.

MEERSBURG 7758 Baden-Württemberg **Map 13**

Hotel-Gasthof zum Bären *Tel* (07532) 60 44
Marktplatz 11

Meersburg is the prettiest town on Lake Constance: it has half-timbered houses, a romantic old castle and a newer pink baroque castle, crowded together in the *Altstadt* on a hill above the lake. Here in the lovely market square is the *Hotel-Gasthof zum Bären*, a stunning old building with flower-pots and carvings on its quaint corner-tower, an inn since the 17th century. Visitors have admired the beamed ceilings, the Alpine furniture and the charm of the owners, the Gilowsky-Karrer family. "A spacious, comfortable room facing the square, with a charming sitting-alcove *in* the quaint old tower." "*Gemütlich* and friendly; food homely but good." "Everything delightful, including room, view, meals and attention by the staff. Fish wonderfully prepared." Be warned that the stairs are fairly steep and there is no lift; also the quieter back rooms lack a view. (*JA and KA, DR Brumley, Ronald A Lennon*)

Open 15 Mar–10 Nov. Restaurant closed Mon.
Rooms 13 double, 3 single – all with shower.
Facilities 2 restaurants. Sailing and windsurfing on the lake. English spoken.
Location Central (back rooms quietest). Parking and garages.
Restriction Not suitable for ♿.
Credit cards None accepted.
Terms B&B: single 50 DM, double 84–98 DM. Set lunch/dinner 22–32 DM; full alc 40 DM. Extra bed for child in parents' room 20 DM; special meals.

MUNICH 8000 Bayern **Map 13**

Gästehaus Englischer Garten *Tel* (089) 39 20 34
Liebergesellstrasse 8
Munich 40

Hard to find but well worth the effort, this small medium-priced bed-and-breakfast hotel is only four kilometres from the city centre, yet idyllically rural. It is a creeper-covered 18th-century millhouse, beside a stream at the edge of the big Englischer Garten and on the eastern fringe at Schwabing. Thick carpets, antiques, a quiet garden by the stream and a pretty rustic breakfast room, complete the picture. The place is much frequented by artists and writers, who book months ahead. "Irene Schlüter-Hübscher runs it as a family concern. In summer you can enjoy a generous breakfast in the secluded garden with a view of the park, which you can also explore on a bicycle loaned by the hotel. The house has atmosphere and the rooms are cosy: but if you want a lift, ask for a room in the annexe 50 metres down the road, where all rooms have their own kitchen." (*John David Morley; endorsed this year by Dr F Peter Woodford, Alison Patey*)

Open All year.
Rooms 1 suite, 21 double, 5 single – 20 with bath, 1 with shower, all with telephone and TV; radio on request. 15 with kitchenette (some on ground floor) in annexe (with lift) across road.
Facilities Breakfast room; terrace. Small garden by stream. Small lake 5 minutes' walk. English spoken.
Location On W edge of Englischer Garten, 6 minutes' walk from Metro. By car, approach from Leopoldstrasse, not Mittlerer Ring. Parking.
Credit cards None accepted.
Terms Rooms: single 74–126 DM, double 99–172 DM, suite 152–172 DM. (No restaurant.)

Marienbad Hotel *Tel* (089) 59 55 85
Barerstrasse 11, Munich 2

Friendly and serviceable little bed-and-breakfast hotel, centrally and quietly located near Alte Pinakothek. Good breakfasts, clean rooms, but no frills or graces. A bit too basic? More reports please. Closed 3 weeks Christmas/New Year. 27 rooms, most with shower. B&B 60-90 DM.

Gästehaus Monopteros *Tel* (089) 29 23 48
Oettingerstrasse 35, Munich 22

An American reader this year endorses our entry for this "very friendly and unpretentious little *pension*", only two kilometres from either the city centre or Schwabing, and next to the southern end of the Englischer Garten ("Monopteros" is the name of a Greek-style temple in the Garten). An earlier account: "It is run with a warm personal touch by exuberant Frau Kellenbach who puts fresh flowers in the bedrooms each Saturday. She has installed a public mini-bar on the main landing, with wine and soft drinks in a fridge, and trusts her guests to sign their names for what they take. Her copious breakfasts are excellent, too. My little room, with TV set and bright lamps for reading, was incredible value in this expensive city. Hot baths down the corridor, for no extra charge. The only snag: front rooms suffer from tram noise. Good Yugoslav and Bavarian restaurants within 200 metres." (*Pamela Pierce, JACA*) Essential to book.

Open All year.
Rooms 8 double, 3 single – 3 with shower, all with TV.
Facilities Breakfast room. Some English spoken.

Location Adjoining Englischer Garten, near *Hilton Hotel*. Residents' parking permits supplied (free) by hotel.
Restriction Not suitable for ♿.
Credit cards None accepted.
Terms B&B: single 47 DM, double 88–122 DM. (No restaurant.)

Hotel an der Oper *Tel* (089) 22 87 11
Falkenturmstrasse 10 *Telex* 522588
Munich 2

Useful modernised bed-and-breakfast hotel in side-street off fashionbable Maximilianstrasse; much used by Opera-goers; very central. French restaurant, La Bouillabaisse, *in same building. Closed at Christmas. 54 rooms, all with bath, B&B 87.50-140 DM.*

Hotel am Sendlinger Tor *Tel* (089) 23.18.80
Blumenstrasse 40

Brand new and very central, on Inner Ring. Bed-and-breakfast only; comfortable rooms, some with solarium. Moderate prices. Indoor garage. 33 rooms, all with bath and shower. B&B 52.50-125 DM [1987].

Trustee Parkhotel *Tel* (089) 51 99 50
Parkstrasse 31, Munich 2 *Telex* 5218 296 TRUP

Brand-new upper-medium-priced hotel, west of city centre and close to main station, exhibition centre and Theresien park (where Oktoberfest is held). Very quiet, built around its own courtyard. Simple evening meals. Garage. 36 rooms, all with bath, many with balcony and/or facing garden. B&B double 185-270 DM. New nomination: more reports welcome.

MÜNSTER-HILTRUP 4400 Nordrhein-Westfalen Map 13

Waldhotel Krautkrämer *Tel* (02501) 80 50
Am Hiltruper See *Telex* 892140 WALDH

This attractive family-owned hotel stands on the edge of a small lake six kilometres south of the historic city of Münster, Westphalia's former capital. It is not far from the Hamburg-Cologne motorway, and a good base too for exploring the *Wasserburgen* country (these "water castles" were built in the Middle Ages surrounded by moats or ponds, and later turned into residences). "The hotel is a large chalet-style building, quite modern from the outside but with traditional and antique furniture inside. The atmosphere is peaceful, personal and cosy and the staff are very welcoming and efficient. Our pleasant bedroom had a picture window and balcony overlooking the lake. The dining room, with the same view, was both elegant and comfortable, with soft lighting and lots of plants and flowers. Dinner (*Michelin* rosette) was good quality but not cheap: lobster in champagne sauce and fresh duck served in two sections, one with honey sauce, one with green pepper sauce. Lavish breakfast buffet. Large indoor swimming pool, and an open-air one within walking distance." (*Steve and Kate Murray-Sykes*)

Open All year, except 23-26 Dec.
Rooms 3 suites, 44 double, 28 single – 47 with bath and shower, 28 with shower only, all with telephone, radio, TV, baby-listening.
Facilities Lift. Salon, bar, dining room; conference room; indoor heated swimming pool and sauna. Garden with terrace and tennis court; bicycles available to hotel guests.
Location 8 km S of Münster.
Terms Rooms: single 165–220 DM, double 200–270 DM, suite 370–420 DM. Breakfast 18 DM. Set lunch/dinner 40–130 DM; full alc 100 DM. Reduced rates and special meals for children.

NUREMBERG 8500 Bayern — Map 13

Hotel Am Schönen Brunnen — *Tel* (0911) 22 42 55
Hauptmarkt 17

Bed and breakfast hotel on second floor of office block, with entrance on Nuremberg's main square directly opposite one of the city's glories, the Beautiful Fountain, from which the hotel takes its name. Only the breakfast room faces the square; bedrooms are on the side of a quite busy street, but have double glazing. Reasonable prices, rooms and bathrooms well-maintained and spacious, owners friendly. And no other hotel in Nuremberg is so central. 25 rooms, most with bath or shower. B&B double 100–140 DM. New nomination: more reports please.

Burghotel — *Tel* (0911) 20 44 14
Lammsgasse 3 — *Telex* 623567 BURG

This newcomer is "in the old town, below the castle and very near the Albrecht Dürer House which escaped wartime damage. It has a *gemütlich* quality and is obviously popular. Some rooms are on the small side, but cosy. Breakfast is plentiful and good, served in a room with a marked Bavarian decor where you can also take a drink in the evening. There is a small swimming pool and bar in the basement, decorated in tropical style (with temperature to match). No restaurant, but the nearby *Südhaus* is famous for its Franconian food. The *Burghotel* has a small annexe 600 metres away." (*Eileen Spencer*)

Open All year.
Rooms 4 suites, 26 double, 15 single – all with bath, telephone, radio and TV. Some ground-floor rooms.
Facilities Lift. Bar, breakfast-room; terrace; indoor heated swimming-pool, sauna. English spoken.
Location Central, 500 metres from Hauptmarkt. Garage and parking.
Credit cards All major cards accepted.
Terms B&B: single 85 DM, double 120–130 DM, suite 150–170 DM. (No restaurant.)

OBERAMMERGAU 8103 Bayern — Map 13

Gasthof "Zur Rose" — *Tel* (08822) 47 06
Dedlerstrasse 9

"The little town of the Passion Play (next performed in 1990) is unashamedly touristy, with every other shop a *Holzschnitzerei* selling wood-carvings, mostly of a religious or religiose character. But it is also the setting for the major cross-country König Ludwig marathon each February, and is becoming popular as a *Langlauf* resort in winter and for walking holidays in summer. Among its amenities is an exceptionally good swimming-pool complex. The "*Zur Rose*" (new to the Guide this year) "is the quintessence of the *gemütlich*. It has the lowest *Michelin* rating, promising a night's shelter, a snack and not much else, but in fact it's a fine example of a friendly Alpine inn and has been in the Stückl family for two generations. They speak good English and are warmly hospitable (see the Introduction, page 9). The rooms, well heated, are simple but not spartan. In the big attractive dining-room, meals are substantial meaty affairs; public rooms are full of fine furniture and old paintings (family heirlooms)."(*HR*)

Open All year except 2 Nov–15 Dec. Restaurant closed Mon.
Rooms 24 double, 4 single – 4 with bath, 2 with shower. 10 self-catering units for 2-6 people with shower, kitchenette, telephone and TV.
Facilities Salon, dining room. Garden. English spoken.
Location In town centre. Parking. Oberammergau is 19 km N of Garmisch.
Terms B&B: single 29 DM, double 54 DM; dinner, B&B 17 DM added to B&B rate. Set lunch 10-20 DM, dinner 15-30 DM; full alc 25 DM. Reduced rates and special meals for children.

OBRIGHEIM 6952 Baden-Württemberg — Map 13

Hotel Schloss Neuburg — *Tel* (06261) 70 01

A tall red-roofed Schloss *high in the trees above the Neckar river, with lovely views. Spacious rooms nicely furnished in local style. Excellent food. Conference facilities. Closed first two weeks January. 13 rooms all with bath or shower. B&B 47.50-70 DM. Full alc 60 DM. New nomination: more reports needed.*

OEVERSEE 2391 Schleswig-Holstein — Map 13

Historischer Krug — *Tel* (04630) 3 34
An der B76 — *Telex* 22714 HISTO

Just south of Flensburg and near the Autobahn, this stylish modernised inn (one of the *Romantik Hotels* fraternity) might make a useful stopover on the journey from Hamburg to Copenhagen. It dates from 1519 and has been much patronised over the centuries by Danish royalty; many guests today are Scandinavian. Badly damaged in a fire in 1980, it has been carefully restored in local "rustic" style, with much use of reed-thatching and repro furniture; the pleasant bedrooms, in light Scandinavian style, are in annexes set quietly around a patio. Owned and run by the Hansen-Mörck family since 1815, it was voted "Schleswig-Holstein's loveliest inn" in 1984 and has been eagerly nominated for us this year: "A bustling, lively popular hotel with a warm personal welcome. Excellent bathrooms, with a profusion of quality towels. The cosy dining-room is hung with local paintings and engravings; food traditionally inspired, with some *nouvelle* touches and good local fish." (*Dudley Wilson*) Endorsed with reservations: "Much esteemed locally and run with terrific self-confidence, but some might find it a little pretentious and soulless. The ambitious restaurant has nice alcoves and does herring in many interesting ways". (*JA and KA*)

Open All year.
Rooms 2 suites, 43 double – all with bath and/or shower, telephone, radio and TV. Some ground-floor rooms.
Facilities Bar, 4 dining rooms; conference room; indoor swimming pool, sauna, whirl pool, beauty farm. Garden. Boating. English spoken. ♿
Location 9 km S of Flensburg on D 76. Leave *Autobahn* at Oeversee exit.
Credit cards All major cards accepted.
Terms B&B: single 69-79 DM, double 125-139 DM, suite 169-189 DM; dinner, B&B: 25 DM per person added; full board 50 DM added. Set lunch 17 DM, dinner 62.50 DM; full alc 40 DM. Reduced rates for children.

OFFENBURG 7600 Baden-Württemberg — Map 13

Hotel Sonne — *Tel* (0781) 7 10 39
Hauptstrasse 94

This industrial town is so near to Strasbourg, the Black Forest and the Frankfurt/Basel *Autobahn* that it makes a useful stopover. The *Sonne*, on its main street, is a typical small-town coaching-inn: the Schimpf-Schöppner family claim to have been running an inn here since 1350, and though much rebuilt in the 19th century, the hotel still has many much older antiques. Napoleon stayed here, and you are shown the pewter tureen he used. A visitor this year endorses this earlier picture: "Despite this weight of history, the *Sonne* is utterly unpretentious; no foyer, the front door leads straight into the big beamed *Stübe*, which today is very much a social centre. At its big round *Stammtisch*, elderly local worthies were tippling and speechifying in true German style, while we enjoyed sound Baden cooking and local wine from the Schimpfs' own vineyards. Our room was modernised, with good bathroom (some older rooms have more character, but lack baths). All excellent value." (*JA and KA; Harry Robinson*) "You can choose a room of the 18th or 19th century if you are an early arrival. We stayed in the new wing – very quiet and comfortable, but not such a delight for our antiquarian eyes." (*HC and Else Robbins Landon*)

Open All year. Restaurant closed Sat.
Rooms 2 suites, 14 double, 21 single – 7 with bath, 13 with shower, all with telephone; 1 with TV.
Facilities TV room, 2 dining rooms. English spoken.
Location Central; in pedestrian zone in old part of town. Parking.
Restriction Only restaurant suitable for ♿.
Credit cards Amex, Visa.
Terms B&B: single 44-48 DM, double 65-85 DM, suite 110-160 DM. Full alc 28 DM.

OPPENAU-RAMSBACH 7603 Baden-Württemberg — Map 13

Höhengasthof Kalikutt — *Tel* (07804) 6 02

High up in the Black Forest, with fine mountain views, this well-built modern chalet-style hotel stands to the west of the little resort of Oppenau on the old Strasbourg–Stuttgart main road, and is three miles up a winding road off the main highway. It has a heavily-beamed rustic interior, and a terrace for summer eating with glorious panoramic views. "Splendid food, *echte Deutsch*, in lavish helpings," runs one recent report, "and it's worth booking well ahead for one of the rooms with the best views, usually full." "The hiking trails, and the cuisine and marvellous appointments, make the place entrancing. Herr Schmiederer is thorough and gracious, and his wife speaks English." (*AJC Brennan, Lois and Arthur Hansen*)

Open All year.
Rooms 2 suites, 16 double, 6 single – all with shower, telephone, radio, TV and balcony.
Facilities Lift. Lounges, TV room, bar, dining room; conference room; sauna, solarium, games room; terrace-café. English spoken.
Location 4 km W of Oppenau which is 40 km E of Strasbourg.
Credit card Diners.
Terms B&B: single 42–55 DM, double 76–110 DM; dinner, B&B: single 58–70 DM, double 108–140 DM; full board: single 66–78 DM, double 124–156 DM. Full alc 26–54 DM. Reduced rates and special meals for children.

PEGNITZ 8750 Bayern — Map 13

Pflaums Posthotel — *Tel* (09241) 72 50
Nürnberger Strasse 14 — *Telex* 642433 PPP

An old posthouse in a small town between Bayreuth and Nuremberg, now a very stylish and fairly expensive hotel. It has been in the hands of the Pflaum family since 1707, but its Guide debut is dated 1988, amid fanfares: "If you like a country house style hotel with an international and musical flavour, this one is very much worth a detour, though during the Bayreuth Festival or the Nuremberg trade fairs it is hard to find a room there. One brother Pflaum is the charming manager of house and another is considered one of the best chefs in Germany (*Michelin* rosette). Pretty girls in *Tracht* serve delicious food in the two restaurants (kid and game are specialities). Drinks by the fire in winter with dense snow outside, and delicious strawberry cake for tea in summer, stay in the memory. A *Relais et Châteaux* place, but with more personal charm than some." (*John and Eileen Spencer; also HR*) Some rooms are in a modern block.

Open All year.
Rooms 25 suites, 25 double, all with bath and shower, telephone, radio and TV. 1 ground-floor suite.
Facilities Lounge, bar, 2 restaurants; indoor swimming pool, sauna. Garden.
Location 1 km SW of Pegnitz, 33 km N of Nuremberg.
Credit cards All major cards accepted.
Terms Rooms: single 105-210 DM, double 140-370 DM, suite 190-650 DM. Buffet breakfast 15 DM. Set lunch/dinner 30 and 130 DM; full alc 75 DM.

REICHENAU (Insel) 7752 Baden-Württemberg — Map 13

Romantik-Hotel Seeschau — *Tel* (07534) 2 57
Schiffslände 8

West of the city of Konstanz, Reichenau is a very pastoral low-lying island in the western part of the Bodensee, linked to the mainland by a causeway. In the Middle Ages it was a major monastic centre, and two glories survive from that time: the late 9th-century Carolingian church of St George (amazing wall paintings of c. 1000 AD), and the Romanesque abbey at Mittelzell. Today the island is given over to market gardening and tourism, and its best hotel is the *Seeschau*, a sturdy gabled building by the water's edge, run by the Winkelmann-Roser family for 60 years and new to the Guide this year: "A delightful small hotel in a lovely situation. Helpful staff, rooms a bit on the small side, food well deserving its *Michelin* rosette but not cheap. (*RM Sparkes*) Local vegetables and lake fish form the basis of many of the best dishes.

Open All year, except 1–25 Jan and 20 Oct–15 Dec. Restaurant closed Sun night and Mon.
Rooms 2 suites, 12 double – all with bath or shower, telephone and TV.
Facilities Salon, 2 restaurants; conference facilities. Garden, terrace. English spoken.
Location 10 km W of Konstanz. Reached by ferry or causeway. Parking.
Credit cards Access, Amex, Diners.
Terms [1987 rates] B&B: single 70-110 DM, double 130-160 DM. Suite 110 DM. Alc meals (excluding wine) 55-90 DM [*Winkelmann*] and 36-69 DM [*Kamin-Stube*].

RETTENBACH 8449 Bayern — Map 13

Kurhotel Gut Schmelmerhof — *Tel* (09965) 5 17
St Englmar–Rettenbach — *Telex* 996580

On the edge of a village in lovely hilly wooded country between the Danube and the Czech border. A large chalet-style building in the local genre (wood panelling, etc), much modernised, but run as a hotel by the Schmelmer family since 1630. Courteous staff; interesting restaurant with vaulted ceiling; heated pool, jacuzzi and sauna. 37 rooms, all with bath and shower. B&B double 104-141 DM. Set meals from 30 DM. No recent reports: more welcome.

ROTHENBURG OB DER TAUBER 8803 Bayern — Map 13

Hotel Eisenhut — *Tel* (09861) 20 41
Herrngasse 3-7 — *Telex* 61367

Enclosed within its 14th-century ramparts above the winding river Tauber, this famous old town of cobbled streets, fountains and tall gabled houses is as picturesque as any in Germany. It was badly bombed in the war, but has been faultlessly reconstructed. The famous old *Eisenhut* is very much in character with the town. As a hotel it is little more than 100 years old, but the four houses that form it date from the Middle Ages. It is in a superb old street leading off the market place, and has been developed as a luxury hotel in ways that enhance its historic nature. The public rooms are furnished with antiques and original paintings. It must be reported that the hotel, much in demand today with package tours, may be falling victim to its renown. Some recent visitors have been very satisfied. But there have been complaints of "garish bedroom decor" (hardly in keeping with the hotel's character) and one visitor found the food "very average". However, the owners tell us that they recently spent 1.5 million DM redecorating 30 rooms and putting marble in the bathrooms. They also stress that they take only "de luxe" groups. More reports please.

Open All year.
Rooms 4 suites, 56 double, 20 single – all with bath and/or shower, telephone and TV. 20 in annexe across road.
Facilities Lift. Lounge, piano bar, TV room, restaurant; conference room; terrace. Garden. English spoken.

Location Central (front rooms could be noisy). Parking. Rothenburg is 62 km S of Würzburg. *Warning:* town is closed to traffic Whit Sun and Mon 0900–1700 hours.
Credit cards All major cards accepted.
Terms B&B: single 150-165 DM, double 210-285 DM; dinner, B&B 50 DM added to B&B rate; full board 100 DM added. Full alc 75 DM. Children under 10 in parents' room free.

Hotel-Gasthof Glocke *Tel* (09861) 30 25
Plönlein 1 *Telex* 61381

Nominated this year as a cheaper and simpler alternative to our other entries in the town, and just as central: "For discriminating travellers who are not Package Tour Persons and prefer a quiet hotel off the tour circuit where one can meet the nationals, enjoy their traditional food and wine, and relax in comfortable and quiet rooms. The host and staff speak English and made us very welcome. They have their own vineyard and their red wine is excellent. So is the food and service." (*RMJ and FMJ*)

Open All year.
Rooms 21 double, 7 single – 10 with bath, 12 with shower, all with telephone; some with radio; TV on request.
Facilities TV room, 4 restaurants, wine-bar with wine tasting, children's games room; terrace. English spoken.
Location Central. See also under *Eisenhut* entry, above.
Restriction Not suitable for ♿.
Credit cards All major cards accepted.
Terms B&B 54-89 DM; dinner, B&B 25 DM added to B&B rate; full board 43 DM added. Set lunch 15-35 DM, dinner 20-45 DM; full alc from 37.50 DM. Reduced rates and special meals for children.

Hotel Goldener Hirsch *Tel* (09861) 20 51
Untere Schmiedgasse 16-25 *Telex* 61372

This old hostelry is not as picturesque as the *Eisenhut* (see above), but its prices are a little lower, and it too has plenty of character. It also has the better setting of the two, being built over the ramparts, with superb views of the deep valley below, from the dining room and some bedrooms. It has been renovated, elegantly if maybe too formally, in a style that is part château, part coaching inn. Several recent visitors have spoken well of the view, the antique furnishings and the hospitality, backing this earlier account: "Our spacious bedroom was well equipped, yet preserved a rustic touch. The food was a little disappointing, as so often in German hotels of this kind. But we enjoyed the view as dusk fell over the lovely wooded valley. In summer you can eat out on a flowery open terrace. Dignified old-style service." (*JACA; also John F Kozlowski Jr, Ruth Kaye, and others*)

Open All year except Dec and Jan.
Rooms 80 – 66 with bath or shower; most with telephone, radio and TV.
Facilities Lift. Salons, TV room, bar, restaurant *"Die Blaue Terrasse"*, café-restaurant on terrace; conference facilities. Garden.
Location Central, near the Weiberturm. Garage parking. *Warning:* town closed to traffic on Whit Sun and Mon 0900-1700 hours.
Credit cards All major cards accepted.
Terms [1987 rates] B&B: single 80-210 DM, double 145-260 DM. Reduced rates for children.

RÜDESHEIM-ASSMANNSHAUSEN 6220 Hessen — Map 13

Hotel Krone *Tel* (06722) 20 36
Rheinuferstrasse 10

An old Rhineside inn, dating from 1541, where many German writers have stayed and worked. It is now a sizeable hotel in two buildings: many bedrooms have balconies overlooking the gardens and river. "Don't be put off by the stags' antlers and gloom of the 19th-century furnishings in the main halls," writes one devotee this year. "The bedrooms are clean, new and well plumbed, with pretty views. The small swimming pool, surrounded by climbing roses, is the prettiest I have ever seen. The food was exquisite (a perfect classic veal dish), served by a helpful elderly waiter on the famous vine-shaded terrace above the river. Of the three concierges I met, one was drunk and the other almost rudely brusque – but how lovely to watch the westering sun in peaceful isolation!" (*FP Woodford*) Others too have heaped praise on the food, the wines, the vine-covered terrace, the river views, the garden and the pool, and the comfortable bedrooms.

Open 15 Mar–15 Nov.
Rooms 2 suites, 48 double, 32 single – 36 with bath, 12 with shower, all with telephone; some with TV; many with balcony. 55 in annexe. Some ground-floor rooms.
Facilities Lift. Salon, TV room, bar, restaurant; riverside terrace/restaurant; conference facilities. Garden with lawn and swimming pool. English spoken.
Location Central, on the Rhine. Front rooms are quietest. Parking.
Restriction Not suitable for ♿.
Credit cards All major cards accepted.
Terms Rooms: single 40–95 DM, double 80–200 DM, suite 225 DM. Extra bed in room 25 DM. Breakfast 12 DM. Set lunch 38 DM, dinner 60–90 DM; full alc 55 DM.

ST BLASIEN 7822 Baden-Württemberg — Map 13

Hotel Sonnenhof *Tel* (07675) 5 01
Vorderdorfstrasse 58
St Blasien-Menzenschwand

"Suffering from jet-lag insomnia (we had flown from Texas), I awoke and stood on our balcony above the beautiful valley, all aglow in the moonlit mist, as the stream in front of the hotel whispered softly. A most peaceful place – and delicious and generous food." That was one recent report on this small family-run hotel in a quiet Black Forest valley, with many walking trails in the area. Others have liked it too: "An excellent restaurant where ravenous German walkers attack their food with the authority of a Mercedes diesel lorry. The particular glory of *Hotel Sonnenhof* is the joyial manager, Herr Wilhelm Jalowicki, who could not possibly be more helpful to his guests. His English is so idiomatic that he can make excellent puns in both languages." (*Sandra Martin*)

Open All year except mid-Nov–20 Dec.
Rooms 3 apartments, 24 double, 4 single – 8 with bath, 20 with shower, all with telephone and radio; TV on request.
Facilities Salon, TV room, restaurant; indoor swimming pool, sauna, solarium. Garden. Horse-riding nearby. English spoken.
Location 9 km NW of St Blasien, which is 62 km SE of Freiburg. Parking.

Restriction Not suitable for ♿.
Terms B&B: single 50-65 DM, double 130 DM; dinner, B&B 69-84 DM per person; full board 82-97 DM. Set lunch 20 DM, dinner 25 DM; full alc 30-50 DM. Weekly packages including ski parties 10 Jan–31 Mar. Reduced rates for children.

SCHARBEUTZ 2409 Schleswig-Holstein — Map 13

Kurhotel Martensen - Die Barke — *Tel* (04503) 71 17
Strandallee 123 — *Telex* 261445 KAMA

One of our few recommendations in this northern part of Germany, the *Martensen* is a typical seaside hotel. White-walled, red-roofed and well-modernised, with a new extension, it stands right beside the Baltic in a charming little family bathing resort. "The swimming pool with an ozone filtration plant was excellent, a really super swim in warm water. The prices of both meals and room were modest, the food, especially fish, was delicious, and the buffet breakfast of Holstein specialities made a good start to the day." The delights of Hanseatic Lübeck are only 15 kilometres away. (*Richard Whiting*)

Open Mar–Nov.
Rooms 15 single, 26 double – 7 with bath, 34 with shower, all with telephone; TV on request. 6 self-catering units.
Facilities Salons, reading room, library, games room, 2 restaurants; conference facilities; indoor heated swimming pool, sauna and massage. Access to fine sandy beaches. English spoken.
Location 15 km N of Lübeck, on the sea.
Restriction Probably not suitable for ♿.
Credit cards None accepted.
Terms B&B: single 75-90 DM; double 150-180 DM; dinner, B&B: 105-120 DM per person. Set lunch/dinner 15-35 DM; full alc 30-50 DM. Off-season reductions. Reduced rates for children.

SCHÖNWALD 7741 Baden-Württemberg — Map 13

Hotel Zum Ochsen — *Tel* (07722) 41 24 and 30 18
Ludwig-Uhland Strasse 18 — *Telex* 792606

Yet another Black Forest stunner – in this region where average hotel standards are arguably Europe's highest. It consists of a group of modern black-and-white chalet-like buildings, set amid rolling meadow-land backed by woods, between Triberg and Furtwangen. The interior decor is both spruce and folksy, in the local style, and the ambience at once informal and sophisticated – you can arrive in a rough old jersey with a rucksack, or dressed by Lagerfeld, and in either case feel at ease. "Just about the best hotel we have stayed in anywhere at any price – and here the charges are modest for what one gets," states one recent report. "The hotel is run with boundless enthusiasm by Horst Martin and his French wife – she speaks good English, too, and her welcome has to be experienced to be believed. He cooks – and we fed like kings from the table d'hôte. Our room was spotless and beautifully appointed. There's a heated swimming pool, and large garden with plenty of sun-loungers." (*Charles and Netta Mercer*) "Excellent local cooking, served by waitresses in Baden costume. I had lovely fresh trout in the patio, where they also do barbecues. In winter, the dining room has a log fire." (*KA*)

Open 15 Dec–10 Nov. Restaurant closed Tue and Wed to non-residents.
Rooms 2 suites, 32 double, 6 single – all with bath and/or shower, telephone and TV.
Facilities Salons, 3 restaurants; indoor heated swimming pool, sauna and solarium; table tennis. Large grounds with grill once a week in summer, terrace and tennis court, lake with fishing. Cross-country skiing in winter. English spoken.
Location 8 km S of Triberg. Hotel is central; garages and parking.
Restriction Not suitable for ♿.
Credit cards All major cards accepted.
Terms B&B: 50–86 DM; double 90–180 DM. Set lunch/dinner from 22 DM; full alc 50 DM. Reduced off-season rates; sporting, health and beauty weeks. Reduced rates and special meals for children.

SCHWARZWALD-HOCHSTRASSE 7580 Baden-Württemberg — Map 13

Höhen-Hotel Unterstmatt — *Tel* (07226) 2 04 and 2 09
Bühl

The Black Forest High Road winds along the high hillcrest from Freudenstadt to Baden-Baden, with wide views over the Rhine plain below. Several good holiday hotels are here: the *Unterstmatt*, by no means the smartest, is one of the most appealing. It's a family place, owned and run since 1905 by the Reymanns, and catering for families who come to ski in winter or hike in summer. Circled by deep pine forests, it has its own ski-slope (for beginners) rising from its back terrace: this is floodlit for night skiing and has a snow-machine using up to 100,000 litres of water a day. Bedrooms are simple, in rustic style, with bright colours; some have Baden painted wardrobe and four-poster. The lively cellar *Stübe* has harmonica music and once a month a pantomime. Joviality reigns: yet the food, starred in *Michelin*, is unusually good for a ski-hotel, pleasantly served by girls in pink dirndls. Superb local smoked ham served with kirsch and crispy country bread; good Baden white wines. "A warm and informal hotel in the best local tradition, with a breezy après-ski charm," says an inspector. (*KA, JA, Harry Robinson*) More reports, please.

Open All year except Nov. Closed Mon in summer.
Rooms 1 suite, 12 double, 6 single – 6 with bath, 9 with shower, all with telephone; TV on request.
Facilities Hall, rustic bar, restaurant. Music on Fri evening. Garden with terrace, lawn and ski lift. English spoken.
Location 15 km S of Baden-Baden.
Restriction Not suitable for ♿.
Credit cards All major cards accepted.
Terms [1987 rates] B&B: 50-80 DM; half board 20 DM added; full board 38 DM added. Reduced rates and special meals for children.

SEEG 8959 Bayern — Map 13

Pension Heim — *Tel* (083 64) 2 58
Aufmberg 8

Several correspondents in 1986/7 have endorsed earlier praise for this family-run private *pension* set on a small hilltop north of Füssen and the castle of Neuschwanstein. It has fine views of the Allgäu Alps to the south and over lakes and forests to the north; south-facing rooms have balconies. "Every superlative applies. A modern building in whitewashed Bavarian style. Herr Heim is a genial friendly host, breakfasts include eggs and cold meats, the rooms are spacious and there is a nice lounge." "Cooking simple but excellent." "Some bedrooms have furniture carved by Herr Heim himself, a real craftsman." As this is a private *pension*, menus offer no choice and the cooking is fairly plain. It is a quiet place and most guests are elderly. (*S and S Pons, BW Ribbons; also RM Sparkes and others*)

Open 20 Dec–1 Nov. Restaurant closed for lunch.
Rooms 14 double, 4 single – all with bath and shower, and telephone; some with balcony; TV on request.
Facilities Salon, restaurant; sauna, table tennis. Terrace and lawns.
Location On hilltop outside Seeg which is 15 km NW of Füssen.
Restrictions Not suitable for ♿. No children under 5.
Credit cards None accepted.
Terms B&B: single 47-52 DM, double 82-92 DM; dinner, B&B: single 57-62 DM, double 102-112 DM.

STUTTGART 7000 Baden-Württemberg — Map 13

Gaststätte zum Muckenstüble — *Tel* (0711) 86 51 22
Solitudestrasse 25
Stuttgart 31–Weilimdorf

Excellent Swabian cuisine served on garden-terrace (or in rustic Stüble) *at this sympathetic and unpretentious inn, a modern building in traditional half-timbered style. Ten kilometres west of city centre, between a quiet suburb and forests leading up to hilltop Schloss Solitude. Children's play area in garden. Closed three weeks July/August. 20 rooms all with bath and/or shower. B&B 44.50-52 DM. Few recent reports: more please.*

Hotel Royal — *Tel* (0711) 62 50 50
Sophienstrasse 35, Stuttgart 1 — *Telex* 722449

"Probably the most agreeable of the smarter hotels in downtown Stuttgart", this one is ten minutes' walk from the city's main tourist sights – the Schillerplatz, Neues Schloss, lovely Schlossgarten with its lake and swans, and James Stirling's exciting extension to the Staatsgalerie. "The *Royal* is somewhat functional, but well appointed in a modern style, with thick carpets, dark pine, soft lighting, and a general air of plushness. My room was well equipped and quiet (the hotel is in a side-street). The restaurant serves standard Swabian-cum-international dishes, carefully prepared, rather rich. For true Swabian cooking (probably Germany's best) at modest cost, try the *Stüble* of the *Zeppelin Hotel*." (*JACA*)

Open All year except 3 days at Christmas.
Rooms 2 suites, 30 double, 70 single – all with bath and shower, telephone, radio and TV.
Facilities Lift. Lounge, TV room, bar, restaurant; conference facilities. English spoken.
Location Central, near Österreicher-Platz. Limited parking.
Restriction Not suitable for ♿.
Credit cards All major cards accepted.

Terms Rooms: single 150–220 DM, double 230–250 DM, suite 250–280 DM. Breakfast 12.50 DM. Set lunch/dinner 20-35 DM; full alc 40–45 DM. Reduced rates and special meals for children.

TIEFENBRONN 7533 Baden-Württemberg — Map 13

Ochsen Post — *Tel* (07234) 80 30
Franz-Josef-Gall-Strasse 13

Tiefenbronn (its ancient Gothic church deserves a visit) is a big village near Pforzheim, at the heart of an exceptionally prosperous area devoted to jewellery-making. Here the *Ochsen Post* is suitably lavish and ornate – an old 17th-century inn, black-beamed and flower girt outside, opulently folksy inside, in the south German manner, and with modern comforts. "I enjoyed Dorothea and Theodor Jost's hospitality, also their seven-course meal for 98 DM [1987]. Tables were set for dinner with silver platters edged with gold, silver cutlery and crystal glass. The cosy bedrooms all have wooden beams, chintzy drapes and solid furniture; one has a four-poster honeymoon bed. A new cocktail bar does not fit in with the hotel's character: but on warm evenings you can sit in the courtyard with a cool beer." (*Brian Aisbitt, confirmed this year by AC Bourne*) "Irritatingly pretentious in some ways, but the food *is* first-rate and the welcome genuinely warm." (*Katinka Ardagh*) *Michelin* rosette for such dishes as carpaccio of beef with crab and caviar.

Open Feb–Dec.
Rooms 12 double, 7 single – 7 with bath, 12 with shower, all with telephone, radio and TV.
Facilities Lounge, bistro/bar, restaurant, winter garden. English spoken.
Location Leave Autobahn A8 (E52) at Heimsheim exit. Continue to Heimsheim and turn right at Tiefenbronn sign. Hotel is central; parking.
Restriction Not suitable for ♿.
Credit cards Amex, Diners.
Terms B&B single 69-98 DM, double 89-138 DM, suite from 138 DM. Set lunch 58 DM, dinner 78 DM.

TRIBERG IM SCHWARZWALD 7740 Baden-Württemberg — Map 13

Parkhotel Wehrle — *Tel* (07722) 86020
Gartenstrasse 24

Triberg is a famous watch- and cuckoo-clock-making centre, as well as a popular Black Forest skiing and hiking resort. The *Parkhotel*, in the town centre, is a fairly luxurious and sumptuously furnished old hostelry; it has been owned and run by the Wehrle/Blum family since 1707. Some rooms are in the old building, others in two more modern ones in a park to one side. Both have been enjoyed recently by visitors who also praise the cooking (*Michelin* rosette): "*Nouvelle cuisine* but with much better helpings than is usual with this kind of menu." Earlier reports: "Klaus Blum is a warm and civilised host and imparts a cultivated atmosphere; service is skilled and stylish, and the cuisine is excellent (20 ways with trout, a speciality). Delightful outdoor and indoor swimming pools. Many rather grand people come here for special occasions, such as groups of Arab sheikhs or Stuttgart tycoons." "Scrupulously managed in old-fashioned style but with plenty of space-age plumbing and a full complement of rest and recreation facilities." (*C and J Campari, Katinka Ardagh, Jonathan Williams*)

Open All year.
Rooms 58 double or suite, 2 single – 57 with bath and/or shower, all with direct-dial telephone, radio and TV. 20 in annexe.
Facilities Lounge, TV room, dining rooms, billiard room; conference room with projector and video. Indoor and outdoor heated swimming pools; sauna, solarium, massage. Large garden. English spoken.
Location Central, near market place (quietest rooms overlook garden). Parking.
Restriction Only dining rooms suitable for ♿.
Credit cards All major cards accepted.
Terms B&B: single 79–124 DM, double 138–232 DM. Set lunch 35 DM, dinner 49–67 DM; full alc 55 DM. 15% reductions in low season. Reduced rates and special meals for children.

TRIER 5500 Rheinland-Pfalz — Map 13

Petrisberg Hotel — *Tel* (0651) 4 11 81
Sickingenstrasse 11-13

The proud city of Trier has many claims to fame. Under the Emperor Diocletian it was the capital of Gaul (a lost grandeur evoked by the Porta Nigra, the finest Roman relic in Germany). It was also the birthplace of Karl Marx (his house is a museum) and is today the centre of the Mosel wine trade. One great merit of the *Petrisberg*, a modern family-run bed-and-breakfast place, is that it stands in a splendid position amid vineyards, high on a hill above the city with a view of the Roman ruins - and rooms facing the city have balconies. Approved again this year, it has recently drawn such comments as "easily the pleasantest hotel in town"; "superb, with magnificent rooms"; "personal service by the English-speaking owner"; and "first egg-and-bacon breakfast I've had on the Continent". (*DE Jennings, Ruth Kaye, and others*)

Open All year.
Rooms 3 suites, 30 double – all with bath or shower and telephone; many with balcony; radio and TV on request. 13 in annexe. 3 ground-floor rooms.
Facilities Salon, TV room, breakfast room, wine bar. Garden and terraces. Forest nearby. English spoken.
Location 20 minutes' walk from town centre (near Roman amphitheatre). Parking area and garages (4.50 DM).
Restriction Not suitable for ♿.
Credit cards None accepted.
Terms B&B: single 70 DM, double 100–105 DM, suite 150–160 DM. (No restaurant, but light evening meals available.)

TÜBINGEN 7400 Baden-Württemberg — Map 13

Hotel Krone — *Tel* (07071) 3 10 36
Uhlandstrasse 1 — *Telex* 7262762 KRON

"Solid, well-appointed and very comfortable", the leading hotel in this ancient university city is again commended this year: "Our enormous room, double-glazed to absolute silence, had a whole breakfast room of its own, entirely (including walls and *ceiling*) upholstered in linen and silk in that combination of dusky rose and apple-green inherited from medieval South German wall paintings. And the luxurious pink bathroom contained no fewer than 14 fluffy towels, for a one-night stay." Others, without encountering quite such splendour, speak of "an excellent family-run hotel of style and character, with very good food." As for student life, "on the Neckar, girls laze in punts in summer, as pretty as any on the Cherwell". (*Dr F Peter Woodford, GM Morrison, JA*)

Open All year except 22-30 Dec.
Rooms 5 suites, 15 double, 31 single – 48 with bath and/or shower, all with direct-dial telephone and TV.
Facilities Lift. Lounge, TV room, bar, restaurants. English spoken.
Location Central (windows are soundproofed), just S of main bridge over Neckar.
Credit cards All major cards accepted.
Terms B&B: single 108 DM, double 175 DM, suite 230 DM. Set meals from 25 DM. Reduced rates for children sharing parents' room; special meals.

WARTMANNSROTH-NEUMÜHLE 8781 Bayern — Map 13

Hotel Neumühle — *Tel* (09732) 80 30
Neumühle 54 — *Telex* 72559025 RZ

An unusual hotel in the north of Bavaria, just off the Würzburg–Fulda road: "A wonderful experience, and our most interesting find in years. It consists of a complex of half-timbered houses all joined together, including a swimming-pool, sauna etc, forming its own little 'village' on the banks of the Saar river. This fascinating collection of old buildings is furnished with genuine 17th–19th-century antiques, paintings, etc, which the owners spent ten years collecting. Most of the rooms are on two floors, so you feel you are staying in your own little maisonette: we had a sitting room with spiral staircase leading to the bedroom, and all mod cons discreetly hidden inside country-style antiques. The beamed houses, cobbled courtyards, rural views, sound of water from the mill-wheel, and the lovingly displayed antiques, add up to a harmonious ensemble. There are several dining rooms, all lovely to look at but informal, and an interesting choice of food – e.g. a soup of shrimps and quail egg, or boned duck with fruits, broccoli and rösti. The panelled breakfast room is pretty and cosy. The hotel provides rowing boats for use on the river. A lovely place for a few quiet days away from it all." (*Stephen and Kate Murray-Sykes*)

Open All year except 4–28 Jan.
Rooms 5 suites, 12 double, 9 single – all with bath and/or shower, direct-dial telephone, radio and TV. Ground-floor rooms.
Facilities Salons, breakfast room, restaurant; conference facilities; indoor swimming pool and sauna. Gardens with tennis. English spoken.
Restriction Not suitable for ♿.
Location 6 km W of Hammelburg.
Credit cards None accepted.
Terms Rooms: single 120-155 DM, double 175-200 DM, suite 200-300 DM. Breakfast 15 DM. Set dinner 35-50 DM; full alc 60 DM.

> Our italicised entries are different this year. There are more of them and they indicate hotels which are worth considering, but which, for various reasons – inadequate information, lack of feedback, ambivalent reports – do not at the moment warrant a fully entry. We should particularly welcome comments on these hotels.

WEIKERSHEIM 6992 Baden-Württemberg **Map 13**

Hotel Laurentius *Tel* (07934) 70 07
Marktplatz 5

Newly-opened hotel in old building beside the pretty market square, in attractive old town with Hohenlohe castle on river Tauber. Good food served in vaulted cellar; breakfast on flowery patio. Closed February. 12 rooms, all with bath or shower. B&B 40-70 DM. No recent reports; please send some.

WEITENBURG 7245 Baden-Württemberg **Map 13**

Hotel-Restaurant Schloss Weitenburg *Tel* (07457) 80 51

A large 16th-century castle on a hilltop, with sweeping views over the Neckar valley between Horb and Tübingen. Owned since 1720 by the Barons of Rassler, it is one of a number of such *Schlösser* in this area that have been turned into hotels by their baronial owners as the best way of keeping the family estates together. It is run by a manager, but the Baron still lives there and is much in evidence, a charming and cultivated man and a great hunter. He has sensibly kept the hotel in its original style, modernising only those aspects that need it (e.g. bathrooms). "He manages to give his customers the feeling that they really are guests in a private castle. The food is good, too." "Our bedrooms were sumptuously furnished with antiques, and the corridors were filled with beautiful chests." The hotel is in extensive grounds, with riding school, swimming pool and sauna. There is a balcony over the valley where you can have drinks and meals. The dining room is massive. (*KA, NEG*)

Open All year, except 23-25 Dec.
Rooms 1 suite, 18 double, 16 single – 13 with bath and shower, 18 with shower only, all with telephone and radio.
Facilities Lift. Hall, 4 lounges, bar, TV room, dining room; chapel for weddings and christenings; conference facilities; big balcony for drinks and meals. Large grounds with riding school, heated enclosed swimming pool, sauna and solarium. English spoken.
Location 12 km E of Horb; from A81 motorway take Rottenburg exit, drive 5-10 minutes in the direction of Ergenzingan then follow signposts to Weitenburg.
Credit cards Access, Diners.
Terms B&B: single 86 DM, double 150 DM, suite 200 DM; dinner, B&B: single 128 DM, double 234 DM, suite 284 DM. Set lunch/dinner 30-40 DM; full alc 60 DM. Special meals for children.

WERTHEIM 6980 Baden-Württemberg **Map 13**

Hotel Schwan *Tel* (09342) 12 78
Mainplatz 8

A turreted castle stands on the wooded slopes above this pretty town of half-timbered houses at the confluence of the Main and Tauber rivers, west of Würzburg. The *Schwan*, an attractive traditional inn in the main square, has received one brickbat this year from a reader who found his bed uncomfortable and the traffic noisy, but otherwise it is again praised, especially for its good food and friendly owners: "Gourmet fare in the unpretentious restaurant." "Comfortable room with excellent bathroom.

Good local wines and an interesting menu (some Franconian specialities) with delicious fish dishes." "Exceptionally helpful owners." (*Ann Marie and Frank Giraldi, Mr and Mrs Hervey C Merrill, and others*)

Open 15 Jan–15 Dec.
Rooms 20 double, 7 single – all with bath and/or shower and telephone; some with radio and TV. Some ground-floor rooms.
Facilities Bar, TV room, restaurant; conference room; large terrace. River nearby; fishing rights. English spoken.
Location Central; parking. Wertheim is 42 km W of Würzburg.
Restriction Not suitable for ♿.
Credit cards All major cards accepted.
Terms B&B: single 62-90 DM, double 80-145 DM; dinner, B&B: single 82-112 DM, double 130-185 DM. Set lunch/ dinner 15-39 DM; full alc 65 DM. Reduced rates for children; special meals.

WERTHEIM-BETTINGEN 6980 Baden-Württemberg — Map 13

Hotel-Restaurant Schweizer Stuben — *Tel* (09342) 43 51
Geiselbrunnweg 11 — *Telex* 689190 CHSTU

This spacious and luxurious new country hotel, built in chalet style, stands in a quiet village by the river Main, west of Würzburg. "Our room was large, very comfortable and well equipped, furnished in traditional style with painted country furniture. There are pleasant views of the river valley. Dinner in the *Schweizer Stuben* restaurant was superb, with modern and inventive food, well deserving its two *Michelin* rosettes; the hotel's other restaurant is country style, more informal and less expensive. Our gourmet breakfast, included in the room price, began with Bucks Fizz and went on to scrambled quails' eggs with smoked salmon. Expensive, but a good treat. There is a large tennis school, as well as swimming pool, saunas, etc." (*Pat and Jeremy Temple*)

Open All year. Restaurant closed 1–28 Jan.
Rooms 2 suites, 15 double – all with bath and/or shower, telephone, radio and TV. 8 in villa 100 metres from main building. 5 ground-floor rooms.
Facilities Salon, 2 restaurants; conference facilities. Garden with tennis park (indoor and outdoor court and school); swimming pool, sauna. English spoken.
Location 6 km E of Wertheim; 3 km from *Autobahn* (exit Wertheim).
Credit cards Access, Diners.
Terms B&B: single 195–295 DM, double 235–370 DM, suite 450–850 DM. Set meals: in *Schober* restaurant 39–58 DM, in *Schweizer Stuben* 150–175 DM.

HOTEL GANIMEDE, GALAXIDION

ATHENS **Map 17**

Herodion Hotel
4 Rovertou Galli Street
Makriyanni, Athens 11742

Tel (01) 9236832
Telex 219423 HERO

The cradle-city of Western civilisation hardly distinguishes itself by its hotels (just see how few entries we have). The Herodion *is at least above average: it is modern and impersonal but comfortable, clean and friendly, and has a useful location in a quiet street quite close to the Akropolis and the Plaka. Patio garden where drinks are served beneath the trees; roof terrace with views of Akropolis. 90 rooms, almost all with bath and shower, many with balcony. B&B double 7,700-11,100 drs. Set meals 1,800 drs. Back in Guide this year: more reports please, especially on the restaurant.*

Italicised entries are for hotels on which we need more feedback – either because we are short of reports or because we have had mixed or inadequate reports.

CHANIA Crete — Map 17

Hotel Contessa — *Tel* (0821) 23966 and 57437
Theofanous 15, Palio Limani

Many Cretophiles regard Chania as the most attractive town on the island, a fascinating mixture of Turkish and Venetian architecture. The *Contessa* will suit those who like to be at the centre of things. It is an old family house down by the harbour, carefully converted into a small bed-and-breakfast hotel, and now very popular. "We found it most welcoming, full of charm and atmosphere," says a visitor this year. Others too have stressed the courtesy of the owner and staff and the impeccable taste of all the decor and fittings. Don't miss the room with the painted ceiling! Booking essential.

Open 1 Apr–1 Nov.
Rooms 2 triple, 4 double – all with shower, telephone and radio; baby-listening on request. All in annexe.
Facilities Bar, breakfast room. Swimming pool at *Xenia* hotel nearby. 15 minutes' walk to beach. English spoken.
Location Overlooking old Venetian harbour; 1 km from town centre. Parking 150 metres.
Restriction Not suitable for ♿.
Credit cards Diners, Visa.
Terms [1987 rates] B&B: single 4,234 drs, double 5,650 drs, triple 6,624 drs. 10% reductions for children. (No restaurant.)

Hotel Doma — *Tel* (0821) 21772
124 El. Venizelou

"We were so pleased to find this oasis among the Benidormitories of Crete that we made a prolonged stay," wrote one grateful visitor to Irène Valiraki's recently renovated guest house a kilometre from the centre of town on the coast. The house, neo-classical in style, was once a British consulate. There are balustraded stairs leading to a terrace with fragments of broken statuary. All the rooms have a shower; some have a balcony overlooking Chania and the rocky seashore, though light sleepers should ask for a garden room, since the coastal road tends to get noisy after 7 am. It is a house of character, and the public rooms have many antiques and antiquities, old photographs, interesting pictures and suchlike. The breakfast room doubles as a bar in the evening and you can normally get drinks and hot snacks during the day; Greek and Cretan specialities are available on an à la carte menu in the evenings. A reader who spent a week this year found the food excellent but expensive and the service slow. Another has added: "Mme Valiraki was quite charming and her staff were obliging. The food was very good – a small variety of beautifully-cooked superior Greek dishes." (*Ms JAV Rose, Yvonne Warren*)

Open Mid-Mar–end Oct.
Rooms 1 suite, 26 double, 2 single – all with shower and telephone; some with balcony overlooking sea. Some ground-floor rooms.
Facilities Lift. Lounge, breakfast room/snack bar; terrace; laundry facilities. Garden, small rocky beach. English spoken.
Location 20 minutes' walk from town centre. Main beach 20 minutes' drive. Parking available near hotel. Buses stop directly outside.
Credit cards None accepted.

Terms Rooms: single 4,680 drs, double 5,090-8,250 drs, suite 12,000 drs. Breakfast 50 drs. Alc meals. 10% added to room rate for stays of less than 2 days 15 July–30 Sept.

FERMA Crete — Map 17

Coriva Village — *Tel* (0842) 61263
Ierapetra — *Telex* 262508 CORV

Not far from the port of Ierapetra, and just outside the village of Ferma, here is a hotel and not-too-large bungalow complex on the south coast of Crete where new hotels are sprouting fast. A recent visitor has liked it very much, especially the restaurant and large clean swimming pool. An earlier view: "It is quiet and many of the rooms are in bungalows surrounded by flowering shrubs. The beach is not impressive, but nearby are small secluded coves excellent for swimming." (*LR, Stephanie Sowerby*) More reports would be welcome.

Open March–Nov.
Rooms 42 double – 37 with bath, 5 with shower, all with telephone and air-conditioning. 11 in main house, 31 in bungalows with terrace.
Facilities Salon with TV, bar, taverna, restaurant. Lawns and swimming pool; private beach with water sports; Cretan evenings once a week. English spoken.
Location 8 km E of Ierapetra; 1 km from Ferma. Parking.
Restriction Not suitable for ♿.
Credit cards None accepted.
Terms [1987 rates] Rooms: single 3,500 drs, double 4,950 drs. Breakfast 450 drs. Set lunch/dinner 1,050 drs.

FIRA Santorini, Cyclades — Map 17

Atlantis Hotel — *Tel* (0286) 22232 and 22111
Telex 293113 ATRA

The volcanic island of Santorini is a striking crescent shape. You sail into a wide bay, thought to be the crater of a volcano which erupted in Minoan times, throwing up the spectacular cliffs of pumice and lava that surround the bay. The white-washed town of Fira is perched on the cliffs, 800 steps up from the harbour: you can ride up by mule or take a cable car. The *Atlantis Hotel* is perched above Fira: "We arrived in inauspicious circumstances. Our priority was sleep, but we were able to appreciate the large and spacious room. We also had a balcony almost as large as the room itself, with a stunning view of the town of Fira winding its way up the hillside, the clear blue sea and the island of Nea Kamani, the only live volcano in Greece. The hotel has an airy lounge with the same view, a helpful desk staff with tireless patience, and, best of all, an elegant facade with rows of white arches, visible from most of Fira." (*Susan de Mont*) One possible drawback: loud nocturnal music from the restaurant next door.

Open 1 Apr–31 Oct.
Rooms 19 double, 8 single – 6 with bath, 21 with shower, all with telephone; most with balcony.
Facilities Living room with TV, bar, breakfast room; meeting room; terrace. Beach 6 km.
Location Central. Parking.
Credit cards None accepted.

Terms [1987 rates] B&B: single 6,750-8,100 drs, double 9,300-11,250 drs. Breakfast 600 drs. (No restaurant.)

GALAXIDION Central Greece — Map 17

Hotel Ganimede — *Tel* (0265) 41328

An enticing discovery by two readers in 1987: an Italian-owned *pensione* in a small, ancient town on the Gulf of Corinth near Delphi. "The sort of place one dreams of finding in Greece but never does. Quiet, relaxed, informal, all-round idyllic. It is formed of two houses back-to-back, one a 19th-century captain's house, the other a modern facsimile of it, with a large garden-cum-patio in between – trees, flowers, comfortable chairs. Breakfasts, claimed to be the best in Greece (and probably they are), are served here. Rooms simply furnished, comfortable, dark and cool. Bruno Perocco, the owner, speaks good English." "If Bruno does not like the look of you, you will not get a room. In winter he runs courses on making icons. The British and American embassies have found the place, but he is careful to spread the nationalities." No restaurant, but *To Steki* and *To Galaxidi* are recommended among the harbourside tavernas. (*Peter Bowen, Gordon Wrigley*)

Open Apr–Oct.
Rooms 10 – some with bath or shower.
Facilities Bar, dining room. Garden and courtyard. 10 min walk to sea.
Location Central; Galaxidion is 33km SW of Delphi, via Itea and the coast road. Parking.
Credit cards None accepted.
Terms Rooms: double 3,330 drs. Breakfast 583 drs.

GEROLIMIN Peloponnesus — Map 17

Hotel-Restaurant Akrogiali — *Tel* (0733) 54204

Gerolimin (or Yerolimin), the "sacred harbour" of Mani, is a far cry from the commercialised Mykonos. It is here that a reader found the *Akrogiali*, overlooking the fishing boats tied up against the quay. "At night it is silent, except for the sea; clean bedrooms, all with balconies, breakfast on demand, delicious fresh fish – vegetables depend on when the travelling greengrocer arrives. You can swim from a pebbly beach in clear water right outside the hotel. Altogether 'unpretentious comfortable' – a centre from which to tour the Mani with its tower villages, crumbly medieval Byzantine churches and empty beaches." (*M Baron*) More reports please.

Open All year.
Rooms 14 double, 2 single – 6 with shower, all with balcony. 4 in old building next door to new one.
Facilities Bar, restaurant. English spoken.
Location On W coast of Mani peninsula. 50 km S of Gythion.
Restriction Not suitable for ♿.
Credit cards All major cards accepted.
Terms Rooms: single 1,300 drs, double 2,300 drs. Breakfast 250 drs.

> "... had all the ambience of a chiropodist's waiting-room without the charm."

HERMOUPOLIS Syros, Cyclades — Map 17

Hotel Vourlis — *Tel* (0281) 28440 and 23750
Mavrogordatou 5 — *Telex* 293206 MIT

Syros is in the centre of the Cyclades ("circle") islands, reached by boat from Piraeus or by air to Mykonos and then on by boat. The island itself has no special charm, but Hermoupolis (or Ermoupolis) is a picturesque town of predominantly neo-classical architecture with houses that rise tier after tier on the slopes of two hills. The *Hotel Vourlis* is a 19th-century mansion in this neo-classical style, transformed into what one reader calls a small, elegant hotel or guest house. It is owned by Alexandra Mavrogordatou Petritzh, a well-known Greek artist, and was strongly praised by a recent visitor: "A real oasis and sheer luxury. We were warmly welcomed and given two very elegant rooms in pink and blue, with lots of space and beautiful pictures. The bathroom was big, and we found chocolates and Metaxa brandy by the bed. Service was excellent and breakfast superb, including fruit salad and scrambled eggs." (*Antoinette and John Geake*). No restaurant, but snacks available. *Note:* Since we received the above report, the former Dutch managers have left and a new one, Nikolaos Halaris, has arrived: verdicts on his regime, please.

Open All year.
Rooms 1 suite, 5 double, 1 single – all with bath and/or shower and telephone. 3 ground-floor rooms.
Facilities Hall, lounge/breakfast room, bar. Small front garden and patio. 100 metres from shingle beach with safe bathing and fishing. Windsurfing, waterskiing, sailing, tennis and mini-golf nearby. English spoken.
Location Hermoupolis is capital of Syros, capital of the Cyclades. Daily boat connections from Piraeus and Rafina. Hotel is central. Parking.
Credit cards All major cards accepted.
Terms B&B: single 3,850-4,850 drs, double 5,200-6,700 drs, suite 6,150-8,350 drs. Reduced rates for children. (No restaurant, but snacks available.)

IA Santorini, Cyclades — Map 17

Atlantis Villas — *Tel* (0286) 71214 and 71236
Ia, Nr Fira — *Telex* 293179 ATVI

Near the northern tip of Santorini, by the sea at the edge of the village of Ia (or Oia), a young Athenian couple have tastefully restored a group of 20 island dwellings, some of them caves in the volcanic hillside, and equipped them as holiday homes, quite spacious, with kitchenettes and up-to-date bathrooms. Nice breakfasts. No restaurant, but tavernas in village. Open 15 Mar–31 Oct. 20 rooms, all with bath or shower. B&B double 14,280-16,224 drs. No recent reports: please send some.

KASTRON ILIAS 27050 Peleponnesus — Map 17

Hotel Chryssi Avgi — *Tel* (0623) 95224 and 95380
9 Loutropoleos

A new discovery, this simple C-class hotel near the western tip of the Peloponnese: it is run by a Frenchwoman who speaks (and writes to us in) perfect English and her Greek husband. It is an hour's drive from Patras or from Olympia and is close to Killini where boats leave for the lovely Ionian islands. "The hotel is small but has public rooms and a delightful shady garden for breakfast and drinks. The restaurant next door serves pizzas and good Greek food (hotel guests get a 10 per cent discount). Kastron is an attractive village dominated by a medieval Frankish castle, with superb views out to the Ionian isles. Excellent beach of golden sand two miles away." (*RJ Brown*)

Open End Apr–Mid-Oct.
Rooms 10 double – all with shower, WC and direct-dial telephone.
Facilities Bar, lounge, library. Terrace. Beach 3 km. English spoken.
Location 60 km SW of Patras towards Pyros.
Restriction Not suitable for ♿.
Credit cards None accepted.
Terms Rooms: single occupancy 3,000 drs, double 3,700-drs; with extra bed 4,500 drs. Breakfast 350 drs. Full alc 1,000 drs.

KORONI Peloponnesus — Map 17

Logga Beach Hotel — *Tel* (0725) 31583 amd 31165
Paliokabos
Logga 24010, Messinias

New to the Guide, this is a small modern family-run hotel just north of Koroni, a town with a Venetian castle at the south-east tip of the Messinian peninsula. "Still quite new and in some aspects a little amateurish, but Mr Drakopoulos and his family create a relaxed, friendly atmosphere. Meals are relatively simple but of a high quality. Most rooms face the sea which is just a few yards away (the hotel has its own small beach with views across the gulf to Mani). An extremely cheap place, good value." (*RJ Brown*) More reports welcome.

Open 1 Apr–end Oct.
Rooms 1 suite, 12 double, 2 single – all with shower and WC.
Facilities Lounge with TV, bar, restaurant. Garden; beach bar and restaurant. English spoken.
Location 1.5 km N of Koroni, on main road from Kalamata.
Restriction Not suitable for ♿.
Credit cards Some may be accepted in 1988.
Terms B&B: single 1,800-2,600 drs, double 2,600-3,600 drs, suite 4,700-5,400 drs. Full alc 1,000 drs. Reduced rates for children; special meals.

MONEMVASSIA Peloponnesus — Map 17

Hotel Malvasia — *Tel* (0732) 61323 and 61435

A characterful old hotel in an old town on the south-eastern corner of the Peloponnese, with a famous castle dating from the 6th century. "There is only one hotel inside Monemvassia, and it is completely in keeping with the rest of the old town, which has no wheeled traffic (car parking just outside the main gate) and which until recently was derelict. The hotel is several converted old houses with barrel-vaulted ceilings, low doors and small windows. My room was very spacious. The windows had mosquito screens but I was badly bitten. The sitting/dining area had comfortable chairs. The furniture was old, stripped pine style, and had been carefully chosen. I found it delightful but the place needed dusting. The shower and loo were standard Greek, which meant drenching floor, walls and towel. At night there was heavy quiet all around, and utter blackness. It was possible to get snacks in the hotel, but there are plenty of restaurants within a 100 yards or so. A charming hotel with a sense of history – delightful despite the midges and dust." (*Anne-Marie Sutcliffe*)

Open All year.
Rooms 6 double – most with shower. Also 5 furnished apartments.
Facilities Salon, breakfast room.
Location On SE coast of Peloponnesus, near the tip. Parking.
Terms [1987 rates] Double room 1,800 drs, suite 4,200-9,000 drs.

MYRINA Lemnos, Aegean Islands — Map 17

Hotel Akti Myrina — *Tel* (0254) 22681
Myrina Beach — *Telex* 297173 MYRI
Myrina 81400

Overlooking a bay just outside Myrina, the tiny capital of the lovely island of Lemnos, the *Akti Myrina* is a large, fairly luxurious and quite original holiday venture, long popular with readers (a report this year praises especially the food and service). "The concept is brilliant," ran an earlier account, "125 bungalows spread over the hillside, each hidden by greenery from its neighbour. The central services (pool, beach etc) are all within two minutes' pleasant walk. The design assures privacy from one's neighbours, and most units have a little patio/garden with a view, ideal for breakfast and an evening drink. Lunch is an irresistible garden buffet, and dinner is in one of three intimate and cool restaurants. Over three weeks there was no monotony of dishes. There are beach and poolside bars for snacks and drinks, and typical beach sports and excursions in the hotel's caïque. As with any hotel, faults exist – maintenance is not perfect – but the *Akti Myrina*'s supreme attribute is the hospitality of the amicable Greek islanders and of the hotel staff in particular." "The gardens are a joy, and the cuisine was of a very high standard. We liked best the quiet, unobtrusive but firm grip the management clearly had on the whole operation. Everything ran like clockwork." (*JF Greenhough, Conrad Dehn, Anthony Rota, and others*)

Open 7 May–10 Oct.
Rooms 15 suites, 110 double – all with bath and/or shower, telephone, refrigerator, veranda and small garden. All in bungalows.
Facilities Lounge, 3 bars, TV lounge, bridge room, library, 3 indoor restaurants, taverna; hairdresser, boutique. 25-acre grounds with private sandy beach with restaurant; fishing, bathing, water sports, 3 tennis courts, swimming pool, pool for children, mini-golf, ping-pong and other games. Disco and Greek evenings. English spoken.
Location 2 km (about 15 minutes' walk) from Myrina Town. Lemnos is reached by direct flight from Athens, or by boat from Piraeus. Transport to and from Lemnos airport to hotel. Parking.
Restriction Not suitable for ♿.
Credit cards All major cards accepted.
Terms [1987 rates] Dinner, B&B: single 9,896-22,272 drs, double 17,140-32,610 drs, suite 22,665-38,135 drs; full board 2,500 drs per person added. Set lunch/dinner 4,200 drs; full alc 5,000 drs. Reduced rates for children sharing parents' room; special meals on request.

MYRTIES Kalymnos, Dodecanessus Islands — Map 17

Marilena — *Tel* (0243) 47289

In the small seaside resort of Myrties, seven kilometres from Kalymnos town and backed by a mountain range, this is a simple but very clean little hotel, well run by its charming resident owners (she is Belgian). Some rooms are in bungalows with shower and veranda. Breakfast only, but there are tavernas near by; good swimming. Open Apr–Oct. 10 rooms. Prices on application. No recent reports: more needed.

NAFPLION Peloponnesus — Map 17

Hotel Leto — *Tel* (0752) 28093
28 Zygomala

"Very basic but wonderful" is a recent comment on this pleasant hotel on a hill with good views over the rooftops of the old town but only five minutes' walk from the seafront of this lively resort. Rooms are simple but comfortable and quite cool (all face north or east), and some have a balcony facing the sea. The Rekoumis family owners are friendly and a good breakfast is served on a pretty terrace with scented jasmine and honeysuckle. Some noise from motorbikes at night. (*Allan Murray-Garner*) More reports please.

Open All year.
Rooms 8 double, 3 single – 7 with bath; some with balcony.
Facilities Salon; terrace, Rocky beach nearby. English spoken.
Location Central, near *Amfitryon* and *Dioscouri* hotels. Parking.
Terms [1987 rates] Rooms: single 1,400-2,200 drs, double 1,600-2,400 drs. Breakfast 225 drs. (No restaurant.)

Xenia's Palace Hotel — *Tel* (0752) 28981
Akronafplia — *Telex* 298154 XENI

Regarded by some as the queen of the chain of government-run Xenias, this one is elegant and fairly luxurious, and has a splendid location inside the old Venetian fort above the historic peninsular city of Nafplion. Reports on it this year are mixed. "The most comfortable hotel in the Peloponnese, expensive by Greek standards but not by others in Europe. Service was good and very amiable. An excellent place for the weary traveller who wants a respite from Greek plumbing and those peculiarly uncomfortable Greek pillows stuffed with lead." "Management helpful, breakfast best of any hotel we found in Greece." So ran two reports, but a third did find the plumbing noisy and thought the facilities poor, the pool too small and the staff indifferent. The set meals are dull, as in most big Greek hotels: one reader found the fish "delicious" on the à la carte, but it's probably best to try the tavernas in town. Package tours are prevalent in summer, less so out of season. An earlier view: "You can reach the hotel either by car, driving up through the fortifications, or by a lift ascending rather James Bondishly from a corridor off a car park. The main building is overwhelmingly built of grey stones, but the bungalows in lovely gardens by the swimming pool are more luscious. Our luxurious room had a balcony with fabulous views. The public rooms seemed rather cold and 'airport lounge' in decor." (*Nina Bawden and Austen Kark, Jasper Salisbury-Jones, MF-C*)

Open All year.
Rooms 54 bungalows, 3 suites, 48 double – all with bath or shower; some with air-conditioning; many with veranda or balcony.
Facilities Lounges, 3 bars, TV room, 2 restaurants; conference facilities; disco nightly. Garden with swimming pool. Private beach. English spoken.
Location Inside Venetian fort above Nafplion. Parking.
Credit cards Access, Diners, Visa.
Terms [1987 rates] Half board (obligatory): single 7,774-8,926 drs, double 11,229-12,668 drs, suite 16,767-19,314 drs. Set lunch/dinner 1,350 drs.

OLYMPIA Peloponnesus — Map 17

Hotel Amalia

Tel (0624) 22190
Telex 215161 AMAL

The ancient site of Olympia is on one side of the modern village, while the large modern luxury-class *Amalia* is on the other, amid fields. It is admired this year by a reader who brings it back to our pages after a period when we had no news of it: "Being outside the town, away from the main road, it is a haven of peace in this noisy country. Large open spaces, up-market (i.e. pricey) boutiques, an outdoor pool and bar (somewhat crowded), big comfortable rooms, air-conditioning throughout. My room was excellent, with two large beds. International cuisine, offensive to no one and everyone, with a token nod to Greece in the form of the ubiquitous horiatiki salad: but I heard high praise of the lunchtime buffet. Breakfast OK. Inevitably a hotel of this size is impersonal, but service is good. Fine for a night or two's halt, and not hysterically expensive." (*PB; also RJ Brown*)

Open All year.
Rooms 150 – all with bath or shower, telephone and radio; many with balcony.
Facilities Lounges, TV room, bar, dining room; conference facilities. Garden with swimming pool.
Location 2 km outside village. Parking.
Credit cards None accepted.
Terms [1987 rates] Rooms: single 5,500 drs, double 7,500 drs. Breakfast 500 drs. Set lunch/dinner 1,400 drs.

Hotel Kronion

8 Tsoureka

Tel (0624) 22502 and 22188

Built to serve the needs of tourists to the archaeological site, Olympia is an ungainly village full of souvenir shops. In its main street is the modern C-class *Kronion*, no beauty but useful, excluded from our last edition for lack of reports, but now again commended: "Creaking staircases but good balconies and plumbing reliable. Rooms simple but adequately furnished, clean, comfortable and cool; rooms on the side-street are quieter than front ones. Good breakfast. Staff friendly and helpful: they speak French but little English." Earlier visitors, who had a superb bathroom, warned that the food is monotonous, unless you happen to be there for the traditional midnight Easter meal – red-dyed hard-boiled eggs, lemon-and-herb-flavoured lamb-offal soup, huge chunks of Easter lamb. (*PB*)

Open All year.
Rooms 3 triple, 35 double, 3 single, – all with bath, shower and telephone.
Facilities Lift. Salon, bar, TV room, restaurant. Beach 17 km. English spoken.
Location Central, on main road. Parking.
Credit cards All major cards accepted.
Terms B&B: single 2,200-2,700 drs, double 3,400-3,900 drs; dinner, B&B: single 3,000-3,700 drs, double 5,400-5,900 drs. Full alc 1,200 drs. Reduced rates for children.

PALEA EPIDAVROS Peloponnesus — Map 17

Paola Beach Hotel — *Tel* (0753) 41397

In a fishing-village 12 km from the classical theatre at Epidaurus, a modern hotel facing a sandy beach, clean and (rarity in Greece) with plumbing that works. Open 1 Apr–30 Oct. 27 rooms, all with bath, shower and balcony facing sea or farmland. B&B double 3,000-4,000 drs. No restaurant: tavernas in village. New nomination: more reports welcome.

PIGHADIA Karpathos, Dodecanessus Islands — Map 17

Hotel Romantica — *Tel* (0245) 22460

"A small, very clean, friendly modern hotel on an unspoilt Dodecanese island. The atmosphere is that of Greece 15 years ago, but the facilities are now better. If you want a drink, you help yourself and write a chit. The friendliness and concern are genuine. The room was fairly small but had – still unusually for Greece – a very good shower and big towels. Small balconies looking out to sea or over lemon groves. At Easter only breakfast was available and it was plentiful but boring – milk was the dreaded canned. The hotel is used by at least two English specialist package tour firms but as the island does not appeal to standard packagees that doesn't seem to me a drawback; though the presence of heavily organised Swiss-German walking groups might be. There is a superb beach opposite and buses will stop there. The road is little used and the hotel is quiet – even on Easter Sunday I could hardly hear the fireworks." (*Anne-Marie Sutcliffe*) 12 bedrooms have been added since last year.

Open 1 Apr–31 Oct.
Rooms 29 double, 3 single – all with bath and shower, telephone and radio; some with balcony.
Facilities Breakfast room, bar. Large garden. Opposite beach. English spoken.
Location 1 m from Pighadia on road to Aperi.
Credit cards All major cards accepted.
Terms Rooms: single 1,883-2,215 drs, double 2,326-2,770 drs. Breakfast 300 drs. Reduced rates for children. (No restaurant.)

PLANOS Zakynthos, Ionian Islands — Map 17

Caravel Hotel — *Tel* (0695) 25261
Alexandra Beach

The beautiful Ionian island of Zakynthos (or Zante) was known as "the flower of the Levant" by the Venetians, because of the softness of its climate, the luxuriance of its flora, and the gentleness of its people; in Byron's day it was an important centre of poetry and the arts. Today the poets may be fewer but the other attractions remain, bringing tourists to its many hotels. The *Caravel*, a modern building three miles from Zakynthos town, makes its Guide debut: "Finding idyllic Greek islands is no problem (this one is specially delightful); finding comfortable quiet hotels is quite another. This is the only 'A' hotel on the island: indifferent beach but lovely views, and plenty of creature comforts, including good bathroom. A haven of peace and cleanliness. We did not try the restaurant, preferring to sample the local tavernas." (*DH Bennett*) All rooms have sea views. More reports welcome.

Open Apr–Oct.
Rooms 74 – all with bath, shower, direct-dial telephone, radio, air-conditioning and balcony.
Facilities Lounges, bar, restaurant. Terraces and swimming pool. Water sports nearby. English spoken.
Location On coast 4.5 km NW of Zakynthos town.
Credit cards None accepted.
Terms [1987 rates] Rooms: single 5,200-7,000 drs, double 6,700-9,600 drs. Breakfast 500 drs. Set lunch/dinner 1,300 drs.

TOLON Peloponnesus — Map 17

Hotel Minoa — *Tel* (0752) 59207 and 59416
56 Aktis Street — *Telex* 298157 MINO

Once just a simple fishing-village near Nafplion, Tolon is now a sizeable seaside resort, popular with Britons and others. One of the many hotels along the beach is the sympathetic *Minoa*, dropped from last year's Guide for lack of feedback, now restored by this report: "Run by a large family of Cretan emigrants, it is also very suitable for a family holiday, being right on the beach. It is just fine – lots of space in the delightfully furnished public rooms, a covered garden bar by the water (popular with locals, too), and large comfortable rooms, many with canopied balcony facing the sea (my single one was tucked in at the back, but otherwise OK). The polyglot staff are cheerful, helpful, generally good news. Breakfast was good, especially the coffee. The food at main meals is quite good; there are also lots of tavernas nearby." (*PB*)

Open 15 Mar–31 Oct.
Rooms 56 double, 6 single – 8 with bath, 54 with shower, all with telephone and radio. 18 in annexe (Hotel *Kronos*).
Facilities Lounge with TV, bar, restaurant. Garden. Sandy beach. English spoken.
Location Near old port; parking. Tolon is 12km SE of Nafplion.
Restriction Not suitable for ♿.
Credit cards All major cards accepted.
Terms B&B: single 2,850-3,350 drs, double 3,800-4,400 drs; dinner, B&B: single 3,550-4,050 drs, double 5,500-6,200 drs. Set lunch 600 drs, dinner 800 drs. Reduced rates for children; special meals.

> If you have had recent experience of a good hotel that ought to be in the Guide, please write to us at once. Report forms are to be found at the back (or use your own stationery if you prefer). Procrastination is the thief of the next edition.

XYLOKASTRON Corinth **Map 17**

Apollon Hotel *Tel* (0743) 22239
105 J. Ioannou

A B-class hotel in a town west of Corinth on the south shore of its gulf. Impressive main building (a former presidential residence) and modern annexe. Rooms comfortable (front ones can be noisy). Good food; pleasant garden for drinks. 27 rooms, all with bath. Double 3,500 drs. No recent reports: more welcome.

Hungary

BUDAPEST **Map 17**

Hotel Erzsébet *Tel* (1) 38.21.11
Károlyi Mihaly utca 11-15
1053 Budapest

In a fairly quiet street in Pest Inner City, this famous old 1900s hotel has been completely rebuilt and refurbished and is now very comfortable, with a good restaurant and well-patronised beer-hall. Service outstanding: apprentice hotel staff do a "practical" stint here. Hotel named after Franz Joseph's wife, Queen Elizabeth, assassinated in 1897. 123 rooms, all with shower, 58-82 DM (low season), 103-142 DM (high season). More reports welcome.

We asked hotels to estimate their 1988 tariffs. About a quarter of the hotels in Part Two failed to reply, so prices in that section are often more approximate than those in Part One.

Hotel Gellért
Szt Gellért tér 1
Budapest 1111

Tel (1) 85.22.00
Telex 224363

The *Gellért* lies in its baroque deco glory at the foot of the Gellért hill, overlooking the river. It was the city's premier hotel when it first opened, and its decor and furnishings, and the style of service inside, complement the confident and the grand-and-proud-of-it stance of the facade. The furnishings may seem outmoded by Hilton standards, but the size of the rooms, the solidity of the walls between the rooms, the large towels, the splendid corridors and stairways recall the great days of grand hotels. The art deco Turkish baths adjoining the hotel are on no account to be missed. The *Gellért* still scores high for impeccably attentive and cheerful service, for a very good restaurant (naturally with a diligent gypsy band), a superb coffee shop replete with rich Hungarian pastries, and much else to cheer the traveller. The front rooms have fine views of the city, but a visitor this year found that their double-glazing was not adequate to blot out all the noise of car traffic and clanging trams. He also thought the furniture "rather tacky". And he notes that the hotel's indoor swimming pool is part of a spa complex used by the health services and the place gets crowded with queues of ill people waiting for treatment, though hotel residents get priority. In summer, there are outdoor pools. More reports please.

Open All year.
Rooms 14 suites, 82 double, 139 single – all with bath and/or shower, telephone, radio and TV.
Facilities Large foyer, lounges, bar, brasserie, coffee shop, dining room; banquet hall, night club; 6 conference rooms; indoor swimming pool; terraces. 3 outdoor swimming pools. English spoken.
Location At the foot of Gellért hill, in city centre. Parking.
Credit cards All major cards accepted.
Terms B&B: single US$36–US$56, double US$48–US$82, suite US$111. Set lunch US$8, dinner US$12; full alc US$15. Weekend packages; 1-week "Thermal" packages. Children under 12 sharing parents' room free; special meals.

Thermal Hotel
Margitsziget
Budapest 1138

Tel (1) 32.11.00 and 11.10.00
Telex 225463

"An oasis of peace in a large and busy city. Despite its ultra-modern appearance, the five-star *Thermal* provides all the traditional Hungarian comforts. It is a spa hotel with every facility for treating rheumatic ailments. Located on the Margitsziget (Margaret Island), in the Danube, which is carefully preserved as a park, it is surrounded by charming gardens with great trees, lawns and flowers. The bedrooms have balconies with lovely views and the public rooms are spacious. The large, bright restaurant is sheer enchantment: a bower of flowers and shrubs. The food is good and an excellent three-course table d'hôte very reasonably priced. Above all we liked the warm personal welcome and the efficient and kindly service." (*E George Maddocks*)

Open All year.
Rooms 8 suites, 154 double, 44 single – all with bath and shower, direct-dial telephone, radio, mini-bar, TV and balcony; 1 suite with kitchenette; baby-sitters available. Some rooms suitable for ♿.

Facilities Lifts. 2 lounges, 3 bars, coffee shop, restaurant; 3 function rooms; night club daily except Sun; heated indoor swimming pool and thermal bath; hairdresser. Medical centre with diagnostic unit adjoins the hotel. Garden. English spoken.
Location On N part Margitsziget (Margaret Island); free bus shuttle service centre to city centre. Parking.
Credit cards All major cards accepted.
Terms B&B: single US$57–US$65, double US$81–US$92, suite US$116–US$133. Set lunch/dinner US$8; full alc US$11. 1- and 2-week packages; thermal package. Children under 12 sharing parents' room free; special meals on request.

VISEGRÁD — Map 17

Hotel Sylvanus — *Tel* 361/13.60.63
Feketehegy — *Telex* 225720
2025 Visegrád

Modern, purpose-built hotel perched high above the Danube Bend north of Budapest, along with ruined castle and look-out tower. Popular with skiers, walkers. Large restaurant serving good honest Hungarian food. Accommodation adequate – useful overnight stop. 79 rooms, most with bath and shower. Dinner, B&B US$20–US$31.

We give below a short list of some other hotels in Hungary which have been recommended to us, though without sufficient information to make possible a full entry. Of necessity, these citations do not carry the same authority as those of which we give full information above. The grades – from 5-star down to 1-star – are those of the official Hungarian Hotel List.

We have mentioned only three hotels on Lake Balaton – at the interesting resorts of Balatonfüred, Keszthely and Tihany – as the lakeside hotels have recently, at least from late May till early September, become grossly overcrowded with large and often noisy package-tour groups from both East and West Europe. Nor are most of the hotels enticing; they form an almost unbroken line of uniform, box-like structures along much of the lakeside. In the rest of provincial Hungary, the visitor will almost everywhere find a warm welcome, a comfortable room and good food – all at a very reasonable price.

BALATONFÜRED **Annabella** (3-star), Beloiannisz utca 25, 8231 Balatonfüred. *Tel* (86) 42.222. Finely situated on lake front in famous spa resort. 390 double rooms, all with bath. Private beach and tennis nearby. The spa specialises in diseases of the heart.

BUDAPEST **Budapest Hilton** (5-star), Hess András tér 1-3, 1014 Budapest. *Tel* (1) 751.000. One of the better Hiltons, in a splendid position in the historic Castle district of Buda, with a splendid view. It incorporates the remains of an old monastery. 323 rooms. Attractively furnished. Casino.

BUDAPEST **Forum** (4-star), Apáczai Csere János utca 12–14, 1052 Budapest. *Tel* (1) 178.088. On the Danube bank in the Inner City of Pest, with a magnificent view. Every luxury and convenience for the (wealthy) businessman – or tourist, for that matter. Underground garage. 408 rooms.

BUDAPEST **Taverna** (3-star), Váci utca 20, 1056 Budapest. *Tel* (1) 384.999. New hotel in the Inner City's pedestrian precinct. Garage. 224 rooms, all with bath.

BUDAPEST **Metropol** (2-star), Rákóczi út 58, 1074 Budapest. *Tel* (1) 421.175. Small, old-fashioned but comfortable hotel in main shopping street; ask for back rooms. 102 rooms, some with bath.

BÜK **Kastély** (Castle), 9737 Bük. *Tel* 150, *telex* 37258. Simple 1-star hotel in small west Hungarian spa. Charming old Baroque castle, with period furniture. 22 rooms, all doubles with bath. Inexpensive.

DEBRECEN **Arany Bika** (3-star), Vörös Hadsereg utca 11–15, 4025 Debrecen. *Tel* (52) 16.777. The oldest inn in Hungary, now enlarged and modernised. 300 rooms, many singles and doubles with bath. Praised for its food.

EGER **Park** (2-star), Klapka György utca 8, 3300 Eger. 40 rooms and **Eger** (3-star), Szálloda utca 1–3, 3300 Eger. 170 rooms. *Tel* (for both) (36) 13.233. The *Park* is elegant but old-fashioned, the *Eger* modern but without charm. The hotels adjoin and are under one management. Both have private baths. Eger is a lovely old Baroque town.

FERTÖD **Kastély** (Castle), Bartók Béla utca 2, 9431 Fertöd. *Tel* (99) 45.921. Very simple, but attractive hotel in part of magnificent Esterházy Palace. 19 rooms; no private baths.

HÉVÍZ **Thermál**, (4-star) Kossuth L. utca 9–11, 8380 Hévíz. *Tel* 11.190. Luxurious hotel in what is probably Hungary's most famous spa. 202 single and double rooms, all with bath. Casino. Hévíz specialises in disorders of the nervous system.

KESZTHELY **Helikon**, (3-star), Balatonpart 5, 8360 Keszthely. *Tel* 11.330. Very comfortable hotel on shore of Lake Balaton in interesting town, famous for the Festetics Palace and its concerts. 240 doubles with bath, swimming pool, tennis courts.

PÉCS **Pannónia** (3-star), Rákóczi utca 3, 7621 Pécs. *Tel* (72) 13.322. New; 118 rooms, many with private bath. Famous old town, with Romanesque cathedral and Vasarély museum. Also **Kastély** (Castle) (3-star), some way out, at Üszögpuszta; address 7676 Pécs. Classified as "inn". Old castle, with period furniture. 18 rooms, some with private bath. Riding school attached. Inexpensive.

SOPRON **Palatinus** (3-star), Uj utca 23, 9400 Sopron. *Tel* (99) 11.395. New hotel in charming old house in centre of highly picturesque town. 32 rooms, many with bath. **Sopron** (3-star), Fövényverem út 9, 9400 Sopron. *Tel* (99) 14.254. New hotel on outskirts of town, with open-air swimming pool and tennis court. 112 rooms, all with bath.

SZIRÁK **Kastélyszálló** (Castle), (3-star), Petöfi utca, 3044 Szirák. *Tel* 37. Late 17th-century castle-hotel in north Hungarian hills, refurbished and decorated to a high standard. 13 rooms, all with bath. Riding facilities available.

TIHANY **Club Tihany** (4-star), Tihany rév, 8237 Tihany. *Tel* (80) 44.170. 330 double rooms with bath. This is part of a large complex which includes bungalows. Tihany is famous for its site and its historic abbey, which contains the tomb of King Andrew I, dating from 1055.

TOKAJ **Tokaj** (2-star) Rákóczi út 5, 3910 Tokaj. *Tel* 201. 30 double rooms, 20 with bath. Near famous Rákóczi wine-restaurant and cellar.

VESZPRÉM **Veszprém** (2-star), Budapesti utca 6, 8200 Veszprém. *Tel* (80) 12.345. 92 rooms, 42 with bath. The town is extremely picturesque, the hotel strictly utilitarian, though said to be comfortable and well run.

Italy

HOTEL VIRGILIO, ORVIETO

ALPE FAGGETO 52033 Arezzo **Map 16**

Fonte della Galletta *Tel* (0575) 793925
Caprese Michelangelo

This idiosyncratic little rural hotel, really a restaurant-with-rooms, lies secluded amid woodlands in the wild Apennines. Readers have long enjoyed the robust cooking of its jovial and well-named proprietor, Signor Boncompagni, who uses local mushrooms and funghi in various fascinating and unusual ways. It dropped out of the Guide recently as we had no news of it, but now a reader begs us to restore it: "Staying here is an experience. It is as unlike any British hotel as could be imagined – one of the reasons why our stay was so enjoyably stimulating! We didn't even get a proper bill: the Signor just jotted down some figures on a scrap of paper, but he did not overcharge us at £15 [1986] per head for dinner, bed and breakfast! Signor Boncompagni is intensely energetic and kind. Once dinner began the whole place roared into tremendous activity, and it was necessary to eat rapidly (and not to allow attention to wander from one's food) in order to keep up with the vigorous service, led by the Signor himself. After dinner the staff not surprisingly appeared to collapse with exhaustion and all the clearing up was left till morning. There were big parties for local weddings, evidence of the place's popularity. Above the hotel are some interesting walks and the great monastery of La Verna is not far away."(*BW Ribbons*)

There is no menu but guests are asked for their approval of the night's dinner in advance – this could include mushroom soup, various pastas stuffed with mushrooms and truffles, and zuppa inglese. The local wine is "deep purple and delicious". Clearly the place is more of a "typically Italian experience" than a conventionally dependable hotel – no one speaks English, the local guests make cheerful noise, the TV dominates the lounge where the lighting is inadequate for reading, the bedrooms can be rather cold. But oh! the compensations: "The charm of the staff," ran one earlier report, "the beautiful countryside, the roads winding down to Michelangelo's birthplace between quantities of wild flowers." (*BA*)

Open All year.
Rooms 3 suites, 18 double, 2 single – 20 with bath, shower and telephone; 3 with TV.
Facilities Lounge with TV, bar, restaurant; banqueting facilities. Garden. Lake nearby.
Location 5 km SW of Caprese Michelangelo; 50 km NE of Arezzo.
Credit card Amex.
Terms B&B: single 22,000-24,000 L, double 43,000 L; dinner, B&B: 30,000 L per person; full board 38,000-40,000 L. Full alc 15,000 L. Reduced rates and special meals for children.

AMEGLIA 19031 La Spezia — Map 16

Paracucchi-Locanda dell'Angelo — *Tel* (0187) 64391

A sophisticated country hotel just inland from Lerici and La Spezia: "It is a modern, low building, set back from the main road. The owner, Angelo Paracucchi, is one of Italy's finest chefs (*Michelin* rosette) and the main attraction here is the spacious restaurant which offers a large daily menu based on the best local ingredients. The cooking is adventurous and modern, far removed from the usual idea of Italian cooking. The wine list is superb. Rooms are comfortable and adequately furnished in cool style with well-fitted bathrooms. They each have a small balcony with views to the hills or over the plain. There is a comfortable bar and lounge area, and many interesting paintings hang throughout the building." (*Pat and Jeremy Temple*)

Open All year.
Rooms 37 – most with bath or shower and telephone; many with balcony.
Facilities Salons, lounge/bar, restaurant.
Location 3 km SE of Ameglia on Sarzana–Marinella road.
Credit cards All major cards accepted.
Terms B&B: 70,000 L per person; full alc 66,000 L.

In all continental European and Scandinavian countries except France, Hungary, Malta, Spain and Turkey, the dialling codes begin with a 0. Omit this when dialling from outside the country in question. Spanish codes begin with a 9, which should also be omitted.

ANCONA 60020 — Map 16

Hotel Emilia — *Tel* (071) 801145
Collina di Portonovo

This beautiful modern hotel, eight miles south-east of Ancona, stands on a cliff above the sea with open field behind. Dropped from the Guide last year for lack of reports, it is now borne back by a reader who was welcomed with a "delicious" meal at 11.30 pm, when arriving late, and who much enjoyed the "delightfully situated" swimming-pool and the meals on the clifftop terrace. Earlier reports praised the "very drinkable wine from the owner's vineyard", the "cool white bedrooms and pretty rosebud-tiled shower-rooms", and the "outstanding" service. "Fellow guests tend to be slightly trendy Italians, but the atmosphere is informal. Portonovo beach is only a few kilometres down (and I mean down) the road." Some readers have praised the set menus, but one found them disappointing. (*Rosemarie Powell; also Robert D Hill, and others*)

Open Mar–Oct.
Rooms 5 4-bedded, 23 double, 2 single – 3 with bath and shower, 27 with shower, all with telephone, TV and frigo-bar. Ground-floor rooms.
Facilities Lift. Lounge, TV room, bar, restaurant; conference facilities; video films shown nightly in high season. Garden with swimming pool. Rocky beach 2 km by road (transport by hotel's mini-bus). English spoken.
Location On coast at Portonovo, 12 km SE of Ancona.
Credit card Amex.
Terms B&B: single 56,000-66,000 L, double 85,000 L; dinner, B&B: 70,000-80,000 L per person; full board 85,000-95,000 L. Full alc 50,000 L. 1-night bookings sometimes refused in high season. Reduced rates for children under 6; special meals.

ASOLO 31011 Treviso — Map 16

Hotel Villa Cipriani — *Tel* (0423) 55444
Via Canova 298 — *Telex* 411060 CIPRAS

An old town of arcaded streets and Venetian palaces and villas. One of them is the *Cipriani* which used to belong to Robert Browning (he lived in it) and is now a luxurious hotel, quite unconnected with its even grander homonym in Venice (q.v.). "A lovely hotel, quiet and relaxing, with highly efficient service." "Our room was excellent, in the garden annexe, with fresh flowers and fruit every day. Housekeeping is exemplary and all the staff are cheerful and friendly, remembering us from previous visits." "The restaurant is good and although very expensive it is possible to eat well without having the more elaborate, costly dishes. Wine list excellent but pricey." "It is the most absolutely heavenly spot in the world. The food and atmosphere are what you dream of when you think of Italy." (*Pat Clinch, Diana Warburton-Lee, Philip Gill, Ruth Kaye, and others*) Be sure to ask for a room with a garden view.

Open All year.
Rooms 31 double, 1 single – all with bath and/or shower, telephone and TV. 11 in garden annexe.
Facilities Lift. Lounges, bar, restaurant; pianist during dinner. Garden. English spoken.
Location 35 km NW of Treviso. 300 yards from town centre. Parking.
Credit cards All major cards accepted.

Terms [1987 rates] (Excluding taxes) Rooms: single 160,000 L; double 280,000 L. Breakfast 21,000 L. Alc (excluding wine) 62,000-85,000 L.

ASSISI 06081 Perugia — Map 16

Hotel Umbra — *Tel* (075) 812240
Via degli Archi 6 — *Telex* 66122 AZIENTUR

Down an alley just off the main square, a small reasonably-priced family-run hotel with a touch of Italian elegance about the public rooms, and a pleasant patio at the back where you can eat out under the trees. It is again liked this year: "Staff helpful, room comfortable, though plumbing erratic." "Lovely sunny rooms, peaceful and clean," runs another report, while one of Britain's most distinguished hotelier/chefs has found the food "excellent". " (*Harrison Gardner, Marie Earl, Kenneth Bell, and others*)

Open All year, except 16 Nov–14 Dec, 16 Jan–14 Mar. Restaurant closed Tue.
Rooms 22 double, 5 single – 16 with bath, 7 with shower, all with telephone. Some ground-floor rooms.
Facilities 3 lounges, bar with TV, 2 restaurants. Garden with terraces for meals in fine weather. English spoken.
Location In town centre, near main square.
Credit cards All major cards accepted.
Terms B&B: single 46,000 L, double 68,000 L. Full alc 25,000-30,000 L.

BELLAGIO 22021 Como — Map 16

Hotel du Lac — *Tel* (031) 950320
Piazza Mazzini — *Telex* 326299 DULAC

Not as sleekly superior as Anita Brookner's *Hotel du Lac*, this one is a decent middle-of-the-road family-run place, with the benefit of a splendid view over Lake Como stretching below. This year and last it has been praised for its efficiency and good food, and for the congenial atmosphere. "Lovingly polished traditional furniture, and real Italian food served in a dining room with a view second to none. If the weather is bad, you are offered a 'bad day drink' on the house." "The food is delicious and the dining room so situated that you dine as if on the bridge of a ship looking across the beautiful lake." The buffet breakfasts and the roof-garden facilities have also been admired, though some readers this year have found the food lacking in variety, and one complained of a cool reception. While some rooms overlook the lake, others have a view of "typical Italian backyards". (*J Broadhurst, Peter Moscari, Dr Paul Fincham*)

Open Mid-Apr–mid-Oct.
Rooms 38 double, 10 single – 39 with bath, 8 with shower, all with telephone; some with private terrace.
Facilities Lift. Lounge, tea room, bar, TV room, indoor and outdoor restaurants. Large roof garden for sun bathing. 300 metres from beach with safe bathing. English spoken.
Location In the centre of the village, opposite landing stage. 4 lock-up garages.
Restriction Not suitable for ♿.
Credit cards All major cards accepted.
Terms B&B: single 63,000 L, double 90,000-97,000 L; dinner, B&B 62,000-68,000 L per person; full board 68,000-74,000 L per person. Set lunch 24,000 L, dinner 25,000 L; full alc 30,000-40,000 L. Reduced rates for children in parents' room; special meals.

Grand Hotel Villa Serbelloni *Tel* (031) 950216
Via Roma 1 *Telex* 380330 SERBOT

Stendhal found the views "sublime and charming" from the promontory above Lake Como where Bellagio stands. The *Villa Serbelloni*, which enjoys those views, is a huge, ornate villa of grand-operatic splendour, with a superb position on the lake, and is backed by a large park famous for its display of magnolias, camellias and pomegranates. Inside, the palatial public rooms are hung with gold chandeliers and decorated with original frescoes. The staircase is flanked by gilt *putti* on giant candelabra, and the bedrooms, large enough for regal *levées*, have wonderful views over the lake or the gardens at the back. There is a heated swimming pool and a private beach. Rooms vary from "a bit shabby" to "de luxe – more than we could ask for". This year, one American visitor found the front desk inefficient about delivering an urgent message, but other reports have again been very positive: "Excellent." "One of the finest hotels we have ever stayed in." Front rooms are the ones to go for: the ones at the back look on to a steep bank and those facing the road can be noisy. (*Mr and Mrs G Sparrow, M and T Goodger, DE Jennings, and many others*)

Open Mid-Apr–mid-Oct.
Rooms 21 suites, 50 double, 11 single – all with bath and shower, telephone and mini-bar; radio and TV on request. Some ground-floor rooms.
Facilities Lifts. Lounges, TV/reading room, writing room, games room, bar, breakfast room, restaurant; banqueting and conference facilities; hairdressing salon, boutique; terrace (also for meals), evening orchestra with dancing. Gardens with tennis courts, heated swimming pool with snack bar; private beach with boating, windsurfing, waterskiing, boating excursions. English spoken.
Location Central. Private garage and large parking place.
Credit cards Amex, Diners, Visa.
Terms B&B: single 185,000-205,000 L, double 260,000-290,000 L; dinner, B&B: single 215,000-235,000 L, double 320,000-350,000 L. Set lunch/dinner 65,000 L. Reduced rates for children; special meals on request.

BOLOGNA Map 16

Hotel Nettuno *Tel* (051) 260964
Via Galliera 65, Bologna 40121

A useful and comfortable B&B hotel in a narrow and relatively quiet street between the station and Bologna's wonderful historic centre. An old building discreetly modernised, with fairly large rooms and a pleasant management that provides touching little gifts (miniature bottles of aperitifs, etc). Average breakfast, pleasant English-speaking staff. Closed 20 July–20 Aug. 38 rooms, all with bath or shower, 53,000-78,000 L [1987]. No recent reports: more welcome.

Hotel Roma *Tel* (051) 274400
Via Massimo d'Azeglio 9 *Telex* 583270
Bologna 40123

Dropped from the 1986 Guide for lack of reports, but now back with three new plaudits, this sizeable hotel is very centrally located, in a narrow street just off the magnificent Piazza Maggiore, heart of the historic core of medieval Bologna. "The air-conditioning was bliss and the room was enormous with every amenity." "Room 425 is one of very few with access to a delightful roof-garden." The decor has been variously described as "charming" and "hectic". Quiet, save for sonorous clock chimes. The restaurant's food is "acceptable" though expensive: but there are masses of good cheap places all around, in the world capital of good pasta. (*Lord Vernon, Sally and Chris Davis, P and I Leslie*)

Open All year. Restaurant closed 1–23 Aug.
Rooms 80 – most with bath or shower, telephone, TV and air-conditioning.
Facilities Lift. Restaurant; roof garden.
Location Central: by car, go to the back entrance which is not in pedestrian zone. Garage.
Credit cards All major cards accepted.
Terms [1987 rates] Rooms: single: 60,000 L, double 90,000 L. Breakfast 8,000 L. Full board 102,000-117,000 L per person. Set lunch/dinner 25,000-28,000 L.

BRESSANONE 39042 Bolzano — Map 16

Hotel Dominik — *Tel* (0472) 30144
Via Terzo di Sotto 13 — *Telex* 401524 DOMNIK

A bright and breezy modern hotel, all orange and yellow colours, set close to the Rienz river on the edge of this busy resort (good centre for exploring Dolomites and Tyrol). Friendly staff, good food, nice rooms (decor a bit garish). Indoor/outdoor pool, covered garage, pretty gardens. 29 rooms, all with bath and/or shower. B&B double 140,000-180,000 lire. Set meals 20,000–35,000 L. New nomination: more reports please.

CAMAIORE 55043 Lucca — Map 16

Peralta — *Tel* (0584) 951230
Reservations in UK (01) 736 5094

First an Etruscan settlement, then a hamlet growing olives and chestnuts, *Peralta* fell into ruin. But it has now been restored by the sculptress Fiore de Henriquez and turned into an out-of-the-ordinary holiday haunt, run somewhat on the lines of an informal house-party. Many of its guests are English, and its managers are London-based. Several visitors this year have enjoyed it, thus endorsing this earlier account: "We went up and up, and came to *Peralta* after a hair-raising drive. The road finally runs out and you have to walk. It is a collection of houses and studios, all simple, some primitive, all with white walls and beams, and a shower of sorts – we had the only bath. Water is a problem since it has to be pumped up. You have an open bar, everyone writes down what they take. Meals are in the open (when fine). The cook is a Cordon Bleu; the food was excellent: no choice, but alternatives could be found. You are moved around at dinner to sit with different people. The small swimming pool, overlooking Tuscany, has plenty of places to sit and sunbathe.

"It was one of the most beautiful places I have ever been to. Lovely walks in the country and olive groves, amid wild flowers. Our room had views as far as the sea. We had our own small garden to sit in, with lavender bushes and an orange tree. But it's an isolated place – a car is advisable – and it is important to get along with your fellow guests." (*Heather Sharland; also Curtis B Wilmot-Allistone, and others*)

Open 1 May–10 Oct. Hotel open, but no arrivals accepted on Thur. Restaurant closed Thur.
Rooms 15 – 1 with bath, 14 with shower. All in 4 separate buildings.
Facilities Lounge, bar, restaurant. 2-acre grounds with terraces and unheated swimming pool; *boules* area and olive groves. Safe sandy beaches 25 minutes' drive. English spoken.
Location SE of Camaiore which is 30 km NW of Lucca, 10 km NE of Viareggio. Carpark is 200 metres from village.
Restriction Not suitable for ♿. No children under 16.
Credit cards None accepted.
Terms B&B £16; dinner, B&B £26. Set lunch £5, dinner £10. Half board compulsory in July and Aug. (Reservations in UK: Harrison Stanton & Haslam Ltd, 25 Studdridge Street, London SW6 *Tel* (01) 736 5094)

CANNERO RIVIERA 28051 Novara — Map 16

Hotel Cannero — *Tel* (0323) 788046
Lunga Lago 2 — (in winter) 788113

The mild climate of Cannero Riviera, which encourages lemons and oranges to grow in great proliferation, also entices travellers to the health and holiday resort on Lake Maggiore, and to the hotels situated along the water's edge. The *Hotel Cannero* is well away from noisy roads, right on the edge of the lake beside the landing stage, and readers this year continue to enjoy it: "A charming place, with a genuinely warm welcome from the Gallinotto family and their staff. The lake view rooms were all booked, but our side room was very comfortable. The swimming pool was inviting, the pleasant terrace made breakfast alfresco a real treat, and the table d'hôte menu provided excellent fresh pasta for a modest sum." Other visitors have enjoyed the fresh fish and vegetables and the mountain scenery, though one reader points out that the sun goes off this east-facing hotel just after lunch, also that the balconies lack privacy. The nearness of the landing-stage can be regarded as a boon (useful for lake excursions) or a nuisance (noisy Italians late and early). (*KW George, RCJ Gordon, AE Pow, KL Gillott*)

Open 15 Mar–5 Nov.
Rooms 30 double, 6 single – all with bath and/or shower, and telephone; some with balcony. Some ground-floor rooms.
Facilities Lift. 2 lounges (piano player every night in high season), TV room, bar, restaurant. Lakeside terrace, garden with tennis court (7,000 L per hour), swimming pool; bathing and water sports in lake. English spoken.
Location Central, on Lake Maggiore. Garage and parking.
Credit cards Access, Amex, Visa.
Terms B&B: single 40,000-43,000 L, double 64,000-66,000 L; dinner, B&B 47,000-50,000 L per person; full board 53,000-56,000 L. Set lunch/dinner 22,000 L. 30% reduction for children under 10 sharing parents' room; special meals.

CAPRI 80073 Naples — Map 16

Hotel Flora — *Tel* (081) 8370211
Via F. Serena 26

A friendly little modern bed-and-breakfast pensione *near the main square of Capri town. Antiques and tiled floors; all rooms spacious, front ones have fine views; balconies with bougainvillaea; no lounge, but a sun-terrace. Good value in expensive, crowded Capri. Open 1 Apr–31 Oct. 23 rooms, most with bath and shower. B&B double 110,000-140,000 L. Few recent reports: more, please.*

CASTELLINA IN CHIANTI 53011 Siena — Map 16

Pensione Salivolpi — *Tel* (0577) 740484
Via Fiorentina

"We were looking for somewhere to stay comfortably for several days at a modest price, and we found it," writes a reader about the family-run *Salivolpi*, a converted Tuscan farmhouse located on a hill that was once the site of the Etruscan Castellina, now simply affording a panoramic view from Siena to Volterra and San Gimignano. "The hotel consists of three buildings set in a pretty garden with quite a large swimming pool. The chief building is small enough to have a family atmosphere and yet large enough to offer excellent accommodation. Our ground-floor bedroom had a very large bathroom, done in that elegant manner characteristic of Italian bathrooms. We breakfasted in the garden and ate dinners out, since the *Salivolpi* has no restaurant. However, things like coffee and beer were freely available whenever we were sitting outside or in the little entrance hall." (*Esther Wilson*)

Open All year.
Rooms 18 double, 1 single – all with bath, shower and telephone. 7 in different buildings.
Facilities Reception, salon with TV. Garden with swimming pool. English spoken.
Location 1 km NW of Castellina towards San Donato.
Restriction Not suitable for ♿.
Credit cards None accepted.
Terms B&B: single 30,000 L, double 50,000 L. (No restaurant.)

COGNE 11012 Aosta — Map 16

Hôtel Bellevue — *Tel* (0165) 74825
Rue Grand Paradis 20

The village of Cogne is a summer and skiing resort, high up in a mountain valley south of Aosta, facing the Gran Paradiso massif. "One could have a wonderful holiday here, with many delights and comforts," says a visitor this year to the *Bellevue*, while another has spelled it out: "Simple but comfortably furnished, and well kept. All rooms have a bathroom, and though not large are warm, clean and well equipped. Good traditional local food. The hotel is modest, but has a warm comfortable feeling, is run by a family that cares, and is in a beautiful area." Other recent reports also speak well of the "affable" staff, "excellent" food, and of the views and walks in the mountains. (*Ann Lawson Lucas, and others*)

Open 22 Dec–6 Jan, 30 Jan–5 Apr, 9 June–25 Sept.
Rooms 4 suites, 38 double, 7 single – all with bath and/or shower, telephone and radio. Suites, in separate building, have TV and tea-making facilities.
Facilities Salons, TV room, pub with video and music, games room, restaurant; conference room. Garden; swimming pool planned for 1988. Tennis, fishing, walking and winter sports nearby.
Location 27 km S of Aosta. Hotel is central; parking.
Credit cards None accepted.

Terms B&B: single 58,000 L, double 80,000 L, suite 114,000 L; dinner, B&B 63,000-86,000 L per person; full board 70,000-110,000 L. Set lunch/dinner 26,000-30,000 L. Reduced rates for children sharing parents' room; special meals.

ERICE 91016 Sicily — Map 16

Hotel Moderno — *Tel* (0923) 869300
Via Vittorio Emanuele 67

Apart from a few gripes (a "disappointing" dinner, prices a bit high), most readers continue to endorse this earlier recommendation of a family-run hotel in a lovely town: "Erice is an atmospheric sun-bleached town at the very tip of a breathtakingly high pinnacle of rock, a village in the clouds, with views of the sea and, almost straight down, western Sicily. The medieval atmosphere is stronger than virtually anywhere we've seen. The streets are paved with stones laid in striking patterns – ribbons, basket-weaves, checker-boards. The castle and churches are marvellous. The *Moderno* is charming, snug and friendly. Its owner fixed our car, and his pink-cheeked lads scampered after bags, drinks, dinner. No bath in our room, and the showers were not completely enclosed – but no big problem." (*Tom and Connie Congdon*) More reports, please.

Open All year.
Rooms 6 suites, 28 double, 6 single – 8 with bath and shower, 32 with shower, all with telephone. Some ground-floor rooms.
Facilities Lift. Lounge, bar, TV room, dining room; terrace. English spoken.
Location Central. Parking.
Credit cards Amex, Diners, Visa.
Terms B&B: single 43,000-45,000 L, double 70,000-75,000 L, suite 90,000-100,000 L; dinner, B&B 65,000-90,000 L per person; full board 85,000-110,000 L. Set lunch/dinner 30,000 L; full alc 40,000 L. Reduced rates and special meals for children.

FASANO DEL GARDA 25080 Brescia — Map 16

Hotel Villa del Sogno — *Tel* (0365) 20228

"A serpentine ascent off the main road of Lake Garda, through beautifully landscaped gardens, takes you to the scenic perch of the *Villa del Sogno*, located in the village of Fasano, just north of Gardone Riviera. Grand, but quirky enough not to overwhelm, the buildings built in the 1920s evoke both Renaissance villas and Californian kitsch. It has 30 good-sized rooms, some with private balcony, a pleasant dining room serving huge meals that range from adequate to great, a bar, splendid gardens, a pool and, best of all, an impressive flower-filled terrace with tables and chairs facing a spectacular view of the mountain-ringed lake – the view, incidentally, shared by most of the bedrooms. The staff can be wayward, but are mostly helpful and efficient. *Villa del Sogno* means 'Villa of the Dream'. Gazing from the magnificent terrace certainly gave me a lot of good ones." (*Felicity Rubinstein*) Since last year, the hotel has acquired a new tennis court.

Open Apr–Oct.
Rooms 25 double, 5 single – 11 with bath, 19 with shower, all with telephone; some with balcony.

Facilities Lift. Lounges, TV room, bar, restaurant; large terrace. Garden with swimming pool and tennis court. English spoken.
Location 2 km NE of Gardone, on lake shore.
Credit cards Access, Diners, Visa.
Terms [1987 rates] B&B: 50,000-70,000 L; half board: 75,000-100,000 L; full board (min 3 days) 80,000-110,000 L per person. Set lunch/dinner 40,000 L. Supplement of 10,000 L for room with balcony. Reduced rates for children under 8.

FIESOLE 50014 Florence — Map 16

Hotel Villa Bonelli — *Tel* (055) 59513 and 598941
Via F. Poeti 1/3

Many visitors to Florence prefer to stay up in the peace and quiet of Fiesole, a lovely old town on a cypress-clad hill five miles north of the busy city. Here the *Villa Bonelli*, a modern unpretentious family-run place with a pleasant top-floor restaurant, partakes of that famous view down to the spires and palaces, and what is more it is served by regular buses to the city. "Excellent value for a short stay," runs a report this year. "The rooms were not large, but scrupulously clean and comfortable, with really effective bed-lights, the staff were friendly, and the Tuscan cooking was excellent, with a wide choice on the table d'hôte. The measures of after-dinner sambuca were the most generous we have found in a hotel." Others too have praised the food and the rooms, though it is pointed out that there is nowhere much to sit after dinner except in the foyer which has TV. The owners, the brothers Boninsegni, are much admired for their cordiality and effective regular presence. (*WK Reid, Alan W Barraclough, Sandra Martin*)

Open All year. Restaurant closed Nov–Mar.
Rooms 1 suite, 16 double, 7 single – 1 with bath, 13 with shower, all with telephone. Some ground-floor rooms.
Facilities Lift. Foyer with TV, bar, restaurant; terrace. English spoken.
Location Coming from Florence turn right at Piazza Mino; hotel is 300 metres on right. Garage. Regular bus link with Florence.
Restriction Not suitable for ♿.
Credit cards All major cards accepted.
Terms B&B: single 36,500-44,500 L, double 57,000-69,500 L; dinner, B&B: single 61,500-69,500 L, double 107,000-119,500 L. Set lunch/dinner 25,000 L; full alc 30,000 L. Reduced rates for children; special meals on request.

FLORENCE — Map 16

Hotel Villa Belvedere — *Tel* (055) 222501
Via Benedetto Castelli 3 — *Telex* 575648 VILBEL
Florence 50124

A recent impression of this often praised modern hotel on the Poggio Imperiale hill: "An oasis of peace and tranquillity. I remember driving down through a tunnel of trees to the delightful villa, seemingly asleep in the afternoon sun. Only the cicadas disturbed the silence. The roar of traffic from nearby Florence faded to a distant hum once we were inside the walled grounds. The interior of the hotel lived up to its promise. Cool, shiny marble floors, and simply but elegantly furnished rooms. Outside, in the colourful garden, a swimming pool awaited. Breakfast is served in a glass-walled veranda which looks down onto the Duomo, the roofs of Florence and the hills beyond. Even after a late return from dinner in a *trattoria*, the staff (who, in five years, have remained the same) will willingly serve drinks or coffee, which you can sip in the garden, the sound of cicadas filling the night, the perfume from Giorgio's roses scenting the air and the lights of Florence twinkling below." (*Mrs JD Edwards*) However, some other recent visitors have been less starry-eyed. They have found the bar service "fierce" or non-existent and the promise of "snacks al bar" erratically fulfilled (if these do arrive, they can be well-prepared simple dishes such as pasta and omelettes). One reader this year thought the hotel friendly but its prices too high; another thought it penny-pinching; a third, however, declared it "very pleasant and very inexpensive". No consensus but the pros clearly have it. (*Michael Peretz, Jane Dorrell, and others*) More reports please.

Open 1 Mar–30 Nov.
Rooms 2 suites, 22 double, 3 single – 25 with bath and shower, 2 with shower only, all with telephone and baby-listening; some with balcony overlooking the garden. Ground-floor rooms.
Facilities Lift. Sitting rooms, TV room, bar with veranda. Large garden with swimming pool, tennis court, children's play area. English spoken.
Location 2 km S of centre; leave Florence by Porta Romana, turn E off Via Senese.
Credit cards Amex, Visa.
Terms B&B: single 120,000-135,000 L, double 170,000-200,000 L. (No restaurant, but light meals available.) Reduced rates for children sharing parents' room.

Hotel Calzaiuoli — *Tel* (055) 212456
Via Calzaiuoli 6 — *Telex* 580 589
Florence 50122

Centrally situated on a pedestrian street leading from the Duomo to the Palazzo Vecchio, a recently modernised little hotel that is clean and well run, fairly quiet, and with a friendly staff who speak English. Some upper rooms have views of the Duomo. Street parking not easy; garage nearby, expensive. 37 rooms, most with bath, 65,000-96,000 L [1987]. No restaurant. New nomination: more reports would be welcome.

Grand Hotel Villa Cora — *Tel* (055) 2298451
Viale Machiavelli 18 — *Telex* 570604 VICORA
Florence 50125

On the lovely hill-road south of the Arno, overlooking the city, here is a small 19th-century palace of almost unbelievable sumptuousness, now a very superior luxury hotel. It was built by Baron Oppenheim in the 1860s in pure neo-classical style, and later was a residence of the ex-Empress Eugenia. It is nominated by the distinguished *padrone* of *Miller Howe*, Windermere (q.v.): "A beautifully restored château with fine parquet flooring and ornate Napoleonic decor, set in lovely large plain grounds. Splendid swimming pool, superb views of Florence from the second-floor rooms. Good air-conditioning. Excellent front desk staff, very good room service with breakfasts produced in four minutes flat. The food served is first-class, so do not be put off by the slovenly restaurant staff." (*John Tovey*) The glossy brochure is a connoisseur's treasure of page upon page of elaborate frescoes, statues and chandeliers. But we should welcome more reports, especially on the *Taverna Machiavelli* and its Florentine cuisine.

Open All year. Restaurant closed 1–20 Aug.
Rooms 16 suites, 28 double, 4 single – all with bath and/or shower, telephone, radio, TV, mini-bar, air-conditioning and baby-listening. 18 in 2 different annexes.
Facilities Lift. Salons, bar, restaurant. Large grounds with gardens, heated swimming pool, solarium. English spoken.
Location 3 km S of city centre, via Porta Romana.
Credit cards All major cards accepted.
Terms [1987 rates] Rooms: single 154,000-224,000 L, double 215,000-356,000-L, suite 408,000-678,000-L. Breakfast 16,000 L. Set lunch 60,000 L, dinner 70,000 L; full alc 55,000 L. Reduced rates for children.

Hermitage Hotel *Tel* (055) 287216
1 vicolo Marzo (Ponte Vecchio)
Florence 50122

Readers this year have been pleased with the *Hermitage*, which is splendidly situated beside the Ponte Vecchio, backing onto the Uffizi. "Clean, friendly and informal, and its central location is a prime advantage for sightseeing." "Pleasant and relaxed atmosphere, comfortable bedrooms with interesting furniture; breakfast in the sunny morning-room was delightful." The roof-terrace has also been enjoyed. An unusual feature is that lounge, reception and breakfast rooms are up on the fifth floor. Rooms facing the small square are quiet, but those on the Arno side could be noisy. Contrary to a report last year, visitors this year found the place well heated in winter (the heating system has been changed). (*Eileen Bye, Mary Lawrence, Harrison Gardner, and others*)

Open All year.
Rooms 14 double, 2 single – 13 with bath, 2 with shower, all with telephone.
Facilities Lift. Reception, lounge with bar, TV room, breakfast room; roof garden.
Location Central, near Ponte Vecchio. Front rooms double-glazed. Garage and parking facilities nearby.
Restriction Not suitable for ♿.
Credit cards None accepted.
Terms B&B: single 80,000 L, double 120,000 L. (No restaurant, but snacks available.)

Hotel Loggiato dei Serviti *Tel* (055) 219165 and 298280
Piazza SS. Annunziata 3
Florence 50122

This lovely building in the heart of Florence was built in 1527 for a religious order, the Serviti, and has been newly and sympathetically restored. An inspector brings it into the Guide this year: "Probably the city's most elegant small hotel, combining the best of old (Renaissance building, antique furnishings) and new (including the plumbing). The lovely piazza has been mercifully rescued from its undignified role as a parking lot (but the hotel will park your car for you) and so tranquillity is added to the *Loggiato*'s other virtues. Bedrooms are calm and uncluttered; no restaurant, but breakfast room and small bar." (*FR*) More reports welcome.

We depend on detailed fresh reports to keep our entries up-to-date.

Open All year.
Rooms 2 suites, 12 double, 5 single – all with bath and/or shower and direct-dial telephone; TV on request. 11 more planned for 1988.
Facilities Lift. TV room, bar, breakfast room. English spoken.
Location Central; parking.
Restriction Not suitable for ♿.
Credit cards All major cards accepted.
Terms B&B: single 80,000 L, double 125,000 L, suite 295,000 L. Reduced rates for children under 3. (No restaurant.)

Pensione Rigatti *Tel* (055) 213022
Lungarno Diaz 2, Florence 50121

Those who enjoyed the film of *A Room with a View* will be glad of news of the large rooms with a view of the Arno at this "unique" *pensione*, enthusiastically commended by two recent visitors and very central ("five minutes from the Duomo and only two minutes' skip to *Viroli*, the world's best *gelateria*"). "Signora di Benedetti and her brother have owned this *palazzo* for always, and their elderly hall porter looked too frail for me to let him carry our bags to our room with its three big windows over the river. He also showed us round the beautiful antique-filled reception rooms. At dinner (food simple but good) we were placed by Nanny (I'm sure) who told us all exactly where to sit, but later she mellowed and was friendly, as were the other ancient retainers. All in all a really Florentine experience. Downstairs are the apartments of a mysterious count whose shutters are always drawn, thus adding to the Henry James atmosphere." Forsterian, too: "A sitting room with various sofas, and a little upright piano should Lucy Honeychurch drop by. Our room was tiny, but the lovely view of the Arno made up for it. Breakfast in another large reception room overlooking a courtyard garden was presided over by an elderly and quite batty retainer. But the members of this family enterprise, though antiquated, are charming and helpful – even though guests in all languages were making little jokes about Fawlty Towers." (*Rachel Macdonald, Felicity Rubinstein*)

Open Apr–Oct.
Rooms 33 – most with bath or shower.
Facilities Lift. 2 lounges; courtyard.
Location Central; 3 minutes' walk from Piazza della Signoria.
Terms [1987 rates] Rooms: single 30,000-38,000 L, double 44,000–56,000 L. Breakfast 8,000 L.

Hotel Tornabuoni Beacci *Tel* (055) 268377 and 212645
Via Tornabuoni 3
Florence 50123

This hotel has a lot going for it: it is in a 14th-century palace, it is on the top floor so suffers very little from street noise, it is centrally situated near the Palazzo Strozzi, it has a "homelike atmosphere", and a splendid roof-terrace, with trees, plants, tables and chairs, where guests take breakfast. Bedrooms are mostly large; bathrooms old-fashioned but well-maintained. There is a small restaurant with a basic menu. One visitor this year enjoyed cocktails in the drawing room and found the basic menu "not bad at all". Another has written: "There is a comfortable sitting room filled with tapestries, plants, bookcases and wonderful old furniture. The guest books are filled with messages from people all over the world, many considering their stay here to be one of the highlights of their trip to Italy. I agree." (*JB, Ann H Kearton, Donna Cuervo*) Not everyone, though, is equally enchanted. Some have written of high prices, small rooms and uncomfortable beds. One thrust this year: "Mixed feelings about this hotel. It's quite tacky in some ways. Staff welcoming, but the display of ancient plaudits from previous guests is a bit over the top. At the end of our quite pleasant meal, the solo waiter hovered impatiently, then flung open the windows to let in a blast of December air. We asked him to close them. He pretended not to hear and disappeared muttering Latin threats."

Open All year.
Rooms 31 double – all with bath and telephone; TV on request. 5 in annexe.
Facilities Lift. Salon, bar, restaurant; roof-terrace. English spoken.
Location Central, close to Palazzo Strozzi. Parking.
Credit cards Amex, Diners, Visa.
Terms [1987 rates] Dinner, B&B 96,000-112,000 L; double 192,000-224,000 L. 20% reduction for children; special meals.

FORTE DEI MARMI 55042 Lucca — Map 16

Hotel Tirreno — *Tel* (0584) 83333
Viale Morin 7

Forte dei Marmi is a traditional seaside resort of villas with shady gardens, a wide traffic-free promenade, a pier and a long golden beach – one of the most attractive towns on the Versilian Riviera, north of Pisa, and very Italian in atmosphere. This year, a new chorus of praise has come our way about the *Tirreno*, a family-run hotel with a "lovely and peaceful" garden, well equipped with deckchairs and tables: "Lovely everything – excellent room, food, service, garden and situation." "Extremely good value, bedroom simple but adequate, they are so anxious to please and would cook anything you requested at a few hours' notice." "Our room afforded a lovely view of both the sea in front of the hotel and the mountains behind. We luxuriated on our balcony." Another reader had a marble bathroom "as big as a bedroom in some hotels". One feature of the hotel is that most guests receive a complimentary bottle of Italian champagne with dinner on the night before their departure. One dissident this year enjoyed the warm welcome and the "beautiful uncrowded clean beach", but thought the food mediocre and the bedroom decor garish. (*DS Rampton, BJ Barry, Sheila Shaw, and others*)

Open Easter–Oct.
Rooms 49 double, 10 single – 12 with bath, 47 with shower, all with telephone; 20 have balcony with sea views. 21 in villa in garden.
Facilities Lounge, TV room, games room, bar, dining room; dancing. Garden. 50 metres from fine, safe beach with bathing and boat rental. English spoken.
Location Central; parking. Town is 35km NW of Pisa.
Restriction Not suitable for ♿.
Credit cards Amex, Diners.
Terms [1987 rates] B&B: single 57,000 L, double 89,500 L; dinner, B&B 80,000-105,000 L per person; full board 86,000-113,000 L. Reduced rates for children sharing parents's room; special meals.

GAIOLE IN CHIANTI 53013 Siena — Map 16

Hotel Cavarchione Toscanum *Tel* (0577) 749550

A converted stone farmhouse in the Chianti country, high in the Tuscan hills, now making its Guide debut: "At the end of a short steep drive, a mile up a country road from the township of Gaiole, the front gate is operated electronically: this initiates the visitor into the idiosyncratic efficiency and friendly charm of this small hotel and of its German owners, Adrian Dabriel and his mother, who are meticulously attentive hosts. Most of the bedrooms have stunning views, suitable furnishings, and toilet facilities which in some cases are cramped. The public rooms are traditionally and comfortably furnished and on various levels. In mid-October sunshine we breakfasted, and sometimes had light snack lunches, on the garden terrace. There are plenty of good restaurants within 20 minutes' car drive. The house bar, the shelter beside the swimming pool and the bedrooms are all provided with stocks of wine, other drinks and snacks, from which guests help themselves and sign for it; the house telephone is available on the same basis." (*Helen and Jack Thornton*)

Open 15 Mar–31 Oct.
Rooms 10 double, 1 single – all with shower, radio and frigo-bar.
Facilities Lounge with fireplace, bar, reading-room, TV room. Large garden with sun terrace, swimming pool and mini-golf. English spoken.
Location Towards Vertine, 1 km NW of Gaiole which is 28 km NE of Siena.
Restriction Not suitable for ♿.
Credit cards None accepted.
Terms B&B: 70,000-115,000 L. (No restaurant, but cold lunches available.)

GARGONZA 52048 Arezzo — Map 16

Castello di Gargonza *Tel* (0575) 847021 and 847053
Monte San Savino *Reservations* in Florence: (055) 296151
Telex 571466 REDCO

"Enchanting", "wonderful", "superb" and other superlatives continue to roll out for this unusual paradise which is not exactly a hotel. On a hilltop in the Tuscan woodlands above the Chiana valley, it is an intact 13th-century walled village which Count Roberto Guiccardini's family have owned for centuries and which he has recently converted into a partly-self-catering hotel-cum-conference centre and rural community. Below the *Castello* itself with its tall turreted tower are a score of red-roofed cottages that cluster round it for ramparted protection, archetypally Tuscan. The Count has turned these village homes into bedrooms and suites, which can be hired either for a week or more on a self-catering basis, or else per night as hotel rooms. He and his wife have done the conversion most elegantly, with true Italian flair – clean stone walls, beamed ceilings, pretty rustic decor, neatly cobbled alleys.

One enraptured report this year: "You enter the village through its single great portal, surmounted by a plaque commemorating Dante's stay here in 1302 at the start of his exile from Florence. You may bring your horsepower into the village only for loading or unloading baggage: there is parking below the walls in the shade of forest trees. When the Count inherited it, Gargonza was falling into ruin and nearly all the villagers had left. His restoration has been a labour of love, aiming at the recreation of a living community (there are concerts, exhibitions, study-groups, etc). The cottages are furnished in individual style, and there are always flowers when you arrive. Inside the village are two small gardens, one shady under pines, the other an enclosed hanging garden embellished with lemon-trees and grapevine. At the foot of the old mule-track down from the village is the restaurant, whose pleasures are country ones. Calves' liver, brains, fillet of beef with green peppercorns, spatchcocked bantam and other meats grilled over charcoal are delicious. Wild boar stew is tough: try the beast as raw ham or in a sauce on pasta. They have excellent wines, Chianti and others. In winter you eat indoors with a blazing log fire and the wrought-iron candelabra lit; on warm summer evenings you can sit in the open on the long roofed terrace above the wooded valley, with bats flitting through the rafters." (*Ann Lawson Lucas; also Jenny Towndrow, Curtis B Wilmot-Allistone, and others*) Those booking just for a night or two should be warned that hotel service as such hardly exists. A swimming pool is still "in project", writes the Count.

Open All year except Jan. Restaurant closed Mon.
Rooms 33 double, 7 single – 32 with bath, 8 with shower, all with telephone and self-catering facilities; TV on request. All in 20 separate houses.
Facilities Lounge, TV room, restaurant; auditorium, meeting halls, conference rooms. Large grounds with children's play area, woods and farm; swimming pool planned. English spoken.
Location 8 km W of Monte San Savino on SS73 towards Siena (35 km). From *autostrada* A1, exit 27, Monte San Savino is 10 km.
Restriction Not suitable for ♿.
Credit card Amex.
Terms [1987 rates] B&B 55,000-85,000 L; dinner, B&B 80,000-105,000 L; full board 105,000-130,000 L. Full alc 25,000-27,000 L. 1-night bookings sometimes refused. 10% discount for children under 14.

GIARDINI NAXOS 98035 Messina, Sicily — Map 16

Hotel Arathena Rocks — *Tel* (0942) 51348
Via Calcide Eubea 55

Naxos is a busy little coastal resort just below Taormina. Here the much-lauded *Arathena Rocks* has a central but quiet location down a private road – "a lovely peaceful place". It is a family-run hotel in traditional style with white plaster walls and much of the furniture and doors painted with local scenes. Fresh flowers from the large garden decorate all the rooms – Signora Arcidiacono, who speaks excellent English, also has an Englishwoman's enthusiasm for gardening! The free-form swimming pool hewn out of lava rocks is an extra luxury with "gloriously clear, warm sea swimming only 20 yards away". A report this year: "An excellent place, with some remarkable Italian antique furniture and ornaments. Food was good but not quite the very best of Italian. Bar drinks were very expensive. Many guests are Scandinavian and we met some amusing people." Other recent comments: "Spotless, bright, quiet and cheerful, and far fewer mosquitoes than on our previous visits. Ask for a room overlooking the sea and garden." "We had delicious food – the pasta was always unusual and beautifully cooked." (*Edwin Shipley, Richard Wiersum, DW, and others*)

Open Apr–Oct inclusive.
Rooms 2 suites, 42 double, 10 single – 47 with bath, 10 with shower, all with telephone. 3 apartments in annexe.
Facilities Lift. 2 salons, bar, restaurant; folk music once a week. Gardens with sea-water swimming pool and snack bar, tennis court; man-made private beach. English spoken.
Location In Naxos, 5 km S of Taormina. Hotel has mini-bus to take guests to Taormina.
Credit cards Amex, Diners, Visa.
Terms [1987 rates] Dinner, B&B 69,000-75,000 L. Set lunch/dinner 25,000 L; full alc 25,000-35,000 L. Reduced rates for children sharing parents' room; special meals on request.

JESOLO PINETA 30017 Venice — Map 16

Hotel Mediterraneo — *Tel* (0421) 961175
Via Oriente 106

At the quieter end of Venetian lagoon, six kilometres beyond the big noisy popular resort of Lido di Jesolo, the Mediterraneo *is modern-looking, secluded and countrified. Rooms fairly basic, clean and comfortable. Generous buffet lunch served outside. Car advisable. In italics as no recent feedback. Open Apr–Sept. 57 rooms, all with bath or shower. B&B 45,000–60,000 L. Set lunch/dinner 25,000 L.*

LIPARI 98055 Aeolian Islands, Sicily — Map 16

Villa Meligunis — *Tel* (090) 9812426
Via Marte — *Telex* 912499
Messina

If beautiful volcanic islands are for you, then try this one. The Aeolian isles are so named because the Greeks believed that Aeolus, the God of the Winds, lived there: Vulcano and Stromboli are perhaps the best known, but Lipari is the largest, and like the others it is made of volcanic rock dipping sheer and majestic into the sea. The vines on the terraces produce a strong red wine, tasting a bit like sherry. In the town of Lipari, just behind the port, is this very stylish little hotel, brought to the Guide this year by an English hotelier: "A 17th-century house, totally refurbished in excellent taste with summery decor (tiled floors, etc). The restaurant occupies the roof and has lovely views of the port. The bedrooms are spacious (ours had sofa, writing table, etc). There's a piano-bar, and on our visit the pianist's style was a cross between Gilbert and Sullivan and Elton John – rather good, we thought. Good service: the *direttore* and his team were trying to please." (*Tim Hart*) More reports welcome.

Open All year.
Rooms 4 suites, 27 double, 1 single – all with shower, telephone, radio, TV, mini-bar and air-conditioning.
Facilities Lounge, bar, piano-bar, restaurant. Garden and roof-terrace. Shuttle service to beach. English spoken.

Location Lipari is 45 mins by hydrofoil from Milazzo, Sicily; 2 hours by ferry from Palermo, 4 from Naples.
Restriction Not suitable for ♿.
Credit cards All major cards accepted.
Terms B&B: 77,000-114,000 L, suite 114,000-174,000 L; full board 115,000-135,000 L per person.

MANTUA 46100 — Map 16

Albergo San Lorenzo — *Tel* (0376) 327153
Piazza Concordia 14

One of the two best hotels in this somewhat severe city on the Po plain. Comfortable and friendly; rooms well furnished, cool and quiet, except for church bells (some have views of the fine Piazza delle Erbe). Very central. No restaurant or lounge. 42 rooms, all with bath and/or shower. B&B double 144,000 L [1987]. More reports please.

MERANO 39012 Bolzano — Map 16

Hotel Fragsburg (Castel Verruca) — *Tel* (0473) 44071
Via Fragsburg 3a (PO Box 210)

This small but handsome chalet-style hotel with its two names stands high on a hill overlooking the well-known spa town of Merano in the Alto Adige. It is surrounded by woods, meadows and mountains, and it's only a 20-minute walk to the highest waterfall in the country. There is a heated, open-air swimming pool and a game reserve. Each room has a balcony and meals are served on an open-air terrace in summer. The proprietor Hubert Ortner keeps his own bees and has fresh honey on hand. He tells us that his hotel gets two hours more sunshine a day than in the valley. A helpful report this year: "We were the only non-Germans. Everyone was amicable. We had two quite good meals and one poor one: we wish we'd tried the à la carte which looked interesting. Do *not* drink the local wine: the red in particular is dreadful. And ask for a room with a view or you may overlook the car park as we did." (*Gillian Seel, GN Hobson*)

Open April–Nov.
Rooms 13 double, 5 single – all with bath and/or shower, balcony and telephone; TV on request.
Facilities 6 lounges, bar, TV room, café, dining room; terrace for summer meals. Private park with heated swimming pool, children's play area, ping-pong, chess tables. Tennis nearby. English spoken.
Location 6 km NE of Merano. From Merano take road to Bolzano (Bozen), turn left towards Schenna; after 2.5 km turn right at Rametz. Hotel is 5.5 km along this road.
Restriction Not suitable for ♿.
Credit cards None accepted.
Terms [1987 rates] Dinner, B&B: 48,000-70,000 L; full board 50,000-80,000 L. Set lunch/dinner 15,500-22,000 L.

> Important reminder: terms printed must be regarded as a rough guide only to the size of the bill to be expected at the end of your stay. For latest tariffs, check when booking.

Hotel Villa Mozart *Tel* (0473) 30630
Via San Marco 26

This splendid place about ten minutes' walk from the town centre has drawn this comment from an English hotel-owner: "I cannot think of a hotel that combines luxury, good service and excellent cuisine in such abundance. The attention to detail is astounding." Veteran appreciators of luxury hotels concur: "The building, outside as well as in, is immaculately designed and furnished in the style of the Viennese Secession to designs by Josef Hoffman, Charles Rennie Mackintosh, Liberty and others of the period. This includes everything – carpets, curtains, door fittings, cutlery, crockery, glasses and even the waitresses' uniforms! For architects and interior designers the hotel is worth a detour. Our room was large and comfortable with a small sitting area and a marble-clad bathroom. Large windows gave a pleasant view of the garden and sun terrace. The restaurant is the other attraction for a stay here (one *Michelin* rosette). Andreas Helrigl, the owner, whose personal taste dominates the hotel, is a very accomplished chef. His style is modern and light, and the beautiful table settings and stunning surroundings made every meal an absolute delight. Breakfasts were equally impressive." (*Audrey Simpson, Pat and Jeremy Temple*)

Open 1 Apr–end Oct.
Rooms 8 double, 2 single – 8 with bath, 2 with shower, all with telephone, radio and TV.
Facilities Lift. Lounges, library, bar, restaurant. Large grounds with sun terrace, covered heated swimming pool, sauna, solarium. English spoken.
Location Coming on main road from Bolzano, via Roma, take third street on right. Private parking.
Restriction Not suitable for ♿.
Credit cards None accepted.
Terms [1987 rates, likely to increase by 10% in 1988] B&B 110,000 L; dinner, B&B 150,000 L. Breakfast 20,000 L. Extra bed in room 20,000 L.

Park Hotel Mignon *Tel* (0473) 30353
Grabmayrstrasse 5 *Telex* 401011 Amparc

Nominated this year as a very friendly modern hotel in beautiful grounds, with lovely heated swimming pool, jacuzzi, massage, etc. Generous breakfast buffet, help-yourself salads at main meals. Quite close to town centre. Open Mar–Nov. 55 rooms, all with bath or shower, many with balcony. Half board 94,000-108,000 lire per person. More reports welcome.

MILAN — Map 16

Hotel Gran Duca di York *Tel* (02) 874863
Via Moneta 1/a
Milan 20123

When with 10,000 other tourists you have marched up to the top of the Duomo's roof and then marched down again, you might well be glad of this nearby *Duke of York*, not grand but medium-range: "Quite a find, cheerful and well run, with a positive atmosphere and a large turnover of customers. It is friendly and central, but quiet. Paintings of various past aristocracy, and a suit of armour outside the lifts in the hall. Large, clean bedroom, clean green-tiled bathroom, but poor reading lights. No car park, and parking in the area is tricky." (*Natalia Forde*)

Open All year except Aug.
Rooms 33 – some with bath or shower, all with direct-dial telephone and TV.
Facilities Lift. Conference facilities.
Location Central; just W of Duomo. No private parking.
Credit cards None accepted.
Terms [1987 rates] Rooms: single 72,000 L, double 105,000 L. Breakfast 8,000 L. (No restaurant.)

Hotel Manzoni *Tel* (02) 705700
Via Santo Spirito 20
Milan 20121

A modern, pleasantly quiet and friendly hotel in a small side street a block from the Via Manzoni which leads to the Piazza della Scala, the Vittorio Emanuele shopping arcade and the cathedral. It is well run, comparatively cheap (hotels in Milan are expensive), and has been liked again this year: "Superb room with fantastic bathroom; good breakfast and service. But a headache to reach by car." (*BJ Barry; also Linda Stoner, MD Watts, and others*)

Open All year.
Rooms 52 – most with bath or shower and telephone.
Facilities Lift. Breakfast room.
Location In central zone, not far from public garden. Garage parking.
Credit cards None accepted.
Terms [1987 rates] Rooms: single 81,000 L, double 118,000 L. Breakfast 10,000 L.

NATURNO 39025 Bolzano — Map 16

Hotel Feldhof *Tel* (0473) 87264

Up in the foothills of the Dolomites, a Tyrolean village on the river Adige where the unpretentious *Feldhof* has clean, well-appointed rooms, large bathrooms, and balconies with mountain views. Most guests are German. Reports this year: "All was elegance and restfulness. The Pirhofers are superb hoteliers and all is well designed. The restaurant is faultless." "The best thing about the hotel is charming Signora Feldhof, a lovely lady who speaks good English and takes special care and interest. Our rooms were nice and we liked the meals, especially the buffet breakfast." One reader found the staff helpful but the food too bland, and mentions road noise at night. (*BW Ribbons, Bernadette Murray, and others*)

Open Approx Mar–10 Nov, 18 Dec–15 Jan.
Rooms 28 – most with bath or shower, all with TV and air-conditioning; some with balcony.
Facilities Lift. Dining room; indoor swimming pool. Garden. Riding nearby. English spoken.
Location 15 km W of Merano.
Credit cards None accepted.
Terms On application.

Sterling and dollar equivalents of foreign currencies at the date of going to press will be found on page 712.

ORTA SAN GIULIO 28016 Novara — Map 16

Hotel La Bussola — *Tel* (0322) 90198

Orta San Giulio is an old village delightfully situated on a peninsula that juts into Lake Orta, in Piedmont. This comfortable hotel, on a low hill with a fine view of the lake, makes a cheaper alternative to the San Rocco, *often full. Restaurant and terrace, flowery garden, swimming pool. Excellent food, welcoming staff. Closed 15–30 Jan. 16 rooms, all with bath or shower, 51,000-77,000 L [1987]. Set meals 23,000-32,000 L. No recent reports: more welcome.*

Hotel San Rocco — *Tel* (0322) 90222

A former 17th-century monastery, right by the lake's edge. San Rocco was the patron saint of plague victims, but today there is little suffering in this lovely place, save for annoyance caused by recent building work. "The situation is enchanting, the lake and view to the little island magical and the nearby village gorgeous," writes one visitor. Another rates it "perfect for honeymooners". The hotel's origins are now apparent only in the cell-like dimensions of some of the rooms. Readers are unanimous in their praise for the obliging management and staff. "Elegant and cheerful service," says a visitor this year. "Even a power cut during a psychodelic storm on the lake caused not a ruffle in the calm atmosphere, and candles appeared as quick as the lightning." The food has sometimes been criticised, but latest reports have been positive: "If you don't like the menu, just ask for something different." (*Stanley and Minda Alexander, and others*) A heated swimming pool has just been added. The building work was due to have been completed by the end of 1987.

Open All year.
Rooms 39 double, 1 single – all with bath and shower, telephone and balcony overlooking lake; TV on request; air-conditioning.
Facilities Lift. Hall, salon, TV room, bar with piano, dining room; 2 banqueting rooms. Garden with bar, swimming pool, lakeside terrace. Boating, waterskiing, tennis and mini-golf nearby. English spoken.
Location 5 minutes from centre of town, signposted from main road. Parking.
Credit cards All major cards accepted.
Terms [1987 rates] Rooms: single 84,000 L, double 105,000 L. Breakfast 15,000 L. Full board 95,000-115,000 L per person. Alc meals (excluding wine) 35,000-50,000 L.

ORVIETO 05018 Terni — Map 16

Hotel Virgilio — *Tel* (0763) 41882
Piazza del Duomo 5/6

Inspectors in 1987 have reaffirmed the qualities of the *Virgilio*: "The kind of small city hotel one always hopes to find but rarely does. On the outside it is an unspoiled and shuttered old building, inside it is designed and furnished in good modern Italian style – gleaming chrome, white and pink marble. In the reception area, a large piece of Roman sculpture is flanked by good modern original drawings; a beautiful old tapestry is hung alongside delightful puppets. The hotel faces the side of the glorious Duomo, and our room had a side view of its richly decorated front. The bedroom was not large but attractively furnished, with a big bed, and the bathroom was elegant. Breakfast, as in most Italian hotels, was minimal and expensive. This apart, the hotel is marvellous value. Ask for room 15. Parking under trees across the square." No restaurant, but the *Maurizio*, close by, is "very good, especially for grilled lamb". (*Kenneth Bell*).

Open All year.
Rooms 14 double, 2 single – 14 with bath, 2 with shower, all with telephone. 2 doubles in annexe. Some ground-floor rooms.
Facilities Lift. Bar. English spoken.
Location Central, near *Duomo*. Parking.
Credit cards None accepted.
Terms B&B: single 59,000 L, double 88,000 L. (No restaurant.)

OSPEDALICCHIO DI BASTIA 06080 Perugia — Map 16

Lo Spedalicchio — *Tel* (075) 809323

A reader this year "highly recommends" this attractively converted old fortified manor house, halfway between Perugia and Assisi (buses stop outside the door). Another recent visitor found the staff charming and the food delicious, backing up this earlier account: "The management are particularly friendly and helpful, and offered to drive us anywhere we liked. The decor is a combination of modern and medieval, with lots of natural stonework and no carpets. The food was good Italian and the local wines pleasant and cheap; it seemed to be a favourite eating place for Perugians." (*Curtis B Wilmot-Allinstone, Sarah Whitfield*)

Open All year. Restaurant closed Mon.
Rooms 3 suites, 20 double, 2 single – all with bath, telephone, TV, and tea-making facilities.
Facilities Lift. Hall, salon with bar and TV, restaurant; conference room. Garden. English spoken.
Location 12 km E of Perugia, N of main road to Assisi.
Restriction Not suitable for ♿.
Credit cards Amex, Diners, Visa.
Terms B&B 32,500-49,000 L; dinner, B&B 53,000-73,000 L; full board 70,000–89,000 L. Full alc 25,000 L. Special rates for long stays negotiable. Reductions for children under 2; special children's meals.

PALESTRINA 00036 Rome — Map 16

Albergo Stella — *Tel* (06) 9558172 and 9558637
Piazzale della Liberazione 3

Birthplace of the 16th-century composer Palestrina, this ancient town in the hills east of Rome has a fine panoramic setting and contains the ruins of a classical Roman temple dedicated to Fortune. Here the cheap and unpretentious *Stella* is a new find this year: "One drives along the tiny walled streets of medieval Palestrina, and there in the tiny piazza is this delightful hotel, its restaurant very popular with locals (red "*Pas*" in *Michelin* for good value). We loved the place. Our room was large and clean, the bathroom modern, and only the church clock disturbed the peace. Ideal as a night stop." (*Paul Palmer*)

Open All year.
Rooms 28 double – 2 with bath and shower, 24 with shower, all with telephone.
Facilities Lift. Lounge, bar, TV lounge, restaurant. English spoken.

Location Central. Town is 38km E of Rome, off S6 to Frosinone. Parking.
Credit cards Amex, Diners, Visa.
Terms Rooms: single 23,000 L, double 38,000-40,000 L. Breakfast 4,000 L. Half board 32,000-36,000 L; full board 45,000-50,000 L. Full alc 18,000-25,000 L. Reduced rates for children; special meals on request.

PANZANO IN CHIANTI 50020 Florence — Map 16

Villa Le Barone — *Tel* (055) 852215
Via San Leolino 19

A graceful villa – more of a sophisticated *pensione* than a hotel – high on a hilltop between Florence and Siena. Spread out below is the hilly Tuscan landscape of vineyards, olive groves and cypress trees – "as lovely as any view in the world, especially under a full moon". The grounds are dotted with venerable trees and there is a swimming pool and a terrace. The villa is the former home of the famous Della Robbia family whose classic blue and white has been used as a theme in the decoration. The Duchessa Visconti is the present owner; she only lives here from time to time, but her villa retains the atmosphere of a cared-for private home. Most rooms are elegantly furnished with good antiques, carefully arranged flowers and fine linen sheets. A report this year: "Blissfully quiet after the Italian cities. The public rooms are charming, the staff helpful, the rooms very neat (ours was lovely) and the 'honour system' with the evening drinks most pleasant. But the service is languid and the food, while attractively served, is not inspired." Others have variously described the food as "bland and international" (to suit the mainly Anglo-American and German clientèle?) and "a small range of simple dishes well cooked". The service, says one reader, is "always available but never noticeable". (*Harrison Gardner, Patricia Roberts, and others*)

Open 1 Apr–31 Oct.
Rooms 27 double, 1 single – 24 with bath, 4 with shower; 3 with tea-making facilities. 3 garden annexes.
Facilities 4 sitting rooms (1 with TV), bar, dining room. 5-acre grounds with swimming pool and table-tennis. Golf nearby. English spoken.
Location Off SS222 to Siena, 31 km S of Florence. Hotel is SE of Panzano.
Credit card Amex.
Terms [1987 rates] Dinner, B&B 110,000-135,000 L; full board 140,000-165,000 L. Set lunch/dinner 30,000 L. Min stay 3 days. Reduced rates for children according to age; special meals.

PERUGIA 06100 — Map 16

Hotel La Rosetta — *Tel* (075) 20841
Piazza Italia 19

Perugia's second largest hotel enjoys a prime situation at the top of the main street, Corso Vannucci, near to all the main sights. It has been commended again this year as comfortable, friendly and efficient, and readers have especially praised the food, though one found the vaulted dining room "a bit bleak" and the ambience a little impersonal. "The decor is not always alluring – our bathroom in shiny bronze was a bit much – but the bedrooms were large." "There is an attractive shady courtyard where you can lunch or dine. The food is delicious." The nightly *passeggiata* takes place outside the hotel, and a reader warns that "this non-stop cocktail party" makes sleep in the front rooms difficult – "bring earplugs, or ask for rooms at the back, which are less attractive". (*S and C Davis, Robert Saxon, AG Don, and others*)

Open All year. Restaurant closed Mon.
Rooms 64 double, 32 single – 51 with bath, 34 with shower/wc, all with telephone and radio. Some ground-floor rooms.
Facilities Lift. Salons (2 with TV), bar, games room, reading room, restaurant; conference facilities. Courtyard where meals are served in fine weather. English spoken.
Location Central; some traffic noise. Parking and 2 garages (extra charge).
Credit cards All major cards accepted.
Terms [1987 rates] Rooms: single 48,000 L, double 80,000 L. Breakfast 6,000 L. Full board (min 3 days) 95,000-100,000 L per person. Alc meals (excluding wine) 20,000-30,000 L.

PETTENASCO 28028 Novara — Map 16

Hotel Giardinetto — *Tel* (0323) 89118
Via Provinciale 1, Lago d'Orta — *Telex* 200206 SIMTUR

A biggish white-walled family hotel on the eastern shore of little Lake Orta, with an oblique view onto the island of San Giuglio and its Romanesque basilica. Views from the rooms, which directly adjoin the lake, and from the restaurant are enchanting, and this year our readers have again been mainly enthusiastic. "Our rooms, nicely furnished though deficient in some small details, were in a new wing with balconies facing the lake. The owners, Oreste and Caterina Primatesta, were very helpful and their table d'hôte was so good that we did not go à la carte." "On this our sixth visit we found the service as good as ever, and the food varied and enjoyable." Another visitor enjoyed the well-maintained swimming-pool and found the breakfast "decent by Italian standards". Swiss readers comment: "It is still an unspoilt area, with no bright lights or loud music. In the evenings there are lovely walks. As the sun sinks across the lake below the dining-room, throwing a glow of red across the calm water, one almost forgets to eat the delicious food." (*ME Wood, Jonathan Palfrey, E Ryf, and others*)

Open 1 Apr–end Oct.
Rooms 2 suites, 45 double, 7 single – all with bath and/or shower (2 with jacuzzi), telephone and baby-listening; 2 with tea-making facilities; TV on request.
Facilities Lift. Lounge, 2 bars, restaurant and coffee shop, both with terrace on lake; conference room; gala evening every Thur in summer with buffet, music and dancing. Garden with large lakeside beach, safe bathing, boats, pedalos, waterskiing; heated swimming pool and table tennis. English spoken.
Location 4 km S of Orta San Giulio. Hotel is 200 metres from town centre, on lake shore. Private parking.
Credit cards Access, Amex, Visa.
Terms B&B: 45,000-120,000 L; dinner, B&B 50,000-80,000 L; full board 65,000-90,000 L. Full alc 30,000 L. Reduced rates and special meals for children.

Do you know of a good hotel or country inn in the United States or Canada? Nominations please to our sibling publication, *America's Wonderful Little Hotels and Inns*, PO Box 150, Riverside Avenue, Riverside, Conn. 06878, USA.

PORTO ERCOLE 58018 Grosseto — Map 16

Hotel Il Pellicano — *Tel* (0564) 833801
Cala dei Santi — *Telex* 500131 PELICA

A devotee of this very expensive hotel, in a lovely coastal setting, returned this year and found it as good as ever: "Beautiful rooms, furnishings with lots of glamour, classy bar service but patchy food. The operation is now run by Nadia and Ennio Emili, a young couple who bring an Italian warmth to their very personal style of management." Earlier he had written, lyrically: "Leaving the village of Porto Ercole, we climb towards the coast road to the hotel. The air is scented with herbs and pines. This is Argentario, a rocky outcrop into the Tyrrhenian Sea – a region of outstanding beauty mercifully free of the ravages of mass tourism. The familiar cluster of red-tiled roofs appears from amongst the pines and olive trees. The silence is total apart from birdsong. In the cool, stylish entrance hall we are greeted and conducted to our room – with a vast terrace lined with huge pots of geraniums – one side looking across the gardens and up to the mountain, the other over tiled roofs to the pool and sea. Breakfast includes a glass of delicious red orange juice. The hotel is scrupulously maintained in first-class nick. The gardens are similarly immaculate, the setting one of timeless beauty and the staff efficient and welcoming. We also like the relaxed atmosphere of smart informality. The cooking is not about to win any rosettes but it is honest Tuscan food using first-class fresh produce." Endorsed by another reader this year: "In this beautiful hotel we had a large pretty room and a first-class dinner with good service." (*David Wooff, MD Janson*)

Open 16 Apr–2 Nov.
Rooms 4 suites, 30 double – all with bath, shower and telephone; TV and radio on request. 15 in cottages in garden.
Facilities Lounge, piano bar, restaurant; conference facilities; dinner-dance Fri July and Aug; terrace. Large grounds with restaurant, heated swimming pool with bar and barbecue; tennis, ping-pong and bowls; boats available; riding, sailing and waterskiing; rocky beach with safe bathing, Beach Club and fishing rights. Golf 1 hour's drive. English spoken.
Location 4 km S of Porto Ercole on Monte Argentario coast. Parking.
Restriction Not suitable for ♿.
Credit cards Amex, Diners.
Terms [1987 rates] Double room 160,000-435,000 L, suite 365,000-750,000 L. Breakfast 20,000 L. Set lunch/dinner 70,000 L. Reduced rates for children sharing parents' room.

PORTOFINO 16034 Genova — Map 16

Hotel Splendido — *Tel* (0185) 69551
Viale Baratta 13 — *Telex* 281057 SPLEND

This famous little resort's most grandiose hotel – five red turrets in *Michelin*, etc. "The situation is most spectacular. The hotel is perched on the side of the bay overlooking the promontory opposite, with yachts moving in and out. Our small suite had a large balcony from which one could sit and gaze at the beautiful sight of water and unspoilt wooded peninsula (visit the château at the top of the latter for views of the little port). The *Splendido* is a successful top class international hotel while also retaining its character as the old private house it used to be. The rooms are beautifully furnished, the bathrooms excellent. The swimming pool is on a terrace on the side of the hill, with its share of views. Restaurant on the terrace in summer lacks the personal touch of good Italian, although the food is very good. Hotel service excellent and very helpful." (*DC Eastwood*)

Open 28 Mar–28 Oct.
Rooms 13 suites, 48 double, 6 single – all with bath, shower, telephone, radio, TV and baby-listening; many with balcony.
Facilities Salon, piano bar (music every evening), bridge room, TV room, 2 restaurants; conference facilities; beauty salon, hairdresser, boutique. Large grounds with tennis court and heated swimming pool with bar and grill. English spoken.
Location 5 minutes' walk from centre of Portofino. Garage and parking.
Restriction Not suitable for ♿.
Credit cards All major cards accepted.
Terms B&B: single 182,800-245,800 L, double 329,300-420,300-L, suite 465,600-540,600 L. Set lunch/dinner 75,000 L; full alc 90,000 L. Reduced rates for children sharing parents' room.

PORTOVENERE 19025 La Spezia — Map 16

Hotel Royal Sporting — *Tel* (0187) 900326
Via dell'Olivo 345

This ancient Ligurian port on a rocky peninsular inspired Byron to write the lyrical poem *Corsair,* and has since inspired a Guide correspondent too: "No question that it is picturesque, with marvellous citadel arches which frame the setting sun kissing the sea. Also a great base for taking the winding, climbing, perennially 'just-completed' single track road to Cinqueterre villages such as Corniglia and Vernazza, strikingly set on or under steep cliffs which fall into the sea, impossibly covered with grapes. Great place to get away from crowds, since most people seemed scared silly of the narrow road. Oh yes, the hotel – four official stars, maids who come in to put away scattered shoes, turn sheets and lay out pyjamas, supercilious (in that Latin way) bartenders, polite buffet waiters, a surprisingly romantic dining room with spacious window view of the harbour and twinkling lights; salt-water swimming pool that maddeningly closes at 7.30 pm. The hotel is Portovenere's class act. It's not exactly an inexpensive gem full of character and charm, but it's an honest four-star establishment, with many positive advantages, especially its location." Visitors this year found that description "spot-on" and added: "Buffet lunch excellent, restaurant staff charming and interested, our room a bit clinical but very clean and with all we needed." (*TC Seoh; Mr and Mrs Neil Biggs*)

Open 1 Apr–30 Oct.
Rooms 57 double, 5 single – 2 with bath, 60 with shower, all with telephone and baby-listening; TV on request.
Facilities Lift. Lounge, 2 bars, TV room, restaurant. Small garden, salt-water swimming pool, tennis. Beach with safe bathing. English spoken.
Location On peninsula 14 km S of La Spezia. Garage.
Credit cards All major cards accepted.
Terms B&B: single 80,000-100,000 L, double 130,000-170,000 L; full board (min 3 days) 120,000-150,000 L per person. Set lunch/dinner 40,000-45,000 L; full alc 50,000 L. Reduced rates for children; special meals.

POSITANO 84017 Salerno — Map 16

Hotel Casa Albertina
Tel (089) 875143
Via della Tavolozza 3

"It is the nearest we shall ever get to being treated like royalty!" writes one gratified recent guest about an enchanting, medium-priced hotel in this justly renowned but trendy and expensive resort town. The lobby and sitting rooms have cool white walls and vaulted ceilings, while the rooms and dining room are decorated in pastels. There is a lovely terrace overlooking coast and sea. Another lyrical account: "I must recommend this utterly authentic family-run hotel with commanding views over the sea. It has style, intimacy, friendliness, great quality and good value. Grandmother cooks – 'you eat what we eat' – and it is perfect Italian *cuisine paysanne*. Quiet, the rustle of the sea, spotless tiled bedrooms, clean sheets every other day – and cheap, by Positano prices. Breakfast with squeezed orange juice and hot croissants, brought in by Maestro Michele Cinque himself, a smiling bear-like man, whose wife helps in the kitchen and who discusses Raphael and Italian politics in the lounges with us all. I can't wait to come again." (*TM Stephens, TP; also Professor Richard Lamb*)

Open All year.
Rooms 2 suites, 18 double, 1 single – all with bath, most also with shower, all with telephone.
Facilities Lift. Sitting room, TV room, bar, dining room, open-air restaurant; terraces. 10 minutes' walk to beach. English spoken.
Location Central, but quietly situated. Parking 200 metres.
Credit cards Amex, Diners, Visa.
Terms B&B: 45,000-65,000 L per person. Set lunch/dinner 35,000-38,000 L. Full alc 45,000-60,000 L. Reduced rates for children.

Hotel Villa Franca e Residence
Tel (089) 875035
Via Pasitea 318
Telex 660077 attn Villa Franca

"One of the nicest hotels I've ever stayed in," says a visitor to this cool, spacious villa. "The theme is white walls and arches, with oak woodwork and, of course, tiles – the latter throughout the public rooms and bedrooms. Our room had a private bathroom and small terrace. Breakfast is on a bamboo-roofed terrace overlooking the sea (plus bougainvillaea!); dinner in a candlelit, arched room with huge windows overlooking the southern part of the town. Food tasted freshly prepared and was traditional Italian fare. The friendly staff made us feel welcome guests. It's quite a long climb from the beach if you take the back stairs. A bus is quicker, and the hotel is said to have its own in season." (*Will Peskett*) Could we hear from other guests please?

Open All year.
Rooms 42 double – 35 with bath, 7 with shower, all with telephone, radio and baby-listening; TV on request; some with terrace. 12 in building 20 metres from hotel. Some ground-floor rooms.
Facilities Lift. Hall, lounge, TV room, bar, dining room; breakfast terrace. Beach nearby (hotel has private bus).
Location 17 km E of Sorrento on coast road.
Credit cards All major cards accepted.
Terms B&B: single 45,500-51,500 L, double 75,000-84,000 L. Full board 60,000-74,000 L per person. Set lunch/dinner 29,000 L.

RAVELLO 84010 Salerno — Map 16

Hotel Marmorata
Strada Statale 163

Tel (089) 877777
Telex 720667 HOTMAR

The *Marmorata*, once a paper mill, is six kilometres from Ravello itself, nestled in the cliff face beneath the coastal road to Amalfi. "A lovely hotel in a beautiful position, with good varied food, helpful staff, excellent bedrooms, and hygiene of a high standard." So runs a report this year, endorsing an earlier one: "The cool, restful interiors designed in the style of a ship, the seafront terraces and the friendly, helpful service are simply superb. We had a comfortable bedroom with a sea view. The food was well cooked and presented. There is a steep slope from the road down to the hotel and about 30 steps down to sea level, so not suitable for the infirm." (*Mrs AM Coppin, Mrs Noreen Redfern*)

Open 1 Apr–end Oct.
Rooms 5 suites, 36 double, 3 single – 3 with bath, 36 with shower, all with telephone, radio, TV, mini-bar and air-conditioning.
Facilities Hall, lounge, 2 bars, restaurant. Small grounds with terraces down to sea, sea-water swimming pool, private rocky beach with safe bathing and fishing. English spoken.
Location 1 km W of Minori, 3 km E of Amalfi. Parking.
Restriction Not suitable for ♿.
Credit cards All major cards accepted.
Terms B&B: single 70,000-100,000 L, double 100,000-160,000 L; half board 80,000-130,000 L per person; full board 90,000-140,000 L. Alc (excluding wine) 40,000 L. Reductions of 25% for children under 6, 15% for children over 6 sharing parents' room.

Hotel Palumbo
Via S. Giovanni del Toro 28

Tel (089) 857244
Telex 770101 VUILLE

There is a strange story attached to this startlingly beautiful hotel, owned and run by Pasquale Vuilleumier. In the mid-19th century his grandfather, from Switzerland, bought a 12th-century episcopal palace up the road and on the advice of Wagner (who was writing bits of *Parsifal* in a nearby villa) turned it into a hotel. Over the years his guests there included Longfellow, Grieg, DH Lawrence (he worked on *Lady Chatterley* in one of the rooms), Garbo, Bogart and the Kennedys. But about six years ago Signor Vuilleumier transferred the hotel to his own residence, the Palazzo Confalone, also 12th-century. The original *Palumbo* is now deserted save for its illustrious ghosts, but the newer *Palumbo* he has converted with exquisite taste. Its high-ceilinged central foyer is a miracle of cool white arches, plants and flowers, and vistas of the azure sea far below. The canopied dining-room terrace and the lemon-tree-shaded lounge terrace have the same miraculous view. "The most romantic place I have ever stayed in," says a visitor this year. "The view from our bedroom balcony was breathtaking, literally between sea and sky, and the bedroom itself was stunning with its blue and white tiles. The food in the elegant dining-room was good without being remarkable, but the wines were excellent. Signor Vuilleumier, now in his seventies, was very amiable although regretting the grandeur of the past." (*Stefan and Yvette Wiener*)

Open All year.
Rooms 3 suites, 17 double – all with bath and shower, telephone, TV and baby-listening. 7 in annexe 50 yards from main building.
Facilities Salons, bar, TV lounge, restaurant; sun terrace. Garden; solarium. Beaches 10-15 minutes by car. English spoken.
Location Above the Amalfi Drive, overlooking Ravello. Parking.
Restriction Not suitable for ♿.
Credit cards All major cards accepted.
Terms B&B: double 206,000-336,000 L, suite 326,000-486,000 L; half board 148,000-288,000 L per person; full board 150,000-315,000 L. Set lunch/dinner 45,000 L. Reduced rates for children; special meals.

ROME — Map 16

Hotel Cesàri

Tel (06) 6792386 and 6797504

Via di Pietra 89a, Rome 00186

A remarkable discovery this year, in the heart of old Rome, just off the strident via del Corso. According to its brochure, the *Cesàri* has been a hotel since the early 18th century, and former guests have included Stendhal, Mazzini and Garibaldi: but (believe it or not), though it was once a palace, today it is a modest and quite low-priced hotel, rating just one gable in *Michelin*. Our reporter: "This is as near as you will get in central Rome to a *Relais du Silence*: we had a pleasant room overlooking the small street, but as it is a cul-de-sac the curse of the Lambretta is relieved. The phones would have been instantly recognisable to Alexander Graham Bell, and the lift reminded me of Fellini's *Giulietta degli Spiriti*, but it did work. The beds were comfortable and the staff charming. Breakfast was typical of Italy – delicious *hot* coffee with UHT milk pulverised to atoms and reconstituted à la milk-shake, fresh rolls like cannon-balls and revolting soggy Motta buns tasting of some chemical (probably in contravention of some EEC law), but the jams even in their pre-packaged tubs tasted good and fruity. No restaurant, but nearby try *Il Falchetto*, fairly priced, or – for a splurge – *Da Bologna*." (*Paul Palmer*) More reports please on this quirky idyll.

Open All year.
Rooms 42 double, 8 single – all with bath and/or shower, and telephone.
Facilities Lift. Lounge with TV, bar. English spoken.
Location Central, off via del Corso.
Credit cards All major cards accepted.
Terms [1987 rates] Rooms: single 37,000-71,000 L, double 65,900-85,700 L. Breakfast 10,000 L. (No restaurant)

Hotel Forum

Tel (06) 6792446
Telex 622549

Via dei Fori Imperiale
Rome 00184

So many of our Roman entries were dropped from the Guide last year that we are glad now to welcome the *Forum*, a solid classic ochre-coloured building, fairly smart and upper-medium in price. As its name implies, it is very close to the Foro Romano, but tucked away down a small street: "The ideal place to stay in Rome if you want to explore the pagan monuments and leave the Christian ones alone. It is not a tourist-trap but a hotel of obvious quality with a rooftop restaurant to match, half indoors, half out. Somehow, amid the swarming sightseers and the teeming traffic, the *Forum* keeps its cool. The lobby, all polished wood, period furniture, and bits of Roman wall and marble column, offers a welcome respite. There is a clubby, aristocratic but far from stuffy atmosphere in the public areas that is appealing. Rooms are on the small side, but ours was very clean and comfortable. Noise is a serious problem in Rome, but two sets of shutters and two sets of curtains proved an adequate baffle. The service is obliging. But prices are fairly steep." (*Adrian Turner*) We should welcome reports on the cuisine.

Open All year. Restaurant closed Sun.
Rooms 79 – all with bath or shower, telephone, radio, TV, teamaking-facilities and baby-listening.
Facilities Hall, bar, TV room, panoramic restaurant; roof garden. English spoken.
Restriction Not suitable for ♿.
Location Central, just E of Via dei Imperiali and Forum.
Credit cards All major cards accepted.
Terms B&B: single 166,000-214,000 L, double 262,000-307,000 L. Full alc 55,000 L. Reduced rates for children sharing parents' room; special meals.

Hotel Gregoriana *Tel* (06) 6794269
Via Gregoriana 18, Rome 00187

A former convent near the top of the Spanish steps has been turned into a sophisticated little hotel with unusual decor – a landing with black satin walls and leopardskin cushions, etc. Despite its location it is quiet: "Our room, with two broad windows overlooking a little courtyard, was *silent* from midnight until dawn. It was a generous and comfortable room in a mixture of Erté and American Chinese, with a big, sunny bathroom in blues and mauves. Because it is so small, the *Gregoriana* might be a bit claustrophobic for a long stay but for a few nights it's near perfect." "The staff are extremely friendly and helpful. Breakfast would arrive in our room almost immediately after we had telephoned." "The owner is so welcoming; our third-floor room at the back looked out over rooftops with beautiful roof gardens and orange and lemon trees in fruit." Book well ahead. No lounge and no resaturant, but there are lots of good ones close by. (*Lady Macdonald, D and C Rivers, and others*)

Open All year.
Rooms 16 double, 3 single – 12 with bath, 7 with shower, all with telephone; TV on request. 4 ground-floor rooms.
Facilities Lift. Hall. English spoken.
Location Central, above Spanish Steps. Parking.
Credit cards None accepted.
Terms B&B: single 100,000 L, double 155,000 L. Reduced rates for children. (No restaurant.)

Hotel La Residenza *Tel* (06) 463271 and 460789
Via Emilia 22 *Telex* 410423 GIOTEL
Rome 00187 attn La Residenza

A small but luxurious hotel in a good location, around the corner from the Via Veneto and near the Villa Borghese. "We found this hotel from your Guide and were delighted with it," runs a letter this year. "Comfortably furnished with pleasing decor and ambience, staff most courteous and helpful." An earlier visitor had a huge double room complete with refrigerator, sofa and writing desk, while the bathroom had its own telephone and a heated towel rack. Some rooms are quite small, however, and the hotel faces a night-club which could be noisy; rooms at the back are preferable. No restaurant: but there are good ones in the area, such as the small family-run *Tempio di Bacco,* via Lombardia. (*Angus Sibley, Ann Mattingley, Kathleen McCleery, Ann Kearton, Robert Martinez.*)

Open All year.
Rooms 24 double, 3 single – 24 with bath and shower, 3 with shower, all with direct-dial telephone, radio, TV and mini-bar.
Facilities 2 halls, 3 lounges, breakfast room; terrace and patio. Air conditioning. English spoken.
Location Central, near the Via Veneto and American Embassy (back rooms quietest). Parking.
Restriction Not suitable for ♿.
Credit cards None accepted.
Terms B&B: single 95,000 L, double 147,000 L. 1-night bookings sometimes refused. Reduced rates for children sharing parents' room. (No restaurant.)

SAN GIMIGNANO 53037 Siena — Map 16

Bel Soggiorno — *Tel* (0577) 940375
Via S. Giovanni 91

San Gimignano seems unchanged since the Middle Ages but, although on the tourist trail, it has escaped the pretentiousness of other "museum" towns. Its 14 straight towers rising above the rooftops are indeed an extraordinary sight. The *Bel Soggiorno* is a lovely 13th-century building, just inside the town walls, recommended again this year for its very reasonable prices, good food and efficient service. The top floor of the hotel is to be avoided if possible: hot, and noisy with plumbing. The remaining rooms, though small, are adequate, some with terraces and most with magnificent views. There is a TV salon but no garden, and if hot water is a priority, you had better think twice; otherwise, "a good find!" "The menu," says one reader, "is permanently unchanged but always excellent. Best of all is risotto di Bel Soggiorno with nutmeg and cream, but it is always tempting to order pollo al diavolo which comes aflame! One wall of the restaurant is glass and the views of the Tuscan hills and olive groves are spectacular." (*BW Ribbons, Nina Bawden, Lord Vernon, P Vischer, and others*)

Open All year. Restaurant closed Mon.
Rooms 25 double – all with bath and shower, telephone and tea-making facilities.
Facilities Lift. Salon with TV, restaurant. English spoken.
Location 30 km from Siena; cars allowed in for loading and unloading only. Car-park nearby.
Restrictions Not suitable for ♿. No children under 8.
Credit cards All major cards accepted.
Terms B&B: single occupancy 42,000 L, double 58,000 L. Set lunch/dinner 25,000-34,000 L; full alc 30,000 L. 1-night bookings sometimes refused.

Hotel La Cisterna — *Tel* (0577) 940328
Piazza della Cisterna 24 — *Telex* 575152

A palazzo with a 14th-century facade, fronting the main square where the townsfolk gather in the evening. Many rooms have balcony facing either this urban animation or the wide Tuscan landscape. Rooms quite large, some simple, some more luxurious. Splendid church-like lounge; beamed restaurant with stunning view but variable cooking. Open 10 Mar–10 Nov. 46 rooms, all with bath and/or shower. B&B double 84,000 L. Full alc from 25,000 L. Little recent feedback: more reports welcome.

Hotel Pescille *Tel* (0577) 940186
Località Pescille

An old farmhouse converted into a country inn, outside the town and just off the road to Siena. "The spotlessly clean rooms are comfortably furnished in 'rural modern' style and each has a magnificent view of the surrounding countryside. Those in the front have a view of San Gimignano while those on the back overlook extensive gardens, vineyards and a pool. A good breakfast is served in a charming room and light lunches are available on the outdoor terrace. A peaceful, comfortable place in beautiful countryside." (*Elizabeth Ring*) A 1987 visitor reports electricity failures and water problems. Isolated instances? More reports please.

Open 1 Dec–7 Jan, 1 Mar–4 Nov. Restaurant closed Wed.
Rooms 31 double, 2 single – all with bath and telephone.
Facilities 2 lounges, TV room, 2 bars, breakfast room. Garden with terrace, tennis court and swimming pool.
Location 3 km from San Gimignano, on provincial road from Castel San Gimignano to Volterra.
Restriction Not suitable for ♿.
Credit cards Amex, Diners, Visa.
Terms B&B: single 45,000 L, double 80,000 L. Light lunches available for 35,000 L.)

SAN MAMETE 22010 Como — Map 16

Hotel Stella d'Italia *Tel* (0344) 68139
Piazza Roma 1
(postal address: PO Box 3,
San Mamete, Valsolda
6976 Castagnola, Switzerland)

A small hotel with a very special quality, right on Lake Lugano and close to the Swiss border. The English-speaking owners, the Ortellis, have been running it for decades, and have won a faithfully returning clientele, many of them English. The bedrooms, each with its own balcony on which you can breakfast, all have views across the lake to the green slopes and the mountains in the distance. There is a garden leading down to a "lido" for swimming or sunbathing. In good weather, dinner is served on the pretty trellised terrace, with the water at one's feet, but the indoor dining room also has fine views.

More praise has come in this year. For example: "The somewhat restrained un-Italian aura is more than compensated for by the fat delights of the beautiful veranda restaurant, the attentive service, the tranquil lido by the lake (but beware Germans bearing huge lilos) and a library which must have the largest collection of Warwick Deeping in north Italy." But we receive the occasional complaint, too. For example, that the *en pension* food is a little plain and boring, or that the evening meal is served sharp at 7.30 (but there is a later sitting), or that the hotel is not for light sleepers. One family this year received curt treatment, and thought it might be because they had come with young children: but the Ortellis assure us they welcome children and offer them special meals and reduced rates. (*Prof Laurie Taylor, Sandra Martin, Bernadette Murray, and many others*)

Open Apr–Oct.
Rooms 31 double, 5 single – all with bath or shower, balcony and telephone.
Facilities 2 lounges, bar, restaurant. Garden with easy chairs and open-air restaurant. Lake bathing, fishing, surfing, boating. 18-hole golf course 10 km away. English spoken.
Location 10 km NE of Lugano on Lake Lugano between Gandria and Menaggio. Garage for 14 cars.
Restriction Not suitable for ♿.
Credit cards All major cards accepted.
Terms B&B: single 42,000-52,000 L, double 63,000-76,000 L; dinner, B&B 44,000-58,000 L per person; full board 52,000-66,000 L. Set lunch/dinner 24,000 L; full alc 30,000-40,000 L. Reduced rates and special meals for children.

SELVA DI VAL GARDENA 39048 Bolzano — Map 16

Hotel Dorfer — *Tel* (0471) 75204

"Selva, also known as Wolkenstein, is a village in the highest part of the Val Gardena: the Austrian name comes from a 13th-century castle that was the birthplace of the *Minnesinger* Oswald von Wolkenstein. The country people speak Ladinisch and German in preference to Italian. Spring is earlier here than in the northern Alps and the flowers are magnificent. There is good skiing, and chairlifts for those who want them.

"The meadow has been built up with ski chalets but the *Dorfer* preserves an uninterrupted view of nearby woods, a church spire and the distant mountains. It is very quiet and the air is like peppermint. Over the years the *Dorfer* has become increasingly comfortable, but it remains an essentially homely place. The food is very good indeed and the breakfast table has everything the most diet-conscious person could want, including a variety of fresh local breads. The sitting rooms are not large but are cheerful and many bedrooms have a balcony. But what makes the *Dorfer* special is Frau Dorfer herself. Her guests become her friends, and are treated as such, though she never intrudes. She has a warm sense of hospitality that is shared by the staff. The hotel has never let me down." (*Jean Rowntree*)

Open 18 Dec–15 Apr, 4 June–Sept. Restaurant closed to non-residents.
Rooms 30 – most with bath and/or shower and telephone; many with balcony.
Facilities Salon, bar, restaurants; jacuzzi, sauna and gym. Garden with terrace for alfresco meals and table tennis. Tennis and winter sports nearby.
Location 42 km E of Bolzano.
Credit cards None accepted.
Terms [1987 rates] Rooms: single 35,000 L, double 70,000 L. Breakfast 12.000 L. Full board (min 3 days) 70,000-100,000 L per person. Alc (excluding wine) 24,000-35,000 L.

If you feel we have done a hotel an injustice
If we have failed to mention salient details
If you consider we have got it about right
} please let us know.

SESTRI LEVANTE 16039 Genova — Map 16

Hotel Helvetia — *Tel* (0185) 41175 and 47216
Via Cappuccini 43 — *Telex* 272003 HELVET

An attractively positioned hotel overlooking the Bay of Silence – the oldest and most interesting part of an otherwise rather tatty Riviera resort. "We enjoyed this hotel, its food and above all the friendliness and helpfulness of the owners," runs a recent report. "Our room was small but adequate and clean. There are pretty terraces outside, and a private 'beach' opposite, which consisted of a very small area of dirty grey sand." Another report endorsed the friendly atmosphere and scenic situation: "Complimentary beverages of choice on arrival and a *very* drinkable bottle of wine on departure. Gardens and terrace with great view." (*J and CL, ME, Alan Murray-Garner*) More reports please.

Open 15 Mar–15 Oct.
Rooms 28 double, – 14 with bath, 14 with shower, all with direct-dial telephone, and radio.
Facilities Lift. Lounge, TV lounge, restaurant with terrace looking over the sea. Large terraced garden, solarium. Private beach. English spoken.
Location 100 metres from town centre, overlooking the Bay of Silence. Garage.
Credit cards None accepted.
Terms [1987 rates] B&B: double 60,000-80,000 L. Set lunch/dinner 25,000-30,000 L. Full alc 35,000 L. Reduced rates for children; special meals.

SIENA 53100 — Map 16

Hotel Certosa di Maggiano — *Tel* (0577) 288180
Via Certosa 82 — *Telex* 574221 CERMAG

Of the oldest Carthusian monastery in Tuscany (built 1314) just the cloister and tower remain, and these now form part of this luxurious and well-converted little hotel, lying a mile outside the city walls in a bucolic setting. It is an unusual place with a powerful personality which may not suit everyone. "Some might find the intimacy, relentless good taste and attention to detail a little precious," writes one devotee returning this year, "but others, myself included, are enchanted by the beautiful old building, the sumptuous bedrooms, the recorded Mozart in the library, the swimming pool looking over the vineyards to the walls of Siena, and the formal but *nice* service. Food is modern Italian: dishes may sound dull (veal with herbs, etc) but most of them look and taste superb. Meal prices are high, but include a free aperitif." Others have joined in the praise: "The swimming pool is in a natural garden with peach and apricot trees overlooking the vineyard which supplies the excellent house wine. Our room was large, furnished with antiques, chintz curtains and wall coverings. The bathroom was bright and modern with green and white tiles." "We breakfasted and dined in the central courtyard, but could have eaten in a ravishingly pretty dining room (only residents may dine). Our dinner was, gastronomically speaking, the best in ten days of intensive Italian eating. While we were lounging by the pool, a bowl of freshly picked figs and grapes was put in our room; while we dined, a dish of sweets was placed by the bedside. All in all, the manners and civilised charm of an earlier epoch, bolstered by 20th-century plumbing – but alas at 20th-century prices. Our stay was a joy to remember." (*David Wooff, Anthony Rota*)

Open All year. Restaurant closed to non-residents.
Rooms 9 suites, 5 double – all with bath and shower, telephone, radio, TV. Ground-floor rooms.
Facilities Lift. Salon, library, TV room, games room, bar, dining room. Garden with heated swimming pool and tennis court. English spoken.
Location 1 km SE of Siena outside gate of Porta Romana. Parking.
Credit cards All major cards accepted.
Terms B&B: double 240,000-280,000 L; suite 400,000-490,000 L. Set lunch 60,000 L, dinner 85,000 L. Reduced rates for children; special meals.

Hotel Garden *Tel* (0577) 47056
Via Custoza 2 *Telex* 574239

A comfortable hotel with a large well-kept garden and a good-sized pool, on a hill overlooking the city, two kilometres from the centre to the north-west. Very quiet, pleasant lounges and terraces; food nothing special. 67 rooms, many with shower, 48,000-80,000 L. Alc meals (excluding wine) 26,000-37,000 L [1987]. New nomination: more reports please, on food and bedrooms.

Pensione Palazzo Ravizza *Tel* (0577) 280462
Pian dei Mantellini 34 *Telex* 575304

This 17th-century palace in the old city, just a short walk from the Duomo and famous piazza, has been in the Grottanelli family for two centuries and is today a resolutely traditional "class 1" *pensione*, much admired by some readers but maybe not to all tastes. Much of the original antique furniture is still in place; there is a grand piano in the drawing room and a tea room opening onto a terraced garden. Some rooms have lovely views over the Sienese countryside and most are huge and high-ceilinged. "We could have given a dance in ours. No private bathroom, but we had a demurely screened-off corner with large basins and bidets. Our waiter served us with enormous charm – and with white gloves!" Others have enjoyed the hotel's patrician grace, lovely setting and friendly owners. Some have found its grandeur a little *too* run-down and the food unexciting, so it lost its place in recent Guides. But several visitors this year have liked it a lot, and found the food much improved: "A wonderful hotel full of history, and its guest books are full of poetry." "The atmosphere is delightful – dark passages with improving Latin inscriptions over the doors, intense Germanic and Anglo-Saxon visitors, a feeling of plain living and high thinking. The food is in the same style, robust and solid, with huge helpings. A splendid elderly couple seem to be in charge. One can imagine Virginia Woolf or EM Forster in a *pensione* like this." Guests are expected to take dinner, which can be a drawback. Rooms at the back are quietest and have the best views. (*Andrew and Jan Palmer, Robert Stevens and Alexa Grace*)

Open All year.
Rooms 3 suites, 23 double, 4 single – 18 with bath, 3 with shower, all with telephone. Some ground-floor rooms.
Facilities Lift. 3 lounges (1 with TV, 1 with piano, 1 with library), tea room, bar, restaurant. Large garden with terrace for breakfast. English spoken.
Location 500 metres from centre; enter Siena by Porta San Marco; parking.

Credit cards All major cards accepted.
Terms Dinner, B&B: single 82,900 L, double 149,000 L, suite 171,000 L. Reduced rates for children under 3.

Villa Scacciapensieri *Tel* (0577) 41441
Via di Scacciapensieri 10 *Telex* 573390 VI SCA

A Tuscan villa on a hillside outside Siena, surrounded by vineyards and olive trees (but industrial suburbia is encroaching). Admired over the years for its lovely garden, tastefully furnished rooms, quiet and relaxing atmosphere, and the friendliness of the Nardi family owners; good food served indoors or under the trees. Clientele mainly German. Open 20 Mar–5 Nov. 29 rooms, all with bath and shower. B&B double 190,000 L. Set meals 35,000–40,000 L. Recent reports few and lukewarm: new ones welcome.

SINALUNGA 53048 Siena Map 16

Locanda dell'Amorosa *Tel* (0577) 679497
Telex 580047 AMOR

This entrancing Guide newcomer is a cluster of old stone buildings on the edge of the lovely Sienese hills, transformed from a private residence into a select and expensive little country inn – "one of the nicest hotels we have found in Italy", say the expert travellers who nominate it: "Converted from an old estate, it is still a working farm, producing its own wines, jams and honey. The beautiful old buildings of various shapes and sizes surround a central courtyard with a huge well. The estate chapel has some superb frescoes. Our room was really a suite, its beamed rooms comfortably furnished with antiques; floors were red Tuscan tiles, with rugs. The restaurant, in the old stables, is a fascinating room in very rustic style. The food is excellent (*Michelin* rosette), and the menu includes traditional Tuscan dishes and unusual fish from lake Trasimeno. Service, by local girls, is quiet and efficient. Breakfast was also excellent, with lovely hot fresh-baked brioches. There is a comfortable lounge, and chairs under giant umbrellas in the courtyard. The pleasant staff mostly spoke English. Siena, Arezzo and Perugia are all within easy reach." (*Pat and Jeremy Temple; also Patrick Gale*)

Open All year. Restaurant closed Mon and Tue midday, and 20 Jan–28 Feb.
Rooms 7 – all with bath and shower, telephone, TV and refrigerator.
Facilities Hall, lounge with fire-place, restaurant. Garden and courtyard. English spoken.
Location 2 km S of Sinalunga which is 45 km E of Siena. Parking.
Credit cards Amex, Diners, Visa.
Terms [1987 rates] Rooms 180,000 L. Breakfast 10,000 L. Alc (excluding wine) 44,000-64,000 L.

SORRENTO 80067 Naples Map 16

Pensione La Tonnarella *Tel* (081) 8781153
Via del Capo 31

An unusual little *pensione*, spectacularly sited on a cliff above the sea, and sharply assessed by a visitor this year: "An odd place. We were greeted by the charming elderly 'hall porter' who was sitting on a chair in the doorway and led us down past an astonishing assortment of 19th-century engravings to meet the owner, Carlo Gargiulo, who runs the place very efficiently. Nearly all the rooms face away from the noisy main road. Ours was clean and bright but designed for the hot summer, so was cold in April. The dining room with its huge windows had a panoramic view of one of the world's finest views – the bay of Naples. Service was helpful and the food appetising, though there was a tendency to serve octopus at every meal. The beach is rather small and littered, but the lift down the cliff-face does work and the *pensione* supplies deckchairs you can take down with you. A pleasant place, certainly different from Sorrento's many big hotels." Another 1987 guest also appreciated the stunning site, but was less complimentary about the management and staff (some were "haughty and abrupt"), and about the food. More reports would be welcome.

Open 1 Apr–30 Oct.
Rooms 18 double – 8 with bath, 10 with shower; 9 with terrace. Some ground-floor rooms.
Facilities Lift. Lounge, bar, TV room, restaurant; terrace. Garden. Lift to private beach with cabins and bar; motor and rowing boats available.
Location 1 km W of centre. Parking.
Credit cards Amex, Diners, Visa.
Terms Double room: dinner, B&B 45,000 L; full board 55,000 L. Set lunch/dinner 15,000 L; full alc 25,000 L. Reduced rates for children; special meals.

SYRACUSE 96100 Sicily — Map 16

Grand Hotel Villa Politi

Via M Politi Laudien 2 — *Tel* (0931) 32100
Telex 970205

This imposing hotel is set directly above the deep limestone quarries where, in ancient times, thousands of invading Greeks were held captive and left to die. Today the quarries are full of trees and flowers, but the memory remains. The *Villa Politi* was built in the pompous late 19th-century style with vast shutters, high rooms, antique plumbing and peeling paint, but a recent visitor found it "a delightful place to stay". Another view: "This hotel once must have been glorious. It's somewhat run-down now, but for those who care about character, and who have a sense of humour and some patience, it's acceptable. In fact, for all its faults, we loved it. Our rooms were spacious and comfortable, even if the furniture was mismatched. The bathroom was nothing short of majestic." (*David H Clark, Tom and Connie Congdon*)

Open All year.
Rooms 2 suites, 55 double, 35 single – all with bath and/or shower and telephone; some with radio and mono TV; many with balcony.
Facilities 2 lifts. Large reception hall, TV room, bar, restaurant; conference and function facilities. Large garden and park; terrace restaurant; swimming pool. Rocky beach with fishing rights 200 metres; sandy beach 17 km. English spoken.
Location 2 km N of centre, near Piazza Cappuccini. Parking.
Restriction Not suitable for ♿.
Credit cards Access, Amex, Diners.
Terms B&B: single 51,000-56,000 L, double 80,000-206,000 L; dinner, B&B 58,500-75,000 L per person; full board 77,500-95,000 L. Full alc 36,000 L. Reduced rates for children.

TAORMINA 98039 Messina, Sicily — Map 16

San Domenico Palace Hotel — *Tel* (0942) 23701
Piazza San Domenico 5 — *Telex* 980013 DOMHOT

This famous and palatial hotel on its high promontory began life as a monastery. In 1943 Kesselring used it as his headquarters and much of the original 15th-century building, apart from the miraculously intact cloister, was destroyed by Allied bombs. "The reception area," ran our initial report on it, "is like a discreet Mayfair bank, but just beyond is the interior courtyard and it is here that you begin to believe this may be the world's most beautiful hotel. The staircase is grand and straight; the corridor is incredibly long and wide; the view from the balcony is sensational. Below are the gardens, ablaze with colour and punctuated by palms, and beyond is the smoky profile of Mount Etna, sometimes clear and proud, sometimes hazy and mysterious." Some have described it as "the queen of Sicilian hotels". But we have had tales of dull food and persistent mosquitoes, while this year a sharp-eyed British hotelier gave what may be the definitive view: "Lovely cloister and courtyards to which have been added an ill-proportioned, gloomy and ill-furnished Edwardian block. We much preferred the old section, though the rooms lack the large balconies of the Edwardian part. Garden beautifully kept – unusual for Sicily. Housekeeping poor – some passages neglected. Staff not instructed by management to be nice to clients. Would be a wonderful place if properly managed. As it is, passable." Go, then, for the historic splendour, but don't expect a "good hotel".

Open All year.
Rooms 10 suites, 80 double, 28 single – all with bath, direct-dial telephone, radio, TV and air-conditioning.
Facilities Lift. Hall, 4 lounges, bar, TV room, games room, dining room; conference facilities; mandolin group every night in bar; courtyard terrace. Garden with heated swimming pool and snack bar. Private beach (car service). Tennis nearby. English spoken.
Location On promontory on W side of town, but close to centre.
Restriction Not suitable for ♿.
Credit cards All major cards accepted.
Terms [1987 rates] B&B: single 207,000 L, double 354,000 L, suite 474,000-534,000 L; full board 250,000-310,000 L per person. Set lunch/dinner 60,000 L. Reduced rates for children sharing parents' room.

Villa Fiorita — *Tel* (0942) 24122
Via L. Pirandello 39

Just next to the cable car station that takes you down to the beach, *Villa Fiorita* is a *simpatico* hotel with a large garden, sunny verandas and a fine view of the coast. A reader this year enjoyed all this, as well as the lovely swimming pool and breakfast on the flowery terrace. Inside the hotel there are several sitting rooms – plenty of nooks and crannies to hide away with a book. "Our room was a decent size and included such modern amenities as a refrigerator, TV and large bathroom. The decor was somewhat quaint. We had a brass bed, and a balcony with a panoramic view of the town and the sheer cliff leading down to the water." (*Anne and David Gray, and others*)

Please make a habit of sending a report if you stay at a Guide hotel.

Open All year.
Rooms 2 suites, 22 double – 21 with bath and shower, 3 with shower, all with telephone, radio, TV, mini-bar and air-conditioning; some doubles have terrace or balcony.
Facilities Hall, 2 lounges, bar, restaurant (for breakfast and snacks), games room. Large garden with terraces, swimming pool and sauna. 50 metres to sandy beach (cable car down). English spoken.
Location Central, near Greek theatre, but quiet. Garage (5,000 L).
Restriction Not suitable for ♿. No children under 10.
Credit card Amex.
Terms [1987 rates] Double rooms 67,000 L, suite 86,950 L. Breakfast 5,500 L. 1-night bookings sometimes refused in high season. Reduced rates for children sharing parents' room. (No restaurant.)

Hotel Pensione Villa Paradiso *Tel* (0942) 23921
Via Roma 2

More approval this year (with reservations) for this pleasant class I *pensione* close to the centre of town. The public rooms are decorated in traditional Sicilian style and the fourth-floor restaurant with its many windows takes full advantage of the spectacular view of Etna and the coast, as does the sun terrace. "Beautifully located next to the enchanting little public park. Good taste carried through to nearly every detail – very pretty interiors. An accommodating staff, led by the owner, the gracious, soft-spoken Salvatore Martorana. A pleasant restaurant, with good food." Others too have admired the location, the food and the friendly service, though one reader this year found his room noisy and the hot water inadequate (*DT White, T and CC, EL*) The hotel now has its own lido down at Letojanni, with free minibus transport to and fro.

Open All year, except 5 Nov–19 Dec.
Rooms 9 suites, 21 double, 3 single – 28 with bath, 5 with shower, all with balcony, telephone, radio, air-conditioning and baby-listening; 9 with TV. 1 ground-floor room.
Facilities Lifts. Lounges, TV lounge, library, bars, panoramic restaurant; facilities for small conferences; sun terraces with tables. Next door to public gardens with free tennis courts. Free mini-bus transport to private lido. English spoken.
Location 5 minutes to town centre; hotel is signposted. Some town-view rooms are close to road. Public parking 200 metres.
Credit cards All major cards accepted.
Terms B&B 40,000-56,000 L; dinner, B&B 60,000-88,000 L; full board 72,000-105,000 L. Set lunch 27,500 L, dinner 27,500-30,000 L. 15% discount for stays of 10 days or more; also for honeymoon couples and elderly couples (min 7 days).

TELLARO DI LERICI 19030 La Spezia — Map 16

Il Nido di Fiascherino *Tel* (0187) 967286 and 966429
Via Fiascherino 75

A modern hotel in a splendid location, above a cove in a small village near Lerici on the Gulf of Spezia, with fine views over beach, rocks and pine trees. The small private beach is crowded in summer, and rooms in the main building are preferred to those in the annexe across a busy main road. These limitations, plus some critical reports on main meals and breakfasts, caused the the *Nido* to lose its place in the 1986 Guide, but four accounts this year are more enthusiastic: "An excellent choice for a few days in September. Coast is as idyllic now as it must have been when

Shelley drowned here. The beach facilities have room for improvement, but the dining room is cool, white and spacious with lovely views of the bay, and food was good and plentiful – good fish and seafood, and salads etc from a self-service buffet. Breakfast is also self-service, with cheese, ham etc: sybarites who opt for breakfast in bed do less well on packaged toast. Other guests included a Sloane-ish couple and an English judge and his wife." "A lovely hotel with friendly staff, excellent food and coffee; our room large and spotless." "Very good service, hot fresh croissants." An earlier view: "Our room with balcony overlooked the bay where waves crashed thrillingly day and night over the rocks below." (*A Rozenberg, Dr and Mrs GA Jones, Nina Bawden; also Eric Dodson*)

Open All year.
Rooms 1 suite, 33 double, 5 single – 1 with bath, 37 with shower, all with telephone and baby-listening; some with balcony. 23 in annexe nearby.
Facilities TV room, bar, 2 dining rooms; terraces. Garden. Small private beach. English spoken.
Location 2 km SE of Lerici; follow signes for Lerici and Tellaro. Parking.
Restriction Not suitable for ♿.
Credit cards All major cards accepted.
Terms B&B: single 52,500-54,600 L, double 80,850 L; dinner B&B 73,500-94,500 L per person. Set lunch/dinner 35,000 L; full alc 45,000 L. Reduced rates for children; special meals.

TORGIANO 06089 Perugia — Map 16

Le Tre Vaselle — *Tel* (075) 982447
Via Garibaldi 48 — *Telex* 564028 TREVAS

"Peaceful and quiet, in a side-street of a charming Umbrian village south of Perugia and near the E7 *autostrada.* The interior is fascinating, with broad white arches and large and comfortable lounge and dining room, and the rooms are attractively decorated, with textiles, rugs and flowers suggesting a woman's careful touch. Our bedroom was spacious, and its window looked onto the countryside. The staff were friendly, and on *demi-pension* we were served delicious Umbrian specialities – the best food we had in Italy, south of Milan. The hotel, much used for conferences of oenologists, is owned by Lungarotti wine which operates an interesting wine museum in the village." (*Sally and Ken Burt*)

Open All year.
Rooms 1 suite, 47 double – all with bath and/or shower and telephone.
Facilities Lift. Reading room, piano bar (music every evening), TV room, breakfast room, restaurant; terrace where meals are served.
Location 15 km S of Perugia, just E of *autostrada.*
Restriction Not suitable for ♿.
Credit cards All major cards accepted.
Terms Dinner, B&B: single 155,000 L, double 280,000 L, suite 400,000 L. Full alc 48,000 L. Reduced rates for children under 8.

TORNO 22020 Como — Map 16

Villa Flora — *Tel* (031) 419922

No beauty from the outside, but splendidly located right by the lake, this unpretentious little hotel in a village just north of Como comes new to the Guide this year: "We stayed three days and loved this place, which is run by a rather camp male duo who cannot do enough to please their guests. The rooms are simple and blessedly quiet, save for the lapping of the water just below, and the beds let us sleep undisturbed. The food was excellent (small wonder that locals use the place for wedding parties): one member of the duo cooks, the other takes orders in a multitude of Eurospeak (including perfect English). Our shower was separated from the rest of the bathroom by what can only be described as a huge umbrella, so after a shower it looked as if Gene Kelly had just performed *Singing in the Rain*. I was stunned by the beauty of the view from the terrace, and almost as stunned by the reasonableness of the prices." (*Paul Palmer*) More reports please.

Open Mar–Oct. Restaurant closed Tue.
Rooms 20 double – all with shower, WC and telephone.
Facilities Lounge, bar, TV room, restaurant; conference facilities; terrace. Small garden with private beach on lake, bathing. English spoken.
Location 6 km N of Como. Take road to Bellagio: hotel is down road on left just past centre of Torno. Private parking.
Restriction Not suitable for severely ♿.
Credit card Visa.
Terms Rooms: 60,000-65,000 L. Set lunch 20,000-25,000 L, dinner 25,000-30,000 L; full alc 30,000-35,000 L. Special meals for children.

TORRI DEL BENACO 37010 Verona — Map 16

Hotel Gardesana — *Tel* (045) 7225411
Piazza Calderini 20

Very crowded in summer, especially with German tourists, this little resort on the eastern shore of Lake Garda boasts a 14th-century castle; boat services ply to Catullus' romantic Sirmione and other spots around the lake. The *Gardesana* faces the little harbour, a traditional hotel with arcades and orange-brown stucco walls, but modernised inside. "An ideal honeymoon-style hotel," writes an enthusiast this year. "We spent a delightful week, enjoying the very comfortable rooms, above-average food and friendly service." "Our balcony had a view across the lake. An enormous breakfast was brought up to our room at no extra charge. Everyone in the hotel was most helpful and the price was amazingly reasonable." The dining room has an outdoor terrace facing the harbour. Front rooms facing the lake can be noisy at night, and one visitor this year has complained that the groups of musicians who play in the evenings may well consist of "a loud band with a Frank Sinatra impersonator singing Italian favourites such as *My Old Kentucky Home*", which might not be quite what honeymooners would want. (*Allison Bretherton, Pat Clinch, and others*)

Open Mar–Oct, Christmas and New Year.
Rooms 31 double, 3 single – 4 with bath, 30 with shower, all with telephone and air-conditioning; some with balcony. Some ground-floor rooms.
Facilities Lift. TV lounge, bar, dining room with outdoor terrace; conference room; portico with dancing in summer. Private cabins at lido 300 metres from the hotel. Water sports, golf, tennis and riding nearby. English spoken.
Location In centre of Torri del Benaco which is 45 km NW of Verona. Private parking.
Credit cards All major cards accepted.
Terms B&B: single 48,000-60,000 L, double 75,000-100,000 L; dinner, B&B: single 58,000-75,000 L, double 100,000-150,000 L. Set dinner 25,000 L; full alc 30,000 L.

TRICESIMO 33019 Udine — Map 16

Hotel Ristorante Boschetti — *Tel* (0432) 851230 and 851531
Piazza Mazzini 10

To the north of the delightful city of Udine, Tricesimo is a small town on the main road to Austria. Here stands the *Boschetti*, an old inn, much enlarged and modernised and now a smart hotel with a distinguished gastronomic reputation (two *Michelin* rosettes). "Family-owned and run, it is immaculately kept, with excellent public rooms and a small panelled bar. Service is most hospitable and the staff speak English. Bedrooms, simple but pleasantly furnished in 1950s style, are in a wing to the rear of the main building, thus alleviating some of the traffic noise (also, a new motorway opened in 1987 has now taken much of the heavy traffic away from the town). An excellent restaurant – traditional dishes with many modern touches – and a superb wine list with many local Friuli wines." (*Pat and Jeremy Temple*)

Open All year, except 1–15 Aug. Restaurant closed Mon.
Rooms 32 double – all with bath or shower, and telephone; 16 with TV.
Facilities Lift. 3 salons, bar, restaurant. English spoken.
Location 10 km N of Udine.
Credit cards Amex, Diners, Visa.
Terms B&B: single 69,000 L, double 106,000 L; dinner, B&B: 100,000 L per person. Full alc 50,000-70,000 L.

VENICE — Map 16

Pensione Accademia — *Tel* (041) 5237846 or 710188
Fondamenta Maravegie
Dorsoduro 1058-1060
Venice 30123

A perennially popular bed-and-breakfast pensione *housed in a delightful 17th-century villa facing a side canal only a few yards from the Grand Canal at the Accademia bridge. Rooms vary in size: some are quite small. A bonus is the patio garden – for breakfasts, tea, post-prandial drinks. For many a Venetian home-from-home, and always booked well ahead. But there have been recent complaints about poor housekeeping and offhand service. 26 rooms, 20 with bath or shower. B&B double 81,000-107,500 L. More reports would be welcome.*

Casa Frollo — *Tel* (041) 5222723
Guidecca 50, Venice 30123

Reports this year ("we loved it") corroborate this earlier classic description: "If you are prepared to forfeit the busy, bruising delights of a Piazza San Marco filled in equal parts with crabby tourists trailing after officious guides, and sad pigeons trailing after everything, escape across the water to the Giudecca and the elegant calm of the *Casa Frollo*: a terraced 17th-century palace with a soothing, uninterrupted view of the square and the Doge's Palace. Enter a cool, ordered courtyard running the whole of the ground floor and leading into a neat, narrow garden. Take the stairs to the right and ascend to a vast room liberally stocked with the kind of polished Renaissance furniture you generally meet behind red ropes. Several dozen minor modern masters' works – personally inscribed to Madame – hang along one wall, while the facing wall props up an older school. This is where breakfast is served and the interior competes distractingly well with the postcard views of the Palace to be glimpsed through the windows. Seventeenth-century swank, however, does not always spell 20th-century comfort, and it is a brisk baronial step down lofty corridors to the nearest virginia-creeper-veiled bathroom if you are not in one of the rooms favoured with a private bath. Still, it is an historical treat and remarkably reasonable: stay there!" (*PT*)

Other visitors chime in: "Being seated at the large flower-bedecked table with the superb view, together with the extraordinary variety of water traffic in the foreground, is one of our enduring memories." The small rooms at the back, facing the garden, lack the splendid view but are "amazingly quiet". (*Tom and Linda Baldwin, G O'Reilly and B Vinson, and others*)

Open 20 Mar–20 Nov.
Rooms 18 double, 8 single – 2 with bath and shower, 7 with shower, all with telephone; some with balcony.
Facilities Bar, lounge, salon, breakfast room. Garden.
Location On waterfront, on La Giudecca.
Restriction Not suitable for ♿.
Credit cards None accepted.
Terms B&B: single 41,000-53,000 L, double 75,000-93,000 L.

Hotel Cipriani — *Tel* (041) 5207744
Guidecca 10 — *Telex* 410162 CIPRVE
Venice 30133

Set on the tip of Giudecca island, facing towards the Lido, this famous luxury palace turns its back on the hurly-burly of Venice. Superior bedrooms with thick carpets and high-quality fabrics, overlooking the gardens or lagoon; stylish public rooms; terraces, sea-water pool, tennis court, piano bar. Lunch served in a pretty courtyard. A relaxing atmosphere and delicious food: but room and restaurant service have both been sharply criticised, and the vertiginous prices bring value-for-money into doubt. Open Mar–Nov. 98 rooms, all with bath and shower. B&B double 470,000-660,000 L. Full alc 90,000 L. More reports please.

Hotel Flora — *Tel* (041) 5205844
Calle larga 22 Marzo 2283/a — *Telex* 410401 FLORA
Venice 30124

This is the only medium-priced non-palatial hotel in Venice on which *Michelin* bestows its accolade of red print for special quality, and some of our own readers tend to feel likewise, as witness this account: "Ask anyone English where to stay in Venice and they'll probably say the *Flora* (unless they're in the *Gritti/Cipriani/Danieli* league). It's quiet, central (just west of St Mark's) and very inviting. Perhaps its greatest attraction is the garden – ivy-clad walls, stone fountains, handsome pots of flowering shrubs, and plenty of tables and chairs for breakfasts and Camparis. In poor weather you take breakfast in the salon, decorated in floral pinks and dark wood furniture. Bedrooms can be something of an anti-climax. You may be lucky and get one of the spacious, traditional doubles with pretty *Veneziana* painted furniture; the alternative is something much smaller and simpler, saved only by views of the garden. Breakfast is a lot more substantial than in most smaller hotels." Others have commended the helpful staff and pleasant ambience. (*SB, E Clark, Helen E Land*)

Open 1 Feb–20 Nov.
Rooms 38 double, 6 single – all with bath or shower, and telephone. 2 ground-floor rooms.
Facilities Lift. Lounge, TV room, bar, small breakfast room. Courtyard/garden where breakfast and drinks are served. English spoken.
Location Central, just off the Calle larga 22 Marzo.
Credit cards All major cards accepted.
Terms B&B: single 110,800 L, double 173,000 L. (No restaurant.)

Hotel Monaco & Grand Canal — *Tel* (041) 5200211
Calle Vallaresso, 1325 San Marco — *Telex* 410450 MONACO
Venice 30124

The elegant *Monaco* would make a slightly cheaper (but still expensive) alternative to the *Cipriani* or *Gritti*: "Right on the Grand Canal, near San Marco, and you can dine, breakfast etc on the terrace watching the world go by. Public rooms impeccable, staff friendly and mostly English-speaking, and food the best we had in Venice where we tried several highly-rated restaurants." Classic cooking, with some Venetian dishes. Pleasant leafy inner courtyard. (*RA Dubery*)

Open All year.
Rooms 4 suites, 51 double, 20 single – 63 with bath, 8 with shower, all with telephone, radio, TV and mini-bar.
Facilities Lifts. 2 lounges, piano bar with singer, 2 restaurants; conference room; terrace. Walled garden. English spoken.
Location Central, near Piazza San Marco. Quietest rooms overlook garden.
Credit cards Amex, Visa.
Terms B&B: single 110,000-210,000 L, double 170,000-320,000 L, suite 330,000-560,000 L. Full alc 80,000-95,000 L. Special meals for children.

Hotel Do Pozzi — *Tel* (041) 5207855
Calle larga 22 Marzo 2373 — *Telex* 410275 attn Do Pozzi
Venice 30124

Down an alleyway off a smart shopping street just west of San Marco, the *Do Pozzi* continues to be praised as a good-value, well-located place to stay. "A delightful B&B hotel, very central, inexpensive for Venice, where prices are high, with a staff who are charming and helpful. My room was compact, but not cramped. The meal we had at the nearby *Raffaele* (under the same management) was very enjoyable, and again pretty reasonable for Venice. In the evening the atmosphere is enchanting – the restaurant is adjacent to a canal and you can enjoy awful Italian tenors and accordions sailing past in gondolas as you tuck into your pasta." (*Roy Tipping; endorsed by TM Wilson, Mrs PD Tindley, and others*) *Note:* If coming by *motoscafo* (water taxi), ask to be taken to the *Ristorante da Raffaele*, not the *Hotel Do Pozzi*.

Open All year except Jan.
Rooms 25 double, 10 single – 10 with bath, 25 with shower, all with direct-dial telephone, air-conditioning and frigo-bar.
Facilities Breakfast room, TV room; courtyard. English spoken.
Location Central, near San Marco.

Restriction Not suitable for ♿.
Credit cards All major cards accepted.
Terms B&B: single 78,000-100,000 L, double 115,000-250,000 L. Set lunch/dinner 20,000 L; full alc 40,000-50,000 L (in restaurant *Raffaele*). Special meals for children.

Hotel Saturnia e International *Tel* (041) 708377
Calle larga 22 Marzo 2398 *Telex* 410355
Venice 30124

"Courteous, comfortable, unpretentious, and very well done in all details," is a recent plaudit for this 14th-century *palazzo*-cum-hotel about three minutes' walk from St Mark's. The reception area makes quite an impact: a Gothic patio with an elaborate inlaid ceiling. Another letter: "We thought this a perfect place to stay in Venice. We liked the ambience, the friendly staff and, in particular, our room – on a back canal with two large windows and a huge Venetian glass chandelier." Readers have never quite agreed about the hotel's two restaurants: the *Michelin*-rosetted *Caravella* and the more modest *Cortile*. Of the *Caravella* we hear a range of views from "in our opinion one of the best in Venice, but not cheap" to "disappointing and service off-hand". *Il Cortile*, with outdoor seating in the summer, is said to serve the same food at lower prices and tends to receive warmer praise.

Open All year. Restaurants closed Wed.
Rooms 79 double, 19 single – 87 with bath, 11 with shower, all with telephone and air-conditioning; some with TV.
Facilities Lift. 2 lounges, bar, TV room, 2 restaurants; conference facilities. English spoken.
Location Central, W of St Mark's Square.
Restriction Not suitable for ♿.
Credit cards All major cards accepted.
Terms [1987 rates] Rooms: single 180,000 L, double 270,000 L. Breakfast 17,000 L. Full alc 48,000-69,000 L.

Pensione Seguso *Tel* (041) 5222340
Dorsoduro, Zattere 779
Venice 30123

One main attraction of this modest and amiable *pensione* on the Zattere is the stunning view from the front-facing windows of the Giudecca canal with its Venetian craft of all sizes; the side rooms have pleasing views over a smaller canal. It has the virtues of a high-class, old-fashioned establishment – fine old Venetian furniture, dining room with embroidered silk wall covering and friendly service. One visitor this year was quite seduced: "I found it comfortable and quaint, full of character and of characters – charming people who keep returning. I enjoyed the quiet, the Venetian glass windows and chandeliers, the heating, the service, the food and the position." Another reader this year found the dinners "unexciting" (meals have sometimes been criticised in the past) but loved the "warm and courteous service" and "the charm that outweighs the slight shabbiness." (*Consuelo Phelan, GD Paterson, Nicholas Powell*)

Open 1 Mar–30 Nov. Restaurant closed Wed.
Rooms 31 double, 5 single – 9 with bath, 9 with shower, all with telephone.
Facilities Lift. Lounge, restaurant; breakfast terrace. English spoken.

Location 15 minutes from the centre, overlooking the Giudecca canal.
Credit cards Access, Amex, Visa.
Terms Dinner, B&B: 67,000-82,000 L.

VERONA 37121 **Map 16**

Hotel Colomba d'Oro *Tel* (045) 595300
Via Cattaneo 10 *Telex* 480872 COLOMB

A serviceable and very central hotel, near the Arena in a traffic-restricted zone. Lots of polished wood and comfortable chairs in the salon. Bedrooms well modernised, service cheerful, breakfast adequate. No restaurant but a garage. 51 rooms, 88,000-120,000 L [1987]. Some recent criticism: more reports welcome.

Hotel Torcolo *Tel* (045) 8007512
Vicolo Listone 3

"A real find in the heart of Verona", this small bed-and-breakfast hotel is in a side street near the Arena. "It is conveniently above a popular restaurant, but is not noisy by Italian standards. The rooms are tastefully furnished and air-conditioned. Signora Ponari is charming, speaks some English and is anxious to help her guests." Confirmed by a reader this year who had a large room furnished with antiques (many are more modern in style) and found breakfasts "delightful", with apricot juice and unlimited coffee. (*Dilys Pinion, VH and MC Whiting*)

Open All year except 7–18 Jan.
Rooms 19 – all with bath or shower; TV on request.
Facilities Lift. Breakfast room, TV room. English spoken.
Location Central, off Piazza Bra, near Arena. Parking for 10 cars.
Credit cards None accepted.
Terms B&B: single 45,000-52,000 L, double 70,000-80,000 L. Extra bed 3,000 L. Meals in the *Torcolo* restaurant [1987 rates] 23,000-34,000 L plus 15% service charge.

VICENZA 36100 **Map 16**

Hotel Campo Marzio *Tel* (0444) 545700
Viale Roma 21

A very good businessman's hotel, usefully situated between the station and the wonderful centre of this old city, beside a canal and facing a park. Comfortable rooms, good service. Food unremarkable, but try the superb Cinzia e Valerio. *35 rooms, 69,000-110,000 L. Set meals 22,000-36,000 L [1987]. New nomination: more reports please.*

ZERMAN 31020 Treviso **Map 16**

Villa Condulmer *Tel* (041) 457100
Zerman, Mogliano Veneto

This beautiful 18th-century Venetian villa, in a pleasant rural setting on the misty plain between Venice and Treviso, has been warmly praised again: "Lovely rooms, attentive service, very good restaurant – try the swordfish – and reasonable prices." An earlier view: "We had a large and grand room – it is almost like staying in an English stately home. The staff are discreet and you are made to feel special. Good quality food. No air-conditioning, so you may have to choose between the heat and the flies." (*Anne S Wolff, Kate and Steve Murray-Sykes*)

Open Apr–Oct.
Rooms 33 double – all with bath and/or shower; most with telephone; 8 with radio. Some in annexe. Some ground-floor rooms.
Facilities Salon, reading room, TV room, 3 restaurants, bar (with piano); conference room. Park with unheated swimming pool, tennis court, 18-hole golf course and riding. English spoken.
Location Outside village, which is 4 km NE of Mogliano Veneto and 22 km N of Venice.
Credit cards Access, Amex, Diners.
Terms On application.

"I had booked the best suite for my sister and her husband on their wedding night. However, on arrival, the newly-married couple were told in an abrasive and aggressive manner by the receptionist that this suite was no longer available for their use and 'had been given to someone else'. They had been allocated a small room at the end of the hotel annexe and received a half-bottle of very ordinary champagne as compensation."

Luxembourg

HOTEL SIMMER, EHNEN

BERDORF 6550 **Map 9**

Hôtel l'Ermitage *Tel* 79184
44 route de Grundhof

Warm words again this year for *l'Ermitage*, a modern white-walled building in incongruous Spanish-Moorish style, set in a big garden on the outskirts of a small town near the German frontier in the hilly wooded area known as the "Luxembourg Suisse" (interesting rock formations). It is run by two sisters who speak good English; one of them is chef. "They welcome you personally and run a most efficient holiday place. Most rooms are in a purpose-built annexe where radiators made us cosy on a wet day. Spacious bathroom and smaller but comfortable bedroom. Food delicious, notably the smoked quail, quenelles, veal with grapes, and soufflés, all beautifully presented." "Lots of good vegetables – after a week in Belgium we welcomed this change from the ubiquitous chip." However, there is no choice and dinner is sharp at 7.30 pm. (*PM Turner, Fiona Dick, and others*)

Open Easter–Oct. Restaurant closed for lunch.
Rooms 14 double, 2 single – all with bath and/or shower, telephone, TV and mini-bar. 9 in pavilion opposite main building. 9 ground-floor rooms. Self-catering units.
Facilities 2 lounges, bar, loggia, restaurant. Park and garden. Swimming, tennis, mini-golf nearby.
Location Berdorf is 6 km W of Echternach. Hotel is 1 km from Berdorf, towards Grundhof.
Credit cards Amex, Diners, Visa.
Terms B&B: single 1,500 Lfrs, double 2,500 Lfrs; half board 2,000-2,180 Lfrs per person. Set dinner 850-1,100 Lfrs.

ECHTERNACH 6409 — Map 9

Hôtel Bel-Air — *Tel* 729383
Route de Berdorf 1 — *Telex* 2640 BELAIR

This rather grand country house hotel, with modern extensions, stands on the edge of the popular and pretty resort town of Echternach in the wooded and hilly "Luxembourg Suisse" area near the German frontier. It is a palatial kind of place, with extensive and imposing gardens full of pools, flowering shrubs and Doric columns. Pity that the facade facing the gardens is so ugly, in such a jumble of styles. "Most of the bedrooms are in the modern part, each with a balcony where you can take breakfast looking down over the grounds towards the river. The restaurant has a *Michelin* rosette and the food is excellent but fairly expensive." That report was confirmed this year by one reader who found the place delightful, but another thought the decor gloomy and the prices excessive. Panoramic dining room, offering such dishes as pigeon aux gousses d'ail en chemise. (*Kate and Steve Murray-Sykes; also RS McNeill*)

Open All year. Restaurant closed Jan.
Rooms 10 suites, 32 double, 2 single – all with bath and shower, telephone, radio and TV; baby-listening on request.
Facilities Bar, 2 salons, TV room, 2 dining rooms; conference facilities. 1½-acre grounds with tennis and children's playground. Fishing nearby. English spoken.
Location On western side of Echternach, off Diekirch road; follow river Sure to Berdorf turn-off. 35 km NE of Luxembourg city. Parking.
Credit cards All major cards accepted.
Terms B&B: single 2,200-3,000 Lfrs, double 3,000-4,000 Lfrs, suite 4,000-5,000 Lfrs; dinner, B&B: 2,600-3,500 Lfrs per person; full board 3,000-3,800 Lfrs. Set lunch/dinner 1,350-2,000 Lfrs; full alc 1,700-3,000 Lfrs. Reduced rates and special meals for children.

EHNEN 5416 — Map 9

Hôtel Bamberg — *Tel* 76022 and 76717
131 Route du Vin

Formerly known as the Hôtel de la Moselle *but still owned and run by the Bamberg family, this neat modern hostelry lies across a busy road from the Moselle river. Hospitable owners, comfortable rooms, and excellent food in the restaurant with its river views. Some night noises from traffic and striking clocks. Closed mid-Dec to mid-Jan. 18 rooms, all with bath and/or shower. B&B double 1,850-2,100 Lfrs. Set meals 400-1,100 Lfrs. Reinstated in Guide: more reports welcome.*

Hôtel Simmer *Tel* 76030 and 76010
117 route du Vin

Again this year readers have praised the "delightful" family owners and the excellent food (*Michelin* rosette) at this venerable little hotel almost next to the *Bamberg*. It has a 15th-century dining room (with soft lighting and quiet recorded music) which is much frequented by locals and by EEC officials. "Our comfortable room was sombrely furnished but met our needs: there was even a chamber-pot in the bedside locker. A homely atmosphere and good local wines." "Our room at the back was very quiet: those at the front have the river views." (*Angela Pearse, WH Bailey*)

Open 15 March–Jan. Closed Tue in low season.
Rooms 19 double, 4 single – 18 with bath (4 also have shower), all with phone.
Facilities Salon with TV, bar, dining room; banqueting facilities; terrace. Garden. Watersports and fishing. English spoken.
Location 10km N of Remich, 10 km S of Greuenmacher. Hotel is central. Parking.
Restriction Not suitable for ♿.
Credit cards Access, Amex, Visa.
Terms B&B: single 1,750 Lfrs, double 2,250 Lfrs; dinner, B&B: 2,250 Lfrs per person. Full alc 1,500-1,800 Lfrs. Reduced rates for children.

ETTELBRÜCK 9010 Map 9

Hôtel Central *Tel* 82116
25 rue de Bastogne

In a small town pleasantly situated at the confluence of two rivers, the *Central* has an unattractive outward appearance but plenty of inner virtues. Reports this year: "The dinner was worthy of its *Michelin* rosette and the service faultless. We had a comfortable, recently refurbished room with large bathroom, but it was on the street side and noisy at night." "Pleasant staff, excellent food, all good value especially as breakfast is Dutch in size and content, not French." Upper rooms have the best views. (*Angela Pearse, ME Kirk*)

Open 15 Jan–15 Aug, 1 Sept–23 Dec. Restaurant closed Sun and public holidays.
Rooms 16 double – 7 with bath, 9 with shower, all with telephone, TV, minibar.
Facilities Lift. Lounge/bar with TV, restaurant. English spoken.
Location Central. Ettelbrück is 28 km N of Luxembourg city. Garage and parking.
Credit cards All major cards accepted.
Terms B&B: single 1,200-1,500 Lfrs, double 1,800-2,400 Lfrs; dinner B&B: 1,700-1,900 Lfrs per person; full board 2,000-2,300 Lfrs. Set lunch/dinner 800-1,200 Lfrs; full alc 2,000 Lfrs. Reduced rates and special meals for children.

LUXEMBOURG 1453 Map 9

Hostellerie du Grünewald *Tel* 431882 and 436062
10-16 Route d'Echternach *Telex* 60543 HGRWD
Luxembourg–Dommeldange

In the northern outskirts of Luxembourg city, this Romantik hotel is a sedate country hostelry, stronger on comfort and opulence than on personal charm, but friendly enough. Elegant dining room with good food (e.g. chevreuil au Chablis); pleasant garden. Restaurant closed 5–26 Jan. 28 rooms, all with bath or shower. B&B double 2,800 Lfrs. Full alc 1,800–2,300 Lfrs. More reports welcome.

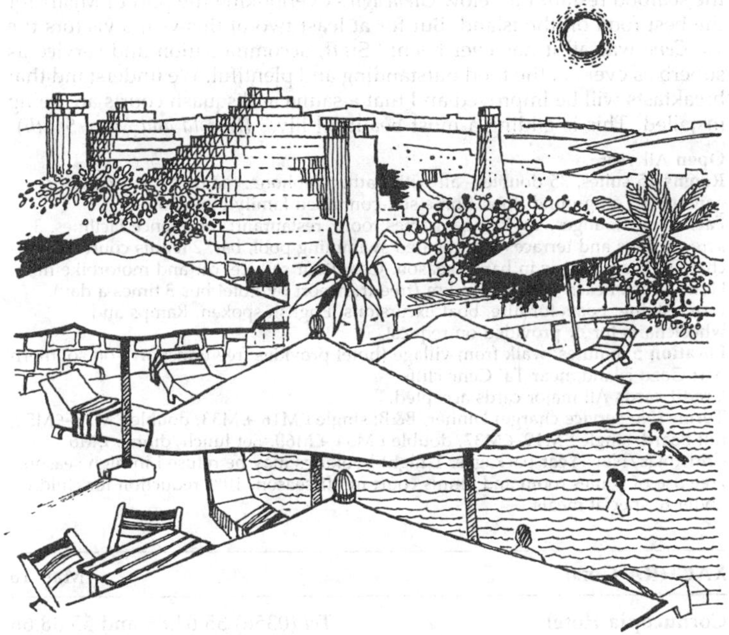

HOTEL TA'CENC

SANNAT Gozo **Map 16**

Hotel Ta' Cenc *Tel* (00356) 55.68.19 and 55.68.30
Telex 1479 REFINZ

For many years past, the *Ta' Cenc* has been the one dependably good hotel on Gozo – or maybe in the whole archipelago. The island of Gozo is one of two small islands off the north-eastern corner of Malta, a quarter the size of the main island. The ferry takes half an hour, but a five-kilometre strip of sea makes a world of difference. The *Ta' Cenc* is beautifully sited on a high promontory, built in the local honey-coloured limestone on a low-profile principle: it's all one storey and cunningly terraced to blend into the hillside. Some rooms are bungalows, most with their own small patios for breakfast or sun-worship. They are ranged round a central pool, with plenty of space between for oleanders, fig trees and cacti. The pool itself offers a breath-taking view of the sea and Malta beyond, and many residents are content to brown and browse there all day. But for the more adventurous, there is lots to see on Gozo – on foot, by bus or by cheap rented car. There is plenty of good rock bathing all round the island, but only one first-class sandy beach, ten kilometres away. The hotel has had a number of changes of manager in recent years and some regulars feel it is no longer as cheerful a place as formerly. The cooking, too, is said to have become erratic, and one reader recommends the seafood restaurant below *Gleneagles* overlooking the port of Mgarr for the best food on the island. But for at least two of this year's visitors the *Ta' Cenc* was all it has ever been: "Staff, accommodation and service as superb as ever . . . the food outstanding and plentiful. We understand that breakfasts will be improved and that a sauna and squash courts are being installed. This is gilding a most beautiful lily." (*Harold and Mary Smith*)

Open All year.
Rooms 15 suites, 35 double – all with bath, telephone, radio, TV and patio or garden. All on ground floor. Some self-contained family bungalows.
Facilities 2 lounges, TV lounge, games room, restaurant; conference facilities. 3-acre gardens and terraces with heated swimming pool, bar, 2 tennis courts (small charge). Disco; music in bar in season. Chauffeur service, car and motorbike hire. Hotel's rock beach with bar 2½ km (free transport by hotel bus 3 times a day), water-skiing, boats for hire, boat excursions. English spoken. Ramps and wheelchairs for ♿ provided on request.
Location 5 minutes' walk from village (hotel provides free transport), on southern part Gozo island, near Ta' Cenc cliffs.
Credit cards All major cards accepted.
Terms (No service charge) Dinner, B&B: single £M16–£M33, double £M28–£M52; full board: single £M19–£M37, double £M34–£M60. Set lunch/dinner £M6. Christmas/New Year packages. 1-night bookings may be refused in high season. Free use of games room and tennis court in off-season. 10% reduction for children under 6; special meals.

XAGHRA Gozo — Map 16

Cornucopia Hotel — *Tel* (0356) 55.64.86 and 55.38.66
10 Gnien Imrik Street — *Telex* 1467 VJB

Cheerful family hotel in converted farmhouse two miles inland, run by Victor Borg and family, offering cheaper alternative to Ta' Cenc *above. Attractive pool, fine views. Rooms simple but well-maintained. Generous portions of freshly-cooked food. Recently enlarged: more reports needed. 38 rooms, all with private facilities. Dinner, B&B £M5.75–£M10.75.*

"I asked for breakfast to be delivered to my room. The waiter knocked once at the door and immediately walked in. He found me completely naked, standing in the middle of the room. The following day I ordered breakfast to be delivered to my room between 8.30 and 9 am. At 9.30 I telephoned the kitchen to see what was going on since my breakfast hadn't been delivered. At 10 am I called the kitchen again. At last at 10.15 my breakfast arrived. Unfortunately I couldn't eat it because I didn't have a knife to cut and spread butter or marmalade on my bread. On my departure day I ordered breakfast to be in my room between 8 and 8.30 am. Once again it arrived only at 10 am and for this I had to phone the kitchen twice. Although a knife and some more sugar were requested they were not brought; consequently once again I couldn't have my breakfast."

The Netherlands

HOTEL-RESTAURANT HOFSTEDE
SLANGEVEGT, BREUKELEN

ALMEN Gelderland **Map 9**

De Hoofdige Boer *Tel* (05751) 1744
Dorpsstraat 38
Almen 7218 AH

Almen is a village in eastern Holland, not far from Arnhem and the famous Kröller-Müller museum (splendid Van Goghs), and close to the charming old town of Zutphen. This old-established hotel with its unusual beamed decor (its name means "the stubborn farmer") continues to please most readers. "Staff friendly, food and wine excellent, rooms very comfortable – nice touches like fruit in the room." "Ideal for a quiet holiday. Modern bedrooms and comfortable lounge: tea garden in summer." "A charming place. At the back is a pleasant garden giving on to open fields. The food is somewhat unimaginative, but the restaurant is professionally run and not pretentious. Breakfast was copious." "The owners are lovely people who make every effort to accommodate their guests." That last bit of praise sounds somewhat ironic in the light of an odd incident reported to us this year. A reader and his wife arrived on spec, took the last room available, settled down in it, and two hours later were told by the owner that they must leave at once, as he had made a mistake and the room had already been booked by other guests who had now arrived. So scandalised, they left (but not before they had been given a free dinner by way of apology). The Guide then wrote to the *hoofdige* hotelier, but got no reply. (*David Blomley, Susan Hayes, Geoffrey Sharp, and others*)

Open All year, except early Jan.
Rooms 18 double, 2 single – all with bath and/or shower and TV; 12 with telephone; baby-listening arranged. 2 ground-floor rooms.
Facilities Bar, lounge, TV room, restaurants; functions room; table tennis. Garden with tea garden and dinner terrace. 5 minutes' walk to heated swimming pool; fishing nearby. English spoken.
Location Central, near the church. Parking. About 1½ hours' drive from Amsterdam via E8 Deventer and Eefde.
Credit cards Amex, Diners.
Terms B&B: single 75 glds, double 100-130 glds; dinner, B&B: single 115 glds, double 160-180 glds. Full alc 45 glds. Off-season and Christmas packages. Reduced rates for children sharing parents' room; special meals.

AMSTERDAM Noord-Holland — Map 9

Hotel Ambassade
Herengracht 341
Amsterdam 1016 AZ

Tel (020) 262333
Telex 10158 AMBAS

This is much the most popular of all our Dutch recommendations, and with one striking exception (see below) it has again been smothered with praise in 1986/7 – "super", "delightful", "excellent value", "just like being in your own home", "a warm and friendly atmosphere". It is a bed-and-breakfast hotel on a grand stretch of the Herengracht, Amsterdam's grandest canal, and it consists of seven 17th-century patrician town houses, side by side and linked together: their rooms, varying in size according to their altitude in these tall buildings, are all furnished in period and all have a bathroom. The public rooms have many items from the owner's own collection of antiques – old china, clocks, paintings. The efficient room service, quiet yet central location and excellent bathroom furnishings are all admired. A common complaint is of the very steep steps to upper floors (normal in these old Amsterdam houses) and of the "spiral staircases everywhere" (the elderly or less than athletic should ask for ground-floor rooms). "The great asset is Mr Van der Velden, the manager – nearly always there, courteous, friendly, inviting questions and apparently running the whole show without effort or tension. The relaxed friendly atmosphere is striking." Breakfasts have sometimes been criticised as "just ordinary", but most readers this year have liked them and one found them lavish – "it makes you quite needless of luncheon". (*Robin and James Rosen, GK Needham, Gillian and Geoffrey Trevelyan, and many others*) One sharp dissenter this year liked the setting and the public rooms, but found the bedroom furnishings mediocre, the bathrooms lacking in amenities and the staff less than helpful.

Open All year.
Rooms 4 suites, 36 double, 3 single – all with bath (12 also have shower), telephone and TV; baby sitters available; 24-hour room service. 20 in annexe. 9 ground-floor rooms.

Facilities Lounge, TV lounge, breakfast room. English spoken.
Location Central, but quietly situated on Herengracht canal. Parking.
Credit cards Access, Amex, Visa.
Terms B&B: single 150-170 glds, double 170-195 glds, suite 240-265 glds. Drinks and light refreshments available all day. Reduced rates for children sharing parents' room.

Amstel Inter Continental Hotel *Tel* (020) 226060
1 Prof. Tulpplein *Telex* 11004 AMSOT
Amsterdam 1018 GX

Beautifully situated on the river Amstel, this large hotel is a favourite choice with film-stars and other celebrities visiting the city. "The interior is certainly very grand and the double rooms are like suites, with very plush furnishings. Service is good and discreet. Prices are high, but you are paying for the surroundings and the setting. One possible drawback of the hotel is its distance from the centre of Amsterdam, a good 20 minutes' walk." (*John H Wilson, Catherine Steele-Kroon*) The restaurant, formerly much praised, has just acquired a new chef and we should welcome reports on this change.

Open All year.
Rooms 7 suites, 94 double, 10 single – all with bath and shower, radio and TV. 2 rooms suitable for ♿.
Facilities Lift. Salon, TV room, bar, restaurant, terrace. Garden. Air-conditioning. English spoken.
Location On Amstel river, 20 minutes' walk from centre.
Credit cards All major credit cards accepted.
Terms Rooms: single 415 glds, double 525 glds. Breakfast 30 glds. Set lunch from 65 glds, dinner from 80 glds.

Het Canal House *Tel* (020) 225182
Keizersgracht 148 *Telex* 10412
Amsterdam 1015 CX

A former 18th-century merchant's house on a quiet canal, close to city centre and Anne Frank's house. Comfortable modernised rooms with antiques; friendly English-speaking staff and owners. Bar, but no restaurant. Hotel being expanded, 1987-8. 27 rooms, all with bath or shower. B&B double 165-190 glds. No recent reports: more welcome.

Hotel de l'Europe *Tel* (020) 234836
Nieuwe Doelenstraat 2-8 *Telex* 12081
Amsterdam 1012 CP

One of the city's grander hotels, built on the Amstel in 1895 with beautiful rooms, luxury fittings and an ideal location. "Service was as pleasant as ever," say visitors returning this year. "Our room was not so very spacious, but prettily decorated in cream and blue. All the public rooms are attractive, but breakfast for 15 florins is very basic." Rooms at the back, facing the river, are quietest. The restaurant has a fine reputation both for food and cellar. (*Kate and Steve Murray-Sykes, Catherine Steele-Kroon*)

Report forms (Freepost in UK) will be found at the end of the Guide.

Open All year.
Rooms 12 suites, 62 double, 40 single – all with bath and shower, telephone, radio and TV. Baby-listening on request. 24-hour room service.
Facilities Lift. Lounge, bar, 2 restaurants; banqueting and conference facilities; indoor heated swimming pool, sauna, solarium; terrace overlooking Amstel serving meals and drinks in summer. English spoken.
Location Central, opposite the Mint Tower and Flowermarket (rooms double-glazed: quietest ones at back of hotel). Limited private parking, public garage nearby.
Credit cards All major cards accepted.
Terms B&B: single 370-470 glds, double 490-590 glds, suite 690-990 glds. Set lunch 65 glds, dinner 75 glds; full alc 100 glds. Reduced rates for children; special meals on request.

Hotel Pulitzer *Tel* (020) 228333
Prinsengracht 315-331 *Telex* 16508
Amsterdam 1016 GZ

Again admired this year, this large and sophisticated – and, one reader found, slightly anonymous – hotel straddles a terrace of 17th-century houses, some facing the Prinsengracht and some the neighbouring canal, the Keizersgracht. The old beams and brick walls have been preserved in all the bedrooms. "A hotel of considerable charm. The atmosphere is of a tastefully well-modernised building in which all the original features of the old warehouse have been retained. There is a garden with a glass walkway connecting the front half of the hotel with the back. Our room, facing a canal, was well furnished and spacious with comfortable chairs, a desk and good reading lights – important, as there is no lounge. We decided against visiting the main restaurant (expensive); there are plenty of places to eat within walking distance." (*Mr and Mrs Oppenheimer; also Richard G Shifrin, Claire Enders*)

Open All year. Restaurant closed 15 July–15 Aug.
Rooms 5 suites, 220 double, 25 single – all with bath and shower, direct-dial telephone, radio, TV, mini-bar; baby-listening arranged. 25 ground-floor rooms.
Facilities Lift. Lobby, lounge, bar, 2 restaurants; conference facilities; gift shop; live music in bar or garden; terrace for light meals, drinks, concerts in summer. Large garden. English spoken.
Location Central, near Wester Church; garden rooms best for light sleepers. Garage 8 minutes' walk; valet parking.
Credit cards All major cards accepted.
Terms Rooms: single 275-325 glds, double 325-375 glds, suite 750 glds. Breakfast 21 glds. Dinner, B&B: single 342-392 glds, double 392-442 glds. Full alc 60 glds. Extra bed in room 50 glds, baby cots free; special meals for children on request.

BREUKELEN Utrecht — Map 9

Hotel-Restaurant Hofstede Slangevegt *Tel* (03462) 61525
Straatweg 40, Breukelen 3621 BN

A recently-nominated hotel 15 miles south of Amsterdam, in the middle of "one of the loveliest regions in the Netherlands – fairytale castles, rich merchants' country houses, old Dutch farms, windmills and draw-bridges". The *Slangevegt* is a merchant's house with gardens dating from 1850. It exudes slight eccentricity, with mounted antlers, stuffed birds and a wilderness of plants. "Service during my stay was by just one man and in a word he was perfect. The two double bedrooms with balconies overlooking the river at the back are worth asking for; others are rather characterless with small separate but private bathrooms. Very clean, very neat, towels a bit mingy. There was some noise, but in an old house like this you hear every footstep. The dining room has the atmosphere of a grand drawing room. Dinner was excellent: French, basically *nouvelle*, good use of seasonal produce. Breakfast was a let down. But the hotel is very fair value for money, the location is superb, with a real country feel, and the owners are friendly." (*CS-K*)

Open All year, except 2 weeks in Feb, 5–31 Dec. Restaurant closed Tue.
Rooms 4 double, l single – all with shower, radio and baby-listening.
Facilities Reception/bar, 2 restaurants. Garden with riverside terrace. English spoken.
Location 2 km S of Breukelen, off A2/E9.
Restriction Not suitable for ♿.
Credit cards All major cards accepted.
Terms B&B: single 80 glds, double 90 glds; dinner, B&B: single 130 glds, double 190 glds. Set lunch 42.50 glds, dinner 50-70 glds; full alc 62.50 glds. Extra bed for child 25 glds; special meals.

DELFT Zuid-Holland — Map 9

Delft Museumhotel — *Tel* (015) 140930
Oude Delft 189 — *Telex* 38026 MUSHL
Delft 2611 HD

This recently-opened hotel, converted from 17th-century canal houses, is situated in the heart of Delft's old quarter next to the Prinsenhofmuseum and opposite the Oude Jan church tower. "Three visits of a week each have proven to be more than satisfactory. It is delightfully situated and is managed and staffed by a young and enthusiastic team who work with efficiency and courtesy. The bedrooms are very comfortable with all amenities. There is a bar where light meals are served, and a small but neat breakfast room." (*John S Wright*)

Open All year, except Christmas and New Year.
Rooms 2 suites, 25 double, 3 single – all with bath and shower, direct-dial telephone, radio, TV and mini-bar. 4 ground-floor rooms.
Facilities Lift. Lounge, breakfast room, bar; conference/functions room. Car and bicycle hire. English spoken.
Location Next to Prinsenhofmuseum and opposite Oude Jan church. Parking.
Credit cards All major cards accepted.
Terms [1987 rates] B&B: single 117.50-177.50 glds, double 162.50-197.50 glds. Set lunch/dinner 35-50 glds. Reduced rates for children sharing parents' room.

Hotel Leeuwenbrug — *Tel* (015) 123062 and 134640
Koornmarkt 16 — *Telex* 33756 ref. no. 013
Delft 2611 EE

The prices are reasonable, the welcome friendly and the buffet breakfasts plentiful at this small hotel in one of the finest parts of Delft. The best rooms are in the front, overlooking the canal, a picturesque footbridge and gabled houses opposite, "the loveliest view from a European hotel bedroom that I've ever had" (there is at least one large room with a delightful flower-decked balcony). Other rooms are smallish but warm, adequately furnished and comfortable. Many have been recently renovated. Only limited space in the lounge but a pleasant little bar. (*TM Loveday*)

Open All year.
Rooms 26 double, 8 single – all with bath and/or shower, telephone, radio, TV and baby-listening. 6 ground-floor rooms.
Facilities Lift. Bar with TV, breakfast room; conference facilities. Sandy beach 15 km. English spoken.
Location Take Delft Zuid turning off Rotterdam–Amsterdam highway, and follow signs to Centre West. Paid parking next to hotel.
Credit cards All major cards accepted.
Terms B&B: single 105-135 glds, double 130-160 glds. (No restaurant.)

HEEZE Noord-Brabant — Map 9

Hostellerie du Château — *Tel* (04907) 3515
Kapelstraat 48 — *Telex* 59355
Heeze 5591 HE

Those going on business to the big, ugly industrial town of Eindhoven, headquarters of Philips, might prefer, if they have time, to stay out in the pleasant wooded country to the south-east where the little town of Heeze contains this ambitious restaurant-with-rooms. "The food (*Michelin* rosette) is still brilliant," writes our inspector in 1987, confirming her 1986 account: "An attractive long two-storey yellow building with a Mediterranean touch: dark green shutters, flower-boxes, and lots of tables for outside eating and drinking. Service is formal but not standoffish. The food was magnificent – really creative dishes, best of all being the terrine of layers of duck liver mousse and raw meat of young pigeon breast. The feel of the place grows on you – faded, relaxed abundance. Only drawback: muzak seeps through into the bedrooms at all hours." The *Château* has been extensively renovated in 1986/7. Reports on its new look please.

Open All year except New Year. Restaurant closed Sat midday.
Rooms 14 – all with bath and shower, direct-dial telephone, radio, TV, mini-bar and baby-listening.
Facilities Lounge, café, restaurant; conference facilities; covered terrace. Garden. Golf, tennis, riding, walking and cycling nearby. English spoken.
Location 11 km SE of Eindhoven, between E3 and E9 motorways.
Restriction Not suitable for ♿.
Credit cards All major cards accepted.
Terms Rooms: single 140 glds, double 170 glds, suite 200-240 glds. Breakfast 18.50 glds. Set lunch 52.50 glds, dinner 77.50-105 glds; full alc 75-85 glds. Reduced rates and special meals for children.

LEUSDEN Utrecht — Map 9

Hotel Huize den Treek — *Tel* (03498) 1425
Trekerweg 23

This 17th-century mansion in a wooded area near Amersfoort was dropped from the Guide two years ago after a poor report, but is now again well liked by recent American visitors: "A most romantic setting. Our room had gold brocade bedspreads and antique furniture; its windows overlooked a small lake with white geese on an island in it. You can take drinks on a patio by the lake. The sumptuous and elegant lounge with its deep velvet chairs made us feel pampered, and breakfast in the library was wonderful. An incredibly posh place for the money." Another reader found his Dutch-French meal a little too elaborate and the menu too ambitious. (*Jodi Homann, D and K Perry*) More reports, please.

Open All year.
Rooms 1 suite, 10 double, 7 single – all with bath and/or shower, telephone, radio, TV and baby-listening.
Facilities Lift. Lounge with TV, restaurant, bar. Garden with terrace. English spoken.
Location 5 km SW of Leusden, which is 4km SE of Amersfoort
Credit cards Amex, Diners.
Terms B&B: single 67.50 glds, double 115 glds, suite 230 glds; dinner B&B: single 103.25 glds, double 186.50 glds. Set lunch 22.50 glds, dinner 30.75 glds; full alc 72.50 glds. Reduced rates and special meals for children.

OISTERWIJK Noord-Brabant — Map 9

Hotel-Restaurant De Swaen — *Tel* (04242) 19006
De Lind 47 — *Telex* 52617
Oisterwijk 5061 HT

"Absolutely the best restaurant in the Netherlands," is our local inspector's authoritative 1987 verdict on this very elegant and sophisticated little hostelry on the tree-lined main street of the pleasant shady town of Oisterwijk. It has a terrace in the front and a beautiful formal garden at the back. "Recently converted by a local furniture maker, from the outside it looks like many other pleasant Dutch provincial hotels. But inside it's a veritable Aladdin's cave. Rooms are smallish but very adequate, bathroom in marble and the bath itself warm! Food is excellent and beautifully served." "Rooms are modern, comfortably furnished, each with a small balcony. Welcoming chocolates and all the other little extras. Shoes are cleaned overnight if required." "The bathrooms have gold-plated fittings!" A visitor this year, who had "an exquisite and memorable meal", found the staff extremely solicitous and efficient in helping to deal with an urgent car repair. (*Alan Greenwood, Pat and Jeremy Temple, Mary Jo Fleig, M Alexander*) They are be-toqued in *Gault Millau*, and two-rosetted in *Michelin*.

Open All year except first 2 weeks Jan, last 3 weeks July. Restaurant closed Mon.
Rooms 18 suites, 1 single – all with bath and/or shower, telephone, radio, TV and baby-listening.
Facilities Lift. Bar, lounge, restaurant; 2 conference rooms. Formal garden. Swimming, fishing, woods and lakes nearby. English spoken.
Location Central. Parking. Oisterwijk is 10 km NE of Tilberg.
Credit cards All major cards accepted.
Terms B&B: single 225 glds, double 275 glds. Set lunch 90 glds, dinner 120 glds; full alc 130 glds. Weekend package. Special meals for children.

> Hotels often book you into their most expensive rooms or suites unless you specify otherwise. Even if all room prices are the same, hotels may give you a less good room in the hope of selling their better rooms to late customers. It always pays to discuss accommodation in detail when making a reservation.

OOTMARSUM Overijssel — Map 9

De Wiemsel
Winhofflaan 2
Ootmarsum 7631 HX

Tel (05419) 2155
Telex 44667

To the east of the pretty little town of Ootmarsum, in gentle pastoral country near the German frontier, *De Wiemsel* is a sophisticated ranch-style hotel with attractive modern decor, light and spacious. It is a place where leading Dutch politicians and businessmen come to relax. "Set quietly in its own grounds, it is really a number of low bungalow-style buildings attached to the main block which houses the restaurant. Most of the rooms are in fact apartments. We arrived to a welcoming smile and the offer of tea or coffee with fruit bread (on the house) to revive us. The room was lovely with a view over fields, and the bathroom luxurious. Service was good, and so was the food." The chef has changed this year, but according to our inspector the cooking remains as good as ever, though it is better still at *De Wanne* (*Michelin* rosette) which is down in the town and under the same management. (*K and SM-S, CS-K*) The hotel has a stable of horses for the use of guests, as well as a floodlit tennis court and a big indoor pool. It is 20 minutes' drive to the German casino across the border at Bad Bentheim.

Open All year.
Rooms 42 suites, 5 double (also let as single) – all with bath, shower, direct-dial telephone, radio, TV, and baby-listening; suites have kitchenette and terrace. 2 in garden house, 50-metres from main building. 37 ground-floor rooms.
Facilities Hall, lounge, 2 bars, restaurant; conference facilities; indoor heated swimming pool, sauna, solarium and billiard room. Large garden with terrace, tennis court and stables. Bicycles for hire. English spoken.
Location 1 km E of Ootmarsum, which is 28 km N of Enschede.
Credit cards All major cards accepted.
Terms B&B: single occupancy 141 glds, double 211 glds, suite 254.50-309.50 glds. Set lunch 40-70 glds, dinner 75-140 glds. Alc (excluding wine) 90 glds. Reduced rates and special meals for children.

WITTEM Limburg — Map 9

Kasteel Wittem
Wittemerallee 3
Wittem 6286 AA

Tel (04450) 1208 and 1260
Telex 56287 KAWIT

"In the Eighty Years' War Wittem Castle played an important part, and the eleventh couplet of the Dutch national anthem recalls this period in the Netherlands' battle for freedom," says the hotel's brochure. Indeed, steeped in history and keeping its stately tradition, this medieval castle with its 12-foot-thick walls surrounded by ancient trees has a lot to offer – including *Michelin*-rosetted cuisine. The dozen rooms, each with its own bathroom, have been successfully gouged out of these cyclopean walls. Veteran travellers found it as good as ever in 1987: "Always friendly and relaxing. Our warm and comfortable room had a bowl of fruit, magazines, good lighting. Breakfast was lavish and excellent, wines are reasonably priced for Holland, the cooking is fairly *nouvelle* (e.g. caille et foie de canard à la marmelade de concombres) but portions are large and puddings elaborate." An earlier view: "We enjoyed walking around the grounds, imagining the history the castle had witnessed. Superb food, excellent service, friendly and charming, and the unforgettable twinkling eyes of the cordial owner, always in evidence. A totally delightful experience." (*Pat and Jeremy Temple, IE, CS-K*)

Open All year.
Rooms 12 double – all with bath, shower and telephone.
Facilities Lounge, bar, restaurant; conference/banqueting facilities; terrace. Park with garden, river. Golf, cycling, walking, tennis and trout fishing nearby. English spoken.
Location Between Maastricht (17 km) and Aachen (15 km). 2 km SW of Gulpen on Maastricht road.
Restriction Not suitable for ♿.
Credit cards All major cards accepted.
Terms B&B: single 110 glds, double 180 glds. Set lunch 52.50 glds, dinner 75 glds; full alc 110 glds. Gastronomic weekends; weekend and mid-week breaks; Christmas package. Reduced rates and special meals for children.

ZEDDAM Gelderland — Map 9

Montferland
Montferland 1
Zeddam 7038 EB

Tel (08345) 1444
Telex 45765 HCHAM

"A perfect hotel, if you are rich, love luxury and good food, prefer formal to family-style treatment, and rural pursuits to city night-life." So runs an inspector's recent report on the very stylish *Montferland*, just outside the hamlet of Zeddam, south-east of Arnhem and close to the German border. "It is set like a fortress on the top of a small hill, with terrific views over the surrounding flat countryside. There are lots of tables outside for summer eating, and the area is great for walking or cycling – you can visit mills or go to see clogs and cheeses being made at nearby farms. The hotel building is unremarkable, but inside all is spacious and elegant. My bedroom and bathroom were superb, stylishly furnished in white and grey, everything brand new and in working order. Shower cap, sewing kit, hairdrier etc – everything you might need and lots you might not. The restaurant has huge windows with extensive views. The young head waitress was very knowledgeable, leading a team of friendly girls. Chef Hans de Bout is young too, just 26 – and very talented: *nouvelle cuisine* with an adventurous and creative touch. The wine list is extensive. Breakfast was also excellent, and sumptuous by Dutch standards. The owners, the Aalderlings, care for their guests with impeccable professionalism but not with warmth."

Open All year.
Rooms 8 – all with bath, shower, telephone, TV and mini-bar.
Facilities Lounge, bar, restaurant; conference facilities. Large grounds with sun terrace. English spoken.
Location On hilltop just W of hamlet of Zeddam which is about 20 m SE of Arnhem.
Credit cards All major cards accepted.
Terms B&B: single 90 glds, double 150 glds; dinner, B&B: single 140 glds, double 250 glds. Set lunch/dinner 35-50 glds; full alc 50 glds. Reduced rates and special meals for children.

Norway

BALESTRAND 5850 **Map 7**

Midtnes Pensjonat *Tel* (056) 91133

This trim white-fronted hotel is in the pleasant small resort of Balestrand at the heart of Sognefjord, north-east of Bergen. It has its own pier and bathing area, and boats and bicycles are available to its guests. "The *Midtnes* is a family concern, with Mr Gjeraker working in the kitchen and his son as receptionist. Like most hotels in the area, it is built on a slope. The older part contains the dining room and lounge; the new part another lounge, fitness room and bedrooms, some of which face the fjord. The accommodation is of a very high standard and the charges are reasonable. Clean towels were supplied each day and there were generous helpings of well-cooked food. The service was excellent and all the staff were very helpful and spoke English fluently." (*JS Morrison*)

Open All year, except Christmas and New Year.
Rooms 30 double, 6 single – all with bath and shower; many with balcony. Some ground-floor rooms.

Facilities Lift. 3 lounges, bar, TV room, dining room; fitness room, billiard room. Garden and sun terrace; private pier with boats, rocky beach, free fishing, safe bathing; bicycles for guests' use. English spoken.
Location Central, next to the English church of St Olav. Parking.
Credit cards None accepted.
Terms Rooms: single 250 Nkr, double 310-350 Nkr. Breakfast 40 Nkr. Full board (min 3 days) 310-370 Nkr per person. Set lunch 80 Nkr, dinner 95 Nkr. Children under 3 free; 50% reduction for children aged 3-12.

BERGEN 5000 — Map 7

Augustin Hotel — *Tel* (05) 23.00.25
C. Sundtsgt. 24 — *Telex* 40923 AUGUS

A spruce little town hotel near the harbour, in this busy city girt by fjords and wooded hills. "Recently renovated, it contains a handsome breakfast room where lavish Scandinavian breakfasts are available buffet style. The bedrooms are small but very neat and clean. The staff are accommodating: we had a small child, and they provided crib facilities. This is not a de luxe inn, but it is centrally located with a friendly staff and with some design quality which a discerning visitor would appreciate." (*Ronald Lee Fleming*) The hotel's brochure says that it has won a prize for "good coffee and ambience".

Open All year, except 24-27 Dec. Restaurant closed 17 May.
Rooms 26 double, 11 single – all with shower, telephone, radio and TV.
Facilities Lounge with TV, coffee shop serving light meals, residents' breakfast room, dining room. English spoken.
Location Central, near aquarium and fish market. Public parking.
Restriction Not suitable for ♿.
Credit cards All major cards accepted.
Terms B&B: single 490 Nkr, double 640 Nkr; dinner, B&B 400-570 Nkr per person. Set lunch/dinner 70 Nkr, dinner 80 Nkr.

Myklebust Pensjonat — *Tel* (05) 31.13.28
Rosenbergsgt. 19

"In a quiet street not too far from the centre (though it wouldn't suit people who can't cope with steep hills!), and in an upper floor of what seems to be a block of private flats. Loo and shower across a landing, though spotlessly clean. Our room was delightful: a large, attractively-furnished bed-sitting room, complete with a pine dining table and chairs we'd love to have taken home, very comfortable, and a built-in washbasin. Wonderful breakfast – every item one could think of from a Norwegian breakfast selection, brought to our room. Service by the friendly son of the house speaking good English. Excellent value at half the price of some Bergen hotels." Endorsed this year ("attractive rooms, owner's son most helpful"). (*J and JW, Mr and Mrs W Bentsen*)

Open All year except Christmas.
Rooms 1 family room, 4 double, 2 single – 2 with shower; most with TV.
Facilities No public rooms. English spoken.
Location Central. Street parking.
Restriction Not suitable for ♿.
Credit cards None accepted.
Terms Rooms: single 140 Nkr, double 280 Nkr. Breakfast 35 Nkr. Reduced rates for children. (No restaurant.)

Hotell Neptun *Tel* (05) 32.60.00
Walckendorffsgt. 8 *Telex* 40040 NEPTUN

A well-equipped and comfortable modern hotel, central but quiet, overlooking market and harbour. Attractive restaurant, good cooking, splendid buffet breakfasts. Closed Christmas and New Year. 122 rooms, all with bath and/or shower. B&B double 1,165 Nkr. No recent reports: more welcome.

FJÆRLAND 5855 Map 7

Hotel Mundal *Tel* (056) 93101
Telex 74745 POLAR attn ORHEIM

Fjærland lies at the head of an arm of Sognefjord, Norway's longest and deepest fjord. Until recently it has been accessible only by the thrice-daily ferry from Balestrand. Now a road tunnel has opened up the valley to motorists. The trim white clapboard-fronted *Mundal* sits at the head of the fjord in the shadow of Norway's largest glacier, the Josteldalsbreen. It has been run by the same family since it was built in 1891.

"The owners have updated the bathrooms, but the hotel has not been spoiled in any way. The bedrooms are all different and all Norwegian in atmosphere. There is a good library containing many English books, a billiard room and a music room with a piano (and a beautiful ceiling). All the family speak English. The food is plentiful and very good. One of the highlights of our stay was the fjord trout with butter sauce and cucumber salad. Many of the elegant old traditions are carried on here – beds turned down every night, damask napkins, even breakfast butter balls fashioned by the kitchen ladies. There are many antiques and beautiful furnishings, made by past members of the family. Even the stair carpet is hand woven." (*E and S Sandham, who have endorsed that account after returning this year*) The valley is a walker's paradise and Olav Orheim, a grandson of the hotel's founder, and a glaciologist who led Norway's last three expeditions to Antarctica, will take guests to visit the glacier at some 5,000 feet.

Open 1 May–1 Oct.
Rooms 4 suites, 28 double, 8 single – 36 with bath, 4 with shower – all with telephone.
Facilities Hall, lounge with fireplace, TV room, music room, library/billiard room, bar, 2 restaurants. Garden on shore of fjord; rowing boat free of charge; fishing (equipment can be borrowed); swimming possible, but very cold. English spoken.
Location 180 km NE of Bergen. Reached by express boat service, ferry and bus.
Restriction Not suitable for ♿.
Credit card Visa.
Terms B&B: 305-460 Nkr; half board (min 3 days) 70 Nkr added. Set lunch 60-130 Nkr, dinner 140 Nkr. Reduced rates for children.

There is inevitably less feedback from Scandinavia than from other more touristy parts of Europe. If you have been to Scandinavia and stayed in a good hotel, whether in the present Guide or not, please write and tell us.

JELØY 1501 — Map 7

Hotell Refsnes Gods — *Tel* (032) 70411
Godset 5 — *Telex* 74353
Moss

On the green and leafy island of Jeløy, in the Oslofjord, a fairly luxurious hotel looking like a French château. Sizeable modern bedrooms, many overlooking the fjord. Good food, heated outdoor pool. Closed Christmas and Easter. 60 rooms, all with bath and shower. B&B double 790 Nkr. Set meals 285-345 Nkr. Few recent reports: more welcome.

LOEN 6878 — Map 7

Alexandra Hotel — *Tel* (057) 77660
Telex 42665 ALEX

A large modern six-storey hotel with "a touch of luxury", in a valley surrounded by majestic mountains and fjords, waterfalls and glaciers. Not really our sort of place perhaps, but if you're travelling as far north as Loen for summer skiing, mountain climbing or fishing, this could be a find. "During three weeks spent touring Norway, this was the high spot of our visit and easily surpassed any other hotel we stayed in, offering both parents and children the facilities required. Beautiful situation, spacious and well-equipped bedrooms and public rooms, and friendly and helpful staff. Endless activities available and good food." (*JE Stapleton; endorsed in 1987 by KB Mowle*)

Open All year, except 3 weeks in Jan.
Rooms 210 – all with bath, shower, telephone and radio.
Facilities Lift. 3 bars, 4 lounges, café, restaurant; conference facilities; hairdresser; indoor heated swimming pool, sauna, gym; dancing nightly in bar. Garden with tennis and mini-golf. Near sea with fishing and water sports. English spoken.
Location 10 km E of Olden. Nearest station at Otta (200 km); bus connection.
Credit cards All major cards accepted.
Terms [1987 rates] Rooms: single 530-1,050 Nkr, double 720-1,760 Nkr. Breakfast 50 Nkr. Set lunch 120 Nkr, dinner 190 Nkr. Reduced rates and special meals for children.

OSLO — Map 7

Hotel Bristol — *Tel* (02) 41.58.40
Kristian IV's gt. 7 — *Telex* 71668 BRIS
0164 Oslo 1

Like other grand hotels with this name, the *Bristol* commemorates the travels of the eccentric 4th Earl of Bristol (1750-1803). This one, "perhaps the most sympathetic of the bigger Oslo hotels", is commended again this year as pleasant and quiet. "It has touches of genuine class. Bedrooms are spacious and comfortable and some public rooms have kept an aura of old-fashioned luxury. The staff were helpful." Recent visitors have found the food pedestrian and poorly served, though an earlier one had been more enthusiastic: "Here I had one of my finest gastronomic experiences – fresh trout prepared in sour cream. Next morning, I had a long breakfast from a loaded buffet starting with several kinds of pickled herring and ending with limitless coffee. That, too, was an experience. To eat well in Norway one could do worse than breakfast three times a day. The dining room was dark, old-fashioned, rather like a set from an Ibsen play. In fact, the same may be said of the hotel, at least the public parts." (*Eric Clyne, M Wane, NB*)

Open All year.
Rooms 3 suites, 90 double, 47 single – all with bath, shower, telephone, radio and tv.
Facilities Lift. Large lobby with winter garden, library/bar, TV room, Trafalgar Bar, restaurants, grill; conference/banqueting facilities; night club disco. English spoken.
Location In city centre, near harbour (front rooms may be noisy). Parking.
Credit cards All major cards accepted.
Terms [1987 rates] B&B: single 910-980 Nkr, double 1,110 Nkr, suite 2,360 Nkr. Full alc from 300 Nkr. Large reductions for weekend stays. Reduced rates for children; special meals on request.

Hotel Continental — *Tel* (02) 41.90.60
Stortingsgt. 24-26 — *Telex* 71012 CONTI
0161 Oslo 1

Opposite the National Theatre, a large solid-looking building dating from the turn of the century, very much in the grand style, particularly its restaurants. It has been in the same family for four generations. The dining room is formal, with chandeliers and serious waiters. Bedrooms vary in size and style; front rooms are noisy with passing trams. "Oslo has, more than any other European capital, preserved the traditions and atmosphere of the 19th century. The *Continental* retains the grave dignity, courtesy and friendly warmth which visitors to Norway so much appreciate. I could wax even more lyrical over the breakfast's cold table." And of the hotel's famous *Theatercafféen*, another correspondent writes: "The last really Viennese-style restaurant in Scandinavia – a large room, with stained wood, mirrors and a stuccoed ceiling supported by tall white columns with decorated capitals. Food was super, and the Norwegian beer was very fine too. People were having a good time, including us." (*John Wilson, D Steven McGuire*) The hotel writes to say that more than 100 of its room have been renovated this year.

Open All year except Easter.
Rooms 12 suites, 127 double, 40 single – all with bath, shower, telephone, radio and TV.
Facilities 2 lifts. Lounge, bar, restaurant, grill, café; conference/banqueting facilities; discothèque daily except Sun and Mon; terrace. English spoken.
Location Central, between Royal Palace and National Theatre. Underground carpark.
Restriction Not suitable for ♿.
Credit cards All major cards accepted.
Terms B&B: single 950 Nkr, double 1,100 Nkr. Children under 15 sharing parents' room free.

> Set dinner refers to a fixed price meal (which may have ample, limited or no choice on the menu). Full alc is the hotel's own estimated price per person of a three-course meal taken à la carte, with a half-bottle of house wine.

Gabelshus Hotell *Tel* (02) 55.22.60
Gabelsgt. 16 *Telex* 74073 GABEL
0272 Oslo 2

Recommended again this year as a quiet, comfortable and friendly hotel on a tree-lined residential street not far from the centre of Oslo, with the city's excellent public transport only three minutes' walk away. The hotel is popular with visitors from overseas and booking is usually essential. The lobby, decorated in dark wood, is reminiscent of a hunting lodge in the country. "The restaurant offers good, reasonably-priced meals, and the bedrooms are considerably cheaper than those in the large city-centre hotels." (*M Wane; also Mr and Mrs RG Shifrin*)

Open All year, except Easter and Christmas.
Rooms 36 double, 10 single – all with bath and shower, telephone, radio and TV.
Facilities Lift. 2 lounges, TV lounge, dining room; conference facilities. Garden. English spoken.
Location Between Bygdøy alle and Drammensv. 15 minutes' walk from city centre; bus and tram nearby. Parking.
Restriction Not suitable for ♿.
Credit cards All major cards accepted.
Terms B&B: single 700 Nkr, double 900 Nkr. Extra bed 160 Nkr. Full alc from 250 Nkr.

Stefanhotellet *Tel* (02) 42.92.50
Rosenkrantzgt. 1 *Telex* 19809 STEFA
0159 Oslo 1

An inspector jauntily restores to the Guide this large 1950s cube-shaped edifice, centrally located: "Forget charm. It was to the airport lounge that the owners of the *Stefan* must have turned when seeking a model – prioritising functionalism and efficiency – and in these terms it fares pretty well. Scandinavian black leather chairs, lots of sleek pine, homely touches like fresh flowers, and the nattiest lift I've ever seen. Of bedrooms: my assigned sleeping quarters (all rooms are identical) had enormous suicide-proofed windows, pale green walls, horrible red upholstery, a white white white bathroom with lots of extras, and some delicious chocs which I ate instantly. The hotel's best feature is the eighth-floor dining room with large windows all round where they lay out the best breakfast in Oslo – at least ten different cold meats. Apparently it's quite OK in Norway to fill the pockets in order to feed yourself at lunchtime, but British reserve held me back. In sum, not a place you'd want to stay more than a couple of nights – but then Oslo isn't that sort of place either." More reports please on this brave new world.

Open All year.
Rooms 131 – all with bath or shower, telephone and TV. Some adapted for ♿.
Facilities Lounges, dining rooms; conference facilities; childrens'playroom, gymnasium.
Location Central, parking.
Credit cards All major cards accepted.
Terms [1987 rates] Rooms: single 415-475 Nkr, double 580-700 Nkr. Breakfast 75 Nkr. Set lunch 160 Nkr; dinner alc.

White House Hotell *Tel* (02) 44.19.60
President Harbitzgt. 18
0259 Oslo 2

A spruce little hotel in a pleasant suburb, ten minutes' walk from centre. Clean, quiet, comfortable; modestly priced by local standards. Restaurant specialises in fondues and serves lavish buffet breakfasts. Staff young and friendly. 20 rooms, some with bath, all with shower. B&B double 600-900 Nkr. New nomination: more reports welcome.

SKJOLDEN 5833 Map 7

Skjolden Hotel *Tel* (056) 86606
Telex 40654

Situated at the end of the Lusterfjord (a branch of the long Sognefjord), this square flat-roofed hotel, owned by the Galde family for 75 years, is popular as a base for hiking, fishing and other sports. Large lounge, open terrace, fairly big garden; rooms simply furnished but comfortable. Food good, including large buffet breakfast. Open 1 Jan–30 Sept. 54 rooms, almost all with bath and/or shower. B&B double 285-360 Nkr. New nomination: more reports welcome.

UTNE 5797 Map 7

Hotel Utne *Tel* (054) 66983

Founded in 1722, this "gem" of a small hotel on the Hardangerfjord, south of Bergen, is the oldest in Norway and has been run by the same family since 1787. It is a white clapboard building, lovingly maintained, with flowers in all the public rooms, embroidered cushions and lace curtains, and lots of old painted Norwegian furniture. "Its setting is splendid: the foot of a steep promontory where the Hardanger branches into two small fjords; high blue mountains across the water; sheer cliffs above it; a waterfall plunging down the cliff face and rushing through the village; apple orchards on each side. There are fine walks along the fjord in both directions or you can climb paths to the high pastures. The village is small and tranquil. It has a folk museum, a collection of old farm buildings in the medieval style. The *Utne* stands in the centre of the village, opposite the boat landing. Behind it, on the hillside, is a small modern annexe. Inside, the hotel is like a charming country home, with fine old furniture, painted wood, brass and copper. Meals (taken communally) are hearty and excellent. On Sundays you have a magnificent *koldtbord*. Fru Aga Blokhus and her staff, wearing the Hardanger costume, look after you with grace and enthusiasm." (*EWD*) A devotee who has visited the hotel six times tells us this year: "The food this time was the best ever, with excellent salmon, various versions of potato, and splendid sweets." (*E and P Sandham*)

Open All year except Christmas and New Year.
Rooms 20 double, 4 single – 3 with bath, 16 with shower. 7 in nearby annexe (1 single).
Facilities 3 sitting rooms, basement café, dining room, games room; some off-season conference facilities; badminton. Garden and terrace; safe bathing in fjord in front of hotel; sailing, fishing, boating, cycling and good walks. English spoken.

Location At tip of Folgefonn Peninsula; at Odda cross bridge on to peninsula, or take ferry from Kvanndal or Kinsarvik.
Restriction Not suitable for ♿.
Credit cards Access, Amex, Diners.
Terms B&B 240-410 Nkr; dinner, B&B 390-560 Nkr. Set lunch 90-120 Nkr, dinner 120-150 Nkr. Reductions for long stays. 50%-70% reduction for children under 12 in parents' room.

"The brochure had advised us that the food was exceptional. From this we deduced a hint of complacency and smug satisfaction. Our forebodings were confirmed. The owner was quick to assure us of his attainments to the extent that he was *surprised* it had taken him so long to be included in all the guides. By day three, we had become weary of the constant reminder of how fresh, how good, how real everything was. We kept our eyes well averted from the plastic flowers all about. 'If he says it once more,' I growled through clenched teeth, 'there will be a massacre.'"

Portugal

VILLA HOSTILINA, LAMEGO

ARCOS DE VALDEVEZ 4970 Braga **Map 12**

Paço da Gloria *Tel* (058) 94.14.77

A 17th-century manor house in northern Portugal, near the Spanish frontier, now converted into a stylish hotel, owned by the Hon. Colin Clark (son of the late Kenneth Clark, the art historian) and managed by his brother-in-law, James Li. Honeymooners report to us this year: "A striking old building, set high on the side of the Lima valley. The atmosphere is sublime – distant murmurs of voices, slapping of naked feet on stone floors, the splatter of the fountain of the pool. The house is wonderful, full of beautiful statues, antiques, ancient books, paintings . . . is that a *real* Cézanne? The service is charming and idiosyncratic, the food local in style and you all eat round one table *en famille*, with conversation general. An excellent centre for a holiday in beautiful unspoilt countryside." (*Mr and Mrs Ian-Peter Macdonald*) Last year's views: "That countryside, with its rock lanes, hanging vines, terraced hills of pine, citrus and olive groves, can only be described as arcadian. Life in the hotel is conducted with easy informality and mild eccentricity. Quite simply one of Europe's really magical places." "Every modern luxury, excellent food." (*R Wilkin, Richard and Wendy Kahlenberg, Mrs André Lewis, and many others*). We have had several complaints of unanswered letters: but Mr Li explains that from October to March, when the hotel is closed, he is in Germany, at Jakob-Haspel Strasse 49, 7100 Heilbronn, tel (07131) 21978. So a ticket to paradise could well be worth the cost of a phone call to *ultima* Swabia.

Open 1 Apr–30 Sep.
Rooms 1 suite, 9 double – all with bath and/or shower. 7 in annexe. Some ground-floor rooms.
Facilities 2 salons, library, music/billiard room, TV room, dining room. 15 acre grounds with swimming pool. River 1 km, sea 25 km. English spoken.
Location 2 km N of N202 between Arcos de Valdevez and Ponte de Lima; about 34 km N of Braga. Ask for Jolda Madalena.
Credit card Visa.
Terms B&B: single 5,500 esc, double 6,500-8,500 esc, suite 10,000 esc. Snacks 800 esc, set dinner 1,200 esc. 1-night bookings sometimes refused.

AZEITÃO 2925 Setúbal — Map 12

Estalagem da Quinta das Torres — *Tel* (065) 208.00.01

Azeitão, consisting of two small villages about 1.5 kilometres apart, is on the old Lisbon–Setúbal main road, surrounded by vineyards and olive orchards. It is a good base for the Arrabida peninsula with its beautiful coastline, attractive beaches and the resorts of Sesimbra and Portinho. You approach the *Quinta* up a long overgrown drive between flowering shrubs. It is a beautiful rather shabby old house in its own grounds with a small ornamental lake against one wall. The whole place is beautifully furnished with old family furniture, portraits, prints, etc. Rumoured to have been the scene of many elegant parties and a gathering place for the wealthy residents of Lisbon before the Revolution, the *Quinta* is now warmly praised by readers for its old-world charm, tinged with gentle melancholy. "Visiting was like stepping back in time; the whole place has something of the air of an abandoned (but not neglected) palace. The room we had was in one of the tower wings round the courtyard with its Renaissance fountain and orange trees. It featured a four-poster bed worthy of Catherine of Braganza and a fireplace in which we were invited to light a log fire (and did so). Dinner was excellent and exquisitely served; breakfast taken in one's room." (*Shirley and Alan Day; endorsed by many others*)

Open All year.
Rooms 2 suites, 6 double, 2 single – all with bath, shower and tea-making facilities. 2 bungalows in grounds with kitchenette and lounge. Some ground floor rooms.
Facilities Lounge, bar, restaurant; terrace. 30-acre grounds;
Sandy beaches 15 km. English spoken.
Location 27 km W of Setúbal off N10; in village centre. Parking.
Credit cards None accepted.
Terms B&B: single 3,500 esc, double 5,500 esc, suite 6,000 esc. Set lunch/dinner 1,500 esc; full alc 2,500 esc. Reduced rates for children under 8; special meals.

> In your own interest, always check latest tariffs with hotels when you make your bookings.

BUÇACO 3050 Aveiro — Map 12

Palace Hotel do Buçaco *Tel* (032) 931.01
Floresta do Buçaco *Telex* 53049 BUCACO

The *Palace* is a 19th-century royal hunting lodge, built with extreme examples of Manueline architecture. It stands in a large park on the Buçaco ridge, which is planted with a magnificent selection of trees, particularly cedars of Buçaco (*Cupressus lusitanica*), which are world-famous. The park was created by Carmelite monks, whose monastery stands beside the hotel. Wellington spent the night in one of the monastery cells before the battle of Buçaco when he defeated the French attempt to capture Lisbon and throw the English out of Portugal.

"Food remarkable (we had jugged hare) and impeccable old-fashioned service," writes a returning visitor this year, "but the decaying elegance is more decaying now. We expect cobwebs next time." Others too have written of "a faded passé air about the place, like a sepia photograph of a Victorian club". But the general view is that the experience is worth it, especially for the location and the very good service – "charming, gracious and hospitable", "exquisite furnishings". A reader this year thought the rooms in the main palace "dearer but nicer" than those in the old monastery. (*M Richardson, PL Aston, Betty Silander, and others*)

Open All year.
Rooms 2 suites, 58 double – all with bath and telephone. Some ground-floor rooms.
Facilities Lift. Salon, TV room, bar, restaurant; conference facilities. Garden and park; tennis courts. English spoken.
Location 20 km N of Coimbra on N234. Parking.
Credit cards All major cards accepted.
Terms [1987 rates] B&B: double 12,000 esc; full board 15,600-24,000 esc per person. Set lunch/dinner 3,000 esc. Reduced rates and special meals for children.

CANIÇADA 4850 Braga — Map 12

Pousada de São Bento *Tel* (053) 571.90
Telex 32339

This small but very welcoming *pousada*, high above the Caniçada dam in the mountains of the Minho, provides welcome rest after exploration of the cathedral town of Braga, the rococo gardens of the pilgrimage centre of Bom Jesus, and other local splendours. It is at the south-western end of the Peneda-Geres National Park, with a stupendous view of the river valley and reservoirs and the surrounding mountain ranges. Built as an alpine chalet, it has a smell of pine and eucalyptus that wafts everywhere. An earlier visitor thought the food dull, but this year it was much approved. Other impressions: "Our room was modest in size but very clean and had a pretty view through the ivy-clad windows." "One should ask for a room looking outwards, as those facing the courtyard can be rather noisy. There is a pleasant terrace overlooking the lake and a comfortable sitting room; also a well-maintained garden." "The view across the valley to the mountains was breathtaking, the sunset was spectacular, and coffee on the terrace overlooking the attractive garden was a moment of pure magic. Reception staff were unsmiling but dining room staff were pleasant." (*F Durham, Mrs RB Richards*)

Open All year.
Rooms 18 – most with bath and telephone.
Facilities Lounge with TV, restaurant; terrace. Garden with swimming pool and tennis court; sailing and riding nearby.
Location 2 km SW of Vieira do Minho on N304.
Credit cards Probably all major cards accepted.
Terms [1987 rates] B&B: single 4,500-8,600 esc, double 5,900-9,500 esc. Set meals from 1,700 esc.

CASCAIS 2750 Lisbon — Map 12

Albatroz — *Tel* (01) 28.28.21
Rua Frederico Arouca 100 — *Telex* 16052

Cascais is a relatively unspoiled fishing port west of Lisbon, watched over by a picturesque 17th-century citadel on a rocky cape. If you get up early you can watch the fishermen tinkering down at the shore, painting their small boats in bright reds and yellows. The hotel is on a rocky headland by the sea, fairly near the station but not noisy. "Our room in the new building was comfortable, except for soiled carpet," writes a visitor in 1987. "Restaurant service and bar lunches were excellent, but meals a little stereotyped. Bed linen changed daily." Earlier views: "One of the most pleasant hotels we have stayed in – elegantly furnished and decorated yet extremely comfortable. The bedroom and bathrooms were well equipped and clean. The staff were well trained and unobtrusive. The restaurant was good but expensive." "An attractive setting. We had a lovely bedroom with three balconies in the old part of the inn, and found the service very good." Rooms in the older part of the hotel are preferred to those in the new wing. (*B and J Goodenough, RA Dubery, and others*)

Open All year.
Rooms 40 – most with bath or shower, telephone and TV.
Facilities Lift. Salon, bar, dining room; conference facilities. Swimming pool. English spoken.
Location On bay, near station. Parking.
Credit cards All major cards accepted.
Terms [1987 rates] B&B double 20,500 esc. Alc (excluding wine) 3,000-4,500 esc.

Estalagem Senhora da Guia — *Tel* (01) 28.92.39 and 28.97.85
Estrado do Guincho — *Telex* 42111 GUIA

This enticing white-walled holiday hotel, amid the trees and right by the sea, was once a villa built by a brewer, and is about ten minutes' drive west of Cascais. There are sometimes *fado* singers in the restaurant. "The friendliness of the place is gentle and infectious. Some of the rooms have been converted from the stables, other have views of the coast and terracotta-tiled balconies where one can breakfast or have drinks as the sun goes down. Large, comfortable lounge/bar and restaurant; drinks and meals are also served on the terraces in the garden by the ample but unheated sea water swimming pool." (*Martin Page*)

Open All year.
Rooms 4 suites, 24 double – all with bath, shower and telephone; 10 with TV. 13 in 2 annexes.

We depend on detailed fresh reports to keep our entries up-to-date.

Facilities Lounge/bar with fire-place and balcony, restaurant; *fado* singers once a week. Garden with swimming pool and bar/restaurant. Beach 3 km (bus from hotel). Golf, tennis and riding nearby. English spoken.
Location 5 km from Cascais on road to Guincho.
Restriction Not suitable for ♿.
Credit cards All major cards accepted.
Terms B&B 6,000-20,000 esc; dinner, B&B 9,000-21,600 esc; full board 12,000-25,200 esc. Set lunch/dinner 2,000 esc; full alc 3,000 esc. Children under 2 in parents' room free; special meals.

ESTREMOZ 7100 Évora — Map 12

Pousada de Rainha Santa Isabel — *Tel* (66) 226.18
Largo D. Diniz — *Telex* 43885

Estremoz, on the road east from Lisbon to Badajoz, is a busy market town with a bull-ring, interesting local pottery, and many marble quarries. Its *pousada*, one of the most famous in Portugal, has been converted from a 13th-century castle, the chief residence of King Diniz, and is named after his wife Isabel who was both queen and saint. The building has been expertly restored to its former glories: all rooms are furnished with real antiques and the restaurant is a beamed and vaulted baronial hall. The hotel went through a very bad patch recently and was dropped from the Guide after accounts of appalling service. But reports this year indicate a change for the better. One reader who lives locally says: "The *pousada* seems to have overcome its problems. The dining room was the trouble and that has really improved, the several meals we have had there recently have been very good." Another visitor has written: "A magnificent hotel with good four-poster bedrooms and plumbing much improved. The lounges, bar, etc are medievally impressive. Staff a little reticent, but a smile and a friendly approach will thaw them out. Small begging kids around the palatial entrance can be a nuisance, but a stern '*vamos*' despatches them rapidly." (*RA Dubery, H Bramwell*) So let's withdraw our own stern *vamos* from this *pousada* and give it another chance – but more reports would be welcome.

Open All year.
Rooms 3 suites, 18 double, 2 single – all with bath, shower and telephone.
Facilities Lift. Lounge, TV room, bar, restaurant.
Location In town centre. Parking.
Credit cards All major cards accepted.
Terms B&B: single 9,250-11,450 esc, double 10,850-13,100 esc, suite 14,200-26,150 esc. Reduced rates for children.

ÉVORA 7000 — Map 12

Pousada dos Lóios — *Tel* (066) 240.51
Largo do Conde de Vila Flor — *Telex* 43288

The Upper Alentejo is one of the prettiest and least spoilt parts of Portugal, and here Évora is one of the country's loveliest old towns, pleasantly Moorish in style, with clean white buildings, hanging gardens and tiled patios – many of the best of Alentejo coloured tiles come from this area. There is much to see, including a Roman temple, a museum of ancient art, and a fine Gothic cathedral. The *pousada* has a choice position in the centre of the walled city, next to the temple of Diana. Rooms were originally monks' cells, and tend towards the pokey or cosy depending on your mood. The restaurant is in the old cloisters around the central courtyard, complete with fountain. Readers this year have found the place "very attractive, comfortable and enjoyable", though the food, formerly praised, has come in for some criticism, and so has the service. But one recent visitor has mentioned a charming head waiter with good English. (*Betty Silander, Kathleen and Dennis Perry, H Bramwell, and others*)

Open All year.
Rooms 32 double – all with bath, shower and telephone.
Facilities Salons, bar, dining area in cloisters. English spoken.
Location Central, near cathedral. Évora is 145 km SE of Lisbon.
Restriction Not suitable for ♿.
Credit cards All major cards accepted.
Terms B&B: single 8,000-13,500 esc, double 11,000-15,500 esc, suite 19,000-26,000 esc. Set lunch/dinner 2,950 esc; full alc 3,500 esc. Reduced rates for children.

FUNCHAL 9000 Madeira — Map 12

Quinta Penha de França — *Tel* (091) 290.87
Rua da Penha de França 2

A small hotel of character, surrounded by huge new ones (Sheraton etc). Charming garden; attractive terrace where snacks are served. Rooms in the new wing are best. 35 rooms, all with bath and/or shower. No restaurant. B&B double £38-£44. Reports this year of noisy building work, poor food and service, too many package tours – so more reports urgently needed on what has always been a delightful hotel.

Reid's Hotel — *Tel* (091) 230.01
Estrada Monumental 139 — *Telex* 72139

On the outskirts of Madeira's strident, ugly capital, set gracefully apart on a cliff above Funchal Bay with magnificent semi-tropical gardens, here is a large, grand and very famous hotel that tries hard to keep up the old traditions (e.g. formal dress at dinner). It has its critics, but also its devotees who return year after year, many of them British and elderly, and our mailbag this year has been voluminous. "Service, manners (both of staff and guests) and decor all belong to the 1930s; so do the band that plays every night, the dancing and the food. They do have a modern swimming pool but I can't remember seeing a bikini. The staff seem to have worked at *Reid*'s for years, and as well as being very professional their care and kindness seem genuine. As for guests, the elderly couples were very noticeable every night at dinner, in immaculate evening dress, sweet and courteous. The traffic at the back is dreadful, but all is peace in front and you can walk down through the gardens to swim in the sea or in a rock pool." "A beautifully run hotel, impeccably clean, with endless sitting space and the most delightful willing staff. The ladies' loo is the most glamorous I have ever seen and the garden is my idea of Eden. We enjoyed the poolside buffet lunches too. *Reid*'s is like a club, full of congenial like-minded people." "Our bathroom was gloriously large and old-fashioned. Dinner with a pianist remembering the tunes of yesteryear helped to create a nostalgic atmosphere."

However, a few caveats seem to be in order. Not every room has a balcony, and side and road-facing ones can be noisy. The food in the main formal restaurants is not as good as in the more expensive grill-room, which at lunch has fine views of the sea and at night is candle-lit. And the otherwise much-admired staff seem to bestow their charming attentions more readily on private guests whom they know than on newcomers or package tourists (the latter are numerous, in season). One visitor this year had a small, ill-kept room and felt that the hotel's legend was tarnished, adding "The President of South Africa and the Queen of Sweden were fellow guests during our stay and the staff protected their anonymity superbly. As for us, their attitude to room service promptly changed when they realised we were a private booking." (*Myrtle Allen, Rosemary Bowmer, Donald and Shirley Grimwood, Dulcie Baxter, and others*)

Open All year.
Rooms 165 – most with bath and/or shower.
Facilities Lifts. Salons, TV room, card room, restaurant, grill room; tea terrace. Large garden with 2 heated swimming pools, 2 tennis courts; lift down to sea with swimming pool, changing rooms and bathing platform. English spoken.
Location 1 km from town centre. Parking.
Restriction Not suitable for severely ♿.
Credit cards All major cards accepted.
Terms [1987 rates] B&B: single 15,000 esc, double 25,000 esc; full board 20,000-23,000 esc per person. Set lunch/dinner 4,000 esc.

GUIMARÃES 4800 Braga — Map 12

Pousada da Santa Maria de Oliveira — *Tel* (053) 41.65.54, *Telex* 32875
Largo de Oliveira

This ancient town at the foot of the mountains north-east of Oporto was the birthplace in 1109 of Portugal's first king, Alfonso Henriques. The *pousada*, a remodelled 17th-century castle, has again been much admired this year: "It is reached through a maze of squares and narrow streets. There is no garden, but the furnishings are elegant and comfortable; there are only 16 rooms, but meals and service are of a quality you might expect to find in a much grander place." Others have appreciated the hand-made beds, embroidered spreads and fine local linen. One reader had "a magnificent suite" and enjoyed the good and plentiful regional cooking: the dining room overlooks the market-place. (*Blake Pinnell, Betty Silander, Mr and Mrs Staples, and others*)

Open All year.
Rooms 14 double or suites, 2 single – all with bath and shower.
Facilities Lift, 2 salons, TV room, 2 bars, dining room; terrace.
Location Central, near church of the Santa Maria da Oliveira. Private parking.
Credit cards Access, Diners, Visa.
Terms [1987 rates] B&B: single 4,500-8,600 esc, double 5,900-9,750 esc. Set meals from 1,700 esc.

> In Portugal, reservations for *pousadas* can be made direct or through Enatur, Avenida Santa Joana Princesa, 10-A, 1700 Lisbon. *Tel* (01) 88.12.21. *Telex* 63475.

LAMEGO 5100 Viseu — Map 12

Villa Hostilina — *Tel* (054) 623.94

This "exceptional place" (to quote a 1987 report) is an old farmhouse now reincarnated as a rural hotel, on a hill overlooking the attractive old town of Lamego, in a wine-growing area near the Douro Valley in northern Portugal. "From the little tiled terrace that leads off your bedroom, gentle hills covered with vines roll and fold into the blue distance. Immediately below is the house's own vineyard where, if you're up early enough, you can watch the workers tend the vines. It is the most peaceful prospect imaginable. Downstairs a breakfast awaits you not only generous but gorgeous to behold – figs, peaches, quince jelly . . . Thus nourished, you may set off to explore lovely Lamego – a gem. The villa, right on the edge of town, is comfortable and up-to-date, with its own health centre and gym, and the welcome is very warm." (*Shelley Cranshaw*) That earlier report has been warmly endorsed this year: "Spotlessly kept. Senhor and Senhora are naturally friendly, courteous, not over-attentive; maids are neat and obliging. Not much English spoken, but French serves. There's no restaurant, but you can eat *en famille* by arrangement (dinner good, varied)." "Excellent value. If you *can* persuade the staff to give you meals, you are probably better off doing so, for Lamego is badly supplied with restaurants. You should visit the amazing staircase of over 600 steps leading up to the shrine of Our Lady of the Cures, a flowering of the Baroque concept surrounded by lush woodland." (*Brian Williams, TJH, and others*)

Open All year.
Rooms 6 double, 1 single – all with bath and shower, telephone, radio, mono TV and baby-listening.
Facilities Lounge, TV room, bar, dining room; health centre with gymnasium, massage, sauna etc. Garden with swimming pool and tennis courts. River with fishing rights nearby. English spoken.
Location 500 metres from centre; private parking.
Credit cards None accepted.
Restriction Not suitable for ♿.
Terms [1987 rates, likely to go up 25% in 1988] B&B: single 5,000 esc, double 6,000 esc; dinner, B&B: single 7,500 esc, double 10,000 esc. Extra bed 1,500 esc. (No restaurant, but meals by arrangement.)

LISBON — Map 12

Hotel Principe Real — *Tel* (01) 36.01.16
Rua da Alegria 53, Lisbon 1200

Praised again in 1987, the *Principe Real* has a good central location, only a couple of blocks off the Avenida da Liberdade in a charming area full of older buildings serving as residences, groceries and small shops. "The hotel is spotlessly maintained, the staff very courteous and helpful. The rooms are somewhat small but comfortable and well furnished. Some have a balcony. Ours was at the back and very quiet. The hotel offers only breakfast, served on the top floor with a memorable view overlooking much of central Lisbon." "Nice lounge, but orange juice was a rip-off price". (*Robert Young; also William Bentsen*) Since last year individually controlled air-conditioning has been installed in half the bedrooms.

Open All year.
Rooms 24 double – all with bath, shower and telephone; some with air-conditioning.
Facilities Lift. Bar, lounge with TV, breakfast room. English spoken.
Location Central; 300 metres from Avenida da Liberdade (back rooms quietest). Parking in street or nearby garage.
Credit cards All major cards accepted.
Terms B&B: single occupancy 6,750-9,600 esc, double 8,250-12,000 esc. 50% reduction for children under 8. (No restaurant.)

Hotel Tivoli Jardim *Tel* (01) 53.99.71
Rua Julio Cesar Machado 7 *Telex* 12172 JARDIM
Lisbon 1200

A modern multi-storey hotel, catering for the business and package trade as well as the individual traveller, just off the main central avenue of Lisbon, the Avenida da Liberdade. (*Note*: it should not be confused with its sister hotel, the *Tivoli* next door.) A visitor to the *Jardim* this year found it very friendly, with excellent food, while others too have written of good value for money, comfort and high standards, notwithstanding the package tours. A frequent customer stresses: "Friendly but not elegant. The restaurant is quite good, though better quality can be found at a quarter of the price in restaurants five minutes' walk away." (*RA Dubery, Trevor Phillips, MA Atkinson*)

Open All year.
Rooms 119 double – all with bath and shower, telephone, radio, TV with video, mini-bar and air-conditioning.
Facilities Lift. Hall with bar, restaurant. Gardens with Tivoli club, heated swimming pool, tennis and bar. 12 km to beach. English spoken.
Location 10 minutes from town centre, NE of Botanical Garden. Garage and carpark.
Credit cards All major cards accepted.
Terms [1987 rates] B&B double 11,000 esc; full board 9,200-11,700 esc per person. Set lunch/dinner 2,000 esc. Reduced rates for children sharing parents' room.

MANTEIGAS 6260 Guarda Map 12

Pousada de São Lourenço *Tel* (075) 471.50
Telex 53992 PSLOUR

Recommended again this year, the *São Lourenço* is high on the Serra da Estrela, about 4,200 feet above sea level, and a few kilometres up the mountain from the old town of Manteigas, with unparalleled views. Best for a summer visit: it can be pretty bleak in winter. "We had a room with balcony and a mountain view, and enjoyed two memorable nights. The staff are mostly young girls and they were all charming and most attentive. The food in the delightful Alpine-style restaurant was among the best we had, the wine equally good, and the prices were moderate. We visited the town and experienced a friendly welcome from its people. We also visited a local beauty spot, a mountain lake near Penhas Douadas, about two kilometres away: there is a small beach surrounded by wooded slopes, and the water was clear and like warm milk to bathe in." A report this year: "Good and copious food, and a surprisingly varied menu. In summer the town is hot, but in winter the snow can be nine feet deep." (*DS McBain, Blake Pinnell*)

Open All year.
Rooms 14 double – all with bath, shower, and telephone; some with balcony. 7 ground-floor rooms.
Facilities Bar, restaurant. Garden. Lake with beach and safe bathing nearby. English spoken.
Location 13 km N of Manteigas on estrada de Gouveia.
Credit cards Access, Diners, Visa.
Terms B&B: single 3,500-6,500 esc, double 4,600-7,500 esc. Set lunch/dinner 1,600-2,100 esc. Reduced rates for children.

MARVÃO 7330 Portalegre — Map 12

Pousada de Santa Maria

Tel (045) 932.01
Telex 42360

"Marvão is an enchantment" – a tiny village near the Spanish border, six kilometres north of the main Lisbon–Madrid road, thus useful for a stopover. Its small white houses and narrow cobbled streets are entirely inside the walls of a castle over which the keep stands guard. You can walk round the ramparts, looking within at the roofs, gardens, chicken runs, kitchens and television sets, or without over the Sierra de Torrico in Spain and the valleys below in Portugal. The *pousada*, like everything in Marvão, is tiny: it is built of stone with tile floors, the public rooms are well furnished, the beds comfortable, you can see to read, and the hot water is dependable. The staff are few but young and amiable. The view from the bar is fine, and the local wine excellent. Prices are very reasonable. "The local cockerel announces the sun early every morning, but that fits beautifully," says a reader this year. "The restaurant serves good local food – try the best bacalau (dried cod) I have had in Portugal, or try the goat-meat soup (if you can forget the resentful looks the mountain goats gave you when you photographed them over the castle walls)." Others too this year have praised the food, the quiet and the location – "a delightful place". The new rooms, with air-conditioning and bathrooms, are said to be very attractive. (*David Wainwright, RA Dubery, Fiona Dick, and others*)

Open All year.
Rooms 21 double – all with bath and telephone.
Facilities Lounge, bar, restaurant. Garden. Riding. English spoken.
Location 22 km N of Portalegre on N521.
Credit cards All major cards accepted.
Terms [1987 rates] B&B: single occupancy 4,500-8,600 esc, double 5,900-9,750 esc. Set lunch/dinner from 1,700 esc. Reduced rates for children under 12; special meals.

MONCHIQUE 8550 Faro — Map 12

Estalagem Abrigo da Montanha

Tel (082) 921.31

Corte Pereira/Estrada de Foia

Halfway between the hill town of Monchique and the peak of Foia, this *estalagem* in the Algarve has fine views over green hills, lush valleys and the coastline. There is a main building and a long tier of separate apartments at the other end of a pretty flowery garden. It is a restaurant-with-rooms, family-owned and run and good English is spoken. One visitor this year dubbed it "a must for any visitor to Monchique for it sets a bench mark in value for money". An earlier report: "I could dine on the black olives, fresh white fish and green wine at the *estalagem* for a long, long time before I'd get bored with it. And lunch on the terrace there, under the chestnut trees with the sweeping view of the valley below, is a memorable experience. The peacefulness of the surroundings is slightly marred (but very slightly) by the rock quarry down the hillside. The staff couldn't be warmer or more hospitable, the surrounding forests of cork, chestnut and eucalyptus trees are lovely, and the inn itself, with its flower-filled garden, is most beautiful. It was one of the cheapest places we have stayed in, and perhaps the most wonderful." (*Helen Wallis, Dr Jacob Brynes*) *Warning:* It can be cold and wet in Monchique even when blazing on the coast. And one reader has cautioned that the peace can be shattered when coach parties arrive for lunch.

Open All year.
Rooms 3 suites, 5 double – all with bath, shower, telephone. 2 suites in annexe.
Facilities Lounge, bar with TV, dining room; terrace. Garden. English spoken.
Location About 25 km inland from Portimão. Hotel is 2 km from Monchique on road to Foia.
Restriction Not suitable for ♿.
Credit cards All major cards accepted.
Terms B&B: double 4,000-6,000 esc, suite 5,000-7,000 esc; dinner, B&B: double 5,800-8,200 esc, suite 6,800-9,200 esc; full board: double 7,600-10,400 esc, suite 8,600-11,400 esc. Set lunch/dinner 1,200 esc; full alc 1,800 esc.

MURTOSA 3870 Aveiro — Map 12

Pousada da Ria — *Tel* (034) 483.32
Bico do Muranzel, Torreira — *Telex* 37061

About 50 kilometres south of Oporto, Murtosa is a fishing village on the Aveiro lagoon, a wide inlet full of every kind of small ocean-going vessel. The *Pousada da Ria* is in an isolated position to the south-west, near Praia da Torreira, and has been clearly summed up by a visitor this year: "It is very comfortable, spacious and well appointed, but has some drawbacks. First, it is actually *on* the lagoon, and thus suffers from mosquitoes at some seasons. Secondly, the young staff though charming are some of them trainees and do not yet know their job well. Thirdly, the large airy restaurant has uninspiring food, and service by those trainees is very slow. This *pousada* is in an unusual and inviting spot: with a little effort it could be first class." Others have written: "The design of the reception area with its indoor garden and pool is welcoming and cool." Each room has a covered balcony and a good view. (*B Williams, Daphne and Frank Hodgson*) More reports please.

Open All year.
Rooms 3 suites, 16 double – all with bath, shower, telephone and balcony.
Facilities Salon, TV room, bar, restaurant. Garden with outdoor swimming pool. Near river with fishing; beach 3 km (but sea a bit rough). English spoken.
Location On N327 15 km SW of Murtosa, near Praia da Torreira.
Credit cards All major cards accepted.
Terms B&B: single occupancy 3,800-6,500 esc, double 5,000-7,500 esc, suite 7,000-10,500 esc. Set lunch 1,600 esc, dinner 2,100 esc.

ÓBIDOS 2510 Leiria — Map 12

Pousada do Castelo — *Tel* (062) 951.05
Paço Real — *Telex* 15540 POSOBI

This *pousada* was built from the ruins of a 15th-century castle destroyed by the 1755 earthquake. "We approached this perfectly walled hilltop village, crowned with its small and beautiful castle, late one sunny winter afternoon. It was breathtaking and magical (out of season, at least). Óbidos is one of the prettiest towns we have seen in Portugal. The *pousada* in the castle has enchanting views over the village and surrounding countryside. Our room looking into the courtyard was adequately furnished and we found the beds comfortable. The food was good and offered interesting regional dishes. (We also greatly enjoyed eating in the village with the local people.) The staff were friendly and helpful. Breakfasts were especially good with a wide choice of breads, cakes, yoghurt, honey and jam in dishes." (*John C Gillett*) More reports please.

Open All year.
Rooms 3 suites, 6 double – all with bath, shower, telephone, radio and tea-making facilities; 3 with TV.
Facilities Lounge, TV room, bar, restaurant. English spoken.
Location Central. No private parking.
Restriction Not suitable for ♿.
Credit cards All major cards accepted.
Terms B&B: single occupancy 8,000-12,000 esc, double 10,500-14,500 esc; suite 15,000-25,000 esc; dinner, B&B: single 10,000-14,500 esc, double 15,500-18,500 esc. Set lunch/dinner 2,500-3,500 esc.

Estalagem do Convento — *Tel* (062) 952.17 and 952.14
Rua Dom João de Ornelas — *Telex* 44906

This unusual hotel lies just outside the walls of a medieval town full of cobbled alleys and flower-girt piazzas. "We were housed in a tiny building next to the church as ancient as the hotel itself. Table and chairs and other bits and pieces I'm sure were medieval too! The beds were below in another tiny room reached by a delightful 18-inch wide spiral staircase. The bedroom, although small, was entirely adequate and there was an efficient shower room attached. We really felt we were back in historic Portugal. The hotel itself is quite fascinating with lots of dark rooms and pretty cobbled courtyards. The food and service generally were good. We would not recommend this hotel to anyone preferring light, modern, plush comfort. It was, after all, built a long time ago for purposes very different from the pampering of today's finicky travellers, but if, like us, you want to feel the past as much as it is possible to do then the hotel will suit you down to the ground." (*JO Nairn*) "Very impressed by comfort, food and value for money – half the price of the *pousada*. Altogether delightful." (*Michael Richardson*)

Open All year.
Rooms 6 suites, 21 double – all with bath, shower, telephone and radio; suites have TV.
Facilities 2 lounges, 2 bars (1 with TV), dining room. Garden. English spoken.
Location In town centre. Parking.
Restriction Not suitable for ♿.

Credit cards Access, Visa.
Terms B&B: 2,000-6,000 esc; dinner, B&B 3,320-7,600 esc. Set lunch/dinner 1,600 esc; full alc 3,000 esc. 20% reduction for children; special meals.

OPORTO Map 12

Castelo Santa Catarina *Tel* (02) 49.55.99
Rua Santa Catarina 1347
Oporto 4000

This former seigneurial mansion, much turreted, is only 500 metres or so from the city centre but remarkably quiet. Ground-floor rooms, in an annexe, look past vine-covered trellises to green lawns. More French spoken than English. Parking. 24 rooms, many with bath and shower. B&B double 3,500 esc [1987]. No restaurant: lots nearby. New nomination: more reports please.

Hotel Infante de Sagres *Tel* (02) 281.01
Praça D. Filipa de Lencastre 62 *Telex* 26880 SAGRES
Oporto 4000

Oporto's grandest hotel has been described as "a splendid old-style Anglo-Portuguese hotel where the British connection is still appreciated, and where you can find superb ports and the best vinho verde outside the Tras es Montes". This year an American reader found it "charming, beautifully appointed and finely managed, with superb food and service", while last year an experienced traveller wrote: "Wonderfully comfortable and personal. The general manager, who started in the hotel as a bellboy, welcomed us very warmly and even got up at 6 am on our last day to see us off. The hotel was originally built by a textile magnate as a private place in which to put up his clients. Excellent food, exquisitely served – and prices very reasonable." (*Betty Silander, Stefan and Yvette Wiener*)

Open All year.
Rooms 4 suites, 70 double, 10 single – all with bath and shower, telephone, radio and TV.
Facilities Lift. Lounges, bar, restaurant. Garden. 15 km from sandy beach with safe bathing. English spoken.
Location In city centre, near Avenida dos Aliados. Parking.
Credit cards All major cards accepted.
Terms [1987 rates] B&B: single 9,000-11,000 esc, double 10,000-12,500 esc, suite 13,000-33,000 esc. Set lunch/dinner 3,000 esc; full alc 5,000 esc. 50% reduction for children under 8 in parents' room; special meals.

Malaposta *Tel* (02) 262.78
Rua de Conceição 80
Oporto 4000

Sympathetic hotels in Portugal's second city seem in short supply, so we were glad to get more news this year of the modest *Malaposta*: "Central and very quiet, simple but comfy, staff *very* friendly and helpful. Bathroom overlooks flat roof with lots of cats. No restaurant, but there are plenty a sharp walk away." (*Mr and Mrs F Stapley; NF*)

Open All year.
Rooms 37 – some with bath; some with telephone.

Facilities Lift. Salon, breakfast room. English spoken.
Location Central, 600 m NW of main station; parking.
Credit cards Most major cards accepted.
Terms On application. (No restaurant.)

PALMELA 2950 Setúbal — Map 12

Pousada do Castelo de Palmela — *Tel* (01) 235.04.10
Telex 42290

Palmela, 43 kilometres south of Lisbon, stands in tiers on the northern slopes of a hillside, a small and very pretty white-walled town. Here this state-run *pousada* is a recently transformed convent inside a 1,000-year-old castle. Readers remain enthusiastic about the location, ambience and other qualities. "As comfortable as ever – superb interior, lovely room and views, staff helpful, restaurant good though the food is not exceptional, save for the very good breakfast." All recent reports on the service and food are favourable. An earlier portrait: "High above the beautiful white-walled town with its houses jumbled together and cascading down the slopes, surrounded by the plains and olive groves, and in the distance the port and coastline in clear view. Reception is a little forbidding but the public areas and rooms are opulent. Our room afforded splendid views over the plains towards Évora. The standard of furnishings and comfort was about the best we encountered. The swimming pool is in a delightful location, in a low walled courtyard with locked access guarded by a young porter. The cloisters are wonderful, full of the most exotic and vivid array of plants." (*BH and MR Robinson, David and Brenda Evans, DS McBain, RA Dubery*)

Open All year.
Rooms 2 suites, 25 double – all with bath, telephone and radio. Some ground-floor rooms.
Facilities Lift. Lounge, breakfast room, bar, TV room, dining room; art gallery. Large grounds with heated swimming pool and children's play area. Sandy beaches with safe bathing nearby; river 7 km with fishing and sailing. English spoken.
Location 7 km from Setúbal in centre of village. Parking for 40 cars.
Credit cards All major cards accepted.
Terms [1987 rates] B&B double 13,900 esc. Set lunch/dinner 2,860 esc. Reduced rates for children.

SAGRES 8650 Faro — Map 12

Pousada do Infante — *Tel* (082) 642.22
Telex 57491 PINFA

A modern purpose-built *pousada* on the most south-western tip of Europe, the centre for Henry the Navigator's school from which came all the great Portuguese discoveries in the 15th century. "There are stunning views, and Sagres makes a good base from which to explore the Algarve, though the early or late season could be chilly with strong Atlantic winds. Worth making sure you get a room commanding the Atlantic prospect. Average *pousada* fare in a large cheerless restaurant, but there is an excellent fish restaurant above the small beach and port of Sagres where fish is landed every day. Another small beach, sandy, isolated and safe, is five minutes' walk from the *pousada* and has a beach-style café/restaurant." (*DS McBain*)

Open All year.
Rooms 2 suites, 21 double – all with bath, shower, telephone and balcony.
Facilities Lounge, bar, restaurant. Swimming pool. Sandy beach 100 metres, safe bathing and fishing. English spoken.
Location 35 km W of Lagos. Follow "pousada" signs in Sagres.
Credit cards All major cards accepted.
Terms B&B: single occupancy 8,300-13,200 esc, double 11,000-15,000 esc, suite 13,800-20,000 esc; dinner, B&B: single 11,300-16,200 esc, double 17,000-21,700 esc, suite 19,800-26,000 esc. Set lunch/dinner 3,000 esc; full alc 2,300 esc. Reduced rates for children.

SÃO BRÁS DE ALPORTEL 8150 Faro — Map 12

Pousada de São Brás — *Tel* (089) 423.05
Telex 56945

About 12 miles north of the coast town of Faro in the Algarve, this small *pousada* is on a hill, with beautiful views all round. "Its initial impression is a little depressing," wrote a nominator last year, "with the exterior paintwork in a poor state and bedroom furnishings much the worse for wear. Two drawer knobs in the chest-of-drawers came off in our hands. Now, here is the joy! The drawer knobs, weary furniture, flaking paint and creaky stairs were utterly eclipsed by the comfort, warmth, superb service, smiling friendliness and attention which we received throughout our stay. We like simple food done in the regional style: the menu here is certainly simple, but the variety and character were most enjoyable. Their local fish dishes are excellent. Don't miss caldeirada de borrego (stewed lamb) or ameijoas na cataplana (clams with ham, sausage, onion, tomato and paprika). And the place is excellent value for money." (*John C Gillett*) This year the editor of our sister, *The Good Food Guide*, qualifies that panegyric: "The staff are formally dressed in black, the dining room has fine views and a terrace. The menu was disappointingly international and overcooked, in the way that has given Portuguese food a bad reputation. But local people seem to get local dishes of much greater interest. The wines are good. All round, I don't think you would lose readers by sending them here, especially given what I have seen of the local competition." (*Drew Smith*)

Open All year.
Rooms 23 – most with bath.
Facilities Restaurant.
Location 2 km N of São Brás de Alportel on the Lisbon road.
Credit cards All major cards accepted.
Terms [1987 rates] B&B double 7,900 esc; full board 8,950-11,900 esc per person. Set lunch/dinner 2,500 esc.

SERPA 7830 Beja — Map 12

Pousada de São Gens — *Tel* (084) 903 27
Telex 43651

Set amid rolling wheatfields just south of the little town of Serpa, in the lower Alentejo between Beja and the Spanish frontier, this small pousada *is off the main road and very peaceful. A dullish custom-built building but the warmth of welcome compensates; most bedrooms have pleasant views; food less bland than in many* pousadas, *with regional specialities. 18 rooms, many with bath. B&B double 7,500 esc. Set meals 1,600 esc. New nomination: more reports welcome.*

SETÚBAL 2900 **Map 12**

Pousada de São Filipe *Tel* (065) 238.44
Telex 44655

This *pousada* is a 15th-century fortress perched high above the port of Portugal's fourth biggest city, with fine views over the fishing fleet and the Atlantic. Visitors in November found the staff a bit uncooperative, but a summer customer reports that service was helpful and cheerful. The appointments of the rooms been appreciated, also the choice of food both on the set menus and à la carte, but "the service was so formal that by the time my wife's grilled sole was exquisitely deboned at the table it was stone cold". Prices of food and wine seemed on the high side. (*DS McBain, John C Gillett*)

Open All year.
Rooms 15 – some with bath or shower.
Facilities Restaurant.
Location 1 km W of Setúbal.
Credit cards All major cards accepted.
Terms [1987 rates] B&B double 10,850 esc. Set lunch/dinner 2,000 esc.

SINTRA 2710 Lisbon **Map 12**

Quinto São Thiago *Tel* (01) 923.29.23

A most civilised white-walled 16th-century manor house open to guests, secluded in its own grounds in the hills just west of Sintra. Antiques, large library, music room: but modernised amenities. Gracious hostess, Teresa Braddell, and her English husband. Lavish breakfasts; main meals served too; after-dinner dancing. Swimming-pool and tennis court. 10 rooms, nearly all with bath and shower. B&B double 10,000-11,000 esc. Attractive new nomination: more reports please.

Hotel Palácio de Seteais *Tel* (01) 923.32.00
Rua Barbosa do Bocage 8 *Telex* 14410 HOPASE

Immortalised by Byron in *Childe Harold* this famous hill town is set dramatically against the north face of the *serra*. The *Palace of Seteais*, built a year before the poet's birth, sits regally about a mile away down the Colares road. It is one of the few de luxe country houses in Portugal. "One of the most beautiful houses we have ever seen, with fantastic views over the château and Moorish castles from the front rooms, and over the plain from back ones. Lovely gardens, gallery and drawing room, all enchanting and very quiet. Service excellent, rooms large and well furnished." "High ceilings, delicately painted walls and antique furniture give a feeling of bygone elegance and graciousness. The bar opens onto a terrace with tables and chairs. Bathrooms are as large as many hotel bedrooms." So far, so good. But while some readers this year have warmly praised the cooking, others have been highly critical – "at best erratic and at worst pretentious". For the latter group it would be best to stay here and eat elsewhere in this town with several good restaurants. (*Stefan and Yvette Wiener, Harrison Gardner, B and J Goodenough, D Baxter, and others*)

Open All year.
Rooms 1 suite, 17 double – all with bath and shower. Some ground-floor rooms.
Facilities Lift. Salons, bar, TV room, restaurant; terrace. Garden. Beach 10 km with bathing and water sports. English spoken.
Location 1 km W of Sintra on Colares road. Parking.
Credit cards All major cards accepted.
Terms [1987 rates] B&B: single 14,000-17,000 esc, double 15,000-18,000 esc. Set lunch/dinner 2,900-3,200 esc. Reduced rates for children sharing parents' room; special meals on request.

VALENÇA DO MINHO 4930 Viana do Castelo — Map 12

Pousada de São Teotónio — *Tel* (051) 222.52 and 222.42
Telex 32837 PSTEOT

A welcoming and efficiently run *pousada* built on the 17th-century ramparts of a Vaubanesque frontier fortress and commanding a splendid view of the Minho river-frontier with Spain and the Spanish cathedral citadel of Tuy. Valença itself is pretty if trippery but the Minho valley offers gentle classical landscapes and vinho verde. As for the hotel, its pleasant modern rooms share the view with the airy and comfortable lounge and restaurant. A visitor this year thought the place very comfortable and attractive but found the food poor. Another writes: "In the Portuguese tradition, everything starts late in the morning – the hot water as well as the 8 o'clock breakfast – but we can heartily recommend this beautifully-located and well-managed *pousada*. The beautiful linen table scarves were brought here from Viana do Castelo. I especially recommend the Minho river salmon and broa, the local bread made with cornmeal. The Dão wines were excellent." (*Betty Silander; also MW Atkinson, and John C Gillett*)

Open All year.
Rooms 1 suite, 14 double – all with bath, shower and telephone. 4 in annexe.
Facilities 2 lounges, bar, restaurant. Garden. River 1 km; fishing. Sea 25 km. English spoken.
Location On Portuguese/Spanish frontier, 37 km NE of Viana do Castelo, on E50.
Restriction Not suitable for ♿.
Credit cards Access, Diners, Visa.
Terms [1987 rates] B&B single 4,500-8,600 esc, double 5,900-9,750 esc. Set lunch/dinner from 1,700 esc. Children under 8 half price; special meals.

"We asked the manager for some coffee a little stronger than the rather watered-down communal pot available on the bar. He replied 'Do you think we run this place on a commercial basis?' and 'Why should you not like it – it's free isn't it?'. The fact that he was slightly drunk might have had a bearing on this."

Spain

ALMAGRO 13270 Ciudad Real **Map 12**

Parador Nacional de Almagro *Tel* (926) 86.01.00
Ronda de San Francisco

A small town 190 kilometres south of Madrid, a short detour off the main road south to Granada. It has a 14th-century theatre, the oldest of its kind in Europe, maybe giving some idea of what the Globe in London used to be like. The *parador*, a converted 15th-century convent, has been commended again this year: "Its various small gardens are pleasant and secluded. Nice pool with grounds. A little lady sits in the hotel busy with her lace-making – it made me quite dizzy to watch. Good churros (sugared fritters) with breakfast." Others have praised the air-conditioned bedrooms and the pleasant staff. But about the food there is some dissent (as so often with *paradores*). Two visitors this year thought it "better than *parador* average" (not saying much), but in past years comments have ranged from "marvellous" to "a great disappointment". (*KE Smith, James Joll, Osmond Edwards, and others*)

Open All year.
Rooms 1 suite, 48 double, 6 single – all with bath and/or shower and telephone; some with air-conditioning. 5 ground-floor rooms.
Facilities Bar, 3 salons, 2 restaurants; conference room. Garden with swimming pool. English spoken.
Location Central (*parador* is sign-posted). Parking.
Credit cards All major cards accepted.
Terms B&B: single 5,400-6,600 pts, double 7,200-8,700 pts, suite 10,380-12,770 pts; dinner, B&B 2,500 pts added. Set lunch/dinner 1,900 pts.

ANTEQUERA 29200 Málaga — Map 12

Parador Nacional de Antequera — *Tel* (952) 84.02.61
Paseo Garcia del Olmo

The old white-walled town of Antequera, up in the hills behind Malaga, could be a useful base for exploring the Andalusian countryside without enduring the frenzy of the Costa del Sol. This *parador* is not a converted Moorish castle, for once, but a rather new building: "It is furnished in modern style, without suits of armour and tapestries on the walls, and is comfortable, clean and welcoming. There is a fine view over the valley with its rows of olive trees. The town museum with Roman relics is within easy walking distance. The newly created garden contains a swimming pool and the hotel's public rooms are large and comfortably furnished. Meals are excellent and, with one exception, we found the service good." (*LB Pinnell*) More reports please.

Open All year.
Rooms 55 double – all with bath, shower, telephone and air-conditioning.
Facilities 3 lounges, TV room, bar, dining room; conference room. Garden with swimming pool. English spoken.
Location Off N342 between Granada and Jerez de la Frontera. Hotel is on the outskirts of the town. Parking.
Credit cards All major cards accepted.
Terms (Excluding 6% tax) Double room 6,000-7,500 pts. Breakfast 600 pts. Full board 3,740-3,995 pts. Set lunch/dinner 2,000 pts.

BAGUR 17255 Gerona — Map 12

Hotel Aigua Blava — *Tel* (972) 62.20.58
Playa de Fornells, Aigua Blava — *Telex* 57077 UNHO ref HABIT

Playa de Fornells, at the northern end of the Costa Brava, is a beautiful landscape, and the *Aigua Blava* has annexed an especially lovely corner of it. It occupies nooks and crannies amid trees, on rocks, at all sorts of levels. For some years now it has been a special favourite among readers. who have called it "the best hotel on the Costa Brava", "one of the best-run hotels in Spain", "unique, of exceptional quality", and "it has the knack of creating the atmosphere of a country house party". Since last year, it has had a major refurbishment – new beds, new bathrooms, four new de luxe suites and two new lounges.

The following report, now some years old, still holds good: "The *Aigua Blava* (which is Catalan for Blue Water) has literally grown from a fisherman's hut. Xiquet (pronounced Chickee) Sabater, who owns it, is quarter-Japanese, quarter-French, half-Spanish, and married to a local woman. He is a great charmer. Some of his first guests are still coming back after more than 30 years. The buildings have just developed round a small fishing beach and harbour – a rather random aggregation. Marvellous staff – friendly and bright." (*AS*)

Señor Sabater is an anglophile and his hotel is something of a traditional British stronghold. But a visitor this year found it "less encroachingly anglophilic than I had feared" and admired the "good food and superb service". Another reader this year found it "living up to its reputation", but warns that – perhaps inevitably – in high season the warm personal touch gives way in the restaurant to a "hurried mass-catering air". Maybe it is best to go out of season. (*J McGillivray, Brian Williams, and others*)

Open 25 Mar–24 Oct.
Rooms 14 suites, 67 double, 8 single – all with bath and/or shower, telephone and air-conditioning; 4 with TV, some with balcony. All in 5 different buildings.
Facilities 4 lounges, 2 bars, 4 restaurants, TV room; conference and banquet rooms; boutique, hairdresser. Gardens with tennis, volleyball, paddling pool, swimming pool (disco by pool every night); children's play area. Sand and rock beach with safe bathing and water sports. Golf 7 km. English spoken.
Location 4 km SE of Bagur, 8 km E of Palafrugell. Garage and parking.
Restriction Not suitable for ♿.
Credit cards Access, Visa.
Terms (Excluding 6% tax) B&B: single 4,500-5,400 pts, double 6,600-9,600 pts; half board: single 5,700-6,900 pts, double 10,000-14,000 pts; full board: single 6,300-7,500 pts, double 11,000-15,200 pts. Set lunch/dinner 2,200 pts; full alc 2,800 pts. Reduced rates for children under 7; special meals.

BAÑALBUFAR Mallorca — Map 12

Hotel Mar I Vent — *Tel* (971) 61.00.25
José Antonio 47-49

A deluge of praise has reached us in 1986/7 for this small, inexpensive hotel in a fishing-village on the rugged west coast of Mallorca, popular with readers since our first edition. Run by a delightful brother and sister, Tony and Juanita Vives, it has been in the same family for four generations and was built in the 18th century: though much modernised, it still retains some older features. There is antique furniture, and the comfortable lounges have English books (the Vives speak excellent English). Bedrooms are furnished in local style: some are smallish, but all are bright and airy. There are fine views of the sea and cliffs from the hotel and its swimming pool on the sun terrace below. You can also bathe from a tiny cove about 15 minutes' stroll by winding paths through the terraced tomato fields, and the hills behind offer exhilarating walking country.

An inspector who went with her family of five in October reports: "In friendliness and kindness Tony Vives and his sister would be hard to beat – for example, Tony bought newspapers specially for us in town each day. They work very hard, were always up at breakfast time and much in evidence in the dining-room in the evening. The food was always good, not elaborate but fresh-tasting, not the chips-with-everything so common in Mallorca. Breakfast was nice too, and included melon. There is no beach to speak of, but the sea was beautifully warm, warmer in fact than the swimming pool which is unheated and gets little sun owing to the hotel's north-facing position. Our rooms were simply but prettily furnished and hot water was plentiful. The other guests, many of them English, were mostly middle-aged to elderly." Another reader this year had a light room with balcony in the new annexe and thought the ambience first-class. But there are just a few quibbles about this otherwise delightful hotel. Bedroom and bathroom fittings not always in perfect repair, strange smells in some of the bathrooms, the insulation in the new annexe far from ideal; and one visitor found the house wine over-priced. (*Mr and Mrs WM Lee, Marie and Hans Haenlein, Patrick Briggs, Eardley Knollys, James Lees-Milne, and others*)

Open 1 Feb–25 Nov.
Rooms 16 double, 3 single – all with bath, telephone and balcony. 8 in adjoining annexe. Some ground-floor rooms.
Facilities Lift. 2 salons (1 with TV), bar/restaurant. Terrace with swimming pool; tennis court. Sea-bathing. English spoken.
Location 24 km NW of Palma, at entrance of village. Parking.
Restriction Not really suitable for ♿.
Credit cards None accepted.
Terms B&B: single 2,795 pts, double 4,050 pts; dinner, B&B: single 4,250 pts, double 6,950 pts. Set lunch/dinner 1,475 pts. 10% reduction for children sharing parents' rooms; special meals.

BARCELONA — Map 12

Hotel Colon — *Tel* (3) 301.14.04
Avenida Catedral 7 — *Telex* 52654
Barcelona 08002

"Do you know a good hotel in Barcelona?" was our appeal last year. The response has brought us this one, rather on the large side for our Guide, but with the merit of being very central (right opposite the cathedral): "The manager told me that permission to build it in 1951 was given on condition that it should not clash with the cathedral by looking like a hotel, inside or out. Indeed, its amazing collection of antiques and paintings in the public rooms gives it more the feel of an historic house. Picasso's widow was staying when we were there. Our comfortable room had a balcony looking onto the cathedral; service was good and friendly, but little English was spoken." (*Mark Paterson*) More reports, please, especially on the restaurant.

Open All year.
Rooms 5 suites, 80 double, 60 single – all with bath and/or shower, telephone, radio and TV.
Facilities 2 lifts. Bar, lounges, TV room, 2 restaurants; conference facilities. English spoken.
Location Central, opposite cathedral.
Credit cards All major cards accepted.
Terms (Excluding 6% tax) Rooms: single 5,700 pts, double 10,100 pts, suite 16,950 pts. Breakfast 500 pts. Dinner, B&B: single 8,600 pts, double 15,900 pts, suite 21,750 pts; full board: single 9,850 pts, double 17,475 pts, suite 25,250 pts. Reduced rates for children; special meals.

In Spain, reservations for state-run establishments can be made direct or through their central booking office:
Central de Reservas de los Paradores de España,
Calle Velazquez 25, Madrid 28001.
Tel (91) 435.97.00.

BAYONA 36300 Pontevedra — Map 12

Parador Nacional Conde de Gondomar
Carretera de Bayona

Tel (986) 35.50.00
Telex 83424 RRPP

It was into this Atlantic port, south of Vigo, that the good ship Pinta sailed in 1493 with the news of Columbus' discovery of the New World. The white-walled *Conde de Gondomar* stands high above the sea, in a former fort and governor's palace. "This is a favourite *parador* with many people. It has a splendid setting on a romantic shoreline. The *parador* is a mock *pazo* in the grounds of the Monte Real fortress – the old walls and tower remain, though the hotel itself is thoroughly modern. There are splendid views from the ramparts, and lovely beaches very close. The *parador* has its own pool and other facilities which put it squarely in the four-star bracket, so it's one of the more expensive ones. It's certainly comfortable and in very good order." (*LH*) More reports welcome.

Open All year.
Rooms 2 suites, 106 double, 20 single – all with bath, shower, telephone, radio and baby-listening. 20 with TV. Some ground-floor rooms.
Facilities 4 salons, TV room, bar, 2 restaurants; conference facilities. Park with swimming pool, tennis court and children's play area. Beach nearby with bathing and fishing. English spoken.
Location On coast, 18 km SW of Vigo by C550. Garage and parking.
Credit cards All major cards accepted.
Terms [1987 rates] (Excluding 6% tax) Rooms: single 4,100-5,900 pts, double 7,000-10,000 pts, suite 11,000-15,000 pts. Breakfast 600 pts. Set lunch/dinner 2,350 pts; full alc 2,500 pts. Reduced rates and special meals for children.

BURGOS 09000 — Map 12

Landa Palace Hotel
Carretera de Madrid

Tel (947) 20.63.43
Telex 39534

Out on the Madrid road, this hotel is one of Spain's most magnificent, in a classically regal style. The main hall is an impressive tower reconstructed from a country castle dating from the 14th century. Above it is the King of Spain's suite, with gold fittings in the bathroom, Isabel II's bed, sumptuously comfortable sofas and English prints. Almost everything that can be made in marble is. Parts are like a museum: there are collections of beds and cribs from many places, wall clocks of various kinds, a teapot collection and much else besides. There is also a remarkable indoor swimming pool in a vault, surrounded by plants. You can swim out one end to an outdoor pool surrounded by lawns. "The finest hotel we stayed at in a month in Europe: all services and rooms first class and spotless," wrote recent visitors *Bill and Kathy Reece*, and others have felt much the same way. But this year a reader who had a pleasant suite in the tower had to keep the windows closed because of traffic noise; and there is reported to be a five per cent charge for changing traveller's cheques. (*Ralph Clark*)

Open All year.
Rooms 7 suites, 28 double, 6 single – all with bath and shower, telephone and air-conditioning.
Facilities Lift. Hall, TV room, 3 salons, bar, restaurant; conference/banqueting facilities. Garden, swimming pool. English spoken.

Location 1.5 km S of Burgos on Madrid road.
Credit cards Access, Visa.
Terms [1987 rates] Rooms: single 7,500-9,500 pts, double 9,000-13,500 pts, suite 17,500 pts. Breakfast 720 pts. Set lunch/dinner 3,900 pts. Special meals for children.

CALONGE 17251 Gerona — Map 12

Hostal Los Porches — *Tel* (972) 50
Cinco de Febrero 51

In the Costa Brava area but four kilometres from the sea, the *Hostal Los Porches* is recommended by regular visitors as "clean, well run, modest and cheap", a good base for a family holiday for those wanting to avoid the "architectural monstrosities" along this touristy coast. Recent visitors found it a little impersonal, though they did enjoy "delicious" meals, and they liked the relaxed warmth of the Laviña family owners. All rooms are double, all have private bath (primitive tub and shower but decent plumbing by Spanish standards) and half of them have beautiful views over the elegant hotel garden and the distant hills. The hotel's restaurant, across the road, is basically Catalan but Alberto Laviña is Swiss-trained and can produce anything to order. Breakfast is first-class, usually including some cold ham, and prices are very reasonable. (*TGR*) More reports please.

Open 1 May–30 Sept.
Rooms 36 – all with bath and radio.
Facilities Breakfast room, restaurant (across road). Garden.
Location 15 km SW of Palafrugell. Hotel is central.
Credit cards None accepted.
Terms On application.

CAMBADOS 36630 Pontevedra — Map 12

Parador Nacional del Albariño — *Tel* (986) 54.22.50
Paseo de Cervantes

On the indented west coast of Galicia, not far from Pontevedra and the white sandy beaches of La Toja, here in the small modern port of Cambados is an attractive *parador* new to the Guide this year: "It has been converted from a beautiful aristocratic manor house set within a large walled and tree-shaded garden, and has been furnished with taste: the bedrooms have polished pine floors and luxurious bathrooms. The central courtyard with its sunshades captures the cooling breezes off the sea. Service is good, and so is the seafood. Some traffic noise at night." (*Blake Pinnell*)

Open All year.
Rooms 51 double, 12 single – all with bath, shower and telephone; some with TV. Ground-floor rooms.
Facilities Lift. 3 salons, TV room, restaurant, cafeteria. Garden. English spoken.
Location Central; parking. Town is 53 km S of Santiago.
Credit cards All major cards accepted.
Terms B&B: single 4,950-5,940 pts, double 7,920-9,570 pts; full board 4,115 pts per person added. Set lunch/dinner 2,090; full alc 2,600 pts. Reduced rates for children; special meals.

CARMONA 41410 Seville — Map 12

Parador Nacional Alcázar del Rey Don Pedro — *Tel* (954) 14.10.10, *Telex* 72992

A very superior *parador* that is admired on every account – location, furnishing, friendly service *and* (unusual in *parador*-land) cuisine, which three lots of readers this year found excellent. It was formally opened by the King and Queen of Spain in 1976, and it certainly seems worthy of a royal opening. It has been built inside the massive walls of the ancient Moorish *alcázar* on the top of a hill, from which there are marvellous views over the wide green plain of the Guadalquivir valley, with mountains on the horizon. Although the hotel itself is new, it has been built in the Spanish Renaissance manner, with Moorish influences: pierced wooden shutters and doors in the public rooms, a patio with a fountain in the middle. The walls, whitewashed or of honey-coloured brick, are sparingly punctuated with black or brown wooden and leather furniture. There is a sumptuous sitting room; the dining room is a cool, lofty hall. There is also a swimming pool – a model of good taste, with natural brick and grass surrounds, arcades to protect you from the sun, and white-painted garden furniture and colourful flowers. "Food of quality, graciously served: as one studies the menu, a glass of sherry, a cup of consommé and other trimmings are brought to the table. It is only the top-floor rooms that have the desirable balconies with views. Some traffic noise if windows are opened." (*Andrew and Anita Kirkby, Lord Vernon, Philip Gill, and others*)

Open All year.
Rooms 51 double, 8 single – all with bath and/or shower, and telephone; 25 with radio and TV; some with balcony. 6 ground-floor rooms.
Facilities Lifts. Hall, sitting room with TV, bar, dining room; room for functions and banquets; air-conditioning. Patio and garden with swimming pool. English spoken.
Location In town centre (hotel is signposted). Parking.
Credit cards All major cards accepted.
Terms [1987 rates] (Excluding 6% tax) B&B: single 6,975 pts, double 9,700 pts; dinner, B&B: single 9,175 pts, double 14,100 pts; full board: single 10,625 pts, double 17,000 pts. Set lunch/dinner 2,200 pts; full alc 2,500 pts. Reduced rates for children; special meals.

CERVERA DE PISUERGA 34840 Palencia — Map 12

Parador Nacional de Fuentes Carrionas — *Tel* (988) 87.00.75 and 87.01.05

In the mountains between Santander and León, a large and fairly luxurious *parador* on a plateau above a lake, with magnificent views. It is interestingly designed in a sort of chalet style with large terrace-balconies – a particularly attractive feature – and a steep roof. Inside it is well though not luxuriously furnished. Bedrooms are rather better than the public rooms – very large and well equipped, with polished tile floors. A popular *parador* with walkers because of the local scenery (the wild flowers are fantastic in May), and there are water sports on nearby reservoirs. The food has disappointed some, but a reader this year was pleased, while another warns: "It is fashionable to be dismissive about Spanish food and wine. We've been to a number of *paradores* and the food, in the main, was excellent." (*LH, Walter Baxter; endorsed this year by Blake Pinnell*)

Open All year except 1 Dec–1 Feb.
Rooms 72 double, 8 single – all with bath, shower, telephone and baby-listening; many with balcony. Ground-floor rooms.
Facilities Lift. Salons (one with TV), bar, games room, bar/cafeteria, dining room. Lake with watersports and fishing nearby. English spoken.
Location 2 km from Cervera – the parador is signposted from Cervera.
Credit cards Amex, Diners, Visa.
Terms [1987 rates] (Excluding 6% tax) Rooms: single 4,400-5,600 pts, double 5,500-7,000 pts. Breakfast 600 pts. Half board: 2,500 pts per person added; full board 3,740 pts added. Set lunch/dinner 1,900–2,000 pts. Reduced rates for children; special meals.

CHINCHÓN 28370 Madrid — Map 12

Parador Nacional de Chinchón — *Tel* (91) 894.08.36
Avenida del Generalisimo 1 — *Telex* 49398 RRPP

The village of Chinchón is 30 minutes' drive from Madrid, in lovely rolling countryside with vines and olive groves. The *parador* has been converted from a 17th-century convent, and it stands in the village square – actually a circle, used as a bullring in the summer and surrounded by houses with balconies. "This is a charmer – refreshing and utterly different from other *paradores*. The former convent still has a church within its confines and a cloistered but somehow cheerful air, full of *azulejos* (tiles) and pretty painted furniture. Nice views. Service is helpful and courteous, and the staff speak some English." An earlier description ran: "The *parador* is probably one of the best we stayed at in Spain – light, airy and homely. Reception is small, but the corridors nearby form a square around a beautiful garden with a working fountain. There is also a large garden at the back on several different levels with fruit trees, shrubs, benches, fountains and a swimming pool. It is very secluded and rather romantic. The bedrooms all have a bathroom, enormous single beds (no doubles) and adequate furnishings. Food was superior *parador* fare, and the wine cheap, but there are also some fine restaurants up the hill." (*LH, J and K Archer*)

Open All year.
Rooms 2 suites, 36 double, – all with bath and shower, telephone, radio, TV and baby-listening. Some ground-floor rooms.
Facilities Bar, salon, restaurant; conference facilities in cloisters. Garden with swimming pool. English spoken.
Location Central. Chinchón is 52 km SE of Madrid.
Credit cards All major cards accepted.
Terms (Excluding 6% tax) B&B: 4,850–8,200 pts; half board 7,050–10,600 pts; full board 8,500–12,200 pts. Set lunch/dinner 1,950–2,200 pts.

CIUDAD RODRIGO 37500 Salamanca — Map 12

Parador Nacional Enrique II — *Tel* (923) 46.01.50
Plaza del Castillo 1

Archetypal parador: *an imposing 14th-century Moorish fortress on a hill, inside this historic little town near the Portuguese border. Austere masonry, but lovely beamed dining room and beautiful sheltered garden overlooking river.*

Some bedrooms small, service erratic, and food usual unexciting parador *fare. 27 rooms, all with bath and shower. B&B double 3,850-4,600 pts. Set meals 1,900 pts. More reports please.*

CÓRDOBA 14000 — Map 12

Parador Nacional de la Arruzafa — *Tel* (957) 27.59.00
Avenida de la Arruzafa 33

A modern building set quietly amid orange-groves in the hilly northern suburbs. Most rooms are large, with wide balconies and views. Large well-landscaped swimming-pool amid oleanders, popular also with locals. Meals include self-service buffet dinner. Some criticisms this year of food and management. 86 rooms, all with bath and shower. B&B double 9,200-10,200 pts. Set meals 2,200 pts [1987]. More reports please.

Hotel Residencia Marisa — *Tel* (957) 47.31.42
Cardenal Herrero 6

A bed-and-breakfast hotel in the old district of the *Juderia,* which boasts a marvellous situation facing the *Mezquita* itself. The *Marisa* is recommended for its very attractive, clean and well-furnished rooms, its friendly and helpful staff, and its decent breakfasts. Best of all, however, is its excellent value for money. A 1987 visitor reports: "One of my favourite Guide discoveries this year . . . Picturesque inside and out. And the people who work there are so very welcoming, and seem to appreciate every guest. I hated to say goodbye to them." (*Donna Cuervo*)

Open All year.
Rooms 23 double, 5 single – all with bath, shower and telephone. Some ground-floor rooms, accessible for ♿.
Facilities Salon, bar. English spoken.
Location Central. No private parking.
Credit cards Amex, Diners, Visa.
Terms B&B: single 2,500 pts, double 4,250 pts. (No restaurant)

CUENCA 16001 — Map 12

Cueva del Fraile — *Tel* (966) 21.15.71

Roman in origin, Cuenca is an unspoiled medieval town situated on the rocky spur of San Cristóbal. The old walls and towers overhang streams and from seven gates narrow lanes wind upwards to the cathedral in the Plaza Mayor. It is worth a detour from almost anywhere in Spain. A short distance away is this 16th-century farm/convent, set amidst fantastic eroded mountains. "Only the sound of frogs and birds," ran a report last year, "and then nothing, once the diners' cars have left. Spacious rooms, all with bath *en suite,* overlook a pretty courtyard. Meals in the restaurant or on a terrace where there is an excellent, cheap barbeque with friendly (if not hasty!) service. Good breakfast (for Spain)." (*J Streets*) One recent visitor was less lyrical, finding the night silence impaired by a chorus of barking dogs and the peace of the dawn polluted at 8 am by coach-drivers revving their engines; there were some plumbing problems too – though none of these niggles would prevent a return visit.

Open All year.
Rooms 40 (some suites) – all with bath and telephone.
Facilities Restaurant; conference facilities. Terrace and courtyard.
Location 7 km NE of Cuenca by the Palomera road.
Credit cards All major cards accepted.
Terms [1987 rates] (Excluding 6% tax) Rooms 3,300-4,400 pts. Breakfast 310 pts. Full board 4,400-5,780 pts per person. Set lunch/dinner 1,400 pts.

DEYÁ Mallorca — Map 12

Hotel Es Molí — *Tel* (971) 63.90.00
Carretera de Valldemossa — *Telex* 69007 SMOLI

This village, at the foot of the Teix mountains on the rugged coast of north-west Mallorca, has one of the loveliest settings in the Mediterranean, close to a beautiful coastline, with sunny valleys of oranges and lemons. And it is this setting above all that draws our readers back again and again to the *Es Molí*, still one of the most popular hotels in this book. A report this year: "As luxurious as ever, with its attentive and caring management, informally efficient staff. The gardens, dazzling with blossom and fruit, fragrant with scents galore, huge colourful butterflies, and the cheerful gossipy frogs shouting across the lily ponds. The stunning views to the sea and the marvellous meandering walk through olive, orange and lemon groves down to the rocky cove of Port Deya." Meals in summer on the terrace overlooking the gardens; the swimming pool is "bedazzling in its beauty", while the hotel also provides a minibus to its private beach at Muleta, 20 minutes' drive away, for deep-water bathing from a rocky platform.

Others have referred to "the courtesy of Mr Peters and his staff" and "this terraced oasis of shady trees and cascading flowers, below a semicircle of towering crags". The one weak point, it would seem, is the food, which is "made of fresh and plentiful ingredients", but dishes are mostly unimaginative. However, the owners have now opened a much better restaurant a short walk away, which offers a 10 per cent discount to hotel guests (but for those on *pension* terms this might be an expensive alternative) It should also be said that this paradise-hotel is much used by package tours, and one reader this year felt that decor and furnishing could do with a face-lift. (*RJ Barker, Patricia Fenn, Air Cdr and Mrs HM Pearson, and many others*)

Open 1 Apr–27 Oct.
Rooms 1 suite, 62 double, 10 single – all with bath and shower, telephone, radio, piped music and air-conditioning; most with terrace (300 pts supplement). Annexe with 9 rooms 50 metres from main buildings.
Facilities Lift. Several lounges (1 with TV), 2 bars, video room, card and reading room; dining terrace, dancing by the pool weekly in summer. Large gardens with heated swimming pool, tennis court, ping-pong, pétanque. Rock beach with bar; restaurant (not hotel's) 6 km away (free hotel minibus). English spoken.
Location 1 km from Deyá; Palma 29 km; airport 37 km. Parking in front of hotel.
Restriction Not suitable for ♿.
Credit cards Access, Diners, Visa.
Terms B&B 6,000-14,000 pts; dinner, B&B 7,000-15,000 pts. Reduced rates for children sharing parents' room.

> When hotels have failed to return their questionnaire, we have quoted 1987 prices, with a note to that effect.

La Residencia *Tel* (971) 63.90.11
Telex 69570 DEYA

"Without a doubt the best hotel on the island," writes a travel expert this year. "It's an idyllic place, the site is beautiful, the staff welcoming and the food excellent." The hotel would make a good alternative to the often fully booked *Es Molí*. It is in the heart of the village, and according to an earlier report has been "converted from two adjoining manor houses at what must have been staggering expense: its faultless elegance and stylishness is almost in danger of being its only fault. The furnishings are discreet and timeless, many are antique, and the public rooms are used as a gallery to display the work of local artists. There are huge solid oak doors, small open quadrangles, a pleasingly shaped pool and well-watered gardens. The most delightful of continental breakfasts, with home-made jam, butter served in silver dishes, massive coffee pots. This is served either ceremoniously in one's room, in the breakfast room, or on the terrace where there are glorious vistas of mountains and village. At night the terrace is even more magical by candlelight." (*PM Jackson, Mrs Elizabeth Syrett*) A private beach some ten minutes' drive away, with transportation provided, has just been opened.

Open Approx 20 Mar–15 Jan.
Rooms 7 suites, 19 double, 8 single – all with bath and/or shower and direct-dial telephone. 2 ground-floor rooms.
Facilities 5 salons, 3 bars, restaurant, snack bar (summer); conference room; live music, poetry readings, fashion shows etc in summer. 32-acre grounds with gardens, tennis court, swimming pool with grill bar. 10 minutes from sea (private beach), boats, sailing, windsurfing. English spoken.
Location On edge of village on road to Valldemossa.
Credit cards All major cards accepted.
Terms (Excluding 6% tax) B&B: single 9,000-11,000 pts, double 16,000-18,000 pts, suite 21,000-24,000 pts. Set lunch 4,500 pts, dinner 6,500 pts; full alc 6,000 pts. Reduced rates for children; special meals.

ELCHE 03203 Alicante — Map 12

Hotel Huerto del Cura *Tel* (965) 45.80.40
Federico Garcia Sanchiz 14 *Telex* 66814 PMHO

Just outside the large town of Elche, between Alicante and Murcia, stands the largest palm forest in Europe (100,000 trees), and on the edge of it is this breezy modern hotel. It is privately owned, but the government has awarded it the status of *parador colaborador* ("associate *parador*") because of its "special qualities" (lots of red print in *Michelin*). Our nominator this year is also enthusiastic: "Absolutely first-class. The rooms are in little individual bungalows under the palms. A lovely dining-room set among the trees beside the pool, where service and cuisine are excellent. For dinner we enjoyed the *tapas*, spiced omelette, delicious sole en croûte and a dream of a seafood vol-au-vent. Most flavoursome dinners we ever had in Spain. This place is miles away in spirit from the awful coastline around Benidorm. I guess it would be crowded with trippers in summers, but it was utter peace in early October." (*Kenneth E Smith*)

Open All year.
Rooms 4 suites, 56 double, 10 single – all with bath and shower, telephone, radio, TV and mini-bar. All in different buildings in gardens. Many ground-floor rooms.

Facilities 5 lounges, 2 restaurants, bar, TV room; conference facilities; discotheque. Garden, 2 swimming pools (one for children), sauna, tennis. Sandy beach 16 km. English spoken.
Location in SE suburbs, on edge of forest. Elche is 24 km W of Alicante.
Credit cards None accepted.
Terms [1987 rates, likely to go up about 10%] (Excluding 6% tax) B&B: single 6,550-7,050 pts, double 8,600-9,600 pts, suite 12,100-13,100 pts; dinner, B&B: single 8,300-8,800 pts, double 12,100-13,100 pts. Set lunch/dinner 2,000 pts. Full alc 2,500 pts.

ENCAMP Andorra — Map 12

Hotel Residencia Belvedere — *Tel* (628) 312.63

This little bit of England in high Andorra remains as popular as ever – a friendly, informal and inexpensive guest house, run by an English couple, Terry and Jo Dixon. It is away from the main road, just outside Encamp above the town, and has a sun terrace with fine Pyrenean views. In winter people come for skiing, and in summer for the walking. "A warm greeting," writes one visitor this year, "and Jo's wonderful cooking provided a different menu each night. It gave us something to look forward to, after our daily walks amid beautiful scenery, with wild flowers and butterflies of every kind. The *Belvedere* is clean and attractive, with a log fire to welcome home skiers in winter." "A nightingale sang every night." "If you want a drink, you help yourself and enter it in the book. Although the hotel offers half board, bar lunches and afternoon teas are supplied willingly." "Welcoming proprietors, delicious dishes. Bedrooms a little spartan, but attractive and very clean." "Atmosphere is like a house party." (*Joan and George Hodgson, William A Howard, PLC, and many others*)

Open 19 Dec–16 Apr, 21 May–30 Sep.
Rooms 9 double, 1 single – 1 ground-floor room with bath and shower.
Facilities Lounge, bar, dining room. Small grounds with sun terrace and lawn. Convenient for ski slopes. Pony-trekking in spring, mountain walking, trout fishing; open-air swimming pool in town; winter sports nearby. English spoken.
Location 1 km from Encamp, just off road to Soldeu and France. Parking.
Credit cards None accepted (but UK cheques accepted).
Terms Dinner, B&B: single £17–£18.25, double £16.50–£19. Bar snacks £8–£9. 1-night bookings sometimes refused Christmas, New Year and Easter. Reduced rates for children sharing parents' room; high teas.

FUENTE DÉ 39588 Cantabria — Map 12

Parador Nacional del Río Deva — *Tel* (942) 73.00.01

This *parador* is magnificently sited in the Picos de Europa, a wild, mountainous region two-and-a-half hours' drive from Santander. "It is not a difficult drive, but for the last hour and a half the road twists up 3,000 feet along the river Deva, where people were fishing for salmon. In May the wildflowers are splendid with many species rare to Europe. The road ends at the *parador*, a large modern hotel at the bottom of a 4,000-foot grey rock cliff with a cable car to the top. The views from the hotel were of snow-capped peaks. The bedroom was well lit and comfortably furnished, with a small glass-enclosed balcony. The bathroom was large.

There was the usual magnificent *parador* buffet breakfast, excellent value." (*Walter Baxter; also LH*)

Open All year.
Rooms 72 double, 6 single – all with bath, telephone and balcony.
Facilities Lounges, TV room, bar, 2 restaurants. Garden. River with fishing nearby.
Location On the N621 25 m W of Camaleno.
Restriction Not suitable for ♿.
Credit cards Amex, Diners, Visa.
Terms (Excluding 6% tax) B&B: single 6,200, double 8,200 pts. Set lunch/dinner 2,000 pts. Children under 3 free; special meals.

GOMERA 38800 Canary Islands — Map 12

Parador Nacional Conde de la Gomera — *Tel* (922) 87.11.00
Orilla del Llano de la Villa 5
San Sebastián de la Gomera

The island of Gomera, neglected by the tourist hordes, is a far cry from its extrovert sister Tenerife, although only 1½ hours by ferry. It has a mountain, El Alto de Garajonay (1,487 m), valleys and a forest or two, and hidden beaches along the coast. In the capital port of San Sebastián, Christopher Columbus prepared his ships to sail for the New World. Above the town, on its own cliff, sits the *parador*, a fine example of an aristocratic island mansion surrounded by a garden of date palms. A devotee writes: "Food and service have improved from very good to excellent. All the staff smile; the rooms are clean and comfortable; and they provide real, delicious Spanish cooking. An innovation is the buffet breakfast when you can have local delicacies like gofio, miel de palma, chorizo, freshly-baked cakes and the local dates and figs. The swimming pool is kept clean and the garden is a delight; the situation perfect and the view over the harbour is fascinating." A new extension, with a new courtyard, was opened early in 1987, and a subsequent visitor has written: "Alterations seem complete. Our main memory of a peaceful holiday is of many secluded spacious rooms, balconies, courtyards, garden areas, abundant birdsong and tropical trees, and an uncrowded clean swimming pool. As for food: fish OK, meat so so, breakfast good. Staff mainly good, but waitresses indifferent." (*J MacGillivray*)

Open All year.
Rooms 38 double, 4 single – all with bath and shower, telephone, radio, TV, and air-conditioning.
Facilities 3 large salons (one with TV), bar, restaurant. Large garden with orchard and unheated swimming pool. Sea 15 minutes' walk. English spoken.
Location 700 metres from centre of San Sebastián, overlooking the port. Parking.
Restriction Not suitable for ♿.
Credit cards All major cards accepted.
Terms [1987 rates] (Excluding tax) Rooms: 7,600-9,500 pts. Breakfast 600 pts. Full board: 9,000-11,850 pts per person. Set lunch/dinner 2,200 pts. Reduced rates for children; special meals on request.

> We asked hotels to estimate their 1988 tariffs some time before publication so the rates given are often arbitrary. Please always check terms with hotels when making bookings.

GRANADA 18009 **Map 12**

Hotel América *Tel* (958) 22.74.71
Real de la Alhambra 53

A tiny hotel of character, in a delightful position inside the Alhambra, in a street quiet at night. Preferred by some to the nearby parador, *it has small but clean rooms, friendly service, and reasonable food served under a canopy in a charming courtyard to the strains of piped Vivaldi and Mozart. Open Mar–9 Nov. 13 rooms, 3,670-5,950 pts [1987]. Parking. Enticing new nomination: please tell us more.*

Parador Nacional de San Francisco *Tel* (958) 22.14.40
Alhambra

This harmonious modern building on the site of an historic Franciscan monastery on the Alhambra hill has lovely formal gardens and a unique view from its terrace across to the Generalife. The hotel is delightfully furnished and rooms, though small, are warm and cosy. But the service is variable and the food by common consent poor, especially the set menus: à la carte is a little better. 35 rooms, all with bath, 9,600-12,000 pts [1987]. More reports needed.

GUADALUPE 10140 Cáceres **Map 12**

Hospedería Real Monasterio *Tel* (927) 36.70.00
Plaza Juan Carlos I

This small picturesque town lies some 2,000 feet up in the mountains between Toledo and Cáceres, and is approached by a winding minor road through splendid scenery. It is dominated by its medieval monastery, with some marvellous 17th-century baroque rooms, and the hotel is right inside it – in fact, the old pharmacy. During the Middle Ages, this was a pilgrimage centre: there is a cult still of the Virgin of Guadalupe whose image is kept within the church. The present occupants of the monastery are the Franciscans who have restored the buildings. There are some fine paintings, gorgeous decorations and many treasures. One recent visitor, who "loved the place", was so moved as to write: "Our tour through the monastery galleries showed such wonders we almost converted to Catholicism!" Local people use the hotel for midday banquets in the picturesque courtyard.

An earlier view: "This was the best hotel we stayed in during our Spanish tour. We may have had better meals, better bedrooms and better views, but never all at the same time – and we certainly never had better value for money. The approach from the east over the *sierras* during May, when the wild flowers flood down the hills and bank up against the road, is astonishingly beautiful. You need to book in advance, and ask for a room with a view. Ours was extremely comfortable, with good bedside lighting and a large bathroom. The main feature is an enormous cloister/courtyard, cool and full of plants, where you sit for coffee or drinks. The hotel is managed by Franciscan monks, but the restaurant is staffed by girls; the food is very good by Spanish standards. Only criticism: the muzak." (*Walter Baxter; also Gertrude and Gerhard Cohn*)

Open All year except 12 Jan–12 Feb.
Rooms 2 suites, 35 double, 3 single – all with bath, shower and telephone.
Facilities Lift. Hall, 2 salons, TV room, bar, 2 restaurants; cloisters and courtyard.
Location Central. Parking.
Credit card Access, Visa.
Terms [1987 rates] (Excluding tax) B&B: single 2,900 pts, double 4,450 pts; dinner, B&B: single 4,400 pts, double 7,450 pts. Set lunch/dinner 1,300 pts; full alc 1,600 pts. Reduced rates for children; special meals.

Parador Nacional Zurbarán *Tel* (927) 36.70.75
Marqués de la Romana 10

A *parador* named after the 17th-century artist Zurbarán, whose paintings can be seen in the sacristy of the nearby monastery at Guadalupe. "A beautiful 16th-century building. Lovely courtyards with orange trees, wide staircases and passages full of mosaics. Luxurious bedrooms, mine with intricate wooden shutters that had little openings and a spy window that intrigued me. Good balcony with lovely views of the mountains and of the roofs of the church and monastery. Good bathrooms. Breakfast the first morning looked like a children's tea party, with every imaginable kind of cake and sweet biscuit, the toast arriving slice by slice. Staff were all very friendly and the monastery and church were well worth the horrific climb up the mountain." (*Mrs MD Prodgers*)

Open All year.
Rooms 40 – most with bath, telephone and radio; some with balcony.
Facilities Lift. Restaurant; courtyards. Garden with swimming pool and tennis court.
Location Central. Parking.
Credit cards All major cards accepted.
Terms [1987 rates] (Excluding 6% tax) Rooms 6,000-7,500 pts. Breakfast 600 pts. Full board 7,490-9,740 pts per person. Set lunch/dinner 1,900 pts.

GUALCHOS 18614 Granada — Map 12

Hotel La Posada *Tel* (58) 64.60.34
Plaza Constitucion 9 *Reservations* in UK (0223) 323618

Just out of reach of the madding crowds of the Costa del Sol, Gualchos is a still unexploited inland village in the foothills of the Sierra de Lujar, in a region of almond groves. Here two adjacent 18th-century houses in the main square have been restored to create this *posada* (inn), an intriguing discovery new to the Guide this year: "In an area characterised by full *paradores,* coastal 'scrot' and mediocre 'anywheresville', *La Posada* represents an oasis of Spanish elegance. Gualchos is unspoilt Spain – the square outside the hotel (almost inaccessible by car) is alive with children playing, old men talking, others drinking at the bar till 1 am. Yet the coast and fabulous Granada are only short drives away. The restoration of the old houses is exemplary – a maze of inner courtyards and gardens on many levels provides enchanting private rooms: ours had its own large balcony/terrace and a view of mountains and Med from the bed. The owner/chef José Gonzalez and his staff provide a warm welcome, in our case overlooking their general rule to exclude children. The food is excellent, so is the value for money, and the atmosphere is one of laid-back elegance." (*Alan Hildon; and others*)

Open All year. Restaurant closed Mon.
Rooms 7 double, 2 single – all with bath, 5 also with shower.
Facilities Lounge, bar, restaurant; patio. Garden with swimming pool. Pebble beach 20 minutes' drive. English spoken.
Location 9 km inland from coast at Castell de Ferro which is E of Motril. Hotel is in village centre. Parking.
Restriction Not suitable for ♿.
Credit cards None accepted.
Terms B&B £19; dinner, B&B £33. Full alc £15.

JAÉN 23000 — Map 12

Parador Nacional Castillo de Santa Catalina — *Tel* (953) 26.44.11
Carretera del Castillo

"A splendid place to stay, stunningly situated," is a comment this year on the recently modernised *Santa Catalina,* two miles outside the city of Jaén. It is a colossal eagle's nest of a castle perched precariously on a mountain above the town with dizzying views. Only southern-facing rooms have a balcony, but all have remarkable vistas. "The best of all the nine *paradores* we visited," is another recent verdict. "It had better food and views, a more exciting site and ambience. And reception was unusually friendly." An earlier visitor was equally enthusiastic: "Jaén represents the *parador* system at its best: the vision of the architect, his respect for the original structure, the harmonious, almost imperceptible blending of old and new, as well as the skill of the builders. The ante-room to the dining room has an arch springing from each of the four corners of the room to meet 60 or 70 feet above your head, and is worthy of a cathedral. The dining room itself, with its priceless tapestries, is only slightly less grand. Oh, for a marriage of Spanish accommodation and French cuisine, and I don't think I would ever leave the place. Still, at the price I am not complaining." (*Philip Gill, MA Goulding, JAD*)

Open All year.
Rooms 37 double, 6 single – all with bath and shower and telephone; some with balcony. 11 ground-floor rooms.
Facilities Lift. 2 lounges, chess and card room, TV room, bar, 2 restaurants; air-conditioning. Large garden with trees; swimming pool. English spoken.
Location 3 km SW of Jaén.
Credit cards All major cards accepted.
Terms [1987 rates] Rooms: single 7,740 pts, double 10,140 pts. Breakfast 600 pts. Set lunch/dinner 1,900 pts.

LEÓN 24001 — Map 12

Hotel de San Marcos — *Tel* (987) 23.73.00
Plaza de San Marcos 7 — *Telex* 89809 HSML

The glory of the proud city of León, part modern, part medieval, is its great Gothic cathedral, one of Europe's finest. Its second glory is the former 16th-century monastery of San Marcos, with a staggering Renaissance facade: today part of it is an archaeological museum, and part is a *very* grand hotel (five red *Michelin* gables). There are three-quarters of a mile of carpeted corridors, lined on both sides with exquisite reproductions of Spanish furniture through the ages – a museum in itself.

The smaller restaurant gives on to a summer terrace, with the river beyond; the main lounge, 84 feet square, has a polished marble floor and one huge painting across its ceiling. The hotel provided a "pleasant memory" for one visitor this year who preferred it to *paradores*: "As you know, they lack the personal touch, whereas this is a proper hotel and its staff are prepared to put themselves out for guests." (*RB Clark, H Bramwell, and others*)

Open All year.
Rooms 195 – all with bath and/or shower, telephone and radio; most with TV.
Facilities Lift. Salons, restaurants; conference facilities; night club; hairdresser and beauty parlour. Garden. Archaeological museum in building. English spoken.
Location On river. Parking.
Credit cards All major cards accepted.
Terms [1987 rates] Rooms: single 6,750 pts, double 10,700 pts. Breakfast 600 pts. Full board 9,770-11,170 pts per person. Reduced rates for children; special meals.

MADRID — Map 12

Hotel Liabeny — *Tel* (91) 232.53.06 and 231.46.09
Salud 3, Madrid 28013 — *Telex* 49024 LBNY

This sizeable hotel, efficient rather than beautiful, is again praised this year not only for its own qualities but for its good central location, in the heart of old Madrid between the Puerta del Sol and Gran Via, and close to Metro stops and good shops. "A gem – our room was spacious and spotless, the staff courteous, breakfast arrived promptly and included hot toast and squeezed orange juice. The only snag was someone rehearsing opera outside our window." Very comfortable beds, useful coffee-shop, English-speaking staff." "The hotel maintains a money exchange, where we got rates better than at most banks." (*Paul Palmer, John Worth, Carol Hahn*)

Open All year.
Rooms 10 suites, 166 double, 41 single – all with bath, telephone, TV and air-conditioning.
Facilities Lift. Salon, bar, restaurant.
Location Central, but quietly situated, between Gran Via and Puerta del Sol. Garage.
Credit cards Amex, Visa.
Terms [1987 rates] (Excluding 6% tax) Rooms: single 4,800 pts, double 7,400 pts. Breakfast: continental 550 pts, English 1,100 pts. Set lunch/dinner 1,400 pts.

Hotel El Prado — *Tel* (91) 429.35.68
Calle del Prado 11, Madrid 28014

A small modern five-storey hotel, upper-medium-priced, very centrally placed between the Prado and the Puerta del Sol. Rooms small but clean, recently decorated (top floor ones have balcony with rooftop views). Small rather dull salon; foyer with copies of Prado pictures. Pleasant staff. No restaurant; garage. 45 rooms, all with bath, 6,300-8,000 frs [1987]. New nomination: more reports welcome.

Sterling and dollar equivalents of foreign currencies at the date of going to press will be found on page 712.

Hotel Suecia *Tel* (91) 231.69.00
Marqués de Casa Riera 4 *Telex* 22313 SUECOTEL
Madrid 28014

Plenty of favourable comment in 1986/7 on this Swedish-run hotel, located in a quiet side-street in central Madrid, between the Prado and the Puerta del Sol. It is patronised by foreign journalists and visiting opera singers, though a report just in qualifies this: "Clean, efficient and pleasantly run, catering mainly for Scandinavian tour groups. Not much character, but ideal for those who prefer Scandinavia to Spain." Other comments: "The porter actually ran down the street as he saw me taking luggage out of the car, and everyone was helpful and efficient. Public areas are stylish-modern, designer-look café-bar and reception, and posh restaurant" (the well-known *Bellman*). "We spent a happy week here." "Because of its location and excellent restaurant, it is our favourite place to stay in Madrid." (*LH, Joan Williamson and Ruth Kaye*)

Open All year. Main restaurant closed Sat night, Sun and Aug.
Rooms 5 suites, 62 double – all with bath and shower, direct-dial telephone, air-conditioning and mini-bar; TV (with satellite broadcasts from English-speaking countries) and baby-listening on request.
Facilities Bar/breakfast room, restaurant; conference facilities; sun terrace. English spoken.
Location Central, but quietly situated, close to banking/commercial district, just off Calle de Alcalá. Public parking nearby.
Credit cards All major cards accepted.
Terms [1987 rates, likely to go up about 10% in 1988](Excluding 6% tax) Rooms: single occupancy 7,250-8,375 pts, double 8,975-10,275 pts, suite 13,975 pts. Breakfast 675-850 pts. Set lunch/dinner 2,400 pts.

Hotel Villa Magna *Tel* (91) 261.49.00
Paseo de la Castellana 22 *Telex* 22914 VIMA
Madrid 28046

A modern "block" hotel, fairly central (near Plaza de Colon), with private parking. It is expensive, luxurious and quiet, with eye-catching decor that may not please all tastes. Sumptuous bathrooms, very comfortable public rooms and bedrooms; service outstandingly efficient. Huge buffet breakfasts. 198 rooms, all with bath and shower, 22,000-30,000 pts. Few recent reports: more welcome.

MÁLAGA 29016 Map 12

Parador Nacional de Gibralfaro *Tel* (952) 22.19.02
Apartado de Correos 274

A panoramic parador *of stone arcades and terraces, on a hill above Málaga, with magnficent views of city, coast and mountains from bedroom balconies and public rooms. Bedrooms large, with heavy carved wood furniture; set dinner copious and above* parador *average; bar popular with locals and noisy with* TV. *12 rooms, all with bath, 6,400-8,000 pts. Few recent reports: more welcome.*

> If you have kept brochures and tariffs for foreign hotels, *please* enclose them with your reports.

MOJÁCAR 04638 Almeria **Map 12**

Parador Nacional Reyes Católicos *Tel* (951) 47.82.50
Playa de Mojácar

Just outside a tiny ancient town on a rocky hill, dominating the coast and plain between Almeria and Murcia. This very modern white-walled parador *is liked for its pleasant spacious design, huge terraces, gardens and swimming pool overlooking the sea; bedrooms large, comfortable, correctly heated. But food is said to be poor even by* parador *standards, and service and ambience are also criticised this year. 98 rooms, all with bath and shower. B&B double 7,200-9,200 pts. Set meals 1,900 pts. New reports needed, please.*

NUÉVALOS 50210 Zaragoza **Map 12**

Hotel Monasterio de Piedra *Tel* (976) 84.90.11

This "unique" hotel between Madrid and Zaragoza began its life in the 12th century as a Cistercian monastery, and is enjoyed for its lovely location in a park of beautiful waterfalls and lakes completely walled off from the arid stony countryside which surrounds it. "The hotel is most impressive. The vestibule is enormous and has a beautiful romanesque plastered ceiling with paintings and gilded rib vaulting. The halls are wide with polished floors and round alabaster windows. There are some Roman parts to the adjoining cloisters. The rooms are large with *en suite* bathrooms and each has a large tiled terrace. The dining room is lovely also. The food was average, but not expensive. Staff were friendly, efficient and courteous. *Parador* standards but at half the price." (*Mrs M McMillan*)

Open All year.
Rooms 7 suites, 45 double, 9 single – all with bath, shower, telephone and private terrace. Ground-floor rooms.
Facilities Salon, bar, TV room, restaurant. Large park with gardens, swimming pool, tennis court. Fishing and shooting nearby. English spoken.
Location Turn off main Zaragoza–Madrid road at Catalayud; hotel is 28 km S.
Credit cards Amex, Diners, Visa.
Terms (Excluding 6% tax) B&B: single 4,050 pts, double 5,100 pts. Set lunch/dinner 1,350-1,500 pts; full alc 2,250-2,500 pts.

OROPESA 45560 Toledo **Map 12**

Parador Nacional Virrey de Toledo *Tel* (925) 43.00.00
Plaza del Palacio 1

This old and graceful little town between Madrid and Badajoz has a feudal castle part of which is now a parador *with a flower-decked courtyard. Public rooms are super-baronial; many bedrooms and bathrooms are enormous too; some have balcony with fine views; air-conditioning. 44 rooms, all with bath. B&B double 8,200 pts. Recent reports contradictory, both on service (standoff-ish, say some) and on food (rather good, say some): more views, please.*

RIBADEO 27700 Lugo — Map 12

Parador Nacional de Ribadeo *Tel* (982) 11.08.25

A slightly younger than usual *parador* overlooking a huge inlet of the sea on the Galician coast, with an unusual feature: you go down by lift from the ground floor to the bedrooms below – the more expensive have fine views over the estuary. "Just on the outskirts of this once quite elegant town, it offers a variety of very good rooms, large and airy: those facing the bay are very quiet. Our large balcony had a view over the lawn. The bathroom was superb even by *parador* standards. Add to this helpful staff and more than adequate local food. The bay of Ribadeo and the scenically magnificent river valley with a glorious road climbing to the central plateau make this a very attractive stop on the long north coast of Galicia." A visitor this year agreed about the rooms but thought the food "just average *parador*". (*Angela and David Stewart, PL Aston*)

Open All year.
Rooms 41 double, 6 single – all with bath, shower and telephone; many with balcony.
Facilities Lift. 2 salons, bar with gallery, dining room. Beach 200 metres. English spoken.
Location On outskirts of town. Parking.
Restriction Not suitable for ♿.
Credit cards All major cards accepted.
Terms (Excluding 6% tax) B&B: single 5,400-6,600 pts, double7,200-8,700 pts; full board: single 8,540-9,740 pts, double 13,480-14,980 pts. Set lunch/dinner 1,900 pts; full alc 2,300 pts.

SANTIAGO DE COMPOSTELA La Coruña — Map 12

Hostal de los Reyes Católicos *Tel* (981) 58.22.00 and 58.23.00
Plaza de España 1 *Telex* 86004 HRCS
Santiago de Compostela 15705

This very large, grand and famous hotel stands in the heart of medieval Santiago and was built by Ferdinand and Isabella in the 15th century as a hostel for pilgrims to the shrine of St James ("Imagine staying at a cross between Hampton Court and All Souls', furnished with the best pieces from the Victoria and Albert Museum," wrote one reader). It is built in the shape of an Etruscan cross, with four cloisters, and forms one side of the plaza on which the cathedral sits. "Very memorable, expensive but worth it," is one recent comment. "Our room had twin canopied beds, 20-foot ceilings and medieval Spanish furniture." (However, rooms vary greatly in size and furnishings.) The dining room is an enormous gracefully vaulted crypt, but some have found the food disappointing, and you can eat much more cheaply in the elegant cafeteria. There has also been disagreement about the quality of the service. But these are mere quibbles to those impressed by the sheer magnificence: "For a knock-out hotel experience (honeymoon or something), you really couldn't do much better in Spain." (*Carol Hahn, Shelley Cranshaw, LH and others*)

Open All year.
Rooms 3 suites, 142 double, 12 single – all with bath and/or shower, telephone, radio and TV. Some ground-floor rooms.

Facilities Lifts. Reception hall, salons, TV room, bars, dining room, cafeteria; conference facilities; beauty parlour/hairdressing salon, boutiques; nightclub; Chapel Royal with occasional concerts. Gardens. English spoken.
Location In town centre, by cathedral. Garage parking. Special bus to station.
Credit cards All major cards accepted.
Terms (Excluding 12% tax) B&B: single 6,250-7,350 pts, double 8,450-15,200 pts; dinner, B&B 2,650 pts per person added; full board 5,300 pts added. Set lunch/dinner 2,650 pts; full alc 4,000 pts. Reduced rates and special meals for children.

Hostal Windsor *Tel* (981) 59.28.22 and 59.29.39
República de El Salvador 16
Santiago de Compostela 15701

Nothing special, but useful for a short stay, this hotel is half the price of the *Hostal de Los Reyes Catolicos* (see above) and lies in the newer part of town, only five minutes' walk from the historic quarter (there is a good cheap garage around the corner). Readers this year have found the rooms clean and the Italian manager and his staff very helpful, though one complained of plumbing and other noises in the night. "Though modern, it has been attractively decorated in traditional Spanish style, using wood, glass and brasswork to great effect. Our bedroom was attractive, quiet and comfortable, though the bathroom was tiny." (*PD Scott, Nicolette Comport, Valerie Eden, and others*)

Open All year.
Rooms 40 double, 10 single – all with bath and/or shower, telephone, radio and tea-making facilities.
Facilities Lift. Lounge, TV room, bar; conference facilities. English spoken.
Location Central, near the Alameida. Parking.
Restriction Not suitable for ♿.
Credit cards None accepted.
Terms Rooms: single 2,000-2,900 pts, double 3,800-4,400 pts. Breakfast 400 pts. (No restaurant.)

SANTILLANA DEL MAR 39330 Cantabria — Map 12

Parador Nacional Gil Blas *Tel* (942) 81.80.00
Plaza Ramón Pelayo 11

In this showplace village of narrow cobbled streets and fine old seigneurial mansions, 18 miles west of Santander, the Gil Blas *is itself a large old manor house, well furnished, with polished oak floors and oak beams. But the rooms have up-to-date comforts such as modern bathrooms. 57 rooms, all with bath and shower. B&B double 8,700-10,700 pts. Set meals 2,200 pts [1987]. Reports this year of cooking smells and poor food: news also needed of the 29 rooms in the newly-added extension.*

Hotel Los Infantes *Tel* (942) 81.81.00
Avenida Le Dorat 1

Useful cheaper alternative to the parador *(often full). Cool, pleasant building, full of antique clocks, etc, with orchard next door where drinks are served. Rooms very clean, staff efficient. Simple food; breakfasts poor. 30 rooms, all with bath and shower. B&B double 4,700-7,200 pts. Set meals 1,200 pts. New nomination: more reports welcome.*

SANTO DOMINGO DE LA CALZADA 26250 La Rioja — Map 12

Parador Nacional Santo Domingo de la Calzada
Plaza del Santo 3

Tel (941) 34.03.00

Santo Domingo was an 11th-century anchorite who built a bridge across the Glera river and a causeway (*calzada*) to help pilgrims on their way to Santiago. A town grew up (in what is now Rioja wine country) and for the pilgrims a hostel was built whose imposing main hall forms the kernel of today's *parador*. Readers generally approve of the place: not a paragon among *paradores* but serviceable, with clean, rather small rooms and well-cooked food. The staff speak little English. Some visitors have complained of loud bells from the *campanile* next door and the click-clack of people's shoes along the stone-flagged corridors, a complaint echoed at many *paradores*.

Open All year.
Rooms 25 double, 2 single – all with bath and telephone.
Facilities Lift. 2 lounges, TV room, bar, restaurant.
Location Central (no private parking). Town is on main Logroño–Burgos road.
Restriction Not suitable for &.
Credit cards All major cards accepted.
Terms [1987 rates] (Excluding 6% tax) Rooms 6,000-7,500 pts. Breakfast 600 pts. Full board 7,490-9,740 pts per person. Set lunch/dinner 1,900 pts.

SEGOVIA 40003 — Map 12

Parador Nacional
Apartado de Correos 106
Carretera de Valladolid

Tel (911) 43.04.62
Telex 47913 RRPP

"One of the very best *paradores* in Spain", "an oasis in the country's dry interior" – two recent comments on this modern hotel on a hill above the town, with superb views of the golden cathedral and the romantic *alcázar*. "It should be ugly since it is only concrete beams and brick walls. But lines in every direction give pleasure to the eye, and the place is full of small gardens, lit by light traps from the roof to keep them flourishing." "It is palatial, stylishly designed and sumptuously furnished. Bedrooms are ultra-modern, excellently-equipped with huge terraces – all with stunning views of the city. But it's not the place to absorb the atmosphere of Segovia, which can be done better from the simpler hotels within its walls. Staff are highly trained in the business of being nice and efficient to guests."

The restaurants of Segovia, with their ancient Guild of Meat Roasters, are famous all over Spain. If you say you have been to Segovia, at once you are asked whether you ate at *Candido* or *Casa Duque*. But in fairness to the *parador*, we should add that one visitor who ate on the premises thought its menu offered some of the best *parador* food at a very reasonable price. (*A and P Grant, LH; also Carol Hahn, and MP*)

Open All year.
Rooms 5 suites, 70 double, 5 single – all with bath, shower, telephone, radio, TV; air-conditioning throughout. Some ground-floor rooms.
Facilities Salons, library, TV room, bar, 2 dining rooms; conference facilities; indoor swimming pool, sauna. Garden with outdoor swimming pool. English spoken.
Restriction Not suitable for ♿
Location 2 km N of Segovia on N601.
Credit cards All major cards accepted.
Terms [1987 rates] Rooms: single 6,400-7,200 pts, double 8,000-9,000 pts, suite 10,800-12,115 pts. Breakfast 600 pts. Set lunch/dinner 2,200 pts.

SIGÜENZA 19250 Guadalajara — Map 12

Parador Nacional Castillo de Sigüenza — *Tel* (911) 39.01.00, *Telex* 22517
Plaza del Castillo

This small town north-east of Madrid is built in steep tiers on a hillside and is dominated by its bishops' castle. It also has a very fine old cathedral, damaged in the Civil War. "The *parador,*" writes an inspector, "is set in the medieval fortress of a beautifully restored town. Marvellous dramatic scenery all around – splendid views from the ramparts. The interior is well kept and attractively furnished in traditional *parador* style (suits of armour in the lounge guarding the TV, local ceramics used to good effect, dark wood fittings). The bedrooms and bathrooms are excellent – ours had magnificent views from the balcony. There are some small gardens, too. The food is no worse than average for a *parador.*"

Open All year.
Rooms 6 suites, 68 double, 3 single – all with bath and telephone.
Facilities Lift. Lounge with TV, bar, dining room; conference facilities. Small garden. English spoken.
Location 129 km NE of Madrid. Take C204 off N11.
Credit cards All major cards accepted.
Terms [1987 rates] (Excluding 6% tax) Rooms: single 5,200-6,000 pts, double 6,500-7,500 pts, suite 7,500-8,500 pts. Breakfast 600 pts. Set lunch/dinner 1,900 pts.

TOLEDO 45004 — Map 12

Hostal del Cardenal — *Tel* (925) 22.49.00
Paseo de Recaredo 24

Residence of the Archbishop of Toledo in the 18th century, this "true Toledan palace" reflects the historic *riqueza* of the small city. It abuts the city walls and some of the rooms overlook the terraced garden, which extends down to one of the city gates. A 1987 visitor writes: "The furnishings throughout are most distinguished and in total keeping with the surroundings. The walk through the gardens and along the inner walls is a delight – a haven from the crowded streets outside. Excellent regional cooking." (*Ann Mathias*)

Open All year.
Rooms 2 suites, 22 double, 3 single – all with bath, shower, telephone and baby-listening.
Facilities Lounges, TV room, dining room. Garden, patios and courtyards. English spoken.

Location 10-15 minutes' walk from centre; by the old walls at Puerto de Bisagra. Parking.
Restriction Not suitable for ♿.
Credit cards Amex, Diners.
Terms [1987 rates] (Excluding 6% tax) Rooms: single 3,600 pts, double 5,900 pts, suite 8,500 pts. Breakfast 325 pts. Full alc 1,800 pts. Special meals for children.

Parador Nacional Conde de Orgaz — *Tel* (925) 22.18.50
Paseo de los Cigarrales — *Telex* 47998 RRPT

Despite tourist spoliations, Toledo remains a fascinating and beautiful city, full of narrow winding streets and crammed with historic buildings and churches. Overlooking the city is the *Conde de Orgaz*, one of the showpiece *paradores* of the Spanish state tourist organisation. The first impression is of 16th-century Spain at its most baronial: coats of arms, shields and antique weapons forged from Toledo steel abound in halls and corridors, hung with banners and portraits of grave-faced bearded grandees. In fact, it's all a big cheat, though carried out with panache. The hotel was built in 1968, and the rooms, although furnished in the old style, have every modern amenity including a fridge. It is on the site where El Greco executed his famous painting of Toledo, high on a hill to the north. Ask for a room with a view of the city, it is well worth the extra money. "Lots of locals use the restaurant, so it has a bustling atmosphere," says an inspector, "and what's more I had one of the best and most polished *parador* meals I've ever eaten. Service is excellent, too – this is a place where porters race for your bags and kiss your hands Sevillian-style, muttering Spanish gallantries in your ear." (*Carol Hahn, LB Pinnell*) A new wing opened in 1986.

Open All year.
Rooms 2 suites, 69 double, 6 single – all with bath, telephone and radio; 23 with TV.
Facilities Lift. 3 salons, TV room, restaurant, bar – all with air-conditioning. Extensive landscaped grounds with terraces and unheated swimming pool. Hunting and fishing nearby. English spoken.
Location 3 km S of town centre. Parking.
Credit cards All major cards accepted.
Terms Rooms: single 4,700 pts, double 10,000-14,000 pts.Breakfast 600 pts. Set lunch/dinner 2,200 pts.

TORDESILLAS 47100 Valladolid — Map 12

Parador Nacional de Tordesillas — *Tel* (983) 77.00.51

This old town south-west of Valladolid has a fine ancient convent, Santa Clara. It was converted from a royal palace by Peter the Cruel, and in 1506 Juana the Mad locked herself away in it on the death of her husband, Philip the Fair, and stayed there for 44 years in her despair. In 1987, however, Dubery the Discerning, whose clearly-argued reports have led many an unworthy *parador* or *pousada* to be expunged from these pages, wrote to say that this is one of the best of the whole uneven bunch (untypically of *paradores*, it is not the old convent now converted, but a large low-rise 1950s building just outside the town): "The decor is attractive traditional Spanish repro, the rooms are large and well furnished, and by any standards the food was excellent. Best soup of our whole trip and the roast sucking pig melted in the mouth. Buffet breakfast very good, including a superb tortilla. Very friendly and efficient staff." (*RA Dubery; also Ann Price*)

Open All year.
Rooms 65 double, 8 single – 65 with bath, 8 with shower, all with telephone and air-conditioning.
Facilities Lifts. Lounge, TV room, bar, dining room; conference facilities. Garden with swimming pool. English spoken.
Location 2 km SW of Tordesillas on N620 to Salamanca.
Credit cards All major cards accepted.
Terms [1987 rates] B&B: single 3,600-4,300 pts, double 6,700-8,200 pts; dinner B&B: single 5,500-6,200 pts, double 10,500-12,000 pts. Full alc 2,280 pts. Special meals for children.

TORTOSA 43500 Tarragona — Map 12

Parador Nacional Castillo de la Zuda — *Tel* (977) 44.44.50 and 44.44.58

On a hilltop dominating this historic town on the banks of the Ebro, a massive feudal castle dating from Moorish times, now much restored in true parador *style. Pleasant public rooms with baronial decor; rooms fairly simple, with remarkable views. Helpful staff. 82 rooms, all with bath and shower. B&B double 7,700-8,700 pts. Set meals 2,000 pts. New nomination: more reports welcome.*

TRUJILLO 10200 Cáceres — Map 12

Parador Nacional — *Tel* (927) 32.13.50
Plaza de Santa Clara

Trujillo is the birthplace of Pizarro, whose magnificent statue stands in the town square. On top of a hill in its ancient citadel is this new *parador* (opened 1985), built within the ancient convent of Santa Clara. "The rooms in the old convent setting are tastefully modern but well in keeping with the nun-like courtyards and character of the rambling old building. The bathrooms were well fitted and spotless; the plumbing excellent. The food is average *parador* fare and the absent-minded waiter one so often gets in these places did not disappoint us by being too efficient. There is a modern annexe also used for conferences: but get a room in the old part – not difficult as it is a large *parador*." (*H Bramwell*)

Open All year.
Rooms 1 suite, 41 double, 4 single – all with bath, telephone and minibar. Some in annexe.
Facilities TV room, dining room; conference facilities. Garden with swimming pool. English spoken.
Location 47 km E of Cáceres. Hotel is central. Garage.
Restriction Not suitable for ♿.
Credit cards All major cards accepted.
Terms (Excluding 6% tax) Double room 7,500 pts. Breakfast 600 pts. Set lunch/dinner 1,900 pts. Reduced rates and special meals for children.

> If you think we have over-praised a hotel or done it an injustice, please let us know.

VALVERDE 38900 Canary Islands — Map 12

Hotel Boomerang — *Tel* (922) 55.02.00
Calle Doctor Gost 1
Valverde, Hierro

Hierro, the smallest and most remote of the Canaries, is not yet infected by the tourist traffic that has invaded the other islands; its few inhabitants raise sheep and goats and produce a very drinkable white wine as well as figs and even bananas. Here in the tiny inland capital, Valverde, is the unusual and appealing *Boomerang*, its name deriving from the fact that its owner, Fernando Padron, lived in Australia for 15 years and then returned and built this hotel himself. It is a low white building with pine shutters and marble floors – and this year several readers, kindly answering our 1987 appeal for more reports on this out-of-the-way Eden, have written to express their delight. One of them, who was even sent a four-page explanatory letter by Sr Padron in advance of his visit, says: "Wonderfully friendly and spotlessly clean. An away-from-it-all holiday with unpaved roads and water delivered daily to the hotel. The anglophile Sr Padron makes his own wine from his vineyard: it was delicious." Others have spoken of the "piping hot water from solar panels" and the "excellent food in the pretty dining room, a meeting-place for the local notables". The *pension* meals are said to be erratic and uninteresting: it is better to eat à la carte, though dishes available will depend on the day's fishing catch. *Note*: (a) while the Señor speaks perfect English, his wife speaks none, and he is often away all day; (b) English-speaking visitors receive a 10% discount. (*MN Samson, AW Thomas, Peter Wilson, and others*)

Open All year.
Rooms 2 suites, 17 double – all with bath, shower and telephone; radio and TV in some ground-floor rooms.
Facilities Reception, lounge, bar, TV room, dining room; night club under construction. English spoken.
Location Hierro is 30 minutes by air from Tenerife.
Credit cards Amex, Diners, Visa.
Terms B&B: single 2,575 pts, double 3,850 pts, suite 4,800 pts; dinner, B&B: single 3,525 pts, double 5,750 pts; full board: single 4,475 pts, double 7,650 pts. Set lunch/dinner 950 pts; full alc 1,500 pts. 10% discount for English speakers. Reduced rates for children; special meals.

VERÍN 32600 Orense — Map 12

Parador Nacional de Monterrey — *Tel* (988) 41.00.75

Verín is on the wide vine-covered slopes of the Tamega Valley, a few kilometres north of the Portuguese border. It is a well-preserved medieval town, with narrow streets and attractive old houses. The *parador* adjoins Monterrey Castle, just outside the town. "The charm of this *parador* next to its hilltop castle is hard to resist. It's modern, but built in local style (*Michelin* calls it 'sumptuous regional') with lovely views of burnt Castilian countryside all around. There is a pool in the grounds which must be very welcome on a hot day. Public rooms are spacious and pleasant, and bedrooms are attractively furnished in traditional style. The town lies in the valley below, so it's a very peaceful setting." (*LH*)

Open All year.
Rooms 1 suite, 22 double – all with bath, and telephone. 8 in annexe.
Facilities Lounge with TV, bar, dining room. Garden with swimming pool. English spoken.
Location 71 km SE of Orense on N525. *Parador* is 4 km NW of Verín.
Restriction Not suitable for ♿.
Credit cards All major cards accepted.
Terms (Excluding 6% tax) Rooms: single 4,400-5,600 pts, double 5,500-7,000 pts. Breakfast 600 pts. Set lunch/dinner 1,900 pts; full alc 2,200 pts. No charge for children under 6.

VICH 08500 Barcelona — Map 12

Parador Nacional — *Tel* (93) 888.72.11

Nominated this year as an above-average parador, *14 kilometres outside this thriving industrial town with a fine cathedral. A splendid site above a lake, with views of the far Pyrenees. Comfortable beds, edible food. Swimming and tennis. 36 rooms. B&B double 7,200-9,200 pts. Set meals 1,900 pts [1987]. More reports please.*

VILLALBA 27800 Lugo — Map 12

Parador Nacional Condes de Villalba — *Tel* (982) 51.00.11
Valeriano Valdesuso s/n

This small *parador* on the plains of Galicia could be a useful staging post between Gijon and Santiago. It is a medieval bastion with an intriguing octagonal tower reached by crossing a drawbridge. Traditional high-quality comfortable furnishings emphasise the hotel's historic features and flatter the enormously thick stone walls. A recent visitor comments: "What super big baths! The beds are especially comfortable. We still dream of that romantic bedroom and its fantastic bathroom. It was like a second honeymoon! In the restaurant the soup and wine were especially good and the service was excellent." (*JC Gillett; also LH*)

Open All year.
Rooms 6 double – all with bath and shower, telephone, tea-making facilities and baby-listening.
Facilities Salon with TV, bar/cafeteria, dining room. Gardens. English spoken.
Location Villalba is 36 km N of Lugo. Hotel is central. Parking.
Restriction Not suitable for ♿.
Credit cards All major cards accepted.
Terms (Excluding 6% tax) B&B: single 7,000 pts, double 9,200 pts; dinner, B&B: single 8,900 pts, double 13,000 pts; full board single 10,140 pts, double 15,480 pts. Set lunch/dinner 1,900 pts; full alc 1,600 pts.

VITORIA-GASTEIZ 01000 Álava — Map 12

Parador Nacional de Argómaniz — *Tel* (945) 28.22.00
Apartado 601 Vitoria

Just off the main Pamplona–Vitoria road in the heart of Basque country, this *parador* is a converted 18th-century country mansion. Its best features are its peaceful, isolated location surrounded by the Navarre hills and its raftered barn-like restaurant on an upper floor. "Helpful reception, slightly rushed. Our double room had a good view over the wide valley to the distant mountains. Furnishings and bathroom showing signs of wear, but the beds were exceptionally comfortable. Food was simple and fresh, well presented. Breakfast was also good. A useful stopover." (*JC Gillett, LH*)

Open All year.
Rooms 53 double – all with bath, shower and telephone.
Facilities Lift. Salon, TV room, games room, bar, restaurant. Garden.
Location 12 km E of Vitoria by N1 to Irun.
Restriction Not suitable for ♿.
Credit cards All major cards accepted.
Terms B&B: single occupancy 5,000 pts, double 6,700 pts; full board: single 8,140 pts, double 12,980 pts. Set lunch/dinner 1,900-2,100 pts. Special meals for children.

ZAFRA 06300 Badajoz — Map 12

Parador Nacional Hernán Cortés — *Tel* (924) 55.02.00
Plaza de Maria Cristina

In a small town just off the Badajoz–Seville road, this Guide newcomer like many other *paradores* is a converted castle with massive grey walls – austere from outside, but cool and inviting inside: "An inspired conversion, modern enough for convenience but retaining the best of the period (tapestries everywhere). My bags were cheerfully carried up to my eyrie in a tower – ornate black ironwork, heavy furniture and tiles – I would not have been surprised if Cortes himself had appeared in full armour. Till dinner I collapsed by and in the pool, in a shady garden. The food makes little concession to 'international' style – a plus in my view." "Food adequate, rooms spacious, service charming." (*Ann Price, M Barratt Brown*)

Open All year.
Rooms 28 – most with bath or shower, all with telephone.
Facilities Lounge, dining room. Garden with swimming pool.
Location Central; parking. Town is 76 km SE of Badajoz.
Credit cards All major cards accepted.
Terms [1987 rates] Rooms: single 5,600 pts, double 7000 pts. Breakfast 600 pts. Full board 7,240-9,340 pts per person. Set lunch/dinner 1,900 pts.

ZAMORA 49001 — Map 12

Parador Nacional Condes de Alba y Aliste — *Tel* (988) 51.44.97
Piazza de Viriato 5

By the banks of the upper Duero, in the heart of an old city north of Salamanca, this parador *occupies a beautiful old 15th-century palace, carefully restored, with a fine inner court. Rooms furnished with antiques, splendid dining room with above-average food; service slow. Swimming pool with fine view. 27 rooms, all with bath and shower. B&B double 8,300-9,800 pts. Reinstated in Guide after period of closure for repairs: more reports please.*

Sweden

HOTEL ÅKERBLADS, TÄLLBERG

ARILD 260 43 Skåne **Map 7**

Rusthållargården *Tel* (042) 462.75

This handsome 17th-century stone building, well modernised within, stands just outside the picturesque fishing-village of Arild on Sweden's west coast, with good views of the bay. Lack of feedback kept it out of the 1987 Guide, but inspectors have now been there: "The hotel has a strong individuality, feels cosy and unpretentious. Decoration is fresh, unsophisticated but pleasant, furniture solid and traditional. Bedrooms are not spacious. Each is furnished in its own personal style and has its own name – Grandmother's Room, the Major's Room, etc. We had the Poet's Room (pale gold wallpaper) which is allotted to the British because they prefer a bath to a shower. We enjoyed our meal in the 'blue' dining room (the large 'green' one was occupied by a merry gathering of gentlemen having a whale of a time at their business conference). Our little waitress was charming and the food cooked with care, while the breakfast table served a vast assortment." An earlier visitor had praised the fresh fish and the wine cellar, and the friendly feeling given to the hotel by Peter

Malgren, fourth generation of the family that owns it. The peninsula from Arild to Kulla is a national park, excellent for walking and with lovely views; good sandy beaches are not far away. (*JS*)

Open All year except 22 Dec–7 Jan.
Rooms 5 suites, 29 double, 13 single – all with bath and/or shower, telephone, radio and TV; baby-sitter available. 30 in nearby annexes.
Facilities Lounges, TV room, library, bar, restaurant; conference facilities; terrace. Garden with tennis, swimming pool and sauna. Beach nearby. English spoken.
Location Take road from Helsingborg to Höganäs; after 4 km turn right to Arild. Parking.
Restriction Not suitable for ♿.
Credit cards All major cards accepted.
Terms [1987 rates] B&B 240-440 Skr; dinner B&B 365-425 Skr. Set lunch 75 Skr, dinner 135 Skr. Reduced rates for children; special meals.

BORGHOLM 387 00 Öland — Map 7

Halltorps Gästgiveri — *Tel* (0485) 552.50
Hogsrum

A four-mile bridge, Europe's longest, goes from the mainland to the very long island of Öland, where about midway down stands this country inn converted from a 17th-century royal stable. Removed from the 1987 Guide through lack of reports, it is now borne back in some triumph by this inspectorial assessment: "Öland is covered with windmills, standing singly or in twos and threes. Just a few hundred metres from the imposing ruins of Borgholm castle is *Halltorps Gästgiveri*, a typical Swedish inn with its mansard roof. In the invading dusk, how welcoming the Olympic-style torches on each side of the blue door! How cheering the airy entrance hall with its spot-lit modern furniture! The owner then carried my heavy suitcase for me (the only time in my two weeks in Sweden that anyone had offered to do that). The amazing and palatial bedrooms are on two levels, with a smart sitting room and, up under the roof, a large bedroom area with vast double bed, the whole decorated in warm wooden tones, with traditional woven rugs, fresh flowers and a bowl of fruit. Sauna and beauty parlour are along the corridor. Dining-rooms are spectacular, in pale pastel shades with bold modern oil paintings. In one stands an old carriage, bearing the lavish salad bar in the evening and the breakfast spread in the morning. Tables were candle-lit, and our gentle middle-aged waitress (who spoke no English) was superbly efficient. On the set menu, raw smoked beef and reindeer filet were both superb. Breakfast was a feast – several sorts of pickled fish, peaches, grapes, etc. We cannot praise this place too highly – friendly, generous, and for Sweden amazingly good value."

Open 8 Mar–22 Dec.
Rooms 6 suites, 2 double, 2 single – 9 with shower, all with telephone, radio and TV.
Facilities Restaurant, bar. Garden. Beach 3 km. English spoken.
Location 10 km S of Borgholm. Parking.
Credit cards All major cards accepted.
Terms B&B: single 400-440 Skr, double 540-590 Skr; dinner, B&B: 490-680 Skr per person. Full alc 250 Skr. Reduced rates and special meals for children.

Give the Guide positive support. Don't just leave feedback to others.

GOTHENBURG 416 66 — Map 7

Tidbloms Hotel — *Tel* (031) 19.20.70
Olskroksgt. 23 — *Telex* 27369 TIDBLO

A turn-of-the century, turreted, red-brick house, close to the centre of Sweden's second city. "It looks like an old warehouse," writes an acute hotel-watcher this year, "and though a member of the Romantikhotel association it is not very romantic – but good value, quiet and well situated, with bedrooms comfortably furnished in modern contract style. The restaurant and bar are built into the rocky hillside and have a cavernous feel, softened by handwoven rugs, real oil lamps and rustic furniture. A good selection of Swedish specialities (snow goose, reindeer filet, etc) with carefully prepared sauces. The flambéed cloudberries were delicious – and the head waiter is quite a character." Others too have found the place pleasant and friendly. The restaurant-cavern was formerly a bicycle repair shop. (*Francine and Ian Walsh; also Susan Ruff, J Goeller*)

Open All year.
Rooms 3 suites, 14 double, 20 single – all with bath or shower, telephone, radio, TV and baby-listening. 3 rooms equipped for ♿.
Facilities Lift. Cocktail bar, restaurant; conference facilities. Rock and sand beach 20 minutes. English spoken.
Location In E part of Gothenberg, within a pedestrian housing area (take small access road behind filling station). Parking.
Credit cards All major cards accepted.
Terms [1987 rates] B&B: single 580 Skr, double 735 Skr. Set meals 40 Skr. Reduced rates in low season. Children under 7 sharing parents' room free.

GRÄNNA 563 00 Småland — Map 7

Hotel Gyllene Uttern — *Tel* (0390) 108.00
Telex 70856

A stylish modern hotel on the eastern shore of Lake Vättern, Sweden's second largest lake, about half way between Stockholm and Malmö. "Though it looks like a medieval castle, in fact it is entirely mock, built in the 1930s. But the location and atmosphere make you feel like a lord, and the service and food match the surroundings – fish from the lake is a speciality. To dine with the sun setting over the lake was an unforgettable experience. It is a chain hotel, but this is not noticeable." The hotel was built and is owned by the Gyllensvaan family who were raised to the peerage in 1756. The paintings in its dining room are copies of the great masters. Thirteen bedrooms are in individual cottages on a slope by the lake. You can get married in the chapel. (*Richard O Whiting*)

Open All year.
Rooms 53 rooms, 13 cottages – all with bath and/or shower, telephone, radio and TV. 1 specially adapted for ♿.
Facilities Lobby, lounges, restaurant; chapel; sauna. Grounds on shores of lake.
Location 3km from Gränna.
Credit cards All major cards accepted.
Terms [1987 rates] B&B: single 450-560 Skr, double 540-660 Skr. Alc (excluding wine) 200-250 Skr.

GRYTHYTTAN 710 60 Västmanland — Map 7

Grythyttans Gästgivaregård — *Tel* (0591) 143.10
Prästgt. 2

In a village off the beaten track just north of huge Lake Vanern, this rather unusual country house hotel is run with showmanlike *brio* by Carl Jan Granqvist and is well known in Sweden for its French-influenced gastronomy. Originally built in 1640 in the heart of the then flourishing iron-mining district, it fell into disuse with the arrival of the railway, and slowly decayed. In 1972 it was reopened; Mr Granqvist bought up the surrounding 18th-century shops and cottages, converted them into comfortable bedrooms, filled the rooms with antique furniture and art, dressed the staff in period clothes, and successfully recreated the atmosphere of 150 years ago. "It is a delightful experience," says one visitor this year, "to stay in the lovely old village houses which now contain the lavish bedrooms furnished with the Swedish sense of colour. Service by the dedicated young staff is outstanding, wines are marvellous in quality and range." (*Dudley Wilson; also Keith and Mary Weller*)

Our inspector-at-large in Sweden this year gives a slightly different slant: "One of the most expensive hotels in expensive Sweden, with a charm less rural than sophisticated. Carl Granqvist leaves no stone unturned: his hotel is one of the *Relais et Châteaux* (top of the market) but also a Romantikhotel (middle of the market) *and* a *Bitur Logi* (bottom of it), with rooms which range from the sybaritic to the two-bunked youth hostel type. The place has panache, smartness and idiosyncrasy. Our bedroom, with its green Chinese lacquered furniture, dark red wallpaper and curtains, and dramatic black and mother-of-pearl antique panels, looked extremely smart. But oddly the bath had no taps and I had to fill it from the shower-head which took ten minutes and left me with luke-warm water (some designer's bright idea, very unpractical). Worse, the bathroom's beautiful slate floor sloped the wrong way so that water from the shower flooded into the bedroom. In the maze of connecting dining rooms (one of them filled with a merry gathering of businessmen, smoking heavily) the Scandinavian atmosphere was at its strongest. This was gourmet cooking for the masses and we were satisfied with our set menus – trout caviar, turbot in white sauce, a large selection of mainly French cheeses. Service was slow but effective – the waitresses were like bats out of hell with the ties of their Victorian pinnies flapping behind them. Breakfast was impeccable – loads of food. Despite the floods and foibles, keep this place in the Guide."

Open All year.
Rooms 9 suites, 53 double, 18 single – 26 with bath, 52 with shower, all with telephone and radio. 52 in cottages and houses in grounds; 18 in annexe (15 min drive away). Some ground-floor rooms.
Facilities Lounges, bars, TV room, restaurant; conference facilities. Dancing on Sat. 2-acre grounds with tennis court and children's playground. 150 lakes in area; boats for hire, bathing, fishing and golf nearby. English spoken.
Location 70 km W of Orebro. In centre of village. Parking.
Restriction Not suitable for ♿.
Credit cards All major cards accepted.
Terms B&B 350-1,020 Skr; dinner, B&B 600-1,370 Skr. Full alc 375 Skr. Children under 4 free, 5-12 50% reduction; special meals.

SIGTUNA 193 00 Uppland — Map 7

Stadshotellet-Mälarens Pärla — *Tel* (0760) 501.00
Stora Nygt. 3

Sigtuna, between Stockholm and Uppsala, is a picturesque little lakeside town of wooden 18th-century houses and has the ruins of very early Christian churches. The *Stadshotellet*, dropped from last year's Guide for lack of reports, has now been visited by inspectors: "It stands on an embankment at the end of the main street, with spectacular views from the restaurant and upper back rooms. The bedrooms have recently been redecorated in pastel shades by a new management and are very pleasant; some have adjoining sitting-rooms. The attractive restaurant, separately managed, is very well known and people drive out to it from Stockholm: on our visit, there was a wedding party of people in authentic 18th-century costume dancing the minuet. The food was very good, with spectacular sweets. Breakfast was adequate, below the high Swedish average. Everyone speaks good English." (*Also David Callow*)

Open All year.
Rooms 26 – 24 with bath or shower, all with telephone, radio and TV.
Facilities Salons, restaurant; sauna, solarium. English spoken.
Location About 45 km NW of Stockholm. Parking.
Credit cards All major cards accepted.
Terms [1987 rates] B&B: single 440 Skr, double 550 Skr. Special weekend rates.

STOCKHOLM — Map 7

Hotell Anno 1647 — *Tel* (08) 44.04.80
3 Mariagränd — *Telex* 12550
Stockholm 116 46

In 1647 a red-brick house was built on the site by a master tailor, so this small hotel takes its name from this. "Not easy to find, but well worth it when we did! A beautiful old house, with a small courtyard, furnished with due regard for its period. The *pièce de résistance*, which crowned the sense of gracious living, was the huge and magnificent sitting room forming part of our suite (there are two of these in the hotel). We felt like 18th-century aristocrats. There were fascinating views from the windows over the Old Town and across the water. The hotel has no restaurant but there is a pleasant breakfast room downstairs. The staff were friendly and obliging." (*J and JW*) *Warning*: stairs are steep.

Open All year.
Rooms 2 suites, 16 double, 24 single – 21 with shower, all with telephone, radio and TV. Some ground-floor rooms.
Facilities Breakfast room, TV room. Garden. Sea within walking distance, fishing. English spoken.
Location Central, in side street at Götgatan 3,, by Slussen on the island of Södermalm. Garage parking.
Restriction Not suitable for ♿.
Credit cards All major cards accepted.
Terms B&B: single 295-600 Skr, double 385-750 Skr, suite 375-1,075 Skr. (No restaurant.)

Hotel Diplomat
Strandvägen 7C
Stockholm 104 40

Tel (08) 663.58.00
Telex 17119

Like any good diplomat, this one wears an air of discretion yet quietly absorbs all the gossip (its attractive ground-floor tea-house is a smart local rendezvous, as well as serving lavish buffet breakfasts). With a fine central position by the waterfront, the hotel is expensive, fashionable and placidly comfortable. Bedrooms vary in price: the better ones face the harbour; service variable. 132 rooms, all with bath or shower. B&B double 1,075-1,200 Skr. Few recent reports: more welcome.

Lady Hamilton Hotel
Storkyrkobrinken 5
Stockholm 111 28

Tel (08) 23.46.80

Lord Nelson Hotel
Västerlånggt. 22
Stockholm 111 29

Tel (08) 23.23.90
Telex 10434 NELSHAM
(for both hotels)

Both much admired, here are two small hotels of character, jointly owned and very close to each other in the old town. They were made by knocking together some old houses dating from the 15th century, and each carefully portrays its historical theme. Models of ships, and nautical pictures and prints, provide a backdrop; there are also items taken from boats, such as coloured prows and brass rails. The bedrooms are modern but not large. "Apart from the very small bedroom, I much enjoyed it," says a visitor this year to the *Lord Nelson*. "In an area of fascinating cobbled streets and little shops, it has lighted ship models in the comfortable bedrooms, a sauna in the basement and an open-air rooftop which is nice for a drink while viewing the city skyline. The self-service breakfast is exceptionally good and the young staff pleasant and helpful." "If you can pretend that the very small rooms are cabins, it helps." The basement plunge pool in the *Lady Hamilton* was a well in the 15th century. (*Donna Cuervo, Ann and Sidney Carpenter, and others*)

Lady Hamilton Hotel
Open All year.
Rooms 3 triple, 18 double, 13 single – 6 with bath, 28 with shower, all with telephone, radio and TV.
Facilities Bar; conference facilities; sauna, plunge-pool. English spoken.
Location Central, in pedestrian zone, near royal palace. (Front rooms might be noisy.) Street parking.
Credit cards All major cards accepted.
Terms B&B: single 1,010 Skr, double 1,190 Skr. Reduced prices mid-Jun–early Aug and some weekends. (No restaurant.)

Lord Nelson Hotel
Open All year.
Rooms 9 double, 22 single – all with shower, telephone, radio and TV.
Facilities Bar; conference facilities; rooftop terrace; sauna. English spoken.
Location Central, in pedestrian zone, near royal palace. Street parking.
Credit cards All major cards accepted.
Terms B&B: single 760 Skr, double 1,010 Skr. Reduced prices mid-Jun–early Aug and some weekends. (No restaurant.)

Sara Hotell Reisen
Skeppsbron 12-14
Stockholm 111 30

Tel (08) 22.32.60
Telex 17494 REISEN

Very highly esteemed alike for cuisine and accommodation, the *Reisen* has just undergone a major renovation programme. A visitor scrutinising the results this year was much impressed: "The view of the harbour from the restaurant and front bedrooms is breathtaking; behind lie the quaint and narrow streets of the old city. We were given one of the newly-finished rooms on the sixth floor and found it elegant and luxurious, with smoked glass mirrors behind the bed and a large bathroom in honey-toned marble. Our only quibble: rather noisy air-conditioning. On the first floor is a cosy sitting room with interesting old books, some in English; in the cellars are saunas and jacuzzis. In the restaurant, dynamic and stylish English-speaking waiters and waitresses serve food that is as good as can be found in Sweden, with French presentation of local ingredients. Salmon in dill sauce, scallops and roast goose breast were all outstanding. As for the buffet breakfast, it was the most extensive, imaginative and tasteful that I have ever come across – superlative, even by Sweden's high standards. This impeccable hotel's only drawback is that parking is difficult." (*F and IW, endorsed by Moyra Beaves*) An earlier view: "If you like ships you will certainly like the *Reisen*, three 17th-century merchants' houses sympathetically joined together. Not only is the decor generally maritime, but the hotel stands bang on the quayside, and looks across to the elegant white three-master *Chapman*, floodlit at night. Almost next door is the Royal Palace, a short walk away is the Opera House; but best of all, it is one of the very nicest places I know for watching the boats go by." (*Jan Morris*)

Open All year except Christmas.
Rooms 12 suites, 95 double, 8 single – all with bath and shower, telephone, radio and TV.
Facilities Lobby, 2 bars (1 with piano), grill room, restaurant; conference/banqueting facilities; indoor heated swimming pool, sauna. On harbour with free salmon fishing. English spoken.
Location Central, in old town. (Light sleepers may be disturbed by traffic noise.) Meter parking only.
Restriction Not suitable for ♿.
Credit cards All major cards accepted.
Terms B&B: single 900-2,000 Skr, double 1,150-3,000 Skr, suite 3,000 Skr. Children under 15 in parents' room free; special meals.

Strand Hotel
Nybrokajen 9
Stockholm 103 27

Tel (08) 22.29.00
Telex 10504

This de luxe hotel, recently renovated within a Scandinavian *beaux-arts* building, enjoys a waterside position on the Nybroviken (of which many rooms have splendid views) and is just minutes from two of the treasure houses of Stockholm: the National Museum and the Moderna Museet. It changed hands in October 1986. First report since the new ownership: "Staffed by flaxen-haired young Swedes, the *Strand* is as homely as a 21st-century hotel can be. Liquor, as everywhere in Sweden, is hideously expensive – £9 for a glass of Chablis. But the food is tasty and prettily served. Room service is polite and prompt and ungrasping." (*Tony*

Thomas) Breakfast and light meals are served in a pretty glass-roofed winter garden.

Open All year.
Rooms 19 suites, 65 double, 53 single – 131 with bath, 6 with shower, all with direct-dial telephone, radio and TV; baby sitters available. 6 rooms (with bath) specially adapted for ♿.
Facilities Lift. Lobby, bar, restaurant, winter garden with glass roof for light meals. English spoken.
Location Central; near National Museum. Garage and parking.
Credit cards All major cards accepted.
Terms B&B: single 525-1,100 Skr, double 950-1,500 Skr, suite 2,500-3,000 Skr. Full alc 365 Skr. Special meals for children.

SVARTA 71011 Svarta — Map 7

Svarta Herrgard — *Tel* (0585) 50003

A Guide newcomer, outside a small town by a lake some 250 kilometres west of Stockholm: "This handsome manor house hotel is Gustavian (Swedish version of Georgian), in a fine lakeside setting worthy of Bergman's *Smiles of a Summer Night*. The interior has a sense of provincial opulence and stylish elegance – gilded stucco over the doors, a blue dining room with parquet floors. Owner/managers Nils and Marianne Frantzen (who speak excellent English) have indulged their passion for antiques in restoring the house, and the care they have lavished on it shows everywhere. The ambience is never chilly or starchy, as in some country house hotels. The former basement kitchens are now conference areas, sauna, etc. Some bedrooms in the main building are magnificent, some in the wings are far from spacious. Lunch is usually smorgasbord and dinner a decent table d'hôte: standards are high without being *haute cuisine*. The hotel would make a good base for exploring, *inter alia*, the 12th-century wooden church with murals at Sodra Rada, the Picasso sculpture on lake Vanern, Alfred Nobel's house at Karlskoga and Sveafallen, an intriguing area of gorges and rocks." (*Dudley Wilson*) More reports please.

Open All year
Rooms 20 double, 20 single – all with bath or shower, telephone and radio.
Facilities Salons, TV room, billiards room, restaurant; conference facilities. Garden. Lake with boating and fishing nearby, also tennis and golf.
Location About 250 km W of Stockholm. Outside Svarta on road 205.
Credit cards All major cards accepted.
Terms [1987 rates] B&B: single 425 Skr, double 520-560 Skr; full board 520 Skr per person.

TÄLLBERG 793 03 Dalarna — Map 7

Hotel Åkerblads — *Tel* (0247) 508.00

Tällberg is halfway between Leksand and Rättvik on Lake Siljan. The Åkerblad family have been here since the early 18th century, and Christina and Arne claim to be the 19th and 20th generations – probably the oldest reigning hotel family in Europe. The hotel, the oldest part of which is a 17th-century farmhouse, is a comfortable and spacious building in the old style, with a fine view of the lake. The bedrooms are pleasantly furnished, hardly any two being alike. A fresh account this year: "A remarkable place for a rural holiday, amid incredibly neat and tidy countryside. We did not think the food all that outstanding, but our little bedroom was nicely decorated, the staff were friendly, and the sauna and pool are of a very high standard." This chimes in with an earlier report that caught the charm of the place: "We had a delightful bedroom with verandas. It felt very Swedish, painted in different shades of green and orange. The atmosphere in the hotel is easy and informal. We loved the meals too – also very Swedish. People helped themselves from a central table. Lunch seemed to be the main meal – often with several kinds of fish and potatoes with dill. It always ended with cake and excellent coffee in the upper hall. Local parties coming for meals often included men and women in national costume. Christina and Arne Åkerblad made us very welcome – it was a pleasant and somehow particularly *Swedish* experience." (*Ann and Sidney Carpenter, JA Wainwright, SB*) Since last year, the hotel has added 15 individually-styled suites in an adjoining building.

Open All year except 20-27 Dec.
Rooms 15 suites, 29 double, 15 single – 15 with bath, 36 with shower, all with radio, and baby-listening; most with telephone; some with TV. 39 in 3 annexes in garden.
Facilities 2 sitting rooms, bar, 2 TV rooms, coffee/dancing room, 2 dining rooms; facilities for parties and functions. Large garden with tennis, badminton, table-tennis, skating rink; bicycles; sauna, warm brine-bath. Skiing, sleigh-rides in winter; lake with beach 400 metres away, bathing, fishing, boating in summer. English spoken.
Location 12 km from Leksand; on road between Leksand and Rättvik. Parking.
Restriction Not suitable for ♿.
Credit cards Access, Diners, Visa.
Terms B&B: 230-390 Skr; dinner, B&B 360-495 Skr. Set lunch 85-135 Skr, dinner 90-135 Skr. 50% reduction for children under 12; special meals.

TANUMSHEDE 457 00 Bohuslän **Map 7**

Tanums Gestgifveri *Tel* (0525) 290.10

The *Gestgifveri*, which means "guest house", is a charming, two-storey building with yellow-painted wooden walls, and it has been serving travellers since 1663. One of them in 1987 has endorsed this earlier account: "An elegant and charming hotel with an air of sophistication unusual in Sweden. Lounge and bedrooms are in the modern part, the restaurant in the converted 17th-century inn, close by. It is prettily furnished throughout with warm fabrics, soft lamp lighting, a profusion of prints and paintings. No two bedrooms are alike, some feminine and flowery, others plainer and more sophisticated, all comfortable. The restaurant has earned a reputation for French food, and a lot of the dishes are very rich, but of good quality. The wine list was one of the better ones I have seen in Sweden, but with high mark-ups." One visitor stayed in a "splendid suite" used by royal guests. Despite double-glazing, there may be some noise from the main road. Interesting Bronze Age rock carvings in the area. (*Dudley Wilson, also SB*)

Open All year, except Good Friday. Restaurant closed 1 May.
Rooms 2 suites, 22 double, 7 single – 4 with bath, 25 with shower, all with telephone, radio and TV. 15 ground-floor rooms.

Facilities Lift. Lobby, salon with TV, bar, cafeteria; pool room; small sauna with dip pool. Beach, fishing and sea bathing 4-6 km; golf 20 km. English spoken.
Location On E6 near village centre. Parking. Village is 150 km N of Göteborg.
Restriction Not suitable for ♿.
Credit cards All major cards accepted.
Terms B&B: single 430 Skr, double 500-675 Skr, suite 950 Skr. Set lunch 100 Skr, dinner 175 Skr; full alc 250 Skr. Reduced rates for children; special meals.

TOFTAHOLM 340 15 Vittaryd — Map 7

Toftaholm Herrgårdshotell — *Tel* (0370) 440 55

This trim turn-of-the century hunting-lodge in south central Sweden, just north of Ljungby, is new to the Guide this year: "Previously a simple guesthouse, it was taken over in 1984 by Jan and Lisbeth Boëthus who refurbished it with real flair ('we have tried to restore its manor house qualities'). It is a wooden building, painted in the bright yellow that the Swedes love, and the warmth of the large entrance hall (featuring a basking labrador) raised our spirits after a long dull drive. The *patronne* speaks good English and is pleasant and cheerful. The design of the public rooms shows panache – polished parquet floors, crystal chandeliers, beautiful old china, lots of flowers. Bedrooms are simply furnished, with pastel-shaded decor; there are showers but no baths. Through the large dining-room windows we saw the sun setting romantically over the lake. Service is by charming waitresses in quaint Victorian uniforms. The menu is simple and the food, though good, not quite up to the lovely surroundings. Breakfast was an excellent Swedish buffet. Friendly staff and pets." (*Francine and Ian Walsh*)

Open All year.
Rooms 40 rooms – 33 with shower and telephone.
Facilities Salons, dining rooms; conference facilities; terrace. Garden. Lake with swimming, fishing and rowing. Winter sports, golf nearby. English spoken.
Location N of Ljungby, just off the E4 Malmö-Stockholm highway. Parking.
Credit cards All major cards accepted.
Terms [1987 rates] B&B: single 200-450 Skr, double 300-540 Skr.

"As we passed the desk, the manager wished us a good night, 'If you can sleep . . .'. He assured us that the party starting in the courtyard would end at midnight. Warning bells began to ring in our heads. Soon they were accompanied by the whining and squealing of numerous untuned violins from a violinists' convention. For hours we listened to loud, atonal fiddle tunes, murdered over and over and over again. The racket did not end until 2.30 am, when, at the urging of several exhausted hotel guests standing at their courtyard windows, the last fiddlers left...But wait! The ringing in our heads began again at 6 am as the electric alarm clock, unbidden by us, came to life. Fumbling to find the 'off' switch, my exhausted, cursing husband finally unplugged it. Ten minutes later it rose from the dead and began clamouring again. This time we disembowelled it by yanking out the back-up batteries. By this time we felt like the dead, struggling to wake up from Hotel Hell."

Switzerland

HOTEL BELLEVUE, ISELTWALD

AROSA 7050 Graubünden **Map 14**

Hotel Hof Maran *Tel* (01) 31.01.85
Telex 74329

There is praise again this year for the food and friendliness at the fairly large and very well equipped *Hof Maran*, a modern hotel grafted onto the old chalet from which it has developed. It stands high above Arosa, beside the golf-cum-cross-country-ski course. An earlier report: "Half board is almost inevitable as it is a long way down to the town, but food, as so often in Switzerland, lacked that vital touch of imagination. Breakfast in the bedroom looking out to distant snow-covered peaks was a good start to the day. The bedroom door was nearly a foot thick and totally soundproof; the bedroom furniture in honey-gold wood veneer was superbly finished. The beds were wonderfully hard; the bathroom beautifully fitted with all the latest gadgets. Dinner at 7 pm – ushered in and out with Swiss efficiency – did mean rather a long evening, but on our second night the small band set up and the lounge fairly rocked with music and dancing. Surprisingly, the only thing missing was a swimming pool and sauna." (*Angela and David Stewart; endorsed by John and Valerie Harrison*)

Open Dec–Apr, June–Sept.
Rooms 52 double, 20 single – 55 with bath, 9 with shower, all with telephone and radio; TV on request.
Facilities Lifts. Lounges, TV room, 2 *Stübli*, dining room; conference facilities; dancing in the bar; children's games room with ping-pong; sun terrace on roof. Large grounds with 5 tennis courts (pro available), and children's play area; skating rink in winter, 4 curling rinks. Ski-lift and ski school behind hotel; 9-hole golf course nearby.
Location Above Arosa, about 10 minutes' drive. Bus service every 20 minutes. Parking.
Restriction Not suitable for ♿.
Terms [1987 rates] B&B: single 58-198 Sfrs, double 115-400 Sfrs; full board 20 Sfrs per person added. Children under 2 in parents' room free, 2-6 50% reduction, 6-15 30% reduction; special meals on request.

ASCONA 6612 Ticino — Map 14

Hotel Casa Berno

Tel (093) 35.32.32
Telex 846167

The animated little town of Ascona calls itself "the St-Tropez of Switzerland": it lies beside Lago Maggiore, possibly the loveliest of the north Italian lakes. *Casa Berno* itself, a modern four-star hotel, stands on the hillside between Monte Verità and Ronco, about 30 minutes' walk from the centre up a steep winding road (so a car is an asset). The views from its terraces and swimming-pool are stunning; all rooms face south and have a balcony. The pool is heated, and there are secluded meadows for those who prefer solitude. "Efficiently managed by the Goetschis – she is a charming front-of-house and her staff are impressively well trained," runs a report this year, backing up earlier ones: "enchanting", "rooms excellent, food first-class". "The public rooms are spacious and attractively furnished and our bedroom was light and airy, with a mini-bar disguised in the writing desk. Breakfast is an extensive buffet which can be taken on the terrace, and we found the *en pension* dinner to be consistently good." "Useful wardrobe compartments for storing valuables." (*RS McNeill, Elisabeth Lambert and Cesar Ortiz-Tinoco, Arnold Horwell, and others*) One reader found that, even here in the Italian-speaking Ticino, the lingua franca in the restaurant seemed to be German (for touristic reasons, clearly).

Open Mar–Oct inclusive.
Rooms 11 suites, 43 double, 7 single – all with telephone, radio and balcony or terrace.
Facilities Lift. Lounges (1 with TV), bar on roof-garden, grill room, restaurant with terrace; sauna, massage, solarium, fitness room, ladies' hairdresser. Garden with heated swimming pool. Golf, tennis nearby. English spoken.
Location Between Monte Verità and Ronco; c. 20–30 minutes' walk from Ascona. Parking.
Credit card Amex.
Terms B&B: 120-150 Sfrs; half board 140-180 Sfrs; full board 160-190 Sfrs. Reduced rates for children sharing parents' room; special meals.

> Don't let old favourites down. Entries are dropped when there is no endorsement.

BASLE 4058 — Map 14

Hotel Merian am Rhein — *Tel* (061) 25.94.66
Greifengasse/Rheingasse 2 — *Telex* 963537

Centrally located beside the Rhine, an efficient and well-equipped but no-frills hotel, with excellent café-restaurant and outdoor café by the river. Good value in an expensive country. 63 rooms, all with bath and shower. B&B 75-108 Sfrs. Set dinner 22 Sfrs. More reports welcome.

CHÂTEAU-D'OEX 1837 Vaud — Map 14

Hostellerie Bon Accueil — *Tel* (029) 4.63.20
Telex 940083 HOST

Château-d'Oex is a wide and sunny Alpine village on the French side of the Bernese Oberland about 45 minutes' drive from Lake Geneva and ten minutes from the ski resort of Gstaad. The *Bon Accueil* continues to be enjoyed by regular visitors who describe it thus: "An 18th-century chalet, up quite a steep road from the village, so a car would be advisable. We received a warm welcome in English and were brought a pre-dinner drink in our bedroom to enjoy with that glorious view over lush green meadows and snow-capped peaks. Our room was wood-panelled, with rustic but comfortable furnishings. There are several attractive public rooms, and tables and chairs were set out in the pleasant gardens. Dinner in another wood-panelled room with a roaring log fire was very enjoyable and good value." (*S and K Murray-Sykes*) There's a new annexe with eight rooms.

Open 15 Dec–31 Oct.
Rooms 1 suite, 16 double, 2 single – 19 with bath and shower, 1 with shower, all with telephone. 8 rooms in annexe.
Facilities Lounge, cellar bar, dining room. Garden. Winter sports. English spoken.
Location 1 km from town centre. Parking.
Restriction Not suitable for ♿.
Credit cards Amex, Diners, Visa.
Terms B&B: single 80-95 Sfrs, double 130-160 Sfrs; dinner, B&B: 25–30 Sfrs per person added. 30% reduction for children under 12; special meals on request.

DAVOS DORF 7260 Graubünden — Map 14

Hotel Flüela — *Tel* (083) 6.12.21
Bahnhofstrasse 5 — *Telex* 853100 FLUA

"One of the best hotels we've stayed at in years," runs a recent comment on this sizeable ski-hotel, owned and run by the Gredig family for over a century, and now much modernised. Open only in the winter, it is close to the Parsenn Bahn, the largest ski-lift in this big and bustling resort. "Herr Gredig sets the tone for all the staff, who tidy your bedroom twice a day and will even clean your boots. Food is outstanding."

"The hotel excels in general comfort – super lounges, with pianist every evening, open log fire, indoor swimming pool, sauna, solarium; and quite outstanding breakfast and dinner, really the best food I have ever had during a skiing holiday." (*Mrs YC Holding, Dr TJ David*) Davos has many connections with the British: Arthur Conan Doyle was among those who helped to introduce skiing here, and RL Stevenson, who was sent here in 1880 because of lung trouble, completed *Treasure Island* here. He also introduced ice-skating and tobogganing.

Open 28 Nov–10 Apr.
Rooms 10 suites, 55 double, 25 single – 80 with bath and shower, 5 with shower only, all with telephone, radio and TV.
Facilities Bar lounge (with pianist), sitting rooms, several restaurants; function rooms. Indoor heated swimming pool with sauna, solarium, massage, fitness-room; ski boutique, barber, hairdresser; Swiss Credit Bank. Winter sports facilities nearby. English spoken.
Location In town centre. A few roadside rooms may be noisy. Parking.
Restriction Not suitable for ♿.
Credit cards All major cards accepted.
Terms B&B: single 115-195 Sfrs, double 105-370 Sfrs; dinner, B&B single 155-245 Sfrs, double 290-470 Sfrs; full board single 180-270 Sfrs, double 340-520 Sfrs. Set lunch 35 Sfrs, dinner 50-60 Sfrs; full alc 60-100 Sfrs. Reduced rates and special meals for children.

LES DIABLERETS 1865 Vaud — Map 14

Hotel Les Lilas — *Tel* (025)531134

"Les Diablerets is a charming unspoilt village in a valley between Aigle and Gstaad, in the Vaud. Jean-Pierre Matti was born here, and he took over *Les Lilas* in 1986. He and his delightful wife give a warm welcome and speak fluent English. Their rustic bedrooms are comfortable and the dining room most attractive – candle-lit dining with a log fire, surrounded by wooden beams. Delicious specialities." (*Michael Forrest*) The menu features such dishes as poulet à la bière and filet de boeuf aux morilles. This small chalet-like roadside hotel is new to the Guide this year, and we'd welcome more reports.

Open All year.
Rooms 15 – most with bath and shower.
Facilities Bar, TV room, 2 restaurants. Garden. English spoken.
Location On edge of village, which is 20 km E of Aigle on road to Gstaad.
Credit cards Access, Amex, Visa.
Terms B&B: single 50–60 Sfrs, double 90–100 Sfrs; dinner, B&B: single 75–80 Sfrs, double 150–160 Sfrs; full board: single 100–105 Sfrs, double 180–190 Sfrs. Set lunch 12 Sfrs, dinner 30 Sfrs; full alc 50 Sfrs. Reduced rates and special meals for children.

ENGELBERG 6390 Unterwalden — Map 14

Hotel Eden — *Tel* (041) 94.32.94

Plenty of renewed enthusiasm – especially for the food – has arrived this year for Thomas Reinhardt-Waser's small and friendly hotel, in a well-known resort high up in a lovely isolated mountain valley south of Lucerne. The squat white building may look unprepossessing, but inside all is quality and *Gemütlichkeit*. "The friendly proprietors were always ready to enjoy a drink and a chat after dinner. Our room was simple, but adequate; each floor has its own sitting-room with TV and multilingual bookshelf. You need a hearty appetite to appreciate fully the good cooking." "Yes, a real Eden, this *Eden* – delightful public rooms, atmosphere, rocking-chairs, a nursery which would keep any child quiet on a wet day, and the best Swiss meal I have ever eaten." Others have enjoyed the mountain views from room-balconies and sun terrace, but have found the furnishings a little basic. (*J and R Davidson, Rev M Bourdeaux, J and B Flowers, NCC Trench*)

Open Mid-Dec–mid-Apr, early June–early Oct.
Rooms 10 double – 8 with shower, 6 also with WC, all with telephone, radio and mini-bar.
Facilities Sitting room, TV room, games room for children, restaurant, residents' dining room. Garden and terrace where meals can be taken in summer. Swimming pool and sports centre nearby; close to ski-school and mountain walks. English spoken.
Location Central, near station. Garage and outdoor parking.
Restriction Not suitable for ♿.
Credit cards All major cards accepted.
Terms B&B: single 50-65 Sfrs, double 100-120 Sfrs; dinner, B&B: single 68-83 Sfrs, double 136-156 Sfrs. Set lunch/dinner 15-20 Sfrs (on Sun 30-35 Sfrs); full alc 45-55 Sfrs. Reduced rates for family holidays in summer and skiing holidays in winter (1 or 2 weeks). Reductions for children under 15; special meals.

Hotel Hess — *Tel* (041) 94.13.66
Telex 866 270 HESS

Confident, traditional 19th-century holiday hotel, well modernised; more expensive alternative to the Eden. *Large rooms with balconies facing mountains; cosy restaurant with good Swiss food; large swimming pool, sauna, tennis, dancing, etc; big garden. Open 18 Dec–30 Apr, 10 May–31 Oct. 44 rooms, all with bath and/or shower. B&B 75-108 Sfrs. Set meals 25 Sfrs. New nomination: more reports please.*

GENEVA 1204 — Map 14

Hôtel L'Arbalète — *Tel* (022) 28.41.55
3 rue de la Tour Maıtresse — *Telex* 427293 ARBA

A small de luxe hotel, well located near the lake and the best shops, recommended for the quality of its furnishings, its excellent reasonably priced restaurant and pleasant staff. Reports this year: "Clean and comfortable, with a homely feel; quiet, because windows double-glazed; good food." "Good bedrooms: nice touches like an umbrella in the bedroom to help with Geneva showers." An earlier view: "Reception was charming. Our bedroom had a small balcony, overlooking nice rooftops. Good furniture. Breakfast arrived with flowers and pretty china. Not cheap but nothing is in Geneva." (*Lena Pycroft, S Carpenter*)

Open All year.
Rooms 20 double, 12 single – all with bath and shower, telephone, radio, TV, mini-bar and baby-listening.
Facilities Lift. Hall, 2 bars, pub with pianist 9–12 pm, 3 restaurants. Lake Geneva 2 minutes' walk, with sandy beach, safe bathing, fishing. English spoken.
Location Central. Windows double-glazed. Garage and parking.
Credit cards All major cards accepted.
Terms [1987 rates] B&B: single 200-260 Sfrs, double 270-350 Sfrs. Set lunch/dinner 20-50 Sfrs. Reduced rates for children in parents' room; special meals on request.

Hôtel Les Armures *Tel* (022) 28.91.72
1 rue du Puits St-Pierre *Telex* 421129

This elegant little hotel in a small square near the cathedral, up in the old town, makes a pleasant contrast to the grand, impersonal places down by the lake: but like them it is not cheap (indeed, what is, in Geneva?). It is an old stone building and its restaurant is said to be the city's oldest – and excellent too. A visitor this year enjoyed the hotel and the location, but thought the prices charged for breakfast extras were excessive. Another complaint is of the noise from children at night. But one reader had a very quiet room. "Beautifully furnished with a small roof-garden outside its window. The finest, lightest duvet. All here is comfort and perfection." (*Konstanze Crüwell, Mrs KM Plowden*)

Open All year. Restaurant closed public holidays.
Rooms 4 suites, 16 double, 8 single – all with bath, telephone, radio and TV.
Facilities Lift. Lobby, salon, breakfast room, bar, lounge, restaurant, *Stüberl* (rustic bar/restaurant). English spoken.
Location Central, near St-Pierre Cathedral. No special parking facilities.
Restriction Not suitable for ♿.
Credit cards All major cards accepted.
Terms B&B: single 175-205 Sfrs, double 265-285 Sfrs, suite 350 Sfrs.

GRINDELWALD 3818 Bern Map 14

Hotel Fiescherblick *Tel* (036) 53.44.53

"Grindelwald, whose main street contains everything from immaculate Japanese to scruffy-booted walkers hoping to pass as climbers, has its compensations in the beauty of the Jungfrau group and the Jungfraujoch railway. Grindelwald sports mainly characterless would-be chalet type hotels but we fell gratefully into this one on the main street. It is an old chalet, with attractive antiques to give atmosphere. The charming dining room is panelled, and the food is satisfying." (Try the poached perch with Pernod, and try saying it too). "No porter or lift – the age and structure of the building makes the latter impossible. But in a town where much is bogus we found it clean, unpretentious and good value." (*Catherine Green; also Patrick Till*) A reader this year found even this haven to be in a somewhat noisy setting. More reports welcome.

Open 15 Dec–15 Apr, 1 June–20 Oct. Restaurant closed Tues.
Rooms 20 double, 3 single – all with bath or shower, telephone, radio and mini-bar; many with balcony.
Facilities Lounge, TV lounge, bar, dining room, restaurant. Garden and terrace. Winter sports and mountain climbing. English spoken.
Location Centre of village, near church. Parking.
Restriction Not suitable for ♿.
Credit cards Access, Diners, Visa.
Terms B&B 55–80 Sfrs; dinner, B&B 78–103 Sfrs. Set lunch 10–30 Sfrs, dinner 14–75 Sfrs; full alc 42 Sfrs. 30–50% reductions for children; special menus.

If you have had recent experience of a good hotel that ought to be in the Guide, please write to us at once. Report forms are to be found at the back (or use your own stationery if you prefer). Procrastination is the thief of the next edition.

GSTAAD 3780 Bern — Map 14

Hotel Christiania — *Tel* (030) 4.51.21
Hauptstrasse — *Telex* 922250 CHRI

Small four-star hotel in main street of fashionable Gstaad. Rooms comfortable and attractively furnished; very good food in a small cosy restaurant. 18 rooms, most with bath or shower. B&B double 120-350 Sfrs. No recent reports: new ones welcome.

GUARDA 7545 Graubünden — Map 14

Hotel Meisser — *Tel* (084) 9.21.32

This picturesque village, once an important staging-post on the old main road between Munich and Milan, lies high above the Inn valley of the Lower Engadin in a splendidly isolated position. Bell-laden cows are herded down the narrow cobbled main street at milking time, and all around are snow-capped mountains. The *Meisser*, an old house nicely restored, has again been admired this year: "We had a lovely room, though a little dark. *Demi-pension* meals very good, excellent young waitresses. Great location for walking, spectacular views." An earlier report: "We were fortunate enough to stay in what had been the upstairs living room. It was large, and had kept its original wooden walls and hand-carved ceiling. The glass-enclosed restaurant section of the dining room offers panoramas in every direction. The owners speak excellent English. The food was delicious and the service outstanding." (*Bernadette Murray, BS*) Rooms vary greatly in size.

Open June–Oct.
Rooms 17 double, 3 single – all with bath, shower, telephone and radio.
Facilities Salon, dining rooms; terrace café. Garden. Winter sports, walking etc.
Location E of Davos; 2 km from Guarda station. Parking.
Credit cards All major cards accepted.
Terms [1987 rates] Dinner, B&B: single 60-85 Sfrs, double 120-174 Sfrs; full board 16 Sfrs per person added. 1-night bookings sometimes refused.

INTRAGNA 6655 Locarno — Map 14

Hotel Ristorante Antico — *Tel* (093) 81.11.07

Intragna, which has a music summer school and the highest *campanile* in the Ticino, is a quiet hill-village only five miles from the bustle of Locarno down by the lake. Here the cheerfully rustic *Antico*, a Guide newcomer, has been made up from several old houses. "These old buildings have been skilfully restored, and the bedrooms are all individual, whether in the main building or the various annexes. Nearby are two small swimming pools reserved for hotel guests. The Ticinese cooking is excellent (notably the rabbit dishes) and the wine very fairly priced. Lovely walks through woods, streams and gorges." (*WP Jaspert*) More reports welcome.

Open All year.
Rooms 4 suites, 20 double, 8 single – 25 with bath, 3 with shower, all with TV. Some in annexes.

Facilities Bar, restaurant; disco; terraces. 2 swimming-pools, sauna. English spoken.
Location 8 km W of Locarno; hotel is in the direction of Domodossola.
Restriction Not suitable for ♿.
Credit cards All major cards accepted.
Terms B&B: 30-65 Sfrs; dinner B&B: 47-82 Sfrs; full board 60-95 Sfrs. Full alc 30 Sfrs. Reduced rates for children.

ISELTWALD 3807 Bern **Map 14**

Hotel Bellevue *Tel* (036) 45.11.10

"The charming summer resort of Iseltwald," writes a connoisseur enthusiastically, "is a picturesque hamlet on a peninsula beside the lake of Brienz, east of Interlaken. You can sail or water-ski, or go for mountain walks or climbs; the beautiful Giessback falls are worth a visit. The *Bellevue*, a *Relais du Silence*, is in a delightful position close to the lake and has two terraced gardens for drinks and light meals. The hotel's design is typically Swiss, with much use of wood and folkweave fabrics for the interiors. The bedrooms are smallish but with good cupboard space and some have balconies with wonderful views; bathrooms are tiny but functional. Our main criticisms were of poor sound-proofing and the worst bedroom lighting we've ever met. The hotel's main emphasis is on the food, under the aegis of the hardworking owners, the Kinners. There are two restaurants, one of them being also used for breakfast which is a sumptuous buffet affair. The other, the *Fischgrill*, is more sophisticated. Here Herr Kinner can be seen cooking a superb choice of local fish or steaks over an open fire. Our excellent meal included fish soup made from lake fish, and a local fish called fera cooked in a light creamy basil sauce. A bottle of Swiss Aigle went well with the meal. Coffee was superb and all dishes were strikingly presented." (*Padi Howard*)

Open Feb–Dec. Closed Tue.
Rooms 9 double, 1 single – 5 with bath, 6 with shower.
Facilities Salon, 2 restaurants. Garden. On lake shore with beach and sailing. Indoor swimming pool, tennis courts and golf nearby.
Restriction Not suitable for ♿
Location On S shore of Lake Brienz, 10 km E of Interlaken.
Terms B&B 43–53 Sfrs. Set lunch/dinner 20–35 Sfrs; full alc 45–60 Sfrs. Reduced rates and special meals for children.

Hotel Bernahof *Tel* (036) 45.11.07

The *Bernahof* (with its restaurant *Ländte*) is a small shore-fronted building on the same quiet peninsula. "Many of the simple but comfortable rooms give marvellous balcony views. The hotel is run informally but efficiently by the Wagner family who are warm and hospitable. The restaurant offers a range of high-quality traditional dishes and fresh fish from the lake, and of course the helpings are in the true Swiss tradition. Dining can be either on one of the numerous terraces or indoors. It is tempting to sit by the lake all day long eating their home-made pastries." (*Tom and Gillian Brent*) Some modernisation and expansion is planned for 1988/9.

Open 1 May–31 Oct. Restaurant closed Wed in low season.
Rooms 4 triple, 14 double, 3 single – 1 with shower and WC; 4 triple and 7 double in Pension Kreuz under same management.

Facilities Salon, restaurant; banqueting room; terrace. Garden restaurant by lake. Fishing (no permit necessary), surfing, sailing, safe bathing. English spoken.
Location On S shore of Lake of Brienz, 10 km E of Interlaken (10 minutes' drive); hotel is near landing stage.
Restriction Not suitable for ♿.
Terms B&B 32–35 Sfrs; dinner, B&B 42–48 Sfrs. Full alc 30 Sfrs. Reduced rates for children under 12; special meals.

KANDERSTEG 3718 Bern — Map 14

Hotel Ermitage

Tel (033) 75.15.12

A returning fan confirms his earlier assessment: "The first attraction of the *Ermitage* is that it stands half a mile from the main road, amid meadows and woods, so it is quiet. A pleasant walk leads in ten minutes to the village; the woods and the closeness of the mountain slopes keep the air beautifully fresh. If you love the sound of rushing water to go to sleep by, several waterfalls and a steep brook provide that. The hotel is run by Mrs Hirschi and her family – staff were among the friendliest I have met in Switzerland. Rooms are beautifully furnished, with well-equipped bathrooms; the front-facing rooms all have a large balcony with deckchairs, while at the other end is a fully-equipped kitchenette. Breakfast is a buffet of a high standard. The hotel has a lovely garden restaurant and this was used all day long. Really excellent cakes are made on the premises. The hotel's only snags: no separate lounge for guests, and bedside reading lamps badly placed." (*Richard Pinner; warmly endorsed by Angela and David Stewart*) The owners are awaiting planning permission to build a new bar area, perhaps rectifying the need for more public space for guests.

Open 20 Dec–10 Apr, 21 May–23 Oct. Restaurant closed Mon.
Rooms 1 suite, 12 double – 10 with bath and shower, 3 with shower, all with telephone, radio, TV and mini-bar; many with balcony; 6 with kitchenette.
Facilities Restaurant, grill room, breakfast room; sun terrace. Garden with restaurant and children's play area. Winter sports, heated swimming pool, tennis, walking, climbing, fishing etc nearby. English spoken.
Location Turn left off road from Spiez and Thun, near the Oeschinensee chairlift. Hotel is quietly situated. Parking.
Restriction Not suitable for ♿.
Credit cards Access, Diners, Visa.
Terms B&B 42–70 Sfrs; dinner, B&B 60–90 Sfrs. Set lunch 12–17 Sfrs, dinner 18–26 Sfrs; full alc 32 Sfrs. Reduced rates for children; special menus.

KLOSTERS 7250 Graubünden — Map 14

Hotel Chesa Grischuna

Tel (083) 4.22.22
Telex 853348 CHESA

In the centre of this busy resort, an attractive old-style hotel with lots of mellow character, but nicely modernised: bright rugs on polished floors, hand-woven bedspreads, etc. Rooms smallish but very clean; staff pleasant. Good food served by girls in local costume; lively ambience in the cellar-bar where locals and après-skiers meet. Open early June to mid-Apr. 26 rooms, all with bath and/or shower. Half board: double 170-360 Sfrs. No recent reports: please send some.

LACHEN 8853 Zürich **Map 14**

Hotel Bären *Tel* (055) 63.16.02
Marktstrasse 9

Pleasant traditional hotel in a pretty lakeside village 25 miles east of Zürich. Warm welcome, excellent food including breakfast, but some rooms very small. 16 rooms, most with bath or shower. Dinner, B&B double 68-75 Sfrs. More reports welcome.

LAUSANNE-JORAT 1000 Vaud **Map 14**

Hôtel-Restaurant Les Chevreuils *Tel* (021) 91.61.09
Route du Jorat 80
Vers-chez-les-Blanc

A stylishly converted hunting lodge, run by an Italian manager and his wife, with a garden in front and modern bedrooms in an annexe: it is in sub-alpine country about 1000 feet above Lake Geneva, outside Lausanne. It overlooks the lake and has a large elegant restaurant and garden patio. Two correspondents this year found the welcome on the cool side, but others have endorsed the entry: "Very good value. Rooms and baths spacious and clean, atmosphere quiet and elegant. Good provincial cooking on the set menu." And *a fortiori*: "Wonderful. Bliss. Everything a hotel should be. Service impeccable and dinner excellent." This follows up earlier praise: "Lovely walks, peace and quiet; a terrace shaded by chestnut trees for meals in front; good bourgeois cooking. Views to the range of mountains opposite; behind are rolling farmland and woods. Good bus connections to Lausanne in 30 minutes or so." (*S and S Pons, David Wurtzel, PB*)

Open All year.
Rooms 2 suites, 28 double, 1 single – all with bath or shower, telephone, radio, TV and mini-bar. 15 in annexe. 15 suitable for ♿.
Facilities Hall, salon, bar, bistro, restaurant; conference facilities. Large park with garden and children's play area. English spoken.
Location 8 km from Lausanne on Lausanne–Berne road. Take exit for Vers-chez-les-Blanc.
Credit cards All major cards accepted.
Terms [1987 rates] B&B: single 65-70 Sfrs, double 80-90 Sfrs; half-board 25 Sfrs per person added; full board 50 Sfrs added. Set meals 26-50 Sfrs.

MEGGEN 6045 Lucerne **Map 14**

Hotel Sonnegg *Tel* (041) 37.21.64

Just east of Lucerne, beside its lovely lake, the *Sonnegg* is brought to the Guide this year by regulars who have stayed there often: "Don't expect great luxury, but this is a good family hotel, popular and busy, with good service and modern comfort combined with Swiss rustic touches. Most bedrooms look towards the lake and are quiet; the railway is near, but not noisy. Good coffee shop-cum-*Stübli*; excellent restaurant, where you can give the children pizzas and salad in one part, and eat delicious fresh lake-fish dishes (not cheap) in another. The helpful staff will baby-listen or even supervise our teenage sons. There is a small park on the lake's edge." (*Ann Carr and Martin McKeown*)

Open All year. Restaurant closed Sun, and Mon lunch.
Rooms 18 double – 9 with bath, shower and TV.
Facilities Lift. Bar, restaurant. English spoken.
Location On lake Lucerne, 5 km E of Lucerne towards Rigi, Gotthard on old road.
Credit cards All major cards accepted.
Terms B&B: single 50–55 Sfrs, double 80–95 Sfrs. Set lunch/dinner 12–35 Sfrs; full alc 30 Frs. Reduced rates for children under 6.

MURTEN 3280 Fribourg — Map 14

Le Vieux Manoir Au Lac — *Tel* (037) 71.12.83
Meyriez — *Telex* 942026

Le Vieux Manoir sits on the outskirts of Murten (Morat in French), a charming medieval ramparted city built by the Zähringers. "In the 'expensive-but-worth-it' category, this hotel on the shores of Lac Morat affords lovely views, including the vineyards on the opposite side of the lake. The rooms are large and tastefully decorated, well furnished in period style. Our room was almost a lounge with additional bedroom area, bathroom and separate toilet. Most rooms overlook the lake. The staff are pleasant, friendly and professional. Breakfasts were of the Germanic style, even though Murten is just into the French-speaking zone. They take our prize for the best Swiss breakfasts ever, with freshly-squeezed and peeled fruit, proper muesli, real jams and excellent coffee served in a fabulously decorated room overlooking the lake. The cooking, presentation and service at dinner were well up to the standards one would expect from this type of establishment. Excellent wine list." (*Iain and Liz Elliott*)

Open All year except mid-Dec–mid-Feb.
Rooms 5 suites, 14 double, 4 single – all with bath and/or shower, telephone and radio; TV for hire.
Facilities Lift. Lounge, TV room, restaurant, veranda, terrace restaurant; conference facilities. Lakeside garden, beach, swimming and fishing. English spoken.
Location 1 km SE of Murten right on road to Avenches.
Credit cards Amex, Diners, Visa.
Terms B&B: single 80-110 Sfrs, double 150-230 Sfrs, suite 290-320 Sfrs; dinner, B&B 50 Sfrs per person added. Full alc 70 Sfrs. Reduced rates for children sharing parents' room; special meals.

NEUHAUSEN 8212 Schaffhausen — Map 14

Hotel Bellevue — *Tel* (053) 2.21.21
Bad Bahnhofstrasse 17

Just two kilometres from the attractive medieval town of Schaffhausen are the Rhine Falls, not the highest waterfalls in Europe but the most powerful, and 500 feet wide. Here the *Bellevue* is aptly named and splendidly situated: "Its position is breathtaking. Our bedroom overlooked the falls. The hotel staff were pleasant and everything was well appointed." "We had good large rooms and dinner in a splendid lofty dining room with spectacular views. Dinner was a splendid meal with lots of choice and breakfast was cooked." (*PS*) One reader this year was less impressed by the food and ambience. We should welcome more reports.

Open All year, except 24 Dec–26 Jan.
Rooms 24 double, 3 single – 13 with bath, 7 with shower, all with telephone, radio and mini-bar.
Facilities Lift. Lounge, restaurants; functions room. Large garden with terrace. English spoken.
Location By the Rhine on outskirts of Neuhausen, 2 km SW of Schaffhausen. Parking.
Credit cards Access, Amex, Visa.
Terms [1987 rates] B&B: single 95 Sfrs, double 160 Sfrs. Alc meals 50 Sfrs. Reductions for children's meals.

NYON 1260 Vaud — Map 14

Hôtel du Clos de Sadex — *Tel* (022) 61.28.31

A dignified creeper-covered house on Lac Léman, formerly the home of Major and Madame Louis de Tscharner, who now run it as a hotel. The atmosphere of the aristocratic family whose seat it was (and is) is carefully preserved in the furnishing of the public rooms and the restaurant. Beautiful lakeside garden, with breakfast and lunch served on the terrace overlooking the lake and mountains. Our most recent report: "We thought the room expensive, but the hotel is only 23 kilometres from horrendously expensive Geneva and is used by visitors to the city. The food is acceptable but not exceptional: best stick to the plats du jour." Another reader had a ground-floor room in the annexe and found it to be superior to the main hotel: "I lived like a princess, in a huge beautifully-furnished room with its own entrance hall. First-floor rooms are smaller. Breakfast in bed was like old times. The maid was also very helpful." (*I and LE, KP*) The management tell us that the sitting room, restaurant and entrance hall have all been redone recently.

Open All year except Feb.
Rooms 13 double, 5 single – 12 with bath, 2 with shower, all with telephone. 5 in annexe 10 metres away. 2 ground-floor rooms.
Facilities Hall, salon with TV, restaurant; conference room. Gardens with terrace for meals, leading directly to lake (hotel has small harbour); swimming, boating, waterskiing. English spoken.
Location 1 km from Nyon towards Lausanne on lake road; the hotel is on right. Parking.
Credit cards All major cards accepted.
Terms [1987 rates] B&B: single 60-145 Sfrs, double 100-210 Sfrs; half board 40 Sfrs per person added. Set lunch/dinner 50 Sfrs; full alc 70 Sfrs. Reduced rates for children sharing parents' room; special meals.

PONTRESINA 7504 Graubünden — Map 14

Hotel Garni Chesa Mulin — *Tel* (082) 6.75.75

Via de Mulin

Non-skiers may be relieved to learn that Pontresina is an anagram of "inane sport": but that will not deter the thousands of addicts who make for the highly-reputed ski-slopes around this village-resort and adjacent St Moritz. Pontresina is the smaller and quieter place of the two, and its dry bracing air is less polluted. Here the *Chesa Mulin* is recommended as a hotel without a restaurant (but there are many good ones near by): "The breakfast room, like the bedrooms, is furnished beautifully in a modern Engadin style; all is light and airy. There is an embarrassingly large buffet from which you help yourself each morning. Bedrooms have comfortable beds and armchairs. The writing desk even has a small safe. Lights are sensibly arranged and you can read in bed. There is a lovely garden with a fine view. Led by Mr and Mrs Schmid, the staff are most polite, friendly and helpful." In summer there are walks in woods and across meadows and glaciers. (*Richard Pinner*)

Open Dec–Apr, June–Oct.
Rooms 23 double, 4 single – all with bath and/or shower, direct-dial telephone, radio and mini-bar; TV on request. 1 room (with bath) specially designed for ♿.
Facilities Lift. Lounge, bar, TV room; breakfast room, sauna, solarium; terrace. Garden. English spoken.
Location Central; turn off main road towards station. Garage and parking.
Credit cards All major cards accepted.
Terms B&B: single 70-95 Sfrs, double 114-170 Sfrs. 1-week bookings (Sat–Sat) preferred in winter; ski packages in winter low season. Reduced rates for children sharing parents' room. (No restaurant).

Grand Hotel Kronenhof *Tel* (082) 6.01.11
Telex 74488

Utterly palatial, Pontresina's only five-star hotel is first glimpsed sitting regally behind its wrought iron gates and courtyard. "The lounge just inside the door is rather jaded Edwardiana," writes a visitor, "but persevere because it is a very comfortable hotel with really excellent service. On our arrival we were brought glasses of orange juice – a very nice touch. Our climbing boots were cleaned within an hour of putting them outside our bedroom and nothing was too much trouble for the staff. We had large bedrooms and the whole hotel is very spacious. Nice dining room with excellent food. And the hotel has a very much better garden than most Swiss hotels." (*C Smith*)

Open 18 Dec–8 Apr, 18 June–18 Sept.
Rooms 9 suites, 65 double, 46 single – 92 with bath and shower, 4 with shower only, all with telephone, radio and mini-bar; TV on request.
Facilities Salon, library, 2 TV rooms, bar, dining room, public restaurant; indoor swimming pool, bowling. Large grounds with swimming pool, 2 tennis courts and ice rink. English spoken.
Location Central. Parking.
Restriction Not suitable for ♿.
Credit cards All major cards accepted.
Terms Dinner, B&B: single 120-200 Sfrs, double 220-380 Sfrs; suite 420-600 Sfrs. Set lunch 30-45 Sfrs, dinner 45-60 Sfrs; full alc from 50 Sfrs.

SAANENMÖSER 3777 Bern — Map 14

Hotel Hornberg *Tel* (030) 4.44.40

This typical chalet-style hotel stands alone at the foot of the Hornberg and looks out over the valley, beyond which lies neighbouring Gstaad. Run by the family von Siebenthal "who take a very friendly interest in their guests". "The bedrooms are extremely comfortable and well equipped. The food is imaginative, artistically presented and *hausgemacht* (home-made). The breakfast buffet is the best I've ever seen. Children are made welcome and are well provided for. One of the outstanding aspects of this hotel is the excursions run by the von Siebenthals at no extra charge: the trip may be to the family cheese-making hut high up in the mountains, a mountain lake or some remote local beauty spot." (*MJ Woodward*)

Open 28 May–6 Oct, Dec–Apr.
Rooms 7 suites, 20 double, 8 single – 27 with bath, 6 with shower, all with telephone and radio; some with balcony.
Facilities Lounge, bar with TV, children's playroom, restaurant, dining room; terrace. Large garden, indoor and outdoor swimming-pool, sauna. Winter sports. Trips, barbecues, picnics etc organised for guests. English spoken.
Location 20 km N of Gstaad.
Restriction Not suitable for ♿.
Credit cards Amex, Diners, Visa.
Terms Dinner, B&B: single 75-130 Sfrs, double 150-300 Sfrs; full board 7 Sfrs per person added. Set lunch 17-23 Sfrs, dinner 30-40 Sfrs; full alc 45-55 Sfrs. Reduced rates for children; special meals.

ST-LUC 3961 Valais — Map 14

Hôtel Bella Tola et St-Luc

Tel (027) 65.14.44
Telex 472094 PONT

Long popular with Guide readers, this venerable hostelry stands in a mountain village high up the slopes of a sunny valley west of Zermatt. It dates from 1859, when it could be reached only by mule-track, and for four generations it has been owned and run by the Pont family. "The sight of sunrise over the Matterhorn while breakfasting in bed" is one visitor's special memory. Others speak of the "beautifully furnished cottage-style rooms" and value for money. A distinguished musician writes: "We cannot praise this hotel enough. M. Pont is a most efficient and charming young man. Excellent food – the helpings at table were more than generous – lovely rooms and good and willing service. Blissfully quiet, and the reception rooms furnished in perfect taste. We hope to return this year." (*Louis Kentner, M and M Peretz, I and L Elliott*) One visitor warns prospective guests with vertigo that the hotel can only be reached by a very winding and steep road.

Open June–Sept, Dec–Apr.
Rooms 28 double, 14 single – 21 with bath and/or shower.
Facilities Lift. 3 salons (1 with TV), bar, restaurant, children's playroom; sauna. Garden, terrace. English spoken.
Location Coming from Sierre, at entrance to resort, on left.
Restriction Not suitable for ♿.
Credit cards Amex, Visa.
Terms [1987 rates] B&B 30–75 Sfrs; dinner, B&B 45–90 Sfrs. Set dinner 25 Sfrs. Low season 7-day package. Reduced rates for children; special meals.

ST MORITZ 7500 Graubünden — Map 14

Hotel Chesa Sur L'En

Tel (082) 3.31.44 and 3.64.74

"One of the most delightful and unusual hotels in the Alps, a surprising and welcome contrast to the rather styleless lavishness of some of the big

St Moritz hotels." So ran a recent report on this "archetypal Swiss chalet", very soigné but most reasonable in price for this swanky resort. This was one reader's introduction to it: "We glimpsed its upper storeys through the pines from the main road at St Moritz Bad. A side turning led across a tiny bridge over the river Inn (En). Up a steep winding drive deep with snow, a sharp turn, and facing you is a stone tower with great overhanging eaves topped by a glassed-in watch-tower and the Swiss flag. Steps to a massive front door opened into a stone-flagged entrance hall – and beyond more massive steps to a richly-panelled, ornately-carved and utterly superb main hall. We were warmly welcomed by the proprietor, Herr Schwarzenbach, who spoke good English, and did his own cooking." "The hotel is short on rooms with baths: it would be almost impossible to provide bathrooms throughout without destroying the proportions of most of the main bedrooms, though two more rooms have been given *en suite* bathrooms since last year, and two more *en suites* are planned. Meanwhile: "We had rooms right at the top in the watch tower which *did* include a bathroom and also had spectacular views on all four sides over the rooftops to the snow-clad mountains. Central heating was of venerable age and infirmity, but a mobile heater provided adequate back-up. The furniture here was basic, but other bedrooms had furniture to match the house, in Germanic proportions." The house was for some time the home of ex-king Faroukh during his exile. (*Adam Ruck, Angela and David Stewart*)

Open 15 Dec–20 Apr, 1 July–30 Oct.
Rooms 11 double, 2 single – 4 with bath and shower, 2 with shower; 5 with TV.
Facilities Hall, salon with TV, breakfast room, dining room; functions room. Ski run to hotel entrance. Winter sports, indoor swimming pool, sauna, tennis and squash courts, skating rink and riding nearby. English spoken.
Location In St Moritz Bad; 5 minutes by bus to St Moritz: Private parking.
Restriction Not suitable for ♿.
Credit cards All major cards accepted.
Terms B&B 43-90 Sfrs; dinner, B&B 66-113 Sfrs. Set dinner 29 Sfrs. Minimum stay of 14 days at Christmas/New Year. 50% reduction for children sharing parents' room; special meals on request.

SCHAFFHAUSEN 8200 — Map 14

Rheinhotel Fischerzunft — *Tel* (053) 5.32.81
Rheinquai 8 — *Telex* 897162 FZFT

This picturesque old town on the upper Rhine has some medieval streets and houses with painted and richly decorated facades. The Rhine Falls, Europe's most powerful waterfall, are close by. The *Fischerzunft* is a former fishermen's guildhouse converted into a chic restaurant-with-rooms. One visitor this year thought it "expensive, impersonal and not our cup of tea", but others have lavished more superlatives than ever. "Everything is perfect at this gem of a small hotel. Flowers everywhere. Our bedroom was the largest and most beautiful we have ever used, beating the *Dorchester*. Pale marigold silk walls, beds which had switches to raise and lower head and feet, marble coffee table, dining table with a large basket of fruit and box of chocolates. The loo had a warm water jet if you pressed one lever, a warm air jet if you pressed another. Marvellous views of the Rhine through the big windows. After all this bliss, it was quite endearing to find a chipped plate at dinner." This rave does not mention the food, but others have done so – "a must for the adventurous gourmet" – and *Gault Millau* continues to award two red *toques*. The owner/chef André Jaeger met his Chinese wife Doreen in Hong Kong, and the Chinese influence is apparent both in the delicate cuisine and in the decor (you take breakfast in the Chinese Room). "Dinner by soft candlelight." (*S and M Alexander; also Patrick J O'Donnell, Iain Elliott, and others*)

Open All year, except last week in Jan, first two weeks in Feb, 23 and 24 Dec.
Rooms 3 suites, 9 double – all with bath and/or shower, telephone, radio, TV and mini-bar.
Facilities 2 Lounges, card room, restaurant; conference facilities. Terrace for alfresco dining in summer. English spoken.
Location On banks of Rhine, 5 minutes' walk from centre (all windows triple-glazed). Parking.
Restriction Not suitable for ♿.
Credit cards All major cards accepted.
Terms B&B: single occupancy 110–180 Sfrs, double 150–220 Sfrs, suite 260–305 Sfrs. Set lunch/dinner 88–118 Sfrs; full alc 80 Sfrs. Children under 6 sharing parents' room free.

SCHÖNRIED-GSTAAD 3778 Bern — Map 14

Hotel Alpin nova — *Tel* (030) 8.33.11
Hauptstrasse — *Telex* 922230

Just outside glossy Gstaad, a smart new hotel in traditional Swiss chalet style. Many bedrooms very large, with luxurious bathrooms and balconies overlooking Bernese Oberland. Intimate dining-rooms, with varied en pension *menus. Heated swimming pool, sauna, fitness centre, children's playroom, dancing, videos, conference facilities, etc. Open 15 Dec–15 Apr, 15 May–5 Nov. 64 rooms, all with bath, some with shower. Half board 82-160 Sfrs. More reports please.*

SCHWANDEN 3657 Bern — Map 14

Gasthof-Restaurant Rothorn — *Tel* (033) 51.11.86

A mountain village high above the resorts of Sigriswil and Gunten, facing across the beautiful lake of Thun to the Bernese Alps. Here much enthusiasm is still generated by the *Rothorn*, a big brown chalet amid meadows, backed by pinewoods. "A splendid *Gasthof*," is one report this year. "Our host and hostess, the Amstutzes, were delightful, the food was excellent, and our large and virtually new room was the nicest in which we have ever stayed, with a magnificent view of the Alps." "A fairytale come true. The hotel is in a quiet location, the only noise being the cow bells. Excellent food, both in quality and quantity, including traditional Swiss breakfast. Friendly staff. In the bar, local yodellers yodelled just for us." Others too comment on the musicians in the restaurant frequented by locals. (*Janet and Carl Campbell, Paul and Jude Spencer-White*)

Open All year, except Nov. Restaurant closed Mon.
Rooms 13 double – 2 with bath, 8 with shower; some with balcony. 4 in annexe.
Facilities Lounge, TV room, dining room, restaurant with occasional folk music. Overlooking mountains and lake; tennis, water sports and ski schools nearby. English spoken.

Location 20 minutes NW of Interlaken, 15 minutes NE of Thun.
Credit cards None accepted.
Terms B&B: single 38–49 Sfrs, double 62–94 Sfrs; dinner, B&B: single 53–64 Sfrs, double 92–124 Sfrs; full board: single 63–74 Sfrs, double 112–144 Sfrs. Set lunch/dinner 12–23 Sfrs. Children under 6 sharing parents' room half price, 6–12 30% reduction.

SILS-MARIA 7514 Graubünden — Map 14

Edelweiss Hotel — *Tel* (082) 4.52.22
Dorfstrasse — *Telex* 74835

This village-resort in the upper Engadin valley contains a small Nietzsche museum, in the house where the philosopher used to spend his summers. And today the supermen and supergirls of sport and high society frequent the ski-slopes and smart cafés of nearby St Moritz. Sils-Maria, though less grand, is also quite elegant, and lies between two crystal-blue lakes in this, one of the loveliest of Swiss mountain valleys, where the curious Romansch language is spoken. The *Edelweiss*, a sedate and confident four-starrer, dates from 1875, though most of the building is more modern and all of it is modernised. It continues to be popular with readers: "Friendly staff, excellent food," runs a 1987 report; earlier ones singled out the breakfasts, and the "beautiful dining room". Good skiing, and good walking too in a valley that in summer is filled with wild flowers. (*Lord Vernon, Jean Rowntree, and others*)

Open Mid-June–mid-Oct, 20 Dec–early Apr.
Rooms 54 double, 24 single – all with bath and shower, telephone and radio. 28 in annexe linked to main building.
Facilities Salon, TV room, children's games room, rôtisserie/bar with pianist, dancing in winter, bar/restaurant. Garden with tables and chairs. Winter sports. English spoken.
Location On edge of village which is 8 km SW of St Moritz. Large car park, garages.
Credit cards Access, Visa.
Terms B&B: single 80-140 Sfrs, double 160-190 Sfrs. Half board: single 95-155 Sfrs, double 190-320 Sfrs. Set lunch 22 Sfrs, dinner 35 Sfrs; full alc 55-60 Sfrs. Cross-country skiing course in winter, surfing and other courses in summer. Reduced rates for children on request; special meals.

SOGLIO 7649 Graubünden — Map 14

Hotel Stüa Granda — *Tel* (082) 4.16.66

This high mountain village is reached by a steep and narrow road from the main valley highway running from St-Moritz to Chiavenna in Italy. "The delightful young owners, the Nasses, made our stay most pleasant at the *Stüa Granda*," runs a report this year on this "impeccably maintained, totally unpretentious and charming little hotel". An earlier view: "Time seems to stand still here. Chestnut trees surround the village and the air is unusually crisp and clean. The sunny terrace restaurant is a favourite meeting place for hikers and the fare is hearty and fresh. Guest rooms (some small) are beautifully furnished. High-beamed ceilings, lace curtains, soft pine, and heavenly eiderdown quilts. Every room is different and the aroma of fresh bread and local specialities such as bundner gerstensuppe fill the air. A romantic hotel for those who love out of the way places in beautiful settings." Other recent visitors commend the "superb" restaurant, the spotless rooms and magnificent views. (*Richard H Proctor, Bill and Kathy Reece, and others*)

Open All year except 10 Nov–10 Dec.
Rooms 31 double – 23 with bath; 14 with telephone and radio; some with balcony. 22 in annexe, *Pension Soglina*.
Facilities 2 sitting rooms, restaurant. Garden terrace. English spoken.
Location On edge of village, just N of route N3 between Chiavenna (to W) and Maloja pass (to E). Nearby parking.
Credit cards None accepted.
Terms [1987 rates] Double room from 62 Sfrs. Other prices on application. 10% reduction for children under 12; special meals.

TRIESENBERG 9497 Liechtenstein — Map 14

Hotel Kulm — *Tel* (075) 2.87.77

Though tiny, Liechtenstein is far from twee, but very modern and go-ahead: the municipally-owned *Kulm*, though also small, has been making a strong bid to attract the business and conference trade, so you might be sharing its casual, friendly charm with 50 neat-suited executives. Perhaps this deterred our readers, who were silent for two years about the *Kulm*, so it lost its place in the 1987 Guide. But visitors this year have again found it charming and very clean, in a quiet village with "breathtaking" alpine views. The food is still good, though one report mentions "somewhat arrogant" waiters. "Our balcony overlooked the curving Rhine valley, with mountains beyond. Food was very good, in a casual restaurant. The peace of farming country was enjoyable after the hassle of Vaduz." Local skiing and good summer walking. (*Hervey C Merrill, Jean Dennerline*)

Open All year.
Rooms 7 suites, 12 double, 1 single – all with telephone, radio, TV and baby-listening. Some ground-floor rooms suitable for ♿.
Facilities Lift. Hall with TV, lounge, bar, restaurant; *Stübe*; conference/functions facilities; terrace. English spoken.
Location 5 km S of Vaduz. Hotel is central but quiet; parking.
Credit cards Access, Amex, Visa.
Terms B&B: single 60 Sfrs, double 80-90 Sfrs, suite 110-125 Sfrs; dinner B&B: single 75 Sfrs, double 110-120 Sfrs. Set lunch 12 Sfrs; full alc 26 Sfrs. Reduced rates for children; special meals.

VEVEY 1800 Vaud — Map 14

Les Trois Couronnes — *Tel* (021) 51.30.05

49 rue d'Italie — *Telex* 451148

Complete with lakeside promenade and a number of exclusive girls' finishing schools, Vevey is a smart and busy resort on the northern shore of Lac Léman. In the centre stands the five-star late-Victorian *Trois Couronnes* ("one of the 'great' hotels of Switzerland," said one visitor): it is old-fashioned but in a fine position overlooking the lake. The rooms have large French windows and balconies facing the lake. A recent report: "We were welcomed graciously by the staff with a basket of fruit in our spacious, quiet room furnished with antiques and a comfortable bed. Our balcony was draped with wistaria and overlooked fountains and flowers on the terrace below. Public rooms are comfortable and elegant – carved, gilded, marbled and with an abundance of fine furniture and fresh flowers. Food was excellent." Others too have praised the efficient and courteous service, the food in the beautiful Louis XV-style dining room, and even the breakfasts ("11 different jams to choose from"). (*Sally R Burt; also B and R Kenyon Glover*) More reports please.

Open All year.
Rooms 7 suites, 41 double, 27 single – all with bath and shower, telephone, radio and TV; baby-listening on request.
Facilities Lift. Salons, TV room, bar, restaurant; conference facilities; large terrace with open restaurant. Pianist several evenings a week. Beach, lake, swimming, fishing nearby. English spoken.
Location Central, but quietly situated. Parking in courtyard.
Restriction Not suitable for ♿.
Credit cards All major cards accepted.
Terms [1987 rates] B&B: single 135-200 Sfrs, double 230-350 Sfrs; dinner, B&B: 40 Sfrs per person added; full board 75 Sfrs added. Set lunch/dinner 50-60 Sfrs. Reduced rates for children; special meals on request.

VILLARS 1884 Vaud — Map 14

Hotel du Golf et Marie-Louise

Tel (025) 35.24.76
Telex 456212 HOML

In this popular French-Swiss mountain resort, a sizeable and excellent four-star hotel in traditional style (chalet-like buildings, rustic decor). Rooms in new annexe are large and have balconies with mountain views. Service friendly, good food including breakfast buffet. Tennis, ping-pong, putting green, garden; piscine *planned for 1989. Open 12 Dec–10 Apr, 29 Apr–30 Oct. 62 rooms, most with bath. B&B double 200 Sfrs. Set meals 30-48 Sfrs. New nomination: more reports please.*

VITZNAU 6354 Lucerne — Map 14

Hotel Floralpina

Tel (041) 83.13.86

A handsome modern lakeside hotel just outside Vitznau, which is one of the more elegant resorts on Lake Lucerne: for a really stunning view, take Europe's oldest mountain rack-railway (1871) up to the Rigi-Kulm summit. "Along the lake, at Weggis, under an oak-tree there, Mark Twain was moved to write, 'this is the most charming spot'." So begins a letter nominating the *Floralpina* this year. "So magnificently situated that a millionaire could not buy this view. Huge grounds, direct access to swimming in the lake (private beach), and unbeatable views from the terrace, where you can eat. Some of the largest double bedrooms one can find these days in Europe, and it's well worth paying extra for a lakeview room. A limited menu with good solid Swiss meals; nice cream cakes and good cheeseboard." (*WP Jaspert*)

Open 15 Apr-15 Oct.
Rooms 6 suites, 49 double, 9 single – all with shower and WC.
Facilities Lounges, bar, restaurant, TV room; indoor whirl pool, sauna. Terrace, park, private beach.
Location 2 km S of Vitznau on Brunnen road.

Credit cards Amex, Diners, Visa.
Terms B&B 48 Sfrs. Set lunch/dinner 13 Sfrs; full alc 25 Sfrs. Reduced rates and special meals for children.

WEGGIS 6353 Lucerne — Map 14

Hotel Beau Rivage — *Tel* (041) 93.14.22, *Telex* 862982

Weggis is a delightful resort some 30 minutes by road or 45 by steamer from Lucerne; other lake pleasures are easily accessible, as are the heights of Rigi, served by Weggis's funicular. The *Beau Rivage* has a choice position right on the lake, a few minutes' walk from the quay, with its own garden and swimming pool. It continues to be very popular, as witness reports this year and last: "Food beautifully prepared, rooms very comfortable, friendly personal attention by the owners, the Geerings." "The rooms are lovely with pleasant lake views and the personal were friendly and very helpful. We enjoyed the boat trip to Lucerne for shopping and the return to this lakeside haven." (*Sylvia Hollis, Frank Mattinson, Ronald S McNeill, Cathy Bassiouni, and others*) Some package tours, out of season only.

Open End Mar–mid-Oct.
Rooms 5 suites, 31 double, 10 single – all with bath and/or shower, telephone, radio; TV in suites, in rooms on request (5 Sfrs). Some rooms suitable for ♿.
Facilities Lift. Hall, 2 lounges, TV room, bar, garden room, restaurant; lakeside terrace; band twice a week. Garden with swimming pool, beach, fishing. English spoken.
Location 20 km E of Lucerne; on lake, near quay. Garages and parking.
Credit cards All major cards accepted.
Terms B&B: single 75-110 Sfrs, double 120-200 Sfrs, suite 260-290 Sfrs; half board: single 95-135 Sfrs, double 170-250 Sfrs, suite 310-350 Sfrs; full board: single 115-155 Sfrs, double 210-290 Sfrs, suite 350-390 Sfrs. Set lunch 36 Sfrs, dinner 42 Sfrs; full alc 60 Sfrs. Reduced rates for children.

WORB 3076 Bern — Map 14

Gasthof Zum Löwen — *Tel* (031) 83.23.03
Enggisteinstrasse 3

In a village just east of Berne, a Romantik hotel, small and spruce, run by the same family for 11 generations. Large, comfortable rooms; restaurant much admired locally; jovial staff. Closed July. 14 rooms, most with bath or shower. B&B double 72-120 Sfrs. No recent reports: please send some.

ZERMATT 3920 Valais — Map 14

Hôtel-Garni Metropol — *Tel* (028) 67.32.31, *Telex* 427137

More praise again this year for this unpretentious, medium-sized family establishment in the centre of the town on the banks of the fast-flowing Vispa. "We had a lovely room facing south with a clear view of the Matterhorn, and the Taugwalder family were just as welcoming and helpful as on our first visit three years ago." A reader who has been going to Zermatt since 1948 reports: "The hotel remains as good as ever, with splendid rooms (sensible beds, reading lights, spacious cupboards, well-equipped bathrooms, glass-topped writing desk, comfortable easy chairs); the constant rush of the river next door – so soothing at night; and, directing it all tirelessly, the friendly Taugwalder family." The lively bar and the buffet breakfasts are also praised. The best bedrooms are the dozen on the south side, each with a private bathroom and a roomy balcony facing the Matterhorn. Main meals are available by order only, but in the evening these can include meat dishes such as veal in cream and mushroom sauce, much approved. (*Byron A Eliashof, Alex and Beryl Williams, Neil and Jacqueline Britton, and others*)

Open 1 Dec–10 May, 10 June–20 Oct.
Rooms 20 double, 4 single – 16 with bath and shower, 4 with shower, all with telephone, radio and TV.
Facilities Lift. Lounge, bar, TV room, dining room. Garden and terrace.
Location Central; near station. Hotel porter will fetch you. (No cars in Zermatt.)
Credit cards All major cards accepted.
Terms B&B: single 52-87 Sfrs, double 95-174 Sfrs.

Hotel Nicoletta *Tel* (028) 66.11.51
Telex 472108

This modern four-star hotel in the centre of Zermatt has one regular devotee amongst our readers who finds it "much the best hotel we have stayed at in some 35 years' skiing, with almost everything for a middle-aged couple". Last year it was dropped from the Guide for lack of recent reports, either from him or others, but now he has again sprung to its defence: "I have just spent a fortnight there and confirm my past recommendation. The hotel has now moved up-market and so have its prices (I noticed at least four very well-dressed women, including my wife). It has been redecorated in lighter colours, with a large mural in the dining-room which looks rather nice from a distance but less so closer to (no one could tell me what it depicted). The quality of the food has improved and so has the service. Friendly middle-aged music in the rooftop bar continues (you can dance to a piano there without losing your hearing), and the lighting in the bedrooms has been made more tasteful. The situation cannot be bettered: quiet at night yet close to the main shopping street. Oddly, the cheaper north-facing rooms have a more interesting view than those facing south with a balcony and the Matterhorn. In sum, a very comfortable hotel which sets out to look modern and not dreadfully 'olde-worlde'." (*AV Chute*) Could we hear whether others agree with Mr Chute?

Open 28 Nov–10 Apr and 4 Jun–2 Oct.
Rooms 7 suites, 52 double – all with bath and/or shower, telephone, radio and TV. Some with balcony.
Facilities Lifts. Lounge, bar, childrens' playroom, restaurants; conference facilities. Piano player nightly in rooftop bar. Swimming pool, sauna, solarium. Tennis in summer, winter sports. English spoken.
Location Central (no cars in Zermatt).
Restriction Not suitable for ♿.
Credit cards Amex, Diners, Visa.
Terms [1987 rates] B&B: 78-120 Sfrs; half board 30 Sfrs per person added; full-board 55 Sfrs added. Reduced rates for children.

ZUOZ 7524 Graubünden — Map 14

Posthotel Engiadina

Tel (082) 7.10.21
Telex 852100

Zuoz is a summer resort in the Engadin, in the Inn valley that leads north-west from St Moritz. It is a picture-postcard little village in true Engadin style (barns are built into the houses and many are illustrated with wall murals). "Switzerland at its best," says one reader. Here the five-storey pink-fronted *Engiadina* is outwardly sedate-looking but much less formal within: "A very warm welcome, beautifully decorated rooms with every convenience, and marvellous food especially the sumptuous breakfast. Although over 100 years old, the hotel has been faithfully restored by its owners, the Arquints, he a local architect (his family has lived in Zuoz for 600 years). There was a friendly house-party atmosphere among the guests. Nice small pool." (*Maryanne Menk*) More reports please.

Open Dec–Apr, June–Oct.
Rooms 1 suite, 30 double, 9 single – all with bath or shower, telephone and radio. TV on request.
Facilities Lift. Lounge, 2 bars, 2 restaurants, ballroom; terrace. Garden with swimming pool, sauna. Tennis and winter sports nearby. English spoken.
Location 10 m NE of St Moritz. Hotel is central. Parking.
Credit cards Amex, Diners, Visa.
Terms B&B: single 82-109 Sfrs, double 133-188 Sfrs, suite 170-208 Sfrs; dinner, B&B: single 105-132 Sfrs, double 176-234 Sfrs. Set lunch/dinner 28-38 Sfrs. Golf, walking, skiing packages. Reduced rates and special meals for children.

Hotel-Confiserie Klarer

Tel (082) 7.13.21

"What a charming little inn! Spotlessly clean, efficient, friendly with good local food and marvellous service." "The house is beautifully and imaginatively converted and we had a lovely room with bathroom and view." "The whole atmosphere of the house with its unobtrusive efficiency behind the pleasing, relaxed comfort is notable. It is difficult not to be lyrical about a stay here – one must go back." Those are some recent reports. Not everyone thinks very highly of the cooking, but all enjoy the pastries and chocolates made by Herr Klarer and his son and sold in the shop below the hotel. There's been one complaint of early morning cowbells – "but remember," says one reader, "this is a working village, so, while peaceful, allow for country noises."

Open All year, except May and Nov, and Tue in Jul, Sept and Oct.
Rooms 14 double, 4 single – 3 with bath and shower, 10 with shower only, all with telephone and radio.
Facilities Lift. Lounge, café restaurant. English spoken.
Location 10 m NE of St Moritz. Hotel is central. Parking.
Credit cards Access, Visa.
Terms B&B: single 50-65 Sfrs, double 90-130 Sfrs; dinner, B&B: single 80-95 Sfrs, double 150-190 Sfrs. Set lunch 30 Sfrs, dinner 35 Sfrs; full alc 50 Sfrs. Reduced rates for children.

> Set dinner refers to a fixed price meal (which may have ample, limited or no choice on the menu). Full alc is the hotel's own estimated price per person of a three-course meal taken à la carte, with a half-bottle of house wine.

ZÜRICH 8001 — Map 14

Hotel Florhof — *Tel* (01) 47.44.70
Florhofgasse 4 — *Telex* 817364

We are still receiving satisfied approval of this well-run, friendly little hotel, in a 16th-century patrician's house with small garden; meals can be taken on the terrace in fine weather. It is in a quiet residential street near the *Kunsthaus*, theatre and university. The music Conservatoire is next door, so you may have Bach fugues and violin lessons for breakfast. (*KJ Salway and others*)

Open All year.
Rooms 23 double, 10 single – all with bath and/or shower, telephone and radio; TV on request. Some ground-floor rooms.
Facilities Lift. Small salon, restaurant. Garden with terrace for lunch and light refreshments in fine weather. English spoken.
Location Near *Kunsthaus*, theatre and university. Parking.
Restriction Not suitable for ♿.
Credit cards All major cards accepted.
Terms B&B: single 110–140 Sfrs, double 165–195 Sfrs. Set lunch 25–35 Sfrs, dinner 30–40 Sfrs; full alc 55–70 Sfrs. Reduced rates and special meals for children.

" 'Drenched with' and 'smothered by' are two of Mr . . .'s favourite phrases, and they sum up his hotel. We were almost smothered by his effusive attentions and our appetites were drenched with the amount of cream in the cooking. This over-the-top, ponced-up, dollified and chi-chi flower-bedecked cuisine contrasts strangely with the under-the-top state of the bedrooms. My room (5′ by 10′) must have been converted from the end of a corridor. Every time I passed between the radiator and the bed to get to the bathroom I grazed my ankles. The windows were frosted over, and no wonder: they looked out on a dustbin and beer crate alley."

Turkey

AYASOFYA PANSIYONLARI , ISTANBUL

ADANA **Map 17**

Zaimoğlu Oteli *Tel* (711) 133.66
Özler Caddesi 72 *Telex* 62875 ZATE

"The city is fat on the fertility of its surrounding plain. Cotton is the most lucrative crop; the man in a good suit you see being chauffeured along the broad central boulevard is, as likely as not, a 'pamuk kralı' (cotton king), or perhaps an executive from one of the myriad high-powered commercial concerns that have been attracted to the area in the last few decades like frogs to a swamp. Visiting hot shots have their tastes pandered to in almost-international-class hotels: the *Divan*, the *Büyük Sürmeli*, or now this place – with its pastel interiors, air-conditioning, elevator-muzak and fixed staff-smiles à la *Hilton* – which made the canny move of opening last year straight opposite the *Bükük Sürmeli* and charging a tiny fraction of its prices (£24 for a palatial double room in April 1987). While such a hotel might not find itself hugged to the very bosom of this Guide's philosophies, it is worth including now for the prospect of a regular night's sleep in a hot, dusty, boisterous city, in which many a gloomy sty has similar rates. Of course, as soon as the establishment catches on, inflation will make it less interesting. Your dilemma is that by visiting the place, you will hasten the process." (*Jeremy Round*)

Open All year
Rooms 2 apartments, 6 suites, 69 rooms – all with bath, telephone, TV, video and mini-bar.
Facilities Bar, restaurant; night-club; hairdresser, gift shop.
Location 10 minutes' walk from main boulevard. Garage parking.
Credit card Visa.
Terms On application.

ALANYA Antalya — Map 17

Hotel Güneş — *Tel* (3231) 1918

A small bed-and-breakfast hotel beside the attractive sandy beach of Alanya "where one just lies in the sun and bakes all day". The building has a distinctive character, with an abundance of pine wood. The pleasant owner and his staff contribute greatly to its friendly ambience. Breakfast and cool drinks are served on a shady terrace in front, or in a new breakfast room and bar on the top floor. Most rooms have a balcony, and they all face the sea. The beach at Alanya is well equipped and the town itself offers many water sports, shops and inexpensive restaurants." (*RW; confirmed this year by F Daley*) We should welcome more reports.

Open Dates not known.
Rooms 21 – all with bath or shower; most with balcony.
Facilities Bar, breakfast room; terrace. Beach with water sports.
Location On the beach at Alanya.
Terms On application.

ANAMUR Akdeniž — Map 17

Anahan Hotel — *Tel* (7571) 1045

"Although there are one or two reasonable resort motels on the long beach ten minutes' drive from Anamur, until now the town itself has had nowhere at all in which to stay where one might have felt happy about walking barefoot in the rooms or even undressing fully before bed. 1987 was this hotel's first season. A visit shortly after opening seemed promising. The rooms are simple but clean and all with showers. Service is enthusiastic, especially in the echoing barn of a restaurant where there is that rarest of Turkish humankind – a waitress. Dust and lack of maintenance may soon play their part in reducing the *Anahan* to the standard of its local competitors, and in the searingly hot summers (this is Turkey's southernmost bulge), the effort of getting from here to the beach, almost perfectly preserved seaside castle, and spooky ruins of Ancient Anameurium, may put off all but the most devoted loiterer around tawdry Eastern centres, but in April 1987 at least, the hotel showed that it could provide a tranquil break in a gruelling area." (*JR*)

Open All year.
Rooms Not known.
Facilities Restaurant.
Location In town centre. Anamur is on S coast.
Terms On application.

ANKARA — Map 17

Bulvar Palas Oteli
Atatürk Bulvari 141

Tel (41) 134.21.80
Telex 42613 BLVD

To establish the right mood, catch a ferry from the Galata bridge across the dusk-reddening Bosphorus to Haydarpaşa (Istanbul's Asian rail terminus); board the nine o'clock sleeper with its French-polished panelling and comfortable sofas; watch the lights along the shore of the Gulf of Nicea as you are served a four-course table d'hôte meal at a white-clothed table in the smoky, noisy dining car; return to your compartment where the bed will have been made up with starched linen sheets and soft blankets; wake again – after a night of rattles and stops – to a glass of tea at seven. Take a cab to this hotel and then breakfast off fat black olives and rose-petal jam in the flaking magnificence of the dining room under a dusty chandelier. The rest of Ankara may try to impress with its modernity, but the *Bulvar Palas* sails through still in the fifties, with its big bedrooms, solid plumbing and comfortable beds. Staff are efficient and abundant, meals are reasonably priced and of fair quality, but it is the atmosphere that is the thing: a "B" movie remake of Istanbul's *Pera Palas*. (That delightful 1986 account endorsed this year by *Mrs Leslie Purdy* who enjoyed that very journey.)

Open All year.
Rooms 177 – 167 with bath or shower, all with telephone, radio, TV, mini-bar and air-conditioning.
Facilities Lift. Lounge, restaurant; conference facilities; hairdressing salon.
Location Central, in area called "Ministries". Next door to Belgian Ministry. Parking.
Credit cards All major cards accepted.
Terms On application.

Keykan Oteli
Fevzi Çakmak Sokak 12

Tel (41) 230.21.95
Telex 44134 KEYN

A friendly modern medium-priced hotel on a quiet side-street near Kizilay (one of the city's hubs). Its brochure promises Selcuk-style architecture, but with plastic pyramid ceiling lights and an undulating concrete garden. Furniture throughout is MFI *à la turque*: varnished light wood, orange carpets and mirrors in curvy plastic frames. Bedrooms have large wardrobes, limited drawer-space and you can forget bedtime reading unless you are standing by the washbasin in your well-equipped bathroom. Meals can be quite good, but one would not make a point of eating here. Rosto (baked meat with a tomato sauce) has been excellent. Westerners may have to ask if they want olives at breakfast. A suitable hotel for a short stay – time enough to explore the Hittite Museum, Gençlik Park, Roman citadel, Baths of Caracalla, Julian Column and Temple of Augustus. We badly need more reports.

Open All year.
Rooms 10 suites, 35 double, 5 single – all with bath or shower, telephone and radio; some with balcony.
Facilities Lift. Restaurant; conference facilities.
Location Central on quiet side street near Kizilay. Parking.
Terms On application.

ANTALYA **Map 17**

Talya Oteli *Tel* (311) 156.00
Fevzi Çakmak Caddesi *Telex* 56111 TATA

"When you have been travelling, it is wonderful to step into the cool luxury of the *Talya*, the good food, the kind staff." Thus a report this year on the city's most luxurious five-star hotel. It is just south of the old town and the splendid park where various fairs and exhibitions are held over the summer. The hotel is modern, tastefully and spaciously set out, and built right on the cliff top with a superb view across Antalya Bay. It is worth getting a room with the spectacular sea view. All have private bath, air-conditioning, and a balcony where one can have breakfast. There is no sandy beach but the hotel has carved its own patio at the base of the cliff, complete with changing rooms, showers, sunbeds and a bar. A lift goes down the side of the cliff to the beach direct from the pool. The food is very good, a mixture of Turkish and international. The restaurant is on the edge of the cliff bounded on three sides by the sea. Lunch can be taken here or else round the pool where there is a daily help-yourself buffet of delicious and beautifully presented food. Two or three evenings a week they also have special dinners around the pool which is lit up for the occasion. A reader this year also recommends the "tiny restaurants with tiny Turkish prices" behind the harbour. As for the *Talya's* far-from-tiny prices, we are told that they have more than doubled in the past year, after refurbishing. And you should get your room bookings confirmed in writing, or you may be shunted off elsewhere to "the worst hotel ever", as happened to one visitor this year.

Open All year.
Rooms 150 double – all with bath, shower, telephone, radio, TV, air-conditioning and balcony.
Facilities Lift. Lobby, 3 bars, 2 restaurants; conference facilities; nightclub, disco, casino; hairdresser. Large grounds with swimming pool, tennis court. Lift to beach patio with swimming area, changing rooms and bar; waterskiing, windsurfing, boating, sailing, skin-diving off rocky beach. English spoken.
Location On cliff overlooking Antalya Bay, south of Old Town.
Credit cards All major cards accepted.
Terms On application.

Turban Adalya Oteli *Tel* (311) 180.66
Kaleiçi Yat Limani *Telex* 56241 TBA

Antalya's famous harbour has recently been much restored, and it is now on its way to becoming a showplace resort. "Sleek yachts," we are told, "are moored alongside beautifully preserved Turkish houses with their dark wooden balconies and colourful tiled roofs. The *Turban Adalya* started life in 1869 as the branch office of a bank, and was later used as a warehouse. Eventually it was lovingly converted into the most individual small luxury hotel I have come across in Turkey. The refreshing sound of running water from the fountains in the atrium-patio greets you as you walk into the welcome coolness beyond the entrance steps. The charmingly decorated bedrooms lead off from upstairs galleries. There is a pleasant bar-terrace at the back overlooking the harbour, with another bar and an excellent restaurant on the top floor." Endorsing that earlier report, a reader this year points out that most rooms have no view. His suite was spacious and pleasant, but the toast for breakfast was stale. (*RW; also RSM, Mary P Purdy, and others*)

Open All year.
Rooms 2 suites, 26 double – all with bath and shower, telephone, radio, TV and air-conditioning.
Facilities Lounge, 2 bars, restaurant; patio.
Location Central; parking.
Credit cards Amex, Diners.
Terms On application.

ARSUZ Hatay — Map 17

Arsuz Turistik Oteli — *Tel* (881) 217.82
Uluçīnar,
Arsuz-Iskenderun

"Certainly the best resort-hotel on the eastern Mediterranean coast of Turkey, this clean white block sits like a docked liner on the shore of the tiny fishing village that locals still know as Arsuz (not a Turkish word) despite the Turkish State's having recently renamed it Uluçīnar (great plane tree). The Mistikoglu family have made here the weekend seaside retreat of wealthy Alexandretta (Iskenderun) and Antioch (Antakya). Bedrooms are sparsely furnished but well maintained; public rooms have a relaxed Mediterranean style; the broad paved terrace – with its palms, flower beds, globe lanterns, white wrought-iron balustrades and well-upholstered garden furniture – is worth the front cover of any tourist office hand-out. The brothers who host the operation are unforced charm itself and speak excellent English. Other staff are obliging and professional. Food in the restaurant is fine and unfussy. "High season high jinks extend to an open-air disco – Turkish hotel discos are relatively dressy and sedate affairs; potential hazards are the local mosquitoes and the village itself which has little to offer apart from a good back-drop of distant mountains." (*Jeremy Round*)

Open Apr–Nov.
Rooms 102 – all with shower, telephone and radio.
Facilities TV lobby, bar, restaurant; disco in season. Private beach.
Location 32 km S of Iskenderun.
Terms On application.

BODRUM Muğla — Map 17

Manzara Oteli — *Tel* (6141) 1719
Kumbahçe Mah, Meteoroloji Yani

A returning visitor has again enjoyed this little hotel on a hill above an attractive resort town opposite the Greek island of Kos. "It is only about five minutes' walk from the sea front and ten from the centre of town. Its position gives a stunning view of the bay and of the 'crusader castle', especially when illuminated at night. The accommodation is arranged in the style of small apartments, each with table and chairs, sofa, terrace for outdoor eating, small sink unit and refrigerator. The bedroom was comfortable and clean, if small, and had a private bathroom. There is a small heated swimming pool with an adjoining bar and small restaurant, with service throughout the day. The staff were attentive and helpful without being intrusive. Dinner is served barbecue-style on the poolside terrace and the one meal we had was extremely good. For other meals we went into town." Another visitor this year equally enjoyed the place but found the room service rather sketchy. (*RS Millsum; also WH Bruton, RW, Mary Purdy*) *Note*: the *Manzara* may now be insisting on half board terms despite the self-catering facilities.

Open All year.
Rooms 20 double, including some suites – all with bath or shower, arranged in small apartments with living room, with sink unit and refrigerator, and terrace.
Facilities Restaurant. Terrace with swimming pool and bar.
Location On hill overlooking Bodrum.
Terms On application.

BURSA — Map 17

Çelik Palas Oteli — *Tel* (241) 619.00
Çekirge Caddesi 79 — *Telex* 32121 CEPA

A large purpose-built hotel in Bursa's smart suburbs, overlooking the bustle of the old town. It was built between the wars and opened, it proudly recalls, by Ataturk himself. Recently renovated, it has been recently praised too: "Immediate welcome from baggage boy and reception. Big comfortable room and bathroom up to international standards, plus a balcony with a marvellous view of Ulu Dağ – Mount Olympus (one of the Turkish ones – there are at least two!) to one side and over the fertile valley to the hills around the Sea of Marmara. All immaculately clean, and prices very modest. Splendid breakfast, with dozens of dishes. Dinner had a decent international menu, also violin players and a dance floor. Nice to be spoilt in comfort after a tiring day. A real haven in an area famous for its history rather than for its hotels." (*Col RWH Crawford; also J Murray*) Since last year, the hotel has added 42 new rooms. May we hear, please, from visitors to the new grander *Palas*?

Open All year.
Rooms 173 double – all with bath, telephone, radio, TV and mini-bar; many with balcony.
Facilities Lift. Restaurant; conference facilities; night club, hairdresser; thermal pool and sauna.
Location Central. Back rooms quietest. Parking.
Terms On application.

ÇANAKKALE — Map 17

Truva Oteli — *Tel* (1961) 1024
Yaliboyu — *Telex* 58115

In a quiet part of the town, and with fine views of the Hellespont, a functional modern four-star hotel convenient for Troy (32 km to the south) or for the car ferry across the Dardanelles. Clean, average bedrooms; staff friendly. Clean kitchen where you are taken to choose your own Turkish dishes, delicious and mainly vegetarian. 66 rooms. Double 4,950-5,850 TL [1987]. No recent reports: more welcome.

DATÇA Muğla — Map 17

Perili Köşk — *Tel in Istanbul* (1) 337.10.33
Telex 22279

No more beguiling new Turkish delight has entered these pages in 1988 than this "Fairies' Castle" (literal translation) on the coast opposite Rhodes: "From Marmaris after a tortuous 60 km drive through the hills, a neat sign on the left directs you along a rough track that you'd think only fit for a donkey. After about 700 metres, a lovely tiled roof and chimneys come into view, peering over cascades of oleander and bougainvillaea. It's a secret gem of a hotel facing a beautiful crescent bay and with no other building in sight (Datça village is 17 kilometres away). The design is impressive – a wealth of lovely natural pine, with balconies and latticed windows, and the rooms have stunning traditional framed panelled ceilings. We had a good sized room though some are cramped, but all have private bathroom. There is a terrace-bar and another overlooking the beach. Service was very attentive. You must take full board, but for once this is a bonus and not a recipe for gastronomic boredom. A British diplomat had recommended me the hotel and told me that its food was very close to what you would get if staying with a good Turkish family. Certainly there was variety and every meal was delicious. Wine is included with the meals. There is a tennis court. I feel a pang of conscience in telling you about this place." (*Robert Millsum*) And so do we, in asking for more reports.

Open 1 Apr–30 Nov.
Rooms 2 suites, 18 double – all with bath; many with balcony.
Facilities Bars; restaurants; terrace. Garden with tennis court; beach with water sports.
Location 15 km from Datça towards Dalaman Airport.
Restriction Not suitable for ♿.
Terms On application.

ERZURUM — Map 17

Oral Oteli — *Tel* (011) 197.40
Terminal Caddesi 3 — *Telex* 74117 HAVA

"Hearts generally sink as they enter Erzurum – a wild, bleak city at 6,000 feet where the air scarcely seems to warm even in midsummer. One does not travel here for the ring of suburban army bases or the treeless landscape with its wolves, bears and vultures. But there are Georgian monasteries in the valleys and the magical northern source of the Euphrates is a couple of hours away by jeep. Touring the east of Turkey often necessitates a night in Erzurum. The *Oral*, an abrupt modern block, is the best hotel on this road before Tabriz and is in many ways very comfortable: well-appointed bedrooms, smart bathrooms with the area's fine fresh water, constantly hot, a laundry service, highly competent English-speaking receptionists, friendly and helpful staff. The extensive modern wood-panelling in the public rooms is impressive. The restaurant can be noisy if the television or tape-machine is at the usual Turkish volume, but the food is generally excellent. Et söte, a local dish of fried meat and peas, is not to be missed, also a fine cold green bean starter, zeytin yağli taze fasulya, and the charcoal-grilled offal – juicy kidneys, liver and sheep testicles (koç yumurtasi). Rates are extraordinarily low, perhaps reflecting a degree of military subsidy (visiting NATO brass seem regularly to be in residence). The hotel has efficient heating and solid double-glazing." (*JR*) More reports from these far horizons, please.

Open All year.
Rooms 1 master-suite, 6 suites, 64 double, 19 single – all with bath, telephone and radio.
Facilities Lift. Lobby/lounge area with TV, dining room; laundry service. Palandöken ski-resort nearby; 15 km from thermal springs. English spoken.
Location 10 minutes' walk from centre. On road to airport, just N of westernmost roundabout on main E–W road through city. Parking.
Restriction Not suitable for ♿.
Credit cards None accepted.
Terms On application.

INCEKUM Antalya — Map 17

Alara Oteli — *Tel* (3237) 1146
Yeşilköy, Bay of Incekum — *Telex* 56613 ALRA

As Alanya becomes an ever more popular resort, the attractions of a hotel well away from the main conurbation becomes greater. The *Alara* is 20 kilometres distant but it runs a twice daily mini-bus service into town. "For those who enjoy tranquillity and long unspoilt beaches, this is the place to stay along the southern coast of Turkey. The hotel is in a prime position high up at one end of the bay giving wide vistas over the surrounding area. Built in the Moorish style, it is made up of five separate buildings. The main one houses the reception, lounge, bar and open-air dining room and is ringed by a pleasant patio and pool overlooking the cliffs. There are four other two-storey buildings with bedrooms, set amid the beautifully-tended, lush gardens which run from the top of the cliff down the gentle slope to the sea. The rooms all have a sea view and are clean and fresh though rather unsophisticated. All the staff are helpful, though only the manager spoke English. The food was palatable, if hardly a gastronomic experience, but it was a pleasant and relaxing base for a most enjoyable holiday." (*Susan Petch; confirmed this year by F Daley, RW*)

Open 20 Apr–31 Oct.
Rooms 6 suites, 116 double – all with shower and telephone; many with balcony. Bedrooms in 4 separate buildings in grounds.
Facilities 3 bars, breakfast room, snack bar, restaurant; shops. Belly dancing once a week. Garden with table tennis and swimming pool. Private beach, with water sports. English spoken.
Location 20 km W of Alanya; mini-bus service twice a day.
Credit cards Amex, Diners.
Terms Dinner, B&B: single £18–£33, double £33–£53, suite (for 3 persons) £53–£95. Set lunch/dinner £4. Reduced rates for children.

> Detailed information about many Turkish hotels was not available in mid-1987 when we went to press.

> We get less feedback from smaller and more remote hotels. But we need feedback on all hotels: big and small, far and near, famous and first-timers.

ISTANBUL **Map 17**

Ayasofya Pansiyonlari
Soğukçeşme Sokak
Sultanahmet

Tel (1) 512.57.32 and 512.50.55
Telex 23841 TSAP

Two years ago we welcomed to our Istanbul section the *Yesil Ev Hotel* (formerly known as *Yesil Konak*), an admirable work of restoration by the Touring and Automobile Club of Turkey (see below). Now the same outfit, a hybrid of the Automobile Association and the National Trust, have opened what promises to be another Guide winner – the conversion of a terrace of nine historic houses, with attractive pastel-coloured wooden exteriors, in a narrow lane that lies between Topkapi Palace and Hagia Sophia. Two houses have ground-floor breakfast and tea rooms, and one has been converted into a library, strong on books about Old Constantinople. The brochure tells us that reception provides guests with two keys – one for the outer door of their house and the other for the room. "The traveller entering the house feels as if he is in his own home from then on. Only a knave welcomes him." An intriguing prospect . . . Meanwhile a nominator reports that the indoor dining room was delightful (there is an outdoor area for meals and drinks, too, open in summer), the service excellent and his twin-bedded room had *two* bathrooms, as did several others. The road is sealed off from traffic, so very quiet; only minor murmur of discontent: the recorded muezzin from Hagia Sophia seemed to come from outside his very room. (*Ralph Blumenau*)

Open All year.
Rooms 5 triple, 33 double, 3 single – all with bath and/or shower, telephone and radio.
Facilities Library, bar, breakfast room, tea room, two restaurants. Terrace.
Location Central, near Hagia Sophia.
Credit cards None accepted.
Terms B&B: single US$32–US$65, double US$63.65–US$100.

Divan Oteli
Cumhuriyet Caddesi 2
Şişili 80200

Tel (1) 131.41.00
Telex 22402 DVAN

Modern central hotel recommended as smaller, quieter, cheaper and less touristy than the Hilton *and* Sheraton, *with one of the best restaurants in Istanbul, especially for caviar, fish and baklava. But several readers report discourteous service. 202 rooms, all with bath or shower. B&B double US$96–US$135. Set meals US$16.75. More reports please.*

Hīdiv Kasrī
Çubuklu-Kanlīca

Book through TTOK
Tel (1) 146.70.90

Of the three Istanbul hotels converted from Ottoman mansions (see also *Ayasofya Pansiyonlari* and *Yeşil Ev*), this is by far the most bizarre and spectacular – the old summer palace of the last Viceroy of Egypt, set on a wooded hill on the Asian side of the city above the Bosphorus-shore villages of Çubuklu and Kanlīca (famed for its yoghurt). The palace was built and originally furnished in a fabulous mixture of styles – stolid

Middle-Eastern opulent, Tuscan villa and Belgian *Art Nouveau*. The restoration and refurbishment has kept many of the fittings, including regal mahogany-surrounded loos from a works in Lambeth, bronze cage-lifts from Munich and baths as big as boats with elaborate *fin-de-siècle* shower attachments surmounted by chrome crescent moons and stars.

All the present furniture is fetchingly clumsy reproduction *Art Nouveau*. The master-mind of this enterprise, Çelik Gülersoy, decides on and designs everything according to how he sees the buildings in his dreams. Part of his gasp-inducing fantasy here includes features such as a vast marble fountain in the central hall, a wood-panelled salon hung with a riot of crystal and gilt chandeliers, a field of roses growing through grass outside a marble-floored tea room lit by pastel-coloured blown glass flowers. A piano trio plays in the banana-shaped dining room at night – Mozart, Schubert, then *The Blue Danube*. When the musicians go off for their break, the piped muzak starts up again – perhaps Country and Western, a Beethoven piano concerto or Simon and Garfunkel's greatest hits. The food is never better than unremarkable – and sometimes much worse.

Most rooms have views that it would be hard to better anywhere in the city. The superb Viceroy's suite has a long, wide terrace looking out over the trees to a sumptuous bend in the Bosphorus. On the same floor at the back, where the Tuscan eaves are most harmonious, the bedrooms overlook a rose field framed by cypresses. The cheaper rooms on the second floor are on a more human scale but have no terrace. In order not to destroy the room plan of the palace, bathrooms and loos have not been knocked into the bedrooms – they are shared between two or three rooms but have the advantage of retaining their original impressive proportions. Take the lift up the stubby tower for the best views of this most rural and tranquil portion of the city.

The grounds, with their wooden viewing-pavilions and a glass house selling local honey and preserves, are popular with day-trippers from all around. The terrace and marble hall are open to anyone for tea and cocktails. Part of Mr Gülersoy's success is that his properties make their money by attracting extreme ends of the pleasure-seeking market – the well-heeled tourist who can afford the rooms and the ordinary local family that wants to pass an hour or two in beautiful surroundings.

Getting to the hotel is not that easy. The infrequent boat all the way from the city centre to Kanlīca takes up to two hours – although this is a trip worth taking on its own account; or take the ferry to Uskudar, then bus, dolmuş (shared taxi) or taxi along the Asian shore of the Bosphorus to Kanlīca. (*JR*)

Open All year.
Rooms About 30 – all with telephone and radio.
Facilities Restaurant, tea room; terrace. Wooded grounds.
Location On the Asian shore of the Bosphorus, 2 hours by boat from the city centre (45 minutes by ferry and land transport).
Terms B&B: single US$36–US$67, double US$47–US$86, Viceroy's suite US$143.

> Many Turkish hotels failed to return our questionnaire, and tariffs are not given in the official list of hotels in Turkey, so we have in many cases been unable to give detailed information about facilities, tariffs etc.

Kalyon Hotel
Sahil Yolu
Sultanahmet

Tel (1) 520.13.03
Telex 23364 KLYN

A modern hotel on the edge of the Bosphorus, only ten minutes' walk from the Blue Mosque, Hagia Sophia and Topkapi Palace. "It is clean and comfortable and all the staff were friendly. It is also away from the crowds and enjoys a wonderful view over the waterway, with its constant, silent traffic. Nice walks along the waterfront past the old Byzantine ramparts with several excellent fish restaurants nearby. The *Kalyon* is not as luxurious as the big hotels in the New Town, but its setting is better and it is far cheaper." Endorsed this year, with nuances: "Rooms at the back may be small; front ones are large, with views of the sea of Marmara, but lower floors would hear traffic noise. Prices reasonable." (*RWH Crawford; JR Lloyd*)

Open All year.
Rooms 38 – all with bath, telephone and balcony.
Facilities Lobby/reception, bar, restaurant, cafeteria; conference room, meeting room.
Location Central; on the waterfront; near Blue Mosque. Parking.
Terms On application.

Pera Palas Oteli
Meşrutiyet Caddesi 98-100
Tepebaşi

Tel (1) 151.45.60
Telex 24152 PERA

Set in the old diplomatic quarter of Galata just by the American Consulate General, this used to be *the* hotel for travellers arriving on the Orient Express, in the days when Istanbul was still Constantinople – and today it is the grandest of the city's old hotels still in use. "Those who want the Hilton can go there," runs a report this year, "but the *Pera Palace* evokes the era of the tarboosh and the Turkish cigarette. I liked it. It is run down, but the building has style and the old-fashioned lift is a delight." Some of the bedrooms look out over the Golden Horn; all of them are very comfortable in a solid, 19th-century sort of way. Today, with its souvenir stall and package deals, it does seem to be cashing in on its fading glory, but it still remains highly atmospheric. One wry recent comment: "We had what purported to be one of the best rooms, with lofty ceilings (complete with cobwebs) and imposing doors. But the noise! The traffic in Istanbul is indescribable and we had difficulty sleeping. The food was better than I expected, however." (*David Evans*) An expert on Turkey adds: "The covered central court is worth the visit alone. The comfort of your room depends on the luck of the draw: some (lower floors and facing into the court) are enormous, impressive, cool and quiet; some (higher up at the back) have views of the Golden Horn and over to the Old City; some (higher up at the front and back, facing out) are pokey little heat traps into which all the noise of the race-track main thoroughfares below gets funnelled. All have a ravishing air of faded splendour, with *froid* and *chaud* on the taps and baths big enough to float in. Breakfast is semi-self service and rather disappointing." (*Jeremy Round*)

Open All year.
Rooms 3 suites, 92 double, 25 single – all with bath, shower and telephone.

Facilities Lift. Hall, lounges, bar, restaurants; conference facilities. English spoken.
Location Central, near American Consulate and Galata tower. Some parking.
Restriction Not suitable for ♿.
Credit cards Diners, Visa.
Terms (Excluding 10% tax and 15% service) B&B: single US$66, double US$85, suite US$163; dinner, B&B: single US$76, double US$105, suite US$183; full board: single US$86, double US$125, suite US$203. Set lunch/dinner US$15; full alc US$20. Children under 4 sharing parents' room free.

Yeşil Ev Oteli
Sultanahmet

Tel (1) 528.67.64 and 511.11.50
Telex 30470
Reservations in UK: Savile Travel, Maddox Street, London W1
Tel (01) 499 5101

This charming hotel of real character began life only in 1984 but already has changed its name – from *Yeşil Konak* to *Yeşil Ev* (Green House). What has *not* changed is our readers' enthusiastic endorsement in 1986/7 of this initial description: "Istanbul the magnificent is also Istanbul the exhausting – dusty, hilly and, at first, bewildering; so it is a lucky traveller who can take refuge in this hotel high up in the oldest part of the Old City, 600 metres from the first courtyard of Topkapi Sarayi. It is an old wooden 19th-century mansion, painted a fresh apple green and white, set between a row of ever-hopeful carpet shops. Three years ago it was derelict, but the Touring Club of Turkey has restored it lovingly. Our ground-floor bedroom was almost more bed than room: the huge and well-sprung bed left just enough room to squeeze past an armchair, a polished mahogany wardrobe and a chest of drawers. The room was high and had tall sash windows hung with lace and brocade curtains and fitted with latticed shutters giving what were basically light rooms a pleasantly secretive, Ottoman feeling. Communication with the outside world – and the present century – was via a brass 'candlestick' telephone made in Coventry in 1930; the switchboard operator, like all the staff, speaks enough English to be helpful and friendly. The bathroom, *en suite*, was spotlessly clean. Soundproofing between it and the next bathroom . . . well, there wasn't any.

"The walled, paved garden is the hotel's happiest asset. Water splashes down from a porphyry fountain; fig and plane trees are edged with pansies and stocks, wallflowers and marigolds; roses and vines climb the walls. Two dozen marble-topped tables with cushioned white chairs are set for breakfast, lunch, dinner or tea; there is a dining room inside for less sunny days. On one side of the garden stands a pelargonium-filled conservatory, for cool evenings. The food is very good, typically Turkish, with enough variety for a week's stay. And where better than here to take the last Turkish coffee of the day, turning one's gaze from the great dome of Hagia Sophia to the six slender minarets of the Blue Mosque, with a fond glance at Sinan's elegant Baths of Roxellana in between?"

A reader this year: "That account says it all." But be prepared for the muezzin at 5 am; and maybe for the hotel's three-piece ensemble playing mainly Austrian music in the evening. (*David HM Smith; also WH Bruton, Mary P Purdy, Fred and Pat Wood, and others*)

We are particularly keen to have reports on italicised entries.

Open All year.
Rooms 1 suite, 19 double – 3 with bath and shower, 17 with shower, all with telephone, radio, tea-making facilities and baby-listening; TV in suite.
Facilities Salon, coffee shop, bar, restaurant. Garden with restaurant. English spoken.
Location In Old City, mid-way between Hagia Sophia and the Blue Mosque.
Credit card Visa.
Terms B&B: single US$73, double US$97, suite US$141. Set lunch/dinner US$10; full alc US$19. Reduced rates for children sharing parents' room.

KONYA — Map 17

Başak Palas Oteli — *Tel* (331) 113.38
Hükümet Meydani 3

In the centre of an ancient city between Ankara and the Taurus mountains, a clean and characterful hotel with outstanding service (e.g. breakfast with boiled eggs served at 5 am for an early start). No restaurant, but the staff will advise on good ones near by. 2 star. 40 rooms, some with bath. Prices on application. Upgraded this year from brief note: more reports please.

KUŞADASI Aydin — Map 17

Hotel Club Kervansarayi — *Tel* (6361) 4115

Although 300 years old, this is a much less "batter'd" caravanserai than Edward Fitzgerald's, for it was renovated in 1974 and offers modern comfort and good service, as well as a central location. Ottoman decor and furnishings; cool courtyard with lush tropical trees and a marble fountain; two bars, lounge, night-club with dancing, elegant restaurant; all rooms with private shower, most with balcony. Extensively used by package tours. 38 rooms. Double approx. US$45 [1986]. New nomination: more reports please.

Kismet — *Tel* (6361) 2005
Akyar Mevkii

The pleasant resort of Kuşadasi, convenient for Ephesus and many other ancient marvels, has become a fashionable marina as well as a daystop for Mediterranean cruises. Neither the largest nor the dearest hotel in town, the white modern *Kismet* stands high on a small peninsula above the yacht marina, surrounded by its pleasant palm and pine-shaded gardens. Readers this year have found the management attentive, the service and food very good, the sea breezes refreshing, and the land and water views comprehensive. A novelist's pen earlier drew this picture: "This is one of those confident, never smug establishments which have clearly been 'discovered' for many years by those shrewd enough not to advertise its virtues. The *Kismet* is far from the tavernas and carpet shops which make the evenings agreeable with colour and loud with amiable huckstering. Its small paradise of a garden is liberally set with lounging chairs and with a tennis court for the energetic, niched above the Aegean into which you can plunge from a private, rocky 'beach'. The bedrooms are well maintained and offer remarkable value. The dining room is adequate, but we would not recommend full *pension*. However, the breakfast is self-service and there is a full vat of yoghurt on which to start the day. Nicely served afternoon teas remind one of what one is not missing in Britain, so to speak." (*Frederic and Sylvia Raphael; also Ann Farrow, WH Bruton, Sheila and Uwe Kitzinger, and many others*) Many rooms have a balcony. The hotel gets very full and booking, in writing, is essential.

Open 1 Apr–end Oct.
Rooms 14 triple, 70 double – 15 with bath, 69 with shower, all with telephone, radio and TV. 10 in garden annexe.
Facilities Lift. Hall, salon, TV room, bars, restaurant. Garden with restaurant, swimming pool and tennis court. Beach, waterskiing, boating. English spoken.
Location On peninsula in Kuşadasi bay.
Restriction Not suitable for ♿.
Credit cards Access, Visa.
Terms B&B: single US$31, double US$41; full board single US$47, double US$73. Set lunch/dinner US$10. Reduced rates for children; special meals.

ÖLÜDENIZ Muğla — Map 17

Meri Oteli — *Tel* (6151) 1
Ölüdeniz, near Fethiye

The white beach curving around a turquoise lagoon that features on Turkish travel posters is Öludeniz. The *Meri* is on the lagoon itself at the end of the road, well away from the camping sites on the beach. Its own private beach is calm, with beautiful white sand. You can sit under the trees in the garden or lie on wooden loungers under straw umbrellas. The rooms are built in blocks scattered up a steep ravine. No lift, and close on 150 steps to the top: the *Meri* is not for those who can't climb stairs. The views from the balconies are nice but the rooms are a little dark and the bathrooms a little worse for wear. The restaurant, on the first floor overlooking the garden, is pleasant and breezy: half or full board is obligatory, which is a pity as the food is nothing special. The hotel has a picturesque boat which goes on a tour of the lagoon every afternoon, but most people just lie on the beautiful beach or row out to the sandy spit. A good place for children: very safe swimming. A visitor this year found this state-owned hotel rather impersonal and housekeeping imperfect. *Note:* for good fish, a pretty rooftop bar and taped jazz go to Han Çamping's restaurant on the main beach. (*Catherine Cuthell; RS Millsum*)

Open All year.
Rooms 75 – all with shower and telephone; some with balcony. All in separate blocks.
Facilities Bar, indoor and outdoor restaurants; disco. Garden with play area for children. Private beach with water sports, sailing, fishing.
Location 15 km S of Fethiye.
Restriction Not suitable for ♿.
Terms On application.

PAMUKKALE Denizli — Map 17

Tusan Oteli — *Tel* (621) 1010

Pamukkale (which means Cotton Castle) is one of the seven wonders of Turkey, with its hot springs constantly adding to the striking petrified cascades of gleaming white marble – a weird landscape high above the broad dusty valley of the Meander. It is also the site of ancient Hierapolis, with atmospheric ruins scattered over the hillside. The "clean and well kept" *Tusan* is the best of the half-dozen hotels in the area: it has its own thermal pools on the lip of the escarpment, pleasant if fairly basic rooms in single-storey motel style, and cooking similarly adequate. And there is nothing to stop you walking up the road and taking a dip in the pool of a neighbouring hotel built over the fallen masonry of the old city – one of the more memorable, as well as therapeutic, bathes to be had anywhere. (*Robert Millsum; G Hudson, HR, JR*)

Open All year.
Rooms 47 – all with bath or shower, and telephone.
Facilities Restaurant. Thermal pools.
Location 14 km N of Denizli.
Terms On application.

In addition to the preceding entries, a number of other hotels have been recommended to us by our Turkish correspondent, *Jeremy Round,* though without sufficient information to provide a proper citation. We list these below – with no guarantees. The gradings are from the official listings of the Ministry of Tourism.

ABANT, Bolu Province **Turban Abant Oteli.** *Tel* (462) 5573 *Telex* 84538 ABNT. Graded 3-Star. 94 comfortable rooms in a restful hotel in a beautiful area of woods, hills and lakes. Turks come here for the clear air and fine food (the country's best chefs come from Bolu). Almost the atmosphere of a spa hotel.

ALANYA **Kaptan Oteli** Iskele Cad. 62. *Tel* (3231) 2000 and 1094. *Telex* 56675. Graded 3-star. 45 rooms. Set on a slight rise a few minutes from the fine sandy beach, and close to the shops. Excellent views from the roof-top dining-terrace. Front rooms have a balcony and sea view; most of those at the back overlook the swimming pool.

ANTAKYA **Atahan Oteli** Hurriyet Cad. 28. *Tel* (891) 110.36 and 114.07. Graded 3-star. The French only left in 1938. Many of their grand civic buildings still stand empty and abused and on many streets one might swear one was in Menton. This gracious, long-established hotel by the Orontes has a separately-run restaurant at street level that is the best in the city. On no account stay at the much less attractive hotel by the bus station. It is incomprehensive that the tourist office nave graded it 2-star while giving the splendid *Arsuz Otel* in Arsuz only 1-star.

ANTALYA **Bilgehan Oteli** Kazimözalp Cad. 194. *Tel* (311) 253.24. *Telex* 56004. Graded 2-star. Just by the main bus station with a half-mile walk to the harbour, this large modern hotel (88 rooms) is comfortable if a little characterless. A good stopover, not a resort hotel. Summer eating on the roof can afford spectacular views. Also breakfast at dawn before an early flight.

ANTALYA **Büyük Oteli** Cumhuriyet Cad. 57. *Tel* (311) 114.99 and 125.43. Graded 1-star. This used to be the city's grand hotel (a direct translation of the name). Small (42 rooms) and well run, it has some good views over the tea-gardens and harbour. Recent refurbishment has lent a new lease of life, although the departure of the ground-floor pastry shop to an address up the street means that breakfasts are no longer out of the ordinary.

BURSA **Akdoğan Oteli** 1. Murat Cad. 5. *Tel* (241) 606.10 *Telex* 32229 AKOT. Graded 2-star. 119 beds. Plumbing a little crude, but modest and pleasant. Its bonus is the Turkish baths in the basement. Away from the centre of town at the foot of the approach road to Ulu Dağ, Turkey's famous skiing resort.

DIYARBAKIR **Diyar Büyük Oteli** Inönü Cad. 4. *Tel* (831) 158.32; **Turistik Oteli** Ziya Gökalp Bul. 7. *Tel* (831) 126.62. Both graded 2-star. The *Büyük* has better fitted rooms and bathrooms; the *Turistik* is longer established and more roomy. Eat the kaburga at *Selim Amca,* Ali Emiri Cad. in preference to the overpriced fare at either of the hotel restaurants.

HARBIYE Hatay **Hidro Oteli** Karyer Mah. *Tel* 8983) 6, and **Deliban** Dermaşta Mah. *Tel* (8983) 54. Antioch has always come to ancient Daphne for picnics and dalliance. The best of the extraordinary mosaics from the Roman villas and club-houses that used to fringe the laurel-shaded hillside, with its brooks and falls, are now in the museum at Antioch. No plaque marks the spot where Cleopatra married Mark Antony. Of the present-day hotels, the restful *Hidro* has the best restaurant, with tables outside by a rectangular lake full of carp. The more upbeat *Deliban*, on the main E5 40 km from the Syrian border, has the better rooms, fitted with TV and fridge. Its rooftop restaurant becomes an exotic night-club in the evening.

ISKENDERUN **Güney Palas Oteli** Beş Temmuz Cad. 17. *Tel* (881) 110.20. *Telex* 68105. Old Alexandretta has had a substantial and effective face-lift over the past few years. The sea-front is now all flower beds and tea kiosks but as yet there is no decent hotel from which to admire the prospect. A minute's walk away in the former commercial heart, is this oldest and most solidly built of the port's hotels. The baths are big enough to float in. The dining room and the *Saray Lokantasi* on the front are the two best restaurants in town.

ISTANBUL **Büyük Trabya Oteli** Kefeliköy Cad. Trabya. *Tel* (1) 162.10.00 *Telex* 26203 HTRB. Graded 5-star. A luxury class, 261-room hotel on a splendid stretch of the Bosphorus a few miles out of the centre. A good place for a restful holiday with excellent facilities and good views. One of the few hotels that makes Istanbul feel like a real resort. Expensive food.

ISTANBUL **Olcay Oteli** Millet Cad. 187. *Tel* (1) 585.32.20 *Telex* 23209 OLCA. Graded 4-star. Moderately priced, and close to Topkapi and the Bazaar. Popular with tour parties, but offering the bonus of a pleasant garden. 134 rooms.

IZMIR **Kismet Oteli** 1377 Sok. 9. *Tel* (51) 21.70.50. Graded 2-star. Beautiful decor. Quietly situated. 68 rooms.

MARDIN **Bayraklar** on the main square, no details. Domestic grading only. Standards here are appallingly low but, in order to visit the Aramaic-speaking churches and monasteries nearby, a night or two's stay may be necessary. There is nowhere else even half decent. The views from the rooms at the back stretch way, way down and across the plains of Upper Mesopotamia which – in the green spring, or at night with the lights of Nusaybin in the distance – from this height might easily be mistaken for the sea.

MERSIN **Aktaş Otel** Istiklal Cad. 152. *Tel* (741) 370.07. Laid-back, modern block, with smooth services, set just on the fringe of this prosperous commercial port's city centre. Cheaper than the other three or four establishments here aiming at the sub-executive travelling business client. Eat at the *Fuar* restaurant on the seafront or at the *Liman* on the top floor of the harbour's passenger terminal.

NEVŞEHİR **Orsan Kapadokya Oteli** Kayseri Cad. *Tel* (4851) 1035. The town is a good half hour's drive – in one direction from the lunatic scenery of Cappadocia with its troglodytic churches and wonderful Byzantine frescoes, and in the other, the underground cities of Kaymakli and Derinkuyu. But this hotel, reasonably priced, friendly and adequately comfortable, makes it a pleasant alternative, for a short stay in the area, to the inflated prices and often blasé service of the "good" hotels in Ürgüp or Ortahisar.

TRABZON **Usta Oteli** Iskele Cad.; Telegrafhane Sok. 3. *Tel* (031) 121.95 *Telex* 83124 ATME. Graded 2-star. No restaurant, but *the* place to stay here. Upper floors have views of the Black Sea. Furnishing is spartan and bathrooms are relatively primitive. Staff helpful, with some English. Good breakfasts. 72 rooms. Eat at the *Özgür* on the main square.

URFA **Turban Urfa Oteli** Köprübaşi Yusufpaşa Mah. *Tel* 3520; **Harran Oteli** Atatürk Bulvari. *Tel* (8711) 4743 and 2860. Both graded 2-star. The *Turban* is cheaper, less flashy and has marginally the better restaurant unless you like flambée. Service is more constantly obliging at the *Harran*. Both are comfortable stopovers in this sublime city that was once Edessa.

ÜRGÜP Nevşehir Province **Turban Ürgüp Moteli**. *Tel* (4868) 1490. Graded M1. 160 beds, with chalet-style blocks of 8-10 units in two-storey buildings. Attractively laid out and very clean. Expensive restaurant – eating in the village recommended.

Yugoslavia

VILA BLED, BLED

BELGRADE **Map 17**

Hotel Moskva *Tel* (011) 686.255
Balkanska Ulica *Telex* 11505

An ancient but well-kept hotel in the old part of the city that escaped wartime damage. Rooms old-fashioned but comfortable, clean and quiet. Old-style coffee-shop complete with violin and zither, much frequented by lively locals. Hotel expensive by Yugoslav standards. 140 rooms, all with bath or shower, double US$70–US$110 [1987]. Reinstated in Guide after period without feedback: more reports welcome.

BLED 64260 **Map 17**

Vila Bled *Tel* (064) 77.436
Cesta Svobode 26 *Telex* 34515 VILABL

Not only Yugoslavia's most splendiferous hotel, but a part of history too. This white palace above Lake Bled was erected by President Tito after

World War II and from then until his death he used it as his official summer residence: here he entertained Eden, Nehru, Brandt, Haile Selassie, King Hussein of Jordan and many other world leaders. Then in 1984 the Government turned it into a luxury hotel, which stands in its own 13-acre park, overlooking Yugoslavia's leading inland resort: views of the lake and the Alps are spectacular. Prices for so much pampered splendour are amazingly low by Western standards (a double room with breakfast is a mere US$70-US$90), but quality is not skimped, as our *Heather Sharland* found. Her report, bringing the *Vila Bled* new to the Guide this year, captures its mood of Socialist-imperialist grandeur:

"The place is fenced in all round and stray visitors do not seem to be encouraged. A wonderful display of flowers just inside the big gates. Our taxi deposited us onto the red carpet (yes, a real red carpet), where the commissionaire greeted us warmly. The receptionist rushes to meet you, then you are handed over lovingly to under-manager, then to cocktail-lounge waiter. There's an awful lot of marble, white and black, and lots of chandeliers – all very thirties. A pianist tinkles. Staff excellent. The dining-room has wonderful white linen, good modern prints, good silver and candles – everything glistens. Large menu, too large (most of it must be frozen), but to see such a good menu was a treat in Yugoslavia. Dinner was good (wonderful veal escalope and banana soufflé, good salad which is unusual in Yugoslavia, but bad coffee as Yugoslavia imports inferior stuff). Waiting was very formal and stylised (they all curled their fingers in exactly the same way) but everyone was nice too. Fellow diners included leading TV personalities, some German ministers, and a well-known actress dressed like Alice in Wonderland.

"The bedrooms are well modernised, with bathrooms a miracle of luxury, all gleaming white marble. Flower arrangements dreadful. The rooms don't really have a lake view, I suppose for security reasons. On the top floor is a small concert hall, which Tito used for receptions. When we left, the under-manager told us proudly that the hotel is now a *Relais et Châteaux* member – 'It is a great honour,' he said." (*Endorsed by PL Sugden*)

Open All year.
Rooms 21 suites, 11 double – 24 with bath and shower, 8 with shower only, all with telephone and radio; TV in suites.
Facilities 3 lifts. Lounge, TV lounge, bar with piano music, cafeteria, restaurant; conference room; terrace. Garden with tennis. Private lake beach; rowing boats. Musical events in summer. Golf, riding, hunting, fishing, gliding nearby. English spoken.
Location 1 mile along the lake from Bled, towards Bohinj.
Restriction Not suitable for ♿.
Credit cards All major cards accepted.
Terms B&B: US$35–US$100; dinner, B&B: US$53–US$118; full board: US$71–US$136. Full alc US$40. Reduced rates for children sharing parents' suite; special meals.

Our Yugoslav section is unacceptably short. Please would travellers in Yugoslavia tell us if they come across a good hotel.

Please write and confirm an entry when it is deserved. If you think that a hotel is not as good as we say, please write and tell us.

CETINJE Map 17

Grand Hotel *Tel* (086) 21.211, 21.047 and 21.762
Telex 61294

If you don't like a hotel in this book, don't just complain to us: try to help the manager and his staff to improve it. That is this year's message ringing loud and clear from the grandest modern hotel (there's not much competition) in Montenegro's former royal capital. It is an ancient town with many fine buildings, some of them former embassies and many of them, including King Nikolas' palace, now museums or art galleries. Our nominator/reorganiser reports:

"The *Grand* was built in 1984 to replace two older hotels damaged in the recent earthquake. No expense has been spared; it is a Balkan architect's dream, spacious and comfortable. The bedrooms are well furnished with oak parquet floors, many mirrors and real dressing tables. There is a deep indoor swimming pool, several rather pretty bars and café areas , and a concert hall with a sprung oak floor for dancing. In the large and tranquil restaurant, the service was of a high quality, supervised by a handsome head waiter looking more like an eminent barrister. All the employees are highly trained. But the first evening I was given positively the most revolting meal I have ever tried to eat in my life. I found that I had been dumped among the "Anglais packagers", something we usually manage to avoid on holiday, and the Milan-trained manager installed by the government told me that this food seemed to be what the English liked. But the next day I found that they also had a perfectly good *carte* of beautifully cooked dishes, Yugoslav, French, Austrian etc. The manager asked me to help him improve things, so I devised better menus for the group tours; I also got them to promote their good local wines, so that more people came to use the bar; and I started on the chambermaids, who were not doing their job, and I showed them how to get rid of the cobwebs and polish the lovely oak floors. At the end of my three-week stay my husband and I had two of the best meals we have eaten anywhere." (*Stephanie Sowerby*) Who will kindly report to us on whether Mrs Sowerby's purge has had lasting effects?

Open All year.
Rooms 8 suites, 200 double – all with bath, telephone and terrace.
Facilities Salons, library, reading-room, TV lounge, billiard room, chess room, bars, restaurants; conference facilities; night-club with dancing; bowling-alley; indoor swimming pool, sauna. Hairdresser and various shops. Surrounded by 2 parks with tennis courts and jogging track. 2 tennis courts nearby. English spoken.
Location On edge of town which is 35 km from Titograd.
Credit cards All major cards accepted.
Terms On application.

DUBROVNIK 50000 Map 17

Villa Dubrovnik *Tel* (050) 22.933
Telex 523299

Of the three smart hotels on the south side of Dubrovnik, the *Excelsior*, the *Argentina* and the *Villa Dubrovnik*, it is the last (much smaller than the others) which our readers continue to prefer – "what a spectacular find!" says one this year. It is a modern hotel, perched high on a cliff, with lovely views of the old walled town and harbour, and also over to the island of Lokrum opposite. The hotel is terraced into the cliff with lifts to all floors, except to the bathing rocks. Pine trees, flowers and blue awnings give a Riviera flavour. The bar and dining room both have superb views, and you can eat outdoors in fine weather. Most bedrooms face the front with a small balcony, and are well furnished; it's well worth paying extra for sea-facing rooms. There are high standards of cleanliness. The hotel has its own "concrete" beach with rock bathing in unpolluted water. The food is described this year as "so-so" but the service as "uniformly efficient and friendly". There is no nightlife on the spot, but you can wander down to the city in about 20 minutes or take the hotel's own motor-boat, and it is easy to get a taxi back. Not recommended for the elderly or infirm, as there are steps up from the hotel entrance to the road above. (*Byron Eliashof, N Redfern*)

Open All year.
Rooms 56 – most with bath or shower, all with telephone; many with sea-facing balcony.
Facilities Lifts. Lounge, bar, restaurant. Sub-tropical gardens; own bathing beach, mainly rock, reached by lift; sea-level bar service. English spoken.
Location On S side of Dubrovnik. Garage parking.
Restriction Not suitable for ♿.
Credit card Amex.
Terms [1987 rates] (Excluding tax) B&B: single US$24–US64, double: US$29–US$97; full board (min 3 nights): US$22–US$67 per person.

HVAR 58450 — Map 17

Palace Hotel

Tel (058) 74.966
Telex 26235

Hvar is a charming little harbour town on the island of the same name, about an hour by hydrofoil from Split. It has a gentle winter climate; pines offer shade in summer, olives and vines flourish. Sights include the remains of a Greek colony and a neolithic cave. The *Palace*, a classic white-fronted hotel, is very centrally located just above the busy quay. Dropped from the Guide in 1985 for lack of feedback, it has been renominated by a visitor this year: "Hvar's best hotel. We had a lovely room facing the front. Service is efficient and courteous, food good and varied. There was entertainment every evening and a cocktail party twice a week." Some back rooms may be gloomy. Best avoid high summer and its package tours. (*Noreen Redfern*)

Open All year.
Rooms 2 suites, 70 double, 4 single – all with bath or shower and telephone; some with TV.
Facilities Lifts. Lounge, salon, TV room, bar, restaurant; indoor sea-water swimming pool. Sun terrace overlooking harbour with music and dancing every night during summer. English spoken.
Location Central.
Credit cards Diners, Visa.
Terms B&B: single US$27–US$32.50, double US$30–US$59; dinner B&B: US$20–US$45 per person. Reduced rates for children under 7; special meals on request.

NOVI SAD 21000 — Map 17

Tvrdjava-Varadin — *Tel* (021) 431.122
Telex 14310

A hotel inside the fortress of Petrovaradin, on a hill above the Danube overlooking the city of Novi Sad. Ornately decorated public rooms, central European style. Beds comfortable, plumbing efficient, service pleasant, cuisine good for the area; restaurant has a roof terrace, popular with locals. 52 rooms, all with bath and shower. B&B double US$72. No recent reports: please send some.

PLITVIČKA JEZERA 48231 — Map 17

Hotel Jezero — *Tel* (048) 76.526
Telex 23817 PLITVICE

This large and remarkable holiday complex in the wooded hills of western Croatia lost its place in the Guide two years ago, purely through lack of feedback. Now it is restored by a reader who largely endorses our earlier account: "The Plitvice National Park has a quality of serene beauty. Sixteen lakes, linked by streams and waterfalls, are surrounded by lovely maple trees, firs and beeches which range in colour from blazing autumn crimson to a breathtaking variety of greens. A well-contrived system of paths, often built on stilts, makes walking easy. The forest is so tranquil that even chamois, deer and bear live at ease with the visitors. A few boats commute to hamlets on the largest lake: there is no machinery and no pollution.

"Here the *Jezero* is a huge well-planned wooden chalet-type hotel, and no one looking at it would guess that it held 242 bedrooms, a big lounge with snug bar area, an attractive restaurant, and indoor swimming pool, ladies' hairdresser and souvenir shop. Plus a nightbar with dancing during the high season, and facilities for many sports. The hotel is mainly concealed by the forest, but there are glimpses of several lakes from some bedrooms. On one day every year many young couples come to the hotel in preparation for their wedding, which is celebrated beside the highest of the many waterfalls. These couples usually wear the national dress of their own country or region. Staff in the hotel are efficient; food is good, with lake trout among the specialities. Prices are very moderate and cleanliness ideal. One of our favourite holiday places in Europe." (*Trudie and George Muir*) "A wonderful ambience, comfortable rooms, staff friendly, food good." (*Endorsed this year by Byron A Eliashof*)

Open All year.
Rooms 7 suites, 235 double or triple – all with bath or shower and telephone; TV in suites; many with balcony.
Facilities Large lounge with bar (dancing in high season), 2 bars, 3 restaurants; cinema and conference hall; heated indoor swimming pool, sauna, ladies' hairdresser. Adjoins sports and recreation centre with automatic 4-lane bowling alley. Near lake with safe bathing. English spoken.
Location In National Park, about 120 km SW of Zagreb.
Credit cards Amex, Diners, Visa.
Terms [1987 rates] B&B: £17.40–£18.80; dinner, B&B: £21–£23.30; full board £24–£26.30. Reduced rates for children.

SVETI STEFAN 81315 — Map 16

Hotel Sveti Stefan
Hotel Miločer
Hotel Maestral
Vila Miločer

Tel (all hotels) (086) 41.333 and 41.411
Telex 61188 SV STF

This is the most complex entry in our book, for it is not one hotel but four, all state-run and close together on the lovely Montenegrin coast just south of the old walled city of Budva. Sveti Stefan is a pocket-sized fishermen's island joined to the mainland by a long causeway. Since the war the whole island has been converted into one big eponymous hotel, the individual cottages restored and fitted out in luxury style serving as separate suites. The result is what many claim to be the most sumptuous resort in Yugoslavia. Flowering shrubs, cacti and trees blaze between the little houses and along the narrow alleys. Readers praise the setting, the food in the main dining-room and the friendly and efficient service at meals. A visitor this year speaks of "dinner by candlelight overlooking the sea, swift and courteous service, very good beach restaurant, very calm and warm sea water, a dance band playing nightly on the terrace". (*Conrad Dehn*) But some drawbacks are reported too: there are flights of steps everywhere, not so convenient for the elderly or infirm; the incessant coach tours in high season induce a lack of privacy; the pool is only a small plunge pool; and while some bedrooms are excellent, some are rather cramped.

The *Miločer*, on the mainland, facing the island hotel, is altogether different. Built as a summer palace by Alexander I for his wife, it was unfinished at the time of his assassination in Marseilles in 1934, but still retains an air of opulence. It is much smaller than the other hotels in the complex. The central block has a handsome vine-shaded terrace where meals are served. Most of the rooms are in annexes set discreetly in the grounds. Some readers (as well as the Editor) prefer the *Miločer*: "The *Sveti Stefan* is spectacularly pretty, of course, but to me claustrophobic. What is lovely about the *Miločer* is that it is very private, with big gardens, a fine, if pebbly beach, splendid swimming and a wonderful outdoor restaurant." (*Gitta Sereny*) A reader this year agrees: "Food good by Yugoslav standards. Breakfast under the vines, with toast, toast and more toast, and anything cooked that you want. Bedroom like a suite, with damask linen, fresh flowers, a fireplace." (*Heather Sharland*) The third hotel, on the coast near the *Miločer*, is the *Maestral*: "From the outside it is hideous, like a pile of worn bricks and concrete, but inside it is beautifully furnished, with good sized bedrooms, excellent reception rooms and restaurant, cool marble floors. It has a good private beach and a superb swimming pool. The food is slightly better than at the other two hotels and the service infinitely superior." (*Stephanie Sowerby*) New to the Guide this year is the *Vila Miločer*, between the *Miločer* and the *Maestral*, with its own beach. Our correspondent thought it looked pleasant and quiet, but didn't stay. More reports, please, on the newcomer, and on all this interesting diversity under the umbrella of Socialism.

Hotel Sveti Stefan
Open May–Oct.
Rooms 1 villa, 24 suites, 76 double, 18 single – all in separate houses and all with bath/WC/bidet and telephone; radio in villa; TV on request.

Facilities Salons, cocktail bars, terrace café, restaurant; night club, casino; hairdresser, beauty salon and shops. Spacious gardens with swimming pool and mini-golf. Private sandy beach with water sports. English spoken.
Location 6 km S of Budva on Adriatic coast. Parking.
Credit cards All major cards accepted.
Terms B&B: [1987 rates] B&B: single US$45–US$70, double US$38–US$75.

Hotel Miločer
Open Apr–end Oct.
Rooms 21 single and double – about half with bath or shower. Also cottages in grounds.
Facilities Bar, extensive terrace for meals. Large secluded wooded grounds and gardens; beach nearby; tennis.
Terms On application (cheaper than *Sveti Stefan*).

Hotel Maestral
Open Apr–Oct.
Rooms 156 – most with bath or shower, telephone and terrace.
Facilities Lift. Restaurant, bar, café. Swimming pool, sauna. Private beach.
Terms [1987 rates] B&B: single US$55–US$120, double US$45–US$220; dinner B&B: US$60–US$140, double US$50–US$235.

Vila Miločer
Open May–Oct.
Rooms 4 villas, 55 double.
Terms On application (cheaper than the others).

"We parked. Nobody appeared. We went in. Nobody about. We found the office. The girl, busy with the computer, said: 'Just a minute please', her back to us, and completed her business. The cheerful young porter remarked in a jolly way that his name was Johnnie and that neither he nor the girl were quite certain where any of the rooms were as they were both new there. He bounded up the stairs ahead of us without offering to carry our grips."

Exchange rates

These rates for buying currency are correct at time of printing but in some cases may be wildly awry at the time of publication. It is essential to check with banks or newspapers for up-to-date pound and dollar equivalents.

	£1 sterling	$1 US
Austria (Schillings)	21.00	12.82
Belgium (Belgian francs)	61.70	37.78
Denmark (Danish kroner)	11.20	6.85
France (French francs)	9.94	6.08
Germany (Deutschmarks)	2.97	1.82
Greece (drachmae)	222.00	136.00
Hungary (forints)	75.00	47.65
Ireland (punts)	1.11	1.08
Italy (lire)	2,154.00	1,318.00
Luxembourg (Luxembourg francs)	61.80	37.85
Malta (Maltese pounds)	0.54	0.35
The Netherlands (guilders)	3.35	2.05
Norway (Norwegian kroner)	10.94	6.70
Portugal, Madeira (escudos)	232.00	142.00
Spain, Andorra, Balearics, Canaries (pesetas)	207.00	126.00
Sweden (Swedish kronor)	10.36	6.34
Switzerland (Swiss francs)	2.47	1.51
Turkey (lira)	1,380.00	845.00
Yugoslavia (dinar)	1,049.20	647.07

Good hotels – Czech and Bulgarian style

We are grateful to Mr and Mrs Robert Gooder (magnum winners in 1987) for the following informative note about hotels in Czechoslovakia, and to Mr Antony Fletcher for his report on hotels in Bulgaria. We would like next year to include similar "appreciations" of hotels that travellers may come across in other countries of Eastern Europe. You are unlikely to encounter César winners in the Eastern Bloc, though we have heard rumours of an outstanding hotel in Dresden, but any guidance that readers can offer their fellow travellers would be a real consumer service.

Czechoslovakia

Czech hotels are officially divided into three categories, designated A, B and C. Class A hotels would correspond in western Europe with pretty modest places, as defined by *Michelin* as *assez confortable* or *de bon confort*. As far as we could see, these would be acceptable to users of the Guide, but scarcely worth listing. They are recently built – not very well – and appear to have been designed by the same architect, so that a Class A hotel in Litomyšl is (and feels) exactly the same as a Class A hotel in Banská Bystrica. They are tastelessly decorated, clinical in atmosphere, barely adequate in service, and have all the necessary conveniences (showers and radios in rooms, a bar, a restaurant, etc). They never seem to be fully booked, even at the height of the season, except in or near mountainous regions dear to the hearts of East German tourists. They are not expensive, even at the official rate of exchange. Class B hotels are pretty bad. These seem to be older establishments, often well placed near the centres of towns, and were formerly frequented, probably, by the better class of traveller in the provinces, and by commercial travellers (back in the days when there was such a thing as a better class of person, or commerce, in Czechoslovakia). In the West many such places would have been charmingly done-up; in Czechoslovakia they look grim. With little attention to design or planning they have been modernised higgledy-piggledy, with conveniences added where easily done, and not where not. They appear to be aimed at East European coach parties. They are sometimes fitted out with a bogus restaurant and a pretentious *coktely* lounge. They are dirty, and service is inadequate, to say the least. The best one could hope for in such places would be an Authentic Experience. Class C hotels must be grimmer still, though we may never have stayed in one. Some years ago, as a family of four, we stayed in a dormitory in Česky Krumlov with a family of six East Germans. The place was cavernous and moribund, there was a shower in our "room" that was filthy and didn't drain properly, the food was sparse and poor, and the bed-linen was spotlessly clean. I suspect this was a Class C hotel. At any rate, the experience was a great deal too authentic. Below these classed establishments are inns, called *hostinec,* which are pubs that sometimes have rooms. Czech friends tell us that these can be all right, and that those that are allowed to receive overnight guests are designated by the government. They could be useful in a pinch. Finally, there are establishments that are *hors classe,* like the *Hotel Intercontinental* in Prague, built for the international trade. The *Intercontinental* looks okay but hardly Guide-worthy.

After three visits to Prague we have come to feel that the best hotels, the most *Guide*-like hotels, are the old, and old-fashioned hotels left over from the beginning of the century. There are two of these in Prague that we know of the – *Hotel Europa* on Wenceslas Square, and the *Hotel Esplanade* around the corner at the top in Washingtonova. We are told that the former is the better; and we ourselves stayed in the latter ten years ago and loved it. They are places to which little has been done because they were built to luxury standards decades ago and have somehow endured. The *Esplanade* made efforts to live up to these pretensions, with white-gloved lift operators and uniformed flunkeys to carry your bags. (The white gloves are frequently out and at the ready for a tip. Tipping remains a great blight in Czechoslovakia.) The *Europa,* recently done up at ground floor level in order to take advantage of the newly pedestrianised Wenceslas Square, looks good. Indeed, Wenceslas Square is much improved and very agreeable, if you can suppress your memory that that is where the Russians landed their tanks in 1968. Similar hotels probably exist where a rich clientele once justified them, i.e. at Carlsbad, Marienbad, Brno, and Bratislava. We stayed at a marvellous relic in Marienbad ten years ago (where the toilets were thrones, the baths swimming pools, and the wardrobes built to hold ladies' crinolines for the season).

The Three Ostriches (U Tří Pštrosů in Prague is different from all of these. Originally it was built as a private house by a man who had made his fortune selling feathers to courtiers (hence its name), and the signs of his trade can still be seen on the side of the building. Latterly it degenerated into a low pub, but was taken over by Interhotel (the state chain) and turned into a luxury hotel in 1976. There are a thousand such places in France, but this is the only one we know of in Czechoslovakia. It is comparable (in inspiration, at least) with a place like the *Abbaye St-Germain* in Paris. It has been tastefully converted and decorated. Original features have been retained. Bathrooms have been fitted into all rooms, of which there is a fair variety, from single-bed attic rooms to suites lower down. The standard of accommodation is good, though the beds are the hardest we have ever known, and the tasteful furniture was designed to a high degree of perverse discomfort. Nevertheless, the thought was there, and all the other little things (wardrobe, bedside lights, writing surfaces, chests of drawers, etc) were fine. Room service was said to work all night, but we never tested it. Everyone at the desk spoke English, and managed mail, telephone and telegraph services impeccably. Indeed, their recollection of the telephone numbers we wanted was suspicious and suggested regular communication with the security police. Friends said we could assume our room was bugged, but there was (of course) no evidence. Breakfast was dull and expensive, and involved breakfast tickets, for some reason (presumably because accommodation and catering are separate state bureaucracies). Orange juice was poor and could turn out to be orange squash. Coffee was mediocre, but so it is everywhere in Czechoslovakia. Bread, butter and jam were fine. The actual hotel restaurant is (in the opinion of natives, and in our experience) the best in Prague. This is not to say a lot, as Czech cuisine has disappeared, but it is to say something. We would have eaten there all the time, except that the interiors of other old city restaurants are so splendid to see. Probably the best thing about *The Three Ostriches* is its location. It is at one end of the Charles Bridge (pedestrian) square in the middle of what might be the most beautiful city in Europe. There is easily accessible reserved parking space on the street outside the hotel, but the area round about is largely pedestrianised, so the hotel is unusually quiet, rather like Venice, where the night-time sounds are of human voices and human feet. Views from the hotel rooms are charming rather than spectacular. Pretty well everything there is to see is within easy walking distance, even the Castle, if one is prepared to climb the long, gently inclined flight of stairs that leads up to the Hradcany.

In sum, the *Three Ostriches* is an excellent hotel, of just the sort that users of the Guide would hope to find, but not cheap. Its faults derive from the culture and the economy of which it is a part. It suffers, much less than other establishments in Czechoslovakia, from the sense that the business is there to serve the employees rather than the clientele. It would have deserved a place in the Guide, even if it were not in Czechoslovakia. Readers would need to know, though, that rooms cannot be booked more than two months in advance, and that there are only about 20 of them.

RD AND JM GOODER

Hotel Esplanade Washingtonova 19, Prague 1. *Tel* 222552. 6 suites, 27 double, 29 single – 60 with bath. All major credit cards accepted.

Hotel Europa Vaclavske Namesti 29, Prague 1. *Tel* 263905. 54 double, 59 single – 36 with bath. All major credit cards accepted.

The Three Ostriches Drazickeho Namesti 12. *Tel* 536151. 3 suites, 9 double, 6 single – 7 with bath, 11 with shower. All major credit cards accepted.

Bulgaria

Most visitors from the UK go to Bulgaria's Black Sea coast for a package holiday. These are good value, but fairly rough. Behind the Iron Curtain comfort has a low priority. And – yes – there are no plugs for the baths or basins. Probably Suzopol is the best resort, away from the huge crowds in vast concrete hotels.

If you want to explore Bulgaria, there are formidable difficulties. This is a "hard line" Communist country with many irksome petty restrictions. Do not get caught changing money unofficially; they take a dim view of that. An example we found frustrating was the impossibility of booking hotel rooms direct with a hotel. They simply refer you to the State tourist office. If this is closed, too bad.

We decided to visit our daughter in Sofia. Both the Bulgarian Tourist Office and the national airline said it was impossible to obtain a visa in under a week. But after huge effort, and by mere chance, we discovered a travel agent who told us how it could be done. We booked a cheap package for one week to Drouzhba, an old resort on the Black Sea – very dirty at this point. We then abandoned our room there and flew to Sofia, having been careful to book a room in the capital well in advance, and through the proper channel. After two days in this attractive city, we hired a car (only dollars acceptable), and spent three days visiting some magnificent countryside in central Bulgaria. It is a beautiful country, with "peasant life" still very much in evidence. By chance we came across a charming hotel (by Bulgarian standards) called *The Etara Inn*, near Gabrova. This is quiet, reasonably comfortable, and with adequate food. It is situated in a lush valley next to a major tourist attraction – a restored village showing crafts and other aspect of rural life long ago. The *Etara* was inexpensive, with pleasant staff and a most attractive setting. We found no other hotel worthy of mention in the Guide.

ANTONY FLETCHER

An Innkeeper's Diary

by
JOHN FOTHERGILL

Before World War II, The Spreadeagle *in Thame, near Oxford, under John Fothergill's aegis, was the most exciting hotel in the country. It was in effect the first Good Hotel, just as Fothergill, who described himself in* Who's Who *as "pioneer amateur innkeeper", almost single-handedly made the occupation of hotel-keeping smart as well as respectable and was the inspiration for the present generation of dedicated amateurs who run many of the best hotels in the Guide.*

Fothergill was a dedicated hotelier, but he was far from being the bland or unctuous patron *once described by Bemelmans as "a type whose face is like a towel on which everyone has wiped both hands". He had a short fuse, and was as keen to repel the wrong sort of boarder as he was to attract the kind of people who would appreciate his own highly personal style of hospitality. Like Nico Ladenis, the great prima donna chef of* Simply Nico, *he derided the notion that the customer is always right. Many everyday innkeeping pinpricks raised the Fothergill blood-pressure. He had a particular detestation for those who came in off the street to use his lavatories. He would stop them and ask for their addresses, "just in case I feel like a pumpship when I am passing your door". In many respects, I would not dream of holding up Fothergill as a model of the good hotelier. His behaviour was often so outrageous to those who crossed him that, if the Guide had been going in the 1930s,* The Spreadeagle, *for all its splendours, would doubtless have had to be blackballed some years, only to be restored the following year after a clamour for reinstatement from loyal Fothergill supporters. But I warmly recommend his thirties bestseller,* An Innkeeper's Diary, *now reissued after decades of neglect, both for its entertainment value and also because it conveys so well the tribulations as well as the rewards of running a hotel. You can get some impression of the wit and wisdom of this marvellous bedside book from the following extracts.*

The Commercials

Commercial travellers have been spoilt by their having hotels kept on purpose for them. Once a commercial came and of course asked for a steak. I said, "I've some very good saddle of mutton and jugged hare. Wouldn't you have that for a change?" – "No, I want a steak." – "But I don't keep steaks, and if I got you one I know it would be very tough." – "Look here, I've had a steak five days a week for 30 years, and I want a steak now, if you *please.*" – "But I don't please; I guarantee that it will be utterly tough." –

"Never mind, I'll have it." I had tried to save him and the reputation of the place even amongst commercial travellers, so now I went into the butcher's and asked for the toughest piece of steak out of the freshest animal he had, and between us we got a beauty. I didn't see him again, but he told the parlour-maid that he had had to leave half of it.

A Dining Club

I had a letter from the Queen's College, asking for an elaborate dinner, for two, each dish meticulously described – for instance, pheasant (shooting had begun only the day before) without "bread poultice, gravel or fried counters", and so on. But disliking to have undergraduates spend extravagantly I got ready a very nice meal, though I winkled their oysters, so to speak, all the way through: chicken, for instance, instead of gun-warm pheasant, and for aubergines stuffed cucumber. They arrived and weren't undergraduates at all, but, as I learnt afterwards, TW Allen, Fellow of Queen's College, and Dr Cowley, Curator of the Bodleian, the two undisputed reigning epicures of Oxford. Allen had, at least, his bottle of Château d'Yquem 1914, and "Cowles" his Château Lafite 1907. After dinner, said Allen heavily: "*We* are a dining club, we've dined together for 25 years. Once we had a guest, but never again. This is the first time we've dined out of College, but we shall return." They never did. I couldn't tell them the reason why I had economised, I was so sick about it all.

Face Money

Last Sunday we had 39 folks to tea and I noticed that they were almost all ill-shaped, ugly or ill-dressed. I came into the office and complained at having to work for such people at 1*s.* 6*d.* a head. Charles Neilson said, "That's easy. Put up a notice: 'Buy our masks at 1*s.* each, or pay 6*d.* extra.'" So I went in and told Phyllis to charge 6*d.* face-money each for the worst cases. Thus for the first time in history seven people without knowing it have left an inn having paid 6*d.* each for not being beautiful. Surely this was a more praiseworthy action than the usual one of charging people extra because they *are* beautiful, well bred and dressed?

The Last of the Charabancs

We had 60 charabanc men for "dinner" from the East End. I saw their horrid charabancs coming along the clean and empty Sunday street, swoop down upon us and pull up. The 60-strong great burly black broad-cloth-suited brutes with buttonholes all the same coloured target, leapt out and, already semi-tight, swung round to the back of the charabanc and began to pull cases of beer out of the boot. With quick courage I had the beer put back. They swarmed over the yard and into the big room where they ate, *inter alia,* $1\frac{1}{4}$lb of meat per head and got quite drunk. Later Kate came to tell me they were all out in the yard again, cursing and yelling out for me and at the same time a deputation of three came in to tell me that I had grossly underfed them and that they wouldn't undertake to get the men out of the place unless I knocked off 6*d.* a head. I gave way meekly and out they went. How much better to have called in the police and got their money. Our last charabanc party.

Proper Innkeeping

Here I've determined not only to have proper and properly cooked food but to have only either intelligent, beautiful or well-bred people to eat it. Although barely paying our way, we've declined dozens of applications for rooms simply because we don't know the people, or the writing or the address don't please. To several of the commoner undergraduates I have said that I don't want them here with indiscriminate girls, and yet some people will argue with me that I am compelled by law to take them in or feed them! Few realise what I go through to get and keep for it the atmosphere this place now has. After all, Innkeeping is the only profession where one's business is also one's home. If it be thought eccentric or arrogant to encourage only certain kinds of people to share your roof and floor, is this not, in fact, always done? The beery Innkeeper has beery friends and discourages the others and so on, and the man who has no particular character or leanings but thinks of his hotel first and his home last merely makes a characterless business of it.

A Fine Fellow

A journalist of some repute wrote to me that he wanted to come here and perhaps write about this place. I replied rather deprecating the writing. At lunch-time, today, Sunday, he turned up in the yard with car and a lady. "I didn't know you were coming," I said. – "Didn't you get my second letter?" he snapped – "No." – "You're lying," to which I replied, "Anyhow it's not worth disputing about." – "No, but you're a liar for all that." (No letter reached me even afterwards.) I sent up his bags and then hinted that I be introduced to the lady, the silent witness of this comic advent. "Mrs B––," he grudgingly announced. But somehow, though he had asked for "a room", I began to think that not he alone but both were staying here. "Is the lady staying too?" – "Yes." – "Then you want two rooms?" – "No, I said a 'double room'." – "But really you make it very embarrassing for me." – "Why?" – "Because you're not married and I discourage indiscriminate coupling here." – "That's not your business." – "But it is." – "You mean, you think you can ask everyone who comes here if they are married?" – "Yes, if I want to." – "But the law compels you to take me if I ask for a room." – "Perhaps, but you'd make out a poor case to the magistrates in these particular circumstances." – "Then what about the –– ?" Here the fellow descended to implying that I did a fine trade in a very different kind of couple, for which I gave him what the bully deserved. Then I recounted to him the whole interview, everything of which he denied categorically, and I ended with, "So you're a liar yourself, a cad, and I'll do nothing to help you. I'm only sorry for the lady who's heard all this to her distress." I went back into the kitchen to carve meat, and I suppose he got back his bags, and took his car away. I felt wounded at first, then I rejoiced that the place had escaped a repetition of the dear old things that the average journalist has written about it, but with a novelty, perhaps, a hint that it was a place for a jolly week-end with a lady friend. . . *"Because thy rage against me, and thy tumult, is come up into mine ears, therefore will I put my hook in thy nose, and my bridle in thy lips, and I will turn thee back by the way by which thou camest."* (*Isaiah 37.29*)

"Gastronomic Specialities"

The place with its *spécialité gastronomique* is at least one better than the place with none, but you can't make a meal of écrevisses alone, or Grasmere gingerbread, Rouen duck, Edinburgh rock or Westminster school pancake, or pâté de canard d'Amiens, especially as, in these speciality places, the rest of the food is extra meaningless. But where is it, besides here, that you get intention in *everything*? When I took this shop, I thought round for all the things I had found best wherever I'd been and sent for them. So Kate pays regular bills for foodstuff in Athens, France, Norway, Jaffa and Italy. And of English things we have daily from three bakers three different kinds of bread made from flours that I have forced upon them, besides the breads we make ourselves, cheese from East Harptree, salt from Malden, mustard from Newport Pagnell, sausages, after a romantic search all over England, from Glenthorn in Thame, books from the Book Society, bacon, found by accident, from the International Stores (for their ugly branch here they tore down part of the most remarkable building in Thame, the Bird Cage Inn: an obscenotaph to Lord Devonport), and despite the trouble, the net result upon the patient is that he is alive to something very different in the food. Real food *is* a surprise, and simply because the gastric juices fly out to it, whilst they hold back aching at the aromalessness of synthetic, poor or adulterated products. Surely this is better than buying all your stuff from an "hotel purveyor", making out your quantities required on a big list – butter, coffee, coal, caviare, paraffin, all tasting the same and all wrapped up in Marie Stopes paper, even the coal. Surely this is better and more difficult than having one *spécialité gastronomique?*

Bank Holiday and Lavatory Work

A man led from a big car a good-looking ill lady limping into the house, and pushed past me in my short white steward's coat, and three other people. So I followed up and asked them, it being three o'clock, if they wanted tea or lunch. "No," said the lady, "the ladies' room, if there is such a thing." The absence of a "please" and the suggestion that there was no indoor sanitation in the house irritated me – so I waited on the doorstep. They returned and pushed past me again. When they were back in their car, I went out, signalled to the chauffeur not to start, and asked, "Have you had *everything* you want?" – "Yes, thank you." – "Ah, yes, it was only that 'thank you' that I was wanting." She looked confused towards the big man, who sat speechless and then at me, "But I *did* say 'good afternoon'." This she hadn't done in any case and she began to look more ill and distinguished than ever. "No, you didn't, not even that – you were thoughtless," I replied, as kindly as possible. "Like other people you think a public house is kept up by no one for the public use; I only wanted a 'thank you'." Then I turned and went back. I heard a plaintive voice calling "Waiter." For an instant I wondered whether I should answer to this ridiculous title, but I turned round and held up my hand once more to the chauffeur, who had already started the car. As I got up a thin delicate hand held over to me a shilling, "Please take this." – "No, thank you, I'm not a waiter." Then sweeping my hand across the whole nine-window length of the place, "I – I own *all* this; I *really* don't want it; I only asked for a 'thank you'. Sometimes nice people like you do this thing, and I get irritated" – and then she looked sweeter than ever. "But do take it, I *must* do something – it was horrible, I see it was horrible." And the fool of a man who ought to have done all the work for her in the first instance sat tight. "No," I said, "thank you ever so much – please don't be angry with me – I see you are ever so nice – please forget it, goodbye." And I retired, sad but still convinced that people mustn't go walking into other people's lavatories like this.

Alphabetical list of hotels

England

Abbey Penzance 139
Angel Bury St Edmunds 59
Appletree Holme Farm Blawith 46
Arundell Arms Lifton 116
Ashfield House Grassington 87
Ashleigh House Henley-in-Arden 98
Ashwick Country House Dulverton 77
At Sign Of Angel Lacock 110
Athenaeum London 118
Ayton Hall Great Ayton 88
Basil Street London 119
Bay Tree Burford 58
Beaufort London 120
Bedruthan Steps Mawgan Porth 132
Bell Inn Aston Clinton 31
La Belle Alliance Blandford Forum 45
Bibury Court Bibury 43
Biggin Hall Farm Guest House Biggin-by-Hartington 43
Bishopstrow House Warminster 168
Black Lion Long Melford 128
Black Swan Ravenstonedale 142
Blakes London 120
Boscundle Manor St Austell 147
Bowlish House Shepton Mallet 152
Breamish House Powburn 142
Bridge House Beaminster 41
Bridgefield House Spark Bridge 155
Brookdale House North Huish 136
Buckinghamshire Arms Blickling 47
Buckland Manor Buckland 57
Burleigh Court Minchinhampton 133
Butchers Arms Woolhope 181
Calcot Manor Tetbury 161
Capital London 120
Casterbridge Dorchester 77
Castle Taunton 160
Caterham House Stratford-upon-Avon 157
Cavendish Baslow 34
Chadlington House Chadlington 64
Chedington Court Chedington 65
Cherrybrook Two Bridges 164
Chewton Glen New Milton 136
Chilvester Hill House Calne 60
Claverly London 121
Colestocks House Honiton 101
Collin House Broadway 54
Combe House Gittisham 86
Congham Hall Country House King's Lynn 107
Connaught London 121
Coombe Farm Widegates 173
Corse Lawn House Corse Lawn 72
Cotswold House Chipping Campden 66
Courtlands Hove 101
Cranley Place London 122

Crantock Bay Crantock 73
Crown Southwold 154
Curdon Mill Williton 174
D'Isney Place Lincoln 117
Dalmeny St Anne's-on-Sea 146
Danescombe Valley Calstock 61
Dedham Hall Dedham 74
Downhayes Spreyton 155
Downrew House Barnstaple 33
Duke's London 122
Eagle House Bathford 39
Eastbury Sherborne 153
Ebury Court London 122
Elms Abberley 27
Elvey Farm Pluckley 140
Esseborne Manor Hurstbourne Tarrant 104
Etrop Grange Manchester 132
Fallowfields Kingston Bagpuize 108
Farlam Hall Brampton 50
Farmhouse Lew 115
Feathers Woodstock 180
Feldon House Lower Brailes 129
Felmingham Hall Felmingham 83
Field Head House Hawkshead 96
Fleece Cirencester 69
Flitwick Manor Flitwick 84
Fox's Earth Lewdown 115
Frog Street Farm Beercrocombe 41
Garrack St Ives 148
George of Stamford Stamford 156
Gidleigh Park Chagford 64
Glebe Farm Diddlebury 76
Goring London 123
Grafton Manor Bromsgrove 55
Gravetye Manor East Grinstead 78
Greenriggs Country House Underbarrow 167
Grey Cottage Leonard Stanley 114
Grey Friar Lodge Brathay 51
Grizedale Lodge Grizedale 90
Hall Garth Country House Coatham Mundeville 70
Hambleton Hall Hambleton 92
Hassop Hall Hassop 94
Hazlitt's London 123
Headlam Hall Headlam 97
Heddon's Gate Heddon's Mouth 97
Hell Bay Bryher 56
High Greenrigg House Caldbeck 60
Highbullen Chittlehamholt 68
Higher Faugan Country House Newlyn 135
Higher House West Bagborough 170
Hintlesham Hall Hintlesham 99
Holdsworth House Halifax 91
Holly Lodge Bath 35
Homewood Park Hinton Charterhouse 100
Hope End Country House Ledbury 113
Horn of Plenty Gulworthy 91
Horsted Place Little Horsted 117
L'Hôtel London 125
Howe Villa Richmond 143
Howfield Manor Canterbury 62
Howtown Ullswater 165
Hunstrete House Hunstrete 101
Huntsham Court Huntsham 103
Hurstone Farmhouse Wiveliscombe 179
Island Tresco 163
Ivy House Braithwaite 49
Jervaulx Hall Jervaulx 105
Kemps Country House East Stoke 79
Kennel Holt Cranbrook 73
Kings Arms Chipping Campden 67
Kirkby Fleetham Hall Kirkby Fleetham 109
Kirkstone Foot Country House Ambleside 29
Knightsbridge London 124
Knightsbridge Green London 124
Lamorna Cove Lamorna Cove 111
Langley House Wiveliscombe 179

Lansdowne Leamington Spa 113
Lastingham Grange Lastingham 112
Linden Hall Longhorsley 128
Little Barwick House Barwick 33
Little Hemingfold Farmhouse Battle 40
Little Hodgeham Bethersden 42
Lord Crewe Arms Blanchland 45
Lovelady Shield Alston 28
Low Greenfield Buckden 57
Lower Pitt Guest House East Buckland 78
Lygon Arms Broadway 55
Maiden Newton House Maiden Newton 131
Mains Hall Little Singleton 118
Maison Talbooth Dedham 75
Mallory Court Bishops Tachbrook 44
Malt House Broad Campden 53
Le Manoir aux Quat' Saisons Great Milton 89
Manor West Bexington 170
Manor Arms at Abberley Abberley 28
Manor Farm Barn Taynton 160
Mansion House Poole 141
Marine Salcombe 150
Marlborough Ipswich 105
Mason's Arms Branscombe 50
Masons Arms Inn Knowstone 110
May View Guest House Cambridge 62
Meadow House Kilve 106
Mill Mungrisdale 133
Mill House Kingham 107
Millcombe House Lundy Island 130
Miller Howe Windermere 176
Millstream Bosham 48
Mount Royale York 184
Nare Veryan 167
Netherfield Place Battle 41
Northcote Manor Langho 112
Number Nine Bath 36
Number Sixteen London 126
Oakhill House Oakhill 137
Old Bridge Huntingdon 102
Old Church Watermillock 168
Old Granary Wareham 167
Old House Wickham 173
Old Millfloor Trebarwith Strand 162
Old Rectory Great Snoring 90
Old Rectory Willersey 174
Old Vicarage Malvern Wells 132
Old Vicarage Witherslack 178
Old Vicarage Worfield 182
Old Vicarage Guest House Rye 145
Otley House Otley 138
Painswick Painswick 139
Paradise House Bath 37
Parrock Head Farm Slaidburn 153
Peacock Rowsley 145
Penmere Manor Falmouth 82
Pennyhill Park Bagshot 32
Pheasant Harome 93
Pheasant Inn Bassenthwaite Lake 35
Plough Clanfield 70
Plumber Manor Sturminster Newton 158
Pool Court with Rooms Pool-in-Wharfedale 140
Portobello London 126
Priory Bath 37
Quarry Garth Windermere 177
Ram Jam Inn Stretton 158
Red Lion Weobley 169
Reeds Poughill 141
Rookery Hall Worleston 183
Rose Crown Romaldkirk 144
Rothay Manor Ambleside 29
Royal Oak Yattendon 183
Royal Oak Inn Winsford 177
Russell Harrogate 93
Ryecroft Wooler 181
Ryedale Lodge Nunnington 137
Saffron Saffron Walden 146
Sandringham London 126
Scale Hill Loweswater 129

Seatoller House Borrowdale 47
Seaview Seaview 152
Sharrow Bay Country House Ullswater 166
Ship Inn West Stour 172
Somerset House Bath 38
Stanneylands Wilmslow 175
Star Castle St Mary's 149
Steppes Country House Ullingswick 164
Stock Hill House Gillingham 85
Ston Easton Park Ston Easton 156
String of Horses Faugh 82
Suffolk House Chichester 66
Summer Lodge Evershot 81
Swinside Lodge Newlands 134
Swynford Paddocks Newmarket 135
Sydney Gardens Bath 39
Talland Bay Talland-by-Looe 159
Tanyard Boughton Monchelsea 48
Tarr Steps Hawkridge 95
Teignworthy Frenchbeer 84
Tides Reach Salcombe 151
Topps Brighton 52
Treglos Constantine Bay 71
Tregony House Tregony 162
Twenty One Brighton 52
Uplands Cartmel 63
Wallett's Court Country Guest House West Cliffe 171
Wateredge Ambleside 30
Whatley Manor Easton Grey 80
White Hart Exeter 81
White House Williton 174
White Moss House Grasmere 87
Whitehall Broxted 56
Wilbraham London 127
Woodhayes Whimple 172
Woodmans Arms Auberge Hastingleigh 94
Woody Bank St Lawrence 149

Wales

Bodysgallen Hall Llandudno 194
Castle Cottage Harlech 191
Cnapan Country House for Guests Newport 198
Fairyhill Country House Reynoldston 198
Gliffaes Country House Crickhowell 189
Golden Grove Arms Llanarthney 191
Guest House St-y-Nyll St-Bride's-super-Ely 199
Maenan Abbey Maenan 197
Maes-y-Neuadd Talsarnau 199
Meadowsweet Llanrwst 195
Minffordd Talyllyn 200
Old Rectory Glan Conwy 191
Palé Hall Llandderfel 192
Pen-y-Gwryd Llanberis 192
Penlan Oleu Llanychaer 196
Porth Tocyn Abersoch 187
Rhyd-Garn-Wen Cardigan 188
St Tudno Llandudno 194
Sychnant Pass Conwy 189
Tyddyn Llan Country House Llandrillo 193
Ynyshir Hall Country House Eglwysfach 190

Scotland

Airds Port Appin 236
Altnaharrie Inn Ullapool 244
Amulree Amulree 204
Ard-Na-Coille Newtonmore 234
Ardfenaig House Bunessan 209
Ardsheal House Kentallen 227
Ardvasar Ardvasar 205
Argyll Iona 226
Arisaig Arisaig 205
Auchen Castle Beattock 208
Baile-na-Cille Timsgarry 241
Ballathie House Kinclaven 231

Bellachroy Dervaig 214
Burrastow House Walls 246
Busta House Busta 210
Ceilidh Place Ullapool 245
Clifton Nairn 233
Cozac Lodge Glen Cannich 223
Craigendarroch Ballater 207
Crinan Crinan 214
Cringletie House Peebles 235
Cromlix House Dunblane 216
Cuil-na-Sithe Guest House Kilchrenan 228
Druimnacroish Dervaig 215
Dunain Park Inverness 226
Easdale Inn Easdale 218
Enmore Dunoon 217
Factor's House Fort William 221
Ferniehurst Mill Lodge Jedburgh 227
Foveran St Ola 238
Gleddoch House Langbank 233
Glenborrodale Castle Glenborrodale 224
Glencripesdale House Glencripesdale 225
Golf Crail 213
Howard Edinburgh 218
Inverlochy Castle Fort William 221
Isle of Colonsay Colonsay 212
Isle of Eriska Eriska 220
Isle of Raasay Raasay 238
Kilfinan Kilfinan 229
Killiecrankie Killiecrankie 230
Kinloch House Blairgowrie 209
Kinloch Lodge Sleat 240
Kinlochbervie Kinlochbervie 232
Knipoch Knipoch 232
Knockie Lodge Whitebridge 246
Knockinaam Lodge Portpatrick 236
Mansion House Elgin 220
Old Mansion House Auchterhouse 206
One Devonshire Gardens Glasgow 222
Osprey Kingussie 231
Pittodrie House Pitcaple 235
Polmaily House Drumnadrochit 215
Port-An-Eilean Strathtummel 241
Portsonachan Portsonachan 237
Prestonfield House Edinburgh 218
Putechan Lodge Bellochantuy 208
Riverside Inn Canonbie 211
Roman Camp Callander 210
Scarista House Scarista 239
Summer Isles Achiltibuie 203
Taychreggan Kilchrenan 228
Teviotdale House Edinburgh 219
Tiroran House Tiroran 242
Tobermory Tobermory 243
White House Glasgow 222

Channel Isles

La Frégate St Peter Port 250
La Sablonnerie Sark 253
Longueville Manor St Saviour 251
Midhurst House St Peter Port 251
Petit Champ Sark 252
Stocks Sark 254
White House Herm 249

Ireland

Arbutus Lodge Cork 259
Assolas Country House Kanturk 263
Ballymaloe House Shanagarry 270
Buswells Dublin 261
Cahernane Killarney 264
Cashel House Cashel Bay 258
Cashel Palace Cashel 257
Coopershill Riverstown 268

Currarevagh House Oughterard 266
Drumlease Glebe House Dromahair 260
Gregans Castle Ballyvaughan 257
Gurthalougha House Ballinderry 255
Hilton Park Scotshouse 270
Hunter's Rathnew 267
Kilronan House Dublin 262
Knockmuldowney Country House Culleenamore 260
Lotamore House Cork 259
Marlfield House Gorey 262
Mount Herbert Dublin 262
Newport House Newport 265
Park Kenmare Kenmare 263
Roundwood House Mountrath 265
Sand House Rossnowlagh 269
Sea View House Ballylickey 256
Tinakilly House Rathnew 267

Austria

Alpbacherhof Alpbach 275
Amadeus Vienna 291
Elefant Salzburg 288
Elisabeth Mayrhofen 287
Friesacher Anif 276
Gasthof Deim zum Goldenen Hirschen Freistadt 280
Gasthof Gams Bezau 278
Gasthof Krimmlerfälle Krimml 284
Gasthof Zur Traube Lans 285
Haus Senger Heiligenblut 282
Hotel-Gasthof Gmachl Bergheim 277
Hotel-Gasthof Moawirt Wagrain-Moadörfl 294
Hotel-Gasthof Salome Lech am Arlberg 286
Hotel-Pension Schwarzes-Rössl Windischgarsten 295
Kaiserin Elisabeth Vienna 292
Kasererbräu Salzburg 288
König von Ungarn Vienna 292
Krone Schruns 291
Madrisa Gargellen 281
Minichmayr Steyr 291
Modersnhof Weiz 295
Montana Kitzbühel 284
Museumsverein Schloss Rosenau Schloss Rosenau 290
Muttererhof Mutters 288
Palais Schwarzenberg Vienna 293
Pension Nonntal Salzburg 289
Pension Nossek Vienna 293
Pension Rupertihof Fuschl-am-See 281
Pension Suzanne Vienna 294
Post Lech am Arlberg 285
Richard Löwenherz Dürnstein 278
Romantikhotel Böglerhof Alpbach 276
Schloss Dürnstein Dürnstein 279
Schloss Fuschl Hof bei Salzburg 283
Schloss Mönchstein Salzburg 289
Schlossberg Graz 282
Schlosshotel Rosenegg Fieberbrunn 279
Schöne Aussicht Salzburg 290
Singer Sporthotel Berwang 277
Tannbergerhof Lech am Arlberg 286
Weinhaus Happ Innsbruck 283

Belgium

Adornes Bruges 298
Anselmus Bruges 298
Auberge du Moulin Hideux Noirefontaine 306
Convent Reninge 307
Hostellerie Bellemolen Essene 302
Hostellerie Le Fox De Panne 306
Hostellerie Le Val d'Amblève Stavelot 308

Hostellerie Shamrock Ronse 307
Hostellerie Trôs Marets Malmédy 305
Hostellerie du Prieuré de Conques Herbeumont 304
Hostellerie le Sanglier des Ardennes Durbuy 301
Hôtel Agenda Brussels 300
Hôtel Amigo Brussels 301
Hôtel St Jorishof Gent 302
Mardaga As 297
Moulin de Lisogne Lisogne 304
Orangerie Bruges 299
Oude Abdij Lo 305
Residence Rembrandt Brussels 301
Scholteshof Hasselt-Stevoort 303
Swaene Bruges 299
Ter Duinen Bruges 299

Denmark

Ascot Copenhagen 309
Dagmar Ribe 313
Falsled Kro Falsled 310
Munkebjerg Vejle 314
71 Nyhavn Copenhagen 309
Pension Kirkedal Lønstrup 312
Sønderho Kro Sønderho 313
Steensgaard Herregårdspension Millinge 312
Store Kro Fredensborg 311
Vestersøhus Copenhagen 310

France

A Pasturella Monticello 396
Abbaye La Colle-sur-Loup 354
Abbaye Le Bec-Hellouin 331
Abbaye St-Cyprien 434
Abbaye Talloires 456
Abbaye St-Germain Paris 407
Abbaye de Sainte-Croix Salon-de-Provence 450
Agoult, Château d'Arpaillargues Arpaillargues 324
Aigle Noir Fontainebleau 373
Aiguille du Midi Chamonix 346
Albert Premier et de Milan Chamonix 347
Alisiers Lapoutroie 387
Angleterre Avignon 326
Angleterre Jacky Michel Châlons-sur-Marne 346
Antiques St-Rémy-de-Provence 444
Argouges Bayeux 329
Arlatan Arles 323
Armes de Champagne l'Épine 365
Atalaya Saillagouse 432
Auberge de Vendeuil Vendeuil 464
Auberge sans Frontière Dégagnac 361
Avaugour Dinan 363
Baou Ramatuelle 423
Bayard Lyon 389
Beatus Cambrai 341
Beau Rivage Condrieu 357
Beau-Site Talloires 456
Belle-Rive Najac 401
Bellevue Les Roches-de-Condrieu 428
Bellevue Montrichard 398
Bellier Val d'Isère 462
Benvengudo Les Baux-de-Provence 329
Berceaux Épernay 365
Bon Coin du Lac Mimizan 394
Bonne Étape Château-Arnoux 348
Bonnet Beynac 333
Bordeaux Le Havre 381
Bosquet Pégomas 413
Bourgogne Cluny 354
Boyer "Les Crayères" Reims 424
Brikétenia Guéthary 380
Briqueterie Vinay 470
Brises La Rochelle 427
Cagnard Haut-de-Cagnes 381
Caillère Candé-sur-Beuvron 341
Cap d'Antibes Cap d'Antibes 341

Cap Estel Èze-Bord-de-Mer 368
Capo Rosso Piana 416
Caravelle Peyrat-le-Château 416
Caribou Porticciolo 420
Castel Mailly-le-Château 390
Castel Seurre 454
Cathédrale Rouen 431
Cazaudehore La Forestière St-Germain-en-Laye 436
Cep Beaune 331
Cévenole La Favède 370
Chalet Coulandon 360
Chalet du Lac Gérardmer 376
Chapelle-St-Martin St-Martin-du-Fault 441
Cheneaudière Colroy-la-Roche 356
Cheval Blanc Sept-Saulx 453
Chez Pierre Raguenès-Plage 423
Christiania Villard-de-Lans 468
Château Challes-les-Eaux 345
Château Châteauneuf-en-Auxois 349
Château Fère-en-Tardenois 371
Château d'Artigny Montbazon 395
Château de la Barge Crèches-sur-Saône 361
Château de Castel-Novel Varetz-en-Limousin 463
Château de Castelpers Castelpers 343
Château de la Caze La Malène 391
Château de la Chèvre d'Or Èze-Village 369
Château Hôtel de Coatguelen Pléhédel 416
Château de la Corniche Rolleboise 429
Château d'Esclimont St-Symphorien-le-Château 445
Château de Faverges Faverges-de-la-Tour 370
Château des Fines Roches Châteauneuf-du-Pape 349
Château d'Igé Igé 383
Château de Keravéon Erdeven 366
Château de Locguénolé et Hennebont 382
Château de Marçay Chinon 352
Château de Montreuil Montreuil 397
Château de Nieuil Nieuil 403
Château de Ponderach St-Pons-de-Thomières 443
Château de Pray Amboise 320
Château de Quinéville Quinéville 422
Château de la Râpée Bazincourt-sur-Epte 330
Château de Rigny Rigny 426
Château de Rochegude Rochegude 426
Château de Roussan St-Rémy-de-Provence 444
Château de Teildras Cheffes 350
Château de Trigance Trigance 461
Château d'Urbilhac Lamastre 386
Châtenet Brantôme 337
Châtillon Paris 407
Clos Chablis 344
Clos Normand Martin-Église 392
Clos Saint-Vincent Ribeauvillé 425
Cochon d'Or Beuzeville 333
Colombe d'Or St-Paul-de-Vence 442
Commerce Villefranche-du-Périgord 468
Commerce et Diligences Digoin 363
Coq Hardi Verdun 464
Côte Saint-Jacques Joigny 384
Côte d'Or Nuits-St-Georges 406
Côte d'Or Saulieu 451
Coteau Fleuri Grimaud 379
Cottage Argelès-sur-Mer 323
Couleuvrine Sarlat 451
Cour des Loges Lyon 389
Cro-Magnon Les Eyzies-de-Tayac 367
Daille Florimont-Gaumiers 372
Deux-Iles Paris 408
Deux Rocs Seillans 452

Diana Vence 464
Diderot Chinon 352
Dolce Notte St-Florent 435
Dolce Vita Ajaccio 318
Domaine d'Auriac Carcassonne 342
Domaine de Beauvois Luynes 389
Domaine de Clairefontaine Chonas l'Amballan 353
Domaine de Fleurac Jarnac 384
Domaine de Loselly Ste-Foy-la-Grande 448
Domaine d'Orvault Orvault 406
Eden Roc Ajaccio 319
Entraigues Uzès 461
Équipe Molines-en-Queyras 395
Espérance Vézelay 466
Esplanade Domme 363
Étrier Camarguais Les Stes-Maries-de-la-Mer 449
Europe Avignon 326
Fartoret Bellegarde-sur-Valsérine 331
Ferme-Auberge du Vert Wierre-Effroy 471
Ferme St-Siméon Honfleur 382
Fifi Moulin Serres 453
Fleurie Montsalvy 399
Florets Gigondas 376
Forestière Louvie-Juzon 388
France Mende 393
France et d'Angleterre La Rochelle 428
France et des Fuchsias St-Vaast-la-Hougue 447
France Mercier Montmorillon 397
Galerie des Arcades Biot 334
Georges Blanc Vonnas 471
Glycines Les Eyzies-de-Tayac 368
Grande Chaumière St-Florentin 436
Grand Écuyer Cordes 358
Grands Hommes Paris 408
Grand Hôtel Roquefort-sur-Soulzon 430
Grand Hôtel de Cala Rossa Porto-Vecchio 421
Grand Hôtel Clément Ardres 322
Grand Hôtel de l'Europe Langres 387
Grand Hôtel de l'Opéra Toulouse 458
Grand Hôtel Pélisson Nontron 404
Grand Hôtel de l'Univers Amiens 321
Halle Givry 377
Horizon Cabris 340
Hospitaliers Le Poët-Laval 417
Huchette Replonges 425
Huitrière du Lac Hossegor 382
Jeanne de Laval Les Rosiers-sur-Loire 430
Jules César Arles 324
L'Hôtel Paris 408
Laborderie Tamniès 457
Lameloise Chagny 345
Lancaster Paris 409
Les Griffons Bourdeilles 337
Lièvre Amoureux St-Lattier 439
Lion d'Or Bayeux 329
Lons Foix 373
Lou Calen Cotignac 360
Louisiane Paris 410
Lutèce Paris 410
Lys Lys-Chantilly 390
Madeloc Collioure 355
Madone Peillon 414
Manoir Aix-en-Provence 318
Manoir Bel Air St-Dyé-sur-Loire 434
Manoir Les Prouillacs St-Amand-de-Vergt 432
Manoir-Hôtel Rochecourbe Vézac 466
Maquis Porticcio 419
Marais Coulon 361
Marais St-Jean Chonas l'Amballan 353
Marine Carteret 342
Maritonnes Romanèche-Thorins 429

Maronne St-Martin-Valmeroux 442
Mas Candille Mougins 400
Mas de Chastelas St-Tropez 446
Mas Djoliba Antibes 322
Mas de la Fouque Les Stes-Maries-de-la-Mer 450
Mayanelle Gordes 377
Meijette La Grave 379
Menez-Frost Bénodet 332
Mère Poulard Mont-St-Michel 399
Métairie Neuve Pont-de-Larn 419
Métropole Beaulieu-sur-Mer 330
Midi St-Jean-du-Bruel 437
Midi/Restaurant Lamastre 386
Miquel: l'Oustal del Barry Najac 402
Montrachet Puligny-Montrachet 422
Moulin Flagy 371
Moulin de la Beune Les Eyzies-de-Tayac 368
Moulin de Chaméron Bannegon 327
Moulin de la Gorce La Roche-l'Abeille 427
Moulin de Montalétang St-Moreil 441
Moulin du Roc Champagnac-de-Belair 347
Moulin de la Source Bleue Touzac 460
Moulin des Templiers Avallon 326
Moulin de Villeray Villeray 470
Moulin de Villiers Nouan-le-Fuzelier 405
Munsch: Aux Ducs de St-Hippolyte 437
Musardière Thizy 458
Naulets d'Anjou Gennes 375
Noailles Montpellier 397
Normandie Caudebec-en-Caux 343
Nouvel Hôtel Maison Rouge Strasbourg 455
Noves Noves 405
Ombremont Le Bourget-du-Lac 337
Oustaù de Baumanière Les Baux-de-Provence 328
Parc des Maréchaux Auxerre 325
Paris Moulins 401
Pavillon Paris 411
Pavillon de l'Ermitage Chavoire 350
Pélissaria St-Cirq-Lapopie 433
Pen'Roc La Peinière-St-Didier 414
Pereria Guéthary 380
Pérouse Nice 403
Pescalerie Cabrerets 339
Philippe Million Albertville 319
Pic Valence 462
Pietracap Bastia 328
Pins Sabres 431
Plage Boulogne-sur-Mer 336
Plage Ste-Anne-la-Palud 448
Poids Public St-Félix-Lauragais 435
Pont de l'Ouysse Lacave 385
Pont Romain Sommières 455
Pontoise Pons 417
Port Port-Manech 421
Poste Avallon 325
Poste Corps-la-Salette 359
Poste et Champanne Brioude 338
Poste et du Lion d'Or Vézelay 468
Préjoly St-Vallier-de-Thiey 447
Prés d'Eugénie Eugénie-les-Bains 366
Prés du Lac Talloires 457
Prieuré Chênehutte-les-Tuffeaux 351
Prieuré Villeneuve-lès-Avignon 469
Pullman le Pigonnet Aix-en-Provence 318
Pyrénées St-Jean-Pied-de-Port 439
Régalido Fontvieille 374
Relais Ardres 322
Relais du Bois St-Georges Saintes 449

Relais de Comodoliac St-Junien 439
Relais Fleuri Avallon 325
Relais de la Magdeleine Gémenos 374
Relais de Nantilly Nantilly 402
Relais de St-Jacques de Compostelle Collonges-la-Rouge 355
Remparts Aigues-Mortes 316
Réserve Albi 320
Résidence Narbonne 403
Résidence Chambard Kaysersberg 385
Résidence Hôtel Le Pontot Vézelay 467
Résidence "Les Aloës" Calvi 340
Résidence du Bois Paris 411
Résidence les Cèdres Villeneuve-lès-Avignon 469
Résidences Le Petit Nice et Marseilles 391
Rhône Seyssel 454
Richelieu La Flotte 372
Rivage Gien 376
Roches Fleuries Cordon 359
Rohan Strasbourg 456
Rostaing Passenans 413
Royal Champagne Champillon 348
Royal-Lieu Compiègne 357
Rustica Pons 418
Saint-Pierre La Bouille 335
Saint-Pierre St-Pierre-du-Vauvray 443
Sainte-Foy Conques 358
San Giovanni Porto-Vecchio 421
Sarthe Châteauneuf-sur-Sarthe 349
Scandinavia Paris 411
Scierie Aix-en-Othe 317
Sélune Ducey 364
Solognote Brinon-sur-Sauldre 338
Sombral St-Cirq-Lapopie 433
St-Georges Chalon-sur-Saône 346
St-Merry Paris 411
St-Pierre Tourtour 459
Suède Paris 411
Table du Comtat Séguret 452
Taillard Goumois 378
Tamarissière Agde 315
Templiers Les Bézards 334
Terminus Cahors 340
Terrasse au Soleil Céret 344
Tête Noire Montrichard 398
Thermes Bourbon-l'Archambault 336
Ti al-Lannec Trebeurden 460
Tour de l'Esquillon Miramar 394
Tour du Roy Vervins 465
Touring Hôtel St-Léonard-des-Bois 440
Treizain St-Tropez 446
Trois Barbus Anduze 321
Trois Mousquetaires Aire-sur-la-Lys 316
Trois Roses La Petite Pierre 415
Ty-Pont St-Jean-du-Doigt 438
U Castagnetu Bastelica 327
Univers Dieppe 362
Université Paris 412
Val Suzon Val Suzon 463
Val d'Or Mercurey 393
Valmarin St-Malo 440
Vannes et sa Résidence Liverdun 388
Varenne Paris 412
Vieux Logis Lestelle-Bétharram 387
Vieux Moulin Bouilland 334
Vieux Moulin Centuri Port 344
Vieux Puits Pont-Audemer 418

Germany

Abtei Hamburg 494
Adler Asperg 474
Adler Gutach Im Breisgau 493
Alpenhof Grainau 493
Alte Rheinmühle Büsingen 484
Badischer Hof Amorbach 474
Bären Meersburg 501

Bayerischer Hof Bayreuth 479
Bayerischer Hof Lindau im Bodensee 500
Bellevue Hamburg 495
Belvedere Berlin 480
Böttingerhaus Gästehaus Steinmühle Bamberg 477
Bristol Cologne 485
Burghotel Geislingen an der Steige 492
Burghotel Nuremberg 504
Deidesheimer Hof Deidesheim 486
Dittberner Berlin 481
Eisenhut Rothenburg ob der Tauber 508
Engel Horben-Langackern 497
Erbguth's Landhaus Hagnau 494
Erbprinz Ettlingen 487
Fischerwirt Ismaning 498
Fürstenhof Endtenfang Celle 485
Gästehaus Englischer Garten Munich 501
Gästehaus Monopteros Munich 502
Gasthof Glocke Rothenburg ob der Tauber 509
Gasthof "Zur Rose" Oberammergau 504
Gaststätte zum Muckenstüble Stuttgart 513
Goldener Hirsch Rothenburg ob der Tauber 509
Greifen-Post Feuchtwangen 488
Hanseatic Hamburg 495
Haus Lipmann Beilstein 480
Haus Lyskirchen Cologne 485
Historischer Krug Oeversee 505
Höhen-Unterstmatt Schwarzwald-Hochstrasse 512
Höhengasthof Kalikutt Oppenau-Ramsbach 506
Kaiser's Tanne-Wirtshus Breitnau 483
Kleine Prinz Baden-Baden 477
Krone Rüdesheim-Assmannshausen 510
Krone Tübingen 515
Kurhotel Gut Schmelmerhof Rettenbach 508
Kurhotel Martensen – Die Barke Scharbeutz 511
Landhaus Louisenthal Bremen 484
Laurentius Weikersheim 517
Lauterbad Freudenstadt 490
Marienbad Munich 502
Mehn "Zum Niederberg" Lieser-an-der-Mosel 500
Mertens Bonn 482
Molitors Mühle Eisenschmitt-Eichelhütte 487
Mönchs Posthotel Bad Herrenalb 475
Neumühle Wartmannsroth–Neumühle 516
Ochsen Schönwald 511
Ochsen Post Tiefenbronn 514
Oper Munich 503
Parkhotel Wehrle Triberg im Schwarzwald 514
Pension Heim Seeg 512
Pension Sassenhof Hinterzarten 496
Petrisberg Trier 515
Pfälzer Wald Bad Bergzabern 475
Pflaums Posthotel Pegnitz 507
Posthotel Partenkirchen Garmisch-Partenkirchen 491
Prem Hamburg 495
Ritter St Georg Heidelberg 496
Romantik-Bierhütte Hohenau 497
Romantik-Seeschau Reichenau 507
Romberg-Park Dortmund 486
Roten Bären Freiburg im Breisgau 489
Royal Stuttgart 513
Sankt Nepomuk Bamberg 478
Schaumberger Hof Bonn 483
Schloss Heinsheim Bad Rappenau 476
Schloss Hugenpoet Kettwig 498
Schloss Neuburg Obrigheim 505

Schloss Weitenburg Weitenburg 517
Schlosshotel Gehrhus Berlin 481
Schlosshotel Kommende Ramersdorf Bonn 482
Schlosshotel Kronberg Kronberg im Taunus 499
Schnellenburg Düsseldorf 486
Schönen Brunnen Nuremberg 504
Schwan Wertheim 517
Schweizer Stuben Wertheim-Bettingen 518
Seegasthof Weissensee Füssen-Weissensee 491
Sendlinger Tor Munich 503
Sonne Göttingen 492
Sonne Offenburg 506
Sonnenhof Königstein im Taunus 499
Sonnenhof St Blasien 510
Stern Bad Hersfeld 476
Strandcafé Heinzler Immenstaad am Bodensee 497
Töpferhaus Alt-Duvenstedt 473
Trustee Parkhotel Munich 503
Vier Jahreszeiten Hamburg 496
Wald-und Schlosshotel Friedrichsruhe 490
Waldhotel Krautkrämer Münster-Hiltrup 503
Waldhotel Stein Bayreuth-Seulbitz 479
Westend Frankfurt-am-Main 489
Wiesenhof Eutin-Fissau 488
Zens Manderscheid 501
Zimmermann Limburg an der Lahn 500

Greece

Akti Myrina Myrina 525
Amalia Olympia 527
Apollon Xylokastron 530
Atlantis Fira 521
Atlantis Villas Ia 523
Caravel Planos 528
Chryssi Avgi Kastron Ilias 523
Contessa Chania 520
Coriva Village Ferma 521
Doma Chania 520
Ganimede Galaxidion 522
Herodion Athens 519
Hotel-Akrogiali Gerolimin 522
Kronion Olympia 527
Leto Nafplion 526
Logga Beach Koroni 524
Malvasia Monemvassia 524
Marilena Myrties 526
Minoa Tolon 529
Paola Beach Palea Epidavros 528
Romantica Pighadia 528
Vourlis Hermoupolis 523
Xenia's Palace Nafplion 526

Hungary

Annabella Balatonfüred 533
Arany Bika Debrecen 534
Budapest Hilton Budapest 533
Club Tihany Tihany 534
Eger Eger 534
Erzsébet Budapest 531
Forum Budapest 533
Gellért Budapest 532
Helikon Keszthely 534
Kastély Bük 534
Kastély Fertöd 534
Kastély Pécs 534
Kastélyszálló Szirák 534
Metropol Budapest 534
Palatinus Sopron 534
Pannónia Pécs 534
Park Eger 534
Sopron Sopron 534
Sylvanus Visegrád 533
Taverna Budapest 533
Thermal Budapest 532
Thermál Hévíz 534
Tokaj Tokaj 534
Veszprém Veszprém 534

Italy

Accademia Venice 576
Albergo San Lorenzo Mantua 552
Albergo Stella Palestrina 556
Arathena Rocks Giardini Naxos 550
Bel Soggiorno San Gimignano 565
Bussola Orta San Giulio 555
Calzaiuoli Florence 545
Campo Marzio Vicenza 580
Cannero Cannero Riviera 541
Casa Albertina Positano 561
Casa Frollo Venice 576
Castello di Gargonza Gargonza 549
Cavarchione Toscanum Gaiole in Chianti 549
Certosa di Maggiano Siena 568
Cesàri Rome 563
Cipriani Venice 577
Cisterna San Gimignano 565
Colomba d'Oro Verona 580
Do Pozzi Venice 578
Dominik Bressanone 540
Dorfer Selva di Val Gardena 567
Emilia Ancona 537
Feldhof Naturno 554
Flora Capri 541
Flora Venice 577
Fonte della Galletta Alpe Faggeto 535
Forum Rome 563
Fragsburg (Castel Verruca) Merano 552
Garden Siena 569
Gardesana Torri del Benaco 575
Giardinetto Pettenasco 558
Gran Duca di York Milan 553
Grand Villa Cora Florence 545
Grand Villa Politi Syracuse 571
Grand Villa Serbelloni Bellagio 539
Gregoriana Rome 564
Helvetia Sestri Levante 568
Hermitage Florence 546
Hôtel Bellevue Cogne 542
Lac Bellagio 538
Locanda dell'Amorosa Sinalunga 570
Loggiato dei Serviti Florence 546
Manzoni Milan 554
Marmorata Ravello 562
Mediterraneo Jesolo Pineta 551
Moderno Erice 543
Monaco Grand Canal Venice 578
Nettuno Bologna 539
Nido di Fiascherino Tellaro di Lerici 573
Palazzo Ravizza Siena 569
Palumbo Ravello 562
Paracucchi-Locanda dell'Angelo Ameglia 536
Park Mignon Merano 553
Pellicano Porto Ercole 559
Peralta Camaiore 540
Pescille San Gimignano 566
Residenza Rome 564
Rigatti Florence 547
Ristorante Boschetti Tricesimo 576
Roma Bologna 539
Rosetta Perugia 557
Royal Sporting Portovenere 560
Salivolpi Castellina In Chianti 542
San Domenico Palace Taormina 572
San Rocco Orta San Giulio 555
Saturnia e International Venice 579
Seguso Venice 579
Spedalicchio Ospedalicchio di Bastia 556
Splendido Portofino 559
Stella d'Italia San Mamete 566
Tirreno Forte dei Marmi 548
Tonnarella Sorrento 570
Torcolo Verona 580
Tornabuoni Beacci Florence 547
Tre Vaselle Torgiano 574
Umbra Assisi 538
Villa Belvedere Florence 544

Villa Bonelli Fiesole 544
Villa Cipriani Asolo 537
Villa Condulmer Zerman 580
Villa Fiorita Taormina 572
Villa Flora Torno 574
Villa Franca e Residence Positano 561
Villa Le Barone Panzano in Chianti 557
Villa Meligunis Lipari 551
Villa Mozart Merano 553
Villa Paradiso Taormina 573
Villa Scacciapensieri Siena 570
Villa del Sogno Fasano del Garda 543
Virgilio Orvieto 555

Luxembourg

Bamberg Ehnen 584
Bel-Air Echternach 584
Central Ettelbrück 585
Ermitage Berdorf 583
Grünewald Luxembourg 585
Simmer Ehnen 585

Malta

Cornucopia Xaghra 588
Ta' Cenc Sannat 587

Netherlands

Ambassade Amsterdam 590
Amstel Inter Continental Amsterdam 591
Canal House Amsterdam 591
Delft Museumhotel Delft 593
Europe Amsterdam 591
Hoofdige Boer Almen 589
Hostellerie du Château Heeze 594
Hotel de Swaen Oisterwijk 595
Hotel-Hofstede Slangevegt Breukelen 592
Huize den Treek Leusden 594
Kasteel Wittem Wittem 596
Leeuwenbrug Delft 593
Montferland Zeddam 597
Pulitzer Amsterdam 592
Wiemsel Ootmarsum 596

Norway

Alexandra Loen 602
Augustin Bergen 600
Bristol Oslo 602
Continental Oslo 603
Gabelshusl Oslo 604
Hotell Neptun Bergen 601
Hotell Refsnes Gods Jeløy 602
Midtnes Pensjonat Balestrand 599
Mundal Fjærland 601
Myklebust Pensjonat Bergen 600
Skjolden Skjolden 605
Stefanhotellet Oslo 604
Utne Utne 605
White Housel Oslo 605

Portugal

Albatroz Cascais 610
Castelo Santa Catarina Oporto 619
Estalagem Abrigo da Montanha Monchique 616
Estalagem Senhora da Guia Cascais 610
Estalagem da Quinta das Torres Azeitão 608
Estalagem do Convento Óbidos 618
Infante de Sagres Oporto 619
Malaposta Oporto 619

Paço da Gloria Arcos de Valdevez 607
Palace do Buçaco Buçaco 609
Palácio de Seteais Sintra 622
Pousada da Ria Murtosa 617
Pousada de Rainha Santa Isabel Estremoz 611
Pousada da Santa Maria de Oliveira Guimarães 613
Pousada de Santa Maria Marvão 616
Pousada de São Bento Caniçada 609
Pousada de São Brás São Brás de Alportel 621
Pousada de São Filipe Setúbal 622
Pousada de São Gens Serpa 621
Pousada de São Lourenço Manteigas 615
Pousada de São Teotónio Valença do Minho 623
Pousada do Castelo Óbidos 618
Pousada do Castelo de Palmela Palmela 620
Pousada do Infante Sagres 620
Pousada dos Lóios Évora 611
Principe Real Lisbon 614
Quinta Penha de França Funchal 612
Quinto São Thiago Sintra 622
Reid's Funchal 612
Tivoli Jardim Lisbon 615
Villa Hostilina Lamego 614

Spain

Aigua Blava Bagur 626
América Granada 638
Boomerang Valverde 650
Colon Barcelona 628
Cueva del Fraile Cuenca 633
Es Molí Deyá 634
Hospedería-Real Monasterio Guadalupe 638
Hostal del Cardenal Toledo 647
Hostal los Porches Calonge 630
Hostal de los Reyes Católicos Santiago de Compostela 644
Hostal Windsor Santiago de Compostela 645
Huerto del Cura Elche 635
Infantes Santillana del Mar 645
Landa Palace Burgos 629
Liabeny Madrid 641
Mar I Vent Bañalbufar 627
Monasterio de Piedra Nuévalos 643
Parador Nacional Segovia 646
Parador Nacional Trujillo 649
Parador Nacional Vich 651
Parador Nacional Alcázar del Rey Don Pedro Carmona 631
Parador Nacional del Albariño Cambados 630
Parador Nacional de Almagro Almagro 625
Parador Nacional de Antequera Antequera 626
Parador Nacional de Argómaniz Vitoria-Gasteiz 651
Parador Nacional de la Arruzafa Córdoba 633
Parador Nacional Castillo de Santa Catalina Jaén 640
Parador Nacional Castillo de Sigüenza Sigüenza 647
Parador Nacional Castillo de la Zuda Tortosa 649
Parador Nacional de Chinchón Chinchón 632
Parador Nacional Conde de Gondomar Bayona 629
Parador Nacional Conde de Orgaz Toledo 648
Parador Nacional Conde de la Gomera Gomera 637
Parador Nacional Condes de Alba y Aliste Zamora 652
Parador Nacional Condes de Villalba Villalba 651
Parador Nacional Enrique II Ciudad Rodrigo 632

Parador Nacional de Fuentes Carrionas Cervera de Pisuerga 631
Parador Nacional de Gibralfaro Málaga 642
Parador Nacional Gil Blas Santillana del Mar 645
Parador Nacional Hernán Cortés Zafra 652
Parador Nacional de Monterrey Verín 650
Parador Nacional Reyes Católicos Mojácar 643
Parador Nacional de Ribadeo Ribadeo 644
Parador Nacional del Río Deva Fuente Dé 636
Parador Nacional de San Francisco Granada 638
Parador Nacional Santo Domingo de la Calzada Santo Domingo de la Calzada 646
Parador Nacional de Tordesillas Tordesillas 648
Parador Nacional Virrey de Toledo Oropesa 643
Parador Nacional Zurbarán Guadalupe 639
Posada Gualchos 639
Prado Madrid 641
Residencia Deyá 635
Residencia Belvedere Encamp 636
Residencia Marisa Córdoba 633
San Marcos León 640
Suecia Madrid 642
Villa Magna Madrid 642

Sweden

Åkerblads Tällberg 660
Diplomat Stockholm 658
Grythyttans Gästgivaregård Grythyttan 656
Gyllene Uttern Gränna 655
Halltorps Gästgiveri Borgholm 654
Hotell Anno 1647 Stockholm 657
Lady Hamilton Stockholm 658
Rusthållargården Arild 653
Sara Reisen Stockholm 659
Stadshotellet-Mälarens Pärla Sigtuna 657
Strand Stockholm 659
Svarta Herrgard Svarta 660
Tanums Gestgifveri Tanumshede 661
Tidbloms Gothenburg 655
Toftaholm Herrgårdshotell Toftaholm 662

Switzerland

Alpin nova Schönried-Gstaad 678
Arbalète Geneva 667
Armures Geneva 668
Bären Lachen 672
Beau Rivage Weggis 682
Bella Tola et St-Luc St-Luc 676
Bellevue Iseltwald 670
Bellevue Neuhausen 673
Bernahof Iseltwald 670
Bon Accueil Château-d'Oex 665
Casa Berno Ascona 664
Chesa Grischuna Klosters 671
Chesa Sur L'En St Moritz 676
Chevreuils Lausanne-Jorat 672
Christiania Gstaad 669
Clos de Sadex Nyon 674
Edelweiss Sils-Maria 679
Eden Engelberg 666
Ermitage Kandersteg 671
Fiescherblick Grindelwald 668
Floralpina Vitznau 681
Florhof Zürich 685
Flüela Davos Dorf 665
Garni Chesa Mulin Pontresina 674
Garni Metropol Zermatt 682
Gasthof Zum Löwen Worb 682
Gasthof-Rothorn Schwanden 678

Golf et Marie-Louise Villars 681
Grand Kronenhof Pontresina 675
Hess Engelberg 667
Hof Maran Arosa 663
Hornberg Saanenmöser 675
Klarer Zuoz 684
Kulm Triesenberg 680
Lilas Les Diablerets 666
Meisser Guarda 669
Merian am Rhein Basle 665
Nicoletta Zermatt 683
Posthotel Engiadina Zuoz 684
Rheinhotel Fischerzunft Schaffhausen 677
Ristorante Antico Intragna 669
Sonnegg Meggen 672
Stüa Granda Soglio 679
Trois Couronnes Vevey 680
Vieux Manoir au Lac Murten 673

Turkey

Akdoğan Bursa 701
Aktaş Mersin 702
Alara Incekum 694
Anahan Anamur 688
Arsuz Turistik Arsuz 691
Atahan Antakya 701
Ayasofya Pansiyonlari Istanbul 695
Başak Palas Konya 699
Bayraklar Mardin 702
Bilgehan Antalya 701
Bulvar Palas Ankara 689
Büyük Antalya 701
Büyük Trabya Istanbul 702
Çelik Palas Bursa 692
Club Kervansarayi Kuşadasi 699
Deliban Harbiye 702
Divan Istanbul 695
Diyar Büyük Diyarbakir 701
Güneş Alanya 688
Güney Palas Iskenderun 702
Harran Urfa 702
Hīdiv Kasrī Istanbul 695
Hidro Harbiye 702
Kalyon Istanbul 697
Kaptan Alanya 701
Keykan Ankara 689
Kismet Kuşadasi 699
Kismet Izmir 702
Manzara Bodrum 691
Meri Ölüdeniz 700
Olcay Istanbul 702
Oral Erzurum 693
Orsan Kapadokya Nevşehīr 702
Pera Palas Istanbul 697
Perili Köşk Datça 693
Talya Antalya 690
Truva Çanakkale 692
Turban Abant Abant 701
Turban Adalya Antalya 690
Turban Urfa Urfa 702
Turban Ürgüp Ürgüp 703
Turistik Diyarbakir 701
Tusan Pamukkale 700
Usta Trabzon 702
Yeşil Ev Istanbul 698
Zaimoğlu Adana 687

Yugoslavia

Grand Cetinje 707
Jezero Plitvička Jezera 709
Moskva Belgrade 705
Palace Hvar 708
Sveti Stefan Sveti Stefan 710
Tvrdjava-Varadin Novi Sad 709
Vila Bled Bled 705
Villa Dubrovnik Dubrovnik 707

Maps

1 South-West England and South Wales
2 Wessex and the Cotswolds
3 South-East England
4 North Wales, the Midlands and the North of England
5 Scotland
6 Ireland
7 Southern Scandinavia
8 North-West France
9 Benelux and North-East France
10 Central and Southern France
11 The South of France and Corsica
12 Spain and Portugal
13 Germany
14 Switzerland
15 Austria
16 Italy and Malta
17 Greece, Hungary, Turkey and Yugoslavia

British Isles Maps

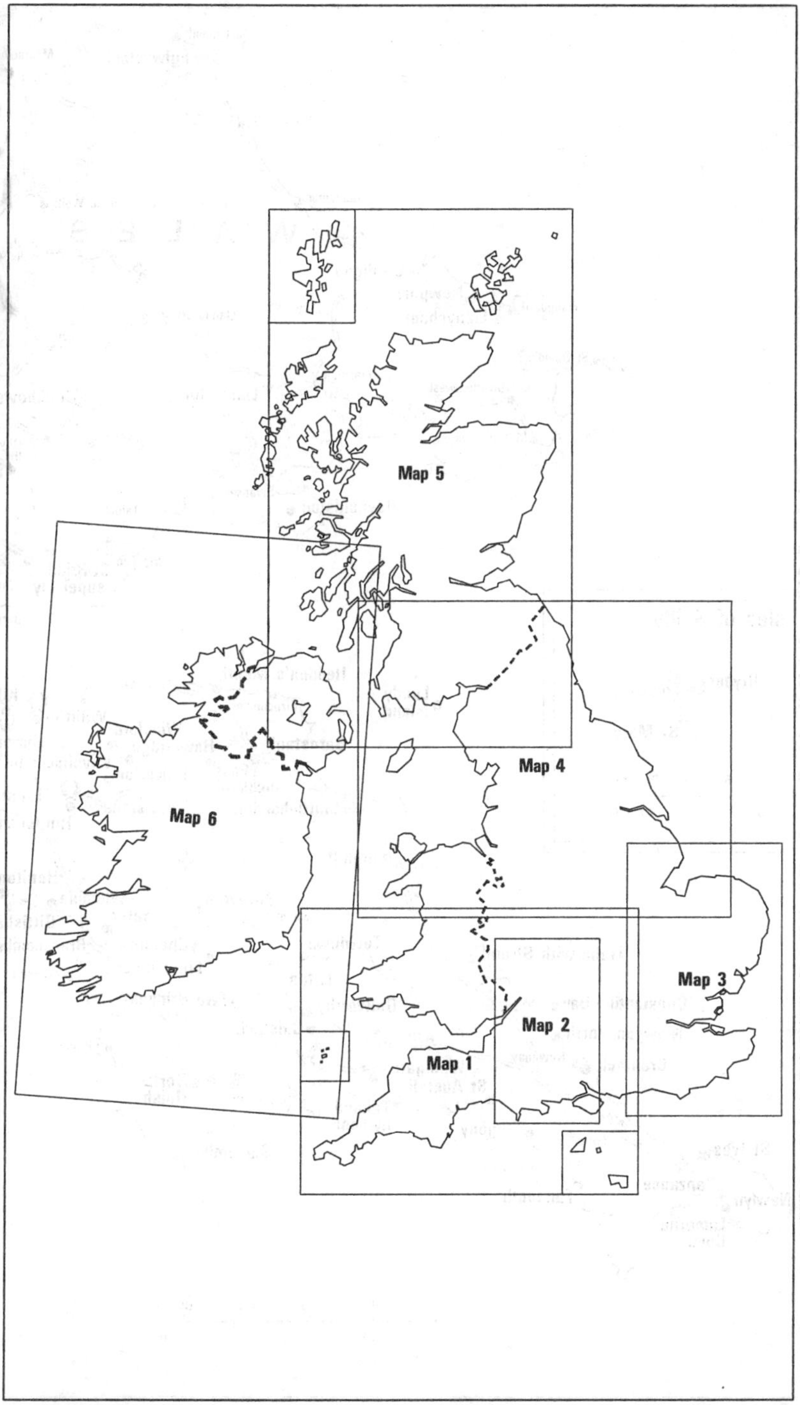

Map 1 South–West England and South Wales

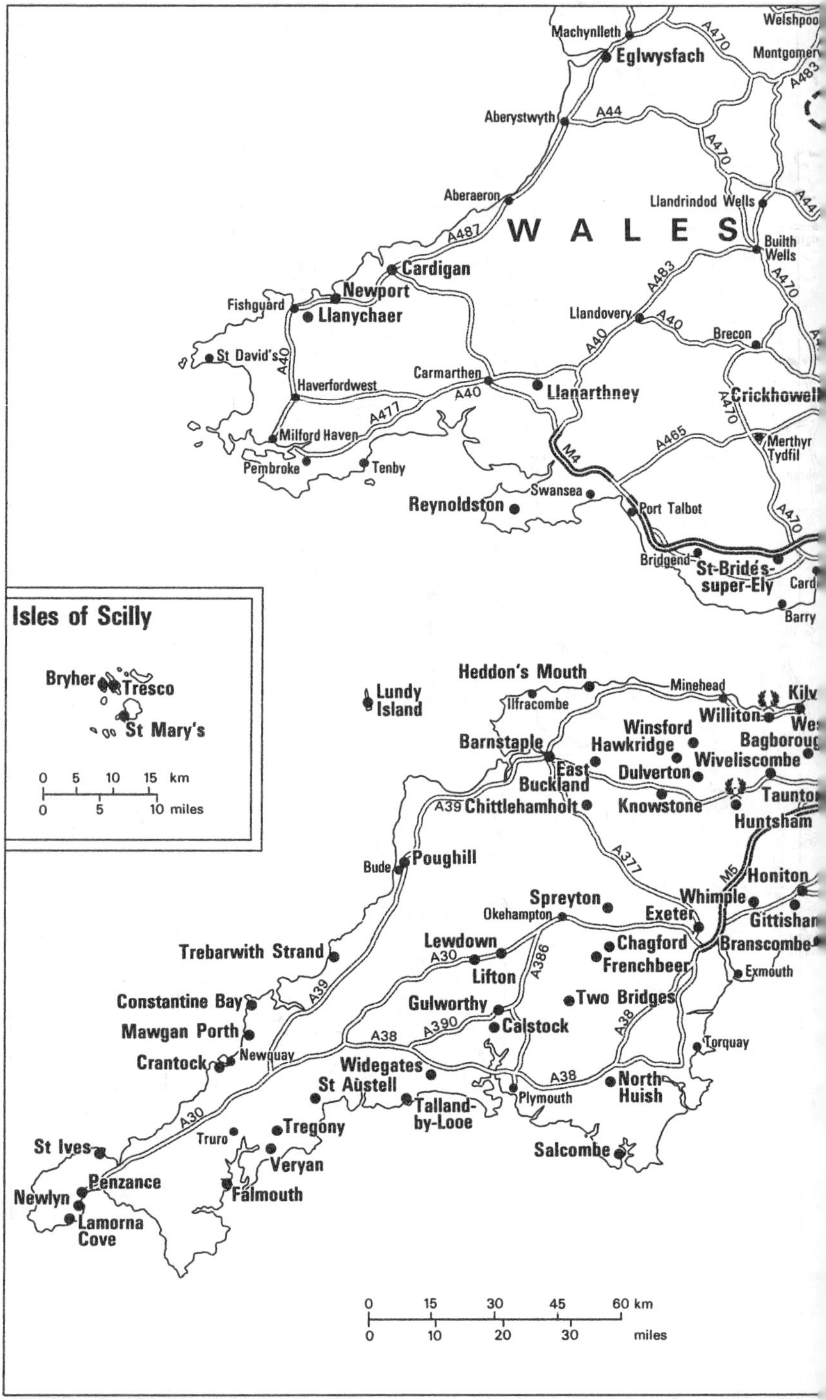

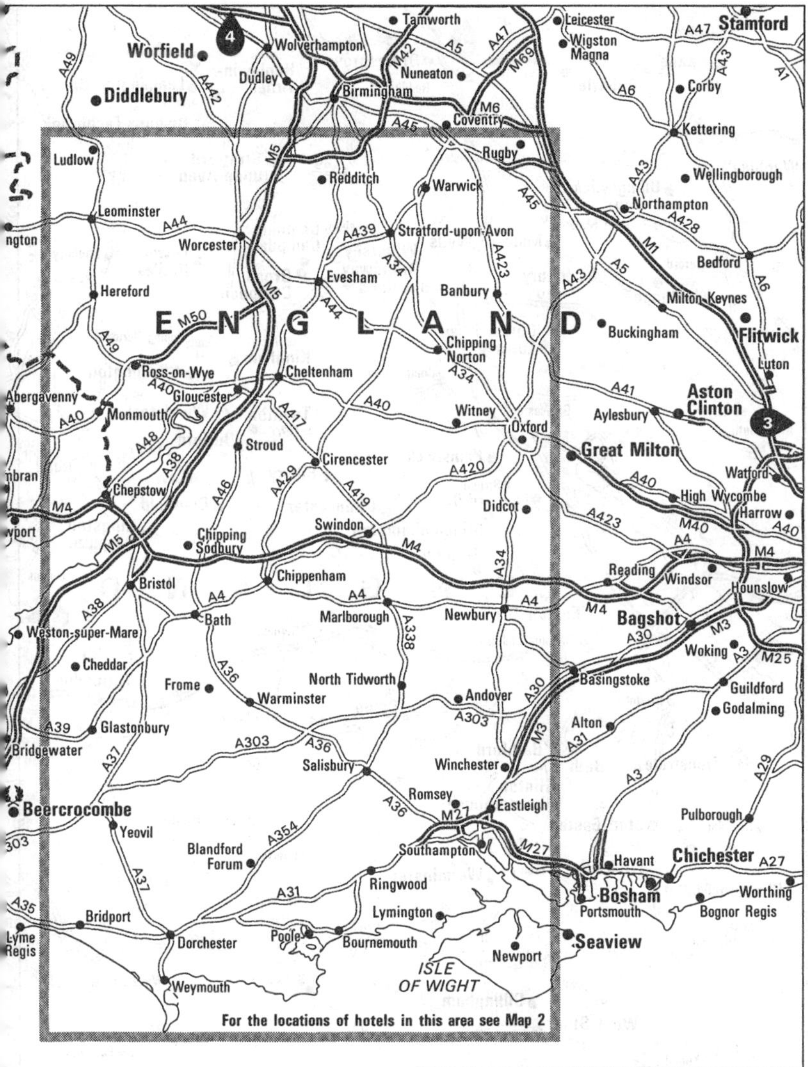
Tamworth
Leicester
Wigston Magna
Stamford
Worfield
Wolverhampton
Dudley
Diddlebury
Birmingham
Nuneaton
Coventry
Corby
Kettering
Ludlow
Rugby
Redditch
Warwick
Wellingborough
Northampton
Leominster
Worcester
Stratford-upon-Avon
Bedford
Hereford
Evesham
Banbury
Milton Keynes
Flitwick
ENGLAND
Buckingham
Chipping Norton
Luton
Ross-on-Wye
Cheltenham
Gloucester
Abergavenny
Monmouth
Witney
Oxford
Aylesbury
Aston Clinton
Great Milton
Stroud
Cirencester
Chepstow
Watford
High Wycombe
Harrow
Didcot
Swindon
Chipping Sodbury
Bristol
Chippenham
Reading
Windsor
Hounslow
Bath
Marlborough
Newbury
Bagshot
Woking
Weston-super-Mare
Cheddar
Frome
North Tidworth
Warminster
Andover
Basingstoke
Guildford
Godalming
Glastonbury
Alton
Bridgewater
Salisbury
Winchester
Beercrocombe
Yeovil
Romsey
Eastleigh
Pulborough
Blandford Forum
Southampton
Havant
Chichester
Ringwood
Bosham
Worthing
Portsmouth
Bognor Regis
Bridport
Lymington
Lyme Regis
Dorchester
Poole
Bournemouth
Seaview
Newport
ISLE OF WIGHT
Weymouth
For the locations of hotels in this area see Map 2
4
3
M1
M4
M5
M6
M40
M42
M50
M69
M3
M25
M27
A1
A3
A4
A5
A6
A27
A29
A30
A31
A34
A35
A36
A37
A38
A39
A40
A41
A43
A44
A45
A46
A47
A48
A49
A303
A338
A354
A417
A419
A420
A423
A428
A429
A439
A442

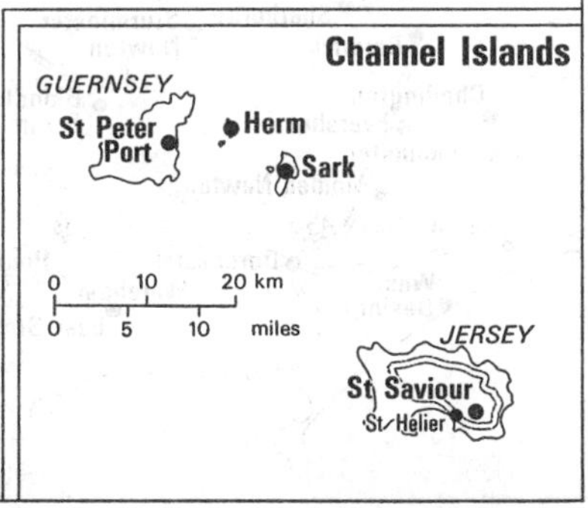
Channel Islands
GUERNSEY
St Peter Port
Herm
Sark
JERSEY
St Saviour
St Helier
0 10 20 km
0 5 10 miles

Map 2 Wessex and the Cotswolds

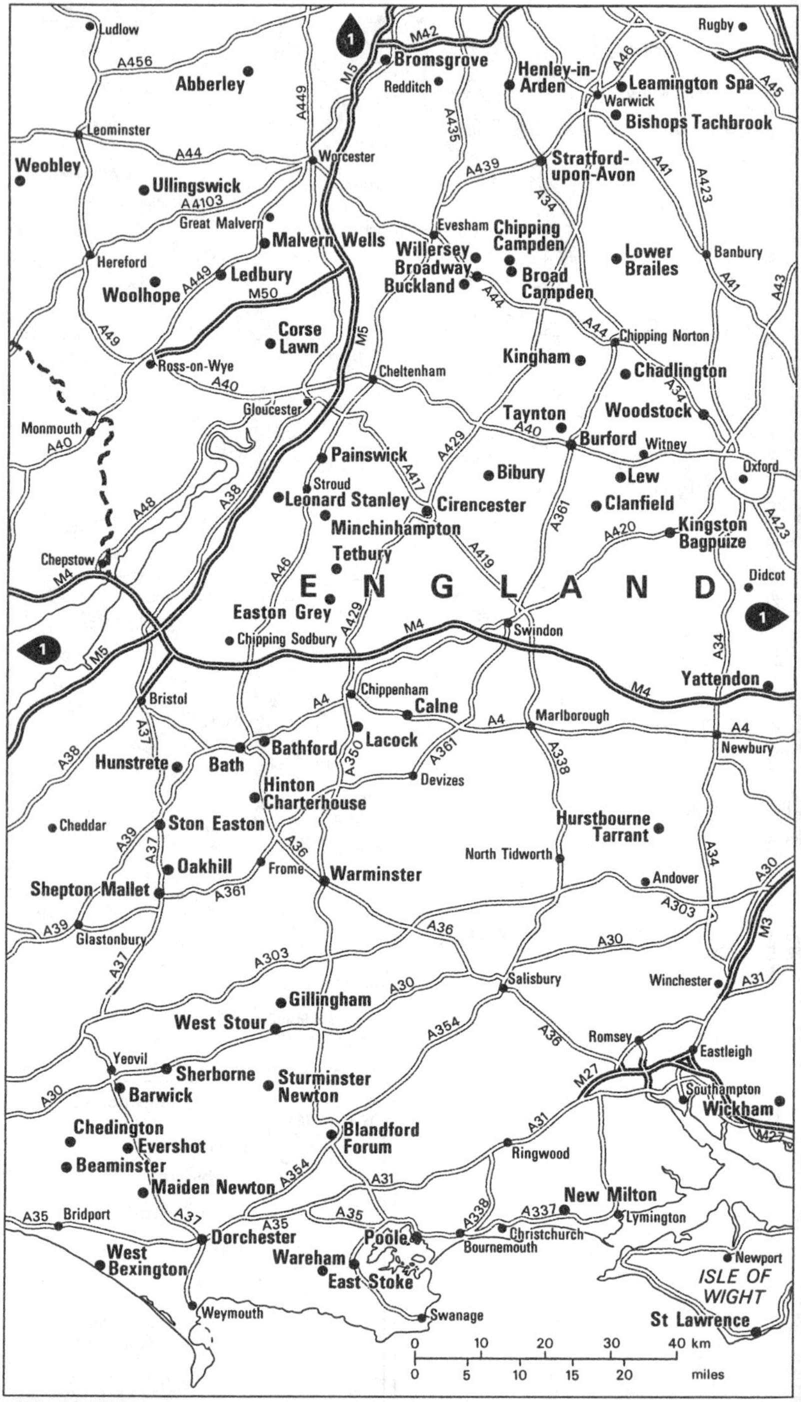

Map 3 South–East England

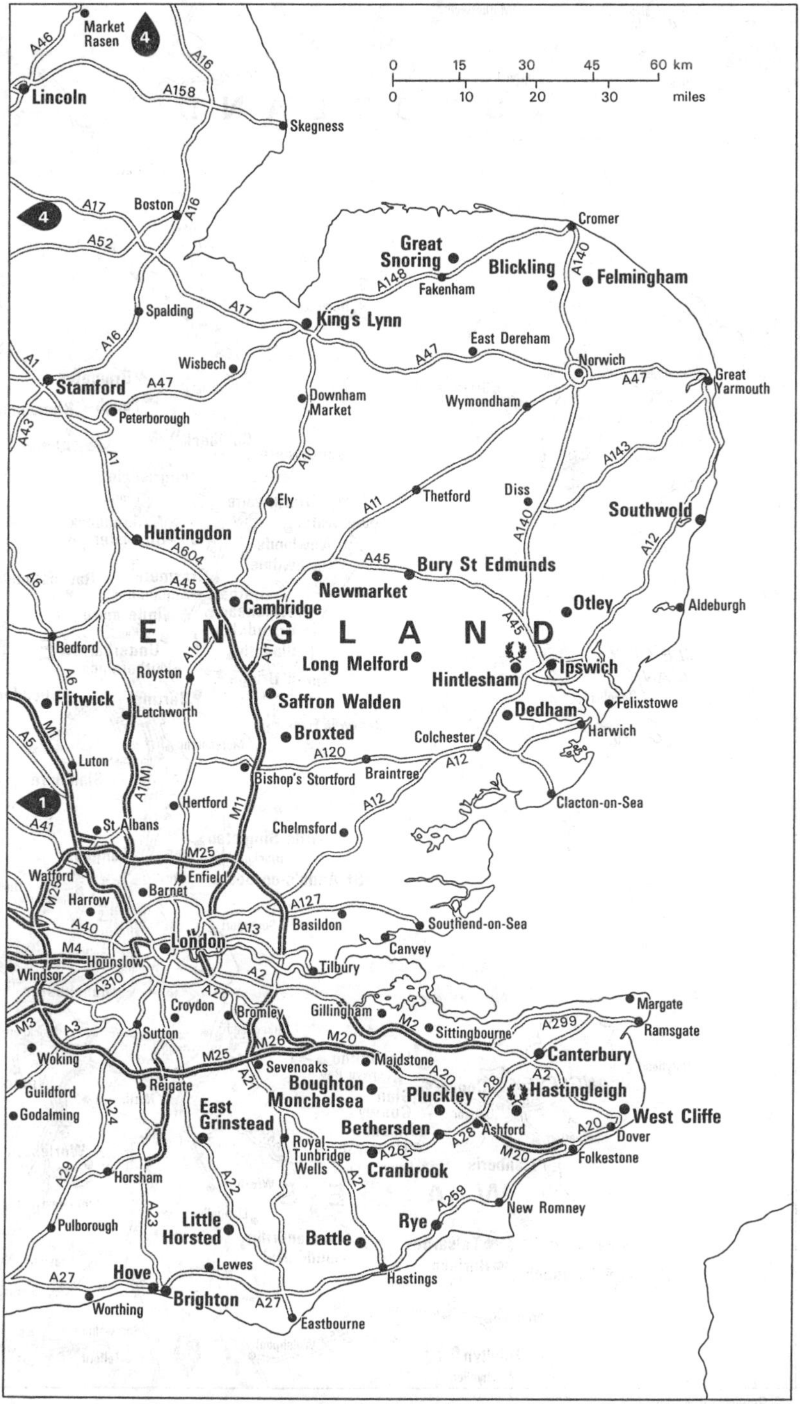

Map 4 North Wales, the Midlands and the North of England

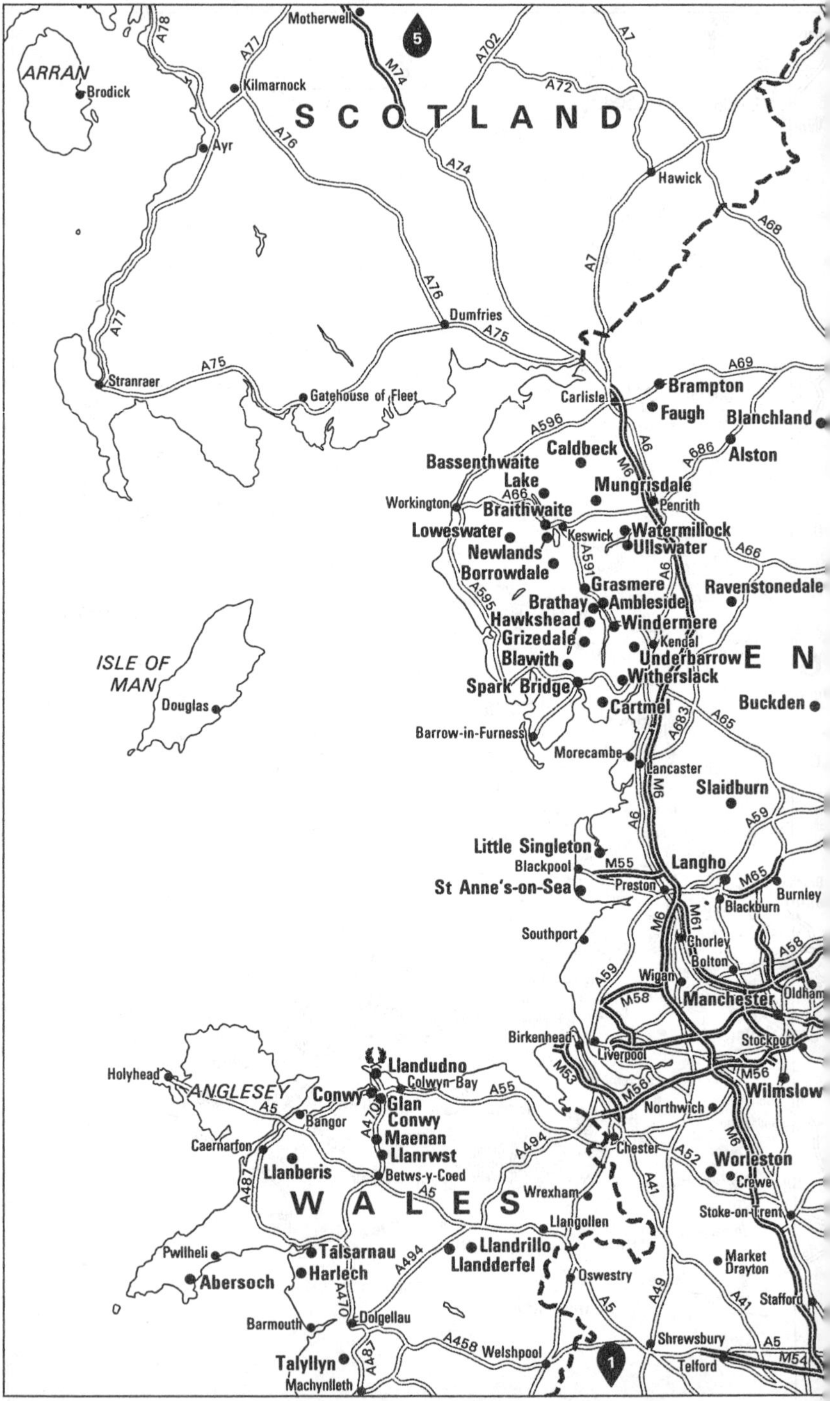

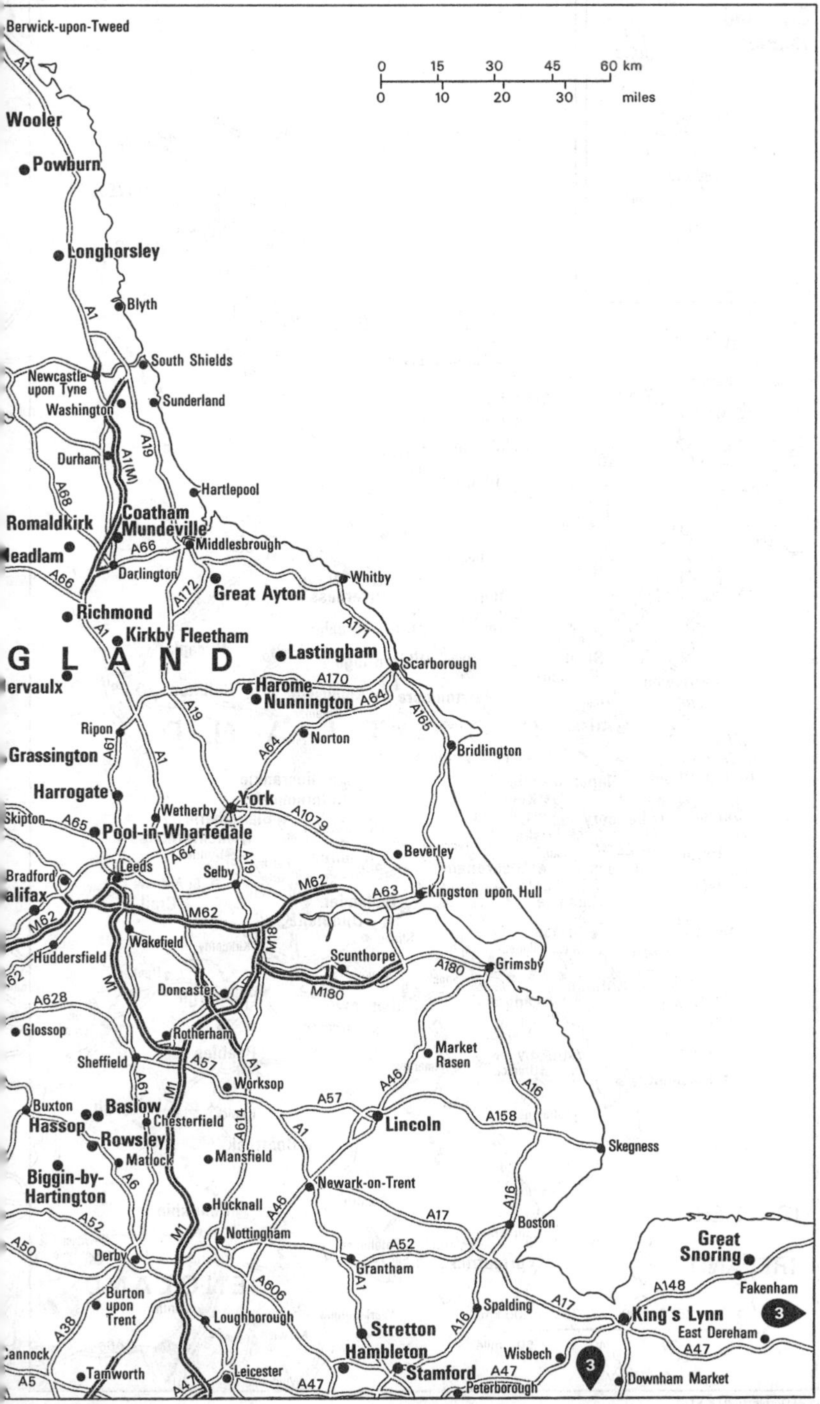

0 15 30 45 60 km
0 10 20 30 miles
Berwick-upon-Tweed
Wooler
Powburn
Longhorsley
Blyth
South Shields
Newcastle upon Tyne
Washington
Sunderland
Durham
Hartlepool
Romaldkirk
Coatham Mundeville
Middlesbrough
Darlington
Great Ayton
Whitby
Richmond
Kirkby Fleetham
G L A N D
Lastingham
Scarborough
Harome
Nunnington
Norton
Ripon
Bridlington
Grassington
Harrogate
York
Wetherby
Skipton
Pool-in-Wharfedale
Beverley
Leeds
Selby
Bradford
Kingston upon Hull
Wakefield
Huddersfield
Scunthorpe
Grimsby
Doncaster
Glossop
Rotherham
Sheffield
Market Rasen
Worksop
Buxton
Baslow
Hassop
Chesterfield
Lincoln
Rowsley
Skegness
Matlock
Mansfield
Biggin-by-Hartington
Newark-on-Trent
Hucknall
Boston
Nottingham
Great Snoring
Derby
Grantham
Fakenham
Burton upon Trent
Loughborough
Spalding
King's Lynn
Stretton
East Dereham
Hambleton
Wisbech
Stamford
Tamworth
Leicester
Downham Market
Peterborough
A1
A1(M)
A19
A68
A66
A172
A171
A170
A64
A165
A61
A65
A1079
A63
M62
M18
A180
M180
M1
A628
A57
A614
A46
A16
A158
A6
A52
A17
A50
A606
A148
A38
A47
A5

Map 5 Scotland

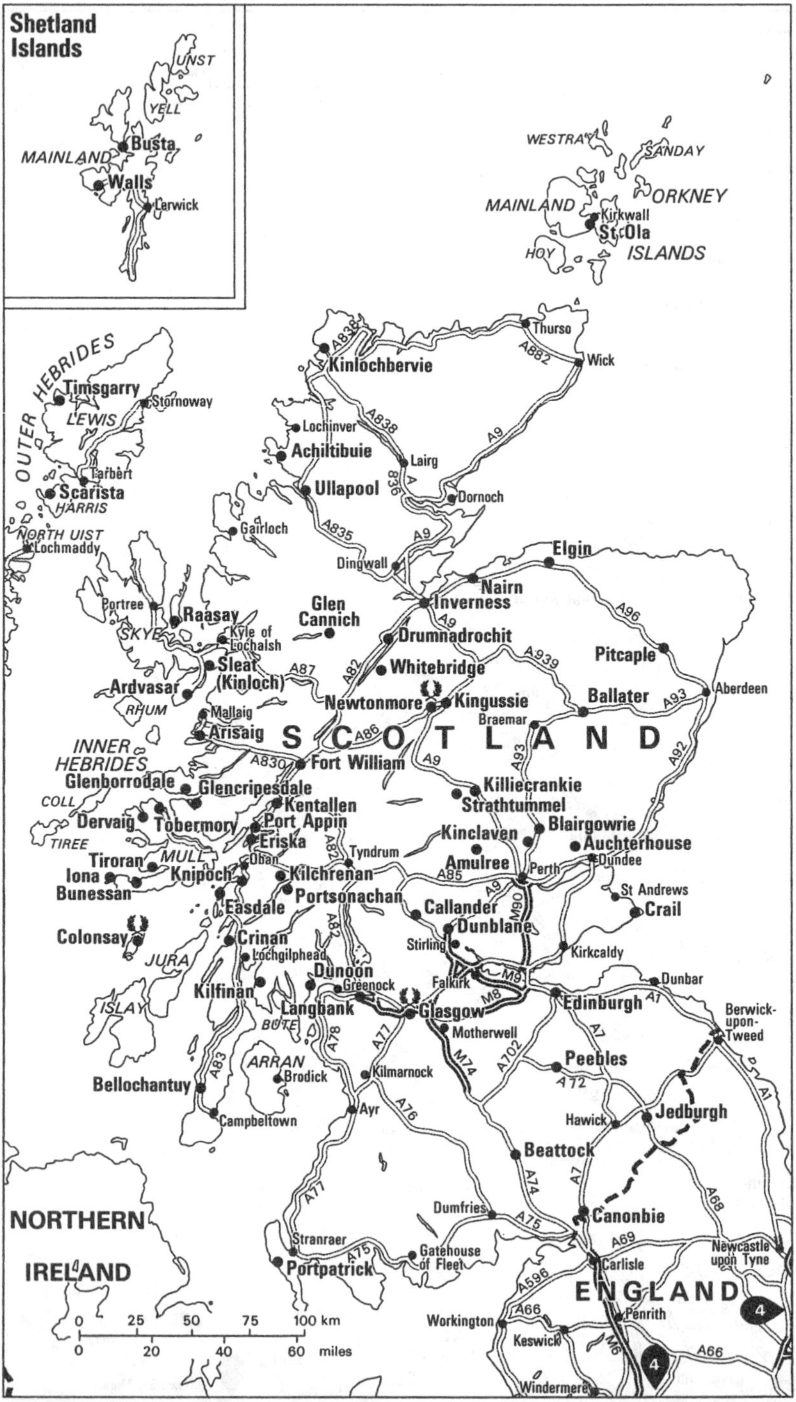

Map 6 Ireland

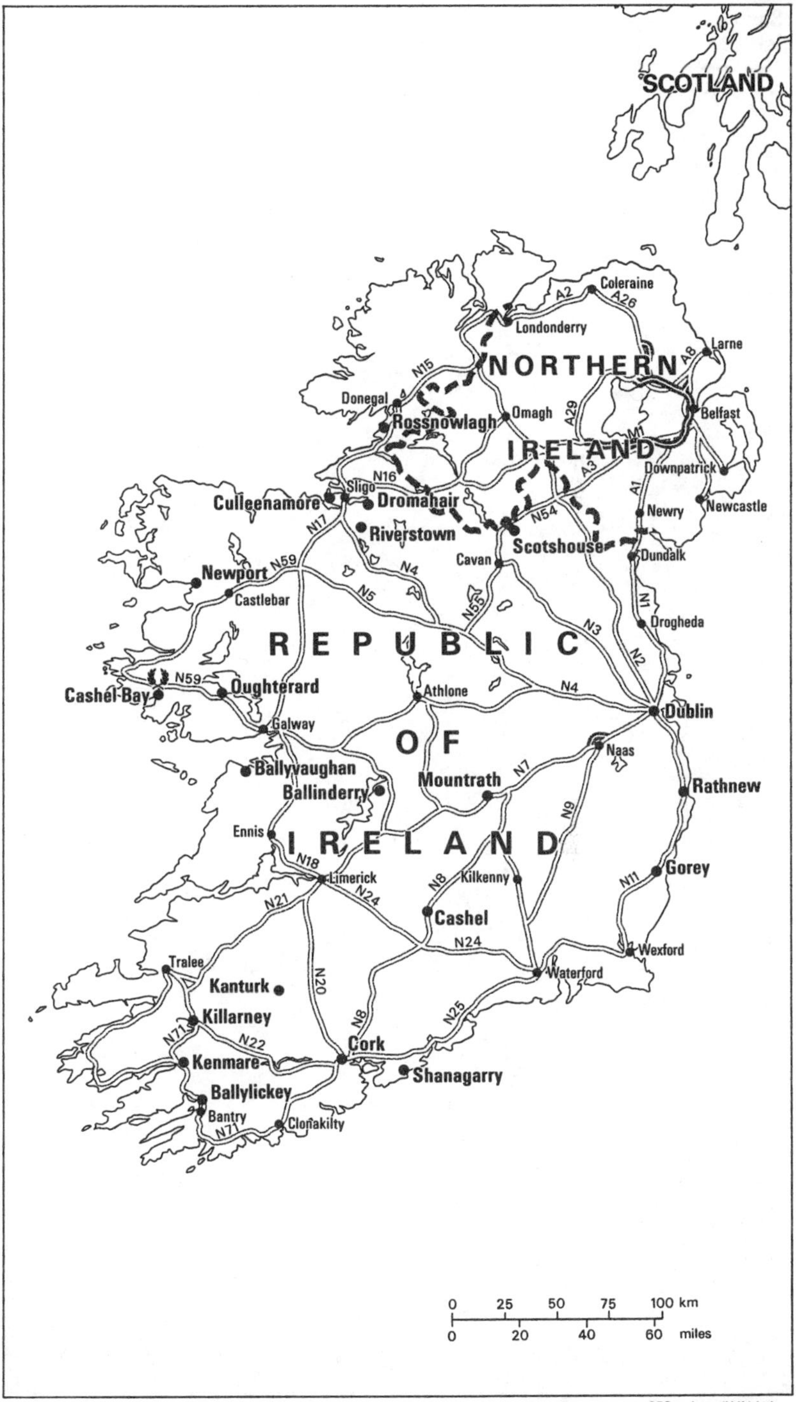

Europe Maps

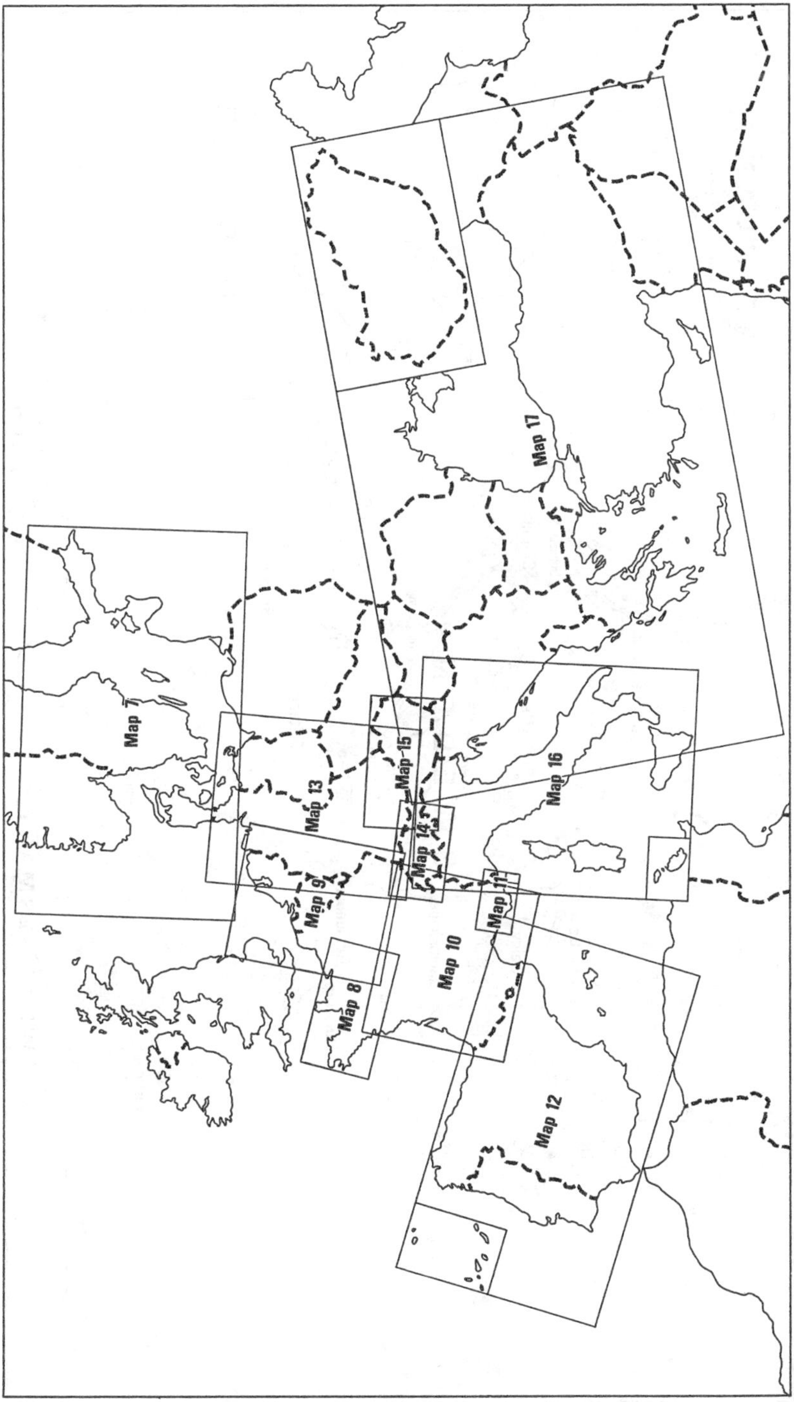
Map 7
Map 8
Map 9
Map 10
Map 11
Map 12
Map 13
Map 14
Map 15
Map 16
Map 17

Map 7 Southern Scandinavia

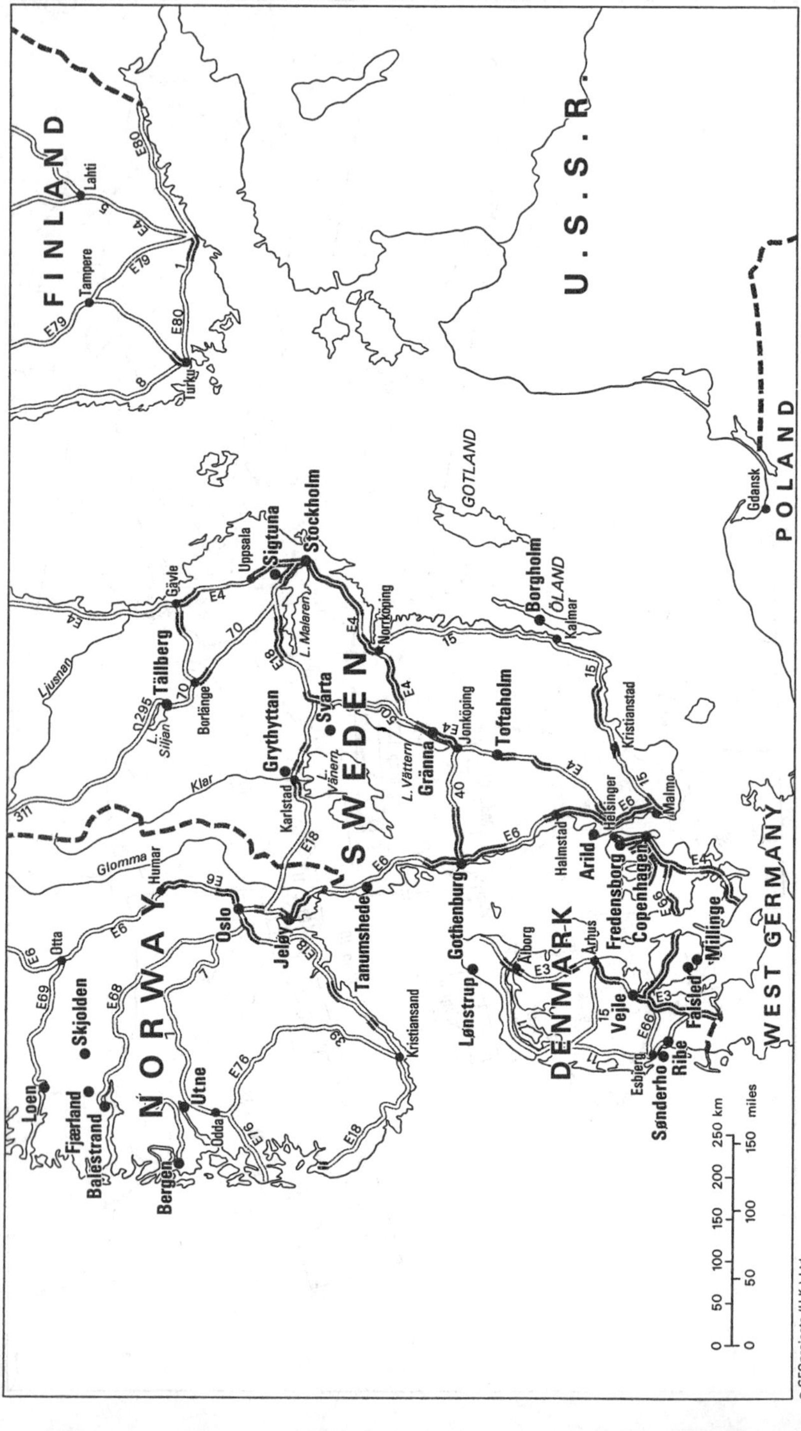

Map 8   North–West France

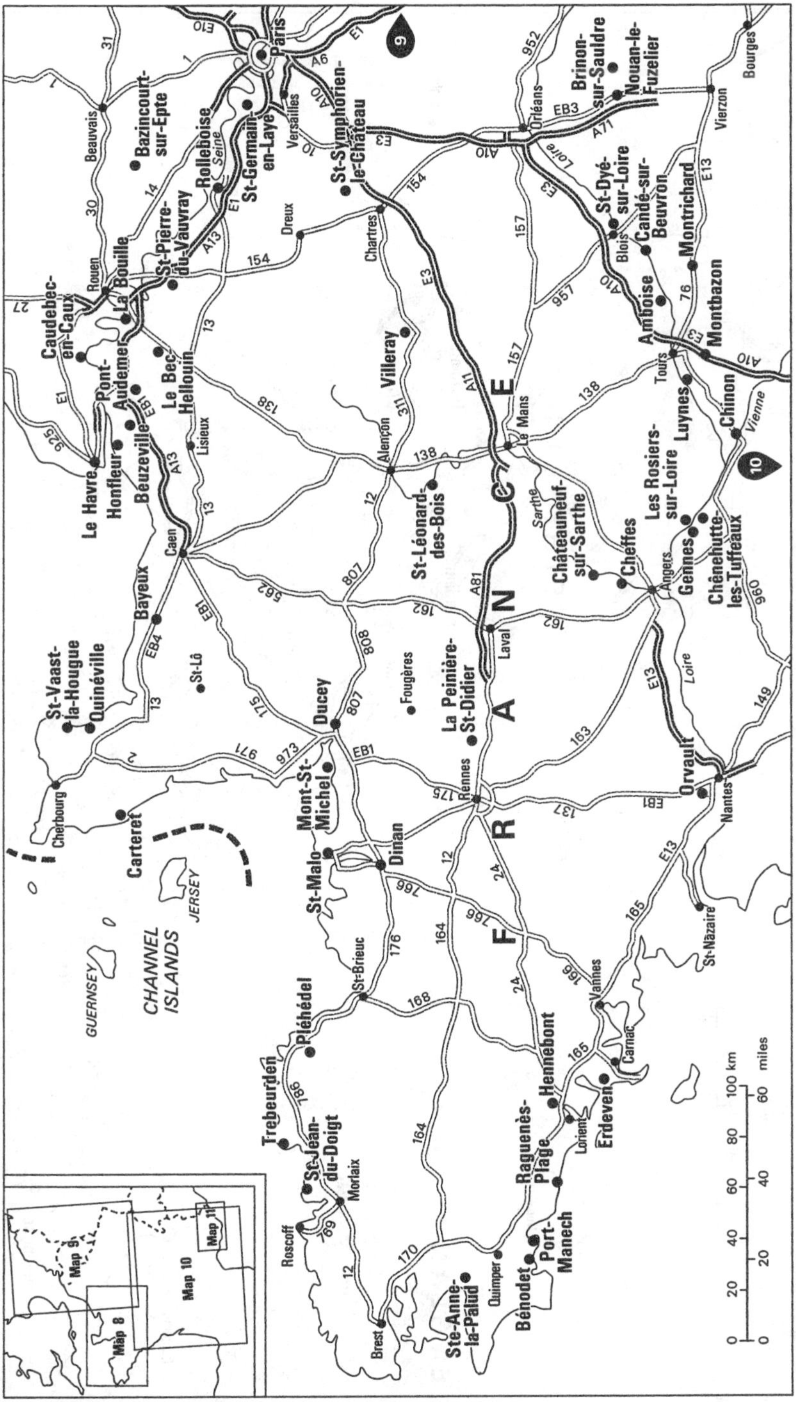

Map 9 Benelux and North–East France

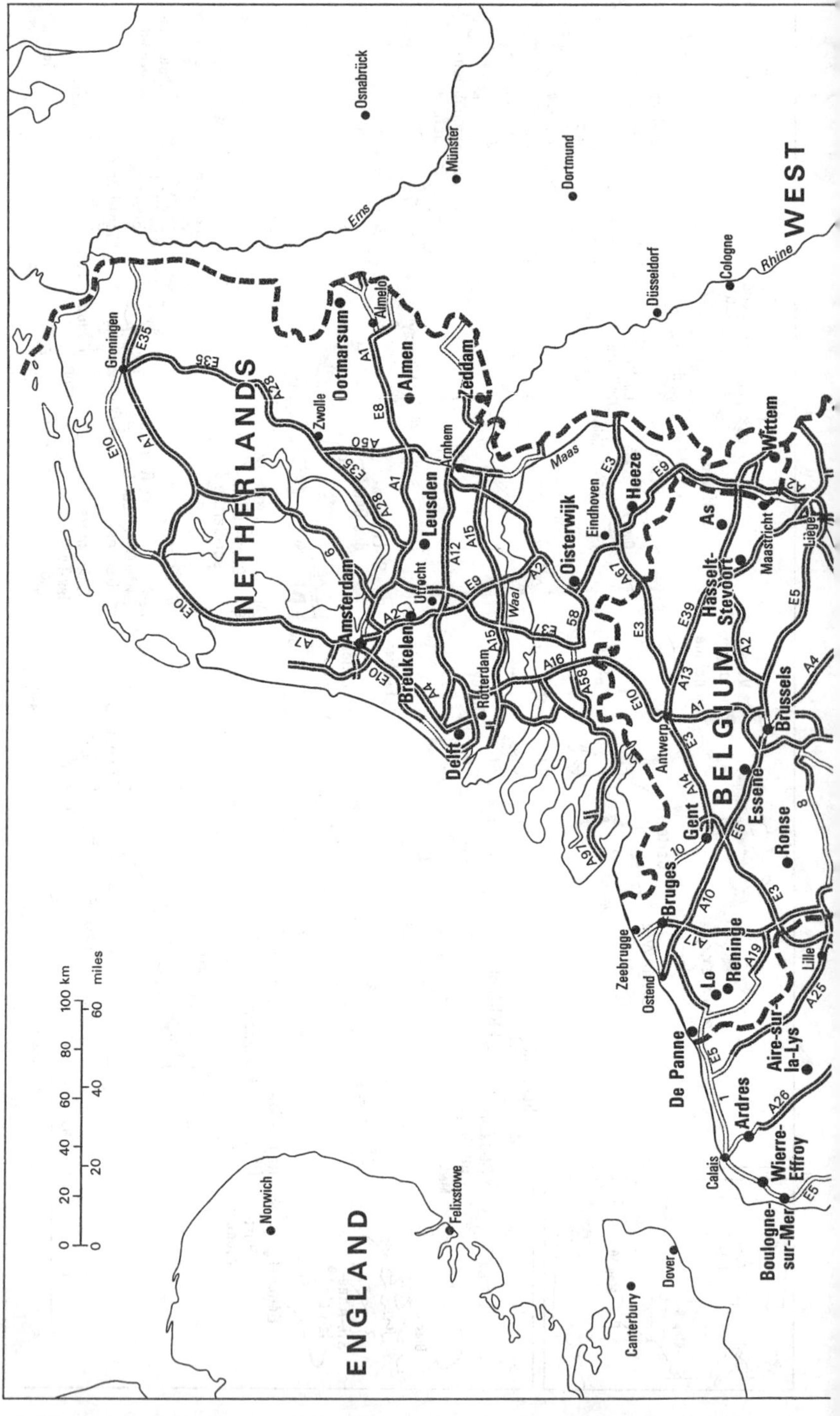

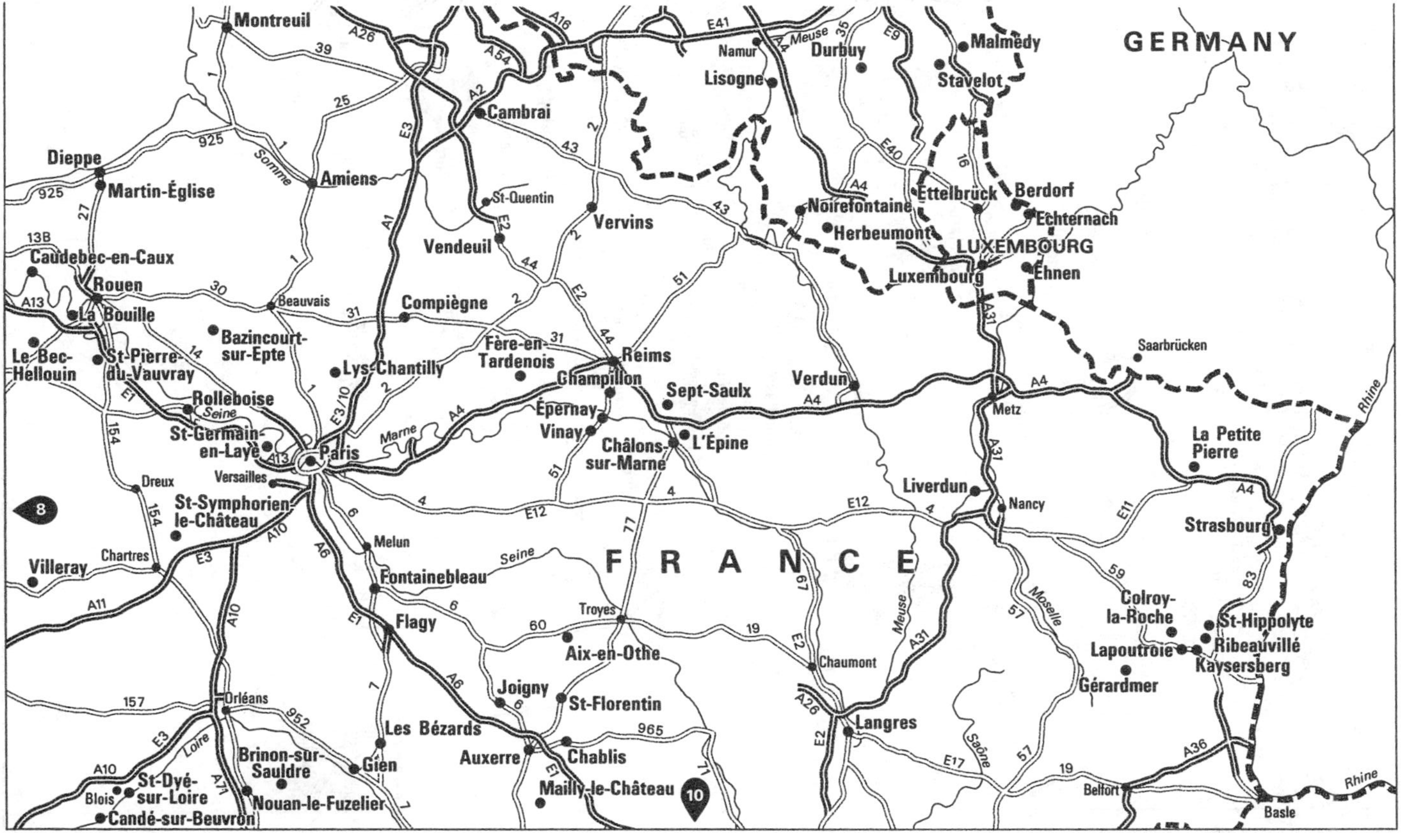
GERMANY
FRANCE
LUXEMBOURG
Montreuil
Dieppe
Martin-Église
Caudebec-en-Caux
Rouen
La Bouille
Le-Bec-Hellouin
St-Pierre-du-Vauvray
Bazincourt-sur-Epte
Rolleboise
St-Germain-en-Laye
Versailles
Dreux
St-Symphorien-le-Château
Chartres
Villeray
Amiens
Beauvais
Lys-Chantilly
Paris
Cambrai
St-Quentin
Vendeuil
Compiègne
Vervins
Fère-en-Tardenois
Reims
Champillon
Épernay
Vinay
Châlons-sur-Marne
L'Épine
Sept-Saulx
Verdun
Namur
Lisogne
Durbuy
Malmédy
Stavelot
Noirefontaine
Herbeumont
Ettelbrück
Berdorf
Echternach
Ehnen
Luxembourg
Saarbrücken
Metz
Liverdun
Nancy
La Petite Pierre
Strasbourg
Colroy-la-Roche
Lapoutroie
Gérardmer
St-Hippolyte
Ribeauvillé
Kaysersberg
Belfort
Basle
Melun
Fontainebleau
Flagy
Troyes
Aix-en-Othe
Joigny
St-Florentin
Chaumont
Langres
Les Bézards
Auxerre
Chablis
Mailly-le-Château
Orléans
Gien
Brinon-sur-Sauldre
Nouan-le-Fuzelier
Blois
St-Dyé-sur-Loire
Candé-sur-Beuvron
Somme
Seine
Marne
Meuse
Moselle
Saône
Loire
Rhine
8
10

Map 10 Central and Southern France

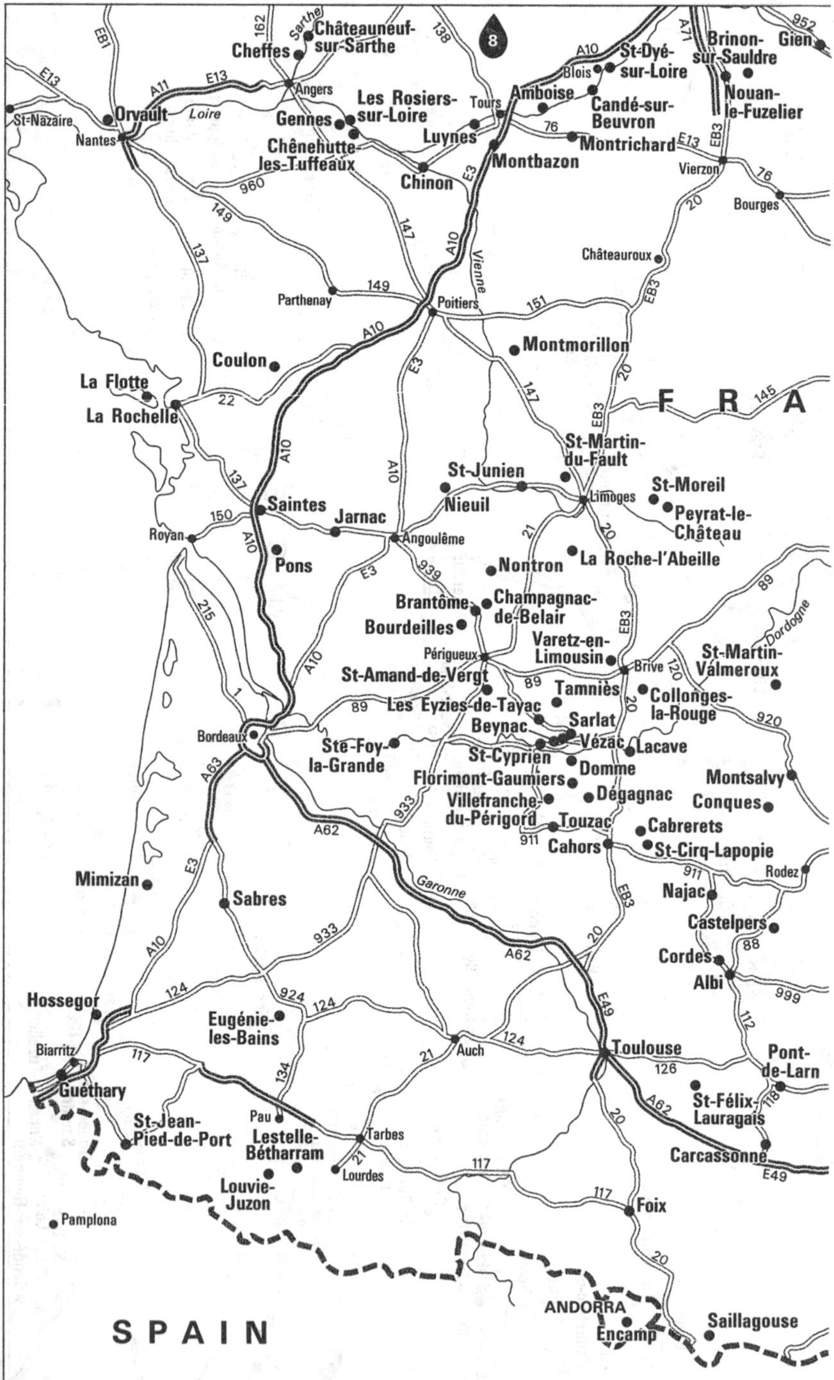

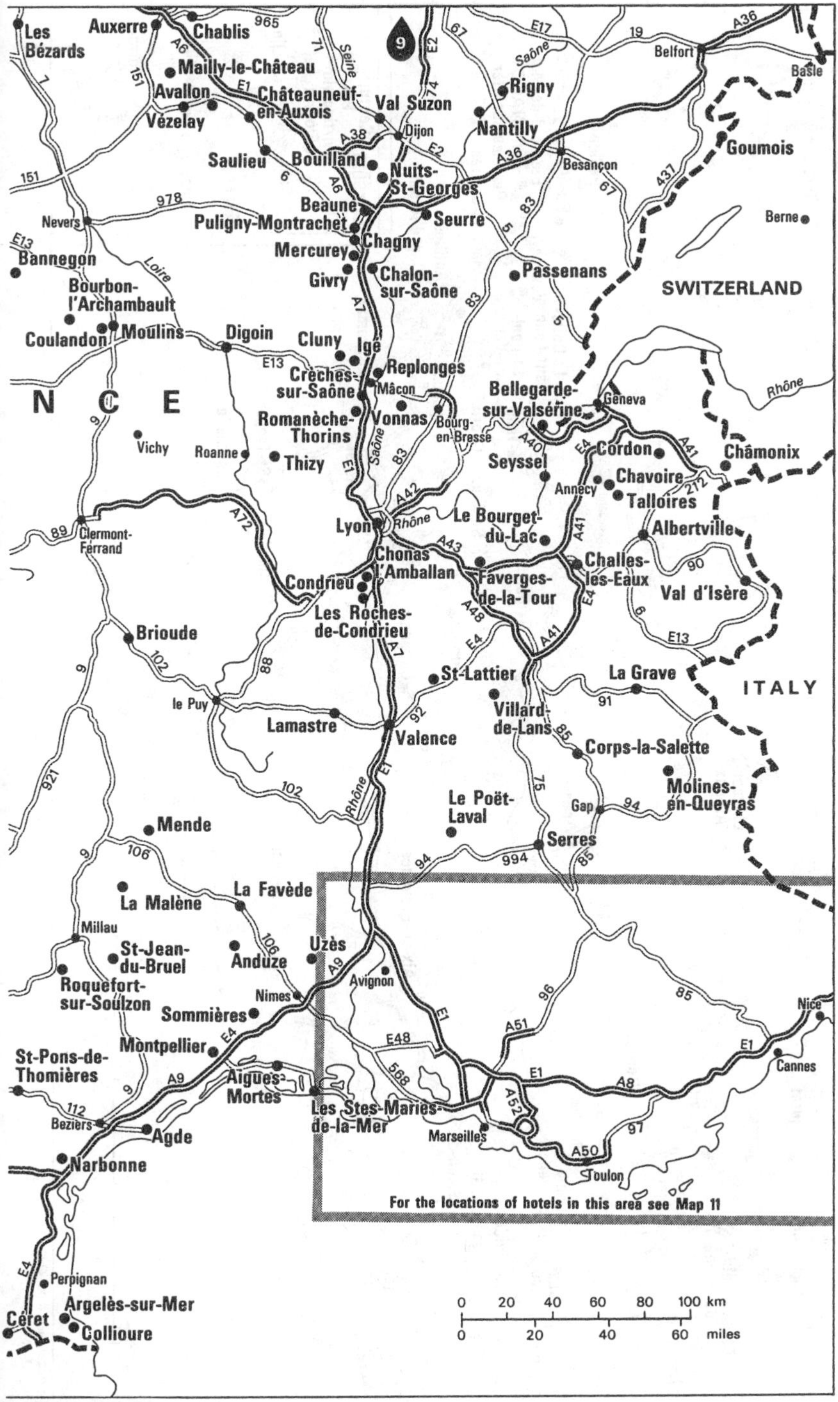

Les Bézards
Auxerre
Chablis
Mailly-le-Château
Avallon
Vézelay
Châteauneuf-en-Auxois
Val Suzon
Dijon
Saulieu
Bouilland
Nuits-St-Georges
Beaune
Puligny-Montrachet
Seurre
Chagny
Mercurey
Givry
Chalon-sur-Saône
Nevers
Bannegon
Bourbon-l'Archambault
Coulandon
Moulins
Digoin
Cluny
Igé
Replonges
Crèches-sur-Saône
Mâcon
Vonnas
Romanèche-Thorins
Bourg-en-Bresse
Vichy
Roanne
Thizy
Lyon
Clermont-Ferrand
Chonas-l'Amballan
Condrieu
Les Roches-de-Condrieu
Brioude
le Puy
Lamastre
Valence
St-Lattier
Villard-de-Lans
Rigny
Nantilly
Besançon
Belfort
Basle
Goumois
Berne
Passenans
SWITZERLAND
Bellegarde-sur-Valsérine
Geneva
Seyssel
Cordon
Chamonix
Chavoire
Annecy
Talloires
Le Bourget-du-Lac
Albertville
Faverges-de-la-Tour
Challes-les-Eaux
Val d'Isère
La Grave
ITALY
Corps-la-Salette
Molines-en-Queyras
Gap
Le Poët-Laval
Serres
Mende
La Malène
La Favède
Millau
St-Jean-du-Bruel
Anduze
Uzès
Avignon
Roquefort-sur-Soulzon
Nimes
Sommières
Montpellier
St-Pons-de-Thomières
Aigues-Mortes
Les Stes-Maries-de-la-Mer
Beziers
Agde
Narbonne
Marseilles
Toulon
Nice
Cannes
Perpignan
Argelès-sur-Mer
Céret
Collioure
N C E
Loire
Saône
Seine
Rhône
For the locations of hotels in this area see Map 11
0 20 40 60 80 100 km
0 20 40 60 miles

Map 11 The South of France

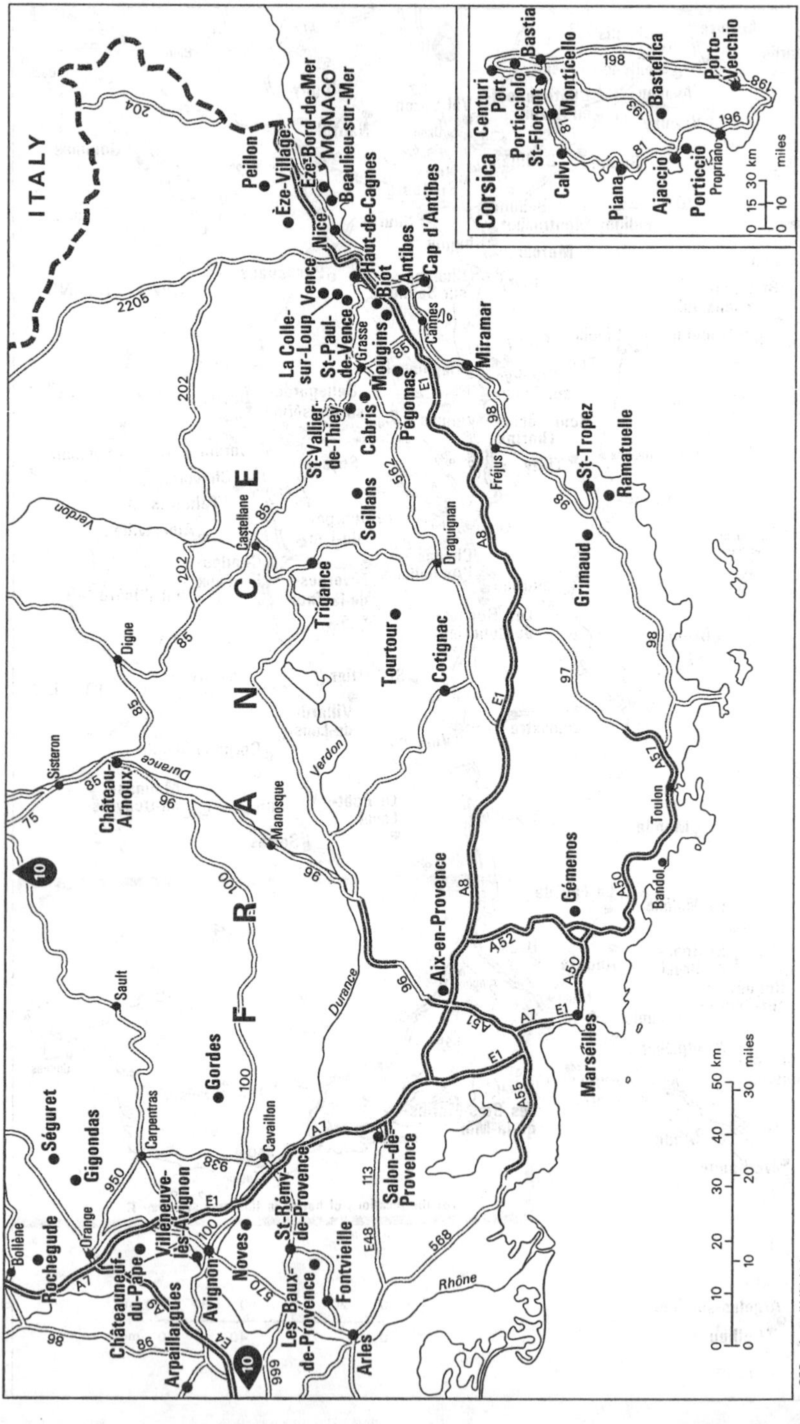

Map 12 Spain and Portugal

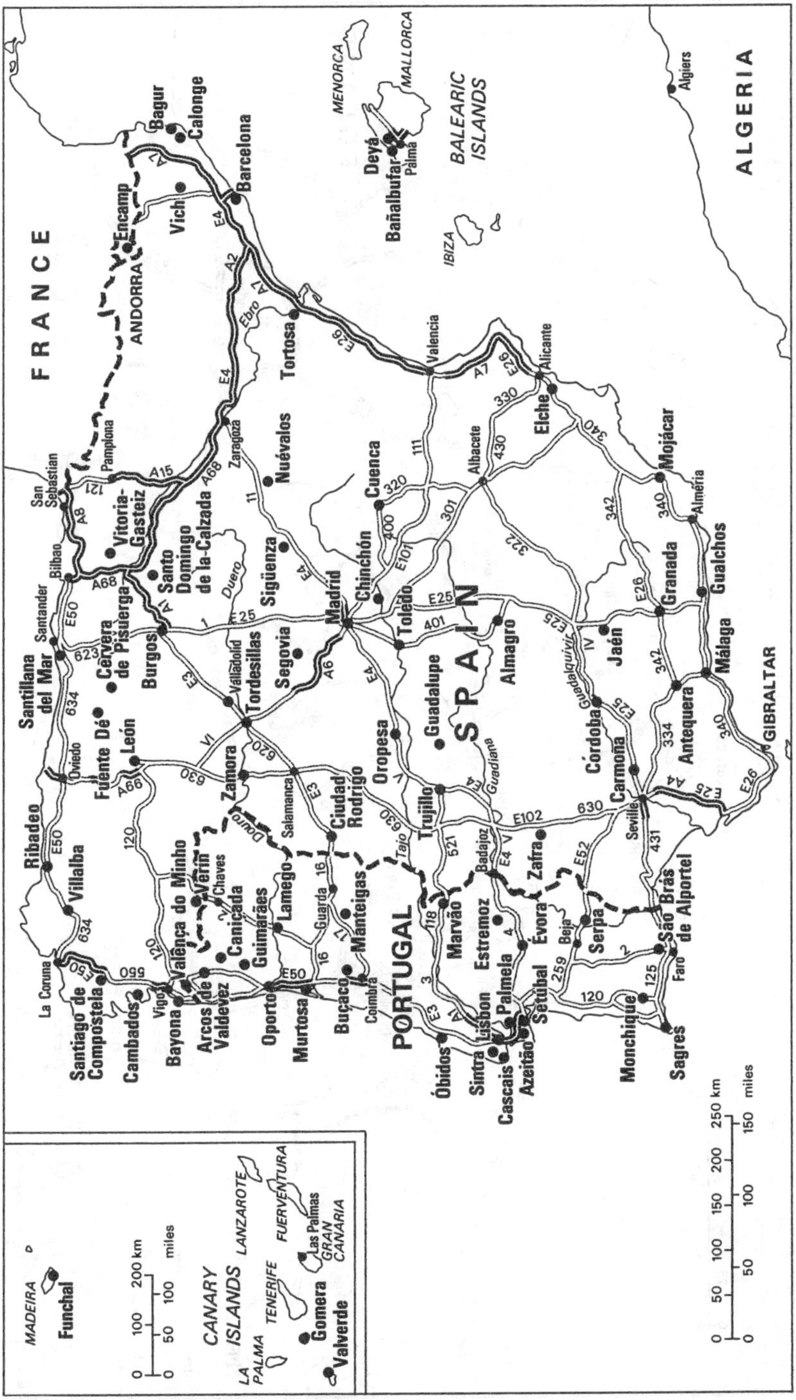

Map 13 Germany

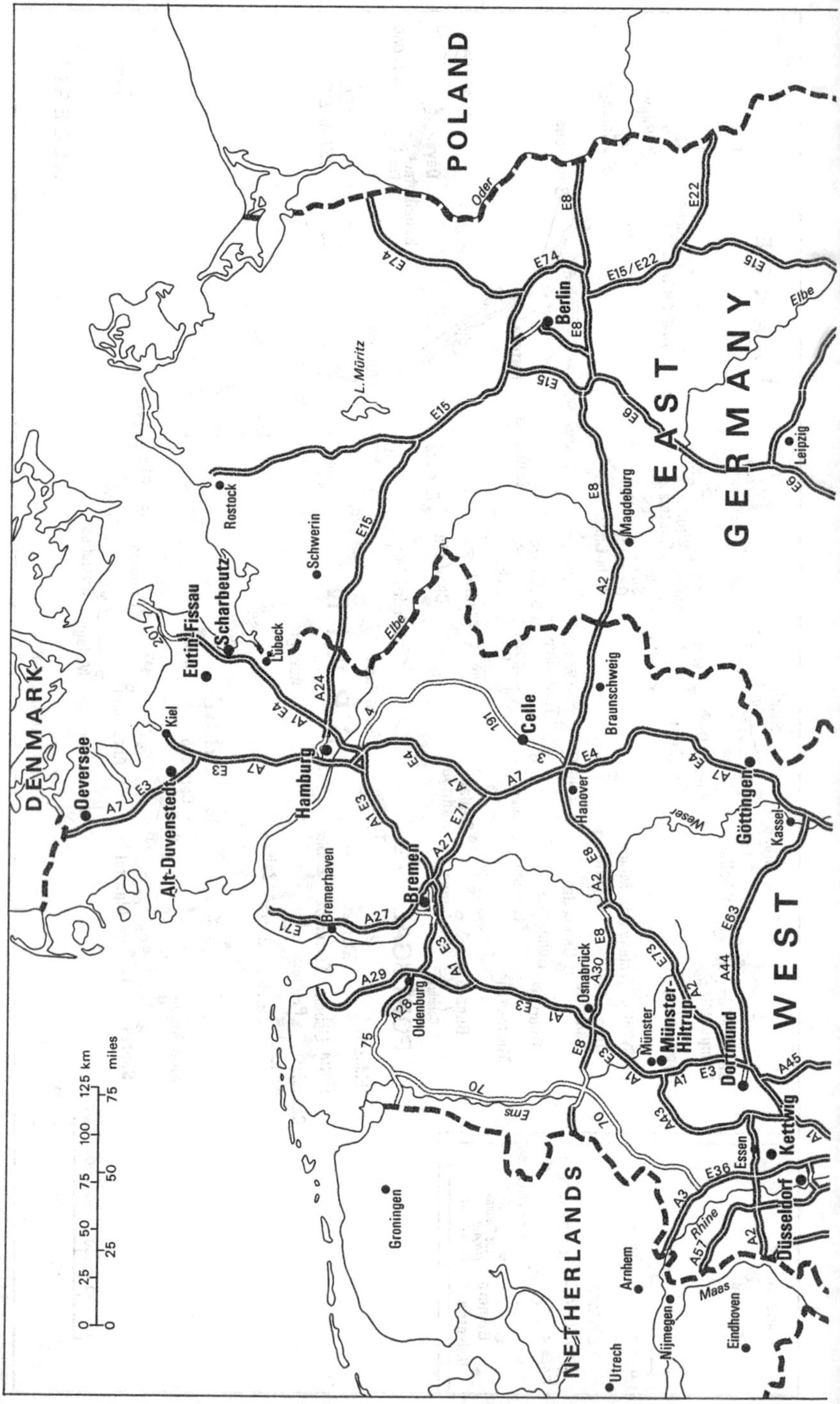

© GEOprojects (U.K.) Ltd.

Map 14 Switzerland

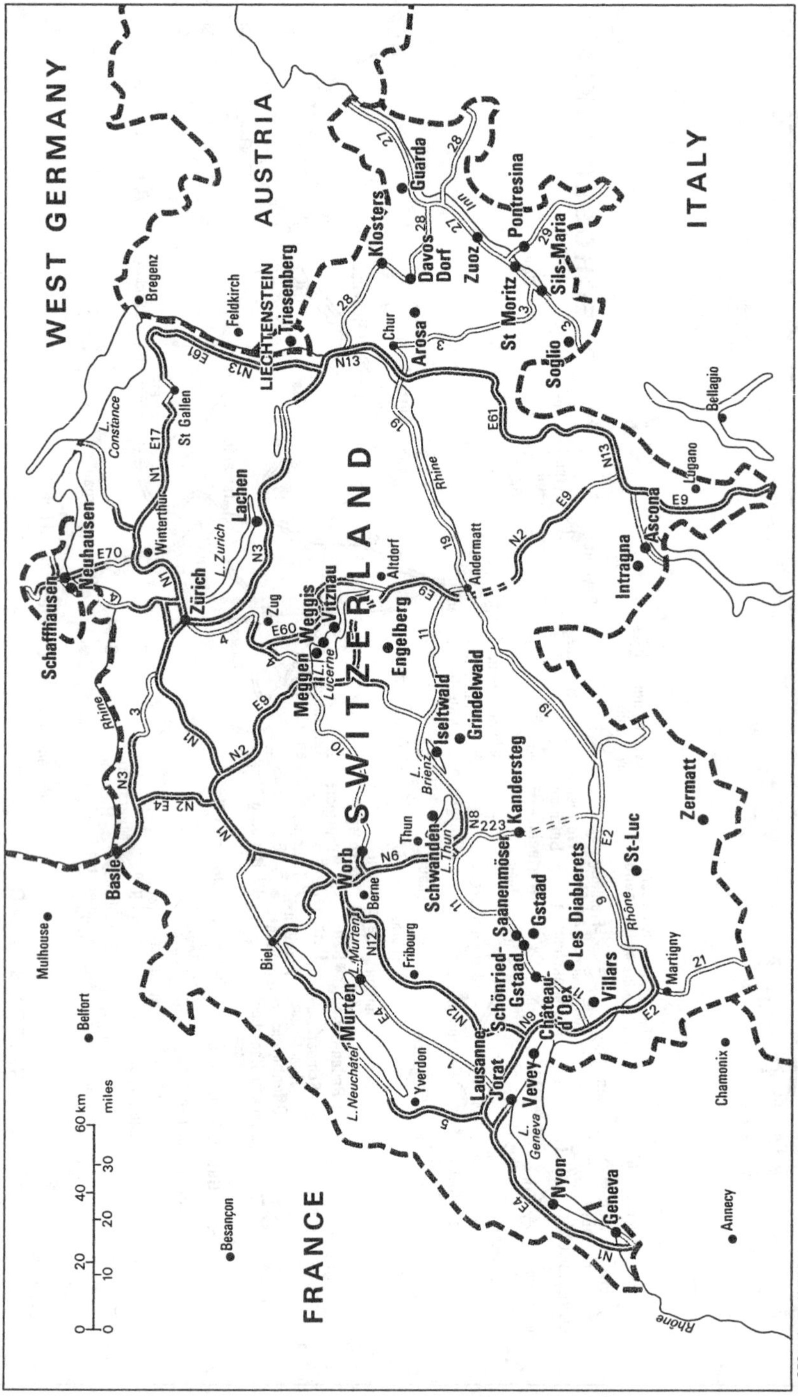

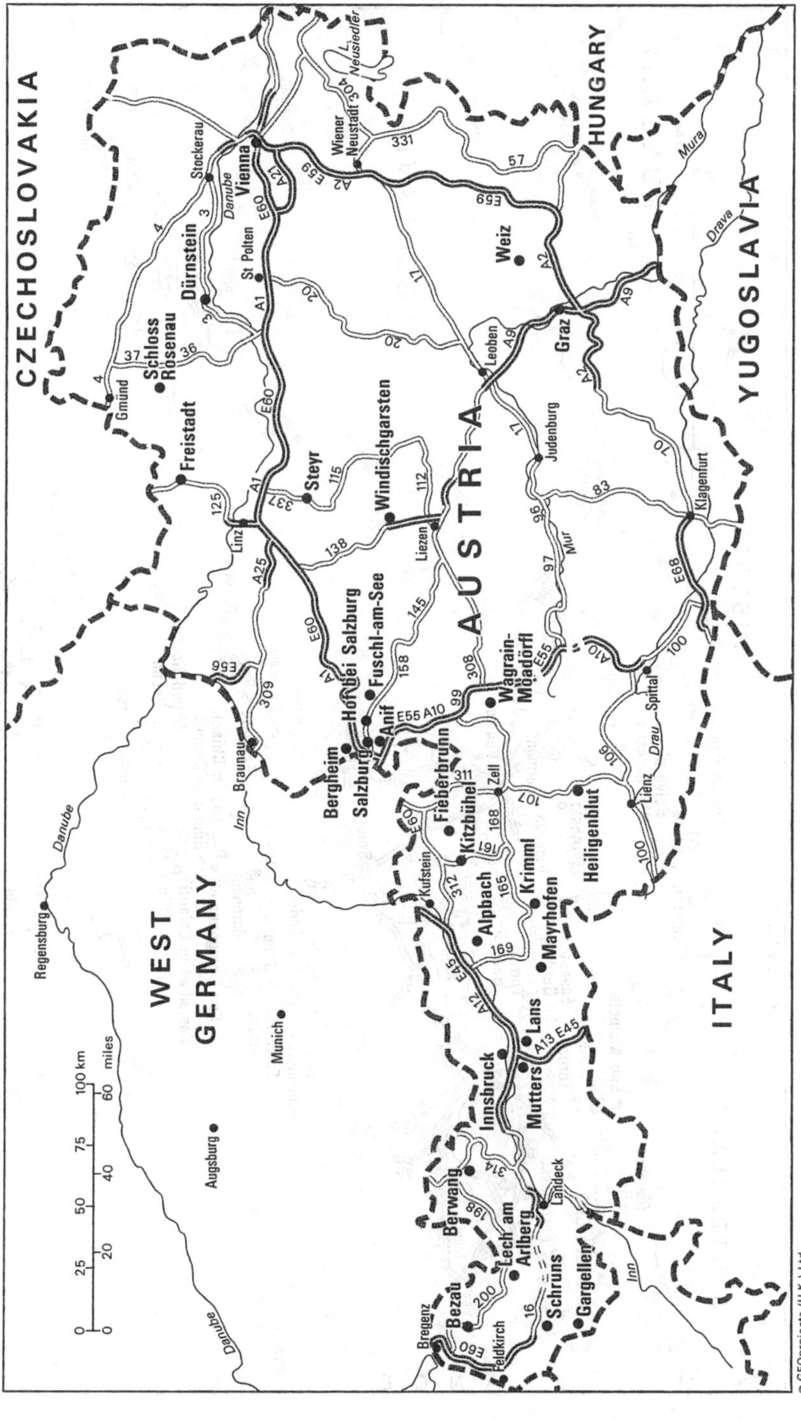

CZECHOSLOVAKIA
HUNGARY
YUGOSLAVIA
ITALY
WEST GERMANY
AUSTRIA
Vienna
Stockerau
Wiener Neustadt
L. Neusiedler
Dürnstein
St Polten
Schloss Rosenau
Gmünd
Freistadt
Linz
Steyr
Windischgarsten
Liezen
Leoben
Graz
Weiz
Judenburg
Klagenfurt
Spittal
Lienz
Heiligenblut
Wagrain-Moadörfl
Bergheim
Salzburg
Hof bei Salzburg
Fuschl-am-See
Anif
Braunau
Fieberbrunn
Kitzbühel
Zell
Krimml
Mayrhofen
Alpbach
Kufstein
Innsbruck
Lans
Mutters
Landeck
Berwang
Lech am Arlberg
Schruns
Gargellen
Bezau
Bregenz
Feldkirch
Regensburg
Munich
Augsburg
Danube
Inn
Mur
Mura
Drava
Drau
0 25 50 75 100 km
0 20 40 60 miles

Map 16 Italy and Malta

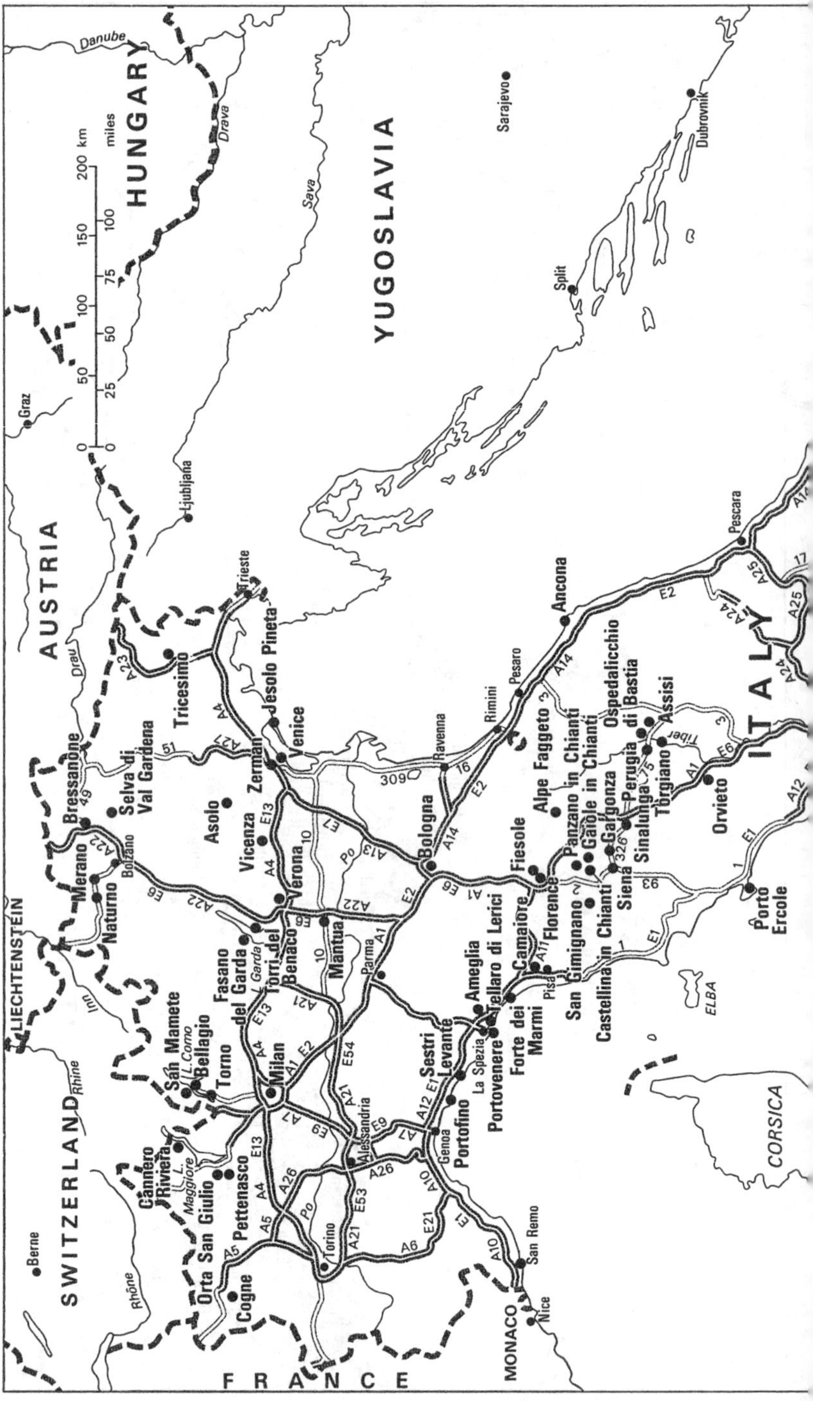

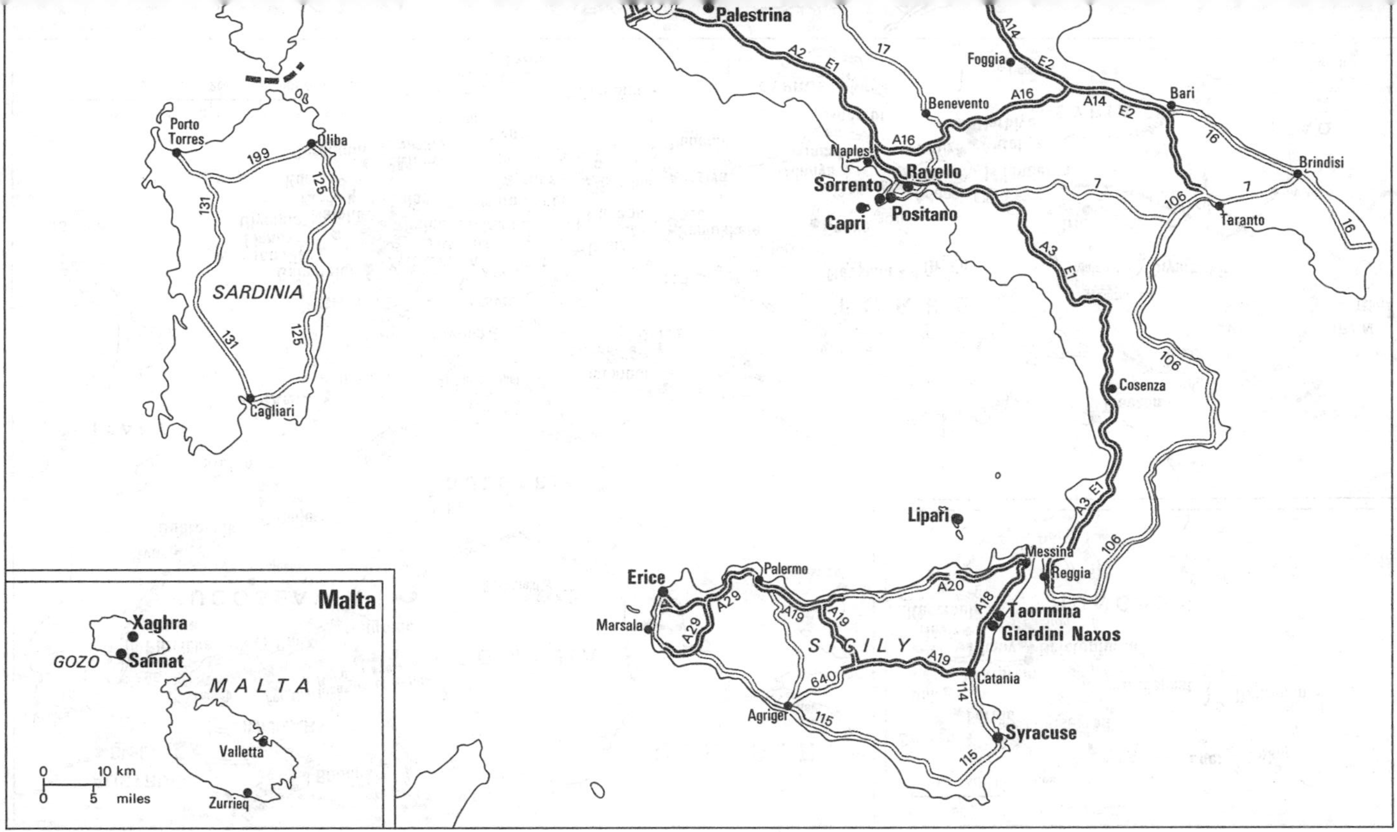
Palestrina
A2
E1
17
Foggia
A14
E2
Benevento
A16
A14
E2
Bari
16
Brindisi
Naples
A16
Ravello
Sorrento
Capri
Positano
7
106
7
Taranto
16
A3
E1
106
Cosenza
A3 E1
Lipari
106
Messina
Reggia
Porto
Torres
Oliba
199
125
131
SARDINIA
131
125
Cagliari
Erice
Palermo
A29
A29
Marsala
A19
A19
A20
A18
Taormina
Giardini Naxos
SICILY
A19
640
Catania
114
Agriger
115
Syracuse
115
Malta
Xaghra
GOZO
Sannat
MALTA
Valletta
Zurrieq
0
10 km
0
5
miles

Map 17 Greece, Hungary, Turkey and Yugoslavia

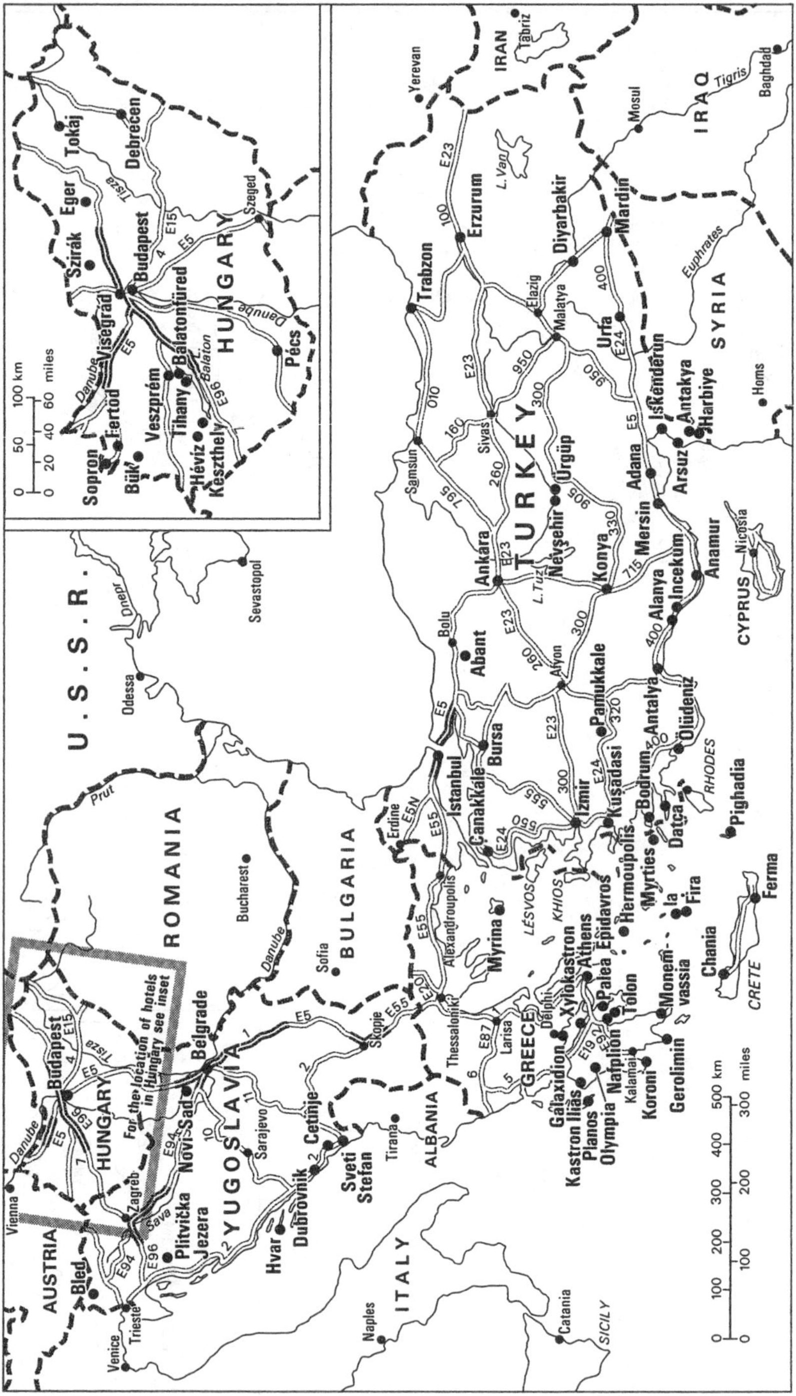

Hotel reports and champagne winners

The report forms on the following pages may be used to endorse or criticise an existing entry or to nominate a hotel that you feel deserves inclusion in next year's Guide. Either way, there is no need to use our forms, or, if you do, to restrict yourself to the space available. All nominations (each on a separate piece of paper, please) should include your name and address, the name and location of the hotel, when you stayed there and for how long. Please nominate only hotels you have visited in the past 12 months unless you are sure from friends that standards have not fallen off since your stay. And please be as specific as possible, and critical where appropriate, about the character of the building, the public and bedrooms, the meals, the service, the night-life, the grounds. We should be glad if you would give some impression of the location as well as of the hotel itself, particularly in less familiar regions.

You should not feel embarrassed about writing at length. More than anything else, we want the Guide to convey the special flavour of its hotels; so the more time and trouble you can take in providing those small details which will help to make a description come alive, the more valuable to others will be the final published result. We mind having to pass up a potentially attractive hotel because the report doesn't really tell us enough. There is no need to bother with prices or with routine information about number of rooms and facilities. We obtain such details direct from the hotels selected. What we are anxious to get from readers is information that is not accessible elsewhere. And we should be extremely grateful, in the case of foreign hotels, to be sent brochures if you have them available. Nominations for the 1989 edition should reach us not later than 1 May 1988. The latest date for comments on existing entries is 1 June 1988.

As usual, we have awarded a dozen bottles of champagne for the best reports of the year. Stephanie Sowerby, Barnard Castle, and Paul Palmer, Surbiton, have won a magnum apiece, and the following runners-up will each receive a bottle: Michael Bourdeaux, AV Chute, Rosemary Davidson, Rosamund Hebdon, Ann Lawson Lucas, Bernadette Murray, BW Ribbons, FP Woodford.

A further case will be on offer for 1988 reports. No special entry form is required: everything we receive in the course of the year will qualify. A winner may be someone who nominates a new hotel or comments on an existing one. And we also award champagne to those whose reports are consistently useful as well as to individually brilliant examples of the art of hotel criticism. Please let us know if you would like more report forms. Our address is *The Good Hotel Guide,* Freepost, London W11 4BR, for UK correspondents (no stamp needed). For letters from outside the UK, the address of the Guide is 61 Clarendon Road, London W11 4JE, stamped normally.

These report forms may also be used, if you wish, to recommend good hotels in North America to our equivalent publication in the States, *America's Wonderful Little Hotels and Inns.* They should be sent adequately stamped (no Freepost to the United States), not to *The Good Hotel Guide,* but to *America's Wonderful Little Hotels and Inns,* PO Box 150, Riverside, Conn. 06878, USA.

To: *The Good Hotel Guide*, Freepost, London W11 4BR

NOTE: No stamps needed in UK, but letters posted outside the UK should be addressed to 61 Clarendon Road, London W11 4JE and stamped normally. Unless asked not to, we shall assume that we may publish your name if you are recommending a new hotel or supporting an existing entry. If you would like more report forms please tick ☐

Name of Hotel ____

Address ____

____

Date of most recent visit | Duration of visit

☐ New recommendation | ☐ Comment on existing entry

Report:

I am not connected directly or indirectly with the management or proprietors
(Continue overleaf if you wish or use separate sheet)

Signed ____

Name and address (capitals please) ______________________

____

To: *The Good Hotel Guide,* Freepost, London W11 4BR

NOTE: No stamps needed in UK, but letters posted outside the UK should be addressed to 61 Clarendon Road, London W11 4JE and stamped normally. Unless asked not to, we shall assume that we may publish your name if you are recommending a new hotel or supporting an existing entry. If you would like more report forms please tick ☐

Name of Hotel ______________________________

Address ______________________________

____

Date of most recent visit

Duration of visit

☐ New recommendation

☐ Comment on existing entry

Report:

I am not connected directly or indirectly with the management or proprietors
(Continue overleaf if you wish or use separate sheet)

Signed ______________________________

Name and address (capitals please) ______________________________

____

To: *The Good Hotel Guide*, Freepost, London W11 4BR

NOTE: No stamps needed in UK, but letters posted outside the UK should be addressed to 61 Clarendon Road, London W11 4JE and stamped normally. Unless asked not to, we shall assume that we may publish your name if you are recommending a new hotel or supporting an existing entry. If you would like more report forms please tick ☐

Name of Hotel ______________________________

Address ______________________________

____

Date of most recent visit

Duration of visit

☐ New recommendation

☐ Comment on existing entry

Report:

I am not connected directly or indirectly with the management or proprietors
(Continue overleaf if you wish or use separate sheet)

Signed ______________________________

Name and address (capitals please) ______________________________

____

To: *The Good Hotel Guide*, Freepost, London W11 4BR

NOTE: No stamps needed in UK, but letters posted outside the UK should be addressed to 61 Clarendon Road, London W11 4JE and stamped normally. Unless asked not to, we shall assume that we may publish your name if you are recommending a new hotel or supporting an existing entry. If you would like more report forms please tick ☐

Name of Hotel ______________________________

Address ______________________________

____

Date of most recent visit

☐ New recommendation

Duration of visit

☐ Comment on existing entry

Report:

I am not connected directly or indirectly with the management or proprietors
(Continue overleaf if you wish or use separate sheet)

Signed ______________________________

Name and address (capitals please) ______________________________

____

To: *The Good Hotel Guide*, Freepost, London W11 4BR

NOTE: No stamps needed in UK, but letters posted outside the UK should be addressed to 61 Clarendon Road, London W11 4JE and stamped normally. Unless asked not to, we shall assume that we may publish your name if you are recommending a new hotel or supporting an existing entry. If you would like more report forms please tick ☐

Name of Hotel ______________________________

Address ______________________________

____

Date of most recent visit

☐ New recommendation

Duration of visit

☐ Comment on existing entry

Report:

I am not connected directly or indirectly with the management or proprietors

(Continue overleaf if you wish or use separate sheet)

Signed ______________________________

Name and address (capitals please) ______________________________

____

To: *The Good Hotel Guide*, Freepost, London W11 4BR

NOTE: No stamps needed in UK, but letters posted outside the UK should be addressed to 61 Clarendon Road, London W11 4JE and stamped normally. Unless asked not to, we shall assume that we may publish your name if you are recommending a new hotel or supporting an existing entry. If you would like more report forms please tick ☐

Name of Hotel ______________________________

Address ______________________________

____

Date of most recent visit

Duration of visit

☐ New recommendation

☐ Comment on existing entry

Report:

I am not connected directly or indirectly with the management or proprietors
(Continue overleaf if you wish or use separate sheet)

Signed ______________________________

Name and address (capitals please) ______________________________

____